DICTIONARY OF AMERICAN BIOGRAPHY
AMERICAN COUNCIL OF LEARNED SOCIETIES
CSS
C0-AUD-780

DICTIONARY OF AMERICAN BIOGRAPHY

Prompted solely by a desire for public service the New York Times Company and its President, Mr. Adolph S. Ochs, have made possible the preparation of the manuscript of the Dictionary of American Biography through a subvention of more than $500,000 and with the understanding that the entire responsibility for the contents of the volumes rests with the American Council of Learned Societies.

Printed in the United States of America

The Dictionary of American Biography is published under the auspices of the American Council of Learned Societies and under the direction of a Committee of Management which consists of J. FRANKLIN JAMESON, *Chairman*, JOHN H. FINLEY, DUMAS MALONE, FREDERIC L. PAXSON, IPHIGENE OCHS SULZBERGER, CARL VAN DOREN, CHARLES WARREN.

The editorial staff consists of DUMAS MALONE, *Editor;* HARRIS E. STARR, *Associate Editor;* GEORGE H. GENZMER, ELEANOR R. DOBSON, MILDRED B. PALMER, *Assistant Editors.*

The American Council of Learned Societies consists of the following societies:

American Philosophical Society
American Academy of Arts and Sciences
American Antiquarian Society
American Oriental Society
American Philological Association
Archaeological Institute of America
Society of Biblical Literature and Exegesis
Modern Language Association of America
American Historical Association
American Economic Association
American Philosophical Association
American Anthropological Association
American Political Science Association
Bibliographical Society of America
American Sociological Society
History of Science Society
Linguistic Society of America
Mediaeval Academy of America

CONTRIBUTORS TO VOLUME XII

Charles G. Abbot . . . C. G. A.
Mather A. Abbott . . . M. A. A.
Thomas P. Abernethy . . . T. P. A.
Evelyn Abraham . . . E. A.
Adeline Adams . . . A. A.
James Truslow Adams . . . J. T. A.
Nelson F. Adkins . . . N. F. A.
Cyrus Adler . . . C. A.
Robert Greenhalgh Albion . . . R. G. A.
William F. Albright . . . W. F. A.
Carroll S. Alden . . . C. S. A.
Freeman H. Allen . . . F. H. A.
Gardner W. Allen . . . G. W. A.
John Clark Archer . . . J. C. A.
Edward C. Armstrong . . . E. C. A.
Charles F. Arrowood . . . C. F. A.
Percy M. Ashburn . . . P. M. A.
Clifford W. Ashley . . . C. W. A.
Horace B. Baker . . . H. B. B.
Ray Palmer Baker . . . R. P. B—r.
Hayes Baker-Crothers . . . H. B–C.
William W. Ball . . . W. W. B.
Thomas S. Barclay . . . T. S. B.
Claribel R. Barnett . . . C. R. B.
Adriaan J. Barnouw . . . A. J. B.
Harold K. Barrows . . . H. K. B.
Robert Duncan Bass . . . R. D. B.
Ernest Sutherland Bates . . . E. S. B.
G. Philip Bauer . . . G. P. B.
Albert C. Baugh . . . A. C. B.
William G. Bean . . . W. G. B.
Mary R. Beard . . . M. R. B.
Elbert J. Benton . . . E. J. B.
Percy W. Bidwell . . . P. W. B.
Theodore C. Blegen . . . T. C. B.
Ernest Ludlow Bogart . . . E. L. B.
Robert W. Bolwell . . . R. W. B.
Leonard Napoleon Boston . . . L. N. B.
Archibald L. Bouton . . . A. L. B.
Witt Bowden . . . W. B—n.
Sarah G. Bowerman . . . S. G. B.
Walter Russell Bowie . . . W. R. B.
F. E. Bowman . . . F. E. B.
Julian P. Boyd . . . J. P. B.
William L. Boyden . . . W. L. B.
William Joseph Bradley . . . W. J. B.
William Bridgwater . . . W. B—r.
John E. Briggs . . . J. E. B.
Lyman J. Briggs . . . L. J. B.
Ruth Lee Briscoe . . . R. L. B.
Jean Lambert Brockway . . . J. L. B.
Robert Preston Brooks . . . R. P. B—s.
Van Wyck Brooks . . . V. W. B.
L. Parmly Brown . . . L. P. B.
Oswald E. Brown . . . O. E. B.
Carleton L. Brownson . . . C. L. B.
John S. Brubacher . . . J. S. B.
Kathleen Bruce . . . K. B.
Robert Bruce . . . R. B.
G. MacLaren Brydon . . . G. M. B.
Paul H. Buck . . . P. H. B.
F. Lauriston Bullard . . . F. L. B.
William Mill Butler . . . W. M. B.
Isabel M. Calder . . . I. M. C.
Robert G. Caldwell . . . R. G. C—l.
Harry J. Carman . . . H. J. C.
William S. Carpenter . . . W. S. C.
Louise Fontaine Catterall . . . L. F. C.
Zechariah Chafee, Jr. . . . Z. C., Jr.
Arney R. Childs . . . A. R. C.
Russell H. Chittenden . . . R. H. C.
O. P. Chitwood . . . O. P. C.
Hubert Lyman Clark . . . H. L. C.
Robert Glass Cleland . . . R. G. C—d.
Oral Sumner Coad . . . O. S. C.
Frederick W. Coburn . . . F. W. C.
Rudolph I. Coffee . . . R. I. C.
Fannie L. Gwinner Cole . . . F. L. G. C.
Christopher B. Coleman . . . C. B. C.
Henry T. Colestock . . . H. T. C.
John R. Commons . . . J. R. C.
Royal Cortissoz . . . R. C.
Edward S. Corwin . . . E. S. C.
Robert Spencer Cotterill . . . R. S. C.
George S. Cottman . . . G. S. C.
E. Merton Coulter . . . E. M. C.
Isaac J. Cox . . . I. J. C.
Owen C. Coy . . . O. C. C.
Katharine Elizabeth Crane . . . K. E. C.
Verner W. Crane . . . V. W. C.
Frederic R. Crownfield . . . F. R. C.
Edward E. Curtis . . . E. E. C.
Virginius Dabney . . . V. D.
Stuart Daggett . . . S. D.
Edward E. Dale . . . E. E. D.
Charles B. Davenport . . . C. B. D.
Donald Davidson . . . D. D.
Henry C. Davis . . . H. C. D.

Contributors to Volume XII

Richard E. Day	R. E. D.
Edward S. Delaplaine	E. S. D.
D. Bryson Delavan	D. B. D.
William H. S. Demarest	W. H. S. D.
Everett N. Dick	E. N. D.
Irving Dilliard	I. D.
Lee Wilson Dodd	L. W. D.
Leonidas Dodson	L. D.
Dorothy Anne Dondore	D. A. D.
William Howe Downes	W. H. D.
Stella M. Drumm	S. M. D.
Raymond S. Dugan	R. S. D.
Lionel C. Durel	L. C. D.
Frank L. Dyer	F. L. D.
Edward Dwight Eaton	E. D. E.
Walter Prichard Eaton	W. P. E.
Edwin Francis Edgett	E. F. E.
Joseph D. Eggleston	J. D. E.
Katharine S. Eisenhart	K. S. E.
L. Ethan Ellis	L. E. E.
Milton Ellis	M. E.
John Erskine	J. E.
Paul D. Evans	P. D. E.
Charles Fairman	C. F.
Paul Patton Faris	P. P. F.
Hallie Farmer	H. F.
Harold U. Faulkner	H. U. F.
George Haws Feltus	G. H. F.
Gustav J. Fiebeger	G. J. F.
Edward Fitch	E. F.
William Foster	W. F.
John H. Frederick	J. H. F.
John C. French	J. C. F.
Claude M. Fuess	C. M. F.
George W. Fuller	G. W. F.
Joseph V. Fuller	J. V. F.
John F. Fulton	J. F. F.
Franklin DeR. Furman	F. DeR. F.
Charles B. Galbreath	C. B. G.
W. Freeman Galpin	W. F. G.
Herbert P. Gambrell	H. P. G.
William A. Ganoe	W. A. G.
Lee Garby	L. G.
Richard Cecil Garlick, Jr.	R. C. G., Jr.
Curtis W. Garrison	C. W. G.
George Harvey Genzmer	G. H. G.
W. J. Ghent	W. J. G.
Robert W. Goodloe	R. W. G.
Armistead Churchill Gordon, Jr.	A. C. G., Jr.
Dorothy Grafly	D. G.
Walter Granger	W. G.
Ruth Shepard Granniss	R. S. G.
John N. Greely	J. N. G.
Edwin L. Green	E. L. G.
Ernest S. Griffith	E. S. G.
Ernest Gruening	E. G.
Le Roy R. Hafen	L. R. H.
Marguerite Bartlett Hamer	M. B. H—r.
Philip M. Hamer	P. M. H.
J. G. deR. Hamilton	J. G. deR. H.
Talbot Faulkner Hamlin	T. F. H.
Lloyd C. M. Hare	L. C. M. H.
Alvin F. Harlow	A. F. H.
George M. Harper	G. M. H.
John W. Harshberger	J. W. H.
Edward Hart	E. H.
Freeman H. Hart	F. H. H.
Mary Bronson Hartt	M. B. H—t.
Daniel C. Haskell	D. C. H.
Frank Wilson Cheney Hersey	F. W. C. H.
John L. Hervey	J. L. H.
Rufus P. Hibbard	R. P. H.
Granville Hicks	G. H.
John Donald Hicks	J. D. H.
Helen Hill	H. H.
Edward M. Hinton	E. M. H.
M. M. Hoffman	M. M. H.
Oliver W. Holmes	O. W. H.
A. Van Doren Honeyman	A. V-D. H.
Walter Hough	W. H.
William I. Hull	W. I. H.
Augustus E. Ingram	A. E. I.
Asher Isaacs	A. I.
Joseph Jackson	J. J.
M. C. James	M. C. J.
Charles F. Jenkins	C. F. J.
T. Cary Johnson, Jr.	T. C. J., Jr.
Theodore F. Jones	T. F. J.
James R. Joy	J. R. J.
Louis C. Karpinski	L. C. K.
Louise Phelps Kellogg	L. P. K.
Rayner W. Kelsey	R. W. K.
Benjamin B. Kendrick	B. B. K.
John Kieran	J. K.
Fiske Kimball	F. K.
James Gore King, Jr.	J. G. K., Jr.
Max J. Kohler	M. J. K.
Alois F. Kovarik	A. F. K.
Kenneth S. Latourette	K. S. L.
Charles H. LaWall	C. H. L—l.
H. Barrett Learned	H. B. L—d.
Harvey B. Lemon	H. B. L—n.
William R. Leonard	W. R. L.
Allen F. Lesser	A. F. L.
William S. Lewis	W. S. L.
William E. Lingelbach	W. E. L.
Ralph G. Lounsbury	R. G. L.
Selden Gale Lowrie	S. G. L.
William T. Lyle	W. T. L.
Charles H. Lyttle	C. H. L—e.
Eugene I. McCormac	E. I. McC.
Nelson Glenn McCrea	N. G. M.
Joseph McFarland	J. M.
Walter M. McFarland	W. M. M.
W. J. McGlothlin	W. J. M.

Contributors to Volume XII

Reginald C. McGrane	R. C. M.	James H. Peeling	J. H. P—g.
Douglas C. McMurtrie	D. C. M.	James M. Phalen	J. M. P.
John H. T. McPherson	J. H. T. M.	Francis S. Philbrick	F. S. P.
M. D'Arcy Magee	M. D. M.	Paul Chrisler Phillips	P. C. P.
James C. Malin	J. C. M.	David deSola Pool	D. deS. P.
W. C. Mallalieu	W. C. M.	Julius W. Pratt	J. W. P—t.
Dumas Malone	D. M.	Edward Preble	E. P.
Kemp Malone	K. M.	Richard J. Purcell	R. J. P.
H. A. Marmer	H. A. M.	Lowell Joseph Ragatz	L. J. R.
Frederick H. Martens	F. H. M.	Charles W. Ramsdell	C. W. R.
Frank Jewett Mather, Jr.	F. J. M., Jr.	Harrison Randolph	H. R.
Shailer Mathews	S. M.	P. O. Ray	P. O. R.
Lawrence S. Mayo	L. S. M.	Thomas T. Read	T. T. R.
Robert Douthat Meade	R. D. M.	Charles Dudley Rhodes	C. D. R.
Newton D. Mereness	N. D. M.	George L. Ridgeway	G. L. R.
Robert L. Meriwether	R. L. M—r.	Robert E. Riegel	R. E. R.
George P. Merrill	G. P. M.	Donald A. Roberts	D. A. R—s.
Gerrit S. Miller	G. S. M.	David A. Robertson	D. A. R—n.
Edwin Mims, Jr.	E. M., Jr.	Burr A. Robinson	B. A. R.
Harvey C. Minnich	H. C. M.	Doane Robinson	D. R.
Samuel Chiles Mitchell	S. C. M.	William A. Robinson	W. A. R.
Carl W. Mitman	C. W. M.	William M. Robinson, Jr.	W. M. R., Jr.
Fulmer Mood	F. M.	William Rosenau	W. R.
Robert E. Moody	R. E. M.	A. S. W. Rosenbach	A. S. W. R.
Albert B. Moore	A. B. M.	Lois K. M. Rosenberry	L. K. M. R.
Charles Moore	C. M.	Victor Rosewater	V. R.
Samuel Eliot Morison	S. E. M.	Frank Edward Ross	F. E. R.
Richard L. Morton	R. L. M—n.	George Y. Rusk	G. Y. R.
Kenneth B. Murdock	K. B. M.	John A. Ryan	J. A. R.
H. Edward Nettles	H. E. N.	George H. Ryden	G. H. R.
Lyman C. Newell	L. C. N.	Joseph Schafer	J. S.
A. R. Newsome	A. R. N.	Louis Bernard Schmidt	L. B. S—t.
Jeannette P. Nichols	J. P. N.	Charles Schuchert	C. S.
Robert Hastings Nichols	R. H. N.	Frederic C. Sears	F. C. S.
Roy F. Nichols	R. F. N.	Benjamin F. Shambaugh	B. F. S.
John Scholte Nollen	J. S. N.	Bertha M. H. Shambaugh	B. M. H. S.
Walter B. Norris	W. B. N.	William Bristol Shaw	W. B. S.
Alexander D. Noyes	A. D. N.	Guy Emery Shipler	G. E. S.
George C. D. Odell	G. C. D. O.	Lester B. Shippee	L. B. S—e.
Herman Oliphant	H. O.	Enoch W. Sikes	E. W. S.
Louis A. Olney	L. A. O.	Kenneth C. M. Sills	K. C. M. S.
Vincent O'Sullivan	V. O.	Francis Butler Simkins	F. B. S.
Frank Lawrence Owsley	F. L. O.	David Eugene Smith	D. E. S.
Francis R. Packard	F. R. P.	Marion Parris Smith	M. P. S.
Victor H. Paltsits	V. H. P.	William E. Smith	W. E. S.
John I. Parcel	J. I. P.	William Roy Smith	W. R. S.
Stanley M. Pargellis	S. M. P.	George Franklin Smythe	G. F. S.
Henry B. Parkes	H. B. P.	George A. Soper	G. A. S.
Francis Parkman	F. P.	James P. C. Southall	J. P. C. S.
Julius H. Parmelee	J. H. P—e.	Oliver L. Spaulding, Jr.	O. L. S., Jr.
S. Howard Patterson	S. H. P.	Harris Elwood Starr	H. E. S.
James W. Patton	J. W. P—n.	Bertha Monica Stearns	B. M. S.
Charles O. Paullin	C. O. P.	George M. Stephenson	G. M. S.
Frederic Logan Paxson	F. L. P.	Witmer Stone	W. S.
Charles E. Payne	C. E. P.	Tracy E. Strevey	T. E. S.
Haywood J. Pearce, Jr.	H. J. P., Jr.	R. H. Sudds	R. H. S.
C. C. Pearson	C. C. P.	Fletcher Harper Swift	F. H. S.
Henry G. Pearson	H. G. P.	Charles S. Sydnor	C. S. S.

Contributors to Volume XII

David Y. Thomas	D. Y. T.
Milton Halsey Thomas	M. H. T.
C. Mildred Thompson	C. M. T.
Ernest Trice Thompson	E. T. T.
Irving L. Thomson	I. L. T.
Edward Larocque Tinker	E. L. T.
Richard F. F. Tyner	R. F. F. T.
William T. Utter	W. T. U.
John R. Vance	J. R. V.
John G. Van Deusen	J. G. V–D.
Irene Van Fossen	I. V–F.
Bertha Van Hoosen	B. V–H.
Francis Preston Venable	F. P. V.
Henry R. Viets	H. R. V.
Eugene M. Violette	E. M. V.
Albert T. Volwiler	A. T. V.
James Elliott Walmsley	J. E. W.
W. Randall Waterman	W. R. W.
Mabel L. Webber	M. L. W.
Frank Weitenkampf	F. W.
F. Estelle Wells	F. E. W.
Allan Westcott	A. W.
Joseph L. Wheeler	J. L. W.
Arthur P. Whitaker	A. P. W.
Melvin J. White	M. J. W.
Harry Emerson Wildes	H. E. W.
Allen Sinclair Will	A. S. W.
James F. Willard	J. F. W.
Mary Wilhelmine Williams	M. W. W.
Walter Williams	W. W.
Louis B. Wilson	L. B. W.
Helen Sumner Woodbury	H. S. W.
Maude H. Woodfin	M. H. W.
C. P. Wright	C. P. W.
Helen Wright	H. W.
Walter L. Wright, Jr.	W. L. W., Jr.
Robert Sterling Yard	R. S. Y.
Donovan Yeuell	D. Y.
Harold Zink	H. Z.

DICTIONARY OF

AMERICAN BIOGRAPHY

McCrady — Millington

McCRADY, EDWARD (Apr. 8, 1833–Nov. 1, 1903), lawyer, Confederate officer, historian, was born at Charleston, S. C., the second son of Edward and Louisa Rebecca (Lane) McCrady and a great-grandson of Edward McCrady who emigrated from the north of Ireland about the middle of the eighteenth century. On Feb. 24, 1863, he was married to Mary Fraser Davie. They had no children. He was graduated in 1853 from the College of Charleston, read law in his father's office, and was admitted to the bar in 1855. In his profession—as, indeed, in his later avocation of history—he seems to have made his way by energy and persistence rather than by the possession of exceptional talents. During the Civil War he achieved a creditable record in the Confederate service, rising from captain to lieutenant-colonel in the Virginia campaigns, 1861–62. Severely wounded at Second Manassas, he fought again at Fredericksburg but was injured by an accident early in 1863, and in March 1864 he was detailed to command a camp of instruction at Madison, Fla. His military concerns, which colored his writings, continued after the war; in 1882 he was appointed major-general in the South Carolina militia. Through the agency of the Survivors' Association he began to collect the state military records in the late conflict, his first service to South Carolina history. These collections were the foundation of the South Carolina war records.

McCrady's interest in writing history developed late in an active career. During Reconstruction he built up a legal reputation in the political trials and in bank and railroad cases. After working for Wade Hampton's election (1876) he launched the movement to disfranchise the negro without resort to open fraud and intimidation and drafted the "Eight Ballot Box Law" of 1882. Between 1880 and 1890 he sat for Charleston County in the South Carolina House of Representatives. He had already published a number of pamphlets on public questions when his first historical essay appeared in 1883. *Education in South Carolina Prior to and During the Revolution* (reprinted in the *Collections of the South Carolina Historical Society,* vol. IV, 1887) was a spirited reply to a passage in McMaster. It set the tone of much of McCrady's later writing—a tone of aggressive state-loyalty, justified in some measure by the neglect of Southern history on the part of American historians. In 1889 he was invited to supply the volume on South Carolina in the American Commonwealth Series. Although he later withdrew from the engagement, this was the genesis of his detailed narrative of South Carolina through the War of Independence. Completed in thirteen years, it was a remarkable *tour de force* for an amateur whose studies of local history had hitherto been desultory, and who until a few years before his death did all his literary work after office hours.

In 1897 appeared the first volume, *The History of South Carolina under the Proprietary Government, 1670–1719.* It met a favorable reception even in those professional journals which called attention to its too exclusively chronological arrangement, its concentration on political annals, neglect of manuscript sources, and pedestrian style. Though McCrady developed in skill, he never quite overcame these faults. In his first volume he had leaned heavily upon his able predecessor, W. J. Rivers; in the next, *The History of South Carolina under the Royal Gov-*

ernment, 1719–76 (1899) he followed the earlier chroniclers, Alexander Hewat and David Ramsay, but less slavishly, and drew upon the colonial gazettes as well as other contemporary printed sources. But he always slighted the state archives and preferred calendars to the voluminous transcripts from the Public Record Office. Consequently he revealed little consciousness of the place of the province in the empire, or of its frontier rôle in the international struggles, which he treated only episodically. In this volume there were a number of chapters devoted to economic and social conditions, but these were somewhat antiquarian, and too little correlated with the political themes. Toward the approaching Revolution he adopted Lecky's views rather than Bancroft's: he was eminently fair to the Loyalists, so numerous in South Carolina. His patriotic bias, indeed, was not continental but Carolinian. This stood out strongly in *The History of South Carolina in the Revolution, 1775–80* (1901), and especially in its sequel (1902), a work of the same title covering the years 1780–83. But despite his failings, he wrote one of the best narrative histories which exist for any of the original commonwealths. Recognition came locally in his election to the presidency of the South Carolina Historical Society (1899), and nationally when he was chosen in 1902 second vice-president of the American Historical Association.

[Memoirs of McCrady were written by A. S. Salley, Jr., for the *S. C. Hist. and Geneal. Mag.*, Jan. 1904, and by the historian's brother, Louis deB. McCrady, for the Charleston *Year Book* of 1904 (reprinted, 1905), with bibliography. See also: *Who's Who in America*, 1901–02; *Proc. Mass. Hist. Soc.*, 2 ser. XVIII (1905); *News and Courier* (Charleston), Nov. 2, 1903. Reviews of McCrady's works appeared in the *Am. Hist. Rev.*, Apr. 1898, Jan. 1900, Oct. 1901, Apr. 1903, and in the *Nation*, June 2, 1898, Jan. 11, 1900, Jan. 30, 1902, Apr. 16, 23, 1903. Information for this sketch was supplied by the late Joseph W. Barnwell of Charleston, S. C.] V. W. C.

McCRARY, GEORGE WASHINGTON (Aug. 29, 1835–June 23, 1890), jurist and congressman, was born near Evansville, Ind., the son of a hard-working farmer, James McCrary, and a religious mother, Matilda (Forest) McCrary. In 1837 the family settled in what is now Van Buren County, Iowa, where the Indians were still roaming and settlers were widely scattered. Hard drudgery with brief intervals at school and academy marked the boy's early life. Nevertheless he obtained a good training and at eighteen was teaching a country school. He studied law in Keokuk with John W. Rankin and Samuel F. Miller, the latter of whom became a justice of the United States Supreme Court in 1862, at which time McCrary entered partnership with Rankin. In the meantime he was admitted to the bar in 1856, began practice in Keokuk, and the next year was married to Helen Gelatt and was elected state representative. From 1861 to 1865 he was state senator, serving as chairman of the committees on Indian affairs and on the judiciary. At thirty-three he began eight years of active congressional services, from 1869 to 1877. His experience as chairman of the committee on elections, which he became in the Forty-second Congress, enabled him to publish in 1875, *A Treatise on the American Law of Elections,* which went through four editions. He also acted on the committee of investigation for the Crédit Mobilier scandal, where his presence helped "guarantee that the inquiry would not result in a whitewashing report" (J. F. Rhodes, *History of the United States,* vol. VII, 1906, p. 2). As chairman of the committee on canals and railroads in the Forty-third Congress he reported a bill to regulate commerce among the states that would have created a commission to make a schedule of rates for each road. After a memorable debate it passed the House but died in the Senate. It became, however, a basis for later legislation. In the Hayes-Tilden election controversy his wisdom and moderation helped avert a grave crisis. In the creation of the Electoral Commission, Rhodes says that he was "prominent in sympathetic co-operation" (*Ibid.*, p. 256). Before that body, as one of Hayes' counselors, Garfield wrote that he made "a very powerful argument . . . making his points with great clearness and force" (T. C. Smith, *The Life and Letters of James Abram Garfield,* 1925, vol. I, p. 634).

Upon the inauguration of Hayes he became secretary of war and was in full sympathy with Hayes's reform of the civil service and with his more generous attitude toward the South. By the President's orders he withdrew the support of federal troops from the remaining Carpet-bag governments in South Carolina and Louisiana. In the railway strike of 1877 the new secretary used the federal troops, and, during Mexican disturbances, he ordered the troops to pursue marauding Mexicans across the Mexican border. The latter act resulted in American recognition of the Diaz government. The war department also began in this administration the publication of the *War of the Rebellion: Official Records.* In December 1879, he resigned from the cabinet to become federal judge of the Eighth Judicial Circuit. He had a judicial mind and his opinions were clear, sound, and comprehensive. During his years on the bench he reported and published the cases tried before his court (*Mc-*

Crary's Reports, 5 vols., 1881–84). After five years he left the bench, moved to Kansas City, Mo., and acted as general-counsel for the Atchison, Topeka & Sante Fé Railroad for the rest of his life. He had an unusually well-balanced nature, singularly devoid of weakness or pretension. While his interests were chiefly intellectual he was an excellent story teller and an ardent trout-fisher. In faith he was a Unitarian. An original Frémont Republican he was always a stanch party supporter, but his opponents conceded that he honestly tried to subordinate partisan to public interests.

[Pioneer Lawmakers Assoc. of Iowa, *Reunions of 1890 and 1892* (1890–93); B. F. Gue, *Hist. of Iowa,* (copr. 1903), vols. I, III, IV; E. H. Stiles, *Recollections and Sketches of Notable Lawyers and Public Men of Early Iowa* (1916); C. R. Williams, *The Life of Rutherford B. Hayes* (2 vols., 1914).] C. E. P.

McCREARY, JAMES BENNETT (July 8, 1838–Oct. 8, 1918), governor of Kentucky, representative, and senator, was born in Madison County, Ky., the son of Sabrina D. (Bennett) and E. R. McCreary, a physician. He was educated in the common schools, at Centre College, from which he graduated (A.B.) in 1857, and in the law department of Cumberland University, where he received the degree of LL.B. in 1859. Admitted to the bar in 1859, he practised in Richmond, Ky. During the Civil War he enlisted in the 7th (later the 11th) Kentucky Cavalry, C.S.A., and was commissioned major on Sept. 10, 1862. Under General John H. Morgan, his regiment took a prominent part in the battle of Hartsville, Tenn. He raided Monticello, Ky., and Burkesville, Ky., and rendered distinguished service in the battle of Greasy Creek. On July 4, 1863, he was commissioned lieutenant-colonel. Captured at Cheshire, Ohio, during Morgan's raid, he was sent to the Ohio penitentiary and then to Morris Island, near Charleston, S. C. Later he was exchanged and, after a short furlough, took command of a battalion in Virginia under Gen. J. C. Breckinridge. Resuming practice at Richmond, Ky., he was married on June 12, 1867, to Katherine Hughes of Lexington. He joined the conservative Democrats, was chosen a delegate to the national convention in 1868, was a member of the Kentucky House of Representatives from 1869 to 1875, and speaker from 1871 to 1875. He favored the much-discussed charter of the Cincinnati Southern Railroad, and his election as speaker facilitated its passage. Then he won the gubernatorial nomination over the popular Gen. John Stuart Williams and defeated the Republican candidate, John M. Harlan. As governor from 1875 to 1879 he devoted himself to suppressing mountain feuds and establishing an independent agricultural college, a normal school, a health board, and an agricultural department. Beginning in 1884, he was six times elected to Congress, usually with little or no opposition. In the House, he served on the coinage and foreign affairs committees and was also interested in the tariff. He introduced the bill authorizing the first Pan-American conference. As a delegate to the International Monetary Conference at Brussels in 1892 (*Report of the Commissioners on Behalf of the U. S., and Journal of the Sessions of Nov. 22, 1892 to Dec. 17, 1892,* 1893) he favored international bimetallism and opposed the Rothschild silver-purchase plan. After the failure of the conference, he favored the repeal of the silver-purchase act and allied himself with the Sound-Money Democrats, who supported him for the Senate in 1896. But the Silver Democrats prevented even his nomination for the House. In 1900 he was made state chairman and was delegate to the four national conventions from 1900 to 1912. In 1902 he was elected to the Senate but was defeated in 1908 and 1914. In the Senate he served on the committees for foreign affairs, for immigration, and for military affairs. In 1911 he easily won the gubernatorial nomination and election on a platform of progress and county option. To fulfill his platform he recommended county option, a longer school term, cheaper textbooks, campaigns against tuberculosis and illiteracy, departments of banking, public roads, fish and game, and forests, workmen's compensation, restriction of campaign funds, and direct primaries. These recommendations, except the last three, were heeded by the legislature. He spent his last years in Richmond, Ky., where he died. He was survived by his one son.

[Misc. Military Papers, 1875–77, in MSS. of Governors' Papers in Ky. State Hist. Soc.; H. Levin, *The Lawyers and Lawmakers of Ky.* (1897); *The Biog. Enc. of Ky.* (1878); J. J. McAfee, *Ky. Politicians* (1886); W. E. Connelley and E. M. Coulter, *Hist. of Ky.* (1922), vol. II; *Bulletin of the Pan American Union,* Oct. 1918; *Biog. Directory of Am. Cong.* (1928); *Who's Who in America,* 1916–17; *War of the Rebellion: Official Records (Army),* ser. 2, vol. VIII; *Report of the Adjutant-General of the State of Ky.,* vol. II (1919), esp. pp. 96–99; *Courier-Journal* (Louisville), Oct. 9, 1918; *Evening Post* (Louisville), Oct. 8, 9, 1918.] W. C. M.

McCREERY, CHARLES (June 13, 1785–Aug. 27, 1826), pioneer Kentucky physician, was born near Winchester, Clark County, Ky., to Robert and Mary (McClanahan) McCreery, both of Scotch-Irish descent, who had moved to Kentucky from Maryland. After such an education as he could obtain in the local schools he studied medicine under Dr. Goodlet of Bardstown and in 1810 he settled in Hartford, Ohio County, for the practice of his profession. The remainder of his life was spent in this community where he covered an area of several counties, mostly on horseback. He built up a large practice among a clientele that was devoted to him. No distance was too long nor pains too great for him to respond to a call. From the beginning of his career he had a bent for surgery. In 1813, his third year of practice, at the age of twenty-seven, he performed the operation upon which rests his greatest claim to remembrance. It involved the complete extirpation of the clavicle, the first operation of its kind performed in the United States. The patient, a boy of fourteen, had been suffering for a long time from a tubercular infection of the right collar bone. Not only was the condition relieved, but the loss of the clavicle did not seriously impair the function of the corresponding arm. It was not until a similar operation performed by Valentine Mott of New York in 1828 attracted country-wide attention that the brilliant surgical feat of McCreery was made generally known. The technique of Mott was practically the same as that of McCreery and the operation still follows much the same procedure. (McCreery's case is reported by James H. Johnson in the *New Orleans Medical and Surgical Journal,* January 1850.)

In the midst of an exacting practice McCreery found time for lectures to his own students, and to those of others. He was a ready speaker and a good instructor. By diligent reading he developed from a meagerly educated youth to a scholarly man. He is described as being a tall, well-formed, handsome man with dark hair and fine dark eyes. He married in 1811 Ann Wayman Crowe of Hartford whose parents were from Maryland. They had seven children. McCreery died at the early age of forty-one of cardiac dropsy at West Point, Ky. He is buried at Hartford.

[See the *Am. Practitioner and News* (Louisville), July 1, 1901; H. A. Kelly and W. L. Burrage, *Am. Medic. Biogs.* (1920).] J. M. P.

McCREERY, JAMES WORK (July 13, 1849–Feb. 20, 1923), lawyer, legislator, authority on irrigation law, came of Scotch-Irish ancestry. His grandfather, William McCreery, emigrated to America in 1793 from County Donegal, Ireland. James was born in Indiana County, Pa., the son of William G. and Mary (Work) McCreery, and was reared on his father's farm. He attended public school and graduated from the State Normal School at Indiana in 1877. After teaching for a time he took up the study of law in the offices of Judge Silas M. Clark and George Shiras, Jr., in Pittsburgh and was admitted to the Pennsylvania bar in 1880. Feeling that the West afforded good opportunities for a legal career, he went to Colorado in 1881 and settled in Greeley. The country was agricultural, the farming was done on irrigated lands, and the young lawyer's chief practice had to do with water rights. Many phases of irrigation law had not as yet received definite formulation and McCreery came to be an important influence in working out and establishing sound principles of law regarding the new questions that arose. He became an authority in this branch of law, writing several papers on the subject and lecturing on irrigation law at the University of Colorado (1905–23). He also contributed the section on "Irrigation and Water Rights" to Volume VI of *Modern American Law,* edited by E. A. Gilmore and W. C. Wermuth. His specialized practice, devoted to water-rights cases, brought him before the courts of several western states and before the Supreme Court of the United States.

McCreery was active in political life and was twice elected to the state Senate on the Republican ticket (1888 and 1896). During his eight years in the legislature, he was a leader in matters relating to farm interests, finance, and especially to water rights. He was the author and the chief force in effecting the enactment of the bill which created the State Normal School (later the State Teachers' College of Colorado) at Greeley. From 1891 to 1897 he was on the board of trustees of this institution and served for four years (1893–97) as president of the board. In 1907–08 he was president of the Colorado Bar Association. In addition to his legal practice he developed and operated large farming properties east of Greeley. During the World War he worked effectively for the various welfare organizations and for the conservation of resources. He had married, on Aug. 27, 1883, Mary M. Arbuckle of Greeley. They had four children. Until a few months before his death he remained active in his law practice. Temperamentally, he was an advocate rather than a judge; his inherited persistency made him loath to yield a point. By nature conservative, he was not a champion of pure democracy but emphasized the constitutional safeguards to the rights of minorities and to individual liberty.

[*Portrait and Biog. Record of the State of Colo.* (1899); J. C. Smiley, *Semi-Centennial Hist. of the State of Colo.* (1913), vol. II; W. F. Stone, *Hist. of Colo.,* vol. II (1918); J. H. Baker and L. R. Hafen, *Hist. of Colo.* (1927), vol. V; *Report Colo. Bar Asso.:*

Twenty-Sixth Ann. Meeting (1923); Greeley *Tribune and Republican*, Feb. 20, 1923; Denver *Post*, Feb. 21, 1923; information from relatives and associates of McCreery.] L. R. H.

McCULLAGH, JOSEPH BURBRIDGE (November 1842–Dec. 31, 1896), journalist, was born in Dublin, Ireland, one of the sixteen children of John and Sarah (Burbridge) McCullagh. At eleven he left home and worked his way to New York on a sailing vessel. Little is known of the next five years except that for a time he worked as an apprentice in the printing office of the *New York Freeman's Journal*. In 1858 he moved to St. Louis and became a compositor in the office of the *St. Louis Christian Advocate*. The next year he obtained a position on the local staff of the *St. Louis Democrat*, and his proficiency in stenography gained for him an assignment to report the proceedings of the State General Assembly during the session of 1859–60. Accepting an offer at an increased salary he left the *Democrat* early in 1860 to become a reporter for the *Cincinnati Daily Gazette*, but at the outbreak of the Civil War he entered the Union army as a lieutenant in the Benton Cadets, Gen. John C. Frémont's body guard. After Frémont's retirement he became war correspondent for the *Gazette*. He fought at Fort Donelson where he was one of the first men who volunteered to go on board the gunboat *St. Louis*, the first boat to pass the fire of the Fort. When the *Gazette* refused to publish his report of the first day's fighting at Shiloh, discrediting the conduct of the Union forces, he resigned his position but was immediately taken on by the *Cincinnati Commercial* at twice the salary he had been receiving. His war correspondence was widely popular and gained for him as a writer a reputation for fairness and reliability.

After the capture of Vicksburg he left the army in 1863 to become Washington correspondent of the *Commercial*, and for several years he was also the Senate reporter for the New York Associated Press. He made special use of the interview and gained added fame by his interviews with Alexander H. Stephens and with President Andrew Johnson in 1867–68. Writing over the name of "Mack" he proved popular with public officials and with the public. President Johnson often called on him to talk with him and to "give out" interviews. In 1868 he resigned as Washington correspondent for the *Commercial* to become managing editor of the *Cincinnati Enquirer*, a position held for some months. He then went to Chicago with a brother, John W. McCullagh, to take charge of the *Chicago Republican*. His personality was beginning to be felt when the fire of 1871 swept Chicago and destroyed his paper, his library, and his small fortune. Undaunted he went to St. Louis and became editor of the *Democrat*, the first newspaper on which he had been employed. After the founding of the *St. Louis Daily Globe* he edited the new paper from 1873 to 1875 when the two papers were combined as the *St. Louis Globe-Democrat*, of which he was editor until his death. As an editor he possessed a biting wit and frequently engaged in controversy through the columns of the *Globe-Democrat*. His newspaper was strongly Republican in a state largely Democratic, but his readers were of all political parties, brought to the paper by the brightness of its editorial page and the comprehensiveness of its news service. McCullagh was killed by falling out of his bedroom window during an illness. He had never married.

[Walter B. Stevens, "Joseph B. McCullagh," *Mo. Hist. Rev.*, Oct. 1930, and "The New Journalism in Mo.," *Ibid.*, Apr. 1923–July 1925; H. L. Conard, *Encyc. of the Hist. of Mo.* (1901), vol. IV; J. T. Scharf, *Hist. of St. Louis City and County* (1883), vol. I; *St. Louis Globe-Democrat*, Jan. 1, 1897; personal recollections.] W. W.

McCULLOCH, BEN (Nov. 11, 1811–Mar. 7, 1862), Texas and Confederate soldier, was born in Rutherford County, Tenn., an elder son in a family of six sons and six daughters. His parents were Maj. Alexander McCulloch, an aide-de-camp to Gen. James Coffee in the Creek War and War of 1812, and Frances LeNoir of Virginia. In 1820 the family moved to Alabama, and in 1830, when Ben was nineteen, they moved to Dyersburg, a village in western Tennessee some twenty miles from the Mississippi. Here a cabin was built and a clearing made in the forest. Two years later, after a visit to Missouri, Ben joined his younger brother Henry in the business of cutting cypress logs and floating their rafts in the spring to a market at Natchez or New Orleans. The McCulloch family lived only thirty miles from that of the celebrated David Crockett [*q.v.*] and, after the fashion of the woods, they regarded one another as neighbors. So when "Davy" Crockett went to Texas to meet a glorious death at the Alamo, he was soon followed by his young friend, Ben McCulloch, and shortly after by Henry and other members of the family. Ben McCulloch went in time to see service at the battle of San Jacinto, where he was in charge of one of the two little cannons called the "Twin Sisters," which were the only pieces of artillery in Houston's army.

After the battle, McCulloch returned to Tennessee to study surveying under his father but was back in Texas before the opening of the

Texas land office in February 1838. The young surveyor established himself at the frontier town of Gonzales. Unmarried and unencumbered with a family, he relieved the tedium of his professional duties by exploits against the Indians. His resourceful activity during the great Comanche raid of August 1840 especially added to his growing reputation. Of medium height and slender, with quiet manners, he was not the type which one associates with heroic deeds on the frontier. On horseback and leading a band of Texas rangers, however, he was the idol of his men and one of the most popular figures in Texas. At the outbreak of the Mexican War, he organized a company of mounted men which rendered effective and daring service to Taylor's army in the campaigns of Monterey and Buena Vista. His exploits caught the attention of the newspaper correspondents, and the reports of George Wilkins Kendall in the New Orleans *Picayune* had soon made the fame of McCulloch's rangers familiar through the South. McCulloch emerged from the war a major. He returned to surveying and devoted his spare time to reading of the campaigns of the great captains of history.

In 1849 he joined in the gold rush to California, where he became for a time sheriff of Sacramento. He does not appear to have made his fortune and in 1852 he was again in Texas. In March 1853 he was appointed by President Pierce marshal for the coast district of Texas, a position which he continued to hold by reappointment of President Buchanan until his resignation in the spring of 1859. In 1858 he was sent as one of two commissioners to conciliate the Mormons in Utah, a task which he seems to have performed with reasonable success. In February 1861, with the rank of colonel, he was in command of the Texas troops which received the surrender of General Twiggs at San Antonio. He was subsequently commissioned brigadier-general in the Confederate army and was assigned to the command of the troops in Arkansas. Later, under General Price in Missouri, he had the chief command of the Confederates at the battle of Wilson's Creek (Aug. 10, 1861) and won an important victory. In the spring of 1862, under the command of General Van Dorn, he led his brigade against Union troops at Elkhorn Tavern, and at the opening of that engagement, while reconnoitering the Federal lines, rode into a party of sharp-shooters and was fatally wounded in the breast.

[V. M. Rose, *The Life and Services of Gen. Ben McCulloch* (1888); S. C. Reid, Jr., *The Scouting Expeditions of McCulloch's Tex. Rangers* (1847); C. A. Evans, ed., *Confed. Mil. Hist.* (1899), vol. XI; *War of the Rebellion: Official Records (Army)*, 1 ser. III, pp. 104–07, and VIII, pp. 283–301; H. H. Bancroft, *Hist. of Utah, 1540–1886* (1889), p. 531.]

R. G. C—I.

McCULLOCH, HUGH (Dec. 7, 1808–May 24, 1895), comptroller of the currency, secretary of the treasury, was born at Kennebunk, Me., to which place his parents had moved from Kennebunkport in 1802. A grandson of Adam McCulloch who came to Maine from Scotland about 1766, he was the son of Hugh and Abigail (Perkins) McCulloch. His father was a ship-builder and West India merchant. Hugh entered Bowdoin College, but left during his sophomore year. In 1863 Bowdoin gave him the honorary degree of A.M., and in subsequent catalogues he was listed among the graduates of 1829 (information from office of Alumni Secretary, Bowdoin College). After leaving college he taught school, studied law in Boston, and was admitted to the bar in 1832. In 1833 he moved to Fort Wayne, Ind., where he began the practice of law and in 1838 married Susan Mann. In 1835 he was appointed cashier and manager of the Fort Wayne branch of the State Bank of Indiana, a position which he accepted with some hesitation because he possessed "no practical knowledge" of banking. Until 1856 he managed the Fort Wayne branch, and then, until 1863, the State Bank itself, of which he had been made president. The bank weathered the panic of 1837, though not without suspending specie payments; but in the panic of 1857 it was the only state bank in the country, except the Chemical at New York and isolated Kentucky institutions, to avoid such suspension.

McCulloch's larger field of achievement opened to him unexpectedly, as a result of the high repute won through his Indiana career. He visited Washington in 1862 to oppose, on behalf of the old state banks, the projected national banking legislation. When the law had been enacted, in March 1863, he was asked by the secretary of the treasury, Salmon P. Chase [*q.v.*], to launch the new system himself as comptroller of the currency. After some hesitation he consented, and in his arduous task he was completely successful, largely because of his influence with the existing state banks. With the Secretary, whom he greatly respected, he seems to have had but one dispute: he disapproved positively Chase's plan of requiring numerical titles for all state banks rechartered as national institutions. The Comptroller insisted that compulsory relinquishment of well-known titles or "trade names" such as Bank of Commerce or Chemical Bank, in exchange for designation as Tenth or Twentieth National, would seriously impede the acceptance of national charters, and the Secretary had eventually to yield through visible force of circumstances.

McCulloch remained in charge of the national banking system until March 1865. Chase had resigned the Treasury portfolio in 1864 to become chief justice of the Supreme Court; W. P. Fessenden [*q.v.*], his successor, withdrew at the beginning of Lincoln's second term; and Lincoln thereupon offered the place to McCulloch, who thus succeeded to the administration of the Treasury virtually at the moment when the Civil War ended. He was confronted immediately with the question of what to do with the government's war-time issues of paper money, irredeemable in gold. Of this, $450,000,000 was in existence, and its value in gold had ranged early in 1865 from 42¾ cents per dollar in January to 77⅞ cents in May, when the war was definitely over.

In his official declarations, the new Secretary at once recommended retirement of the United States notes and return to the gold standard. In his first report to Congress he took the advanced ground that authority for the government "to issue obligations for a circulating medium as money, and to make these obligations a legal tender," could be found "only in the unwritten law" which warrants assumption in war-time of powers ordinarily withheld and that, since the "present legal tender acts were war measures," he believed that "they ought not to remain in force one day longer than shall be necessary to enable the people to prepare for a return to the constitutional currency" ("Report of the Secretary of the Treasury . . . 1865," *House Executive Document No. 3,* 39 Cong., 1 Sess., pp. 3, 4). He referred to the abnormally high prices, reduction of which was imperative, and declared that "there is more danger to be apprehended from the inability of government to reduce its circulation rapidly enough, than from a too rapid reduction of it." He did not believe "that return to specie payments will bring prices back to the standards of former years," but held that "the longer contraction is deferred, the greater must the fall eventually be and the more serious its consequences" (*Ibid.,* p. 12).

McCulloch's clear and cogent reasoning in this report won him a pledge from the House of Representatives, in a resolution adopted by a handsome majority, for cooperation in his program, "with a view to as early a resumption of specie payments as the business interests will permit" (*Congressional Globe,* 39 Cong., 1 Sess., p. 75), but the bill authorizing issue of bonds for early and progressive retirement of the United States notes failed to get a majority. Congress in 1866 authorized the retirement of only $10,000,000 in the first six months under the law and $4,000,000 per month thereafter. Two years later it revoked even these powers. Resumption was destined not to be actually achieved until eleven or twelve years afterward.

Although failing in his primary purpose, McCulloch continued to conduct the Treasury until March 1869. The policy of regular and large-scale reduction of the funded public debt, the task of readjusting the public revenue and carefully re-introducing federal taxation in the South, occupied all his energies. The Secretary was as bold when occasion warranted as he was habitually cautious. He did not hesitate, for instance, to purchase United States bonds on the market with Treasury funds, in order to support the price when panic was threatened in Wall Street on the news of Lincoln's assassination. With President Andrew Johnson he was able to maintain cordial relations; though he criticized severely Johnson's ill-judged public speeches. Indeed McCulloch described Johnson as one who "in intellectual force had few superiors" (*Men and Measures,* p. 406) and held that his official attitude on public questions of the day was justified by the event and by subsequent Supreme Court decisions.

After his retirement from the Treasury in 1869, McCulloch was for several years a partner in the London banking house of Jay Cooke, McCulloch & Company. The firm survived the failure in 1873 of the affiliated American house of Jay Cooke & Company, continued to meet all payments, and was in due course reorganized under the title McCulloch & Company. McCulloch made one brief reappearance in public life when, in October 1884, at the age of seventy-six, he was asked by President Arthur to resume the office of secretary of the treasury to succeed W. Q. Gresham [*q.v.*], resigned. He held the post until the end of the Arthur administration in the ensuing March. In this brief time he had little opportunity for constructive effort; his chief contribution was the warning, in his "Annual Report . . . on the State of the Finances," in December 1884, of what was happening to the currency. As a result of the compulsory Silver Coinage Act of 1878, he wrote, "It is evident . . . that silver certificates are taking the place of gold, and later a panic or an adverse current of exchange might compel the use in ordinary payments by the Treasury of the gold held for redemption of the United States notes, or the use of silver or silver certificates in payment of its gold obligations" (*House Executive Document No. 2,* 48 Cong., 2 Sess., p. xxxi). The first conditional prediction actually came true in 1894; fulfilment of the second was narrowly averted.

In his last years McCulloch lived in retirement in the neighborhood of Washington, D. C. In 1888 he published *Men and Measures of Half a Century,* containing reminiscences of his early Western career and his official experiences, together with personal impressions of American life and opinions concerning public questions of the period. He died at "Holly Hill," Prince George's County, Md., survived by two sons and two daughters.

[*Men and Measures of Half a Century* and a review in the *Nation* (N. Y.), Mar. 7, 1889; annual reports of the Secretary of the Treasury, 1865–68; E. P. Oberholtzer, *Jay Cooke, Financier of the Civil War* (2 vols., 1907); William Henry Smith, *Hist. of the Cabinet of the U. S.* (1925); E. E. Bourne, *Hist. of Wells and Kennebunk* (1875); Charles Bradbury, *Hist. of Kennebunk Port* (1837); *A Biog Hist. of Eminent and Self-made Men of the State of Ind.* (1880), vol. II; obituary in *Evening Star* (Washington), May 24, 1895.]

A. D. N.

McCULLOCH, OSCAR CARLETON (July 2, 1843–Dec. 10, 1891), Congregational clergyman, son of Carleton B. and Harriet (Pettibone) McCulloch, was born at Fremont, Ohio. After a common-school education, he entered the occupation of his father, that of a drug-salesman. Soon he was covering most of the West for a Chicago firm at a high salary. In 1867, however, although twenty-four years old, he entered the Chicago Theological Seminary, from which he graduated in 1870. Ordained at Sheboygan, Wis., on Oct. 19, 1870, he was pastor of the Congregational church there until 1877. He was then called to Plymouth Church, Indianapolis, Ind., with which he was connected for the remainder of his life. He had unusual executive and business ability, and gave himself tirelessly to the work of organization. As a result his sermons were usually prepared on Saturday evening, or even Sunday morning, and were chiefly straightforward talks, reflecting wide reading, contact with diverse classes of people, and much knowledge of human character. In a few years he had succeeded in building a great institutional church, dedicated Jan. 27, 1884. He discarded the confession of faith as a requirement for admission, and the membership became a group of "friends associated for Christian work and worship." As one of its departments he established Plymouth Institute, in connection with which lecture courses were given; classes conducted in various subjects, including manual training, with work benches in the neighboring high school; and a saving and loan association operated. To aid in worship and services of song, he compiled *Hymns of Faith and Hope* (1884).

His genius for organization was exercised not only through his church, but also in behalf of the charitable needs of the city and state. Practically all the philanthropical enterprises in Indianapolis for a generation were his creations—the Charity Organization Society (1878–79), the Friendly Inn, with its woodyard (1880), Children's Aid Society (1881), Flower Mission Training School for Nurses (1882), Dime Savings and Loan Association (1885–87), free baths (1885), district nursing (1885), and the Summer Mission for Sick Children (1890). He was prominent in the National Conference of Charities and Correction and was its president at the Indianapolis meeting in 1891. His paper on the "Tribe of Ishmael" (*Proceedings,* 1888), read at the Buffalo meeting, July 1888, embodied more than eight years' investigation of six generations of a degenerate inheritance, involving 1,692 individuals and 250 families with intensive studies of thirty. In cooperation with others, he drafted and, in 1889, secured the passage of a law creating the Board of State Charities, of which he was appointed a member; also a law providing for a Board of Children's Guardians for Center Township, Indianapolis (later extended to all counties of the state), to take charge of children of vicious or incompetent parents.

He was married, first, Sept. 8, 1870, to Agnes Buel of Chicago, by whom he had two sons; she died Aug. 31, 1874, and May 8, 1878, he married Alice Barteau of Appleton, Wis., by whom he had three daughters. He died of Hodgkin's disease after a lingering illness and was buried in Crown Hill Cemetery, Indianapolis. In 1892 his widow published *The Open Door,* containing some of his sermons and a biographical sketch.

[In addition to the above, see J. P. Dunn, *Indiana and Indianans* (1919), vol. II; "Plymouth Church," *Ind. Quart. Mag. of Hist.,* Sept. 1911; *Proc. of the Nat. Conference of Charities and Correction,* 1892; *Congregational Year Book,* 1892; *The Advance,* Dec. 17, 1891; *Indianapolis Sentinel,* Dec. 11, 1891; McCulloch file, Indiana Board of State Charities.]

C. B. C.

McCULLOUGH, ERNEST (May 22, 1867–Oct. 1, 1931), structural engineer, editor, author, and soldier, was born on Staten Island, N. Y., the son of James and Caroline (McBlain) McCullough. His formal education was obtained in the high school of Wyandotte (now Kansas City), Kan., the Institute of Technology in Chicago, Ill. (1884–85), and the Van der Naillen

School of Practical Engineering in San Francisco, where he took courses in engineering and architecture. Upon graduation, in 1887, he engaged in municipal engineering work in San Francisco until 1898. During this period he acted as consulting engineer of the Merchants' Association, served as chief engineer for the Midwinter Exposition, built the Sutro Baths, and for three years was editor of *Engineer and Contractor*. Removing to Lewiston, Idaho, he continued his municipal work there, as city engineer and in private practice. In 1903 he became chief engineer of the Municipal Engineering & Construction Company, in Chicago. During his two years in this position he had charge of putting in one-half mile of reinforced concrete storm conduit, being one of the first American engineers to do reinforced-concrete work. As a specialist in reinforced concrete and structural steel, he acquired a large practice. More than sixteen miles of sewers were constructed by him in St. Louis, Mo., and he superintended the establishment of water purification plants for the Union Stock Yards in Chicago. For a time he served as city engineer of Cedar Rapids, Iowa. From February 1916 to March 1917 he was in charge of the fireproof construction bureau of the Portland Cement Association, being one of the first experts employed by that organization. He was one of a committee of three engaged by the city of Chicago to prepare regulations for concrete flat-slab design. Owing largely to his initiative and aggressiveness, moreover, the state of Illinois, July 5, 1915, passed a law for the licensing of structural engineers. In 1909 while in Chicago, McCullough was editor of *Engineering-Contracting* (later, *Engineering and Contracting*), and in 1910 associate editor of *Railway Age Gazette* (later *Railway Age*). He also taught night classes in engineering at the Young Men's Christian Association College and at Lewis Institute, where he was well liked by his students, for he shared with them the "short cuts" he had learned from long and varied experience.

In June 1917, after a few months' connection with the Stone & Webster Corporation of Boston, Mass., he began service in the World War, going to France as acting chief engineer of the American Red Cross. Later, he entered the chemical warfare service, in which branch he attained the rank of lieutenant-colonel. He was gassed at the battle of Cambrai in 1917. Returning to the United States in August 1919, he became assistant commandant of the Lakehurst Proving Grounds and director of the School for Officers of the Chemical Warfare Service.

McCullough resigned from the army in July 1920. After being connected for a short time with the Semet-Solvay Company, Syracuse, N. Y., as structural engineer, he became, in 1921, associate editor of *The American Architect and the Architectural Review.* In 1923 and 1924 he was associated with the construction firm of Dwight P. Robinson & Company, Incorporated, in New York. He then went to London, and for two years was chief structural engineer for Vickers and International Combustion, Limited. Returning to New York City in 1925, he became an editor of *Building Age* (later *American Builder and Building Age*), and served as such until 1928, the last year as editor-in-chief. He resigned to engage in writing and in practice as a consultant.

McCullough was the author of numerous books, among the best known of which are: *Engineering Work in Towns and Small Cities* (1906, 1908); *Reinforced Concrete* (1908); *Engineering as a Vocation* (1911); *Practical Surveying* (1915, 1921); *Practical Structural Design* (1917, 1921, 1926); *How to Spend Your Money* (1931). He was likewise a frequent contributor to magazines on engineering and economic topics. For his paper on "The Structural Engineer in America" (*Structural Engineer,* March 1925) he received in 1925 the medal of the Institution of Structural Engineers, London. He was twice married: first, in 1891, to Elizabeth Townsend Seymour of Troy, N. Y., who died in 1918, survived by their four children; second, in 1919, at Tours, France, to Thérèse Claquin.

[*Who's Who in America,* 1930–31; *Who's Who in Engineering,* 1931; *Trans. Am. Soc. Civil Engineers,* vol. XCVI (1932); *N. Y. Times,* Oct. 2, 1931; letters from a son, Capt. G. S. McCullough, and from a friend, B. F. Affleck, president of the Universal Cement Co.]

B. A. R.

McCULLOUGH, JOHN (Nov. 14, 1832–Nov. 8, 1885), actor, made his way in the world and on the stage through his own individual efforts, aided by an innate talent for his profession. He was born of peasant parentage in a little village not far from Coleraine, Londonderry, near the northeast coast of Ireland. His father, James McCullough, was a poor farmer, and his mother, Mary, left at her death in 1844 a family including also three daughters and her husband. John McCullough emigrated to the United States in the spring of 1847 some weeks after one of his sisters had made the trip. He went to Philadelphia, where resided a cousin, with whom he obtained employment as a chairmaker. His father, with his two other sisters, followed soon afterward. At the age of fifteen he could neither read nor write, but he soon overcame that handicap, and within a few years by reading and study, by practical experience as an amateur with a Philadelphia dramatic club, and by taking lessons with a teacher, he found himself well equipped in body and mind for the profession he followed almost uninterruptedly for twenty-seven years. He made his first professional appearance on Aug. 15, 1857, as Thomas in *The Belle's Stratagem* at the Arch Street Theatre, Philadelphia. His advance was slow but always forward and was the undeniable result of close study and hard work. He remained in Philadelphia until the summer of 1860, and was then engaged by Edward L. Davenport for the company at the Howard Athenæum in Boston, acting there through the season of 1860–61. Again in Philadelphia, he reached the turning point in his career when he was chosen by Edwin Forrest to act second parts with him. He first acted with Forrest while on tour with him in Boston in October 1861, as Pythias to the star's Damon in John Banim's famous play. He was soon, as Forrest's leading man, playing Laertes, Macduff, Iago, Edgar, Richmond, Icilius, and Titus, also seconding him in those dramas that were Forrest's personal property, *Metamora, The Gladiator, Jack Cade,* and *The Broker of Bogota.*

After traveling with Forrest for several seasons, McCullough spent two years at McGuire's Theatre in San Francisco then entered a partnership with Lawrence Barrett at the California Theatre which continued until November 1870. He remained in San Francisco as sole manager of the theatre until a heavy financial loss in 1875 compelled his permanent abandonment of theatre management. In 1873 he had begun a series of tours over the country, and for season after season he was everywhere received with a continuous favor that did not abate until his compulsory retirement on account of illness. Frequent engagements in New York added to his reputation not merely as Forrest's successor in robust characters, but also through his own merits. In 1881 he played a brief engagement in London. At the height of his career he was one of the most eminent and popular actors of his day. The word noble was frequently, and justly, applied to his characterizations. He found in the tragedies of Shakespeare, in the classic plays of our language such as *Virginius, Richelieu,* and *Damon and Pythias,* and also in the melodramas first made famous by Forrest, a fitting and expressive means for the denotement of a dramatic skill that was always effective even though it fell short of inspiration and genius. Like Forrest, he was imposing in stature, forceful in voice and action, and although he lacked the finer powers that gave spiritual significance to the interpretations of other actors, he was in many ways the real embodiment of a long line of theatrical figures. William Winter has said (*Brief Chronicles,* part 2, p. 215): "He played many parts, but the parts in which he was best—in which his nature was liberated and his triumph supreme—were distinctly those which rest upon the basis of the genial human heart and proceed in the realm of the affections. He displayed artistic resources, intellectual intention, and sometimes a subtle professional skill in such characters as Hamlet and Richelieu; but he never was in sympathy with them, and he did not make them his own. He was an heroic actor."

The last days of McCullough were pathetic. After vainly seeking renewed health in Germany, he returned to the stage for a brief period, his final mental and physical breakdown occurring at McVicker's Theatre in Chicago, Sept. 29, 1884, during a performance of *The Gladiator.* The audience, not realizing the cause of his failure to go on with his part, broke out into laughter, and when he was helped before the curtain by two members of his company, he said: "Ladies and gentlemen, you are the worst mannered audience I ever saw. If you had suffered tonight as I have, you would never have done this. Good night." He never acted again. After a while he was placed by friends in a sanitarium, remaining there from June 27 to Oct. 25, 1885, being removed thence to his home in Philadelphia, where he died two weeks later. He was married on Apr. 8, 1849, to Letitia McClain (or McClane) who survived him. They had two sons, James and William F. Johnson McCullough. In 1888 an ornate monument was erected with elaborate ceremonies in Mount Moriah Cemetery, Philadelphia.

[William Winter, *Brief Chronicles,* part 2 (1889); Susie C. Clark, *John McCullough as Man, Actor and Spirit* (1905); *In Memory of John McCullough* (1889); Percy MacKaye, *Epoch: The Life of Steele MacKaye* (1927), vol. I; John R. Towse, *Sixty Years of the Theatre* (1916); *Daily Inter Ocean* (Chicago), Nov. 9–11, 1885; *Boston Transcript, N. Y. Tribune, N. Y. Times,* Nov. 9, 1885.] E. F. E.

McCULLOUGH, JOHN GRIFFITH (Sept. 16, 1835–May 29, 1915), lawyer, attorney general of California, governor of Vermont, railroad president, was born in Newark, Del., of Scotch and Welsh ancestry, the son of Alexander and Rebecca (Griffith) McCullough. At the age of seven he was left an orphan. He graduated with honors from Delaware College (University of Delaware), in 1855 and for the next three years studied law at the University of Pennsylvania, receiving the degree of LL.B. in 1858. A complete failure of health drove him to California. Here, at Mariposa, in the foothills, he opened a law office. Political honors came quickly in the early days of California, and in 1861 the newcomer was elected to the legislature by a coalition of Republicans and Union Democrats. The following year he was sent to the state Senate. By this time the Union men had control of the state government. Several Republicans aspired to the United States Senate, among them Trenor W. Park [*q.v.*], a Vermonter who had come to San Francisco and made a considerable fortune at the bar and by wise investments. McCullough supported Park, and in the caucus just before the election exposed the attempt of a rival to buy off one of Park's adherents. This incident led to recriminations, and eventually the legislature chose a war Democrat. In 1863 McCullough was elected attorney general and served one term of four years. While in office he represented the state in some 250 cases, his experience in enforcing ill-considered statutes leading him in one of his reports to declare that "too much legislation is one of the curses of the country." He urged revision and codification, provided the legislature would employ competent legal talent; he criticized the code of criminal procedure and especially the rule making inadmissible the testimony of Asiatics; he urged a conservative policy in grants to railroads. Defeated for reëlection along with the entire ticket, for the next five years he had a lucrative practice in San Francisco.

By 1863 Park had returned to Bennington, Vt., and here, Aug. 30, 1871, McCullough was married to his daughter, Eliza. Shortly thereafter, Park became president of the Panama Railroad, and in 1875 McCullough, having moved to Bennington, became the vice-president. Upon Park's death in 1883, with the support of Ferdinand de Lesseps, whose company now controlled the road, McCullough was made president and served as such until 1888. In the meantime he was elected to the directorates of other roads, among them the New York, Lake Erie & Western. Of the executive committee of its board he was made chairman in 1888. "The company was bankrupt *de facto*" (not an unusual experience for the Erie), and only by the "tact and resourcefulness" of the new régime was it kept out of the bankruptcy court (Mott, *post*, p. 273). Finally in 1893 it was unable to renew its floating debt of nine millions, and to preclude attachments and the sacrifice of collaterals a friendly suit was brought and President John King and McCullough were appointed co-receivers. After some disagreement among the various interests, a reorganization was effected late in 1895. It has been called "the best that had ever been applied to the rehabilitation of Erie's affairs" (Daggett, *post*, pp. 72–73). For some years thereafter the road was prosperous. McCullough was also interested in the Central Vermont and the Bennington & Rutland railroads, serving as president of the latter from 1883 to 1900.

During all this time he took a part in politics. As a delegate to the Republican national convention of 1880 he favored the nomination of Senator George F. Edmunds for the presidency, and in the conventions of 1888 and 1900, as a delegate-at-large, he supported the successful candidates from the start. He was a member of the Vermont Senate in 1898 and for a time hoped to head the state ticket. In matters of national policy he favored active competition for world markets and a "broader reciprocity" in the tariff; the growing friendliness with England met his hearty approval; he was mistrustful of the strain which the acquisition of the Philippines put upon American political institutions. In 1902 he entered upon what proved a lively scramble for the office of governor. Since 1852 Vermont had had prohibition; those favoring it and those opposed were about evenly balanced. In the pre-convention canvass Percival W. Clement, one of McCullough's rivals for the nomination, made an attack on prohibition. The convention adopted a plank calling for a referendum, and nominated McCullough for governor. Clement bolted his party, charging the Republicans with insincerity. McCullough received only a plurality of the votes, but was chosen by the legislature. The next year a license–local option referendum was carried by a narrow margin. In his messages as governor McCullough advocated a primary election law, the development of roads without federal aid, and the conservation of the esthetic and economic values of forests and rivers. After the expiration of his term he continued his railroad and banking connections until his death, which occurred in New York City.

[T. H. Hittell, *Hist. of Cal.*, vol. IV (1897); W. H. Crockett, *Vermont: The Green Mountain State*, vol. IV (1921); E. H. Mott, *Between the Ocean and the Lakes: the Story of Erie* (1899); Stuart Daggett, *Railroad Reorganization* (1908); *National Mag.* (N. Y.), Mar. 1892; *Proc. Vt. Hist. Soc., 1915–16* (1918); *Who's Who in America*, 1914–15; *N. Y. Times*, May 30, 1915.] C. F.

McCURDY, RICHARD ALDRICH (Jan. 29, 1835–Mar. 6, 1916), insurance official, was born in New York City, a son of Robert H. and Gertrude Mercer (Lee) McCurdy. His father, a leading drygoods importer in his day, was descended from John McCurdy who emigrated from County Antrim, Ireland, in 1745 and became a merchant in New York City. The son grew up in New York, enjoying many advantages. At twenty-one he was graduated from Harvard Law School and at once entered practice in his native city. Such interest in his profession as he may have had at first seems to have yielded to the demands of a business career. His father was director of the Mutual Life Insurance Company and in 1860 Richard was appointed counsel for the organization. After serving five years in that capacity he was asked to fill a vacancy in the office of vice-president. Thereafter administrative matters absorbed his energies and he never returned to law practice. From the time he was thirty until he was seventy his activities were completely centered in the affairs of the insurance company. In the first half of this period his rôle, so far as the public knew, was subordinate; he was supposed to be acquiring a knowledge and grasp of details. After his election as president, in 1885, he gradually emerged as a dominant, even autocratic personality. His administration was marked by unparalleled gains in business and resources: huge reserve funds were credited to the company, and statisticians busied themselves with the computations of the Mutual Life's assets.

Meanwhile, rumor-mongers were equally busy circulating reports that the policy-holders' money had been squandered by the executives. Finally came the investigation of the New York life-insurance companies by the Armstrong committee of the state legislature in 1905–06, in the course of which Charles Evans Hughes as counsel elicited from testimony given by McCurdy himself, by his son John, and by other officers of the Mutual Life, many sensational facts for which no satisfactory explanation was forthcoming. It remained for a committee appointed by the company's trustees to verify the most damaging of the disclosures and to complete the "house-cleaning." It was found that McCurdy, having taken office as president at a salary of $30,000, had received repeated increases until by 1905 his yearly stipend was $150,000, while a group of relatives also on the company's payroll brought the total, in salaries and commissions, annually paid out to the family, to more than $500,000. Large contributions had been made to political campaign and legislative corruption funds, while policy dividends had decreased. The trustees concluded that McCurdy and officers intimately associated with him were in debt to the company in the sum of $8,000,000 and brought suit to recover that amount. McCurdy had at first offered to take a cut in salary to $75,000 and then resigned. The suit was withdrawn, however, McCurdy paying $815,000 as a refund—$750,000 in cash. He escaped criminal prosecution. During the years 1906–07 he lived in France but returned in 1908 to Morristown, N. J., where in his years of large income he had built a house supposed to have cost $1,000,000. There he died in his eighty-second year. He had outlived his wife, Sarah Ellen Little of Boston, Mass., and was survived by two daughters and a son.

[*Testimony Taken Before the Joint Committee of the Senate and Assembly of the State of N. Y. to Investigate . . . Life Insurance Companies* (10 vols., 1905–06); B. J. Hendrick, *The Story of Life Insurance* (1907); H. S. Beardsley, "The Despotism of Combined Millions," *Era Mag.*, Nov. 1904, Oct. 1905; *Campaign and Other Contributions Made by Life Insurance Companies Doing Business in Tenn.* (1906); G. T. Little, *Descendants of Geo. Little* (1882), p. 209; *Nation* (N. Y.), Oct. 26, 1905; the *Eastern Underwriter,* Mar. 10, 1916; *Weekly Underwriter,* Mar. 11, 1916; *World* (N. Y.), and *N. Y. Times,* Mar. 7, 1916.] W. B. S.

McCUTCHEON, GEORGE BARR (July 26, 1866–Oct. 23, 1928), novelist, eldest of three sons of John Barr and Clara (Glick) McCutcheon, was born in Tippecanoe County, near Lafayette, Ind. His father, descended from Scotch ancestors who settled in Virginia and Kentucky, was a drover with literary tastes, which evinced themselves in the authorship of a play, produced by a cast of his neighbors. George's childhood was spent at farm chores and study at a country school. He taught himself to draw and then taught his brother John, who became a cartoonist. At the age of eight he wrote his first tale of adventure, "Panther Jim," which was never finished. When the McCutcheon family moved into Lafayette, the boys had a better school and continued their writing and drawing in secret, often by candlelight in the cellar. They were also athletic and played football and lacrosse. In 1882–83 George was a student at Purdue University at Lafayette, where his chums were his brother John and George Ade. He reported Purdue news for the *Lafayette Journal* and before long left college and took a regular reporter's post on the paper at six dollars a week. In 1893 he went to the *Lafayette Daily Courier* as city editor and remained until 1901.

McCutcheon's first published short story was "The Ante-Mortem Condition of George Ramor," which appeared in the *National Magazine,* October 1896. His letters in dialect, "Waddleton Mail," had previously had newspaper publication. In spare moments at the editorial office he wrote a romance, *Pootoo's Gods,* which at first sold poorly, but later, under the new title *Nedra* (1905), became a season's success. *Graustark*

(1901), written in the same way and sold for $500, brought McCutcheon his first fame and is said to have cleared over $250,000 for publishers and theatrical producers. The publishers later voluntarily paid him royalties. This tale of a mythical Balkan country, whose name was a combination of the German words *grau* and *stark,* with its capital Edelweiss and its Princess Yetive, actually deceived many readers who wrote to ask McCutcheon for the best route to Graustark. His next romances were *Castle Craneycrow* (1902), *Brewster's Millions* (1902), and *The Sherrods* (1903). To test the sales value of his name he published *Brewster's Millions* under the pseudonym Richard Greaves. It became a best seller when *The Sherrods* had only moderate sales. His other romances, many of them Graustark tales, include: *The Day of the Dog* (1904), a story in which a dog is the villain; *Beverly of Graustark* (1904); *Jane Cable* (1906); *The Daughter of Anderson Crow* (1907); *Mary Midthorne* (1911), a realistic Indiana story and his own favorite work; *The Hollow of Her Hand* (1912); *A Fool and His Money* (1913); *The Prince of Graustark* (1914); *Sherry* (1919); *Anderson Crow, Detective* (1920); *West Wind Drift* (1920); *East of the Setting Sun* (1924); *The Inn of the Hawk and Raven* (1927); and *The Merivales* (1929).

McCutcheon wrote with zest and lived for the time in his own romances. For *Graustark* he prepared a complete geographical and genealogical plan. He wrote only one draft, with pencil, from an elaborate outline, and produced about a thousand words a day. He worked best in the afternoon, but he frequently wrote in the evenings. Though his success was in the realm of romance, he much preferred realism. With an output of almost two books a year, he published much that was hasty and slight. Even at his best, he can hardly be called a great romanticist, but he furnished wholesome, not too extravagant, romances to a public weary of extreme realism and materialism. One editorial at the time of his death said that he supplied innocent happiness for "many college boys, kitchen maids, and daughters of millionaires" (*New York Times,* Oct. 24, 1928). On Sept. 26, 1904, he was married to Mrs. Marie Van Antwerp Fay. They made their home in New York City. He died suddenly, at a luncheon of the Dutch Treat Club at the Hotel Martinique, and his ashes were buried in Lafayette, Ind.

[*Who's Who in America,* 1928–29; Arnold Patrick, "Getting into Six Figures: George Barr McCutcheon," *Bookman,* May 1925; A. B. Maurice, "The History of their Books: Concerning George Barr McCutcheon," *Bookman,* Jan. 1929; John T. and G. B. McCutcheon, "Brothers Under the Pen," *Collier's,* Apr. 11, 1925; "Buying a Ticket to Graustark," *Lit. Digest,* Nov. 17, 1928; *Indianapolis Star,* Oct. 24, 1928; *N. Y. Times,* Oct. 24, 25, Nov. 15, 1928.] S. G. B.

McDANIEL, HENRY DICKERSON (Sept. 4, 1836–July 25, 1926), lawyer, Confederate soldier, governor of Georgia, industrialist, was born in Monroe, Ga., at the home of his mother's parents. His father, Ira Oliver McDaniel, a native South Carolinian of Virginian ancestry, had come to Georgia as an instructor at Mercer University, then located at Penfield, in Green County, and had married Rebecca J. Walker, member of an important Georgia family. About 1850 the McDaniels removed to Atlanta, at that time a small town at the meeting point of three principal railway systems of the state. There Ira McDaniel became a merchant and a leading citizen. After passing through the schools of Atlanta, Henry enrolled as a student in Mercer University, which by that time had been removed to Macon. After his graduation, in 1856, he settled in Monroe and began the practice of law. He was the youngest member of the secession convention of 1861. Though opposing secession, when hostilities began he joined the army as a lieutenant and during the next two years was promoted to major. He commanded Anderson's brigade on the third day at Gettysburg, and on the retreat through Maryland was wounded and captured. He was sent to a military hospital for five months, and from December 1863 to July 28, 1865, was imprisoned on Johnson's Island, Lake Erie.

On the close of the war he returned to Monroe, resumed his law practice, and was a member of the constitutional convention of 1865. During the next seven years he was prevented by political disability from taking any overt part in the political life of the state, but there is reason to believe that he wielded large influence in a quiet way. Bitterly opposed to the reconstruction policies and to the control of the state government by those who furthered them, he labored indefatigably for the restoration of home rule and for the material rehabilitation of Georgia. On the passage of the General Amnesty Act he was elected to the lower house of the General Assembly (1872) and became acting chairman of the finance committee, which at that time included the ways and means and appropriations committees. In 1874 he became a member of the state Senate, and was twice reëlected. In that body he was chairman of the finance committee and of the judiciary committee. On the death of Gov. Alexander H. Stephens (1883), McDaniel was chosen governor to fill the unexpired term and was reëlected in 1884. In this office he displayed financial ability of a high order and managed the affairs of Georgia with conspicuous success. The state bonded debt was reduced by a million dollars, and the tax rate was lower than at any time since 1865.

McDaniel was much interested in railroads. He was the author of the act of 1874, providing for the taxation of railroads in the same manner as other property, and was co-author of the act of 1879 creating the state railroad commission. For forty years he was a director of the Georgia Railroad and Banking Company. A memorial presented to the board on the occasion of his death attributed the success of the corporation largely to his wise leadership. He was also director of several other banking and railroad corporations, and of manufacturing enterprises. Always noted for his sound judgment in business matters, through careful management and wise investment he amassed a considerable fortune.

Not the least of McDaniel's public services were those rendered during his thirty-eight years as a member of the board of trustees of the University of Georgia. For twenty-four years he was chairman of the board. To the management of university affairs he brought the same ability that had characterized his public and business career, and it was during his chairmanship of the board that the modern expansion of the university began. On Dec. 20, 1865, he married Hester C. Felker, daughter of Stephen Felker, of Monroe, Ga., by whom he had two children. He died at his home in Monroe.

[W. J. Northen, *Men of Mark in Ga.*, vol. IV (1908); *Biog. Souvenir of the States of Ga. and Fla.* (1889); P. W. Meldrim, "Memorial of Henry D. McDaniel," *Report of the Forty-fourth Ann. Session of the Ga. Bar Asso.* (1927); *Who's Who in America*, 1926–27; L. L. Knight, *Ga.'s Bi-Centennial Memoirs and Memories* (1923), vol. II; *Atlanta Constitution*, July 26, 1926; information from a son, Sanders McDaniel.]

R. P. B—s.

McDILL, JAMES WILSON (Mar. 4, 1834–Feb. 28, 1894), representative, senator, and member of the Interstate Commerce Commission, the son of Frances (Wilson) and John McDill, who was a graduate of Miami University and a United Presbyterian minister, was born in Monroe, Ohio. He was taken by his parents to Hanover, Ind., where his father died in 1840. He attended the preparatory department of Hanover College in 1844 and 1845. In that year his mother went back to Ohio to live at South Salem with her father, the Rev. Robert G. Wilson, who had been a Presbyterian minister at Chillicothe and president of Ohio University at Athens. Here the boy profited by the teaching of his grandfather and attended Salem Academy. In 1853 he graduated from Miami University. After a year of teaching in Jefferson Academy at Kossuth, Des Moines County, Iowa, he studied law in the office of Samuel Galloway [*q.v.*] at Columbus, Ohio, and was admitted to the bar in 1856. The next year he began practice in Afton, Iowa, and, in August 1857, was married to Narcissa Fullenwider. They had five children. He went to Iowa when pioneer conditions still prevailed and when Eastern settlers led by James Grimes were turning the state from Democracy to Republicanism on the slavery issue. In this movement, as friend and admirer of Grimes, he played his part and has left a vivid picture of the period and its leaders in "The Making of Iowa," which was published in the *Iowa Historical Record* for October 1891. He became judge of Union County and during the war held minor federal offices in Washington, D. C. Returning to Iowa in 1866, he practised law in Afton, which remained his home until his removal to Creston in 1885. After presiding over the circuit and district courts he was a member of Congress from 1873 to 1877, where he did useful service on the committees on the Pacific railroad and on public lands.

Declining a third term he hoped to return to the practice of law, but a new factor in Iowa politics soon brought him into public service again. Ever since their construction the railroads had been regulated only by the common law. Their officials regarded them "from a purely proprietary standpoint" (*Report, post*, II, p. 944), and grave abuses had developed. Impelled by the Grange and similar organizations, Iowa in 1874 had passed a law fixing a maximum tariff and forbidding discriminations. The law was sustained by the courts, but it lacked provision for effective enforcement. In consequence there was substituted in 1878 a board of railroad commissioners empowered to supervise the roads, investigate all alleged violations of state laws, and modify unreasonable charges. Governor Gear desired a strong commission and appointed McDill one of the Board. After filling out Samuel J. Kirkwood's unexpired term in the Senate, which extended to Mar. 4, 1883, he was reappointed to the railroad commission for another three years. In 1885 a committee, with Shelby M. Cullom [*q.v.*] as chairman, was appointed in the United States Senate to investigate the regulation of freight and passenger transportation. As an Iowa commissioner, McDill testified that the chief objection to the Iowa method of regulation was that the commission lacked power to enforce its decisions. He maintained that the only method by which there could be any intelligent and sufficient control would be through a federal commission authorized to lower rates when too high, while the right of appeal to the courts was reserved to the railroads only after they had complied with the orders of the commission (*Ibid.*, II, pp. 948–50). The result of this investigation was the creation of the Interstate Commerce Commission, to which McDill was appointed in 1892 by President Harrison. He died at Creston, while serving in this capacity. As a man he was unpretentious, deliberate in thought and action. As a lawyer he was regarded as a safe counselor, who always tried his cases on law and evidence. On the bench he was fair and approachable though not lacking in dignity. He exercised great care in considering cases and measures and had the confidence of his associates.

["Report on Interstate Commerce, with Testimony, and Establishment Recommended," *Sen. Rept. 46*, 49 Cong., 1 Sess. (1886), pt. II; E. H. Stiles, *Recollections and Sketches of Notable Lawyers and Public Men of Early Iowa* (1916); B. F. Gue, *Hist. of Iowa* (copr. 1903), vols. II, III, IV; *Biog. and Hist. Record of Ringgold and Union Counties, Iowa* (1887); L. S. Evans, *A Standard Hist. of Ross County, Ohio* (1917), vol. I; *Illustrated Centennial Sketches, Map and Directory of Union County, Iowa* (1876); A. M. Antrobus, *Hist. of Des Moines County, Iowa* (1915), vol. II, p. 534; *General Cat. of the Grads. and Former Students of Miami Univ.* (1910?); *Iowa State Register* (Des Moines), Mar. 1, 1894; information from McDill's daughter, Mrs. Elmer Bradford, Watkins, Colo.] C. E. P.

McDONALD, CHARLES JAMES (July 9, 1793–Dec. 16, 1860), jurist, governor of Georgia, was born in Charleston, S. C., the son of Charles and Mary (Glas) Burn McDonald. The elder McDonald had emigrated from Scotland in 1761 and about 1794 he took his family to Georgia and settled in Hancock County. The son was sent to South Carolina College (now the University of South Carolina) and was graduated in 1816. After studying law for a short time under Joel Crawford, an eminent Georgia lawyer, he was admitted to the bar in 1817 and began practice in Milledgeville, Ga. In a few years he entered upon a career of public service and held office successively as solicitor-general (1822–25) and judge (1825–30) of the Flint circuit; as a member of the General Assembly of Georgia (1830, 1834–37); as governor (1839–43); and as justice of the supreme court of the state (1855–59). His terms as governor occurred during a period of economic distress following the crisis of 1837. The state in 1828 had set up a bank of issue known as the Central Bank, entirely state-owned, and for a number of years Georgia enjoyed the enviable situation of being able to dispense with state taxation, the profits of the bank being more than sufficient to meet the state's obligations, which at that time were small. The "general tax" usually collected was remitted to the counties for their support. With the coming of economic difficulties in the late thirties, the bank's profits were inadequate to finance the state, but the legislature could not be induced to resort to taxation. Instead, the bank was required to borrow money to meet the legislative appropriations. The capital stock of the bank was in this way consumed and when McDonald came into office a $300,000 obligation of the bank had been protested for non-payment. It became McDonald's duty to devise means for rehabilitating the state financially. He finally prevailed upon the legislature to resume its taxing function and the general tax was reënacted in 1841 for the first time in six years. The legislature also empowered the Governor to issue $1,000,000 of state bonds for the redemption of state bank notes. In this way the state's credit was restored.

In national politics McDonald was a Democrat of the strict-construction school. He was an advocate of secession in 1850 and went as the leader of the Georgia delegation to the Nashville Convention where he was vice-president of the first session and president of the second session. Along with Rhett, Barnwell, and Colquitt, he attempted to commit the convention to extreme action. Unionists considered it of prime importance that Georgia should set the example to other Southern states of acquiescing in Clay's compromise measures. Toombs, Stephens, and Cobb organized a Constitutional Union party on that issue with Cobb as the gubernatorial candidate. McDonald was nominated by the opposing group, which took the name Southern Rights party. Its platform denounced Clay's compromise measures and specifically upheld the sovereign right of secession. In the election McDonald was overwhelmingly defeated, carrying only twenty-one of the ninety-five counties. In 1819 McDonald had married Anne Franklin, of Macon, Ga., by whom he had five children. After her death he was married to Mrs. Ruffin, of Virginia. Some time after his term as governor he removed to Marietta, Ga., and there he died.

[See R. H. Shryock, *Ga. and the Union in 1850* (1926); St. George L. Sioussat, "Tenn., the Compromise of 1850, and the Nashville Convention," *Miss. Valley Hist. Rev.*, Dec. 1915; R. P. Brooks, "Howell Cobb and the Crisis of 1850," *Ibid.*, Dec. 1917; U. B. Phillips, "Ga. and State Rights," *Ann. Report of the Am. Hist. Asso. for the Year 1901* (1902), vol. II, and "The Correspondence of Robert Toombs, Alexander H. Stephens, and Howell Cobb," *Ibid.* for the year 1911 (1913), vol. II; and W. J. Northen, *Men of Mark in Ga.*, vol. II (1910). The facts bearing on lineage and the dates used in this sketch were taken from the family Bible of Mrs. Mary Ann Atkinson, eldest daughter of McDonald.] R. P. B—s.

MACDONALD, JAMES WILSON ALEXANDER (Aug. 25, 1824–Aug. 14, 1908), a sculptor often signing his works Wilson MacDonald, was born in Steubenville, Ohio, the son of Isaac MacDonald. In childhood he showed an aptitude for art by drawing caricatures, but he was without advantages for art study. At sixteen he saw for the first time a plaster bust of Washington and resolved to become a sculptor. His father wished him to be a blacksmith. The outcome was that he ran away to St. Louis, Mo., where he worked by day in a publishing house and at night studied art, encouraged and instructed by the painter Alfred Waugh. Within eleven years he became the senior partner in the publishing firm. Meanwhile he was pursuing art as well as business. At twenty-one he modeled his first bust in clay, a likeness of a business associate. He studied anatomy in St. Louis and is said to have had a year's study in New York in 1849. Five years later, having given up business, he became well known as a sculptor through his bust of Thomas H. Benton, senator from Missouri. This work was studied from life and was said to have been the first portrait-bust cut from marble west of the Mississippi. His early attempts in ideal figures were his "Italia" and "Joan of Arc." Later came "La Somnambula," a life-size marble figure.

After the Civil War, MacDonald settled permanently in New York City. Among his portrait-busts are those of the jurist Charles O'Conor, ordered by the New York bar and presented to the supreme court of the state (now in the Appellate Court Building, New York City); of Thurlow Weed, of the poet Bryant, "Prince" John van Buren, and James T. Brady, the last a posthumous work. His heroic bronze bust of Brig.-Gen. Winfield Scott Hancock, given to the city in 1891, is in Hancock Square. In New York's Central Park, near the head of the Mall, is his heroic seated bronze statue of the American poet and wit, Fitz-Greene Halleck, placed in 1877. It does not suffer greatly in comparison with the adjacent contemporary but more monumental effigies of Robert Burns and Sir Walter Scott, by Sir John Steell, but it is distinctly inferior to two neighboring works by J. Q. A. Ward, the "Indian Hunter" and the "William Shakespeare." It is fair to consider these five works together, since all were made in practically the same decade. Other important productions by MacDonald are bronze statues—the "Edward Bates," Forest Park, St. Louis, the "General Custer," West Point, N. Y., and the "General Nathaniel Lyon." Committees on monumental projects have valued his sculpture for its realistic correctness. Besides sculpturing, he painted a few portraits and landscapes, wrote art criticism, and lectured on anatomy. Several accounts state that he possessed the original model of the Houdon bust of Washington, and that he received many orders for bronze copies. Expert criticism has rejected the attribution to Houdon of MacDonald's model, and the matter remains controversial (C. H. Hart and Edward Biddle, *Memoirs of the Life and Works of Jean Antoine Houdon,* 1911, p. 224). MacDonald died at Yonkers, N. Y.

[H. T. Tuckerman, *Book of the Artists* (1867); Clara E. Clement Waters and Laurence Hutton, *Artists of the Nineteenth Century and Their Works* (1879); *Cat. of the Works of Art Belonging to the City of N. Y.* (1909); *Biog. Sketches of Am. Artists* (1924), pub. by the Mich. State Lib.; Edna Marie Clark, *Ohio Art and Artists* (1932); *Am. Art News,* Sept. 12, 1908; *N. Y. Herald,* Aug. 15, 1908.]

A. A.

MCDONALD, JOHN BARTHOLOMEW (Nov. 7, 1844–Mar. 17, 1911), contractor and railway builder, was born in Fermoy, County Cork, Ireland, the son of Bartholomew and Mary McDonald. In 1847 his parents emigrated to America and settled on the West side in New York City. From small beginnings the elder McDonald built up a successful contracting business, and with the *flair* for politics that characterized so many Irish immigrants he became an active worker in Tammany Hall and eventually attained a position of considerable influence, serving as a member of the Board of Aldermen for many years. John McDonald received a common-school education in the New York public schools and at eighteen started his business career as a clerk in the office of the register of deeds, a position obtained through his father's influence. In the same manner he obtained somewhat later a position as time-keeper on the construction of the dam at Boyd's Corners, a part of the Croton water-supply project. He rose from this position to inspector on the construction of the Vanderbilt tunnels of the New York Central and Hudson River railroads located above Forty-second Street. He was a keen observer and made the most of his experience on the two construction projects. When still in his early twenties, he resigned his position as inspector to make his first venture in contracting on a small subcontract of the New York Central's improvements at Ninety-sixth Street. In this undertaking he had the benefit of his father's financial backing and business experience, and he completed his contract with marked success.

Shortly afterward his father died and McDonald took over his contracting business. While this was a well-established and prosperous business, it was limited in scope, and the younger

McDonald had both the ambition and the technical qualifications for success in a larger field. This was the great period of railway expansion in the United States and Canada, and into this field he threw his entire energy, rising during the two decades following 1870 to a position in the front rank of railroad constructors. Among the important projects on which he was engaged during this period were: the line of the West Shore Railroad from Weehawken to Buffalo; the Potomac Valley Railroad; the Illinois Central from Elgin, Ill., to Dodgeville, Wis.; the Trenton cut-off of the Pennsylvania Railroad; and the Baltimore & Ohio from Baltimore to Philadelphia. He also executed subcontracts on the Boston, Hoosac Tunnel, & Western Railway, the Georgian Bay branch of the Canadian Pacific Railway, and the Delaware, Lackawanna & Western line from Binghamton to Buffalo. His most remarkable achievement and the one which gained him a national reputation was the Baltimore belt-line railroad—a project to connect the Baltimore & Ohio lines by a tunnel, some two miles long, through the heart of the city of Baltimore. This was a most difficult and expensive piece of work, involving a contract in excess of $8,000,000. The plan was originated and promoted by McDonald (who had taken residence in Baltimore), and the construction was successfully carried out by him (1890–94) through the firm of Ryan & McDonald.

Between 1890 and 1900 McDonald became identified with several important business ventures in addition to his large contracting business. He was president of the Eastern Ohio Railroad, 1894–95; of the Maryland Bolt and Nut Company; and of the South Baltimore Car Works. In 1900 he was the successful bidder on the New York subway project ($35,000,000) and entered upon the final achievement of his career as a constructor. He was vice-president of the Interborough Rapid Transit Construction Company, especially organized by August Belmont to finance the work, and he took personal charge of the construction from start to finish, and though the project was one of the most difficult in the history of engineering construction, it was completed well within the time limit. He also built the Jerome Park Reservoir in New York City, which, at the time of its completion, was the largest artificial reservoir in the world. With W. J. Oliver of Knoxville, Tenn., he prepared a bid for the construction of the Panama Canal before it was decided that the United States government should handle the work directly.

McDonald was married in 1869 to Georgeann Strang, by whom he had a son, born 1870, and a daughter, born 1878. From the late nineties until his death he resided in New York City. He was a quiet, unassuming man, of retiring habit and disposition, and his personality was little known to the world. He was a born executive with a talent for mastering and handling details, however intricate and diverse, which was little short of genius. He died shortly after completing the New York subway—"burned out," in a manner, by the prolonged and strenuous exactions of the project. He was buried from St. Patrick's Cathedral with all the pomp and circumstance befitting the passing of a great public figure, and as the funeral service began, the power on all subways in the city was turned off for two minutes as a tribute of respect to the man whose skill and energy had been so largely responsible for their completion.

[*Who's Who in America*, 1910–11; *Engineering News*, Mar. 23, 1911; *Iron Age*, Mar. 23, 1911; J. C. Frost, *The Strang Geneal.* (1915), p. 86; *Evening Post* (N. Y.), Mar. 17, 20, 1911; articles relating to railway and tunnel construction in various technical journals, 1890 to 1910.]

J. I. P.

McDONALD, JOSEPH EWING (Aug. 29, 1819–June 21, 1891), Indiana lawyer and politician, was born in Butler County, Ohio, of Scotch and Huguenot ancestry. His father, John McDonald, died while Joseph was an infant, and his mother, Eleanor (Piatt) McDonald, was soon married to John Kerr, who removed with his family in 1826 to Montgomery County, Ind. There young Joseph worked on his step-father's farm, attended school, and when he was twelve years of age began a term of apprenticeship to a saddler. He learned his trade well, but his ambitions led him to attend first Wabash College, Crawfordsville, Ind., then Asbury College (now De Pauw University), at Greencastle, where he was graduated in 1840. After leaving college he read law and in 1843 was admitted to the bar. In 1845 he moved to Crawfordsville. He showed early his talent for politics. He was twice nominated and elected by the Democrats prosecuting attorney for the LaFayette circuit, and in 1848 he was elected to Congress from the eighth district, which was normally Whig. He thus sat in the Congress made famous by its adoption of the compromise measures of 1850, and he was later gratified to recall that he had joined with Clay, Webster, Cass, and "a whole band of conservative men" in their efforts to forestall sectional strife (Foulke, *post,* I, p. 338). In 1856 and again in 1858 he was the successful Democratic candidate for attorney-general of Indiana. His widening law practice led him to move to Indianapolis in 1859.

During the Civil War McDonald stood loyally by the Democratic party. He was a caustic and consistent critic of the Lincoln administration, and of the Morton administration in Indiana. He believed that the war might and should have been avoided, and he was "utterly opposed" to making it an anti-slavery crusade. He branded the methods used by Morton to thwart the will of the Democratic majority in the legislature as revolutionary and indefensible. These views he stated freely and fearlessly during the stormy campaign of 1864 when, as Democratic candidate for governor, he met Morton, the Republican candidate, in joint debate. McDonald always counseled obedience to law, however, and he never stooped to the extreme methods of the peace-at-any-price men. Morton was reëlected, but by a smaller majority than he had received in the preceding election. It was to the credit of both men that they were able to hold their turbulent adherents in leash during the campaign, and to maintain their friendship and respect for each other.

After 1874 McDonald came again to the front in Indiana politics. He was chairman that year of the Democratic state committee and did much toward reorganizing the party for the successful campaign that followed. In 1875 he was sent to the United States Senate, where, much to the distress of some of his Democratic colleagues, he warmly advocated hard-money measures and a protective tariff. He served on the Senate judiciary committee, and more spectacularly on a special committee to investigate the frauds in the Southern states that occasioned the Hayes-Tilden election dispute. His argument before the electoral commission in defense of the Democratic position demonstrated his ability as a constitutional lawyer. In 1881, however, he was succeeded in the Senate by a Republican, Benjamin Harrison, and soon afterward dropped out of politics. McDonald was three times married: on Dec. 25, 1844, to Nancy Ruth Buell, who died in 1872; on Sept. 15, 1874, to Araminta W. Vance, who died in 1875; and on Jan. 12, 1880, to Mrs. Josephine F. Bernard, who survived him. He was the father of four children. His strong features, his unmistakable talent as an orator, his courageous championing of the causes in which he believed, and his humble beginnings —he was sometimes called "Old Saddle-Bags"— made him deservedly popular with the people. Even his political adversaries admired him. He died in Indianapolis.

[See: *A Biog. Hist. of Eminent and Self-Made Men . . . of Ind.* (1880), vol. II; *Biog. Dir. Am. Cong.* (1928); *Proc. of the Electoral Commission . . . Relative to the Count of Electoral Votes Cast Dec. 6, 1876* (1877); J. A. Woodburn, "Party Politics in Ind. During the Civil War," *Ann. Report of the Am. Hist. Asso. for the Year 1902* (1903), vol. I; W. D. Foulke, *Life of Oliver P. Morton* (2 vols., 1899); *Appletons' Ann. Cyc.*, 1891; the *Indianapolis Jour.*, June 22, 1891.]

J. D. H.

MACDONALD, RANALD (Feb. 3, 1824–Aug. 26, 1894), adventurer, early teacher of English to the Japanese, was born of an Indian mother, Princess Sunday, at the old Hudson's Bay Company post, Fort George (formerly Astoria), where his father, Archibald McDonald (*sic*), was a chief trader in the company's service. After some home schooling of a kind he was sent in 1834 across the Rocky Mountains to the Red River Missionary School at Fort Garry (now Winnipeg, Canada), where he spent five years. He was there apprenticed as a bank clerk to Edward Ermatinger, an early banker of St. Thomas, Ontario.

Tiring of the tedium of bank book-keeping, in 1841, at the age of seventeen, he threw down his pen, vacated his bank stool, and ran away to sea. After seven years of adventure, he carried out a long-cherished and carefully planned purpose to push his way into Japan, from whose shores all foreigners were at the time rigorously excluded. He reached the Japan Sea on the American whaler, *Plymouth.* Leaving ship in a boat prepared for the purpose, he capsized it when near shore and entered the country under the guise of a shipwrecked sailor. His strategy availed him little, for he was confined in a bamboo prison cage during most of his stay in the Flowery Kingdom. The awakening interest of the Japanese in world affairs caused the Japanese officials secretly to utilize MacDonald as a teacher of English to government interpreters. A few years later some of his pupils were the Japanese interpreters in the negotiations between Commodore Perry and the Mikado's representatives that resulted in the treaty of 1854 between the United States and Japan.

In 1849 MacDonald with a number of other shipwrecked American sailors was rescued from further imprisonment in Japan and taken to Macao, China, by Commodore James Glynn of the American sloop-of-war, *Preble.* Later wanderings and adventures took him to the Australian gold fields, and into British Columbia during the Cariboo "gold rush" of the sixties, where with his brother he ran a supply store for prospectors at Douglas, Harrison Lake, and a ferry across Fraser River to Lilloet. Finally, in his declining years, he settled on a homestead adjoining the site of the old trading post, Fort Colville, Stevens County, Wash. He died near Toroda P. O., Ferry County, Wash., poor and unknown; his remains were buried in an unmarked grave in an old Indian cemetery on Kettle River in that neighborhood. He never married, and the social prejudice against his mixed blood, together with his secret resentment thereof, probably prevented him from taking his proper position in the world. His Japan exploit marks him as one of the adventurous spirits of his century.

[W. S. Lewis and Naojiro Murakami, *Ranald MacDonald . . . 1824–1894* (1923) contains MacDonald's account of his Japan adventure; E. M. Dye, *McDonald of Oregon* (1906) is an historical romance based upon MacDonald's life. See also, Richard Hildreth, *Japan as It Was and Is* (1855); W. E. Griffis, *The Japanese Nation in Evolution* (1907) and *America in the East* (1899); *Senate Exec. Doc. 59*, 32 Cong., 1 Sess.; *China Mail* (Hong Kong), May 31, 1849; E. R. Custer, "An Out-of-the-Way Outing," *Harper's Weekly*, July 18, 1891; *Morning Oregonian* (Portland), Feb. 12, 1891; *Spokesman-Review* (Spokane, Wash.), Aug. 31, 1894).]

W. S. L.

McDONOGH, JOHN (Dec. 29, 1779–Oct. 26, 1850), merchant and philanthropist, was born in Baltimore, Md., the son of John and Elizabeth (Wilkins) McDonogh. He was of Scotch-Irish stock, descended from ancestors who settled in York County, Pa., early in the eighteenth century. His father moved from that region to Baltimore several years before the son's birth. At an early age the boy was placed with the house of William Taylor, a Baltimore merchant who had an extensive trade with Europe, the West Indies, and Spanish America. At the age of twenty-one he was sent by Taylor to New Orleans to act as his agent in receiving consignments, and he continued in this capacity for several years, at length beginning business also on his own account. With the rapid expansion of trade at this port, influenced in 1803 by the purchase of Louisiana, he became eminently successful. About this time he began to transfer his capital into West Florida and Louisiana lands, and in 1806 he retired from mercantile business to attend to his properties. His holdings were gradually increased until they grew to enormous proportions. Though private affairs absorbed him principally he was, in 1806, elected director in the Louisiana State Bank. Like most of his fellow citizens, he took part in Jackson's defense of New Orleans against the British and was enrolled in a volunteer corps called Beale's Rifles. In 1818 he was an unsuccessful candidate for the United States Senate.

McDonogh's active participation in the social life of New Orleans came to an end in 1817 with his removal to one of his plantations across the river. Tradition represented this withdrawal from society as a dramatic seclusion from the pleasures of the world because of unfortunate affairs of the heart. This is probably untrue. The increasing detail of business connected with his estates made the change natural. He was a self-contained man and gradually his retirement deepened until, in the popular imagination, he became the miser millionaire, eccentric, parsimonious, and unsociable. Contrary to the general opinion of the day, however, he was a benevolent man, and his thoughts were wrapped up in various philanthropic enterprises. One, a scheme for the emancipation of his slaves, was most unique and practical. To prevent a "desecration" of the Sabbath he gave his slaves one-half of Saturday to labor for themselves and to enable them to purchase little necessities which their master did not supply. From this he was led to calculate how long it would take a slave to purchase his entire working time if he had his half-Saturdays as a start and devoted every day he added to his freedom to working for his total liberty. Calling his slaves together he laid before them a plan for their emancipation. They accepted it, and the contract was completed in fifteen years as McDonogh had planned. In June 1842, about eighty were sent to Liberia on a ship provided by the American Colonization Society. McDonogh was no abolitionist; on the contrary he purchased more slaves when these departed. He disliked to see human bondage but did not think the two races could live happily together. In his later years he matured a splendid but visionary plan for the education of the youth of New Orleans and Baltimore, based on his large properties which he felt he held as trustee for this one great purpose of his life. Unfortunately the lands were overvalued, but enough was saved after the depreciation caused by the Civil War to found schools in New Orleans and an industrial school near Baltimore which bears his name.

[William Allan's *Life and Work of John McDonogh* (1886), is an excellent biography, based on all available papers and other sources. *Some Interesting Papers of John McDonogh* (1898), edited by J. T. Edwards, contains the well-known letter on African colonization which appeared in full in the *African Repository and Colonial Jour.*, Feb. 1843. See also: D. M. Benham, *A Useful Life* (1899); J. S. Kendall, *Hist. of New Orleans* (1922), II, 643–44; Baltimore and New Orleans newspapers for several weeks following McDonogh's death.]

C. W. G.

MACDONOUGH, THOMAS (Dec. 31, 1783–Nov. 10, 1825), naval officer, was born at The Trap (now Macdonough), Del., sixth of the ten children of Maj. Thomas McDonough (*sic*), a physician, and of Mary (Vance) McDonough. His grandfather, James, who was of the Protestant faith, had emigrated from County Kildare, Ireland, to America about 1730. On Feb. 5, 1800, Thomas entered the navy as a midshipman, and that year made his first cruise in the West Indies against the French. He next participated in the war with Tripoli, first on the *Constellation* and later on the *Philadelphia.* When the last-named ship captured the Moorish vessel *Mirboka,* he was ordered to the prize as second officer. Later he joined the *Enterprise,* Capt. Stephen Decatur [*q.v.*], and took part in the two daring exploits of that officer, the burning of the captured *Philadelphia* and an attack on the Tripolitan gunboats. In 1805 he was made first lieutenant of the *Enterprise* and two years later filled the same office on the *Syren,* on which vessel he returned to America. In January 1807, he received a permanent appointment as lieutenant.

He was ordered to Middletown, Conn., in October 1806, to assist Capt. Isaac Hull [*q.v.*] in the construction of some gunboats. This proved to him an exceedingly important tour of duty, although it lasted only three months, for in Middletown he found a new home among new friends, joined the Episcopal church, and on Dec. 12, 1812, married Lucy Ann Shaler after six years of courtship. As first lieutenant of the *Wasp* he spent the years 1807–08 in a voyage to England and in cruises along the Atlantic coast enforcing the Embargo. Since the navy at this time offered little chance for advancement, he requested and obtained a furlough, in 1810, in order to make a voyage to the East Indies. He sailed from New York in command of the brig *Gulliver,* bound for Liverpool and Calcutta, and returned home with a cargo of mixed merchandise. A second venture of a similar character as commander of the ship *Jeannette* was interrupted early in 1812 by the passage of the Non-Intercourse Act.

On the outbreak of the War of 1812 Macdonough applied for active duty and was ordered to Washington to join the *Constellation* as first lieutenant. Finding this vessel not ready for sea, he sought and obtained command of the naval station at Portland, Me. A few weeks later he was ordered to take command of the fleet on Lake Champlain, and early in October arrived at the scene of his new duties. Here he was confronted with the task of fitting out a small fleet and maintaining a superiority in naval force over the enemy. He worked at a great disadvantage, since armament, naval stores, artisans, and seamen had to be moved from the seacoast to the lake. By the time he was ready for operations, the season was too far advanced to undertake them and he went into winter quarters at Shelburne, Vt. Soon after the cruising season of 1813 opened, he lost two of his vessels through the bad judgment of one of his officers, and the balance of naval power shifted to the enemy. September arrived before he could assemble another fleet and contest the possession of the lake. As he sailed down the lake, the British retreated into Canadian waters and a decision was postponed until the coming year.

The season of 1814 opened with naval superiority on the side of Macdonough. By energetic efforts he had built or otherwise obtained a fleet of thirteen small vessels, of which his flagship *Saratoga,* 26 guns, was the largest and most powerful. By September the British commander, Commodore George Downie, had regained the naval advantage, chiefly by the construction of the *Confiance,* 37 guns. A formidable British army cooperating with the navy had advanced to the vicinity of Plattsburg. Its further movements awaited the destruction or capture of the American fleet, confidently expected. Outclassed in a contest in open water, Macdonough made his dispositions in an advantageous position in Plattsburg Bay, with his vessels riding at anchor, and awaited the arrival of the enemy. The action began about 9 A.M. on Sept. 11. After a sanguinary and indecisive fight of an hour and a half, in which both sides suffered severely, Macdonough wound his ship, a maneuver that he had anticipated and prepared for, and brought to bear on the *Confiance* an uninjured broadside. The enemy was too much damaged to make a similar maneuver, and was forced to surrender. The American loss was fifty-seven; the British, more than a hundred.

The battle of Plattsburg was one of the most decisive engagements ever fought by the American navy. Before it took place the British planned to make the Great Lakes British waters. Macdonough's victory caused the enemy's army to retreat into Canada and left the government of Great Britain no ground upon which to claim territorial adjustments at Ghent (Mahan, *post,* 355–57, 381–82). Macdonough's action has been cited as an illustration of foresight and accurate reasoning in preparation for battle and of undaunted perseverance, gallantry, and skill in fighting (J. H. Ward, *A Manual of Naval Tactics,* 1859, p. 108). For his great services he received many honors, including the thanks of Congress, and promotion (Nov. 18) to a captaincy, with rank from Sept. 11, the date of the battle. Previously, on July 24, 1813, he had attained the rank of master-commandant.

After serving as commandant of the Portsmouth (N. H.) navy-yard for three years, he took command in 1818 of the frigate *Guerriere* and convoyed to Russia the newly appointed American minister, G. W. Campbell. Thence he joined the Mediterranean Squadron. Differences with his commander over a question of precedence respecting a court martial led to his return home. In 1820 he was assigned to the command of the *Ohio,* 74 guns, under construction at New York, and four years later once more visited the Mediterranean, this time as the commander of the squadron. His health, which had been seriously impaired in the War of 1812, now rapidly declined, and, moved by a longing to see his native land, he gave up his command and sailed for home on the merchantman *Edwin.* He died at sea some six hundred miles from the American coast. His body was received in New York City with military honors and after a funeral service there was conveyed to its last resting place in Middletown, Conn. In person, Macdonough was tall and slender. If one may judge from the pleasing portrait of him (*c.* 1816) by Gilbert Stuart, his disposition was amiable and generous. His son, Charles S. Macdonough, died in 1871, a captain on the retired list of the navy.

[Record of Officers, Bureau of Navigation, 1798–1825; Rodney Macdonough (a grandson), memoir in *Papers of the Hist. Soc. of Del.,* no. XVIII (1897), *Life of Commodore Thomas Macdonough* (1909), and *The Macdonough-Hackstaff Ancestry* (1904); A. T. Mahan, *Sea Power in Its Relations to the War of 1812* (1905, 1919); J. F. Cooper, *Hist. of the Navy of the U. S. A.* (1839); *Am. State Papers, Naval Affairs,* vol. I (1834); N. Y. *Spectator,* Nov. 25, Dec. 2, 1825; *Commercial Advertiser,* Dec. 1, 1825.] C. O. P.

McDOUGAL, DAVID STOCKTON (Sept. 27, 1809–Aug. 7, 1882), naval officer, was born in Chillicothe, Ohio. His father, Dr. John McDougal, born in Dumbarton, Scotland, was a member of the Ohio legislature from 1813 to 1815; his mother, Margaret Stockton, was a descendant of Robert Stockton of Lancaster County, Pa. In later life David discarded his middle name. He entered the navy as a midshipman in 1828, was promoted through the various grades, and was made rear admiral, Sept. 27, 1873. He served first on the *Natchez* in the West India Squadron (1829–31), and while at Pensacola he is said to have gained reputation for heroism by rescuing a sailor from waters infested with sharks. Various assignments to shore and sea duty followed, and the Mexican War found him a lieutenant on the *Mississippi* at the capture of Vera Cruz.

Soon after the Civil War began, he was given command of the *Wyoming,* a wooden screw sloop, the former commander of which had been dismissed for disloyalty. Following a cruise to South America, the ship was sent to the Far East to seek Confederate privateers, especially the *Alabama.* On this duty McDougal cruised about the China Sea and the Straits of Sunda till 1864, but, although at one time the *Alabama* was only twenty-five miles away, she learned of his presence and escaped. The chief incident of the cruise occurred in Japan on July 16, 1863. McDougal had been informed in Yokohama that an American steamer, the *Pembroke,* had been fired on by Choshu clansmen in the Straits of Shimonoseki, in obedience to a decree of the Emperor that foreigners should be excluded from Japan—a decree which the friendlier Shogun at Tokyo had refused to promulgate. In retaliation for this violation of treaty promises, the *Wyoming,* single-handed, attacked the entire Japanese force at Shimonoseki, consisting of land batteries and three armed vessels—in all about forty guns—and by clever maneuvering and rapid firing was able to destroy the ships and do much damage to the batteries. The engagement was at close range and lasted for an hour, after which the *Wyoming* withdrew with a loss of four killed and seven wounded. McDougal's action without orders was approved by Seward and Lincoln, and, with a later attack by an international fleet, secured better protection for foreigners.

After bringing the *Wyoming* back to Philadelphia in 1864, McDougal was sent to Mare Island as commandant, but by 1868 he was at sea on the Pacific in the *Powhatan.* From 1870 to 1872 he commanded the South Pacific Squadron. His last days were spent in the vicinity of San Francisco, where he died. His wife, whom he married in 1833, was Caroline Sterrett of New York City.

[Records of the Navy Department; name of wife and date of marriage from a grand-daughter, Mrs. Ralph Rainsford; L. R. Hamersly, *The Records of Living Officers of the U. S. Navy and Marine Corps* (3rd ed., 1878); *Official Records of the Union and Confederate Navies in the Civil War,* 1 ser., vols. I, II, III; P. J. Treat, *Diplomatic Relations Between the U. S. and Japan, 1853–1895* (1932), vol. I; Tyler Dennett, *Americans in Eastern Asia* (1922); *Army and Navy Jour.,* Aug. 12, 1882; *Daily Examiner* (San Francisco), Aug. 8, 1882.] W. B. N.

McDOUGALL, ALEXANDER (July or August 1732–June 9, 1786), Revolutionary agitator, soldier, son of Ronald and Elizabeth MacDougal (*sic*), was born in the parish of Kildalton, Islay, Inner Hebrides, the second of five children. He accompanied his parents to America when, in 1738, they came over with the first party of Lachlan Campbell's colonists to establish a settlement near Fort Edward, N. Y. (*Historical Magazine,* October 1861, p. 302). The project failed to materialize and Ronald MacDougal settled in New York City as a milkman. The son early evinced a fondness for the sea, and during the years 1756–63 commanded the privateers *Tyger* and *Barrington.* Having accumulated a competence, he returned to New York, where he became a merchant and "gave himself to hard Study & made very singular Advancem[ts] in the Cultivation of his Mind" (Stokes, *post,* VI, 31).

He came into prominence in 1769 as the author of a broadside addressed "to the Betrayed Inhabitants of the City and Colony of New York," issued Dec. 16, which violently attacked the General Assembly (reprinted by O'Callaghan, *post*). The broadside was declared libelous, and he was arrested Feb. 8, 1770, on the testimony of the printer. He remained in jail until after his indictment in April, refusing to give bail. "The Arm of Power could not perhaps, have fallen on a Subject more fearless of its Menaces" was the self-confident conclusion to his defense, issued from prison (*New York Journal,* Feb. 15, 1770). He was looked upon by supporters and opponents as the "Wilkes of America." So numerous were the visits of his partisans that he was obliged to appoint visiting hours. William Smith, historian of New York, wrote of him: "[He] possesses great presence of mind, is methodical & connected in the Arrangement of his Ideas, writes well speaks (tho' with some small Impediment) yet with tolerable Ease—Has great Fire & Vehemence without Hurry and Precipitation" (Stokes, VI, 31). Because of the death of the principal witness, the case was never tried, but in December McDougall was summoned by the General Assembly for questioning concerning the authorship of the broadside. On his refusal to answer, he was committed for contempt and was kept in confinement until March 1771.

He was one of the most prominent of the radical leaders as an accelerator of public opinion during 1774–75 in the New York Committee of Fifty-one and in the first and second Provincial congresses. He presided over the famous mass meeting in the "Fields," July 6, 1774. In 1775 he was appointed colonel of the first New York regiment and was later made a Continental brigadier-general (1776) and major-general (1777). He participated in the battles of White Plains and Germantown, but rendered his most important military service in the Highlands of the Hudson, where he was stationed the greater part of the war, much of the time as commanding officer. Washington wrote him in 1778: "The vast importance of it [control of the Hudson] has determined me to confide it in you" (W. C. Ford, *The Writings of George Washington,* vol. VI, 1890, p. 429). On the discovery of Arnold's treason, Washington placed McDougall in command of West Point. In 1781 he declined appointment as minister of marine. In 1782 a quarrel with General Heath led to his arrest and court-martialing for insubordination. In the winter of 1782–83 he headed the delegation sent by the officers of the army to confer with the Continental Congress upon questions of pay.

He represented New York in the Continental Congress, 1781–82 and 1784–85, and served as state senator, 1783–86. He was one of the organizers and the first president of the Bank of New York. Another indication of the increasingly conservative attitude of his later years was his service as president of the New York State Society of the Cincinnati from its organization until his death. By his first wife he had two sons and one daughter. Both sons died without issue; the daughter, Elizabeth, became the wife of John Laurance [*q.v.*]. In 1767 he was married to Hannah Bostwick, who survived him.

[Birth record from manuscript register, New Register House, Edinburgh. Other material from McDougall MSS. (N. Y. Hist. Soc.); a few McDougall letters and William Smith's diary (MS.), in N. Y. Pub. Lib.; C. L. Becker, *The Hist. of Political Parties in the Province of N. Y.* (1909). I. N. Phelps Stokes, *The Iconography of Manhattan Island,* vols. IV–V (1922–28); *Public Papers of George Clinton* (10 vols., 1899–1914); E. B. O'Callaghan, *The Doc. Hist. of the State of N. Y.,* 4to ed., III (1850), 317–21; "Heath Papers," *Mass. Hist. Soc. Colls.,* 5 ser. IV (1878) and 7 ser. IV, V (1904–05); C. S. Hall, *Life and Letters of Samuel Holden Parsons* (1905); James Thacher, *A Mil. Jour. during the Am. Rev.* (1823); H. W. Domett, *A Hist. of the Bank of N. Y.* (1884); obituary in *Daily Advertiser* (N. Y.), June 12, 1786.] D. C. H.

McDOUGALL, ALEXANDER (Mar. 16, 1845–May 23, 1923), inventor, ship-builder, eldest child of Dougald and Ellen (McDougall) McDougall, was born in Port Ellen on the Island of Islay, just off the southwest coast of Scotland. His father was a carpenter and storekeeper in very poor circumstances, and as his family increased it became necessary for him to seek employment elsewhere. Accordingly, when Alexander was seven years old, his parents moved to Glasgow and two years later, in 1854, the family emigrated to Canada. They settled at Nottawa, a Scotch community near Collingwood at the southern end of Georgian Bay, Ont. Here the boy continued his common-school education, begun in Scotland; but within a few months, upon the death of his father in a grist-mill accident, he went to work as a farm hand. After several years he became a blacksmith's apprentice but at the age of sixteen ran away, to ship as deck hand on a Lake vessel bound for Chicago, Ill. For twenty-one years he sailed the Great Lakes. He became a second mate at the age of eighteen and at twenty-five was made captain of the *Thomas A. Scott,* one of the finest ships then on the Lakes. Until 1871 he made his home in Nottawa, but in that year established his mother and sisters in

Duluth, Minn. He continued a resident of this city until his death.

When he was twenty-six years old he helped to build for the Anchor Line the three passenger ships, *China, Japan,* and *India,* which were for years the "queens" of the Great Lakes. This experience spurred him on to develop his radical design for a freight ship which came to be known as the whaleback. He patented the basic design in 1881. In that year he gave up navigation and took charge of stevedoring for ship owners at a number of lake ports, meanwhile endeavoring to interest capital in his whaleback steamship. His efforts resulted after seven years in the organization of the American Steel Barge Company (1888), and in the construction of the first whaleback, in the company yard at Duluth. Seven vessels were launched from this yard and forty from that at Superior, Wis., established in 1891. These ships were used principally for transporting iron ores, grain, and coal. Although within a generation they became obsolete, they revolutionized the architecture of Great-Lakes freighters.

In 1892 McDougall built the first steel-ship yard in the Pacific Northwest and founded the city of Everett, Wash. Five years later he sold his interest in the American Steel Barge Company, and in 1899 organized the Collingwood Shipbuilding Company at Collingwood, Ont. Later he acquired control of the Kingston Shipbuilding Company at Kingston, Ont. In 1899, also, he organized the St. Louis Steel Barge Company of St. Louis, Mo., which built three vessels suitable for the navigation of the lower Mississippi River. While managing these several widely scattered enterprises, he patented, between 1888 and 1900, forty inventions pertaining chiefly to ship construction and equipment, ore and grain loading apparatus, and dredging machinery. From 1900 to 1903 he was one of the prime movers in establishing the Great Northern hydro-electric power plant at Duluth, and during the four years following gave much attention to perfecting and patenting a successful process for washing and cleaning the sand iron ores of the western Mesabi Range. During the last few years of his life (1920–22) he was plaintiff in one of the largest suits for damages ever filed in the federal courts—a claim against the Oliver Iron Mining Company, a subsidiary of the United States Steel Corporation, for $40,000,000 for alleged infringement of his ore-washing patents (Case No. 6061). The court gave an opinion in favor of the defendant, which was later affirmed by the United States circuit court of appeals, eighth circuit. During the World War, as president of the McDougall-Duluth Ship Building Company, he directed the work of constructing a large fleet of freighters and steamers for both Lake and ocean service, and just prior to his death he had completed and opened the McDougall Terminal at Duluth. Even toward the end of his career he continued his inventive work. With his son he invented a sea-going canal boat in 1914; he also devised a variety of mining machinery, apparatus for destroying submarines, improved ship's equipment, and a peat fuel machine which was patented a few months before his death. He married Emmeline Ross of Toronto, Canada, in January 1878, and at the time of his death in Duluth was survived by a son and a daughter.

[W. B. Kaempffert, *A Popular Hist. of Am. Invention* (1924), vol. I; *Who's Who in America*, 1922–23; *Riverside Review* (McDougall-Duluth Co.), Apr. 1918; Walter Van Brunt, *Duluth and St. Louis County, Minn.* (1921), vol. I, *Duluth Herald*, May 23, 1923; *N. Y. Times*, May 24, 1923; Patent Office records.]

C. W. M.

McDOUGALL, FRANCES HARRIET [See GREEN, FRANCES HARRIET WHIPPLE, 1805–1878].

McDOWELL, CHARLES (*c.* 1743–Mar. 31, 1815), Revolutionary soldier, was born in Winchester, Va., the son of Joseph McDowell and Margaret O'Neal or O'Neil. Joseph McDowell is said to have been a grandson of Ephraim McDowell, who emigrated from Ireland to America (1735) at the age of sixty-two. With his family, Ephraim settled first in Pennsylvania, then in 1737 migrated to the Valley of Virginia. Joseph, the father of Charles, moved to Quaker Meadows (near Morganton), Burke County, N. C. After the outbreak of the Revolution Charles McDowell was named captain and in April 1776 was commissioned lieutenant-colonel of a militia regiment. He was never attached to the regular Continental armies, but in the backwater region of the South, continually subject to attack from hostile Indians and zealous Loyalists, he rendered valuable aid to the patriot cause as commander of one of the rear-guards of the Revolution. He occupied himself with the repression and destruction of Loyalists and took part in the successful expedition of Brigadier-General Griffith Rutherford against the Cherokees (1776). In 1780 Patrick Ferguson, major, 71st Highlanders, invaded the Carolinas with a large army of Loyalists. McDowell promptly sent word over the mountains to Col. Isaac Shelby [*q.v.*] asking immediate aid. Even with Shelby's force, McDowell's army was too small to deal with Ferguson and so the mountaineers began guerrilla warfare. They hung upon the flanks of the Loyalist army and destroyed small groups coming to join Ferguson. It was a warfare in which Shelby's restless activity brought immediate result. Three times he was detached from McDowell's army for hasty sallies. Finally, McDowell sent him to disperse a Loyalist encampment at Musgrove's Mill. He circled Ferguson's camp, which intervened, and routed the Loyalist forces. An express from Gov. Richard Caswell informed McDowell of the defeat of Gates at Camden and the mountaineers withdrew to the frontier and dispersed. A few weeks later Ferguson sent word by a paroled prisoner that he would lay waste the entire countryside if submission were refused. McDowell and Shelby at once sent out an alarm and the "backwater men" assembled again in September 1780. McDowell was in command of the military district, but the colonels feared his slowness and elected Col. William Campbell [*q.v.*] commander. McDowell, leaving his brother Joseph [*q.v.*] in charge of his regiment, went to obtain a general officer for the command from General Gates. Although the battle of King's Mountain (Oct. 7, 1780) was fought in McDowell's absence, it was his and Shelby's initiative that brought the forces together and made possible the first Continental victory in the South after Gates's defeat, a victory which prevented lukewarm patriots from becoming Loyalists and helped to stem the flow of recruits to the British armies. McDowell was commissioned brigadier-general by the North Carolina legislature and placed in command of an expedition sent against the Cherokees (1782). He sat in the North Carolina Senate in 1778 and from 1782 to 1788. Toward the close of the war he married Grace or Grizel (Greenlee) Bowman, widow of Capt. John Bowman.

[*The Colonial Records of N. C.* (10 vols., 1886–90) and *The State Records of N. C.* (20 vols., 1895–1914); David Schenck, *N. C., 1780–'81* (1889); Isaac Shelby, *Battle of King's Mountain, To the Public* (1823); *American Review*, Dec. 1848; L. C. Draper, *King's Mountain and Its Heroes* (1881); J. H. Wheeler, *Hist. Sketches of N. C.* (1851); J. R. Gilmore, *The Rear-Guard of the Revolution* (1886); J. H. McDowell, *Hist. of the McDowells and Connections* (1918); T. M. Green, *Hist. Families of Ky.* (1889); *N. C. Booklet*, July 1904; S. A. Ashe, *Biog. Hist. of N. C.*, vol. VII (1908).]
F. E. R.

MACDOWELL, EDWARD ALEXANDER (Dec. 18, 1861–Jan. 23, 1908), distinguished American composer, was born in New York City, the son of Thomas and Frances (Knapp) MacDowell and the grandson of Alexander MacDowell, born in Belfast of Scotch parents, who emigrated to New York early in the nineteenth century. His father was a business man with an aptitude for painting. His mother had no talents in art, but was high-spirited, witty, and ambitious. Thomas MacDowell was a Quaker. His wife was not. Blest with remarkable parents, Edward McDowell escaped the misunderstandings and the lack of sympathy which often shadow the early years of genius. He spent his boyhood in a home rich in culture and affection. Though he was a sensitive and imaginative child, he had his share of fun and mischief, and with his brother Walter, three years his senior, he exercised all the instincts which belong to normal and happy children. When he began his piano studies he showed the usual reluctance to practise. On one occasion the family were astonished at the noises he was making, and discovered at the piano not Edward but Walter, whom Edward had hired to do his practising for him, at two cents an hour, while he read a story book. His first piano teacher was a friend of his father's, Juan Buitrago, a native of Colombia. Buitrago brought the talented boy to the attention of Teresa Carreño, who became his next teacher. He seems to have studied at about the same time with Paul Desvernine. Since all these teachers were of the Latin tradition, it is not surprising that when he was later taken abroad to study, it was to France rather than to Germany. He went to the public schools, and after his tenth year, when his father removed to East Nineteenth Street, near Third Avenue, close to Gramercy Park, he attended a French school, the *Institution Elie Charlier,* on East Twenty-fourth Street. Coming home from this school one day he exhibited to his astonished Quaker father a revolver which he had won in a public contest at a local shooting gallery.

McDowell's education became exactly what it should have been for his art. He spoke the modern languages and knew more about the ancient ones than most college graduates. He was widely read in literature and history, and he had a passion for ideas. Few artists have been more in touch with the philosophical and political currents of their times, as well as with the artistic. His dreams for American music and for music in American education in his day seemed impractical. But he had no opportunity to know the educational system in America, the obligations or the traditions of faculties and curricula, and to his innocence of such matters may be ascribed some of his disappointment later at Columbia University. His early teachers were impressed more by his versatility than by his excellence in any one direction. Though he disliked practising, he liked to play and he liked to compose. He also liked to draw, and there are portraits of his father and of himself, reproduced in Abbie Farwell Brown's *The Boyhood of Edward Mac-*

Dowell, which show convincing talent. It is no disparagement of his achievements in music to say that all his life he gave the impression of greater powers than he ever fully developed.

In April 1876 his mother took him to Paris, where he passed his examinations for the Conservatoire, and studied the piano with Marmontel and theory and composition with Savard. He also took private lessons in French. Some of his drawings came to the attention of Carolus Duran, who offered free instruction if he would give up music for painting, but Marmontel persuaded him without much difficulty to continue in the art of his first choice. His stay in France influenced him deeply, but his temperament was not at home with French music. Later on he cared little for Debussy, a fellow student at the Conservatoire, or for César Franck, and one cannot imagine him enthusiastic about D'Indy, or Ravel. At the end of three years in Paris he followed his natural bent and turned to Germany. After nearly a year at Wiesbaden (1878–79), where he studied composition with Louis Ehlert, he entered the Frankfort Conservatory, attracted by the brilliant pianist Carl Heymann, then at the height of his tragically brief career. Joachim Raff, the director of the Conservatory, took charge of MacDowell's studies in composition, and with Heymann gave him prompt recognition and encouragement. When Heymann retired because of failing health in 1881, he suggested the young American, barely twenty, as his successor, and Raff seconded the nomination. Though the faculty refused to make the appointment, on the ground that the candidate was as yet unproved, the confidence which these two master musicians showed in him gave MacDowell a place of respect in the musical world. He began to take private pupils, among them Marian Nevins, whom he later married. Appointed head piano teacher at the Darmstadt Conservatory in 1881, he continued to live in Frankfort, giving his private lessons, and commuting to Darmstadt. Most of his composing at this period he did on the train. This program soon proved too great a tax on his strength, and he resigned the Darmstadt post.

In 1882, at Raff's suggestion, he called upon Liszt at Weimar, with the manuscript of his first concerto, in A-minor (*opus* 15). This work, afterward revised, had been improvised in little more than a fortnight, though the themes had been gathered in advance. MacDowell arrived on Liszt's doorstep in such a condition of nervousness and self-distrust that he could not ring the bell. One wonders now why he had not gone directly to that doorstep when he began his European studies. Liszt received him with characteristic generosity, told one of his pupils, Eugen d'Albert, to play the orchestral part on the second piano, and listened to the concerto with approval. Immediately after this visit he recommended MacDowell's First Modern Suite (*opus* 10) for the program of the nineteenth annual convention of the Allgemeiner Deutscher Musik-Verein, at Zürich, July 1882. MacDowell himself played the Suite with success, on July 11. He still thought he was primarily a pianist, and set little value on his compositions. Some of the German critics objected to his playing the Suite with the notes before him. Years later he explained to Henry T. Finck that until his appearance before the Musik-Verein he had not considered his notes worth memorizing (*Century Magazine,* January 1897, p. 451). In 1883 Breitkopf & Härtel brought out this Suite, together with the Second Modern Suite (*opus* 14). Nothing of MacDowell's had previously been published, and this beginning he owed to Liszt.

For the next two years he devoted himself seriously to composition, chiefly in orchestral forms, seizing the opportunity to hear his experiments rehearsed by the local orchestras of Baden-Baden and Wiesbaden. To this period belong the five songs of *opus* 11 and *opus* 12, the Prélude and Fugue (*opus* 13), the "Serenata" for piano (*opus* 16), the "Two Fantastic Pieces" (*opus* 17), the "Barcarolle" and "Humoresque" (*opus* 18), and "Forest Idyls" (*opus* 18). In June 1884, he returned to America to marry Miss Nevins. After their wedding, July 21, at Waterford, Conn., they went to London and Paris, and settled in Wiesbaden for the winter of 1885–86, to complete, among other things, his second concerto, in D-minor (*opus* 23), and his symphonic poem, "Hamlet and Ophelia" (*opus* 22). Later he bought a small cottage outside of Wiesbaden, near the forest, and settled down for one of the happiest periods of his life, storing up inspiration for much that he composed later, as well as for the orchestral works, the piano pieces, and the songs which belong to this fertile time—among them the symphonic poems "Lancelot and Elaine" (*opus* 25), "Lamia" (*opus* 29), "The Saracens," and "The Lovely Alda" (*opus* 30); the six songs, "From an Old Garden" (*opus* 26), Four Compositions for Piano (*opus* 24), and the "Romance" for cello and orchestra (*opus* 35). It was the devotion and sympathy of his wife which provided MacDowell with this ideal opportunity to develop his genius.

In September 1888 he gave up his Wiesbaden cottage and sailed for Boston. The growth of his reputation, the success of his works at home as well as in Europe, made this step natural, but with it the tragic chapters of his life began. Some of his admirers regret for his sake that he did not stay in Europe, others lament that in his youth musical conditions in America were such that for even these few years he had to expatriate himself. Undoubtedly he missed some of the contacts with national life which are helpful to creative art. The deep emotions of his early manhood were bound up with Europe, with a tradition and an atmosphere not to be found on this side the ocean. Perhaps he was always looking for it here, wistfully and tragically. He gave the impression, against his will, of being a visitant in his own land, trying to establish himself in alien conditions. His interest in America was genuine and deep, reaching far beyond the field of music, but it is doubtful whether he knew how close he was to his country, how ready it was to welcome him, how instinctively it looked to him to be its spokesman in his art. On the other hand, the Europe he loved was a dream country, suggested by the great poets and artists and by ancient monuments, by folk-lore, by enchanting forests. Had he remained abroad he would probably not have been happy. He was by temperament energetic and surprisingly active, needing the society of his fellows as well as creative solitude. He came a little late for Europe and a little early for America.

In Boston the MacDowells lived first in Mt. Vernon Street, then at 13 West Cedar Street, then at 38 Chestnut Street. For eight busy and successful years he composed, taught his pupils, gave frequent performances and recitals. On Nov. 19, 1888, he appeared with the Kneisel Quartet in Chickering Hall, Boston, playing the Prelude, the Intermezzo, and the Presto from his First Piano Suite, and the piano part in Goldmark's B-flat Quintet. On Mar. 5, 1889, he played his Second Concerto for the first time in public at Chickering Hall, New York, Theodore Thomas conducting. A few weeks later he repeated the same concerto in Boston, under Gericke, and in July he made a flying trip to France to play the same work in an American concert at the Paris Exposition, with Frank Van der Stucken conducting. The critics acclaimed him at once as the leading American pianist and composer. During these years he wrote, among other works, the First Suite for Orchestra (*opus* 42), the Second, or Indian, Suite (*opus* 48), "Eight Songs" (*opus* 47), the Sonata Eroica (*opus* 50), the Sonata Tragica (*opus* 45), and the popular "Woodland Sketches" (*opus* 51). The performance of his larger compositions by the American and European orchestras became frequent. No American musician before him had achieved, or perhaps deserved, such recognition.

In 1896 MacDowell accepted a call to the recently established professorship of music at Columbia University. The intention of the endowment was "to elevate the standard of musical instruction in the United States, and to afford the most favorable opportunity for acquiring instruction of the highest order." McDowell took these words at their face value, not knowing that universities, like other institutions, must interpret their trusts in terms of their general policy. He assumed that he was to train musicians, just as his colleagues might be training historians or mathematicians. By January 1904 he found out his mistake, and resigned. Much has been said and written about this episode in MacDowell's life. (For an intelligent discussion see John Tasker Howard, *Our American Music*.) The tragedy was one of misunderstanding, a conflict not of personalities but of educational ideals. MacDowell threw himself into his work with enthusiasm and extreme conscientiousness. His name attracted large classes, of whom only a few were prepared for the kind of instruction he could give. He organized an excellent orchestra, he gathered a male chorus to sing serious music, perhaps the earliest attempt to interest a college glee club in art, he composed six Columbia Songs (published in 1901 but afterward withdrawn), as an experiment in the improvement of undergraduate music, he held departmental concerts and tried to make music function in the academic community. When his work became too much even for his devotion, he had an assistant for his classes, Leonard McWhood, and a conductor for the orchestra, Gustav Hinrichs. But the students in his classes received no academic credit for music courses. Music in those days was an "extra."

MacDowell also learned to his disappointment that the best musical talent rarely goes to college, nor does the best talent, with some exceptions, in painting and sculpture. He tried to persuade his colleagues to open the academic doors to the arts. "I have tried," he wrote, "to impress the 'powers that be' with the necessity of allowing no student to enter the university without some knowledge of the fine arts. Such knowledge may be very general, and not technical. This would force upon the preparatory school the admission of fine arts to its curriculum . . . I proposed that music be taken out of the faculty of philosophy, and architecture out of the School of Mines, and with Belles Lettres form a faculty of fine arts, to complete which, painting and sculpture would be indispensable. Owing to my inability to persuade rich men of New York into endowing a chair of painting and sculpture, the scheme, though approved by the 'powers that be,' was not realized" (New York *Evening Post,* Feb. 10, 1904, p. 9, quoted by Howard, *post,* p. 400). His resignation was a sad blow for his Columbia students, even for many who were not in his classes but who knew instinctively that he had stood in the community for something ideal. He was in some respects a great teacher, certainly a great musician and a scholar, as his lectures, published after his death, indicate. Given a student who was already well prepared, with something of the professional attitude toward the arts, MacDowell was one of the most stimulating of lecturers. But many of the pupils in his Columbia classes, though charmed by his personality and impressed with his genius, did not know what he was talking about, and their distress bewildered him. If part of the teacher's mission is to diagnose ignorance, MacDowell was not a teacher at all. Perhaps he failed to recognize some talent because it did not take the forms he was accustomed to in European conservatories.

During his Columbia years he lived in Eighty-eighth Street, near Riverside Drive, then at the Majestic Hotel, then at Ninety-sixth Street and Central Park West. For two seasons he conducted the Mendelssohn Glee Club, he gave occasional performances, he taught private pupils, and he composed—though this was chiefly during the vacations. His schedule was enough to crush a giant. But he was a singularly healthy figure, above medium height, who walked vigorously, dressed usually in brown or grey tweeds, with heavy brown shoes—an out-of-doors person, strongly Nordic. His blue eyes were alternately merry and dreamy. When he spoke, his listeners were caught by the quiet beauty of his voice and by the exquisiteness of his speech. It was not apparent that he was killing himself by overwork. To this period belong his Norse Sonata (*opus* 57) and his Keltic Sonata (*opus* 59), many of his finest songs and part songs, and a suite for stringed orchestra which he left unfinished. That he was able to accomplish so much in these years of teaching, he owed to his wife's foresight in securing, in 1896, the little farm at Peterboro, N. H., which became his happiest refuge and home. There, in a log cabin, at a distance from the main house, he spent his summers composing. After his resignation from Columbia he resumed his private teaching. In 1905 his health began to break. A nervous collapse was succeeded by an obscure brain trouble which proved incurable. He died Jan. 23, 1908, at his New York home in the Westminster Hotel, Irving Place, in the neighborhood where his boyhood had been passed. After the funeral at St. George's Church, he was buried at Peterboro, on a favorite hilltop. As a tribute to his memory his widow developed the farm into a large and beautiful estate, incorporated as a memorial to the composer, and equipped with studios for the use of poets, musicians, painters, and sculptors.

MacDowell's music is highly original and extremely colorful. The popularity of some of his small things, such as "To a Wild Rose," or the song, "Thy Beaming Eyes," threatened for a while to obscure his large qualities, but in time competent musicians showed increasing respect for the orchestral works, for the greater piano pieces, the sonatas particularly, and the second concerto, and for the best of the songs. In all his work the quality is lyrical, a quality revealed in his poems written for his songs (*Verses,* 1903, 1908), as well as in his music. He once said that he would never compose an opera, since the form always seemed to him unreal. His temperament was for song, not for drama. Though his work is harmonically rich, he deliberately turned away from the extreme experiments of the music of his day. He understood them and could say illuminating things about them, but he believed that art progresses by developing national and racial impulses, by developing hints supplied by the folk, rather than by imposing on the folk a new idiom intellectually arrived at. Even in the popular rhythms of dance music he recognized a significant development. Whatever the course of American music, he will remain one of its first great figures.

[See Lawrence Gilman, *Edward MacDowell: A Study* (1909), containing a bibliography of MacDowell's works; Wm. H. Humiston, *Little Biogs.: MacDowell* (1921); Abbie Farwell Brown, *The Boyhood of Edward MacDowell* (1924); O. G. T. Sonneck, *Cat. of First Editions of Edward MacDowell* (1917), and *Suum Cuique: Essays in Music* (1916); J. F. Porte, *Edward MacDowell* (1922); R. W. Brown, *Lonely Americans* (1929); J. T. Howard, *Our Am. Music* (1930); Paul Rosenfeld, *An Hour with Am. Music* (1929); Jas. G. Huneker, *Unicorns* (1917), ch. II; Hamlin Garland, *Roadside Meetings* (1930); T. P. Currier, "Edward MacDowell as I Knew Him," *Musical Quart.,* Jan. 1915; H. F. Gilbert, "Personal Recollections of Edward MacDowell," *New Music Rev.,* Nov. 1912; the *Musician,* Mar. 1908; New York newspapers at the time of MacDowell's death. MacDowell's *Critical and Historical Essays* (1912) is a volume of lectures delivered at Columbia University. Some of his letters and papers, not yet available to investigators, are in the music division of the Library of Congress.]

J. E.

McDOWELL, EPHRAIM (Nov. 11, 1771–June 25, 1830), physician, pioneer in abdominal surgery, was born in Rockbridge County, Va., the son of Samuel and Mary (McClung) McDowell. He was the ninth of eleven children.

His father, a veteran of the French and Indian War and a colonel in the Revolution, went to Kentucky in 1784, taking his family with him. He was a prominent man in the history of Kentucky, where he presided over the first organized court and also over the convention which framed the constitution of the state. The family settled in Danville, and Ephraim received his premedical education at the seminary of Worley and James, located first at Georgetown and afterward at Bardstown. Soon after leaving that school he went to Staunton, Va., and entered the office of Dr. Alexander Humphreys as a medical student. In 1793–94, he attended lectures at the medical school of the University of Edinburgh, where his preceptor had graduated, and at the same time took a course with John Bell, a brilliant private teacher.

He returned to America in 1795 without having secured a degree, but with a broadened understanding of the medicine of that day and particularly of anatomy and surgery. He settled in Danville, and established a reputation as the best surgeon west of Philadelphia. In 1802 he married Sarah Shelby, daughter of Gov. Isaac Shelby [*q.v.*]. Six children were born to this union. McDowell is said to have had an excellent library; he was always a student and, with the young men studying in his office, carried on dissections during each winter. It is to his credit that he cautioned his students against too free a use of medicines and gave it as his opinion that the employment of medical drugs was more of a curse than a blessing to the human race. This was his doctrine at a time when Benjamin Rush [*q.v.*], the leader of American medicine, was teaching the opposite principle.

McDowell was not a writer and did not even keep notes on his cases. He published but two papers, in an obscure journal (*Eclectic Repertory and Analytical Review,* April 1817, October 1819), which together described inadequately the first five cases upon which he performed ovariotomy. Recognition of his work was consequently slow in coming, and his reports attracted practically no attention until one contained in a letter addressed to John Bell of Edinburgh, but never received by him, was published by John Lizars in the *Edinburgh Medical and Surgical Journal* for October 1824, seven years after it was written. A similar report sent to Philip Syng Physick in Philadelphia was never acknowledged, if received, and never published.

Nevertheless McDowell was doing bold surgery. In a letter dated Jan. 2, 1829, to Robert Thompson, a student of medicine in Philadelphia, he described vividly the circumstances under which he performed his first operation for diseased ovaria. "I was sent for in 1809," he wrote, "to deliver a Mrs. Crawford near Greentown of twins; as the two attending physicians supposed. Upon examination per vaginam I soon ascertained that she was not pregnant; but had a large tumor in the Abdomen which moved easily from side to side. I told the Lady I could do her no good and candidly stated to her her deplorable situation; Informed her that John Bell Hunter Hey and A Wood four of the first and most eminent Surgeons in England and Scotland had uniformly declared in their Lectures that such was the danger of Peritoneal Inflammation, that opening the abdomen to extract the tumour was inevitable death. But notwithstanding this, if she thought herself prepared to die, I would take the lump from her if she could come to Danville; She came in a few days after my return home and in six days I opened her side and extracted one of the ovaria which from its diseased and enlarged state weighed upwards of twenty pounds; The Intestines, as soon as an opening was made ran out upon the table remained out about thirty minutes and, being upon Christmas day they became so cold that I thought proper to bathe them in tepid water previous to my replacing them; I then returned them stitched up the wound and she was perfectly well in twenty-five days." (The letter is published in full by J. N. McCormack, *post,* pp. 20–33, and in the *Military Surgeon,* April 1928.) At the date of this writing McDowell had performed ovariotomy twelve times, with but one death, and he had repeatedly performed radical operative cures for non-strangulated hernia. This last fact was unknown to Samuel D. Gross [*q.v.*], whose excellent sketches of McDowell are the most reliable and accurate to be found. Gross states that McDowell performed at least thirty-two operations for stone in the bladder, without a death. He used the lateral perineal incision. One patient upon whom he successfully operated for both stone and hernia was James K. Polk, afterwards president of the United States.

McDowell was a large man, vigorous and athletic, as he needed to be to withstand the hardships of the long journeys he took on horseback. He did much professional work for charity, but from those who could pay them he demanded fees large for that day. He was a religious man, and assigned as a reason for his preference for operating on Sundays his desire for the prayers of the congregation. He helped to found and gave the ground for the Episcopal Church in Danville, and was one of the founders and first trustees of Centre College. In June 1830, he was seized with an acute attack of illness marked by violent pain and nausea at the outset, then fever; and his death occurred on June 25. His disease at the time was referred to as inflammatory fever, but it is an interesting speculation, and not improbable, that the founder of abdominal surgery died of appendicitis. In 1879 a monument to him was erected in Danville, and McDowell and his wife were buried beside it.

[*Some of the Medic. Pioneers of Ky.* (1917), ed. by J. N. McCormack, pub. as supp. to vol. XV, *Ky. Medic. Jour.*; Mary Young Ridenbaugh, *Biog. of Ephraim McDowell, M.D.* (1890); August Schachner, *Ephraim McDowell* (1921); S. C. Swartzel, in *Lancet-Clinic*, Dec. 25, 1909; L. S. McMurtry, in *Surgery, Gynecol. and Obstetrics*, Feb. 1923; S. D. Gross, "Origin of Ovariotomy," in *Trans. Ky. Medic. Soc., 1852* (1853), *Lives of Eminent American Physicians and Surgeons of the Nineteenth Century* (1861), and *Memorial Oration in Honor of Ephraim McDowell* (1879); H. A. Kelly and W. L. Burrage, *Am. Medic. Biogs.* (1920), with additional references.] P. M. A.

McDOWELL, IRVIN (Oct. 15, 1818–May 4, 1885), soldier, was born at Columbus, Ohio, the son of Abram Irvin McDowell, and Eliza Selden Lord, his wife. The family was Scotch-Irish; its founder in America, Ephraim McDowell, came to Pennsylvania in 1735 and later migrated to the Valley of Virginia, whence his descendants crossed the mountains into Kentucky. Irvin McDowell received his early education in France, at the Collège de Troyes. Returning home, he was appointed a cadet at the Military Academy in 1834, and graduated in 1838, as No. 23 in a class of forty-five. Assigned to the 1st Artillery as brevet second lieutenant, he became second lieutenant almost immediately (July 7, 1838), upon the occurrence of a vacancy in his regiment. His first service was on the Canadian frontier, from Niagara to Maine, in connection with the border disturbances then in progress. In 1841, however, he was brought back to the Military Academy as a tactical officer, and served in that capacity and as adjutant until the outbreak of the Mexican War. Meanwhile (Oct. 7, 1842) he had been promoted first lieutenant. On Oct. 6, 1845, he was detailed as aide-de-camp to General Wool, and served with that officer's command throughout the war and in the Army of Occupation, most of the time acting as his adjutant general. For his services at the battle of Buena Vista he was made captain by brevet, and on May 13, 1847, was transferred with that rank to the Adjutant General's Department. He returned to the United States in 1848, and until 1861 served at headquarters of the Army and of various territorial departments, except for the year 1859, which he spent on leave in Europe. He was promoted major in 1856.

At the outbreak of the Civil War he was serving in Washington. Through General Scott, who had known him since his graduation and thought highly of him, he became acquainted with the leaders of the new administration, and particularly with Secretary Chase, whose confidence and esteem he immediately won. On May 14, 1861, he was promoted brigadier-general and assigned to duty with the forces assembling in Washington under the command of Gen. J. K. F. Mansfield. As these troops were transferred across the Potomac, it became necessary to organize those south of the river into a separate command, later known as the Army of the Potomac; and McDowell received this assignment, together with command of the Department of Northeastern Virginia. Although neither he nor most other officers concerned considered the army in any condition to operate in the field, both the political and the military situation seemed to demand a move to dislodge the Confederate forces at Manassas Junction, where the rail line from the West joined that from the South—for at that time the direct railway from Washington to Richmond did not exist. He was therefore required to undertake the brief campaign which ended in the disastrous battle of Bull Run (First Manassas), a campaign of which it has been well said that "although foredoomed to failure, yet it came within inches of success" (Johnston, *post*, p. 269).

He was now superseded by McClellan in command of the army, but remained with it as a division commander. In March 1862 he was made major-general of volunteers, and assigned to command the I Corps, Army of the Potomac. When McClellan moved to Fort Monroe to open his Peninsular campaign, this corps was retained, against the judgment of both generals, for the direct defense of Washington; it was later separated from McClellan's command entirely, and designated as the Army of the Rappahannock, McDowell retaining command of the troops and of the territorial Department of the Rappahannock. When, after the Peninsular campaign, most of McClellan's troops were transferred to General Pope's new Army of Virginia, McDowell's force became the III Corps of that army. At the second battle of Bull Run (Second Manassas), McDowell's conduct was severely criticized, and he was relieved of his command. He at once applied for an inquiry, and was ultimately exonerated, but was never afterward employed in the field. In 1864 he was assigned to territorial command in San Francisco; in 1868 he was transferred to the Department of the East, and in 1872 to that of the South. In that year he was promoted major-general in the regular army.

In 1876 he returned to San Francisco, where he remained until his retirement in 1882. He then took up his residence in that city, and interested himself in local affairs, serving as park commissioner until his death in 1885. In this capacity he planned the park improvement of the Presidio reservation, and laid out its roads overlooking the Golden Gate. He was buried on the reservation. He was married in 1849 to Helen Burden, of Troy, N. Y., and had four children, three of whom, a son and two daughters, survived him.

Although able, energetic, and devoted to his profession, McDowell was always unfortunate as a field commander. His previous service, while most creditable, had been entirely as a staff officer; until he took over the Army of the Potomac he had never held a command of his own, not even the smallest. In the preparation of his plans for Bull Run, he seemed instinctively to assume the position of a staff officer or second in command to General Scott, not that of the commander of an army; and in their execution he perhaps deferred too much to the views of his subordinates, and accepted situations instead of controlling them. But to control the situation that existed at that time would have required a most exceptional man, and no such man was found until much later in the war.

In person, McDowell was squarely and powerfully built. His manner was frank and agreeable. An appreciation of him by Secretary Chase exists, written Sept. 4, 1862, just after the second battle of Manassas. According to this estimate he was loyal, brave, truthful, and capable; a good disciplinarian. Contrary to the usual customs of the time, he used neither alcohol nor tobacco. He was serious and earnest, never sought popularity, and had no political aims. In official relations, his manner was purely military; he seemed to disregard individuals, and did not as a rule arouse warm personal sentiment in officers or men.

[Personal and family information is taken chiefly from a letter to the writer from Mrs. Maud Appleton McDowell, a daughter-in-law, and from W. H. Russell, *My Diary North and South* (1863). An outline of McDowell's military career is found in G. W. Cullum, *Biog. Reg. Officers and Grads. U. S. Mil. Acad.* (3rd ed., 1891); his reports and dispatches appear in *War of the Rebellion: Official Records (Army)*; analyses of his action in command in R. M. Johnston, *Bull Run: Its Strategy and Tactics* (1913), J. B. Fry, *McDowell and Tyler in the Campaign of Bull Run* (1884), Thomas Worthington, *A Correct Hist. of Pope, McDowell and FitzJohn Porter at the Second Battle of Bull Run* (1880), and in his own *Statement . . . before the Court of Inquiry* (1863). See also memoir by G. W. Cullum in *Sixteenth Ann. Reunion, Asso. Grads. U. S. Mil. Acad.* (1885); T. M. Green, *Hist. Families of Ky.* (1889); "Report of the Joint Committee on the Conduct of the War," *Senate Report No. 108*, 37 Cong., 3 Sess.; *Battles and Leaders of the Civil War* (4 vols., 1887–88); *Daily Alta California* (San Francisco), May 5, 1885.]

O. L. S., Jr.

MCDOWELL, JAMES (Oct. 13, 1795–Aug. 24, 1851), governor of Virginia, congressman, was of Scotch-Irish ancestry. His father, Col. James McDowell, was the great-grandson of Ephraim McDowell who, coming from Ulster, was a pioneer settler of Rockbridge County, Va., in 1738. His mother, Sarah Preston, was the grand-daughter of John Preston, who that same year emigrated from Londonderry to Augusta County, Va. His sister, Elizabeth, was the wife of Thomas H. Benton [*q.v.*]. In the character of James McDowell the pioneer spirit and the Presbyterian faith were dominant, though he had no taste for agricultural pursuits. Born at the ancestral home, "Cherry Grove," Rockbridge County, he was educated in private schools, attended Washington College (now Washington and Lee University) for one year, and in 1813 was sent to Yale. After a year here, he entered the College of New Jersey and graduated in 1816, delivering the Latin salutatory for his class. He was considered the most talented writer in college and had early developed a gift for public speaking, which led him into the study of law. On Sept. 7, 1818, he was married to his cousin, Susanna Smith Preston, grand-daughter of Gen. William Campbell [*q.v.*] and Elizabeth Henry, sister of Patrick Henry [*q.v.*]. At this time his father burdened him with the gift of two thousand acres of land near Lexington, Ky., where he tried to give himself to the farm as well as to the law, with the result that he soon abandoned both. Returning to Virginia, he established himself at "Colalto," an estate about a mile from Lexington.

Following the course of the Virginia gentleman of the day, he entered the legislature in 1830, and was concerned with local matters, mostly road building, until the Nat Turner Insurrection of 1831. When the legislature was asked by Gov. John Floyd [*q.v.*], McDowell's uncle, to turn its deliberations "to the melancholy subject which has filled the country with affliction" (Miller, *post*, p. 81), McDowell prepared and delivered one of his greatest speeches (*Speech of James M'Dowell, Jr., . . . on the Slave Question*, 2nd ed., 1832). He maintained that slavery was a cause of national dissension, that separation could not be peaceful, and that the separate existence of the slave states would be disastrous to their own welfare. He also advocated, in this session, a state-controlled canal connecting the tide-water of the James with the Ohio River. In 1832, owing to a division in the ranks of the Jackson Democrats, McDowell was defeated for the United States Senate by John Tyler. He strongly opposed Nullification and stated in 1833 that the doctrine "that each state had the right 'peaceably to secede' is wholly unwarranted by the Constitution" (Miller, *post,* p. 115). He canvassed southwestern Virginia in the interests of Van Buren's election as president, but in 1838 was defeated for reëlection to the legislature. His address at the College of New Jersey in 1838 (*Address Delivered before the Alumni Association of the College of New Jersey,* 1839) was ranked by many with Patrick Henry's orations.

In 1842 he was elected governor and served for the three-year term beginning Jan. 1, 1843. During his administration he gave himself largely to the problems of internal improvement, especially the James River and Kanawha Canal. He anticipated later developments by thirty years in recommending that the canal be abandoned above Lynchburg and a railroad be built at once to the Ohio. A few weeks after the expiration of his term as governor, his brother-in-law, William Taylor, died, and McDowell was elected in his place as representative in the Twenty-ninth Congress; he also served through the Thirtieth and Thirty-first congresses (1846–51). He supported the bill to create a lieutenant-general for the prosecution of the Mexican War, with the understanding that his brother-in-law, Thomas H. Benton, would receive the appointment. This act probably contributed to his defeat for the Senate in 1847 by a combination of Whigs and Calhoun Democrats. The remaining four years of his congressional service were marked by failing health, but three of his speeches during this period are considered among his best—his memorial tribute to John Quincy Adams (*Congressional Globe,* 30 Cong., 1 Sess., p. 386), and two speeches on the Wilmot Proviso, Feb. 23, 1849, and Sept. 3, 1850 (*Ibid.,* 2 Sess., Appendix, pp. 212–19 and 31 Cong., 1 Sess., Appendix, pp. 1678–85). In speaking against the Proviso, he reconciled his position with that which he had taken in 1831 by the argument that Virginia had the right to abolish slavery within the limits of the state, but that Congress in adopting the proposed act would create the very conditions which he had tried to avert in Virginia. His death occurred at his home near Lexington and he was buried in the Presbyterian Cemetery. He had ten children, three sons and seven daughters. A sidelight on his character is the fact that he was the first governor of Virginia to ban wine at official entertainments.

[His speech of 1849 on the Wilmot Proviso is reviewed in *Southern Literary Messenger,* May 1849; that on the slave question is discussed in *Richmond Whig,* Jan. 23, 1832; Henry Wilson, *Hist. of the Rise and Fall of the Slave Power* (3 vols., 1872–77) gives many details of McDowell's speeches, especially in vol. I, p. 205, and vol. II, pp. 194–97; see also, S. C. P. Miller, "James McDowell," *Washington and Lee Univ., Lexington, Va., Hist. Papers,* no. 5 (1895); D. X. Junkin, *The Christian Statesman: A Discourse Occasioned by the Death of the Hon. James McDowell* (1851); *Richmond Enquirer,* Aug. 29, 1851.]

J. E. W.

McDOWELL, JOHN (Feb. 11, 1751–Dec. 22, 1820), lawyer and educator, was born in Peters Township, Cumberland, now Franklin, County, Pa., the second of the twelve children of William and Mary (Maxwell) McDowell. His grandfather, William, born in Ireland, had emigrated to America about 1715 and settled in Chester County, Pa. The second William was a man of standing in his community, a justice of the peace and a Presbyterian elder. With other families of the neighborhood, the McDowells were several times driven from their home during the French and Indian wars, and on one occasion their dwelling was burned. John seems to have received a good elementary education and when he was seventeen years old he entered the College of Philadelphia, from which he graduated in 1771, being assigned the part of English orator on the Commencement program. Before his graduation he had served as tutor and in this capacity he continued his connection with the college until 1782. He joined Capt. Samuel Patton's company as a private in 1777, but was not rugged enough to undergo the hardships of army life. A rather frail constitution, in fact, was more or less a factor in his whole career.

Going to Cambridge, Dorchester County, Md., in 1782, he taught, took up the study of law, and was admitted to the bar. He was successful as a practitioner and had some of the prominent people of the state as his clients. Teaching still attracted him, however, and on Aug. 11, 1789, at a meeting of the visitors and governors of St. John's College, soon to be opened at Annapolis, he appeared and accepted the professorship of mathematics, which had been tendered him on the 14th of May preceding. The institution began to give instruction in November, with McDowell acting as principal. The original plan to bring over some one from England to head the college failed, and on May 14, 1790, McDowell was formally elected principal. He served in this capacity for the next sixteen years, during which time the institution drew students from at least eight of the states, not a few of whom later became nationally prominent. In 1806 the Maryland legislature withdrew its support, and the board of visitors and governors voted that the principal and faculty "be discontinued." They were offered reappointment, however, but McDowell declined to serve longer. He was made a member of the board but soon resigned owing to his connection with the University of Pennsylvania, where in 1806 he became professor of natural philosophy, and the following year, provost. In 1810 ill health caused him to relinquish both these offices. Returning to Maryland in 1815, he was again offered the principalship of St. John's College. This he declined, but he accepted an election to the board of visitors and governors and seems at times to have acted as principal. He is described as "a man of fine presence, and of pleasing and winning address, combining in a remarkable degree great firmness and dignity of character with an almost feminine gentleness" (*Commemoration of the One Hundredth Anniversary of St. John's College,* 1890, p. 88). He never married, and the last two years of his life were spent in Peters Township, Pa., with a sister, Margaret, widow of Matthias Maris. Here he died and was buried. That he was a man of sagacity and frugality is indicated by the fact that he left an estate of $40,000. His Latin and Greek books, and his books on mathematics and natural philosophy, he bequeathed to the University of Pennsylvania.

[In addition to source cited above, see *Gen. Alumni Cat. of the Univ. of Pa.* (1917); *The Alumni Reg., Univ. of Pa.,* Oct. 1903; *Old Mercersburg* (1912); *Biog. Annals of Franklin County, Pa.* (1905); W. B. Norris, *Annapolis: Its Colonial and Naval Story* (1925); *The Kittochtinny Hist. Soc. . . . Papers . . . 1901–03* (1904).] H. E. S.

McDOWELL, JOHN (Sept. 10, 1780–Feb. 13, 1863), Presbyterian clergyman, was born in Bedminster, Somerset County, N. J. He was the son of Matthew and Elizabeth (Anderson) McDowell, whose parents were of Scotch descent and had migrated to America from the north of Ireland. His schooling was more or less interrupted by work on his father's farm, but he secured sufficient preparation at a classical school, conducted by Rev. William Boyd about two miles from the McDowell home, to enable him in 1799 to enter the junior class of the College of New Jersey. After graduating with honors in 1801, he studied theology, first, under Rev. H. W. Hunt of Newton, N. J., and later, under Rev. John Woodhull of Freehold. He was licensed to preach by the Presbytery of New Brunswick, at Basking Ridge, Apr. 25, 1804, and was ordained by the Presbytery of New York and installed pastor of the Presbyterian Church in Elizabethtown, N. J., on Dec. 26 of the same year. On Feb. 5, 1805, he married Henrietta, daughter of Shepard Kollock [*q.v.*]. Although called to a number of important churches elsewhere, he remained in Elizabethtown for more than twenty-eight years, during which time his church had large growth, and from its membership the Second Presbyterian Church was formed. In 1833 he took charge of the newly organized Central Church, Philadelphia. Resigning in 1845, he became pastor of the Spring Garden Church, constituted by some of his former parishioners. The duties of this office he performed until he was past eighty, when a colleague was called.

A practical mind, executive ability, exactitude, methodical industry, and a thorough acquaintance with Presbyterian procedure, made him a valuable member of church boards, and of the General Assembly. The latter body he served as clerk, trustee, and, in 1820, as moderator. During the controversy which resulted in the division of 1837, he did not approve of the extreme measures taken by the conservatives, but after the division was effected he loyally supported the Old School branch of the church. He was an enthusiastic promoter of education, religious and secular. Early in his first pastorate he formed a class for the study of the Bible and church history, and in 1814 his congregation united with the Methodists and Episcopalians in establishing the first Sunday school in Elizabethtown. He published, probably the next year, a system of Bible questions, a fourth edition of which, 1820, bears the title, *Questions on the Bible for the Use of Schools,* said to have been the earliest work of its kind in this country. It circulated to the extent of 250,000 copies before being superseded by publications of the American Sunday School Union. He also issued in 1838 *Bible Class Manual: or, a System of Theology in the Order of the Westminster Shorter Catechism, Adapted to Bible Classes.* He was a member of the Presbyterian General Assembly in 1812, which determined to establish a theological seminary at Princeton, and was chosen one of the first directors. Two years later he became a trustee of the College of New Jersey, and in 1822, a trustee of the Seminary. These positions he held until his death, serving as secretary of the Seminary Board from 1824 to 1860. On several different occasions, notably in 1818 when he visited the Southern states, he solicited funds for the Seminary, and once he made a tour in the interests of the College. His most ambitious publication was *Theology, in a Series of Sermons in the Order of the Westminster Shorter Catechism* (2 vols., 1825–26). In 1828 he declined an appointment by the General Assembly as professor of ecclesiastical history and church government in Western (Allegheny) Theological Seminary, and in 1831 accepted the chair of church history and polity in Union Seminary, Va., but later withdrew his acceptance. On Dec. 31, 1854, he preached a sermon, published under the title, *Fifty Years a Pastor: a Semi-Centenary Discourse Delivered in the Spring Garden Presbyterian Church* (1855), which contains much biographical material. Several of his sermons were printed separately; two appear in *The New Jersey Preacher* (1813), and three in the *American National Preacher* (vol. V, no. 6, 1830; and vol. XI, no. 8, 1837).

[W. B. Sprague, *Memoirs of the Rev. John McDowell, D.D., and the Rev. Wm. A. McDowell, D.D.* (1864); *Gen. Cat. of Princeton Univ., 1746–1906* (1908); *The Presbyt. Hist. Almanac,* 1864; *N. Y. Observer,* Feb. 26, 1863; *The Presbyterian* (Phila.), Feb. 21, 28, 1863; *Phila. Inquirer,* Feb. 17, 1863.]

H. E. S.

McDOWELL, JOSEPH (Feb. 15, 1756–Aug. 11, 1801), Revolutionary soldier, congressman, was born at Winchester, Va., the son of Joseph McDowell and Margaret O'Neal or O'Neil and the brother of Charles McDowell [*q.v.*]. His father settled at Quaker Meadows (near Morganton), Burke County, N. C., where Joseph's youth was spent. After the outbreak of the Revolution he was attached to Charles McDowell's militia regiment and accompanied his brother on the Rutherford expedition against the Cherokees (1776). He took part in the numerous battles in North Carolina against the Loyalists—including Ramsour's Mill (June 20, 1780), the Pacolet River skirmish, and Musgrove's Mill. When the "backwater men" assembled in September 1780 to oppose the Loyalist invasion of Maj. Patrick Ferguson of the 71st Highlanders, McDowell was major in his brother's regiment. During the absence of Charles McDowell on a mission to General Gates, Joseph commanded the McDowell regiment in the battle of King's Mountain, Oct. 7, 1780 (Isaac Shelby, *Battle of King's Mountain, To the Public,* 1823). At the battle of Cowpens (Jan. 17, 1781) he commanded a detachment of 190 mounted riflemen from Burke County. In the same year he was active in attacking the Cherokees and later commanded the McDowell regiment during his brother's expedition against the Cherokees (1782). He was a member of the North Carolina House of Commons (1785–88), of the North Carolina Senate (1791–95), and of the North Carolina conventions of 1788 and 1789 that met to consider ratification of the Federal Constitution. He opposed ratification because the Constitution lacked a bill of rights. A leader of the Democratic-Republicans in western North Carolina, he was elected to the Fifth Congress (1797–99), where he joined other Democratic-Republicans in opposing the Alien and Sedition acts. He is usually said to have been a member of the Third Congress (1793–95), but the *Biographical Directory of the American Congress* (1928) credits the term to his cousin Joseph, known as "Pleasant Gardens Joe." The descendants of the latter insist that it was he who commanded the McDowell militia at King's Mountain, but the claim is disproved by the testimony of other officers. "Quaker Meadows Joe" married Margaret Moffett of Virginia, by whom he had six daughters and two sons, one of whom was Joseph Jefferson McDcwell, member of Congress from Ohio.

[*The Colonial Records of N. C.* (10 vols., 1886–90) and *The State Records of N. C.* (20 vols., 1895–1914); David Schenck, *N. C., 1780–'81* (1889); J. W. Moore, *Hist. of N. C.* (2 vols., 1880); J. H. Wheeler, *Hist. Sketches of N. C.* (1851); *Proc. and Debates of the Convention of N. C.* (Hillsborough, N. C., 1788); L. C. Draper, *King's Mountain and Its Heroes* (1881); T. M. Green, *Hist. Families of Ky.* (1889); J. H. McDowell, *Hist. of the McDowells and Connections* (1918); *N. C. Booklet,* July 1904; S. A. Ashe, *Biog. Hist. of N. C.,* vol. VII (1908).]

F. E. R.

MACDOWELL, KATHERINE SHERWOOD BONNER (Feb. 26, 1849–July 22, 1883), short-story writer and novelist under the pen name Sherwood Bonner, was born in Holly Springs, Miss. Her father, Dr. Charles Bonner, early in life came from Ireland to Pennsylvania, where he studied medicine, and then moved to Mississippi, where he married Mary Wilson of Holly Springs. Katherine grew up with her younger brother and sister under the devoted care of a negro mammy whose superstitious lore and lovable personality are reflected in many stories. Her father supervised her early reading, and later she attended a private school in Holly Springs, leaving at the age of fourteen for six months at a fashionable boarding school in Montgomery, Ala. The Civil War left a deep impression on her mind. The siege of Vicksburg and Port Hudson, the passage of Johnston's army through Holly Springs, and nearby raids and skirmishes were the outstanding events of her life in 1863. Her attitude, revealed in her later writings, was one of love for the South, hatred of slavery, and admiration for the intellectual standards of the North. Her first story was published in 1864 in the *Massachusetts Ploughman,* whose editor, Nahum Capen, saw the promise of her pen and became her friend and adviser. In 1871 she married Edward MacDowell of Holly Springs, by whom she had a daughter, but her high-strung temperament and literary ambitions were incompatible with domestic routine, and not long after the birth of her child she separated from her husband.

Leaving her daughter with a relative, she went

to Boston, where she served at first as secretary to Nahum Capen. Through him she became acquainted with important literary figures. Longfellow engaged her as an amanuensis and encouraged her in her writing. Under this stimulation she contributed articles, letters, and verses to the Boston *Times, Memphis Avalanche,* and other papers. From 1875 on, her stories of Southern life and character appeared in periodicals; most of them were later collected in two volumes, *Dialect Tales* (1883) and *Suwanee River Tales* (1884). These stories place her in the midst of the local-colorist movement which was part of the drift toward realism in her generation. She made a tour of Europe in 1876, spending most of her time in Italy. Her novel *Like unto Like,* dedicated to Longfellow, appeared in 1878 and was favorably received. This story with its background of the Civil War and the reconstruction era is autobiographical in nature and is of value for the interpretation of her character and her marital experience. She returned to Holly Springs to nurse her father and brother who died of yellow fever in August 1878; then once more threw herself into the writing of short stories and produced several dialect tales of Tennessee mountain life and of the "Egypt" district of Illinois. Her work shows a further increase in realism during this period, making use of gloomy scenes from her experience with the yellow fever and vivid details of Mississippi life. The intensity and frankness of "The Volcanic Interlude," published in *Lippincott's Magazine* in April 1880, caused many readers to cancel their subscriptions. Under the strain of absorbing work her health began to give way. In 1882 she was urged to have an operation for cancer, but refused. She worked with undiminished energy into the spring of 1883 and then, accompanied by her friend Sophia Kirk, returned to Holly Springs, where she died.

[Monograph by Dorothy L. Gilligan, "Life and Works of Sherwood Bonner" (MS.), in George Washington University library; accounts by friends: A. L. Bondurant, in *Pubs. Miss. Hist. Soc.*, vol. II (1899) and Sophia Kirk in preface to *Suwanee River Tales* (1884); B. M. Drake, article in *Southern Writers,* vol. II (1903); *Appletons' Ann. Cyc.,* 1884; M. L. Rutherford, *The South in Hist. and Lit.* (1907); *Harper's Weekly,* Aug. 11, 1883.] R. W. B.

McDUFFIE, GEORGE (Aug. 10, 1790–Mar. 11, 1851), representative and senator, was probably born in Columbia County, Ga. There is some doubt as to the date and the place of his birth. His parents were John and Jane McDuffie, both natives of Scotland who came to Georgia after the Revolution and settled in the pinelands about thirty miles from Augusta. The father was a man of fine mind and character but very poor, and the boy began life with no prospect of education beyond that offered by an old-field school. At the age of twelve he was a clerk in a country store and, two years later, obtained a similar place in Augusta, where he boarded with his employer, James Calhoun, who, seeing the boy's capacity, in 1810 persuaded William Calhoun, a brother, to take him to live with him while attending Moses Waddell's school at Willington, which was close by. There McDuffie remained for a year and then entered the junior class at South Carolina College, where he was graduated in 1813 with a reputation as a debater and orator. He was admitted to the bar a year later and began practice at Pendleton, S. C. In 1815 he moved to Edgefield and became the partner of Eldred Simkins, who had a large practice. McDuffie was soon elected to the lower house of the legislature and served two terms. In 1818 Simkins succeeded to Calhoun's seat in Congress and, after a second term, retired in favor of McDuffie, who remained in the House from 1821 until 1834, when he resigned to become governor of South Carolina. Returning to the bar after two terms as governor, he at once built up a large practice. In 1842 he succeeded William C. Preston in the Senate. He resigned in August 1846 and returned to private life. About 1829 he moved to "Cherry Hill," a plantation in the Sumter District, S. C., near the Savannah River and there ended his days. Although he came from poverty and obscurity, he won admission into exclusive South Carolina society. He married in 1829 Mary Rebecca, the daughter of Col. Richard Singleton, who died on Sept. 14, 1830. Their only child married the younger Wade Hampton, 1818–1902 [*q.v.*].

McDuffie entered Congress a strong nationalist. In the same year he wrote as a newspaper article a "Defence of a Liberal Construction of the Powers of Congress," directed against state sovereignty and strict construction, which, amusingly enough in the light of later events, James Hamilton, Jr., had reprinted in pamphlet form with laudatory comment (1821). In discussing the right of a state to judge of its own powers, McDuffie said, "No climax of political heresies can be imagined, in which this might not fairly claim the most prominent place" (see Magoon, *post,* 246). But his nationalism did not long endure. He was attacking the tariff in a short time, opposing internal improvements with almost equal vehemence in 1825, advocating a prohibitory tax on Northern goods in 1828, and in 1831 declaring that a Union made by the majority was a foul monster whose deformity could be worshiped only by those worthy of their chains. In

1830, while fulminating against the protective tariff, he developed what was known as the "forty-bale" theory. Holding that the tariff affected cotton growers particularly and that it subtracted from their profits by forcing them to sell their produce in exchange for a reduced purchasing power, he argued that the producer and not the consumer paid the duty on imports, and that, as a result, the Southern planters gave to the government, or to Northern manufacturers, forty out of every hundred bales of cotton they produced (*Register of Debates in Cong.*, 21 Cong., 1 Sess., 1830, pp. 842–62). Like most of his contemporaries in South Carolina, he was utterly unable to perceive how far slavery was an economic handicap to the South.

He favored nullification, although he was inclined to regard it, if not a revolutionary remedy, at least one outside of the Constitution. Nor would he agree that it was a peaceful one but believed that secession would probably follow it, a prospect that aroused no terrors in his soul. His speech of May 19, 1831, at Charleston is frequently said to have brought Calhoun to open advocacy of nullification. He was a delegate to the nullification convention in 1832 and wrote the address to the people of the other states in which, after severe condemnation of the protective tariff, he warned them that secession might follow and declared that, if the federal government employed force, South Carolina would rather be "the cemetery of freemen, than the habitation of slaves" (*Journal of the Convention of the People of S. C. . . . 1833*, 1833, p. 78). He was disappointed at the success of the compromise and frankly scornful of the nullification of the Force Bill in 1833, which he thought an empty and impotent gesture.

In Congress he quickly acquired reputation as a ready, eloquent, and sensational debater, and the news that he intended speaking rarely failed to fill the galleries. His speeches, usually extemporaneous, were always delivered as if he were in a frenzy of passion. They were characterized by their noise and fury, extravagance of phrase, and denunciatory quality, though on occasions he could also be persuasive. His voice was fine and powerful, his memory unfailing, his face expressive, his fluency never failed, and always he "pounded the air with his fists." All of this was in striking contrast to his normal manner, for he was ordinarily quiet and reserved, almost to taciturnity, with a somber cast to his thought, which made a smile almost a stranger to his face. John Quincy Adams said he had a "gloomy churlishness" (*post*, vol. IX, p. 119) in his character. The explanation of this characteristic probably lies in his physical condition. He was a confirmed dyspeptic. During the session of Congress of 1821–22 he became involved in a quarrel with William Cumming of Georgia growing out of the Calhoun-Crawford rivalry for the presidency. After they had extensively abused each other in the press, Cumming challenged McDuffie and came to Washington for the duel, which occurred after the close of the session. McDuffie suffered a permanent injury to the spine and was never again a well man. His health grew steadily worse, and he suffered from severe fits of depression, which finally amounted to attacks of melancholia. He also grew increasingly irritable, during his last years was a pitiable wreck, and finally died insane. The Cumming duel was not his only affair of the kind. In fact, Cumming again challenged him, but the duel was never fought. At the same session McDuffie had a quarrel with James M. Wayne of Georgia, later associate justice of the United States Supreme Court, which led to a challenge, but the matter was adjusted. During the Twentieth Congress he challenged Thomas Metcalfe of Kentucky, who chose rifles as the weapons for the encounter. James Hamilton, Jr., McDuffie's second, horrified at this breach of the code, refused to let his friend appear and later made it known that McDuffie, as a result of his wound, could not fire a rifle. McDuffie also challenged Joseph Vance, of Ohio, who declined to meet him.

In Congress McDuffie became the most radical of the opponents of the protective tariff. He was venomous in his hatred of the Adams administration, and in the first session of the Nineteenth Congress he made furious charges of a corrupt bargain between Adams and Clay and proposed an amendment to the Constitution providing for a more direct election of president in order to prevent a recurrence of such a thing. During the Adams administration he was chairman of the ways and means committee. He had supported Jackson strongly in 1821 in the Florida matter and from 1825 to 1829 was an enthusiastic advocate of his election as president, and it was confidently expected in 1829 that he would be in the cabinet. But his support was soon lost. He broke with Jackson on the questions of nullification and the bank. McDuffie was as enthusiastic in his support of the bank as he was of nullification, and in 1832 he presented to the House the bank's memorial for recharter. During his brief senatorial career he favored the annexation of Texas, although as governor of South Carolina he had opposed it, and introduced a resolution for it. He opposed the occupation of Oregon as impracticable, declaring that never, even in the sanguine dreams of youth, had he conceived of having under the same government people who lived 3,000 miles apart (*Congressional Globe,* 27 Cong., 3 Sess., p. 200). After the expiration of his term as governor he lost influence in South Carolina, as Calhoun gained it. Up to that time he was in high popular favor and genuinely beloved. He was a little above medium height with a large, spare figure. He had prominent, striking features, brilliant and deep-set blue eyes, and black hair. Always he was grim-looking with the "fierce earnestness" of passionate conviction. His temperament was nervous, he was easily moved emotionally, and his motives seem not to have been selfish. He was as frank as he was bold, clear-headed, and strikingly consistent for a politician. He relaxed somewhat with his intimates and, when in good health, enjoyed cards, checkers, and backgammon.

[Some letters in Lib. of Cong.; family records and MSS. in private hands; *Trinity Archive,* Sept. 1892; *Memoirs of John Quincy Adams,* ed. by C. F. Adams, vols. V–IX (1875–76); J. B. O'Neall, *Biog. Sketches of the Bench and Bar,* 1859, vol. II; E. L. Magoon, *Living Orators in America* (1849); B. F. Perry, *Reminiscences of Public Men* (1883); *Hist. of S. C.,* ed. by Yates Snowden (1920), vol. II; C. S. Boucher, *The Nullification Controversy in S. C.* (copr. 1916); D. F. Houston, *A Critical Study of Nullification in S. C.* (1896), pp. 35–49; *Charleston Daily Courier,* Mar. 13, 1851.]

J. G. deR. H.

McELRATH, THOMAS (May 1, 1807–June 6, 1888), publisher, partner of Horace Greeley in the publication of the *New York Tribune,* was born at Williamsport, Pa. After an early apprenticeship on the *Harrisburg Chronicle,* he pushed on to Philadelphia, finding employment in a book-printing establishment. He later returned to Williamsport and studied law. Equipped now for a struggle with fortune, he went to New York City, where he was employed as proof-reader and head salesman by the Methodist Book Concern, and subsequently he engaged on his own account in the publication of school books and religious works. In 1828 he was admitted to the bar, formed a partnership with William Bloomfield and Charles P. Daly, and entered upon a lucrative practice. In 1833 he was married to Elizabeth Price of New York City. His ability and attractive personal qualities brought him advancement. Elected as a Whig to the New York Assembly, he won attention by a minority report on the petition for removing the state capital from Albany to Utica, his report closing with a recommendation to transfer the seat of government to New York. During the same session he presented for the judiciary committee an adverse report on a petition for the abolishment of capital punishment. He was also among those who protested against the action of Congress in resolving to table without debate, printing, or reference, all petitions affecting slavery.

In 1841 McElrath became business manager of the *New York Tribune,* then in its uncertain infancy. On July 31 Horace Greeley made this terse announcement over his name: "The principal Editorial charge of the paper will still rest with the subscriber; while the entire business management of the concern henceforth devolves upon his partner." McElrath declared "his hearty concurrence in the principles, Political and Moral" on which the *Tribune* had been conducted. Surveying this combination of sanctum and counting-room, James Parton, in his life of Greeley, exclaimed: "Oh! that every Greeley could find his McElrath! and blessed is the McElrath that finds his Greeley!" (*post,* p. 162). Although the business manager did not share every enthusiasm of his partner's flaming pen, the steady course of the *Tribune* as a publishing concern insured a constant enlargement of its influence and prosperity. When muscular men of the "bloody sixth" ward, in resentment of plain language, swore to wreck the *Tribune* building, McElrath did his share to put the office in a state of defense. When he withdrew from the *Tribune* in 1857, to become corresponding secretary of the American Institute, the paper had risen to a position of social and political leadership.

McElrath had numerous official trusts. He was a master of chancery for New York City in 1840; state director of the Bank of America in 1841; New York alderman in 1845–46; appraiser-general of the New York district in 1861, by appointment of President Lincoln; custom-house officer in 1866; United States commissioner to the Paris Exposition in 1867; commissioner to the Vienna Exposition in 1873 and superintendent of American exhibitions; general executive officer of the New York state commission at the Centennial Exposition in Philadelphia in 1876; and commissioner of the World's Fair in New York in 1884. In 1864 he had resumed the post of publisher of the *Tribune* and was associated with Greeley in the publication of works issued by the firm. He himself was the author of a standard work of reference, *A Dictionary of Words and Phrases Used in Commerce* (1871).

[James Parton, *The Life of Horace Greeley* (1889); Frederic Hudson, *Journalism in the U. S. from 1690 to 1872* (1873); J. C. Derby, *Fifty Years Among Authors, Books, and Publishers* (1884); *N. Y. Tribune,* June 7, 1888.]

R. E. D.

McELROY, JOHN (May 14, 1782–Sept. 12, 1877), priest and missionary, was born in Enniskillen, County Fermanagh, Ireland, where as a barefooted boy, carrying his daily ration of turf, he obtained a scant education in a hedge-school. A gigantic fellow, wiry, and red faced, he spoke with the nasal twang of Ulster and committed treason with the Presbyterian United Irishmen. Like many of his associates who were "on the run after the troubles," McElroy found relief in emigration to America and took passage on a flax ship returning to Baltimore (1803). Within a year he was in business in the port of Georgetown, D. C., but he soon experienced a religious call and joined the partially restored Society of Jesus as a lay brother (1806). At Georgetown College he served as a buyer and bookkeeper for a number of years until Father Grassi, who recognized his natural cleverness and fine qualities, urged him to study for the priesthood and assisted him by patient tutoring in preparation for his theological studies. It was as a seminarian that he witnessed from the college windows the wanton burning of Washington with all the pent-up hatred of an Irish rebel. Although tempted to enlist, he remained in the cloister and was finally ordained by Archbishop Leonard Neale (May 21, 1817) whom strangely enough he prepared for death within a month. For a few years he remained at the college and attended nearby stations in Maryland and Virginia, when on the petition of Roger B. Taney and others, he was stationed as pastor at Frederick, Md. (1822–46). In this capacity he built a church at Liberty (1828), a new church of St. John at Frederick, an orphanage under the Sisters of Charity (1824), and established the first local free school which attracted Protestant children to such an extent that the ministers became exercised. In 1829 he founded St. John's Literary Institute or College which at one time rivaled Georgetown. Despite the lack of a thorough education, Father McElroy was winning fame as a forceful preacher and a retreat-master who gave missions throughout Virginia, Maryland, and Pennsylvania. In 1842 he was invited by Bishop Hughes to preach at the latter's diocesan synod, and he also conducted the first clerical retreat in the Boston diocese. In 1846, probably at the suggestion of Hughes who was called upon by the government for chaplains for the Mexican War, McElroy and Anthony Rey were commissioned chaplains. McElroy served in Taylor's army with considerable success. He won the soldiers' favor and became a living argument to the Mexicans that the war was not being waged against their Catholic religion.

After the war, McElroy was assigned to St. Mary's Church in north Boston by Bishop Fitzpatrick, who found its congregation factious. As the first Jesuit pastor in Boston, he virtually made St. Mary's a city church. In 1853 he bought the old jail lands for a college, but when the city council learned the purpose of the purchase it imposed impossible restrictions upon the property. After vexatious litigations, he purchased another site where the Church of the Immaculate Conception (1859) and Boston College (1860) were erected. As rector of the largest Catholic church he became an influential leader in Boston despite his age. A patron of the Sisters of Notre Dame, whom he introduced into the diocese (1849), he assisted them in their establishment at Lowell (1852), and in the foundation of an academy in Boston. In 1854 he gave the first retreat for the Hartford diocesan clergy. Archbishop Hughes called him to his death bed. At ordinations, episcopal consecrations, cornerstone ceremonies, and at anniversaries, he was a favorite preacher partly because of his almost legendary prestige, his favor with Irish-American bishops, his reputed refusal of three bishoprics, and, toward the end, as the world's oldest Jesuit both in point of years and of service in the Society. Sightless, he retired to Frederick, Md., where he finally succumbed to death, the victim of an accident in which he had broken several ribs.

[*Woodstock Letters,* vols. III (1874), V (1876), VI (1877), and X (1880); *Records of the Am. Cath. Hist. Soc. of Philadelphia,* vols. VI (1895), VIII (1897), XII (1901), and XXII (1911); Wm. Byrne, ed., *Hist. of the Cath. Ch. in the New Eng. States* (2 vols., 1899); J. G. Shea, *Hist. of the Cath. Ch. in the U. S.,* vols. III and IV (1890–92); *Sadliers' Cath. Directory,* 1878; *N. Y. Freeman's Jour.,* Sept. 22, 1877.] R. J. P.

McELROY, JOHN (Aug. 25, 1846–Oct. 12, 1929), soldier and editor, was born in Greenup County, Ky., the son of Robert McElroy, a builder of blast furnaces, and Mary (Henderson) McElroy, both of Scotch-Irish ancestry. He was given his mother's maiden name as a middle name but, throughout his career, he was known as John McElroy. His formal schooling was fragmentary. In 1855 his father died, his mother remarried, and young John, leaving home, went to St. Louis, where he became a printer's devil at the age of ten. Aided by sympathetic journeymen printers, he succeeded in setting the type for popular songs and sold the sheets on the streets of St. Louis. Later he moved to Chicago, where he enlisted in McClernand's body-guards after the outbreak of the Civil War. On Mar. 29, 1863, he enlisted in Company L of the 16th Illinois Cavalry and served through the various enlisted grades in that organization. On Jan. 3, 1864, after he had been appointed sergeant-major, he was captured by the Confederates at Jonesville, Va.

He spent more than a year in various Confederate prisons, chiefly at Andersonville, which had been established the previous November. His story of this camp, *Andersonville* (1879), is remarkable for its force and, aside from the compelling nature of its narrative, is a noteworthy document from a historical as well as a literary standpoint.

At the close of the Civil War, after release from Andersonville, he went to Ottawa, Ohio, where he studied pharmacy in a drugstore and in February 1866 married Elsie Pomeroy, the daughter of the owner. They had two children, a son and a daughter. Moving to Chicago in 1868, he became a reporter on the *Inter Ocean* and later became an editorial writer. His private reading was enormous, and his memory was of the photographic kind that imprints entire pages indelibly upon the mind. In 1874 he was called to Toledo, Ohio, by D. R. Locke (Petroleum V. Nasby), to be an editor of the *Toledo Blade.* He filled this post with distinction for ten years. Then he became an editor of the *National Tribune* of Washington and, upon the death of George Lemmon, editor and publisher. He continued to be active in this position until his death. Perhaps his most important literary contribution was his book, *Andersonville,* although Champ Clark was said to have considered the *Struggle for Missouri* (1909) the finest history of that state ever written. His writings were numerous, including the *History of Slavery in the United States* (1896), and the well-remembered "Si Klegg" series, among the most popular of which were *Si Klegg, his Development from a Raw Recruit to a Veteran* (1897) and *Further Haps and Mishaps to Si Klegg and Shorty* (1898). He also wrote numerous pamphlets and monographs. He became a national figure by his efforts to obtain aid for veterans of the Civil War, and his pocket and pen were unfailingly at their service. In 1901 he was senior vice-commander-in-chief of the Grand Army of the Republic, was many times commander of the Kit Carson post of that organization, was three times commander of the Department of the Potomac, and was a member of the legislative committee of the Grand Army of the Republic for fifteen years. He was a charter member of the Press Club in Washington and a member of the Board of Trade. Some years after the death of his first wife he married, on May 16, 1925, Isabel (Worrell) Ball, a member of the staff of his own newspaper, who attained some distinction as a newspaper writer and interested herself in many patriotic organizations and projects, especially in the details of the history and etiquette of the flag as a national emblem.

[Private papers of McElroy in the possession of his son, K. P. McElroy, Washington, D. C.; *Who's Who in America, 1928–29*; *Report of the Adjutant General of the State of Ill.*, vol. VIII (1867), p. 512; *Evening Star* (Washington), Oct. 12, 1929; *National Tribune* (Washington), Oct. 17, 1929.]

D. Y.

McELWAIN, WILLIAM HOWE (Feb. 11, 1867–Jan. 10, 1908), shoe-manufacturer, was born in Charlestown, Mass., the son of John Allen McElwain, a Baptist minister, and Susan Gilbert McElwain. Leaving high school at the age of sixteen, he obtained employment with George H. Burt, a shoe-manufacturer, as office boy and order clerk, at a salary of $100 a year. In the course of the next eleven years he acquired a thorough knowledge of the business in all its details; he also perceived the changes that must be made in the manufacture and the distribution of shoes to meet the changed conditions created by the use of new machinery and constantly increasing competition. Severing his connection with Burt, he borrowed $9,000, to which he added $1,500 of his own savings, and started a shoe factory at Bridgewater, Mass., in October 1894. At the end of nine months he bought out his partner. His purpose was to make a man's shoe, retailing for two dollars, that would have the attractive qualities of higher priced shoes and that could be manufactured profitably by the methods of quantity production. He had worked out for himself principles of scientific management, and he applied these principles to the manufacture and the distribution of his product. Thus he perfected the technique of quantity production at the moment when it was necessary to meet the new demand.

As a result of his boldness in putting his conclusions into effect, his business went ahead by leaps and bounds. Within five years he had established himself as a successful shoe-manufacturer; from 1902 to 1906 he built several new factories in Manchester, N. H.; for the year ending May 31, 1908, the production reached 5,716,955 pairs of shoes, the largest output of any shoe factory in the United States. This volume was attained by what McElwain called the "sheet system," which, based upon a searching analysis of every operation, consisted of a time schedule which controlled strictly the work of the factory. The application of scientific methods in the field of production was followed by a study of the methods by which jobbers placed their orders, as a result of which seasonal employment was eliminated and the cost of manufacture reduced; and by the establishment of a labor department to determine with accuracy the piece rate for each operation. Working in a period when the principles of scientific management as formulated by

F. W. Taylor were but little known, McElwain, without knowledge of Taylor's work, created a model large-scale industrial organization based on those principles. The intensity of his labors for thirteen years in building up and perfecting his business precluded his giving very much attention to anything else. He died suddenly at the age of forty, following an operation for appendicitis, and was survived by his wife, Helen (Merriam) McElwain, and four children.

[H. G. Pearson, *Wm. Howe McElwain* (1917); L. D. Brandeis, *Business: A Profession* (1925); *Shoe and Leather Reporter*, Jan. 16, 1908; *Boot and Shoe Recorder*, Jan. 15, 1908; *Shoe and Leather Facts*, Feb. 1908; *Boston Transcript*, Jan. 10, 1908.] H. G. P.

McENERY, SAMUEL DOUGLAS (May 28, 1837–June 28, 1910), jurist, governor of Louisiana, United States senator, the son of Henry O'Neil and Caroline H. (Douglas) McEnery, was born in Monroe, Ouachita Parish, La. His father, originally from Ireland, emigrated to Virginia when quite young, and after living there for some years, removed to Louisiana in 1835 and settled in Monroe, where he became a planter and for eight years was register of the Land Office. His knowledge of land matters enabled him to give valuable information regarding locations for settlement to immigrants from other states, and in this way he contributed greatly to the settlement of northern Louisiana. Samuel attended the public schools of Monroe, Spring Hill College in Mobile, Ala., the United States Naval Academy, the University of Virginia, and in 1859 graduated from the State and National Law School at Poughkeepsie, N. Y. For a year following his graduation he practised law at Marysville, Mo. Soon after the outbreak of the Civil War he entered the Confederate service as a member of a Louisiana volunteer company known as the Pelican Grays. In 1862 he was commissioned a lieutenant under General Magruder in Virginia. Later he was placed in charge of an instruction camp at Trenton, La., and here it seems he was when the war ended.

After the war McEnery returned to Monroe, was admitted to the Louisiana bar in 1866, and began to practise his profession, but while he was successful as a lawyer, the bar proved only a stepping-stone to his political career. A democrat in politics, he was in 1879 nominated by that party for the office of lieutenant-governor on a ticket with L. A. Wiltz for governor. They were elected and upon the death of Wiltz in October 1881, McEnery succeeded him as governor. He was reëlected governor in 1884 but four years later was defeated for the office by Francis T. Nicholls, who appointed him an associate justice of the state supreme court for the term of twelve years. In 1892, during the struggle for the recharter of the Louisiana Lottery, he was the candidate of the lottery wing of the Democratic party for governor but was defeated by the anti-lottery candidate. On May 28, 1896, he was elected to the United States Senate for the term beginning Mar. 4, 1897, to succeed N. C. Blanchard, and by reëlection served until his death in 1910.

McEnery was a well-proportioned man, with a ruddy face and keen blue eyes. He walked with a slight stoop or forward bend of neck and head. During his later years he was troubled by deafness. His legal opinions are said to indicate an impatience with detail but a thorough knowledge of principles; his messages and papers while governor, repressed and condensed to the point of dryness, are not marked by the literary distinction which takes such matters out of the ordinary. His greatest gift, perhaps, was his ability to handle men. He kept no diary and left no reminiscences. After a brief illness he died in New Orleans, where he was buried in Metairie Cemetery. He had married, on June 27, 1878, Elizabeth Phillips of Monroe, La.

[*Biog. Dir. Am. Cong.* (1928); *Who's Who in America*, 1910–11; 127 *La. Reports*, xxvii–xxix; Alcée Fortier, *Louisiana* (1914), vol. II; *Biog. and Hist. Memoirs of La.* (1892), vol. II; *Biog. Sketches of Louisiana's Governors from D'Iberville to McEnery, By a Louisianaise* (1885); *Senate Doc. 871*, 61 Cong., 3 Sess.; New Orleans newspapers for June 29, 1910; information as to certain facts from McEnery's niece, Mrs. Henry Baumgarten, New Orleans, La.] M. J. W.

McENTEE, JERVIS (July 14, 1828–Jan. 27, 1891), landscape painter, born at Rondout, N. Y., the eldest child of James S. and Sarah Jane (Goetcheus) McEntee, came of Irish and Huguenot stock. His father, an engineer, had charge of the construction of the Delaware & Hudson canal and the terminal docks at Rondout. Jervis McEntee received his early education at Clinton Institute, Clinton, N. Y., and soon after leaving this school he became (1850–51) a pupil of Frederick E. Church in New York City. In 1854 he married Gertrude, daughter of the Rev. Thomas Jefferson Sawyer. For three or four years he engaged in business at Rondout, but without much success, and in 1858, at the age of thirty, he definitely turned to art and opened a studio in the metropolis. In 1859, with his friend Sanford R. Gifford [*q.v.*], he went to Europe, visited all the leading art galleries, and sketched from nature in Italy and Switzerland. In 1861 his "Melancholy Days" was bought by James A. Suydam, N. A., who left it to the National Academy. McEntee was elected an Academician the same year.

As a rule he spent his summers and autumns at Rondout, whence he made frequent painting excursions to the nearby Catskills. A place especially endeared to him was Lanesville, where many of his best studies were made. He soon became noted for his winter and autumn scenes, which were his best productions and have a marked poetic character. Tuckerman found in his landscapes "a subtle feeling, a latent sentiment, and a delicate touch . . . rarely found even among the most skilful scenic limners" (*post,* p. 545); but Isham, less lenient, wrote that he "had no thorough training, and his works sometimes show the lack of it" (*post,* p. 245). It is perhaps just to say that he shared the technical weaknesses as well as the engaging personal qualities of the men of the Hudson River school. Their work, in spite of its lack of substance and depth, has a historic significance. In the eyes of their compatriots, at least, it was peculiarly winning because of its native ingenuousness.

McEntee had many warm friends and ardent patrons in the New York of the late nineteenth century. At the Paris Exposition of 1867 he exhibited two landscapes. At the Centennial Exposition, Philadelphia, 1876, he was represented by eight pictures. He exhibited also at the Royal Academy, London, 1872, and at the Paris Exposition of 1878. His "Eastern Sunset Sky" was in the Thomas B. Clarke collection, and his "November Days" was in the J. Taylor Johnston collection. The "Autumn Landscape with Figures," from the Borden collection, is in the Metropolitan Museum of Art, New York. A work of dramatic interest, outside the customary range of his subjects, was "The Danger Signal." In a driving snow-storm a passenger train has been brought to a sudden stop by a red lantern swung by a track-walker in the foreground. The snow lies in drifts on the track, and the glare of the locomotive headlight illuminates the wintry scene with strong effect. McEntee died at his old homestead at Rondout, at the age of sixty-two. He left no children. His wife had died some twelve years before him.

[The *Kingston* (N. Y.) *Daily Freeman,* Jan. 27, 1891; H. T. Tuckerman, *Book of the Artists* (1867); Samuel Isham, *The Hist. of Am. Painting* (1905); *Bull. of the Metropolitan Museum, N. Y.,* Apr. 1913; *Internat. Exhibition, 1876: Official Cat.,* Part II; *Cat. of the Thos. B. Clarke Coll. of Am. Pictures* (1891); Sadakichi Hartmann, *A Hist. of Am. Art* (1902), vol. I; G. W. Sheldon, *Am. Painters* (1881); *N. Y. Times,* Jan. 28, 1891.] W. H. D.

McFARLAND, JOHN THOMAS (Jan. 2, 1851–Dec. 22, 1913), Methodist Episcopal minister and educator, was born at Mount Vernon, Ind. His parents were Sylvanas and Elizabeth (Ginn) McFarland, pioneer settlers, who later moved to the prairies of Iowa, where he spent his boyhood on a farm. His father was of a deeply religious nature, and the son used to tell of his own conversion, when a college junior, after an earnest conversation with his parent in an old farm wagon on a country road. He studied at Iowa Wesleyan University, but received the degree of A.B. at Simpson College, Indianola, Iowa, in 1873. In that year he was ordained as a Methodist minister and began to serve a rural Iowa charge. Ambitious, however, for thorough ministerial preparation, he soon entered Boston University School of Theology, graduating in 1878. He had already married, in 1873, Mary Burt, of Mount Pleasant, Iowa, a college mate. They had two sons and a daughter. For years he devoted himself to the round of pastoral duty —in Iowa till 1880, and in Peoria, Ill., from 1880 to 1882. During the latter year he was called to Iowa Wesleyan University as vice-president, succeeding in 1884 to the presidency, which he held until 1891. The institution was limited in resources, but he somewhat enlarged its physical equipment and liberalized and strengthened its cultural courses. Subsequently he served as pastor of three large churches—Grace Church, Jacksonville, Ill. (1891–96), New York Avenue Church, Brooklyn, N. Y. (1897–99), and the First Church, Topeka, Kan. (1899–1904).

Always a keen student of philosophy and educational theory, he had success in applying the principles derived from these to the training of the young people of his churches. In 1904, he was elected editor of the Sunday-school literature of the Methodist Episcopal Church. He inherited an elaborate system of Biblical and religious lesson periodicals, which had wide circulation but which reflected the scholarship as well as the pedagogical theories and methods of a former generation. With patience and courage he devoted himself to the task of reforming the lesson material in such a way as to bring it into harmony with the advances in pedagogy, archeology, and Biblical criticism. As signs of new life in the periodicals began to appear, the editor became the object of bitter attacks from conservatives in his own denomination who accused him of "putting poison in the milk." He persevered in his course, however, with serene confidence in its essential rectitude. At the General Conference of 1912 an attempt was made by the conservative ministers and laymen to censure him, and, if possible, to prevent his reëlection as editor. His dignified speech in defense of his course is one of the high points in his career (see *Daily Christian Advocate,* Minneapolis, Minn., May 23, 1912) and is a landmark in the history of the development of progressive thinking in the denomination. The result was his complete vindication and reëlection. Eventually the strain of incessant labor, coupled with the hostility of his enemies, wore him down. His health gave way; partial paralysis set in; yet he toiled at his task, and gave to the churches the first complete system of lessons scientifically adapted to the needs and capacities of the developing mind of childhood, adolescence, youth, and maturity. Other Protestant churches acknowledged his leadership and adopted or imitated the system which he had worked out. After the summer of 1913 he continued to work, though some of his bodily powers were seriously impaired, and in December at Maplewood, N. J., he died.

His writings were largely fugitive editorials in Sunday-school periodicals, but some of the convictions for which he stood he embodied in *Preservation vs. the Rescue of the Child* (1906), and in *The Book and the Child* (1907). The vein of genuine poetry that lay deep in his fine nature found occasional expression in verse, a volume of which, *Poems,* was published in 1914. The spiritual yearnings of his nature are seen in his *Etchings of the Master* (1909). He was one of the editors of *The Encyclopedia of Sunday Schools and Religious Education* (3 vols., 1915).

[Memoir of McFarland by L. H. Murlin, in the *Jour. of the Twenty-seventh Delegated General Conference of the M. E. Ch.,* 1916; *M. E. Ch. Official Record, Kan. Conference,* 1914; *Who's Who in America,* 1912–13; *Christian Advocate* (N. Y.), Dec. 25, 1913; *Northwestern Christian Advocate* (Chicago), Dec. 31, 1913; *N. Y. Tribune,* Dec. 23, 1913.] J. R. J.

McFARLAND, SAMUEL GAMBLE (Dec. 11, 1830–Apr. 25, 1897), a Presbyterian clergyman who served in Siam first as a missionary and later in the educational department of the Siamese government, was born in Washington County, Pa., the son of William and Mary (McKenahan) McFarland and the grandson of Samuel McFarland who emigrated from the North of Ireland to Pennsylvania about 1793. He graduated from Washington (now Washington and Jefferson) College in 1857 with the degree of A.B., studied theology in the Western Theological Seminary, Pittsburgh, 1857–60, and was ordained by the Presbytery of Washington (Pa.) and commissioned for Siam in April 1860. On the 3rd of May following he married Jane E. Hays, daughter of John Hays of Canonsburg, Pa. To this union four children were born.

McFarland reached Bangkok Sept. 15, 1860. After a year of language study he was assigned, together with Rev. Daniel McGilvary [*q.v.*], to open at Petchaburi the first station outside the capital. It fell to his lot to construct the early buildings for the mission, in fulfillment of which task he found it necessary not only to draw plans but to supervise the brick-making and lumber mill and to direct the workmen item by item in the process of construction. When funds failed for the school building he appealed to the Siamese who were sympathetic with the work and in response received half the required amount from the king and the balance from princes and nobles. The first Siamese to be licensed to the gospel ministry was trained by him. McFarland became a thorough scholar in the Siamese language, mastering both the idiom and the pronunciation so that in its oral use he was as proficient as an educated native. His versatility is further shown in the publication (1876) of a Siamese hymnbook, the first to include tunes. In this undertaking it was necessary for him to teach the translator each separate tune to enable him to provide the correct meter; he then supervised the making of the plates in the United States, and finally printed the book at Petchaburi on a wooden press which he himself had made.

His acquaintance with the language and his achievement in his school work commended him to King Chulalongkorn, who was then purposing to initiate the work of education by the government. As the first step in the realization of his plan, he appointed McFarland, in 1878, principal of the proposed royal school for princes and sons of nobles. To accept this appointment McFarland resigned his commission as missionary. His new task involved the laying out of a curriculum together with a standard of grades and examinations, the enlistment of a faculty and provision for future training of teachers, and the adaptation and translation of suitable textbooks. All this had to be accomplished despite the opposition of a conservative council which was imbued with reactionism against the progressive policies of the king. He succeeded, however, by the exercise of tact and a sympathetic understanding of his co-workers, who at the same time had confidence in his wisdom. Sharing the king's vision of a future national system of education, in developing the royal school he laid the foundations for the system of universal compulsory education which was eventually established. On account of broken health, however, he was obliged to resign, in 1896, before the scheme was completed. He died in Canonsburg, Pa., the following year.

The literary work accredited to him includes *An English-Siamese Dictionary* (1865), which went through a number of editions; the hymnbook previously mentioned; translations into Siamese of the Pentateuch, the Minor Prophets, the Westminster Shorter Catechism, and a Bible textbook; together with original works, written in Siamese, on Church history, Christian evidences, botany, geology, bookkeeping; and numerous sermons and tracts.

[*Biog. and Hist. Cat. of Washington and Jefferson Coll.* (1889); *Commemorative Biog. Record of Washington County, Pa.* (1893); J. F. McFarland, *20th Century Hist. of the City of Washington and Washington County, Pa.* (1910); Daniel McGilvary, *A Half Century Among the Siamese and the Lāo* (1912); G. B. McFarland, *Hist. Sketch of Protestant Missions in Siam 1828–1928* (1928); S. S. Gilson, "Thirty-six Years in Siam," *Presbyterian Banner* (Pittsburgh), Feb. 17, 1897; *Pittsburgh Post and Pittsburg Press,* Apr. 27, 1897; biographical notes by McFarland's son, George B. McFarland, M.D., in Presbyterian Foreign Missions Library, New York.] G. H. F.

McFARLAND, THOMAS BARD (Apr. 19, 1828–Sept. 16, 1908), California jurist, was born in the Cumberland Valley, near Mercersburg, Pa., the son of John and Eliza (Parker) McFarland. His paternal ancestry was Scotch-Irish, his maternal English. Little is known of his education until his graduation in 1846 from Marshall College at Mercersburg (now Franklin and Marshall College at Lancaster). He then moved to Chambersburg and began the study of law under the tutelage of Robert M. Bard, a relative as well as a distinguished lawyer. He was admitted to the bar in 1849 and immediately made plans to join one of the numerous caravans then making its way across the plains to the Pacific Coast. He reached California in September 1850, and influenced by the success of others, staked for himself a small claim in the gold region. This venture proved so successful that he followed mining for a period of three years in Eldorado, Placer, Nevada, and Yuba counties, before beginning the practice of law in Nevada City in 1853. In 1856 he served as a member of the California General Assembly. On Nov. 20, 1861, at Nevada City, he was married to Susie Briggs, a native of New York. In the same year, 1861, he was elected to the judgeship of the fourteenth judicial district, at that time consisting of Nevada County. Two years later, his term having ended prematurely because of changes in the constitution, he was reëlected to the judgeship and given an enlarged judicial district including both Nevada and Placer counties. He served the full term of six years in this capacity, resuming private practice in 1870 in Sacramento. From 1874 to 1878 he served as the register of the United States Land Office in that city, though he accepted the appointment with reluctance and resigned within two months after his reappointment for a second term. During his residence in Sacramento he was also a member of the board of education.

McFarland served as a member of the convention which in 1878–79 formulated the constitution of the state of California, but he consistently opposed numerous provisions of the constitution itself and the adoption of that instrument by the people. Considering the influences active in the convention, which to many of that day seemed exceedingly radical, it is not hard to understand his opposition. In December 1882 he was appointed by Governor Perkins judge of the superior court of Sacramento County, and in 1884 he was elected by a large majority to succeed himself. Nominated in 1886 by the State Republican Convention, he was elected justice of the supreme court of California in the same year. He served in this capacity twenty-two years, having been reëlected in 1898 for a second term, which was cut short by his death in 1908. As a young man McFarland had been an ardent Whig, but with the election of Lincoln he had transferred his allegiance to the Republican party. This he served with intense loyalty for the remainder of his life. He was regarded as a man of scholarly attainments in his profession, of high personal integrity, kindly and genial, with an enormous capacity for work. He was a member of the board of trustees of Stanford University, for which he had been chosen by Senator Stanford, from the foundation of the University until his death. He died at his home in San Francisco at eighty years of age.

[*Who's Who in America,* 1908–09; O. T. Shuck, *Hist. of the Bench and Bar of Cal.* (rev. ed., 1901); *The Bay of San Francisco . . . A Hist.* (1892), vol. I; *Cal. Blue Book,* 1907; 154 *Cal. Reports,* 807–09; G. O. Seilhamer, *The Bard Family* (1908); *San Francisco Chronicle,* Sept. 16, 17, 1908.] R. G. C—d.

MACFARLANE, CHARLES WILLIAM (Nov. 5, 1850–May 15, 1931), engineer, builder, economist, was born in Philadelphia, Pa., of Scotch ancestry, the youngest son of David and Catherine (Macfarlane) Macfarlane. After preparatory work in the Philadelphia Central High School, he attended Lafayette College for a year, then transferred to Lehigh University, from which institution he received the degree of civil engineer in 1876. He remained at Lehigh University for postgraduate work in analytical chemistry, later entering the employment of a Philadelphia manufacturing concern, William Sellers & Company. His first two years were spent at manual labor in the shops, after which apprenticeship he served as superintendent of the foundry department for seven years. During these days he spent his evenings in study and writing, particularly on *Canons of Criticism* (1885). Eventually he entered business for himself. His operations were chiefly confined to the building of residences in West Philadelphia; he was his own architect, supervisor of building operations, and business manager. When he had attained a small fortune he decided to retire from business and to devote his time to intellectual pursuits and in 1888–89 he engaged in graduate study at the University of Pennsylvania, emphasizing philosophy, history, and economics. He then continued his studies in Germany, receiving the degree of Ph.D. at Freiburg, Baden, in 1893. The remainder of his life was spent in study and writing.

During his collegiate years at Bethlehem, Macfarlane made the acquaintance of Kathleen Selfridge, a gifted singer, whom he married on Mar. 8, 1883. He and his wife spent most of their lives in Philadelphia, but long visits were made to Europe, especially to France. He died in Philadelphia after years of failing health. His chief theoretical work in economics was *Value and Distribution,* published in 1899 and republished in 1911. It was an exposition of the Austrian School, attempting a reconciliation of this new approach with the older one of the British classical economists. His best-known work in applied economics was *The Economic Basis of an Enduring Peace* (1918) which was chiefly devoted to a discussion of the distribution of the coal lands of Germany, France, and Belgium. His other works include: *Pennsylvania Paper Currency* (1896); *The Three Primary Laws of Social Evolution* (1902); *The Place of Philosophy and Economics in the Curriculum of a Modern University* (1913); *Economic Interpretation of Early Roman History* (1915); *Les Défenses du Sanglier* (1915); and numerous small essays. In 1893 he published *The Ultimate Standard of Value,* translated from the German of the Austrian economist, Eugen Böhm von Bawerk. Several of his monographs on economic subjects were published by the American Economic Association and the American Academy of Political and Social Science. The later years of his life he devoted to the collection of material for an economic history of Rome. Unable to finish the work, he directed that his library and source material be given to Lehigh University with the understanding that this project be brought to completion. He also endowed at that institution chairs of philosophy and economics. In February 1931, a few months before his death, several of his works were collected by his wife and published under the title *Science and Literature.*

[See the Foreword by Isaac Pennypacker in *Science and Lit.*; *Who's Who in America,* 1926–27; *Jour. of Commerce* (Phila.), May 23, 1931; *Lehigh Alumni Bull.,* Oct. 1931; *N. Y. Times, Pub. Ledger* (Phila.), May 17, 1931. There is some doubt about the date of Macfarlane's birth. The date given here appears on his tombstone and is believed by his widow to be correct.]

S. H. P.

MACFARLANE, ROBERT (Apr. 23, 1815–Dec. 20, 1883), dyer, writer on scientific subjects, was born in Rutherglen, near Glasgow, Scotland. His educational advantages in youth were limited. He learned the art of dyeing at his father's works in Paisley; but, dissatisfied with the prospect of advancement in his native country, he emigrated at the age of twenty to America and in 1840 he settled in the city of Albany, N. Y. The scientific cast of his mind declared itself gradually and in 1846, with Joel Munsell, he began the publication of the *Mechanics' Mirror.* To this periodical he contributed a series of scientific papers which brought him a reputation as an expositor of mechanical principles and opened a larger field to him. Called in 1848 to the editorial chair of the *Scientific American,* in New York City, he devoted seventeen years to the journal, becoming a recognized authority on mechanical devices and kindred subjects. He was also an acceptable lecturer in the field. In 1851 he published a *History of Propellers and Steam Navigation with Biographical Sketches of the Early Inventors,* which ran into several editions. In the preface to this work, he stated his leading design in its preparation: "The arrangement and description of many devices which have been invented to propel vessels, in order to prevent many ingenious men from wasting their time, talents and money on such projects."

Macfarlane's connection with the *Scientific American* embraced a period of the Civil War in which the attention of the country was fixed on the machinery of marine warfare, in particular on the competing types of armored vessels; and his journal was among the stoutest champions of effective naval construction. Threatened with failure of eyesight, he resigned his editorship, and, returning to Albany, purchased a dyeing establishment. He had not lost his interest in the industry and in 1860 had published *A Practical Treatise on Dyeing and Calico-Printing.* During his years in America his remembrance of Scotland and the fascination of Scottish history and romance had kept their hold on his mind. His birthplace was not remote from the ancient possessions of the clan Macfarlane. He returned twice to his native land, and there found employment for his pen in sketches of travel, which appeared, under the name "Rutherglen," in the *Scottish American Journal.* If Scottish antiquities and scenery appealed to him, hardly less did the story of Scottish emigration to America. In Albany he was active in the St. Andrew's Society, serving at one time as its president, and was president of the Burns Club. Late in life he removed to Brooklyn, where he died. His wife was Anna Garth Macfarlane.

[A. J. Parker, *Landmarks of Albany County, N. Y.* (1897), pt. 3; G. R. Howell and others, *Bi-Centennial Hist. of Albany: Hist. of the County of Albany* (1886); Mrs. C. M. Little, *Hist. of the Clan MacFarlane* (1893), pp. 227–30; Peter Ross, *The Scot in America* (1896); *Sci. American*, Jan. 5, 1884; *Albany Evening Jour.*, Dec. 20, 1883; *Brooklyn Daily Eagle*, Dec. 21, 1883.]
R. E. D.

McFAUL, JAMES AUGUSTINE (June 6, 1850–June 16, 1917), Roman Catholic prelate, son of James and Mary (Heffernan) McFaul, was born in the village of Larne, County Antrim, Ireland. At the age of six months, he was brought to New York by his parents, who soon afterward settled permanently at Bound Brook, N. J. As a child, he attended the local schools of Weston and Millstone, journeying to New Brunswick or Raritan for mass and religious instruction under Benedictine missionaries. Through the influence of the Benedictines, he was sent to St. Vincent's College, Beatty, Pa., and later completed his classical education at St. Francis Xavier College, New York. Having studied theology at Seton Hall College, South Orange, N. J., he was ordained, May 26, 1877, by Archbishop Corrigan [*q.v.*]. He served as curate at Paterson, Orange, St. Patrick's Church in Jersey City, St. Peter's Church in New Brunswick, and finally at St. Mary's Church, Trenton, where he was under the distinguished Vicar General, Anthony Smith. St. Mary's Church was selected as a cathedral by Bishop M. J. O'Farrell, when, in 1881, he was named first bishop of the newly created diocese of Trenton. Hence the young assistant and secretary came into intimate contact with his ordinary, who appreciated his zeal and mental equipment. In 1884 McFaul was promoted to the rectorship of the Star of the Sea Church at Long Branch, where he paid off a heavy mortgage and built St. Michael's Church in the neighboring town of Elberon. Called back as pastor of the cathedral in 1890, he acted as the bishop's secretary and chancellor, and in 1892 became vicar general. On Bishop O'Farrell's death, he served as administrator and was soon appointed to the see, being consecrated by Archbishop Corrigan on Oct. 18, 1894.

Bishop McFaul proved a capable leader who gained the whole-hearted support of his priests and people. During his rule the diocese advanced rapidly, the number of priests, teaching and nursing sisters, and churches and chapels greatly increasing. About twenty-five parochial schools were erected, largely because of his insistence on Catholic education. In addition to five academies, he gave unstinted patronage to Mount St. Mary's College, Plainfield, which cared for the higher education of women. Interested in the newer immigrant groups, he exerted himself to provide churches for the Poles and Hungarians and especially for the Italians, who presented a discouraging problem. Deeply concerned in social welfare work, he gave close attention to two hospitals, to Morris Hall (the home for the aged at Lawrenceville), and to St. Michael's Orphan Asylum and Industrial School at Hopewell. His interests, however, were not bounded by his diocese.

An active friend of Irish societies and the Home-Rule movement, he served as the arbiter of differences between two factions of the Ancient Order of Hibernians, welding them together into a united fraternal society (1897–98). He was equally successful in organizing the American Federation of the Catholic Societies with a total membership of about 2,000,000, though his inspiration failed to make this organization as effective in Catholic social and civic action as might have been anticipated. Liberal in spirit, he took an active part in municipal and state reforms, supported labor, and served on the state tuberculosis commission. As a Catholic controversialist and lecturer, he was able and courageous, but popular in tone. An energetic, self-denying man, he labored to the end despite a year of ill health. In 1916, *Pastoral Letters, Addresses, and Other Writings of the Rt. Rev. James A. McFaul*, edited by J. J. Powers, was published.

[W. T. Leahy, *The Cath. Ch. of the Diocese of Trenton* (1907); J. M. Flynn, *The Cath. Ch. in N. J.* (1904); J. H. Fox, *A Century of Catholicity in Trenton, N. J.* (1907); T. F. McGrath, *Hist. of the Ancient Order of Hibernians* (1898); annual Cath. directories; *Am. Cath. Who's Who*, 1911; *Who's Who in America*, 1916–17; *Daily State Gazette* (Trenton, N. J.), May 24, June 18–22, 1917; *N. Y. Times*, June 17, 1917; *Messenger of the Sacred Heart*, Apr. 1910; *Ill. Cath. Hist. Rev.* (later *Mid-America*), 1927–29.]
R. J. P.

McFERRIN, JOHN BERRY (June 15, 1807–May 10, 1887), Methodist clergyman, was born in Rutherford County, Tenn., and throughout his entire life was a citizen of that state. Emigrating to America from Ireland about 1750, the McFerrins were a family of fighters. The grandfather of John served during the American Revolution; his father, James, saw service under General Jackson in the War of 1812, and attained the rank of colonel in the Indian wars; through his mother, Jane Campbell Berry, he was directly related to the Col. William Campbell [*q.v.*] of King's Mountain celebrity. Their militant characteristics John McFerrin manifested throughout his long career as a leader in the affairs of his denomination. Never was he more at home than when under the fire of criticism or questions on the floor of public assemblies. Of large frame, heavy features, standing square on his feet, he was a typical son of the West. Although of Presbyterian stock, with his father he was converted under the preaching of a Methodist circuit rider and, also with his father, entered the Methodist ministry. He was never enrolled in an institution of higher learning, being of that group of pioneers who felt that a call to preach did not mean a call to go to school to get ready to preach.

In 1825 he was admitted to the Tennessee Conference on trial and spent two years as a circuit rider. Ordained deacon in 1827, he was appointed missionary to the Cherokee Indians in the territory where Chattanooga and Fort Oglethorpe now stand. He was ordained elder in 1829, and was a stationed preacher and presiding elder until 1840, when he became editor of the *Southwestern Christian Advocate,* Nashville. This paper he conducted with ability for eighteen years. In the meantime the Methodist Church divided over the question of slavery and McFerrin, who had been a delegate to the General Conference of 1844, was also a delegate to the Louisville Convention of 1845 at which the Methodist Episcopal Church, South, was organized. In 1858 he reluctantly relinquished his editorship to take charge, as book agent, of the publishing interests of his denomination, continuing in this office until 1866, though during the Civil War he also had charge of all the Methodist missionary work in the Army of the Tennessee. At the General Conference of 1866 he was elected secretary of the board of domestic missions; four years later the domestic and foreign boards were consolidated, and McFerrin directed the work of both until 1878. During his term of service he cleared away a depressing indebtedness, yet, because he lacked the faculties and sympathies necessary for successful missionary propagation, this period gave him less satisfaction than others in his long official career. The nine years from 1878 to 1887, when he again served as book agent, proved the climax of his labors. As a result of the war and bad management, the Methodist publishing house was in an almost hopeless struggle with debt. Shaping a plan of bond sales similar to that in use at the time by the federal government, he raised within a remarkably short time $350,000, and before his death saw every obligation met, every bond refunded, and the publishing house flourishing again. His business ability is indicated by the fact that he owned real estate and bank stock, and was at one time president of a street railway company.

In the midst of his many activities he found time to write *History of Methodism in Tennessee* (1869–73), a three-volume work which gives a first-hand account of life in Tennessee during the first quarter of the nineteenth century. He was twice married: first, in 1833, to Almyra Avery Probart; second, in 1855, to Cynthia Tennessee McGavock. The second wife and four children survived his death.

[O. P. Fitzgerald, *John B. McFerrin* (1888); *Christian Advocate* (Nashville), May 14, 21, 28, 1887; *General Minutes of the Methodist Episcopal Church, South* (1887); S. A. Steel, *Eminent Men I Met Along the Sunny Road* (1925).] R. W. G.

MACGAHAN, JANUARIUS ALOYSIUS (June 12, 1844–June 9, 1878), war correspondent, son of James and Esther (Dempsey) MacGahan, both of Irish descent, was born in Perry County, Ohio, on a small farm near the home of his cousin, Philip Sheridan [*q.v.*]. During his boyhood his father died, but the widowed mother managed to keep her children in school for some years, and after a period in St. Louis as a bookkeeper MacGahan resolved to go abroad to improve his general education and to continue his study of law. He lived in Brussels, in Paris, and in Germany, acquiring several languages, and on the outbreak of the Franco-Prussian War he obtained, partly through the influence of General Sheridan, an appointment as a special correspondent for the *New York Herald.* At once his adventurous disposition and his facility as a vivid descriptive writer with an eye for drama, manifested themselves. He had found his vocation. He followed the campaign of General Bourbaki, returned to Paris in time to witness the opening of the Commune, was imprisoned by the Versailles troops, and released through the efforts of the American minister. In the course of the next eight years he saw service in places widely distant from each other. During a summer in the Crimea he became a favorite with the Czar's court and conceived a warm liking for Russia. He "covered" the Caucasus expedition of General Sherman (1872) and the sittings of the Alabama Claims tribunal at Geneva.

There followed his ride into the desert of Central Asia (1873), which, according to Eugene Schuyler [*q.v.*], American secretary of legation at St. Petersburg, was "spoken of everywhere . . . as by far the most wonderful thing that ever had been done there" (Schuyler, *Turkistan,* 1885, I, 66). He defied the Russian embargo on newspaper men to find the expedition sent out under General Kauffmann to reduce the Khanate of Khiva. Cossacks pursued him almost a thousand miles. After twenty-nine days, with two attendants who could not understand his language, sometimes forced to wade to his knees in sand and several times "lost," he reached the camp. As an American he was allowed to stay; as a *molodyetz,* a hero, he instantly became popular. With the army he remained through the campaign against Khiva and the war with the Turkomans. At Khiva he met General Skobelev and they became affectionate friends. Later in the same year he reported the *Virginius* complications in Cuba; after that, the Carlist campaign in the Pyrenees (1874); and then, the expedition to the Arctic of the barque *Pandora* (1875) promoted by the younger James Gordon Bennett [*q.v.*].

Back in London, he found the Eastern Question the absorbing subject of the day. Rumors of the *bashi-bazouk* massacres in Bulgaria filtered through Europe. The opportunity for MacGahan's greatest service came when the *Daily News* sent him to make an independent investigation and write the exact truth. His Bulgarian letters of July and August 1876 wrought a great change in British sentiment and did much to produce the political reaction which made war inevitable between Russia and Turkey. Since that war gave Bulgaria her independence, he came to be known in that country as "the Liberator." For his London paper he followed the campaign, much of the time as a comrade of Skobelev, rendering distinguished service even when almost fully disabled. After the fall of Plevna, he went to Constantinople to nurse Francis Vinton Greene [*q.v.*] through typhoid, only himself to fall a victim to typhus. The burial was at Pera, with Skobelev as a mourner. In 1884, on the initiative of the General Assembly of his native state, his body was brought to America on a United States cruiser. A monument now marks his grave near New Lexington, to which the Bulgarian envoys at Washington make ceremonial visits at times.

At Yalta, MacGahan had met Barbara Nicholavna Elagin, of an ancient Russian family, whom he married in Paris in 1872. They had one son. MacGahan was very popular among his fellow correspondents and with army officers, who respected him both for his personal qualities and his professional abilities. His most important writings appeared in book form as follows: *Campaigning on the Oxus and the Fall of Khiva* (1874); *Under the Northern Lights* (1876), on the cruise of the *Pandora*; *The Turkish Atrocities in Bulgaria* (1876), and articles in *War Correspondence of the Daily News* (2 vols., London, 1877–78).

[Archibald Forbes, *Souvenirs of Some Continents* (1885); F. L. Bullard, *Famous War Correspondents* (1914); *Ohio Archaeol. and Hist. Quart.*, Apr.–July 1912; *N. Y. Herald,* June 11, 1878; *Daily News* (London), June 11, 12, 1878; references in the works of Frederick Boyle, Frederic Villiers, Frank Millet, and Gen. F. V. Greene; documentary material furnished by the family.]

F. L. B.

McGARVEY, JOHN WILLIAM (Mar. 1, 1829–Oct. 6, 1911), minister of the Disciples of Christ, educator, and writer, was born in Hopkinsville, Ky., where his father, John, a native of Ireland, conducted a small dry-goods business. His mother, whose maiden name was Sallie Ann Thomson, born near Georgetown, Ky., was of Virginia stock. After her husband's death in 1833, she married Dr. G. F. Saltonstall, and when John was about ten years old the family moved to Tremont, Tazewell County, Ill. Here he received a good preparatory training, and in 1847 entered Bethany College, graduating in 1850 with high rank as a classical scholar. Going to Fayette, Mo., where his family was then living, he conducted a boys' school for about a year. In September 1851 he was ordained by the Fayette church of the Disciples, and afterwards preached for that and neighboring churches, until, in February 1853, he accepted a call to Dover, Lafayette County, Mo. On Mar. 23, he married Ottie F. Hix of Fayette.

During the next nine years he became widely known throughout Missouri as a man of scholarly tastes, interested in education, alive with missionary zeal, and keen for theological controversy. He secured funds to establish a school in Dover and conducted it for a time, made preaching tours, and debated publicly with representatives of other denominations. At the time of the Civil War he was one of the ministers of his order who signed the circular "Concerning the Duties of Christians in this Conflict," which declared that Christians ought not to go to war. In 1862 he was called to Lexington, Ky.; and the following year he published *A Commentary on Acts of Apostles with a Revised Version of the Text.* Several other commentaries by him appeared later. In 1865 he was made professor of sacred history in the College of the Bible affiliated with Kentucky University, but for a number of years still carried on his pastoral work. His insistence upon larger support for the College brought him into conflict with President J. B. Bowman [*q.v.*] of the University and in 1873 he was dismissed. Two years later he was reinstated. Finally, in 1877, the College of the Bible became an independent institution, with McGarvey as professor, although it used the University classrooms and ultimately erected buildings on the University campus. From 1895 until his death McGarvey was president of the College.

Over a long period he was one of the most

prominent of the Disciples. His influence was thrown entirely on the side of conservatism. In the earlier part of his career he strenuously combated all modern methods and organization in church work. He was one of those who established (1868) and edited the *Apostolic Times,* designed to oppose the more liberal Isaac Errett [*q.v.*], editor of the *Christian Standard.* Later his guns were trained chiefly on the higher criticism. Through a department in the *Christian Standard,* which he began to edit in 1890, he familiarized the Disciples with the views of the critics, and fought them with both argument and ridicule. He published *Evidences of Christianity* in two volumes (1886, 1891), of which the first discusses the integrity of the New Testament text and the genuineness of the New Testament books, while the second treats of the credibility and inspiration of the New Testament; *Jesus and Jonah* (1896); *The Authorship of the Book of Deuteronomy, with its Bearing on the Higher Criticism of the Pentateuch* (1902); *The Standard Bible Commentary* (4 vols., 1905–08), with P. Y. Pendleton; *Short Essays in Biblical Criticism* (1910). In 1879 he made a tour of Egypt and Palestine, one of the results of which was *Lands of the Bible* (1881), which had a considerable circulation. He also published *Sermons, Delivered in Louisville, Kentucky, June–September 1893* (1894), and was for half a century a constant contributor to periodicals. His death occurred in Lexington in his eighty-third year.

[W. T. Moore, *The Living Pulpit of the Christian Church* (1869); J. T. Brown, *Churches of Christ* (1904); Errett Gates, *The Disciples of Christ* (1905); M. M. Davis, *How the Disciples Began and Grew* (1915); A. W. Fortune, *The Disciples in Ky.* (1932); *Who's Who in America,* 1910–11; *Christian Standard,* Oct. 14, 21, 1911; *Evening Post* (Louisville), Oct. 7, 1911; *Courier-Journal* (Louisville), Oct. 8, 1911.]

H. E. S.

McGEE, WILLIAM JOHN (Apr. 17, 1853–Sept. 4, 1912), geologist, anthropologist, and hydrologist, was born in a log-cabin near Farley, Iowa, the fourth of nine children of James and Martha Ann (Anderson) McGee. His father was a native of Antrim, Ireland, who came to America in 1831; his mother, born in Kentucky, was also of Scotch-Irish descent. The boy spent the first years of his life on a farm. His mind early took its bent toward science and he studied by himself, with some assistance from an elder brother who had attended Cornell College. The habit of self-help led him into studies far beyond anything to be furnished on the frontier in the sixties. His formative years saw him striving for knowledge and material support. He tried blacksmithing and studied surveying. Becoming greatly interested in the structure of the earth, he made surveys of the geology of Iowa which he reported in the *American Journal of Science* (1878–82). During these investigations, mounds and other traces of former inhabitants of the prairies also came under his observation. The work he carried on independently attracted the attention of the United States Geological Survey, and in 1883, at the age of thirty, he was invited by Maj. J. W. Powell [*q.v.*] to become a member of that force. Soon he was given charge of the branch of the survey dealing with the geology of the Atlantic Coastal Plain, and during the years 1883–94 he conducted important studies of this area. His geological publications include more than a hundred papers, notable among them being: "The Geology of the Head of Chesapeake Bay" (*Seventh Annual Report of the United States Geological Survey . . . 1885–'86,* 1888); "Three Formations of the Middle Atlantic Slope" (*American Journal of Science,* February, April, May, June 1888); "The Pleistocene History of Northeastern Iowa" (*Eleventh Annual Report, United States Geological Survey . . . 1889–'90,* pt. 1, 1891); "The Lafayette Formation" (*Twelfth Annual Report . . . 1890–'91,* pt. 1, 1891); "The Gulf of Mexico as a Measure of Isostasy" (*American Journal of Science,* September 1892). In 1888–91 he edited the *Bulletin* of the Geological Society of America.

McGee's official connection with anthropology began with his transfer in 1893 to the post of ethnologist in charge, in the Bureau of American Ethnology, of which his chief, Major Powell, was director. Bringing to the new work a genius for essential classification and the ability to inspire his younger helpers and colleagues, he gave the Bureau an impetus which was felt for years. His anthropological writings include some thirty titles. Noteworthy among the papers which he published in the *Annual Reports* of the Bureau were: "The Siouan Indians" (*Fifteenth . . . 1893–'94,* 1897); "Primitive Trephining in Peru" (*Sixteenth . . . 1894–'95,* 1897); "The Seri Indians" (*Seventeenth . . . 1895–'96,* 1898, pt. I); and "Primitive Numbers" (*Nineteenth . . . 1897–'98,* pt. I, 1900). During Powell's last illness he assumed the administrative work, and at the time of Powell's death in 1902 was serving as acting director.

The following year he resigned and took charge of the anthropological and historical exhibit at the Louisiana Purchase Exposition in St. Louis. He was subsequently appointed by President Roosevelt to the Inland Waterways Commission, and by the Secretary of Agriculture to take charge of the study of the water resources of the United States, an investigation begun in his surveys of Iowa. A report on this subject ("Wells and Subsoil Water," *Department of Agriculture Bulletin No. 92,* 1913) was his last contribution to science. His death, from cancer, occurred in his sixtieth year.

In 1888 he was married to Anita Newcomb, daughter of Simon Newcomb [*q.v.*] the astronomer. His wife survived him. Throughout his mature life he was known even to his friends by the initials only of his given names, and always signed himself W J McGee, without periods. Facile in expressing the stores of his mind, he delivered unnumbered addresses and discussions. Approachable, benevolent, willing to impart and to learn, he filled an important place in the scientific life of his time.

[F. H. Knowlton, in *Bull. Geol. Soc. of America,* Mar. 1913; F. W. Hodge, in *Am. Anthropologist,* Oct.–Dec. 1912; *The McGee Memorial Meeting of the Washington Academy of Sciences . . . Dec. 5, 1913* (1916); *Who's Who in America,* 1910–11; Emma R. McGee, *Life of W. J. McGee* (1915), which is eulogistic and does not treat of his scientific work; *Evening Star* (Washington), Sept. 4, 1912; personal recollections.]

W. H.

McGHEE, CHARLES McCLUNG (Jan. 23, 1828–May 5, 1907), financier, was born in Monroe County, Tenn. He was the fifth and youngest child of Betsy Jones (McClung) McGhee, the daughter of Charles McClung, and John McGhee, the grandson of Irish emigrants who had settled in Lancaster County, Pa. From his father he inherited a large estate in lands and slaves. In 1846 he graduated from East Tennessee University, which is now the University of Tennessee. On June 10, 1847, he was married to his cousin, the daughter of Hugh A. M. White of Knoxville, Isabella McNutt White, whose only child died shortly after her own death on May 13, 1848. On Apr. 14, 1857, he was married to his first wife's sister, Cornelia Humes White. They had five children. During the Civil War he served as colonel in the commissary department of the Confederate army. The war over, he devoted his energies to the financial rehabilitation of his section. He served his alma mater for a number of years, from 1869 to 1884, in the several offices of trustee, treasurer, and secretary and treasurer. He helped to maintain the institution on the meager revenue furnished by the state, which was financially so embarrassed that, instead of paying interest on its bonds held by the university, it issued depreciated warrants. He succeeded in marketing these advantageously by virtue of his financial connections as president of the People's Bank of Knoxville. He further served his university and his city as a member of the Tennessee legislature in the session of 1871–72. Finding the representatives from western Tennessee opposed to the giving of state support to the university in the eastern section, he placated them by a resolution that resulted in the granting of free transportation by the railroads to state students on their way to and from Knoxville. This effort seems the more commendable when it is noted that he already had a controlling interest in Tennessee railroads.

When the railroads (for the financing of which the state had gone heavily into debt) proved unprofitable, were thrown into receiverships, and advertised for sale, he and his business friends enlisted the financial support of such northern capitalists as Thomas A. Scott of Pennsylvania and obtained the formation of the Southern Railway Security Company. The various roads running out of Knoxville were consolidated into the East Tennessee, Virginia & Georgia Railroad, of which he became one of the directors. They purchased the state's interest in certain delinquent roads and acquired the Knoxville & Ohio, the Memphis & Charleston, and the Rogersville and Jefferson railroads. The South was joined by one more railway when a road to Macon, Ga., was built and consolidated. The Alabama & Chattanooga Railroad, too, became another link in the great southern combination. The Atlantic, Mississippi & Ohio Railroad (Norfolk and Western) was added and equipped with a highly ornamented train of red coaches. From the end of the Civil War until his death he was concerned with every railroad that affected the life of East Tennessee. Until his retirement about ten years before his death he was active in the organizations, reorganizations, receiverships, and changes in control of the network of railroads that, completely bankrupt, passed to the J. P. Morgan interests in 1894 and were rehabilitated under the control of the Southern Railway Company. In spite of the collapse in the financial structure of the railroads, in these years he amassed a fortune, from which he endowed many Knoxville enterprises, notably the Lawson-McGhee Library.

[W. T. Hale and D. L. Merritt, *A Hist. of Tenn.* (1913), vols. III, V; John Allison, *Notable Men of Tenn.* (1905), vol. I; Henry Hall, *America's Successful Men of Affairs,* vol. I (1895); *War of the Rebellion: Official Records (Army),* 2 ser., vol. I; *University of Tenn. Record,* July 1898; H. V. and H. W. Poor, *Manual of the Railroads of the U. S.* (1877–96), esp. 1886 and 1894; Stuart Daggett, *Railroad Reorganization* (1908); *Jour. House of Representatives of . . . Tenn.,* 37 Gen. Assembly, 1 Sess. (1871), joint resolution no. 119, p. 363. Wm. McClung, *The McClung Geneal.* (1904), pp. 36–37; *Journal and Tribune* (Knoxville), May 6, 1907.]

M. B. H—r.

McGIFFIN, PHILO NORTON (Dec. 13, 1860–Feb. 11, 1897), naval officer, was born in Washington, Pa. His great-grandfather, who came from Scotland, fought in the Revolution. His father, Col. Norton McGiffin, served in the Mexican and Civil wars. His mother was Sarah Houston (Quail). After preliminary schooling in Washington, Pa., where he attended the Washington and Jefferson Academy, Philo McGiffin entered the United States Naval Academy in his seventeenth year. Here he distinguished himself not so much in scholarship as by the many escapades in which he was involved. He spent several months on the station ship *Santee* in punishment, and took five years to complete the four-year Academy course. On graduation in 1882 he was assigned to duty in the *Hartford,* the flagship of the Pacific Squadron. Two years later he was examined for the grade of past midshipman. It was a time when commissions in the service could be granted only as vacancies occurred. Thus, with many of his classmates, instead of being promoted, he was given an honorable discharge with a year's pay. He is said to have long treasured the hope that Congress might reinstate the naval cadets who had been denied commissions, but such an act was never passed.

In the spring of 1885 the Tongking affair in China induced him to go to the East. Applying in person to the viceroy Li Hung-Chang, he was given a commission in the Chinese navy. Upon the conclusion of peace with France, he was made professor of seamanship and gunnery at the Naval College in Tien-tsin. When four Chinese ironclads were ordered in England, he was sent to superintend their construction. Serving for ten years as naval constructor and during the same time as profesor of gunnery and seamanship, he taught most of the Chinese officers that were destined to serve in the Sino-Japanese War.

On the beginning of hostilities McGiffin was the executive and second in command on board the *Chen Yuen,* a seven-thousand-ton battleship, the sister ship of the *Ting Yuen,* flagship of Admiral Ting. In the decisive naval engagement fought off the Yalu River, Sept. 17, 1894, the two Chinese battleships withstood the main Japanese squadron until the Japanese steamed away. "It was due to the *Chen Yuen's* skillful manœuvers that the Chinese flagship did not suffer more," wrote a Japanese (*United States Naval Institute Proceedings,* XX, 812). The Chinese captain of this ship having failed utterly in the crisis, everything devolved on McGiffin. Although the *Chen Yuen* was miserably equipped with ammunition and was on fire eight different times, he carried her through to safety. He was so severely wounded and burned, however, that he was left a physical and mental wreck. Resigning from the Chinese service he returned to America. For two years he lived in New York City, suffering in the extreme. In a state of intense nervous prostration, a victim of hallucinations, he was cared for by a life-long friend, Col. Robert M. Thompson, and sent to the Post Graduate Hospital. For a while he seemed much improved; then, eluding his attendants, he secured his revolvers and committed suicide. He was absolutely fearless, and when given the opportunity excelled in action; but he seems to have been impelled not so much by a spirit of patriotism or self-sacrifice as by a love of adventure. Richard Harding Davis, a boyhood friend, gave him a proper characterization by including him in his *Real Soldiers of Fortune* (1906).

[Davis, *Real Soldiers of Fortune*; Park Benjamin, in *Army and Navy Jour.*, Feb. 20, 1897; McGiffin's article, "The Battle of Yalu, Personal Recollections by the Commander of the Chinese Ironclad *Chen Yuen*," *Century Magazine*, Aug. 1895; *U. S. Naval Inst. Proc.*, XX (1894), 803–18, and XXI (1895), 479–521; letter from Alumni Secretary, Washington and Jefferson College; *Evening Post* (N. Y.), Feb. 11, 1897; the *Sun* (N. Y.), Feb. 12, 1897.] C. S. A.

MCGILL, JOHN (Nov. 4, 1809–Jan. 14, 1872), Roman Catholic prelate, son of James and Lavenia (Dougherty) McGill, was born in Philadelphia, where his father, an immigrant from County Derry (1788), was engaged in business. About 1819 the McGills moved westward, finally settling in Bardstown, Ky. Here John completed his elementary schooling and in 1828 graduated from St. Joseph's College. Having read law under Gov. Charles A. Wickliffe [*q.v.*], he was admitted to the bar and practised with success in New Orleans and in Bardstown. Dissatisfied in this profession, he studied theology at the neighboring St. Thomas Seminary and under the Sulpicians at St. Mary's, Baltimore. Ordained at Bardstown by Bishop David [*q.v.*], June 13, 1835, he was assigned to St. Peter's Church, Lexington, Ky., and later as an assistant to Dr. I. A. Reynolds of St. Louis' Church, Louisville, whom he succeeded as pastor when the latter was named to the See of Charleston. An assistant editor of *The Catholic Advocate* under Dr. M. J. Spalding [*q.v.*], whom he also served as vicar general, he won reputation as a somewhat aggressive controversialist. To a local disputation, he contributed a brochure on the origin of the Church of England and a translation of J. M. V. Audin's *History of the Life, Works, and Doctrines of John Calvin* (1845). On Oct. 10, 1850, he was named bishop of Richmond, Va., and a month later consecrated at Bardstown by Archbishop P. R. Kenrick [*q.v.*].

Bishop McGill found Richmond an impoverished diocese with only eight priests. Within ten years, however, he paid the bulk of the diocesan debt, built several churches, established a number of missions, assigned St. Mary's German Church in Richmond to the Benedictines, founded schools at Richmond, Norfolk, Petersburg, and Harpers Ferry, erected a hospital at Norfolk, and neutralized the evil effects of the Know-Nothing agitation by his judicious carriage and a series of letters in refutation of charges made by Robert Ridgway in nativist papers. The Civil War threw all into chaos. A strong Southern sympathizer, the Bishop urged enlistments, especially in the Emmett and Montgomery Guards, furnished chaplains for the Confederate forces, ministered personally at Libby Prison, and detailed Sisters of Mercy and of Charity as military nurses. Unable to visit the churches of the diocese, he utilized his time in writing *The True Church, Indicated to the Inquirer* (1862) and *Our Faith, the Victory: or a Comprehensive View of the Principal Doctrines of the Christian Religion* (1865), which in revised form appeared in several editions. In the latter work he was inclined to view the war as a punishment for the treatment of slaves and hoped "that by the present convulsions, his providence is preparing for them at least, a recognition of those rights as immortal beings, which are required for the observance of the paramount laws of God."

On Lee's surrender, Bishop McGill visited his war-torn diocese and entered upon the arduous labor of reconstruction: churches were rebuilt and scattered congregations mobilized; academies were established by the Visitation nuns, Sisters of Charity, and Sisters of Notre Dame; and orphan asylums were provided. At the Second Plenary Council of Baltimore he depicted to the assembled bishops the needs of the Church in the South and pled for its support. In 1867 he visited Rome for the second time in the interest of the diocese, and two years later attended the Vatican Council, at which he preached a public discourse. His active career was then practically at an end, though as an invalid, dying of a cancer, he lived on bravely for several years.

[F. J. Magri, *The Cath. Ch. in the City and Diocese of Richmond* (1906); R. H. Clarke, *Lives of the Deceased Bishops of the Cath. Ch. in the U. S.*, vol. III (1888); J. G. Shea, *Hist. of the Cath. Ch. in the U. S.*, vol. IV (1892); B. J. Webb, *The Centenary of Catholicity in Ky.* (1884); *U. S. Cath. Mag.*, July 1845; *The Metropolitan Cath. Almanac*, 1851, pp. 120 f.; *Sadliers' Cath. Directory*, 1873, p. 39; *Richmond Daily Enquirer*, Jan. 16, 1872; *Freeman's Journal*, (N. Y.), Sept. 29, 1855.]
R. J. P.

McGILLIVRAY, ALEXANDER (*c.* 1759–Feb. 17, 1793), Creek chief, belonged to the Wind clan of the Upper Creek Indians, among whom descent was traced on the maternal side. His mother is said to have been Sehoy Marchand, a French-Indian halfbreed (Pickett, *post*, I, 32); his father was Lachlan McGillivray, a prominent trader and politician of Georgia. Probably until the age of fourteen, Alexander lived with the Indians at his father's trading post on the Tallapoosa River. He was then taken to Charleston and Savannah, where he is said to have worked in a counting-house and to have spent his spare time reading history. Upon the outbreak of the American Revolution the McGillivrays became Loyalists and their property was confiscated. Father and son each returned to his childhood home, Lachlan to Scotland and Alexander to the Creek country, where he spent the rest of his life. During the Revolution he served as a British agent among the Southern Indians, sent out war parties against the American frontier, and formed a connection with the Loyalist traders, Panton, Leslie & Company. After the Revolution, this connection was of great value to both parties, for each advanced the other's interests with the Spanish government, which had acquired the Floridas in 1783. At the same time, McGillivray seems to have been genuinely devoted to the welfare of his people. His immediate purpose was to form a confederation of the Southern Indians and, with the aid of Spain or perhaps Great Britain, compel the Americans to restore the Indian line as it existed in 1773; in other words, to evacuate a large part of Georgia, Tennessee, and Kentucky. Since he also sought the cooperation of the Northern Indians, he may be regarded as the prototype of Tecumseh, whose mother was a Creek woman of McGillivray's generation.

From 1784 to his death in 1793, McGillivray touched the life of the Old Southwest at many of its most important points, and his career possessed international significance. He was courted by merchants, land speculators, and filibusters and by the governments of Georgia, the United States, and Spain. In June 1784 the Spanish governor, Esteban Rodríguez Miró [*q.v.*], concluded a treaty with the Creek Indians at Pensacola, and through the aid of Panton, Leslie & Company, McGillivray was appointed Spanish commissary to enforce Spain's monopoly of trade with the Creeks. His salary was fifty dollars a month. In the following year he rewarded the Loyalist traders by helping them to obtain Spain's permission to establish a branch at Pensacola. In 1786 he first precipitated a war with the American frontiersmen and then forced the reluctant Spaniards to provide him with munitions with which to prosecute it. One of the causes of the war was his resentment at the confiscation of his family's property by Georgia. It was waged for the purpose of annihilating American competition in the southern Indian trade and driving back the American frontier within the line of 1773. In 1785 he had opposed Georgia's effort to establish Bourbon County on the Mississippi, and his war parties now harried the outlying settlements from Georgia to Cumberland. His power was probably at its height in 1787, when his warriors' attacks almost succeeded in destroying the stations on the Cumberland River; when men under his orders murdered a Georgia agent in the midst of the friendly Chickasaws; and when he himself was visited by the agent of Congress, James White, to whom he is said to have expressed the wish that the Creek towns might be organized as a state and admitted into the Union.

Two sources of his strength were Spanish aid and the weakness of the United States government. At the end of 1787 the cautious Spaniards stopped furnishing him with munitions; and, although his intrigue with the adventurer William Augustus Bowles [*q.v.*] frightened them into renewing the practice in 1789, mutual confidence was never restored. In the latter year a stronger government was established in the United States. President Washington immediately gave his attention to Creek relations and the dangerous designs of the Yazoo land speculators, who were bidding for McGillivray's support. After one abortive effort at peace, when David Humphreys, Benjamin Lincoln, and Cyrus Griffin [*qq.v.*] were sent to negotiate a treaty with the Creek nation, Col. Marinus Willett persuaded McGillivray to come to New York, where a pension of $1,200 to him obtained a treaty (Aug. 7, 1790) satisfactory to the United States but contrary to the Creek treaty of 1784 with Spain. Returning to the Indian country, McGillivray was induced by the resentment of the Indians, the return of the hostile Bowles, the arguments of William Panton [*q.v.*], and the increase of his Spanish pension to $2,000 and ultimately to $3,500, to sign a convention (July 6, 1792) with Governor Carondelet [*q.v.*] repudiating the Treaty of New York. During the progress of further negotiations for the formation of a confederation of the Southern Indians in alliance with Spain against the United States, McGillivray died at Pensacola of a complication of "gout in the stomach" and pneumonia. He is said to have been buried with Masonic honors in the garden of William Panton at Pensacola.

McGillivray was not a warrior and almost never took part in the incessant fighting on the southern frontier. His chief interests were diplomacy, trade, and planting. Far better educated than most of the leading American frontiersmen of his day, he wrote clearly and forcefully in both his private and public correspondence. Although closely associated with Panton, Leslie & Company and financially dependent upon them, he was not a member of the company. He had three plantations and about sixty slaves, engaged extensively in stock raising, set a good table, lived well, and was never out of debt. He was a heavy drinker and frequently suffered from blinding headaches. He had two wives at least and his involved estate was left to his two children, Alexander and Elizabeth, who later brought suit to recover it from the executors, William Panton and John Forbes, 1769–1823 [*q.v.*]. McGillivray was a relative of John Weatherford, another well known halfbreed, and a nephew of the Creek chief, Red Shoes.

[*Am. State Papers, Indian Affairs,* vol. I (1832); A. J. Pickett, *Hist. of Ala.* (2 vols., 1851); John Pope, *A Tour through the Southern and Western Territories of the U. S.* (1792); A. P. Whitaker, *The Spanish-American Frontier* (1927) and two articles, "Alexander McGillivray, 1783–1789," in which the date of his birth is discussed, and "Alexander McGillivray, 1789–1793," *N. C. Hist. Rev.,* Apr. and July 1928, both giving copious references to manuscript and printed sources.]

A. P. W.

McGILVARY, DANIEL (May 16, 1828–Aug. 22, 1911), missionary in Siam, was born in Moore County, N. C., son of Malcolm McGilvary and his wife, Catharine McIver. He received his academic education in the private academy of Rev. William Bingham at Hillsboro, from which he graduated in 1849. He served as principal of a new academy at Pittsboro for four years, then entered Princeton Theological Seminary, where he graduated in 1856. After a brief pastorate at Carthage, in his native state, he was appointed to the Siam mission of the Presbyterian Church, and was ordained, Dec. 11, 1857, by the Presbytery of Orange, N. C. He reached Bangkok in June of the following year. On Dec. 6, 1860, he married Sophia Royce Bradley, eldest daughter of Rev. Dan Beach Bradley, pioneer medical missionary in Siam. To this union were born two sons and three daughters.

In 1861, with Rev. Samuel G. McFarland [*q.v.*], he was appointed to open a new station at Petchaburi. There he came into contact with a colony of Lao war captives and discovered that their language varied but slightly from the Siamese, although they used a different written character. Finding that these people were more willing to receive his message than the Siamese, he made an exploratory trip into the Lao States and thereupon decided to establish a mission among them. With the consent of the Prince of

Chieng-mai, the Siamese government issued the necessary passports. McGilvary and his family reached Chieng-mai in the winter of 1867, and were joined the following year by the Rev. Jonathan Wilson and his family. Thus these two men became the founders of the mission to the Lao. In token of goodwill the Prince donated land for a permanent establishment.

McGilvary was a man of clear vision, quick intuition, candor, and honor; furthermore, he had courage to the point of daring. When on the occasion of the first Christian marriage ceremony the family patriarch refused to consent to the new form unless the customary "spirit-fee" should be paid to him, McGilvary was quick to perceive that acquiescence would not only appear to condone spirit worship in the eyes of the people but would set a precedent for future demands. Accordingly, when the Prince, fearing to oppose custom, excused himself from interference on the pretext that only the King of Siam could regulate religious matters, McGilvary promptly took him at his word and made an appeal to the King for religious freedom on behalf of the native Christians. In response, the Royal Commissioner resident at Chieng-mai received instructions from Bangkok to issue in the King's name an "edict of religious toleration" (Oct. 8, 1878). The turning of this crisis by the statesmanship of McGilvary proved to be all but the last step in the passing of the feudal power of the Prince of Chieng-mai. When the reigning price died no successor was appointed and the Lao provinces were brought fully under the Siamese government.

Undeniably McGilvary had a love of adventure. He early made several elephant tours through the provinces to learn the state of affairs. In 1884 he gave his services as interpreter for Holt S. Hallett, who was prospecting for a British rail route from Maulmain into southwest China. Subsequently he made an annual tour through various parts of the region covered by the upper watershed of the Menam and the central watershed of the Mekong. He was among the first to investigate the several aboriginal tribes in the mountains of that region. Through these tours he came to know personally all the provincial governors and to be on friendly terms with many of the village chiefs. He was more widely acquainted with the geography, ethnography, and travel routes than any other Westerner up to his time and than most of the government officials of that day.

Of his fifty-three years in Siam, McGilvary spent forty-three among the Lao, coming to be known as "the Apostle to the Lao." On several occasions he received expressions of royal favor for his labors. Toward the end of his life he prepared his autobiography, *A Half Century among the Siamese and the Lāo,* which was published in 1912, the year after his death. In the Preface to this book McGilvary's superior officer, Dr. A. J. Brown, summarized his achievements in the following words: "He laid the foundations of the medical work, introducing quinine and vaccination among a people scourged by malaria and smallpox, a work which has now developed into five hospitals and a leper asylum. He began educational work, which is now represented by eight boarding schools and twenty-two elementary schools. He was the evangelist who won the first converts, founded the first church, and had a prominent part in founding twenty other churches." He died in Chieng-mai in his eighty-fourth year.

[McGilvary's autobiography, mentioned above; H. S. Hallett, *A Thousand Miles on an Elephant in the Shan States* (1890); Lilian J. Curtis, *The Laos of North Siam* (1903); G. B. McFarland, *Hist. Sketch of Protestant Missions in Siam* (1928); *Princeton Theol. Sem. Bull.; Necrological Report,* Aug. 1912; *Minutes of the Gen. Assembly of the Presbyterian Church in the U. S. A.* (1912); *Assembly Herald,* Oct. 1911.] G. H. F.

McGIVNEY, MICHAEL JOSEPH (Aug. 12, 1852–Aug. 14, 1890), Roman Catholic priest, a founder of the Knights of Columbus, was the eldest of the thirteen children born to Patrick and Mary (Lynch) McGivney. On completion of his elementary education in the parochial and public schools of his native town, Waterbury, Conn., he worked in the spoon factory of Holmes, Booth & Haydens. On discerning a religious vocation in their son, his parents, though recent immigrants from Ireland, managed to send him to the college of St. Hyacinth in Canada, a preparatory institution, and then to Niagara University at Niagara Falls, where he was graduated in 1873. That autumn, he enrolled as a theological student in St. Mary's Seminary, Baltimore, where on Dec. 22, 1877, he was ordained by Archbishop Gibbons. Early in the following year, he was assigned by Bishop Thomas Galberry [*q.v.*] as an assistant to Father P. A. Murphy of St. Mary's Church, New Haven, Conn. An energetic, zealous priest, he organized a parochial total-abstinence society and unstintingly gave his time to sodalities and to a social organization known as the Red Knights, which, after the Civil War, had grown out of the Sarsfield Guard, an Irish military unit. Since the Red Knights died a natural death and Catholics were not permitted to join the various attractive secret societies, Father McGivney grew interested in the establishment of an acceptable

Catholic fraternal order which would bring men together in mutually helpful association. As a result of a series of meetings at the parochial house commencing Jan. 16, 1882, he and nine lay associates established the Knights of Columbus, a fraternal insurance society of a semi-secret character, which was chartered by the State of Connecticut Mar. 29, 1882. McGivney assisted in composing the ritual, and as an advocate of total abstinence insisted that members of the order must be recognized practical Catholics who were in no way directly connected with the liquor traffic. Through his good offices the order was approved by Bishop Lawrence S. McMahon of Hartford, and soon spread its local councils throughout the diocese, though its extension beyond the state of Connecticut, in the face of clerical suspicion, was slow until it was approved by the papal delegate. As national chaplain and a member of the supreme council, McGivney remained the inspiring force in the society until his death in Thomaston, Conn., where for six years he had been pastor of St. Thomas' Church. His inspiration was continued through two brothers, Monsignor P. J. and Father John J. McGivney, who in turn succeeded him in the national chaplaincy of the order, which at its high tide during the World War approached a million members.

[M. F. Egan and J. B. Kennedy, *The Knights of Columbus in Peace and War* (2 vols., 1920), vol. I; *Souvenir of Twentieth Anniversary, Sheridan Council, K. of C., Waterbury, Conn.* (1905), ed. by C. Maloney; information furnished from the files of the Knights of Columbus and by Rev. J. J. McGivney; New Haven *Daily Morning Journal and Courier,* Aug. 15, 19, 1890.]

R. J. P.

McGLYNN, EDWARD (Sept. 27, 1837–Jan. 7, 1900), Catholic priest, social reformer, was born in New York of Irish parents, Peter and Sarah McGlynn, and educated in the public schools of his native city. At the age of thirteen he was sent by Bishop Hughes to the Urban College of the Propaganda, Rome, and there he was ordained priest, Mar. 24, 1860. Immediately after ordination he became assistant to Rev. Thomas Farrell at St. Joseph's Church, Sixth Avenue, New York.

Inasmuch as Father Farrell had been an ardent opponent of slavery and left five thousand dollars in his will for a colored Catholic church, he probably was in large measure responsible for the charitable and humanitarian views and practices for which his young assistant became and remained conspicuous. In 1866 McGlynn was appointed pastor of St. Stephen's parish, one of the most populous in New York. Here he worked with great energy and zeal, not only in the various fields of parochial activity, but on behalf of every worthy public cause. After a time he began to feel that life was made a burden "by the never-ending procession of men, women and little children coming to my door begging, not so much for alms as employment." "I began to ask myself," he wrote, " 'Is there no remedy?' . . . I began to study a little political economy, to ask, 'what is God's law as to the maintenance of his family down here below?' " (Malone, *post,* p. 4).

He thought that he had found the answer in the teachings of Henry George, 1839–1897 [*q.v.*]. With his accustomed fervor, energy, and eloquence he expounded the Single-Tax doctrine as the universal and fundamental remedy for poverty. In the year 1886 he took an active part in the campaign of Henry George for the office of mayor of New York. This brought him into open conflict with Archbishop Corrigan.

About four years previously, Cardinal Simeoni, prefect of the Congregation of the Propaganda, had directed the authorities of the Archdiocese to compel McGlynn to retract his views on the land question. Cardinal McCloskey [*q.v.*], at that time the head of the Archdiocese, merely required McGlynn to refrain from defending these views in public. After the death of Cardinal McCloskey, McGlynn considered himself free again to advocate the Single-Tax doctrine. On Sept. 29, 1886, Archbishop Corrigan [*q.v.*] forbade him to speak on behalf of Henry George's candidacy at a scheduled public meeting. McGlynn replied that to break this engagement would be imprudent, but promised to refrain from addressing any later meeting during the political campaign. The Archbishop immediately suspended him from the exercise of his priestly functions for a period of two weeks. Toward the end of November a second temporary suspension was imposed. On Jan. 14, 1887, Archbishop Corrigan removed McGlynn from the pastorate of St. Stephen's. Two days later a cablegram arrived from Cardinal Simeoni commanding McGlynn to retract publicly his land theory and to come immediately to Rome. On Feb. 18 Cardinal Gibbons [*q.v.*], who was then in Rome, sent word that McGlynn ought to go to Rome as soon as possible. On Mar. 11 Dr. Burtsell, as McGlynn's canonical advocate, cabled a reply that his client would do so on certain conditions. At the same time he wrote a long letter to Cardinal Gibbons explaining fully the canonical situation from McGlynn's viewpoint. For reasons which seemed good, Cardinal Gibbons did not present either the cablegram or the letter to the Roman authorities, contenting himself with an oral statement of their contents. Failing to receive any written reply from McGlynn, the Pope ordered him to come to Rome within forty days under penalty of excommunication. Holding that he had been guilty of no contumacy, and unaware that the reply made on his behalf by Dr. Burtsell had never reached the Holy Father, McGlynn, on the score of health, refused to obey the order, and the excommunication became effective July 4, 1887. For more than five years following this censure he defended the Single-Tax doctrine at the Sunday afternoon meetings of the Anti-Poverty Society, of which he was the first president. He lived at the home of his widowed sister in Brooklyn.

In December 1892, upon the assurance of four professors at the Catholic University that McGlynn's Single-Tax views were not contrary to Catholic teaching, Msgr. Satolli, the Papal Ablegate in the United States reinstated him in the ministry. On Christmas Day 1892 McGlynn said mass for the first time since his excommunication in 1887. The following June he visited Rome and was cordially received in private audience by the Holy Father. In his description of this event shortly afterwards, McGlynn reported that the Pope had said to him, "But surely you admit the right of property," and that he had answered in the affirmative as regards "the products of individual industry." Apparently the Pope was satisfied with this answer.

In January 1894, McGlynn became pastor of St. Mary's at Newburgh, N. Y., where he died Jan. 7, 1900. In the years following his restoration to his priestly functions he frequently spoke at Single-Tax meetings and made it quite clear that he had not been required by the Pope to retract his view on the land question. His funeral occasioned widespread expressions of sorrow and appreciation in all walks of life, both within and without the Catholic Church.

[Some of the details contained in the foregoing sketch were taken from a long letter written by Bishop Moore of St. Augustine, Fla., to Cardinal Manning in November 1887. The principal printed sources concerning McGlynn are: the daily papers of New York City from 1886 to 1900; the *Cath. Encyc.*, XI (1911), 24, 25; John Talbot Smith, *Hist. of the Cath. Ch. in N. Y.* (1905), II, 420–23, 432–36; S. L. Malone, *Dr. Edward McGlynn* (1918); and Arthur Preuss, *The Fundamental Fallacy of Socialism* (1908). See also *N. Y. Freeman's Jour.*, Apr. 9, May 7, 1887; *N. Y. Times*, Jan. 8, 1900.]

J. A. R.

McGOVERN, JOHN (Feb. 18, 1850–Dec. 17, 1917), journalist and author, was born in Troy, N. Y., the eldest of three children of James and Marion (Carter) McGovern. In 1854, when his father and sister died of cholera, his mother took him to Ligonier, Ind., where she died four years later. The boy then lived with Judson Palmiter, a printer, in Ligonier, where he attended school and worked during the summer months on the farm of his uncle, Henry Carter, at Lima, Ind. In 1862 when Palmiter moved to Kendallville, Ind., to publish the *Noble County Journal*, McGovern began his journalistic career by working in the printing office. Under the kindly influence of Palmiter he developed an appreciation of music and poetry which colored his later life. He worked as a printer in Sturgis, Mich., in 1866, returning the following year to Kendallville, and thence going to Kalamazoo to join the staff of the *Michigan Telegraph*. In 1868 he moved to Chicago, became a typesetter on the *Chicago Tribune*, and gradually advanced to proof-reader, telegraph editor, and night editor. In these years he began to write poetry, some of which was published in the *Tribune*. In 1877 he was married to Kate C. Van Arsdale of Philadelphia, who bore him two sons and a daughter. For two years (July 1884–July 1886) he was associate editor and for a few weeks (July–October 1886) sole editor of the *Current*, a literary magazine, which printed poems, essays, and editorials by him, and from 1887 to 1889 he was chief editorial writer for the *Chicago Herald*.

Encouraged by his growing literary experience, he gave up newspaper work to devote his time to literature. His writings fall into several categories; all show his understanding of public taste in easy reading, sensational matter, and moral emphasis. Four published novels and two still in manuscript, two volumes of poetry, along with other lyrics printed in newspapers, and nearly twenty volumes of moral and literary essays and miscellaneous writings make up the bulk of his work. Numerous philosophic and moral essays still remain unpublished, also several dramas and manuscripts of personal experiences. McGovern was always confident of his literary powers and wrote with the conviction that posterity would value his unpublished works more than his contemporaries did his printed volumes. The manuscripts were preserved by his daughter, Mary Harriet McGovern, whom he made his literary executrix. His novel, *David Lockwin; The People's Idol* (1892), is of interest because McGovern accused the British novelist, Gilbert Parker, of taking its plot for his novel, *The Right of Way* (*Chicago Evening Post*, May 23, 1902, May 24, 1903). In 1899 McGovern served as literary expert for Samuel Eberley Gross in his plagiarism case against Edmund Rostand, and studied texts of *Cyrano de Bergerac* and the *Merchant Prince of Cornville* for similarities. His testimony and evidence won the case for Gross (May 21, 1902). After 1902 he became an occasional lecturer on literary and biographical subjects. He was a genial person, was referred to as the "grand old man" of the Chicago Press Club, where he gave many lectures, and was the leading spirit of the Old Printers Club. The last two years of his life were dark with sickness. He died in Chicago.

[Andrew F. Leiser, "The Life and Writings of John McGovern" (1930), an unpublished thesis at the library of George Washington University; *Who's Who in America,* 1916–17; *Chicago Tribune,* May 21, 1902, Dec. 18, 19, 1917; *Chicago Herald,* Dec. 18, 1917.]
R. W. B.

McGOWAN, SAMUEL (Oct. 9, 1819–Aug. 9, 1897), jurist and Confederate soldier, was born in the Crosshill section of Laurens District, S. C., the son of William and Jeannie (McWilliams) McGowan, Irish Presbyterians who in 1801 emigrated to South Carolina from Ireland. His father became a prosperous farmer, able to fulfil the ambition to send his sons to college. The younger McGowan attended the school of Thomas Lewis Lesly and was graduated from the South Carolina College in 1841. He then went to Abbeville, where he studied law under T. C. Perrin and was admitted to the bar in 1842. This son of Irish emigrants possessed personal qualities that made possible his rise to positions of distinction. Although not brilliant, he was studious and ambitious and endowed with a fund of simple humor. He was powerful in body, commanding in personal appearance, and possessed of a degree of physical courage and sense of civic duty that won admiration. His rise in the somewhat exclusive social and professional circles of Abbeville was facilitated by his conduct in an affair of honor. He reprimanded John Cuningham, an experienced duelist, for slurring remarks about a young woman, accepted Cuningham's challenge, and was slightly wounded in the duel that followed at Sandbar Ferry, S. C. He became the partner of Perrin and was soon recognized as a popular politician and eloquent advocate. He was elected a major-general of militia and for thirteen years before 1865 represented Abbeville District in the state House of Representatives. He married Susan Caroline, the daughter of David L. Wardlaw, a distinguished judge of Abbeville. They had seven children.

His civil career was interrupted by military services. In 1846 he entered the famous Palmetto Regiment as a private in the Mexican War, rose to the rank of staff captain, and was complimented for gallantry in action near Mexico city. In 1861, as commander of a South Carolina brigade, he assisted in the capture of Fort Sumter. In 1862 he became colonel of the 14th South Carolina Volunteers, which was attached to Maxcy Gregg's famous brigade. When in 1863 Gregg was killed, he was made commander of the brigade. He served in that capacity until the surrender at Appomattox. In many of the bloodiest battles in Virginia he displayed extraordinary bravery. He was wounded at least four times. After the Civil War he resumed the practice of law at Abbeville as the partner of William H. Parker. He was a member of the state constitutional convention of 1865 and was elected to Congress in the same year, but he was denied a seat by the Republican majority. He was a leader in the struggle to redeem South Carolina from Republican rule in 1876. In 1878 he was again elected to the legislature, and a year later he was made an associate justice of the state supreme court, where he won a high reputation as a jurist. In 1893 he was defeated for reëlection through the influence of Ben Tillman, the Democratic boss of the state, whom he had antagonized by casting the deciding vote in a supreme-court decision declaring the proposed liquor dispensary unconstitutional. He died at his home in Abbeville and after services in Trinity Episcopal Church was buried in upper Long Cane Cemetery in that town.

[*Cyc. of Eminent and Representative Men of the Carolinas* (1892), I; C. A. Evans, *Confederate Military Hist.* (1899), vol. V; *Hist. of S. C.,* ed. by Yates Snowden (1920), vol. II; J. E. J. Caldwell, *The Hist. of a Brigade of South Carolinians, Known First as "Gregg's" and Subsequently as "McGowan's Brigade"* (1866); *South Carolina Reports,* esp. speeches made before the supreme court at his death, in vol. LI; F. B. Simkins, *The Tillman Movement in S. C.* (copr. 1926); *Proceedings of the Reunion of the McGowan Family Held at Liberty Springs Church* (1915); J. G. Wardlaw, *Geneal. of the Wardlaw Family* (1929), p. 87; U. R. Brooks, *S. C. Bench and Bar,* vol. I (1908), quoting the *News and Courier* (Charleston), Aug. 10, 1897.] F. B. S.

McGRATH, JAMES (June 26, 1835–Jan. 12, 1898), Roman Catholic priest, was born in Holy Cross, County Tipperary, Ireland, and received his early training in the local schools and in the University of Dublin. While a student at the University, he was professed in the Oblates of Mary Immaculate at Inchicor (1855), and the following year was sent to Canada, where he completed his theological studies at the University of Ottawa. Ordained in 1859, he was assigned to a curacy in St. Patrick's Church, Ottawa, for three years and was then transferred to the Texan missions. In 1864, he returned to Ottawa, where he built the Church of the Immaculate Conception. Subsequently, while attached to the Holy Angels' Apostolic School of Buffalo, he preached missions throughout New York and New England, winning recognition as a preacher in both French and English. In 1870 he was appointed pastor at St. John's Church, Lowell, Mass., and there erected the Church of the Immaculate Conception (1872), one of the largest in the archdiocese of Boston. One of the first New England priests to introduce parochial education, he organized a school under the Canadian Grey Nuns of the Cross (1880).

In the belief that Canadian control was preventing the normal growth of his community in the United States, McGrath successfully urged the creation of an American province of the Oblate Fathers. In 1883 he was elected first provincial, with authority over the community's churches and monasteries in Lowell, Buffalo, and Plattsburg, as well as in Texas and Mexico. During his administration of ten years, the Sacred Heart house was opened in Lowell, and monasteries were founded in Eagle Pass and Rio Grande, Tex. In 1883 a novitiate was established at Tewksbury, Mass., to which in 1888 was added a juniorate for recruiting novices. Three years later, the Provincial transferred the juniorate to Buffalo. On the completion of his term, Father McGrath returned to Buffalo where he was superior of the Holy Angels' Church and Apostolic School, until his sudden death of heart failure in the Albany railway station while on his way to a chapter meeting in Lowell.

[*Albany Argus*, Jan. 13, 1898; *Buffalo Courier*, Jan. 13–16, 1898; material contributed from the community archives at the Tewksbury Novitiate; annual Catholic directories.] R. J. P.

McGRAW, JOHN HARTE (Oct. 4, 1850–June 23, 1910), governor of Washington, was born in Penobscot County, Me., soon after the arrival from Ireland of his parents, Daniel and Catherine (Harte) McGraw. His father was drowned about two years later. His mother remarried, and he left home at the age of fourteen. Earning his living as a clerk in a general merchandise store, he became manager at seventeen, and at twenty-one he and a brother opened a grocery store. They failed in the panic of 1873. He decided to go west and reached San Francisco by ship on July 10, 1876, drove a horse-car a few months, and then sailed for Seattle arriving on Dec. 28. After working as a clerk in the Occidental Hotel, he went into the hotel business with a partner. He was left stranded again when their place, the American House, burned in 1878, and he joined the police force of four men. Fearlessness and ability won his election as city marshal from 1879 to 1882 and as sheriff of King County for two terms. During the Anti-Chinese riots in 1886 he became unpopular by performing his duty, and he lost his office at the next election. He had studied law while sheriff, and after his defeat he became a member of the law firm of Greene, Hanford & McGraw. He was admitted to the bar in 1886. In 1888 he accepted election as sheriff in vindication of his previous actions. He was elected president of the First National Bank of Seattle before the completion of this term and retained the position until 1897. He was elected governor of Washington in 1892, and his four-year term, falling in a time of financial depression, was a stormy period of railway and mining strikes and of riotous conditions in Tacoma and elsewhere attending the march of Coxey's Army. He went alone into mining districts to reason with the strike leaders. The legislature was extravagant, and he vetoed many appropriation bills and defeated a raid on the capitol building fund. During these years he neglected his private affairs, and at the end of his term he was left bankrupt.

In 1897 he borrowed money to go to Alaska, and he returned in two years with enough gold to pay all his debts. Though active in Republican politics, he refused further political honors. His private fortunes improved steadily, and he devoted much time to public enterprises, notably the Lake Washington canal and the Alaska-Yukon-Pacific Exposition. He was greatly interested in the University of Washington and in Whitman College, of which he was an overseer. While still a policeman, he gave books to the new library of the university. He was president of the Seattle Chamber of Commerce from 1905 to 1909 and was the first president of the associated chambers of commerce of the Pacific Coast. On Oct. 12, 1874, he married May L. Kelley of Bancroft, Me. He was survived by a son and daughter.

[Seattle Chamber of Commerce, *In Memoriam John Harte McGraw* (1911); Elwood Evans, *Hist. of the Pacific Northwest* (1889), vol. II; C. A. Snowden, *Hist. of Washington*, vol. V (1911); Clarence B. Bagley, *Hist. of Seattle* (1916), vol. II; E. S. Meany, *Governors of Washington* (1915); *Seattle Daily Times*, June 24, 1910.] G. W. F.

McGREADY, JAMES (*c.* 1758–February 1817), pioneer Presbyterian preacher, and revivalist, was born in western Pennsylvania of Scotch-Irish parents. In his early childhood they moved South and he spent the greater part of his boyhood in Guilford County, N. C. There was a quality about him as a youth which convinced a visiting uncle that he ought to be educated for the Christian ministry. Accordingly he accompanied his uncle to Pennsylvania to prepare for the work of a preacher. He began his study in the autumn of 1785 in a Latin school conducted by Rev. Joseph Smith at Upper Buffalo, Pa., and completed his literary and theological education at Canonsburg, Pa., under Rev. John McMillan, and on Aug. 13, 1788, was licensed to preach by the Presbytery of Redstone, Pa. Soon he decided to move to North Carolina, and on the way spent some deeply significant days at Hampden-Sidney College in Virginia, with Dr. John Blair Smith [*q.v.*], who at the time was the leading spirit in a great revival of religion. It was here that McGready was first deeply impressed with the value of evangelistic preaching and felt the kindling of revival zeal in himself.

Settling in North Carolina, he preached with such effect that he soon brought about a religious awakening "in which ten or twelve young men were brought into the fold, all of whom became ministers of the gospel" (Beard, *post,* p. 9). One of these was Barton W. Stone [*q.v.*]. About 1790 McGready became pastor of a church in Orange County. Possessed of great physical stamina and a voice which won for him the title Boanerges, he was so vehement in his denunciation of sin and hypocrisy that the community was divided into two factions: his ardent supporters and his blood-thirsty enemies. "A letter was written to him in *blood,* requiring him to leave the country at the peril of his life" (*Ibid.*). Partly because of this hostility and partly for the sake of following the migration of his North Carolina converts, he went to Kentucky in 1796, and there took charge of the three small congregations of Gaspar, Red, and Muddy rivers in Logan County. Here he soon induced his people to sign the following covenant: "We bind ourselves to observe the third Saturday of each month, for one year, as a day of fasting and prayer for the conversion of sinners in Logan County and throughout the world. We also engage to spend one half hour every Saturday evening, beginning at the setting of the sun and one half hour every Sabbath morning from the rising of the sun, pleading with God to revive his work" (*Ibid.,* p. 11). With this covenant as a background, at each of McGready's three churches, in connection with sacramental services, remarkable revivals broke out in 1797, 1798, and 1799. These were the forerunners of the Great Revival of 1800. Although many were converted during these three preceding years, yet all that work, McGready wrote later, was "but like a few scattering drops before a mighty rain, when compared with the overflowing floods of salvation . . . poured out like a mighty river" in the year 1800 (*New-York Missionary Magazine,* April 1803, p. 154). Beginning in Logan County, Ky., the revival swept over the western and southern states, affecting all the denominations on the frontier. It was marked by the highest degree of religious excitement, accompanied by violent physical demonstrations, trances, and visions. In connection with it the camp meeting originated, families coming to meeting places in wagons from miles around and camping out together for several days as they took part in the revival exercises. McGready wrote "A Short Narrative of the Revival of Religion in Logan County in the State of Kentucky, and the Adjacent Settlements in the State of Tennessee, from May 1797 until September 1800," which was published serially, February–June 1803, in the *New-York Missionary Magazine.*

One of the consequences of the Great Revival was the organization of the Cumberland Presbyterian Church, which separated from the older Presbyterian body on two issues: the denial that a classical education is prerequisite to ministerial ordination, and renunciation of the fatalism in the Westminster standards. McGready allied himself with the Cumberland Presbytery in its policy regarding licensing preachers who do not have classical training, but finally (1809) refused to go with them in their renunciation of the strict Calvinism of the Westminster Confession. After a period of discipline and silence he was restored to the orthodox Transylvania Presbytery. In 1811, he was sent as a pioneer preacher to found churches in southern Indiana. In the fall of 1816, at a camp meeting near Evansville, Ind., he preached with such effectiveness that he exclaimed, "I this day feel the same holy fire that filled my soul sixteen years ago, during the glorious revival of 1800" (Beard, p. 14). Just a few months later, February 1817, he died at his home in Henderson County, Ky. According to his biographer, Beard (*post*), he was married about 1790, but the name of his wife is not recorded. A number of years after his death there appeared *The Posthumous Works of the Reverend and Pious M'Gready* (2 vols., 1831–33), edited by James Smith.

[Richard Beard, *Brief Biog. Sketches of Some of the Early Ministers of the Cumberland Presbyt. Ch.* (1867); T. C. Blake, *The Old Log House* (1878); E. H. Gillett, *Hist. of the Presbyt. Ch. in the U. S. A.* (2 vols., 1864); W. B. Sprague, *Annals Am. Pulpit,* III (1859), 278; B. W. McDonnold, *Hist. of the Cumberland Presbyt. Ch.* (1888); R. V. Foster, "A Sketch of the History of the Cumberland Presbyterian Church," *Am. Church Hist.,* vol. XI (1894); Joseph Smith, *Old Redstone; or, Hist. Sketches of Western Presbyterianism* (1854); Robert Davidson, *Hist. of the Presbyt. Ch. in the State of Ky.* (1847); C. C. Cleveland, *The Great Revival in the West, 1797–1805* (1916).]

O. E. B.

McGROARTY, SUSAN [See Julia, Sister, 1827–1901].

McGUFFEY, WILLIAM HOLMES (Sept. 23, 1800–May 4, 1873), educator, compiler of school-readers, was born near Claysville in Washington County, Pa. He came from Scotch-Irish stock; his grandfather, William McGuffey, emigrated from Scotland to America in 1774 and settled in Pennsylvania; his father, Alexander, became an Indian fighter, served under both St. Clair and Anthony Wayne, and in 1794 married Anna Holmes. When the "Connecticut Reserve" was opened in Ohio in 1802, the young couple with their son settled near Youngstown. On this pioneer homestead, William Holmes McGuffey spent sixteen years. His mother gave him instruction in the rudiments, and he attended the intermittent sessions of the rural schools. In his teens his parents sent him to take private lessons in Latin from the pastor of the Presbyterian Church at Youngstown. His striking capacity to memorize marked him as a prodigy; he committed to memory entire books of the Bible, and much other literature. In 1818 he entered the Old Stone Academy of Darlington, Pa., under the Rev. Thomas Hughes, and thence proceeded to Washington College, from which he graduated with honors in 1826. Between his periods of college attendance, he taught school, chiefly in Kentucky.

On Mar. 29, 1826, he was elected by the Board of Trustees to the position of professor of languages in Miami University, Oxford, Ohio. In the following year he married Harriet Spinning of Dayton, to which union two daughters and three sons were born. He was licensed to preach in the Presbyterian church in 1829, but never held a regular ministerial appointment; while in Oxford, however, he preached every Sunday at Darrtown, four miles distant. He always spoke extemporaneously and in later life often said that he had preached three thousand sermons and had never written one of them. In 1832 he became head of the department of mental philosophy and philology at Miami and four years later (1836), was called to the presidency of Cincinnati College. During this period his fame as a lecturer on moral and Biblical subjects spread rapidly; with Samuel Lewis [*q.v.*] and others he took part in organizing the College of Teachers, an association formed to promote the interests of education; and with Lewis he labored to secure the passage of the law under which the common schools of Ohio were first organized. On Sept. 17, 1839, he was elected president of Ohio University at Athens, Ohio, and served until the institution closed its doors in 1843. He then returned to Cincinnati to become a professor in Woodward College. Here he remained until his election as professor of moral philosophy in the University of Virginia, July 1845, a post which he held for the rest of his life, teaching until within a few weeks of his death. He soon became ranking professor and was widely remembered and quoted. In Virginia as in Ohio he was an earnest advocate of a public-school system. His wife died in 1853 and in 1857 he married Laura Howard, daughter of Dean Henry Howard of the University. One daughter, who died at the age of four, was born of this second marriage. Through the lean years of the Civil War and Reconstruction he was noted for his philanthropy and generosity among the poor and the negroes.

Despite his long career as a college and university professor, McGuffey is most widely known for his *Eclectic Readers* for elementary schools. While he was professor at Miami University he began, at the solicitation of the Cincinnati publishers, Truman & Smith, to compile the series of schoolbooks which have made his name a household word. The First and Second Readers were published in 1836, the Third and Fourth in 1837. These books—with the Fifth, added in 1844, the *Eclectic Spelling Book,* added in 1846 by McGuffey's brother, Alexander Hamilton McGuffey, and a Sixth, added in 1857—went through edition after edition, were revised and enlarged, and reached the fabulous sale of 122,000,000 copies. Even the simplest lessons, although containing obvious, sometimes explicit, morals, were designed to win the pupil's interest, and the more advanced selections included well-chosen extracts from the greatest English writers. The *Readers* served to introduce thousands of boys and girls to the treasures of literature. Their influence, moral and cultural, upon the children in the thirty-seven states in which they were used contributed much to the shaping of the American mind in the nineteenth century.

[H. H. Vail, *A Hist. of the McGuffey Readers* (1910); H. C. Minnich, *Wm. Holmes McGuffey and the Peerless Pioneer McGuffey Readers* (1928); M. Tope, *A Biog. of Wm. Holmes McGuffey* (1929); Mark Sullivan, *Our Times,* vol. II (1927); P. A. Bruce, *Hist. of the Univ. of Va., 1819–1919* (5 vols., 1920–22); *Ohio Archæol. and Hist. Quart.,* Apr. 1927; Daniel Read, in *Addresses and Jour. of Proc. Nat. Educ. Asso.,* 1873; *Daily Dispatch* (Richmond), May 6, 1873.]

H. C. M.

McGUIRE, CHARLES BONAVENTURE (Dec. 16, 1768–July 17, 1833), Franciscan friar, was born of a gentle family in Dungannon, County Tyrone, Ireland, the name of which is often given as Maguire. Charles obtained his rudimentary education from a refugee master in a "hedge-school." Forced by the penal laws to flee the land, he was educated in a French or Belgian college and at Louvain. Ordained a Franciscan friar, he served in the Low Countries until proscribed by the French Revolutionists. Dragged to the guillotine, he was rescued by a cooper, who was instantly cut to pieces by the infuriated mob, while McGuire made his escape. Thereafter he dwelt in Rome until the arrival of Napoleon's soldiers. Again escaping, he traveled over the Continent making observations and conducting confidential work for his order and, presumably, for the papacy. Commissioned by the king of Bohemia to perform a religious office for a member of the royal family then in Brussels, he was on hand to attend the wounded from Waterloo and to collect battle relics, which he preserved. An adventurous friar, he sought service in the American missions, for which he was warmly recommended to Archbishop Maréchal [*q.v.*], by Cardinal Litta. Arriving in Pennsylvania in 1817, he was assigned to the Western missions, to Sportsman's Hall or Latrobe, and in 1820 to the pastorate of the diminutive church of St. Patrick's in Pittsburgh.

Aided by Col. James O'Hara, one of the founders of the Pittsburgh glass industry, and the donations of the increasing number of German artisans and Irish laborers, Father McGuire enlarged the church. Within a few years, 1829, he laid the corner-stone of St. Paul's Church on Grant Hill, which, when completed by his successor, was one of the largest in America. A year earlier, he was named superior of the Poor Clare nuns, who opened a convent and academy in the town of Allegheny. Catholicism in Western Pennsylvania found a worthy expositor in this simple religious, whom Bishop Fenwick [*q.v.*], of Cincinnati, was anxious to have named bishop of a proposed see in Indiana in 1823 (J. H. Lamott, *History of the Archdiocese of Cincinnati,* 1921, p. 55). His fluent use of several languages, intimate knowledge of Europe, cosmopolitan character, commanding appearance, ready wit, and urbanity added to the prestige of the uneducated Catholic minority and made him a social favorite in Pittsburgh. Without episcopal ambition, he remained a pastor to his death. Buried in a vault in St. Paul's his remains were later moved to St. Mary's cemetery.

[A. A. Lambing, *Hist. of the Cath. Ch. in the Dioceses of Pittsburg and Allegheny* (1880) ; *Records of the Am. Cath. Hist. Soc.,* vol. III (1891) ; *The Am. Cath. Hist. Researches,* Oct. 1894 ; *N. Y. Weekly Register,* Apr. 19, 1834 ; *The Jesuit,* Aug. 10, 1833, reprinting obit. in *Pittsburg Manufacturer* ; *U. S. Cath. Almanac,* 1834.]

R. J. P.

McGUIRE, HUNTER HOLMES (Oct. 11, 1835–Sept. 19, 1900), surgeon, was born in Winchester, Va., the son of a physician and surgeon, Dr. Hugh Holmes McGuire, and of Ann Eliza (Moss) McGuire. He was a descendant of Edward McGuire of County Kerry, Ireland, who settled in Virginia in 1747. Hunter McGuire received his premedical education at Winchester Academy and later studied at the Winchester Medical College, from which he received his diploma in 1855. The year following, he matriculated at both the University of Pennsylvania and Jefferson Medical College, Philadelphia, but was forced to return home because of an attack of rheumatism. In 1857 he was elected professor of anatomy in the College at Winchester, but he resigned the position after one session and went once more to Philadelphia, where he established a quiz class and pursued further studies. John Brown's raid gave rise to such intense sectional feeling in 1859 as to lead to a mass meeting of Southern medical students in Philadelphia and a resolution that they go South. McGuire was the leading spirit in this movement and assumed the expenses of such of the three hundred students as could not pay their own way to Richmond. He resumed studies there and acquired a second medical degree. He then went to New Orleans, where he established a quiz class in connection with the medical department of the University of Louisiana.

When Virginia seceded from the Union, he volunteered as a private soldier and marched to Harpers Ferry. He was soon commissioned as a medical officer, and in May 1861 he was made medical director of the Army of the Shenandoah, then under command of "Stonewall" Jackson. Later, when Jackson organized the First Virginia Brigade, he asked that McGuire be made its surgeon. Thereafter he served as chief surgeon of Jackson's commands until the latter's death. He was also his personal physician. Subsequently he was surgeon of the II Army Corps, under General Ewell, medical director of the Army of Northern Virginia under General Ewell, and medical director of the Army of the Valley of Virginia, under General Jubal Early. It is said that he organized the "Reserve Corps Hospitals of the Confederacy" and that he perfected the "Ambulance Corps." The latter consisted of a detail of four men from each company to assist the wounded from the field to hospitals in the rear. The men wore conspicuous badges, and no other soldiers were permitted to leave the ranks during battle for the purpose of rendering aid. Just what constituted the "Reserve Corps Hospitals of the Confederacy" does not appear from any available records. McGuire was always active in securing the release of captured Union medical officers, and when he was himself captured by General Sheridan's troops in March 1865, he was at once paroled and in two weeks released.

In 1865 he was elected professor of surgery in the Virginia Medical College, and served as such until 1878, when he resigned; in 1880 he was made professor emeritus. He was actively connected with the establishment at Richmond in

1893 of the College of Physicians and Surgeons, later named the University College of Medicine, and was its president and professor of surgery at the time of his death. He also organized St. Luke's Home for the Sick, with a training school for nurses. He wrote a great variety of articles, mostly upon surgical matters, but also upon such subjects as "Nervous Troubles Following Organic Urethral Stricture" (*Virginia Medical Monthly,* October 1890), "Sexual Crimes among the Southern Negroes, Scientifically Considered" (*Ibid.,* May 1893), "Cases of Tuberculosis Cured by Cancrum Oris" (*Kansas City Medical Record,* April 1897), "The Treatment of Acute Exudative Nephritis Following Infectious Diseases" (*Bi-monthly Bulletin of the University College of Medicine,* March 1898). He also contributed to John Ashhurst's *International Encyclopædia of Surgery* (6 vols., 1881–86), to William Pepper's *System of Practical Medicine* (5 vols., 1885–86), and to the American Edition of Timothy Holmes's *System of Surgery, Theoretical and Practical* (3 vols., 1881–82).

Always an ardent Southerner, when in his later life his attention was called to the "efforts of Northern writers and their friends to pervert the world's judgment and secure a world verdict in their favor," he at once undertook a campaign which resulted in the appointment of a committee to examine the school histories in use in Virginia, in the reorganization of the Virginia School Board, and in the condemnation of offending books. His account of the death of his own good friend, "Stonewall" Jackson (*American Medical Weekly,* Jan. 6, 1883), is touching and beautiful in its simplicity and in the pictures which it evokes so vividly. In 1866 he married Mary Stuart, by whom he had nine children. His death, after six months of invalidism, resulted from cerebral embolism. Always an outstanding and honored figure in his community, McGuire was also the recipient of many honors from his professional fellows. In Capitol Square, Richmond, a bronze statue of heroic size, which is a remarkable likeness, perpetuates his memory.

[W. G. Stanard, *The McGuire Family in Va.* (1926); H. A. Kelly and W. L. Burrage, *Am. Medic. Biogs.* (1920); *The Clinic Bull.,* Sept.–Oct. 1910; *Revue de Chirurgie,* Nov. 1900; *British Medic. Jour.,* Sept. 29, 1900; *Medic. News,* Sept. 29, 1900; *Va. Medic. Monthly,* Oct. 1877; *Richmond and Louisville Medic. Jour.,* Oct. 1877; *Dublin Jour. of Medic. Science,* Nov. 1, 1900; *New England Medic. Monthly,* Jan. 1885; *Trans. of the Thirty-first Ann. Session of the Medic. Soc. of Va., 1900* (1901); *Trans. of the Southern Surgic. and Gynecological Asso., 1902* (1903); *Annals of Gynecology and Pediatry,* Nov. 1900; *Pacific Medic. Jour.,* Nov. 1900; *Jour. Am. Medic. Asso.,* Sept. 29, 1900; *Boston Medic. and Surgic. Jour.,* Sept. 27, 1900; *N. Y. Medic. Jour.,* Sept. 22, 1900; *Medic. Record,* Sept. 22, 1900; *Surgery, Gynecology and Obstetrics,* Jan. 1923; the *Times* (Richmond), Sept. 20, 1900.]

P. M. A.

McGUIRE, JOSEPH DEAKINS (Nov. 26, 1842–Sept. 6, 1916), anthropologist, was born in Washington, D. C., the son of James C. and Margaret (Deakins) McGuire. After studying at Georgetown College, he entered the College of New Jersey in 1859, but left at the opening of the Civil War with the intention of enlisting in the army. On account of his youth, however, his family sent him abroad to complete his education. After studying languages and scientific farming in France and Germany for two years, he returned to the United States and settled at Ellicott City, Md. Having prepared himself for the practice of law, he was admitted to the bar in 1876. From 1884 to 1900 he held the office of state's attorney for Howard County. In 1901 Princeton University conferred upon him the honorary degree of A.M. and at the same time awarded him the degree of A.B. as of the class of 1863.

Stone implements and other archeological relics scattered over his estate at Ellicott City attracted his interest, and for years he collected these, amassing a large number of objects now in the Smithsonian Institution. At times his explorations were carried on further afield. Moving to Washington in 1900, he occupied his time in investigations conducted at the Smithsonian, where he was appointed honorary collaborator. The study of aboriginal technology was then being pursued and McGuire applied himself to some of the problems involved. He was the first white man to shape a stone axe with stone tools and to carve in stone by aboriginal methods. As a result of his studies and experiments, he published "Materials, Apparatus, and Processes of the Aboriginal Lapidary" (*Anthropologist,* April 1892); "The Development of Sculpture" (*Ibid.,* October 1894); "On the Evolution of the Art of Working Stone" (*Ibid.,* July 1893); "The Stone Hammer and Its Various Uses" (*Ibid.,* October 1891); and "A Study of the Primitive Methods of Drilling" (*Report of the United States National Museum* for 1894). Following explorations in Maine, he published "Ethnological and Archeological Notes on Moosehead Lake, Maine" (*American Anthropologist,* October–December 1908). Ethnological papers of his which attracted much attention were: "Ethnology in the Jesuit Relations" (*Ibid.,* April–June 1901), and "Pipes and Smoking Customs of the American Aborigines" (*Report of the United States National Museum* for 1897). These papers, written by McGuire in his mature years, are considered valuable contributions to anthropological science, because of their empirical character and the light they throw on the fundamental shaping arts of primitive man. His trained legal mind was an asset in his scientific work, bringing to it acumen and judgment in weighing facts, and habits of keen observation. His compeers in science considered him an earnest, fair-minded worker with the saving grace of humor. On Dec. 19, 1866, he married Anna Chapman of Staunton, Va.

[*Princeton, Sixty-three: Fortieth Year Book of the Members of the Class of 1863* (1904); *Am. Anthropologist*, July–Sept. 1916; *Who's Who in America*, 1916–17; *Evening Star* (Washington), Sept. 7, 1916; personal recollections.] W. H.

MACHEBEUF, JOSEPH PROJECTUS (Aug. 11, 1812–July 10, 1889), Roman Catholic prelate, son of Michael Anthony and Gilberte (Plauc) Machebeuf, was born at Riom, in the heart of Auvergne, France. Since his family was in comfortable circumstances, he was privileged to attend a private school, a Christian Brothers' college, and the old Oratorian College of Riom, which had become secularized. In 1831 he entered the Sulpician Seminary of Montferrand, where his theological studies were interrupted by forced vacations in the Volvic Mountains for the preservation of his health. Ordained on Dec. 21, 1836, Abbé Machebeuf was named curate at Cendre, where he was inspired with missionary zeal by Dr. J. M. Odin and Bishop B. J. Flaget [*qq.v.*], traveling through their native France in the interest of American missions. Along with Abbé J. B. Lamy [*q.v.*], he accepted the call of Bishop John Purcell and accompanied him and Bishop Flaget to Cincinnati in 1839. Though only slightly acquainted with German and English, he was immediately sent to Tiffin, which served as a mission center for northern Ohio and was being settled by Germans with a sprinkling of Irish and French. In 1841 he was assigned to Lower Sandusky (Fremont), and Sandusky City, where he built three churches, made extensive visitations to railroad camps, and labored for temperance among hard-drinking navvies. He journeyed to Montreal and Quebec soliciting financial aid, and on behalf of Bishop Purcell went back to France and Rome seeking helpers and bringing back in 1844 a colony of Ursuline nuns and the first American group of sisters of Notre Dame de Namur. In 1849 Father Pierre-Jean De Smet [*q.v.*], learning of Machebeuf's disinterested missionary zeal, visited him in the hope of obtaining his services for the Rocky Mountain missions; but while he longed for a wider field, he hesitated to go unless Father Lamy would accompany him, for on leaving France they had pledged themselves to remain together. The desire for a frontier field was soon answered, for in 1850 Lamy was appointed vicar apostolic of New Mexico and Machebeuf went with him to Santa Fé.

He learned Spanish and the Mexicans turned out in mass to meet the itinerant *señor vicario* when he visited the scattered stations with his muleteam. At Albuquerque in 1852, he replaced the popular but irregular José Gallegos, later a delegate to Congress, and quieted a tumultuous congregation by sheer personal courage. As vicar general, he administered the vicariate during Mgr. Lamy's absence, and in 1856 journeyed to France for additional priests. As pastor of the adobe cathedral of Sante Fé he ministered to 5,000 souls and yet found time to attend missions at Arroyo Hondo and Taos, where with Kit Carson's aid he put down an uprising caused by a Mexican priest who did not relish the new American jurisdiction. Sent to care for Arizona, he barely escaped assassination, but neither Indians nor desperadoes could deter one who boasted the Auvergne motto *Latsin pas.* At Tucson he erected a rude chapel and undertook the preservation of the historic mission of San Xavier del Bac.

Since the newly developing region of Colorado could not be cared for from Santa Fé, Lamy sent him in 1860 to Denver along with Father John B. Raverdy. Soon his strange wagon loaded with supplies, cooking utensils, bedding, and books was known in all gulches, boom towns, mining camps, and army posts of Colorado and Utah. It was a desperate field for a lone missionary, yet he was everywhere, even fraternizing with Brigham Young and his elders in Salt Lake City. Alive to the future of Colorado and Denver, he bought church sites when land values were low, though he invested little in mining properties. On small plots of land, at a time when few men looked beyond gold diggings, he demonstrated that Colorado valleys were suitable for agriculture. Within a few years he built churches, in Denver, Central City, and Golden City, besides establishing a dozen chapels and stations in mining towns and the new agricultural villages. Under his direction the Sisters of Charity erected hospitals in Denver and Pueblo, the Sisters of Loretto founded St. Mary's Academy in Denver and a school in Pueblo, and the Sisters of St. Joseph erected a school at Central City.

In 1868 when Colorado and Utah were made a vicariate, Machebeuf was named vicar apostolic with the title of Bishop of Epiphania. Consecrated in Cincinnati by Archbishop Purcell, Aug. 16, 1868, he traveled through the East visiting the chief seminaries in a vain effort to obtain volunteers. A year later he sought aid in France from the Propagation of the Faith and finally obtained three French missionaries and an Irish priest for his distant diocese. A boom in Colorado was followed by hard times. Rumors reached the East and even Rome that Machebeuf was insolvent, although the only danger lay in frightened creditors driving him to the wall by forcing property sales at auction prices. Going to Rome he offered to resign, but his resignation was refused. Instead, he was made a bishop (1887), and his friend, Nicholas C. Matz, was named coadjutor with the right of succession. Meanwhile a holding company had been established, some properties were sold, and in time the financial tangle was straightened out, leaving a surplus besides some of the finest church sites in the state. Active to the end despite injuries received in mountain wrecks, he journeyed to Washington for the foundation of the Catholic University in 1888, the year the Jesuits removed their college from Morrison to Denver and his dearest friend, Archbishop Lamy, died. Within a year, after an illness of a few days, Machebeuf, too, passed away.

[W. J. Howlett, *Life of the Rt. Rev. Joseph P. Machebeuf* (1908); *Cath. Encyc.*, vol. IV (1908); J. G. Shea, *Hist. of the Cath. Ch. in the U. S.*, vol. IV (1892), *The Hierarchy of the Cath. Ch. in the U. S.* (1886); R. H. Clarke, *Hist. of the Cath. Ch. in the U. S. with Biog. Sketches of the Living Bishops*, vol. II (1890); Sadliers' *Cath. Directory for 1890* (1890); *Denver Republican*, July 10, 11, 1889.]
R. J. P.

McHENRY, JAMES (Nov. 16, 1753–May 3, 1816), Revolutionary soldier, secretary of war, son of Daniel and Agnes McHenry, was born in Ballymena, County Antrim, Ireland, and received his classical education in Dublin. In 1771, he joined the immigrant crowds who left Ulster for Philadelphia; and on his insistence, the remainder of the family emigrated the following year. His father and his brother John established a profitable importing business in Baltimore and built up a considerable estate, to which ultimately (in 1790) James fell heir. He attended the Newark Academy, Delaware (1772), where he displayed a weakness for poetry, and then studied medicine in Philadelphia under Dr. Benjamin Rush.

An ardent patriot because of his pronounced hostility to England, he hurried to Cambridge in 1775 to volunteer for military service. In January 1776, he was assigned to the medical staff of the military hospital in Cambridge, where he won recognition from the Continental Congress and assurance of advancement. On Aug. 10, he was named surgeon of Col. Robert Magaw's 5th Pennsylvania Battalion. Captured at the fall of Fort Washington in November, he was paroled Jan. 27, 1777, and remained in Philadelphia and Baltimore until a complete exchange was arranged, Mar. 5, 1778. For a short time, apparently, he acted as "Senior Surgeon of the Flying Hospital, Valley Forge," and on May 15 was appointed secretary to Washington. With this appointment, according to one of his biographers (Steiner, *post,* p. 17), he abandoned the practice of medicine for the rest of his life. Winning the confidence of Washington for ability and prudence, McHenry was transferred to Lafayette's staff in August 1780. Ever afterward he gloried in his association with Lafayette, and some years later contributed an account of the French general's services to Dr. William Gordon [*q.v.*], for use in his *History of the Rise, Progress and Establishment of the Independence of the United States of America* (1788). With characteristic loyalty he urged Washington to aid Lafayette when the latter was a prisoner at Olmütz. Commissioned a major, May 30, 1781, McHenry continued in active service until he was elected to the Maryland Senate (September 1781), where he sat for five years.

In May 1783, he was appointed to Congress and through later elections and reëlections served until 1786. During this period he wrote (1784) three articles, published five years later under the general title, "Observations Relative to a Commercial Treaty with Great Britain," in Mathew Carey's *American Museum* (April, May, June 1789). A Maryland delegate to the Convention of 1787, which drafted the federal Constitution, he attended from May 28 to June 1, when the illness of his brother recalled him to Baltimore, and was again in attendance from Aug. 6 until the convention adjourned. He was a conscientious worker, but for one of such varied training and experience added little to the debates. He kept a private record of the proceedings of the Convention, however, which is one of the valuable sources for its history (*American Historical Review,* April 1906; Max Farrand, *The Records of the Federal Convention of 1787,* 1911). A stout Federalist, he campaigned for state adoption of the Constitution and served as a member of Maryland's ratifying convention. Subsequently, in a warm contest, he defeated Samuel Chase for a seat in the Assembly, in which he sat until 1791, when he entered the state Senate for a period of five years. As an intimate associate of the President-Elect, he was named to the Maryland commission which formally welcomed Washington on his journey to New York for the inauguration in April 1789.

In January 1796, fourth choice for the post, he was offered the secretaryship of war, to succeed Timothy Pickering [*q.v.*], who had become secretary of state. As a member of the cabinet, he won the President's esteem and apparently considerable influence in the distribution of patronage. He retained his portfolio into Adams' administration. Like his colleague Pickering, he regarded Hamilton as his political leader and on all major matters of policy reflected Hamilton's opinions. Consequently, with the increasing difficulty of the question of war with France, his relations with President Adams [*q.v.*] became more and more strained. When Hamilton, Pinckney, and Knox were appointed generals, under Washington, to provide for the event of war, Adams suspected McHenry of machinations in Hamilton's favor; later he believed McHenry guilty of intriguing against his reëlection, but this McHenry denied. In May 1800, on Adams' demand, he resigned from the cabinet. His troubles were not over, however, for the Republicans violently assailed his administration of the department of war. Yet a congressional committee (Apr. 29, 1802), reported against undertaking an investigation of his expenditure of funds. Keenly sensitive to criticism, McHenry prepared an elaborate defense which was read from the floor of the House on Dec. 28, 1802, and privately printed under the title, *A Letter to the Honourable Speaker of the House of Representatives of the United States,* early in 1803.

Thereafter, he lived in retirement on his pleasant estate at Fayetteville, near Baltimore, with his wife, Margaret Allison Caldwell, whom he had married Jan. 8, 1784. As a Federalist, he was opposed to the War of 1812; though his son John volunteered in the defense of Fort McHenry (named for McHenry during his secretaryship) and of Baltimore. Of other activities he had but few. He served as president of the first Bible society founded in Baltimore (1813), and published a Baltimore directory (1807). A brochure, *The Three Patriots* (1811), dealing with Jefferson, Madison, and Monroe, has been attributed to him, though not conclusively (Steiner, p. 572). Without marked ability as an orator, a legislator, a surgeon, or a soldier, he was a high-minded gentleman, a conservative politician, and an associate of great men in stirring days. He died in his sixty-third year. Of his children, only two, a son and a daughter, survived him.

[B. C. Steiner, *The Life and Correspondence of James McHenry* (1907); F. J. Brown, *A Sketch of the Life of Dr. James McHenry* (1877); *Biog. Dir. Am. Cong.* (1928); *Pubs. Southern Hist. Asso.,* Sept., Nov. 1905, Jan., Mar. 1906, Jan. 1907; James McHenry Papers, MSS. Div., Lib. of Cong.]

R. J. P.

McHENRY, JAMES (Dec. 20, 1785–July 21, 1845), poet, novelist, was born at Larne, County Antrim, Ireland, where he studied first for the Presbyterian ministry, but being disinclined to the pulpit because he was a hunchback he became a student of medicine at Belfast and later at Glasgow. Sensitive and deeply impressionable, he turned to poetry and wrote many lyrics to celebrate the valley of the Larne and the blue Scottish hills. For some years after his certification he practised medicine in his native town of Larne and Belfast; but in 1817, with his wife and infant son, he emigrated to the United States, living in Baltimore, Butler County, Pa., and in Pittsburgh until 1824 when he settled in Philadelphia. In that city for eighteen years he was prominent as a physician, merchant, political leader, magazine editor, poet, and critic. With the assistance of his wife he established and kept a draper's shop near his home at 36 Second Street: in addition to this he very soon met with some success in professional and literary circles.

As early as 1822, while in Pittsburgh, he had brought out a volume of miscellaneous verse, *The Pleasures of Friendship,* and a year later his first exclusively American work, *Waltham,* a poetic legend of Revolutionary days. About the same time, his first novel, written under the pseudonym of Solomon Secondsight, was published in London. *The Wilderness; or The Youthful Days of Washington* (1823), is an account of the adventures of Protestant Ulstermen in America during the Revolutionary days of the West. In 1824 McHenry began his brief career as an editor when he founded the *American Monthly Magazine* as a Philadelphia rival of the *North American Review.* This magazine, devoted to criticism, essays, poetry, and social satire, failed within its first year for reasons principally financial. He had already published his second novel, *The Spectre of the Forest* (1823), to be followed in 1824 by *O'Halloran, or the Insurgent Chief,* and in 1825 by *The Hearts of Steel,* an Irish historical tale. In 1827 he undertook to launch his sole venture in the dramatic field, *The Usurper,* a tragedy of Druidical times in blank verse and interesting as having been the first attempt to place Irish legendary history upon the American stage. *The Usurper* appeared at the Chestnut Street Theatre Dec. 26, 1827, but was received without enthusiasm. McHenry now turned again to novel writing, producing American historical tales of which *The Betrothed of Wyoming* (1830) and *Meredith, or the Mystery of Meschianza* (1831) are types.

In the meantime the success of his earliest and perhaps his best work, *The Pleasures of Friendship,* which had reached a seventh edition in 1836, led McHenry, whose views upon poetry were highly conservative, to attack Wordsworth, Scott, Byron, and other romanticists of their respective schools in the most unmeasured terms. As leading poetry reviewer for the *American*

Quarterly Review, he was led by his bias into extravagances so effectively rebutted by writers for *Blackwood's Edinburgh Magazine* and the *Athenæum* as to discredit him as a critic. He now turned once more to prose fiction and verse. Ambitious like Pope, to whom he has been not very happily likened, he attempted an epic and in 1839 published *Antediluvians, or the World Destroyed,* a blank verse chronicle of the Flood. It was scathingly reviewed in *Blackwood's* (July 1839). Undoubtedly he was at his best with the Irish lyric. For all his many talents, his sole contribution to American letters was his portraiture of the Ulster Irishman who in conduct, beliefs, and religious tenets resembles the lowland Scot. In 1843 he was appointed to the consulate in Londonderry. He assumed his duties and after two years in office died in his native town of Larne.

[E. P. Oberholtzer, *The Lit. Hist. of Phila.* (1906); F. L. Mott, *A Hist. of Am. Mags., 1741–1850* (1930); F. C. Wemyss, *Twenty Six Years of the Life of an Actor and Manager* (1847); A. H. Quinn, *A Hist. of the Am. Drama from the Beginning to the Civil War* (1923); the *Knickerbocker,* July 1834, Apr. 1859; *Pub. Ledger* (Phila.), Aug. 12, 1845.] E. M. H.

McILVAINE, CHARLES PETTIT (Jan. 18, 1799–Mar. 13, 1873), Protestant Episcopal bishop, son of Joseph and Maria (Reed) McIlvaine, was descended on his father's side from the McIlvaines of Ayrshire, Scotland; his mother's family was of English origin. Joseph McIlvaine, a lawyer by profession, was from 1823 until his death in 1826 a member of the United States Senate. Charles was born at Burlington, N. J.; he studied at the Burlington Academy, graduated with high honors from the College of New Jersey at Princeton in 1816, and subsequently pursued theological studies there and in private. Ordered deacon on July 4, 1820, he at once took charge of Christ Church, Georgetown, D. C., where he remained until 1824. He was ordained priest Mar. 20, 1823. On Oct. 8, 1822, he married Emily, daughter of William Coxe [*q.v.*], whom he had known in childhood. At Georgetown his preaching attracted the attention of many leading statesmen in Washington, and in the year 1821–22 he served as chaplain of the Senate. In January 1825 he was appointed chaplain and professor of geography, history, and ethics at West Point, where he remained until December 1827. Here he instituted revivals of religion that profoundly affected many officers and cadets—something unusual at the Military Academy, and not altogether pleasing to those in authority.

McIlvaine's theology was of the most evangelical school and he received calls to several churches of that type, while on the other hand he incurred the strong opposition of some prominent high-churchmen. He was rector of St. Ann's, Brooklyn, N. Y., from December 1827 until 1833, and was also for part of the same time professor of the evidences of Christianity at the University of the City of New York. In the winter of 1831–32 he delivered a series of lectures which were published under the title, *The Evidences of Christianity in Their External Division* (1832).

Elected bishop of Ohio in 1831, he was consecrated to that office Oct. 31, 1832, and the next year moved to Gambier, Ohio, the seat of Kenyon College and its divinity school, of which institutions he became president *ex officio.* As bishop he was incessant in his labors, incurring cheerfully the hardships involved in traveling over miserable roads in primitive conveyances. Never robust, he often sought rest by visits to Europe, especially to England. Both at home and in England he was recognized as a leader of the evangelical cause in the war on the tractarian doctrines. His activity in this connection brought him into unhappy controversies in Ohio, although he had the steadfast support of a strong majority of his diocese. In controversy he was strenuous but without asperity. In the administration of affairs he was decided and imperative. He ruled the institutions at Gambier with a strong hand, and by obtaining money for them at several times rescued them from bankruptcy and secured the erection of many buildings. In 1846 he moved to Clifton, near Cincinnati, which was thereafter his home.

In 1861 when British opinion was greatly inflamed because of the *Trent* affair, he visited England at the request of President Lincoln and exerted himself, particularly among the higher clergy, to make friends for the United States. He was most cordially received and his efforts were in a considerable degree successful. On a subsequent visit to England he was presented to the Queen at her request, and was shown marked attentions by the Prince of Wales. He died in March 1873, at Florence, Italy, to which place he had gone in search of health. His body was taken to England, where a funeral service was held in Westminster Abbey, and was then brought to America and buried at Clifton, Ohio.

In addition to his *Evidences of Christianity,* McIlvaine published many books and pamphlets, the majority of them in exposition and defense of evangelical doctrines, the most important being *Oxford Divinity Compared with That of the Romish and Anglican Churches* (1841). Although a decided Episcopalian, he was on friendly terms with evangelical Christians of all denominations, and was a member of many interdenominational societies. He was tall, stately, handsome, of impressive appearance. His manners were reserved, and he was thought by many to be "cold," yet he was of a very affectionate and sympathetic nature, and was greatly loved by all who knew him well. He was famous as an eloquent and effective preacher. His opinions when once formed seldom changed. His religious faith, clear and unwavering, was the sustaining and controlling power in his life.

[William Carus, *Memorial of the Right Rev. Charles Pettit McIlvaine* (London, 1882); G. F. Smythe, *A Hist. of the Diocese of Ohio* (1931); McIlvaine papers, including letters, journals, memoranda, etc., in the library of Kenyon College, Gambier, Ohio; letters at Trinity Cathedral, Cleveland; annual journals of the Diocese of Ohio, esp. *Jour. of the Fifty-sixth Ann. Conv.* . . . (1873); N. N. Hill, *Hist. of Knox County, Ohio* (1881); Harriet Weed, *The Life of Thurlow Weed* (1884), vol. I; *Cincinnati Commercial,* Mar. 15, 1873.] G. F. S.

MCILWAINE, RICHARD (May 28, 1834–Aug. 10, 1913), Presbyterian clergyman, college president, was the son of Archibald Graham and Martha (Dunn) McIlwaine, of Petersburg, Va. He entered Petersburg Classical Institute at the age of ten, and in January 1850 enrolled in Hampden-Sydney College, where he was an honor graduate with the degree of A.B. in 1853. He studied law at the University of Virginia, 1853–55; was enrolled at Union Theological Seminary, Hampden-Sydney, 1855–57, and in 1857–58 studied in the Free Church College, Edinburgh, Scotland. On May 14, 1857, he married Elizabeth, daughter of Clement Carrington Read of Farmville, Va. From 1858 to 1861 he was pastor of the Presbyterian Church at Amelia Court House, Va. At the outbreak of the Civil War he became lieutenant and chaplain of the 44th Virginia Volunteers, continuing in this capacity until 1862, when precarious health caused him to retire from active service. Returning to Farmville, Va., he became volunteer chaplain of the army hospital located there, and was pastor until 1870. From September 1870 till 1872 he was pastor of the First Presbyterian Church of Lynchburg, Va.; from 1872 to 1882 he was coördinate secretary of the Executive Committee of Foreign Missions and the Executive Committee of Home Missions of the Southern Presbyterian body (Presbyterian Church in the United States). In 1882–83 he was sole secretary of the latter committee. These positions he filled with signal ability, greatly stimulating interest in mission work.

From 1883 to 1904, he was president of Hampden-Sydney College and filled also the chair of moral philosophy and Bible studies. His administration was one of sustained vigor. The curriculum was broadened; the endowment was enlarged; the faculty was increased. He had marked gifts as a teacher. In 1901, without seeking the position, and without opposition, he was elected by the citizens of Prince Edward County as a member of the state constitutional convention, and became chairman of the committee of that body on education and public instruction. In this capacity he was instrumental in the establishment of a central Board of Education with large powers, under which the public-school system of the state has made its greatest progress. He retired from the presidency of Hampden-Sydney College in 1904 and thereafter lived in Richmond, Va., until his death. He was buried at Petersburg. McIlwaine was a prolific writer for church and secular papers. Many of his sermons and addresses were collected in a volume, *Addresses and Papers Bearing Chiefly on Education* (1908). He also published an autobiography, *Memories of Three Score Years and Ten* (1908), and several biographical sketches in the Hampden-Sydney *Kaleidoscope,* a student publication.

[McIlwaine's *Memories*; Hampden-Sydney *Kaleidoscope,* 1895, 1907; L. G. Tyler, *Men of Mark in Va.* (1909), V, 282; *Who's Who in America,* 1912–13; *Times-Dispatch* (Richmond, Va.), Aug. 11, 12, 1913; personal acquaintance.] J. D. E.

MCINTIRE, SAMUEL (January 1757–Feb. 6, 1811), architect, wood-carver, who was to fix the characteristic aspect of his native town of Salem, Mass., was the son of Joseph McIntire, a housewright, and his wife, Sarah (Ruck). He was baptized on Jan. 16, 1757. In his father's shop he learned the family trade with his brothers, Joseph and Angier, before the death of the elder McIntire in 1776. At twenty-one, in 1778, he married Elizabeth Field.

Already, apparently, he had a skill and inspired a confidence beyond his years, for his was the major share in the design of the great house built by Jerathmeel Peirce on land bought in 1779. In general scheme it did not differ from a number of fine houses built in Massachusetts before the Revolution—four-square, three stories in height, with tall pilasters at the corners; but it did differ from all but a very few buildings by cultivated amateurs such as Peter Harrison and John Smibert in its more literate adherence to academic profiles and proportions in the pilasters and other classical details, and thus in its total effect. This was one of great solidity and dignity, not a little enhanced by the formality of its stable court and elaborate fence. The details come from a work long familiar to the colonial carpenters, Batty Langley's *City and Country Builder's and Workman's Treasury of Designs,* first published in 1740, but they are followed with unusually literal faithfulness. The young designer clearly was beginning to know his books, and had taught himself to draw better than any of his predecessors among the builder-architects.

The success of the Peirce house brought him the patronage, which was to be lifelong, of the greatest of Salem merchants at that time, Elias Hasket Derby [*q.v.*], and of his wife, Elizabeth Crowninshield, whose love of display was responsible for a series of commissions. The first was for a great house near the Derby wharf, begun in 1780, on which work was abandoned in 1783. In its plan it had little that was unusual except a screen of columns parting the front hall from the stairs, a feature new to New England; its façade, however, was remarkable for a portico of four Ionic columns opposite the ground story, with a Palladian window and a great lunette marking the center of the two stories above. For the Derbys also the house on Washington Street built about 1764 by Benjamin Pickman was enlarged and remodeled about 1790 on a design by McIntire very similar to that of the Peirce house, but with pilasters Ionic instead of Doric.

It is probably safe to infer from the accounts that Samuel McIntire designed the fine house built by Francis Boardman on Salem Common in 1782–89. This house, likewise three stories and four-square, had quoins at the corners instead of pilasters, a charming small porch of the Roman-Doric order, and a bold staircase with columns for balusters. Many Salem porches and doorways recall the Doric boldness and simplicity of these features in the Peirce and Boardman houses. In the Forrester house, finished after 1791, there is a unique specimen of McIntire's early carving, the rich adornment of the parlor chimneypiece.

McIntire's skill was meanwhile laid under contribution for public and semi-public buildings. The earliest was the Assembly House or "Concert Hall" as built in its first form about 1782. It was succeeded in 1792 by Washington Hall, also from McIntire's drawings. In 1785 he provided the design for the Salem Court House, demolished in 1839. One of the first of the governmental edifices built in New England after the Revolution, it was in its early days one of the most ambitious. A Doric portico below, Ionic pilasters above, adorned the front; a tall cupola in three stages rose over the center.

These successes emboldened McIntire to submit in 1792 a competitive design for the Federal Capitol—one by no means unworthy of consideration among the majority of those received (F. Kimball, in *Journal of the American Institute of Architects,* March 1920). It showed a noble palace with a great central frontispiece of six tall Corinthian columns above a high basement, itself fronted along the wings by Doric colonnades. The suggestion came, obviously, from a plate of James Gibbs, published as Plate 41 in his *Book of Architecture* (1728), a work from which James Hoban [*q.v.*] derived his winning front for the President's House. This plan for the Capitol, his most ambitious attempt, closed the early period of McIntire's work.

A new sun had meanwhile risen in New England architecture; a new style had been revealed in the first designs of Charles Bulfinch [*q.v.*]. McIntire was quick to recognize and study the new fashion. By 1793 he was following it in his own practice. Several of his works in the new manner date from that year. The Nathan Read house, long destroyed, was typical of many to follow. Although it preserved the plan and the shape of the earlier great houses, their massive dignity gave way in it to more refined elegance. The tall pilasters and corner quoins disappeared. The cornice, the balusters above, were thinner and more delicate, as were the columns of the porch, here a reduced echo of the large semicircular portico of Bulfinch's Barrell house. Within, the mid-Georgian detail of fireplace and doorway, with their heavy architraves, was replaced by slender Adam forms, reeded or paneled pilasters, with capitals and friezes delicately enriched. The ornaments cast in composition, characteristic of the style abroad and used in Bulfinch's work and many of McIntire's later houses, were evidently not available for this one, and the native craftsman was stimulated to supply the lack by his own carvings. They included not only fine Corinthian capitals, but baskets of fruit, horns of plenty, and sprays of grape, motives which became typical of McIntire's decorative work.

A house of exceptional qualities, in which Bulfinch's innovations in planning had an influence, was the Theodore Lyman house in Waltham, the only building outside the Salem vicinity from McIntire's designs. The land was bought in March 1793, and by 1798 Mr. Lyman's "elegant seat," with its beautiful grounds in the landscape style, was an object of admiration to travelers. The front was adorned in the upper story with pairs of small Ionic pilasters; below, with rustic blocks about the openings. The hall, ending in a screen of columns, led into an oval drawing room projecting toward the garden as in the

Barrell house. Wings to left and right for kitchens and ball room, connected by lower passages, gave the house something of the air of the Maryland houses of the period. The Assembly House in Salem, remodeled as a private dwelling at this time, was given a similar front of Ionic pilasters.

Mrs. Derby, although she had occupied the remodeled Pickman house for but three or four years, could not be left behind by the change of fashion. Great preparations were made, and local talent was not alone considered. Bulfinch himself was called on for a set of drawings, and others were got even from New York. Features of Bulfinch's design and of his Barrell and Russell houses were then combined in the final plans drawn by McIntire and executed in 1795–98. (F. Kimball, in *Essex Institute Historical Collections*, vol. LX, 1924, pp. 273–92.) A vista from the entrance on the north ran through the central stair-hall with curved ends, and through an oval drawing-room which formed the center of a suite along the southern garden front. Over the central bow toward the garden rose a majestic curved portico. The front in general followed Bulfinch's sketch, itself based on the Provost's House in Dublin, and thus was a distant descendant of Burlington's famous house for General Wade in London. To left and right were formal outbuildings; a summer house in the form of a temple adorned the landscape garden which ran down to a terrace toward the water. All told, the Mansion—by which name it was distinguished among other houses of the Derbys—seemed to contemporaries "more like a palace than the dwelling of an American merchant." In the decoration of the interior there was the greatest lavishness. For every room McIntire carved capitals, medallions, roses, draperies, cabling on beads. The single chimneypiece which survives shows an almost overladen richness, its columns wreathed in sprays of laurel. In the oval room the stucco worker Daniel Raynerd executed a sumptuous Adam ceiling. The owners had but a few months to inhabit and enjoy the house, for Mrs. Derby's death on Apr. 19, 1799, was closely followed by that of her husband, Sept. 8. In 1815, "the convenience of the spot for other buildings brought a sentence of destruction," wrote the Salem diarist William Bentley, "& before the world it was destroyed from its foundations" (*Diary, post,* IV, 362).

On the death of the great merchant, those of his children who had not received one of the fine existing houses as part of their inheritance began to build in feverish rivalry. Thus by 1800 Elizabeth Derby, who had married Capt. Nathaniel West, built "Oak Hill" from McIntire's designs on her tract in Peabody. The richness of decoration rivaled even that of her father's mansion, Samuel McIntire's carvings being supplemented in 1813, after his death, by further ornaments executed by his son. The interior has now lost its principal features, three of the principal rooms being installed in the Museum of Fine Arts, Boston. The third son, Ezekiel Hersey Derby, secured plans for his house on Essex Street from Bulfinch, but the execution of the carved detail was left to McIntire. The mantels were enriched with figural ornament; the great semicircular stair hall, with carved archways and a stucco ceiling. Degraded to business uses, the house has now been stripped of its decorations, the principal ones being incorporated in the Pennsylvania Museum of Art (*Pennsylvania Museum Bulletin,* April 1930, pp. 11–17). Anstis Derby, who had married Benjamin Pickman, Jr., contented herself with adding a new porch, a new bow, and new mantel-pieces to the fine old Pickman house on Essex Street. Meanwhile many other clients were coming to McIntire for their houses, among them Benjamin Carpenter in 1796 (the house now much remodeled), Samuel Cook about 1804, and John Gardner, 1804–05. The Cook and Gardner houses are among the finest of the architect's works still preserved. The great parlor of the Peirce house, remodeled for the wedding of Sally Peirce to George Nichols in 1801, is rightly considered one of McIntire's masterpieces in the Adam manner.

He was also commissioned to do work for several churches during these middle years. In 1796 he replaced the old steeple of the North Meeting House with a plain octagonal cupola. In 1804 the South Church was begun from his designs. The steeple had three stages above the tower, one square and two octagonal, with a tall spire above—certainly one of the most graceful in New England. The tower rested on a broad porch fronted by four Ionic pilasters with festooned capitals. The church was gutted by fire in 1903 and demolished. The Branch Church, built in 1804–05, was removed to Beverly and rebuilt in 1867. In the emulation among the churches even the old Tabernacle had to have a new steeple, which was built in 1805. McIntire was now well recognized as a local celebrity, whom the Town Clerk was to describe at his death as "The Architect of Salem." Thus when the Common was leveled and fenced as Washington Square in 1802 he was called on to design the several gateways—the principal one a little wooden triumphal arch adorned with sculpture and crowned by an eagle. Hamilton Hall, to which the Salem Assemblies were transferred about 1805, was a very admirable and dignified solution of the problem: the great hall above with a row of five Palladian windows under simple brick arches.

The houses of his last years, from 1805 to 1811, are all of brick. For Benjamin March Woodbridge he designed and ornamented the fine square mansion still standing (1933) on Bridge Street; for the Recorder of Deeds, in 1807, a house of which only a single mantelpiece, carved with an eagle, survives. The Gideon Tucker house (1809) was closely similar to the Gardner house opposite; the Joseph Felt house, with a square Doric porch to the street, was one of the architect's last works. In all this group, and especially the two latest, there was an increasing note of austerity, as the growing classicism of the time laid its restraint on the craftsman's facile hand. With the growth of trade and of communication certain newer and larger tasks were imposed upon him—hotels and business buildings of a larger scale. The Archer (Franklin) Building in Salem (1809–10) was perhaps his most extensive undertaking. The treatment was sober, of admirable proportion, depending only on the skilful grouping of the openings in the brick walls and on a rich balustrade at the eaves. There were McIntire carvings in many houses not otherwise known to be his: particularly the Joseph Hosmer house, the David P. Waters house, and the Clifford Crowninshield house. His carving was lavished not only on interior woodwork but on furniture. Some scores of pieces showing his handiwork survive—sofas, chairs, tables of various sorts, beds and their canopies, mirror frames, and chests of drawers—preserved by Salem families, by certain museums (the Essex Institute, Boston Museum of Fine Arts, Yale University, Metropolitan Museum, Pennsylvania Museum) and by a very few private collectors. They show all his characteristic motives of ornament: eagles, baskets and dishes of fruit, urns, rosettes, festoons of drapery and of husks, horns of plenty, sprays of grape and of laurel, executed with a brilliance which has never been surpassed in America (F. Kimball, in *Antiques,* November 1930–March 1931; corrected, *Ibid.,* January 1932, and M. M. Swan, *Ibid.,* November, December 1931).

Although McIntire's achievements in sculpture cannot compare in intrinsic value with those in architecture and furniture carving, he has in this field the merit of a pioneer. Little enough had been done in sculpture anywhere in America, less by native talent. In New England, John and Simeon Skillin of Boston carved in 1793 four figures for the Derby summer house and garden. McIntire, who had perhaps already carved some of his famous eagles, was stimulated to take up figural sculpture, both in relief and in the round, all executed in wood. In 1798 he made a bust of John Winthrop, which the Rev. William Bentley exhibited in the East Church. In 1802, for the Common gates, he carved several bas-reliefs, now preserved by the Essex Institute, among them a profile medallion of Washington (F. Kimball, in *Art in America,* December 1923). The figure of a Canton merchant, clothed, in the Peabody Museum, has head and hands carved by McIntire in 1801; and a small ship's figurehead there, holding a medallion portrait, is believed to be his work (*Old-Time New England,* October 1921, p. 67). His eagles in the round adorned the Pickman (Derby) house, the Common gateway, the Peirce house, and other buildings. Eagles in relief formed part of the external ornament of the Custom House and Hamilton Hall, and of the interior decoration of the Registry of Deeds and a number of private houses, all executed after 1805.

When McIntire died of congestion of the lungs, after rescuing a child from drowning, William Bentley wrote in his diary: "This day Salem was deprived of one of the most ingenious men it had in it. Samuel McIntire, *aet.* 54, in Summer St. . . . By attention he soon gained a superiority to all of his occupation . . . indeed all the improvements of Salem for nearly thirty years past have been done under his eye. In Sculpture he had no rival in New England. . . . To the best of my abilities I encouraged him in this branch. In music he had a good taste, & tho' not presuming to be an original composer, he was among our best Judges & most able performers. All the Instruments we use he could understand & was the best person to be employed in correcting any defects, or repairing them. He had a fine person, a majestic appearance, calm countenance, great self command & amiable temper. He was welcome but never intruded" (*Diary,* IV, 6). No likeness of his features is known.

He was survived by his wife, and by his son Samuel Field McIntire (1780–1819), who carried on the work in carving until his own death, and whose works have often been confused with his father's (F. Kimball, in *Antiques,* February 1933). Samuel's brother Joseph (1748–1825) and the latter's son Joseph, Jr., were carvers as well as carpenters, and continued the business until the death of the last of the line after 1850, when the contents of his shop—still including some of the characteristic eagles—were sold. No architectural designs drawn by these successors are known, however, and none of them approached in distinction the founder of the house.

[Many of McIntire's drawings and bills, as well as his carving-tools and certain of his carvings, are preserved by the Essex Institute in Salem, which also has an extensive archive of photographic negatives and prints of his work. These form the primary basis of Fiske Kimball's "Mr. Samuel McIntire, Carver, The Architect of Salem," in preparation. Some of them are reproduced (partly with incorrect captions) in Frank Cousins and P. M. Riley, *The Woodcarver of Salem* (1916). A paper on McIntire is also to be found in W. A. Dyer, *Early American Craftsmen* (1915). *The Diary of William Bentley, D.D., 1784–1819* (4 vols., 1905–14), contains many references to McIntire and his works and forms an important source. Obituaries appeared in the *Salem Gazette*, Feb. 8, 12, 1811, and *Essex Register*, Feb. 9, 1811. J. B. Felt's *Annals of Salem* (2nd ed., 2 vols., 1845–49), H. W. Belknap, *Artists and Craftsmen of Essex County, Mass.* (1927), and many papers in the *Essex Inst. Hist. Colls.* and in the *Essex Antiquarian* contain allusions to him of documentary value.] F.K.

McINTOSH, JOHN BAILLIE (June 6, 1829–June 29, 1888), Union soldier, was born in Florida, the son of Col. James Simmons McIntosh, United States Army, and the brother of James McQueen McIntosh, later a brigadier-general in the Confederate army. His mother, Eliza (Matthews) Shumate McIntosh, was the daughter of James Matthews of Brooklyn, N. Y. The last of an illustrious fighting family, John entered the navy during the Mexican War and served aboard the U. S. S. *Saratoga* as a midshipman. Upon his return home after the war, he learned of his father's death in Mexico as the result of wounds received in the battle of Molino del Rey. He thereupon resigned from the navy and went to live with an uncle at New Brunswick, N. J. Here, in 1850, he married Amelia Stout. One child, a daughter, was born to this union. For the next decade McIntosh engaged in business with his father-in-law.

When the Civil War began, he declared for the preservation of the Union and applied for a commission in the Regular Army, notwithstanding the many family and social influences tending to enlist his sympathies with the South. He considered as a blot on his family honor the resignation from the Federal service of his brother, who had been educated at West Point and now took up arms against the government.

In June 1861, he entered the Federal service as a second lieutenant of cavalry. Serving in the Shenandoah Valley in 1861 and later with the Army of the Potomac, he at once drew the attention of his commanders and was frequently commended in orders. In July 1862 he was assigned temporarily to the command of the 95th Pennsylvania Volunteers, whose colonel had been killed. For gallant and meritorious services at White Oak Swamp (August 1862) he was brevetted major; he participated in the battles of South Mountain and Antietam, and in November 1862 was appointed colonel of the 3rd Pennsylvania Cavalry. When the Union cavalry was reorganized by Gen. Alfred Pleasanton in the spring of 1863, McIntosh was given the command of a brigade, with which he distinguished himself at Kelly's Ford (March 1863). He fought at Chancellorsville and played a significant rôle in the cavalry fighting of the Gettysburg campaign, demonstrating that as a brigade commander he had no superior (letter of General W. W. Averell, War Department files). While recuperating from a fall from a horse, he was placed in charge of the Cavalry Depot in Washington. Returning to the command of his brigade in May 1864, he took part in the great cavalry operations of that year, ending with the battle of Winchester, where he received wounds necessitating the amputation of his right leg. He received in succession every brevet grade from major to major-general for bold, valiant, and gallant action under fire.

After the war, he was commissioned a lieutenant colonel in the Regular Army upon the special recommendation of General Grant. He commanded the 42nd Infantry 1866–67, was deputy governor and governor of the Soldier's Home at Washington 1867–68, and superintendent of Indian affairs in California, 1869–70. He was retired in 1870 with the rank of brigadier-general, and made his residence in New Brunswick, N. J., where he took an active interest in public affairs. McIntosh was a born fighter, a strict disciplinarian, a dashing leader, and a polished gentleman. He represents the highest type of volunteer soldier.

[Navy records; War Dept. records; Pension Office records; *War of the Rebellion, Official Records (Army)*; J. G. B. Bulloch, *A Hist. and Geneal. of the Family of Baillie of Dunain . . . with a Short Sketch of the Family of McIntosh . . .* (1898); L. R. Hamersly, *Records of Living Officers of the U. S. Army* (1884); F. B. Heitman, *Hist. Reg. U. S. Army* (1890); *Army and Navy Jour.* and *Army and Navy Reg.*, July 7, 1888; *N. Y. Herald*, July 1, 1888.] J.R.V.

McINTOSH, LACHLAN (Mar. 17, 1725–Feb. 20, 1806), Revolutionary soldier, born at Raits in Badenoch, Scotland, was the son of John Mohr and Marjory (Fraser) McIntosh, who came to Georgia with other Highlanders in 1736 and settled at Inverness (later Darien). In 1748 Lachlan moved from bankrupt Georgia to Charleston, S. C. (*Georgia Historical Quarterly*, September 1919), where he is said to have worked as a clerk in a counting-house and to have lived with Henry Laurens.

Little is known of his life before July 1775, when he appeared at Savannah as a member for the Parish of St. Andrew of the Provincial Congress. On Jan. 7, 1776, he was appointed colonel of a battalion of Georgia troops. This force was later increased and incorporated in the Continental Army, and McIntosh was appointed brigadier-general as of Sept. 16, 1776. The efforts of Button Gwinnett [*q.v.*] to bring the Continental troops under local control, and an investigation of the failure of a military expedition into Florida in 1777 which vindicated the civil authority at the expense of the military, together with personal differences and the bitter factional disputes of the Georgia patriots, led to a duel (May 16, 1777), between the two men in which both were wounded, Gwinnett mortally. Though acquitted when brought to trial, McIntosh suffered from the hostility of Gwinnett's friends. Alleging this as his reason, George Walton, Georgia delegate in Congress, obtained McIntosh's transfer to Washington's headquarters (*Letters of Members of the Continental Congress,* vol. II, 1923, p. 439). After a winter at Valley Forge, he was appointed in May 1778 to command the Western department, with headquarters at Fort Pitt. His plans for an expedition to Detroit and an attack on the Northern Indians were not carried out; his subordinates, Daniel Brodhead and George Morgan [*qq.v.*], complained of his conduct; Gouverneur Morris described him to Washington as "one of those who excel in the Regularity of still Life from the Possession of an indolent uniformity of soul" (Kellogg, *post,* 252–53); and on Mar. 5, 1779, Washington directed him to turn over the command to Brodhead. On May 18 he was ordered south again by Congress, and commanded the 1st and 5th South Carolina regiments in the disastrous attack on Savannah (October 1779). Taken prisoner by the British at the capture of Charleston (May 12, 1780), he was exchanged for General O'Hara under an agreement dated Feb. 9, 1782. In the meantime his enemies in Georgia, led by George Walton, had induced Congress to suspend him from active service by a resolve of Feb. 15, 1780. The resolve was repealed on July 16, 1781, and he was brevetted major-general Sept. 30, 1783; but his final vindication was delayed until Feb. 24, 1784, when a committee of Congress, of which James Monroe was a member, quoted with approval a resolution of the Georgia Assembly charging Walton with forgery, and praised McIntosh for his Revolutionary services.

When he returned to Georgia in 1783 he was, according to his own statement, "incredibly poor." He took little part in public life thereafter, devoting much of his time to the management of his deceased brother George's estate. He was a charter member of the Society of the Cincinnati of Georgia (1784); was elected a delegate to Congress on Feb. 23, 1784, but apparently never attended its sessions; was twice appointed a commissioner to adjust the boundary dispute between Georgia and South Carolina; and was one of the four commissioners of Congress to treat with the Southern Indians (1785–86). In 1791 he was a member of the committee that welcomed President Washington at Savannah. He married Sarah Threadcraft. His death occurred in Savannah and he was buried in the Colonial Cemetery there.

[*Jours. of the Continental Cong.,* Feb. 11, 15, June 23, Sept. 25, 1780, July 16, 1781; *Calendar of the Correspondence of George Washington . . . with the Officers* (4 vols., 1915), see Index; Jared Sparks, ed., *Writings of George Washington,* V (1834), 361–62, 382; W. B. Stevens, *Hist. of Ga.* (2 vols., 1847–59); C. C. Jones, *Hist. of Ga.* (2 vols., 1883); L. P. Kellogg, *Frontier Advance on the Upper Ohio* (1916); J. G. B. Bulloch, *A Hist. and Geneal. of the Family of Baillie of Dunain . . . with a short Sketch of the Family of McIntosh . . .* (1898); *Charleston Courier,* Feb. 26, 1806.] A. P. W.

McINTOSH, WILLIAM (*c.* 1775–May 1, 1825), Creek Indian chief, brigadier-general of the United States Army, was born in the Coweta country, Creek Nation, on the east bank of the Chattahoochee River, in the present limits of Carroll County, Ga. His father was William McIntosh, captain in the British army, and agent to the Creek Indians; his mother, a full-blooded Indian woman of unknown name. The sister of his father, Catherine, became the mother of George M. Troup [*q.v.*], and with the career of his cousin that of the Indian chief was closely intertwined. He emerges from obscurity as leader of the Lower Creeks, friendly to the Americans in the War of 1812, in which the Upper Creeks sided with the British. As a reward for notable service in this war he was commissioned brigadier-general in the United States Army, and served with Jackson in the campaigns against the Seminoles, 1817–18 (*Historical Collections of Georgia, post,* pp. 170–73).

After the Indian wars McIntosh was known as the friend of the white man and of Georgia. Troup became governor in 1823 and endeavored to secure the removal of the Creek and Cherokee Indians still occupying choice lands in the western part of the state. The Upper Creeks or "Red Sticks," resident in Alabama and long hostile to the whites, were determined to make no cession of tribal lands. The Lower Creeks, on the Georgia side of the river, influenced by McIntosh, were disposed to conclude treaties of cession. McIntosh was proscribed by the hostile faction of Creeks, and expelled from the Cherokee council as a renegade (he had married a Cherokee wife). After the failure of treaty negotiations at Broken Arrow, Ala., Dec. 1, 1824, United States commissioners arranged a council at Indian Springs, Ga., Feb. 7, 1825. Here the Upper Creeks continued to oppose any cession and succeeded in breaking up the council. On Feb. 12, however, the McIntosh party signed a treaty of cession. Its fairness was at least doubtful, and McIntosh's disinterestedness was called in question. The Upper Creeks, supported by the United States agent, Crowell, protested the treaty; but eventually its provisions went into effect. The vengeance of the Upper Creeks was not long delayed. McIntosh's house on the east bank of the Chattahoochee River was surrounded during the night of Apr. 30, and set on fire, and in the ensuing mêlée McIntosh was slain. In person he is described as "tall, finely formed and of graceful and commanding manner." He had much of the polish of the gentleman. In his life and death he illustrates the not infrequent tragedy of the American half-breed Indian. He had several Indian wives, and left Indian progeny.

[*Am. State Papers. Indian Affairs,* vols. I, II (1832–34), contain the documents bearing on McIntosh's public career; the best secondary account is E. J. Harden, *The Life of George M. Troup* (1859); other sources are: George White, *Statistics of the State of Ga.* (1849), and *Hist. Colls. of Ga.* (1854); A. J. Pickett, *Hist. of Ala.* (2 vols., 1851); U. B. Phillips, *Ga. and State Rights* (1902); J. G. B. Bulloch, *A Hist. and Geneal. of the Family of Baillie of Dunain . . . with a Short Sketch of the Family of McIntosh . . .* (1898).] H. J. P., Jr.

MCIVER, CHARLES DUNCAN (Sept. 27, 1860–Sept. 17, 1906), Southern educator, the son of Matthew Henry and Sarah (Harrington) McIver, was born on a farm in Moore County, N. C. He was of Scotch Presbyterian descent, and as a youth lived amidst the austere surroundings which characterized the poverty-stricken era of reconstruction in the South. In 1881 he graduated from the University of North Carolina, and after a few years of teaching in private and public schools decided to make education his life work. At this time in North Carolina, as in the South generally, the idea that higher education, or even elementary education, should be at public expense found little acceptance. Except at the University, which each year received a few thousand dollars from the state treasury, such higher education as was afforded was paid for either by the churches or privately, and even this was wholly inadequate both in quality and quantity. McIver saw that wider opportunities for higher education would be distinctly advantageous to the state, and, despite the depleted condition of the state treasury, he urgently recommended that a system affording such opportunities, supported largely by taxation, be inaugurated. Inasmuch as the University of North Carolina already constituted a skeleton for the widening of the advantages open to men, he turned his attention to the establishment of a similar institution for women. Since the greater part of elementary and high school teaching is done by women, he argued, it is the part of wisdom for the commonwealth to provide advantages that will better fit women to fulfil the function of teaching or the equally important function of motherhood. In arriving at these views he was aided largely by his wife, Lula (Martin) McIver, herself a teacher, to whom he was married in 1885 and by whom he had five children.

Having been appointed by the Teachers' Assembly of North Carolina chairman of a committee to appear before the legislature in 1889 and urge the adoption of a bill for the establishment of a training school for teachers, he argued eloquently for its approval. Although the measure did not pass, his earnestness reduced the opposition from a huge to a very scant majority. In that year the state board of education transferred its appropriation from the short-term summer normal schools to a system of county institutes, and appointed McIver and Edwin A. Alderman co-conductors. They at once commenced a remarkable campaign. Beginning in September 1889, McIver appeared in virtually every county in the state, and almost every town and hamlet, urging the dual causes of universal public education for all children in the state and the higher education of women. In 1891 a bill was again presented to the legislature for the establishment of a college for women and this time it passed with little opposition. At the initial meeting of the board of directors of the newly formed North Carolina State Normal and Industrial College (later North Carolina College for Women), located at Greensboro, McIver was elected president.

Despite numerous tempting offers of more remunerative employment in the business and educational world, he continued in this position for the remainder of his life. During the fourteen years of his presidency he built the college upon such firm foundations that it has become one of the outstanding women's colleges in the South. This achievement, however, was by no means the sum of his accomplishments. Assisted by a few kindred spirits, he gave unstintedly of his time and energy to the further awakening of North Carolina from the lethargy into which it had fallen at the close of the Civil War. As a prime mover in the organization of the Conference for Education in the South, as secretary of the Southern Education Board, and as a public-spirited citizen, he carried on his crusade throughout the South for the extension of educational facilities. Although he died in the prime of life, he lived to see his section well on the way toward that educational renaissance which has been notable in recent years. He had well earned the tribute, "educational statesman," which was universally bestowed upon him after his untimely death.

[Information derived from associates of McIver and particularly his widow; *Charles Duncan McIver* (1906), privately printed; *Program of Exercises for N. C. Day —McIver Memorial Day* (1906), compiled by R. D. W. Connor; *Report of the Commissioner of Education* (1908); B. J. Hendrick, *The Life and Letters of Walter H. Page* (1924), vol. I; *Charlotte Daily Observer*, Sept. 18, 1906.] B. B. K.

McKAY, DONALD (Sept. 4, 1810–Sept. 20, 1880), naval architect and master ship-builder, was born on a farm on the east side of Jordan River in Shelburne County, Nova Scotia, second of sixteen children (W. L. Kean, *The Genealogy of Hugh McKay*, 1895, p. 6) of Hugh and Ann (McPherson) McKay. His paternal grandfather, for whom he was named, was a Scottish army officer who took up the farm among United Empire Loyalists in 1783. Equipped only with a common-school education, Donald emigrated in 1827 to New York where he was apprenticed ship-carpenter to Isaac Webb [*q.v.*]. When his indenture was up and he became a free-lance shipwright, his talents were noticed and encouraged by the leading New York ship-builders. Jacob Bell [*q.v.*] sent him to Wiscasset, Me., in 1839 to finish a vessel; he then found employment at Newburyport, Mass., where in 1841 he formed a partnership with William Currier as master ship-builder. There he quickly made a reputation by building two New York packet ships, and after forming a new partnership, with William Pickett, was chosen in 1844 to design and build the *Joshua Bates* for the Boston-Liverpool line. The owner, Enoch Train, induced McKay to come to Boston, and aided him in establishing a shipyard at East Boston.

Here, for five years, he concentrated his attention on packet ships. On Dec. 7, 1850, he launched the *Stag Hound* (1,534 tons), his first clipper ship; and on Apr. 15, 1851, the *Flying Cloud* (1,783 tons), which made San Francisco in less than ninety days from New York, a passage but twice equaled, once by herself. Three other great clippers left his yard that year. In 1852 he built the *Sovereign of the Seas* (2,421 tons) on his own account, since no one would order so great a vessel, and placed her in command of his brother Lauchlan (1811–1895), who was a practical builder as well as master mariner. After two remarkable voyages the *Sovereign of the Seas* was sold to British purchasers, and gave her builder an international reputation. In the same year he built the clippers *Westward Ho!* and *Bald Eagle*. In 1853, with amazing courage, Donald McKay built on his own account the *Great Republic*, registering $4,555\frac{3}{5}$ tons, $334\frac{1}{2}$ feet long (Boston Vessel Registry, MS., 1853, no. 457), with a 120-foot yard arm and a main skysail truck over 200 feet above her deck. Although burned before going to sea, the *Great Republic* as razeed and rebuilt was the pride of the American merchant marine. The *Empress of the Seas, Star of Empire, Chariot of Fame,* and *Romance of the Seas* were also of that year. In 1854–55 McKay again surpassed himself with six clipper ships built for the Liverpool-Australia trade, two of which, the *James Baines* (2,515 tons) and *Lightning* (2,084 tons), hold world records for speed under sail. The *Baines* made the fastest transatlantic port-to-port passage, twelve days six hours Boston to Liverpool, and the round-the-world record of 134 days; at times she attained a speed of twenty-one knots. The *Lightning* made the greatest day's run in the annals of sail, 436 nautical miles. In fact ten out of twelve recorded days' runs of 400 miles and upward were made by McKay's ships.

McKay designed all these and many other vessels, superintended every detail of their construction, and invented several labor-saving devices. A man of indefatigable industry, a skilful draftsman and a practical builder, he had an innate sense of beauty and proportion, and intuitive perception of both how and what to build. A characteristic declaration was, "I never yet built a vessel that came up to my own ideal; I saw something in each ship which I desired to improve" (*Boston Daily Advertiser*, Oct. 29, 1864). At prime of life he was a fine figure of a man, with strong features, and dark hair curling back from a high forehead. He loved music and played the violin. His character won the affection of his employés and the respect of his competitors; in the Boston of Webster and Everett he was one of the most prominent citizens. In religion he was a Methodist. His two wives did much for his career: Albenia Martha Boole (m. 1833, d. 1848), a ship-builder's daughter, assisted his education; Mary Cressy Litchfield (m. 1849, d. 1923) acted as his adviser and secretary in business matters, and named his famous clippers. He had fifteen children, most of whom survived him.

By 1855 the day of extreme clipper ships was over, and McKay turned to a more economical type, but the panic of 1857 left his yard vacant. Having obtained a contract to furnish 500 loads of ship timber to the British Admiralty, he spent over a year (1859–60) in Europe, where his reputation gave him access to the leading government dockyards. He watched the construction of the new ironclads, and assisted at armor tests, which convinced him that the United States navy was obsolete, and made him a vigorous advocate of steam screw ironclads of the largest class. These views, coming from the supreme master builder of wooden sailing ships, made a deep impression. In March–April 1861, he proposed to build an ironclad corvette of 2,390 tons displacement, mounting twelve 9-inch guns in casemates (J. P. Baxter 3rd, *post,* pp. 239–40). These and other plans were not accepted, largely for want of funds, and as McKay obtained no orders, he returned to England in July 1861 and remained until April 1863, again doing business with the Admiralty. After his return to America he equipped his yard to produce iron ships and marine and locomotive engines, and in 1864–65 built at considerable financial loss the monitor *Nausett* and three other naval vessels for the government; in 1866–69 he built a few steamers and sailing ships, of which the last, the *Glory of the Seas* (2,102 tons), although a loss to her builder, proved a fast and profitable vessel, and lasted until 1923. Although in 1869 he sold his shipyard, he built elsewhere for the government the wooden sloops-of-war *Adams* and *Essex* in 1874–75 (Bradlee, *post,* pp. 317–18). Being threatened with tuberculosis he retired in 1877 to a country estate at Hamilton, Mass., where, with characteristic energy, he endeavored by scientific farming to recoup health and fortune. Both suffered, and on Sept. 20, 1880, he died.

[The only biography is Richard C. McKay, *Some Famous Sailing Ships and Their Builder Donald McKay* (1928), with list of vessels; the best brief account is the introduction to John Robinson and G. F. Dow, *The Sailing Ships of New England,* ser. 2 (1924), which is in part based on information in F. B. C. Bradlee, "The Ship 'Great Republic' and Donald McKay, Her Builder," published in *Hist. Colls. of the Essex Inst.,* vol. LXIII (1927) and separately. A. H. Clark, *The Clipper Ship Era* (1911), gives a personal impression, the background, and an account of McKay's ships, which may be supplemented by O. T. Howe and F. C. Matthews, *American Clipper Ships* (2 vols., 1926–27), and C. C. Cutler, *Greyhounds of the Sea* (1930). McKay's letters on naval policy are printed in the Boston *Commercial Bulletin,* Nov. 17 and Dec. 1, 1860, Mar. 16, 1861, and *Boston Daily Advertiser,* Oct. 29, 1864. Letters from and about him are in the Navy Department Archives, the Welles Papers, Lib. of Cong., and the Admiralty papers in the Public Record Office, London. His relation to naval policy is described in J. P. Baxter 3rd, *Introduction of the Ironclad Warship* (1933), and "Report of the Joint Committee on the Conduct of the War" (*Sen. Doc. No. 142,* 38 Cong., 2 Sess.), vol. III, pt. 2. A prospectus of a work by Donald McKay on naval architecture was issued in 1859, but the book was never written; his brother Lauchlan published *The Practical Ship-Builder* in 1839.] S. E. M.

McKAY, GORDON (May 4, 1821–Oct. 19, 1903), industrialist, inventor, was born in Pittsfield, Mass., the son of Samuel Michel and Catherine Gordon (Dexter) McKay. His father, the son of Samuel Mackay, a captain in the British army and afterwards professor of French in Williams College (1795–99), was a cotton manufacturer, amateur farmer, and a politician of some prominence in the western part of Massachusetts; his mother, the daughter of Samuel Dexter [*q.v.*] of Boston, an eminent lawyer who in 1800 served as secretary of war and afterwards as secretary of the treasury. McKay was a delicate youth and what little schooling he had was directed toward an outdoor occupation. He studied engineering and for eight years, beginning when he was sixteen, he worked with the engineer corps of the Boston & Albany Railroad and of the Erie Canal. At the age of twenty-four he returned to Pittsfield and established a machine shop for the repair of paper and cotton mill machinery. This he operated profitably for seven years and then, in 1852, accepted the position of treasurer and general manager of the Lawrence Machine Shop at Lawrence, Mass. In 1859 he became interested in the machine recently invented by Lyman R. Blake [*q.v.*] for sewing the soles of shoes to the uppers. McKay bought the patent, paying Blake $70,000 for it, $8,000 in cash and $62,000 to be paid from future profits. He then set to work to improve the machine so that it would stitch the soles around the toes and heels. With the great material assistance of R. H. Matthies, an expert machinist, the attempt succeeded after several years of effort, and on May 6, 1862, McKay obtained a patent (No. 35,165) for a "process of sewing soles of boots and shoes." He immediately organized the McKay Association to manufacture the machine, and since the Civil War was creating a demand for army shoes, he experienced little difficulty in securing the necessary capital. Within a few months he was filling a government contract for 25,000 pairs of army shoes in his two factories at Rayham and Farmington, N. H., and was also manufacturing his shoe machine for other firms. The machines were not sold outright but leased to other manufacturers on a royalty basis. By the end of 1862 McKay was drawing royalties from over sixty shoe factories in the East and Middle West, and by 1876 he was receiving more than a half million dollars annually in royalties. During this time he not only directed the business of his association and worked out the details for manufacturing the machine, but also kept in close touch with the experimental work for the further perfection and application of shoe machinery. He was the joint patentee with Blake for five patents on sewing-machine improvements in 1864, and in 1865 on a machine for manufacturing shoes with turned soles. In 1874 he and Blake fought to secure the extension of the latter's patent, and upon the winning of this battle he paid Blake a large sum of money for the reassignment of the patent to the McKay Association. Meanwhile, the welt-shoe sewing machine controlled by Charles Goodyear, 1833–1896 [*q.v.*], was coming to the fore, and by 1876 the McKay and Goodyear interests were in bitter competition and for four years constantly involved in litigation. In 1880, however, they joined forces, McKay turning over his turned-shoe machinery patents to Goodyear, who, in turn, assigned his rights in welt-and-turned-shoe machinery to McKay. McKay then confined his attention to the development and manufacture of machinery for making the heavier grades of shoes, but fifteen years later, 1895, he sold all of his interests to the Goodyear Company. McKay was also interested in the perfection of machines for nailing and pegging soles on shoes, in improvements in metallic fastenings for shoes, and in machinery for the manufacture of the stouter grades of boots and shoes. In the course of his life he was the patentee or joint patentee of more than forty inventions, which brought him wealth estimated at $40,000,000.

Following his retirement in 1895, he lived quietly in Cambridge and Newport, devoting his time to philanthropic work. His benefactions were many. He established the McKay Institute at Kingston, R. I., for the education of colored boys, and he bequeathed a trust fund of $4,000,000 to Harvard University for the establishment of a department of applied science, with the condition that it should not be used until the last annuitant of the McKay estate died. It is estimated that by that time the fund will amount to about $20,000,000. He was twice married: first, in 1845, to Agnes Jenkins, of Pittsfield, Mass., from whom he was divorced several years later; second, in 1878, to Marian Treat of Longwood, Mass., which marriage likewise terminated in a divorce (1890). He died in Newport, R. I., after a year's illness, and was buried in Pittsfield.

[W. B. Kaempffert, *A Popular Hist. of Am. Invention* (2 vols., 1924); O. P. Dexter, *Dexter Geneal., 1642–1904* (1904); Hennen Jennings, *The McKay Endowment and Applied Science at Harvard* (1918); J. D. Van Slyck, *Representatives of New England* (1879); J. E. A. Smith, *Hist. of Pittsfield*, vol. II (1876); *Sewing Machine Advance*, Feb. 1904; *Sewing Machine Times*, Oct. 25, 1903; *Shoe and Leather Reporter*, Oct. 22, 1903; *Springfield Daily Republican*, Oct. 20, 1903; Patent Office records.]

C. W. M.

MACKAY, JAMES (1759?–Mar. 16, 1822), explorer, was born in the Parish of Kildonan, County of Sutherland, Scotland, the son of George and Elizabeth (McDonald) Mackay. He came of a family that produced many distinguished men. He was well educated, spoke French and Spanish fluently, and was a surveyor by profession. About 1776 he emigrated to Canada, where he joined a fur-trading expedition. He was employed by the British to explore the region of the upper lakes and the far West, hoping to open communication with the South Sea. After some years in this perilous occupation, which carried him as far as the Rocky Mountains, he went to Spanish Louisiana to partake of the privileges extended by the Spanish government to foreign settlers. Although a Scotchman, he grew rapidly in favor with the Spanish government. In 1795 Baron de Carondelet appointed him director of the third expedition sent by the Spanish commercial company to explore the vast country on both sides of the Missouri River and across the continent to the Pacific Ocean and, incidentally, to construct forts for the protection of the Spanish trade. In August 1795, with thirty-three men, he started from St. Louis on this enterprise which cost the Spanish government 104,000 pesos. Thus engaged for two years, he brought about peace among the Indian tribes and between them and the Spanish, took possession of a British fort at the Mandan village, prepared a map of the region explored, and furnished the Spanish government with a journal of the expedition (journal printed in Houck, *Spanish Régime, post,* II, pp. 181–94). Lewis and Clark made use of Mackay's map on their famous expedition to the Pacific Ocean.

In 1797 Mackay was appointed deputy surveyor by Antoine Soulard, the Spanish surveyor-general. As a reward for his services he was made captain of the militia and commandant of San Andres, a settlement on the south bank of the Missouri River, in St. Louis County, to which many Americans were attracted. He was given thirty thousand arpens of land, but this property became a burden to him, as only a small part was productive. On May 20, 1799, Governor Manuel Gayoso de Lemos, at New Orleans, wrote to him and commended him for opening roads and establishing good regulations of military and civil police. He promised him great things in the future through Lieutenant-Governor Delassus and the Court. Mackay remained commandant until the transfer of Upper Louisiana to the United States in 1804, when he was appointed one of the judges of the Court of Quarter Sessions. Delassus's comments on his subordinates to the United States authorities described him as "an officer of knowledge, zealous and punctual . . . a recommendable officer with many good qualities" (F. L. Billon, *Annals of St. Louis,* vol. I, 1886, p. 367). In 1816 he was a member of the legislature of Missouri Territory from St. Louis County and served as major of militia. He was married to Isabella, daughter of John Long, on Feb. 24, 1800, at St. Charles.

[Mackay Papers and Documents from Spain in possession of the Mo. Hist. Soc.; *House Exec. Doc. 59,* 24 Cong., 1 Sess. (1836?), pp. 31–37; Louis Houck, *A Hist. of Mo.* (1908), vols. II, III and *The Spanish Régime in Mo.* (2 vols., 1909); *Mo. Hist. Soc. Colls.,* vol. IV (1912), pp. 20–21; *Am. Hist. Assoc. Report 1908,* vol. I (1909); *Miss. Valley Hist. Review,* Mar. 1924, Mar.); *St. Louis Enquirer,* Mar. 23, 1822.]

S. M. D.

McKAY, JAMES IVER (July 17, 1792–Sept. 14, 1853), congressman, was born in Bladen County, N. C., the son of John and Mary (Salter) McKay and the grandson of Bladen Iver McKay who emigrated from Scotland to North Carolina about 1780. His only academic training, of which there is authentic record, was received at the Raleigh Academy, but he bore every evidence of a liberal education. He studied law and was admitted to the bar and in 1815 was elected state senator. Serving four consecutive terms, he was again elected in 1822, 1826, 1829, and 1830. On Mar. 6, 1817, he was appointed federal district attorney for North Carolina. Elected to Congress, he served from 1831 until 1849, when he declined reëlection.

His congressional career was distinguished. His voice was harsh and unpleasant, but, fluent though terse in speech, and convincing because of the wealth of his carefully prepared information, he was regarded as one of the most influential debaters in the House. Public honesty and economy became his passion, and, as an untiring and profane enemy of claim agents and extravagant members, he won the reputation of being an "Old Money Bags," to whose eyes a dollar seemed as big as a cart-wheel. While chairman of the ways and means committee he would not allow the appointment of a clerk and did all the work himself. Yet in spite of economical notions he favored military preparations and obtained the establishment of Fort Caswell on the Cape Fear and the arsenal at Fayetteville. He was chairman of the committee on ways and means from 1843 to 1847 and was the author of the tariff bill of 1843 that failed to pass Congress. His report on the tariff in 1844 was an important state paper, and in 1846 he introduced the Walker tariff bill, which he had helped prepare.

He rarely smiled and had the reputation of great severity, but he was warm-hearted, charitable, personally generous, and exceedingly popular. He was much interested in the welfare of his constituents and is said to have spent more than his salary every year of his congressional service in buying government publications, chiefly concerning agriculture, and in distributing them in his district. He inherited property and amassed more. On Dec. 3, 1818, he married Eliza Ann Harvey the daughter of Travis and Sarah (Robeson) Harvey, a woman of wealth, who died in 1847. They had one son who died in infancy. By his will McKay provided that his valuable plantation, "Belfont," should become a county home and experimental farm for Bladen. His negroes, numbering between two and three hundred, were freed and sent to Liberia. He died suddenly at Goldsboro and was buried at "Belfont."

[Some McKay Papers in the possession of the Univ. of N. C.; files of the Congressional Joint Committee on Printing; S. A. Ashe, *Biog. Hist. of N. C.,* vol. IV (1906); James Sprunt, *Chronicles of the Cape Fear River* (1914); *Memoirs of John Quincy Adams,* ed. by C. F. Adams, vols. IX–XII (1876–77); *The Diary of James K. Polk* (1910), vols. I, IV; *Daily Journal* (Wilmington, N. C.), Sept. 15, 1853; date of marriage and other information from McKay's grand-niece.]

J. G. deR. H.

MACKAY, JOHN WILLIAM (Nov. 28, 1831–July 20, 1902), miner, capitalist, was born in Dublin, Ireland, one of four children. Desperately poor, his family emigrated to America in 1840. For a short time after their arrival, Mackay attended a public school, but the death of his father ended his formal education, and he became an apprentice in the office of the New York ship-builder, William H. Webb [*q.v.*]. In 1851 he determined to try his fortune in the mines of California and reached the west coast by way of New Orleans and the Isthmus of Panama. For the next seven years, with indifferent success, he worked as a drift and placer miner in various California mines, then went to Virginia City, Nev., where, as a timber man at six dollars a day, he developed expert knowledge and facility in timbering mines.

Having accumulated much practical experience and a small amount of money, he struck out for himself. His first venture at the Esmeralda, Aurora, was a failure, but the Petaluma mill which he built with J. M. Walker at Gold Hill, Nev., turned out profitably. In 1864 Walker and Mackay joined their resources with those of James C. Flood and William S. O'Brien, saloon keepers of San Francisco, and in 1868 the group was joined by James G. Fair [*q.v.*], later United States senator from Nevada. Some time later Walker retired, selling his interest to Mackay. It was the belief of Fair and Mackay that the old workings of the Comstock Lode would reveal a considerable amount of low-grade ore which might be profitably utilized with up-to-date machinery. Following this theory they obtained control in 1865 of the Hale and Norcross Mine, from which they made profits of half a million. The profits were immediately sunk into nearby mines, one of which was the Virginia Consolidated. Here, in 1873, they struck the "Big Bonanza," from which more than a hundred million dollars in gold and silver was taken. Mackay, who at this time had a two-fifths interest in the concern, became a millionaire almost over night. To the end of his life he retained a controlling interest in several of the Comstock ventures and for many years reaped from them a large income. Of all those who sought their fortunes in the western mines, Mackay achieved the most spectacular success.

He acquired important real estate holdings in San Francisco and elsewhere in the West, became a director of the Southern Pacific, and with Flood and Fair organized the Bank of Nevada, San Francisco (from which he withdrew in 1887), but his interests, as time went on, became less concerned with the region from which he had drawn his fortune. In 1867 he had married, at Virginia City, Marie Louise (Hungerford) Bryant, widow of Dr. William C. Bryant and daughter of Col. Daniel E. Hungerford of New Orleans; they had two sons. In 1874 the Mackays took up their residence in San Francisco, and in 1876 moved to New York, but they spent most of their remaining years in Europe, and maintained palatial establishments in London and Paris. The activities of few other millionaires of Mackay's day were more constantly chronicled by the public press. The marriage of his step-daughter to Prince Ferdinand Colonna, and later her divorce; a spectacular attempt to assassinate him in San Francisco in 1895 by an unwise speculator who blamed him for his misfortunes; the lurid reports of the vast sums spent by his wife for jewelry and of their extravagant living, all kept his private life before the public.

More than all this, however, his spectacular battle during the eighties to break the telegraph and cable monopoly built up by Jay Gould [*q.v.*] commanded the attention and admiration of the entire business world. With James Gordon Bennett [*q.v.*], against an almost universal opinion that it would never succeed, he founded the Commercial Cable Company in 1883 and in the following year laid two submarine cables to Europe. A bitter eighteen months' struggle ensued between the strongly entrenched Gould monopoly and the new lines, but the latter won, and in 1886 Mackay organized the Postal Telegraph Cable Company and commenced the construction of telegraph lines to fight the Gould–Western-Union monopoly on land. This was the great constructive work of his career. As a third step in the building of his Postal Telegraph–Commercial Cable system, he planned the laying of a cable across the Pacific and was engaged in this project when he died, in London, in July 1902.

"Of all the bonanza millionaires," said a San Francisco dispatch, "Mackay was the only one who could be called popular" (New York *Sun*, July 21, 1902). As a practical miner, he worked with his hands long after he was rich, and was well liked by his workmen, who looked upon him as an honest and fair employer. In personal appearance, he was tall, slender, well-knit, and active, with a rapid gait, a gentle, measured voice, but a prompt and hearty address (*New York Times*, July 21, 1902). His presence made him distinguished in any gathering. Although he mixed freely with his friends, he shunned interviews and detested publicity. The Prince of Wales is reported to have described him as "the most unassuming American I ever met" (New York *Sun*, July 22, 1902). He twice refused the Republican nomination for senator from Nevada. In religion he was a Roman Catholic.

[James Burnley, *Millionaires and Kings of Enterprise* (1901), inaccurate; S. P. Davis, *The Hist. of Nevada* (1913), vol. I; H. H. Bancroft, *Hist. of Nevada, Colorado, and Wyoming* (1890); J. J. Powell, *Nevada: the Land of Silver* (1876); C. H. Shinn, *The Story of the Mine* (1896), ch. xvi; Don C. Seitz, *The James Gordon Bennetts* (1928); *Who's Who in America*, 1901–02; *The Times* (London), July 21, 1902; *N. Y. Times*, July 21, 22, and *Sun* (N. Y.), July 21–23, 1902.]

H. U. F.

MACKAYE, JAMES MORRISON STEELE (June 6, 1842–Feb. 25, 1894), dramatist, actor, and inventor, better known as Steele MacKaye, was born in Buffalo, N. Y., the son of James Morrison McKay (as the name was then spelled) and Emily Steele. His father was a legal associate of Millard Fillmore and a friend of many of the leading men of the day. The son, in his youth, had as playmates Winslow Homer and William and Henry James. At sixteen he entered the École des Beaux-Arts in Paris, with "unlimited funds at his disposal," and perhaps thereby failed to learn the use and value of money; at any rate, he had an obvious disregard for it in later life. In Paris he worked especially with Troyon. In 1859 he returned to America. His father now lived in New York, a friend of many artists as well as public men. The Civil War soon broke in on American life, Steele joined the 7th Regiment, and made his first stage appearance as Hamlet in a regimental performance in 1862. At this period William James declared he was "effervescing with inco-ordinated romantic ideas of every description." After the war, his incoördination led him into many fields in an attempt to find himself. He was a painter and an art dealer; he invented "photo-sculpture" and launched a company to commercialize it. In 1869 his father set him adrift financially, so he went to Paris, where he met Delsarte and became his enthusiastic disciple. To spread the Delsartian philosophy of expression, he returned to America to give lectures, one of them at Harvard in 1871, and to try to establish a school.

On Jan. 8, 1872, MacKaye made his début in New York as an actor, in *Monaldi,* supported by his pupils, and in a theatre rented and reconstructed by himself. The next autumn he studied acting in France and acted Hamlet in Paris in French that year, and in London in English the following spring—the first American to play the rôle in England. A year of acting and play-writing followed, and then he returned to America, opening a "school of expression" at 46 East Tenth Street, lecturing, and trying to get a foothold on the American stage for himself and his plays. His *Rose Michel,* an adaptation of the French play by Ernest Blum, was produced in 1875, in sets designed by himself. *Won at Last* was acted at Wallack's, Dec. 10, 1877, with a notable cast and much success. Finally he succeeded in having a small theatre on West Twenty-fourth Street, N. Y., rebuilt in accordance with his ideas, and it opened as the Madison Square Theatre in 1879, one of the earliest of American "intimate" playhouses. During his occupancy MacKaye invented for it a double, or elevator stage (anticipating German inventions by a generation), artificial ventilation, and overhead and indirect lighting of the scene. Here, in 1880, his play *Hazel Kirke* was presented and ran for more than a year—a phenomenal run at the time. The play was acted everywhere, for two decades, and should have made him a large fortune, had he not been so childlike and improvident in all business matters that he signed contracts which gave most of the profits of both inventions and plays to others. Forced from the control of this theatre, he built the Lyceum Theatre on Fourth Avenue, and established there the first dramatic school in America (later the American Academy of Dramatic Art). This school influenced many future players and was an important development in the American theatre.

MacKaye continued to write plays, invent mechanical and electric stage devices (he was the first to light a New York theatre entirely by electricity—the Lyceum, in 1884), to preach the gospel of the social value of drama and the educational value of its study, and to fight against constant debt. When the Chicago World's Fair came, he dreamed his biggest dream, rallied capital to his support, and began the erection, outside the Fair grounds, of a vast auditorium, with a still vaster stage, called a Spectatorium, wherein was to be enacted a gigantic scenic spectacle of his devising, called *The World Finder*—a tale of Columbus. Financial disaster prevented the completion of this scheme, and MacKaye's end was hastened by his frantic work and worry. He did, however, live long enough to see the scheme realized in a large working model, so that a few audiences in Chicago were able to vision what had been his conception. This conception included a vast cyclorama background, a flexible proscenium, which was instantly adjustable to the size of the picture desired, and scenic and light effects, such as dawn, sunset, moonlight, clouds, at that time revolutionary in depth and illusion but later in common use. MacKaye died of complete nervous exhaustion at Timpas, Colo., while he was on his way to California. He was the author of more than twenty plays, seven of them in collaboration with others, but only *Hazel Kirke* is remembered. Many were spectacular in nature and foreshadowed the so-called "crowd movies" of today. MacKaye was tall, dark, slender, and oddly resembled, in face, Edgar Allan Poe. He was intensely dynamic, worked sometimes for twenty hours on a stretch, was indifferent to food and creature comforts (including money), idealistic to the point sometimes of fanaticism (so it seemed to those working with him), and a bit lacking in the humor which makes for corrective self-criticism. On June 30, 1862, he was married to Jennie Spring but was later divorced. On June 6, 1865, he was married to Mary Keith Medbery, of Portsmouth, N. H., a descendant of Roger Williams. One of their sons, Percy MacKaye, later became well known as a dramatist.

[Percy MacKaye, *Epoch: The Life of Steele MacKaye* (2 vols., 1927); Wm. Winter, *The Life of David Belasco* (1918), vol. I; I. F. Marcosson and Daniel Frohman, *Chas. Frohman, Manager and Man* (1916); *Chicago Daily Tribune,* Feb. 26, 1894.] W. P. E.

MACKAYE, STEELE [See MacKaye, James Morrison Steele, 1842–1894].

MCKEAN, JOSEPH BORDEN (July 28, 1764–Sept. 3, 1826), jurist, son of Thomas [*q.v.*], signer of the Declaration of Independence, and Mary (Borden) McKean, was born in New Castle, Del. He graduated from the University of Pennsylvania in 1782, studied law, and was admitted to the Philadelphia bar in 1785. His marriage, Apr. 13, 1786, to Hannah, daughter of Col. Samuel Miles, increased the opportunities for legal preferment he already enjoyed as son of the chief justice of Pennsylvania. For some years, in addition to his law practice, he was active in the militia. In 1799 he and fellow officers of the 1st City Troop became involved in a suit for assault for administering a sound beating to William Duane [*q.v.*], because his *Aurora and General Advertiser* had printed an article impeaching the conduct of the troop in the Fries Rebellion. The case dragged on until 1809, when the defendants were acquitted. Although the incident disturbed Republican harmony, having occurred when McKean's father was running for governor, Duane nevertheless supported the elder McKean with undiminished enthusiasm. He never forgot the episode, however, and it remained to plague the McKeans.

From May 10, 1800, to July 22, 1808, Joseph was attorney-general of Pennsylvania, previously having been register of wills of Philadelphia. The Governor was bitterly assailed for appointing his son, whom many regarded as inferior to other Philadelphia lawyers. Despite the assertions of his enemies to the contrary, he was a lawyer of parts, but his aristocratic bearing and domineering manner did not help party harmony. He scorned the attacks of the Jacobins on the judiciary, and incurred their animosity by refusing legal aid in the impeachment trial of the three supreme-court judges (1805). He was an active promoter of the moderate Republican-Federalist coalition which elected his father governor in 1805. In some quarters his influence over his father's administration was regarded as tantamount to domination (*Norristown Register*, quoted in the *Aurora*, May 18, 1805). He was ambitious to be chief justice, and his father would have appointed him in 1806, had reasons of expediency not forbidden his doing so (McKean Papers, III, 104). After 1808, in which year he resumed his law practice, he had little prospect for political office, for he was out of favor with the state administration. He was likewise *persona non grata* to President Madison, because in a legal opinion (1803) he had upheld the contention of the Marquis Casa de Yrujo, his brother-in-law, that Spain was not responsible for damages inflicted by the French on American citizens in Spanish waters. On Mar. 27, 1817, however, Gov. Simon Snyder, a former enemy, appointed him associate judge of the district court for the city and county of Philadelphia, of which he was named president judge Oct. 1, 1818. His commission as associate judge was renewed Mar. 17, 1821. Reappointed president judge on Mar. 21, 1825, he held this post until his death. He was a trustee of the University of Pennsylvania (1794–1826), a member of the Pennsylvania Academy of the Fine Arts, the American Philosophical Society, the Philadelphia Law Association, and the State Fencibles, a military company organized in 1813. On his father's death (1817) he came into possession of the family mansion at Third and Pine Streets, where he died.

[The McKean Papers in the Hist. Soc. of Pa., Philadelphia, contain source material; see also Roberdeau Buchanan, *Geneal. of the McKean Family of Pa.* (1890); *Pa. Mag. of Hist. and Biog.*, Jan. 1925; J. H. Martin, *Martin's Bench and Bar of Phila.* (1883); J. H. Peeling, "The Public Life of Thomas McKean, 1734–1817" (1929), doctor's thesis (MS.), Univ. of Chicago; J. T. Scharf and Thompson Westcott, *Hist. of Phila.* (1884), vols. I, II; *Poulson's Am. Daily Advertiser*, Sept. 4, 5, 1826.]

J. H. P—g.

McKEAN, SAMUEL (Apr. 7, 1787–Dec. 14, 1841), congressman, senator, son of James and Jane (Scott) McKean, was born in Huntingdon County, Pa., of Scotch ancestry, the eighth of ten children. James McKean, a native of Cecil County, Md., moved to Pennsylvania about 1774, served with Washington's army in the Revolution, and later settled near Elmira, N. Y. Finding his land title fraudulent, about 1791 he took up a tract of land on Sugar Creek near Burlington, Pa. Samuel's opportunities for education were meager until he was sixteen. At that age he visited an uncle in Maryland who gave him a thorough education. At his uncle's death, falling heir to part of the estate, he established himself as a merchant in Burlington and did a flourishing business. In 1814 he was elected county commissioner of Bradford County, and, with other Republicans, founded the *Bradford Gazette*, published at Towanda, to further his political fortunes. From 1815 to 1819 he was in the state legislature. In 1822 he was elected to Congress where (1823–29) he was identified with the group favoring high tariff and internal improvements. In 1829 he was a strong contender for the nomination for governor in Pennsylvania. Elected state senator the same year, he resigned almost immediately to become secretary of the commonwealth. While secretary (1829–33) he drafted a bill providing for the taxation of all property for free school purposes, which subsequently became a law. He was a presidential elector on the Jackson ticket in 1832.

In 1833, assisted by his opposition to constitutional and national conventions, he was elected United States senator after a long and bitter struggle. As senator, although opposed to Van Buren and the "kitchen cabinet" and steering a middle course on the question of the deposits, he was an enemy of the United States Bank and generally supported Jackson. He voted against the resolutions (1834) declaring the Treasurer's reasons for removing the deposits unsatisfactory and censuring the president, because they were "exclusively censorious," but he denounced the subsequent expunging of the censure as unconstitutional (*Niles' Weekly Register,* Feb. 25, 1837). While sanctioning the removal of the deposits, nevertheless, he voted to restore them because of "sheer expediency" and to satisfy his constituents (*Register of Debates in Congress,* 23 Cong., 1 Sess., p. 1895). He disapproved of anti-slavery agitation and on Jan. 6, 1838, presented two resolutions: that Congress possessed no power to abolish slavery in the states where it existed; and that it was inexpedient to legislate on slavery in the District of Columbia (*Congressional Globe,* 25 Cong., 2 Sess., p. 80). He was chairman of the committee on contingent expenses and was a member of the committees on militia, public lands, pensions, commerce, roads and canals, and agriculture. In 1839 severe neuralgia in the head caused him to become an opium addict, and in a delirium suffered as a consequence he cut his throat with a razor. He never fully recovered from the wound. He was an adroit politician and a power in local politics for many years. Van Buren regarded him as "an honest, but exceedingly prejudiced man" (Fitzpatrick, *post,* p. 763). He was a major-general of militia. He died at West Burlington, Pa., survived by his wife, Julia McDowell, whom he had married on Jan. 7, 1812.

[David Craft, *Hist. of Bradford County, Pa.* (1878); C. F. Heverly, *Hist. of the Towandas, 1776–1886* (1886); Cornelius McKean, *McKean Geneals.* (1902); *Biog. Dir. Am. Cong.* (1928); J. C. Fitzpatrick, "The Autobiog. of Martin Van Buren," *Ann. Report of the Am. Hist. Asso. for the Year 1918* (1920), vol. II; *Daily Nat. Intelligencer* (Washington, D. C.), Dec. 23, 1841; *Niles' Weekly Reg.,* Jan. 17, 1824, Nov. 9, Dec. 21, 1833.]

J. H. P—g.

McKEAN, THOMAS (Mar. 19, 1734–June 24, 1817), statesman, second son of William and Letitia (Finney) McKean, was of the fourth generation from William McKean of Argyleshire, Scotland, who emigrated to Londonderry, Ireland, about 1674. Coming to Pennsylvania with his mother at an early age (*c.* 1725), William, the father of Thomas, lived on a farm in Chester County and later became a tavern keeper. His wife, Letitia Finney, belonged to a wealthy and prominent family of Scotch-Irish settlers in Pennsylvania. Thomas was born in New London Township, Chester County. After spending seven years at Rev. Francis Allison's academy, New London, he went to New Castle, Del., to study law with his cousin, David Finney. His connections there soon put him on the road to success as a lawyer and politician. First a prothonotary's clerk, in 1752 he was appointed deputy prothonotary and recorder for the probate of wills for New Castle County. He was admitted to the bar in the Lower Counties at twenty, and within the next decade acquired a wide practice in Delaware, Pennsylvania, and New Jersey.

The same period saw many of his ambitions for a political life realized. He was appointed deputy attorney-general in 1756; was clerk of the Delaware Assembly, 1757–59; and in 1762 began the first of seventeen years' successive service in the latter body. A leader of the country party, he assisted in compiling the provincial laws in 1762 and was a trustee of the New Castle County loan office, 1764–72. He was an uncompromising foe of the Stamp Act, was among the most radical delegates to the Stamp Act Congress, and as justice of the court of common pleas and quarter sessions (1765) ordered business to proceed as usual on unstamped paper. He was also chief notary and tabellion officer in 1765, collector of the port of New Castle in 1771, and speaker of the Assembly, 1772–73. His marriage on July 21, 1763, to Mary, eldest daughter of Joseph and Elizabeth Borden of Bordentown, N. J., further widened his legal and political connections. After her death in 1773, he married Sarah Armitage of New Castle, Sept. 3, 1774, and in the fall of that year established a home in Philadelphia.

The widening breach between the American colonies and the mother country in 1774 offered McKean a political oportunity which he was quick to grasp. He led the movement in Delaware for a colonial congress and, excepting the period between December 1776 and January 1778, represented that colony in the Continental Congress continuously until 1783. Prior to July 4, 1776, he was on five standing committees (secret, qualifications, prisoners, claims, and treasury), and on more than thirty others. At first hopeful for reconciliation, he became early in 1776 an ardent advocate of separation. As chairman of the Philadelphia committee of observation he played a conspicuous part in engineering the popular movement in Pennsylvania for a new state government and for independence. In Delaware he effected the repudiation of the Crown and support for independence by his personal appearance in the Assembly. In Congress he voted for Lee's resolution for independence (July 1). His vote being tied with that of his colleague George Read [*q.v.*], he dispatched an express for Cæsar Rodney [*q.v.*], third Delaware delegate, who arrived in time (July 2) to vote for the resolution. McKean seems to have been the first man to challenge the later popular impression that the Declaration of Independence was signed on July 4. Finding that his name did not appear as a signer in the early printed journals of the Congress, he asserted in a letter to Alexander J. Dallas (Sept. 26, 1796; McKean Papers, III, 10), what the corrected Journals and contemporary letters have since substantiated, that no one signed on July 4. The exact date of his signing is not known. Although he later insisted it was in 1776, it is almost certain that it was after Jan. 18, 1777. That it was as late as 1781, as some writers aver, is doubtful.

During July and August 1776, McKean, as colonel, commanded a battalion of Philadelphia associators at Perth Amboy, N. J., but saw no action. He then participated (Aug. 27–Sept. 21) in framing Delaware's first constitution, the authorship of which tradition ascribes to him, relying on his statement made years later to Cæsar A. Rodney (Sept. 22, 1813; Burnett, *post,* I, 535). Although his influence in the convention was considerable, the *Proceedings* of that body indicate that the constitution was not solely his work. In the fall of 1776, failing, through conservative opposition, of reëlection to the Congress, he transferred his exertions to the Assembly, was elected speaker shortly thereafter, and in that capacity became acting president of Delaware for two months in 1777 (Sept. 22–*c.* Nov. 17).

During all this time his major interests had been gravitating toward Philadelphia, and on July 28, 1777, he was commissioned chief justice of Pennsylvania. Nevertheless, he remained active in Delaware politics, and for the next six years (1777–83) held office in both states, enjoying the anomalous position of being assemblyman, acting president, or congressman for one state and chief justice of another. In Congress (1778–83) he supported the Articles of Confederation, favored a federal court of appeals, attacked administrative inefficiency and corruption, decried the dangers of military and financial dictatorships, and was close to the Adams-Lee faction. From July 10 to Nov. 5, 1781, he was president of Congress, despite the protests of his Pennsylvania enemies who were eager to force him to relinquish either the presidency or his judicial position.

Decidedly less liberal after independence had been declared, McKean opposed the radical Pennsylvania constitution of 1776, although he accepted the chief justiceship of the supreme court under it and served for twenty-two years, being convinced that failure to support the new government would endanger the American cause. As a Federalist, he was active in securing ratification of the Federal Constitution in the Pennsylvania convention of 1787. Comparing the arguments of the opposition to "the feeble noise occasioned by the working of small beer," he pronounced the frame of government "the best the world has yet seen" (J. B. McMaster and F. D. Stone, *Pennsylvania and the Federal Constitution,* 1888, pp. 378–79). In the Pennsylvania constitutional convention (1789–90), he manifested his belief in government by the few to an even greater extent, and at the same time was the author of a clause providing education for the poor at state expense.

As chief justice (1777–99) his frequent conservative decisions and his struggle for judicial sanctity and against the encroachments of the military on the civil authority brought numerous conflicts with the Assembly, council, or military authorities. He upheld the proprietors in their property rights (1779), interpreted the law of libel rigorously, sanctioned the doctrine that courts can punish for contempt (*Respublica* vs. *Oswald,* 1788, 1 *Dallas,* 319), and in 1798 created a sensation by appearing as witness against William Cobbett and later sitting as judge in the same case. Although somewhat harsh and domineering, his decisions were unmistakably to the point and reflected honesty and a high sense of justice. McKean also rode the circuit and, from its establishment in 1780, was a judge of the Pennsylvania court of errors and appeals.

After 1792 Federalist foreign policy forced him into the ranks of the Jeffersonians. His friendship for France and his aversion for England made him a favorite of the Republicans, and in 1799 they nominated him for governor. A strong candidate because of his prestige and moderate republicanism, he defeated James Ross, Federalist, after a bitter campaign, his victory entailing a revolution in state politics. As governor he removed his political enemies from office, giving their places to his Republican friends, thereby winning the appellation of "the father of political proscription" and fastening the spoils system on Pennsylvania. He adhered to the principle of giving "a preference to real republicans or whigs, having equal talents and integrity, and to a friend before an Enemy . . . for it is not right to put a dagger in the hands of an assassin" (McKean to Jefferson, Jan. 10, 1801; McKean Papers, III, 46). He warmly espoused Jefferson's election (1800), and later urged on the

President, with some success, a policy of removing Federalists from office.

In 1802 McKean was reëlected by more than 30,000 majority. Personal and factional jealousies, however, soon threatened Republican harmony. William Duane [*q.v.*] whose *Aurora and General Advertiser* had rendered invaluable service in the campaign of 1799, found the state administration disinclined to heed his advice. Chafing at his failure to control the executive in appointments and other matters, he started a movement through the *Aurora's* columns late in 1802 to shunt McKean into the vice-presidency, but this design failed, for the latter could not be moved to relinquish his responsibilities and influence in Pennsylvania. Revolts by friends of the administration against Duane's dictatorship over the party in Philadelphia added further irritation. Moreover, McKean, a consistent advocate of a strong executive and an independent judiciary, was the chief means of frustrating the attacks made by the radical Republicans on the executive's prerogatives, and on judges, lawyers, and judicial practices. He repeatedly vetoed bills extending the jurisdiction of justices of the peace and other "giddy innovations," opposed attempts to impeach three supreme-court judges (1804–05), and refused to sanction pleas for a convention to revise the constitution. Violent schism now disrupted party ranks. The radicals, under Duane's leadership, determined to achieve their ends by shelving the governor, and in 1805 nominated Simon Snyder [*q.v.*], farmer and arch-Jacobin, attacking relentlessly lawyers, judges, courts, and all semblances of aristocracy. Friends of the constitution, denominated Constitutionalists—moderate Republicans and Federalists alike, the former styled Quids by the radicals—united, and elected McKean by 5,000 majority, thus preserving the constitution.

Construing his reëlection as a vindication, the governor now drove from office his Republican enemies, giving their places to his more recent Federalist supporters. The *Aurora* accused him of nepotism, and on Jan. 15, 1806, published the names of twelve relatives appointed to office, under the title, "The Royal Family," dubbing Joseph [*q.v.*], the Governor's eldest son, "heir apparent." Libel suits were instituted against his more violent opponents, and the Assembly was urged to fix more drastic penalties for the punishment of libel. His enemies in the legislature (1806–07) retorted with impeachment proceedings, charging him with having violated the constitution by avoiding a sheriff's election in Philadelphia, assuming unwarranted judicial authority, abusing his power of appointment and removal, stamping his name on state papers, and using his influence improperly to discontinue two court actions involving his son (*Report of the Committee Appointed to Enquire into the Official Conduct of the Governor of Pennsylvania,* 1807). The charges were based on trivialities or absurdities, magnified into high crimes and misdemeanors through spite. By clever strategy, however, the coalition behind the administration secured a general postponement of them (Jan. 27, 1808), and the Governor completed his term in comparative quiet.

Although active in promoting education and internal and other improvements, Governor McKean's main achievement lay in restraining the excesses of the Pennsylvania Jacobins. Throughout his gubernatorial career he was a veritable storm center in state politics. Cold in manner, energetic, independent, proud and vain, too tactless for a practical politician, he had a personality which readily aroused antagonisms. Yet he possessed many admiring friends, and even his enemies in their cooler moments admitted his ability, candor, and honesty. After his retirement he lived in Philadelphia, his tall, stately figure being a familiar sight in the city. These sunset days were spent in reading, writing, and reminiscing, and in following with watchful eye the trend of current affairs. He had six children by his first wife and five by his second, of whom only four, with his second wife, survived him. His will disposed of a considerable estate consisting of stocks, bonds, and large tracts of land in Pennsylvania. He compiled *The Acts of the General Assembly of Pennsylvania* (2 vols., 1782) and collaborated with Edmund Physick in *A Calm Appeal to the People of the State of Delaware* (1793), a plea for a fair settlement of the proprietary interests. Another volume, James Wilson and Thomas McKean, *Commentaries on the Constitution of the United States of America* (1792), contains his speeches in the Pennsylvania convention of 1787.

[McKean's correspondence and papers, including an incomplete autobiographical sketch begun in his eightieth year, are in the library of the Hist. Soc. of Pa. Some of his judicial decisions appear in A. J. Dallas, *Pa. Reports* (4 vols., 1797–1807). Other sources include E. C. Burnett, *Letters of Members of the Continental Congress* (1921–); *Journals of the Continental Cong.*; *Proc. of the Convention of the Delaware State . . . 1776* (1776, repr. 1927); "Governor McKean's Papers," *Pa. Archives,* 4 ser. IV (1900); Roberdeau Buchanan, *Geneal. of the McKean Family of Pa., with a Biog. of the Hon. Thomas McKean* (1890); *Poulson's Am. Daily Advertiser,* June 26, 1817; J. H. Peeling, "The Public Life of Thomas McKean, 1734–1817" (1929), doctor's thesis (MS.) at Univ. of Chicago.]

J. H. P—g.

McKEAN, WILLIAM WISTER (Sept. 19, 1800–Apr. 22, 1865), naval officer, was the son of Judge Joseph Borden McKean [*q.v.*] and grandson of Thomas McKean [*q.v.*], the signer of the Declaration of Independence; his mother was Hannah (Miles). Born in Philadelphia, he became a midshipman on Nov. 30, 1814, and was promoted lieutenant (1825), commander (1841), captain (1855), and commodore (1862). He made his first cruise in the *Java* under O. H. Perry to the Mediterranean. For the most of the time between 1822 and 1824 he was in the West Indies fighting pirates, first on the *Alligator* and then on the *Terrier*. Later, he served on the *Warren* in the Mediterranean and on the *Natchez* off South America. In 1843–44 he was in charge of the Naval Asylum, Philadelphia, then the chief place for the instruction of midshipmen. When George Bancroft [*q.v.*] proposed the establishment of a regular naval school, McKean and his first cousin, Franklin Buchanan [*q.v.*], were on the board that recommended locating it at Annapolis. During the Mexican War he commanded the *Dale* on the west coast till invalided home; but in 1852 he assumed command of the *Raritan*. By 1860 he had secured the finest ship in the navy, the *Niagara*, and in that year carried the Japanese embassy back home. Returning to Boston in April 1861, he had his first news of the Civil War, and promptly refitted his ship, eliminating Southerners by exacting a new oath of allegiance, and sailed to blockade off Charleston, where, on May 12, he made his first capture. In October of the same year he was in charge of the Gulf blockading squadron and occupied the Head of the Passes of the Mississippi. In November he took part in the attack on Pensacola, but by the next June ill health had forced him to relinquish his command, and his naval career was practically over. He died at his home, "The Moorings," near Binghamton, N. Y., and was buried in Spring Forest Cemetery. On Aug. 25, 1824, he had married Davis Rosa Clark, who survived him. They had twelve children, one of whom became an officer in the navy and another in the Marine Corps. In addition to his other sterling qualities he was noted for his piety. When an able chaplain on the *Niagara* stirred up a great revival of religion, he was strongly seconded by McKean. Commodore Schley, who served under him on the same ship, called him "noble old Captain McKean" (*post*, p. 11).

[McKean's naval records and dispatches, as well as some of his letter-books, are in the custody of the Navy Department. See also Roberdeau Buchanan, *Geneal. of the McKean Family of Pa.* (1890); G. W. Allen, *Our Navy and the Barbary Corsairs* (1905), and *Our Navy and the West Indian Pirates* (1929); C. L. Lewis, *Admiral Franklin Buchanan* (1929); W. S. Schley, *Forty-Five Years Under the Flag* (1904); *Official Records of the Union and Confederate Navies in the Civil War*, 1 ser. IV, V; *Army and Navy Jour.*, May 6, 1865; *Daily National Intelligencer* (Washington, D. C.), Apr. 25, 1865.] W. B. N.

McKEE, JOHN (1771–Aug. 12, 1832), Indian agent and congressman, was the son of John (or James) and Esther (Houston) McKee and the cousin of Sam Houston and John Letcher [*qq.v.*]. He was born in Rockbridge County, Va., and attended Liberty Hall Academy, now Washington and Lee University. In 1792 he was appointed by Gov. William Blount of Tennessee as a commissioner to the Cherokee in order to agree on the line designated by the treaty of Holston and, with the other two commissioners, reported that, when the Cherokee did not appear, the line had been measured according to instructions. The next year he was appointed by Blount to try to conciliate the Cherokee and was sent to accompany a deputation of five Chickasaw to visit the president at Philadelphia. In 1794 he was appointed temporary agent of the Cherokee. He signed the treaties of December 1801 and of November 1805 with the Choctaw and appears on the official roll sent to Congress on Feb. 17, 1802, as agent to that tribe. During the Creek War he was active in persuading the other tribes to remain at peace with the United States and in 1814 led an expedition of six or seven hundred Choctaw and Chickasaw to the Black Warrior River. After the war he bent his energies toward the final removal of the Five Civilized Tribes to reservations beyond the Mississippi. He helped to negotiate the treaty of October 1816 with the Choctaw, but in 1818 he was on a commission that failed in its attempt to win their consent to removal. He was one of the first settlers in Tuscaloosa County, where he had charge of the land office. In 1823, as an ardent admirer of Andrew Jackson, he was sent to represent the Tuscaloosa district in Congress. There he spoke but rarely, and after three successive terms he retired. He was a member of the commission to settle the boundary between Kentucky and Tennessee. In 1830 he was one of the commissioners to negotiate the treaty of Dancing Rabbit Creek, whereby the Choctaw ceded their claim to all their eastern lands except such small parcels as might be granted to individual Indians who would undertake to accept allotment and citizenship rather than emigrate across the Mississippi. He died at his plantation home, "Hill of Howth," which he had built about 1818 near Boligee, Ala. He was said to have been legally married to an Indian wife, and he provided that after his death his friend and heir, William P. Gould, should make a quarterly payment in gold to his half-breed son.

[Some papers and diary in possession of J. McKee Gould, Boligee, Ala.; date of death from the diary of Wm. P. Gould; files of the Congressional Joint Committee on Printing; files of the Indian Office; *Am. State Papers*: *Indian Affairs* (2 vols., 1832–34); *Biog. Dir. Am. Cong.* (1928); *Trans. Ala. Hist. Soc.*, vol. III (1899); A. H. Abel, "The Hist. of Events Resulting in Indian Consolidation West of the Mississippi," *Am. Hist. Asso. Report . . . 1906*, vol. I (1908); W. R. Smith, *Reminiscences of a Long Life* (copr. 1889); S. R. Houston, *Brief Biog. Accounts of the Houston Family* (1882), pp. 46–47.] K. E. C.

McKEEN, JOSEPH (Oct. 15, 1757–July 15, 1807), Congregational clergyman, first president of Bowdoin College, was born in Londonderry, N. H., of Scotch ancestry. His grandfather, James, came to America from County Antrim, Ireland, in 1718 and was one of the founders of Londonderry. He brought with him his son, John, who later married his first cousin Mary McKeen. Their son, Joseph, was prepared for college under Rev. Simon Williams of Windham, N. H., and graduated from Dartmouth in the class of 1774 with first honors. For the next eight years he taught school in his native town, undisturbed by the turmoil of the Revolutionary War, except for a brief period when he was in military service under General Sullivan. By nature a student, he proceeded to Cambridge in 1782 and studied natural philosophy, mathematics, and astronomy under Prof. Samuel Williams of Harvard. Later he was tutored in theology by his old teacher, Simon Williams, and licensed to preach by the Londonderry Presbytery. After a short time as assistant at Phillips Academy, Andover, and some practice in preaching at Boston, he was called to the First Congregational Church at Beverly, Mass., as successor to Rev. Joseph Willard, who had been chosen president of Harvard. Here, in May 1785, he was ordained and remained for seventeen years, becoming one of the most eminent divines of New England. He was reputed to have been "not quite orthodox in the opinion of some of his parishioners, nor so liberal in his theological views as others would have liked. But he was candid, upright, prudent and conciliatory" (Hatch, *post,* p. 15)—qualities not always found in college presidents, but traits so harmoniously combined in him as to commend him to the authorities of Bowdoin when they were looking for someone to preside over that infant college.

Though his administration was brief, lasting only five years (1802–07), he won the regard of students, officers, and the public. He laid broad and sound foundations. With a wise boldness he insisted on making the requirements for admission equal to those of Harvard; he argued for a reasonably broad curriculum; he was a stout advocate of liberal education. In his very excellent inaugural address he stated that "literary institutions are founded and endowed for the common good, and not for the private advantage of those who resort to them for education"; and "that every man who has been aided by a public institution to acquire an education, and to qualify himself for usefulness, is under peculiar obligations to exert his talents for the public good." As a teacher he broke away from the older formal methods of his time, using models in mathematics and illustrations from actual life in moral philosophy. He brought to Bowdoin several excellent teachers, among them Parker Cleaveland [*q.v.*], and gave the new-born college worthy standards of scholarship. His promising career was cut short by a most painful illness, dropsical in nature, which ended in his death at Brunswick in his fiftieth year.

In appearance the first president of Bowdoin College was tall, of robust frame, and athletic vigor. He was a man of sound judgment, cool decision, kindly spirit, moral and religious fervor combined with a love of science, and notable tolerance. His scientific attainments gave him membership in the American Academy of Arts and Sciences, to the publications of which he made occasional contributions. In 1785 he married Alice Anderson, by whom he had three sons and two daughters.

[Nehemiah Cleaveland, *Hist. of Bowdoin Coll.* (1882); G. T. Little, "Hist. Sketch of Bowdoin Coll.," in *Gen. Cat. Bowdoin Coll. 1794–1894* (1894); L. C. Hatch, *The Hist. of Bowdoin Coll.* (1927); G. H. Wheeler, *Hist. of Brunswick, Topsham, and Harpswell, Me.* (1878); G. T. Chapman, *Sketches of the Alumni of Dartmouth Coll.* (1867); E. L. Parker, *The Hist. of Londonderry* (1851); *The Repertory* (Boston), July 24, 1807; W. B. Sprague, *Annals Am. Pulpit*, vol. II (1857).] K. C. M. S.

MACKELLAR, PATRICK (1717–Oct. 22, 1778), British military engineer, was born in Scotland, probably in Argyllshire. After entering the ordnance service in 1735 he acted for seven years, the last three at Minorca, as a clerk. From 1742, when he was commissioned as engineer extraordinary, to 1754, he remained at Minorca, attaining in 1751 the rank of engineer in ordinary. Selected as engineer *en second* under James G. Montrésor [*q.v.*] for service in America, he accompanied Braddock's expedition to its defeat at the Monongahela in 1755. His two detailed maps of that battle-field, which delineate accurately the position of the troops at the important stages of the attack, show him to have been a cool, self-possessed observer, better fitted temperamentally than any of his colleagues for the direction of siege operations under fire. He was rated the most competent engineer in

America as early as 1756, when he was sent to Oswego to strengthen the works there. His journal of the summer's proceedings—the most elaborate British account extant—clears him from any responsibility for the disaster of August, when Montcalm stormed the place in four days, and took the captured garrison, among them Mackellar, to Canada. At Quebec the engineer was able to make observations on the fortifications, embodied in a report to the ordnance board, that were invaluable two years later. After being exchanged in England in 1757, and after repairing batteries in the north of Scotland, he returned to America, a sub-director and major, but in the capacity of engineer *en second* under J. H. Bastide, in Amherst's expedition against Louisbourg. When Bastide was wounded, Mackellar assumed charge of siege operations. The following year he served as chief engineer under Wolfe at Quebec, and is credited with having dissuaded his commander from attempting a frontal attack on the citadel from the lower town. He remained in Canada under General Murray, and in 1760 was wounded at the battle of Sillery. Late in 1760, as chief engineer at Halifax, he organized a training school for engineers. He was Monckton's chief engineer in 1762 in the admirably planned and executed capture of Martinique. The next year, a lieutenant-colonel, he acted as Albemarle's chief engineer at the siege of Havana, where he directed elaborate approaches against Morro Castle. Wounded, he returned to England, and published a journal of the siege. In 1763, as chief engineer, he returned to the scene of his early labors at Minorca, where he remained in active service until his death. In 1777 he became director and colonel.

[A. G. Doughty, *The Siege of Quebec,* contains a journal of the siege, attributed to Mackellar; his report of 1757 on Quebec is printed as an appendix to the Champlain Society edition of Capt. John Knox's *Hist. Jour. of the Campaigns in North America* (1916), ed. by A. G. Doughty; a map of Sillery is in *Report Concerning Canadian Archives for the Year 1905,* vol. I, pt. 4; his maps of Braddock's field are in the Public Record Office; his journal and map of Oswego, in the Royal Archives at Windsor. See also R. H. Vetch in *Dict. of Nat. Biog.*; Whitworth Porter, *Hist. of the Corps of Royal Engineers* (1889).] S. M. P.

MACKELLAR, THOMAS (Aug. 12, 1812–Dec. 29, 1899), printer, type-founder, and poet, was born in New York City, the son of Archibald and Harriet (Andrews) MacKellar. His father, who was a native of Greenock, Scotland, had been a midshipman in the British navy; his mother traced her ancestry back to Henry Brezier, one of the original settlers in New Amsterdam. Young MacKellar attended McGowan's Classical Academy until he was fourteen, when his father's circumstances suffered a change and the boy had to go to work. He was first given employment in the office of the *New York Spy* as a compositor, but after a year he entered the publishing house of John and James Harper, where he soon was promoted from setting type to reading proof. Although he was fascinated with the work, his eyesight suffered, and he devoted himself during the remainder of his time with the firm to the practical work of printing. Shortly before he had reached his majority he went to Philadelphia and took a position as proof-reader in the type foundry of Lawrence Johnson and George F. Smith who, in addition to manufacturing type, also set and stereotyped composition for books.

In 1845 MacKellar was taken into partnership, as were the two sons of Smith, who had then retired. The business grew extensively and rapidly. After Johnson died, in 1860, MacKellar and John F. and Richard Smith bought out his interest and formed the firm of MacKellar, Smiths & Jordan, Peter A. Jordan having been admitted to the business. MacKellar succeeded in making the foundry the leading manufactory of type in the United States. In 1855 he began the publication of the *Typographic Advertiser,* of which he was editor until 1884, when he was succeeded by his son, William B. MacKellar. In its pages he proposed an asylum for aged printers, which subsequently was endowed by George W. Childs and Anthony J. Drexel [*qq.v.*]. The Specimen Book of the Johnson Type Foundry, which cost $40,000 to produce, was largely the work of MacKellar, and he is said to have "elevated the prosaic theme of a business catalogue into a work of art" (Ringwalt, *post,* p. 289). "The matter was mostly original, and being uniquely adapted to the conformation of the differing styles of the types exhibited, attracted the attention of printers everywhere" (Scharf and Westcott, *post,* III, 2325). In 1866 he wrote *The American Printer,* a book for the craft, which "proved to be the most popular work on typography ever printed" (*Ibid.*). The eighteenth edition was published in 1893.

In his maturer years, MacKellar developed into a graceful poet. His first volume was *Droppings From the Heart* (1844), which was followed by *Tam's Fortnight Ramble and Other Poems* (1847), *Rhymes Atween-Times* (1873), *Hymns and a Few Metrical Psalms* (1883), and *Faith, Hope, Love, These Three* (1893). He wrote with earnestness and fluency, and his poetry is "inspired by a devotional spirit and a tender feeling to the claims of family and friendship, expressive of the author's hopeful and hearty struggle with the world" (Duyckinck, *post,* II, 566). The Memorial Ode read at the unveiling of the Soldiers' Monument, in Germantown, Philadelphia, July 4, 1883, was written by him. He took a deep interest in religious affairs and for twenty-five years was corresponding secretary of the Philadelphia Bible Society; he also established one of the earliest mission schools in that city. He was president of the Type Founders Association of the United States, and of the Philadelphia Book Trade Association. On Sept. 27, 1834, he was married to Eliza Ross, by whom he had two sons and eight daughters.

[J. T. Scharf and Thompson Westcott, *Hist. of Phila.* (1884), vol. III; J. L. Ringwalt, *Am. Encyc. of Printing* (1871); *One Hundred Years: MacKellar Smiths and Jordan Foundry, Phila., Pa.* (1896); R. W. Griswold, *The Poets and Poetry of America,* (1855); E. A. and G. L. Duyckinck, *Cyc. of Am. Lit.* (1875), vol. II; *Public Ledger* (Phila.), Dec. 30, 1899; *Who's Who in America,* 1899–1900.] J. J.

McKELWAY, ST. CLAIR (Mar. 15, 1845–July 16, 1915), editor, was born at Columbia, Mo. His father was Alexander J. McKelway, a physician who had emigrated from Scotland in early childhood, and his mother was Mary (Ryan) McKelway. In 1853 the family removed to New Jersey. The boy's education was chiefly under private tutelage. While his father was absent at the front as a surgeon in the Civil War he was instructed by his grandfather, John McKelway, who lived in Trenton. For a short time he was a student of the New Jersey State Normal School at Trenton. Having an inclination to write, he contributed to local newspapers and at the age of seventeen sent to the *New York Tribune* an account of the activities of Confederate sympathizers in and near Trenton, for which Horace Greeley sent a check and wrote him a letter of appreciation. Yielding to the wish of his family he studied law, but he never practised that profession and on the day after his admission to the bar in 1866 became a reporter for the New York *World.* In 1868 he was sent to Washington as correspondent for the *World* and for the *Brooklyn Daily Eagle.* He was an editorial writer for the *Eagle* from 1870 to 1878 and then became editor of the *Albany Argus,* whose position on public questions helped to pave the way for the election of Cleveland to the presidency.

After the death of Thomas Kinsella in 1884, he was made editor-in-chief of the *Eagle* and held that post during the remainder of his life. His writing gave distinction to the editorial page of the paper. He was fearless and independent in expression, and the influence of the *Eagle* became national. His name and personality were identified in the public mind with his more striking editorials, which were widely quoted. He had for the background of his utterances an extensive acquaintance among public men, insight into national and local affairs, and wide reading. Under his editorship, the *Eagle* became an intensely local paper, presenting fully the news and interests of Brooklyn, yet at the same time neglecting no part of the general news field. It had a long period of financial as well as journalistic success. Both he and the paper became thoroughly identified with Brooklyn. He was active in demanding the prosecution of John Y. McKane for the frauds in the Gravesend election in 1893, for which McKane was sentenced to imprisonment.

He had rare gifts as a public speaker and was called upon to use them often. His speech on the occasion of a dinner given in his honor by the Lotos Club of New York in 1906 is printed in *After Dinner Speeches at the Lotos Club* (arranged by John Elderkin and others, 1911). From 1883 to 1915 he served as one of the regents of the University of the State of New York, being chancellor of the university at the time of his death. He wrote a memorial volume on *William C. Kingsley* (1885), the contractor for the Brooklyn Bridge and one of the owners of the *Eagle.* He was also the author of an introduction to *Random Recollections of an Old Political Reporter* (1911) by William C. Hudson, for many years a staff writer for the *Eagle.* On one occasion he remarked that journalism "is served as loyally, bravely, unselfishly, intelligently and honestly as Church or State, army or navy, university or sovereign" (*Memorial, post,* p. 45). He was chosen by Pulitzer as one of the first members and, after 1913, was chairman of the advisory board of the Columbia University School of Journalism. He was married in 1867 to Eleanor Hutchinson, who died in 1884. There were two sons from this marriage both of whom died before their father. In 1888 he was married to Virginia Brooks Thompson, who survived him.

[St. Clair McKelway, *Regent of The University of the State of N. Y. . . . Memorial* (1915?); D. C. Seitz, *Joseph Pulitzer* (1924); *Outlook,* July 28, 1915; *New York Times,* July 17–21, 1915; *Brooklyn Daily Eagle,* July 17–20, 1915.] A. S. W.

McKENDREE, WILLIAM (July 6, 1757–Mar. 5, 1835), first American-born bishop of the Methodist Episcopal Church, was a native of Virginia, the oldest of the eight children of John and Mary McKendree. At the time of William's birth his father was a small planter in King William County, but in 1764 he removed to James City County, and six years later to Greenville County. Not until he was thirty-one did the future bishop become a preacher. His schooling had been most elementary, and his experience only such as an unimportant planter might acquire, augmented by that which came from service in the Revolutionary War, during which he is reputed to have risen from the ranks to the office of adjutant, and been present at the surrender of Cornwallis. Whatever early religious training he had received had been in connection with the Established Church. When about nineteen he had joined a Methodist society on probation, but it was not until more than ten years later that, under the evangelistic activities of Rev. John Easter in Virginia, he was thoroughly converted. Without consulting him, through the recommendation of Easter, the Virginia Conference, meeting at Petersburg, June 1788, appointed McKendree a helper on the Mecklenburg circuit. Though he undertook the work with many misgivings, the year's experiences convinced him that he was divinely called to spread the knowledge of salvation. In June 1790 Bishop Asbury ordained him deacon, and in December of the following year, elder.

Hardly had his ministry begun when a crisis arose which almost separated him from the Methodist Episcopal Church. Under the influence of James O'Kelly [*q.v.*], later a seceder and founder of a new sect, he became distrustful of Asbury, and at the General Conference of 1792 supported O'Kelly in his attempt to secure a limitation to the powers of the bishops. When the attempt failed he left the Conference with O'Kelly and his followers, and at the succeeding session of the Virginia Conference declined to take an appointment. Soon afterward, however, at Asbury's invitation he accompanied him for a time on his travels, and as a result of this association McKendree's views changed and he accepted an appointment to Norfolk. Scanty as his early advantages had been, he had the character, the whole-souled consecration to his calling, and the natural gifts which his time and place required. He was tall and attractive physically, with all the graces of the gentleman; he preached with a sincerity, simplicity, force of illustration, and evangelistic zeal which were highly persuasive; he had business sense and skill as a parliamentarian, acquiring as the years went on a knowledge of Methodist government and discipline second to none; he was wise and prudent. Never marrying, he had no ties to interfere with complete surrender to the cause he had espoused.

For twenty years he served on circuits as a traveling pastor or as presiding elder. Until 1800 his labors were chiefly in Virginia. Tireless and diligent, he frequently preached every day in the week. It was said of him that he "kept house in his saddlebags," and that "he could pack more in them and in better order than other men." In 1800 he accompanied Asbury and Whatcoat on their journey west of the Alleghanies, and was put in charge of that vast region which included western Virginia, Ohio, Kentucky, and sections of Illinois, Tennessee, and Mississippi. He was an important factor in the Great Revival in the West, and for eight years was the life and soul of the army of itinerants in this pioneer field. Elected bishop at the General Conference of 1808, he was Asbury's only associate until the latter's death, Bishop Coke being out of the country. Although treating his senior with great deference and affection, McKendree was no mere assistant. In spite of Asbury's disapproval, he inaugurated consultation with the presiding elders in the making of appointments, and the "cabinet" has remained an institution of the Conference down to the present time. At the General Conference of 1812, much to Asbury's amazement, he presented a written statement of his views on prevailing conditions, and the episcopal address became a fixed custom. He was a strict constitutionalist, and when the question of how presiding elders should be selected came to a crisis at the General Conference of 1820 he took extreme grounds in opposition to limiting the bishops' power of appointment. Although relieved of the fixed duties of his office after 1820 because of physical infirmities, he continued to make long journeys and contributed to the superintendency of the work until his death. In 1830 he gave 480 acres of land to Lebanon Seminary, Illinois, the name of which was changed to McKendree College (J. M. Buckley, *A History of Methodists in the United States,* 1896). He died at the home of his brother, Dr. James McKendree, Sumner County, Tenn., in his seventy-eighth year, and was buried nearby. Later his body was taken up and re-buried on the campus of Vanderbilt University.

[Robert Paine, *Life and Times of William M'Kendree* (2 vols., 1869); E. E. Hoss, *William McKendree, a Biog. Study* (1914); Joshua Soule, *Sermon on the Death of the Rev. William M'Kendree* (1836); Nathan Bangs, *A Hist. of the M. E. Church* (1840); J. J. Tigert, *A Constitutional Hist. of Am. Episcopal Methodism* (1904); J. M. Buckley, *Constitutional and Parliamentary Hist. of the M. E. Church* (1912); T. O. Summers, *Biog. Sketches of Eminent Itinerant Ministers . . . of the M. E. Church, South* (1858); J. B. Wakeley, *The Heroes of Methodism* (1856); T. L. Flood and J. W. Hamilton, *Lives of Meth. Bishops* (1882); P. D. Gorrie, *The Lives of Eminent Meth. Ministers* (1852); W. B. Sprague, *Annals Am. Pulpit,* vol. VII (1859); *National Banner and Nashville Whig,* Mar. 13, 1835.]

H. E. S.

McKENNA, CHARLES HYACINTH (May 8, 1835–Feb. 21, 1917), Catholic missionary, eighth child in Francis and Anna (Gillespie) McKenna's family of ten, was born in Fallalea, County Derry, Ireland. His mother was a McDonald, her grandfather having assumed the name Gillespie for reasons of prudence, since he had supported the cause of the Pretender. Her husband's death and the famine forced her in 1848 to take five of her children to her brother in Lancaster, Pa. Charles, who was left with an older brother on the farm in Ireland, was tutored by a kinsman, Father John McKenna, and attended a national school until 1851, when he joined his mother. Two years in a public school, where he was ridiculed because of his brogue, corrected his speech, for which benefit he was later thankful. From 1853 to 1859 he labored as an apprentice and journeyman stone-cutter in Lancaster, Philadelphia, St. Louis, and finally in Dubuque, Iowa, near which place the McKennas had settled in an Irish rural colony. McKenna, however, never abandoned the hope of studying for the priesthood as soon as he had provided a competence for his mother. Through his zeal in parochial societies, he became a friend of Bishop Clement Smyth, who tutored him in Latin and brought his case to the attention of the Dominican provincial, Joseph A. Kelly, who sent him to the college at Sinsinawa Mound.

The self-trained artisan learned rapidly, spending his spare time in the study of Latin and hagiology or in labor on the grounds. Completing his novitiate at St. Joseph's Priory, Somerset, Ohio, he was professed as Brother Hyacinth, Apr. 20, 1863. His course in theology was broken and hurried because of the burning of St. Joseph's and the ravages of war, but on his transfer to St. Rose's Priory, Springfield, Ky., he read widely and was ordained priest in Cincinnati, on Oct. 13, 1867, by Archbishop Purcell. Returning to St. Rose's as assistant master of novices, he soon became master and sub-prior as well as pastor of the local congregation. Recognizing his latent possibilities as a preacher, his superiors ordered the young friar to the priory and church of St. Vincent Ferrer in New York, where the mission band made its headquarters. As a missionary, Father McKenna gradually developed into a powerful preacher who appealed especially to the laboring class with whose problems he sympathized. Association with the noted Irish Dominican, Father Tom Burke, schooled him in the orator's devices of dramatic appeal. For forty-four years he preached the fundamentals of Catholicism in Catholic missions throughout the land, led retreats in colleges and seminaries, gave lectures for non-Catholics, and delivered occasional addresses on Irish historical subjects.

A man of deep piety, he compiled a number of religious manuals which passed through several editions: *The Manual of the Holy Name* (1871); *How to Make the Mission* (1873); *The Dominican Manual* (1875); *St. Dominic's Tertiaries' Guide* (1883); *The Angelic Guide* (1899); and *The Rosary, the Crown of Mary* (1900). A Methodist neighbor, writing of Father McKenna's days at St. Vincent Ferrer's, described him as "a holy man entirely separate from the world, night and day either before the altar or among the most miserable of the living and dying" (A. E. Barr, *All The Days of My Life,* 1913, p. 384), while Cardinal Gibbons considered him one of the greatest American missionaries. His special concern was Catholic societies—the Catholic Knights of America, St. Vincent Ferrer's Union in New York, of which he was a founder, the Angelic Warfare Society, and the Junior Holy Name Society. Director general (1900–1906) of both the Rosary Confraternity and the Men's Holy Name Society, he so popularized the latter society at all his missions that he became known as its apostle. Within his order, he received a number of honors, including the appointments of prior (1878–81) and preacher-general of the Louisville priory (1881) and director of Eastern American missions (1880–92); but outside, he sought no honor, though few priests were more widely known or respected. In 1886, he was worried lest he be named bishop of Providence. At various times, as a relief from overwork, he visited the shrines of Europe and the Holy Land; but finally in 1914, he was forced to retire to the Dominican House of Studies in Washington. He died in Jacksonville, Fla.

[V. F. O'Daniel, *Very Rev. Charles Hyacinth McKenna, O. P.* (1917), a full biography based upon community records and memoirs; *Am. Cath. Who's Who* (1911); *N. Y. Times,* Feb. 23, 1917; material furnished by Father McKenna's associates.] R. J. P.

McKENNA, JOSEPH (Aug. 10, 1843–Nov. 21, 1926), jurist, was born in Philadelphia, the son of John and Mary (Johnson) McKenna, of Irish lineage. His parents moved to Benicia, Cal., in the winter of 1854–55. He was chiefly educated in Catholic seminaries and was graduated from Benicia Collegiate Institute in 1865, having turned to law after an original destination for the priesthood. The same year he was admitted to the bar. His practice, begun in Fairfield, Solano County, was varied by two terms as county attorney (1866–70), and by service for one term (1875–76) as a representative in the state legislature, where he was the unsuccessful Republican candidate for the speakership. Politics continued to attract him. Thrice defeated, apparently because he was a Catholic, as a candidate for the national House of Representatives (1876, 1878, 1880), he was thereafter four times successful, serving from Mar. 4, 1885, to Mar. 28, 1892, when he resigned to accept appointment by President Benjamin Harrison as United States circuit judge for the 9th circuit (Pacific coast). Throughout his residence in Washington he was intimate, politically and socially, with Leland Stanford, then senator from California; and during his third term in the House he served on the committee on ways and means under William McKinley, with whom he formed an abiding friendship. These relations—the latter evidently, the former presumptively (for in California his appointment to the circuit bench was generally ascribed to the influence, or insistence, of Senator Stanford)—were determinative of his later fortunes.

In February 1897, President-Elect McKinley announced his selection as attorney-general, and he was nominated and confirmed Mar. 5. He held the office only a few months, then became associate justice of the Supreme Court of the United States, nominated Dec. 16, 1897, and confirmed Jan. 21, 1898, in succession to Stephen J. Field [*q.v.*]. McKenna had practised only in or about Solano County, where he lived, and had apparently appeared very little in the local federal courts or in the supreme court of the state; contrary to a general impression, therefore, he could not have been associated in any important way with the legal interests of the Southern and Central Pacific railways. He had been, however, one of the small minority who voted against the creation of the Interstate Commerce Commission in 1887 (*Congressional Record,* 49 Cong., 2 Sess., p. 881). His appointment as circuit judge was rather long delayed, and his nomination for the Supreme Court (though not that for the attorney-generalship) aroused remarkably violent opposition (the *Examiner,* San Francisco, Dec. 3, 4, 5, 6, 1897, and the *San Francisco Chronicle,* Dec. 5, 1897, Jan. 22, 1898; the *World,* New York, Dec. 4, 7, 1897, Jan. 22, 1898). To a large degree this opposition seems to have been due to the rivalry of certain railway systems, and to his personal differences with other federal judges on the Pacific coast, or to their ambitions; in addition, however, his service as a circuit judge had been marked by dilatoriness, and by indecision in certain cases politically important. On the other hand, he was reversed in but few cases. On the Supreme Court he did not often speak for the Court, but did speak for it in some exceedingly important cases. His mental processes were slow, and, according to his critics, confused. At best he had no clear general legal philosophy that made his attitude on new cases readily predictable. His final opinions, however, were characterized by practical sense and clear expression. On the whole, his record was thoroughly respectable, and special students of constitutional law refer to some of his decisions and enunciations of principle as commendable for political vision and sound social judgment with reference to labor, the development of federal power, and its relation to the states (184 *U. S. Reports,* 540; 194 *U. S.,* 338; 203 *U. S.,* 192; 227 *U. S.,* 308; 233 *U. S.,* 389). He resigned on Jan. 25, 1925, and died in Washington in November 1926. On June 10, 1869, he married Amanda F. Borneman of San Francisco, and he left a son and three married daughters.

[O. T. Shuck, *Hist. of the Bench and Bar of Cal.* (1901); H. L. Carson, *The Hist. of the Supreme Court of the U. S.* (1902); vol. II; A. G. Feather, *The Supreme Court of the U. S.* (1900); *Sunday Star* (Washington), Nov. 21, 1926; San Francisco *Examiner* and the *World* (N. Y.), Nov. 22, 1926; *Biog. Dir. Am. Cong.* (1928); *Who's Who in America,* 1926–27.]

F. S. P.

McKENNAN, THOMAS McKEAN THOMPSON (Mar. 31, 1794–July 9, 1852), congressman, railroad president, was born at Dragon Neck, New Castle County, Del. His grandfather, Rev. William McKennan, emigrated from Ireland about 1730 and lived and died in Delaware. Thomas' father, Col. William McKennan, was a soldier of the Revolution; his mother, Elizabeth (Thompson) McKennan, was a niece of Thomas McKean [*q.v.*], chief justice of Pennsylvania. In 1797 the family moved to western Virginia, and soon thereafter to Washington, Washington County, in southwestern Pennsylvania. In 1810 Thomas graduated from Washington College (later Washington and Jefferson), and afterwards studied law in the office of Parker Campbell, Washington, Pa. He was admitted to the bar in 1814, and the following year, when only twenty-one, became deputy attorney-general for Washington County, holding this office till 1817. From 1818 to 1831 he was a member of the Washington town council. This office he resigned to assume his duties as a member of the federal House of Representatives, in which capacity he served continuously from Mar. 4, 1831, to Mar. 3, 1839. From May 30, 1842, to Mar. 3, 1843, he was again a member of Congress, completing an unexpired term. In politics he was a Whig, and his influence was exerted in furthering typical Whig policies, such as national banking, internal improvements, and protective tariffs. He was particularly active in connection with the tariff of 1842. In 1840 he was a presidential elector on the ticket of Harrison and Tyler, and in 1848 he headed Pennsylvania's presidential electors. His political prominence led to his selection by President Fillmore as secretary of the interior. This post he held, however, only from Aug. 15 to Aug. 26, 1850.

He had long been interested in promoting internal improvements, having been as early as 1831 an official of the Washington (Pa.) & Pittsburgh Railroad Company. The Baltimore & Ohio Railroad Company secured legislative authority to build a line through Pennsylvania to the west at Pittsburgh or Wheeling, but found it necessary to ask for extensions of time. Meanwhile, opposition developed on the part of the Pennsylvania Railroad Company and also on the part of vested interests associated with the National Road. Washington, lying between the Baltimore & Ohio and the Pennsylvania lines, set about securing connections with the main arteries of trade by building the Hempfield Railroad to Wheeling. The company was incorporated in 1850 and in February 1851 McKennan became its first president. In 1871 the line passed, under foreclosure sale, to the Baltimore & Ohio as an important part of its plan, frustrated earlier, for tapping Pennsylvania traffic. McKennan's incidental activities included his life-long support of Washington College, of which he was a trustee from 1818 to 1852, and his promotion of such local enterprises as the Washington Female Seminary and the Agricultural Society of Washington County. On Dec. 6, 1815, he married Matilda Bowman, by whom he had eight children. His death occurred in Reading, Pa.

[Roberdeau Buchanan, *Geneal. of the McKean Family of Pa.* (1890); Boyd Crumrine, *The Courts of Justice, Bench and Bar of Washington County* (1902) and *Hist. of Washington County, Pa.* (1882); *Commemorative Biog. Record of Washington County, Pa.* (1893); *Biog. and Hist. Cat. of Washington and Jefferson Coll.* (1902); *Biog. Dir. Am. Cong.* (1928); *Am. Railroad Jour.*, 1851–52, see index; *Daily National Intelligencer* (Washington, D. C.), July 12, 17, 1852.] W. B—n.

McKENNEY, THOMAS LORAINE (Mar. 21, 1785–Feb. 20, 1859), author and administrator of Indian affairs, was born in Hopewell, Somerset County, Md. He attended school at Chestertown, Md., and, after preliminary experience in his father's counting-house, opened stores in Georgetown and in Washington, D. C. During the War of 1812 he was adjutant and aide with militia and volunteer companies. His first government appointment, made by President Madison in April 1816, was as superintendent of the Indian trade. He continued in this office until that attempt at federal control of the Indian trade was abolished in 1822, largely owing to the opposition of private fur-traders, merchants, and manufacturers who had not profited by the administration. Charges of favoritism and abuse of trust were brought against him at the same time, particularly by Thomas H. Benton, and, although he considered himself triumphant in the congressional investigation, nevertheless, contemporary slanders were long in dying out, and he appears to have been indiscreet in permitting his notes to be indorsed by John Cox, a merchant from whom he bought large quantities of goods, as well as in persuading the Columbian College to take over his own notes to the amount of $11,958 (*House Report 104,* 17 Cong., 2 Sess., n.d., *Sen. Doc. 103,* 20 Cong., 1 Sess., n.d., see also *Sen. Doc. 60,* 17 Cong., 1 Sess., 1822). On Aug. 7, 1822, he began the publication of a semi-weekly newspaper, the *Washington Republican and Congressional Examiner,* devoted to the interests of John C. Calhoun. After some months of bitter attack he gave up the editorship on May 31, 1823.

Disappointed in his desire to be appointed first assistant postmaster-general, he was, on Mar. 11, 1824, given charge of the newly organized bureau of Indian affairs under the War Department. While superintendent of the Indian trade he had been instrumental in obtaining an annual appropriation of $10,000 for the civilization of the Indian tribes adjoining the frontier settlements. Most of this sum was distributed to the mission schools of the various denominations, which developed steadily during the years he was in charge of the Indian bureau so that, when he was forced out of the Indian department in 1830, about 1800 children were in mission schools. As joint commissioner with Lewis Cass, he negotiated the treaty of Aug. 11, 1827, at Butte des Morts on the Fox River with the Chippewa, Menominee, and Winnebago. His *Sketches of a Tour to the Lakes* (1827) described this expedition. Continuing down the Mississippi on a second expedition, he helped to influence the Chickasaw and Creeks to agree to migrate west of the Mississippi, and he negotiated the agreement of Nov. 15, 1827, with the Creek Indians. Although his *Memoirs, Official and Personal* (*post*) are lavish in defense of his own motives and actions and although all of his reports express his philanthropic interest in the Indian, he seems rather to have been a man hard pressed financially, holding desperately to his jobs, promising impossible things from the languishing Indian trade, constantly prating of Indian betterment, yet siding eagerly with politicians in their argument of state rights and in their desire to move the natives westward. Besides other controversial writings he published *Essays on the Spirit of Jacksonism as Exemplified in its Deadly Hostility to the Bank of the United States* (1835), and with James Hall, a *History of the Indian Tribes of North America, with Biographical Sketches and Anecdotes of the Principal Chiefs* (1836–44), three folio volumes chiefly valuable for the 120 portraits, in color, from the Indian gallery in the War Department. He died from typhoid fever in New York City.

[T. L. McKenney, *Memoirs, Official and Personal* (2 vols. in 1, 1846); a different estimate of motives and accomplishment in A. H. Abel, "The Hist. of Events Resulting in Indian Consolidation West of the Mississippi," *Am. Hist. Assoc. Report . . . 1906*, vol. I (1908); *Memoirs of John Quincy Adams*, ed. by C. F. Adams, vols. VI, VII, VIII (1875); *Bibliographical Soc. of America Papers*, vol. XIX (1925), p. 63; spelling of middle name taken from Lib. of Cong. on authority of niece; transcript of death certificate by department of health with date of Feb. 21 but death notice in *N. Y. Times*, Feb. 21, 1859, with date Feb. 20.] D. A. D.

McKENZIE, ALEXANDER (Dec. 14, 1830–Aug. 6, 1914), Congregational clergyman, was born in New Bedford, Mass., the son of Daniel and Phebe Mayhew (Smith) McKenzie. His father was captain of whaling vessels, a man of dauntless spirit, well-balanced mind, and a gift of eloquent speech. During the War of 1812, when he was nineteen years of age, the whaling ship in which he was serving as boat-steerer was captured by the British and he suffered extreme hardships for many months at Capetown and later in Dartmoor prison. The devoted and courageous wife trained their children during her husband's long absences on the sea. Graduating at sixteen from the New Bedford high school, Alexander found business positions in Cambridge and Boston. His mind turned increasingly, however, to thoughts of an education and the profession of the ministry, and at twenty-three years of age he entered Phillips Academy, Andover, where he made rapid progress and graduated in 1855. Entering Harvard College, he was asked by Edward Everett to be roommate of his gifted son William. He graduated at Harvard in 1859, and at Andover Theological Seminary in 1861, and on Aug. 28, 1861, he was ordained and installed pastor of the Congregational church in Augusta, Me., where James G. Blaine and Lot M. Morrill [*qq.v.*] were among his parishioners. On Jan. 25, 1865, he was married to Ellen Holman Eveleth, daughter of John H. and Martha (Holman) Eveleth of Fitchburg, Mass.

In 1866 he was called to the pastorate of the First (Congregational) Church in Cambridge, Mass. Founded in 1636, this church was a leading one in the Massachusetts Bay Colony and had always exercised a wide influence. Installed Jan. 24, 1867, McKenzie held this pastorate over forty-seven years, the last four as pastor emeritus—a term longer than that of any of his predecessors save one. Of fine physique, never absent from his pulpit because of illness, eloquent in address, often with touches of latent humor, a wise counselor and guide and a public-spirited citizen, he occupied a place comparable to that of the leading ministers of colonial New England. His preaching was not so much argumentative as strongly affirmative, with rich diction, poetic allusion, and penetrating insight. For years during his ministry Harvard students were grouped on Sunday mornings in the east transept of the church.

McKenzie was an overseer of Harvard, 1872–84; and secretary of the board of overseers, 1875–1901. In 1886 he was made one of the first board of preachers to the University. He was also a trustee of Bowdoin College, Phillips Andover Academy, Wellesley College, and Hampton Institute; president of the Boston Seaman's Friend Society and of the Boston Port Society; a trustee of the Cambridge Hospital; and for seven years one of the Cambridge school committee. He was lecturer at Andover Seminary, 1881–82, and at Harvard Divinity School, 1882–83. Besides historical monographs and single sermons, he published *The Two Boys* (1871); *Lectures on the History of the First Church in Cambridge* (1873); *Cambridge Sermons* (1883); *Some Things Abroad* (1887); *Christ Himself* (copr. 1891); *A Door Opened* (1898); *The Divine Force in the Life of the World* (1898), Lowell Institute lectures; *Getting One's Bearings* (1903); *Two Ends of a Houseboat* (1909).

[*Harvard Coll. Records of the Class of 1859* (1896); *Cat. of Officers and Students of the Andover Theological Sem.*, 1881–82; *Proc. Mass. Hist. Soc.*, Feb. 1914; James Schouler in *Ibid.*, Oct. 1914; *Manual of First Ch. in Cambridge, Congl.* (1920); *Who's Who in America*, 1914–15; *Boston Transcript*, Aug. 7, 1914; *Congregationalist and Christian World*, Aug. 13, 1914; letters to the writer from Frank Gaylord Cook.] E. D. E.

MACKENZIE, ALEXANDER SLIDELL (Apr. 6, 1803–Sept. 13, 1848), naval officer and author, was known as Alexander Slidell until 1838, when, under authorization of the New York legislature, he added Mackenzie to his name out of regard for a maternal uncle. He was a son of John Slidell, a New York City merchant, and a brother of John Slidell [*q.v.*], the Confederate diplomatic agent. His mother, Margery or May (Mackenzie) Slidell, was a native of the Highlands of Scotland. After a period of attendance at a boarding school, he continued his education in the navy, which he entered on Jan.

1, 1815, as a midshipman. Fond of books, he applied himself to the study of literature and the rudiments of his profession. From 1818 to 1821 he was with the *Macedonian* in the Pacific Ocean, and later, obtaining a furlough, commanded a merchant vessel. Returning to the navy, he aided in the suppression of piracy in the West Indies in 1824, being attached to the *Terrier*. In January 1825 he was promoted to a lieutenancy and soon thereafter, on leave from the navy, visited France and made a tour of Spain, the main incidents of which he embodied in a two-volume book entitled *A Year in Spain*, which appeared first in Boston in 1829 and later in London. Favorably noticed by some of the leading American and English reviewers and translated into Swedish, it started its author upon a literary career that henceforth absorbed all the time that he could spare from the active duties of his profession.

In 1830–33 he made a cruise in the Mediterranean on the *Brandywine*, and upon his return home published his second book, *Popular Essays on Naval Subjects* (1833). He next toured England and again visited Spain and gathered the material that appeared in *The American in England* (2 vols., 1835) and *Spain Revisited* (2 vols., 1836). In 1837–38 he served as lieutenant on the *Independence* and visited Russia. Thence he proceeded to Brazil, and, taking command of the *Dolphin*, witnessed the siege and surrender of Bahia and other important events in that region, some of which he described in a pamphlet published at this time. Soon after he returned to the United States in 1839, he wrote a *Life of Paul Jones* (2 vols., 1841). In the previous year his *Life of Commodore Oliver Hazard Perry*, in two volumes, had appeared. He was promoted commander, September 1841, and soon thereafter took command of the steamer *Missouri* of the home squadron. From this vessel he was transferred to the brig *Somers*, then used as a training ship for apprentices, and in September 1842 sailed for the African squadron with dispatches. While on the return voyage, plans for a mutiny were discovered and Midshipman Philip Spencer, a boatswain, and a seaman were executed for their complicity therein. When the brig reached the United States this extreme act of discipline caused much public excitement, and in circles friendly to Spencer, who was a notorious scapegrace but a nephew of the secretary of war, the feeling against Mackenzie was bitter. A court of inquiry and a court martial that investigated his conduct exonerated him, and all attempts to indict him in civil courts failed. The official judgment has been justified by the verdict of posterity. (Benjamin, *post*, p. 138.) Mackenzie now retired to his home on the Hudson near Tarrytown, N. Y., and occupied himself with writing *The Life of Stephen Decatur* (1846). In May 1846 President Polk sent him on a special mission to General Santa Anna at Havana. In the Mexican War he acted as one of the two representatives of the navy at the surrender of Vera Cruz and as a commander of artillery at the second attack on Tabasco. In 1847–48, he commanded the steamer *Mississippi* of the home squadron, his last naval service.

Mackenzie was a popular writer and several editions of most of his books were published. He had considerable talent for description and wrote readily, in a sprightly, humorous style. On Oct. 1, 1835, he was married in New York City to Catherine Alexander Robinson. Ranald S. Mackenzie [*q.v.*] was his son; another son, Lieutenant Commander Alexander S. Mackenzie, died gallantly in battle on the island of Formosa in 1867.

[Record of Officers, Bureau of Navigation, 1818–58; L. M. Sears, *John Slidell* (1925); Park Benjamin, *The U. S. Naval Acad.* (1900); J. H. Smith, *The War with Mexico* (1919), vol. I; *Mag. of Am. Hist.*, Feb. 1887; *Proc. of the Naval Court Martial in the Case of Alexander Slidell Mackenzie . . . to which is Annexed an Elaborate Review by James Fennimore Cooper* (1844); *Case of the Somers' Mutiny: Defence of Alexander Slidell Mackenzie* (1843); E. A. and G. L. Duyckinck, *Cyc. of Am. Literature* (1875), vol. II; *N. Y. Herald*, Sept. 14, 1848.]

C. O. P.

MACKENZIE, DONALD (June 15, 1783–Jan. 20, 1851), fur-trader, was born in Scotland, a brother of Roderic Mackenzie of the North West Company, and a cousin of Alexander Mackenzie, the explorer. He was educated for the ministry, but instead of entering that profession went to Canada and joined the North West Company. On June 23, 1810, after ten years' experience, he was engaged by John Jacob Astor to be one of his partners in the Pacific Fur Company. With Wilson P. Hunt [*q.v.*], he led a band of adventurers by the overland route to the mouth of the Columbia River. Mackenzie with his group arrived at Fort Astoria Jan. 18, 1812. He later became the head of a large party which engaged in hunting and trapping. His journeys took him to the rivers Willamette, Columbia, and also the Snake, where he established a post. He left Astoria again in March 1813, and in June returned with 140 packs of furs from Okanagan post, and Spokane River. While carrying supplies to the interior that fall he was robbed by Indians. Returning to Astoria, he occupied himself storing salmon until his party learned of the war with Great Britain. Concluding that Astoria would be captured and goods confiscated, he and his partners there sold out to the North West Company the following spring. On Apr. 14, 1814, Mackenzie set out for New York, where he remained for some time seeking reëmployment by Astor. Failing to obtain it, he returned to Canada and again entered the service of the North West Company. In 1816 he was on the Columbia River, spending his time at Fort George and Fort William, and Spokane House. He rendered valuable service to his company in developing the rich trade of southern Idaho. His brigade of 1817 was the first to report a year without casualties, and the quantity of furs obtained was considerable.

Mackenzie was retained when the Hudson's Bay and North West Companies consolidated, and the following year, 1822, established Chesterfield House. In 1824 he was made chief factor at Fort Garry, on the Red River of the North, and the same year was appointed councilor of the governors. Soon thereafter he was made governor of Red River Colony, the highest post in the country next to the governor-in-chief, which vast province he ruled judiciously and with kindness. To him is due credit for the peace and progress which prevailed during the following eight years. He retired in August 1833, and took his family to Mayville, N. Y., where he had an estate. There he lived until his death.

Donald Mackenzie was eminently fitted, both physically and mentally, for life in the wilderness. His knowledge of the Indians was remarkably keen and accurate, and his influence over them was great. His boldness and prompt decision, in times of danger, helped to awe and conquer them. His ways and accomplishments astonished his associates; he weighed over 300 pounds, but was so active that he was called "perpetual motion." In August 1825, at Fort Garry, he married Adelgonde Humbert-Droze, by whom he had thirteen children.

[Mackenzie MSS. in Mo. Hist. Soc.; "Reminiscences by Hon. Roderic McKenzie," in L. R. Masson, *Les Bourgeois de la Compagnie du Nord-Ouest,* vol. I (Quebec, 1889); Alexander Ross, *The Fur Hunters of the Far West* (1855), and *The Red River Settlement, Its Rise, Progress, and Present State* (1856); William Anderson, *The Scottish Nation,* vol. III, Supp. (1863); Elliott Coues, ed., *New Light on the Early Hist. of the Greater Northwest* (1897); E. Cawcroft, "Donald Mackenzie," in *Canadian Magazine,* Feb. 1918; A. W. Young, *Hist. of Chautauqua County, N. Y.* (1875); *Mo. Republican* (St. Louis), Feb. 13, 1851.]

S. M. D.

MACKENZIE, GEORGE HENRY (Nov. 24, 1837–Apr. 14, 1891), chess-player, was born at Belfield House, North Kessock, Ross and Cromarty, Scotland, the youngest of the four sons of John and Ann (Douglass) Mackenzie. The year after the boy's birth, his father died and the family moved to Inverness and later to Aberdeen. George received his early education in the schools of that city and was then sent to a high school in Southampton, England. In 1853 he returned to Aberdeen and afterward went to Rouen, France, where he entered a business office. Subsequently, he served as ensign in the 60th Rifles, a Scottish volunteer regiment, and with the regulars at the Cape of Good Hope, attaining the rank of lieutenant. In 1861 he sold his commission. The following year he competed in the London handicap chess tournament, winning the first prize by defeating Anderssen, the foremost European chess player, at the odds of pawn and move.

In 1863 he emigrated to New York and on Aug. 27 of that year enlisted as a private in Company F, 83rd New York Infantry. On Apr. 20, 1864, he was promoted to a captaincy in the 10th United States Infantry (Colored) and was honorably discharged, June 16, 1864. Taking up his residence in New York City, he became a professional chess player and writer on chess. He won first prize in the tournaments of the New York Chess Club for 1865 to 1868 inclusive. In the second American Chess Congress (1871), at Cleveland, the third, at Chicago (1874), and the fifth, at New York (1880), he took first prize, winning recognition as the American chess champion. In international tournaments he placed fourth at Paris in 1878; tied for fourth-fifth at Vienna in 1882; tied for fifth-sixth-seventh at London in 1883; placed seventh at Hamburg in 1885; won first place at Frankfort in 1887, which victory made him world champion. He was second at Bradford, England, in 1888, and fourth at Manchester in 1890; only at the tournament in London in 1886 did he fail to place among the prize-winners. In match play he defeated such notable American players as Reichhelm (1866, 1867), Stanley (1868), Judd (1881), and Lipschuetz (1886). In matches with English experts he defeated Bird in 1876 and Blackburne in 1882, tied with Amos Burn in 1886, and lost to Blackburne in 1888. He also won three minor matches in Havana in 1887 and 1888.

Mackenzie made a somewhat precarious living by his success in tournaments, matches, and exhibitions in various parts of the United States and Cuba. He was found dead in his room at Cooper Union Hotel, New York, having died apparently of pneumonia. He was tall and handsome in appearance and genial in manner; with his Vandyke beard and slouch hat he resembled more the typical Southern "colonel" than a former British army officer.

[London *Times*, Apr. 16, 1891; *N. Y. Times* and *N. Y. Herald*, Apr. 15, 1891; G. A. MacDonnell, *The Knights and Kings of Chess* (London, 1894); *New York in the War of the Rebellion* (1912), vol. V; *Schach-Jahrbücher*, 1894–1901; *British Chess Mag.*, May 1891.] L. C. K.

MACKENZIE, JAMES CAMERON (Aug. 15, 1852–May 10, 1931), educator, was born in Aberdeen, Scotland, the son of Alexander and Catherine (Cameron) Mackenzie. After the death of his father, the child was brought to America by his mother, who settled in Wilkes-Barre, Pa. For the first twelve years of his life practically all his schooling consisted of one winter term in a public school. He was subsequently a clerk in the town's largest bookstore and by reading and study educated himself. Intending to prepare to teach in the public schools, he entered the normal school at Bloomsburg, Pa., and a year later went to Phillips Academy, Exeter, N. H., where he graduated at the head of his class in 1873. After a year of teaching and administrative work in Wilkes-Barre Institute, a girls' school, he entered Lafayette College, where he graduated as valedictorian in 1878. Several teaching positions were open to him and he accepted the first principalship of the newly founded Wilkes-Barre (later Harry Hillman) Academy. Here his work attracted the attention of the legatees of the estate of John Cleve Green [*q.v.*], who were looking for a man to build a thoroughly equipped academy at Lawrenceville, N. J., along the lines of the schools at Andover and Exeter. On Oct. 5, 1880, he married Ella Smith, daughter of Robert C. Smith of Wilkes-Barre. In 1882 he went to Lawrenceville, where, using the land and buildings of the old proprietary school there which had been purchased by the legatees of Green's estate, he organized the present Lawrenceville School, in accordance with their desires. During the session of 1882–83 he attended Princeton Theological Seminary, and in 1885 he was ordained to the Presbyterian ministry.

Under his far-sighted, revolutionary method of administration the Lawrenceville School attracted much attention in the outer world; it grew in numbers and its graduates distinguished themselves at college. The English house system was established and in 1893, against the determined opposition of the faculty, Mackenzie organized the Upper House, where the older boys should live and have the greater freedom that would prepare them for the transition from school to college. This was a revolutionary step in the administration of boys' boarding schools. Andover and Exeter had always been like colleges in their treatment of their boys, and other schools had kept the pupils under the strictest discipline even through their graduation year. Lawrenceville became, in spite of financial difficulties, a large and famous school, with a modern plant. As a result, Mackenzie was offered many excellent positions. Exeter and Lafayette both wanted him, and he was tendered the superintendency of the Philadelphia public schools.

In 1891 the United States Commissioner of Education appointed him to membership on the Committee of Ten on Secondary Education, and in 1893 appointed him chairman of the congress on secondary education to be held at the World's Columbian Exposition in Chicago. He was president of the Schoolmasters' Association in the early nineties, and in 1893, in Boston, was instrumental in the formation of the Headmasters' Association, of which he was later president. He was also a president of the Association of Colleges and Preparatory Schools of the Middle States and Maryland.

After the death of the last of Green's legatees, and upon certain changes in the board of trustees, Mackenzie resigned from the headmastership of Lawrenceville School in 1899 (*New York Times*, May 11, 1931) and became director of Jacob Tome Institute, Port Deposit, Md. Here he reorganized the school and supervised the erection of new buildings. In 1901, finding that his plans were not approved by the relatives of Tome (*Ibid.*), he resigned and founded a school of his own, the Mackenzie School, at Dobbs Ferry, N. Y., moving it later to Monroe, N. Y. There he remained as director until 1926, when he retired from active work. He made his home thereafter in New York City, where he died.

[Roland J. Mulford, history of Lawrenceville School, soon to be published; *Who's Who in America*, 1930–31; *Who's Who in N. Y.*, 1907; *N. Y. Times*, May 11, 1931; letters and documents in the possession of the family and of T. Dean Swift, N. Y.] M. A. A.

MACKENZIE, JOHN NOLAND (Oct. 20, 1853–May 21, 1925), physician, pioneer laryngologist, was born in Baltimore, Md., of the fourth generation of a medical family. His father, John Carrere Mackenzie, was a physician, as was his grandfather, John Pinkerton Mackenzie; and his great-grandfather, Colin, was a surgeon. His mother, Eleanor (Noland), was the daughter of Lloyd and Elizabeth (Wynn) Noland of Loudoun County, Va. Part of his boyhood was spent in France and England. In 1872 he entered the academic department of the University of Virginia, but two years later transferred to the Medical Department, graduating (M.D.) in 1876. He took a second medical degree from the University of the City of New York in 1877, and was subsequently interne at

Bellevue Hospital, 1877–79. Meanwhile, he sought the instruction of Dr. Clinton Wagner, then at the full tide of his well-deserved popularity as founder of the pioneer school of advanced laryngology at the Metropolitan Throat Hospital. In 1879 Mackenzie went abroad for an extended course of study, devoting himself principally to laryngology, first under Oertel and as assistant to Von Ziemssem at Munich; then under Von Schroetter and Stoerk at Vienna. Finally he spent a year as chief of clinic at the London Throat Hospital, Golden Square, under Sir Morell Mackenzie, the distinguished master of laryngology. Here he rendered material assistance in the preparation of Mackenzie's great *Manual of the Diseases of the Throat and Nose* (2 vols., 1880–84), work which afforded a discipline rich and productive in the development of his literary gifts. He improved his unusual opportunities to the utmost, gaining an amount of knowledge and experience unusual for one of his years.

Returning to Baltimore, he inaugurated a brilliant career. As a practitioner, he was a founder and surgeon of the Baltimore Eye, Ear and Throat Charity Hospital, surgeon to the nose and throat department of the University of Maryland Hospital from 1887 to 1897, and to the Johns Hopkins Hospital from 1889 to 1912; and consulting laryngologist to a number of different hospitals. He was clinical professor of rhinology and laryngology in the University of Maryland, 1887–97, and clinical professor of laryngology in the Johns Hopkins University Medical School, 1889–1912. He was a co-editor of the *Maryland Medical Journal,* American editor of the British *Journal of Laryngology and Rhinology,* and connected in some capacity with various other special journals, American and foreign. As investigator and author, beginning in 1880, he covered the full range of laryngo-rhinology. His most important original contributions were a number of papers upon the vaso-motor neuroses of the nose and upper air passages. In this field he was a pioneer and his writings formed the basis of many of the accepted theories relating to the subject. From 1895 onward his original studies relating to the accessory sinuses were also of great importance. After 1900 he became a leader in the study of laryngeal cancer. He opposed excessive surgery, showing a conservatism in the treatment of nose and throat conditions which was much needed at the time. He contributed a number of special articles to *A Reference Handbook of the Medical Sciences* (8 vols., 1885–89), edited by A. H. Buck, and to other standard publications.

Quickly recognized everywhere as an authority of the first rank, he was elected a fellow of the American Laryngological Association in 1883 and became its vice-president in 1886 and its president in 1889. Widely known and appreciated abroad, he was a corresponding fellow of the leading British, French, and German associations. Attractive in appearance as in intellect, he had a charm of manner and a bouyancy of spirit that made him a beloved companion. He was married, Feb. 2, 1887, to Rachel Pratt Clark, grand-daughter of Thomas G. Pratt, a governor of Maryland and a United States senator for many years. He died at his home in Baltimore.

[Memoir by D. B. Delavan, in *Trans. of the Forty-Eighth Ann. Meeting of the Am. Laryngological Asso.* (1926), with bibliography; *Who's Who in America,* 1924–25; *Jour. Am. Medic. Asso.,* June 13, 1925; the *Sun* (Baltimore), May 22, 1925; personal acquaintance.]

D. B. D.

MACKENZIE, KENNETH (Apr. 15, 1797–Apr. 26, 1861), fur-trader and merchant, was born in the shire of Ross and Cromarty, Scotland, son of Alexander and Isabella (Mackenzie) Mackenzie. He received a good education. In 1816, at the suggestion of Sir Alexander Mackenzie, a kinsman, he went to Canada and entered the employ of the North West Company. In February 1822 he appeared in St. Louis and immediately applied for citizenship. Here he organized the Columbia Fur Company with a rather small capital stock. The principal power of the company was in the personnel—bold, experienced, and energetic men, including several former North-Westerners. Their trade extended north to the headwaters of the Mississippi, east to the Great Lakes, and west to the Missouri River.

When the Western Department of the American Fur Company was organized, its promoters found Mackenzie's outfit such a strong rival in the Sioux and Omaha countries that they could not operate without a loss of at least ten thousand dollars annually. After a bitter fight the American Fur Company tried to buy out the Mackenzie group. For almost a year efforts were made to prevent competition by agreement, and finally, in July 1827, there was an amalgamation of the two companies. Kenneth Mackenzie and two of his partners were given separate shares in the Upper Missouri Outfit of the American Fur Company. By this arrangement Mackenzie and these partners got control of the Upper Missouri and became as independent as if they had remained in a separate company.

Mackenzie carried on the trade in regions made dangerous by hostile Indians, from which other traders had been driven. Within four years he had posts on the Yellowstone, Bighorn, and Marais rivers. He built Fort Union, the best-equipped post west of the Mississippi. Here he reigned, feared and loved by his men and by the Indians, coming to be called "King of the Missouri," "Emperor Mackenzie," and "Emperor of the West." In 1834, he was charged with having erected a distillery at Fort Union, contrary to law. This unfortunate occurrence threatened the Company's charter and forced Mackenzie to leave the country for a time. In the winter of that year he went abroad to study wine making, and while in Germany was the guest of Prince Maximilian. During this same year he joined the firm of Chouteau & Mackenzie, commission and forwarding merchants, which firm dissolved in July 1841. After returning from Europe in the summer of 1835, he went back to Fort Union. His last trip seems to have been made a decade later. Until about 1850, he was connected with Pierre Chouteau, Jr. & Company in the fur trade, although he spent little time at his old post. He continued his business as commission merchant and importer of foreign liquors until 1854, and then, for the rest of his life, dealt solely in liquors. He invested largely in lands in Missouri, Illinois, and Minnesota, as well as in railroads and other industries, and by the time of his death in St. Louis, he had amassed a fortune.

Mackenzie married Mary Marshall, June 26, 1842, at St. Louis. He had six children, two of whom died in infancy.

[H. M. Chittenden, *The Am. Fur Trade of the Far West* (1902); Richard Edwards and M. Hopewell, *Edwards's Great West* (1860), p. 98; *St. Louis Enquirer*, July 19, 22, 1824; *Daily Missouri Democrat* (St. Louis), Apr. 27, 1861; St. Louis Probate Court Records, Estate of Kenneth Mackenzie; Naturalization Papers, Mo. Hist. Soc.; Fort Union Letter Book, Pierre Chouteau Collection, Mo. Hist. Soc.] S. M. D.

MACKENZIE, RANALD SLIDELL (July 27, 1840–Jan. 19, 1889), soldier, elder son of Alexander Slidell Mackenzie [*q.v.*] and Catherine Alexander (Robinson), was born in New York City. He matriculated at Williams College with the class of 1859, but withdrew to go to West Point, where he graduated No. 1 in the class of 1862. Assigned to the Corps of Engineers, he went promptly to the front, taking part, as an engineer officer, in the battles of Manassas, Fredericksburg, Chancellorsville, Gettysburg and the subsequent campaigns, the Wilderness, Spotsylvania, and the siege of Petersburg (June–July 1864), and receiving during that time two wounds and four brevets for gallantry. In July 1864 he was made colonel of the 2nd Connecticut Heavy Artillery Volunteers, with which he helped defend Washington against Early's raid. In command of a brigade during the Shenandoah campaign, he was wounded at Cedar Creek in October, but returned to duty in time to take part in the siege of Petersburg, February–March 1865. With the further brevets of colonel and brigadier-general, United States Army, and major-general of volunteers, he commanded a highly efficient cavalry division with the Army of the James during the Five Forks-Appomattox campaign in the spring of 1865, and was stationed in and about Appomattox while the details of Lee's surrender and the dispersion of the Army of Northern Virginia were carried out. In his *Personal Memoirs* (II, 541), General Grant said, "I regarded Mackenzie as the most promising young officer in the army. Graduating at West Point, as he did, during the second year of the war, he had won his way up to the command of a corps [division] before its close. This he did upon his own merit and without influence."

After the war he was transferred to the South and Southwest in lower rank, owing to the reduction of the military establishment. As colonel of the 4th Cavalry, he took the leading part in the campaigns of the early 1870's against marauding Indians in West Texas and along the Rio Grande, and was severely wounded (1871) while engaged in a cañon of the "Staked Plains," Texas Panhandle. In 1873 he crossed the Rio Grande, made a forced night march, attacked and destroyed an Indian camp, precipitating a situation which was finally settled by diplomatic exchanges with the Mexican government. As a result of these operations and his subsequent military supervision, large areas in Texas—particularly the "Staked Plains"—were opened to permanent settlement. Mackenzie was then transferred to the Indian Territory, where he was equally successful in coping with the hostile Indians of that region.

When, after the Custer fight at the Little Big Horn, June 25–26, 1876, Gen. P. H. Sheridan, commanding the Military Division of the Missouri, planned large-scale operations against the Sioux and Cheyennes, he relieved Mackenzie from command at Fort Sill, Indian Territory, and brought him with six companies of the 4th Cavalry up into Nebraska to form part of the Powder River Expedition. Before starting on that campaign, Mackenzie, with his own companies, two from the 5th Cavalry, and a detachment of Pawnee Indian scouts, surrounded and disarmed the Red Cloud and Red Leaf bands on Chadron Creek, Nebr., Oct. 23, and then became the mounted column of Gen. George Crook's winter campaign into and up through an extensive district in Wyoming Territory. Locating the

Northern Cheyennes in the Big Horn Mountains, Mackenzie thoroughly defeated them in the battle of Nov. 25, 1876, dispersing and breaking the fighting power of Dull Knife's formidable band. This campaign, with corresponding successes by troops operating in Montana under Col. Nelson A. Miles [*q.v.*], led to the surrender of Crazy Horse without further hostilities in Wyoming.

Transferred back to the Indian Territory in 1877, and thence again to Texas, Mackenzie completed the work of pacifying the region extending down to the Mexican border. At the outbreak of the Ute disturbances in Colorado and Utah in 1879 he was sent into that district, and was engaged for about two years in military operations and administration, with marked success. Later Indian troubles in Arizona and New Mexico required short tours of duty in both these territories. After comparatively brief periods of command in the departments of New Mexico and Texas, he was retired on Mar. 24, 1884, for disability incurred in the line of duty; already failing in health, he died at New Brighton, Staten Island, N. Y., as brigadier-general, United States Army, although he had held the brevet rank of major-general of volunteers since Mar. 31, 1865, for gallant and meritorious services during the Civil War.

Mackenzie was slightly above medium height, very active, somewhat nervous, often impetuous and exacting; he had a reputation in the old army for being a severe disciplinarian, but his officers and men became much attached to and had complete confidence in him as a leader. "I really classed him," writes Capt. Robert G. Carter, who served under him in Texas, "as our best, most reliable and dependable Indian fighter. He had an indomitable will, wonderful powers of endurance, and unsurpassed courage." Several times he was in the forefront of battle; one of the three wounds received in the Civil War resulted in the loss of fingers, which led the Indians to call him "Bad Hand." His particular interest was in the tactical handling of troops in the field, of which he was one of the acknowledged masters. He was, withal, a conserver of forces, and several times—notably in the Dull Knife fight—went through to the point of assured victory, without pressing an advantage at too great sacrifice. His fame has been circumscribed by his temperamental aversion to publicity; all of the military operations under his command were followed by brief reports and immediate retirement to his station or other duties. No act of his ever brought censure from his superiors, and the only incident of his career resulting in controversy was his crossing of the Rio Grande with United States troops in 1873, and that was at least tacitly approved by the government. Mackenzie never wrote for publication and was never married, but devoted all of his energies to the profession of a soldier.

[G. W. Cullum, *Biog. Reg. Officers and Grads., U. S. Mil. Acad.* (3rd ed., 1891); J. H. Dorst, in *Twentieth Ann. Reunion, Asso. Grads., U. S. Mil. Acad.* (1889); James Parker, *The Old Army Memories 1872–1918* (1929); D. L. Vaill, *The County Regiment; a Sketch of the Second Regt. of Conn. Vol. Heavy Artillery* (1908); Col. C. A. P. Hatfield, "Army Life on the Texas Plains in the 1870's," MS. in the possession of Robert Bruce, New York; letter from Capt. R. G. Carter, U. S. A., retired, Sept. 27, 1932; *Personal Memoirs of U. S. Grant* (2 vols., 1885–86); J. G. Bourke, *On the Border with Crook* (1891); *Army and Navy Jour.*, Jan. 26, 1889.]
R. B.

MACKENZIE, ROBERT SHELTON (June 22, 1809–Nov. 21, 1881), author, journalist, was born at Drew's Court, County Limerick, Ireland, second son of Capt. Kenneth Mackenzie of the Kaithness Fencibles, later postmaster of the small military town of Fermoy. His mother was Maria (Shelton) Mackenzie. Robert received his early education at Fermoy and taught school there in 1825. Before he reached his majority he had become editor of a county journal at Hanley, Staffordsville, England, thus beginning a career in newspaper work which lasted until his death. In 1830–31 he wrote a large number of biographies for the *Georgian Era.* From 1831 to 1833 he conducted the *Derbyshire Courier* and shortly thereafter became editor of the *Liverpool Journal.* In 1834 he was appointed English correspondent of the New York *Evening Star,* and is said to have been the first paid European correspondent of any American paper (*Ballou's Pictorial,* Jan. 12, 1856). To the *Star* he contributed letters on politics, literature, fashion, and gossip of high life until 1851. During this period he was also connected with the Liverpool *Mail* and (from about 1840 to 1843) with the *Salopian Journal* in Shrewsbury. The statement is made in biographical sketches published during his lifetime that he received the degree of D.C.L. from Oxford in 1844, but there is no record of it at the University. From 1845 to 1851 he is variously stated to have been editor of a railway journal in London and the London secretary of a railway company. In 1848 he was active in securing publicity in the London *Sun* and the weekly *Times* for Lord Brougham's Law Amendment Society, in recognition of which service he was appointed by Brougham official assignee of the Manchester bankruptcy court, an appointment which came to an end in October 1852 (*Law Times,* London, Oct. 30, 1852). In 1851 he married Georgiana Dickinson, by whom he had one child.

Because of financial difficulties, after the premature death of his wife in 1852 Mackenzie came to New York, where for a time he was literary editor and political writer on a daily, and music and dramatic critic for a Sunday paper. In July 1857 he removed to Philadelphia and in August, upon the establishment of the Philadelphia *Press,* became its literary and foreign editor and dramatic critic. This position he retained for over twenty years. In 1858 he married, in Philadelphia, Adelheid Zwissler (the author of several romances), by whom he had three children. In 1862 he was one of the organizers of the Philadelphia Dental College (now a part of Temple University) and became its secretary. Toward the end of his life he was literary editor of the Philadelphia *Evening News.* He died Nov. 21, 1881 (not Nov. 30, 1880, as frequently stated), and was buried in Philadelphia.

His original literary work began with *Lays of Palestine* (1828), and included a three-volume novel, *Titian: A Romance of Venice* (1843); *Mornings at Matlock* (3 vols., 1850) and *Bits of Blarney* (1854), collections of stories; *Tressilian and His Friends* (1859), in part autobiographical; *Life of Charles Dickens* (1870), written in five weeks; and *Sir Walter Scott: the Story of His Life* (1871). The biographies are interesting accounts, enlivened by numerous reminiscences and anecdotes. Mackenzie is probably best remembered, however, for his five-volume edition of the *Noctes Ambrosianae* (London, 1854; 2nd ed., revised, 1863), the first adequate collection of these papers, accompanied by a valuable commentary. He likewise edited R. L. Sheil's *Sketches of the Irish Bar* (1854), William Henry Curran's *Life of the Right Honorable John Philpot Curran* (1855); *Miscellaneous Writings of the late Dr. Maginn* (5 vols., 1855–57), the last volume containing a 110-page memoir; Lady Morgan's *The O'Briens and the O'Flahertys: A National Tale* (1856); and the *Memoirs of Robert-Houdin, Ambassador, Author, and Conjurer* (1859), of which he seems also to have been the translator. Numerous other works appeared, especially after the publication of the *Noctes Ambrosianae,* with brief introductions or memoirs by Mackenzie, among them *Father Tom and the Pope, or a Night at the Vatican* (1868), by Sir Samuel Ferguson, which Mackenzie attributed to John Fisher Murray. Mackenzie seems not to have taken too seriously his relation of literary god-father to these works and the introductions are often perfunctory. They are useful chiefly as indicating that his name on the title-page of a book had commercial value.

[Sketch by D. J. O'Donoghue, in *Dict. Nat. Biog.*; Frederic Boase, *Modern English Biog.* (1897); *Ballou's Pictorial Drawing-Room Companion,* Jan. 12, 1856; *Public Ledger* (Phila.), Nov. 22, 1881; *Notes and Queries,* Sept. 28, 1907, p. 247; occasional references in his books; a few letters in the Pa. Hist. Soc. and the N. Y. Pub. Lib.; certain data from a daughter, Dr. Marion Mackenzie, of Philadelphia.]
A. C. B.

MACKENZIE, WILLIAM (July 30, 1758–July 23, 1828), bibliophile and book-collector, was probably the only child of Kenneth Mackenzie and his wife Mary, daughter of Edward Thomas of Barbados. His parents were married at Christ Church, Philadelphia, on Dec. 12, 1754. It is possible that his father was of Scottish birth, since William later became an active member of the St. Andrew's Society and bequeathed money to it in his will. The fact that he was entered a student at the Philadelphia Academy in 1766 by one Captain Morrell suggests that his father had died before that time. At the Academy he formed a lifelong friendship with his classmate, James Abercrombie, afterwards an associate pastor of Christ Church and principal of the Episcopal Academy for many years. After leaving the school he entered the counting-house of John Ross, one of the most eminent shipping merchants of the city and muster-master of the Pennsylvania navy. Here he acquired an extensive knowledge of mercantile and shipping affairs, in which he never entirely lost interest; at his death he bequeathed one thousand dollars for the relief of distressed ship-masters.

By temperament, however, he was little adapted to a business life, and when about thirty years of age, he inherited an income sufficient to enable him to devote himself to scholarship and the collecting of books. In time he built up a library which, when he died, was one of the largest in the United States. He never married, and by his will bequeathed "to the Library Company of Philadelphia, 500 volumes, to be chosen by the directors, from his English books printed since the commencement of the eighteenth century; to the same, in trust for the Loganian Library all his books printed before the commencement of the eighteenth century, and 300 volumes more, to be chosen by the trustees, from his Latin and French books printed since that period" (*Daily Chronicle,* July 28, 1828). Large bequests to libraries were not common at that time and the generosity of William Mackenzie to his native city attracted much attention. His wishes were punctiliously fulfilled, and furthermore, all of his books which had not been bequeathed were purchased for the libraries, which thus, by purchase and bequest, acquired a total of 7,051 volumes, including examples of printing from the earliest European presses. Many of the important incunabula left to the Loganian Library are listed in the *Census of Fifteenth Century Books Owned in America* (1919) as being the only copies in America. Among these are Gratian's *Decretum,* printed at Nürnberg by Koberger in 1483; *Les Oeuvres de Senecque translatez de latin en francoys* printed by Verard at Paris without date; *Nicolaus Bessarion, Oratzione . . . contra il Turcho, vulgarizate,* Venice, 1471. Included also are a Pliny on vellum printed by Jenson in 1476, and other works from that important press, and the *Biblia latina cum postillis Nicolai de Lyra,* printed by Paganinus at Venice in 1495. The library is rich, moreover, in early English printing, and in this section is included a fine Caxton, the first edition of the Golden Legend in English, printed about 1485 (Seymour De Ricci, *A Census of Caxtons,* 1909, p. 103). There is a vast quantity of miscellaneous literature, both English and European, and much valuable Americana.

Mackenzie's portrait, painted by John Neagle in 1829 and presented to the Library Company of Philadelphia by Dr. James Abercrombie, now hangs in the Reading Room of that institution. It suggests a gentle and scholarly personality. Abercrombie described him as being without an enemy, adding: "at least, from the purity of his principles and correctness of his conduct, I am sure he never deserved one." The author of the short account prefixed to the catalogue of his books in the Loganian Library (possibly Judah Dobson who printed the pamphlet), thus describes him: "His constitution, though vigorous, was not robust, his manners plain and conciliatory, his hand and his purse were ever open and ready to relieve individual and domestic distress, and contribute to public requisitions; in short, in every relation which he bore to society, he exhibited a truly estimable and exemplary character. . . . He was an accomplished Belles Lettres and classical scholar, and the tenor of his life was an uniform illustration of his principles and the benevolence of his heart."

[Official records at City Hall and Christ Church, Phila., and at the Univ. of Pa.; minutes of the Library Company of Phila.; *Catalogue of the Books Belonging to the Loganian Library,* vol. II (1829); *Daily Chronicle* (Phila.), July 24, 1828, and *Democratic Press* (Phila.), July 29, 1828.] A. S. W. R.

MACKEY, ALBERT GALLATIN (Mar. 12, 1807–June 20, 1881), Masonic writer and encyclopedist, was born in Charleston, S. C., the youngest son of Dr. John Mackey, also a native South Carolinian, of Scotch descent. The latter was a physician, editor, and teacher. He conducted *The Investigator* from its establishment in 1812 to 1817, and in 1826 published *The American Teacher's Assistant and Self-Instructor's Guide.* Albert received a good English education and an elementary classical one, which later he extended greatly by private study. After teaching school for a time, he entered the South Carolina Medical College, Charleston, and graduated in 1832, receiving the first prize for his Latin thesis. On Dec. 27, 1836, he married Sarah Pamela Hubbell, daughter of Sears Hubbell, a sea-captain of Connecticut ancestry. He practised medicine in Charleston and became demonstrator of anatomy in the Medical College. In 1854, however, his increasing interest in Freemasonry impelled him to relinquish his profession and devote his entire time to the interests of the Masonic fraternity. When South Carolina seceded from the Union he espoused the latter's cause and remained steadfast throughout the Civil War, although practically all the citizens of Charleston were Southern sympathizers. Confined within the city limits he gave his time, his energies, and his substance to the succor of his brethren, little heeding whether they belonged North or South. After the war he made a journey to the North, where he was received with enthusiastic and substantial manifestations of gratitude and appreciation. In July 1865 he was appointed by President Johnson collector of the port of Charleston.

Mackey was a Mason in St. Andrew's Lodge, No. 10 of Charleston in 1841, shortly thereafter joining Solomon's Lodge, No. 1 of the same city, of which he became master in 1842. He was a member and presiding officer of practically all the subordinate bodies of the various rites of Freemasonry, eventually becoming grand secretary of the Grand Lodge, grand high priest of the Grand Chapter, grand master of the Grand Council, and general grand high priest of the General Grand Chapter of the United States. The last decade of his life was spent in Washington, D. C., where he devoted himself to the continuance of his work as secretary general of the Supreme Council of the 33rd Degree, having held this office since 1844. While Mackey attained high official positions in Freemasonry, it is chiefly through his literary labors for the fraternity that his name has been perpetuated. Most of his writings are still in constant demand, and his *Encyclopædia of Freemasonry* is a standard authority, which, with slight revisions, continues to be republished at frequent intervals. His first book was *A Lexicon of Freemasonry* (1845), after which appeared in quick succession *The Mystic Tie* (1849), *The Ahiman Rezon, or Book of Constitutions of the Grand Lodge of South Carolina* (1852), *Principles of Masonic Law* (1856), *The Book of the Chapter* (1858), *A*

Text Book of Masonic Jurisprudence (1859), *History of Freemasonry in South Carolina* (1861), *Manual of the Lodge* (1862), *Cryptic Masonry* (1867), *Mackey's Masonic Ritualist* (1869), *The Symbolism of Freemasonry* (1869), *Encyclopædia of Freemasonry* (1874), *Masonic Parliamentary Law* (1875). He was the editor of a number of Masonic magazines, a contributor to many others, and some of his many Masonic addresses have been printed.

Mackey was of stalwart and commanding presence with somewhat harsh but striking features, replete with intelligence and amiability; he conversed well and was liked as a genial and companionable man, of cheerful, tolerant and kindly nature, who, if he had quarrels with individuals, had none with the world (Pike, *post*, p. 203). His death occurred at Old Point Comfort, Va., and he was buried in Glenwood Cemetery, Washington, D. C.

[Mackey's *Encyc. of Freemasonry* (1929), revised by R. I. Clegg; T. A. W. Melcher, *A Hist. Sketch of S. C. Commandery, No. 1, K. T.* (1900); Albert Pike, *Ex Corde Locutiones: Words from the Heart . . . 1860–1891* (copr. 1899); *Freemasons' Monthly Mag.*, vols. I–VI, VIII, X, XIII, XXII (1841–63); *Masonic Eclectic* (Washington), July 1881; *Masonic Rev.* (Cincinnati), Aug. 1881; Walter Hubbell, *Hist. of the Hubbell Family* (1915); *Washington Post*, June 21, 27, 1881; *News and Courier* (Charleston), June 21, 1881.]

W. L. B.

McKIM, CHARLES FOLLEN (Aug. 24, 1847–Sept. 14, 1909), architect, born at Isabella Furnace, Chester County, Pa., was the second of the two children of James Miller McKim [*q.v.*] and Sarah Allibone (Speakman) McKim, who made their home in Philadelphia. He was named for Charles Follen [*q.v.*], the first professor of German at Harvard, who lost his position on account of his anti-slavery activities. McKim's father spent his life in promoting the abolition of slavery and the education of freedmen; his mother, a Quaker, was an ardent advocate and helper in the same cause. Yet the rancor and strife of the bitter struggle did not cross the threshold; there was neither plenty nor meagerness; and the amenities of life were cultivated in the home. Trained in the school of that ardent abolitionist, Theodore D. Weld, at Perth Amboy, N. J., and in the Philadelphia public schools, Charles McKim prepared for the Lawrence Scientific School at Harvard, with the purpose of becoming a mining engineer. Entering in 1866, he spent a year in Cambridge and longed for the better training of French schools. His father persuaded him to enter the architectural office of Russell Sturgis, in New York, because he had "a positive talent" for drawing. Still determined to go to Paris, McKim now bent his desires toward the École des Beaux Arts. In September 1867, he entered the Atelier Daumet; there he stayed until the spring of 1870, during which time he visited England, Germany, Austria, and northern Italy.

The threatened outbreak of the Franco-Prussian War sent American students from Paris. The McKim family were now settled in Orange, N. J., and Charles was taken into the New York office of Charles D. Gambrill and Henry H. Richardson [*q.v.*]. He was put in charge of the drawings at $8.00 a week, which meant independence and joy. Trinity Church, Boston, was then the chief work in the office. McKim's proclivities were towards early rather than modern French architecture; and the romantic element in Richardson's work appealed to him. He was bent on establishing a practice of his own, and, when several small commissions came to him, he took rooms near the Richardson offices for his special work. Thither by chance came William Rutherford Mead [*q.v.*], fresh from European study, and for several years they worked together on their individual commissions, until in 1878 a partnership was formed by McKim, Mead, and William B. Bigelow. The next year Bigelow gave way to Stanford White [*q.v.*], who had succeeded to McKim's place in the Richardson office.

Even before the partnership, McKim, Mead, Bigelow, and White had made a walking trip to New England, visiting Boston, Salem, Marblehead, Newburyport, and Portsmouth in order to measure and draw specimens of colonial architecture. They had become convinced that the style of architecture based on classical precedents developed in England by Sir Christopher Wren, brought to America by the English colonists, and practised in New England by Charles Bulfinch [*q.v.*] was fundamentally the style best suited to the life of the American people, in both their homes and their public buildings. From this conviction the firm of McKim, Mead & White has not departed during more than half a century. The further tendency towards the Italian Renaissance came largely from Joseph M. Wells, who entered the office in 1879 and who, in spite of an unsocial nature, became the intimate friend and companion of the three partners and of Augustus Saint-Gaudens as well. Having reached their own conclusions, these men had the ability to win over their clients, for each of whom they created a distinct, individual work of art. It would have been easy and natural to follow the then popular Richardson tradition. McKim has made plain the point of departure from it. He wrote deliberately in 1905 that Richardson, "an artist and a man of genius," finding the methods of the École des Beaux Arts slow and laborious, "coined for himself a style eclectic, personal and romantic—Gothic in spirit, Romanesque in detail—robust, virile, ingenious, but wholly barbaric: remarkable for its absence of proportion and sense of real beauty; in the hands of his followers lawless, and now happily extinct" (Charles Moore, compiler, *The Promise of American Architecture,* 1905, p. 23 note). In Paris, McKim learned the essential value of the plan; he first pondered the problem, the purpose of the structure; when he had mastered that he gave thought to the exterior. The plan of the Century Club, New York, is McKim's; the general design of the unique exterior is Stanford White's; the details, an architectural triumph in themselves, are Joseph M. Wells's. Such cooperation was characteristic of the office.

It took several years, however, for convictions to ripen into actualities. McKim's early predilection for the romantic found vent in the Newport Casino, designed in 1881 at the behest of James Gordon Bennett as the social center of Newport life. The use of the Romanesque marked the McKim group of buildings (1884) at Narragansett Pier, R. I., most of which have disappeared. In 1882, Henry Villard, by marriage a connection of the McKim-Garrison family, commissioned McKim to build the group of houses on Madison Avenue between 50th and 51st Streets. The result (the combined work of McKim, White, Wells, and George F. Babb), designed in the style of the Italian Renaissance, marked a departure in American architecture so novel as to bring to the firm high renown, and led directly to a commission (1887) to design the Boston Public Library, distinctly the work of McKim. The three features of the Boston plan are: a reading room extending across the entire front of the building and giving a maximum of light; an interior arcaded court with pool and accommodations for out-of-doors reading in summer; and a monumental staircase leading from the offices below to the main floor, after the Italian fashion. These elements settled, the exterior design was studied with relation to the picturesque mass of Richardson's Trinity Church opposite and the square-towered New Old South Church at the left, both prominent features of Copley Square. McKim's conviction was that a building based on classical precedents would hold its own in any company, irrespective of size. His direct inspiration for the series of arched windows along the front came from the Coliseum; and in working out the design of the façade the resemblance to the Library of Ste. Geneviève in Paris was immediately remarked in his office when he sent the drawings from Boston. Such resemblance, so far from disturbing McKim, caused satisfaction; it proved that he was working along the lines of the best traditions in architecture. Applying a quotation from Lowell, one may say: "Always he took the coinage of the past and reminted it to suit his own purposes, giving to it his own image and superscription."

As in all McKim's monumental work, the conception of the Boston Library grew both in intensity and extent. He seized the opportunity to create a building that should express the civic consciousness of an old, proud, wealthy city, in which learning was the most valued tradition. So this Library, with its rare collections of books, should give proper setting to these heaped-up treasures, and at the same time provide for the everyday uses of a multitude of readers. Hence the rare marbles, the like of which had never been used in the United States; the obtaining of them in proper sizes and color, and at the proper times, was a triumph in itself. Then he had to surmount the objections to vastly enlarged appropriations as the project grew and expanded, and also criticisms of details so novel as to excite opposition. To McKim the idea of a monumental building without sculpture and painting was unthinkable—painting and sculpture not as mere adornment but as constituent parts, equal to the architecture itself. From the beginning he had the constant advice of Augustus Saint-Gaudens and Stanford White; and it was due to this consensus of minds that John S. Sargent and Edwin A. Abbey were induced to enter the field of mural painting and undertake the works which have come to be among the most important of their achievements. Also, Puvis de Chavannes, greatest of mural painters of his epoch, was brought to decorate the grand stairway with a series of designs of great dignity and beauty. Saint-Gaudens himself was to execute two groups in sculptural harmony with the architecture of the entrance, but, through vicissitudes regrettable but unavoidable, he is represented only by the shields over the doorways. However, Louis Saint-Gaudens, D. C. French, and F. W. MacMonnies contributed vitally to the ensemble. This first masterpiece of McKim embodied characteristic results of his thought and daring afterwards exhibited in many of his works.

For the Chicago World's Fair of 1893 he designed the colossal and highly adorned Agricultural Building and also the exquisite New York State Building (based on the Villa Medici); especially he had to do with perfecting the architectural scheme of the Court of Honor. To this orderly arrangement of monumental buildings and their landscape settings one traces the movement for city planning in the United States, which followed close upon the Chicago Fair. The popular acclaim excited at Chicago by Daniel H. Burnham [*q.v.*] and his associates led Senator James McMillan [*q.v.*] to select Burnham, McKim, and Saint-Gaudens, together with the younger Olmsted, to make the Plan of 1901, according to which the capital of the nation is being developed on a scale previously unequaled. Here McKim's especial part was to design the central composition from the Capitol to the Potomac, including gardens about the Washington Monument, the location of, and tentative sketches for, the Lincoln Memorial (designed by Henry Bacon, for nine years in the McKim office), and for the Arlington Memorial Bridge and the Water Gate, subsequently redesigned and executed by McKim, Mead, and White, under the immediate supervision of William M. Kendall, who began direct association with McKim in 1882. The office of McKim, Mead, and White came to be regarded by young architects as the best training school in America, because of the inspiration that resulted from two such harmoniously different men as McKim and White, and their methods of encouraging and requiring the young men to think for themselves.

McKim's inherent modesty and his respect for the good work of predecessors were manifested in his restoration of the White House (1902–03) at the call of President and Mrs. Theodore Roosevelt. Here he took the work of Hoban and Latrobe, removed from it later excrescences, and carried it on in their spirit to a culmination that the resources at their disposal did not permit. In the design of the Army War College buildings in Washington, about the same time, he took a motive found on the spot (Bulfinch's, as it has since turned out) and developed it as a capable musician develops an indigenous theme, building quite simply in brick and stone. McKim's ingenuity found play in dealing with the problem of locating the new Columbia University on Morningside Heights, in New York. Others would have cut off the top of the hill to make a plateau. McKim built to the height of three stories on the sides of the hill, thereby saving space and creating a platform at the level of the pinnacle. Then he made the central feature a monumental library of stone and built the subordinate buildings of brick, quite in a style of their own, closer to Italy than to England, and designed especially to obtain a maximum of light and air. The Harvard gates and fence, so severely criticized by Charles Eliot Norton at the time of building, have become a standard type for universities. They were a deliberate start "to bring Harvard back to bricks and mortar," now an accomplished feat.

In 1903 it fell to McKim's lot to design at one and the same time the Pierpont Morgan Library, called by President Charles W. Eliot "the most exquisite architectural gem of our country, and among the masterpieces of the world" (Moore, *post*, p. 283), and also the Pennsylvania Railway Station (1904–10), both in New York, the latter the largest building that had ever been erected at one time. The exterior was constructed entirely of pink granite and the interior of travertine from Rome. In both cases, his persuasiveness with his clients overcame obstacles to the creation of structures according to McKim's ideas rather than the original conceptions of the clients. The University Club in New York, considered by many McKim's masterpiece, has, for the decoration of its library, paintings based on those in the Borgia apartments of the Vatican. For the painter, McKim selected H. Siddons Mowbray, with the avowed purpose of having in America an example of the finest decorations in the world.

Feeling keenly his own limitations and lack of early training, and the limitations of the young men who came into his office, McKim was a devout believer in such schools as the French Academy, founded in Rome by Louis XIV. From the time of the Chicago Fair in 1893 till his death his one consuming purpose was to establish an American Academy in Rome, where young men of high promise might have, under competent direction, association with the masterpieces of all time. He felt that such traveling scholarships as he established at Columbia and Harvard were not enough. He aimed to bring into a community of life and endeavor students in architecture, landscape architecture, sculpture, painting, and music, each one sharing with kindred spirits the enjoyment of past achievements as incentives to future mastery of those problems which the increase of wealth and taste in America would inspire. From small beginnings, supported by his own contributions and those of his friends, the school grew year by year, obtained government recognition (but not support) and persisted until it has become the highest embodiment of American training in the fine arts.

McKim was married on Oct. 1, 1874, to Annie Bigelow of New York; one daughter was born to them. On June 25, 1885, he married Julia Amory Appleton of Boston; she died in 1887. The deaths of Stanford White in 1906, and of Augustus Saint-Gaudens in 1907, broke ties that were the essence of McKim's life. In January 1908 he left the office, suffering from overwork;

he retained an intermittent interest in affairs until his death at St. James, Long Island, on Sept. 14, 1909. He was buried with his family in Rosedale Cemetery, Orange, N. J. At the memorial meetings in New York (Nov. 23) and in Washington (Dec. 15) tributes to his work and worth were paid by his friends, Elihu Root, President Taft, and Joseph H. Choate, as well as by his professional associates. He received honorary degrees from Harvard, Columbia, and Princeton, and, in 1903, the gold medal of the Royal Institute of British Architects; he was posthumously awarded that of the American Institute of Architects. An exquisite memorial to him in the American Academy in Rome, an inscription on the pavement in front of the Columbia Library, and a tablet placed by the architects of Boston in their Public Library keep alive the name of a modest man and an architect eminent in the history of his art.

[Photographs and measured drawings of the architectural work of McKim, Mead, and White have been published in a series of sumptuous volumes. The issue of *The Brickbuilder, An Architectural Monthly*, Feb. 1910, is devoted to McKim. It contains a critical sketch by Royal Cortissoz; see also articles by him in *Scribner's Mag.*, Jan. 1910, July 1929. L. G. White, *Sketches and Designs by Stanford White* (1920), shows the contrasting characters of the two sympathetic men. *The Life and Times of Charles Follen McKim* (1929), by Charles Moore, gives the intimate side of his working life, and has lists of the men in the office and the buildings designed by the firm. See also A. H. Granger, *Charles Follen McKim: A Study of his Life and Work* (1913); C. H. Reilly, *McKim, Mead and White* (1924); *N. Y. Times*, Sept. 15, 1909. McKim letters relating to the plan of Washington and the restoration of the White House are in the Lib. of Cong.] C. M.

McKIM, ISAAC (July 21, 1775–Apr. 1, 1838), merchant, congressman, was born in Philadelphia, Pa., the son of John and Margaret (Duncan) McKim. His grandfather, Judge Thomas McKim, came from Londonderry, Ireland, about 1734, and settled first in Philadelphia, then in Brandywine, Del. John McKim established a mercantile business in Baltimore. When Isaac was nine years old, his mother died, leaving two small sons, to whom the father gave his personal care as they grew up. Isaac attended the public schools, and at an early age began to work in his father's office. At twenty-one he went into partnership with his father in the shipping and importing firm of John McKim & Son, and five years later John McKim retired from active business. Under the direction of Isaac McKim the importing business continued to expand and prosper. It was interrupted briefly by the War of 1812, during which he acted as aide-de-camp to Gen. Samuel Smith, commander of the forces defending Baltimore. In this emergency he advanced $50,000 for the city's defenses.

McKim was a leader in the commercial and industrial life of Baltimore. His importing business firmly established, he built in 1822 a large steam flour mill for which he had to import the machinery from England. A few years later he built a great copper rolling and refining works, and was said to be the largest copper importer and manufacturer in the United States. He was one of the organizers of the Baltimore & Ohio Railroad, and was a member of its first board of directors, 1827–31. His ships were on every sea. His life-long passion for them was based on thorough knowledge and early experience. It is said that when he was a young man his father sent him to Europe as a supercargo on one of his ships. After a difficult voyage across the Atlantic, the captain thought the vessel unseaworthy, and had it inspected and condemned. Isaac McKim vigorously protested the judgment; the captain was left ashore, and McKim brought the ship home himself. In his day the fast, small "Baltimore clippers" were famous. After deliberating for some time, in 1832 he took to Kennard & Williamson, a ship-building firm, a plan for a much larger vessel, a "three-skysail-yarder," modeled along the slender lines of the clipper. It was built despite the derision of all the other ship owners, and christened the *Ann McKim* after his wife. He spared no expense upon it. The rails and hatches were mahogany; the cannon were cast of finest brass. For years it was the finest and fastest merchant ship afloat, and though no other ship was ever made just like it, it anticipated the famous Yankee clipper ships which began to appear about a decade later.

McKim gave much time to charitable enterprises and public service. With his brother he established a free coeducational school in 1821, in memory of his father. Later, he built and endowed a second free school. He served on the Baltimore library board and was a charter member of the Protective Society of Maryland, organized in 1816 to protect the liberty of free negroes. In 1821 he was elected to the Maryland Senate as a Democrat, and served from Dec. 4, 1821, to Jan. 8, 1823, when he resigned in order to fill a vacancy in the House of Representatives of the Seventeenth Congress, caused by the resignation of Gen. Samuel Smith. He was elected for the succeeding term, serving Jan. 8, 1823–Mar. 3, 1825, and later returned to the Twenty-third, Twenty-fourth, and Twenty-fifth congresses (1833–38), in which he served on the House ways and means committee. His death, in Washington, followed a brief illness during a session of Congress in 1838, and he was buried in St. Paul's churchyard, Baltimore. His wife, Ann Bowly of Baltimore, whom he married Dec. 21, 1808, survived him some thirty-seven years. They had no children.

[*Biog. Dir. Am. Cong.* (1928); *Baltimore, Past and Present* (1871); *Md. Hist. Mag.*, Dec. 1906, Sept. 1914; A. H. Clark, *The Clipper Ship Era* (1910); Hawthorne Daniel, *The Clipper Ship* (1928); C. C. Cutler, *Greyhounds of the Sea: The Story of the American Clipper Ship* (1930); *Daily National Intelligencer* (Washington, D. C.), Apr. 2, 5, 1838; name of wife and date of marriage from Md. Hist. Soc., Baltimore.]

I. L. T.

McKIM, JAMES MILLER (Nov. 14, 1810–June 13, 1874), anti-slavery leader, born at Carlisle, Pa., was the grandson of James McKim who came in 1774 from the north of Ireland to Carlisle and there married Hannah McIlvaine; he was the son of James McKim (1779–1831) and Catharine Miller (1783–1831), the latter of German descent. Graduating at Dickinson College at the age of eighteen (1828), he studied for a few weeks in 1831 at Princeton Theological Seminary and attended Andover Theological Seminary (1832–33). After ordination by the Wilmington Presbytery in October 1835, he was settled as the first pastor of the Presbyterian church at Womelsdorf, Berks County, Pa., virtually a home-missionary field rather than the foreign field to which he aspired. William Lloyd Garrison's attack on the American Colonization Society led McKim into the movement for the immediate emancipation of the slaves, and in 1833 he represented a Carlisle negro constituency in the Philadelphia convention at which the American Anti-Slavery Society was formed. Being the youngest delegate, he attracted the attention of the leaders, among them Lucretia Mott. His "New School" theology had already closed orthodox Presbyterian doors; his talks against slavery in Carlisle and elsewhere, together with the permanent conversion of the entire membership of his church to the anti-slavery cause, brought him into antagonism with the prevailing public sentiment. Drawn into association and cooperation with James and Lucretia Mott, McKim resigned his charge and, in a letter explaining the growth of his religious convictions, withdrew from the ministry. He became one of the "seventy" gathered from all professions, whom the eloquence of Theodore D. Weld inspired to spread the gospel of emancipation. His stipend of eight dollars a week laid him open to the charge of being bought by "British gold."

In 1838–39 the name of James M. McKim appears on the rolls of the medical school of the University of Pennsylvania. On Oct. 1, 1840, he married Sarah Allibone Speakman (1813–1891), great-grand-daughter of Thomas Speakman, who came in 1712 from Reading, Berks, England, and settled in Chester County, Pa. She was a Quaker beauty who used her feminine attractions to further the anti-slavery cause. They had two children, Charles Follen [*q.v.*] and Lucy, who married Wendell Phillips Garrison; their adopted daughter, McKim's niece, became Garrison's second wife. The McKims found their service mainly in the protection of fugitive-slaves, and in systematic resistance to legalized slave-hunts and slave-captures. William Still wrote from fourteen years' companionship: "James Miller McKim, as one of the earliest, most faithful, and ablest abolitionists in Pennsylvania, occupied a position of influence, labor and usefulness, scarcely second to Mr. Garrison" (*Underground Railroad,* p. 655). At the time of his marriage McKim was publishing agent of the Pennsylvania Anti-Slavery Society, in Philadelphia; he succeeded John Greenleaf Whittier as editor of the *Pennsylvania Freeman*; then as corresponding secretary he had a share in all the anti-slavery work both local and national. These duties were particularly arduous by reason of the fact that, to use his own expression, the Fugitive-slave Law had "turned Southeastern Pennsylvania into another Guinea Coast" (Still, p. 580).

In 1859 McKim and his wife accompanied Mrs. John Brown to Harpers Ferry to take leave of her husband and receive his body. In the winter of 1862 McKim started the Philadelphia Port Royal Relief Committee to provide for the wants of ten thousand slaves suddenly liberated, and the report on his visit to the Sea Islands of South Carolina was used in America and in Europe as the basis of operations (*The Freed Men of South Carolina,* 1862). He urged the enlistment of colored men as soldiers and had part in creating Camp William Penn, which added eleven regiments to the Union army. In 1863 he became corresponding secretary of the Pennsylvania Freedmen's Relief Association, traveling through the South to establish schools and through the North to organize public sentiment. In 1865 he removed to New York as the corresponding secretary of the American Freedman's Union Commission, which he helped to organize with the aim of promoting education among the blacks. On his motion the Commission disbanded (July 1, 1869), its work having been accomplished. In 1865 he raised a portion of the capital required to found *The Nation,* with which his son-in-law Wendell Phillips Garrison was so long connected, first as literary editor and finally as editor-in-charge.

McKim established the family home at Llewellyn Park, Orange, N. J., where he died June 13, 1874.

[William Still, *The Underground Railroad* (1872); Charles Moore, *The Life and Times of Charles Follen McKim* (1929); W. L. Garrison, Jr., *In Memoriam: Sarah A. McKim* (1891), including genealogies; *N. Y. Tribune*, June 15, 16, 1874.] C. M.

McKINLEY, CARLYLE (Nov. 22, 1847–Aug. 24, 1904), journalist, essayist, and poet, was born at Newnan, Coweta County, Ga., the son of Charles G. and Frances (Jackson) McKinley. He was also known as Carl McKinley. He entered the Confederate army with a student company and subsequently saw active service in the battles around Atlanta. After the Civil War he became a cotton broker in Augusta, Ga., and later worked in the United States marshal's office at Savannah, Ga. He entered the Columbia Theological Seminary at Columbia, S. C., where he graduated with distinction in 1874. Shortly after graduation he was married to Elizabeth H. Bryce, the daughter of Campbell R. Bryce. Owing to a change in his theological views he refrained from entering the ministry and became a teacher in the school of Hugh S. Thompson [*q.v.*] at Columbia. During this teaching his interest in literature and writing became aroused, and in 1875 he was made the Columbia correspondent for the Charleston *News and Courier*. In 1879 he went to Washington to be correspondent for the paper and in 1881 went to Charleston to become associate editor. This position he held until failing health just before his death caused his retirement.

He was a brilliant essayist, an editor with a clear insight into public questions, and a poet of considerable ability. His monographs, *An Appeal to Pharaoh* (1889), a powerful analysis of the negro question, "The August Cyclone . . . of 1885," and "A Descriptive Narrative of the Earthquake . . . of 1886," in the *Year Book . . . City of Charleston* for 1885 and for 1886, are noted for their vigorous and highly artistic prose style. His verse, published in *Selections from the Poems of Carlyle McKinley* (1904), is of great beauty. It is mostly subjective and reflective in theme and it exhibits the bravery and the hopefulness of the Southern writers during the Reconstruction period. He sometimes indulged, however, in the romantic, satiric, and humorous types of poetry, but he was always restrained and had a delicate sense of humor. The charm of his expression of his own faith and optimism made for him a place as one of the chief Southern poets of the period.

[*In Loving Memory of Carlyle McKinley*, ed. by W. A. Courtenay (1904); G. A. Wauchope, *The Writers of South Carolina* (1910); W. A. Courtenay, "Carlyle McKinley," in *The Library of Southern Literature*, ed. by E. A. Alderman and J. C. Harris, vol. VIII (copr. 1907); M. L. Rutherford, *The South in History and Literature* (1907); *News and Courier* (Charleston), Aug. 25, 1904.] R. D. B.

McKINLEY, JOHN (May 1, 1780–July 19, 1852), representative, senator, and associate justice of the United States Supreme Court, was born in Culpeper County, Va., the son of Mary (Logan) and Andrew McKinley, a physician. In his early childhood his parents moved to Kentucky, where his mother's family was numerous and well-connected. As a young man, he became a mechanic. After reading law he was admitted to the bar, and practised at Frankfort and at Louisville, Ky. About 1818 he followed the tide of immigration into the Tennessee Valley of Alabama, settled at Huntsville, then the center for a powerful group of planters, lawyers, and politicians, and with his customary vigor plunged into law practice and politics. In 1820 he entered the state legislature, and two years later he was a candidate for the seat in the United States Senate made vacant by the resignation of John W. Walker. The Georgia machine supported him, but his fellow townsman, William Kelly, the leader of the popular cause, defeated him by a majority of one vote. The death of Henry Chambers in 1826 gave him another chance at a much coveted seat in the Senate, and he entered the contest against Clement Comer Clay, of Huntsville, ex-chief justice of the Alabama supreme court and a prominent planter. McKinley had attracted a good deal of popularity by abandoning the moribund Georgia machine after 1824 and attaching himself to the rising star of Andrew Jackson. Even the Huntsville *Democrat*, claiming to be the people's tribune, supported him, though only three years previously it had felt constrained to reject him as an aristocrat. He was victorious over Clay by three votes and served from Nov. 27, 1826, to Mar. 3, 1831. During his senatorial term he moved to Florence, Ala., which had recently been projected on a pretentious scale and promised to become a great city.

When he stood for reëlection he was defeated decisively by Gabriel Moore [*q.v.*] of Huntsville. He represented Lauderdale County in the legislature in 1831, and two years later he was elected to Congress over James Davis of Franklin County. He did not seek reëlection. Instead, he returned to the state legislature in 1836 with a view to succeeding Moore, who had fallen into public disfavor by opposing Jackson's plans to make Van Buren his successor to the presidency. McKinley's own support of Jackson and of Van Buren as his successor had been unflagging, so when Moore made no effort to succeed himself, he was elected to the seat. Before he qualified as senator Van Buren appointed him, on Apr. 22, 1837, as associate justice of the United States Supreme Court. He held this position till his death. He continued to live simply and devoted himself to his work at Washington and on the circuit. He was a conscientious, hard-working judge, and even in his last years when he was ill and increasingly feeble he forced himself to attend to the duties of his office. He died in Louisville, Ky., where he had made his home after his elevation to the supreme bench. He was married twice: first to Juliana Bryan and later to Elizabeth Armistead.

[H. Levin, *The Lawyers and Lawmakers of Ky.* (1897); *The Biog. Encyc. of Ky.* (1878); T. M. Green, *Historic Families of Ky.* (1889); memorial remarks in the Supreme Court in 14 *Howard,* pp. iii–v; T. M. Owen, *Hist. of Ala.* (1921), vol. IV; Willis Brewer, *Ala.* (1872), p. 297; T. H. Jack, *Sectionalism and Party Politics in Ala.* (1919); T. P. Abernethy, *The Formative Period in Ala.* (1922); *The Second Gathering of the Clan MacKinlay at Chicago . . . 1894* (1894), p. 11; *Daily Louisville Times,* July 20, 21, 1852.] A. B. M.

McKINLEY, WILLIAM (Jan. 29, 1843–Sept. 14, 1901), twenty-fifth President of the United States, was born at Niles, Ohio, seventh of the nine children of William and Nancy (Allison) McKinley. A descendant of David McKinley, known as "David the Weaver," who settled in York County, Pa., about 1743, he came of Scotch-Irish stock (F. A. Claypool, *The Scotch Ancestors of William McKinley,* 1897). His father and grandfather, iron-founders on a small scale, followed the ore from the Susquehanna Valley to Columbiana County, Ohio. Schooled at Poland, Ohio, and at Allegheny College, Meadville, Pa., McKinley had taught a rural school before he enlisted at seventeen as a private in the Union army. Short, slight, and serious as a lad, he took on weight and power with years; and like Napoleon, whom the caricaturists thought he resembled, he bore himself so as to make dignity take the place of inches. He served through the Civil War with the 23rd Ohio Volunteer Regiment, under Rutherford B. Hayes, and at Antietam was a commissary sergeant. Shifted to the Shenandoah Valley, he saw duty at Kernstown, and at Cedar Creek where he was a captain. After being mustered out with brevet rank as major, he studied law in the office of Charles E. Glidden in Mahoning County, Ohio, and, for less than a year, in the Albany Law School. In 1867 he opened a law office at Canton, seat of Stark County, where he maintained residence for the rest of his life, and in 1869 he was elected prosecuting attorney. He married, on Jan. 25, 1871, Ida Saxton, daughter of a local banker and a member of a substantial family that had helped to found the town. The marriage was one of devoted affection, with the greater need for devotion when, after the birth and early death of two daughters, Ida McKinley became a chronic invalid (Josiah Hartzell, *Sketch of the Life of Mrs. William McKinley,* 1896; New York *Evening Post,* May 27, 1907).

Major McKinley, as he was generally known, flourished moderately at the Canton bar; and when in 1875 Hayes was for the third time a candidate for the governorship of Ohio McKinley was among his active supporters. The next year he was elected to Congress as representative from the 17th Ohio district. There is a tradition that President Hayes advised McKinley to study the tariff and to grow up with the issue, but there was no need for such advice to a young congressman who was sympathetic with his constituents, in close touch with Republican leaders, and aware that Southern Democrats were talking of tariff revision on the basis of revenue only. A few weeks after he made his first pronouncement upon the tariff (*Chicago Times,* Apr. 16, 1878), his future was threatened by a Democratic gerrymander of the Ohio congressional districts, whereby Stark County was thrown into a new 16th district. Yet he carried the district in 1878, earning distinction when men more prominent than he fell under the Democratic thrust. A Republican legislature restored his old district in 1880, when he was again elected. His plurality in 1882, however, was so low (only eight votes out of 33,000) that a Democratic House of Representatives unseated him (*Congressional Record,* 48 Cong., 1 Sess., pp. 4567–94). In the autumn of 1884 he faced a new adverse gerrymander with success; and in 1886, his old district having been restored, he was again elected. Once more successful in 1888, he had now become a national figure, able to command renomination by acclamation (Chicago *Daily Inter Ocean,* Apr. 18, 1888). His career in Congress was ended with the help of the third Democratic gerrymander that he had to face, and he was overcome in the landslide of 1890 (J. P. Smith, ed., *History of the Republican Party in Ohio,* 1898, vol. I, p. 699).

While McKinley was struggling upon the treacherous footing of Ohio politics, he was growing in public stature. He was made temporary chairman of the Ohio Republican convention in 1880, and at the end of the year Speaker S. J. Randall gave him Garfield's place on the committee on ways and means (*Congressional Record,* 46 Cong., 3 Sess., p. 281). In 1884 he was permanent chairman of the Ohio convention, and chairman of the committee on resolutions of the Republican National Convention (*Cincinnati Commercial-Gazette,* Apr. 25, June 6, 1884). He was active in the state convention that renominated Foraker for governor in 1885. In 1888, with new distinction from his brilliant warfare against the Mills Bill, he was once more made chairman of the committee on resolutions of the National Convention (*Chicago Tribune,* June 20, 1888); he was a Sherman man, but, over his protest, delegates were now voting for him as a nominee for President. He acquired, after the final failure of the Sherman movement in 1888, a loyal friend in Marcus Alonzo Hanna [*q.v.*] of Cleveland, a business man with money to spend for the advancement of protection. With Hanna's active support, McKinley was elected governor of Ohio in 1891, at a time when Republican fortunes seemed low; the governorship was to be his sounding board during two terms beginning in 1892. In that year at Minneapolis he was permanent chairman of the Republican National Convention. Hanna had an organization at work to make him President, but McKinley insisted on the renomination of Harrison and declined to permit a stampede to himself. He had, however, been tried and tested as a party leader, and was becoming "the foremost champion of protection" (*Chicago Tribune,* Jan. 9, 1894).

The Republican party became more closely identified with the protective tariff in each successive year of McKinley's congressional experience. The tariff was to him a national policy and not a cloak for special privilege to favored interests. He sniped continuously at Democratic attempts at revision, and in 1888 he so vigorously backed up the efforts of the venerable William D. [Pig Iron] Kelly, senior Republican on the committee on ways and means, that he outshone him. When a Republican Congress convened in December 1889, McKinley, trained and disciplined by long years in opposition, contested in the Republican caucus for the speakership. Reed, who won, made him chairman of the committee on ways and means, in charge of the new tariff bill (*New York Tribune,* Dec. 11, 1889). McKinley was, throughout the ensuing debate, the moderator and harmonizer. He challenged the influence of Blaine, who now made a plea for reciprocity, and he met the demand of Western Republicans who insisted that something be done for silver before they voted for the tariff. When the McKinley Bill became a law, Oct. 1, 1890, the November elections were so close at hand that there was no time to explain it even to patient constituencies, far less to the exasperated Western voters who resented an increase in retail prices for the benefit of Eastern manufacturers. As a result, a landslide placed the Democrats again in control of the House of Representatives.

Before McKinley was reëlected governor in 1893 his future was brought into hazard by the consequences of his kindness of heart. He had repaid early favors of an old friend, Robert L. Walker of Youngstown, by indorsing notes as an accommodation; so many, indeed, that when Walker failed in February 1893, McKinley was involved for nearly $130,000. This was much more than he possessed, and even with the aid of all of his wife's fortune, which she placed in Hanna's hands at once, the payment of the debt would have reduced them to poverty. His whole property was deeded to a group of trustees, headed by Myron T. Herrick and including Hanna, who raised from unnamed friends the funds needed to meet his deficit, and the estate of Mrs. McKinley was released (Kohlsaat, *post,* p. 10). The misadventure did not injure his political availability; in the congressional campaign of 1894 he was the outstanding campaigner for his party (*New York Times,* Oct. 25, 1894).

The identification of McKinley with the politics of protection, and a personal kindliness of spirit which enabled him to escape the bitter enmities that harassed many of his contemporaries, placed him in a commanding position in the Republican party after the death of Blaine. But as his availability for the presidency as a protectionist candidate increased, the voters turned away from the tariff to discuss free silver; and upon this issue McKinley was worse than unprepared. He did not believe, even after his nomination, that the currency could become a major issue. He had voted for free silver, and for the Bland-Allison Act over the veto of Hayes, in spite of his avowed admiration for Garfield's "greatest effort" of Nov. 16, 1877, against inflation (*Congressional Record,* 49 Cong., 1 Sess., p. 764). When the unrest of debtors was intensified by the depression of 1893 and free silver was urged as a panacea, some of McKinley's speeches might have been interpreted as favoring it. Only by heroic management did Hanna hold together his organization for the nomination of McKinley when the tariff issue yielded to that of silver. Since most of the Democratic state conventions had demanded free coinage of silver, it was clear that the Republicans must oppose this. It was also probable that an open avowal of the gold standard would drive out of the party many Western Republicans whose support would be badly needed. The platform was agreed upon before the convention met in St. Louis, June 16, 1896. Although many of the leaders later claimed the credit of inserting the word "gold" in the currency plank, Hanna was satisfied to have it there, with McKinley as the candidate, and yet to avoid adding to the pain of Western silver Republicans by seeming responsible for its presence. In the remarkable campaign that followed, while his eloquent rival William Jennings Bryan [*q.v.*] toured the country, and his astute manager Hanna collected funds, perfected organization, and distributed literature, McKinley remained in imperturbable dignity at his old home in Canton, reading carefully drafted arguments to the scores of delegations that were brought to his front porch. The fear of loss through payments in a fifty-cent silver dollar intensified Eastern support of the ticket, regardless of party; and a good harvest with an improving price of grain lessened hard times in the West sufficiently to reduce the bitterness of the demand for cheap money as a measure of debtor relief. McKinley was elected President in November 1896, with 271 electoral votes against 176 for Bryan and with more than 7,000,000 popular votes out of about 14,000,000 cast (Edward Stanwood, *A History of the Presidency,* 1898). He was the first President to receive a popular majority since 1872.

The administration that he set up was orthodox in its Republicanism, with little distinction. It did not include Hanna (though McKinley would have welcomed him), because Hanna did not wish an administrative post, and preferred to sit in the Senate in the seat of John Sherman [*q.v.*]. Sherman was accordingly offered the State Department, and invited to make the gesture for international bimetallism that the party had promised to offset its repudiation of free silver. Sherman, in his seventy-fourth year, was willing to make the transfer for he feared the stress of the approaching campaign in Ohio for reëlection, and it was all too possible that Hanna could then take the seat from him by force. He retained the post of secretary of state for a little more than a year, until his physical incompetence grew to be a danger during the war with Spain. In the Treasury, McKinley placed Lyman J. Gage, a hard-money banker who escaped the stigma of Wall Street by coming from Chicago. The remaining departments went to local politicians: Russell A. Alger (War), John D. Long (Navy), Joseph McKenna (Justice), James A. Gary (Post Office), Cornelius Bliss (Interior), and James Wilson (Agriculture). As vacancies later occurred, McKinley brought into his family men of real significance: John Hay as secretary of state, Elihu Root as secretary of war, and Philander C. Knox as attorney-general.

Except for the restoration of the high tariff and the establishment of the gold standard (which had to be deferred), the theory implicit in Republican ideology was that all that was needed was to let business and life alone, and to harmonize the clashing claims of interest with as little loss as possible. For this task McKinley was ideally suited. His long professional career had given him an intuitive knowledge of the psychology of members of Congress. His natural kindliness and consideration had been developed by the need of a protectionist to conciliate everyone in order to attain his own ends. He met angrily insistent men with a smile at his office door, and sent them away beaming, often wearing a red carnation from the presidential desk. He did not pretend to know more than Congress or his party; to him, as to so many in his generation, the Nation and the Republican party seemed merged as one, and he felt that neither could be other than right. He did not surrender his mind to any of his advisers, not even to Hanna, and he could not easily delegate authority to his subordinates, but he rarely allowed himself to stand far in advance of the opinion of his constituents. The new Congress met in March 1897, and carried through at once the tariff measure for which business men were waiting, the Dingley Act (1897).

The choice of Sherman as head of the State Department, "indecent and alarming," the *Nation* thought (Jan. 31, 1897), could be justified only on the score of party balance. Sherman was feeble and failing, and by ignorance and temper had shown unfitness to meet the difficult diplomatic problems growing out of the Cuban insurrection. McKinley soon faced the alternatives of leading the United States into a war which he abhorred, or of fighting the politicians of his party who were yielding to popular clamor and egging war on. He settled the matter when he referred it to Congress, for Congress was incapable of anything but a declaration of war. It directed him, Apr. 20, 1898, to intervene in Cuba in order to establish Cuban independence, disclaiming an intent to aggrandise the power of the United States in so doing. In the short contest with Spain that resulted, "as his own Chief of Staff, McKinley carried on the war" (W. H. Taft, in *The National McKinley Birthplace Memorial,* 1918, p. 78). There was no alternative, for the War Department and the army as erected by law were inadequate, Secretary Alger [*q.v.*] lacked the qualifications of a successful war minister, and there was no available general on the active list upon whom he was willing to rely. In the navy, matters were not so bad, less because of virtue than because any navy, to go to sea at all, must have in time of peace much of the organization that is required in time of war. Secretary John D. Long [*q.v.*] was indifferent to technical matters; but his very indifference gave freedom to his assistant secretary, Theodore Roosevelt, who made an impression upon the training of the fleet and the selection of its commanders. The experiences of mobilization and the management of the army brought mortification to McKinley, while the details of operations occasioned controversies that might have been disastrous had the enemy possessed any capacity for resistance; but before the mind of the government had been adjusted to the fact of war it was turned to the policy of the peace, to the stipulations required for the tutelage of Cuba, and to the situation of that part of the Philippine Archipelago that lay helpless under Dewey's guns. Again McKinley, not desiring annexations and sincere in his philanthropic gesture towards Cuba, was the slave of his technique. When he instructed his commissioners to negotiate peace at Paris (Royal Cortissoz, *The Life of Whitelaw Reid,* 1921, II, p. 226), he was not ready to say whether the Philippines should be returned, released, or kept. At this crisis he turned, as always, to his conscience, for he was devout and earnest; and to his party, which could not well be wrong (J. F. Rhodes, *The McKinley and Roosevelt Administrations, 1897–1909,* 1922, p. 107). From the former he derived a sense of duty to the Filipinos, whom Spain could not recapture, and who lacked the experience in self-government necessary to survive alone in the tempestuous waters of the Far East. From the latter, as he toured the Middle West in the summer, he gathered opinions reminiscent of the traditional Western attitude that expansion was a natural experience. On Oct. 26 he cabled the commissioners to hold the Archipelago. He had once characterized Garfield's determination to decide each question upon its merits, apart from politics, as an "experiment . . . a perilous one" (*Congressional Record,* 49 Cong., 1 Sess., p. 764); he commended its courage without following its example.

Before the treaty was signed at Paris, the voters had strengthened the Republican majorities in both House and Senate, and prosperity had so weakened the lure of free silver as to permit the passage of a gold-standard bill (Mar. 14, 1900). With the return of courage to business had come a renewal of the trust movement, for which no policy was ready, though there is some reason to believe that had McKinley lived he might have turned a constructive imagination upon the problem of the trusts. Congress, in 1900, passed laws for the government of the new insular possessions, knowing that before these could operate their constitutionality would be tested by the opponents of expansion. There could be no delay in the reorganization of the army and the navy, and Elihu Root, who had succeeded Alger in the War Department, guided essential laws through Congress. Nor could there be indifference towards the erection of civil government in the Philippine Islands, whither William H. Taft was sent; or towards the speedy construction of a canal at the Isthmus. John Hay [*q.v.*] negotiated with Great Britain to get rid of the limitations set by the Clayton-Bulwer Treaty (1850), only to be dismayed by a new spirit of nationalism that prevented the ratification of his agreement. He would have resigned in chagrin, but McKinley bade him "bear the atmosphere of the hour" (W. R. Thayer, *The Life and Letters of John Hay,* 1915, II, pp. 226–28), and prepared to negotiate such a treaty as the party leaders in the Senate would approve. While Cuba was working out a constitution under the guiding hand of Leonard Wood [*q.v.*], it was suspected that the Cubans had forgotten their debt to the United States for their existence. Accordingly, there was slipped through as a rider to the Army Act of 1901 the Platt Amendment requiring Cuba to refrain from financial suicide and to concede to the United States a right to protect Cuban independence and good order. The legal beginnings of a new imperialism were laid down in this provision. It was necessary, too, to determine how to hold the Philippines without the use of force, and with this end in view John Hay in 1899 invited the European Powers with interests in Chinese waters to agree to a self-denial of special advantage and to adopt an "Open-Door" policy. Revolution in China soon occasioned a joint intervention which tested the sincerity of all adherents to the new doctrine. Whatever its inclination, the United States could no longer keep aloof from the international issues that were arousing ambitions and jealousies among the Powers of the world.

The campaign of 1900 was noisy but tame; the issue of imperialism which Bryan tried to raise proved less successful in arousing emotion than free silver had been. Had Hobart been living, he would doubtless have been renominated with McKinley (D. Magie, *Life of Garret Augustus Hobart,* 1910); his death brought the nomination for the vice-presidency to Gov. Theodore Roosevelt, for whom McKinley and Hanna had scant liking but who was now too prominent to be openly resisted. McKinley and Roosevelt won easily, and the new administration started Mar. 4, 1901, without a jolt. Its position was strengthened a few weeks later by the decision of the Supreme Court in the Insular Cases, which upheld what had been done respecting the islands and denied the anti-imperialists the constitutional prohibition they sought. A new period of booming prosperity was opening, and the Republican business interests had no fear of adverse interference by the government. There might have developed some concern lest the President should start upon a new course after he announced at Buffalo, Sept. 5, 1901, that "the period of exclusiveness is past," and suggested doubts as to the complete sufficiency of the tariff policy upon which his fame as statesman was grounded. But an anarchist, Leon F. Czolgosz, shot the President during a public reception on the afternoon of Sept. 6, and he died at Buffalo eight days later. On his lips at the end was the phrase "It is God's way. His will, not ours, be done." He believed in "the divinity of Christ and a recognition of Christianity as the mightiest factor in the world's civilization"; and from his youth he had been by conviction a member of the Methodist Episcopal Church. He was buried at Canton, where in 1907 his wife was laid beside him in a great memorial tomb; at Niles, his birthplace, another memorial to his memory was erected. His personal associates maintained for the rest of their lives an affectionate loyalty to his memory such as few American statesmen have inspired; but upon his death the United States passed out of an era in its history.

[The official biography, C. S. Olcott, *The Life of William McKinley* (1916), contains probably as much as can be said about McKinley's private life, for he was not given to expression by the pen and left no private papers of importance. Much of the office file of his administration is in the custody of George B. Cortelyou of New York, who was his secretary. The following are of some value: Thos. Beer, *Hanna* (1929); N. W. Stephenson, *Nelson W. Aldrich, A Leader in Am. Politics* (1930); H. H. Kohlsaat, *From McKinley to Harding: Personal Recollections of Our Presidents* (1923); T. B. Mott, *Myron T. Herrick, Friend of France; An Autobiographical Biography* (1929); C. W. Thompson, *Presidents I've Known and Two Near Presidents* (1929). None of these, however, adds much information to the facts of his early life that were already recorded in the campaign biographies of 1896. The best of these is R. P. Porter, *Life of William McKinley, Soldier, Lawyer, Statesman,* which had fifteen editions before the end of the year. There are no monographs of consequence. The obituaries, long and laudatory, drew their material from the campaign biographies.]

F. L. P.

McKINLY, JOHN (Feb. 24, 1721–Aug. 31, 1796), president of Delaware, was born in the north of Ireland, settled in Wilmington, Del., and began the practice of medicine. In 1747–48 he seems to have been lieutenant of militia and in 1756 was commissioned major in a militia regiment of New Castle County. In three successive years, 1757, 1758, and 1759, he was elected sheriff, and in 1759 he was also elected chief burgess of the borough of Wilmington for a year's term, being reëlected eleven times including the year 1776. Between 1761 and 1766 he was married to Jane Richardson, the twelfth child of John and Ann Richardson, English Friends living near Wilmington. Elected a member of the colonial Assembly in October 1771, he was still a member when, in October 1773, that body appointed a standing committee of correspondence of which he became one of the five members. As chairman of the New Castle County committee he presided over the meeting that, on Nov. 28, 1774, approved the "Association" recommended by the First Continental Congress and over the meeting that in December issued a call for the organization of a county militia the next month. In March 1775 he served on the committee of the Assembly that drew up the instructions for the delegates to the Second Continental Congress. In March 1775 he was chosen colonel of a regiment of the New Castle County militia. At a meeting of the Council of Safety, begun at Dover on Sept. 11, 1775, he was not only elected president of the council but also brigadier-general of the three battalions of New Castle County. In October 1776 he was elected a member of the first state legislature and, when that body assembled in the same month, was elected speaker of the lower house. Although the constitution provided for the election of a governor (called president) by the legislature, no executive was chosen during the fall session of the General Assembly. Instead, the two houses in joint session, in November 1776, elected a Council of Safety to exercise executive authority during the next recess of the General Assembly. He was included in the membership of this council and, when it organized, was chosen its president.

At the following session of the General Assembly he was chosen, in February 1777, president and commander-in-chief of Delaware for a term of three years. He was destined to exercise the authority of the office only a few months, for on the second night after the Battle of the Brandywine several British regiments occupied Wilmington and captured him. He was removed to Philadelphia, kept a prisoner during the British occupation of that city, and then taken to New York. Paroled by General Clinton in August 1778, he proceeded to Philadelphia to obtain the consent of Congress to his exchange for William Franklin, late governor of New Jersey.

In September he returned to Wilmington, resumed the practice of medicine, and took no further part in politics. He assisted in founding the first medical society of Delaware in 1789 and served for a number of years as trustee of the First Presbyterian Church in Wilmington.

[Records of the borough of Wilmington and letters of McKinly in possession of the Hist. Soc. of Del., Wilmington; colonial and state records and letters in Public Archives at Dover; letters from and to McKinly in N. Y. Pub. Lib., Lib. of Hist. Soc. of Pa., Lib. of Cong., and in the private collection of Judge Richard S. Rodney, New Castle, Del.; Minutes of the Privy Council in Lib. of Cong., esp. vol. I, pp 43, 69; *Delaware Archives*, vols. I–III (1911–19); W. T. Read, *Life and Correspondence of George Read* (1870); J. T. Scharf, *Hist. of Del.* (1888), vol. I; *Biog. and Geneal. Hist. of Del.* (1899), vol. I; H. C. Conrad, *Hist. of the State of Del.* (1908), vols. I, III; Richard Richardson, *The Geneal. of the Richardson Family of Del.*, n.d.] G. H. R.

McKINSTRY, ALEXANDER (Mar. 7, 1822–Oct. 9, 1879), lawyer, Confederate soldier, lieutenant-governor of Alabama, was born at Augusta, Ga., the son of Alexander and Elizabeth (Thompson) McKinstry. His father was of Scotch-Irish descent, the great-grandson of Rev. John McKinstry who came from County Antrim, Ireland, to New England in 1718, settling in Connecticut in 1728. Orphaned before he was fourteen, Alexander went to Mobile, Ala., where he had relatives. There he served as clerk in a drugstore, read law in the office of John A. Campbell, and was admitted to the bar when he was twenty-three. He immediately began the practice of his profession and at the same time began to take an active part in local politics. Before 1860 he had held various city and county offices.

Although he was opposed to secession, he accepted the decision of the majority in the state when in January 1861 Alabama withdrew from the Union. Joining the Confederate army, he was commissioned colonel and assigned to the 32nd Regiment of Alabama Infantry when it was organized at Mobile in 1862. This regiment was attached to the Army of Tennessee under Gen. N. B. Forrest. McKinstry was mentioned in dispatches for able service in the field at Bridgeport, Ala., and Battle Creek, Tenn., Aug. 27, 1862, and was in command in Chattanooga in September and October. The following year he was on detached service, acting as provost marshal-general to the Army of Tennessee. On Apr. 6, 1864, he was made colonel of cavalry and assigned to serve on the court of military justice of Forrest's division. He was presiding judge of this court until the end of the war.

Paroled at Gainesville, Ala., May 9, 1865, McKinstry returned to Mobile and resumed the practice of his profession. He continued to take an active interest in politics, identifying himself with the Radical party which was then being formed in the state to oppose the Democratic party. Elected to the state legislature in 1865 and again in 1867, he was chairman of the judiciary committee and largely instrumental in securing the adoption of the Alabama Code of 1867 by the legislature. In 1872 he was elected lieutenant-governor of the state. By virtue of this office, created by the constitutional convention of 1867, he became presiding officer of the state Senate at a critical point in the reconstruction struggle. The Democrats had won a majority in both houses of the legislature, although the Radicals had succeeded in electing their candidates for governor and lieutenant-governor. This situation was particularly displeasing to the Radicals because they were anxious to send one of their number to the United States Senate and it fell to the legislature to elect him in joint session. It was McKinstry who, by the exercise of his authority as presiding officer of the Senate, enabled the Radical group to overcome the Democratic majority and send their candidate to Washington. With the return of the Democrats to power in 1874, McKinstry retired from politics. He died at Mobile in 1879. On Mar. 20, 1845, he had married Virginia Thompson Dade of Mobile, descendant of an old Virginia family; of their eleven children, five lived to maturity.

[T. M. Owen, *Hist. of Ala. and Dict. of Ala. Biog.* (1921), vol. IV; W. L. Fleming, *Civil War and Reconstruction in Ala.* (1905); Wm. Willis, *Geneal. of the McKinstry Family* (1858); *Daily Register* (Mobile, Ala.), Oct. 10, 1879; *War of the Rebellion: Official Records (Army)*.] H. F.

McKINSTRY, ELISHA WILLIAMS (Apr. 11, 1825–Nov. 1, 1901), California jurist, was born in Detroit, Mich., the seventh and youngest child of David Charles and Nancy Whiting (Backus) McKinstry. His great-grandfather, Capt. John McKinstry, had come to America from Armagh, Ireland, in 1740, settling first in Boston and later in Londonderry, N. H.; his grandfather, Charles, served as an officer with the New York troops in the Revolution; through his mother he was descended from Pilgrim ancestors. He was educated in Michigan and New York and at Kenyon College, Gambier, Ohio, and in 1847 was admitted to the bar in New York. The California gold rush of 1849 turned his eyes to the West, however, and he took passage on the S. S. *Panama,* one of the first steamers of the newly organized Pacific Mail Steamship Company, and sailed with her on her maiden voyage around the Horn, arriving in San Francisco June 4, 1849. By 1850 he had opened a law office in Sacramento and was chosen to represent that district in the lower branch of the first California legislature. A year later he removed to Napa, where in the fall of 1852 he again entered public service with his election to the post of district judge for Napa and adjoining counties. He was reëlected in 1858 and served until 1862, when he resigned to become candidate on the Democratic ticket for the lieutenant-governorship. He was defeated, however, and in 1863 moved to Nevada, where in 1864 he was unsuccessful candidate for the position of justice of the supreme court.

After several years' residence in Nevada, he returned to San Francisco (1867), where, as a Democrat, he was elected county judge and served in that capacity from Jan. 1, 1868, until his election as judge of the twelfth district court in October 1869. Four years later, he was chosen justice of the supreme court, in the last two instances having won the election on an Independent ticket. After the reorganization of the supreme court under the new constitution of 1879 he was reëlected and drew a term of eleven years. During his unusually long service on the supreme bench he dealt with some of the most important cases in California's judicial history, among them being the local option case of 1874 (*Ex Parte Wall*, 48 *Cal.*, 279), in which he delivered the opinion of the court, and the great controversy over water-rights, waged in 1886, known officially as the case of *Lux* vs. *Haggin* (69 *Cal.*, 255). On Oct. 1, 1888, he resigned from the bench to become professor of municipal law in Hastings' College of the Law, San Francisco. In 1890 he resumed private practice and was later joined by his son, James C. McKinstry. In 1896, they became members of the firm of Stanly, McKinstry, Bradley & McKinstry, from which in 1899 Stanly was removed by death. McKinstry had an enviable reputation as one of the ablest members of the San Francisco bar. He was a member of the Sons of the American Revolution and in 1900–01 was president of the Society of California Pioneers.

On July 27, 1863, at Marysville, Cal., he had married Annie L. Hedges, and four children were born to them. His death came suddenly at San José, Cal., where he was seeking recuperation in the warmer climate of the Santa Clara Valley.

[Wm. Willis, *Geneal. of the McKinstry Family* (1858); *New-Eng. Hist. and Geneal. Reg.*, Jan. 1859; O. T. Shuck, *Hist. of the Bench and Bar of Cal.* (1901); *San Francisco Chronicle*, Nov. 2, 1901.]

R. G. C—d.

McKNIGHT, ROBERT (*c.* 1789–March 1846), Santa Fé trader, miner, was born in Augusta County, Va., the son of Timothy and Eleanor (Griffin) McKnight. In 1809 he went to St. Louis and joined his brother John and Thomas Brady in a mercantile venture. In May 1812, Robert McKnight and nine others left St. Louis for Santa Fé on a trading expedition. This enterprise was designed to carry goods easy of transport, and expected to derive great profit under the monopolistic conditions then existing in Santa Fé. The descriptions given by Capt. Zebulon M. Pike [*q.v.*] of rich prospects at Santa Fé were attracting general notice to that trade. The McKnight party, greatly enthusiastic, started on their adventure without passports and without arms other than those for defense against the Indians. They proceeded believing that the declaration of independence by Hidalgo, in 1810, had completely removed the previous requirement of a special permit from the Spanish government in cases of foreign intercourse. Unfortunately, they had not learned of the execution of Hidalgo and the restoration of the Royalists, who were suspicious of all foreigners, particularly Americans, and imposed many hardships upon them.

When McKnight and his companions arrived at Santa Fé, they were seized as spies, and their goods confiscated. The captives, destined to be detained nine years, were distributed among several prisons, some being sent to Chihuahua and others to Durango. In 1815, Edward Hempstead, Congressional delegate from Missouri, laid their case before the State Department, but nothing was done in their behalf until Feb. 8, 1817, when Secretary Monroe began an exchange of diplomatic letters with the Spanish minister. John Scott, of Missouri, brought up the case again the following December, and the President addressed a request to the Mexican government for the return of the prisoners, but they were not returned. Although in 1819 a treaty of amity was made between the United States and Mexico, no condition was imposed as to the release of these men, and not until 1821 was their imprisonment ended. McKnight never forgave his native land for this seeming neglect.

He returned to St. Louis in 1822 with his brother John, who had gone to Durango to effect his release. In the fall of that year, Robert and John McKnight and eight others left for the Comanche country on a trading expedition. They joined Thomas James [*q.v.*] and his party of twelve men, by prearrangement, at the mouth of the Canadian River. This expedition was a failure, however; John McKnight was reported killed by the Indians, and Robert McKnight returned to St. Louis in 1824. In the meantime, and thereafter, he sought redress for the wrongs he had suffered in Mexico, but without avail. Thoroughly disgusted, he renounced his allegiance to the United States, and returned to Mexico, where he spent his remaining years. By his wife, a Spanish lady whom he married at Chihuahua, he had two daughters, and a son who died in early youth. In 1828 he gained possession of a rich copper mine, known as Santa Rita del Cobre, in northern Chihuahua. Here he made a fortune, but in 1846 his mining operations were broken up by the Apache Indians. James describes McKnight as very impulsive, courageous, and unyielding in the midst of danger, but lacking that coolness and presence of mind best adapted to leadership.

[Thomas James, *Three Years Among the Indians and Mexicans* (1916), ed. by W. B. Douglas; *Detroit Gazette*, July 23, 1819; *Am. State Papers, Foreign Relations*, IV (1834), 207–09; *House Ex. Doc. 41*, 30 Cong., 1 Sess., p. 58; *Weekly Reveille* (St. Louis), May 18, Aug. 31, 1846; *Santa Fé Republican*, Nov. 20, 1847; D. C. Peters, *The Life and Adventures of Kit Carson* (1858); "The Personal Narrative of James O. Pattie," in R. G. Thwaites, *Early Western Travels*, XVIII (1905), 86, 350; Grant Foreman, *Indians and Pioneers* (1930); McKnight Family History, MSS. in Mo. Hist. Soc.] S. M. D.

MACKUBIN, FLORENCE (May 19, 1861–Feb. 2, 1918), portrait and miniature painter, was born in Florence, Italy, where her parents were living temporarily. Her father, Charles Nicholas Mackubin, and her mother Ellen (Fay), were members of old well-known Maryland families; one of her grandfathers had served as treasurer of the Western Shore in 1839. Developing early in life a talent for drawing and painting, she was placed under the masters of Florence and Nice, later studying in Munich with Herterrich and with Julius Rolshoven and Louis Deschamps in Paris. She also studied miniature painting in Paris with Jeanne Devina. She became thoroughly familiar with the Italian, French, and German languages and read widely in the literature of these countries. Upon returning to America she adopted Baltimore as her home and took a keen interest in its affairs.

Under a commission from the Governor and Board of Public Works of the State of Maryland she made a copy of Van Dyck's portrait of Queen Henrietta Maria, after whom the state of Maryland was named, for the State House at Annapolis. While engaged in this work at Warwick Castle she was asked by Lady Warwick to paint her portrait. She made copies of the portraits of George and Cecilius Calvert, the first and second lords Baltimore, under a special commission from the Baltimore Club. The originals hang in Windlestone Hall, the seat of Sir William Eden at Windlestone, England. She painted portraits and miniatures of several distinguished men of Maryland; among them a portrait of Gov. Lloyd Lowndes for the Maryland State House at Annapolis, a portrait of Prof. Basil L. Gildersleeve for the University of Virginia, which is considered one of her best; another of Prof. Marshall Elliott for the Johns Hopkins University, Baltimore. At the Louisiana Purchase Exposition in St. Louis she exhibited an oil portrait of Cardinal Gibbons which was later taken to the Maryland Historical Society. While staying at her summer home, "Oriole Cottage," St. Andrews, New Brunswick, she painted portraits of several prominent Canadians, among them Sir William Van Horne. She exhibited at the World's Columbian Exposition, Chicago, in 1893; in Paris in 1900, Buffalo in 1901, Charleston in 1902, and St. Louis in 1904. She received a number of awards, including a bronze medal and diploma for miniatures at the Tennessee Exposition in 1897. A number of her miniatures are in the Walters Gallery, Baltimore. Her work won recognition not only in Baltimore but elsewhere for its exquisite quality. Residing in Europe during the early part of the World War, she wrote a number of letters to the Baltimore *Sun* on the war, full always of her Americanism in spite of long periods spent abroad. She was a member of the Maryland Association Opposed to Women Suffrage, and expressed her views on several occasions. She died in Baltimore.

[A portrait miniature of Florence Mackubin appears in the *Century Magazine*, Oct. 1900. See also *Who's Who in America*, 1918–19; *Am. Art Annual*, vol. XV (1918); *Sun* (Baltimore), Feb. 4, 1918; *Baltimore American*, Feb. 3, 1918; *Am. Art News*, Feb. 9, 1918; *Maryland Women* (1931).] H. W.

McLANE, ALLAN (Aug. 8, 1746–May 22, 1829), Revolutionary soldier, father of Louis McLane [*q.v.*], was born in Philadelphia, as he wrote in his diary, of parents "of the midling grade," whose names he failed to set down. Whatever their station in life, his father accumulated an ample property which, on his death in 1775, he left to his son. At the age of twenty-one Allan McLane visited Europe, and several years after his return, in 1769, he married Rebecca Wells, daughter of the sheriff of Kent County, Del. In 1774 he settled in Kent County, near Smyrna. At the outbreak of the Revolution he hastened to aid the Virginians against Lord Dunmore, fighting at Great Bridge and about Norfolk. Returning North, he was commissioned adjutant (Sept. 11, 1775) in Cæsar Rodney's regiment of volunteers, which saw active service at Long Island. When Col. John Patton's Additional Continental Regiment was created, McLane was made one of its captains (January 1777), and in this capacity proved himself an independent and dashing officer of the most gallant type. During the British occupation of Philadelphia he commanded a body of light troops upon the lines for general reconnoitering purposes, but chiefly as "market stoppers," to prevent the smuggling of provisions into the city by Loyalists. Once while scouting for a reconnoitering expedition of Lafayette's he discovered that the enemy were about to surround the General. Acting with celerity, he warned him in time to prevent his capture. When the British evacuated Philadelphia, McLane, being anxious about his properties, and by special permission from Washington, was the first to enter the city. His exceptional scouting abilities were utilized by Benedict Arnold, who was given command in Philadelphia, to follow the enemy movements before and after the battle of Monmouth. In his contacts with Arnold, McLane came to doubt that officer's patriotism, but was apparently unable to convince Washington of the truth of his charges (McHenry to McLane, June 3, 1778, Washington Papers, Library of Congress; W. S. Stryker, *The Battle of Monmouth,* 1927, pp. 58, 64, 236; McLane Papers, see under June 13, 1778).

When Colonel Patton's regiment was disbanded in June 1779, McLane, at his own and Major Henry Lee's request, was given command of the dismounted dragoons in Lee's partisan corps. One of his first assignments under Lee was to reconnoiter the approaches to Stony Point in order to discover the best route for Wayne's celebrated attack (H. P. Johnston, *The Storming of Stony Point,* 1900, pp. 62, 74). The association which both McLane and Lee seemed to desire soon ended in jealousy and discord. Lee's corps, augmented, became the famous "Lee's Legion" and was dispatched South to join Greene, but McLane was detached to purchase supplies in Maryland while a captain, his junior in the same corps, was raised to a majority. McLane wrote in strong terms to Lee, threatening to resign. The letter was forwarded to Washington, who praised McLane highly, saying that he deserved much, but stated that scores of other officers in the army with longer Continental service than McLane also deserved promotion. McLane was then retired on half-pay. Although the subject was a source of bitterness to him for the remainder of his life, he prevailed upon Washington to attach him to Steuben's command in Virginia, which he joined the last of February. In the closing phase of the war his reconnoitering ability was displayed in acquainting the Comte de Grasse and Washington of the movements of the enemy fleet near the Chesapeake.

After the Revolution, his patrimony swallowed up by his war debts, he entered into a trading venture on the Delaware River with Robert Morris [*q.v.*], and in September 1789 was appointed marshal of Delaware, which office was exchanged in 1797 for the more lucrative post of collector of Wilmington. Intercession of powerful friends with Jefferson tided him over the pressure of Republicans for his office in 1801, and he retained the place until his death (*Annual Report of the American Historical Association for the Year 1913,* 1915, II, 128–29; Jefferson Papers, Library of Congress). He also held various state offices, being member of the Delaware House of Representatives in 1785 and in 1791, when he was chosen speaker; member of the Privy Council in 1788; and justice of the peace in 1793. During the War of 1812 he was in charge of the defenses of Wilmington.

[Three bound volumes of letters and papers of McLane, including autobiographical notes, completely calendared, are in the N. Y. Hist. Soc.; about twenty letters of, to, or about McLane are in the Washington Papers, Lib. of Cong. Published sources include W. G. Whitely, "The Revolutionary Soldiers of Delaware," *Papers of the Hist. Soc. of Del.,* No. XIV (1896); H. H. Bellas, "A History of the Delaware State Society of the Cincinnati," *Ibid.,* No. XIII (1895); T. W. Bean, *Washington at Valley Forge* (1876); F. B. Heitman, *Hist. Reg. of Officers of the Continental Army* (1893); H. C. Conrad, *Hist. of the State of Del.* (3 vols., 1908); *Del. Gazette* (Wilmington), May 29, 1829. Signatures in McLane's MSS. give the spelling "Allan."]

C. W. G.

McLANE, LOUIS (May 28, 1786–Oct. 7, 1857), cabinet officer, diplomat, son of Allan [*q.v.*] and Rebecca (Wells) McLane, was born in Smyrna, Del. At the age of twelve he became a midshipman in the navy and cruised for a year on the *Philadelphia* under Commodore Stephen Decatur. He left the navy in 1801, however, and entered Newark College, Delaware, but apparently abandoned his course without taking a degree and began to read law under the direction of James A. Bayard [*q.v.*]. From this preceptor he seems to have acquired federalistic principles which were never fully eradicated. Admitted to the bar in 1807, he practised law in Smyrna, and in 1812 married Catherine Mary, eldest daughter of Robert Milligan.

McLane's political career began in 1817 when he entered the lower house of Congress as a Jeffersonian Republican. He remained for ten years in this branch and was then transferred to the Senate. As a legislator he was sometimes a political non-conformist. Usually he upheld the party program, but he invariably championed the cause of the Bank of the United States. In 1818 he opposed an investigation of its discounts, and he denied the power of Congress to interfere with the operations of the bank. Although he was opposed to slavery, he denied the power of Congress to exclude Missouri from the Union because her constitution permitted slavery; and when the legislature of Delaware instructed him to vote against admission, he refused to obey, on the federalistic ground that he was an officer of the Union and not the agent of his state.

In 1824 he was an ardent supporter of Crawford, and when the presidential election devolved upon the House of Representatives he remarked that "they might as well think of turning the Capitol upside down as of persuading him to vote for Jackson" (E. S. Brown, *The Missouri Compromises and Presidential Politics,* 1926, p. 136). Four years later, however, he supported Jackson and was rewarded by being offered first the position of attorney-general and second, that of minister to England. Resigning from the Senate (1829), he accepted the latter post with reluctance, in order, as he said, "to preserve my chance for what I frankly tell you would make me happier than any other honor—the Bench" (Van Buren, *post,* p. 258). While in London his principal achievement was an agreement regarding trade with the West Indies. In 1831 he was recalled and made secretary of the treasury, because Jackson wished the diplomatic post for Van Buren. McLane's views on finance did not accord with those of the President. He urged Congress to recharter the Bank of the United States, although it was well known that the President was opposed to such action. Jackson overlooked this defection and his friends talked of running McLane for vice-president in 1832; but when the Senate refused to ratify Van Buren's diplomatic appointment, Jackson decided to make Van Buren the presiding officer of the body which had sought to ruin him politically.

Meanwhile McLane's position in the Treasury Department became very uncomfortable when the President, in 1832, vetoed the bill to recharter the bank. His sympathies were with that institution, but he could not hope for the coveted place on the bench unless he could retain Jackson's good will until the first vacancy should occur. He therefore formulated a plan whereby Edward Livingston was to be sent to France, he himself was to succeed to the Department of State and W. J. Duane [*q.v.*] was to take the Treasury portfolio (Van Buren, p. 593). His wishes were gratified in 1833, but within a few months Jackson dismissed Duane for refusing to remove the government deposits from the United States Bank and appointed Roger Brooke Taney [*q.v.*] in his place. Taney removed the deposits, but the Senate refused to confirm his appointment and the "martyred secretary" had prior claim to the first vacant seat on the supreme bench. Foreseeing the success of his rival and the blasting of his own hopes, McLane began to talk of resigning his portfolio and did so when he was overruled on questions concerning the French spoliations.

The principal diplomatic questions which demanded his attention as secretary of state (May 29, 1833–June 30, 1834) were those with Mexico regarding claims and boundaries; with Great Britain on the subject of the Northeast Boundary; and with France concerning spoliation claims. With Mexico he was firm but reasonable. With Great Britain he could accomplish nothing because the views of the two governments were at that time irreconcilable. On the spoliation claims he took a firm stand, and when the French Chambers refused to appropriate the money to pay the claims, he advised the president to ask Congress for authority to issue letters of marque and reprisal against French shipping, but Jackson was dissuaded by Taney and Van Buren from taking so drastic an action. McLane soon resigned from the cabinet in the hope, as Van Buren believed, of becoming the anti-administration candidate for the presidency at the next election (Van Buren, p. 616). His greatest achievement was his introduction of orderly procedure into the operations of the department (Gaillard Hunt, *The Department of State,* 1914, pp. 203–18). He had undoubted ability, but ambition and jealousy ended abruptly what might have been a successful diplomatic career.

After leaving the cabinet, McLane resided for a time in New York, where he was president of the Morris Canal & Banking Company. In 1837 he moved to Baltimore, tempted by what was then considered to be a munificent salary, $4,000 yearly, to accept the presidency of the Baltimore & Ohio Railroad Company, a position which he held for ten years. While still in the employ of this company he was sent as United States minister to England by President Polk to conduct negotiations on the Oregon question (June 1845–August 1846). When Buchanan expressed a wish to relinquish his portfolio for a place on the supreme bench Polk planned to make McLane secretary of state, but the vacillating Buchanan changed his mind and there was no vacancy in that department. McLane retired from the presidency of the railroad in 1847, and a year later refused to go to Mexico as one of the commissioners to procure the ratification of the Treaty of Guadalupe Hidalgo. He performed his last public service as a member of the Maryland constitutional convention of 1850, and died in Baltimore seven years later. Robert Milligan McLane [*q.v.*], his son, attained some distinction in politics and diplomacy.

Louis McLane's principal weakness was his reluctance to cooperate with his fellows. Unless he could dominate, he would refuse to "play the game." His greatest ambition was to be a distinguished jurist; but Jackson doubtless rendered him a service by not elevating him to the bench, for his temperament was far from being judicial. He gave promise as a diplomat, but his precipitate resignation from the cabinet deprived him of an opportunity to demonstrate his abilities in this field of action. He succeeded best as an executive. As such, he could give rather than receive orders, and he was more at liberty to formulate his own plans. As an executive he was capable and systematic. He was an enemy of waste, whether of money or time, and conducted any enterprise entrusted to him with order and efficiency.

[Sketch by E. I. McCormac in S. F. Bemis, *The Am. Secretaries of State and Their Diplomacy,* vol. IV (1928); "The Autobiography of Martin Van Buren," *Ann. Report Am. Hist. Asso. for . . . 1918,* vol. II (1920); J. T. Scharf, *Hist. of Del.* (1888); Beckles Willson, *America's Ambassadors to England* (1928); Edward Hungerford, *The Story of the Baltimore and Ohio Railroad* (1928); *Baltimore American and Commercial Advertiser,* Oct. 9, 1857.] E. I. McC.

McLANE, ROBERT MILLIGAN (June 23, 1815–Apr. 16, 1898), lawyer, congressman, diplomat, was born in Wilmington, Del., the son of Louis McLane [*q.v.*] and his wife, Catherine Mary Milligan of Cecil County, Md. He received his general education in a Wilmington academy, St. Mary's Academy in Baltimore, and the Collège Bourbon, Paris, which he attended for a year while his father was United States minister to England. In 1833 he entered the United States Military Academy, from which he was graduated in 1837. He served in Florida in the Seminole War and in 1838 was with the troops sent to control the Cherokees in connection with their transfer to the region west of the Mississippi. Following this duty, as a member of a corps of topographical engineers he aided in a military survey of the northern lakes. In 1841 he was sent to Europe to study dikes and drainage, and was occupied with the subject for some time in Italy. In the same year he married Georgine Urquhart, in Paris.

McLane did not like military life, and during his winters he studied law in Washington. He was admitted to the bar of the District of Columbia in 1840 and to that of Baltimore in 1843. In the latter year he resigned his commission and settled in Baltimore, where he began the practice of his new profession, quickly gaining distinction. Early in 1851 he went to California as counsel in a contest over possession of the rich quicksilver mines of New Almaden, in the Santa Clara Valley. While in the West he secured other important cases. He was retained by Commodore Vanderbilt in the dispute over possession of the steamship *Pacific* and of the transit route across Nicaragua, and won both cases for his client. For some years, in the fifties and sixties, he was counsel for the Western Pacific Railroad Company, a forerunner of the Central Pacific.

The competence derived from his professional success enabled McLane to devote considerable time to politics, in which, as a Democrat, he began to be active soon after moving to Baltimore. In 1845 he was elected to the Maryland House of Delegates, where he worked hard for the financial reform of the state, then bankrupt. In 1847 he won a seat in the national House of Representatives, and was reëlected in 1849. In Congress he supported and defended Polk in connection with the war with Mexico. During his second term he was chairman of the committee on commerce and stood for tariff for revenue, with protection an incident. A moderate on the slavery question, he favored the compromise measures of 1850, contending that the admission of California as a free state was a proper offset to the admission of Texas as a slave state.

In 1853 he was made United States commissioner to China and accredited also to Japan, Siam, Korea, and Cochin-China. Shortly after he reached Hong-Kong early in 1854 he tried, in cooperation with the diplomatic agents of Great Britain and France, to secure a renewal of the existing commercial treaty with China; but the effort proved futile at this time. Suffering from poor health and discouraged by the situation, in December 1854 he sailed for the United States on sick leave, and resigned his post when he reached Paris.

In 1859 President Buchanan named him minister to Mexico, which was torn by revolutionary factions, with instructions to recognize the Juárez government, then at Vera Cruz, if the extent of its authority seemed to justify such action. McLane recognized Juárez, and labored, but in vain, to make peace between the warring factions. In December 1859 he signed with the Juárez government a treaty of transit and commerce and a convention to enforce treaty stipulations. By request, he went to Washington to explain the measures before the Senate committee on foreign relations, but neither arrangement was ratified by the Senate, and the imminence of civil war at home made him decide not to return to Mexico.

After the Civil War had opened he was a member of the Maryland committee which conferred with President Lincoln regarding the alleged unconstitutional procedure of the Federal authorities in Maryland. For some time following he was chiefly occupied with his law practice, but in 1876 he resumed activity in politics and was a Maryland delegate to the convention which nominated Tilden. The following year he was elected to the state Senate, but resigned in 1878 to take a seat in the national House of Representatives, to which he was reëlected in 1880. In Congress he was especially active in trying to secure the reduction of existing tariffs and endeavoring to bring about laws to prevent the adulteration of foods. He was elected governor of Maryland in 1883, and in that capacity strove to better the conditions of labor, securing the passage of laws in the interest of working women and children. His term was short, however, for he resigned in March 1885, to become minister to France under President Cleveland. In this new office, the last public position that he filled, the most serious question with which he had to deal concerned the rights of naturalized citizens of the United States, born in France, from whom the French authorities tried to exact military service. After being displaced following the election of Harrison, he continued to reside in Paris, where he died.

[McLane's *Reminiscences, 1827–1897* (privately printed, 1903) is the best single authority and forms the basis of the sketch in H. E. Buchholz, *Governors of Md.* (1908). See also G. W. Cullum, *Biog Reg. . . . U. S. Mil. Acad.* (3rd ed., 1891), vol. I; Beckles Willson, *America's Ambassadors to France* (1928); J. J. Conway, *Footprints of Famous Americans in Paris* (1912); *Baltimore Past and Present* (1871); *Foreign Relations of the U. S.*, 1885–89; *N. Y. Herald*, Apr. 17, 1898; Baltimore *Sun*, Apr. 18, 1898.] M. W. W.

McLAREN, WILLIAM EDWARD (Dec. 13, 1831–Feb. 19, 1905), the third bishop of Illinois, and leader of the High-Church party in the Protestant Episcopal Church, was born in Geneva, N. Y., the son of the Rev. John F. McLaren, a Presbyterian clergyman. After graduating from Jefferson College (now Washington and Jefferson), at Washington, Pa., in 1851, he taught for one year and then from 1852 to 1857 was engaged in journalistic work in Cleveland and Pittsburgh. During the years 1857–60 he took a theological course in the Presbyterian Theological Seminary in Pittsburgh with the purpose of becoming a missionary in China. Ordained by the Presbytery of Allegheny City, Pa., in the year of his graduation, he was sent by the Presbyterian Board of Foreign Missions to Bogotá, South America, remaining there a year and a half, until an impairment to health forced him to return to the United States. After acting as assistant minister in the Second Presbyterian Church at Pittsburgh for a few months he was called to the pastorate of the Second Presbyterian Church in Peoria, Ill., where he remained until 1867. In that year he became pastor of the Westminster Presbyterian Church in Detroit, Mich. It was during his ministry in Detroit that he began to question some of the Presbyterian doctrines. He undertook a careful study of the doctrine and worship of the Episcopal Church and was particularly attracted by its sacramental emphasis, as set forth in its Book of Common Prayer and by its leading theologians. Convinced that he should change his ecclesiastical allegiance, he resigned his pastorate and was confirmed at St. John's Church, Detroit. On July 29, 1872, he was ordained to the diaconate by Bishop McCoskry at St. John's and on Oct. 20 at the same place he was ordained by McCoskry to the priesthood.

Following his ordination McLaren received a call to the rectorship of Trinity Church, Cleveland, Ohio. He accepted and served until his election to the episcopate by the Diocese of Illinois in 1875. He was consecrated at the Cathedral Church of SS. Peter and Paul, Chicago, Dec. 8, 1875. Two years after his consecration the agitation to divide the Diocese of Illinois, owing to its growth in population, resulted in the establishment of two new sees, those of Quincy and Springfield. McLaren continued as head of the old diocese, the name of which was changed to the Diocese of Chicago in 1883. He was a gifted executive. In 1881 he founded the Western Theological Seminary in Chicago, which has had a distinguished record as a theological training school in the Episcopal Church, and in 1885 he founded at Sycamore, Ill., Waterman Hall, a school for girls. He became president of the board of trustees of these two institutions, and in addition held the same position in Racine College and at St. Mary's School at Knoxville, Ill. He was also known as a scholar, linguist, and writer, and was a convincing preacher. He possessed marked judicial capacities, which, in combination with his other qualifications, resulted in bringing his jurisdiction into prominence as a leading diocese of the Episcopal Church. It was he who called the first diocesan "retreat" known to the Episcopal Church in this country, thereby establishing a custom which has become increasingly common, adopted by all parties in the church. His writings include *Catholic Dogma: The Antidote of Doubt* (1883) in which he set forth arguments for the so-called "Catholic position"; *Analysis of Pantheism* (1885); occasional sermons, addresses, and charges, and a few ventures in poetry.

[W. S. Perry, *The Episcopate in America* (1895); H. G. Batterson, *A Sketch-book of the Am. Episcopate* (1878); *Biog. and Hist. Cat. of Washington and Jefferson Coll.* (1902); the *Churchman*, Feb. 25, 1905; *Chicago Tribune*, Feb. 20, 1905.] G. E. S.

McLAUGHLIN, HUGH (Apr. 2, 1826?–Dec. 7, 1904), political boss, was born in Brooklyn, N. Y., the son of Hugh McLaughlin, a poor Irish immigrant. He received practically no formal education. At an early age he went to work at rope-making, then handled barrels on the docks, and later ran a fish stand for several years. In 1849 he became a lieutenant of Henry C. Murphy, a local boss, in 1853 attended his first Democratic state convention, and in 1855, as a result of political activity, became master foreman of civilian labor at the Brooklyn navy yard. Here he judiciously disposed of jobs that he controlled and gradually built up a considerable following. Having purchased the "White House," a well-known saloon, he met his followers there until he emerged as boss of the Brooklyn Democracy and established political headquarters on Willoughby Street. In 1860 he was defeated for sheriff of Kings County and sat as a delegate in the National Democratic Convention. The next year he was elected county register, an office that he held, with the exception of three years, until 1873. From 1862 until 1903 he controlled the Brooklyn Democracy, sometimes being absolutely dominant but rather frequently encountering defeat and enjoying only partial control. During this period he gathered around himself a political ring composed of an elder sister, "Aunt Nancy," a nephew, Hugh, and a changeable group of outsiders, among whom W. C. Kingsley, Alexander McCue, solicitor of the treasury and assistant treasurer of the United States under Cleveland, Thomas Kinsella, W. C. Fowler, and Judge Fred Massey stood out. Although definitely preferring local politics to state or national, he maintained cordial relations with Horatio Seymour, Samuel J. Tilden, Grover Cleveland, and especially with David B. Hill. In 1879 and again in 1881 he led the Brooklyn delegation to the state convention. His most successful years in Brooklyn politics were the years 1886 to 1894. In 1881 he had to face a serious revolt led by Thomas Kinsella and handed in one of his famous resignations as boss—there were three altogether. During the years following 1893 Judge William J. Gaynor, John Y. Kane, Patrick McCarren, and Charles F. Murphy proved thorns in the flesh. "Commissioner" Murphy, of Tammany Hall, desiring to control the political affairs of the entire city of which Brooklyn had become a part, inspired McCarren to declare war on McLaughlin and caused the latter's retirement in 1903.

In 1862 McLaughlin married Sarah Ellen Kays, daughter of a Dutch farmer of New Jersey. They had four children. He lived simply and regularly, read the newspapers faithfully, greatly enjoyed the theatre, spoke rarely but fluently, and was unceasingly active, even whittling, and soaking stamps off old letters. Although apparently mild and quiet, he was actually stubborn, stern, and exacting. He devoted himself to fishing, hunting, and fancy dogs, spending from one to six months each year fishing from Maine to Florida and hunting in the Adirondacks. In spite of few visible business connections he had a shrewd business head, particularly in the field of real estate, and accumulated a fortune of almost three million dollars. Both he and his wife gave generously to hospitals, orphanages, and to poor Irish folks, and they were unusually active in the Roman Catholic Church. Shortly before his death he presented Saint James' procathedral with a $15,000 marble altar.

[Harold Zink, *City Bosses in the United States* (1930); *Brooklyn Citizen*, Dec. 8, 1904; *Brooklyn Daily Eagle*, Dec. 8, 1904.] H. Z.

McLAUGHLIN, JAMES (Feb. 12, 1842–July 28, 1923), agent and inspector in the Indian service, was of Scotch-Irish ancestry, the son of Felix and Mary (Prince) McLaughlin, and was born in Avonmere, Ontario. He was educated in the common schools. In 1863 he went to Minnesota, where for eight years he was variously employed. He was married, on Jan. 28, 1864, to Mary Louise Buisson, of French, Scotch, and Sioux ancestry. On July 1, 1871, he entered the United States Indian service as the assistant agent, under Maj. W. H. Forbes, of the newly established Devils Lake Agency, at Fort Totten, in the present North Dakota. Five years later, on the death of Forbes, he was made agent. While in this post he succeeded in abolishing the savagely cruel sun dance of the Sioux. His work attracted official attention, and in the fall of 1881 he was transferred to the important Standing Rock Agency, at Fort Yates, on the Missouri. Here he had the management of some 6,000 Sioux, many of them former hostiles who had been driven back by force or hunger to the reservation. He became greatly attached to Gall [*q.v.*] and Crow King, two of the leaders in the Little

Bighorn battle, and to John Grass [*q.v.*], the outstanding orator and diplomat of the Sioux nation, and was enabled to alter radically the Indian attitude toward peaceful industry and the education of the children. In the negotiations over the proposed agreements of 1882, 1888, and 1889, whereby large land cessions were demanded by the government, he took an active part and was influential both in obtaining concessions for his wards and in persuading the leaders to accept the final proposal. During the Ghost-Dance craze of 1890, when a general Indian uprising was feared, he opposed the use of the military and exerted himself to check the spread of the excitement by peaceful means. He was, however, compelled to order the arrest of Sitting Bull [*q.v.*], an attempt that resulted (Dec. 15) in the death of the chief and eleven other Indians (*Sixtieth Annual Report of the Commissioner of Indian Affairs,* 1891, pp. 325–38).

In January 1895, the office of assistant commissioner of Indian Affairs was offered him. Preferring field service, he declined the offer but accepted instead (Mar. 31) the post of inspector under the personal direction of the secretary of the interior. He traveled widely and thus became acquainted with conditions among the Indians in every part of the country. He was especially valuable in the rôle of negotiator and participated in more than forty formal agreements with the various tribes. He had returned to Washington from a protracted visit to the Dakotas, where he distributed an award to the Santee Sioux, when he suddenly became ill. He died at the National Hotel. The body was taken to his home at McLaughlin, S. Dak. He was survived by his wife, who, by reason of her command of the Sioux tongue, had been of inestimable help to him, and by several children.

McLaughlin was tall, with a dignified bearing and graceful manners. His tastes were refined, and his intellectual interests were broad and varied. It is doubtful whether any one has better understood Indian character. In 1910 he published *My Friend the Indian,* in considerable part an autobiography. Though the composition is largely another's, the substance is all his own, and the book faithfully reflects the man and his work. It is a contribution of high rank to the study of the Indian question, to Sioux history, and especially to the Indian side of the battle of the Little Bighorn.

[An edition of *My Friend the Indian,* published in 1926, contains an introductory appreciation of McLaughlin by Geo. B. Grinnell. See also: the *Washington Post,* July 29, 1923; *Bismarck Tribune,* July 30, 1923; and the *Native American* (Phoenix, Ariz.), Sept. 8, 1923. Information for this sketch was supplied by Charles H. Burke, commissioner of Indian affairs at the time of McLaughlin's death, and others.] W. J. G.

McLAURIN, ANSELM JOSEPH (Mar. 26, 1848–Dec. 22, 1909), senator, governor of Mississippi, was the eldest of the eight sons born to Lauchlin and Ellen Caroline (Tullus) McLaurin. His father, a native of South Carolina, of Scotch descent, was a man of local prominence and represented his county in the legislature of Mississippi four times between 1841 and 1875. His wife was a native Mississippian. Though Anselm was born at Brandon, Miss., the family soon moved to a farm in Smith County. After some training at the hands of local schoolmasters, he entered Summerville Institute. In August 1864 he became a private in Company K, 3rd Mississippi Cavalry, and served through the remainder of the Civil War. He then returned to Summerville Institute and completed the work of the junior class in 1867. The following year he was admitted to the Mississippi bar, having read law at night. On Feb. 22, 1870, at Trenton, Miss., he was married to Laura Elvira Victoria Rauch, and there were ten children born of this marriage.

After serving as prosecuting attorney of the fifth judicial district from 1871 to 1875, he returned the following year from Smith County to his birth place, Brandon. In his legal career he was chiefly notable in criminal cases. In 1879 he was elected to the state legislature. He took part in framing the Mississippi constitution of 1890, and on Feb. 7, 1894, he was elected to the United States Senate to fill the unexpired term of Edward C. Walthall, who had resigned. McLaurin was elected governor of Mississippi in 1895, having defeated Frank Burkitt, Populist candidate, by a vote of three to one. His administration extended from Jan. 21, 1896, to Jan. 16, 1900, a period which included three mild yellow-fever epidemics, the Spanish-American War, and the decline of the Populist movement within the state. The condition of the state treasury was greatly improved during this term. In 1900 he was again elected to the Senate, defeating Congressman "Private" John Allen. He served from 1901 until his death in 1909, having been reelected for the term extending from 1907 to 1913. He was a member of a number of important senatorial committees, including those on civil service and retrenchment, immigration, and interstate commerce. On Feb. 25, 1908, he was appointed a member of the United States Immigration Commission. His death precipitated a bitter fight in Mississippi over the choice of a successor to his seat in the Senate.

McLaurin was a man of sanity, wisdom, and

genial humor. A close associate, Senator Money, stated that he never knew a man more disinclined to speak ill of others. Nevertheless, he was a shrewd politician. He did not hesitate to advocate the disfranchisement of wife beaters, a minimum pension of seventy-five dollars a year to disabled Confederate veterans, and the popular election of the judiciary of Mississippi as matters proper for incorporation in the Mississippi constitution of 1890. He was also a diligent member of numerous Democratic executive committees.

[Dunbar Rowland, *The Official and Statistical Reg. of the State of Miss.*, 1904, 1908, 1912, 1917, and *Mississippi* (1907), vol. II; *Who's Who in America*, 1908–09; *Biog. Dir. Am. Cong.* (1928); *Anselm J. McLaurin . . . Memorial Addresses* (1911); *Daily Democrat* (Natchez, Miss.), Dec. 23, 1909.] C. S. S.

MACLAURIN, RICHARD COCKBURN (June 5, 1870–Jan. 15, 1920), physicist, born at Lindean, Scotland, was the son of the Rev. Robert Campbell Maclaurin and his wife Martha Joan (Spence) Maclaurin. The family was an ancient one in Scotland, the most famous representative of which was the mathematician Colin Maclaurin, the friend of Sir Isaac Newton and author of the *Treatise on Fluxions* (1742). It was his brother John Maclaurin, one of the leading theologians of his day, who had some communications with Dr. Prince, pastor of the Old South Church in Boston, concerning the founding of the College of New Jersey. Robert Campbell Maclaurin was a minister of the Church of Scotland in a small parish near Edinburgh and a man of literary and scientific tastes. Early in life, finding himself unable to subscribe to the tenets of his church, he resolved to make a new start in New Zealand. With his large family he settled in a country district in Auckland where in the course of a few years he was appointed schoolmaster and had a house with a small farm. Thus from the time he was five years old Richard grew up in New Zealand and got his early training there. Both parents were persons of unusual character and attainments and they and their twelve children made a remarkable household. His mother, who was the daughter of a physician in Lerwick, Shetland, exerted a strong influence over his life.

Although his constitution was never very robust, the boy took kindly to the outdoor life of a country farm and at the same time evinced an unusual aptitude for books and study. At school and afterward at college he was uniformly at the head of his class. When he was seventeen years old he led the list of competitors of the whole colony for a scholarship in Auckland University College, and four years later he had graduated from this college with the highest honors in physics and mathematics. A scientific career seemed to be marked out for him. In 1892 he proceeded to the University of Cambridge. Winning scholarships in both Emmanuel College and St. John's College, he preferred to enter the latter on account of its high reputation in mathematics. He took the degree of bachelor of arts in this university in 1895, obtaining the highest rank in the most advanced mathematical examinations. Throughout his life at Cambridge he held a distinguished place and won the most coveted prizes both in mathematics and in law. He was awarded the Smith prize in mathematics in 1897, which had been won previously by such notable scientific men as Sir John Herschel, Sir G. G. Stokes, James Clerk Maxwell, Lord Kelvin, Lord Rayleigh, and others; and the Yorke prize in law in 1898 for his original essay, *On the Nature and Evidence of Title to Realty* (1901). The strain of these studies told upon his health.

In 1896–97 he spent about a year in Canada where he taught for a short time in the University of Montreal and also began to study law. Returning to England in 1897, he was elected a fellow of St. John's College, Cambridge, and was awarded the McMahon law studentship. During this period he also studied six months in the University of Strassburg. In the autumn of 1898, when he was only twenty-eight years old, he was called to take the chair of mathematics in the newly founded Victoria College of the University of New Zealand at Wellington. He held this post until 1905 and during part of the time he also gave courses of lectures in law without additional compensation. When the law school was established in 1905, he became dean of the faculty of law of the University of New Zealand. As a member of the University Senate he strove to promote the advancement of general education throughout the colony, but his ideas were too far ahead of the rural communities around him. In 1904 Cambridge University conferred on him the honorary degree of LL.D. in recognition of his original contributions in law. At the close of this year, Dec. 27, 1904, he was married to Margaret Alice Young of Auckland.

In 1907 he was invited to Columbia University in the city of New York to take the chair of mathematical physics that had been established for advanced researches in this field. The opportunity of resuming his favorite scientific studies under such conditions was not to be resisted, and in February 1908 he gave his first lectures in Columbia University. His lectures on light given at the American Museum of Natural History during the winter of 1908–09 were published under that title by the Columbia University Press in 1909. Although he was almost immediately made head of the department of physics in Columbia University, he was not destined to remain long in New York. In the following autumn he was chosen to succeed President Pritchett as the sixth president of the Massachusetts Institute of Technology, and on June 7, 1909, when he was just thirty-nine years old, he was formally inaugurated in this office. Here he entered upon a notable career. It was a critical period in the development of the school. It had outgrown its old habitations and was cramped for lack of space and facilities, while the demands for trained engineers in all the fields of industry and commerce were growing every year. The new president grasped the situation from the start and was able to stimulate enthusiasm and win support for his projects, for his wide knowledge, broad culture, and experience in two hemispheres "gave him a cosmopolitan quality that carried him over and through many obstacles." Within the short space of ten years he had transferred the institute to its spacious new home across the river in Cambridge.

Maclaurin had applied to become a citizen of the United States in 1913, but the World War followed in 1914, and he never severed his allegiance to his native country. Four years later when the United States also was in the midst of the war, he was selected by the War Department at Washington to be the director of college training for the huge army that was being sent overseas and also for the select few who were to carry on war work at home in scientific fields. He played a leading part in the prodigious task of organizing the Students Army Training Corps throughout all the American colleges, and it was largely due to his wisdom and tactfulness that the colleges were able to carry on in those distracting times and to resume their normal status practically unimpaired when the war ceased. Doing double duty and beset with problems of the most complex kind, he was under a great strain until several months after the armistice was signed, and it is possible that his health was undermined a year before he died. While he did not live to see the fruition of all his dreams for the Institute of Technology to which he had given the best years of his life, "he saw his great endowment secure, his student body doubled, his faculty growing, and the inception of a plan which should give the school permanent and increasing funds and unexampled opportunities for usefulness" (*Technology Review,* January 1920, p. 13). After an illness of five or six days, he died of pneumonia in his fiftieth year, at the height of his powers of accomplishment. One of the foremost scholars of his day, he was also a man of the broadest human sympathies. While slow to express his own views and eager to hear what others had to say, he formed his own decisions and was quick to detect sham in all its forms.

[There are several articles on the life and work of Maclaurin in the *Technology Rev.,* Jan., Apr. 1920. See also: Ernest F. Nichols, "Dr. Maclaurin as a Colleague," *Ibid.,* July 1920; M. A. DeWolfe Howe, *Later Years of the Saturday Club, 1870–1920* (1927); *Outlook,* Nov. 21, 1908, Jan. 28, 1920; *Boston Transcript,* Jan. 16, 1920. Information as to certain facts was supplied by Mrs. Richard Cockburn Maclaurin.]

J. P. C. S.

McLAWS, LAFAYETTE (Jan. 15, 1821–July 24, 1897), soldier, was born in Augusta, Ga., the son of James McLaws of Augusta and his wife, Elizabeth Huguenin of South Carolina. He entered the University of Virginia in 1837 and West Point the following year. Upon graduation in 1842, he was commissioned in the infantry and soon afterward married Emily Allison Taylor, niece of Zachary Taylor [*q.v.*]. Following service in Indian Territory, Mississippi, Louisiana, and Florida, he entered Texas with Taylor's army of occupation and participated in the defense of Fort Brown and the capture of Monterey. He was transferred to Scott's army before Vera Cruz as a first lieutenant, and was present at the capture of that city. Upon his return from Mexico, he was acting assistant adjutant-general of the department of New Mexico, a member of the Utah expedition of 1858, and in 1859 was engaged in protecting emigrants and escorting Mormons to California.

When the secession movement came to a head, he was on an expedition among the Navajo Indians in New Mexico. Resigning his captaincy in the United States army, he entered the Confederate service as a major, was shortly appointed colonel of the 10th Georgia Regiment, and was promoted to brigadier-general, Sept. 25, 1861. As the result of the excellent manner in which he acquitted himself in the Yorktown campaign, he was made a major-general, May 22, 1862. His division took part in all the larger operations of General Lee's Army of Northern Virginia during 1862–63. In 1862 he cooperated with "Stonewall" Jackson in the capture of Harpers Ferry, effecting the seizure of Maryland Heights, the key position. Arriving on the field of Antietam as Hood's troops were being driven back, McLaws' force was quickly thrown into the fight and helped to restore the situation. He heads the list of those mentioned by Longstreet (*post,* p. 266) as making the best tactical moves at Antietam. At Fredericksburg, McLaws' division made a brilliant defense of Marye's Hill against several times its numbers and inflicted appalling losses on the Union troops. After Chancellorsville, it was assigned to Longstreet's corps. At Gettysburg, it fought at the Peach Orchard and the Devil's Den. McLaws went with Longstreet to Bragg's assistance at Chickamauga, and upon the failure of the attempt to capture Knoxville by storm, he was relieved of his command, at the instance of Longstreet, and court-martialed for failing to make proper preparations for the assault. President Davis exonerated him and placed him in command of the district of Georgia and the defenses of Savannah. Because of the exhausted condition of the district, his efforts to oppose Sherman's operations were unavailing. His command was included in the surrender of General Johnston.

McLaws was popular with his men, yet a good disciplinarian; he loyally carried out decisions of higher authority; when assigned a task, he acted with energy and directness. After the war, he engaged in the insurance business in Augusta, and was collector of internal revenue and postmaster of Savannah in 1875 and 1876.

[G. W. Cullum, *Biog. Register of the Officers and Grads. of the U. S. Mil. Acad.* (3rd ed., 1891); *War of the Rebellion: Official Records* (*Army*); War Department Records; *Battles and Leaders of the Civil War* (4 vols., 1887–88); W. J. Northen, *Men of Mark in Ga.*, vol. III (1911); *Confed. Mil. Hist.* (1899), vol. VI; James Longstreet, *From Manassas to Appomattox* (1896); *Morning News* (Savannah), July 24, 1897; names of parents from a son, U. H. McLaws, Esq., Savannah, Ga.]

J. R. V.

MACLAY, EDGAR STANTON (Apr. 18, 1863–Nov. 2, 1919), author, was born in Foochow, China, the son of the Rev. Robert Samuel Maclay [*q.v.*] and Henrietta Caroline (Sperry) Maclay of Bristol, R. I. Edgar prepared for college chiefly under the instruction of his mother in Japan, and in 1881 entered Syracuse College, at Syracuse, N. Y., graduating four years later with the degree of B.A. In 1888, after a year spent in Europe, where he was engaged chiefly in the study of American history, he received from his alma mater the degree of M.A. After serving as a reporter on the *Brooklyn Daily Times,* he held a similar position with the *New York Tribune,* 1891–93, and for a year, 1893–94, was a member of the editorial staff. The following year he was on the editorial staff of the New York *Sun.* In 1895 he became lighthouse keeper at Old Field Point, L. I., and five years later accepted a minor office in the New York navy yard, with the rating of "laborer." In the meantime, utilizing his spare moments, he had established a considerable reputation as a writer of books, chiefly of a naval character. The rapid succession of their publication is indicative of his unusual industry: *The Maclays of Lurgan* (1889); *Journal of William Maclay* (1890); *A History of the United States Navy from 1775 to 1893* (2 vols., 1894); *Reminiscences of the Old Navy* (1898), and *A History of American Privateers* (1899). His naval books were interestingly written and his *History of the United States Navy* was adopted as a textbook for midshipmen by the United States Naval Academy. They reveal however not a few limitations: want of perspective and proportion, carelessness of statement, unfortunate omissions, and unfamiliarity with the naval art.

In 1901 he published a third volume of his *History,* covering the period of the Spanish-American War and containing a partisan account of the conduct of Admiral Schley in the battle of Santiago. He asserted that the admiral "cravenly declined" to pick up the gauntlet thrown down by Cervera. This account precipitated the Schley court of inquiry and led to Maclay's separation from the New York navy yard. On Dec. 20, 1901, under instructions from President Roosevelt, Secretary Long asked for his resignation. When he declined to comply, the President, four days later, dismissed him. His punishment, judged by its tragic results, was excessive. He was not well adapted to win from a niggard world a livelihood for himself and his family, and the fickle public now showed little interest in his writings, which in the years immediately preceding his death almost ceased. Of this later period he has three books to his credit: *Life and Adventures of "Jack" Philip, Rear Admiral, U. S. N.* (1903); *Moses Brown, Captain, U. S. N.* (1904); and *A Youthful Man-O'-Warsman* (1910). In October 1904 he formed a connection with the Brooklyn *Standard Union.* At the time of his death he was living in Washington, D. C., engaged in research work. He had married, on Dec. 22, 1893, Katherine Koerber, by whom he had four sons.

[E. S. Maclay, *The Maclays of Lurgan* (1889); *Who's Who in America,* 1906–07; *Evening Star* (Wash., D. C.), Dec. 21–26, 1901, Nov. 4, 1919.]

C. O. P.

MACLAY, ROBERT SAMUEL (Feb. 7, 1824–Aug. 18, 1907), founder of three colleges and pioneer missionary in China, Korea, and Japan, was born in Concord, Franklin County, Pa., the son of Robert and Arabella (Erwin) Maclay and a descendant of John Maclay who emigrated to Pennsylvania from the north of Ireland in 1734. Graduating from Dickinson College in 1845, he was ordained a Methodist minister in the following year and in October

1847 was included in the first important group of missionaries sent to China, being assigned to Foochow a few weeks after the opening of the Chinese field. Five years later he became secretary and treasurer of the Foochow group and served in this capacity from 1852 to 1872, becoming "practically the founder of Methodist missions in China." He also assisted in the translation of the New Testament into the local dialect and in collaboration with the Rev. C. C. Baldwin published at Foochow *An Alphabetic Dictionary of the Chinese Language in the Foochow Dialect* (1870). Because of his "pre-eminent fitness for responsibility," he was designated to lead the new mission to open Japan to Methodism, and he remained in general charge of the Japanese work from 1872 till his return to the United States in 1888. While serving in Japan, he undertook a special trip to Seoul, Korea, to confer with the ruler of the then "Hermit Kingdom," and in 1884 he secured permission to establish Christian missions in the peninsula. Korea has since been regarded by missionaries as ranking among the regions most responsive to Christian propaganda. As in Foochow, Maclay helped in translating the New Testament into the native language of Japan.

Both in China and in Japan, Maclay was active in educational work. On a temporary furlough in Foochow, in 1881, he organized the Anglo-Chinese College, and two years later he opened the Anglo-Japanese College at Tokyo, serving as its president from 1883 until 1887. He also established the Philander Smith Biblical Institute at Tokyo, in 1884, and was its dean from 1884 until 1887. He served as delegate to the London Ecumenical Conference in 1881, and to the General Conference of the Methodist Church, at New York, in 1888. Upon returning to the United States in 1888, he became dean of the Maclay College of Theology, formerly at San Fernando, Cal., but transferred to Los Angeles when it became the University of Southern California College of Religion. He continued as dean of this institution until it was temporarily closed in 1893. He then withdrew from active church work and lived in retirement at San Fernando until his death in 1907. He was twice married. His first wife was Henrietta Caroline Sperry, to whom he was married at Hong Kong on July 10, 1850. She died in 1879 and on June 6, 1882, he was married to Sarah Ann Barr, at San Francisco. Edgar Stanton Maclay [*q.v.*] was a son by the first marriage. In addition to the works mentioned Maclay's writings include *Life Among the Chinese* (1861); sketches of Japanese Methodist missions for J. M. Reid's *Missions and Missionary Society of the Methodist Episcopal Church* (2 vols., 1879; 3 vols., 1896); and the article on Shintoism for Reid's *Doomed Religions* (1884).

[*Who's Who in America*, 1908–09; J. M. Buckley, *A Hist. of Methodism in the U. S.* (1897), vol. II; L. G. Paik, *The Hist. of Protestant Missions in Korea, 1832–1910* (1929); Matthew Simpson, *Cyc. of Methodism* (1882); E. S. Maclay, *The Maclays of Lurgan* (1889); *Cal. Christian Advocate*, Aug. 29, 1907; *Christian Advocate* (N. Y.), Sept. 12, 1907.] H. E. W.

MACLAY, SAMUEL (June 17, 1741–Oct. 5, 1811), representative and senator from Pennsylvania, was born in Lurgan township, Franklin County, Pa., the son of Charles and Eleanor (Query) Maclay. In 1734 his father and grandfather, John Maclay, had emigrated from the north of Ireland. In 1767–68 Samuel Maclay appears as an assistant to his brother, William Maclay [*q.v.*], who, during a trip to England, had secured the approval of the proprietors of Pennsylvania to his own appointment as deputy surveyor of Cumberland County. In 1769 Samuel began surveying the "Officers' Tract." He became one of the large landowners of this region, settling in Buffalo Valley probably about 1770. On Nov. 10, 1773, he was married to Elizabeth, eighteen-year-old daughter of William and Esther (Harris) Plunket. He engaged in farming and surveying, owned at least one slave, and soon enjoyed a position of leadership in the affairs of the county. On July 29, 1775, he became a justice of the quarter sessions. Being one of the local court circle, he naturally became a member of the local committee of correspondence at the opening of the Revolution. He was commissioned lieutenant-colonel of militia, and on July 4, 1776, was a delegate to the convention of "Associators" at Lancaster, where the state militia was organized.

In 1787 he entered state politics through his election to the lower house of the legislature; he served in this position until 1791. On Feb. 23, 1792, he was appointed an associate judge for Northumberland County. On Oct. 14, 1794, he was elected to Congress as a Republican. Northumberland County, where the noted liberals Joseph Priestley and Thomas Cooper [*qq.v.*], had just settled, was overwhelmingly Republican, and "Samuel Maclay's influence, from his good character and ability, was almost unbounded" (Linn, *post*, p. 296). In 1795, however, the Rev. Hugh Morrison, a Presbyterian minister, led a determined opposition against the Jeffersonians, and, like Father Peto before Henry VIII, he lectured Maclay from the pulpit. Maclay withdrew from the congregation, and most of the members followed him. In 1799 Morrison brought suit for slander, which was finally discontinued. The attack merely increased Maclay's popularity with his own political group. In Congress, with no less ardor than his brother had shown in the Senate in the years 1789–91, Maclay promptly identified himself with the Opposition. The French minister, Adet, wrote that *"nos amis"* in Congress had calculated a plan to defeat the Jay treaty and throw the onus upon the administration. Maclay introduced the resolution, but his strategy failed: "Even the gentleman from Pennsylvania's promptitude failed him," chided one member, adding: "and the promptest man certainly he was he had ever known" (*Annals of Congress,* 4 Cong., 1 Sess., p. 974). But the gesture strengthened his popularity at home.

In 1797 Maclay was again elected to the lower house of the state legislature, and from 1798 to 1802 he held a seat in the state Senate, serving in 1801 and 1802 as speaker of the latter body. On Dec. 14, 1802, he was elected to the United States Senate, but he took little part in the debates. He voted consistently for administration measures, proposed no less than three amendments to the Constitution, and introduced the resolution calling for the investigation of Senator Smith of Ohio, charged with being in collusion with Aaron Burr. In 1809, before his term had expired, he resigned his seat, probably because of ill health. Like his brother, he was an aristocrat of the frontier, an intense individualist who belonged in spirit neither to the "eastern men of property" nor to the frontiersmen. In a speech in Congress he revealed his conflicting leanings (*Annals of Congress,* 4 Cong., 1 Sess., pp. 346–47): he would use the national territory for the advantage of speculators as well as settlers by dividing it into both large and small tracts. He was an expert marksman and a good mechanic, but his frontier environment would no more permit him to embrace Federalist politics than it would allow him to use the handsome coach which he is said to have abandoned when his democratic neighbors objected to such evidences of aristocracy. His training in the classics and his large library also tended to give him less in common with his neighbors. The *Journal of Samuel Maclay* written during a surveying expedition on the western rivers of Pennsylvania in 1790 reveals almost as much of these dual characteristics as the more famous *Journal of William Maclay.* Samuel Maclay had six sons and three daughters. He died at his home in Buffalo Valley.

[*Journal of Samuel Maclay, while Surveying the West Branch of the Susquehanna, the Sinnemahoning, and the Allegheny Rivers in 1790* (1887), ed. by J. F. Meginness; J. B. Linn, *Annals of Buffalo Valley, Pa., 1755–1855* (1877); *Hist. of . . . the Susquehanna and Juniata Valleys* (1886), vol. II; J. F. Meginness, *Otzinachson; or, A Hist. of the West Branch Valley of the Susquehanna* (rev. ed., 1889); F. J. Turner, "Correspondence of the French Ministers to the U. S., 1791–97," *Ann. Report of the Am. Hist. Asso. for the Year 1903* (1904), vol. II; H. V. Ames, "The Proposed Amendments to the Const. of the U. S. During the First Century of Its Hist.," *Ibid.,* for the year 1896 (1897), vol. II; *Hist. Soc. of Pa., Colls.,* I (1853), 94–118; E. S. Maclay, *The Maclays of Lurgan* (1889); P. D. Evans, *The Holland Land Company* (1924); *U. S. Gazette for the Country,* Oct. 7, 1811.] J. P. B.

MACLAY, WILLIAM (July 27, 1734–Apr. 16, 1804), lawyer, senator, diarist, brother of Samuel Maclay [*q.v.*], was the son of Charles and Eleanor (Query) Maclay. His father, a farmer, came to America in 1734 from the north of Ireland, settling first in New Garden township, Chester County, Pa., where William was born, and afterward moving to Franklin County. The Rev. John Blair, successor to his brother Samuel Blair [*q.v.*] as head of a noted school in Chester County, and a prominent guardian of Scotch-Irish discipline in the New World, gave the stalwart youth his classical training.

In 1758 Maclay was a lieutenant with Gen. John Forbes's expedition to Ft. Duquesne; in 1763–64 he participated in the expedition of Col. Henry Bouquet against the Indians. After the French and Indian War, visiting England, he took up the matter of surveys with Thomas Penn; he was engaged in surveying land in 1766, if not earlier. On Apr. 11, 1769, he was married to Mary McClure, daughter of John Harris, founder of Harrisburg, and settled at Mifflintown, where he owned 300 acres of land. He was admitted to the bar of York County in 1760, whether or not he practised there. He held various local offices in the new county of Northumberland, organized in 1772, laid out the town of Sunbury that year, and lived there himself until his removal to Harrisburg in 1786. Though he had been on good terms with the proprietors, he gave his allegiance to the patriot side when the battle for independence opened. He served for a time in the militia, acted as issuing commissary in Sunbury, and played a considerable part in organizing the frontier defense against Indian raids. The successful conclusion of the Revolution carried him to the state legislature, where he represented Northumberland County from 1781 to 1785. He was also a member of the Supreme Executive Council, in 1786 and 1788, a judge of the court of common pleas, deputy-surveyor, and a member of commissions to examine the navigation of the Susquehanna (1783) and to treat with the Indians for the purchase of lands (1784–85).

As United States senator he represented rural Pennsylvania in the first Congress held under the Constitution (1789–91). His colleague was Robert Morris who, in the drawing of lots, secured the long-term seat whereas Maclay got the short term. When he stood for reëlection he lost his seat to a Federalist. His historical significance consequently was lost until 1880, when the publication of a private journal he kept during the time he served in Congress revealed both the extent and nature of the debates in the Senate on the financial proposals of Hamilton and the rôle of Maclay in opposition. His notes are the only continuous report in existence of that early federal period when debates occurred behind closed doors and no official record was prepared for the public. They reveal the diarist as such a stanch antagonist of the Hamiltonian program, such a strong defender of the interests of the small-farming class, such a denunciator of the speculation rife at the time, that Pennsylvania may be called the home of the first Jeffersonian democrat. Jefferson did not reach the seat of government until eleven months after Congress commenced to work and during that time Maclay was at the democratic helm. As his journal discloses, moreover, he was often distressed by Jefferson's attitude when he became secretary of state, particularly with reference to the building up of a navy for an attack on the Algerian pirates and for dealing with the fisheries question. His comments on all the leaders of that critical period, including Washington, are invaluable side-lights on the contest so bitterly fought between the Federalists and their opponents over the interpretation of the new Constitution, the funding of the debt, the tariff, the bank, the excise tax, proper ceremonials and a title for the president, and manners and tastes in the young republic. Since Maclay sat in on conferences with Morris and others relative to the location of the federal capital and attended functions where the ladies of the "republican court" were present, his comments are warm with the personal aspects of the economic struggle. His wit is caustic, perhaps because he suffered from rheumatism, but the journal was meant solely for private release.

His neighbors sent him to the state legislature again in 1795, and in 1803. In the meantime, he had been a presidential elector in 1796 and associate judge of Dauphin County (1801–03). He died at Harrisburg in 1804.

[G. W. Harris, ed., *Sketches of Debate in the First Senate of the U. S., in 1789–90–91, by William Maclay* (1880), with a good biog. sketch in the preface; E. S. Maclay, ed., *Journal of William Maclay* (1890); C. A. Beard, ed., *The Journal of William Maclay* (1927); L. R. Harley, *William Maclay, U. S. Senator from Pa., 1789–1791* (1909); E. S. Maclay, *The Maclays of Lurgan* (1889); J. B. Linn, *Annals of Buffalo Valley, Pa., 1755–1855* (1877); *Pa. Archives*, 1 ser., vols. IV–X (1853–54); E. P. Oberholtzer, *Robert Morris* (1903).]

M. R. B.

MACLAY, WILLIAM BROWN (Mar. 20, 1812–Feb. 19, 1882), lawyer, editor, legislator, was born in New York City, one of twelve children of the Rev. Archibald and Mary Brown Maclay. His father was born in the village of Killearn, Stirlingshire, Scotland; his mother was the daughter of a Glasgow merchant. He matriculated at the University of the City of New York at twenty and graduated with highest honors in the class of 1836, remaining after his graduation to accept a temporary professorship in Latin language and literature. In 1839, having taken up the study of law, he was admitted to the bar and at once formed a partnership with his brother-in-law, Isaac P. Martin. In the same year he was elected to the state Assembly and was reëlected in 1840 and 1841. He, more than any one else, was responsible for the legislation reorganizing the superior court and the court of common pleas of the city and county of New York. He also secured the publication of the *Journals of the Provincial Congress . . . of New York* (2 vols., 1842), covering the years 1775–77 and containing many original unpublished letters of distinguished Revolutionary personages. His most important legislative work, however, related to popular education. As a member of the committee on colleges, academies, and common schools, he obtained the passage of an act which in substance gave the City of New York full benefit of the state law providing for publicly supported, publicly controlled schools. At the time, the Protestants charged that the measure was designed to favor the growing Catholic population of the city, and Maclay was roundly and unjustly denounced, but he was a believer in religious toleration and wished to have the schools of the city and state open on equal terms to all.

In 1842 Maclay was elected to Congress. He served five terms in all, being reëlected in 1844, 1848, 1856, and 1858, after which he declined to be a candidate for reëlection. At Washington he was distinguished for his punctuality and diligent attention to business. He advocated the passage of the bill to aid S. F. B. Morse in demonstrating the practical utility of the telegraph, introduced an unsuccessful bill for the relief of the heirs of John Paul Jones, and was one of those foremost in the movement for the reduction of postal rates. He asserted that the title of the United States to the disputed Oregon territory was "clear and unquestionable," was an earnest advocate for annexation of Texas, and favored the war with Mexico. A pronounced Democrat of the Jacksonian type, he maintained that public lands should be gratuitously conveyed to actual settlers in the form of homesteads rather than be held by the government for sale to private speculators; he did not favor their donation to private corporations for the ostensible purpose of internal improvements. He vigorously opposed the doctrines of the Native Americans or Know-Nothings as contrary to the spirit of republican institutions and incompatible with national unity.

Maclay was a lover of books and libraries, was widely read, could speak or write intelligently and often eloquently on many subjects. His characteristic traits were those of a cultured gentleman. He was proud of his good name, yet modest; he possessed a high sense of honor, loved justice, and was urbane and refined in taste and manner. On Aug. 22, 1838, he married Antoinette Walton, daughter of Mark Walton, a New Orleans merchant. Three children were born of this marriage. In the spring of 1849, at the close of his third term in Congress, he removed with his family to Mount Palatine, Ill. Here, soon after their arrival, his wife died of cholera; he then returned to New York where his youngest daughter died of the same malady. He did not remarry. From 1838 to the time of his death he served as a trustee of the University of the City of New York.

[Orrin B. Judd, *Maclay Memorial Sketching the Lineage, Life and Obsequies of Hon. Wm. B. Maclay* (1884); *Biog. Dir. Am. Cong.* (1928); *N. Y. Times*, Feb. 20, 1882; W. B. Maclay, *Address* [*on civil and religious liberty*] *Delievered at the Democratic-Republican Celebration . . . July 4, 1840* (1840), *A Selection of Letters Written on Various Pub. Occasions* (1859).]

H. J. C.

McLEAN, ARCHIBALD (Sept. 6, 1849–Dec. 15, 1920), clergyman and missionary executive of the Disciples of Christ, son of Malcolm and Alexandra (McKay) McLean, was born on his father's farm near Summerside, Prince Edward Island, Canada. His immediate forebears were of Scotch stock of the island of Skye. His early education was obtained at the near-by Graham's Road public school, which he attended until his fourteenth year. Thereafter he undertook to learn the carriage-builder's trade, first in the service of an uncle, then as apprentice for five years to William Tuplin, a skilful carriage maker of the village of Margate. Afterward he spent one year in Boston as a journeyman mechanic. The spring of 1870 found him again at home, with a desire for a more influential career than that of the tradesman. He had been reared in a strongly religious environment. John Geddie, a Presbyterian minister of New London, P. E. I., who became the first missionary sent abroad from any British colony, made a lasting impression on him, and he also felt the influence of Donald Crawford, a Baptist minister who identified himself with the "Campbellite" movement and founded in 1858 the Summerside Church of Christ. McLean had been baptized by Crawford in 1867 and since then had considered entering the Christian ministry. With this purpose in mind, in the autumn of 1870 he went to Bethany College, West Virginia, an institution founded by Alexander Campbell and conducted by the Disciples of Christ. Here he took the regular four-year classical course and graduated with honors, June 18, 1874. Ordained immediately, he began his ministry on June 21 with the Christian Church of Mount Healthy, near Cincinnati, where after two months he was formally installed. During this pastorate, which continued until 1885, he erected a new church building.

In 1882 he was elected corresponding secretary of the Foreign Christian Missionary Society of the Disciples' brotherhood, and for three years carried on the duties of this office along with his pastorate. In 1885, however, he resigned his pulpit to give the Missionary Society his full time. In 1888 he began the publication of the *Missionary Intelligencer,* first as a quarterly, but soon as a monthly. He represented his Church at the ecumenical conference on foreign missions, held in London June 9–10, 1888. In 1889 he accepted the presidency of Bethany College, in addition to his work as a missionary executive. This office he resigned in 1891—although an emergency required the continuation of his administration through the autumn of that year—and thereafter he devoted his entire time, in one capacity or another, to the work of the missionary society, keeping a connection with the college through a trusteeship.

On July 24, 1895, he left Cincinnati—his headquarters—for a year's tour through all the mission fields, save Africa, in which the Society was working: the Hawaiian Islands, Japan, China, India, Palestine, Turkey, Scandinavia, and England. His observations are admirably recorded in his book, *A Circuit of the Globe* (1897), published soon after his return. He was a delegate to the Ecumenical Missionary Conference held in New York City Apr. 21–May 1, 1900, and in that year was elected president of his Society, in which office he served with distinction until the formation of the United Society in 1919. In 1905 he instituted the policy of missionary "rallies" throughout his denomination, in the interest of missionary education and of support for the missionary enterprise. He served on the committee in charge of arrangements for the centennial of the Church, held in Pittsburgh Oct. 11–19, 1909. In 1910 he attended the Edinburgh World Missionary Conference as a delegate of his denomination. He was chairman of the executive committee of the "Men and Millions" movement (1914–18) of the Disciples, a great financial drive on behalf of missions and the work of the church. He aided in the organization of the Panama congress (1916) on Christian work in Latin America, and attended its sessions as a delegate of his Society. As the movement among the Disciples toward the amalgamation of several of their intra-denominational organizations gathered momentum, he gave it his sympathy and assistance, and on the formation of the United Christian Missionary Society in 1919 he became its first vice-president. As president of the former Foreign Society he had commissioned every missionary sent to non-Christian lands in the entire history of the organization. He died at Battle Creek Sanitarium, Michigan, the best known and most highly esteemed man among the Disciples of Christ. His body was taken first to St. Louis—at that time the headquarters of the United Society—thence to Cincinnati, and finally to Bethany, W. Va., where it was interred in the Campbell Cemetery.

McLean was the author of *Missionary Addresses* (1895); *Handbook of Missions* (1897); *A Circuit of the Globe* (1897), previously mentioned; *Where the Book Speaks* (1907); *Epoch Makers of Modern Missions* (1912); *The Primacy of the Missionary* (1920); *The History of the Foreign Christian Missionary Society* (1921); and many articles in the *Missionary Intelligencer, Christian-Evangelist, Christian Standard,* and other periodicals. Among his tracts were *Intercessory Prayer, Doubling the Preacher's Power,* and *Forty Years of Service for the King*. He was also the author of two memorable addresses, *Alexander Campbell as a Preacher,* and *Thomas and Alexander Campbell,* both of which were published (Cincinnati, no date).

[W. R. Warren, *Archibald McLean* (1923); *Who's Who in America,* 1920–21, inaccurate; *Missionary Review of the World,* Sept. 1921; *Christian Evangelist,* Dec. 23, 1920; *Christian Standard,* Dec. 25, 1920; *Commercial Tribune* (Cincinnati), Dec. 16, 1920.]

J. C. A.

MACLEAN, JOHN (Mar. 1, 1771–Feb. 17, 1814), chemist, educator, was born in Glasgow, Scotland, the son of John and Agnes (Lang) Maclean. His father was a surgeon of the British army, who was present at the capture of Quebec from the French, being the third man to scale the Heights of Abraham. The boy was left an orphan at an early age, and George Macintosh, father of Charles Macintosh who later invented the waterproof cloth, was appointed his guardian. Maclean received his early education in the Glasgow Grammar School and entered the University of Glasgow before he was thirteen years old. He was especially interested in chemistry, natural philosophy, medicine, and anatomy, for it was his purpose to become a surgeon. Under the influence of Charles Macintosh, who was four years his senior, while a student at the university he joined the Chemical Society, before which he read several papers. Leaving Glasgow about 1787, he spent two or three years in study at Edinburgh, London, and Paris, where he was greatly impressed by Lavoisier, Berthollet, and other French scholars. Returning to Glasgow in 1790, he resumed his studies for another year, and then engaged in the practice of medicine and surgery. The diploma authorizing him to practise surgery and pharmacy was dated Aug. 1, 1791, and on the same day he was admitted as a member of the faculty of physicians and surgeons of the university.

Being in sympathy with the political sentiments of the United States, he left Scotland for America in April 1795. In Philadelphia, Dr. Benjamin Rush advised him to settle in Princeton, seat of the College of New Jersey. In the summer of 1795, he delivered there a course of lectures on chemistry, and on Oct. 1 he was chosen professor of chemistry and natural history in the College. Two years later he relinquished his medical and surgical practice to give his full time to his academic duties, which were increased in 1797 by his appointment as professor of mathematics and natural philosophy, with the provision that chemistry and natural history be taught as branches of natural philosophy. He was the first professor of chemistry in any American college other than medical institutions (Benjamin Silliman, Jr., "American Contributions to Chemistry," *American Chemist,* August-September, December 1874), and for a number of years he was the only professor, other than the president, on the faculty of the College of New Jersey. While in Paris, he had been won to the support of the antiphlogistic theory, as the "new chemistry" of Lavoisier was called. In 1797 he prepared *Two Lectures on Combustion: Supplementary to a Course of Lectures on Chemistry Read at Nassau Hall; Containing an Examination of Dr. Priestley's Considerations on the Doctrine of Phlogiston, and the Decomposition of Water,* printed in that year by T. Dobson, at the Stone-House, No. 41 South Second Street, Philadelphia. The lectures displayed ability and learning, and were helpful in the overthrow of the phlogistic theory. The discussion was continued for a time by Maclean, Joseph Priestley, James Woodhouse, and Samuel Mitchill [*qq.v.*] in the New York *Medical Repository.* In 1797, the University of Aberdeen conferred the degree of M.D. upon Maclean. He was elected a member of the American Philosophical Society, Jan. 18, 1805, and two years later became a naturalized citizen of the United States. Meanwhile, in 1802, he had given a reading list to Benjamin Silliman [*q.v.*], who had been appointed professor of chemistry at Yale College despite a scant knowledge of the subject. Silliman (the elder of the name), who later came to be revered as one of the fathers of science in America, left in his diary the following note: "Dr. Maclean was a man of brilliant mind, with all the acumen of his native Scotland; and a sprinkling of wit gave variety to his conversation. I regard him as my earliest master in chemistry, and Princeton as my first starting point in that pursuit; although I had not an opportunity to attend any lectures there" (G. P. Fisher, *Life of Benjamin Silliman,* 1866, I, 109–10).

In 1812, in consequence of certain contemplated changes in the Princeton faculty, Maclean resigned, and shortly thereafter accepted the chair of natural philosophy and chemistry in the College of William and Mary, Williamsburg, Va. After one year, his health being poor, he returned to Princeton, where in February 1814 he died. He was buried in the old cemetery, in a grave adjoining those of the college presidents and professors. On Nov. 7, 1798, he had married Phebe Bainbridge, sister of Commodore William Bainbridge [*q.v.*], and to them were born two daughters and four sons. One son, John Maclean [*q.v.*], became the tenth president of the College of New Jersey at Princeton.

[The chief source is *A Memoir of John Maclean, M.D.* (1876), by his son, John Maclean, privately printed. See also William Foster, "John Maclean—Chemist," in *Science,* Oct. 3, 1924, and "Doctor Maclean and the Doctrine of Phlogiston," in *Jour. of Chemical Educ.,* Sept. 1925, and "Some Letters by Dr. John Maclean," *Ibid.,* Dec. 1929; *Poulson's Am. Daily Advertiser* (Phila.), Feb. 23, 1814. There are in the Princeton University Library seven letters written by Maclean.]

W. F.

McLEAN, JOHN (Mar. 11, 1785–Apr. 4, 1861), congressman, postmaster-general, jurist, was born in Morris County, N. J., the son of Fergus and Sophia (Blockford) McLean. His parents came to America from Ireland, the father being descended from the Scottish clan of McLean. A weaver by trade, he became a farmer, but having a large family and being limited in means, he soon decided to go West. In 1789 the family moved to Morgantown, Va., then to Jessamine, near Nicholasville, Ky., thence to Maysville, Ky., and finally, in 1799, settled on a farm near Lebanon, in what is now Warren County, Ohio. During these wanderings young McLean's education suffered. He attended school as opportunity offered and as the pressing needs of the family permitted. Determined to get further instruction, he worked for wages and at sixteen was able to hire private tutors. Two years later he went to Cincinnati, where he was formally indentured for two years to the clerk of the Hamilton County court. By working part of the day in the office he was able to support himself. Meanwhile, he read law with Arthur St. Clair, one of the best counselors in the West, and the son of General St. Clair. He also joined a debating club, in which he acquired facility of expression.

In 1807 he was admitted to the bar. The same year he married Rebecca Edwards and moved to Lebanon, where he founded the *Western Star,* a weekly newspaper. Commencing to practise in Lebanon, he soon won recognition by his industry and scrupulous care. In October 1812 he was elected as a War Democrat to Congress from the Cincinnati district, which then included Warren County. He was reëlected in 1814 "by the unanimous vote of all the electors who took part in the election. Not only did no one vote against him, but also no one who voted for any office at the election, refrained from voting for him" (Force, *post,* 271–72). He vigorously sponsored the war with England and advocated bills to indemnify persons for property lost in the public service, to grant pensions to officers and soldiers, and to pay congressmen a salary of $1500 per annum instead of the per diem allowance. In 1815 he declined to be a candidate for the United States Senate. The following year he resigned his seat in Congress to become judge of the supreme court of Ohio, to which office he had been elected by the state legislature. He remained upon the bench until 1822, when President Monroe appointed him commissioner of the land office. The next year he was made postmaster-general, and in the direction of this office he acquired a national reputation as an able administrator. Heretofore, this branch of the public service had been inefficient and disorganized. Under his management contractors were held to their agreements and incompetent and unfaithful officials were removed. He was reappointed by President J. Q. Adams and, it is claimed, used his official position to work against the reëlection of his superior (Bassett, *post,* II, 412, 413). McLean was not in sympathy with President Jackson's policy as to removals, and, after declining the portfolios of secretary of war and secretary of the navy, he was nominated by Jackson to be associate justice of the United States Supreme Court. His appointment was confirmed by the Senate on Mar. 7, 1829. "It is a good and satisfactory appointment," wrote Joseph Story, "but was, in fact, produced by other causes than his fitness or our advantage. The truth is . . . he told the new President, that he would not form a part of the new Cabinet, or remain in office, if he was compelled to make removals upon political grounds" (W. W. Story, *post,* I, 564). He was assigned to the seventh circuit, which then included the districts of Tennessee, Kentucky, and Ohio; later, the districts of Ohio, Indiana, Illinois, and Michigan. He took his seat in January 1830 and served until his death. On the bench he was dignified, courteous, painstaking, fearless, and able. Not until his health began to fail, two years before his death, was he absent a single day from his duties. He was not a great judge but his decisions on the circuit were seldom reversed and he was not often in the minority in the Supreme Court. In the celebrated Dred Scott case he dissented from the majority of the court and rendered an opinion of his own, which defined his position upon the slavery question (19 *Howard,* 558, 559). He held that slavery had its origin merely in force and was contrary to right, being sustained only by local law.

During his term on the bench he was frequently mentioned as a possible candidate for the presidency. He maintained that a judge was under no obligation to refrain from the discussion of political affairs and steadfastly defended the propriety of his candidacy. He declined the nomination in the Anti-Masonic Convention of 1831, and was proposed as a candidate by the Ohio legislature in 1836. His name was considered by the convention of "Free Democracy" in 1848 and was before the Whig Convention in 1852. In the Republican Convention of 1856 he received 196 votes, and, although seventy-five years of age, he still hoped for the nomination in the Republican Convention of 1860.

His first wife, by whom he had four daughters and three sons, died in December 1840, and three years later he married Sarah Bella Garrard, widow of Col. Jephtha D. Garrard and the youngest daughter of Israel Ludlow.

[M. F. Force, in *Memorial Biogs. of the New-England Hist. Geneal. Soc.,* vol. IV (1885); Charles Warren, *The Supreme Court in U. S. Hist.* (1922); W. W. Story, *Life and Letters of Joseph Story* (1851); J. S. Bassett, *Andrew Jackson* (1911); B. P. Poor, *Perley's Reminiscences* (1886); *Biog. Dir. Am. Cong.* (1928); 66 *U. S. Reports* (1 *Black*), 8–13; F. H. Hodder, "Some Phases of the Dred Scott Case," in *Miss. Valley Hist. Rev.,* June 1929; *Cincinnati Commercial,* Apr. 5, 1861; *Cincinnati Gazette,* Apr. 5, 1861.] R. C. M.

MACLEAN, JOHN (Mar. 3, 1800–Aug. 10, 1886), president of the College of New Jersey, was born at Princeton, the eldest son of Prof. John Maclean [*q.v.*] and Phebe (Bainbridge) Maclean, a sister of Commodore William Bainbridge [*q.v.*]. His paternal grandfather, a surgeon in the British army, was the third man to scale the Heights of Abraham in Wolfe's attack on Quebec. The boy inherited a strong, active body, great boldness and versatility of spirit, and a scientific turn of mind. His home advantages were such that he entered the College of New Jersey well prepared in the spring of 1813 and graduated, the youngest member of his class, in the autumn of 1816. After teaching for a year at the Lawrenceville preparatory school, he entered the Princeton Theological Seminary. For two years he studied theology, but in 1818 he accepted a position as tutor in the college, and his ordination as a Presbyterian minister did not take place until 1828. He was appointed teacher of mathematics and natural philosophy in 1822 and professor of mathematics in 1823. In 1829 he was shifted to the department of languages and the following year appointed professor of ancient languages and literature; in 1847 he became professor of Greek.

His early and rapid promotions were justified by his natural ability and the ardor of his zeal for teaching. In 1826 he founded the Alumni Association of Nassau Hall, the second oldest college alumni association in America. James Carnahan [*q.v.*], the president of the college, lacked energy, which Maclean possessed in great abundance, and in 1829 the younger man was made vice-president, charged with the duties of a modern dean, with the raising of funds, and with the selection of new members of the faculty. The college was passing through a period of depression. The funds were low; the classes were becoming smaller; the professors were poorly paid. Some of the trustees favored a policy of shrinkage and retrenchment. Maclean, on the other hand, proposed to turn retreat into a bold forward movement. He set forth to raise money for endowment, and came home with a goodly supply. Instead of reducing the faculty, he determined to enlarge it and to offer positions to men of eminence. East College was built in 1832 and West College in 1836. Through his insistence the college calendar was reformed, Commencement being changed from September to June. In 1852 and 1853 he successfully resisted a movement to place the college under the control of the Presbyterian church.

Upon Dr. Carnahan's retirement, Maclean was elected to the presidency on Dec. 20, 1853, and inaugurated on June 28, 1854. His courage was severely tried the next year, when the interior of Nassau Hall, the oldest and largest college building, was ruined by fire, and his task of soliciting money began again. The Civil War caused more loss of students to Princeton than to the New England colleges, but by skilful management Maclean held the faculty together through those years of trial. The students, though amused by his eccentricities, admired and loved the active man, who embodied for them the spirit of the place and time. From 1866 to 1868 he served as professor of Biblical instruction, in addition to his other duties. On Dec. 11, 1867, he resigned the presidency, but remained in office till the Commencement of 1868, when the alumni bade affectionate farewell to him and welcomed his successor, James McCosh [*q.v.*]. No president or professor of Princeton has been regarded with such a harmonious mixture of amusement and affection as "Johnny" Maclean. The men might smile at him as he hurried about in his plaid and, laying aside his dignity, engaged in the performance of some proctorial function; but when they were in trouble he befriended them, when they needed money he gave them his own, when they were sick he visited them.

After his retirement, he employed the rest of his life in works of charity and public service and in writing his history of the college. With the profits from this book he founded scholarships for poor students. He died at Princeton on Aug. 10, 1886; he was never married. Among his numerous pamphlets, sermons, and addresses, may be mentioned his *Lecture on a School System for New Jersey* (1829), and *Letters on the True Relations of the Church and the State to Schools and Colleges* (1853). His chief literary work is his *History of the College of New Jersey,* in two volumes, published in 1877.

[V. L. Collins, *Princeton* (1914); *True American* (Trenton), Aug. 11, 1886; manuscript letters and other records in the office of the secretary of Princeton University; personal recollections.] G. M. H.

McLEAN, WALTER (July 30, 1855–Mar. 20, 1930), naval officer, was born in Elizabeth, N. J. His father was Col. George Washington McLean, who organized, equipped, and commanded a New Jersey regiment in the Civil War; his mother, Rebecca J. McCormick, daughter of James McCormick, whose Maryland estate was Mount Pleasant, now a part of Baltimore, near the site of Johns Hopkins University. Destined by his father for a military career, the boy early decided on the navy, and at fourteen took affairs into his own hands by running away. Going to Washington he called on President Grant, a friend of his father, and applied for an appointment to Annapolis. Though it was necessary for him to spend some time further in study, the appointment was promised, and in June 1872 he entered the Naval Academy.

Graduated in 1876, he had his first duty on the *Trenton,* then fitting out for the European Squadron. After later duty on the North Atlantic Station, he was ordered in 1879 to the Asiatic Station, where he spent three years. On being detached and ordered to Washington for instruction in ordnance, he returned by way of Russia, journeying over the barren wastes of Siberia to Moscow. Varied duties followed, with two assignments in the Coast Survey. In 1891 he received his commission as lieutenant. Four years later he was again sent to the East, and he was there at the outbreak of the Spanish-American War, attached to the old side-wheeler *Monocacy.* Dewey, realizing the need of more officers and men, detached McLean from this ship on Apr. 25, 1898, and ordered him to the *Olympia.* When he reported, May 11, he was placed by Dewey on his staff and became the senior aide. There was need of supplies and also of communications with the United States by way of Hong-Kong. McLean was repeatedly sent in charge of the little supply steamer *Zafiro* to attend to both. Promotion followed rapidly: to lieutenant commander, 1899; commander, 1905; captain, 1908. From 1903 to 1906 he was attached to the Bureau of Ordnance, and then was sent to the Philippines as commandant of the naval station at Cavite and Olongapo. In 1914 he was promoted to the rank of rear admiral. After two years and a half in Washington as a member of the naval examining and retiring boards, he was given a part in the troubled affairs of Mexico by being ordered to relieve Admiral Mayo in command of the fleet off Vera Cruz (1914). The following year he was placed in command of the Norfolk navy-yard and the fifth naval district. When the World War broke out and the United States was finally swept into it, this duty became of great importance. The naval operating base established at Hampton Roads was the scene of intense activity, and large numbers of recruits were there assembled and trained. In addition to this duty McLean was the navy representative in the War Council appointed by the director general of railroads.

On Mar. 15, 1919, after forty-seven years of service in the navy, twenty-two years at sea, he was at his own request placed on the retired list. His last residence was in Annapolis, Md., where he died. He was married in 1887 to Emma Bowne Jarvis of Cooperstown, N. Y., by whom he had a daughter.

[*Register of the Commissioned and Warrant Officers of the Navy of the U. S. and of the Marine Corps* (1901); *The Records of Living Officers of the U. S. Navy and Marine Corps* (7th ed., 1902); *Who's Who in America*, 1928–29; *Army and Navy Jour.*, Mar. 22, 1930; the *Sun* (Baltimore), Mar. 21, 1930; material from friends.]
C. S. S.

McLEAN, WILLIAM LIPPARD (May 4, 1852–July 30, 1931), newspaper publisher, philanthropist, was born at Mount Pleasant, Pa. His father, Robert Caldwell McLean, of Scotch ancestry, head of a furniture factory, was an elder in the Middle Presbyterian Church. His mother, Augusta Dorothea (Voigt) McLean, was the daughter of a clergyman. On both sides, the son profited by examples of industry, thrift, and conscientious rectitude. While at public school, he crossed the threshold of journalism by serving as local carrier for the Pittsburgh *Leader*. At twenty he took a position in its circulation department in Pittsburgh, becoming shortly a subscription solicitor in the outlying districts. One of his early tasks was to help compile the first newspaper almanac published in that city, to which may be traced the annual *Bulletin Almanac and Yearbook* he later established and made a standard statistical reference work. After six years of varied experience, McLean, though only twenty-six, was sent to Philadelphia by Calvin Wells, a Pittsburgh manufacturer who had bought the *Press*, to be its business manager; and he was soon credited with reviving the prestige of that famous journal.

In 1895, he struck out for himself by purchasing, at executor's sale, along with associates whose interests he later secured, the *Evening Bulletin*, the oldest afternoon daily in Pennsylvania. In an editorial in his first issue (*Evening Bulletin*, June 1, 1895), he proclaimed his purpose "to present a complete afternoon paper that will be abreast of every improvement in modern journalism." Promising support of the principles of the Republican party, he added that "on the vital issue of the financial integrity of the nation, it [the *Bulletin*] will oppose all attempts to debase the currency with the free coinage of silver or to alter the existing standard of values. It will register the decrees of no leader or faction and it will reserve to itself the right of independent criticism of men and policies." The circulation, which had ebbed below 6,000 a day, reached 33,625 within a year. McLean molded the *Bulletin* to his journalistic ideals: "Avoid scare heads; treat crime as loathesome; guard against exaggeration." He insisted on honesty above all things. Even when the circulation passed 500,000, he refused to drop the word "nearly" from his slogan, "In Philadelphia, nearly everybody reads *The Bulletin*." To safeguard his independence, he consistently brushed aside public office and corporate directorships, excepting only in organizations of newspapers.

Taking over the *Bulletin* at the height of the bitter news-association war, he was soon active on the side of the victorious Associated Press and shared prominently in its reorganization in 1900. Through him, John G. Johnson [*q.v.*], the noted Philadelphia attorney, was engaged to draft a new charter and bylaws which would stand clear of the court ruling in Illinois that the old Association was "affected with a public interest" and must serve all alike. McLean remained a director of the Associated Press from 1896 until 1924 and was also, for a time, on the Board of the American Newspaper Publishers' Association.

Tall, with a large frame, tireless, deliberate of speech and action, inclined to reticence yet plainspoken on occasion, he was gentle in manner and most considerate of his subordinates, to whom he accorded full confidence and support. He was a lover of nature: hunting, fishing, and camping out filled his vacations. His philanthropy was mostly unobtrusive. In 1919 he established a scholarship at Princeton in memory of his eldest son, who was killed in a military training camp. He presented the "Tudor Room" to the Pennsylvania Art Museum, and gave $100,000 to provide a statue of Benjamin Franklin for the Franklin Memorial Museum. Although a purveyor of publicity, he stubbornly shunned the limelight for himself, refusing interviews and even personal data for biographical compendia. He was married in 1889 to Sarah Burd Warden, daughter of William G. Warden of Philadelphia, who had the same birthday as her husband and died on her fifty-eighth anniversary. Two sons and a daughter survived their parents. McLean had devolved the active conduct of the *Bulletin* gradually upon his sons and, in his closing year, was confined to his home in Germantown, where he died.

[E. P. Oberholtzer, *Phila., A Hist. of the City and Its People* (n.d.), vol. IV; *Who's Who in America*, 1930–31; *Evening Bulletin* (Phila.), July 30, 1931.]
V. R.

McLELLAN, ISAAC (May 21, 1806–Aug. 20, 1899), poet and sportsman, was born in Portland, Me., the son of Isaac and Eliza (Hull) McLellan. When he was thirteen his family moved to Boston. With his friend, Nathaniel P. Willis, he attended Phillips Academy, Andover, Mass., and from there he proceeded to Bowdoin, graduating in 1826. He then returned to Boston and devoted his time to law and journalism. He was associate editor of the *Boston Patriot and Daily Mercantile Advertiser,* merged in 1831 with the *Boston Daily Advertiser,* and he began the publication of a monthly magazine which was consolidated with the *Boston Pearl,* previously edited by Isaac C. Pray. For two years in the forties he traveled in Europe. Upon his return he gave up law and journalism, turning exclusively to the life of an ardent sportsman and poet of sport. He never married. After 1851 he made his home in Greenport, L. I., in an unpretentious board house on Barnegat Bay. He became an active member of the group of New York sportsmen which included William T. Porter, of the *Spirit of the Times,* Henry William Herbert ("Frank Forester"), Genio C. Scott, Edward Zane Carroll Judson ("Ned Buntline"), and Harry Fenwood. He had been a frequent contributor of prose and verse to the magazines of the day, and he now wrote for the sporting journals, principally *Turf, Field and Farm*; *Forest and Stream*; *American Angler*; *Amateur Sportsman,* and *Gameland.*

Most of his poetry, though little of his prose, was from time to time reprinted in book form. His first book, *The Fall of the Indian with Other Poems* (1830), with a timid preface, is heavy with youthful, literary melancholy and elegy, strange perhaps in view of the actual devotion to sport. The graveyard strain is continued in *Mount Auburn and Other Poems* (1843), the title poem being a detailed, annotated elegy over the dead in Mount Auburn Cemetery (where he himself was later buried), and in a fugitive broadside, "Paradise Spring," a poem read before the Phi Beta Kappa society of Bowdoin, Sept. 3, 1835. The outward aspects of Nature do enter these poems, often in expressive epithet, but it is not until the appearance of *Poems of the Rod and Gun, or Sports by Flood and Field* (1886), edited by Frederick E. Pond ("Will Wildwood"), that McLellan became, for the reader familiar only with the collected poems, the sportsman's poet. This and his last volume, *Haunts of Wild Game, or Poems of Woods, Wilds and Waters* (1896), edited by Charles Barker Bradford, are true curiosities in American poetry. They are nothing short of natural histories in verse of the United States and other regions. To invest such subjects as "Bison-hunting in the Far West," "Elephant-hunting in the Island of Ceylon," and "My Parker Gun" with genuine poetry is often beyond his power, as it indeed might be beyond that of any poet, but he was the spokesman in verse of a generation of American sportsmen which, like the noble Indian whom he mourned, has passed away.

[There is a memoir of McLellan by F. E. Pond in the latter's edition of *Poems of the Rod and Gun* and one by C. B. Bradford in *Haunts of Wild Game.* See also: R. W. Griswold, *The Poets and Poetry of America* (1850); G. B. Griffith, *The Poets of Maine* (1888); *Who's Who in America,* 1899–1900; *Obit. Record of the Grads. of Bowdoin Coll.... 1900–09* (1911).]

A. L. B.
F. E. B.

McLEOD, ALEXANDER (June 12, 1774–Feb. 17, 1833), Reformed Presbyterian clergyman, author, and editor, was the son of Rev. Neil McLeod, pastor of two Scottish Established Church parishes on Mull island of the Hebrides, on which isle Alexander was born. Dr. Samuel Johnson refers to the "elegance of conversation, and strength of judgment" of the elder McLeod, by whom the lexicographer was entertained when he visited Mull (*A Journey to the Western Islands of Scotland,* 1775, p. 357). The father having died when Alexander was five years old, care of the boy fell to the mother, Margaret McLeod, daughter of Rev. Archibald McLean, McLeod's predecessor in the parishes. Before he was seven Alexander had mastered his Latin Grammar and had determined to enter the ministry. His mother died when he was about fifteen.

In 1792 he emigrated to the United States and for a time taught Greek at Schenectady, N. Y. He entered Union College in 1796, and was graduated with high honor two years later. During his first year in the United States, through the influence of Rev. James McKinney, who had arrived from Ireland in 1793, McLeod had united with the Reformed Presbyterian Church. After theological studies under McKinney, he was licensed to preach in 1799. The following year he was called to be pastor at Coldenham, near Newburgh, N. Y., and also of the First Reformed Presbyterian Church, New York City. When he objected to the Coldenham call because among its signers were several slave-owners, the presbytery formally forbade communicant membership to slave-holders. A revised call was accepted, but the New York parish grew so rapidly that the young man soon gave all his time to it, and he remained connected with it until his death. Within a few years he was recognized as a leader in his denomination, and as one of America's foremost pulpit orators.

McLeod entered the controversy with the Episcopal Church regarding validity of presbyterial ordination of ministers when, in 1806, he published his *Ecclesiastical Catechism.* In 1814 his *Lectures upon the Principal Prophecies of the Revelation* appeared; and in 1816, *The Life and Power of True Godliness,* which like his *Catechism* was well received in both America and Great Britain. Among his other publications was a sermon in opposition to slavery, *Negro Slavery Unjustifiable* (1802), which pointed toward his active aid, some years afterwards, in organizing the American Colonization Society. His *Scriptural View of the Character, Causes and Ends of the Present War* (1815) accorded with his vigorous defense of the government's war policy. When his synod founded the *Christian Expositor,* a monthly, McLeod became its editor, continuing as such nearly two years. He frequently contributed to the *Christian Magazine,* edited by John M. Mason and John B. Romeyn. He was a member of the New York City Historical Society, and helped organize the American Society for Meliorating the Condition of the Jews and also the New York Society for Instruction of the Deaf and Dumb. Having been in poor health for a long time, he died of heart disease in his fifty-ninth year.

McLeod was a fearless defender of human liberty, whether individual, civic, or religious. Naturally impetuous, he disciplined himself to restraint and was dignified and urbane in manner. In the pulpit, however, he ordinarily followed his calm and reasoned exposition with an application the eloquence of which was vehement, impassioned, and unconfined. One of his distinguished contemporaries characterized his preaching as that of "a mountain torrent, full of foam, but sending off pure water into a thousand pools." In 1805 he married Maria Anne, daughter of John Agnew.

[W. B. Sprague, *Annals Am. Pulpit,* vol. IX (1869); S. N. Rowan, *Tribute to the Memory of Alexander McLeod, D. D.* (1833); R. E. Thompson, *A Hist. of the Presbyterian Churches in the U. S.* (1895); S. B. Wylie, *Memoir of Alexander McLeod, D. D.* (1855); *N. Y. Standard,* Feb. 19, 1833.]

P. P. F.

McLEOD, HUGH (Aug. 1, 1814–Jan. 2, 1862), military leader of the Texan Sante Fé expedition, was born in New York City, but while he was yet a boy his family removed to Macon, Ga. From Georgia he entered the United States Military Academy on Sept. 1, 1831. Four years later he was graduated and was commissioned as second lieutenant of the 3rd Infantry, but before joining his company at Fort Jessup, La., he visited Macon and accompanied the Georgia batallion on its journey to Texas as far as Columbus, Ga. Fired with a desire to join the Texas revolution, he sent in his resignation, which took effect June 30, 1836. He then went to Texas, where he rapidly advanced to prominence. In December 1837, he became adjutant-general and continued as such until Jan. 18, 1841, playing an important part in the Indian wars, particularly the Caddo expedition of 1838, the expulsion of the Cherokee in 1839, and the Comanche troubles of 1840.

In 1841 President Lamar appointed him military head of the expedition sent to Santa Fé to open a trade route and peacefully extend Texas jurisdiction to the Rio Grande. On June 17 he received his commission as brigadier-general. A few days later six companies of soldiers and a band of merchants commenced the journey, without adequate knowledge or adequate equipment. Though delayed by the illness of McLeod and a shortage of provisions, the expedition pushed steadily across the prairies until the end of August, in spite of geographical uncertainty, the infidelity of their Mexican guide, and trouble with the Kiowa, who had been encouraged by Mexican officials. At the Quintufue (Pease River?), the party divided. Almost one hundred men went ahead; the rest, under McLeod, encamped until a guide arrived from the advance party in the middle of September. Joyously, McLeod advanced, only to meet Armijo's hostile army near Laguna Colorada. Treachery, the starving condition of the men, and his officers' insistence forced McLeod to surrender. The party was marched to San Miguel, where the other Texans, also prisoners, were held. All were then marched to distant Mexico city. McLeod, an important prisoner, was always well treated, even during his weary months at Perote fortress, where he remained until the next summer. Released, he returned to Galveston.

In that year he married Rebecca Johnson Lamar, who was the sister of Gazaway Lamar and the cousin of Mirabeau B. Lamar, president of Texas [*qq.v.*]. They had one son, Cazneau. He settled down to a quiet family life, holding several minor offices. He was a member of the Texas Congress, served again as adjutant-general in 1845–46, and later was a member of the state legislature. He may have been the Hugh McLeod who, when Matamoras was occupied by American troops in 1846, began to edit a newspaper there, the *Republic of the Rio Grande.* The editorials, advocating the establishment of an independent republic in the border states of Mexico, aroused the opposition of the military officials, who forced him to resign the editorship. Whether or not he was that editor he was in

Galveston in November of that year and not taking part in the Mexican War (Lamar, *post,* vols. IV, pt. 1, p. 144, V, p. 22). He was in 1850 a member of the company organized to construct the Buffalo Bayou, Brazos, and Colorado Railroad, the first railroad of Texas. In 1855 he was sent as a delegate to the southern commercial convention in New Orleans. He became interested in the Know-Nothing movement but returned to the Democratic fold in 1858. A fat, jovial man, he was personally popular and highly esteemed locally but was chiefly known in state politics for his violent tirades against Sam Houston. After Texas seceded from the Union he enlisted in the Confederate army. As lieutenant-colonel, he assisted in taking over the United States forts on the Rio Grande. Later, as colonel of the 1st Texas Infantry, he went to Dumfries, Va., where he died in camp. His body was taken to Texas and buried in the state cemetery.

[G. W. Cullum, *Biog. Reg. of the Officers and Grads. of the U. S. Mil. Acad.*, 3rd ed., vol. I (1891); G. W. Kendall, *Narrative of the Texan Sante Fé Expedition* (2 vols., 1844); Thomas Falconer, *Letters and Notes on the Texan Sante Fe Expedition* (1930); *Weekly Telegraph* (Houston), esp. Jan.–Mar. 1862; *The Papers of Mirabeau Buonaparte Lamar,* vols. II–IV, VI (1922–27); G. P. Garrison, *Diplomatic Correspondence of the Republic of Texas,* vol. II, pts. 1, 2 (1908–11). W. C. Binkley, *The Expansionist Movement in Texas* (1925); F. R. Lubbock, *Six Decades in Texas* (1900), esp. pp. 185, 199, 233–34, 380; *War of the Rebellion: Official Records (Army)*, 1 ser., vol. LIII (1898), 4 ser., vol. I (1900); Edward Mayes, *Geneal. Notes on a Branch of the Family of Mayes and on the Related Families* (1928?), p. C–34; *Quarterly of the Texas State Hist. Asso.*, July 1897, Apr. 1904; *Southern Hist. Quart.*, Jan. 1917, Apr. 1925, Jan. 1932; *Am. Hist. Review,* Oct. 1932.] W. B—r.

McLEOD, MARTIN (Aug. 30, 1813–Nov. 20, 1860), fur-trader, Minnesota pioneer, was born in L'Orignal, near Montreal, the son of John and Janet McLeod and one of a large family of children. In 1836, impelled by a desire for adventure in the wilds, he resigned a Montreal clerkship and joined a mysterious filibustering expedition under "General" James Dickson, a visionary who planned to cross the continent and establish an Indian kingdom in the Far West. As a major in Dickson's "Indian Liberating Army" of some sixty adventurers, including a few Polish refugees, McLeod endured the rigors of a winter march across northern Minnesota to the Red River colony. Cold, hunger, and fatigue caused the collapse of this fantastic filibuster but failed to break the buoyant spirit of McLeod, who found leisure to study Spanish, to read Xenophon, *The Lady of the Lake, Thaddeus of Warsaw,* and *Scottish Chiefs,* and to keep a remarkable diary, with entries telling of nights when he lay nearly buried in snowdrifts to escape the biting fury of northern blizzards. Late in February 1837, with a guide and some members of the defunct filibuster, he set out from the Red River colony for Fort Snelling. Two of his companions lost their lives on the journey, but McLeod, though he nearly froze to death and so blistered his feet that "at every step," he wrote, "the blood from my toes oozes through my Moccasins," reached his objective.

Soon after his arrival, in April 1837, he engaged in the fur trade, which for two decades led him up and down the Minnesota Valley, braving the perils and loneliness of wilderness winters, equipping Indians, and collecting furs from them at Traverse des Sioux, Big Stone Lake, and Lac qui Parle. He attained great influence over the red men, especially the Upper Sioux, who trusted him. It was due largely to him that the Sioux treaties of 1851 were extremely favorable to the traders. Notwithstanding his growing influence and responsibility and his tireless industry, the evils of the credit system brought him continued losses, and in 1858 he sold his interests.

McLeod identified himself with the frontier commonwealth of Minnesota. He was a member of the territorial council from 1849 to 1853, and president during his last term. As a councilor he worked zealously in behalf of measures for the general welfare and advancement of the territory. Because of his superior education, acquired principally through wide reading, he was made chairman of the committee on schools; and in that capacity, as author of the bill that laid the foundation of Minnesota's school-system, he performed his most important legislative service. He was a vigorous settlement promoter. His letters to Canadian newspapers brought out a considerable number of pioneers. He planned town sites and bought and improved property in various places in the hope that an influx of settlers would enhance its value and bring him fortune. He was one of the founders of Glencoe, and he labored energetically for the development of the county that bears his name. The panic of 1857 dealt a severe blow to these projects, however, and left him heavily in debt and his death three years later forestalled the execution of his plans for the development of the young state.

About 1838 McLeod contracted a union with Mary E. Ortley, the daughter of a trader and a Sioux woman, and they had several children. In 1849 he established his family on a farm at Oak Grove, near Fort Snelling, which remained his home until his death. He is described by a contemporary as "a man of noble form, commanding presence, cultured intellect . . . dignified, eloquent, persuasive, charming" (J. H. Stevens,

Personal Recollections of Minnesota and Its People, 1890, p. 266).

[Further information may be found in McLeod's diary, ed. by Grace L. Nute, in *Minnesota Hist. Bull.*, Aug.–Nov. 1922; see also G. L. Nute, "James Dickson: A Filibuster in Minnesota, in 1836," in *Miss. Valley Hist. Rev.*, Sept. 1923; C. J. Ritchey, "Martin McLeod and the Minnesota Valley," in *Minn. Hist.*, Dec. 1929; papers of McLeod, J. H. Stevens, and H. H. Sibley, in the possession of the Minn. Hist. Soc., St. Paul.]

T. C. B.

McLOUGHLIN, JOHN (Oct. 19, 1784–Sept. 3, 1857), factor of the Hudson's Bay Company on the Columbia River, was born in the parish of Riviere du Loup, province of Quebec, the son of John McLoughlin, a native of Ireland, and Angélique (Fraser), who was born in Canada of Scottish parents. Young John and his brother David were both educated for the profession of medicine under their grandfather Fraser's direction, their father having lost his life early by drowning. David became a physician in Paris. John, after receiving his training in Scotland, returned to Canada and became a partner of the North West Fur Company. At the time of the union of the North West and Hudson's Bay companies in 1821, he was in charge at the important post of Fort William on Lake Superior. In 1824 as chief factor of the Hudson's Bay Company he was given direct supervision of the Columbia District, with headquarters on the Columbia. There he remained in control from 1824 to 1846, the critical period in the history of the Oregon country.

When McLoughlin arrived at Fort George, the former Astoria, there were no American traders regularly established west of the Rockies, notwithstanding John Jacob Astor's attempt —foiled by the War of 1812—to engross the entire commerce of the region, and the fact that the treaty of joint occupation (1818) guaranteed to Englishmen and Americans equal rights to "trade and make settlements" between the crest of the mountains and the Pacific, north of the 42nd parallel and south of the parallel of 54° 40′. The chief factor's duty as manager of the company's affairs in that vast terrain was to monopolize the fur trade as completely as possible, and to exploit it in a way to produce the maximum annual profits for an indefinite period of time. To that end it was necessary to impose permanent peace upon the numerous tribes of Indians and incite them to diligence in collecting furs under strict conservation principles, to keep out rival traders, and to prevent if possible the agricultural settlement of the country. This proved a difficult program for McLoughlin to execute to the satisfaction both of his employers and of his own conscience.

With George Simpson, he fixed upon a location within the present city of Vancouver, Wash., as the most eligible site for the central post, and after 1825 Fort Vancouver was the virtual capital of his far-flung domain. A large farm, gardens, orchards, dairies, a sawmill and flouring mill, a shipyard and mechanics' shops, with the personnel required to man all of these activities, developed around the fort a considerable village. Annual ships from England brought in the supplies of goods for trade, and carried back the furs assembled from all subordinate stations, to the value, it has been estimated, of from $105,000 to $150,000 per year.

McLoughlin was generally successful in keeping peace among the tribes and preventing the murder of white men, whether Englishmen or others. American traders exercised their right of entering the territory, but he succeeded in ruining their business by controlling the Indian customers, underselling, and overbidding. Nevertheless, although his business competition was merciless, he accorded all rivals personally the most generous treatment, furnishing necessaries, entertaining them at his fort, and facilitating their travels. When missionaries began to go to Oregon from the United States in 1834, McLoughlin was their good angel. He encouraged both the Methodist and the Presbyterian missions as well as the later Catholic establishment. He was equally kind to American settlers, whom company policy forbade him to encourage in any way. Being unable to carry more supplies than were imperatively needed on the way, most of the emigrants reached the lower Columbia in a destitute condition. By withholding succor McLoughlin might have delayed the occupation of the country, yet he made it a practice to sell them provisions and wait for his pay till the wheat crop came in the following year. He defended this charitable attitude against the criticism of his superiors on the dual ground of humanity and true policy. He could not let the settlers perish, and had he done so the opposition to the "British monopoly" would have brought upon it swift disaster. Many settlers never paid him, and the Company suffered loss, but not without complaining seriously to him in consequence.

Although through his generosity he gave material aid toward the American occupation of Oregon south of the Columbia, he advised against Americans settling north of that river, thus furthering Canning's policy of making the river itself the future international boundary. When convinced that the 49th parallel and Fuca's Strait were to be the boundary, he quietly prepared to establish the Company's headquarters at Fort Victoria on Vancouver Island. In 1846, the year the boundary treaty was signed, McLoughlin retired from the company under criticism. He had filed with the Oregon Provisional Government a claim embracing the falls of the Willamette, where he built a mill, laid out a town, and proceeded to sell lots. His right to do this was contested by certain Americans, and despite a private adjustment with them and McLoughlin's previous declaration of intention to become an American citizen, Congress in 1850 invalidated his claim under the Donation Land Law, granting the tract to the future state for university purposes. McLoughlin was not ousted, however, and though he died without receiving justice, in 1862 the state released the property to his heirs on the payment of a nominal sum.

This land-claim episode was a *cause célèbre* in Oregon for many years. McLoughlin had gained hosts of friends among the pioneers, notwithstanding his connection with the hated British monopoly. His opponents argued that he was trying to hold his valuable water privilege, with the land adjacent, for his company. Sir George Simpson wrote in 1841 that the claim had been taken in 1829 for the company's benefit (*American Historical Review,* October 1908, p. 80). This seems conclusive, but there is no reason to doubt that McLoughlin later used his own means to develop the tract and that he came to regard it as a support for his old age. How the transfer occurred is not known.

"Doctor McLoughlin," as he was always called, was a man of extraordinary personality. He was six feet four inches tall, splendidly proportioned, dignified and imposing. He had both the air and the gift of command. The Indians called him, on account of his long white locks, the White Eagle. His righteous wrath struck terror to the hearts of his most hardened dependants, whether white or red. He prevailed through character, strict justice, and good judgment, though his personal writings disclose an otherwise ordinary, unimaginative mind. Some manuscripts bearing his signature were written by others possessing higher literary attainments. Probably the "McLoughlin Document" (Holman, *post,* pp. 229–43) was prepared by an attorney, McLoughlin supplying the data for it. Like other traders, he married a half-breed Indian woman, widow of Alexander McKay of the Astoria party, by whom he had four children.

[F. V. Holman, *Dr. John McLoughlin, The Father of Oregon* (1907), which is extremely eulogistic, contains 110 pages of illustrative documents possessing considerable value. Eva Emery Dye's story, *McLoughlin and Old Oregon* (1900), represents much research and supplies an interesting if somewhat idealized picture of life in Oregon under the McLoughlin regime. Three works by Joseph Schafer: "The British Attitude toward the Oregon Question" (*Am. Hist. Rev.,* Jan. 1911), "Oregon Pioneers and American Diplomacy" (*Essays in Am. Hist. Dedicated to Frederick Jackson Turner,* 1910), and *A Hist. of the Pacific Northwest* (1918), and Frederick Merk, "The Oregon Pioneers and the Boundary" (*Am. Hist. Rev.,* July 1924) discuss the political and social backgrounds of McLoughlin's career from somewhat divergent viewpoints. In "Letters of Sir George Simpson," *Am. Hist. Rev.,* Oct. 1908, especially at p. 80, is land-claim testimony. The *Ore. Hist. Soc. Quart.* from 1900 on has valuable material, especially the issues for Sept. 1907 (McLoughlin letter), Mar. 1909 (Warré and Vavasour's report), June 1910 (Minto's recollections), Mar. 1913 (Howison's report), Sept. 1916 (McLoughlin to Simpson, 1844; important), Dec. 1922 (McLoughlin letters), Mar. 1928 (Lieut. Wm. Peel's report). See also Frederick Merk, *Fur Trade and Empire: George Simpson's Jour.* (1931). Letters of McLoughlin, copied from Record Office F. O. Am. 440 and 444, published in the appendix to R. C. Clark, *Hist. of the Willamette Valley* (1927).]

J. S.

MACLURE, WILLIAM (Oct. 27, 1763–Mar. 23, 1840), pioneer geologist, patron of science and education, was born in Ayr, Scotland, the son of David and Ann (Kennedy) McClure. Apparently he was baptized James, but later called himself William and changed the spelling of his family name (Keyes, *post*). He received his elementary education at Ayr, under the tutelage of a "Mr. Douglass, an intelligent teacher, who was especially reputed for classical and mathematical attainments" (Morton, *post,* p. 8). He entered a mercantile house, and at nineteen made his first visit to the United States, to transact some business in New York. Upon his return to Great Britain he became a partner in the London firm of Miller, Hart & Company. He was eminently successful in business, quickly acquiring a fortune which enabled him to retire and devote his life to science and philanthropy.

In 1796 he again paid a visit to America. From boyhood, according to his biographer (Morton, p. 10), the United States "had been to him the land of promise," and at this time he may have taken the first steps toward naturalization. In 1803, having become a citizen of the United States, he was appointed member of a commission to settle spoliation claims between his adopted country and France, a task which engaged him for several years. In 1807 he published *To the People of the United States: A Statement of the Transactions of the Board of Commissioners Appointed in 1803 for the Adjustment of Claims against the French Government.*

During these years in Europe he traveled extensively, studying the geology and natural history of the continent and collecting specimens. Returning to America, he entered upon the task of making a geological map of the United States, the first map of its scope in the history of geology.

The greater part of the country was at this time a wilderness; nevertheless Maclure went forth, for the most part alone and always at his own expense, making observations throughout the entire region east of the Mississippi River. The American Philosophical Society published his colored geological map, with the explanatory "Observations on the Geology of the United States," in Volume I of its *Transactions*. The production was one with which any worker might have been content to rest. Instead, Maclure set about a revision almost at once, completing it in 1817. Published with an accompanying volume, *Observations on the Geology of the United States* (1817), it appeared also in 1818 in Volume I, new series, of the *Transactions of the American Philosophical Society*.

Meanwhile, in 1812, he had become one of the first members of the Academy of Natural Sciences of Philadelphia, and in December 1817 was elected its president, a position to which he was annually reëlected for the remaining twenty-two years of his life. He was heartily interested in the welfare of the Academy and presented to it at different times the greater part of his valuable library, as well as several of his collections of specimens. He supervised the publication of the first volumes of its *Journal,* and by a series of gifts, totaling some $20,000, made possible the erection of a building for its permanent housing. During the winter of 1816–17, with C. A. LeSueur [*q.v.*] as a companion, he visited the West Indies, directing his studies particularly to volcanic phases of their geology, and in the *Journal* of the Academy for November 1817 published his observations.

Another phase of Maclure's activity related to education. In 1805, while in Switzerland, he had visited Pestalozzi's school at Yverdun, and, enthusiastic over what he saw there, had persuaded Joseph Neef [*q.v.*] to come to Amercia to introduce Pestalozzian methods. In 1819 he went to Spain in the hope of establishing a great agricultural school for the common people, in which labor should be combined with instruction. He had purchased some 10,000 acres of land near Alicante and fitted up the necessary buildings when the liberal government of the Cortes was overthrown by revolution, the land was restored to the Church from which it had been confiscated, and he was obliged to relinquish his plan with a complete loss of all the property. This misfortune did not discourage him permanently, however, and after a visit in 1824 to Robert Owen's school at New Lanark, Scotland, he became interested in Owen's projected community at New Harmony, Ind. In his usual whole-hearted manner, he purchased an extensive tract of land in the vicinity and forwarded his library, instruments, and other personal effects that might be useful in carrying out once more, in new territory, his plan for an agricultural school. He succeeded in persuading a number of other scientific men to accompany him to New Harmony, and when he set out, took with him down the Ohio the "boat-load of knowledge," which included LeSueur, Gerard Troost, and Thomas Say [*qq.v.*]. Even after the failure of Owen's venture Maclure persisted in an attempt to organize societies for adult education among the working classes. He founded the New Harmony Working Men's Institute in 1838, and by his will directed his executors to pay $500 to any club of laborers which should establish a library of 100 volumes.

The breakdown of his health led him to spend the winter of 1827–28 in Mexico, with his friend Say. That country, he came to believe, offered a more hopeful field for the realization of the projects near to his heart. Accordingly, after visiting Philadelphia and presiding in November 1828 at the New Haven meeting of the American Geological Society, of which he had been president for several years, he returned to Mexico, in the hope of aiding in the educational uplift of its people. He planned to bring back with him "a considerable number of aboriginal young men" to be trained in his school at New Harmony to "a knowledge of useful arts and the habits that may fit them both to rule and to obey, in a republican government" (*American Journal of Science,* vol. XV, 1829, p. 401), but apparently the design was never carried out. Maclure spent most of the rest of his life in Mexico. Upon the serious failure of his health in 1839 he made an attempt to return to the United States, but was unable to stand the difficulties of the journey and died in the village of San Ángel, near the city of Mexico, early in 1840.

During his residence in Mexico, he had continued to correspond with his scientific friends and contributed a number of letters on political, social, and economic topics to the New Harmony *Disseminator*. These papers were collected and published under the title, *Opinions on Various Subjects, Dedicated to the Industrious Producers* (2 vols., 1831–37). He is described as a man of "above the middle stature and of a naturally robust frame," of conspicuous serenity of mind, singularly mild and unostentatious in manner. He never married.

[Sources include: S. G. Morton, *A Memoir of William Maclure* (1841; 2nd ed., 1844), also pub. in *Proc. Acad. Nat. Sci. of Phila.*, vol. I (1841) and *Am. Jour. Sci.*, Apr.–June 1844; C. R. Keyes, in *Pan American Geolo-*

gist, Sept. 1925. See also G. B. Lockwood, *The New Harmony Movement* (1905); T. J. de la Hunt, *Hist. of the New Harmony Working Men's Inst.* (1927); H. B. Weiss and G. M. Zeigler, *Thomas Say: Early Am. Naturalist* (1931); *A Cyc. of Educ.* (1925), ed. by Paul Monroe; G. P. Merrill, *The First One Hundred Years of American Geology* (1924).] G. P. M.

McMAHON, BERNARD (d. Sept. 18, 1816), Philadelphia horticulturist, was born in Ireland and in 1796 came to America as one of those "Exiles of Erin," driven from Ireland by political motives, who sought and found refuge in the United States. He settled in Philadelphia. William Darlington, the botanist, in a letter written at West Chester, Pa., on June 15, 1857, says: "In the autumn, I think, of 1799, he [McMahon] passed some weeks at my native village of Dilworthtown, in Chester County, in order to avoid the ravages of yellow fever, in Philadelphia, where he resided; and in that rural retreat I first knew him. I renewed the acquaintance in 1802, 3, and 4, while attending medical lectures in the University of Pennsylvania, by which time he had established his nurseries of useful and ornamental plants: and I ever found him an obliging, intelligent, and instructive friend" (*American Gardener's Calendar, post,* p. xiii). These nurseries, including McMahon's greenhouses and experimental gardens, were situated near the Germantown turnpike between Philadelphia and Nicetown. From them "emanated the rarer flowers and novelties such as could be collected in the early part of the present [nineteenth] century," and in them "were performed, to the astonishment of the amateurs of that day, successful feats of horticulture that were but too rarely imitated" (*Ibid.,* p. xi.).

In connection with the nurseries, McMahon had established a seed and general nursery business at 39 South Second Street below Market, on the east side of Philadelphia. Behind the counter was his wife, "with some considerable Irish accent, but a most amiable and excellent disposition, and withal an able saleswoman." The remarkable part of the store was not in its stock, although it was one of the largest seed stores in the United States at that time, but rather the character and prominence of the botanists and horticulturists who were attracted there as a common meeting place for varied scientific discussions. Here Nuttall, Baldwin, Darlington, and other authorities came to impart or receive scientific information. McMahon took an active part in the discussions occurring in his store and his opinion is said to have been greatly respected. As a consequence of his contacts with McMahon, when Nuttall published in 1818 his *Genera of North American Plants,* he named an evergreen barberry *Mahonia,* "in memory of the late Bernard McMahon, whose ardent attachment to Botany, and successful introduction of useful and ornamental Horticulture into the United States, lays claim to public esteem" (vol. I, p. 211, note).

McMahon early began the collection and exportation of American seeds and he was continually soliciting seed and plant exchanges with his many correspondents in the United States and abroad with the purpose of discovering new plants suited for cultivation in the United States. In his catalogue published in 1804, he lists about a thousand species of such seeds. After the Lewis and Clark expedition, Jefferson wrote to La Contesse de Tesse (R. G. Thwaites, ed., *Original Journals of the Lewis and Clark Expedition,* vol. VII, 1905, p. 393): "All Lewis's plants are growing in the garden of Mr. McMahon, a gardener of Philadelphia." According to Bailey (*post,* p. 1586), "M'Mahon and Landreth were instrumental in distributing the seeds which those explorers collected." McMahon was interested in one of the numerous abortive attempts to grow the European wine grape (*Vitis vinifera*) in the eastern United States. In 1806 he gave to America its first notable horticultural book, the *American Gardener's Calendar,* which was a standard cyclopedic work for more than fifty years, the last (eleventh) edition appearing in 1857. After McMahon's death in 1816 his wife conducted his business for a time and then it passed to other hands.

[See Preface to the 1857 edition of the *Am. Gardener's Calendar*; L. H. Bailey, *The Standard Cyc. of Horticulture,* vol. III (1915); *Poulson's Am. Daily Advertiser* (Phila.), Sept. 20, 1816.] R. H. S.

McMAHON, JOHN VAN LEAR (Oct. 18, 1800–June 15, 1871), lawyer and historian, was born in Cumberland, Md. His father, William McMahon, a popular Irish-Presbyterian farmer of Allegany County, was repeatedly elected a member of the Maryland House of Delegates. His mother was a daughter of John Van Lear, a prominent pioneer of Western Maryland. The son was graduated with highest honors, at the age of seventeen, from the College of New Jersey (Princeton). He studied law in his native county, was admitted to the bar in 1819, and began practising in Baltimore the same year. His uncouth manners, unbridled temper, and proud spirit yielded him difficulties with both bench and bar, and in less than two years he closed his office, returned to Cumberland, and took up, in turn, the study of medicine and theology. Resuming the practice of law in Cumberland, he soon won distinction as a public speaker and was elected a representative of Allegany County in the Maryland House of Delegates. He entered this body in 1823 dressed as a mountain huntsman, advocated state aid to the Chesapeake & Ohio Canal, made an effective speech in favor of the removal of the political disabilities of the Jews, was made chairman of the committee on the judiciary, and, before the session closed, won recognition as the House leader. During a second term he supported a measure to allow Baltimore a representation equal to that of a county. Returning, in 1825, to the practice of law in Baltimore he rose rapidly to leadership of the Maryland bar. He represented Baltimore in the House of Delegates for two terms, 1827–28, and subsequently refused to be a candidate for public office.

At a meeting in Baltimore in February 1827, he was appointed a member of a committee to consider a project for the construction of the Baltimore & Ohio Railroad and he subsequently drafted the charter which contributed largely to the success of the undertaking and served as a model for other railroad corporations. McMahon was a leader of the Jackson Democrats of Maryland in the presidential campaign of 1829 but early in Jackson's first administration he affiliated with the National Republicans, alleging dissatisfaction with Jackson's financial and commercial policy. In June 1829, he declined a nomination by his party for a seat in Congress. In November 1837, he could not be persuaded by appeals from every quarter of the state to become a candidate for a seat in the United States Senate. In the presidential campaign of 1840 he was recognized as one of the most powerful speakers in the country. He was rewarded with the offer of a seat in President Harrison's cabinet. This he declined. When Tyler had become president he was urged to accept the post of attorney-general, but again he declined, alleging that he had not the courage to perform duties while the eyes of the whole country were upon him.

At the beginning of his service in the Maryland legislature McMahon undertook the compilation of an elementary treatise on the laws and institutions of the state. The project was revised and expanded and in 1831 he published his *Historical View of the Government of Maryland,* a constitutional history reliable in statement, illuminating in interpretation, and written with some literary merit. After a lapse of more than a hundred years it ranks as one of the most substantial contributions to the historical literature of the state. When, about 1857, McMahon was at the height of his career as a trial lawyer before the Maryland court of appeals he was stricken with partial loss of eyesight. He gradually withdrew from the bar and in 1863 removed to Cumberland where he remained with two sisters until his death, except for an interval with a third sister at Dayton, Ohio. McMahon was known to his friends as a bachelor but he had a son, John A. McMahon (1833–1923), a distinguished lawyer of Ohio, who stated that his mother was Elizabeth (Gouger) McMahon. He possessed an exceptionally retentive memory and a faculty for close observation, and a strong deep voice enhanced his power as a speaker. A mixture of vanity and humility were manifest in his eccentricities.

[John T. Mason, *Life of John Van Lear McMahon* (1879), is a critical review of McMahon's career. Consult also Henry F. Powell, *Tercentenary Hist. of Md.* (1925); J. T. Scharf, *Hist. of Western Md.* (1882), vol. I; and the *Sun* (Baltimore), June 16, 1871. For a sketch of John A. McMahon see Charlotte R. Conover, ed., *Dayton and Montgomery County* (1932), vol. II.] N. D. M.

McMANES, JAMES (Apr. 13, 1822–Nov. 23, 1899), politician, was born in County Tyrone, Ireland, the son of James and Rebecca (Johnson) McManes. He emigrated with his parents to the United States at the age of eight years, and settled in Philadelphia. Because of his family's poverty, he left school before completing the elementary grades and went to work as a bobbin-boy in the cotton-mills. At the age of twenty-five he began spinning for himself on a modest scale, but his mill burned, and he returned to the older mills as an employee. In 1855 he left to establish a real-estate business. Meanwhile, in 1844 he had received naturalization papers and joined the Whigs. In 1852 he was moderately active in support of Winfield Scott; after Scott's defeat he turned to the People's Republican ranks and got himself elected to the ward school board, and by 1858 he controlled the politics of Philadelphia's Seventeenth Ward. In 1860 he sat as a Lincoln delegate in the Republican National Convention and at the state convention helped nominate Andrew G. Curtin [*q.v.*] for governor. Two years later he ran unsuccessfully for a seat in the national House of Representatives. In 1865 he became one of the trustees charged with the management of the municipal gas works and during his twenty years of service had much to do with making the gas trustees a ring which almost completely dominated Philadelphia politics. In 1866 he received election as prothonotary of the district court and a seat on the city board of education. Thenceforward until 1881 his power in Philadelphia politics exceeded that of any other person.

At the Republican National Convention in 1880 McManes favored Garfield, refusing to support Grant for a third term in spite of the state boss, Senator James Donald Cameron [*q.v.*]. As a reprisal, Cameron invaded Philadelphia in 1881 and with the support of a reform movement inflicted on McManes a bad defeat. The next two years were turbulent and in 1883 McManes even temporarily lost his position as gas trustee. By 1884, however, the uprising had sufficiently receded for him to elect the mayor. During the years following 1885, when Matthew S. Quay [*q.v.*] attempted with considerable success to dominate Philadelphia politics, McManes devoted much of his time to private business and to Fairmount Park, which he served as commissioner.

Although gentle to his family and friends, devoted to his wife, Catherine McNamee, simple in habits, taciturn, and of exemplary private life, McManes possessed an imperious nature which together with a pronounced bluntness of manner alienated many, particularly during his later years. He overcame the lack of a formal education by keen powers of observation, dogged perseverance, and ability to judge men. Withal he dealt generously with the poor and faithfully attended the Presbyterian Church. Thrifty and shrewd, he accumulated a fortune of approximately two and a half million dollars. Starting with real estate, he later became interested in street railways and merged the important lines of Philadelphia into the Union Passenger Railway. After helping organize the People's Bank, he became a director and later its president, and although apparently not personally cognizant of the acts that led to its failure, he felt obligated to the depositors and paid out of his own pocket more than half a million dollars. He died in Philadelphia.

[James Bryce, *The Am. Commonwealth* (1888), vol. II, ch. lxxxix; Harold Zink, *City Bosses in the U. S.* (1930); George Vickers, *The Fall of Bossism*, vol. I (1883); S. W. Pennypacker, *The Autobiog. of a Pennsylvanian* (1918); F. W. Leach, "Twenty Years with Quay" and "Philadelphia Politics," appearing in serial form in the *North American* (Phila.), 1904–05; obituaries in *Phila. Inquirer, Public Ledger* (Phila.), and *North American* (Phila.), Nov. 24, 1899; date of birth and maiden names of wife and mother from a grandson.] H. Z.

McMASTER, GUY HUMPHREYS (Jan. 31, 1829–Sept. 13, 1887), jurist and poet, was born in Clyde, Wayne County, N. Y., the son of David and Adeline (Humphreys) McMaster. About a year after his birth his parents moved to Bath, which was thenceforth the family home. After attending Franklin Academy at Prattsburg, N. Y., McMaster entered Hamilton College, where he enjoyed the friendship of Charles Dudley Warner and Joseph R. Hawley [*qq.v.*]. Soon after his graduation in 1847 he began the study of law, but during the next few years varied the tedium of his preliminary studies by literary work. In February 1849 he contributed to the *Knickerbocker* the lyric "Carmen Bellicosum," which was signed "John MacGrom"; and in 1851, to the *American Whig Review*, a poem entitled "The Northern Lights" (September) and some prose essays. In 1853 he published a *History of the Settlement of Steuben County*. In the same year he married Amanda Church; and in succeeding years they had four children.

McMaster was admitted to the bar in 1852. Associated with a succession of partners, he ultimately formed a partnership with his son-in-law, John F. Parkhurst; and the firm of McMaster & Parkhurst continued to function until McMaster's death. In 1863 he became county judge and surrogate, a position which he held until the close of 1883, when the two offices were separated, and he was elected surrogate. As a lawyer and judge, he was greatly respected both for his knowledge of the law and for the fairness of his decisions. His activities were varied in 1877 by a journey to the Pacific Coast, and in 1885 by a trip to Europe. While on these trips, he wrote for the *Steuben Courier* the "Pacific Letters" and the "Other-Side Letters." A member of the Republican party and of the Presbyterian Church, he was one of the most influential citizens of Bath. For many years he was the organist of his church.

To the American public McMaster is known chiefly as the author of "Carmen Bellicosum," which has appeared in many anthologies, including *The Oxford Book of American Verse* (1927). This poem, which was written to the memory of the Continental soldiers, E. C. Stedman regarded as "the ringing, characteristic utterance of an original man" (*post*, p. 52). A similar vigorous note is struck in the descriptive poem "The Northern Lights." During the Civil War he also published in the *Hartford Courant* (November 1864) the half-patriotic, half-humorous "Dream of Thanksgiving Eve" (reprinted in *Army and Navy Journal*, May 5, 1877). Other poems of his include "The Commanders" (1879), later printed in Frederick Cook's *Journals of the Military Expedition of Major General John Sullivan* (1887); and "The Professor's Guest Chamber," published in the *Utica Herald* in 1880. Although the body of his poetry is small, it is nevertheless important in representing a spirited, forceful note in American verse at a period when many native poets found their chief inspiration in the vapid and sentimental.

[Letters from McMaster's daughter, Miss Katherine McMaster, and from J. D. Ibbotson, librarian of Hamilton College; *Hamilton Literary Monthly,* Oct. 1887; *Medico-Legal Jour.,* Sept. 1887; I. W. Near, *A Hist. of Steuben County, N. Y.* (1911); W. W. Clayton, *Hist. of Steuben County* (1879); M. F. Roberts, *Hist. Gazetteer of Steuben County* (1891); H. Hakes, *Landmarks of Steuben County* (1896); E. C. Stedman, "A Belt of Asteroids," *Galaxy,* Jan. 1869; *Critic,* Oct. 22, 1887.]

N. F. A.

McMASTER, JAMES ALPHONSUS (Apr. 1, 1820–Dec. 29, 1886), journalist, son of the Rev. Gilbert and Jane (Brown) McMaster, was born in Duanesburg, N. Y. His strict covenanting Scotch father forced him at an early age to study the classics and Scripture in preparation for the ministry, into which two of his brothers entered. On leaving Union College, 1839, he studied law and commenced its practice. Presumably he preached from a Reformed Presbyterian pulpit and attended the Union Theological Seminary, where he was associated with Isaac Hecker and Clarence Walworth [*qq.v.*] before being received into the Roman Catholic Church by Father Rumpler in 1845. Thereupon, McMaster accompanied Hecker and Walworth to the Redemptorist College at Louvain, Belgium, on the way paying a visit to Newman at Littlemore, England. Here he acquired his vaunted knowledge of Catholic theology, though he agreed with his superiors that he lacked a religious vocation. Returning to New York, he entered journalism as a writer for the *New York Tribune* and the *New York Freeman's Journal.* In 1847 he borrowed enough money from George V. Hecker to buy Bishop Hughes's interest in the *Freeman's Journal,* which he edited until his death. In 1850 he married a Miss Fetterman of Pennsylvania by whom he had four children: Alphonsus, who tried out a vocation at Ilchester, England, and became a New York journalist; and three daughters who entered convents, thus leaving a proud but lonely widowed father to fend for himself.

As an editor, McMaster was honest, able, courageous, and annoyingly frank. Indeed he was a stormy petrel in Catholic circles. A stout supporter of Hughes in the school fight, he so frequently took issue with him that at times the bishop repented of ever selling the journal, though at other times he keenly appreciated McMaster's picturesque service to the Church. A stanch friend of the Redemptorists and Paulists, he was amusingly suspicious of the Jesuits and on occasion violently critical of journalists like Orestes A. Brownson [*q.v.*], Denis Sadlier [*q.v.*], of the *Tablet,* and Thomas D'Arcy McGee, who became a cabinet minister in Canada, and of prelates like Kenrick and Purcell. At times his lack of interest in Irish affairs annoyed extremists, but he made the *Freeman's Journal* the outstanding Catholic organ, which challenged the respect of churchmen and politicians. Without political ambition, and above either flattery or bribery, he was a power in the Democratic party on the side of state rights and against abolition. Even regardless of its nativist associations, Whiggery was detestable to him. While he denounced the South and refuted such clerical "rebels" as Patrick Neeson Lynch and Napoleon Joseph Perché [*qq.v.*], he had little confidence in Lincoln's policies. Criticism of the administration closed the mails to the *Freeman's Journal* and brought about McMaster's arbitrary arrest without warrant or indictment. Imprisoned in Fort Lafayette on Aug. 24, 1861, he was finally freed without trial and resumed the publication of his paper (Apr. 19, 1862) without amending its editorial policy. McMaster to the end gloried in his martyrdom for freedom of the press in war time.

After the war, he paid his compliments to Reconstruction measures, the "godless" schools as he described public schools without training in religion and morals, and to the bishops whose attitude on infallibility he questioned. His journalistic model was Louis Veuillot of *L'Univers Religieux.* He was a stout advocate of the temporal power and a lover of the Eternal City, and he prided himself on his precise Latin and his inauguration of the first American pilgrimage. Archbishop Corrigan he loved; this explained his vicious attacks on Edward McGlynn. He was well characterized by Archbishop Ryan of Philadelphia as "a Scotch Highlander with a touch of Calvinism not yet sponged out of him." Toward the end the *Freeman's Journal* lost influence as more diocesan organs were founded, but its editorials challenged attention even during the last six years when McMaster's fiery rhetoric was toned down by the genial Maurice Francis Egan. Bitter in prejudices, stubborn in support of principles, firm in friendship, and aggressive in religious beliefs, McMaster was a picturesque character. Not until he died was it learned that he had long worn a hair-shirt in mortification.

[M. F. Egan, "A Slight Appreciation of Jas. Alphonsus McMaster," U. S. Cath. Hist. Soc., *Hist. Records and Studies,* vol. XV (1921); J. G. Shea, *Hist. of the Cath. Ch. in the U. S.,* vol. IV (1892); J. T. Smith, *The Cath. Ch. in N. Y.* (2 vols., 1905); *Cath. Encyc.*; files of the *Freeman's Jour.,* especially the issue of Jan. 8, 1887; *U. S. Cath. Hist. Mag.,* Apr. 1887; *N. Y. Herald,* Dec. 30, 1886.]

R. J. P.

McMASTER, JOHN BACH (June 29, 1852–May 24, 1932), historian, was born in Brooklyn,

N. Y., the son of Julia Anna Matilda (Bach) McMaster and Theodore James McMaster, a planter and banker. His grandfather, James McMaster, came from England in 1796, apprenticed to a Mr. Titford, importer and seller of drugs in New York. In 1800 he bought the business, opened a shop at 128 Pearl St., and three years later married Elizabeth Watrous of Balston, N. Y. The grandparents on the mother's side were Robert Bach of Hereford, England, and Margaret Cowan of Newry, Ireland. John Bach McMaster was educated in the public schools of New York, graduating with the B.A. degree from the College of the City of New York in 1872 and remaining for a year longer as instructor in English. It was at this time that he became interested in writing a history of the United States. In 1873 he was appointed chief clerk and civil assistant to Maj. George L. Gillespie of the Engineering Corps, and assigned to make a survey of the battlefield of Winchester for use in the memoirs which General Sheridan was preparing. After a year of map-making at Sheridan's headquarters in Chicago, he returned to New York to practise engineering from 1874 to 1877. During this time he published *Bridge and Tunnel Centres* (1875), and *High Masonry Dams* (1876); he wrote a work on "The Struggle of Man with Nature," the manuscript of which was later destroyed. In 1875 his alma mater conferred upon him the degree of C.E., and in 1877 he was appointed instructor in engineering at the College of New Jersey (Princeton), a position which he held until 1883. In the summer of 1878 he had charge of the Princeton scientific expedition to the Bad Lands of Wyoming in search of fossil remains. The colorful drama of the frontier made a deep impression on him and strengthened his resolve to write the history of the nation while the spirit of growth and expansion was still strong. From the active life of the engineer, he turned to history, spending much of his spare time in research in the Library of Congress, the rooms of the American Antiquarian Society, and the Historical Societies of Pennsylvania, New York, and New Jersey. In 1881, after many years of patient work, the first volume of *The History of the People of the United States* was completed. Written entirely in longhand, the bulky manuscript was sent to Appleton & Company who hesitatingly "ventured its publication" in 1883. The second volume appeared in 1885, and others at irregular intervals until the eighth was published in 1913.

Shortly after the publication of the first volume, the University of Pennsylvania offered McMaster a professorship in American history which he accepted, remaining at that institution for thirty-seven years. On Apr. 14, 1887, he married Gertrude Stevenson of Morristown, N. J., by whom there were three children, a son alone surviving his father. In June 1920, having reached the age of sixty-eight, McMaster was retired as professor emeritus. He continued his researches, however, adding to his larger history another volume, *The History of the People of the United States during Lincoln's Administration* (1927). In the autumn of 1931 he moved from Philadelphia to Darien, Conn., where he died of pneumonia on May 24, 1932. He was slight in physique, reticent and retiring in general society, but his quiet dignity and strength of character marked him as a man of distinction in any group, while in more intimate circles his broad range of information, fund of anecdotes, and genial personality won him the admiration and love of his associates.

McMaster's outstanding work is *The History of the People of the United States.* The earlier volumes in particular hold a unique place in the field of social and economic history, until then so largely neglected for war and politics. Scholars and critics acclaimed them not only because of the shift in historical point of view but also because of the author's originality of thought and realistic narrative style. Working independently and at firsthand in contemporary sources, he made much use of newspapers, magazines, memoirs, books of travel, and letters of prominent men, but he soon found that blazing a new path in historical writing, through materials so voluminous and often unreliable, invited pitfalls and much criticism. Similarly the absence of all hero worship led to dissatisfaction in certain quarters despite the fervent patriotism of the volumes and their strong nationalistic spirit. McMaster was the first professor of American history in the United States to combine research and writing with teaching. Through his advanced students and through his textbooks, his influence upon the study and writing of history was widely disseminated. More than two and a half million copies of the texts, which were carefully graded to meet the needs of primary, grammar, and high school pupils, were sold during his lifetime. Penetrating, and keen in their analysis of men and movements, his texts, like his larger works, show originality and breadth of conception. Seventeen volumes and more than a score of articles, some of which were widely quoted in the press of the time, constitute his contribution to history. In addition to his major work, the following may be cited: *Benjamin Franklin as a Man of Letters* (1887); *With the*

Fathers. Studies in the History of the United States (1896); *Daniel Webster* (1902); "The United States" in *The Cambridge Modern History*, Vol. VII (1903); *The Struggle for Social, Political and Industrial Rights of Man* (1903); *The Life and Times of Stephen Girard* (2 vols., 1918); *The United States in the World War* (2 vols., 1918–20).

He belonged to many learned and social organizations. One of the early members of the American Historical Association, he was an associate editor of the *American Historical Review* from 1895 to 1899, and president of the Association in 1905–06. In 1899 he was elected a member of the National Institute of Arts and Letters.

[Brief "Memoirs" (MS.) written in 1931; scattered family papers in the possession of his son, Dr. Philip D. McMaster; reviews of his writings, at the time of their appearance, in the daily press and historical periodicals; W. T. Hutchinson, "John Bach McMaster, Historian of the American People," in *Miss. Valley Hist. Rev.*, June 1929; *Who's Who in America*, 1930–31; an appreciation by E. P. Cheyney in *Am. Hist. Rev.*, July 1932; E. P. Oberholtzer, "John Bach McMaster, 1852–1932," in *Pa. Mag. of Hist. and Biography*, Jan. 1933; obituaries in *N. Y. Times, N. Y. Herald Tribune*, Philadelphia *Public Ledger*, May 25, 1932; J. L. Chamberlain, ed., *Universities and Their Sons. Univ. of Pa.*, vol. I (1901).]

W. E. L.

McMATH, ROBERT EMMET (Apr. 28, 1833–May 31, 1918), civil engineer, was born at Varick, Seneca County, N. Y., the son of Alla and Elizabeth (Homan) McMath. He graduated from Williams College with the degree of A.B. at the age of twenty-four. Soon after his graduation, he went to St. Louis and was engaged on surveys, designs, and construction to improve the Mississippi and some of its tributaries. In 1862 he became an assistant engineer in the United States Coast Survey. His first important assignment was in Nicaragua, where he made surveys of the San Juan River and Greytown Harbor in connection with an interoceanic canal proposed by a company which had obtained a grant from the Nicaraguan government. Becoming an assistant engineer in the United States Engineer Corps in 1865, he was engaged until 1883 in improving for navigation the Illinois, Arkansas, and Mississippi rivers. Of principal importance was his work on the Illinois. In 1873 he was made principal civil assistant in charge of special physical investigations. From 1880 to 1883 he was employed by the Mississippi River Commission. At the age of fifty, he left the government service and was appointed sewer commissioner of St. Louis, a position which he occupied for eight years. In 1893 he was elected president of the board of public improvements of St. Louis and served in this capacity until 1901. He then closed his official career, although he remained in practice as a consulting engineer until a few years before his death, which occurred at his home, Webster Groves, Mo. On Dec. 29, 1859, he married at Detroit, Mich., Frances Brodie, a native of Berfield, England, who died Feb. 12, 1867.

McMath was held in high esteem among engineers for his personal as well as his professional qualities. During his connection with the Mississippi River, he was looked upon as the best informed engineer on river hydraulics in America. He was a ready and careful writer and contributed to professional engineering literature. He is best known for the formula which he devised to help in determining the proper size for storm-water sewers. Originally the subject of a paper which was read Dec. 15, 1886, and later published in the *Transactions of the American Society of Civil Engineers* (vol. XVI, 1887, p. 179), it was not the first, nor has it been the last, attempt to provide an economical solution for a difficult and common problem. It has been criticized as an empiric, and not a rational, method; yet, after nearly fifty years, it is used more often than any other to determine the size for storm sewers to carry off the water of the great storms of a given locality with no excess of size or cost. His method in arriving at his formula, under St. Louis conditions, was to note every case where a sewer proved inadequate, determine the rainfall in the tributary area, and plot these on a large diagram. A line drawn to represent sewer capacity somewhat greater than indicated by the incapacities so illustrated gave the proper capacity. The formula is applicable elsewhere if certain local data are available. With the help of tables or diagrams such as those proposed by Allen Hazen and published in the *American Civil Engineers' Pocket Book* and elsewhere, rapid determinations of sizes of sufficient accuracy for preliminary estimates can easily be made.

[F. M. McMath, *Memorials of the McMath Family* (1898); *Trans. Am. Soc. Civil Engineers*, vol. LXXXIII (1921); *Am. Men of Science* (1906); *Am. Civil Engineers' Pocket Book* (1912); L. Metcalf and H. P. Eddy, *Am. Sewerage Practice*, vol. I (1914); Emil Kuichling, in *Trans. Asso. of Civil Engineers, Cornell Univ.* (1893); R. E. McMath, "The Waterway Between Lake Michigan and the Mississippi River by Way of the Illinois River," in *Jour. of the Asso. of Engineering Societies*, Aug. 1888; *Jour. of the Engineers Club of St. Louis*, May–June 1918; *St. Louis Republic*, June 1, 1918.]

G. A. S.

McMICHAEL, MORTON (Oct. 20, 1807–Jan. 6, 1879), editor, mayor of Philadelphia, was born in Bordentown, N. J., and educated in the local schools. His family had come to America from the north of Ireland; his father, John McMichael (1777–1846), was employed on the estate of Joseph Bonaparte; his mother was Hannah Maria Masters. Upon the removal of his parents to Philadelphia, McMichael continued his education there. The statement sometimes made that he attended the University of Pennsylvania is apparently an error. He read law with David Paul Brown and was admitted to the bar in 1827. He was already active in journalism, having become editor of the *Saturday Evening Post* the previous year. In 1831 he resigned this position to become editor-in-chief of the newly established *Saturday Courier*. The same year he married Mary, daughter of Daniel Estell of Philadelphia, by whom he had eight children. About this time he began his political career as a police magistrate, displaying early his power of leadership by dispersing a mob in the slavery riot of 1837 and preventing the burning of a negro orphanage. For a number of years he was an alderman and in 1836 was active on the commission for school reform in the city.

The division of his activities between politics and journalism continued throughout his life. He entered upon his career as a newspaper publisher in 1836, when with Louis A. Godey and Joseph C. Neal [*qq.v.*] he started the *Saturday News and Literary Gazette*. Eight years later he associated himself with Neal in editing *Neal's Saturday Gazette*. From 1842 to 1846 he was one of the editors of *Godey's Lady's Book*. In 1847 he became joint owner, with George R. Graham [*q.v.*], of the Philadelphia *North American,* which in July of the same year absorbed the *United States Gazette*. Robert Montgomery Bird [*q.v.*] joined the enterprise at this time. After the withdrawal of Graham in 1848 and the death of Bird in 1854, McMichael became sole owner. He retained his interest in the paper until his death and by a vigorous and progressive editorial policy succeeded in making it the leading Whig journal of the country. During these early years his activity in publishing brought him into intimate association with Leland, Boker, Poe, Richard Penn Smith, and other well-known literary men then in the city. He contributed to the magazines and other occasional publications, and one of his poems was highly praised by Poe in *Graham's Magazine* (December 1841).

From 1843 to 1846 he was sheriff of Philadelphia, again displaying unusual vigor and courage in ending the anti-Catholic or "Native American" riots of 1844. Always active in the cause of civic betterment, he lent his support and that of his paper to the hotly contested movement for the consolidation of various independent districts of Philadelphia under one government, and was in no small measure responsible for the ultimate passage of the Consolidation Act of 1854. As early as 1858 he was mentioned as a possible candidate for mayor and eight years later was elected to that office, filling it from 1866 to 1869. During the Civil War, in which two of his sons served with distinction, he was one of the founders of the Union League, and later became its fourth president (1870–74). When the Fairmount Park Commission was formed in 1867 he was made president and was reëlected repeatedly until his death. He declined the appointment as minister to Great Britain tendered him by President Grant, on the ground that he could not afford to support the office with the proper dignity. In 1872 he was temporary chairman of the Republican National Convention which renominated Grant for president, and at this time was considered for the vice-presidency. He was a delegate at large to the fourth constitutional convention of Pennsylvania in 1873. After a trip to Europe (1874) he was appointed, in 1875, to the board of managers of the Centennial Exposition. In 1876 he declined, on account of ill health, the chairmanship of the Republican National Convention at Cincinnati. In 1877 he was awarded the degree of LL.D. by the University of Pennsylvania.

Although the only public offices McMichael ever held were in Philadelphia, his influence was wide. By concerning himself with issues and refusing to tolerate personal abuse, he did much to improve the tone of the newspaper press. He was a brilliant speaker and hardly a function in Philadelphia passed without finding him its presiding officer or the orator of the occasion. He died in Philadelphia, and was buried in North Laurel Hill Cemetery.

[*North American,* Jan. 7, 8, and *Public Ledger* (Phila.), Jan. 7, 9, 1879; J. T. Scharf and Thompson Westcott, *Hist. of Phila.* (1884); *In re Morton McMichael* (privately printed, 1921), ed. by Albert Mordell; J. W. Forney, *Memorial Address upon the Character and Public Services of Morton McMichael* (1879) and *Anecdotes of Public Men,* vol. II (1881); F. L. Mott, *A Hist. of Am. Mags.* (1930); *Poulson's Am. Daily Advertiser,* Apr. 28, 1831.] A. C. B.

McMILLAN, JAMES (May 12, 1838–Aug. 10, 1902), United States senator from Michigan, was a grandson of a sea-captain of Stranraer, Scotland, who traded to Philadelphia and Russia, and was one of three sons of William McMillan and his wife, Grace MacMeakin of Wigtown, Scotland, who emigrated to Canada in the 1830's, settling at Hamilton, Ontario. Here James was born and attended the provincially famous school of Dr. Tassie. He came to Detroit in 1855, with excellent letters and some training in the hardware business. After a short service under the leading wholesale hardware merchant of the city, he was employed by a contractor who was building an extension of the Detroit & Milwaukee Railroad. He was so successful in handling men that his employer offered him like work in Spain; but he preferred to remain in Michigan as purchasing agent of the Detroit & Milwaukee road. There he was said to have acquired Aladdin's lamp, from which he never parted. On June 7, 1860, at the age of twenty-two, he married Mary, daughter of Charles Wetmore, one of the dominant merchants of the city. Four sons and two daughters were born to them.

About the time of McMillan's marriage, a group of Detroit capitalists organized the Michigan Car Company to build freight cars, and made McMillan their manager. Owing in part to the demands of the Civil War, the company was highly successful. With the president, John S. Newberry [*q.v.*], the leading admiralty lawyer of Michigan, McMillan established a relation out of which grew the firm of Newberry & McMillan, which made successful adventures in railroads, ship-building, steam-ship lines, and kindred enterprises. They established car plants at Hamilton, Ont.; Cambridge, Ind.; and St. Louis, Mo. With the avowed purpose of uniting commercially the upper and lower peninsulas of Michigan, McMillan promoted the building of the Duluth, South Shore & Atlantic Railroad.

His interest in politics began in 1878 with his successful management of the candidacy of his partner, Newberry, for Congress. In 1886 as chairman of the Republican State Committee he reorganized the party, torn by internal dissensions, and thereby attained a leadership which continued during his life—a sort of benevolent authority based on consultation rather than on dictation. Declining to become a candidate for the United States Senate that year, he was the unanimous choice of the Republican members of the legislature in 1889, and by two reëlections he retained his seat in the Senate until his death in 1902. His previous experience in office had been confined to membership on the Detroit Board of Estimates in 1874 and on the Park Commission in 1881–83. In the latter connection, against strenuous opposition, he secured the purchase, for $100,000, of Belle Isle, and then had Frederick Law Olmsted design what has become one of the three leading island parks of the world.

On entering the Senate, McMillan withdrew from active participation in business. His good judgment, fairness, experience with affairs, absence of self-seeking, and conscientious study of the problems presented led to his appointment to those non-official committees having to do with the management of the business of the Senate. His associations naturally were with the active conservatives, and thus it came about that a group of congenial Republicans used to dine together, usually at his hospitable home, on Thursday evenings. Facetiously they called themselves the S. O. P. C. ("School of Philosophy Club"). The membership, varying with the years, included Senators Allison, Aldrich, Hale, Hanna, Hawley, Manderson, Spooner, and Wetmore, and Vice-President Hobart, with Speaker Reed and General Schofield as customary guests; and on rare occasions President Harrison or President McKinley. While cards, billiards, and stories were the ostensible after-dinner diversions, the real interest was Republican policies. Informally it was agreed by this group that President Harrison's Force Bill and Hanna's ship-subsidy bill were bad politics. They supported President Cleveland's successful efforts to repeal the Bland-Allison Act and opposed the free coinage of silver. Above all they succeeded in keeping out of the public eye, and thus escaped arousing needless antagonisms. Just such another influential group has never existed in the Senate. Not adverse to large appropriations to accomplish large purposes, McMillan was influential in securing the "twenty-foot channel" through the Great Lakes; and as a member of the Committee on Commerce his firm opposition to the small economists secured adequate channels to the harbors of New York, Boston, and Philadelphia.

McMillan was drawn into his most conspicuous and enduring service by his casual assignment to the Senate Committee on the District of Columbia. Concerned at the outset with questions of civic economy, he used his experience in revising railroad terminals, eliminating grade crossings, developing the street-railway system, installing filtration for the water supply, opening cardinal streets, and putting the hospitals and reformatory institutions on an adequate basis. Then, public sentiment being propitious, he secured the creation of a commission to make a comprehensive plan for the future development of Washington. To this commission were appointed only artists: D. H. Burnham and C. F. McKim [*qq.v.*], architects; Augustus Saint-Gaudens [*q.v.*], sculptor; Frederick Law Olmsted, Jr., landscape architect. McMillan authorized and personally advanced the money for the preparation and presentation of the plans.

With premeditation the commission returned to the almost forgotten and sadly mutilated L'Enfant plan of 1792, which they restored and extended to meet the growth of a century. Presented to the Senate by McMillan on Jan. 15, 1902, instantly the plans met public favor; but there was criticism and delay in Congress, largely on account of expense. McMillan himself took up the first and most vital task, the removal of the railroads from the Mall to a union station on a new site, and by dint of persuasion and enthusiasm was able to secure the necessary legislation. Then suddenly, in August 1902, he died. Under the National Commission of Fine Arts, subsequently created, the L'Enfant plan as restored and amplified by the McMillan plan (now so-called) is being carried out with a magnitude of scale and an elegance beyond anything ever before undertaken. A fountain, designed by Herbert Adams and Charles A. Platt, the gift of the people of Michigan in memory of the Senator, stands in McMillan Park, in Washington. Grace Hospital, Detroit, a Shakespeare library at Michigan University, a chemical laboratory at Albion College, are among his permanent gifts.

[*In Memory of Hon. James McMillan, . . . Senator . . . from Mich.* (1903); *Senate Report No. 166*, 57 Cong., 1 Sess.; Park Papers, U. S. Senate, 1900–03; and D. C. Committee reports, 1890–1903; Charles Moore, *Daniel H. Burnham, Architect, Planner of Cities* (1921) and *Life and Times of Charles Follen McKim* (1929); *Detroit Free Press*, Aug. 11, 1902.]

C. M.

McMILLAN, JAMES WINNING (Apr. 28, 1825–Mar. 9, 1903), Union soldier, was born in Clark County, Ky., the son of Robert and Nancy (Winning) McMillan. At the age of twenty-one he enlisted for the Mexican War, serving in the 4th Illinois Infantry and in the 3rd Battalion, Louisiana Volunteers, Fiescas Regiment. Upon being discharged he went to Indiana and engaged in business. Here he was twice married: in 1858 to Olivia Ames at Lawrenceburg, and in 1860 to Minerva Foote of Bedford. A daughter, Minerva, was born of the second marriage. When President Lincoln called for volunteers to preserve the Union, McMillan organized the 21st Indiana Infantry Regiment and was sent as its colonel to Louisiana, where he took part in the operations resulting in the opening of the Mississippi River. General Butler, commanding the Department of the Gulf, had a high opinion of McMillan's ability as a leader and placed him in charge of several independent expeditions. In May 1862 McMillan led forces that captured a large quantity of Confederate stores at Berwick Bay, and a blockade runner, the steamer *Fox*. In June he was wounded in an encounter with guerrillas. September found him back with his men and in command of a reinforced brigade that routed Waller's Texas Cavalry near St. Charles Court House. An expedition to Donaldsonville, La., narrowly escaped destruction by being withdrawn under his excellent leadership. His regiment was now stationed at Baton Rouge and reorganized as the 1st Indiana Heavy Artillery.

McMillan was promoted to brigadier-general in November 1862 and assigned to the command of the 2nd Brigade, 1st Division, XIX Corps. In General Banks's Red River expedition in the spring of 1864 the 1st Division arrived on the battlefield at Sabine's Crossroads, La., as the Union troops were fleeing in confusion. McMillan's brigade did its share in stopping the Confederates and driving them from the field. Later, at Pleasant Hill, McMillan's command broke up the attack on the retreating column. Moved to Virginia in July 1864, his brigade took an active part in the Shenandoah Valley campaign. At Winchester he formed line of battle in the midst of disorganized and panic-stricken troops. By keeping control of his regiments, he was able to maneuver in conjunction with the VI Corps in such manner as to drive the Confederates from that part of the field. When, a month later, General Early succeeded in surprising the left and rear of Sheridan's Army near Cedar Creek, Va., McMillan, now commanding the 1st Division, XIX Corps, deployed it at right angles to his former front. It held the position and gained time for troops in rear to get into line. McMillan's men then gave ground, fighting as they went. McMillan was now placed in command of the 1st Division of the Department of West Virginia with headquarters at Grafton. He was brevetted a major-general of volunteers in March 1865 and resigned from the service May 15, 1865. For a time after the war he resided in Kansas, but in 1875 he moved to Washington, D. C., to become a member of the Board of Review in the Pension Office. He held this position until his death in 1903. He was a man of great personal bravery, a tenacious fighter, and a strict disciplinarian.

[*Mil. Order of the Loyal Legion of the U. S., Commandery of D. C., Circular No. 4, Ser. of 1903*; *War of the Rebellion: Official Records (Army)*, 1 ser., VI, XV, XXXIV, XLIII, pt. 1, XLVI, pt. 3; *Personal Memoirs of P. H. Sheridan* (2 vols., 1888); *Army and Navy Jour.*, Mar. 14, 1903; *Evening Star* (Washington, D. C.), Mar. 9, 1903; Pension Office records.]

J. R. V.

McMINN, JOSEPH (June 22, 1758–Nov. 17, 1824), governor of Tennessee, was born in West Marlborough Township, Chester County, Pa., the fifth of ten children of Robert and Sarah (Harlan) McMinn. Early in life he settled in the region that was to be Hawkins County, Tenn. He was a member of the territorial legislature of 1794 and for more than a quarter of a century thereafter was in public office. In 1796 he was a member of the convention that framed the constitution of Tennessee, and it was upon his motion that a bill of rights was incorporated in that document. He served almost continuously in the first eight general assemblies of the state, and was three times speaker of the Senate. In 1815 he defeated four other candidates for governor, and in 1817 and 1819 was reëlected, thus serving the constitutional limit of six successive years. As governor he advocated public education, from which he thought "advantages incalculable would arise to the citizens of the state," and charged the legislature, unsuccessfully, to guard well the lands allotted by Congress for two colleges. He favored improving the navigation of the Tennessee River and sponsored a plan for a canal connecting the Holston and the Tennessee. He championed a project for penal reform, but to no avail. Neither was he successful in his attempt to solve the currency and banking difficulties by the establishment of loan offices.

One of the major problems of his administration was that constituted by the presence of the Indians within the borders of Tennessee. McMinn desired their removal to a region west of the Mississippi, for he believed it an injustice to withhold lands from the white settlers "with no other object than to serve the Cherokee and Chickasaw Indians for a hunting ground" (*Journal of the Senate . . . of Tennessee,* 1817, p. 9). While he was governor, the Chickasaws ceded their claims to the western third of the state. He himself negotiated a treaty by which the Cherokees ceded vast tracts in East Tennessee. In 1823 he was appointed United States agent to the Cherokees, a position that he retained until his death. To the surprise of friend and foe, white man and redskin, he practised "kindness to those miserable Deluded People," his "Red Brethern, the Cherokee." At the solicitation of the Cherokee chief known as the Path Killer, he served notice on intruders from Georgia "to remove their families without the limits of the Cherokee Nation." Then, without awaiting orders from his superior, the secretary of war, thinking that any delay "would prejudice the Public Interest," he burned their houses and cut down their corn. The luckless squatters answered by firing on McMinn's troops: not until October 1824 was quiet restored.

Despite a crowded public life, the democratic ex-governor maintained "a plain but reputable 'hostelry'" at Rogersville, Tenn. Guests found him "affable, kind, and communicative." He was thrice married: on May 9, 1785, to Hannah Cooper of Pennsylvania, who died in 1811; on Jan. 5, 1812, to Rebecca Kincade of Hawkins County, Tenn., who died in 1815; and some time later to Nancy Williams of Roane County, Tenn., whom he sought unsuccessfully to divorce. His name is perpetuated in Tennessee in McMinn County and the town of McMinnville, county seat of Warren County.

[MSS. in Bureau of Indian Affairs, Dept. of the Interior; *Am. Hist. Mag.* (Nashville), vol. IV (1899) and issue of Oct. 1903; A. H. Abel, "The Cherokee Negotiations of 1822 and 1823," *Smith Coll. Studies in Hist.*, vol. I, no. 4 (1916); *Tenn. Hist. Mag.*, Oct. 1930; *Journals* of the Tennessee legislature, *passim*; A. H. Harlan, *Hist. and Geneal. of the Harlan Family* (n.d.); *Knoxville Weekly Register*, 1817; *Knoxville Reg.*, Nov. 26, 1824.]

M. B. H—r.

McMURTRIE, WILLIAM (Mar. 10, 1851–May 24, 1913), chemist, was born on a farm near Belvidere, N. J., the son of Abram and Almira (Smith) McMurtrie. During his boyhood he acquired an interest in chemistry through listening to some lectures by the village pastor. At school, he was an active, ambitious lad, and in 1867 he entered Lafayette College, Easton, Pa., enrolling in the mining-engineering course. Here he was known as an industrious and faithful but self-contained student who had but small interest in the social side of college life.

After his graduation in 1871, he was made assistant to Dr. R. J. Brown, then chief chemist of the department of agriculture at Washington, D. C., and on Dr. Brown's retirement, two years later, McMurtrie was made chief chemist. Resigning in 1877, he became an agent of the department and special commissioner to the Exposition Universelle at Paris. His account of his work there is contained in *Reports of the United States Commissioners to the Paris Universal Exposition, 1878* (1880). In consequence of this appointment he was made a *chevalier du mérite agricole* by the French government. While abroad he studied the beet-sugar industry and made a report which was instrumental in starting beet root sugar manufacture in this country (*Report on the Culture of the Sugar Beet and the Manufacture of Sugar Therefrom in France and the United States,* 1880). While still a special agent of the department in chemical technology he also made investigations which resulted in the publication of *Report on the Culture of Sumac in Sicily and Its Preparation for Market in Europe and the United States* (1880), *On the Mineral Nutrition of the Vine for the Production of Wine* (1882), and *Report on the Examination of Raw Silks* (1883). Several years later he published *Wool—Its Structure and Strength* (1885), *Report Upon an Examination of Wools and Other Animal Fibers* (1886), and "Wools and Other Animal Fibers," in *World's Columbian Exposition* (1901). In 1882 he became professor of chemistry at the University of Illinois; in 1884, chemist of the Illinois State

Board of Agriculture; and in 1886, chemist of the Agricultural Experiment Station.

In 1888 he went to New York as chemist of the New York Tartar Company, manufacturers of Royal Baking Powder. With his customary determination McMurtrie set about improving and cheapening the product. At that time the argols from which the cream of tartar was produced were put into copper-lined pressure cylinders with water and superheated. The solution thus formed was filtered under pressure, and when the pressure was released, steam was given off and the crude cream of tartar precipitated in fine crystals. Copper, however, was dissolved during the process and contaminated the product. After much experimenting McMurtrie succeeded in getting a pure product at a reasonable cost. He then turned his attention to building and equipping a factory for putting the product on the market, completing it to the entire satisfaction of his employers, by whom he was made manager and vice-president of the company. He was not, however, allowed to disclose the manufacturing methods employed, and an interesting chapter of chemical experience was thus lost.

McMurtrie was much interested in the American Chemical Society and the Chemists Club of New York, and devoted much time to them, serving as president of the latter and of the New York section of the former. He was for a number of years a member of the council of the Chemical Society and in 1900 he became its president. On Apr. 5, 1876, he married Helen M. Douglass. His death occurred suddenly in New York.

[C. F. McKenna, in *The Percolator* (N. Y. Chemists Club), June 20, 1913; *Who's Who in America*, 1912–13; H. W. Wiley, in *Jour. of Industrial and Engineering Chemistry*, July 1913, with bibliography by McMurtrie's son, Douglas C. McMurtrie; Edward Hart, in *Science*, Aug. 8, 1913; *N. Y. Times*, May 25, 1913.]

E. H.

McNAIR, ALEXANDER (May 5, 1775–Mar. 18, 1826), the first governor of Missouri, was the grandson of David McNair, a Scotch Covenanter who emigrated from County Donegal, Ireland, before 1737 and settled in what is now Dauphin County, Pa. He was the son of David and Ann (Dunning) McNair and was born on his father's farm in Mifflin (now Juniata) County, Pa. After his father's death in 1777 his mother took him to live near Pittsburgh, where he grew up and obtained some education. In 1799 he became a first lieutenant in the United States Army. When the army was reduced he was discharged in June 1800, and in 1804 he moved to St. Louis. His marriage, in March 1805, to Marguerite Susanne de Reilhe, the well educated and talented daughter of a prominent French merchant who had died three years earlier, gave him standing within the most influential political circles of the city. At the March 1805 term of the court of common pleas he was appointed one of the associate judges and from that time until his death he held public office continuously. Aside from the governorship, the principal offices he held were those of city trustee, sheriff of St. Louis County, colonel, then adjutant and inspector of territorial militia, United States marshal, register of the St. Louis land office, and federal agent to the Osage Indians. He also engaged in various mercantile pursuits and acquired a good deal of property.

Although he was a member of the constitutional convention, he played an unobtrusive part in its deliberations, except in his opposition to the constitutional provision for a high salary schedule for state officials. Before the convention adjourned he announced himself as a candidate for governor against William Clark [*q.v.*]. He had greater gifts of popularity than Clark, and he conducted an extensive personal campaign. His opponents, led by the St. Louis machine, charged that he lacked education and ability for such an office, that he had used his authority in the land office loosely in order to gain popularity, and, as the campaign grew hotter, that he was using the "greatest exertions in the tippling shops" of St. Louis (Shoemaker, *Missouri's Struggle*, *post*, p. 264). Nevertheless, he was elected by a majority of 4,020 in a total of 9,132 votes. As governor from 1820 to 1824 he urged no startling policies. He opposed any restriction on slavery, but in order to hasten her admission into the Union he approved Missouri's adroitly worded "Solemn Public Act." He was careful to observe all the proprieties connected with the inauguration of the new state government and took great pains to study and lay before the assembly copies of the laws of the older states. His messages to the legislature were clear, brief, and conservative in tone, and they dealt with subjects appropriate to a new frontier state, such as fiscal affairs, immigration, relations with the Indians, the militia, and the industrial development of the commonwealth.

Although brought up as a Presbyterian and, during his earlier years at St. Louis, an active member of a Masonic lodge, before his death he received the last rites of the Roman Catholic Church of which his wife was a member. She, with eight of their ten children, survived him.

[McNair Papers in Jefferson Memorial Lib., St. Louis; *The Messages and Proclamations of the Governors of the State of Mo.*, ed. by Buel Leopard and F. C. Shoemaker, vol. I (1922); F. C. Shoemaker, *Mis-*

souri's Struggle for Statehood (1916); W. B. Stevens, *Mo., the Center State*, 2 vols. (1915); Louis Houck, *A Hist. of Mo.* (1908), III; Richard Edwards and M. Hopewell, *Edwards's Great West and her Commercial Metropolis* (1860); F. L. Billon, *Annals of St. Louis in her Territorial Days* (1888); E. H. Shepard, *The Early Hist. of St. Louis* (1870); *Mo. Hist. Rev.*, Oct. 1922; *St. Louis Catholic Hist. Rev.*, July–Oct. 1919; *Wis. State Hist. Soc. Colls.*, II (1856); J. B. McNair, *McNair, McNear, and McNeir Geneals.* (1923); *Mo. Gazette and Public Advertiser* (St. Louis), Apr. 26, 1820; *Mo. Intelligencer* (Franklin), Apr. 7, 1826.]

H. E. N.

MCNAIR, FRED WALTER (Dec. 3, 1862–June 30, 1924), college president, son of Hugh A. Wilson McNair and Mary Jane (Dorland) McNair, was born at Fennimore, Wis. His father, a farmer and surveyor, kindled an early and permanent interest in mathematics and allied subjects in young McNair, who for two undergraduate years was instructor in mathematics at Wisconsin University, and after graduation in 1891 served as assistant professor of mathematics at Michigan Agricultural College, 1892–93, from which he was called to Michigan College of Mines as professor of mathematics and physics in 1893. In 1899 he was made president of Michigan College of Mines, a position which he occupied with distinction for the rest of his life. He married Berta Philbrick of Fennimore, Wis., in 1886. In June 1924, as he was returning from an engineers' meeting in Boulder, Colo., he was killed in a railroad wreck near Buda, Ill.

The deep copper mines of the Lake Superior country gave opportunity for unique physical research, and in cooperation with the United States Coast and Geodetic Survey McNair measured the force of gravity a mile under ground. He also studied the method of transferring the azimuth of a line on the earth's surface to the bottom of a mine by means of two plumb-lines. Extended observations on pairs of plumb-lines over 4400 feet long in vertical mine shafts showed that some pairs hung nearly parallel while others were an inch or more farther apart at the bottom than at the top. McNair found that this divergence was produced by air currents and emphasized the necessity of eliminating air circulation wherever long plumb-lines are used (*Engineering and Mining Journal*, Apr. 26, 1902, p. 578). He next sought to determine experimentally, by means of falling spheres, the easterly deviation which a falling body theoretically undergoes because of the earth's rotation, and to study the air resistance of falling spheres. A steel ball was suspended motionless over the center of a deep shaft and the supporting silken thread was burned away. But the ball was invariably deflected laterally in its downward course, lodging in the timbers lining the walls of the shaft, and never reached the bottom. This was an early demonstration of an aerodynamic principle, now widely recognized, that a slight asymmetry in the air flow around a body produces a lateral force.

When the United States entered the war, McNair was temporarily relieved from his college duties in order to join the staff of the Bureau of Standards, where, in cooperation with J. F. Hayford and L. J. Briggs, he engaged in the successful development of an instrument for directing the gun-fire of battleships. The determination of the proper elevation of the guns formerly depended upon the visibility of the sea-horizon, which was often obscured by fog, or smoke of battle. This instrument, based upon gyroscopic action, provided an artificial horizon and could be used below decks regardless of fog, smoke, or the roll and pitch of the ship.

But it was as an educator that McNair did his greatest work. Slender in physique, he was given an effective presence by his keen mentality and wide, sensitive, and sympathetic understanding of men and their problems. For nearly fifty years he was actively identified with the Society for the Promotion of Engineering Education, of which he was president in 1904–05. He was a fellow of the American Association for the Advancement of Science: vice-president of section D, 1904–05; secretary of the council, 1905–06; general secretary, 1906–07. He was a member of the American Institute of Mining and Metallurgical Engineers; the Mining and Metallurgical Society of America; and the American Physical Society. His chief avocation was biology, and in the company of his four children, he took the keenest delight in roaming the forests near his home in search of *Myxomycetes*, a curious group of slime fungi which possess the remarkable habit of crawling slowly over decaying stumps and logs. His valuable collections of *Myxomycetes* is now deposited with the University of Wisconsin.

[*Who's Who in America*, 1922–23; Hugh McNair, "Fred Walter McNair," *Trans. Am. Inst. Mining and Metallurgical Engineers*, vol. LXX (1924); *Engineering and Mining Journal-Press*, July 5, 1924; Mining and Metallurgical Soc. of America, *Bulletin*, no. 172, Nov.–Dec. 1924; J. B. McNair, *McNair, McNear, and McNeir Geneals.* (1923) and supplement published in 1929; *Detroit Free Press*, July 1, 1924; personal acquaintance.]

L. J. B.

MCNAIR, FREDERICK VALLETTE (Jan. 13, 1839–Nov. 28, 1900), naval officer, was born at Jenkintown, Pa., just north of Philadelphia, the son of John and Mary (Yerkes) McNair, and a descendant of Scotch-Irish settlers in Pennsylvania. On the nomination of his father, who was then representative from the fifth district of Pennsylvania, he was appointed midshipman Sept. 21, 1853. After four years at the Naval Academy he went to the China station in the *Minnesota,* 1857–59; was commissioned lieutenant Apr. 18, 1861; and during the first months of the Civil War was in the *Iroquois,* West Indies. In this ship he subsequently served through the Mississippi River campaign under Farragut, taking part in the battle with the forts below New Orleans, April 1862, the engagement at Grand Gulf, and the running of the batteries at Vicksburg. At Natchez and Baton Rouge he was the officer sent ashore to demand their surrender. After a brief leave in the summer of 1862 he served in the *Juanita* and the *Seminole* on the East Coast until August 1863, and then in the *Pensacola* on the Mississippi until April 1864. Promoted at that time to lieutenant commander, he was for the remainder of the war executive in the *Juanita,* participating in both attacks on Fort Fisher, Dec. 24–25, 1864, and Jan. 13–15, 1865. In connection with a boat accident in March 1865, the commander of the *Juanita,* J. J. Almy, commended McNair as "a most excellent officer, possessing good judgment and . . . more than usual experience" (*War of the Rebellion: Official Records, Navy,* 1 ser., III, p. 450).

Coming through the war with a notable record for dependability and initiative, he was during his later career assigned to positions of unusual responsibility. In 1866–67 he was executive of the flagship *Brooklyn,* Brazil Squadron, and after a year as instructor at the Naval Academy was executive of the flagship *Franklin,* European Squadron. He was head of the department of seamanship at the Naval Academy, 1871–75, and again, after duty on the Asiatic station, at the academy as commandant of cadets, 1878–82. Promoted to captain in 1883, he was at the Mare Island Navy Yard in California, 1883–86; commander of the flagship *Omaha,* Asiatic station, 1887–90; superintendent of the Naval Observatory, 1890–94; and in command of the Asiatic Squadron, 1895–98, during which service he brought his ships to the efficiency in gunnery proved next year under Dewey at Manila. Promotion to rear admiral came in July 1898, and for the next two years he was at the Naval Academy as superintendent. Owing to failing health he resigned from this position in the spring of 1900 and was living in Washington, senior on the active list, at the time of his death from apoplexy. He was married on Oct. 9, 1862, to Clara, daughter of James W. W. Warren of Philadelphia. His son, Frederick Vallette, also became a naval officer.

[L. R. Hamersly, *The Records of Living Officers of the U. S. Navy* (ed. 1898); J. B. McNair, *McNair, McNear, and McNeir Geneals.* (1923), pp. 227–29; Washington *Evening Star,* Nov. 29, 1900.] A. W.

MACNAUGHTAN, MYRA KELLY [See KELLY, MYRA, 1875–1910].

McNEILL, DANIEL (Apr. 5, 1748–1833), privateersman in the Revolution and naval officer, born at Charlestown, Mass., was the son of William and Catherine (Morrison) McNeill, and the grandson of Daniel McNeill who emigrated from Ireland in 1683. On Feb. 10, 1770, he married Mary Cuthbertson, whose early death may be assumed, for not later than 1772 he married Abigail Harvey, of Nottingham, England. The eldest of their ten children was born July 20, 1773. McNeill was doubtless bred to the sea. He first comes into notice as commander of the privateer brig *Hancock,* in November 1776. He commanded five other privateers during the Revolution: the *America, Eagle, Ulysses, Wasp,* and, most noted of all, the *General Mifflin,* a ship of twenty guns and 150 men, in which he cruised in European waters in 1778 and 1779. In this vessel he took thirteen prizes and fought an engagement with a British sloop of war. He has been credited by historians with firing a salute in the harbor of Brest, which was returned by the French admiral, causing international correspondence, but this incident occurred in 1777, when the *Mifflin* was commanded by Capt. William Day. McNeill returned to Boston early in 1779. His privateering ventures were successful and before the end of the war he was part owner of two vessels.

Until the outbreak of hostilities with France in 1798 he was probably employed either as master or owner of ships. On July 17 of that year he was commissioned a captain in the United States navy and given command of the ship *Portsmouth,* of twenty-four guns. She was attached to the squadron of Commodore Barry and until the end of 1799 cruised in the West Indies and off the coast of Surinam, where, with the help of a revenue cutter, she blockaded a French man-of-war and forced her surrender. In April 1800, McNeill was sent in the *Portsmouth* with dispatches to France and brought home the American peace commissioners.

After his return McNeill was given command of the frigate *Boston* and was sent again to France, in October 1801, with the new United States minister, Robert R. Livingston. He then proceeded to the Mediterranean under orders to join the squadron of Commodore Dale, engaged in war with Tripoli. During 1802 he was employed in cruising and in blockading Tripoli. Throughout his stay in the Mediterranean he never fell in with either Commodore Dale or his successor, Commodore Morris, and was supposed to have purposely avoided them. He returned to Boston in October 1802 and was dismissed from the navy on the 27th of that month, under the Peace Establishment Act of Mar. 3, 1801. His son, Daniel McNeill, Jr., entered the navy as a midshipman in 1799 and was dismissed in 1807. McNeill's later years were passed in Boston, where he acquired property in real estate and became a man of substance.

[T. B. Wyman, *Geneals. and Estates of Charlestown* (1879), vol. II; *A Vol. of Records Relating to the Early Hist. of Boston, Containing Boston Marriages from 1752 to 1809* (1903); Nathaniel I. Bowditch's abstracts of Boston titles (manuscript) in the library of the Mass. Hist. Soc.; G. W. Allen, "Mass. Privateers of the Revolution," *Mass. Hist. Soc. Colls.*, vol. LXXVII (1927), and *A Naval Hist. of the Am. Revolution* (2 vols., 1913), *Our Naval War with France* (1909), and *Our Navy and the Barbary Corsairs* (1905).] G. W. A.

McNEILL, GEORGE EDWIN (Aug. 4, 1837–May 19, 1906), leader of American labor movements, and one of the founders of the American Federation of Labor, was born in Amesbury, Mass. He was brought up in the midst of the anti-slavery agitation, of which his father, John McNeill, a friend and neighbor of John G. Whittier, was an active propagandist. His mother was Abigail Todd (Hickey) McNeill. McNeill's formal education came from the public and private schools of Amesbury. He was working in the woolen-mills of his native town at the time of the great strike in 1851. About this time he learned the shoe-maker's trade. He settled in Boston in 1856 and married Adeline J. Trefethen on Dec. 24, 1859. His main renown came through his espousal of the eight-hour philosophy of Ira Steward. As secretary of the Grand Eight-Hour League (1863–64) and president of the Boston Eight-Hour League (1869–74), he was the oratorical, journalistic, and organizing influence which began to place eight-hour legislation on the statute books of state and federal governments as early as 1867, and which, after such legislation was shown to be ineffective, placed the issue at the front in trade-union programs during the eighties. He organized several workingmen's associations, acting as president of one of these, the Workingmen's Institute, from 1867 to 1869. As a member of the school committee of Cambridge, Mass. (1872–75), he succeeded in establishing free evening drawing-schools.

The declaration of principles which was adopted by the Knights of Labor Assembly in 1874 had been written in substance by McNeill for a labor congress at Rochester earlier the same year. It became from this time the platform of the order. Beginning as early as 1865, he was connected in an editorial or associate editorial capacity with the labor papers of the day in New York, Fall River, and Paterson, N. J. On account of his eight-hour philosophy of more leisure for workingmen he opposed vigorously the far more popular greenback and cooperative programs of the labor organizations of his time. While joining with Wendell Phillips in starting a labor party he separated from Phillips when the latter espoused the greenback movement; and with Steward, he organized the hostile Eight-Hour League. The antagonism of the two organizations reached its height in 1872 and meanwhile had much to do with the failure of the political movement led by Phillips. Yet to Phillips and McNeill was due the creation, by the Massachusetts legislature, in 1869, of the first Bureau of Labor Statistics, which has been copied by other states and nations. In 1869 he was appointed the first assistant chief of that bureau but in 1873, on account of his labor activities, he was dropped from the position.

In 1878 McNeill became the president of the newly founded International Labor Union, a precursor in some respects of the American Federation of Labor, in that it eschewed politics and directed its attention to the organization of all classes of labor for strictly economic gains of shorter hours and better wages. It did not reach far beyond the textile industries, but in these industries McNeill showed unusual organizing ability. He was an active member of the Knights of Labor, having joined in 1883, and was treasurer of District 30 of that order, 1884–86. He resigned because he favored the principle of trade autonomy for each trade. When the contest between the Knights and the American Federation of Labor reached its crisis in 1886, it was McNeill, as a member of the Committee on the State of the Order, who, at the special session of the General Assembly of the Knights in May 1886, drafted the plan of cooperation with the Federation. This was destined to failure, and in July of that year he resigned from the Knights and went over to the Federation, whose non-political program fitted his original ideas of labor organization.

Henceforth he was prominent as writer and speaker for that organization, supporting himself as treasurer and general manager of the Accident Insurance Company after 1883. He was successful as arbitrator of differences between employers and employees, notably in the great horse-car strike in Boston in 1885. In 1886 he was the United Labor Party's candidate for mayor of Boston, at which time he was also editor and proprietor of the *Labor Leader,* Boston. From 1886 to 1898 he was a delegate to the conventions of the American Federation of Labor and was sent by it as a fraternal delegate to England in 1898. He served the state of Massachusetts as commissioner of manual training in 1893–94 and on other commissions till his death on May 19, 1906, in Somerville. He edited and wrote the larger portion of *The Labor Movement: the Problem of Today* (1887), the first systematic history of the labor movement in America, wherein he summarized his experiences and views. His other publications include *The Philosophy of the Labor Movement* (1893); *Eight Hour Primer* (1889); *A Study of Accidents and Accident Insurance* (1900); and *Unfrequented Paths: Songs of Nature, Labor, and Men* (1903). In 1903 he contributed to the publications of the American Economic Association a paper on "Trade Union Ideals."

[There is a biography of McNeill, to 1886, in *The Labor Movement,* pp. 611–12. See also: *Who's Who in America,* 1906–07; the *Am. Federationist,* July 1906; John R. Commons and others, *Hist. of Labour in the U. S.* (1918), vol. II, and *A Documentary Hist. of Am. Industrial Soc.* (1910), vol. IX; and the Boston *Transcript,* May 21, 1906.] J. R. C.

McNEILL, HECTOR (Oct. 10, 1728–Dec. 25, 1785), Revolutionary naval officer and privateersman, son of Malcolm and Mary (Stuart) McNeill, was born in County Antrim, Ireland, and came with his parents to Boston in 1737. He was educated in the Boston schools and while still young went to sea, becoming master of a vessel before he was twenty-two. On Nov. 12, 1750, he was married in the Presbyterian church to Mary Wilson. They had four children, three of whom survived infancy. In 1769 his wife died and on Dec. 26, 1770, he was married to Mary Watt, by whom he had one daughter.

McNeill served at the beginning of the French and Indian War as master of a vessel which, in 1755, carried General Monckton to Nova Scotia. Very soon afterward his vessel was captured by Indians and he was sent a prisoner to Quebec. Several years later he was engaged in the coasting trade between Quebec, Boston, and the West Indies. In 1775 he was living in Quebec, but soon entered the service of the United Colonies on the St. Lawrence River. Early in 1776 he returned to Boston and on June 15 was appointed a captain in the Continental Navy. On Oct. 10, 1776, he was placed third on the list of captains (*Journals of the Continental Congress,* Oct. 10, 1776). He was given command of the new frigate *Boston,* of twenty-four guns. On May 21, 1777, the frigate *Hancock,* under Captain John Manley, senior to McNeill, and the *Boston,* accompanied by nine privateers, sailed on a cruise to the eastward. The privateers soon became separated and took no further part in the enterprise. The *Hancock* and *Boston* fell in with and escaped from the British sixty-four-gun ship *Somerset* and the frigate *Mercury.* Soon after this, in June, they captured, after a fight, the British frigate *Fox.* Three small prizes were burned.

On July 7 the little American squadron encountered the enemy's forty-four-gun ship *Rainbow,* the frigate *Flora,* and the brig *Victor.* A severe action followed, first with the *Flora.* The American ships becoming separated, the *Hancock* engaged the *Rainbow* alone and was captured, as was also the prize *Fox.* The *Boston* escaped and went into Wiscasset, later returning to Boston. McNeill was blamed for not coming to the rescue of the *Hancock* when it was attacked by the *Rainbow,* was court-martialed, and was dismissed or suspended from the navy in June 1778. No report of his trial has been preserved. In January 1779, the Marine Committee recommended that the sentence of the court "be not carried into execution." But nothing was done and the captain never again served in the navy. Doubtless one of the contributing factors to the disastrous outcome of this cruise, so auspiciously begun, was the lack of cordial relations between Manley and McNeill; effective cooperation between them was hardly possible.

Later in the war McNeill commanded two privateers—the brigantine *Pallas* and the ship *Adventure*—the bonds of which are dated May 22 and Nov. 22, 1780, respectively. What success, if any, he achieved is unknown. The *Pallas* was supposed to have been lost or captured on her way to Amsterdam, but this is uncertain. After the war the captain returned to the merchant service and on Christmas night, 1785, was lost at sea. McNeill's many letters show strength of character and, despite a somewhat contentious disposition, a kindliness and devotion to the interests of the officers and men who served under him.

[The *Proc. Mass. Hist. Soc.,* vol. LV (1923), contain an article on McNeill by G. W. Allen, an autobiographical sketch dated July 13, 1773, and McNeill's letters, papers, and journal. See also G. W. Allen, *A Naval Hist. of the Am. Revolution* (1913) and "Mass. Privateers of the Revolution," *Mass. Hist. Soc. Colls.,* vol. LXXVII (1927); and E. S. Maclay, *A Hist. of the U. S. Navy* (1894), vol. I.] G. W. A.

McNEILL, JOHN HANSON (June 12, 1815–Nov. 10, 1864), stock-raiser and exhibitor, Confederate ranger, was born in Hardy County, Va., the son of Strother McNeill. His formal education was meager, probably not extending beyond the country schools of the time. In January 1837 he was married to Jemima Cunningham, and the year following he moved to Kentucky where he became a farmer and stock-raiser. After remaining there about six years, he became dissatisfied and returned to Virginia. Relatives in Missouri in time convinced him of that state's promising future, and, in 1848, with his family and slaves, he settled in Boone County and commenced farming operations. He imported from Kentucky and from Ohio blooded short-horn cattle and developed the finest herd in Missouri. He was one of the first and most successful stock-breeders and exhibitors in the state, winning many premiums at the numerous county fairs. He was also vitally interested in various agricultural associations devoted to the care and breeding of the better types of live stock. From 1848 to 1861 he lived the leisurely life of a Virginia gentleman and landowner, acquiring additional holdings in Daviess County, in northern Missouri, whither he had moved in 1855.

By birth and by conviction a Southerner, McNeill urged that Missouri join the Confederacy, and, in 1861, under the governor's commission, he recruited and became captain of a company in Price's army. He and his three sons fought through the Missouri campaigns of 1861–62, serving with devotion and distinction. Severely wounded and captured, he escaped from the federal prison at St. Louis and made his laborious way to Virginia and to the mountainous region of his boyhood. It was by that time evident that Missouri was irrevocably lost to the Confederacy so McNeill decided to remain in the South. Upon authority of the Confederate Congress he organized, late in 1862, the McNeill Partisan Rangers, cooperating with the Southern army but independent in command. His company included friends and relatives selected from the surrounding territory and familiar with every mountain road and bypath. For two years, "Hanse" McNeill and his rangers wrought great havoc among the Northern forces in several West Virginia counties, destroying numerous supply trains, railroad rolling stock and equipment, and capturing some 2600 prisoners. The terrain was admirably adapted to the method of fighting, which was suddenly to attack the enemy, scatter and destroy his supply and ammunition trains, then retreat to the inaccessible mountain fastnesses. Six feet tall and of aristocratic bearing and manner, McNeill possessed a boldness, bravery, and magnanimity which endeared him to his command. He won the commendation of Lee as being "bold and intelligent" and was characterized officially by Sheridan as the "most daring and dangerous of all the bushwhackers" (*War of the Rebellion: Official Records, Army*, 1 ser. XLIII, pt. 1, p. 30). Other Union generals respected and feared the Partisan Rangers and their commander. On Oct. 2, 1864, while leading a surprise daybreak raid into the Shenandoah Valley, McNeill was accidentally and fatally shot by one of his own company. He died on Nov. 10, at Harrisonburg, Va. A minor figure of the Civil War, this intrepid soldier symbolized the best traits of the men who fought on both sides in that conflict.

[W. D. Vandiver, Columbia, Mo., has considerable material relating to McNeill, including an unpublished account of his life by his son, Jesse, and numerous maps. J. W. Duffy, *McNeill's Last Charge* (1912), describes the events of Oct. and Nov. 1864, while W. D. Vandiver, "Two Forgotten Heroes," in *Mo. Hist. Rev.*, Apr. 1927, gives an account of his career. See also C. A. Evans, *Confed. Mil. Hist.* (1899), II, 116–23, and *War of the Rebellion: Official Records (Army)*, 1 ser. XXV, XXIX, XXX, XXXVII, and XLIII.]

T. S. B.

McNEILL, WILLIAM GIBBS (Oct. 3, 1801–Feb. 16, 1853), civil engineer, was born at Wilmington, N. C., the son of Dr. Charles Donald McNeill. His great-grandfather, a member of a Highland clan, after service at the Battle of Culloden, emigrated to North America with the celebrated Flora McDonald in 1746. His father served with the British Army in the West Indies and eventually settled at Wilmington, N. C., where he was a physician of high repute. William Gibbs McNeill was educated near New York, intending to become a minister, but upon visiting West Point with his friend, Joseph Gardner Swift [*q.v.*], he became interested in a military career and succeeded in obtaining a cadet appointment by President Madison. After service at West Point, in 1817 he received a commission as third lieutenant of artillery. Among his comrades at the military academy was George W. Whistler [*q.v.*], who married his sister Anna, and with whom he was professionally associated in many public works.

McNeill's early work, under the Corps of Engineers, was with the United States Coast Survey in the South, although he served as aide-de-camp to General Andrew Jackson during the war in Florida in 1819. In 1823 he was transferred to the corps of topographical engineers, on the general staff. Here he was employed to ascertain the practicability and cost of constructing a railway or canal between the Chesapeake Bay and the Ohio River—across the Alleghany Mountains. He also made surveys for the James River and Kanawha canals, as well as the location survey for the Baltimore & Ohio Railroad. In recognition of his work, he was made a member of the Board of Engineers and in 1828, with his comrades—Whistler, and Jonathan Knight—was deputed to visit Europe to examine the public works, especially existing railroads and those in course of construction. He came into contact with George Stephenson and other noted engineers of the time and became especially impressed with the advantages of railroads as a new mode of transportation. Upon his return to the United States, he took every means to stimulate activity in this field. As a result, McNeill and Whistler became joint engineers upon a majority of the new railways in the eastern part of the country. Among those upon which he was engaged alone or with Whistler, in addition to the Baltimore & Ohio, were the Baltimore & Susquehanna, Paterson & Hudson River, Boston & Providence, Providence & Stonington, Taunton & New Bedford, Long Island, Boston & Albany, and Charleston, Louisville & Cincinnati. His promotion in rank was rapid and in 1834 he became brevet-major of engineers. In 1837 he resigned from the army and became engineer for the state of Georgia, conducting surveys for a railroad from Cincinnati to Charleston.

In 1842 he was appointed major-general of militia in the state of Rhode Island to aid in suppressing the Dorr rebellion. He helped to quell the disturbances, but his vigorous action in the affair made him enemies and resulted in his removal by President Polk in 1845 from his position as chief engineer of the Brooklyn dry dock, for which he had prepared the plans. The same influences were also active in 1846 in causing the declination of his offer of services for the Mexican War. His close application to work severely tried his physical powers, and in 1851 he again visited Europe for the benefit of his health. At this time he was elected a member of the Institution of Civil Engineers of Great Britain—the first American to receive this honor. While in London he was actively engaged in the interests of several large American mining concerns. He returned in 1853 to America, where he died very suddenly at Brooklyn, N. Y., on Feb. 16. His numerous professional reports comprise some of the early history of railways in the United States. He was connected with many public-improvement works of note in Canada and the West Indies—as well as in the United States. He was married to Maria Matilda Camman of New York and had seven children, with whom his family life was especially happy. It has been said of him (Cullum, *post,* pp. 165–66) that his skill as an engineer lay in his ability to "survey the adaptability of ground to practical purposes," and in his ability to manage a project. For the details of construction he was dependent upon his assistants, who were superior to him in technical attainments.

[*Minutes of Proc. of the Inst. of Civil Engineers* (London), vol. XIII (1854); G. W. Cullum, *Biog. Reg. . . . of the U. S. Mil. Acad.,* vol. I (1890); *The Memoirs of Gen. Jos. Gardner Swift* (1890); *N. Y. Times,* Feb. 17, 1853.]

H. K. B.

MACNEVEN, WILLIAM JAMES (Mar. 21, 1763–July 12, 1841), physician, Irish patriot, was born in County Galway, Ireland, the son of Catholic parents, James and Rosa (Dolphin) MacNeven. His father was a country gentleman who lived on his own estate. The family had formerly possessed large holdings in the North of Ireland, but had been expelled by Cromwell and forced to settle in the wilds of Galway. MacNeven's uncle, William O'Kelly MacNeven, finding it necessary to leave Ireland to obtain a professional education, had gone to Austria, where he rose to the post of physician to the Empress Maria Theresa and was made a baron. When William James MacNeven was ten or twelve, since the penal laws which restricted Catholic education were still in force, he went to live with his uncle in Vienna. Eventually he studied medicine at the universities of Prague and Vienna, and received a degree from the latter institution in 1784. Settling at once in Dublin, he began what promised to be a brilliant career.

An earnest patriot and a member of the United Irishmen, he engaged in political activities which led to his internment first in Kilmainham prison and then at Fort George, Scotland, where Thomas Addis Emmet [*q.v.*] was one of his fellow prisoners. During his incarceration he studied extensively, and upon his discharge in 1802 under sentence of banishment, went almost at once to Switzerland, where he spent several months in a walking tour, described in his first book, *A Ramble through Swisserland in the Summer and Autumn of 1802* (1803). In 1803 he went to France, where he sought an interview with Napoleon in regard to a possible invasion of Ireland, but to no effect. For the next two years he served in the Irish Brigade of the French army, and then, apparently convinced that he could no longer aid the cause of Ireland in Europe, he took ship for America, arriving in New York July 4, 1805, with the intention of beginning life anew.

He found a cordial welcome in New York, and soon established himself in practice. Two years after his arrival he delivered a course of clinical lectures at the New York Hospital, and in 1808 was elected professor of obstetrics in the College of Physicians and Surgeons. Three years later he was transferred to the chair of chemistry, and, in addition to this subject, from 1816 to 1820 taught materia medica. His is said to have been the first chemical laboratory in New York. In 1815 he published a *Chemical Examination of the Mineral Waters of Schooley's Mountains,* and in 1819 an *Exposition of the Atomic Theory of Chymistry.* His last scientific publication was an edition, with emendations, of W. T. Brande's *Manual of Chemistry* (1821). He was also coeditor for a time of the *New York Medical and Philosophical Journal and Review.* In 1823 he was elected a member of the American Philosophical Society. Together with his colleagues Valentine Mott, David Hosack, and John W. Francis [*qq.v.*], he withdrew from the College of Physicians and Surgeons in 1826 to found a rival medical school, affiliated with Rutgers College. Although this enterprise was successful, it was short-lived, being abandoned after four years because of legal difficulties.

Meantime, his expatriation did not end MacNeven's interest in his native land. In 1807 he published *Pieces of Irish History*; he also established an employment bureau to find positions for Irish immigrants; he is said to have published a manual of directions for Irishmen arriving in America; he was an organizer and first president (1828–29) of a society known as the Friends of Ireland. An attack of gout in 1838 obliged him to give up his work and move to the country, and the remainder of his life was spent in the home of his step-daughter and her husband, Thomas A. Emmet, Jr., son of his old friend. His death in 1841 followed a long and painful illness. Throughout his life he was a loyal Roman Catholic and the last rites of his Church were administered to him by Bishop Hughes. MacNeven was married in 1810 to Jane Margaret, daughter of Samuel Riker and widow of John Tom. Most of their children died of tuberculosis, an affection to which the children of Irish emigrants were unusually susceptible. Only two sons and a daughter survived their father.

[*N. Y. Medic. Gazette,* Aug. 11, 1841; sketch by J. W. Francis in S. D. Gross, *Lives of Eminent Am. Physicians and Surgeons* (1861); sketch by MacNeven's daughter in R. R. Madden, *The United Irishmen, Their Lives and Times,* 2 ser. (1843); *Cath. Encyc.,* vol. IX (1910); J. H. McCarthy, *Ireland Since the Union* (1887); Robert Dunlop, in *Dict. Nat. Biog.*; H. A. Kelly and W. L. Burrage, *Am. Medic. Biogs.* (1920); *N. Y. Tribune,* July 14, 1841.] E. P.

McNULTY, FRANK JOSEPH (Aug. 10, 1872–May 26, 1926), labor leader and congressman, was born in Londonderry, Ireland, the son of Owen McNulty, a veteran of the Union Army in the Civil War who had returned to Ireland after his marriage to Catherine O'Donnell in New York. When the boy was four years old the family returned to the United States and settled in New York City where he was educated in the public schools. He became an inside electrical wireman, moved to Perth Amboy, N. J., and there assisted in organizing a local of the International Brotherhood of Electrical Workers. Distinguished in appearance, with an excellent tenor voice, a love of sports, great personal courage, undeviating loyalty to his friends, a reputation as a wit, and considerable personal magnetism and charm, he early became a leader in his organization and in 1901 was elected international vice-president of the Brotherhood, with headquarters in Springfield, Ill. Two years later, in 1903, he became president and held this office until 1919 when, after several months' leave of absence, he resigned to continue in the position, in which he had acted since 1917, of deputy director of public safety in Newark. Here he had long made his home with his wife, Edith H. Parker, whom he married in Jersey City in 1893. Upon his retirement, as a mark of appreciation of his services, he was given the title of "president emeritus"—an innovation in the labor movement—and also became chairman of the international executive council of the Brotherhood, a position which he held throughout the remainder of his life. From 1908 to 1913 he carried the organization successfully through one of the most bitter and hard-fought internal struggles that has ever occurred in any American labor union—a socialistic (industrial union) secession movement which involved over half the membership and threatened the entire American labor movement. In the end, supported by the American Federation of Labor and victorious in a series of legal battles with the rival organization, he succeeded in his diplomatic efforts to win back, on liberal terms, the bulk of the seceders and in further increasing the membership until the Brotherhood became the fourth largest American labor organization.

McNulty's chief constructive policies were the promotion of craft improvement to rescue electrical workers from the condition of an unskilled group and the settlement of disputes by reason and negotiation instead of by strikes. In 1906 he was a member of the commission sent to Great Britain by the National Civic Federation to study public ownership. During the war he served as vice-chairman of the Railway Board of Adjustment No. 2, but resigned this office in August 1918 to go to Italy and France for three months with a government commission of five labor leaders, selected by the American Federation of Labor on the request of President Wilson, to strengthen the morale of the Italian working men by showing them that the American labor movement vigorously supported the war. The delegation traveled through the industrial districts of Italy by automobile, addressing sometimes a dozen meetings a day, visited the battle front, dined with the King of Italy, and was entertained by General Diaz. In 1922, after his retirement in 1921 from the city government of Newark, McNulty was elected to Congress from the eighth congressional district of New Jersey as a Democrat and served from Mar. 4, 1923, to Mar. 3, 1925. Always stronger in dealing with individuals than with large groups, he exerted his chief influence in Congress as a member of the committee on labor, though he made short speeches on prison labor and on the railroad labor bill. Defeated for reëlection in the Coolidge landslide of 1924, he spent the remainder of his life in Washington, to which the headquarters of the International Brotherhood of Electrical Workers had been moved, and in Newark, where he died suddenly on May 26, 1926.

[See *Who's Who in America,* 1926–27; *Biog. Dir. Am. Cong.* (1928); notices in New York, Newark, and other newspapers; the *Jour. of the Electrical Workers and Operators,* June 1926; the *Congressional Record,* 68th Cong.; Michael A. Mulcaire, *The Internat. Brotherhood of Electrical Workers* (1923); and the convention proceedings and reports of officers of the International Brotherhood of Electrical Workers.]

H. S. W.

McNUTT, ALEXANDER (*c.* 1725–*c.* 1811), colonial land promoter, the son of Alexander and Jane McNutt, was probably born in Londonderry, Ireland. He came to America before 1753 and settled near Staunton, Va. In 1756, he was an officer in the militia on Major Andrew Lewis's Shawnee expedition. In 1760 he was captain of Massachusetts militia, raising replacements. Representing Apthorp and Hancock of Boston from 1758 to 1761 he canvassed New England for settlers for Nova Scotia. Having persuaded a number, including some Scotch-Irish of Londonderry, N. H., to go there, he proposed direct immigration of Irish Protestants. In 1761, he went to England, where he was well received. At first his project was favored, and he sent some settlers, but later direct Irish settlement was forbidden. He next encouraged immigration from other colonies and interested prominent people in the north, including Benjamin Franklin and the Rev. James Lyon of Trenton, N. J. In 1765 with his associates he was granted about 1,745,000 acres in Nova Scotia, of which probably 1,600,000 acres were in the ill-defined St. John region. Most of this land was escheated between 1770 and 1788 because the promoters did not comply with the terms, and on account of the Revolution. He established New Jerusalem at Port Roseway, now Shelburne, and brought some settlers from New England and Pennsylvania to the St. John.

He sympathized with the revolting colonies and left Nova Scotia in 1778. He lived at Jamaica Plain, Mass., but visited Philadelphia to urge the Congress to try to draw Nova Scotia into the Revolution. Between 1778 and 1781 he advocated invasion of the province and helped foment rebellion. Probably he was still associated with Lyon, who was in Maine. He obtained a grant of $15,000 from Congress to build a road from the Penobscot River to the St. John. About 1780 he published *The Constitution . . . of the Free and Independent State . . . of New Ireland,* a tract containing promises of democratic government but really advertising his lands. "New Ireland" probably embraced eastern Maine and southern New Brunswick. After the Revolution he lived near Lexington, Va. He died unmarried. To the last he claimed his northern lands and bequeathed 100,000 acres to Liberty Hall Academy, now Washington and Lee University, but the title was not good.

His schemes were too ambitious to be practicable. His enthusiasm ultimately inspired distrust rather than confidence. This may be the explanation of his failure to obtain the support of British and provincial officials for his land schemes and was probably the cause of American distrust of his plans for winning Nova Scotia. He was a man of strong personality, not always scrupulous, but an interesting example of the colonial speculator-patriot.

[A. W. H. Eaton, "Alexander McNutt," in *Americana,* Dec. 1913, a critical examination of other biographies from sources carefully cited; *Proc. and Trans. of the Royal Soc. of Canada,* 3 ser., vols. V, VI (1912–13); Beamish Murdoch, *A Hist. of Nova Scotia,* vol. II (1866); George Patterson, *A Hist. of the County of Pictou, Nova Scotia* (1916); H. H. McCormick, *Genealogies and Reminiscences* (rev. ed., 1897), pp. 57–64.]

R. G. L.

MACOMB, ALEXANDER (Apr. 3, 1782–June 25, 1841), soldier, was born at Detroit. His paternal grandfather, John Macomb, had come to New York from Ireland as early as 1742; his father, Alexander Macomb, had built up a prosperous trading business at Detroit, which he did not relinquish until after the close of the Revolution. He then returned to New York, with his wife, Catharine Navarre, daughter of Robert de Navarre, a former French official at Detroit, and with their son, Alexander Macomb the younger. The boy was placed in school at an academy in Newark, N. J., where he received "the rudiments of a classical, mathematical, and French education." At the age of sixteen he was enrolled in a New York City militia company, and during the period of hostilities with France the recommendation of Alexander Hamilton secured him a commission in the regular army as cornet of light dragoons. In the same year (1799), he was promoted to second lieutenant, and after being honorably discharged at the close of hostilities, he was again commissioned (Feb. 16, 1801), this time as second lieutenant of infantry (F. B. Heitman, *Historical Register and Dictionary of the United States Army,* 1903, I, 680). During his period of service in the dragoons he had been designated as assistant to Adj.-Gen. William North, a thoroughly trained veteran of the Revolution, and from North and Hamilton, near whose headquarters he was stationed, he learned much about the organization and administration of an army. In 1801 and 1802 he was attached as secretary to a commission composed of Generals Wilkinson and Pickens and Colonel Hawkins, appointed to treat with the Indians of the Southeast. The commission traveled extensively in the country of the Cherokee, Choctaw, Chickasaw, and Creek Indians. Shortly thereafter (Oct. 12, 1802), Macomb was commissioned first lieutenant in the Corps of Engineers, the newly created unit which at this time constituted the United States Military Academy. Macomb and another lieutenant (James Wilson of Pennsylvania) were the first student officers to receive formal training at West Point and to complete a course of study there (*American State Papers, Military Affairs,* II, 1834, p. 634). After completing his own course of study Macomb remained on duty at West Point till 1805, when he was commissioned captain in the Corps of Engineers and ordered to duty elsewhere. From 1807 to 1812 he was chief engineer in charge of coast fortifications in the Carolinas and Georgia. He became a major in February 1808 and a lieutenant-colonel in July 1810. In April 1812 he was ordered to Washington as adjutant-general, charged with the duty of preparing the army for impending war. When war was declared, and his position in the Corps of Engineers prevented his holding an active command, he was at his own request transferred to the artillery, commissioned colonel (July 6, 1812), and sent to New York to raise a regiment. The following winter he was in command at Sacketts Harbor; in the spring of 1813 he participated in the capture of Fort George on the Niagara River, and in the fall of the same year took a minor part in Wilkinson's St. Lawrence campaign. He was made a brigadier-general in January 1814 and was stationed with his brigade in the Lake Champlain region. When General Izard with the main army at Plattsburg was ordered to Sacketts Harbor in August 1814, Macomb was left with about fifteen hundred regulars fit for duty, and such volunteers as could be mustered in the neighboring country, to confront an invading force of some fifteen thousand British veterans under Gov. Sir George Prevost (H. Adams, *History of the United States,* VIII, 1891, pp. 100–11). His position at Plattsburg had been strongly fortified under Izard's direction, and Macomb worked energetically to make it stronger and to give the British an exaggerated idea of his resources. His defense against the attack of Sept. 11 was skilfully conducted, but the precipitate retreat of the British was probably due rather to the destruction of their fleet by Macdonough and the resulting danger to their communications than to the prowess of the small American army. Nevertheless, Macomb and his troops were signally honored by Congress and by the state and city of New York, and Macomb was given the brevet rank of major-general. After the close of the war Macomb was a member of a board which worked out the plan on which the army was reorganized. He was stationed for a short time in New York in command of the third military district and was then shifted to the fifth district with headquarters at Detroit. In 1821 he went to Washington as head of the Corps of Engineers. On the death of Gen. Jacob Brown in 1828, Macomb was designated to succeed him as senior major-general and commanding general of the United States army—a position which he filled until his death at Washington, June 25, 1841.

Among Macomb's official papers was a "Memoir on the Organization of the Army of the United States" (1826), in which he urged a plan for bringing the militia under more centralized control and better discipline (*American State Papers, Military Affairs,* III, 1860, pp. 458–65). In a letter of Jan. 27, 1829, replying to an inquiry of Secretary of War Peter B. Porter, he recommended the abolition of the whiskey ration in the army and should share in the credit for the general order issued the next year discontinuing that ancient practice (*Ibid.,* IV, 1860, p. 84; *Subject Index of the General Orders of the War Department, from Jan. 1, 1809, to Dec. 31, 1860,* 1886, p. 180). His ability seems to have been primarily of the organizing, systematizing kind, which the army of his day greatly needed. Macomb was married, July 23, 1803, to his cousin, Catharine Macomb, of Belleville, N. J., who became the mother of a large family. After her death he was married in 1826 to Harriet (Balch) Wilson, a widow. His second wife took a lively part in the "Eaton war" in the first administration of Andrew Jackson—"more to his [Macomb's] amusement than annoyance," says Van Buren, "for he took such things lightly." Macomb was the author of *A Treatise on Martial Law and Courts-Martial* (1809) and *The Practice of Courts Martial* (1840), and edited Samuel Cooper's *Tactics and Regulations for the Militia* (1836).

[In addition to works cited above see *Memoir of Alexander Macomb, the Maj. Gen. Commanding the Army of the U. S., by Geo. H. Richards, Esq., Capt. of Macomb's Artillery in the Late War* (1833), and the *Daily Nat. Intelligencer*, June 28, 1841.]
J. W. P—t.

MACOMBER, MARY LIZZIE (Aug. 21, 1861–Feb. 4, 1916), painter of decorative symbolic panels, was born at Fall River, Mass., the daughter of Frederick William and Mary White Poor Macomber. She came of both Pilgrim and Quaker stock. As a child she was fond of drawing. She began to study painting with Robert S. Dunning, an able Fall River painter whose specialty was fruit and flower pieces. Her first efforts were naturally in the same line. After studying with him for about three years she went to Boston and entered the school of the Museum of Fine Arts, where she took up the study of figure painting. In the second year of her course her health failed and for nearly three years she was unable to continue her studies. Later she resumed work for a short time under the direction of Frank Duveneck, and she then opened a studio in Boston. The first of her pictures to be exhibited was "Ruth," in the National Academy exhibition of 1889.

In the early period, that to which the most characteristic works belong, roughly, from 1889 to 1899, she produced a series of symbolic panels which were admirable in a decorative sense and original in conception. Of these perhaps the most interesting example was "Love Awakening Memory" (1892), shown at the Chicago exposition of 1893. Her "St. Catherine" was awarded the Norman W. Dodge prize "for the best picture painted in the United States by a woman" at the National Academy exhibition of 1897. It is now in the permanent collection of the Boston Art Museum. "Love's Lament" (1893) went the rounds of numerous exhibitions. In these early pictures the execution was of a Pre-Raphaelite finish, and the work was essentially decorative. In a period of fourteen years twenty-five of her pictures were seen in the National Academy exhibitions.

In 1898 she made a radical change in her method of painting; she began to stand up while at work instead of sitting. This change of position, with its opportunity for changes of focus, brought about a noticeable broadening of her style. The first work produced in the new manner was "The Hour Glass," exhibited at the Society of American Artists, 1900. "The Lace Jabot," which also made its first appearance in 1900, was a self-portrait. "Night and Her Daughter Sleep," shown at the first exhibition of ideal figure pictures held by the National Arts Club in 1903, is one of the most impressive of her allegories. A fire which occurred in the Harcourt studio building, Boston, in 1903, virtually destroyed Miss Macomber's studio with its contents. Among the paintings ruined was the almost finished "Memory Comforting Sorrow." The artist set to work and painted the motive for the second time, completing it in 1905. This work was bought for $2,500 by the Art and Fortnightly Clubs of Fall River and was hung in the Fall River Public Library.

Coincident with her change of style she began to paint portraits, and, since a number of commissions came to her from New York, she made several lengthy visits to the metropolis. At this period she had her first and only opportunity to go to Europe. She spent a few weeks in England, France, and Holland, and she returned aflame with admiration for Rembrandt, whose work became the most potent influence in her practice. Her portraits showed this dominant influence plainly, more especially in the arbitrary character of the lighting. Her portrait of her mother (1900) is in the Boston Art Museum. A portrait of Dr. Adams, for many years minister of the First Congregational Church of Fall River, hangs in the parish house of that church. Miss Macomber died of pneumonia in a Boston hospital in 1916. At the funeral in the New Old South Church a remarkable company of artists and art-lovers paid homage to her character and achievements.

[W. H. Downes, "Miss Macomber's Paintings," *New Eng. Mag.*, Nov. 1903; A. J. Philpott, article in *Boston Globe*, Feb. 6, 1916; D. M. Cheney, article in *New Bedford Standard*, Feb. 13, 1916; *Boston Transcript*, Feb. 5, 1916; *Fall River Evening News*, Feb. 5, 1916; Mich. State Lib., *Biog. Sketches of Am. Artists* (1916); *Am. Art News*, Feb. 12, 19, 1916; Sadakichi Hartmann, *A Hist. of Am. Art* (1932), vol. I; Boston Museum of Fine Arts, *Cat. of Paintings* (1921); E. S. Stackpole, *Macomber Geneal.* (1908).] W. H. D.

MACON, NATHANIEL (Dec. 17, 1758–June 29, 1837), Revolutionary soldier, speaker of the House, United States senator, was born at "Macon Manor" in Edgecombe (later Bute and now Warren) County, N. C., the sixth child of Gideon and Priscilla (Jones) Macon. He entered the College of New Jersey at Princeton in 1774 and remained there two years. In 1776 he "served a tour" in the New Jersey militia, and late in 1777 left the army and, returning to North Carolina, began to study law. In May 1780 he enlisted as a private in a company commanded by his brother and took part in the battle of Camden. During this period he refused a commission. In 1781 he was elected to the state Senate but ignored the summons until General Greene urged him to accept, on the score of the aid he might render the army.

In the legislature he came under the influence of Willie Jones [*q.v.*], with whom and with whose political doctrines he was thereafter in close accord. He was again elected to the Senate in 1782 and in 1784. On Oct. 9, 1783, he married Hannah Plummer of Warren County, who died leaving three children, on July 11, 1790. In 1786 he was elected to the Continental Congress and declined to serve. He opposed the Federal Convention and advocated the rejection of the Constitution. In 1790 he was a member of the House of Commons, and in 1791 was elected to the federal House of Representatives, taking his seat Oct. 26. He served continuously until December 1815, when he was transferred to the Senate. Here he remained until December 1828, when, having reached the age of seventy, he resigned, giving up at the same time his place as justice of the peace and trustee of the University of North Carolina. He was speaker of the House from 1801 to 1807, and for the last two years of his senatorial service was president *pro tempore.*

A close and devoted friend of Jefferson, except for a period of estrangement after 1806 caused by Macon's support of John Randolph of Roanoke, he was for years the outstanding leader of the Republicans in the House. As such he fought vigorously against the Federalists and their entire program. He detested Hamilton and all his works. He advocated the maintenance of the treaty with France, bitterly opposed the Jay treaty, the Alien and Sedition laws, and the whole movement for war with France in 1798–99. He was a supporter of the purchase of Louisiana and urged upon Jefferson the purchase of Florida as well. Throughout his entire career he opposed building a navy. He supported in its entirety the foreign policy of the Jefferson and Madison administrations, and in 1809 was chairman of the foreign relations committee. In this capacity he reported successively the two bills which bear his name, although he was the author of neither and was definitely opposed to the second. The first, a stroke at British shipping, was defeated, but on May 1, 1810, Macon's Bill No. 2 was passed, giving the president power to suspend intercourse with either Great Britain or France if the other should cease to interfere with United States commerce.

Macon favored the War of 1812, but opposed conscription and the levy of higher taxes. He opposed the recharter of the United States Bank in 1811 and in 1816, uniformly voted against any form of protective tariff, and while favoring road construction by the federal government, opposed the policy of internal improvements. He took part in the Missouri debate and voted against the compromise measure. Throughout his life he was an earnest defender of slavery. Numbered among the opponents of the Adams administration, he fought against the participation of the United States in the Panama Congress. He preferred Monroe to Madison in 1808, and, although he would not enter the caucus, supported Crawford in 1824, in which year he received the electoral vote of Virginia for vice-president. In 1828, while opposing Adams, who wished him as a running mate, he did not want Jackson for president, in spite of their warm personal friendship.

Important and valuable a figure as Macon was in Congress for thirty-seven years, he was not a constructive force. He was a negative radical, and it was said of him that during the entire term of his service no ten other members cast so many negative votes. "Negation was his ward and arm." He was rural and local-minded, and economy was the passion of his public career. "His economy of the public money was the severest, sharpest, most stringent and constant refusal of almost any grant that could be proposed." With him, "not only was . . . parsimony the best subsidy—but . . . the only one" (C. J. Ingersoll, quoted in the *Weekly Raleigh Register,* Sept. 26, 1845). He was a frequent and influential, though not eloquent, speaker. On the floor and in personal intercourse he was genial, human, and inclined to jocularity, and was generally popular in spite of the fact that he was strongly, even dogmatically, opinionated. Of moderate abilities only, he won his way by force of constant integrity, industry, and the entire absence of any personal or selfish motives.

After his resignation from the Senate he spent most of his remaining days in happy retirement at "Buck Spring," his home in Warren County. Constantly asked for political advice, he wrote many letters which are notable for their hard common sense and for their clear revelation of the writer. In 1832, although still a champion of the principles of the Virginia and Kentucky Resolutions, he opposed nullification as unconstitutional, taking the position that secession was the rightful remedy for usurpation of power by the federal government. In 1835 he accepted election as a delegate to the convention called to revise the state constitution, and was unanimously chosen its president. There he opposed such changes as the abolition of annual election of the legislature, and he declined to vote for the amended constitution. The following year he supported Van Buren for president, and as a candidate for elector aided powerfully in winning the last victory the Democrats were to have in North Carolina for many years. He died suddenly at his home the following summer.

["Letters of Nathaniel Macon, John Steele, and William Barry Grove," ed. by K. P. Battle, *James Sprunt Hist. Monograph No. 3* (1902); "Some Unpublished Letters of Nathaniel Macon," ed. by J. S. Bassett, in *Trinity Coll. Hist. Papers,* 6 ser. (1906); "Nathaniel Macon and Bartlett Yancey," in *N. C. Univ. Mag.,* Oct. 1857; E. M. Wilson, "The Congressional Career of Nathaniel Macon," *James Sprunt Hist. Monograph, No. 2* (1900); E. R. Cotten, *Life of the Hon. Nathaniel Macon* (1840); W. N. Edwards, *Memoir of Nathaniel Macon* (1862); W. E. Dodd, "The Place of Nathaniel Macon in Southern History," *Am. Hist. Rev.,* July 1902, and *Life of Nathaniel Macon* (1903); Josephus Daniels, "Nathaniel Macon," in *Proc. . . . State Lit. and Hist. Asso. of N. C. . . . 1912* (1913); *The John P. Branch Hist. Papers of Randolph Macon Coll.,* no. 2 (1902) and *Ibid.,* vol. III, no. 1 (1909); D. H. Gilpatrick, *Jeffersonian Democracy in N. C. 1789–1816* (1931); *Richmond Enquirer,* July 4, 11, 1837.]

J. G. deR. H.

McPHERSON, EDWARD (July 31, 1830–Dec. 14, 1895), member of Congress, clerk of the House of Representatives, author, editor, was born in Gettysburg, Pa., of Pennsylvania colonial stock, the son of John Bayard McPherson and Katharine Lenhart. He attended the common schools of Gettysburg and was graduated from Pennsylvania (now Gettysburg) College in 1848. For a time he studied law, but he left legal studies to enter journalism. From 1851, when he became editor of the *Harrisburg American,* until his death he was connected with various newspapers in Pennsylvania: with the *Independent Whig* of Lancaster, 1851–54; with the Pittsburgh *Daily Times,* 1855; with the Philadelphia *Press,* 1877–80; and as editor and proprietor of the Gettysburg *Star and Sentinel,* 1880–95. In 1862 he was married to Annie Dods Crawford, also a Pennsylvanian. Although he was a member of Congress for two terms and clerk of the House of Representatives for sixteen years, he is best known as a political cyclopedist and statistician. His *Political History of the United States of America During the Great Rebellion* (1864); *The Political History of the United States of America During the Period of Reconstruction* (1871); *Political Manual,* published annually from 1866 to 1869, and the *Handbook of Politics,* published biennially from 1868 through 1894, are invaluable to the student of American history as source books of political material.

McPherson was elected as a Republican to the Thirty-sixth and Thirty-seventh congresses, 1859–63, but was defeated for reëlection in 1862. He was then appointed deputy-commissioner of internal revenue. After six months he resigned to become clerk of the House of Representatives, serving continuously from 1863 to 1875, and again during the years 1881–83 and 1889–91. In fact, he made more of a name for himself as clerk of the House than as member of Congress. His clear knowledge of parliamentary law and his exact command of a wide range of political information made him indispensable to the speaker and to members of Congress. For a brief moment he held the center of the political stage and was the master of destiny of the Southern states. When the Thirty-ninth Congress assembled, Dec. 4, 1865, members from the former Confederate states presented themselves for admission with credentials duly inscribed by the reconstructed governments. The recognition of these representatives from the South was the first trial in the combat now set between Congress and President Johnson. According to the rules of the House, it was McPherson's duty as clerk of the previous House to call the House to order and to call the roll of members. In the midst of the greatest excitement, with floor and galleries of the House crowded, he quickly passed up the aisle, unfolded his papers in a businesslike way, unperturbed by the excitement around him, and began the critical procedure of calling the roll. He had learned his lesson well and carried through completely the agreements reached by the caucus of Republican members of the House two days before. He refused to hear protests from the Southern members whose names were omitted in the roll-call, on the ground that none save those whose names were called had the right to speak. The Civil War was ended, but the Reconstruction battle was only beginning, and in the first skirmish McPherson advanced the standard of the Congressional forces.

McPherson was long an active member of the Republican party. In 1860 he was a member of the Republican National Committee; in 1876 he was permanent president of the Republican National Convention; and in 1880 he was secretary of the Republican Congressional Committee. He contributed a chapter entitled "Rise and Progress of the Republican Party, 1856–88" to *The Republican Party: its History, Principles and Policies* (1888), edited by John D. Long. For a short time in 1877–78 he was chief of the Bureau of Engraving and Printing under appointment by President Hayes. In 1879 he retired to Gettysburg where he bought and edited a newspaper. He also edited the New York *Tribune Almanac and Political Register* from 1877 to 1895, and for several years acted as American editor of the *Almanach de Gotha*.

[*Appletons' Ann Cyc.*, 1895; *Biog. Dir. Am. Cong.* (1928); *The Alumni Record of Gettysburg Coll., 1832–1932* (1932); James G. Blaine, *Twenty Years of Cong.*, vols. I and II (1884–86); E. P. Oberholtzer, *A Hist. of the U. S. Since the Civil War*, vol. I (1917); information as to certain facts from McPherson's son, William L. McPherson.] C. M. T.

McPHERSON, JAMES BIRDSEYE (Nov. 14, 1828–July 22, 1864), Union soldier, was born in Green Creek township, Sandusky County, Ohio, near the present town of Clyde. He was the son of William and Cynthia (Russell) McPherson. Appointed cadet at the United States Military Academy in 1849, he graduated in 1853 at the head of his class, and was assigned to the corps of engineers as brevet second lieutenant. For a year he was retained at the Academy as assistant instructor in practical engineering, and was then assigned to duty in connection with river and harbor improvement and seacoast fortification. Upon duty of this nature he continued, first on the Atlantic and then on the Pacific coast, until 1861; meanwhile, he was promoted second lieutenant, Dec. 18, 1854, and first lieutenant, Dec. 13, 1858.

The outbreak of the Civil War found him in San Francisco. He was ordered East, and employed on fortification work in Boston. Upon the enlargement of the regular army, May 14, 1861, he was offered a commission as captain in the new 19th Infantry, but declined it, and on Aug. 6 reached the grade of captain in his own corps. When General Halleck assumed command in Missouri, he took McPherson with him as an aide-de-camp, with the rank of lieutenant-colonel and later of colonel. He served first as assistant engineer, Department of Missouri, but when General Grant opened his Tennessee campaign in February 1862, he accompanied the expedition as chief engineer, and from that time on was constantly in the field. While before Corinth, May 15, 1862, he was promoted brigadier-general of volunteers; and after the occupation of that place he was made military superintendent of railways in the district of Western Tennessee. Of his services at this period, General Sherman said: "McPherson . . . was one of the most useful staff-officers in the whole army—riding night and day. . . . I think he knew more of the lay . . . of the country around Corinth than any officer of the army" (*Hours at Home,* April 1866, pp. 485–86). His first command, small but unusual in character, resulted naturally from this employment. On Oct. 2, Rosecrans, at Corinth, was heavily attacked by Van Dorn; the situation seemed critical, and Grant, at Jackson, Tenn., made efforts to reinforce him. McPherson, then at headquarters in Jackson, was directed to collect four regiments stationed along the railway between there and Corinth, and report with them to Rosecrans. He moved by rail to within ten miles of Corinth, detrained, and marched the rest of the way, arriving too late to assist in the repulse of Van Dorn, but in time to lead the pursuit. For his conduct in this affair he was made major-general of volunteers, Oct. 8, 1862, and was assigned to command the 2nd Division, Department of the Tennessee; which command, on Nov. 24, became the 2nd Division, XIII Army Corps. Later, Jan. 18, 1863, the army, having been reinforced, was reorganized, and McPherson received command of the XVII Army Corps. He was actively employed throughout the entire Vicksburg campaign, and after the surrender (July 4, 1863) remained in command of the District of Vicksburg until the following March, participating meanwhile in Sherman's raid to Meridian. In recognition of his services before Vicksburg, he was made, Aug. 1, 1863, brigadier-general in the regular army.

On Mar. 18, 1864, Grant went east to assume direction of all the armies; Sherman succeeded him in command of the Military Division of the Mississippi, and began preparations for his Atlanta campaign. McPherson took over Sherman's Army of the Tennessee, assuming command at Huntsville, Mar. 26. At the head of this army he fought the entire campaign, up to the fortifications of Atlanta. At Kenesaw Mountain, the rapid and decisive movements of his force won for it the soldier nickname "the whiplash of the army." On July 22, the armies of the Cumberland and the Ohio were well established north and east of Atlanta. The Army of the Tennessee was directed to connect with the Army of the Ohio on its right, and extend its left to the south. While this movement was in progress, a Confederate turning movement against the left and rear developed. McPherson was at Sherman's headquarters, receiving his orders, and at once started to join his troops. Passing, with a single orderly, through a wood road which had been previously reconnoitered and found clear, he suddenly encountered hostile skirmishers who had penetrated between his XVI and XVII Corps, and was killed.

His death was one of the heaviest individual losses ever suffered by the Union forces. By his superiors, he was recognized as one of the ablest generals in the army. Energetic and ambitious, he welcomed responsibility and active service, but loyally and with no spirit of self-seeking. Grant, in a letter written upon leaving the western army, coupled Sherman and McPherson together as "the men to whom, above all others, I feel indebted for whatever I have had of success" (*Memoirs of Gen. William T. Sherman, post,* I, 399). Sherman was equally emphatic in his praise. In the army at large his talents seemed to be fully recognized, and his advancement to corps and army command gave rise to little or no jealousy. A man of striking and pleasing appearance—over six feet in height, erect and well-proportioned—and possessed in a high degree of the faculty of command, he was able to gain the confidence and loyalty of his subordinates. Young and vigorous, he lived in close association with his troops, and bore his full share of hardship and exposure.

[G. W. Cullum, *Biog. Register of the Officers and Grads. of the U. S. Mil. Acad.* (3rd ed., 1891); *Memoirs of Gen. William T. Sherman* (2 vols., 1875); *Personal Memoirs of U. S. Grant* (2 vols., 1885–86); *Hours at Home,* Mar. 1866; D. R. Keim, "The Life and Character of Maj.-Gen. James B. McPherson," *U. S. Service Mag.,* Oct. 1864; *Biog. Cyc. and Portrait Gallery . . . of the State of Ohio,* vol. I (1883); Basil Meek, *Twentieth Century Hist. of Sandusky County, Ohio, and Representative Citizens* (1909); *Army and Navy Jour.,* July 30, 1864.] O. L. S., Jr.

McPHERSON, LOGAN GRANT (Aug. 11, 1863–Mar. 23, 1925), railway statistician, economist, organizer of railway publicity, was born in Circleville, Ohio, the son of Daniel Workman and Frances Louise (Kinnear) McPherson. The basis for his education, mostly self-directed, was laid in the public schools which he attended until sixteen years of age. After a year's work on a newspaper, he obtained a position with the Pennsylvania Railroad, and remained with the company from 1880 to 1891. Thus began his connection with American railway transportation which was his chief interest for most of his life. In the years from 1892 to 1903 he held various positions with coal companies in Pittsburgh, but he returned to railroading in 1904 when he became statistician for the Rock Island system. At this time the railroads were incurring much public disfavor. They were accused of charging unreasonable rates for unsatisfactory service. Amalgamations and community of interest schemes were denounced as dangerous to the public interest. A greater measure of government control was urged, and bills were introduced into Congress giving the Interstate Commerce Commission wide powers over railway rates, regulations, and practices. It was during this period that the railroad companies were brought to realize the value of well-organized publicity. In 1905 the Associated Railways of the United States was founded by Samuel Spencer, president of the Southern Railway Company, who engaged McPherson as his assistant. In this position he was occupied for two years in collecting railway statistics and in preparing material for use before congressional committees and for dissemination in the public press. The railroads lost their fight, for in 1906 the Hepburn Act was passed.

McPherson's connection with the Associated Railways ended and he was appointed lecturer on transportation at the Johns Hopkins University, 1905–15. For several years he devoted himself to the study of the effects of railway rates on American business conditions and published two books. He had previously published *The Monetary and Banking Problem* (1896). *The Working of the Railroads* (1907) was a modest but distinctly successful attempt to describe the general railroad situation. *Railroad Freight Rates in Relation to the Industry and Commerce of the United States* (1909) contained a wealth of concrete details of rate-making obtained at first hand from traffic officials, but it was not well arranged and it was not an impartial statement of the rate problem from the point of view of public policy. For six months in 1909 McPherson toured Europe making a study of railroads and canals for the National Waterways Commission. After his return he wrote *Transportation in Europe* (1910), an interesting and instructive account of conditions as he observed them. The Bureau of Railway Economics organized by him in Washington in 1910 is a monument to his industry and ability. Its purposes were the exchange of statistics among the cooperating railroads and the creation of public opinion favorable to the railway industry. From 1910 to 1914 he served as director, continuing at the same time his lectures at Johns Hopkins. He also lectured at Harvard and Columbia. After leaving the Bureau he devoted himself to study and writing. He was a frequent contributor to railway journals and to general periodicals; and he also undertook a series of books in the field of general economics: *How the World Makes its Living* (1916), *The Flow of Value* (1919), and *Human Effort and Human Wants* (1923). These books represent an attempt to humanize economics, and to carry its discussions beyond wealth to welfare. They showed wide reading in the literature of economics as well as in history and sociology, but they contributed little to the subject. Lacking the precision of technical works, they also lacked the literary style essential to wide circulation. Their best parts are those drawn from the author's own experience. In 1924 McPherson spent several months in England studying amalgamations of railroads. Shortly after his return to New York City, then his home, he was injured in a street accident, which was a contributing cause of his death a few months later. He never married. Outside his work, his interests were chiefly books which he read constantly and insatiably. Independent, and straightforward in his expressions of opinion, he could be a bitter antagonist in controversies; yet by his thoughtfulness and consideration he attracted the loyalty and affection of those who worked with him.

[The *N. Y. Times*, Mar. 25, 1925; *Railway Age*, Mar. 28, 1925; *Who's Who in America*, 1924–25; E. S. White, *The Kinnears and Their Kin* (1916).]

P. W. B.

McPHERSON, SMITH (Feb. 14, 1848–Jan. 17, 1915), congressman from Iowa and federal district judge, the son of Oliver H. and Polly (Matthews) McPherson, was born and reared on a farm near Mooresville, Ind. Having completed his academic training at the Mooresville academy, he entered the law department at the State University of Iowa in September 1869 and graduated the following June. During the summer of 1870 he worked at Council Bluffs in the law office of his uncle, M. L. McPherson, of whom he many years later wrote a biographical sketch (*M. L. McPherson*, 1913). In November he moved to Redoak, Iowa, where he lived the rest of his life. He was married to Frances H. Boyer of Oskaloosa, on Oct. 2, 1879. They had no children. Beneath his brusque manner was a genial disposition and a sympathetic attitude that attracted many clients and made lifelong friends. Gov. C. C. Carpenter appointed him, in August 1874, to fill a vacancy as prosecuting attorney for the third judicial district. A year later he was elected to the same office and was reëlected in 1878 for a full term of four years. He distinguished himself by winning several important cases and attained sufficient prominence in the Republican party to be elected attorney general of Iowa. Probably the most important episode during his two terms in office, from 1881 to 1885, was the trial of the case of *Koehler & Lange* vs. *Hill* (60 *Iowa Reports*, 543) testing the validity of an amendment to the state constitution prohibiting the manufacture and sale of intoxicating liquor. In spite of his well-reasoned argument before the Supreme Court that the amendment had been adopted in the proper manner and by two successive General Assemblies in substantially identical form, the court decided in favor of the contrary view (*Iowa Journal of History and Politics*, Oct. 1908, pp. 529–33).

Between 1885 and 1900, he established a reputation as an eloquent and aggressive advocate whose services were in great demand, particularly by corporations. Like other successful and conservative lawyers who lived on the Burlington "reservation" in southern Iowa, he was retained as attorney for the Chicago, Burlington, & Quincy Railroad. In 1898 he was nominated for Congress on the 619th ballot after a deadlock that lasted four days (*Iowa State Register*, Des Moines, Aug. 26, 1898, weekly edition). Elected by a majority of nearly 4,000 votes, he found his duties in Congress to be "altogether the most unsatisfactory work in which a public man could engage" (*Iowa Alumnus, post*, p. 18). Consequently when President McKinley offered to appoint him judge for the southern district of Iowa he accepted with alacrity, though he did not resign from Congress until the end of the first session.

During the fifteen years he was on the federal bench, the business of the court increased enormously, particularly in the number of criminal cases, but he had a faculty for expediting procedure and kept his docket fairly clear. His decisions were always influenced by his innate conservatism. He ruled that the Iowa sterilization law as it applied to habitual criminals was unconstitutional (*Davis* vs. *Berry*, 216 *Federal Reporter*, 413). While he was holding court in Missouri, he enjoined the state of Missouri from enforcing maximum freight and passenger rates on the ground that they were confiscatory (*St. Louis & S. F. R. Co.* vs. *Hadley, et al.*, 168 *Federal Reporter*, 317). On appeal the Supreme Court of the United States decided that the Missouri maximum rates were not confiscatory on the basis of assessed valuation of the railroads, and reversed the decrees (*Missouri Rate Cases*, 230 *United States Reports*, 474). Meanwhile popular resentment against judicial frustration of statutory rate regulation found expression in a resolution introduced in Congress by Arthur P. Murphy of Missouri calling for an investigation of the official conduct of Judge McPherson (*Congressional Record*, 61 Cong., 1 Sess., pp. 1689, 1801–1805). The charges proved to be unfounded, however, and no further action was taken.

[*Iowa Jour. of Hist. and Pol.*, Jan., Apr. 1915; E. H. Stiles, *Recollections and Sketches of Notable Lawyers . . . Iowa* (1916); *Iowa Law Bulletin*, Mar. 1915; *Law Notes*, Mar. 1915; *Iowa Alumnus*, Feb. 1915; *Register and Leader* (Des Moines), Jan. 18, 19, 1915; *New York Times*, Jan. 18, 1915.]

J. E. B.

McQUAID, BERNARD JOHN (Dec. 15, 1823–Jan. 18, 1909), first bishop of Rochester, was born in New York of Irish parents, Bernard and Mary McQuaid. His mother died in 1827 and in 1832, following the murder of his father, a laborer in a Paulus Hook glass factory, he found a refuge with the Sisters of Charity. After attending the graded school, he was sent to Chambly College in Canada and then to St. Joseph's Seminary in Fordham, N. Y., where his precarious health kept him apart from fellow-seminarians. He was ordained on Jan. 16, 1848, by Bishop Hughes and assigned to a church in Madison, N. J., from which he worked an area of five counties in addition to teaching in a basement school. Hard and zealous, he sought no ease: he restored isolated Catholics to the fold, instructed the young in doctrine, and built modest chapels at Morristown, Springfield, and Mendham. In 1853 he commenced his long pastorate of St. Patrick's Cathedral in Newark. In 1854 he courageously faced a mob which attacked the German Catholic Church and strove in vain to have the ringleaders brought to justice. He organized relief work in the hungry winter of 1854–55; brought the Sisters of Charity of Mt. St. Vincent to conduct orphanages at Newark and Paterson; developed a cathedral school of 600 pupils; virtually founded and presided over Seton Hall College and Seminary (1857); aided in establishing St. Elizabeth's Convent; organized the Newark branch of the St. Vincent de Paul Society; and promoted a Young Men's Catholic lyceum. During the Civil War he was an aggressive Unionist. In 1864 he rushed to Washington to investigate the care of Catholic soldiers and remained at Fredericksburg to administer the sacraments to the wounded. As a theologian he attended the Second Plenary Council of Baltimore, and as vicar-general (1866–68), he administered the diocese, rigorously handling problems and priests that were wearing out Bishop Bayley.

Named bishop of Rochester, McQuaid was consecrated on July 12, 1868, by Archbishop McCloskey. Immediately he was in conflict with priests who did not relish autocratic discipline and exacting demands. At the Vatican Council he voted against the definition of papal infallibility, July 13, 1870, but he left Rome before the final vote, so anxious was he to reform his diocese. On Aug. 28 he defined and proclaimed the doctrine from St. Patrick's Cathedral. His heart was in Rochester; he had no ambition for elevation but settled down to church-building, giving special attention to educational and charitable institutions. Organizing the Sisters of St. Joseph as a diocesan community, he gave them charge of parochial schools which were built in all well-organized parishes, especially in German centers. In his zeal for Catholic education and in his fear of the "godless school," he drastically refused absolution to parents who failed to send their children to a Catholic school if one was available. Through the East he was regarded as the spokesman for free Christian schools and as such was frequently called upon to lecture. As the diocese grew prosperous, McQuaid established St. Bernard's Seminary (1891), a Catholic Summer Institute (1896) for teacher training, the Nazareth Normal School (1898), a branch of the St. Cecilian Society for the reform of church music, and cathedral schools. His ardor for parish schools accounted in part for his unreasoning bitterness toward Archbishop Ireland, Edward McGlynn, Bishop S. V. Ryan of Buffalo, Sylvester Malone, his successful rival for a regency of the University of New York, and Msgr. Keane of the Catholic University of America, whom he prevented from speaking to the Catholic students of Cornell University lest this give formal sanction to their attendance, which he only tolerated. For girls he did not even tolerate attendance in non-Catholic institutions.

McQuaid rigidly interpreted the ban on secret societies; he was suspicious of the Knights of Labor regardless of Cardinal Gibbons' approbation, and hostile to the Irish Land League, Clan-Na-Gael, and the Ancient Order of Hibernians, who as a body were not allowed to attend Mass in his diocese until 1894. In this respect he emphasized Americanism and boasted of native birth when a majority of the prelates were foreign born. He conducted in 1875 a successful campaign for a chaplain in the Western House of Refuge in Rochester and in 1892 spiritedly aided in the struggle for the law guaranteeing freedom of worship in penal institutions. In addition to building orphanages in Rochester, Canandaigua, and Auburn, he provided chapels at Craig Colony for Epileptics and at the State Soldiers' Home. Toward the end this "venerable but crusty old ecclesiastic who in perfect good faith felt that he alone was fighting the battles of the Church" (Archbishop Dowling of St. Paul in *American Historical Review,* April 1928, p. 702) grew more mild. In an exchange of visits he even found that he had much in common with Archbishop Ireland. In 1908 distinguished guests from the Catholic seminaries of the world attended the dedication of the Hall of Theology at St. Bernard's when McQuaid spoke from an invalid-chair until he collapsed.

The end soon came, and the doughty bishop's remains were consigned to the chapel in Holy Sepulchre Cemetery.

[F. J. Zwierlein, *The Life and Letters of Bishop McQuaid* (3 vols., 1925–27), is a detailed study, biased but startlingly frank. See also J. G. Shea, *The Hierarchy of the Cath. Ch. in the U. S.* (1886), and the *Rochester Democrat and Chronicle*, Jan. 19, 1909.]

R. J. P.

McQUILLEN, JOHN HUGH (Feb. 12, 1826–Mar. 3, 1879), dentist, writer, editor, a son of Hugh and Martha (Scattergood) McQuillen, was born in Philadelphia, Pa., and received his early education in the Friends' schools of that city. At the age of sixteen he became a clerk in an importing house, but in 1847 he began the study of medicine. In 1849 he also became student-assistant to Elisha Townsend, a well-known dentist of Philadelphia, and was shortly enrolled as a member of the Pennsylvania Association of Dental Surgeons. He received the degree of M.D. from the Jefferson Medical College in 1852, and from that year until 1861 he was associated in the practice of dentistry with Daniel Neall. Beginning in 1861, he practised independently in Philadelphia. From 1852 to 1859 he contributed eight articles to the *Dental News Letter,* which periodical was succeeded in the latter year by the *Dental Cosmos,* with McQuillen as one of its editors. He was professor of operative dentistry and dental pathology in the Pennsylvania College of Dental Surgery from 1857 to 1862. In the latter year he severed his connection with this college because of his dissatisfaction with the selection of a new member of the faculty, and in 1863 he founded the Philadelphia Dental College, of which until his death he was dean and professor of anatomy, physiology, and hygiene. During the Civil War he served gratuitously as a surgeon in the military hospitals at Philadelphia, and in that capacity was present at the battle of Antietam.

In 1859 he had been one of the prime movers in the organization of the American Dental Association, for which, under the pseudonym of Junius, he made the original published call, in an article in the *Dental News Letter* (April 1859, p. 184). In 1865 he was president of the association. In 1863 he was one of the organizers and first corresponding secretary of the Odontographic Society of Philadelphia, and served as its president from 1868 to 1870. In 1866 he was the first corresponding secretary of the Association of the Colleges of Dentistry. He also served as president of the Pennsylvania Association of Dental Surgeons, and was a member of several other societies at home and abroad. From 1865 to 1872 he was editor-in-chief of the *Dental Cosmos,* and he contributed many articles to its pages and to other dental journals. His published papers and addresses, some of which were translated into foreign languages, number altogether over one hundred. (See the *Index to Dental Periodical Literature,* vols. I and II.) They relate chiefly to dental anatomy, physiology, pathology, and histology. He was one of the first in America to demonstrate the importance of microscopical knowledge of the human teeth in health and disease, his earliest paper in this connection appearing in 1857, with others following from 1862 to 1874. He was the founder of the biological and microscopical section of the Academy of Natural Science at Philadelphia, of which he was a member for many years.

McQuillen was a skilful practitioner of dentistry and a conscientious teacher. He insisted upon a thorough preliminary as well as professional education for a dentist, and he labored unremittingly in his private practice and at his duties in the college founded by him, until he broke under the strain shortly before his death. He was impulsive and aggressive, but nevertheless generous and hospitable. With liberal religious views, he had due respect for all denominations, but affiliated with none. His one hobby was music, and he enjoyed nothing more than to surround himself with friends for a musical evening. He died in his fifty-fourth year and was interred in Woodland Cemetery, Philadelphia. In 1852 he married Amelia D. Schellenger, and they had five children.

[J. T. Scharf and Thompson Westcott, *Hist. of Phila.* (1884), vol. II; B. L. Thorpe, in C. R. E. Koch, *Hist. of Dental Surgery* (1910), vol. III; *Trans. Am. Dental Asso.*, 1879; *Am. Jour. Dental Sci.*, Mar. 1879; *British Jour. Dental Sci.*, Apr., May 1879; *Dental Cosmos*, Apr. 1879; the *Press* (Phila.), Mar. 5, 1879.]

L. P. B.

McRAE, DUNCAN KIRKLAND (Aug. 16, 1820–Feb. 12, 1888), lawyer, consul, soldier, was born at Fayetteville, (then Campbelltown), N. C., the son of John and Margaret S. Kirkland McRae. His grandfather, Duncan McRae, came to America from Scotland in 1773 or 1774 and became a leader in public affairs in Campbelltown. His father, postmaster and editor in the same city, numbered among his friends many men famous in American history, among them General Lafayette, whom he accompanied through North Carolina on his American tour in 1825 and entertained at his home. Duncan Kirkland McRae was educated at the College of William and Mary, Virginia, and at the University of North Carolina, and was admitted to the bar at twenty-one. As a lawyer he early developed a wide reputation for eloquence and quickness of repartee.

One of the first incidents in his vigorous and varied career was a mission to Mexico city as bearer of dispatches for the Department of State early in 1842. Returning to North Carolina, he was elected to the legislature of 1842, his first and most successful political venture. He subsequently practised law in Raleigh until 1851, when he removed to Wilmington to engage in banking. In 1845 he married Louise Virginia Henry, daughter of Judge Louis D. Henry of Raleigh. In 1853, as an independent candidate for Congress from the third district, he advocated the distribution of the proceeds from the sale of public lands among the states for internal improvements, but withdrew from the campaign to become American consul at Paris under President Pierce. While there he was commissioned to carry the famous Ostend Manifesto from London to Washington. His service at Paris fell in the stirring days of the Second Empire and lasted until ill health compelled his resignation in 1857. A few months after his return to North Carolina, and his establishment of a law office at New Bern, he plunged into politics for the third time, running independently for governor in opposition to John Willis Ellis [*q.v.*] in the campaign of 1858, with the unofficial support of the disorganized remnants of the American or Know-Nothing party. Always individualistic, high-spirited, and undisposed to yield to party restraints or popular sentiment, he favored a positive program of economic development as against what he believed undue emphasis on the slavery question, and was defeated.

At the opening of the Civil War, he was appointed colonel of the 5th North Carolina Regiment by his late political opponent, Governor Ellis. Beginning with the first battle of Manassas, he took an active part in the Virginia and Pennsylvania campaigns of 1861 and 1862. At Williamsburg he led his men in a desperately gallant charge, ranked by an English war correspondent with that of the Old Guard at Waterloo and the Light Brigade at Balaklava. Of this charge General Hancock of the Federal forces said, "The Fifth North Carolina and the Twenty-Fourth Virginia deserve to have the word immortal inscribed on their banners" (Jefferson Davis, *The Rise and Fall of the Confederate Government,* 1881, II, p. 96). Wounded at Williamsburg and again at Sharpsburg (Sept. 17, 1862), he retired from active service. Shortly afterward he was sent by Governor Vance of North Carolina on an important and successful mission to Europe to find a market for Southern cotton and state bonds and to arrange for the purchase of supplies. As a result the North Carolina troops were the best equipped in the Southern army. His European mission occupied almost a year. He then campaigned for a seat in the Confederate Congress, but was defeated. In 1864–65 he edited the *Confederate* at Raleigh, an administration organ to encourage Southern morale. The new political régime in 1865 forced him to leave the state. He practised law for fifteen years at Memphis, Tenn., then, after a few months at Chicago, returned in 1880 to Wilmington, N. C., where he established his last legal practice. He died in Brooklyn, N. Y., Feb. 12, 1888.

[Brief biographical sketches are to be found in Lawrence MacRae, *Descendants of Duncan & Ann (Cameron) MacRae of Scotland and N. C.* (1928), and in the *Confed. Mil. Hist.* (1899), IV, 626–28. His correspondence as U. S. consul at Paris is in the Department of State Archives at Washington (Paris Consulate, vol. X), and military reports by and concerning him are printed in *War of the Rebellion: Official Records (Army)*. An article by himself, "The Battle of Williamsburg—Reply to Colonel Bratton," is in *Southern Hist. Soc. Papers,* Aug. 1879. See also Dunbar Rowland, *Jefferson Davis, Constitutionalist, His Letters, Papers, and Speeches* (1923), IX, 329–33, and the *Morning Star* (Wilmington, N. C.), Feb. 14, 1888.]

I. L. T.

McRAE, MILTON ALEXANDER (June 13, 1858–Oct. 11, 1930), newspaper publisher, was born in Detroit, Mich., the third child of Duncan B. and Helen (Stevenson) McRae, both of Scotch descent. The father had been brought to Canada as a lad; later he went to Detroit, where he engaged in the dry-goods trade. In the public schools, Milton at once manifested noticeable creative talent, particularly in contriving and managing juvenile shows and circuses. After the death of his mother, when he was fourteen, he persuaded his father to let him go to work. For some time he ran a wide gamut—selling groceries, acting on the stage, managing a traveling theatrical troupe, teaching a country school, braking on a railroad, compiling a city directory, newspaper reporting—all the while cherishing an ambition to become a physician, an ambition which he sharpened by industrious reading of books on physiology and anatomy.

The execution of an idea which came to him in connection with his medical studies brought him his first recognition in the newspaper field. A cub reporter on the *Detroit Free Press,* he wormed his way, as an interne, into the pest house during a smallpox epidemic and wrote so realistic a story of his experiences as to cause an increase in his pay. Assigned to help in the promotion of an "Excursions-to-the-Sea" scheme undertaken by the paper, he did so well that he was induced to stay on in the advertising department at a salary which warranted his marriage, in 1880, to Victoria Wallis, of Saginaw, Mich. Closer contact ensued with the publisher, James E. Scripps [*q.v.*], and also with Scripps's brothers, who were interested together in dailies in Cleveland and Cincinnati. McRae was on the point of taking a War Department clerkship at Washington, when Scripps convinced him that a greater opportunity awaited him as advertising manager of the Cincinnati *Penny Paper,* soon renamed the *Penny Post.* He accepted this position and his rise in the newspaper world was thereafter continuous. He became business manager of the *Post* the next year, 1883, and, in 1887, managing director of the *Evening Chronicle,* which Edward W. Scripps [*q.v.*] had started in St. Louis and which McRae consolidated with the *Star.* These papers were the first in each city to sell for one cent. In 1889 McRae entered into a life-partnership agreement with Edward W. Scripps to pool salaries and profits on a division basis of one third and two thirds respectively. They soon began systematic development of their plan for a chain of newspapers of the same popular type as those they had been conducting. Their policy called for the purchase or establishment of papers in many cities. During one period of six months, McRae organized and put into operation six such papers. Not all were successful. Characterizing William R. Nelson as "one of the best newspapermen America has ever produced," he added, "I ought to know—he ran us out of the Kansas City field and cost us several hundred thousand dollars" (Hamby, *post,* p. 68). The enterprise as a whole proved most profitable, however, and, subsequently reorganized, became the Scripps-Howard Newspapers. In 1897 the Scripps-McRae Press Association, with McRae as president, was formed to furnish news to the papers of the Scripps-McRae League. Other evening papers desiring the service were later admitted and the association developed into the United Press Associations, a world-wide news-gathering and distributing agency of the first magnitude.

Forced by ill health into partial retirement at the age of forty-nine, McRae returned to Detroit and directed his energies to civic and philanthropic objects. The Boy Scouts of America, especially, commanded his hearty support and he filled out an unexpired term as its national president. Public office, however, never tempted him. He refused a commission on the military staff of McKinley, when he was governor of Ohio, and was promptly dubbed "Colonel" by his newspaper colleagues. The title thus bestowed clung to him and was proudly borne. His keenest enjoyment came from extensive travels to all quarters of the globe. Newspaper reminiscences and observations abroad constitute the subject matter of his *Forty Years in Newspaperdom,* published in 1924. His death occurred in the Scripps Memorial Hospital at La Jolla, Cal., not far from his winter home in San Diego, in which place he was buried.

[In addition to McRae's book, see W. H. Hamby, "Lifted by Loyalty," in *Sunset: The Pacific Monthly,* Nov. 1919; Victor Rosewater, *Hist. of Cooperative News-Gathering in the U. S.* (1930); *Outlook,* May 12, 1926; N. D. Cockran, *E. W. Scripps* (1933); A. N. Marquis, *The Book of Detroiters* (1914); *Who's Who in America,* 1930–31; *Detroit News,* Oct. 11, 1930.]

V. R.

McRAE, THOMAS CHIPMAN (Dec. 21, 1851–June 2, 1929), lawyer, congressman, governor of Arkansas, was born in Union County, Ark., the son of Duncan L. and Mary Ann (Chipman) McRae. His paternal ancestors emigrated from Scotland to North Carolina in the early part of the eighteenth century. Thomas attended private schools, the Soulé Business College in New Orleans, and the law department of Washington and Lee University, from which he graduated in 1872. He opened a law office in Rosston, Ark., in 1873, but moved to Prescott in 1877, when that town was made the county seat. He was representative in the legislature in 1877, a Democratic presidential elector in 1880, chairman of the Democratic state convention in 1884 and 1902, and a member of the national committee from 1896 to 1900.

In 1885 he was elected to Congress. During his first session (1886) he introduced a bill for a graduated income tax, and again in 1888. He was a member of the committee on public lands for ten years and its chairman for four; for a time he was the ranking Democrat on the appropriations committee. He introduced bills for the recovery of lands previously granted to the Pacific railroads, to preserve the timber on public lands, and to safeguard the national forests. He also worked for the return of the cotton tax, which had been collected after the close of the Civil War. Besides serving on important conference committees, he was several times made chairman of the committee of the whole.

On retiring from Congress voluntarily in 1903 he resumed the practice of law at Prescott and engaged in banking. He was elected president of the Arkansas Bankers' Association in 1909 and of the Bar Association in 1917. In 1917–18 he was a member of the constitutional convention. He secured the Democratic nomination for governor in 1920 by a small plurality, but was elected by a good majority and made an excellent record for two terms. The chief planks in his platform were the abolition of useless offices and a systematic and economical financial administration. He secured the substitution of honorary boards for salaried commissions in four instances. The penitentiary board, which was nearly half a million dollars in debt, he reorganized and put on a firm basis. He secured the abolition of the corporation commission, which exercised jurisdiction "from the greatest railroad to the most insignificant light plant" and restored control of local utilities to the local governments. He was much interested in the common schools and particularly in vocational and agricultural education and had the satisfaction of seeing an increase in funds for their support, partly due to the tobacco tax, and a great improvement in educational conditions generally. Road building had been begun on the mistaken policy of improvement districts, which threw the burden upon the owners of the adjacent real estate; McRae proposed that the roads should be built and maintained by the users and suggested higher fees for motor licenses and a gasoline tax. Throughout his four years he advocated a state income tax and the repeal of the state general property tax. Powerful interests blocked the former measure at the time, but he lived to see such a tax in operation before his death. He secured an appropriation for a tuberculosis sanitarium for negroes, a law giving women the right to hold office, and advocated the creation of a forestry commission. At the expiration of his term he again resumed his law practice at Prescott and engaged in banking. He gave freely to charity, and donated two blocks in Prescott for a park for the negroes, the site of the postoffice, and land upon which to build a county court house. On Dec. 17, 1874, he was married to Amelia Ann White, by whom he had nine children. His death was caused by influenza.

[*Biog. Dir. Am. Cong.* (1928); *Jour. of the House of Representatives of the . . . State of Ark.*, 1921, 1925; *Jour. of the Senate*, 1923; *Jour. of the House of Representatives . . . 1925*; *Proc. of the . . . Bar Asso. of Ark.*, 1929; D. T. Herndon, *Centennial Hist. of Ark.* (1922), vol. II; D. Y. Thomas, *Ark. and Its People* (1930); *Who's Who in America*, 1928–29; *Arkansas Gazette*, June 3, 1929; information furnished by a son, T. C. McRae.] D. Y. T.

MACSPARRAN, JAMES (Sept. 10, 1693–Dec. 1, 1757), missionary of the Society for the Propagation of the Gospel in Foreign Parts, rector of St. Paul's Church in the Narragansett Country, in the extreme southern part of the present township of North Kingstown, R. I., is believed to have been born in Dungiven, County of Derry, Ireland, of Presbyterian parents who had gone there from Kintore, Scotland. He was educated at the University of Glasgow, receiving the degree of master of arts Mar. 5, 1709. He studied for the Presbyterian ministry and received credentials as a licentiate of the Presbytery of Scotland. In 1718 he visited America, stopping at Boston, Barnstable, and Plymouth on the way to the home of the widow Pampelion, a relative, in Bristol, at that time under the jurisdiction of the Colony of Massachusetts. He filled temporarily the vacant pulpit of the Congregational church in Bristol and was invited on Dec. 16, 1718, to become its pastor at an annual salary of £100, an invitation in which the town concurred, Dec. 22, 1718. During his stay in Boston, MacSparran seems to have aroused the enmity of Cotton Mather, who first delayed his ordination and then spread reports that his credentials were fraudulent. He proceeded to Ireland to procure their confirmation but never returned to the Congregational church at Bristol and later wrote that a false charge in his youth had opened the way into the Anglican priesthood for him.

Ordained deacon by the Bishop of London in the chapel of Fulham Palace Aug. 21, 1720, and priest by the Archbishop of Canterbury in the chapel of Lambeth Palace, Sept. 25, 1720, he was licensed to discharge the ministerial office in the province of New England by the Bishop of London on Oct. 3, 1720. The Parish of St. Paul, Narragansett Country, had written to the Bishop of London and to the Society for the Propagation of the Gospel in Foreign Parts, June 15, 1720, asking for a missionary to succeed William Guy, and the Society now sent out MacSparran to officiate there and at Bristol, Freetown, Swansea, and Little Compton at an annual salary of £70. He arrived at Narragansett Apr. 28, 1721, and proved to be one of the ablest of the missionaries sent to America by the Society, serving as rector of St. Paul's and ministering to the surrounding country for a period of thirty-six years. On May 22, 1722, he married Hannah, daughter of William Gardiner of Boston Neck, Narragansett, a sister of Silvester Gardiner [*q.v.*]. He was instrumental in the establishment of an Episcopal church at New London, Conn., in 1725. He entertained Dean Berkeley and John Smibert in 1729, but it was probably at a later date that Smibert's portrait of MacSparran now in the possession of Bowdoin College and that of Mrs. MacSparran now in the possession of the Boston Museum of Fine Arts were painted. During almost his entire ministry at St. Paul's he was involved in a lawsuit to gain possession of three hundred acres of land granted by the proprietors of the Pettaquamscutt purchase to an orthodox ministry but lost the suit by the decision of the Privy Council in 1752. He paid two visits to England; the first, between June 1736 and August 1737, during which the University of Oxford conferred upon him the degree of doctor of sacred theology, and the second, between the autumn of 1754 and February 1756, perhaps to work for the creation of an American bishopric, which he had long favored, and to obtain the office for himself. In the course of this latter visit his wife died of smallpox in London, June 24, 1755.

MacSparran published *The Sacred Dignity of the Christian Priesthood Vindicated* (1752), a discourse delivered at St. Paul's Aug. 4, 1751, intended to correct irregularities among the clergy of his own denomination but which aroused a storm of protest from the non-conforming ministers of New England; and *America Dissected* (1753), an account of the American colonies in a series of letters to friends in Ireland. He contemplated publishing an extended history of New England and is supposed to have written an account of the Narragansett Country, but after his death no trace of the manuscript was found. A diary kept by him during the years 1743, 1744, 1745, and 1751 was discovered and published in 1899. MacSparran died in the present township of South Kingstown at the age of sixty-four. He had no children and bequeathed his farm for the use and support of an American bishop whose diocese should include the Narragansett Country; this provision of his will was not carried out, however, and individuals of the parish of St. Paul bought the farm from his heirs to be used as a perpetual glebe. A monument to his memory was erected in 1869 in North Kingstown, R. I.

[*A Letter Book and Abstract of Out Services, Written During the Years 1743–1751 by the Revd. James MacSparran* (1899), ed. with a sketch of the author and numerous notes by Daniel Goodwin; Wilkins Updike, *A Hist. of the Episcopal Ch. in Narrangansett, R. I., including a Hist. of other Episcopal Churches in the State* (3 vols., 1907), ed. by Daniel Goodwin; *Hist. Colls. Relating to the Am. Colonial Church*, vol. III (1873), ed. by W. S. Perry; *Samuel Johnson, President of King's College, His Career and Writings* (4 vols., 1929), ed. by H. W. and Carol Schneider; A. C. Fraser, *Life and Letters of George Berkeley* (1871); W. S. Perry, *The Hist. of the Am. Episcopal Ch. 1587–1883* (2 vols., 1885); W. B. Sprague, *Annals Am. Pulpit*, vol. V (1859); W. H. Munro, *The Hist. of Bristol, R. I.* (1880); F. M. Caulkins, *Hist. of New London, Conn.* (1852); *Munimenta Alme Universitatis Glasguensis; Records of the Univ. of Glasgow from its Foundation till 1727* (1854), vol. III; Joseph Foster, *Alumni Oxonienses 1715–1886*, vol. III (1888), p. 899; Gordon Goodwin, in *Dict. of Nat. Biog.*]

I. M. C.

McTAMMANY, JOHN (June 26, 1845–Mar. 26, 1915), inventor of the perforated music roll, player-piano, and voting machine, was born in Kelvin Row, a suburb of Glasgow, Scotland, of poor parents, John and Agnes (McLean) McTammany. His father emigrated to America, leaving his two infant sons in the care of their mother, who had to work out, and their grandmother. John enjoyed a few months at school but was soon obliged to help support the family. His ambition was to beome a great pianist when he grew up, but fate decided otherwise. There was not an industry on the Clyde, from rope- and chain-making to ship-building, with which he did not become familiar, and by his work the muscles of his hands permanently lost their pliancy. In 1862 the elder McTammany was able to send for his family. They settled in Uniontown, Ohio, and John, a born inventor, turned his attention to improvements in harvester machinery. According to his own statement he enlisted in 1863 in the 115th Ohio Volunteer Infantry. He was more than once wounded, critically during the fighting around Chattanooga. During his convalescence, at Nashville, while visiting a pawnshop where musical instruments were kept, he volunteered to repair a music box. While thus engaged, the idea of a new musical instrument, to be operated by depressions instead of pins and staples, occurred to him.

Returning to Uniontown, in 1865, he taught music, played in the band, and sold pianos and organs during the day, while he experimented with his piano at night. Within a year he practically mastered his invention. During the next ten years he built, successively, three models of his player and two machines to prepare the perforated sheets. In St. Louis, in the winter of 1876, he gave a public exhibition of his largest model, fitted to an Estey organ (*Boston Herald*, Jan. 28, 1877). Up to that time no instrument had ever been constructed embodying the essential and necessary elements of his invention, such as a flexible sheet on rolls, wind motor, foot pedals, and other important features, suitable for pianos as well as organs. There had been keyboard attachments and other propositions, but even the most pretentious one, of French origin, soon became obsolete.

The musical profession strongly opposed McTammany's innovation from the start. Manufacturers to whom he confided his plans shook their heads but copied his blueprints. In the fall of 1876, considering his invention completed, he had filed a caveat fully describing it. (See illustrated description in McTammany's *Technical History of the Player*, pp. 29–34.) This application gave him two years in which to take out a basic patent. Unfortunately, two years found him in worse difficulties; he let the time in which to obtain his patent go by, and it was declared public property. In due time the manufacturers felt at liberty to apply for and obtain patents. McTammany finally landed in a garret on Tremont Street, Boston, and there, on credit desperately obtained, he built a small instrument embodying his invention, which he named the Organette. After finishing two of these miniature players, which had a special scale of sixteen notes, the inventor tried unsuccessfully to sell them to the music trade. Finally he found buyers for his player and in time he became successful.

Then came a long and costly litigation which once more reduced him to poverty. The patentees of the player stopped him from manufacturing his instrument, but in 1880 he was declared to be the original and prior inventor (*Decisions of the Commissioner of Patents for the Year 1880,* 1881, p. 203). He received three patents on his invention in 1881 and several subsequent patents. Finding themselves defeated in the courts, his competitors, after he had obtained capital to manufacture his player on a large scale, acquired a majority of his company's stock and ousted him. On Sept. 13, 1892, McTammany received a basic patent for a pneumatic registering ballot box, employing the perforated roll. It was the first machine ever used in an election and was adopted in a number of states, but again McTammany was unable to overcome competition. At last the inventor, although of large, robust build, broke down completely and died on Mar. 26, 1915, in the military hospital at Stamford, Conn. The city accorded him a public funeral, at which all the music was played on a grand player-piano. His remains were two years later removed from Stamford, to Canton, Ohio, where elaborate Memorial Day exercises in his honor were held, May 30, 1917, in Westlawn Cemetery, and where the final interment took place near the McKinley monument.

[See John McTammany, *Hist. of the Player* (1913) and *Technical Hist. of the Player* (1915), containing an introduction by Wm. Geppert; W. M. Butler, "Scotch Prodigy's Great Invention," *Presto*, Aug. 23, 1917; *Specifications and Drawings of Patents Issued from the U. S. Patent Office*, June, July, Nov. 1881, Sept. 1892; *Hartford Courant*, Mar. 27, 1915.]

W. M. B.

McTYEIRE, HOLLAND NIMMONS (July 28, 1824–Feb. 15, 1889), bishop of the Methodist Episcopal Church, South, was born in Barnwell County, S. C., and died at Vanderbilt University, Nashville, Tenn. He was of Scotch-Irish ancestry, the son of John and Elizabeth Amanda (Nimmons) McTyeire. His boyhood was spent on the farm in South Carolina. When he was fourteen years of age he began preparation for college at Cokesbury Academy, Abbeville County, S. C., and at twenty he graduated from Randolph-Macon College, Virginia, remaining there one year more as tutor. Admitted to the Virginia Conference of the Methodist Episcopal Church, South, on trial in November 1845, he was appointed pastor of the church at Williamsburg, Va., the seat of William and Mary College. So remarkable was his early intellectual maturity that at twenty-three he was appointed to the St. Francis Street Church, Mobile, Ala., and as a member of the Alabama Conference was ordained deacon Jan. 26, 1848. The preceding year, Nov. 9, he had married Amelia Townsend of Mobile. On Dec. 26, 1849, now a member of the Louisiana Conference, he was ordained elder. He had a large share in pioneering the work of the Methodist Church in New Orleans, and while in charge of a parish there, he also preached regularly to a large negro congregation. In 1851 he founded the *New Orleans Christian Advocate,* through which he became an influential factor in directing the trend of thought in his Church. At the General Conference of 1858 he was elected editor of the *Christian Advocate,* the official periodical of the Methodist Church, South, published at Nashville, Tenn. In this capacity he continued until 1862, when the publication of the *Advocate* was suspended, the Methodist Publishing House being used at that time as an arsenal and hospital by the Federal army.

Transferred to Alabama, he now took charge of the church in Montgomery, with which he remained connected until the General Conference of 1866. In this body he was not only a member, but was probably the master mind. Conditions at this time offered an opportunity for reconstructing the Methodist Episcopal Church, South, and McTyeire was the leader of progressive reforms, winning for himself the name of "fighting elder." The principal reform which he advocated was known as "lay representation." Hitherto the controlling bodies of American Methodism had been exclusively clerical. The measure which McTyeire sponsored provided for laymen in the annual conferences and especially for lay delegates in the General Conferences equal in number to the clerical delegates. At this Conference McTyeire was elected bishop, an office in which he served with statesman-like ability for twenty-three years. It was also decided that in case the negro membership of the Church desired to be organized into an independent body, the bishops should cooperate in providing for such an organization. Four years later Bishop McTyeire was one of the chief commissioners in the formation of the Colored Methodist Episcopal Church as a distinct ecclesiastical body; he shared in turning over to it properties valued at one million dollars, and in committing the mother church to contributing in all possible ways to the support and welfare of the new organization. McTyeire was also one of the chief promoters of the foreign-missionary enterprise of his Church, and when, in 1891, an institution for the higher education of women was founded in China, it was named McTyeire School in recognition of his services. Probably, however, Vanderbilt University will prove the most enduring monument to him, since he was the chief agent in its founding. While he was busy with the plans for establishing such an institution under the auspices of his Church, he was the guest of the elder Cornelius Vanderbilt [*q.v.*], and discussed the enterprise with him. Vanderbilt was so favorably impressed with the plan and with McTyeire's administrative ability that he at once gave him a check for $500,000, and later increased the gift to a million dollars. He insisted that Bishop McTyeire be president of the board of trust and vested with full veto power. During the first fifteen years of the history of the university, therefore, McTyeire had a determining voice in its affairs. He spent his last days in a home especially provided for him on the campus, and there died. He was buried on the campus, and the monument to his memory bears the appropriate inscription:

"A leader of men.
A lover of children."

As an author McTyeire will be known principally for his *History of Methodism* (1884). He also wrote *Duties of Christian Masters* (1859); *A Catechism of Bible History* (1883–84); *A Manual of the Discipline of the Methodist Episcopal Church, South* (1870); *A Catechism on Church Government* (2nd ed., 1880), and a volume of sermons entitled *Passing Through the Gates* (copr. 1890).

[Material for a life of McTyeire is in the custody of his daughter, Mrs. Janie McTyeire Baskerville, Washington, D. C.; published material may be found in the files of the *Christian Advocate* (Nashville), esp. the issue of Feb. 28, 1889; *Jour. of the General Conference, M. E. Ch. South*, 1890; Charles Forster Smith, *Reminiscences and Sketches* (1908); introduction to *Passing Through the Gates*; Gross Alexander, *Hist. of the M. E. Ch., South, in the U. S.* (1894); H. M. DuBose, *Hist. of Methodism* (1916); Richard Irby, *Hist. of Randolph Macon Coll., Va.* (1898), T. L. Flood and J. W. Hamilton, *Lives of Methodist Bishops* (1882); *Daily American* (Nashville), Feb. 16, 17, 1889; records of the proceedings of the Vanderbilt University Faculty, Minute Book, vol. II, p. 190; records of the proceedings of the board of trust of Vanderbilt University, vol. IV, p. 12.] O. E. B.

MACVEAGH, ISAAC WAYNE (Apr. 19, 1833–Jan. 11, 1917), lawyer, diplomat, political reformer, was born near Phoenixville, Chester County, Pa.; his parents were Maj. John and Margaret (Lincoln) MacVeagh. He attended school at Pottstown, Pa., and graduated at Yale, ranking tenth in the class of 1853. Distinction in debate marked him for the law and politics, and he entered the office of J. J. Lewis, prominent lawyer of West Chester, Pa. He was admitted to the bar in 1856 and married Letty Miner Lewis in the same year. He was district attorney for Chester County, 1859–64, adding to his legal duties service during the Civil War in the militia, in which he attained the ranks of captain of emergency infantry (1862) and major of cavalry (1863), attached to the staff of General Couch in reorganizing the local forces. He also became chairman of the Republican State Committee in 1863 and accompanied Lincoln to Gettysburg on the occasion of his address. After the war he transferred his practice to Harrisburg. His first wife had died in 1862 and in 1866 he was married to Virginia Rolette Cameron, daughter of the formidable political boss, Simon Cameron, in alliance with whom he became a figure in the Republican party.

He was appointed minister resident in Turkey, June 4, 1870, reaching his post late in the year. In connection with the Black Sea problem then under discussion among the European powers, he upheld Turkey's right of closure of the Straits against Secretary Fish's disposition to claim freedom of passage for American warships, and warned the Secretary strongly against entangling the United States government in the ulterior designs of other governments in the question. Coming home on leave in June 1871, he found political conditions under the Grant administration so distressing that he resigned his post to begin a lifelong career of "insurgency" by joining the opposition to the Cameron machine in Pennsylvania. He was a delegate to the state constitutional convention, 1872–73. In 1876 he moved to Philadelphia. His opposition to the Grant forces in the Republican National Convention of 1876 marked him for a part in the liquidation of Reconstruction undertaken by President Hayes. He was sent, in 1877, to Louisiana as head of a commission under whose auspices the local Democratic claimants to office were able to make a settlement with their Republican rivals which broke a dangerous deadlock and permitted the withdrawal of Federal troops from New Orleans (*Colonel Alexander K. McClure's Recollections of Half a Century*, 1902, pp. 104, 178). The aftermath of this accomplishment was a classic controversy with Benjamin F. Butler.

MacVeagh's independent position in politics, coupled with his recognized legal ability, won him the post of attorney-general in Garfield's cabinet, in which he was commissioned Mar. 5, 1881. He resigned on the President's death but held office until November, securing the indictment of the assassin, Guiteau, but escaping involvement in the scandalous trial. He then returned to the practice of law in Philadelphia and to his struggle with the powers of darkness in politics. He was especially active in the Civil Service Reform Association, of which he served as state chairman, as well as of the Indian Rights Association. The issues of civil-service reform and tariff reduction finally impelled him to desert the party of his formal allegiance and to support Cleveland's second election to the presidency. On Dec. 20, 1893, he was appointed ambassador to Italy, which post he held for about two years. It imposed upon him the delicate task of helping to preserve good relations in the excitement attending the outrages upon Italians in the United States at the time, although the actual negotiations arising out of these disturbances were conducted at Washington.

In 1897 MacVeagh entered the Washington law firm of McKenney & Flannery, counsel for the District of Columbia and the Pennsylvania Railroad, but he maintained his residence in Pennsylvania and took an active interest in the reform movement which swept the state after the turn of the century. As persistent a non-conformist in his new party as in the old, he opposed the control and policies of Bryan and was on the friendliest terms with Republican presidents and cabinet officers. Roosevelt appointed him chief counsel for the United States in the Venezuela arbitration of 1903. He was intimate with John Hay and Elihu Root and as a conversational foil was found worthy of the steel of Mark Twain. "Rapier-like" he was well called for the spareness of his frame and the penetrating keenness of his wit. By George Harvey, whom he supported against Woodrow Wilson after Harvey's break with Wilson, he was dubbed a "passionate patriot" and compared with Voltaire because of his ardent and tireless warfare against injustice. He was a contributor, chiefly to the *North American Review,* of articles on political reform and international peace. His last literary effort was a plea for the entrance of the United States into the World War ("The Impassable Chasm," *North American Review,* July 1915).

[*Who's Who in America,* 1916–17; *Obit. Record of Grads. of Yale Univ.,* 1917; *Wayne MacVeagh: Proc. of a Meeting of the Phila. Bar* (1917); memoir in *Report of the Twenty-third Ann. Meeting of the Pa. Bar Asso.,* 1917; W. F. Johnson, *Geo. Harvey, 'A Passionate Patriot'* (1929); W. R. Thayer, *The Life and Letters of John Hay* (2 vols., 1915); *Foreign Relations of the U. S.,* 1871, 1894–96; the *Nation,* July 29, 1915; *North Am. Rev.,* Mar. 1917; the *Evening Star* (Wash., D. C.), Jan. 11, 1917; *Pub. Ledger* (Phila.), Jan. 12, 1917.]

J. V. F.

MACVICAR, MALCOLM (Sept. 30, 1829–May 18, 1904), educator, author, was born in Dunglass, Argyleshire, Scotland. When he was six years old his father, John, and his mother, Janet MacTavish, left the Highlands for Canada with their twelve children, settling near Chatham, Ontario. Here frontier conditions and a deeply religious home life gave lasting direction to the boy's future career. His early education was undertaken with a view to his entering the Presbyterian ministry. Since there were no schools in the settlement, the local Presbyterian pastor, a University of Edinburgh graduate, prepared Malcolm for Knox College, Ontario, which he entered in 1850. Three years later he changed his profession of faith and became a Baptist, in which denomination he was ordained in 1856. He never held a pastorate, however, but turned almost immediately to teaching.

After the educational success but financial failure of a private venture in tutoring young men for college, MacVicar left for the United States, where he entered the University of Rochester as a senior. Upon receiving the degree of A.B. in 1859, he engaged in teaching and finally became principal of the Brockport Collegiate Institute, where, excepting for one year at the Buffalo Central High School, he remained till 1867. During this period he so made his mark in secondary education in New York that he was appointed chairman of a committee to report on the operation of the regents' examinations just instituted. He was particularly interested in the "teachers classes" in the academies, which New York State was still utilizing for part of its supply of teachers for the common schools. Believing that the utmost these classes could do was too little, he became largely instrumental in securing in 1866 legislation for four new normal schools. This leadership brought him the principalship of the first normal school under the law, that at Brockport. Owing to the strain of organizing it, his health gave way, but rather than accept his resignation, the state granted him a year's leave of absence. Restored in health by a Western trip, he was appointed, upon his return, to open and organize the Potsdam state normal school. Here from 1869 to 1880 he was at the peak of his normal school career; nevertheless he was glad to accept a call to the Michigan state normal school at Ypsilanti, where he would be free from the unhappy conflict of dual control which characterized New York state educational administration. Again worn out with hard work, he welcomed in 1881 an appointment to the faculty of the Toronto Baptist College, where he might return to his early interest in the philosophy of religion. When this college became the theological department of McMaster University, he reluctantly became its first chancellor (1887–90). After succeeding in its initial organization he resigned to superintend the educational work of the American Baptist Home Mission Society (1890–1900). The last post, and one he held till shortly before his death, was the presidency of Virginia Union University (1900–1904).

His success as an administrator is attested by his succession of offices; his ability as a teacher, however, was no less prominent. His mechanical skill, which had enabled him to earn his college tuition in a ship-carpenter's shop in Cleveland, made him ingenious in inventing mechanical contrivances as aids to classroom exposition, of which his tellurian globe was the most notable. At a later date he was instrumental in instituting a department of manual training in Woodstock College, Canada. Among his publications was *Principles of Education* (1892). Throughout his life he was addicted to hard work without the usual forms of relaxation. Even his year's quest of health in the West was spent in reorganizing the school system of Leavenworth, Kan. In 1865 he married Isabella McKay, a childhood friend, by whom he had three sons and a daughter.

[G. M. Rose, *A Cyc. of Canadian Biog.*, vol. II (1888); *First Quarto-Centennial Hist. of the State Normal and Training School, Potsdam, N. Y., 1869–94* (1895); Daniel Putnam, *A Hist. of the Mich. State Normal School at Ypsilanti, Mich.* (1899); Paul Monroe, *A Cyc. of Educ.*, vol. IV (1913); W. S. Wallace, *The Dict. of Canadian Biog.* (1926); *McMaster Univ. Mo.*, Feb. 1905; *The Baptist Home Mission Monthly*, June 1904; *N. Y. Times*, May 19, 1904; information from a son, John G. MacVicar.] J. S. B.

McVICKAR, JOHN (Aug. 10, 1787–Oct. 29, 1868), Protestant Episcopal clergyman, economist, was the son of John McVickar, born in County Antrim, Ireland, who emigrated to New York in 1780 and there became a wealthy merchant, and his wife Anna, daughter of John Moore of Newtown, L. I. Their son John was born in New York, entered Columbia College, where he ranked at the head of his class throughout his course, and graduated in 1804 at the age of seventeen. Hamilton had died shortly before Commencement, and McVickar's Latin salutatory oration, "Eloquence and Hamilton," was one of the first public eulogies of that statesman. The following year McVickar went abroad with his father, and upon his return began the study of theology with Rev. (afterwards Bishop) John Henry Hobart [*q.v.*], who ordained him deacon in 1811 and priest in 1812. McVickar and Hobart were lifelong friends, and after the bishop's death, McVickar wrote his biography. On Nov. 12, 1809, he married Eliza, daughter of Dr. Samuel Bard [*q.v.*] of Hyde Park, N. Y., and in 1811 he was made rector of the Church of St. James in that town, founded and erected by his father-in-law. He remained there until November 1817, when he was elected to the professorship of moral philosophy in Columbia College. At this time the faculty was composed of the president, three professors, and one adjunct professor; McVickar also gave instruction in rhetoric, belles-lettres, ancient history, and the history of philosophy. He was one of the earliest teachers of political economy in the United States, teaching the subject as a branch of moral philosophy, but the claim that he held the first American chair in that field is not borne out by the records; his title is variously given during his long professorship, some of the changes being official and some his own. In 1857 when Francis Lieber [*q.v.*] was called to Columbia to teach political economy, McVickar was transferred to the more appropriate chair of the evidences of natural and revealed religion, which he held until his retirement in 1864. He died in New York four years later.

During the last illness of President William Harris [*q.v.*] in 1829, and after the resignation of President W. A. Duer [*q.v.*] in 1842, McVickar was acting president of the college. On both occasions, however, he failed to be elected president, due perhaps to "something in his personality which repelled rather than attracted popular approval, an excessive correctness and frigidity, a certain removal from human sympathy" (Dorfman and Tugwell, *post*, p. 371). On the first occasion, his disappointment was so great that he secured leave and took his family to Europe. There he visited Wordsworth, Southey, the Pestalozzis, James Mill, Scott, and other notables; he was particularly impressed by Scott, and upon his death delivered an oration on him in New York (*Tribute to the Memory of Sir Walter Scott, Baronet,* 1833).

Although McVickar is now remembered chiefly as an economist, because of his early teaching of that subject, he was first of all a churchman and a moralist, and his subjects of instruction were merely avenues for the inculcation of sound moral and social precepts. Throughout his career he was active in religious affairs, preaching often, and taking a leading part in denominational activities; in 1835 he issued anonymously *Devotions for the Family and the Closet.* From 1844 to 1862 he was chaplain of the army post at Fort Columbus in New York harbor; there he built the Chapel of St. Cornelius the Centurion, and sent regiments to the Mexican War with individual Bibles and the Church's blessing. In 1860, largely as a result of his labors, St. Stephen's College at Annandale-on-Hudson was established as a training college for Episcopal clergymen.

His biography of Hobart appeared originally in two parts: *The Early Years of the Late Bishop Hobart* (1834) and *The Professional Years of John Henry Hobart* (1836). The two were published together in 1838 under the title *The Early Life and Professional Years of Bishop Hobart.* Other publications, in addition to various sermons and addresses, were: *A Domestic Narrative of the Life of Samuel Bard, M.D., LL.D.* (1822); *Outlines of Political Economy* (1825), a republication of the *Britannica* article of John Ramsay McCulloch, to which McVickar added extensive notes; *Interest Made Equity* (1826), also by McCulloch, with an editorial preface added; *Hints on Banking* (1827), an important tract, reputed to have been responsible for the "Free Banking System" established in New York and elsewhere a decade later; *Considerations upon the Expediency of Abolishing Damages on Protested Bills of Exchange, and the Effect of Establishing a Reciprocal Exchange with Europe* (1829); *A National Bank; Its Necessity and Most Desirable Form* (1841), advocating a national bank fundamentally similar to the second United States Bank. In 1839 he wrote a preliminary essay for the New York edition of Coleridge's *Aids to Reflection.*

[Edward McVickar and W. C. Breed, *Memoranda Relating to the McVickar Family in America* (1906); J. W. Moore, *Rev. John Moore of Newtown, L. I., and Some of His Descendants* (1903); W. A. McVickar, *The Life of the Rev. John McVickar, S.T.D.* (1872); Joseph Dorfman and R. G. Tugwell, "The Rev. John McVickar, Christian Teacher and Economist," *Columbia Univ. Quart.*, Dec. 1931; *N. Y. Times*, Oct. 31, 1868.]

M. H. T.

McVICKAR, WILLIAM NEILSON (Oct. 19, 1843–June 28, 1910), bishop of the Protestant Episcopal Church, was born in New York City, where his great-grandfather, John, an emigrant from County Antrim, Ireland, had been a prosperous merchant and long a vestryman of Trinity Church. One of his sons, John [*q.v.*], was a prominent Episcopal clergyman and professor in Columbia College. William was the grandson of James and the son of Dr. John Augustus McVickar, a well-known homeopathic practitioner, whose wife was Charlotte, daughter of William Neilson, the first president of the New York Board of Underwriters. Young McVickar was prepared for college in private schools and graduated from Columbia in 1865. He entered the Philadelphia Divinity School but later transferred to the General Theological Seminary, New York, where he completed his course in 1868. Ordained deacon in 1867, and priest in 1868, he was for a short time assistant to Dr. Stephen H. Tyng at St. George's Church, New York, but in 1868 became rector of Holy Trinity, Harlem, an infant enterprise with few adherents and no church buildings. During the seven years that McVickar was in charge it became a comparatively large, and well-equipped institution. In 1875 he was called to Holy Trinity, Philadelphia, where he was rector for twenty-two years. Six feet, five inches tall and built on extraordinarily large proportions, of bright and kindly countenance, and possessing a voice of great richness and sweetness, he was impressive in the pulpit and attracted notice and interest wherever he appeared. He and Phillips Brooks [*q.v.*] were intimate friends and kindred spirits, corresponding frequently and traveling abroad together. Like Brooks, McVickar never married. His breadth of sympathies and largeness of heart corresponded with his physical appearance. He exerted much influence in Philadelphia outside the bounds of his parish, and became increasingly prominent in the corporate affairs of the Episcopal Church. He was a deputy to all the General Conventions from 1883 to 1895, and a member of the board of managers of the General Missionary Society. One of those most seriously considered for bishop of Pennsylvania when Dr. O. W. Whitaker was chosen, he was elected coadjutor bishop of Rhode Island in 1897, and became bishop at the death of Bishop Thomas M. Clark [*q.v.*] in 1903. His interest in civic and philanthropic affairs and his catholic spirit soon made him in fact as well as in name one of the first citizens of the state. He was a fearless, yet wise and generous fighter in the cause of righteousness, active in the Watch and Ward Society and president of the Rhode Island Anti-Saloon League, and an outspoken opponent of the political corruption then existing. When his unexpected death from pneumonia at his summer home, Beverly Farms, Mass., was announced, tributes of esteem and affection poured in from people of all classes and faiths.

[*Who's Who in America*, 1910–11; *Providence Daily Jour.*, June 29, 30, and July 2, 1910; *Churchman*, July 9, 1910; *Living Church*, July 9, 1910; *Outlook*, July 9, 1910.]

H. E. S.

McVICKER, JAMES HUBERT (Feb. 14, 1822–Mar. 7, 1896), actor and theatrical manager, was born in New York City, the son of James and Nancy McVicker. With only the most elementary education, he became an apprentice in a printing-shop. In 1837 he went to St. Louis and served for a time as printer on the *St. Louis Republican.* His interest in the theatre, which had been aroused by visits to the local stock company managed by Noah Miller Ludlow [*q.v.*] and Solomon Franklin Smith [*q.v.*], caused him to abandon his trade and go to New Orleans where there was an opening for him at the St. Charles, another Ludlow-Smith theatre. It was there he made his début as an actor, playing the rôle of the old servant in *The Honeymoon,* and it was also under these veteran Western producers that he served his theatrical apprenticeship, at both the St. Charles and the American theatres, in New Orleans. On May 2, 1848, he made his first appearance in Chicago as first low comedian under the management of James B. Rice, prominent political leader and theatrical pioneer of the growing city. For three years he remained a valuable member of Rice's company, becoming eventually stage manager. Having decided, however, to do a more specialized type of acting, McVicker bought from the widow of Danforth Marble [*q.v.*] the rich collection of original Yankee comedies which various authors had written especially for her husband during his lifetime. With a repertory made up of these rôles McVicker built for himself a growing reputation in the Eastern theatres and in London, where with considerable success he opened at the Drury Lane Theatre in 1855. Although throughout his career McVicker continued to appear as an actor in varying rôles, his fame rests much more securely on his activities as manager and producer.

Shortly after his return from England he was invited by George Wood, owner of the People's Theatre in St. Louis, to serve as his manager. McVicker had been in St. Louis but a short time when Wood suggested that they extend their joint activities by opening a theatre in Chicago in opposition to Rice. For most of the financing Wood was to be responsible, while his manager's rôle was that of superintending the construction of a theatre and the assembling of a company. In the midst of carrying out these responsibilities in Chicago, McVicker received word that the financier had withdrawn his support. But overcoming the serious embarrassment which resulted, McVicker was able, with help from other sources, to carry through the original enterprise and in November 1857 to open the New Chicago Theatre with *The Honeymoon* and *The Rough Diamond.* In spite of the many excellent features of the new theatre, McVicker was forced for a number of years to struggle against an accumulation of financial difficulties arising from the panic of 1857 and against rather stiff competition from Rice and others. It was not until the unexpected boom of Chicago during the years after 1862 that the young manager was able to establish his theatre on a profitable basis. In 1864 the building was completely remodeled, and seven years later, thanks to the large receipts which various visiting stars had brought to the box office, McVicker was able to build a still more handsome theatre. Although this was almost immediately destroyed by the great fire of 1871, so firmly was his prestige established that within less than a year, the manager had built his third theatre, which for the next eighteen years, through various developments of the stock, the star, and the combination systems of production, maintained its leadership over its increasingly numerous rivals. This building, remodeled in 1885, was destroyed by fire in 1890, but the following year the final McVicker Theatre opened its doors with a brilliant performance of *The Rivals.*

Owing to ill health, McVicker some years before his death surrendered the direction of this enterprise to the McVicker Company, of which he owned the controlling shares. In Chicago McVicker enjoyed the same prestige as the great New York managers, Lester Wallack, Augustin Daly, and Albert M. Palmer. According to Edward Freiberger, he was "an actor-manager in the fullest and best sense of the word. His stock companies were among the very best in the United States, some of the most accomplished and popular members being members of the same. . . . Mr. McVicker's productions left little to be desired either in the casting of the plays or in the scenic environment. His revivals of *The School for Scandal, A Midsummer Night's Dream* and *The Tempest* were among the most elaborate and correct the American stage has ever known." Imbued with a high civic sense, McVicker was active in numerous phases of Chicago's life, and with outspoken aggressiveness maintained the lofty rôle played by the theatre in the life of society. His first wife was Annie Levering; his second Mrs. Runnion, whose daughter Mary adopted the name of McVicker before her marriage to Edwin Booth.

[N. M. Ludlow, *Dramatic Life as I Found It* (1880); Edward Freiberger, "Theater Beginnings in Chicago," *Theatre Mag.*, June 1911; M. B. Leavitt, *Fifty Years in Theatrical Management* (1912); *Chicago Tribune,* Mar. 8, 1896; *N. Y. Clipper,* Mar. 14, 1896; *N. Y. Dramatic Mirror,* Mar. 14, 21, 1896; A. T. Andreas,

Hist. of Chicago, vols. I and II (1884–85); J. H. McVicker, *The Press, the Pulpit, and the Stage* (1883).]

E. M., Jr.

MACWHORTER, ALEXANDER (July 15, 1734 o.s.–July 20, 1807), Presbyterian clergyman, was born in New Castle County, Del., the son of Hugh and Jane MacWhorter. His father's ancestors, who spelled the family name McWirter or McWhirter, and his mother's as well, had emigrated from Scotland to the north of Ireland. Hugh, a linen merchant in the county of Armagh, came to America and settled in Delaware about 1730. Upon his death in 1748, Alexander went with his mother to North Carolina, where three older children were then living. Here he was awakened to a vivid sense of his sinfulness through the preaching of Rev. John Brown, a "New Light" minister, and for several years experienced great distress of mind. After a time he returned to Delaware and attended an academy in Newark. Later he spent two years at the school of Rev. Samuel Finley [*q.v.*], West Nottingham, Pa., where "he was enabled for the first time to rest his soul on Christ." In May 1756 he entered the junior class of the College of New Jersey, graduating in the autumn of 1757. After studying theology under Rev. William Tennent of Freehold, N. J., in August 1758 he was licensed to preach by the Presbytery of New Brunswick, and in October of the following year he married Mary, daughter of Robert Cumming of Freehold, high sheriff of the county of Monmouth. Ordained at Cranberry, N. J., July 4, 1759, he was soon afterwards installed as pastor of the Presbyterian church, Newark. Here, except for a brief interim, he remained until his death forty-eight years later.

During this period he gathered into his church the fruits of six extensive revivals; rose to leadership in his denomination; and in the days of the Revolution was one of the most conspicuous patriots among the clergy of his locality. While on a visitation to the churches of North Carolina with Elihu Spencer [*q.v.*] in 1764, he developed "a hectick, accompanied with expectoration of blood." After being partially incapacitated for a couple of years, he sought a cure in the climate of Boston, where, strangely enough, he became well, and thereafter was in vigorous health, except for "a paralytick affection in his hands, which he inherited from his father." In 1775, appointed by the Continental Congress, he went to North Carolina to try to win over the Loyalists. His patriotic activities attracted the notice of the British, who, when they invaded Newark in November 1776, inquired for MacWhorter, who had fled, and ransacked the parsonage. In a letter written to Congress Mar. 12, 1777, he describes the unjustifiable conduct of the enemy. When Washington was encamped opposite Trenton, MacWhorter advised with him regarding the safety of New Jersey, and was present at the counsel which recommended the crossing of the Delaware. In the summer of 1778 he became chaplain of General Knox's brigade, but resigned the following year because of the condition of his wife, who had been struck by lightning. Sought by the British and his parish impoverished by the war, in 1779 he accepted a call to the church in Charlotte, N. C., and to the presidency of Charlotte Academy. Scarcely had he settled here, however, when Cornwallis entered the town, and MacWhorter and his family were forced to flee, losing what books and other belongings they still possessed. After a brief stay in Abington, Pa., in April 1781 he resumed his pastorate in Newark.

A man of cool deliberation and sound judgment, never sanguine, always cautious, he was at his best in deliberate assemblies and in the management of large affairs. "He possessed little fancy, but a deep and solid judgment," said the assistant of his later days, Rev. Edward D. Griffin [*q.v.*]. "His genius had no uncommon share of vivacity; it held a stately and even course. It had no wings; but it stood like the pillars of the earth. He never would have gathered laurels in the paths of poetry; but he would have filled with superior dignity the seat of justice" (*A Sermon Preached . . . at the Funeral of the Rev. Alexander MacWhorter, D.D.*, 1807). A member of almost all the important committees of the synod, he was also influential in settling the confession of faith and framing the constitution of the Presbyterian Church of the United States. He was a charter trustee of the General Assembly, serving until 1803. From 1772 until his death he was a trustee of the College of New Jersey, and when the college buildings were burned in 1802, he went to New England and raised $7,000 for their restoration. Yale had conferred the degree of Doctor of Divinity upon him in 1776. On Christmas 1806 he was injured by a fall, and in the following July he died. Several of his sermons were published separately, including one in memory of Washington (1800), and *A Century Sermon* (1807) containing a brief history of the Presbyterian church in Newark; also two volumes of collected sermons, *A Series of Sermons upon the Most Important Principles of Our Holy Religion* (1803).

[J. F. Stearns, *Hist. Discourses, Relating to the First Presbyterian Church in Newark* (1853); Wm. B.

Sprague, *Annals Am. Pulpit,* vol. III (1858); *The Biog. Encyc. of N. J. of the Nineteenth Century* (1877); Jos. Atkinson, *The Hist. of Newark, N. J.* (1878); J. T. Headley, *The Chaplains and Clergy of the Revolution* (1864); S. D. Alexander, *Princeton College During the Eighteenth Century* (1872). MacWhorter's letter to Congress is printed in part in *Archives of the State of N. J.,* 2 ser. I (1901), 350–53. His name is sometimes spelled McWhorter, M'Whorter, or Macwhorter.]

H. E. S.

MACY, JESSE (June 21, 1842–Nov. 3, 1919), prairie philosopher and political scientist, was born, amidst pioneer conditions, near Knightstown, Ind., the son of William and Phoebe (Hiatt) Macy and a descendant of Thomas Macy who emigrated to New England before 1639 and settled later in Nantucket. His parents were Quakers, active in the Underground Railroad. Among the boy's vivid experiences was "hearing stories told by fugitive slaves" at his own fireside. In 1856 the family moved in a covered wagon to another pioneer community near Lynnville, Jasper County, Iowa. Three years later young Macy, "a tall gangling figure in a butternut suit," betook himself to Grinnell, Iowa, to prepare for college. After two years he transferred to a Friends' Institute near Oskaloosa, Iowa, but in September 1864 he was drafted into the army and marched with Sherman to the sea as a non-combatant in hospital service. The war over, he resolved to devote himself to the political reconstruction of his country and, in preparation, spent the years 1866–70 in Iowa (now Grinnell) College. There he encountered Darwin's theory of evolution which completely changed his whole outlook on life. On his graduation he began his forty-two years' career as teacher in his alma mater, first in the academy and then in the college in the chair of political science, created by himself (1884–1912). He believed it "his duty to use every endeavor toward the attainment of a more righteous order in the state and in society, regardless of the prospects of success" (*Autobiography,* p. 25). It seemed to him also that the scientific spirit and method which had accomplished so much in science "would be even more beneficent when applied to political science" (*Ibid.,* p. 33).

He was the first to advocate teaching civil government in the public schools by first-hand observation of the workings of local government. In his college teaching he abandoned textbook and lecture and attempted by the Socratic method to stimulate the students to think for themselves. He was no mere closet-philosopher; he played an active part in local politics and wrote widely in the press and magazines on the tariff, gold standard, public utilities, and woman's suffrage. Isolated in a small college, he worked alone under great handicaps, and his intellectual growth was slow and deliberate. Nevertheless, by the time he was sixty he had won recognition as an original thinker both in America and Great Britain. This achievement was in part due to the devoted cooperation of Mary Maude Little whom he had married on July 25, 1872. The years 1887–88 and 1895–96 he spent abroad, chiefly in England, where he formed a lifelong friendship with James Bryce and was at home in the London Economic Club and the Fabian Society. In his later years he received many honors. He lectured in leading American universities, was Harvard exchange lecturer in the provincial universities of France (1913), and became president of the American Political Science Association (1916).

His political and social philosophies were the fruit of his early pioneer experiences, the study of Darwin and Spencer, and his deep religious convictions. He shared Lincoln's faith in the homely wisdom of the common people and never lost touch with them. He could have as readily doubted "the life-giving air" he breathed as doubt "the continual divine presence" (*Autobiography,* p. 22). To him the "acceptance of evolution and the attempt to carry the scientific spirit and method into the study of politics was a distinctly religious experience" and only the religious motive led him to "persevere against what seemed insuperable obstacles" (*Ibid.,* p. 25). He maintained that science and democracy had come into the world at the same time, that they were mutually related as cause and effect, and that science was fitted to be a determining factor in the establishment of righteousness in government. He was confident too that democracy in the post-war world would achieve a fuller and richer life than it had before achieved and that the democratic nations would "learn to cooperate through a United States of the World" (*Ibid.,* p. 148). His last letter was a plea for the League of Nations as a means of eliminating war.

Tall and erect, with a frank open countenance, Macy had the natural dignity and unconscious simplicity of the pioneer. In an age of theological and political rancor, he remained open-minded and serene. He had the honesty and courage to live his own philosophy while his rich humor and friendliness of spirit disarmed bitterness. Included in his published writings are: *Civil Government in Iowa* (1881); *Institutional Beginnings in a Western State* (1884); *Our Government* (1886); *The English Constitution* (1897); *Political Parties in the United States, 1846–61* (1900); *Party Organization and*

Machinery (1904); *Comparative Free Government* (1915), with J. W. Gannaway; and *The Anti-Slavery Crusade* (1919) in the Chronicles of America Series edited by Allen Johnson.

[The chief source is *Jesse Macy, an Autobiog.* (1933), edited and arranged by Macy's daughter, Katherine Macy Noyes, assisted by Albert Shaw, J. S. Nollen, and Chas. E. Payne. Other sources include: *Who's Who in America,* 1918–19; S. J. Macy, *Geneal. of the Macy Family from 1635–1868* (1868); the *Grinnell Rev.,* Nov. 1919; *Iowa Jour. of Hist. and Pol.,* Jan. 1920; *Annals of Iowa,* July 1920; the *Am. Pol. Sci. Rev.,* Feb. 1920.] C. E. P.

MACY, JOHN ALBERT (Apr. 10, 1877–Aug. 26, 1932), author, literary critic, poet, was born in Detroit, Mich., the son of Powell and Janet Foster (Patten) Macy and a descendant of Thomas Macy who emigrated to New England before 1639 and settled in Nantucket. He was reared in modest circumstances. From Malden High School he entered Harvard in 1895. Dependent largely on his own resources, he achieved a brilliant academic as well as extra-curricular record. Alone in the class of 1899 he received honorable mention on four counts. He won the Phi Beta Kappa key, was editor-in-chief of the *Harvard Advocate* and an editor of the *Lampoon,* was elected to the best clubs, and was chosen class poet. After graduation he was appointed assistant in English at Harvard. Two years later he became advisory master in the Ellet School at Richmond, Va., a connection which he maintained for eighteen years. In 1901 he joined the staff of the *Youth's Companion* and remained as associate editor for eight years. His first serious literary effort, *Edgar Allan Poe* (1907), was followed by *A Child's Guide to Reading* (1909), and *The Spirit of American Literature* (1913). In 1913 he became literary editor of the *Boston Herald.* His articles brought distinction to its book-page, but differences between him and the management brought his retirement after a year.

He had become a Socialist in 1909, "largely through observing the asininities of the present system" (personal conversation). Desiring first-hand experience with what he believed to be the coming social system, he served as secretary in 1912 to the then-Socialist mayor of Schenectady, George R. Lunn. In 1916 Macy published *Socialism in America.* It was this slender volume that caused him to be refused membership in the Harvard Club of New York in 1920 (*Harvard College Class of 1899,* 5th Report, 1924). More gleefully did he record that his views on the folly of war had earned him "the supreme honor of having been reported as a traitor to the . . . fools in Washington, D. C., who were called with unconscious irony the 'Intelligence Department'" (*Ibid.,* p. 428). At the outbreak of the World War in 1914 he had been accepted for an American volunteer ambulance unit, but, as he said, "the armchair patriots . . . were not able to find money for my passage and expenses." He was referring to some of his fellow members of the St. Botolph Club, which for the major part of his Boston residence was in effect his retreat and home. It was here, paradoxically, that he had composed in 1917 his stirring poem "France," read at a banquet in honor of the French military mission to Harvard.

Macy was a vigorous and original thinker. In conservative surroundings he appeared an iconoclast. It was his intellectual pioneering that established his enduring contribution to American letters and criticism. As early as November 1906 in an *Atlantic Monthly* article he extolled Joseph Conrad, then little known. His book, *The Spirit of American Literature,* blazed the trail which has become a well-worn and generally accepted thoroughfare. In lucid and trenchant phrasing Macy pointed out that, excepting Thoreau, Whitman, Mark Twain, and when at their best, Whittier, Lowell, and Emerson, and Mrs. Stowe in *Uncle Tom's Cabin* only, American writers turned "their backs on life" in America. And he plead for and prophesied the subsequent realism. Edith Wharton's *Ethan Frome* and Theodore Dreiser's *Jennie Gerhardt* he signalized as the only contemporary novels that came "to grips with the problems of life."

In 1918 Macy published *Walter James Dodd, a Biographical Sketch,* concerning one of the pioneers and martyrs of roentgenology. This tribute reveals what Macy deemed true service to society. In 1920 he moved to New York. In 1922–23 he was literary editor of the *Nation.* His sympathies for fellow craftsmen in financial distress at times led him to assign books to reviewers against his reasoned judgment. He was impulsively warm-hearted, generous, careless of his own material interests, improvident. A genial sweetness, a deep kindliness, pervaded his personal contacts. His irony and barbed wit he reserved for the shams and injustices of society. From 1926 till his death he was literary adviser to the publishing house of William Morrow & Company. He contributed the article "Journalism" to the symposium *Civilization in the United States* (edited by H. E. Stearns, 1922), and on "Massachusetts" to *These United States* (edited by Ernest Gruening, 1923). He published *The Critical Game* (1922); *The Story of the World's Literature* (1925); *The Romance of America as Told in Our Literature* (1930); *About Women* (1930), and, in collaboration with Blanche Col-ton Williams, *Do You Know English Literature?* (1930). His last work was editing a symposium, *American Writers on American Literature* (1931), in which he called for "a scholarship which shall be both erudite and animated; an unofficial free-and-easy criticism, irreverent, skeptical, watchful of humbug and stupidity, yet not itself lacking in amenity; a sober, aggressive criticism which sees literature as life itself and does not forget that humor and merriment are essential ingredients." That was his own critic's credo. With it he had for a generation infused new light and lightness into the staid academicism that before him had ruled almost unchallenged.

At the time of his instructorship at Harvard, Macy became profoundly interested in Helen Keller, who had entered Radcliffe in 1900. In 1903 he edited her book, *The Story of My Life*. His devotion to the blind deaf-mute prodigy led to his marriage in 1905 to her teacher and life-companion, Anne Mansfield Sullivan of Wrentham, Mass. He was unhappy in this marriage and a separation followed. Unable to secure a divorce he entered into an intensely happy companionship with a deaf-mute, a woman of talent and charm, a sculptor by profession. She died after five years, but their daughter survived. Macy died suddenly of a heart attack after delivering the third of a series of five lectures on rebellious currents in American literature before a gathering of trade union workers at Unity House, Stroudsburg, Pa.

[*Harvard College Class of 1899*, first report (1902); second report (1905); third report (1909); fourth report (1914); fifth report (1924); *Who's Who in America*, 1930–31; *The Publishers' Weekly*, Sept. 3, 1932; *Nation*, Oct. 4, 1922, Oct. 10, 1923, Sept. 7, 1932; *N. Y. Times*, Aug. 27, 1932; G. E. De Mille, *Lit. Criticism in America* (1931); personal recollections and conversations.]

E. G.

MACY, JOSIAH (Feb. 25, 1785–May 15, 1872), merchant captain, founder of the shipping and commission house of Josiah Macy & Son, was born at Nantucket, Mass., the son of Jonathan and Rose (Pinkham) Macy. He was a descendant of Thomas Macy (or Macie), one of the first settlers of Nantucket. Like the majority of the islanders, the Macys were members of the Society of Friends. Josiah received a common-school education, and at the age of twenty, Feb. 6, 1805, he married Lydia Hussey. Beginning his career under his father in a coastwise trading voyage, he engaged in coastwise trade for fifteen years, becoming a shipmaster when hardly out of his teens. On outbound voyages cargoes of sperm and whale oil, whalebone, and sperm candles were carried; these were sometimes consigned, but frequently were peddled from port to port. The proceeds were reinvested in outfits required by the Nantucket whalemen and in provisions needed in the homes of the islanders.

Macy made his first foreign voyage to Gibraltar, Cadiz, and Lisbon with a Nantucket cargo in 1807. In 1808, word of an intended embargo having been brought to Nantucket, he immediately loaded and cleared his one-hundred-ton ship for Spain and was towed out of the harbor and over the bar by a flotilla of whaleboats, according to the practice of that day. After a voyage of continuous anxiety, he reached the island of Fayal, disposed of his cargo, and returned to Nantucket with a load of wine, oranges, and specie. After an interval of coasting, in 1810 he sailed in the brig *Little William* to the Mediterranean. In 1812 he bought the ship *Prudence*, of 243 tons, and sailed for Spain. On his return he made New York and from there was the first to bring to Nantucket the news of the United States' declaration of war against Great Britain. His ship was laid up until the cessation of hostilities.

Nantucket was an unprotected island town of about 8,000 inhabitants, wholly at the mercy of either force. The islanders were non-combatants. Under the circumstances they preserved a tacit neutrality throughout the war, but their trade was gone and there was great difficulty in securing bare necessities. In October 1813 Macy went to Baltimore and commenced buying flour, shipping it in small schooners to Nantucket. A number of these arrived at their destination, but several were captured. Later he commanded one of three vessels, to which the British gave letters of protection, for the purpose of proceeding to Philadelphia for provisions. By accepting British papers the ships were open to capture by American naval vessels; but the plight of the islanders was well understood and sympathized with by the mainlanders, and the ships were not searched. At the conclusion of the war Macy entered the New York-Liverpool trade with a new ship, the *Edward*, of 346 tons. The next fourteen years he spent on the western ocean, concluding his final voyage as shipmaster in 1827.

The following year he founded in New York the shipping and commission house of Josiah Macy & Son, with William H. Macy, his eldest son, as partner. When they came of age, his two younger sons were admitted to the firm. Retiring from business in 1853, having amassed a considerable fortune, he spent the remainder of his life on his farm in Rye, N. Y. A number of men who afterward achieved distinction have testified to the aid given, and the good influence exerted in their early lives by Macy; among them, Capt. Benjamin Morrell [*q.v.*], who was the first American to explore south of the Antarctic circle. Macy served on many business directorates, and was a worthy citizen; but he does not appear to have been concerned with state affairs. He was the founder of a great fortune at a time when great fortunes in the nation were few.

[A long autobiographical letter, dated Dec. 1867, is printed in S. J. Macy, *Geneal. of the Macy Family from 1635–1868* (1868). See also L. S. Hinchman, *Early Settlers of Nantucket* (2nd ed., 1901); *Vital Records of Nantucket, Mass. to the Year 1850* (5 vols., 1925–28); Benjamin Morrell, *A Narrative of Four Voyages . . .* (1832); files of the *Nantucket Inquirer*; N. Y. *World*, May 16, 1872.] C. W. A.

MACY, VALENTINE EVERIT (Mar. 23, 1871–Mar. 21, 1930), capitalist, philanthropist, and public official, was born in New York City, a son of Josiah and Caroline (Everit) Macy. The progenitor of the family in America was Thomas Macy (or Macie), whose settlement on Nantucket Island is commemorated in Whittier's ballad "The Exiles." Most of the Nantucket Macys and their descendants were Friends. Josiah, an official of the Standard Oil Company, had inherited a fortune, the foundation of which had been laid by a group of Nantucket whalers. His grandfather Josiah [*q.v.*] and his father William H. had established in 1828 the firm of Josiah Macy & Son, New York. When Josiah, Jr., died in 1876, he left a large estate to which the son succeeded on reaching his majority. Meanwhile, his education proceeded chiefly under private tutors at home and abroad. At seventeen he was interested in teaching wood-carving to city boys. Later he entered the Columbia University College of Architecture and received the degree of Ph.B. in 1893, but was never active professionally. For many years he was chiefly occupied with the care of his estate, giving much time, however, to public causes, notably the Teachers College of Columbia University, the Metropolitan Museum of Art, and the National Child Labor Committee.

Macy established a residence at Scarboro, Westchester County. In the fall of 1913 a county superintendent of the poor was to be elected and Macy's friends succeeded in placing his name on the Democratic and Progressive tickets. Though strongly opposed by the old-line Republican leaders, he was elected. Upon taking charge of the poor farm and almshouse he at once installed an accounting and purchasing system that within two years reduced the per capita cost of caring for inmates more than twenty per cent., while at the same time he introduced an improved diet that lowered the number of deaths from diabetes and nephritis sixty per cent. For the first time, able-bodied adult inmates were put to work. Macy's chief concern, however, was for the dependent children. He expanded the system under which they were placed in homes throughout the county, and employed a staff of trained social workers in connection therewith. Since public funds were not available at first, he paid the salaries of these workers out of his own pocket for several years, the entire charge being eventually assumed by the county when the value of the service had been fully demonstrated. After three years of his administration Macy, now a candidate of both Democrats and Republicans, was reëlected by a virtually unanimous vote. The title of his office was changed to commissioner of charities and corrections, and later to commissioner of public welfare. The county hospital was separated from the almshouse and a desirable site was acquired for a modern hospital building, to be known as Grasslands; for the purposes of the department of child welfare eight districts were erected in the county; and a county penitentiary was planned for correctional work with first offenders. The World War, during which Macy served as head of the labor-adjustment commission for the United States Shipping Board, delayed the completion of many of his plans for the expansion of county welfare work, but in 1920 the hospital was opened and within three years was so overcrowded that in 1923 its capacity had to be increased from 350 to 500 beds.

When Macy resigned the commissionership, after more than ten years of service, he had clearly shown how a county government may cooperate with enlightened private effort in attacking the causes of dependency. A paper read by him in 1921 before the Congress of the American Prison Association was subsequently published under the title, *Self-Government on a County Prison Farm* (1922). His wife, Edith W. Carpenter, whom he married Feb. 18, 1896, was actively interested in the Girl Scouts, and after her death in 1925 Macy made generous gifts to that organization as memorials to her. As president of the Westchester County park commission he devoted much time in the last four years of his life to the beautification of the county park system, which was placed upon a practically self-supporting basis. He died of bronchial pneumonia near Phoenix, Ariz. Two sons and a daughter survived him.

[S. J. Macy, *Geneal. of the Macy Family from 1635–1868* (1868); D. W. Hoyt, *The Old Families of Salisbury and Amesbury, Mass.*, vol. I (1897); *N. Y. Times*,

Mar. 22, 1930; *Who's Who in America,* 1928–29; Ruth Taylor, "Child Welfare in Westchester County," in *Proc. of the Nat. Conference of Social Work,* 1919; W. D. Lane, "A Rich Man in the Poorhouse," in *The Survey* (N. Y.), Nov 4, 1916; *Reports of the Westchester County Park Commission,* 1926–29; *Milestones of Ten Years of the Westchester Way* (1924), a summary of Macy's work as commissioner of public welfare.]

W. B. S.

MADDEN, JOHN EDWARD (Dec. 28, 1856–Nov. 3, 1929), breeder of race horses, was born in Bethlehem, Pa. He was of Irish descent, his grandfather having been a political refugee who emigrated to the United States with his family. As a boy, after working in the steel mills at Bethlehem, he became a professional athlete, as a foot-racer, broad-jumper, boxer, and oarsman, later retiring to become a manager of other athletes. Having a natural love for horses, he began investing his savings in trotters. His ventures from the first were unusually successful, which he himself attributed to "luck and logic," and he soon accumulated a good working capital. Two of the first horses of note that he acquired, the gelding Class Leader, 2:22¼, and the stallion Warlock, he bought for low prices and sold for $10,000 each.

After establishing himself firmly as a judge of trotting horses, he turned to the thoroughbred. He was not merely interested in race horses because of their financial possibilities but aspired to become a breeder of great horses. Purchasing a farm near Lexington, Ky., in the heart of the blue-grass region, he there embarked in the breeding business, first in a small way; then, by gradual expansion, he became one of the largest breeders in the world, his stud including over four hundred brood mares at one time and a dozen or more famous stallions. He became America's leading breeder of winners in 1916 and remained so annually for eleven years. During the fourteen years preceding his death, horses bred by him had won over 5,000 public races and over $5,000,000 in stake and purse money on both sides of the Atlantic, for many horses of his breeding were sent abroad to race in his own and other colors. Two horses of his breeding were Zev, winner of $313,639, the largest amount of money at that time credited to any horse, in America or Europe, and Princess Doreen, from 1925 to 1931 the leading American money-winning mare, credited with $174,745. He bred also no less than five winners of the Kentucky Derby: Old Rosebud (1913), Sir Barton (1919), Paul Jones (1920), Zev (1923), and Flying Ebony (1925). He continued to breed trotters throughout his career, but on a smaller scale, and produced many famous ones, Periscope, 2:03½, Margaret Parrish, 2:06¼ (the dam of Arion Guy, 1:59½, and grand-dam of Protector, 1:59¼, and The Marchioness, 1:59¼, and others. His sales of both trotters and thoroughbreds for sensational prices were constant and made him facile princeps in the turf world.

Madden was a man of striking personality, combining a Herculean physique with a mentality of great force and acumen. He was celebrated for his epigrams and aphorisms and his quickness in both thought and action. These qualities enabled him to accumulate a tremendous fortune. He was married to Ann Megrue, of Cincinnati, Ohio, from whom he was divorced many years before his death. He died at his hotel in New York City.

[Neil Newman, *Famous Horses of the Am. Turf,* vol. I (1931); L. H. Weeks, *The Am. Turf* (1898); *Daily Racing Form* (N. Y.), Nov. 5, 1929; *Horse Rev.,* Nov. 6, 1929; the *Thoroughbred Record,* Nov. 9, 16, 1929; *Nat. Turf Digest,* Jan. 1930; *N. Y. Times,* Nov. 4, 1929; various manuals of turf statistics, and personal acquaintance.]

J. L. H.

MADDEN, MARTIN BARNABY (Mar. 20, 1855–Apr. 27, 1928), congressman, was born in Darlington, England, the son of John and Elizabeth (O'Neill) Madden. At the age of five he emigrated with his parents and settled in Lemont, Cook County, Ill., where he went to public school. Family necessity forced him to start earning money at the age of ten, and his subsequent education was gained in night school and business college. His first position as waterboy in a quarry at Lemont opened a career in the stone business that carried him to an important position in the Western Stone Company, which became one of the largest concerns of its kind in the world. This prominent position brought to him other offices, such as the presidency of the Quarry Owners' Association of the United States, and of the Illinois Manufacturers' Association, and the vice-presidency of the Builders' and Traders' Exchange of Chicago.

Becoming interested in politics he began in 1889 an eight-year period of service in the Chicago city council, of which he was president from 1891 to 1893. Here he affiliated with the dominant Cook County machine so closely that the Municipal Voters' League frowned upon his activities in behalf of so-called "boodle ordinances" alleged to have conferred franchises without adequate compensation to the city. In the early stages of the campaign for a seat in the United States Senate in 1897, he was supported by the Cook County machine which, however, deserted him when it became evident that he could not win the nomination. Promptly swinging his support to William E. Mason, he helped complete the wreck of the machine and started a realignment in the local Republican party. Later joining the Lorimer faction, he made an unsuccessful race for the House in 1902 but was elected in 1904 to the Fifty-ninth and each succeeding Congress through the seventieth. These activities were punctuated by party service on various local committees, as temporary chairman of the state convention in 1896, and as delegate to the national conventions of 1896 and 1900. At the latter convention he was a member of the committee on resolutions and drafted the plank in the platform that committed the party to the construction of a canal across either Panama or Nicaragua.

In the House he evinced a good deal of ability, rather unusual activity, and a high degree of party regularity, the last marked by occasional streaks of intelligent independence. Much of his early work naturally centered around local interests and his committee assignments, and in these days he showed special solicitude for the welfare of postal workers and the postal service as a whole. He was probably the most progressive member of the Chicago delegation on questions of railroad rate regulation, frequently supporting the various measures intended to increase the powers of the Interstate Commerce Commission. He made repeated efforts to obtain a physical valuation of the roads as a basis for a fair assignment of charges. His interests tended to concentrate more and more upon fiscal and financial matters, and he was made a member of the committee on appropriations in the Sixty-sixth Congress and helped to frame the bill to create the bureau of the budget. In that same Congress he also became a member of the "steering committee." As chairman of the powerful committee on appropriations in the Sixty-seventh Congress, he celebrated his elevation by bringing in the first appropriation bill under the new budget system. His chief claim to fame in the later days lay in the fact that his committee position and his natural bent made him one of the long line of "watchdogs of the treasury," being considered by the contemporary press as, perhaps, the grimmest of them all. In 1925 he published in the *Saturday Evening Post* two articles on "Tax Reduction and the Public Debt" and "The Budget to Date" (Oct. 17, Nov. 7), which are popular expositions of his ideas on the relation of the government to the money acquired by federal taxation. He died from a heart attack at his desk in the room of the appropriations committee at the Capitol. He was survived by his widow, Josephine (Smart) Madden, whom he had married on May 16, 1878, and by their daughter.

[E. W. Brent, *Martin B. Madden* (1901); *Memorial Services Held in the House of Representatives* (1929); *Biog. Directory of the Am. Cong.* (1928); *Who's Who in America*, 1926–27; *Review of Reviews* (N. Y.), Nov. 1925, pp. 459–60, Aug. 1926, pp. 161–62; *Literary Digest*, Nov. 14, 1925; *Evening Star* (Washington), Apr. 27, 30, 1928.]
L. E. E.

MADISON, DOLLY PAYNE (May 20, 1768–July 12, 1849), hostess, is said to have been named Dorothea for Dorothea Dandridge, afterward the second wife of Patrick Henry, but she is known to history as "Dolly." The eldest daughter and apparently the third child of John and Mary (Coles) Payne, she was born in what is now Guilford County, N. C., where her Virginian parents were spending a year with an uncle (Hunt, *post*, p. 351). Her paternal grandfather, John Payne, was an Englishman who settled in Goochland County, Va., and married Anna Fleming of Scotch descent. Her maternal grandfather was William Coles of "Coles Hill," Hanover County, Va., and formerly of Enniscorthy, County Wexford, Ireland. Brought to Virginia by her parents, Dolly grew up at "Scotchtown," in Hanover County. A member of a Quaker family, the little maid lived a restrained country life and received slight schooling. It is said, however, that her fair skin was scrupulously protected from the rays of the Southern sun; her eyes were blue and her hair was black; she was destined to grow tall and to be esteemed beautiful.

Finding the atmosphere of Virginia uncongenial and desiring to provide better educational opportunities for his numerous children, John Payne set free his slaves and in the summer of 1783 removed to Philadelphia, where he engaged unsuccessfully in business and died in 1792. Dolly Payne was married on Jan. 7, 1790, to John Todd, Jr., a lawyer and a member of the Society of Friends. Their son, John Payne Todd, was born on Feb. 29, 1792. Another son was born in the summer of 1793, but his life went out, soon after that of his father (Oct. 24, 1793), during the epidemic of yellow fever. Living thereafter with her mother, who had gentlemen boarders, Dolly Todd was too much admired and sought after to remain a widow long. Senator Aaron Burr introduced to her James Madison [*q.v.*], almost a score of years her elder, and on Sept. 15, 1794, at the home of her sister Lucy, Mrs. George Steptoe Washington, at "Harewood," Jefferson County, Va. (now W. Va.), she became the wife of this noted congressman. The marriage proved to be an unusually happy one, but there were no children.

She became a social figure of the first importance when her husband assumed the secretaryship of state in 1801. Jefferson was a widower and Dolly Madison was in effect the "first lady." Almost invariably she assisted the informal President with his "female guests," and, unwittingly, she was a storm-center in the battle for precedence waged by the British minister, Anthony Merry (Henry Adams, *History of the United States,* 1889, vol. II, 369). Mrs. Merry criticized her dinners as being like "harvest-home" suppers, but few others objected to her generous, unassuming hospitality. She undoubtedly contributed indirectly to political harmony and served to relieve the excessive plainness of the Jeffersonian social régime. With the inauguration of her husband as president, in 1809, she blossomed into more glorious raiment, and, to one observer at least, she met all the requirements of royalty (Hunt, *post,* p. 62). Social life in the Executive Mansion became somewhat more elaborate than it had been in Jefferson's day, though the stiff formality of the Federalist era did not return. She was described by Washington Irving as "a fine, portly, buxom dame," and her "elegance" was much remarked. Her charm, however, was chiefly due to her perennial and inherent friendliness, to her remarkable memory of persons and their interests, to her unfailing tactfulness. Her popularity may have been a minor factor in Madison's reëlection, but essentially she was negative. "She was brilliant in the things she did not say and do" (Goodwin, *post,* p. 101). In August 1814 she had to flee before the British invaders, but she managed to save many state papers and a portrait of George Washington before the Executive Mansion was burned. Living after her return in "The Octagon," she again enjoyed the sunshine of popularity.

From the retirement of Madison in 1817 until his death in 1836, she remained at "Montpellier" (now spelled "Montpelier"), in Orange County, Va., caring for his aged mother (until 1829), reading to her husband and writing for him, living the busy, hospitable life of the mistress of a plantation. In 1837 she returned to Washington with her niece Anna Payne, whom she adopted; she lived at the northeast corner of Lafayette Square in a house formerly owned by Richard Cutts, husband of her beloved sister Anna, and, as "the venerable Mrs. Madison," became again a noted and honored figure. Her last public appearance was at a reception in February 1849, when she passed through the rooms of the White House on the arm of President Polk. Financial difficulties and the waywardness of her son clouded her last days. She was forced to sell "Montpellier." Congress had bought Madison's notes on the Federal Convention for $30,000 in 1837; in 1848 a further appropriation of $25,000 was made for the purchase of other manuscripts of his (*United States Statutes at Large,* V, 1846, p. 171; IX, 1851, p. 235). She died in Washington at the age of eighty-one. After ceremonies at St. John's Church, attended by the highest officials of the Republic, she was buried in the Congressional Cemetery, whence her remains were later removed to "Montpellier." Her reign as a queen of official society may have been benign rather than brilliant, but in length and popular acclaim it has had no parallel in American history.

[The Dolly Madison Collection (13 vols.) in the Lib. of Cong. consists chiefly of private correspondence during her last twenty years. It contains some poetry of her own. She signed her will "Dolley," but the more conventional spelling appears on the certificate of her marriage to Madison in the Account Book of Alexander Balmain, 1782–1821, and has been adopted in this article. Among printed sources may be cited: sketch by Mrs. S. H. Smith, in James Herring and J. B. Longacre, *The Nat. Portrait Gallery of Distinguished Americans,* III (1836); L. B. Cutts, *Memoirs and Letters of Dolly Madison* (1886); J. M. Cutts, "Dolly Madison," in *Records of the Columbia Hist. Soc.,* III (1900); A. C. Clark, *Life and Letters of Dolly Madison* (1914); M. W. Goodwin, *Dolly Madison* (1896); E. L. Dean, *Dolly Madison The Nation's Hostess* (1928); Gaillard Hunt, ed., *The First Forty Years of Washington Society Portrayed by the Family Letters of Mrs. Samuel Harrison Smith* (1906). The best-known of her portraits is the one by Gilbert Stuart, reproduced in Dean and other biographies.] D. M.

MADISON, JAMES (Aug. 27, 1749–Mar. 6, 1812), president of the College of William and Mary and first bishop of the Protestant Episcopal Church in Virginia, was born near Staunton, Va. He grew up at "Madison Hall," purchased by his father in 1851, in Augusta (now Rockingham) County. He was the son of John Madison and a cousin of President James Madison. His mother was Agatha, daughter of William Strother of King George County. After early education at home and at a private school in Maryland he entered the College of William and Mary, from which he graduated in 1771 with high honors. He studied law under George Wythe and was admitted to the bar but did not enter upon practice. In 1773 he was elected professor of natural philosophy and mathematics in the college, and in 1775 he went to England for further study and for ordination to the ministry of the Church of England. Returning to Williamsburg and his professorship, he was in 1777 elected president of William and Mary, though lacking two years of the statutory age. He held this office till his death, being relieved of the teaching of mathematics in 1784 and serving thereafter as professor of natural and moral philosophy. Like the great majority of the clergy of the Established Church in Virginia, he sup-

time, in his seventy-seventh year, Apr. 24, 1902, to Sarah Elizabeth Gardner of New York. During the last part of his life he was occupied with literary labors, including the writing of an autobiography, *Sixty-five Years in the Life of a Teacher, 1841–1906* (1907). His death occurred in New York.

[In addition to Magill's autobiography, see Wm. P. Holcomb, "Swarthmore College," in C. H. Haskins and W. I. Hull, *A Hist. of Higher Educ. in Pa.* (1902); *Who's Who in America*, 1906–07; *Friends' Intelligencer*, Twelfth mo. 21, 1907; *N. Y. Times*, Dec. 11, 1907.] W. I. H.

MAGINNIS, MARTIN (Oct. 27, 1841–Mar. 27, 1919), soldier, Montana politician, congressman, was born in Wayne County, N. Y. His parents, Patrick and Winifred (Devine) Maginnis, had come from Ireland about 1838. In 1851 the family moved to Lasalle, Ill., and in 1853 to Red Wing, Minn. Martin Maginnis attended Hamline University, then at Red Wing. Before graduating, he enlisted in the 1st Minnesota Volunteers and he served throughout the Civil War. He was in most of the battles of the Army of the Potomac and by July 1863 had attained the rank of captain. After Cold Harbor he was sent to Tennessee and assigned to the staff of Andrew Johnson, military governor of the state. At the end of the war he was mustered out with the rank of major. For a while he worked for a newspaper in Red Wing, Minn., but in 1866 he organized a party of about 150 men whom he led from Minnesota along the northern route to Montana. For a year he engaged in mining and then he joined with Peter Ronan in editing the *Daily Rocky Mountain Gazette*, which later became the *Helena Independent* (Henry N. Blake, in *Contributions to the Historical Society of Montana*, vol. V, 1904, p. 255). On Mar. 11, 1868, he was married to Louise E. Mann of Pontiac, Mich.

In a few years he became influential as a politician. His newspaper was the leading Democratic publication of the territory and he was a popular campaign orator. In 1872 he was elected delegate to Congress where he served continuously for six terms. His chief activities in the House were "serving Montana's interests." He persuaded Congress to reduce the size of the Indian reservations and to open the lands to white settlement. He obtained appropriations to build a number of military posts, secured an assay office for Helena, and induced Congress to build a federal penitentiary at Deer Lodge, later turned over to the territory. Through his influence, Congress granted land for a state university and for other state institutions. When the Northern Pacific was under fire on account of the failure of Jay Cooke, he defended its charter and secured an extension of time for the completion of the road. He also took a prominent part in securing legislation granting railways free right-of-way through the public domain and through Indian reservations. He supported appropriations for a large army, and he urged Congress to retain control of the public domain, instead of intrusting it to administrative officials.

After his retirement from Congress in 1885, having been defeated for reëlection, Maginnis engaged in mining but did not lose his interest in politics. In 1889 he was a member of the state constitutional convention. He was again defeated for representative in Congress in 1889 and, in 1890, although chosen for United States senator by one faction calling itself the legal state legislature, he was denied his seat in Washington. Governor Toole appointed him land commissioner, and for the next few years he fought the Northern Pacific's claim to minerals on its land grant, finally winning his suit for independent prospectors and miners. In 1900 he was appointed to fill the unexpired term of William A. Clark in the United States Senate, but he was not seated. A lifelong Democrat, he was delegate to eight successive national conventions. He was quick to comprehend public sentiment and to give it expression, but his popularity outlasted his influence as a politician. He died at Los Angeles, Cal., in his seventy-eighth year.

[*Who's Who in America*, 1918–19; *Biog. Dir. Am. Cong.* (1928); *Progressive Men of the State of Mont.* (n.d.); "A Partial Sketch of the Civil and Mil. Service of Maj. Martin Maginnis," *Contributions to the Hist. Soc. of Mont.*, vol. VIII (1917), and references in *Ibid.*, vols. II–VII (1896–1910); R. G. Raymer, *Montana: The Land and the People* (1930), vol. I; Tom Stout, *Montana: Its Story and Biog.* (1921), vol. I; *Proc. and Debates of the Const. Convention . . . of Mont. . . . 1889* (1921); *Los Angeles Times*, Mar. 28, 1919.] P. C. P.

MAGOFFIN, BERIAH (Apr. 18, 1815–Feb. 28, 1885), lawyer, farmer, governor of Kentucky, brother of James Wiley Magoffin [*q.v.*], was born in Harrodsburg, Ky. His father, Beriah Magoffin, was a native of County Down, Ireland; his mother, Jane McAfee, was a daughter of Samuel McAfee, an early Kentucky pioneer. He attended Centre College at Danville and was graduated there in 1835. Thereupon he began the study of law privately and afterward entered the law department of Transylvania College at Lexington where he finished his course in 1838. Immediately he moved to Mississippi and began the practice of law in Jackson. He remained in Mississippi only about a year, however, returning to Kentucky in 1839 in ill health. He now began the practice of law in his native town, and upon the death of his partner, he succeeded to a remunerative business. In 1840 Gov. Robert P. Letcher, a Whig, appointed him, a Democrat, police judge for Harrodsburg. Ten years later he ran for the state Senate and was elected, but the next year, 1851, he refused to make the race for Congress. He ran for Democratic elector in 1844, 1848, 1852, and 1856, but it was only in the last year that he served since Kentucky was lost by the Democrats in the other years. He was also delegate to the Democratic national conventions in 1848, 1856, and 1860. In 1855 he was nominated for lieutenant-governor, but the Know-Nothings won the state that year.

In 1859 he was nominated for governor and was elected over Joshua F. Bell by a vote of more than 8,000. He took office just on the eve of secession. Realizing the dangers which would beset this strategic border-state, Magoffin did all he could to prevent the disruption of the Democratic party at Charleston. On Dec. 9, 1860, he presented to the governors of the slave states a plan for saving the Union, but it failed to be accepted. He then became an ardent advocate of the Crittenden Compromise. Although a believer in secession as a right, he was opposed to the piecemeal process of leaving the Union. He pleaded for a convention of all the Southern states and declared that a solution could be worked out within forty-eight hours which would suit both sections. Believing that the people of his state should vote on what they wished to do, he called the legislature to meet in January 1861. But the legislature, which had elected John C. Breckinridge United States senator, refused to call a sovereign convention. Magoffin defiantly refused Lincoln's call for troops (Apr. 15, 1861), and a week later he refused Davis' call for troops, though secretly he allowed Confederate recruiting agents to raise their banners in the state. He summoned another session of the legislature in May, which again refused to call a sovereign convention. Instead, it allowed six arbiters, chosen in party caucus, and including Magoffin, to work out a plan which the legislature pledged itself to adopt. This move resulted in the state's declaring its neutrality, the House and Senate passing separate resolutions, and the governor issuing his proclamation on May 20. Magoffin came to terms with McClellan, in command of troops in Cincinnati, and established understandings with both President Davis and President Lincoln. But neutrality was not enough; he sought to secure the adhesion of Ohio, Indiana, Missouri, and Tennessee to a plan for mediation, but the Northern states refused to entertain the idea. Kentucky's position was impossible. By September her neutrality had been broken so many times by both sides that the Confederates decided to march into the state in full force, thereby beating the Federals in by a short time. The legislature passed a resolution (Sept. 11, 1861) calling upon the Governor to order the Confederates out. Magoffin vetoed it, but the legislature, by this time strongly Union in its feelings, passed it over his veto, as indeed it did many other bills looking toward Kentucky's full participation on the side of the Union. Magoffin obstructed this policy wherever he thought the constitution was not being observed and thereby incurred the ill will of the Unionists. Stripped of his power and threatened with assassination he resigned in August 1862, though he was allowed to designate his successor.

He retired to Harrodsburg for the remainder of the war and did not reënter politics except from 1867 to 1869 when he represented his county, Mercer, in the legislature. After the war he took the position that Kentucky should accept with resignation the results of the conflict. He advocated Kentucky's ratification of the Thirteenth Amendment and the granting of civil rights to the negroes. This position lost him the friendship of many Democrats. In 1878 President Hayes appointed him an honorary commissioner to the Paris Exposition. Magoffin had married, in April 1840, Anna Shelby, a granddaughter of Gov. Isaac Shelby, and to them were born five sons and five daughters. Through judicious investments in Chicago, he became one of the wealthiest men in the state. He died on his ancestral estate in Harrodsburg.

[Short sketches of Magoffin can be found in Lewis and R. H. Collins, *Hist. of Ky.* (1874), vol. II, and in *The Biog. Encyc. of Ky.* (1878). For the main facts concerning his public career, see Collins, *supra*, vol. I; R. M. McElroy, *Ky. in the Nation's Hist.* (1909), and E. M. Coulter, *The Civil War and Readjustment in Ky.* (1926). The state archives in Frankfort contain his state papers. Some of the important documents relative to his position in the secession and neutrality movement are in *War of the Rebellion: Official Records (Army)* and *Appletons' Ann. Cyc.*, 1861–63.]

E. M. C.

MAGOFFIN, JAMES WILEY (1799–Sept. 27, 1868), trader, American consul, and early pioneer in Texas, was born at Harrodsburg, Mercer County, Ky., the son of Beriah and Jane (McAfee) Magoffin. The family consisted of seven sons, of whom James was the eldest, and three daughters. Some time prior to 1825 James Wiley Magoffin engaged in trading expeditions into old Mexico, and the records of the Department of State contain the bare announcement (his name being spelled McGoffin) of his appointment as American consul at Saltillo on Mar. 3, 1825, the first appointee at that post. This overland trade, beset by many dangers and hazards, proved very lucrative. Magoffin, who evidently had the brave frontier spirit combined with inherited Irish buoyancy and joviality, became well known and liked in Mexico, and was called by the Mexicans "Don Santiago." He married Mary Gertrude Valdez, of Chihuahua, in 1830, and several children were born to them there. In 1844 he left Chihuahua with his family and settled near Independence, Mo. His wife died there in January 1845. About this time war was declared with Mexico. Senator Thomas H. Benton of Missouri presented Magoffin to President Polk, and on June 18, 1846, Secretary of War Marcy wrote to Gen. Stephen Watts Kearny saying that the President was so favorably impressed with "Colonel Magoffin" that he had engaged him to assist in the expedition (*House Executive Document 17,* 31 Cong., 1 Sess., pp. 240–41). Thereupon Magoffin went in advance of Kearny to Santa Fé and very cleverly induced Gen. Manuel Armijo to retire, thus enabling Kearny with his small army to enter Santa Fé on Aug. 18, 1846, and take possession of all of the Department of New Mexico without firing a shot.

After this success Magoffin, under directions of Kearny, went forward to Chihuahua to render the same service for Gen. J. E. Wool, but the authorities there arrested him as a spy and cast him into prison. He was saved from execution only through his popularity with Mexican officers, whom he entertained lavishly. He was, however, confined at Chihuahua and afterward at Durango until the end of the war (1847). By a provision of an act of Mar. 3, 1849, Congress authorized the payment of $50,000 for secret service rendered during the Mexican War. Although Magoffin was not named, the sum was designed to compensate him for his expenses and losses. After a change of administration he was finally offered $30,000, which he accepted, preferring patriotically to be underpaid rather than to wrangle over finances. He then settled in Texas, opposite the Mexican town of El Paso, and built up and owned the township of Magoffinsville, which is now a part of the city of El Paso, Tex. During the Civil War he furnished supplies to the Confederates. He died at San Antonio, Tex., in 1868. His sons, Joseph and Samuel, served in the Confederate army, the latter giving his life to that cause. His brother Beriah [*q.v.*] was governor of Kentucky.

[W. E. Connelley, *War with Mexico, 1846–47: Doniphan's Expedition and the Conquest of N. Mex. and Cal.* (1907); Stella M. Drumm, ed., *Down the Santa Fé Trail and into Mexico: The Diary of Susan Shelby Magoffin, 1846–47* (1926); T. H. Benton, *Thirty Years' View* (2 vols., 1854–56); P. St. G. Cooke, *The Conquest of N. Mex. and Cal.* (1878); H. H. Bancroft, *Hist. of Ariz. and N. Mex.* (1889); J. H. Smith, *The War with Mexico* (2 vols., 1919); *San Antonio Express,* Sept. 29, 1868.]

A. E. I.

MAGOON, CHARLES EDWARD (Dec. 5, 1861–Jan. 14, 1920), lawyer, civil administrator, was born on a farm in Steele County, Minn., the son of Henry C. and Mehitable W. (Clement) Magoon. After the family had moved to a homestead in Platte County, Neb., he attended the preparatory department 1876–78 and for one year the college of arts of the University of Nebraska. He studied law in the offices of Mason & Wheeler in Lincoln and later he became a member of the law firm of Wheedon & Magoon, practising law in Lincoln from 1882 to 1899. During this period of his life he became interested in military affairs and served as major and judge-advocate, Nebraska National Guard. He also compiled and published a treatise of considerable local value entitled *The Municipal Code of Lincoln* (1889). In the year 1899, at the instance of Assistant Secretary of War Meiklejohn, Magoon became law-officer of the Bureau of Insular Affairs of the War Department, serving in that capacity until 1904 and specializing in matters growing out of the acquisition by the United States of Cuba, Puerto Rico, and the Philippines. As such, he prepared and submitted to the Secretary of War (Feb. 12, 1900), an exhaustive study, *Report on the Legal Status of the Territory . . . Acquired by the United States During the War with Spain.* He also rendered many important interpretations of United States law affecting the country's new possessions, which were ultimately assembled and published under the title, *The Law of Civil Government in Territory Subject to Military Occupation* (1902). In a prefatory introduction to this work, Secretary Elihu Root stated that it was of such value to him in deciding important War Department problems affecting insular possessions, that he ordered the reports printed as a public document for the use of those concerned with the government of the Philippine Islands.

Magoon served as general counsel of the Isthmian Canal Commission, 1904–05, and as a member of the Commission, 1905–06. From May 25, 1905, until Oct. 12, 1906, he served as governor of the Canal Zone and for most of this period also acted as United States envoy extraordinary and minister plenipotentiary to the Republic of Panama. From Oct. 12, 1906, until Jan. 28, 1909, he served as provisional governor of Cuba during a most important period in the Island's recrudescence, in which his administration of affairs was confronted with the difficult problems concerning the maintenance of order, the development of commercial prosperity, and the inauguration of a sound financial system. Not the least of his far-reaching reforms in Cuba was the introduction of adequate sanitary measures throughout the Island and the almost complete elimination of the scourge of yellow fever. Of his administration during this period, Secretary Taft wrote to President Roosevelt, Jan. 14, 1908: "Governor Magoon has conducted matters in a most clear-headed and tactful way. . . . He has successfully handled numerous economic questions. . . . He has had labor troubles which through his conciliatory but impartial attitude have been brought to an end" (Preface to *Annual Report of Charles E. Magoon, Provisional Governor of Cuba . . . 1907*). Withal, Magoon succeeded in winning the high regard and esteem of the Cuban people.

On Feb. 19, 1904, Magoon delivered before the Patria Club of New York City an important address, printed under the title *What Followed the Flag in the Philippines* (1904), dealing in a masterly way with policies governing United States sovereignty over occupied territory, the inauguration in the Philippines of a government of law in which the Filipino people were permitted to exercise certain privileges of citizenship, and the insistence upon a policy of complete religious freedom and tolerance in newly acquired territory. Magoon never married. After his retirement he made his home in Lincoln, Neb., and Washington, D. C., passing away suddenly in the latter city after an operation for appendicitis, in the fifty-ninth year of his age.

[The Bureau of Insular Affairs of the War Department has made available considerable information affecting Magoon's service with the Bureau, up to his incumbency as governor of Cuba. Other sources include: *Who's Who in America*, 1918–19; R. C. Weightman, "Cuba's Am. Gov.," *Rev. of Revs.*, Nov. 1906; *Omaha World-Herald*, and *N. Y. Times*, Jan. 15, 1920; *Evening Star* (Washington, D. C.), Jan. 14, 15, 1920.]

C. D. R.

MAGOUN, GEORGE FREDERIC (Mar. 29, 1821–Jan. 30, 1896), Congregational clergyman, college president, was born at Bath, Me., where his grandfather, Elisha Magoun, a native of Scituate, Mass., was a pioneer ship-builder. His father, David Crooker Magoun, was ship-owner, merchant, bank president, mayor of Bath, member of the Maine legislature in both branches, and one of the authors of the first state prohibitory law; his mother, Hannah (Webb), was the daughter of William Webb, collector of the port of Bath. The Magoun family, of Huguenot descent, had been driven by persecution from France to the North of Ireland, when John Magoun had come to America, settling in 1660 on a farm three miles long on the Massachusetts coast, near Scituate.

George Frederic was graduated from Bath Academy in 1837, received the degree of B.A. from Bowdoin in 1841, and studied theology at Andover and Yale. He is represented in *The Bowdoin Poets* (1840) by a poem on "The Gathering of the Covenanters." In 1844 he went West, serving as principal of a school at Galena, Ill., 1844–45, and of the academy at Platteville, Wis., 1845–46, but then returned to Andover to complete his theological training. He was ordained, Jan. 25, 1848, at Shullsburg, Wis., where he founded a home-mission Congregational church. He was subsequently, for three years, pastor of the Second Presbyterian Church at Galena (1848–51), and served, for five years each, Congregational churches at Davenport and Lyons, Iowa. Between 1851 and 1855 he also studied and practised law.

In 1856 he became a trustee of Iowa College, Davenport, which in 1859 was removed to Grinnell. He was elected president of the college in 1862, but since most of the college men were serving in the Civil War, he continued in his pastorate at Lyons for nearly three years, resigning in 1864 to assume his academic duties. Endowed with superabundant energy, besides carrying on the administrative work of the presidency he taught in the college, wrote many articles, preached and gave public addresses, and spent himself without stint in the raising of funds for the institution after the burning of one of the two buildings in 1871 and the total destruction of all the buildings by a tornado in 1882. He repeatedly declined pastorates and college presidencies at salaries far greater than that paid by the young college at Grinnell. After twenty years' active service, in 1884 he retired from the presidency, but continued for six years longer to teach mental and moral philosophy, a task for which his metaphysical turn of mind peculiarly fitted him.

Magoun was fearless and somewhat combative in temperament, a strong and uncompromising partisan of things be believed in, great-hearted and tender in his affections. A man of large stature, commanding presence, and fine voice, he was recognized, not only as an effective pulpit orator, but also as a powerful advocate of such causes as temperance, anti-slavery, and foreign missions. He was a stanch Republican, having assisted at the forming of the party in 1854. Three times he was a delegate to Peace Congresses in Europe, and in 1882 he represented the Congregationalists of Iowa, Maine, and the National Council at the semi-centennial of the Congregational Union of England and Wales. In 1872 he gave the first of the Boston Lectures, and from 1877 to 1879 lectured on home missions at Andover Theological Seminary. His baccalaureate addresses at Grinnell were events in the life of the community. His publications include contributions to various journals, an address, *The Past of Our College* (1895), and a book on one of the religious and educational pioneers of the West: *Asa Turner, a Home Missionary Patriarch and His Times* (1889). He was twice married: in 1847 to Abby Anne Hyde of Bath, Me., who died at Lyons in 1864; and in 1870, at Waterbury, Conn., to Elizabeth E. Earle.

[*Portr. and Biog. Record of Johnson, Poweshiek and Iowa Counties, Iowa* (1893); B. F. Gue, *Hist. of Iowa* (1903), vol. IV; T. O. Douglass, *The Pilgrims of Iowa* (1911); J. B. Grinnell, *Men and Events of Forty Years* (1891); *Grinnell Herald*, Feb. 4, 1896; *Minutes of the Iowa Congreg. General Assoc.*, 1896, p. 46; *Obit. Record Grads. Bowdoin Coll.*, 1896; *Congreg. Year Book* (1897); *Iowa State Register* (Des Moines), Jan. 31, 1896; also information from family.] J. S. N.

MAGRATH, ANDREW GORDON (Feb. 8, 1813–Apr. 9, 1893), jurist and governor of South Carolina, was born, lived, and died in Charleston. His father, John Magrath, was a soldier in the Irish rebellion of 1798 who, captured by the British, escaped and fled to Charleston; his mother, Maria Gordon, came to Charleston from Scotland in 1792. He received his early education at the private school of Bishop England in Charleston and graduated in 1831 from the South Carolina College. In 1835, after studying law in the office of James L. Petigru and spending a few months at the Harvard Law School, he began the practice of law in Charleston and, with the exception of brief intervals in 1840 and 1842 when he represented the parishes of St. Philip and St. Michael in the South Carolina House of Representatives, continued in this profession until 1856. He insisted on the right of slaveholders to take their property into the newly acquired territory of the United States, and in 1848 he supported Taylor against Cass for president on the ground that the former, although a Whig, was a Southerner and a slaveholder. In 1856 he was elected as a delegate to the National Democratic Convention at Cincinnati, but he resigned before the meeting of the convention to accept an appointment as judge of the United States district court, then in great disfavor in South Carolina and rarely resorted to. He won for the court the confidence of the bar of the state, raised it to a position of commanding distinction, and together with James Connor, the district attorney, won national reputation in the cases of the *Echo* and the *Wanderer*, vessels accused of violating the law against the African slave trade.

He opposed secession as inexpedient when it was advocated by Robert Barnwell Rhett in 1852, but with the election of Abraham Lincoln as president he accepted the view that there were sufficient grounds for separation and that the dissolution of the relations of South Carolina with the Union was necessary to the welfare of the state. On Nov. 7, 1860, he resigned his position as United States district judge with the dramatic declaration that "the Temple of Justice, raised under the Constitution of the United States, is now closed" (*Charleston Daily Courier*, Nov. 8, 1860, p. 1). He was immediately afterward elected a delegate to the secession convention, where he was active in influencing the withdrawal of the state from the Union. On Dec. 30, 1860, he was appointed secretary of state in the executive council of Governor Pickens and directed much of the correspondence of the governor with President Buchanan and Major Anderson regarding the disposition of Fort Sumter. Shortly after the establishment of the Confederate government he was appointed judge of the Confederate district court in South Carolina. Although he upheld the validity of the Confederate sequestration and conscription acts (*Courier*, Nov. 9, 1861, Schwab, *post*, p. 195), some of his decisions, particularly the one declaring the Confederate war tax upon state securities unconstitutional (*Courier*, Apr. 21, 1862), ran counter to the policy of the government at Richmond and appear to have excluded him from its confidence and deprived him of its favor.

In 1864 he resigned from the moribund Confederate court and was elected governor by the legislature, the last governor of South Carolina to be elected in this manner. As governor he took an extreme state-rights position, stating in his inaugural address on Dec. 20 that his efforts would be directed equally toward resisting the invaders from the North and the encroachments of the Confederate government upon the powers of the state. He addressed strong letters to Jefferson Davis criticizing the policy of conscripting South Carolina regiments for the defense of Richmond and even entered into correspondence with Governors Vance of North Carolina and Brown of Georgia with a view to making plans for the defense of their respective states independent of the Confederate government. After the burning of Columbia, however, he was unable to reorganize the state government, and, on May 22, 1865, he issued a proclamation advising submission to the Federal authorities. On May 28 he was arrested and shortly afterward, upon the order of the President, imprisoned at Fort Pulaski. On Nov. 23 the President directed that he be released upon taking the oath of allegiance as prescribed in the amnesty proclamation. He resumed the practice of law and lived quietly in Charleston until his death in 1893. He was a man of unusual personal charm and graciousness of manner. On Mar. 8, 1843, he was married to Emma C. Mikell, by whom he had five children. During his imprisonment at Fort Pulaski he entered into a correspondence with Mary McCord, of Columbia, previously unknown to him, and upon his release they were married. They had no children.

[Leroy Youmans, "A Sketch of the Life of Gov. Magrath," Charleston *Year Book*, 1895, pp. 365–75, is reprinted in U. R. Brooks, *S. C. Bench and Bar*, vol. I (1908). See also: S. W. Crawford, *The Genesis of the Civil War* (1887); J. C. Schwab, *The Confed. States of America, 1861–65* (1901); and *War of the Rebellion: Official Records* (*Army*). The files of the Charleston *Mercury* and the Charleston *Courier* are valuable, and there is an excellent obituary in the *Courier*, Apr. 10, 1893. The Charleston Historical Society possesses copies of several letters written by Magrath to Johnson, Seward, and others while he was confined in Fort Pulaski, and also possesses three large letter-books containing copies of letters and telegrams sent by him while governor.]

J. W. P—n.

MAGRUDER, GEORGE LLOYD (Nov. 1, 1848–Jan. 28, 1914), physician, sanitarian, was the son of Thomas Contee and Elizabeth Olivia (Morgan) Magruder. His earliest American ancestor on the paternal side was Alexander McGruder of the Scotch clan Gregor. His father was paymaster with the Washington aqueduct and capitol extension and later disbursing officer under Quartermaster-Gen. M. C. Meigs. Lloyd Magruder had the advantages of both private and public school training and in 1868 received from Gonzaga College, Washington, D. C., the degree of A.B. In 1870 he graduated in medicine at Georgetown Medical School and remained in Washington to follow his chosen profession until his death. Early in his medical career he was appointed professor of chemistry at Gonzaga College (1871–73); afterward the medical faculty of Georgetown selected him prosector of minor surgery. He rapidly rose to the chair of professor of materia medica (1883–96) and was also dean and treasurer of the medical college. During the year 1871–72 he was physician to the poor and from 1883 to 1887 he administered to the police and fire departments.

Magruder was active as a member of the American Medical Society, the Washington Obstetrical and Gynecological Society, the American Public Health Association, and the Washington Academy of Sciences. He was also a member of the Medical Association of the District of Columbia and of the Medical Society of the District of Columbia. In the latter organization he was corresponding secretary, 1876–77, vice-president, 1895, and a member of the executive committee, 1902–03. He wrote several papers, including *Some Practical Observations Made at the Department of Diseases of Children at the Central Dispensary* (1880); *The Milk Supply of Washington* (1907); and *The Solution of the Milk Problem* (1913). He visualized the need for increased hospital facilities and the necessity of prompt treatment for accident cases. In cooperation with Dr. H. H. Barker and others he founded the Central Dispensary (later Emergency Hospital) and was a member of the consulting staff from its opening, May 1, 1871, until his death. He was also eager to increase clinical facilities for Georgetown medical department and was influential in the founding of Georgetown University Hospital, which opened on Aug. 1, 1898. After thirteen years as dean of the medical school he resigned in 1901. In June 1894 the District commissioners assigned Magruder to draw up a bill to regulate the milk supply for the District of Columbia, and he secured an investigation by the Department of Agriculture of the dairy supply (1906–07). In 1907, at his instigation, a permanent milk commission was established by the District of Columbia authorities.

Magruder's great desire was to make the Capital a healthful place in which to live. He devoted considerable time to ridding the community of all sources of typhoid fever, securing pure water, and closing all city pumps which were a source of infection. He conducted a thorough investigation of the milk supply and the management of dairies which resulted in bringing about the effective legislation regarding the sale of milk. His contribution to humanity was strangely his physical undoing, for the lowered resistance occasioned by the strain of his work exaggerated a glycosuria, with later symptoms of myocarditis, which closed his career. He was survived by his wife, Belle (Burns) Magruder, the daughter of Gen. W. W. Burns, whom he had married on Nov. 22, 1882.

[*Who's Who in America*, 1912–13; *Washington Medic. Annals*, May 1914; *Year Book of the Am. Clan Gregor Soc.*, 1914; J. S. Easby-Smith, *Georgetown Univ. in the District of Columbia* (2 vols., 1907); H. A. Kelly and W. L. Burrage, *Am. Medic. Biogs.* (1920); the *Evening Star* (Wash., D. C.), Jan. 29, 1914.]

M. D. M.

MAGRUDER, JOHN BANKHEAD (Aug. 15, 1810–Feb. 18, 1871), Confederate soldier, was born in Winchester, Va., the son of Thomas Magruder and Elizabeth Bankhead. The Magruders were originally members of the unfortunate Scotch Clan Gregor. After the McGregor name had been proscribed in 1603, some of the disbanded clan assumed the name of McGruder.

In 1651 one Alexander McGruder was captured at Worcester, and was sent to Maryland where he started the numerous Maryland McGruder or Magruder family, with its Virginia offshoot. John Bankhead Magruder's early education was in preparation for West Point. Here he was graduated in 1830 with the brevet rank of second lieutenant of infantry. The next year he transferred to the artillery, and for the following fifteen years served at scattered garrisons, in the occupation of Texas, and in the Seminole War. In 1836 he was promoted first lieutenant. After the outbreak of the Mexican War he was put in charge of the light artillery of Pillow's division. For "gallant and meritorious conduct" he was thrice promoted, finally being appointed, after Chapultepec, lieutenant-colonel. While other officers showed no eagerness to serve under the "restless and hot-tempered Magruder," Thomas Jonathan Jackson bent all his energies and got command under him, for Jackson knew that "if any fighting was to be done Magruder would be 'on hand' " (G. F. R. Henderson, *Stonewall Jackson and the American Civil War,* 1898, I, p. 41).

Magruder later was stationed in Maryland, California, and at Newport, R. I. During this period he devoted himself largely to society, his courtly bearing and "brilliant ability to bring appearances up to the necessity of the occasion" winning him the title of "Prince John" (*Confederate Military History,* III, p. 633). At Newport his entertainments were the envy of fashionable society. On Mar. 16, 1861, having resigned his commission, he was appointed colonel in the Confederate army and was in May put in command of the troops on the Virginia Peninsula. Not only was he one of the best trained of the Virginia officers, but he was the type to attract attention. At Big Bethel in May he won a small engagement, the much-heralded first battle of the Civil War. After Big Bethel he was made brigadier-general and in October 1861, major-general. Upon McClellan's advance in the spring of 1862, Magruder, commanding about 12,000 men, displayed much energy in building defensive works to delay him and in deceiving him in regard to the smallness of his force. While "keeping up a clutter" to fool McClellan, "Prince John" was in his element; indeed his whole conduct so far on the Peninsula won him considerable fame.

But in the Seven Days' Battle around Richmond Magruder's star went into eclipse. His failure to command efficiently was one of the numerous causes of Lee's failure to injure, if not to crush, McClellan. Magruder's force was placed on the south side of the Chickahominy in front of the enemy's left. On June 28, Lee sent orders for him to use the utmost vigilance, and, if the enemy retreated, to pursue vigorously. But Magruder gave no intimation of the Federal withdrawal that day, and it was only discovered the next sunrise by two of Longstreet's engineer officers (Long, *post,* pp. 174–75, and *War of the Rebellion: Official Records* (*Army*), 1 ser. XI, pt. 2, p. 494). On June 29, though there was a serious gap in the opposing forces, Magruder was not quick enough to take advantage of the opportunity, even sending for reinforcements (Ropes, *post,* pt. 2, pp. 191–92). In the late afternoon he attacked gallantly, first at Allen's Farm and then at Savage Station, but was repulsed with heavy loss, and the Federal rearguard continued its retreat. Lee wrote a firm note regretting his slight progress and urging him to press on vigorously (*Official Records,* 1 ser. XI, pt. 2, p. 687). There was some excuse, however, for Magruder in that he erroneously believed that Jackson had been ordered not to support him. At Malvern Hill on July 1 Magruder marched on the wrong road, but made a natural mistake for which he was unduly censured.

Magruder considered himself mistreated in the official reports. He opened a correspondence with Lee, arguing with vigor and not with literal accuracy. He was a disappointment to Lee, who desired not only good generals but men with whom he could work. On Oct. 10, 1862, Magruder was transferred to the command of the district of Texas, later enlarged to include New Mexico and Arizona. He strove to fortify the defenseless Texas coast, and equipped two cotton-clad steamers; on Jan. 1, 1863, he captured Galveston and the revenue cutter *Harriet Lane,* and drove off the blockading fleet. In March 1864 he sent most of his troops to reinforce R. H. Taylor opposing Banks in Louisiana. Upon the close of hostilities, refusing to seek parole, Magruder went to Mexico and became a major-general under Maximilian. He returned to the United States after the downfall of the Emperor and lectured upon his Mexican experiences. In 1869 he settled in Houston, Tex., where he died. He never married.

[C. A. Evans, ed., *Confed. Mil. Hist.* (1899), III, 632–34; G. W. Cullum, *Biog. Reg. . . . U. S. Mil. Acad.* (3rd ed., 1891); J. C. Ropes, *The Story of the Civil War,* pts. I and II (1894–98); A. L. Long, *Memoirs of Robert E. Lee* (1886), and "Memoir of Gen. John Bankhead Magruder," *Southern Hist. Soc. Papers,* vol. XII (1884); B. P. Lee, "Magruder's Peninsula Campaign in 1862," *Southern Hist. Soc. Papers,* vol. XIX (1891); *War of the Rebellion: Official Records* (*Army*), especially 1 ser. XI; *Year Books of Am. Clan Gregor Soc.,* 1913, 1915, 1923; *Houston Telegraph,* Feb. 19, 1871; *Houston Daily Union,* Feb. 20, 1871.] R. D. M.

MAGRUDER, JULIA (Sept. 14, 1854–June 9, 1907), novelist and writer of short stories, was born in Charlottesville, Va., the daughter of Allen Bowie and Sarah Magruder. She was the niece of the Confederate general John Bankhead Magruder [*q.v.*]. When she was three her family moved to Washington where her father practised law and where she and her two sisters were educated by governesses under the supervision of the parents. Throughout her childhood the family returned for frequent residence to Virginia. Her early training was true to the old ideals of Southern culture and taste of the mid-century. While still a young girl she began to write fiction. Her first publication in her eighteenth year, was a serial story which won a prize of three hundred dollars awarded by the Baltimore *Sun*. After the Virginia family home was closed, she lived for several years in North Carolina with her sister. Although she later maintained a home in Washington, she spent a large portion of her life in Europe, traveling and visiting her many friends, among whom were her cousin Lady Abinger of Inverlochy Castle, Scotland, and the Princess Troubetskoy (Amelie Rives) who entertained her in Italy at Lake Maggiore. She had a wide social acquaintance and was highly regarded as a friendly, generous woman with a gift of good conversation.

She was earnest and conscientious in all her literary work, giving to it her best efforts. She read carefully and critically other writers, and many references in her work show especially her interest in Emerson, Eliot, and Tennyson. Upholding the traditions of the old South with ardency, she nevertheless desired the obliteration of sectional feeling. This is well illustrated in her early novel, *Across the Chasm* (1885), which was published anonymously and judged one of the best stories of the year. She wrote about twenty novels, some appearing serially in magazines. They include *A Magnificent Plebeian* (1888); *A Realized Ideal* (1898); *A Beautiful Alien* (1900); and *A Manifest Destiny* (1900). She generally used one of two plot patterns: that of a hero and heroine who overcome fragile barriers to matrimony, or that of a heroine who marries the wrong man and after his death or disappearance joins her true love. Her novels are pleasant reading, but lack a sense of actuality and vigor. Her *Princess Sonia* (1895) was most popular, and best represents her work. This and many of her other books were illustrated by Charles Dana Gibson. She also wrote several juvenile books, one of which, *Child-Sketches from George Eliot* (1895, also in *St. Nicholas Magazine*) shows her interest in popularizing the work of the English novelist. Her numerous short stories were accepted by outstanding magazines and, like her novels, were directed at the feminine reader. Her articles likewise related largely to feminine problems and show a serious and responsible attitude of mind. They discuss such topics as the changing social position of woman and child-labor questions. She was awarded the Order of the Palm by the French Academy a week before her death. Six months before she died she knew of her hopeless illness but continued the writing of a novel, *Her Husband,* which was published posthumously in 1911. She died in St. Luke's Hospital, Richmond, Va., June 9, 1907, and was buried in the family plot at Charlottesville.

[A monograph on Julia Magruder, by Alice Archer Graham, is in the library of George Washington University. Other sources include: *Who's Who in America,* 1906–07; *Lib. of Southern Lit.*, vol. VIII (1909); *Book News,* Mar. 1897; M. L. Rutherford, *The South in Hist. and Lit.* (1907); obituaries in the Richmond *Times-Dispatch, Washington Post,* the *Sun* (Baltimore), and *N. Y. Times.*]

R. W. B.

MAGUIRE, CHARLES BONAVENTURE [See McGuire, Charles Bonaventure, 1768–1833].

MAHAN, ALFRED THAYER (Sept. 27, 1840–Dec. 1, 1914), naval officer, historian, was born at West Point, N. Y. His father, Dennis Hart Mahan [*q.v.*], of pure Irish stock, was for many years professor of engineering at the Military Academy. His mother, Mary Helena Okill, was the daughter of an Englishman who married into the distinguished Jay family of New York. After two years at a private school in Hagerstown, Md., and two years at Columbia University, the boy entered the Naval Academy, and, though just turned sixteen, was granted a year's advanced standing—a concession unique in academy records. He graduated with second honors in 1859. Letters of this period to his classmate and lifelong friend Samuel Ashe of North Carolina reveal the future grave historian as intensely emotional in friendship, fond of reading, a prolific and delightful letter-writer, shy and reserved, as always, yet not averse to social life nor unaware of his good looks and brilliant mind. Slender and over six feet tall, he had light sandy hair, a clear complexion, and grey-blue eyes. By his father and early environment he was imbued with the highest moral and military ideals, his strict observance of which, in reporting a delinquent classmate, led to his being "put in coventry" by part of his class during his graduating year. Right was on his side, yet this affair may help to explain the lukewarm view of Mahan's professional proficiency among many officers of his time. He himself indorsed his father's opinion that he might have done better elsewhere; but, though he was too much a student to be wholly immersed in ship-routine, it is good evidence of his practical attainments that a fellow officer on his first cruise, in the *Congress* to Brazil, 1859–61, asked him to be his "first lieutenant" in an expected command.

Made lieutenant in August 1861, at the outbreak of the Civil War, Mahan came under fire in the *Pocahontas* at Port Royal, and afterward spent many weary months in blockade duty, first in the *Pocahontas* on the Atlantic coast, and later —after eight pleasant months at the Naval Academy, in Newport, and on a midshipmen's cruise in the *Macedonian* (1863)—in the *Seminole* off Sabine Pass, Tex. During the last year of the war he was on Admiral Dahlgren's staff off Charleston. Promoted to lieutenant-commander in 1865, for twenty years thereafter he followed the routine of sea and shore duty. A long cruise in the *Iroquois* (1867–69), to Japan via Rio, Capetown, Aden, and Bombay, was the realization of "a dream of years," and during six months' leave in Europe on his way home he viewed with eager interest the last days of the Empire in Paris and of papal power in Rome. On June 11, 1872, occurred his marriage to Ellen Lyle, daughter of Manlius Evans of Philadelphia, the fortunate outcome of which is attested by Mahan's later comment, "No man can have had a much happier life than I" (Taylor, *post,* p. 23). There were three children, two daughters and a son. In 1883 he wrote for a series dealing with the naval history of the Civil War a short volume, *The Gulf and Inland Waters.* But in 1885, the year he became captain, he had done no other writing; in his own words, he was "drifting on the lines of simple respectability as aimlessly as one very well could" (*From Sail to Steam,* p. 274), when the opportunity came that determined his later career. This was a call from Admiral Luce, which reached him while commanding the *Wachusett* on the west coast of South America, to lecture on tactics and naval history at the newly established War College in Newport.

After over a year's preparation he delivered the first lectures in the autumn of 1886, and in 1886–89 followed Luce as president, fighting for the college with characteristic persistence against a hostile Secretary and an indifferent service. In 1890 the lectures were published as *The Influence of Sea Power upon History, 1660–1783.* This celebrated book contains the essence of Mahan's teaching, the first hundred pages tracing rapidly the rise and decline of the great maritime nations, and pointing out the elements constituting a nation's sea-power, while the remainder treat in detail, over the period indicated, the inter-relation of naval and political history. It won immediate recognition, far greater in Europe than in America. A thirty-two-page article appeared in the *Edinburgh Review* (October 1890), and Theodore Roosevelt wrote enthusiastically of the book, "I am greatly in error if it does not become a classic" (Alden and Earle, *post,* p. 238). Lectures were suspended in 1889–92, and Mahan was sent on a commission to select a navy-yard site on Puget Sound; but he soon returned and devoted two happy, untroubled years to his second, more carefully prepared work, *The Influence of Sea Power upon the French Revolution and Empire, 1793–1812* (2 vols., 1892). These two books were the basis of his fame. There will always be a question what measure of this was due to the fact that the books afforded perfect propaganda for the naval expansion already under way in Great Britain, Germany, and America. British critics hailed them as the gospel of England's greatness; the Kaiser Wilhelm II declared he was "devouring" them, and had them on all his ships (Alden and Earle, p. 243). Something of their success was due also to the fact that they dealt with a relatively unexploited field. There had been naval histories before, but Mahan's power of generalization, his ability to subordinate details to the central theme, and to trace the logic of events and their significance for later times, made him truly the first "philosopher of sea power." He was again president of the War College in 1892–93. When sea-service was due, he pleaded for opportunity to continue writing, but was told it was "not the business of a naval officer to write books" (*From Sail to Steam,* p. 311) and in 1893 was given command of the cruiser *Chicago,* flagship of Admiral Erben in the European Squadron. Between Mahan and Erben there was some friction, for there were drawbacks to having a distinguished author as captain, and in the enthusiastic reception accorded the author during two visits in England the admiral played a secondary rôle. Mahan's modesty, dignity, and courtesy won British hearts. He was dined by the Queen and the Premier, was the first foreign guest of honor ever entertained by the Army and Navy Club, and within a week received degrees from both Oxford and Cambridge. Subsequent degrees from American universities and the presidency of the American Historical Association (1902), were somewhat tardy recognition of this international fame. His reception abroad greatly increased his reputation.

His books as they appeared were translated into many languages, and, as Mahan himself remarks, were nowhere more assiduously studied than in Japan.

He retired in 1896, but during the Spanish-American War was recalled from Italy to become a member of the strategy board directing naval operations, on which he served from May 9 until the close of hostilities. Through his frequent magazine articles and his influence on Roosevelt, Lodge, and others, he undoubtedly had no small share in stimulating the growth of the American expansionist policy throughout this period (J. W. Pratt, "American Expansionists of the Spanish War Period," in MS.). In 1899 he was a delegate to the first Hague Peace Conference, where he stood strongly against immunity of private property at sea and arbitration agreements that would limit American freedom of action under the Monroe Doctrine. Always a conservative, in these and other fields, he defended with great cogency and realism the thought of the school to which he belonged. "When he speaks," wrote the head of the American delegation, "the millennium fades, and this stern, severe, actual world appears" (*Autobiography of Andrew D. White,* 1905, vol. II, 347). Yet only a fanatical advocate of disarmament and universal arbitration would deny the steadying effect of his opposition, based on firm convictions and lifelong study of world politics.

Among books of his not already mentioned were two excellent biographies, *Admiral Farragut* (1892), and *The Life of Nelson* (2 vols., 1897); *Types of Naval Officers* (1901); *Sea Power in Its Relations to the War of 1812* (2 vols., 1905); *Naval Strategy* (1911); *The Major Operations of the Navies in the War of American Independence* (1913); and a number of volumes of collected essays on international politics and naval affairs. A devout Episcopalian, he gave expression to his religious feeling in *The Harvest Within* (1909). *From Sail to Steam* (1907), written just after his promotion to rear admiral, retired, in 1906, is a delightful book of reminiscences, unmarred by the heaviness and over-elaboration into which he was sometimes betrayed in his historical writing by his effort to be perfectly accurate and clear. Of all his books, the sea-power series, covering the years 1660–1815, have the best claim to permanence, not only as sound naval history, but also as affording a definitely new outlook on political history. To future students it may also appear that few other historians by their writings so widely influenced the political thought and policies of their own time as did Mahan.

At the opening of the World War his health suffered from his intense concern in the conflict which he had long foreseen and clearly prophesied. Curbed by governmental restriction from writing on public affairs, he was at Washington engaged in research for a study of American expansion in its relations to sea-power, when his death came suddenly from heart failure. He was buried at Quogue, Long Island, where since 1896 he had made his principal home.

[Aside from the autobiography, *From Sail to Steam* (1907), the chief source is C. C. Taylor, *The Life of Admiral Mahan* (1920), which contains a full list of Mahan's writings and of articles and references relating to him. See also G. K. Kirkham, *The Books and Articles of Rear Admiral A. T. Mahan, U. S. N.* (1929); Allan Westcott, *Mahan on Naval Warfare* (1918), a book of selections with an introduction and notes; C. S. Alden and Ralph Earle, *Makers of Naval Tradition* (1925), pp. 228–46; *U. S. Naval Institute Proc.,* Jan.–Feb. 1915; *Army and Navy Jour.,* Dec. 5, 1914; *N. Y. Times,* Dec. 2, 1914; R. P. Chiles, ed., "Letters of Alfred Thayer Mahan to Samuel A'Court Ashe (1858–59)," *Duke Univ. Lib. Bulletin No. 4,* July 1931. Many of Mahan's letters and papers are in the hands of his family.]

A. W.

MAHAN, ASA (Nov. 9, 1799–Apr. 4, 1889), Congregational clergyman, college president, was born at Vernon, N. Y., the son of Capt. Samuel Mahan and his second wife, Anna Dana, of Worcester, Mass. From his twelfth to his seventeenth year the family lived in western New York, then a pioneer region. Home missionaries from Connecticut were frequently entertained by the Mahans. The mother, who was intensely interested in religious subjects, would propound theological questions to the visitors, and the boy's "heart would leap," he tells us, at the prospect of the discussion. From his eighth year he was much given to religious thought, and as a youth accepted unhesitatingly the high Calvinistic system in which he was trained. When seventeen years old he was appointed to teach a winter school in a district near his home. It was arranged that his father should have the son's wages that winter, after which the latter should be free to apply his earnings to obtaining an education, which it was his consuming desire to secure. During this winter he passed through a period of agony over the question as to whether he was "one of the elect," from which condition he emerged into a free Christian experience, resulting in a radical modification of his Calvinism by the adoption of a doctrine of full moral freedom. Teaching school year after year during the winter months, he pursued his studies at Hamilton College, Clinton, N. Y., graduating in 1824. Entering Andover Theological Seminary, he completed his course there in 1827. He was an active participant in the great revivals from

1824 to 1832. At New Brunswick, N. J., May 9, 1828, he married Mary H. Dix.

He was ordained pastor of the Congregational Church at Pittsford, N. Y., Nov. 10, 1829. Having a naturally weak voice, he subjected it to a self-devised training until it became adequate to the most exacting requirements of public speaking. In 1831 he was called to the pastorate of the Sixth Presbyterian Church, Cincinnati. As trustee of the recently established Lane Theological Seminary, he dissented vigorously from the action of the trustees interdicting discussion of the question of slavery. In 1835 he was elected first president of Oberlin College, founded in 1833. Eighty of the Lane students followed him to Oberlin, which fact led to the establishment of a theological department in the college. For some months the president and his family lived in a log house, the first which had been built in the Oberlin colony.

Mahan threw himself with ardor into the work of the young college, did much speaking and preaching, and taught philosophy with enthusiasm, giving an enduring impetus to this study at Oberlin. In philosophy he was intuitionist of the Scottish "common sense" school. He shared student manual labor, including work on the highway (*Autobiography,* p. 275). His acceptance of the presidency of Oberlin he had made conditional upon its reception of students without discrimination as to color. He was, moreover, always proud of having been the first college president to give degrees to women on the same conditions as to men. A believer in fullest freedom of discussion, he was sometimes suspected of "a greater facility in conviction than in conciliation" (J. H. Fairchild, *post,* p. 278). He was an impressive figure, with solid frame and full-bearded face. His administration in the main was successful; but in 1850 he accepted a call to take the direction of Cleveland University, which friends of his were projecting. Since this enterprise did not succeed, in 1855 he resumed pastoral work, serving Congregational churches, at Jackson, Mich. (1855–57), and at Adrian, Mich. (1857–60). He was connected with Adrian College as professor and from 1860 to 1871 as president. His wife died in 1863 and in 1866 he married Mrs. Mary E. Chase. The later years of his long life he passed in England, preaching to large congregations, advocating Christian perfection, editing a monthly magazine, *The Divine Life,* and issuing volume after volume on philosophy and religion. He died at Eastbourne, England. His published works include *Scripture Doctrine of Christian Perfection* (1839), *A System of Intellectual Philosophy* (copr. 1845), *Doctrine of the Will* (1845), *The True Believer; His Character, Duty and Privileges* (1847), *The Science of Moral Philosophy* (1848), *Election and Influence of the Holy Spirit* (1851), *Modern Mysteries Explained and Exposed* (1855), *The Science of Logic* (1857), *Science of Natural Theology* (1867), *Theism and Anti-Theism in Their Relations to Science* (1872), *The Phenomena of Spiritualism Scientifically Explained and Exposed* (1875), *A Critical History of the Late American War* (1877), *The System of Mental Philosophy* (1882), *A Critical History of Philosophy* (1883), *Autobiography, Intellectual, Moral and Spiritual* (London, 1882).

[In addition to Mahan's *Autobiog.,* see E. H. Fairchild, *Hist. Sketch of Oberlin Coll.* (1868); J. H. Fairchild, *Oberlin, the Colony and the College* (1883); D. L. Leonard, *The Story of Oberlin* (1898), *Oberlin Rev.,* Apr. 30, 1889; *The Times* (London), Apr. 10, 1889.] E. D. E.

MAHAN, DENNIS HART (Apr. 2, 1802–Sept. 16, 1871), educator and soldier, the son of John and Mary (Cleary) Mahan and half-brother of Milo Mahan [*q.v.*], was born in New York City shortly after the arrival of his parents from Ireland, but spent his boyhood in Norfolk, Va. Having begun the study of medicine in Richmond, he wished, also, to take up drawing. Finding no teacher and learning that drawing was taught at the United States Military Academy, he sought and obtained (1820) appointment as cadet. Graduating at the head of his class in 1824, he was assigned as a lieutenant to the corps of engineers. From 1824 to 1826 he was assistant professor, first of mathematics and then of engineering, at the Academy. Because of his native talent and persevering industry he was then sent by the War Department to Europe to study public works and military institutions with a view to improving the course at West Point. He remained abroad four years, during which time he pursued studies at the School of Application for Engineers and Artillery at Metz, France. At the time it was the foremost school of its kind, numbering on its faculty officers who had seen service under Napoleon, and some of the most eminent French scientists.

On his return to the United States he was appointed assistant professor of civil and military engineering at the Military Academy, and in 1832, professor, which position he held until 1871. Instruction at that institution was then in its infancy and as there were no suitable textbooks for his course, he supplied the lack by lectures and lithographic notes, which became the groundwork of subsequent publications. His *Complete Treatise on Field Fortification,* first published in 1836, was the standard work on this subject carried into the field by United States officers in both the Mexican and Civil wars. His *Elementary Treatise on Advance-Guard, Out-Post, and Detachment Service of Troops* (1847) was written during the Mexican War, and utilized by officers in the Civil War. Both were reprinted in Richmond for the use of the officers of the Confederate army. His *Elementary Course of Civil Engineering* was first published in 1837 and, revised from time to time, was a standard text for many years. His other textbooks were *Summary of the Course of Permanent Fortification and of the Attack and Defence of Permanent Works* (1850), *Industrial Drawing* (1852), *Descriptive Geometry as Applied to the Drawing of Fortification and Stereotomy* (1864), *An Elementary Course of Military Engineering* (2 vols., 1866–67). He also edited the American edition (1856) of Henry Moseley's *Mechanical Principles of Engineering and Architecture.*

Though best known as the author of textbooks, he was an accomplished writer in other fields and contributed articles to periodicals on many subjects. His loyalty to his country, its army, and the Military Academy was strong, and his pen was ever ready in their defense. As senior member of the academic board of the Academy his influence in the development of that institution was preëminent through four decades. He was one of the fifty original incorporators of the National Academy of Sciences, a member of the Geographical Society of Paris and many other scientific associations. In 1850 the governor of Virginia appointed him on a board of engineers to decide a controversy between that state and the Baltimore & Ohio Railroad, and in 1871 he was appointed an overseer of Thayer School of Engineering of Dartmouth College. In 1871 the board of visitors of the Academy recommended his retirement. He brooded over the fact and on a trip to New York to visit his physician, he stepped over the side of the boat and was drowned.

In 1839 he married Mary Helena Okill by whom he had three sons and two daughters. His sons all entered either the army or the navy. Frederick A. Mahan graduated at the Military Academy and became an officer of the corps of engineers. Alfred Thayer Mahan [*q.v.*] and Dennis Hart Mahan graduated from the Naval Academy.

[G. W. Cullum, *Biog. Register Officers and Grads. U. S. Mil. Acad.* (3rd ed., 1891); H. L. Abbot, in *Nat. Acad. Sci. Biog. Memoirs,* vol. II (1886); A. T. Mahan, *From Sail to Steam* (1907); *N. Y. Times,* Sept. 17, 1871; names of Mahan's parents from his daughter, Jane Mahan.]

G. J. F.

MAHAN, MILO (May 24, 1819–Sept. 3, 1870), clergyman of the Protestant Episcopal Church, educator, was born in Suffolk, Va., the son of John Mahan, a native of Ireland, by a third wife. His father died when Milo was about two years old and his half-brother, Dennis Hart Mahan [*q.v.*], assumed responsibility for the care and education of the boy, leaving him with his mother for some years and at length placing him in the school at Flushing, L. I., conducted by Rev. William Augustus Muhlenberg [*q.v.*], known after 1838 as St. Paul's College. Here he showed unusual intellectual ability, and in his seventeenth year he went to the Episcopal High School, Alexandria, Va., to teach Greek. During the years he spent there he became affected by the Oxford movement to a degree displeasing to Bishop William Meade, and he returned to St. Paul's College as a teacher. Having carried on studies preparatory to the ministry, he was ordained deacon by Bishop Thomas C. Brownell at New Canaan, Conn., Oct. 27, 1845; and priest, by Bishop Levi S. Ives, at the Church of the Holy Communion, New York, on Dec. 14, 1846. After serving as assistant to Dr. Samuel Seabury at the Church of the Annunciation, New York, in November 1848 he became rector of Grace Church, Van Vorst, Jersey City, organized not long before. In two years, under his leadership, it developed into a flourishing parish, and he then went to St. Mark's Church, Philadelphia, as assistant to Dr. J. P. B. Wilmer. In 1851 he published *The Exercise of Faith in Its Relation to Authority and Private Judgment,* in which, from the Anglican point of view, he set forth the errors of the Roman Catholic position. The same year he was appointed professor of ecclesiastical history at the General Theological Seminary, New York. With two or three other clergymen he started and for several years conducted the *Church Journal,* the first number of which appeared Feb. 5, 1853. On Aug. 23, 1853, he married Mary Griffitts (Fisher) Lewis, widow of Charles Smith Lewis. An intimate friend of Bishop G. W. Doane [*q.v.*] of New Jersey, Mahan cooperated in the bishop's educational projects, serving as a trustee of St. Mary's Hall and of Burlington College. He also represented the New Jersey diocese in the General Conventions of 1856, 1859, and 1862. Bishop Doane, shortly before his death in 1859, expressed the desire that Mahan be his successor, but his election was prevented by those who had been hostile to Doane. In the General Convention of 1862 he made vigorous protest against indorsement of the Union cause, on the ground that the issue was political rather than religious (see *Dr.*

Mahan's Speech, 1862). His Southern sympathies made him uncomfortable in New York and this fact, together with the need of more salary, led him to resign his professorship in 1864, and assume the rectorship of St. Paul's Church, Baltimore.

He had previously published *A Church History of the First Three Centuries, from the Thirtieth to the Three Hundred and Twenty-third Year of the Christian Era* (1860), a useful compendium, but without originality and somewhat influenced by the writer's own ecclesiastical views; and a reply to Bishop John William Colenso's conclusions regarding the Pentateuch, *The Spiritual Point of View: or the Glass Reversed, an Answer to Bishop Colenso* (1863). Obsessed with the idea that the Bible contains elaborate and abstruse symbolisms, he had also published in 1863 an ingenious work on the significance of numbers employed therein, entitled: *Palmoni: or, the Numerals of Scripture a Proof of Inspiration.* His *Comedy of Canonization,* called forth by the *Comedy of Convocation,* a caricature of the Anglican position by a convert to Rome, appeared anonymously in 1868; and his *Church History of the First Seven Centuries,* in 1872. He represented the diocese of Maryland in the General Conventions of 1865 and 1868. On June 30, 1870, he was called back to the General Theological Seminary as professor of systematic divinity. The following month he accepted the appointment, but his death occurred before he entered upon its duties. In 1875 *The Collected Works of the Late Milo Mahan, D.D.,* in three volumes, edited by J. H. Hopkins, was published.

[Memoir in *Collected Works,* vol. III; *Churchman's Year Book,* 1871; *Proc. of the Board of Trustees of the Gen. Theolog. Sem. . . .,* vol. III (1866), vol. IV (1875); *No. Am. Rev.,* Oct. 1860; *Southern Rev.,* July 1875; *The Sun* (Baltimore), Sept. 6, 1870; information from relatives.] H. E. S.

MAHONE, WILLIAM (Dec. 1, 1826–Oct. 8, 1895), railroad president, Confederate soldier, senator from Virginia, was born in Southampton County, Va., the son of Fielding Jordan and Martha (Drew) Mahone. In a region of large slaveholders his father kept tavern and "Billie" rode the mail from Jerusalem (Courtland) to Hill's Ford (Emporia). Tradition has it that the youth was deemed a good mixer and clever at the prevalent sport of gambling. Aided financially by friends he graduated from the Virginia Military Institute in 1847. Continuing the study of engineering while teaching in Rappahannock Military Academy, he became engineer of the Orange & Alexandria road-building project and then (1851) of the Norfolk-Petersburg Railroad. Of the latter—a well-built road for that day—he was in 1861 president, chief engineer, and superintendent. Meantime, in February 1855, he had married Ortelia Butler, who in the course of time bore him three children, and had settled in Petersburg. Though he was apparently little interested in politics, on Virginia's secession he was appointed quartermaster-general. Soon, however, as lieutenant-colonel, then as colonel, of his 6th Virginia Regiment of eastern volunteers, he was taking part in the capture of the Norfolk Navy Yard. He commanded the Norfolk District until its evacuation in May 1862, when he was shifted to the Drewry's Bluff defenses of the James River. Thereafter he was continuously with the Army of Northern Virginia except while recuperating from a severe wound received at Second Manassas. D. H. Hill criticized his conduct at Seven Pines; Magruder and Longstreet praised him at Malvern Hill and Second Manassas respectively. Perhaps because he was not a West-Point man, he was not commissioned brigadier-general until March 1864. In July following, because of the flanking movement in the Wilderness which he commanded, he was recommended by Longstreet for the major-generalship; after his action at the Crater this came quickly, and he was a Southern hero besides (*War of the Rebellion: Official Records, Army,* 1 ser. XI, pts. 1–3, XIV, pt. 1, XL, pt. 3). As a commander Mahone was alert, prompt, precise, and contemptuous of indecision or unnecessary self-exposure in other commanders. Perhaps because he was careful of its equipment and condition "Mahone's Brigade" displayed uncommon *esprit de corps* until and through Appomattox; and in post-war days it held enthusiastic reunions. Not improbable is the report that Gen. Robert E. Lee, who had observed him closely, said after the war that among the younger men he thought William Mahone had developed the highest quality for organization and command (Pearson, *post,* p. 69).

Promptly back at railroading, out of three short and largely state-owned lines from Norfolk to Bristol, Mahone, under legislative authorization of 1867 and 1870, created the privately owned Atlantic, Mississippi & Ohio Railroad, with steamer connections at Norfolk and the right to extend to the Ohio. Of this fine road—later the Norfolk & Western—he was president at a salary (men noted) "as big as the President's." In the sane movements of 1869 for mitigating Reconstruction rigors he helped quietly but powerfully; and thereby secured for governor, Gilbert C. Walter, a director of the Norfolk & Petersburg, whose fiscal ideas were Hamiltonian. Through railroad patronage he dominated the *Richmond Whig* and built himself a strong legislative following. The tavern-keeper's son was traveling far and fast. But everywhere he met obstacles, hostilities: he was dubbed "Railroad Ishmael," "King of the Lobby"; Governors Walker and Kemper successively abandoned him; twice at least he forfeited prestige to escape duels; in the crash of the seventies an unfriendly receivership took away his railroad; and in the Conservative (Democratic) convention of 1877 a combination defeated his gubernatorial aspirations though he led the field on his record for material progress. Undaunted, in 1879 he organized and assumed command of the "Readjusters," who advocated a scaling of the state's huge debt and popular social and economic legislation. Favored neither by the regular party machines nor by wealthy and intelligent people generally, this movement swept the state in 1879 and 1881; and important reforms followed. Aided, perhaps coached, by the Pennsylvania Camerons, Mahone in 1880 was elected to the United States Senate. There he traded his commanding vote for offices and committee assignments, bringing upon his head vials of Southern Democratic wrath for his "treason" but winning great applause from Northern Republicans for his "Anti-Bourbonism," which to them meant protecting the negro's vote. Two years later another senator and a majority of Virginia's representatives, elected as "Coalitionists," were with him in Washington. With the state and federal offices thus secured Mahone built a political machine which thereafter dominated the Republican party of Virginia; and of it he was absolute boss. After 1882, however, though a constant threat, he won no more elections—not even when he himself ran for governor in 1889—owing in part to the rejuvenating effects of the Readjuster Movement on the old dominating elements and in part to defections caused by his own imperiousness. He had shown how to break the "Solid South" but not how to maintain the breach. To the end a unique figure—short, spare, and long-bearded, always in gray slouch hat and peg-top trousers, eyes blue and restless, voice thin and piping—he died in Washington and was buried quietly in Petersburg. There the Daughters of the Confederacy later erected a monument to him.

[See: C. C. Pearson, *The Readjuster Movement in Va.* (1917), for political matters and for biographical references; C. A. Evans, ed., *Confed. Mil. Hist.* (1899), vol. III; P. C. Headley, *Pub. Men of Today* (1882); W. L. Royall, *Some Reminiscences* (1909); R. E. Withers, *Autobiog. of an Octogenarian* (1907); the *Richmond Dispatch*, Oct. 9, 1895; the *Hist. Mag. and Notes and Queries* (N. Y.), June 1870; *The Vital Va. Issues: A Speech by Gen. Wm. Mahone . . . Sept. 23, 1889*; *Characteristic Facts in the . . . Career of Gen. Wm. Mahone* (n.d.); *Special Report . . . to the Stockholders of the Norfolk and Petersburg Railroad Company* (1866). The doctor's thesis of N. M. Blake on Wm. Mahone (Duke Univ., 1932), admirably covers the subject.]

C. C. P.

MAILLY, WILLIAM (Nov. 22, 1871–Sept. 4, 1912), Socialist, journalist, and dramatic critic, was born in the poorhouse in Pittsburgh, Pa., the son of John Mailly and Mary McDowell. His Irish father was a heavy drinker who frequently deserted his mother and the seven children of whom only three boys survived childhood. When William was three his mother took the family back to her native Scotland and his earliest recollections were of Lennoxtown and of a Glasgow close. Afterward she started a laundry in Liverpool and at twelve William left school to become her errand boy. Tips received for delivering laundry he spent for theatre tickets and thus began his lifelong devotion to the drama. He also became interested in socialism. In 1889 his father brought the family again to America and William became a section hand in Illinois and later a coal miner in Alabama. His intelligence, gift for friendship, and keen sense of humor, together with his attractive brown eyes and eager, searching expression, almost immediately made him a leader. At twenty-one he was organizer and the next year state secretary of the United Mine Workers of America. For a time associate editor of the Birmingham *Labor Advocate,* in 1896 he went to Nashville, became secretary of the Tennessee Federation of Labor, and edited the Nashville *Journal of Labor.* Having become an admiring friend of Eugene V. Debs he assisted, in 1898, in forming the Social Democratic (now Socialist) party at Chicago. Shortly afterward he was made organizer for that party in New York City and later went to Massachusetts for the "Social Crusaders." There he edited the Haverhill *Social Democrat,* assisted in electing Socialist mayors in Haverhill and Brockton, and in 1902 became secretary of the state party. His success in that office and as secretary of the "Unity convention" in 1901 led to his choice, early in 1903, as national secretary of the Socialist party, with headquarters first at Omaha and later at Chicago. At a time when the movement was in special need of English-speaking leaders Mailly threw into his task executive ability, forthright sincerity, infectious enthusiasm, and a devotion transferred from the Catholic religion which he early discarded. But he was primarily an idealist and writer and in 1905, having more than doubled the number of organized states, got the party out of debt, and managed the campaign of 1904 in which socialism first became a real factor in American politics, he declined reëlection as secretary though for the next year he was a member of the national executive committee. Meanwhile, on May 15, 1903, at the bedside of his dying mother in Haverhill, he married Bertha Howell, a college-educated woman and an active Socialist. For a time he was joint publisher of a Socialist paper at Toledo, Ohio, but from 1907 to 1909 he was managing editor first of the New York *Worker* and later of the *Evening Call.* In May 1909, he resigned to become dramatic critic for the *Twentieth Century Magazine* and to write articles and stories for the *Arena, Independent, Munsey's Magazine,* and other periodicals. At the time of the Triangle fire he was business manager of the Ladies Waist Makers' Union and the burden of relief work and agitation for better fire protection for workers thrown upon him proved too heavy for his strength, already weakened by diabetes. During the last six months of his life he was associate editor of the *Metropolitan Magazine.* His early death cut short a career of much promise as a writer and pioneer in interpreting the effect of the drama upon social ideals.

[W. P. D. Bliss, *The New Encyc. of Social Reform* (1908), contains a biographical sketch. G. D. Herron, *William Mailly as a Socialist Type* (1912) is a memoir reprinted from the *Coming Nation.* Obituaries were published in a large number of Socialist and other periodicals, including the principal New York and Chicago dailies, the *Springfield Republican,* the *New York Dramatic Mirror,* the *Woman Voter,* the *Milwaukee Leader,* and the *Young Socialists' Mag.* Biographical materials are also contained in the newspapers which Mailly edited and the articles and stories which he wrote for magazines. Other information has been furnished by his widow.] H. S. W.

MAISCH, JOHN MICHAEL (Jan. 30, 1831–Sept. 10, 1893), pharmacist, was born in the ancient German town of Hanau, Hesse, the son of Conrad Maisch, a merchant. He attended a private school, then the *bürgerschule,* entered the *realschule* at twelve, and upon its foundation in 1844 was transferred to the *oberrealschule.* Here he received an excellent fundamental training in natural history, chemistry, physics, and mathematics, as well as instruction in Greek and Latin and in microscopy. His parents wished him to study theology, but his bent was toward a scientific calling, and he selected pharmacy as the study of his preference. Before he had the opportunity to secure training in this subject, however, he took part in the Baden Rebellion of 1849 and was forced to leave Germany.

He came to America in his nineteenth year, without money, influence, or friends, but with so much native ability and industry that he soon made contacts that enabled him to gain practical experience in his chosen profession. He worked in pharmacies in Baltimore, Washington, and New York, and then for some time in the employ of Robert Shoemaker, a pioneer wholesale druggist and manufacturing pharmacist of Philadelphia, who was actively connected with the Philadelphia College of Pharmacy. In May 1854 he contributed his first paper, "On the Adulteration of Drugs and Chemical Preparations," to the *American Journal of Pharmacy.* In 1859 he became associated with another well-known pharmacist, Edward Parrish [*q.v.*], who conducted a pharmaceutical preparatory course for students of medicine, and in this year he revised the chemical section of the second edition of Parrish's *Introduction to Practical Pharmacy.* He profited so well by his contacts with these men that in 1861 he was called to the chair of botany and materia medica in the New York College of Pharmacy. Here he remained for two years, spending his spare time in the laboratory of Dr. Edward R. Squibb [*q.v.*] of Brooklyn, another pharmacist of national repute.

In 1863 he returned to Philadelphia to take charge of the United States Army Laboratory, in which medical and pharmaceutical supplies were made for the Union army. He conducted this work in such a conscientious and thorough manner as to save large sums of money for the government. When the laboratory was discontinued at the close of the Civil War, he opened a pharmacy in Philadelphia. In 1866 he became a professor in the Philadelphia College of Pharmacy, with which he was connected thereafter until his death, occupying several chairs in succession, and finally becoming dean. For many years (1865–93) he was permanent secretary of the American Pharmaceutical Association; he was the chemical, botanical, and pharmaceutical editor of the first three editions of the *National Dispensatory* (1879–84), was editor of the *American Journal of Pharmacy* from 1871 until his death, and was a member of the Committee of Revision of the *Pharmacopoeia of the United States* for three successive decades (1870–90). He also edited and revised R. E. Griffith's *Universal Formulary* (3rd ed., 1874), and published a successful work of his own, *A Manual of Organic Materia Medica* (1882). He was an honorary member of many foreign scientific societies, and just before he died was the recipient of the Hanbury Medal, awarded for distinguished services in pharmacy by the Pharmaceutical Society of Great Britain. His wife, Charlotte Justine Kuhl, whom he married in 1859, predeceased him; but he was survived by five sons and two daughters.

[Files of the *Am. Jour. Pharmacy*; *Alumni Report of the Phila. Coll. of Pharmacy*, Oct. 1893; *Proc. Am. Pharmaceutical Asso.*, 1893, 1894; *The First Century of the Phila. Coll. of Pharmacy* (1922), ed. by J. W. England; *Phila. Press*, Sept. 12, 1893.] C. H. L—l.

MAJOR, CHARLES (July 25, 1856–Feb. 13, 1913), novelist, the son of Stephen and Phoebe (Gaskill) Major, was born in Indianapolis, Ind. His father, who came to the United States in 1829 from his birthplace, Granard, County Longford, Ireland, was descended from ancestors who had gone to Ireland from Scotland in the days of Cromwell. At the age of thirteen Charles removed with his parents to Shelbyville where he lived for the remainder of his life. After attending the public schools he read law in his father's office and was admitted to the bar in 1877. He interrupted a lifelong practice only once, when, in 1885, he was elected to the Indiana legislature on the Democratic ticket. At the end of his first term he refused renomination, and, thereafter, declined to reënter public life. On Sept. 27, 1885, he married Alice Shaw of Shelbyville. A man of quiet demeanor and studious habits, he devoted the greater part of his leisure to reading, especially English and French history of the Renaissance period. He took particular interest in diaries, memoirs, and state papers of the Tudor age, with the result that by the time he came to write his first romance he was an important amateur historian. His best novels were the fruit of his enthusiasm for study.

In 1898 he achieved his widest popularity by the publication of his first book, *When Knighthood Was in Flower*, a novel that reached a sale of over two hundred thousand copies in two years and remained a best-seller for fourteen consecutive months. Told ostensibly by Sir Edwin Caskoden, master of the dance, it recounts the love story of Mary Tudor, sister of Henry VIII, and Charles Brandon against a colorful background of sixteenth-century England. Although accurate in detail the historical setting lacks fullness and does not always succeed in giving life to a somewhat sentimental plot. The principal characters, broadly drawn and glamorous, tend to be the usual romantic types. Major had definite views as to the use of history in fiction; he deplored the practice of attempting contemporary speech, stressed the value of original sources, and advocated a knowledge of the whole life of all the people (*Scribner's*, June 1900). In spite of his theories, however, he seems to put his actors into fancy dress rather than into an actual period atmosphere. He returned to the field of his first success with *Dorothy Vernon of Haddon Hall* (1902). Again, using the first person, he presents a pair of amiable though theatrical lovers, who find happiness after typically fictional difficulties; and again he sketches historic personages, this time chiefly Elizabeth and Mary, Queen of Scots. Like its predecessor the book substitutes sincerity and accuracy of fact for a real portrayal either of character or of history. Continuing in the historical vein with less popular and no greater artistic success, Major published: *Yolanda, Maid of Burgundy* (1905); *A Gentle Knight of Old Brandenburg* (1909); *The Little King* (1910) and *The Touchstone of Fortune* (1912). Meanwhile, though he admitted he knew less about them than he did about historical subjects (*Bookman*, June 1902), he attempted local themes in *The Bears of Blue River* (1901), *A Forest Hearth* (1903), and *Uncle Tom Andy Bill* (1908). *When Knighthood Was in Flower* and *Dorothy Vernon* were made into popular plays by Paul Kester.

Although his importance may be said to be entirely in the historical field, Major made no real contribution to the development of the historical novel created by Scott and Americanized by Cooper. He had their faults but seldom possessed their powers. His books are kept in print chiefly by juvenile readers.

[See *Who's Who in America*, 1912–13; *The Cambridge Hist. of Am. Lit.*, vol. III (1921); J. P. Dunn, *Indiana and Indianans* (1919), vol. III, p. 1366; *Book Buyer*, Mar. 1900; *Current Lit.*, May 1900; *Bookman*, Nov. 1900; F. L. Pattee, *The Hist. of Am. Lit. Since 1870* (1915); *Indianapolis News*, Feb. 13, 1913. The Julia Marlowe edition of *When Knighthood Was in Flower* (copyright 1901) contains an article by Maurice Thompson: "The Author and the Book."]
D. A. R—s.

MAJORS, ALEXANDER (Oct. 4, 1814–Jan. 12, 1900), freighter and promoter of the pony express, the son of Laurania (Kelly) and Benjamin Majors, a native of North Carolina, was born near Franklin, Simpson County, Ky. His father moved to what is now Lafayette County, Mo., about 1819, and he later acquired an extensive farm with saw and flour mills in Jackson County, where the family lived from 1825 to 1858. The boy worked on the farm and served as a miller's boy. On Nov. 6, 1834, he married Katherine Stallcup, having in the meantime started farming on his own account. The returns from farming were not sufficient for his growing family, and on Aug. 10, 1848, with an outfit of six wagons and teams, he undertook the business of carrying freight from Independence to Santa Fé. He made the round trip in ninety-two days and cleared $1,500. He avoided traveling and all unnecessary work on Sunday, and his men had to take the pledge: "While I am in the employ of A. Majors, I agree not to use profane language, not to get drunk, not to gamble, not to treat animals cruelly, and not to do anything else that is incompatible with the conduct of a gentleman" (*Seventy Years, post,* p. 72). In all his operations he persevered in this discipline. He carried freight on his own account for several years, most of the time transporting government supplies to the various forts in New Mexico, Colorado, and Utah. About 1855 he went into partnership with William Hepburn Russell [*q.v.*] and William B. Waddell and continued as Majors & Russell until 1858, when the firm name was changed to Russell, Majors & Waddell. He took complete responsibility for all the business on the road, while the others managed the purchasing and financing. Their operations required the employment of more than four thousand men, forty thousand oxen, and one thousand mules. The shipments were made in trains of about twenty-five wagons each, stationed several miles apart; each wagon had twelve oxen and a teamster; and each train had thirty oxen in reserve, five mules, wagonmaster, and extra men. The partnership agreement required him to move his home from Jackson County to Nebraska City. Their profits in 1855–56 amounted to about $300,000. The business was very hazardous, and they would sometimes lose the profits of several years in one season.

In 1859 the firm took over the operation of a daily stage-coach line from Fort Leavenworth to Denver, begun independently by Russell and John S. Jones, who were, however, unable to carry it financially. Afterward they included in their schedules, St. Joseph, Mo., Atchison, Kan., Salt Lake City, Fort Kearney, Nebraska Territory, and Fort Laramie in what is now Wyoming. On Apr. 3, 1860, they established the famous pony express, a very daring and romantic enterprise, which lasted about eighteen months, and was a financial failure. Nevertheless at the outbreak of the Civil War it performed an important service in maintaining swift communication between the federal government at Washington and the population of the Pacific Coast, and, before the completion of the telegraph, it carried the news of Lincoln's inaugural address, the fall of Fort Sumter, the call for troops, and the battle of Antietam. The old firm of Russell, Majors & Waddell collapsed in the early part of 1861, and, when liquidation failed to provide funds for the debts, Majors, as did his former partners, surrendered his personal estate for that purpose. He had purchased the interests of his partners in the freighting business, and he continued freighting until 1866. In 1868 he worked on the Union Pacific Railroad and later prospected for silver near Salt Lake City until 1872. From 1869 to 1879 he lived in Salt Lake City. In 1893 he published a volume of reminiscences, *Seventy Years on the Frontier,* which was, however, edited by Prentiss Ingraham [*q.v.*], the prolific writer of dime novels. For several years before his death he lived in Kansas City, Mo., and he died in Chicago.

[F. A. Root and W. E. Connelley, *The Overland Stage to Cal.* (1900); L. R. Hafen, *The Overland Mail* (1926); G. D. Bradley, *The Story of the Pony Express* (1913); W. L. Visscher, *A Thrilling and Truthful Hist. of the Pony Express* (copr. 1908); *Collectors Club Philatelist,* Jan., Apr. 1929; *Mo. Republican* (St. Louis), Nov. 14, 1886; *Kansas City Star,* Jan. 15, 1900; *Rocky Mountain News* (Denver), Jan. 15, 1900.]

S. M. D.

MA-KA-TAI-ME-SHE-KIA-KIAK [See Black Hawk, 1767–1838].

MAKEMIE, FRANCIS (*c.* 1658–1708), Presbyterian clergyman, of Scotch parentage, was born near Ramelton, in Donegal County, Ireland. The severe persecution to which the Scotch-Irish Presbyterians were subjected during his boyhood seems to have deepened his allegiance to the church of his fathers. Graduating from the University of Glasgow during Scotland's bloody killing time, he was ordained by Laggan Presbytery, probably in 1682, as a missionary to America. In 1683 he arrived in Maryland—according to tradition, a blue-eyed, brown-haired, fair-complexioned youth, with an intellectual forehead, and the mien of a true Irish gentleman. It was a number of years before he settled permanently. He labored as an evangelist in North Carolina (1683–84), on the Elizabeth River in Virginia (1684–85), on the Eastern shore of Virginia and Maryland (1690–91), in Philadelphia, for a single sermon (1692), and in Barbados (1696–98). Four letters to Increase Mather, two from Virginia and two from Barbados, and one to Benjamin Colman have been preserved (see Briggs, *post,* Appendix X). During these years he published a catechism, popularizing the tenets of the Westminster Confession, of which he was a stanch adherent. The catechism was violently attacked by the Quaker George Keith [*q.v.*], and Makemie defended Presbyterian beliefs and practices against Keith's animadversions in *An Answer to George Keith's Libel* (1694). More serious opposition came to the nascent Presbyterian Church from representatives of the Church of England. In 1699 Makemie published *Truths in a True Light; or a Pastoral Letter to the Reformed Protestants in Barbadoes Vindicating the Non-Conformists from the Misrepresentations Commonly Made of Them, in That Island, and in Other Places,* written in 1697.

The lack of organized churches, and of any stated support, as well as Makemie's own independent spirit, led him to enter the mercantile business. Sometime before 1698 he married Naomi, the daughter of William Anderson, a rich merchant of Accomac County, Va., who died in 1698, leaving to his son-in-law the bulk of his estate. Successful both as a merchant and as a trader in land, Makemie now settled down on the Eastern Shore of Virginia. In 1699 he secured a license to preach at two of his own houses in Virginia. He thus became the first dissenting minister licensed under the Toleration Act to preach in a colony noted for its intolerance. His main service, however, was given to the churches in Maryland, just across the line, particularly Snow Hill and Rehobeth. He remained the pastor of the latter church until his death.

In 1704–05 Makemie made a journey to England. He published here *A Plain & Friendly Perswasive to the Inhabitants of Virginia and Maryland for Promoting Towns & Cohabitation* (1705), in which he displays an intelligent concern for the material needs of the two colonies, and a keen interest in the relation of material welfare to spiritual well-being. He also persuaded the Presbyterian and Independent ministers of London to send two Presbyterian ministers to America, and to assume their support for two years. These young men, John Hampton and George McNish, became pastors of four of the five churches to which Makemie had ministered in Maryland. The following year Makemie and these two ministers united with four others to form the first American Presbytery. It is generally admitted that Makemie was responsible for the organization. He was also its first moderator.

In January 1707 he was arrested by order of Lord Cornbury, governor of New York, and imprisoned for six weeks, for preaching in that colony without a license. Cornbury described him as "Jack of all Trades; he is a Preacher, a Doctor of Physick, a Merchant, an Attorney, or Counsellor at Law, and which is worse of all, a Disturber of Governments" (*Ecclesiastical Records of the State of New York,* III, 1670). Makemie saw that the rights of non-conformists to the Church of England were at stake, not only in New York, but in other colonies as well. He spoke ably and at length himself, and was defended by William Nicoll, James Reignere, and David Jamison [*q.v.*]. The jury acquitted him but he was required by the court to pay all the costs, including that of the prosecution. Being further hounded by Cornbury, Makemie printed in Boston the sermon which caused his arrest, and also published *A Narrative of a New and Unusual American Imprisonment of Two Presbyterian Ministers and Prosecution of Mr. Francis Makemie* (1707). His vigorous action called attention to the conduct of Cornbury and contributed to his recall in 1709. The next legislature made another such persecution impossible in New York.

Makemie died in 1708, survived by his widow and two daughters. He is regarded as the chief founder of the Presbyterian Church in America. He organized or developed some of its earliest churches; was the foremost expounder of its tenets, and its chief literary apologist; defended its liberties; and secured its initial organization. A monument was erected to his memory, May 14, 1908, on the site of his old home in Accomac County, Va.

[L. P. Bowen, *The Days of Makemie* (1885); A. G. Lecky, *In the Days of the Laggan Presbytery* (Belfast, 1908), appendix, pp. 139–42; *Jour. of the Presbyt. Hist. Soc.*, Mar. 1907–Dec. 1907, Dec. 1908; W. B. Sprague, *Annals Am. Pulpit*, vol. III (1858); C. A. Briggs, *Am. Presbyterianism* (1885); *Ecclesiastical Records State of N. Y.*, vol. II (1901), vol. III (1902); W. H. Foote, *Sketches of Va.* (1850); Alfred Nevin, *Hist. of the Presbytery of Philadelphia and Philadelphia Central* (1888); Irving Spence, *Letters on the Early History of the Presbyterian Church in America* (1838); Richard Webster, *A Hist. of the Presbyterian Ch. in America* (1857); L. P. Bowen, *Makemieland Memorials* (1910).]

E. T. T.

MALBONE, EDWARD GREENE (August 1777–May 7, 1807), miniature painter, was born at Newport, R. I., and died in Savannah, Ga. The painter's grandfather, Capt. Godfrey Malbone, went to Newport from Virginia as a young man. He soon claimed a share of Newport's profits in the rum trade, and with his wife, Katherine Scott Malbone, established himself in the community. The artist's father, John Malbone, was the eighth of ten children. For a time he was engaged in the West-Indies trade. At his death in 1795 he left an estate valued at $5,500. His burial was attended with ceremonies conducted by the Marine Society, and an obituary in the *Newport Mercury* referred to his title of brigadier-general in the Rhode Island militia, to his substantial qualities as a citizen, and to his philanthropy. He had several times served as vestryman in Trinity Church. More obscure is the artist's mother, Patience Greene, to whom, tradition says, John Malbone was never married. By her Malbone had five children: Edward, Henry, Harriet, later Mrs. John Whitehorne; Mary, later Mrs. Benjamin Rathbone; and Sarah, later Mrs. John Knight. Their birth dates are not recorded, and it was not until after their father's death that the three sisters were baptized in Trinity Church with the name Malbone.

Harriet Malbone Whitehorne, writing in 1834, said that the family lived in seclusion in Newport and refers to an "accumulation of evils" not of a pecuniary nature (Dunlap, *post,* II, p. 147).

Edward Malbone numbered among these evils the neglect of his early education. It is possible however that this neglect assisted the development of the painter by throwing him upon his own resources. As a small boy he showed an inventive genius and facile hands in fashioning kites with streamers of fireworks, in cutting moulds and in making little lead toys. He early began to draw, copying any picture or illustration at hand. He made his own brushes and paints and at the age of eleven or twelve he started to draw gods and goddesses in India ink on small pieces of ivory or bone. These he cut himself and framed in twisted wire. At one time the local theatre contributed to his artistic education for in it he learned to paint scenery. He finally painted an entire scene which won him a ticket of admission and local renown. But chiefly he painted heads, soon attempted likenesses, and finally devoted himself entirely to portraiture. He kept much to his own room and was somewhat of a trial to his brother and sisters who thought him unsocial and different. His earnestness and passion for work, amounting to a creative fury, were remarkable in a young boy and figured as a source of power in his later career. He used to visit the fascinating shop of Samuel King who made compasses and quadrants and sometimes portraits, and who lent him engravings to copy and helped him with his painting.

In spite of this help, Malbone must be considered a self-taught artist, for by painstaking and constant copying he taught himself to draw and then learned for himself the difficult technique of miniature painting. When at the age of sixteen he painted a head of Thomas Lawrence on paper which was thought a work of genius, his father sent the picture to a painting master in Philadelphia for criticism, but the master sent word back that the boy would take the bread out of his mouth and named an exorbitant fee for giving him lessons, and the question of a teacher was dropped. In the fall of the next year, 1794, Malbone left home without telling anyone but his sister, Harriet, and went to Providence where he set up as a professional miniature painter, an act of considerable rashness in a lad of seventeen. In a letter to his father shortly after his arrival in Providence, he said he expected to succeed in his project and hoped soon to furnish material aid in support of the family. "I must conclude," he wrote, "with making use of that name which I shall study never to dishonor. Your dutiful son, Edward G. Malbone" (*Scribner's Magazine,* May 1910, p. 560). That his confidence in his ability to paint miniatures was justified is shown by his immediate success in Providence. During his stay of a year and a half he drew commissions from the best families and, if an extant receipt is typical, charged $23.33 for his portraits. The few known examples of his first work in Providence were brought together for the first time in 1929 during an exhibition of Malbone miniatures held at the National Gallery of Art. They show the use of fine stipple for modeling the face, scrupulous regard to detail in finishing face and costume, and careful painting in the background.

In October 1795 Malbone was called home to attend the funeral of his father. He returned to Providence, but in the spring of the following year established himself in Boston. There his ability was quickly recognized and his charming manner won him a circle of friends. He renewed his friendship with Washington Allston, then a student at Harvard, whom he had known at Newport. Too much attention from Boston society might have interfered with his career, had he been less determined to perfect his art. He told Dunlap that his average allowance for work each day was eight hours. His self-portrait painted in 1797 (belonging to R. T. H. Halsey) pictures a serious young man possessed of poise and charm, with powdered hair, and wearing the elegant costume of the day. He was tall and slender and Dunlap says by nature of good constitution.

The next two years Malbone divided between New York and Philadelphia. In the autumn of 1800 he went to Charleston, where new friendships included one with the artist Charles Fraser [*q.v.*]. His technique by this time had changed from a stiff, detailed style to a freer method. He used delicate interwoven lines of color which performed the double function of creating form and giving color. The backgrounds are light and simple, kept entirely subordinate to the subject. The miniature of Thomas Lowndes (belonging to C. S. Green), an excellent example of this second style, illustrates Malbone's masterly use of line.

In May 1801 he and Allston went to London. His judgments on what he saw in the galleries and studios are contained in a letter to Fraser: "Mr. West is decidedly the greatest painter amongst them for history. Mr. Lawrence is the best portrait painter . . . Amongst miniature painters, I think Mr. Shelly [*sic*] and Mr. Cosway the best" (Dunlap, *post,* II, pp. 141–42).

Though Malbone admired Shelley and Cosway he was able even at this time to surpass them in portraying individuality. Benjamin West, the president of the Royal Academy, praised Malbone's ability after seeing one of his miniatures and advised him not to "look forward to anything short of the highest excellence." While in London Malbone painted "The Hours" which is now in the Providence Athenæum. He returned to Charleston in December 1801. From this time another or third style is recognizable in his painting, a development of the second period. He used the same delicate lines of color in painting the face but the stroke is even freer and somewhat broader. Subtle transitions give the effect of smoothness. The size of the ivory becomes larger, the largest known portrait being seven inches by five, a beautiful three-quarter-length portrait of Eliza Mason, painted in 1805 (now belonging to Mrs. Samuel Dunn Parker).

It is said that Malbone sometimes painted on hard wood, inlaying pieces of ivory for the face and hands. He always placed his subject on a seat somewhat higher than his own and while at work never conversed. Latterly he received fifty dollars for his portraits. His signature, sometimes a neat and graceful "Malbone," sometimes "E. G. Malbone" or again "E. G. M." or "E. M.," is usually very delicately painted or scratched in some inconspicuous corner of the ivory. Often the date appears. Altogether hardly more than a third of Malbone's miniatures are signed. Most of the years 1804 and 1805 were spent in Boston and in December 1805 he sailed for Charleston, intending to go again to London in the following spring. But in March he contracted tuberculosis and was forced to give up his painting. Neither horseback riding nor a trip to Jamaica gave him relief, and at the home of his cousin, Robert Mackay, in Savannah, Ga., he died on May 7, 1807, at the age of twenty-nine. He was buried in the Colonial Cemetery at Savannah.

Malbone's genius as a technician and as a portrait painter is undisputed. The great variety resulting from his continual and thoughtful experimentation is one of his chief claims to superiority over other miniaturists. This variety is a result not merely of his inventiveness in method but of his ability in characterization, an ability that lifts his art out of the merely good and places it with the most distinguished. He painted perhaps as many as three hundred miniatures in his short professional career of twelve years. Some of these are lost and most of the known examples are privately owned. There are, however, examples in the Metropolitan Museum, the Boston Museum of Fine Arts, the Pennsylvania Academy, the Rhode Island School of Design, and the Providence Athenæum, which has also two oil paintings by Malbone.

[Trinity Church records, Newport, R. I.; Rhode Island records; copies of Malbone family letters belonging to Mrs. W. S. Lovell; anonymous article in *Analectic Mag.*, Sept. 1815; Wm. Dunlap, *A Hist. of the Rise and Progress of the Arts of Design in the U. S.* (1918), vol. II; R. T. H. Halsey, article in *Scribner's Mag.*, May 1910; M. H. Elliott, "Edward Greene Malbone, Rhode Island's Distinguished Miniature Painter," *Providence Jour.*, Sept. 22, 1926; Theodore Bolton, *Early Am. Portrait Painters in Miniature* (1921); Harry B. Wehle, *Am. Miniatures, 1730–1850* (1927); J. L. Brockway, "Malbone, Am. Miniature Painter," *Am. Mag. of Art*, Apr. 1929; R. P. Tolman, "Newly Discovered Malbone Miniatures," *Antiques*, Nov. 1929, and "Other Malbone Miniatures," *Ibid.*, Apr. 1933; and *The Metropolitan Museum of Art Cat. of an Exhibition of Miniatures Painted in America, 1720–1850* (1927). R. P. Tolman, director of the National Gallery of Art, has in progress a definitive study on the life and works of Malbone.]

J. L. B.

MALCOLM, DANIEL (Nov. 29, 1725–Oct. 23, 1769), patriot, merchant, and sea-captain, was descended from the Scottish Clan Malcolm. He was born in Georgetown, Me., the son of Michael and Sarah Malcolm, who came to America a few years before Daniel's birth. His father was one of the selectmen of Georgetown for many years. Two other sons were Allen Malcolm, who fought on the patriot side in the Revolution, and Capt. John Malcolm, a customs officer under the Crown, who was twice tarred and feathered. Daniel became a sea-captain and owned several vessels. He bought two houses in Boston and was a warden of Christ Church. A leader of the Sons of Liberty, he was associated with Otis, Hancock, Revere, and Adams. Believing that the Revenue Acts were unjust, he became the most active antagonist of the customs authorities. On Sept. 24, 1766, the comptroller of customs, having information that a number of casks of uncustomed wine were concealed in Malcolm's cellar, went to his house armed with a writ of assistance, which was presumed by the superior court to give the right to enter and search. Malcolm refused to unlock an inner cellar. He "solemnly swore it should not be [opened] and if any Man attempted it, he would blow his Brains out . . . and took a Pistol in his hand and soon after another and then put on a sword. . . . He said . . . he knew the Laws and that no Body had a right to Come into his House" (*Proceedings of the Massachusetts Historical Society,* vol. LVIII, p. 27). The defeated officers returned in the afternoon with the high sheriff to find Malcolm's gate locked. They besieged him in his house until sunset, but to no avail. Then fearing for their lives from the crowd which had gathered, they abandoned the siege.

"I only wanted for the good of the Country to know whether they would break open Houses," said Malcolm (*Ibid.*, p. 42). When this case was referred to England, the attorney-general ruled that the courts in America had no right to issue writs of assistance.

In February 1768, a schooner of Malcolm's laden with sixty pipes of wines came into Boston harbor. He ordered her to anchor among the islands five miles out, landed the cargo in the night, and had it carried in drays to safety, each load being guarded by men with clubs. A few days later he called and presided at a meeting of the merchants of Boston, at which they entered into an agreement not to import any goods from Great Britain for a year and a half. Of this event Gov. Francis Bernard wrote to London: "This may be said to be the first movement of the merchants against the Acts of Parliament." On June 10, 1768, John Hancock's sloop *Liberty* was seized by the customs officers because her cargo of Madeira wine had been unloaded at night. Malcolm raised a mob at the wharf and attempted to prevent the seizure which was being made by marines from the *Romney*. Thus he led the patriots in the first clash with the armed forces of England. Malcolm married Ann Fudge, by whom he had several children. He died Oct. 23, 1769, at the age of forty-four. His gravestone on Copp's Hill, Boston, records his services: "a true Son of Liberty, a Friend to the Publick, an Enemy to oppression, and one of the foremost in opposing the Revenue Acts on America." This stone still shows the marks of bullets fired at it by British soldiers.

[Sources include: Georgetown, Me., records; Suffolk Deeds; Suffolk Probate Files, No. 14,571; Christ Church records; Lee MSS., Harvard College Lib., I, 15–23; G. G. Wolkins, "The Seizure of Hancock's Sloop 'Liberty'," *Proc. Mass. Hist. Soc.*, vol. LV (1923), and "Daniel Malcom and Writs of Assistance," *Ibid.*, vol. LVIII (1925); *Letters to the Right Hon. the Earl of Hillsborough from Gov. Bernard, Gen. Gage, and . . . Council for the Province of Mass. Bay* (1769); *A Report of the Record Commissioners . . . of Boston Containing the Boston Town Records, 1758 to 1769* (1886). Malcolm's name was sometimes spelled Malcom or Malcomb.] F. W. C. H.

MALCOLM, JAMES PELLER (August 1767–Apr. 5, 1815), line-engraver, author, and antiquary, who in earlier life signed himself James Peller Malcom, was the son of Moses and Mary (Peller) Malcom and was born in Philadelphia, Pa. He began his education in the Friends' School, then presided over by Robert Proud [*q.v.*]. His great-grandfather, James Peller, came over in the ship with William Penn, returned with him to England, but later settled with his family in Pennsylvania. Malcolm never ceased to remember that he had been born a British subject, and continued Loyalist until his death, spending the last half of his life in England. Because of the dangers expected of the Revolution he was taken to Pottstown, Pa., just before the struggle resulted in open warfare, and there his education was continued. He returned to Philadelphia after the war was ended, in 1784, and there he began to devote himself to the study of art. Having a natural aptitude for drawing, he entered the field of engraving. His first published engraving was the frontispiece for Col. John Parke's *Lyric Works of Horace,* which he engraved in line after a sketch by Peter Markoe in 1786. This example is good neither technically nor artistically, but it displayed promise. Under the patronage of the Rev. Jacob Duché and Thomas Willing of Philadelphia Malcolm went to England. He studied three years in the schools of the Royal Academy. His engraving of a view of Bush Hill, the seat of William Hamilton, was published in the *Universal Magazine,* London, in 1787 (vol. LXXXI, Supp., facing p. 361).

In England Malcolm made illustrations for the magazines, especially for the *Gentleman's Magazine.* He is thought to have returned to Philadelphia in 1792 or 1793, though in his own autobiography in the *Gentleman's Magazine* (May 1815), he makes no mention of ever having visited his native land. Originally he intended to become a painter, but after his course in the Royal Academy schools, he received no encouragement and began to devote himself to engraving plates for the London magazines, and to compiling books. For Daniel Lysons' *Environs of London* (4 vols., 1792–96), he engraved seventy-nine plates. He was himself the author and illustrator of many volumes, among them *Londinium Redivivum* (4 vols., 1803–07); *Anecdotes of the Manners and Customs of London, During the Eighteenth Century* (1807); *Excursions in the County of Kent, Gloucester, Hereford, Monmouth, and Somerset* (1807); *Anecdotes of the Manners and Customs of London, from the Roman Invasion to the Year 1700* (1811); and *An Historical Sketch of the Art of Caricaturing* (1813). When his *Manners and Customs of London in the Eighteenth Century* reached a second edition in 1810, he seized the opportunity to refute his critics (the *European Magazine and London Review,* June 1808) by pointing out that for both text and illustrations he had used the great collection of John Nichols, the antiquary. As an engraver Malcolm was careful and painstaking in the interests of accuracy, but his art lacked inspiration. During the last three years of his life, he was ill, and his funds were exhausted. When he died his widow and aged mother were left destitute.

[The basic source for biographies of Malcolm is the autobiographical sketch in the *Gentleman's Mag.*, May 1815. For other printed references see *Ibid.*, Feb., June 1797, Jan., Apr. 1798, Supp. 1800, Apr. 1815; the *Dict. Nat. Biog.*; W. T. Lowndes, *The Bibliographer's Manual of English Lit.* (1834), vol. III; D. M. Stauffer, *Am. Engravers upon Copper and Steel* (1907), vol. I; T. J. Scharf and Thompson Westcott, *Hist. of Phila.* (1884), vol. II; *Phila. Monthly Mag.*, Apr. 1829. The names of his parents were derived from the manuscript records of Christ Church, Phila.]

J. J.

MALCOM, DANIEL [See MALCOLM, DANIEL, 1725–1769].

MALCOM, HOWARD (Jan. 19, 1799–Mar. 25, 1879), Baptist clergyman, author, educator, was born in Philadelphia, Pa., the son of John J. and Deborah (Howard) Malcom. His father had emigrated from Scotland; on his mother's side he was of Welsh ancestry. After the death of his father, his home was with his grandfather, John Howard, a wealthy merchant. He entered Dickinson College but left in his junior year to take a position in a large commission house in Philadelphia. During the following seventeen months of business experience, he passed through a religious experience which resulted in his joining the Sansom Street Baptist Church, where in 1818 he was licensed to preach. There, also, having spent the intervening time at Princeton Theological Seminary, he was ordained a Baptist clergyman on Apr. 23, 1820. On May 1, 1820, he was married to Lydia Morris Shields, who died in 1833. She was the mother of his eldest son. On June 26, 1838, he was married to Ruth A. Dyer, by whom he had two sons and two daughters.

From 1820 to 1826 he was pastor of a Baptist church at Hudson, N. Y., where his capacity for leadership became so well and favorably known that the American Sunday School Union invited him to give all of his time to the field work of that organization. In this service he visited nearly all the principal towns and cities in the United States. In November 1827 he accepted the pastorate of the Federal Street Baptist Church, Boston, which he had to relinquish in 1835 because of a throat disease which made it difficult for him to speak to large audiences. That same year the American Baptist Foreign Missionary Union sent him abroad to visit missionary stations in India, Burma, and China. As a fruitage of three years of travel he published in 1839, *Travels in South-Eastern Asia,* a work which added to his growing reputation as an author, his first venture in authorship, *A Dictionary of Important Names, Objects, and Terms Found in the Holy Scriptures* (1830), having already become the most popular book of its kind.

In 1840 he became president of Georgetown College, Ky., where he remained nine years. When he voted for an anti-slavery amendment to the state constitution, the trustees of the college asked for his resignation. He had been warned that he would have to leave the state if he so voted. Returning to Philadelphia, he soon became pastor of his old home church, but the large auditorium overtaxed his voice and in 1851 he resigned to become president of Lewisburg University, now Bucknell University, Lewisburg, Pa. For six years he made a valuable contribution to the growth of that institution. His literary interests came to absorb so much of his time and strength, however, that in 1857 he resigned his presidency to give them first place. To facilitate his work as a writer he moved to Philadelphia where he became identified with a wide variety of public interests. He was president of the American Baptist Historical Society, of the American Peace Society, of the Pennsylvania Baptist Educational Society, and from 1874 till his death, of Hahnemann Medical College.

In addition to his *Dictionary* and *Travels,* he published about a dozen other books, among them *Extent and Efficacy of the Atonement* (1833), a discourse; *A Brief Memoir of Mrs. Lydia M. Malcom* (1833); *The Christian's Rule of Marriage* (1834); *Theological Index: References to the Principal Works in Every Department of Religious Literature* (1868; 2nd ed., 1870). He also edited several works, including Thomas à Kempis' *The Imitation of Christ* (1830), Matthew Henry's *Communicant's Companion* (1840), William Law's *A Serious Call to a Devout and Holy Life* (1835), and Joseph Butler's *Analogy of Religion* (1857). As his *Dictionary* passed through successive editions, he continued to revise and enlarge it for thirty years. From his royalties he built a home in Lewisburg, Pa.

[*Bucknell Alumni Mo.*, vol. IX; *Dickinson Alumni Record*; *Baptist Memorial and Monthly Record*, vol. X (1851); *The Am. Cyc.*, vol. XI (1875); William Cathcart, *The Baptist Encyc.* (1881); *Princeton Theological Seminary Biog. Cat.* (1909); *Necrological Report . . . Princeton Theological Seminary*, 1879; J. H. Spencer, *A Hist. of Ky. Baptists* (1866), vol. I; *Public Ledger* (Phila.), Mar. 26, 1879.]

H. T. C.

MALCOM, JAMES PELLER [See MALCOLM, JAMES PELLER, 1767–1815].

MALL, FRANKLIN PAINE (Sept. 28, 1862–Nov. 17, 1917), anatomist and embryologist, was born on a farm near Belle Plaine, Iowa, the son of Francis and Louise (Miller) Mall.

His father had emigrated to the United States from Germany in 1848; his mother, who was born in this country, died when he was a young boy. Having obtained his early education in a boarding school near his home, he entered the department of medicine and surgery of the University of Michigan and received the degree of M.D. in 1883. He showed at this time a strong inclination to get knowledge at first hand, rather than through lectures. Victor C. Vaughan [*q.v.*] and Henry Sewall gave him a special inspiration. After graduating he studied at Heidelberg and then at Leipzig under the physiologist K. F. W. Ludwig and the embryologist Wilhelm His. Returning to the United States, he became fellow in pathology at Johns Hopkins Hospital and later instructor in pathology. When Clark University was opened, in 1889, he became adjunct professor of vertebrate anatomy there, but three years later went to the new University of Chicago, as professor of anatomy, with others of his colleagues at Clark. He was soon called back to Baltimore, as head of the department of anatomy in the Johns Hopkins Medical School. In 1914 he was appointed, in addition, director of the department of embryology of the Carnegie Institution, Washington. He maintained close relations with biologists as well as medical men and was a trustee of the Woods Hole Biological Laboratory and member of the advisory board of the Wistar Institute, a member of the National Academy of Sciences, the American Philosophical Society, and a number of other learned societies.

Mall contributed much to the knowledge of human anatomy and embryology. In 1883 American laboratories were adding little to the results of research in these subjects. An English reviewer of Mall's first volume dealing with the accomplishments of the Carnegie Laboratory referred to the remarkable changes which had taken place in the study of anatomy in America during the past twenty-five years, and added: "In effecting this transformation the chief credit must be assigned to one man—Franklin P. Mall. . . . By his personal influence and example, by pupils and disciples, and by reason of the inherent excellence of the Leipzig traditions, he has succeeded in Germanising the majority of the dissecting rooms and anatomical laboratories throughout the length and breadth of North America" (*Nature,* London, Feb. 3, 1916). In medical education Mall stood for freedom of curricula, concentration of courses, broad electives, and freedom for research by the teacher. His department of anatomy at Baltimore was the first to bring into one discipline as correlated studies cytology, histology, embryology, and adult structure. He rarely lectured, insisting that learning from nature was of primary importance and that students should do their own thinking. He was largely responsible for the founding of the *American Journal of Anatomy* in 1901, and was one of its editors until his death. He played a prominent part in the American Association of Anatomists, of which he was president from 1905 to 1907. In 1912 he formulated a plan for an institute of human embryology which so impressed the president and trustees of the Carnegie Institution that they created the department of embryology for him. To increase his already large collection of human embryos he sent a circular letter to physicians of the United States and as far afield as the Orient. As a result the laboratory has ever since been the world repository for specimens. Their study was systematically begun, new methods of research were invented and perfected, and a series of publications, *Contributions to Embryology,* undertaken, which reached seven volumes during Mall's lifetime.

His own researches were numerous and important. He first traced the embryologic origin of the thymus gland, added to knowledge of the structure and function of the intestines, introduced the idea of histological units in organs, worked out the muscular system of the heart, described with unexampled completeness a human embryo of about twenty-eight days, laid the foundation of the science of the development of organs, and placed the subject of the production of human monsters on a scientific basis.

Though shy and retiring in company, and a little tinged with pessimism, he loved association with scientific men. He was too absorbed in his own ideas to converse fluently; but he had broad human interests and a humor that was occasionally a little biting. Behind his whimsical way of saying things, however, was profound wisdom. In 1895 he married Mabel Stanley Glover, who with two daughters survived him.

[Simon Flexner, "Dr. Franklin P. Mall, an Appreciation," and F. R. Sabin, "Franklin Paine Mall; A Review of His Scientific Achievement," in *Science,* Mar. 15, 1918; G. C. Huber, "Franklin Paine Mall," in *Anatomical Record,* Jan. 20, 1918; "Memorial Services in Honor of Franklin Paine Mall, Professor of Anatomy, Johns Hopkins University, 1893 to 1917," *Johns Hopkins Hospital Bull.,* May 1918; *Jour. of the Iowa State Medic. Soc.,* Mar. 1928; H. A. Kelly and W. L. Burrage, *Am. Medic. Biogs.* (1920); *Who's Who in America,* 1916–17; *Evening Sun* (Baltimore), Nov. 17, 1917.]

C. B. D.

MALLARY, ROLLIN CAROLAS (May 27, 1784–Apr. 15, 1831), congressman from Vermont, was born in Cheshire, Conn., the eldest of seven children of Daniel and Martha (Dutton)

Mallary. In 1795 he moved with his father to Poultney, Vt., from which place he entered Middlebury College, graduating in 1805. He studied law with Horatio Seymour at Middlebury and with Robert Temple at Rutland, and, after serving one year (1806–07) as preceptor of Castleton Seminary, was admitted to the bar of Rutland County in March 1807. He practised law with conspicuous success in Castleton until 1818, when he transferred his office to Poultney. While in Castleton he was state's attorney in the years 1810–13 and 1815–16. He was appointed in October 1807 as secretary to the governor and council and held the position intermittently in 1807, 1809–12, and 1815–19.

In 1819 Mallary was a candidate for Congress against Orsamus C. Merrill, of Bennington, the incumbent. Merrill was declared elected, but Mallary claimed the seat, and the House, after a hearing, decided in his favor, Jan. 13, 1820. He proved to be a very effective business member of Congress, mild in manner and unspectacular, but punctual and industrious. He won some distinction as an opponent of the admission of Missouri with slavery, and later became a conspicuous champion of the protective system. At the opening of the Twentieth Congress he was made chairman of the House committee on manufacture and reported the notorious "Tariff of Abominations" in 1828. He was the leader of the debate in the House on this measure and his pertinacity was largely responsible for its passage. At a notable dinner given in his honor at Rutland, on July 6, 1830, he was enthusiastically lauded for his efforts in behalf of the protective system. He was reëlected for six successive terms. Because of overwork, his health failed during the winter of 1830–31 and, after the adjournment of Congress, he was removed to the home of a relative in Baltimore, where he died. Funeral services were held in Baltimore, but he was buried in the old cemetery at East Poultney, Vt., where a marble monument to his memory was erected by the Rutland County Bar. Mallary had married, on Oct. 29, 1806, Ruth Stanley, eldest daughter of John Stanley, by whom he had three children. He was a trustee of Middlebury College from 1825 until his death. His chief distinction was his advocacy of the protective tariff.

[See: Abby M. Hemenway, *The Vt. Hist. Gazeteer*, vol. III (1877); Walter H. Crockett, *Vt., The Green Mountain State*, vol. V (1923); J. S. Ullery, *Men of Vt.* (1894); J. Joslin and others, *A Hist. of the Town of Poultney, Vt.* (1875); *Biog. Dir. Am. Cong.* (1928); *Cat. of the Officers and Students of Middlebury Coll., 1800 to 1900* (1901); *Niles' Weekly Reg.*, Apr. 23, 1831. Mallary's middle name is variously spelled. This sketch follows the spelling given in the *Biog. Dir. Am. Cong.*]

C. M. F.

MALLERY, GARRICK (Apr. 23, 1831–Oct. 24, 1894), soldier, ethnologist, was born in Wilkes-Barre, Pa., the son of Garrick and Catherine J. (Hall) Mallery. His early education was received in private schools, and since his father was a jurist, the son was naturally destined for the legal profession. Accordingly, after graduating from Yale in 1850, he studied law and in 1853 was admitted to the bar in Philadelphia. At the outbreak of the Civil War he immediately enlisted as a private but on June 4, 1861, he was appointed captain in the 71st Pennsylvania Infantry. At the battle of Peach Orchard, Va., the following year, he was wounded and taken prisoner. After his exchange, he was commissioned, Feb. 17, 1863, lieutenant-colonel of the 13th Pennsylvania Cavalry. He was honorably mustered out July 15, 1864, and brevetted colonel of volunteers on Mar. 13, 1865. The following year, July 28, he was commissioned captain in the 43rd Infantry of the regular army, and on Mar. 2, 1867, was brevetted lieutenant-colonel. When in 1870 the system of meteorological observations, which developed into the Signal Service Bureau, was established, Mallery became acting signal officer and remained with this branch of the service for six years. On duty at Fort Rice, Dakota, in 1876, he became interested in the pictography and sign language of the Indians. Later he was engaged on field work with Maj. J. W. Powell in connection with surveys in the Rocky Mountains. Disability from wounds received in the war caused his retirement from the army, July 1, 1879.

This same year he became connected with the Bureau of Ethnology, under the Smithsonian Institution, with headquarters in Washington, D. C. His first paper, "The Former and Present Number of Our Indians" (*Proceedings of the American Association for the Advancement of Science,* vol. XXVI, 1877), was on the moot question that has been raised so many times and not satisfactorily answered. A paper originating from his observations among the Indians, which foreshadowed his future work with the Bureau, was: "A Calendar of the Dakota Nation" (*Bulletin of the Geological and Geographical Survey,* vol. III, no. 1, 1877). This paper related to the conveying of ideas of events by picture writing. Easily the foremost student of the subject, he published: *Introduction to the Study of Sign Language Among the North American Indians as Illustrating the Gesture Speech of Mankind* (Smithsonian Institution—Bureau of Ethnology, 1880), followed by: "Sign Language among North American Indians Compared with That of Other Peoples and Deaf Mutes" (*First*

Annual Report of the Bureau of American Ethnology, 1881). An important feature of this study was the philosophical discussion of the origin of the communication of ideas by the vehicle of language symbols. Mallery's culminating work, requiring years of assiduous collection of data and original investigation on pictography, appeared in 1893—"Picture Writing of the North American Indians" (*Tenth Annual Report of the Bureau of American Ethnology*). As a monumental storehouse of well classified and digested data it is without peer. Through all its overwhelming mass of necessary illustrations the philosophic mind of the author is evident. In only one instance did Mallery's writing evoke controversy. The paper: "Israelite and Indian: a Parallel in Planes of Culture" (*Popular Science Monthly,* November–December 1889), provoked severe and no doubt justified criticism by one of the races thus brought into juxtaposition. As a man of solid attainments Mallery received many high honors. He was an active member of many scientific societies. A tall, erect, dignified man, always well groomed, he gave the impression of capability and directive force. Unmistakably an army man trained in formality, he was nevertheless a pleasant associate and appreciated by his scientific equals. His influence in promoting scientific methods in the formative period of the branch of anthropology was notable. On Apr. 14, 1870, he married Helen W. Wyckoff of New York.

[*Obit. Record Grads. Yale Univ.,* June 1895; F. B. Heitman, *Hist. Reg. and Dict. U. S. Army* (1903), vol. I; S. P. Bates, *Hist. of Pa. Volunteers,* vols. II (1869), III (1870); J. W. Powell, in *Johnson's Universal Encyc.* (1897); Robert Fletcher, *Brief Memoirs of Col. Garrick Mallery* (1895); *Ann. Report of the Board of Regents of the Smithsonian Institution,* 1895; *Evening Star* (Washington, D. C.), Oct. 25, 1894; personal recollections.] W. H.

MALLET, JOHN WILLIAM (Oct. 10, 1832–Nov. 7, 1912), chemist, was born near Dublin, Ireland, the eldest of six children of Robert Mallet, an engineer and fellow of the Royal Society (see *Dictionary of National Biography*), and Cordelia (Watson) Mallet. After studying chemistry (1848) at the Royal College of Surgeons in Ireland, he entered Trinity College in 1849, publishing about this time his first scientific contribution, "Notice of a New Chemical Examination of Killinite," in the *Journal of the Geological Society of Dublin* (vol. IV, 1848–50). In 1852 he graduated (Ph.D.) under Wöhler at Göttingen and in 1853 received the degree of A.B. at Trinity College, Dublin. Meanwhile he had assisted his father in experiments on the velocity of shock-transmission from gunpowder explosions through rock and loose earth, and had commenced the preparation of a "Catalogue of Recorded Earthquakes from B.C. 1606 to A.D. 1842," which was published in the *Report of the British Association for the Advancement of Science* for 1852, 1853, and 1854 (1853–55).

Coming to America in 1853, he was assistant professor of analytical chemistry at Amherst College for several months in 1854, then became chemist to the state geological survey of Alabama (1855–56) and professor of chemistry at the state university (1855–60). From the papers of Michael Tuomey [*q.v.*] he edited the *Second Biennial Report on the Geology of Alabama* (1858). He also undertook an exhaustive scientific study of the culture of cotton. For this work specimens of plants, soils, and rocks were secured from India, Algeria, Africa, and America; soils were analyzed; density, cohesion, capillarity, and absorption of gases were determined; stems, roots, seeds, fibers were separately analyzed. The resulting treatise was published in book form under the title, *Cotton: the Chemical, Geological, and Meteorological Conditions Involved in Its Successful Cultivation* (1862), and appeared the same year in the *Proceedings of the Royal Society of London* (vol. XI, 1862).

Enlisting as a private in the service of the Confederacy shortly after the outbreak of the Civil War, Mallet became in November 1861 an officer on the staff of Gen. R. E. Rodes [*q.v.*], and in 1862 was given general supervision of the ordnance laboratories of the Confederacy. After the war, for a group of Northern capitalists, he made a survey for petroleum in Louisiana and Texas (1865). He was professor of chemistry in the medical department of the University of Louisiana, 1865–67; at the University of Virginia, 1867–83; in the University of Texas, 1883–84; and in Jefferson Medical College, 1884–85. He then returned to the University of Virginia, where he remained, as professor emeritus after 1908, until his death.

As a lecturer Mallet was systematic, concise, clear in his presentation and explanation of facts. He insisted that each of his students make some investigation and so add his fragment to the sum total of knowledge. His own publications comprised more than one hundred papers on new compounds, minerals, and chemical and physical phenomena. In 1881–82 he made investigations of drinking waters, reporting the results in the *Annual Report of the National Board of Health, 1882* (1883). Three times (1886, 1888, 1896) he was a member of the Assay Commission. In 1877–78 he lectured at Johns Hopkins University. He was one of the founders of the American Chemical Society and its president in 1882, a member of several European chemical societies, and a fellow of the Royal Society of London. He served as member of the International Committee on Atomic Weights, 1899; and of the International Congress of Applied Chemistry in Berlin, 1903, and Rome, 1906. He was married in 1857 to Mary Elizabeth Ormond of Tuscaloosa, Ala., who died in 1886; and in 1888 to Joséphine (Pagès) Burthe of Louisiana. Three children were born of his first marriage. Although he was a resident of the United States for more than fifty years, Mallet never relinquished his status as a British subject. He died in Virginia at the age of eighty.

[F. P. Dunnington, in *Am. Chemical Jour.*, Jan. 1913; W. H. Echols, in *Univ. of Va. Alumni Bull.*, Jan. 1913; full bibliography of Mallet's writings, *Ibid.*, Oct. 1923; *Who's Who in America*, 1912–13; *Times-Dispatch* (Richmond), Nov. 8, 1912.] F. P. V.

MALLINCKRODT, EDWARD (Jan. 21, 1845–Feb. 1, 1928), manufacturer of chemicals, benefactor of educational institutions, was born on a farm near St. Louis, Mo., the son of Emil and Eleanor Didier (Luckie) Mallinckrodt. His father, disheartened by conditions in Germany, had emigrated fourteen years before from Westphalia, home of the grandfather, Arnold Mallinckrodt, a Dortmund publisher. Edward's parents had looked forward to his remaining on the farm, but when he was eighteen Liebig's treatises turned him to chemistry. Accordingly his father, who was then visiting in Germany, made arrangements for Edward and Otto, a younger son, to study the subject there, and Edward spent the next three years in Fresenius' laboratory, Wiesbaden, the De Haën works near Hanover, and the University of Berlin.

Returning in 1867, Edward and Otto joined an elder brother, Gustav, under the firm name of G. Mallinckrodt & Company, in what was a pioneer undertaking in the Middle West, the manufacture of chemicals. The enterprise had an unpretentious start, being housed in a small, rough structure on the parental farm. With the West undeveloped and the South prostrated by the Civil War, St. Louis was an unfavorable location. Since it was necessary, moreover, to send products East to compete with established firms, hardships were many in the first decade. Otto and Gustav died six months apart (1876–77), and in 1882 the business was incorporated as the Mallinckrodt Chemical Works, with Edward as president. Although learned in chemical technology, he now devoted himself to the commercial side of the business and the enterprise grew rapidly. Before he died its output included 1,500 chemical products, and it maintained offices or branches in New York, Jersey City, Toronto, and Montreal. In 1889 he formed the National Ammonia Company with subsidiaries as far away as Australia. The press called him the "ammonia king." He was also active in the Phosphorous Compounds Company at Niagara Falls and the St. Louis Union Trust Company, and was an owner of downtown real estate in St. Louis.

Wealth enabled him to indulge a generous nature. His largest single gift, $500,000 to Harvard for its chemical laboratory, named for him, was made because he felt that although chemistry held more potential benefits than any other science, American facilities for its study were inferior to those in some other countries. Further gifts endowed departments in Washington University Medical School and helped to complete its $1,000,000 Mallinckrodt Radiological Institute. He established a ward in the St. Louis Children's Hospital in memory of his wife, formerly Jennie Anderson of St. Louis, whom he married June 7, 1876, and who died in 1913. St. Luke's Hospital, which he helped direct for twenty-five years, as president part of the time, received numerous grants, and the St. Louis College of Pharmacy, which he headed, funds for a scholarship. His will gave approximately $2,000,000 to such "benevolent, scientific, charitable, literary or educational" agencies as his only son should see fit to benefit. He was a member of the Washington University board, a director of the Missouri Botanical Garden, a president of the Mercantile Library, and vice-president of the City Art Museum, to which he donated paintings. The professional and learned societies to which he belonged included British and German organizations. An expert gardener, he was at eighty still caring for the flowers about his homes. He died soon after his eighty-third birthday, of pneumonia following a heart attack, and was buried in Bellefontaine Cemetery, St. Louis.

[Published sources include: *Industrial and Engineering Chemistry*, news. ed., Mar. 10, 1928; W. L. R. Gifford, "Edward Mallinckrodt," in *Harvard Alumni Bull.*, May 22, 1924; *St. Louis Post-Dispatch*, Feb. 1, 1928; *Who's Who in America*, 1928–29. A biographical sketch prepared by George Dumas Stout, of St. Louis, for private distribution is soon to appear.] I. D.

MALLORY, STEPHEN RUSSELL (*c.* 1813–Nov. 9, 1873), secretary of the Confederate navy, was the son of Charles Mallory, a civil engineer, of Reading, Conn., professionally engaged on public work in Trinidad Island, near Venezuela, where he had met and married the sixteen-year-old Ellen Russell, recently of County Waterford, Ireland. They had two children, John, born about 1811, and Stephen Russell Mallory, born in Trinidad about 1813, though it is worth noting that his tombstone in St. Michael's Cemetery, Pensacola, bears no birth date. About 1814 the parents moved first to the United States, then to Havana for Charles Mallory's health. Before settling at Key West around 1820, they entered Stephen at school on Mobile Bay, where he remained six months or a year. In 1822 the father died of tuberculosis, and John did not long survive him. Stephen and his young mother lived on at Key West. Thus the future naval secretary grew up by the sea, loving and learning about ships. When he was fourteen his mother sent him inland to the Moravian school for boys at Nazareth, Pa. Three years in this institution of about eighty youths completed his meager schooling, but not his opportunities to learn and grow. In 1833 he was appointed inspector of customs at Key West. About the same time he began to study law with Judge William Marvin of the local United States district court. Admitted to the bar before 1840, he forged ahead. In 1845 President Polk made him collector of customs at Key West. Meanwhile he had fought in the Seminole War and married Angela, the daughter of Francisca and Josefa Moreno of Pensacola, Fla.

In 1850 Mallory was sufficiently prominent to be picked by his state as a delegate to the Southern convention at Nashville. Though eleven years later a secessionist, he did not attend this abortive convention. In 1851 the Florida legislature elected him to the United States Senate. His opponent, David L. Yulee, with Edwin M. Stanton for attorney, failed to convince the United States Senate that Mallory had been irregularly elected. Mallory was doubtless genuinely interested in the navy. Active in congressional naval reform, he was reëlected senator in 1857 and appointed chairman of the committee on naval affairs. Possibly his ability to speak Spanish correctly, as well as French, had something to do with President Buchanan's offering to send him (if Scharf, *post,* is correct) as United States minister to Spain in 1858. Mallory refused. When Florida seceded he gave up his seat in the Senate, returned to Pensacola, his home since 1858, and took emphatic stand for peace (J. B. Moore, *The Works of James Buchanan,* IX, 1910, pp. 285–86). But in February 1861 he accepted from President Jefferson Davis the office of secretary of the navy of the Confederacy.

Here was a challenge to all of Mallory's ability. Well versed in the advanced naval experiments of the American, Robert L. Stevens [*q.v.*]; aware that England and France were actually building iron fleets, he saw that the confederacy must instantly stimulate her young naval experts to lead the world in naval invention. As early as May 10, 1861, he wrote that the South should fight wood with iron (*War of the Rebellion: Official Records, Navy,* 2 ser. II, pp. 67–69). He dreamed of securing at once two ironclads from England or France. He hurried Lieut. James H. North in May to London, but he did not wait for North's report, or for Congress to sanction the building of an ironclad at home. Having discovered a brilliant naval inventor in John Mercer Brooke [*q.v.*], by March 1862 he had afloat in Hampton Roads that strange murderous craft, the *Merrimac-Virginia.* He pinned greater hope on the *Mississippi,* an ironclad, more like the European models, which in April 1862 the Tift brothers, eagerly aided by the secretary, were feverishly completing at New Orleans. Within about two weeks of a successful launching of the *Mississippi,* the Tifts were forced to burn her to keep her from falling into the hands of the approaching enemy.

Mallory failed to secure a single up-to-date ironclad, but his wide naval horizon, his grasp of naval construction, and his tireless endeavor so stimulated specialists like Brooke and George Minor, chief of ordnance and hydrography, to naval organization and invention that the Confederacy, which started without ships or navy yards, anticipated modern naval invention in deadly torpedoes and submarines to such extent that it terrorized the Federal navy and effectively delayed it from penetrating the great rivers of Virginia. Insight into Mallory's vehement, unconquerable nature, inherited possibly from his Irish mother, may be seen in his ardent wish (not carried out) to burn the Tredegar Iron Works before the Davis government evacuated Richmond.

Retreating with President Davis in April 1865, Mallory joined his wife in La Grange, Ga., and was hauled out of bed there by armed men just past midnight, May 20, 1865, and hustled off half-clothed, a prisoner of state. Until March 1866 he was held in Fort Lafayette, New York Harbor. Released on parole, he returned to Pensacola with his family and resumed his law practice. But he did not have long to live. On Nov. 9, 1873, about the age of sixty, he died at Pensacola and lies buried there in St. Michael's Cemetery. His family consisted of two daughters and three sons, one of whom, Stephen Russell Mallory, Jr., a bachelor until his death, served for years with distinction in the United States House and Senate.

[Mallory has been meagerly treated by historians, and the brief accounts of him in encyclopedias and dictionaries differ astonishingly as to the facts of his life. His only extant papers, according to his grand-daughter, Mrs. Ruby Mallory Fisher of Pensacola, are unpublished letters to his wife, before and after 1865, and a personal manuscript diary which he wrote at Fort Lafayette. The statements in J. T. Scharf, *Hist. of the Confed. States Navy* (1887), pp. 29–30, were probably gained through correspondence with the Secretary's widow in 1886. See also: *War of the Rebellion: Official Records* (*Army* and *Navy*), especially 2 ser. I and II of the latter; *Senate Miscellaneous Doc. 1*, 32 Cong., Special Sess.; *Senate Miscellaneous Doc. 109* and *110*, 32 Cong., 1 Sess.; *Senate Report 349*, 32 Cong., 1 Sess.; Kathleen Bruce, *Va. Iron Manuf. in the Slave Era* (1931); and the *Mobile Daily Reg.*, Nov. 12, 1873. Contemporary local newspaper files are in the Fla. Hist. Soc. at Pensacola.] K. B.

MALONE, SYLVESTER (May 8, 1821–Dec. 29, 1899), Roman Catholic priest, son of Laurence and Marcella (Martin) Malone, was born in Trim, County Meath, Ireland, where his father was a surveyor. Trained in a mixed school kept by two graduates of Trinity College, the boy imbibed a spirit of tactful toleration as well as classical lore. Experiencing a priestly call, in 1839 he accepted the invitation of Father Andrew Byrne [*q.v.*] to come to New York, where he entered St. Joseph's Seminary, Fordham. Ordained Aug. 15, 1844, he was assigned to Williamsburg (Brooklyn), then a town of about 5,000 people. Within three years, he paid off the debt of St. Mary's Church, gathered scattered Catholics into the fold, won the good will of even prejudiced citizens, and commenced the construction of the Church of Saints Peter and Paul, the first Gothic structure in the diocese. Caring for hordes of immigrants, he contracted both the smallpox and the ship's cholera (1848–49). On the eve of his journey to Rome in 1854, however, he could point to a congregation of 5,000, and a well-organized parish.

Regarded as a mild abolitionist, Father Malone suffered some inconveniences on this account; yet even his espousal of Republican principles did not lessen his popularity among Irish Democrats. When Fort Sumter was fired upon, he unfurled a flag from his church, which was soon carried to the front by members of the congregation. Public subscription provided a substitute flag, which waved from the steeple until the war ended. An active war-man, he aided sanitary fairs, quieted turbulent draft-rioters, encouraged enlistments, and donated a fourth of his salary to the fund for soldiers' wives. In 1866, as Bishop Loughlin's theologian, he attended the Second Plenary Council of Baltimore, where he was so impressed with reports of Catholic reconstruction in the South that in 1868 he toured that part of the country, contributing to the press descriptive letters of the conditions he found. On his return he urged Catholic activity among the negroes of the South. At Memorial-Day celebrations of the Grand Army of the Republic, he joined in the exercises with Protestant divines; and in 1870, at a Jewish reception, he aroused comment by demanding equal rights for black and white and for Jew and Gentile.

Returning from a tour through Europe and the Holy Land an ardent Irish Land Leaguer, he later became a liberal with strong labor views. He was deeply interested in civic affairs, clean government, temperance, the improvement of public schools, and the Anti-Poverty Society. Greatly disturbed by the break between Archbishop Corrigan and Edward McGlynn [*q.v.*], he courageously wrote to Pope Leo, in December 1886, that a censure of Dr. McGlynn, "the friend of the poor, the eloquent defender of the doctrines of the Church, the advocate of temperance and of every good cause that works for the public good," unless for a grave irregularity, would set the Church back half a century and raise the question of the rights of a citizen (letter reprinted in Zwierlein, *post,* III, 16). In 1894, urged by Hamilton Fish, Malone stood as a candidate for a regency of the University of New York, and, supported by Archbishop Ireland [*q.v.*], Bishop Ryan of Buffalo, and the Republican press, he was elected by a Republican legislature over Bishop McQuaid [*q.v.*]. Even Democratic papers were not personally hostile, though in some quarters his election was described as an affront to the Catholic Church, since Archbishop Corrigan and most of his suffragan bishops favored McQuaid. This year saw the celebration of Father Malone's golden jubilee as a priest. Congratulations came from Leo XIII, Cardinal Gibbons, the apostolic delegate, and many notable citizens as well as members of the hierarchy and priesthood. The event was considered a vindication of the liberal element in the metropolitan diocese of New York. The *Outlook* (Oct. 27, 1894) pertinently asked: "Why should such a man be allowed to remain in one pastorate? Naturally one would suppose that he would have risen to be a bishop or archbishop" (Oct. 27, 1894); while the *Independent* (Oct. 25) believed that his Republican politics prevented promotion. He continued as pastor of the parish which he had created until his death six years later.

[S. L. Malone, *Memorial of the Golden Jubilee of the Rev. Sylvester Malone* (1895); D. R. O'Brien, "The Centenary of Rev. Sylvester Malone, Great Catholic and Great Citizen," *Jour. Am.-Irish Hist. Soc.*, vol. XX (1921); *Father Malone Memorial, Citizens' Committee Report* (1923), on the occasion of placing a bust of Father Malone in the Brooklyn Institute of Arts and Sciences; H. R. Stiles, *Hist. of the County of*

Kings and City of Brooklyn, N. Y. (1884); F. J. Zwierlein, *The Life and Letters of Bishop McQuaid,* vol. III (1927); *Brooklyn Daily Eagle* and *N. Y. Times,* Dec. 29, 1899–Jan. 2, 1900.] R. J. P.

MALONE, WALTER (Feb. 10, 1866–May 18, 1915), jurist, poet, was born in De Soto County, Miss., near Memphis, Tenn., the son of Dr. Franklin Jefferson and Mary Louisa (Hardin) Malone. During the period of his education, which was principally at the University of Mississippi, where he studied law and was graduated with the degree of Ph.B. in 1887, he did much independent studying and writing. At sixteen he published *Claribel and Other Poems,* tramping the countryside to secure subscribers. In this, as in *The Outcast and Other Poems* (1886), there was, amid much that was grandiloquent and derivative, an unusual facility coupled with a serious predilection for the larger forms of verse and some leaning toward native materials.

Admitted to the bar in 1887, he moved to Memphis and practised law with his brother, James H. Malone, meanwhile serving during 1888 as city editor of the Memphis *Public Ledger* and writing poetry. Of a somewhat reserved, but gentle and sensitive temperament, he matured slowly as a poet. In *Narcissus and Other Poems* (1892), *Songs of Dusk and Dawn* (1894), and *Songs of December and June* (1896) his verse did not escape the savorlessness of current models; but it was precise, serious, and profuse in imagery. There were occasional metrical experiments and frank bursts of passion and melancholy, reflecting his loneliness in the contemporary scene. After writing a volume of short stories, *The Coming of the King* (1897), and three years' residence in New York, only partially satisfactory to him in literary achievement, Malone returned to Memphis in 1900, publishing in that year his *Songs of North and South.* In its seasonal poems and verse sketches full of affectionate observation of Southern scenes, richly described, this volume showed Malone at his best; but his poem "Opportunity," which appeared in 1905, captured the public ear and got him popular fame at a level somewhat lower than his own ideal. In 1904 he published *Poems,* containing his work up to that date with revisions.

Appointed judge of the second division of the Shelby County Circuit Court in 1905, he held this position, universally respected and loved, until his death, and conducted his court according to the best traditions of the Tennessee bench. He experimented a little with play-writing and published *Songs of East and West* (1906), a volume of travel poems. Then for some years he gave his whole creative strength to his epic poem, *Hernando De Soto,* which, notwithstanding his ill health and his fears that it could not be finished, was published in 1914. Though illustrating the difficulty of following epic conventions in modern verse, the poem was one of the most ambitious ever written by an American. The Mississippi River and the historic encounters of Spaniard and Indian had fired Malone's imagination. Despite much that was labored and artificial, his ardor infused magnificence of detail and narrative force into the long tale of De Soto's travels, conquests, and death. In its monumental quality it symbolized the grave intensity of Malone's career, as a jurist and gentleman whose beloved avocation was poetry, and who felt that he owed it to himself and his subject to ignore contemporary trivialities, and that, in the perspective of posterity, only epic dignity could do justice to the history and scenes he loved. He died of an apoplectic stroke in the Peabody Hotel, Memphis. He was never married.

[M. W. Connelly, in *Lib. of Southern Lit.,* vol. VIII (1909); Memphis *Commercial Appeal,* May 19, 1915; Frazer Hood, "Walter Malone—His Life and Works," in Malone's *Selected Poems* (1919); J. T. Moore, *Tenn. The Volunteer State 1769–1923* (1923); J. P. Young, *Standard Hist. of Memphis, Tenn.* (1912); *Munsey's Mag.,* Mar. 1905; information furnished by Dr. F. M. Malone and Judge J. P. Young.] D. D.

MALONEY, MARTIN (Dec. 11, 1847–May 8, 1929), industrialist, philanthropist, was born in Ballingarry near Thurles in Ireland. In 1854 his parents, John and Catharine (Pollard) Maloney, famine-refugees to Scranton, Pa., in 1848, were able to send for him. He had little schooling but developed dependable and thrifty ways as a worker in the mines, as a clerk in a grocer's store, and as an apprentice to a metal worker. As a youth he established a grocery store which failed, and later a plumbing business. In the latter connection he obtained some patents from which he improved a gasoline burner which came to be used widely in street-lighting. He retained his rights and manufactured and marketed this lamp and other lighting devices through the Maloney Manufacturing and Lighting Company. In the meantime (1868), he married Margaret A. Hewittson of Carbondale who maintained a harmonious home for him and their three daughters.

Although only twenty-six years of age when he removed to Philadelphia, he was well on the road to success. He obtained contracts for lighting the grounds of the Centennial Exposition and for the street-lighting of Philadelphia, Pittsburgh, Camden, and Jersey City. In 1880 he organized the Pennsylvania Globe Gas Light

Company. He became an authority on the processes of gas production and thus became interested in chemistry as a business rather than as a science. In 1882 he was an organizer of the United Gas and Improvement Company of Philadelphia which acquired local gas companies in various states. Later he promoted the Pennsylvania Heat, Light and Power Company which absorbed a number of electric companies and in 1899 was reorganized as the Philadelphia Electric Company. The success of this organization made Maloney a factor in promoting the Electric Company of America, one of the earliest holding companies. His interests in time included the Standard Oil Company, the Maloney Oil Company of Scranton, the Pennsylvania Railroad, the Pennsylvania Iron Works Company, and even real-estate and hotel ventures.

Maloney lacked a *flair* for politics, but as a self-made man, he felt his importance and liked adulation. Despite a contentious and suspicious nature, he was kindly, generous in a large way, and amusingly penurious in small matters. A fervent Catholic, he was a supporter of the Catholic Church Extension Society, building chapels in Rock Hill and Florence, S. C., and Rome, Ga., and was a quiet donor to charities and hospitals. He built St. Martin's Chapel for the Seminary of St. Charles Borromeo, Overbrook, Pa., the beautiful Italian Renaissance St. Catherine's Church at his summer home in Spring Lake, N. J., as a memorial to a daughter who died at sea, the Martin Maloney Home for the Aged in Scranton, and the elaborate Maloney Chemical Laboratory at the Catholic University of America in Washington. In Rome he paid for repairing the ancient Church of St. John Lateran, and in France he became identified as the wealthy American who took title to a number of convents and religious institutions which were thus preserved from confiscation as a result of the legislation of 1901. On intimate terms with great prelates, he was created a papal marquis by Leo XIII (1903) and a papal chamberlain by Pius X (1904). Outside the church his gifts included a park for Scranton and the Martin Maloney Memorial Clinic at the University of Pennsylvania. His "White House" by the sea at Spring Lake was modeled on Leinster House in Dublin. Here he retired amid surroundings which conformed to his sense of beauty in the rich, ornate, and massive form. His remains were interred in the crypt of the memorial church at Spring Lake.

[*Records of the Am. Cath. Hist. Soc.*, Dec. 1929; S. M. Lyons, *St. Catherine's Church, Spring Lake, N. J.: A Descriptive Booklet* (n.d.); *Cath. Univ. Bull.*, Nov. 1917, Nov. 1925; clippings of obituary notices in files of Cath. University; notes from his associates; obituaries in *Cath. Standard and Times* (Phila.), the *Phila. Inquirer, Pub. Ledger,* and *N. Y. Times.*]

R. J. P.

MALTER, HENRY (Mar. 23, 1864–Apr. 4, 1925), scholar, teacher, was born in the village of Banse, near Sabno, Galicia (at that time in Austria), the son of Solomon and Rosa Malter. He studied rabbinical literature as a youth, took up secular studies in his eighteenth year, spent four years at the University of Berlin, giving special attention to philosophy and Semitic languages, and received the degree of Ph.D. *cum laude* at Heidelberg in 1894. He then entered the Lehranstalt fur die Wissenchaft des Judentums in Berlin and at the same time the Veitel Heine Ephraimsche Stiftung, studying in the latter under the great Jewish scholar Moritz Steinschneider. For one year he was librarian of the scientific library of the Jewish Community in Berlin. On Sept. 30, 1900, he married Bertha Freund. In the same year he was called to the professorship of Jewish philosophy and Oriental languages in the Hebrew Union College, Cincinnati; this post he resigned in 1907. In 1909 he was elected professor of rabbinical language and literature in the Dropsie College for Hebrew and Cognate Learning, Philadelphia, which position he occupied until his death.

He was one of the leaders of the Hebrew Renaissance, translating into Hebrew Steinschneider's work on Jewish literature, which he greatly expanded and published under the title *Sifrut Yisrael* (1897; 2nd ed., 1923). With Alexander Marx, he edited one volume of the collected writings of Steinschneider, *Gesammelte Schriften von Moritz Steinschneider* (1925). His favorite field was Judeo-Arabic philosophy, and being an excellent scholar in both Hebrew and Arabic, he readily commanded the original sources. In this field he published many articles, but his most distinguished contribution was his *Saadia Gaon: His Life and Works* (1921), which exhibited a profound knowledge of Jewish philosophy and medieval literature, and also a creative imagination that vividly restored an important Jewish figure of the tenth century. Ethiopic was another language with which he was familiar. During the last fifteen years of his life, he undertook the beginning of a great project in Talmudic literature, that of establishing a method for the creation of a critical text of the Talmud. At the time of his death he had completed such a text of one tractate of the Talmud, with an English translation and notes, published in 1928 under the title, *The Treatise Ta'anit of the Babylonian Talmud.* The justification for his method in creating this critical text he put into a separate work, entitled *The Treatise Ta'anit of the Babylonian Talmud . . . Provided with Notes Containing the Critical Apparatus as well as Discussions and Explanations of the Text,* published in 1930 by the American Academy for Jewish Research, of which Malter had been secretary. He also left in manuscript a critical text of the Arabic original of *Emunoth we-Deoth* (Beliefs and Opinions), of Saadia.

He was a painstaking and careful scholar, not prolific, but every work he published was a definite contribution to Jewish or Arabic literature. He was a modest man of simple tastes and had a horror of publicity. He had a genuine passion for learning, a wide interest in men and things outside of his own specialty, and a dry sense of humor that often found delightful expression.

[Alexander Marx, in *Am. Jewish Year Book,* vol. XXVIII (1926); *Who's Who in America,* 1924–25; *Jewish Daily Bull.* (N. Y.), Apr. 7, 1925; *Jewish Tribune* (N. Y.), Apr. 24, 1925; *Jewish Exponent* (Phila.), Apr. 10, 1925; *Ha-Doar* (N. Y.), Apr. 24, May 8, 1925.] C. A.

MANATT, JAMES IRVING (Feb. 17, 1845–Feb. 13, 1915), classicist, till middle life Irving James Manatt, was the son of Robert and Jemima (Gwin) Manatt. His family was Scotch and Scotch-Irish; the name may have a Huguenot origin. His father, a pioneer farmer, moved gradually westward from Pennsylvania. Irving was born at Millersburg, Ohio, but was soon taken to Poweshiek County, Iowa. In 1861 he entered the preparatory department of the recently established Iowa (now Grinnell) College. After a discontinuous school life, he enlisted in May 1864, in the 46th Iowa Infantry, a hundred-day regiment, and spent the summer near Collierville, Tenn., as regimental clerk and picketing a railroad. In 1865 he returned to Iowa College and graduated in 1869. On June 28, 1870, he married Arletta Winifred Clark of Grinnell. Of their children, a son and five daughters attained maturity. After a year on the *Chicago Evening Post,* Manatt went to Yale for graduate study, especially under William Whitney, teaching meanwhile at Hopkins Grammar School in New Haven. His Ph.D. degree (1873) was followed by a Greek professorship at Denison University (1874–76), a year at Leipzig, and a Greek professorship at Marietta College (1877–84).

In 1884 he became chancellor of the University of Nebraska. His selections for the faculty were excellent. He realized that the university was part of the state public school system, and did much to bring it into organic relationship with the high schools. Unfortunately, his four years of administration were marked by difficulties common in the formative stages of universities. He was by nature an inspiring teacher, not an administrator. His policies were good, but he lacked the tact necessary to reconcile divergent groups and he was rendered irritable by asthma, a lifelong affliction. Even so, the charges laid before the regents would have collapsed if he had kept silent at the hearings. The closing argument against him rested on the sole ground that his sarcastic treatment of the professors called as witnesses rendered future harmonious action impossible. On July 19, 1888, the regents "found it necessary to dispense with the services" of Manatt. In 1902 the university made him doctor of laws.

The stormy end of a task Manatt never should have undertaken led to one of the happiest events in his life. Nebraska friends procured his appointment by President Harrison as consul at Athens, where he remained from 1889 until 1893. Those four years gave him a vivid sense of the continuity of the Greek countryside since classical times. In 1892 he completed his edition of Xenophon's *Hellenica* (2 vols., 1888–92). Friendship with Dr. Chrestos Tsountas, who was excavating at Mycenæ, brought about their collaboration in *The Mycenæan Age* (1897), the first complete and systematic survey of primitive Greek culture, not yet wholly superseded by later archeological discoveries. In 1892 he was appointed professor of Greek literature and history in Brown University, where he served from 1893 until his death in Providence, just before retirement. He paid three more visits to Greece. He joined the managing committee of the American School of Classical Studies in Athens and helped organize and attended the First International Congress of Archeology there in 1905. A Greek sabbatical resulted in his *Ægean Days* (1914), a charming union of personal reminiscences with Greek scenery and life, present and past.

Manatt's oratorical powers would never have been guessed from his gaunt appearance, with the heavy gray beard which caused the students to nickname him "Zeus." His addresses used to test some phase of contemporary life by Greek standards, and he would pour out ridicule, invective, eloquence, and paraphrases of classical poetry in a rush of splendid words. In teaching, Manatt delighted especially in the lyric poets and the *Odyssey.* He emphasized philology very little. To him it was the men and women in the poems that mattered, and the land. His later years were depressed by constant asthma, small means, and the abandonment of compulsory Greek, which steadily reduced his classes, but the few students who did know him were much closer to him. To one of them he wrote: "My teaching has fallen so far short of my own ideal, of the pattern shown me in the mount, that I wonder every time I find that some elect spirit like yours has got good from it. It is one thing to have the vision, quite another the vitality to communicate it. With old Socrates, I hold it full reward if among my younger comrades I win a good friend now and then—all the more so if the fathers acquit me of corrupting the youth."

[Manatt's address in *Semi-centennial of the Founding of Grinnell, 1854–1904* (1904); *Ninth Biennial Report of the Board of Regents of the Univ. of Neb., Dec. 1, 1888,* p. 6; *Roster and Record of Iowa Soldiers in the War of the Rebellion,* vol. V (1911), p. 1423; G. E. Barber, "J. Irving Manatt," *Semi-centennial Anniversary Book. The Univ. of Neb.* (1919); H. H. Wilson, "Impeachment of Univ. Chancellor," in *Occasional Addresses* (1929); *Brown Alumni Monthly,* June 1912, Mar., June 1915; the *Providence Sunday Jour.,* Feb. 14, 1915; the *Evening Tribune* (Providence, R. I.), Feb. 15, 1915; catalogues of Iowa College and reports of the regents and chancellor of the Univ. of Neb.; information as to certain facts from members of the family; personal reminiscences.] Z. C., Jr.

MANDERSON, CHARLES FREDERICK (Feb. 9, 1837–Sept. 28, 1911), lawyer, Union soldier, United States senator from Nebraska, was born in Philadelphia, Pa., the son of a Scotch-Irish father, John Manderson, and a German mother, Katharine Benfer Manderson. He obtained a high-school education in Philadelphia, then went to Canton, Ohio, where he read law. He was admitted to the bar in 1859 and was twice elected city solicitor of Canton before the outbreak of the Civil War. In that struggle Manderson quickly demonstrated his capacity for leadership. He enlisted at the outset as a private soldier and shortly afterward helped raise Company A of the 19th Ohio Infantry. His advancement in the service was rapid. He was commissioned first lieutenant, then captain of his company, and thereafter he rose through the various grades to be colonel of his regiment. He saw strenuous fighting from the beginning of the war and participated in all the more important battles fought in the Western theatre of action. While with Sherman in the Atlanta campaign, he commanded a demi-brigade composed of his own and two other regiments. He was severely wounded, Sept. 2, 1864, in a charge on the enemy's works at Lovejoy's Station, Ga., and on this account shortly afterward found it necessary to resign from the army. Before he resigned, however, he was brevetted brigadier-general of volunteers "for long, faithful, gallant and meritorious service." After the war he was an active member of the Grand Army of the Republic, and for three years he was commander of the Military Order of the Loyal Legion of the District of Columbia.

After resigning from the army Manderson resumed his practice of law and his interest in politics. For a few years he remained at Canton, Ohio, where he was twice elected district attorney of Stark County, and once almost nominated by the Republicans for Congress. In 1869, however, he removed to Omaha, Neb. In the new environment he quickly became a prominent political figure. He was a member of the state constitutional conventions of 1871 and 1875, and for over six years was city attorney for Omaha. In 1883 he was elected to the United States Senate, and at the conclusion of his first term was reëlected without serious opposition from within his party—an unusual experience for a Nebraska senator, who could ordinarily count on retirement after a single term. In the Senate Manderson served faithfully on many committees, worked and spoke for high pensions, advocated a more efficient organization of the army, and won considerable notice by introducing a measure, then regarded as novel, for nationally built highways. He foresaw in the nineties a revolution in means of travel, and he predicted confidently "the construction ultimately by this government of great highways or boulevards that shall connect metropolitan centers" (Tipton, *post,* p. 353). He was consistently orthodox and conservative in his votes and speeches, and was rewarded in 1891 by election without opposition to the post of president *pro tempore* of the Senate to succeed Senator John J. Ingalls of Kansas.

After he left public office Manderson became general solicitor for the Burlington Railroad west of the Missouri River. In this capacity he served his client well, but there were those in Nebraska who regretted his course. "What a fine influence he might have exerted," wrote one such critic, "if, after retirement, he had used the knowledge and influence gained at Washington as the representative of the people in their behalf, instead of devoting this experience to the service of a great railroad corporation, to gain legal control of which the people were engaged in a mighty and doubtful struggle!" (Morton and Watkins, *post,* vol. III, p. 289). In 1900 he was chosen president of the American Bar Association. He was a man of varied talents and interests. He knew his way in the fields of literature and art, and he was possessed of a strong collector's instinct. He published in 1902 a romance of Civil-War times, *The Twin Seven-Shooters,* the plot and incidents of which were drawn mostly from his own war-time experience and observation. Many of his addresses on political, legal, and military topics were also published. He was an interesting conversationalist, a skilful after-dinner speaker, and an able orator. In general his tastes were urbane and aristocratic, at once a matter of pride and of suspicion to the unsophisticated country constituency which he represented as senator. His death came in the fall of 1911, on shipboard, as he was returning to America after a summer in Europe. His wife, Rebeckah Brown Manderson, to whom he had been married in 1865, survived him.

[The *Sunday World-Herald* (Omaha), Oct. 1, 1911, gives many Manderson anecdotes, and the *Omaha Daily Bee,* Sept. 29, 1911, contains an excellent obituary notice. His political career is traced in T. W. Tipton, *Forty Years of Neb. at Home and in Cong.* (1902), pp. 333–61, and in J. S. Morton and Albert Watkins, *Illustrated Hist. of Neb.* (3 vols., 1905–13). See also *Who's Who in America,* 1910–11; and the *Report of the Thirty-Fourth Ann. Meeting of the Am. Bar Asso.,* 1911.]

J. D. H.

MANEY, GEORGE EARL (Aug. 24, 1826–Feb. 9, 1901), soldier, lawyer, diplomat, born at Franklin, Tenn., was the eldest son of Thomas and Rebecca (Southall) Maney, and a descendant of James Maney, a French Huguenot, who settled in North Carolina. He attended the Nashville Seminary and in 1845 graduated from the University of Nashville. At the beginning of the Mexican War he entered the United States army, May 28, 1846, as second lieutenant of Captain Foster's Company (subsequently designated Company L), 1st Tennessee Infantry, to serve one year; he was honorably discharged Sept. 7, 1846, at Camargo, Tenn., upon tender of his resignation, due to physical disability. On Mar. 6 of the following year he was appointed first lieutenant, United States Infantry, and in April, first lieutenant, 3rd United States Dragoons, and was honorably mustered out on July 31, 1848.

In 1850 he was admitted to the bar and practised law in Tennessee, but upon the outbreak of the Civil War he entered the Confederate service as captain of Company D, 11th Tennessee Infantry. In May 1861, however, he was made colonel of the 1st (Field's) Regiment, Tennessee Infantry. He took part in the Cheat River campaign under Gen. Robert E. Lee and served at Bath and Romney under General Jackson, one of the few officers of the Army of the Tennessee to have that distinction. He distinguished himself at the battle of Shiloh, Apr. 6–7, 1862, and was made brigadier-general on Apr. 18, the appointment to date from Apr. 16, 1862. He commanded a brigade at the battles of Perryville, Stone's River, Chickamauga, and Chattanooga, where he was wounded in the right arm. In the Atlanta campaign he commanded a division and was engaged in the battle of Atlanta, July 22, 1864. He was paroled at Greensboro, N. C., on or about May 1, 1865.

Maney became president of the Tennessee & Pacific Railroad in 1868. He was the Republican nominee for governor of Tennessee in 1876, opposing James D. Porter [*q.v.*], but withdrew before election. He served in the state legislature and being an able speaker took an active part in presidential campaigns. On May 19, 1881, he was appointed minister resident to Colombia. His predecessor had been recalled at the request of the Colombian government, and since it was a critical period in the relations of the United States with Colombia, owing to an attempt by European powers to establish a guarantee of neutrality over the inter-oceanic canal, Maney's duties were both onerous and delicate. He was transferred to Bolivia Apr. 17, 1882, as minister resident and consul general at La Paz. On June 20, 1889, he was made minister resident to Paraguay and Uruguay, and on Sept. 23, 1890, his rank was raised to that of envoy extraordinary and minister plenipotentiary. He remained at that post until June 30, 1894.

He was married at Nashville, Tenn., June 23, 1853, to Bettie, daughter of F. G. Crutcher, and had two sons and three daughters. His death occurred suddenly in Washington, D. C.

[War Dept. records; State Dept. records; *Reg. of The Dept. of State,* Jan. 1894; *Conf. Mil. Hist.* (1899), vol. VIII; *War of the Revellion: Official Records* (*Army*), 2 ser., 4 ser.; M. J. Wright, *Tenn. in the War, 1861–1865* (copr. 1908); *Washington Post,* Feb. 10, 1901; *Evening Star* (Washington), Feb. 11, 1901; *Nashville Banner,* Feb. 11, 1901; names of parents from James T. Maney, Esq., Nashville, Tenn.]

A. E. I.

MANGIN, JOSEPH FRANÇOIS (fl. 1794–1818), engineer, architect, was of French origin. His letters indicate that he was a cultivated aristocrat, and he may have come to New York as a refugee from the Revolution. He first appears as an assistant to Vincent, another Frenchman, who was engineer-in-chief of the New York fortifications. In 1795 he succeeded Vincent as chief engineer, with another Mangin (probably a younger brother) as his assistant. He was admitted and sworn as a freeman of the city on May 9, 1795, and a week later was appointed one of the city surveyors. As such, in partnership with Casimir T. Goerck, he began in 1797 the preparation of an official city map which was published in 1803. This well-known map, which was a magnificent piece of draftsmanship determined the present shore line and street layout of the entire Corlear's Hook section, of which one street perpetuates his name.

Meanwhile, in 1797 he had designed the monumental prison for the state of New York, on the block now bounded by Washington Street, Christopher Street, and the North River. According to contemporary newspapers (*e.g., New York Daily Advertiser,* Jan. 31, 1798), Mangin Brothers were the architects of the Park Theater, built between 1795 and 1798, the design of which is often credited to Marc Isambard Brunel, who was at this time perhaps a draftsman in their office. During the French war scare of 1798, while Mangin was a technical adviser to Ebenezer Stevens, agent of the War Department in connection with the fortifications of the city, Aaron Burr wrote from Albany to Stevens (Aug. 17) asking that Mangin prepare plans and estimates for an "impregnable castle" two or three stories high, to be erected in about six feet of water and connected with the land by a drawbridge. This is possibly the first appearance of the idea of the fort built later and eventually known as Castle Garden, of which John McComb [*q.v.*] was the architect. Mangin's reports to Colonel Stevens are precise, scholarly, and imaginative.

Mangin is best known for his connection with the New York City Hall. A competition for designs was advertised Feb. 20, 1802, and on Oct. 4, the plan of "Mr. Joseph F. Mangin and John McComb, Jr." was adopted and the premium of $350 awarded to them (Council Minutes, *post*). The plan was curtailed somewhat by request of the committee, and in March 1803 the curtailed plan was approved and McComb appointed architect. When the cornerstone was laid May 26, 1803, McComb, as architect, assisted the mayor, and no mention of Mangin in connection with the building was made in the ceremonies or on the inscribed foundation stone. On June 2, the New York *Evening Post* published a letter signed "Justice," deploring the absence of Mangin from the ceremonies and the denial of credit to him, together with an assertion that a brass plate giving the true state of affairs and naming Mangin as chief designer had been built secretly into the walls. This question of the design of the City Hall is still a matter of controversy. It is significant that certain of the competition drawings now signed "John McComb, Jr., Architect" show unmistakable signs of the erasure of some other name and that, while McComb's work is in every other case distinctly English in feeling, the spirit of the City Hall design is entirely Louis XVI.

Mangin's only other known important work was the design for the first St. Patrick's Cathedral, on Mott Street, 1809–15. This building was famous for its Gothic style, and is without doubt one of the first signs of the beginning of the Gothic revival in America. It was dedicated on Ascension Day 1815, and contemporary views show that the twin towers once intended for the façade were never completed and only carried slightly above the main roof ridge. The original walls and the lower part of the front are still standing (1933). Mangin appears last in the New York Directory for 1818, at Bowery Hill, as a city surveyor. He was probably married, since the Vital Statistics of New York show that a Charles Mangin, aged one year, died on Bowery Hill, Apr. 10, 1818.

[Plans and elevation of N. Y. State Prison in Schuyler Papers, N. Y. Pub. Lib.; McComb Drawings and Papers, Ebenezer Stevens Papers, and Proceedings of the Commissioners for N. Y. and Vicinity, in N. Y. Hist. Soc.; *Minutes of the Common Council of the City of N. Y.* (1917), vols. II–IX, see Analytical Index; I. N. P. Stokes, *The Iconography of Manhattan Island* (6 vols., 1915–28); Thomas Eddy, *An Account of the State Prison or Penitentiary House in the City of New-York* (1801); Montgomery Schuyler, "The N. Y. City Hall," in *Arch. Record,* May 1908; E. S. Wilde, "The N. Y. City Hall," *Century Mag.,* Apr. 1884, and "John McComb, Jr., Architect," in *Am. Architect and Building News,* Aug. 12, 19, 1908.] T. F. H.

MANGUM, WILLIE PERSON (May 10, 1792–Sept. 7, 1861), senator, was born in Orange (now Durham) County, N. C. He was the son of William Person Mangum, a farmer and merchant, and of Catharine (Davis) Mangum, a native of Pennsylvania. Like that of Willie Jones his Christian name was pronounced Wylie. His preparatory education was received at home and at academies in Hillsboro, Fayetteville, and Raleigh, and in 1815 he was graduated from the University of North Carolina. He studied law under Judge Duncan Cameron, while serving as tutor in his family, and was licensed in 1817. Beginning practice at home he was immediately successful, but his mind was set on public life, and in 1818 and 1819 he was a member of the House of Commons, where he actively supported the cause of constitutional reform, thereby winning great popularity in the western part of the state. In 1819 he was elected a judge of the superior court but was compelled for financial reasons to retire at the end of a year. In 1823 he began a service of two terms in the federal Congress. In 1824 he supported Crawford and voted for him when the election was thrown into the House. He resigned in 1826 and was soon appointed to fill a vacancy as judge, but the appointment was not confirmed by the legislature. In 1828 he was a Jackson elector and was again elected judge, but once more he resigned after a year's service. He was a candidate for the United States Senate in 1828 but withdrew, and in 1830 he was elected.

He entered the Senate a Jacksonian Democrat, a strong opponent of the protective tariff, and a champion of state rights. In the House he had been an opponent of the Bank of the United States, but by this time he was converted to its cause, though he objected to making it an issue in 1832 and voted against the rechartering bill. At this time he was distrustful of Clay and in general disapproved of his policies. While opposed to nullification, he was friendly to South Carolina in 1832 and voted against the Force Bill in 1833. This measure and the removal of the deposits led to a definite break with Jackson, and he voted for the resolution of censure and against the expunging resolution. The North Carolina legislature of 1834, in the hands of the Democrats, passed a resolution instructing him to vote to expunge. Mangum, denying the right of instruction, refused to obey, but the succeeding legislature was also Democratic and he resigned. In 1837 he received the electoral vote of South Carolina for president. Except for service in the state Senate in 1840 he remained in private life busily engaged in the practice of law for several years. He identified himself with the Whig party and became one of its chief leaders in the state. He was a Clay delegate to the Whig convention of 1839, and was offered the nomination for vice-president, but refused it. He was elected to the United States Senate in 1840 and served until 1853. He was active in the Whig quarrel with Tyler, directing the caucus, and he offered the resolution reading him out of the party. He was elected president *pro tempore* of the Senate from May 31, 1842, to Mar. 4, 1845, and was thus acting vice-president of the United States. He seldom spoke in the Senate, but when he did so he proved himself an effective debater. He was a most astute political leader, and his personal charm and magnetism as well as his brilliancy in conversation gave him great strength. In North Carolina he was best known for his power as a campaign speaker. He was the intimate of Webster and, with his colleague, George E. Badger [*q.v.*], persuaded him to make his Seventh of March speech. In 1852 he was a supporter of Scott for the Whig nomination.

He was defeated in 1852 and retired to private life. Although in desperate health, he took an active part for Fillmore in the campaign of 1856 but not long thereafter suffered a stroke of apoplexy from which he never recovered. He was not a secessionist, but after Lincoln's call for troops he yielded the point. After the death of his only son in battle a second stroke proved fatal. On Sept. 30, 1819, he married Charity Alston Cain, the daughter of William and Sarah (Alston) Cain of Orange County.

[Mangum Collection in Lib. of Cong.; *Trinity College Hist. Soc. Papers*, vol. XV (1925); J. H. Wheeler, *Reminiscences and Memoirs of N. C.* (1884); S. A. Ashe, *Biog. Hist. of N. C.*, vol. V (1906).]

J. G. deR. H.

MANIGAULT, ARTHUR MIDDLETON (Oct. 26, 1824–Aug. 16, 1886), soldier and adjutant-general of South Carolina, was born in Charleston, the eighth and youngest child of Charlotte (Drayton) and Joseph Manigault. His father, a wealthy rice planter, was the son of Peter Manigault, the grandson of Gabriel Manigault, and the great-grandson of Pierre Manigault [*qq.v.*]. His mother was descended from an English family that had been prominent in Charleston life from the earliest history of the city. He received an elementary education but instead of attending college set out to learn the export trade in Charleston. He became sergeant-major of a local militia company and received his first military experience during the Mexican War when, as first lieutenant of Company F of the Palmetto Regiment, he served under General Scott. This experience he afterward described as "perhaps the happiest and most romantic period" of his life (unpublished memoirs). Upon his return from Mexico in 1848 he entered the commission business in Charleston and, on Apr. 18, 1851, was married to Mary Proctor Huger, grand-daughter of Daniel E. Huger [*q.v.*]. They had five children. In 1856 he removed to Georgetown County, where, having inherited considerable property from his parents, he began rice planting.

Upon the secession of South Carolina in December 1860 he was elected captain of the North Santee Mounted Rifles, a volunteer company organized in his community, and during the following winter he superintended the construction of several batteries for the defense of Winyaw Bay and the North Santee River. Early in April 1861 he became volunteer aide-de-camp on the staff of General Beauregard. He took part in the attack upon Fort Sumter and shortly afterward was commissioned lieutenant-colonel and assigned to duty as adjutant and inspector-general on Beauregard's staff. He was elected colonel of the 10th South Carolina Volunteers on May 31, 1861, became commander of the first military district of South Carolina, and later was ordered to Corinth, Miss., with his regiment. Throughout the remainder of the war he served in the West. On Apr. 26, 1863, he was advanced to the rank of brigadier-general, a promotion which he thought was unjustly delayed through the influence of certain enemies of his family at

Richmond (unpublished memoirs). He was slightly wounded at Resaca, Ga., on May 14, 1863, but he participated in all of the engagements of the Army of Tennessee until the Battle of Franklin, Tenn., in November 1864, when he received a wound in the head so serious as to incapacitate him for the remainder of the war. At the close of the war he returned to rice planting and pursued that occupation with varying success until 1880, when he was elected adjutant and inspector-general of the state. He held this office until his death at South Island, Georgetown County.

[Unpublished Memoirs in the possession of his grandson, Edward Manigault, Charleston, S. C.; *Trans. of the Huguenot Soc. of S. C.*, no. 4 (1897); *Confederate Military Hist.*, ed. by C. A. Evans (1899), vol. V; C. I. Walker, *Rolls and Hist. Sketch of the Tenth Regiment, S. C.* (1881); *News and Courier* (Charleston), Aug. 17, 18, 1886.] J. W. P—n.

MANIGAULT, GABRIEL (Apr. 21, 1704–June 5, 1781), wealthy South Carolina merchant and planter, the only son of Pierre Manigault [*q.v.*] by his first wife Judith (Giton) Royer, was born and died at Charlestown. He was about twenty-five years old when his father died and had for some time been associated in the well-established trade carried on with the West Indies, England, and France. On Apr. 29, 1730, he married Ann Ashby, the daughter of John Ashby, a cassique of Carolina, and of Constantia (Broughton) Ashby, a sister of Thomas Broughton, at one time governor of South Carolina, thus forming an important social and political connection. In the diary that his wife kept from 1754 to 1781 (*South Carolina Historical and Genealogical Magazine,* July 1919–July 1920) was reflected the social life of the times, the rising prosperity of the colony, and the extensive hospitality of the Manigaults, who entertained all visitors of note, the governors, the members of council, and other local gentry. At a time when rice was the leading staple and indigo a profitable crop, the slave trade offered increasingly large returns, but dealing in slaves did not form an important part of Gabriel Manigault's business. He invested his profits in plantations and in slaves to work them. When the British Parliament undertook to investigate the condition of slaves, the situation on his plantations was cited in defense of slavery since it could be shown that in 38 years the number had increased from 86 to 270 with the addition by purchase of only 12 or 14 slaves. By 1754 he had become the wealthiest merchant in the province. He retired from the active management of his commercial business in order to attend particularly to his rice and indigo plantation, "Silk Hope," which he had bought from the heirs of Gov. Robert Johnson.

He entered public life as a member of the Commons House of Assembly. In 1735 he succeeded Alexander Parris as public treasurer and continued in office until 1743. He labored diligently to reduce to order the confused accounts of the unfortunate expedition of 1740 against St. Augustine. He was for many years vice-president of the Charlestown Library Society, of which the governor of the province was always president, and he leased for twenty-one years without charge a convenient building near his counting-house for the books and the librarian. Interested in helping poor French-Protestant immigrants to South Carolina, he advanced £3,500 for that purpose. He was one of the leaders in the Revolutionary movement. During the war he lent the equivalent of $220,000 to the province, most of which was lost since the amount was repaid by the state in the form of indents on which only about $44,000 was realized. Too old to go into the army he did, however, offer his services, along with those of his grandson, Joseph, then a youth of fifteen and later the father of Arthur Middleton Manigault [*q.v.*], to defend the city of Charlestown against the attack of General Prevost in 1779. Two years later he was buried in the French churchyard. His wife died the next year and their only child, Peter Manigault [*q.v.*], already lay buried in the family tomb. He left, chiefly to his grandchildren, a very large estate, including 43,532 acres of land. Among his bequests was one of £5,000 sterling to the South Carolina Society, the interest of which was used to educate a number of children.

[Registers of the parishes of St. Philips, St. Thomas, and St. Dennis; records from the probate court at Charleston; *Trans. Huguenot Soc. of S. C.*, no. 4 (1889); Edward McCrady, *The Hist. of S. C. under the Royal Government* (1899); W. R. Smith, *S. C. as a Royal Province* (1903); David Ramsay, *The Hist. of S. C.* (1809), vol. II; *S. C. Hist. and Geneal. Mag.*, esp. Oct. 1914, Jan. 1917.] M. L. W.

MANIGAULT, PETER (Oct. 10, 1731–Nov. 12, 1773), speaker of the colonial Assembly, business man, and planter, was born in Charlestown, S. C., the only son and heir of Ann (Ashby) and Gabriel Manigault [*q.v.*]. He was educated at a classical school and under a tutor in Charlestown until 1750, when he was sent to study law in England under the care of Thomas Corbett, who had tutored him in Carolina. He lived with Mr. Corbett for two years, then entered the Inner Temple in 1752, residing in chambers there, and was called to the English bar on Feb. 8, 1754. His letters to his parents (*South Carolina Historical and Genealogical Magazine,* July 1914,

July, Oct. 1930) give interesting pictures of fashionable society, the theatre, and his acquaintances at the Carolina Coffee House. While in London he had his portrait painted by Allan Ramsay, later the Court painter. In 1753 he spent ten weeks in France, Belgium, and Holland, staying most of the time in Paris and showing little interest in La Rochelle, the native city of his grandfather, Pierre Manigault [*q.v.*]. He returned to South Carolina in 1754 and began at once to practise law. He was married, on June 8, 1755, to Elizabeth, the daughter of Joseph Wragg. They had, besides three children who died young, two sons and two daughters. The year of his marriage he was elected to the colonial Assembly and was speaker from 1765 until he resigned in October 1772. He opposed the Stamp Act and, when Parliament repealed it, as speaker he wrote to Charles Garth, South Carolina's agent in London, enclosing an address of thanks to the King and to Parliament. During the struggle over South Carolina's contribution to the Wilkes fund, he was a member of the committee, in 1770, entrusted with the £1,500 sterling that the House voted for the support of the Bill of Rights society in spite of the opposition by William Wragg and William Henry Drayton, who maintained that such funds would be used to pay the debts of John Wilkes.

In 1763 he took over the management of the estates and affairs of Ralph Izard [*q.v.*], including rice and indigo plantations on the Goose Creek and Santee River, and also managed the interests in South Carolina of several London business firms. He bought a small estate at Goose Creek and made frequent visits there. His health, always delicate, had grown very much worse with recurring attacks of fever. On May 16, 1773, he sailed for England in the hope that he might benefit by spending a summer in that climate. His letters to his mother from England report his own continued hopefulness as well as the gradual weakening of a body too sick to withstand the medical treatment of the time (*South Carolina Historical and Genealogical Magazine,* Apr. 1920). He died in London at the home of Benjamin Stead. His body was taken back to Charlestown for burial.

[Edward McCrady, *The Hist. of S. C.* (1899); W. R. Smith, *S. C. as a Royal Province* (1903); E. A. Jones, *Am. Members of the Inns of Court* (1924); *Trans. Huguenot Soc. of S. C.,* no. 4 (1897); *S. C. Hist. and Geneal. Mag.,* esp. Jan. 1902, July 1914, Jan. 1919–July 1920, July, Oct. 1930.] M. L. W.

MANIGAULT, PIERRE (d. December 1729), South Carolina merchant, was a native of La Rochelle, France. The son of Gabriel and Marie Manigault, he was a member of a family of good position that had long been Protestant. Pierre with his brother, Gabriel, left France about 1685, after the Edict of Nantes was revoked. They went to London, where they remained for several years, then to South Carolina, arriving in Charlestown (now Charleston) probably early in 1695 since, on June 28, 1695, Gabriel received a warrant for land for the arrival of himself and a negro man named Sambo. On June 22, 1696, Pierre received a warrant for 100 acres. The two brothers seem to have had some means when they arrived, from their earnings in England and from the sale of lands in France. They first settled on the Santee River but, finding the work of planting uncongenial and the climate unhealthy, removed to Charlestown, where Gabriel pursued the trade of carpenter, and Pierre set up in business as a victualler. Gabriel never married and died about ten years after he came to Charlestown as the result of a fall from a scaffold. Pierre was married in 1699 to Judith (Giton) Royer, who with her first husband, Noe (Noah) Royer, came to South Carolina before the Manigaults. (See her letter describing the sufferings she experienced during the journey from France to England and the first hard years of her life in Carolina in David Ramsay, *The History of South Carolina,* 1809, vol. I, pp. 5–8.) She died in 1711, leaving two children by her second marriage. Her son, Gabriel Manigault, her grandson, Peter Manigault, and her great-great-grandson, Arthur Middleton Manigault [*qq.v.*], as well as numerous other descendants, continued to represent her Huguenot blood in the life of South Carolina. Pierre was married in 1713 to Ann Reason, of English parentage, who died on Aug. 10, 1727, leaving no children.

Pierre identified himself with the English colonists, changed his name to Peter, and, although he still kept a connection with the French Church, attended the English Church. He set up a small distillery to make brandy and, about 1719, also became a merchant, conducted trade directly with England, built storehouses, and sold his goods to the colonists. Unlike so many of the French refugees in South Carolina, who arrived in a destitute condition and suffered for some years from the refusal of the colonial government to grant the rights promised before they left England, he prospered greatly and died possessed of a considerable fortune. He was buried, on Dec. 10, in the French churchyard. His will, written in English (printed in full in *Transactions of the Huguenot Society of South Carolina,* No. 30, 1925), left £10 each, Carolina currency, to the English and to the French Church in Charlestown, for their poor.

[*Warrants for lands in S. C., 1692–1711,* ed. by A. S. Salley (1913); Public Records of S. C. in probate court and mesne conveyance office, Charleston, and in possession of the historical commission, Columbia; St. Philip's Register, no. 1; *Trans. Huguenot Soc. of S. C.*, nos. 4, 5 (1897), no. 5 (1897), p. 35, for mother's name.] M. L. W.

MANLEY, JOHN (*c.* 1734–Feb. 12, 1793), naval officer, was born probably in Boston (Greenwood, *post,* p. 17). He was living there in 1757, his occupation being that of mariner. On Feb. 26, 1763, he married Hannah Cheevers of that city. In 1768–69 he commanded the *Little Fortescue,* trading between Boston and St. Eustatius. When, in the fall of 1775, Washington was fitting out a small fleet to operate against British transports, he chose Manley to command the schooner *Lee* and commissioned him a captain in the army. Sailing on one of the last days of October, he captured, a month later, the first valuable prize taken in the war, the brigantine *Nancy,* laden with a cargo of ordnance and military stores. It was a timely capture, for the army at Cambridge was sorely in need of these supplies. Fortune continued to favor him and in December he seized several other ships. He was widely acclaimed as a naval hero, the first of the Revolution to be thus distinguished. In January 1776 Washington made him commander of the fleet, with the schooner *Hancock* as his flagship. He made several successful cruises in this vessel, but on one occasion was forced to beach her to prevent her capture. On Apr. 17, Congress recognized Manley's services by appointing him a captain in the Continental navy, and later fixed his rank, making him the third officer in the service. Taking command of the new frigate *Hancock,* he sailed from Boston on May 21, 1777, accompanied by the frigate *Boston,* Capt. Hector McNeill [*q.v.*], and a small fleet of privateers. On June 7, he captured the frigate *Fox,* 28 guns, but a month later the *Hancock* and her prize were taken by the enemy. Manley was confined on board a prison-ship in New York harbor until exchanged in March 1778. He was tried by a court martial for the loss of his ship and acquitted.

Since Congress had no naval vessel suitable to Manley's rank he entered the privateer service, and in the fall of 1778 made a successful cruise in the *Marlborough.* Early in 1779 he went to sea in the *Cumberland* and near Barbados was forced to surrender to the frigate *Pomona.* Escaping from prison and returning to Boston, he next made two cruises in the *Jason,* the second of which ended with her capture, after a sharp engagement. Manley was committed to Old Mill Prison, England, and confined there two years before he was exchanged. Returning to the navy, he commanded the frigate *Hague* and made a cruise in the West Indies that was marked by a brilliant escape from a superior force and by the capture of the *Baille* in January 1783, the last valuable prize taken by a Continental ship.

After the Revolution he continued to reside in Boston. His wife Hannah died in 1786, and on Dec. 14, 1791, his marriage intentions to Friswith Arnold, his second wife, were recorded. In the last year of his life, in consideration of the severe injuries he had received in the war, Congress granted him a pension of thirty dollars a month. He was buried with military honors.

[I. J. Greenwood, *Captain John Manley* (1915); R. E. Peabody, "The Naval Career of Capt. John Manley of Marblehead," in *Essex Inst. Hist. Colls.*, Jan. 1909; G. W. Allen, *A Naval Hist. of the Am. Revolution* (2 vols., 1913); Peter Force, *Am. Archives* (4 ser., 6 vols., 1837–46; 5 ser., vol. II, 1851); *Jour. of the Continental Cong.*, Apr. 17, Oct. 10, 1776; *Columbian Centinel* (Boston), Feb. 16, 20, 1793; *Mass. Mercury* (Boston), Feb. 16, 19, 1793.] C. O. P.

MANLEY, JOSEPH HOMAN (Oct. 13, 1842–Feb. 7, 1905), politician and journalist, was born in Bangor, Me., where his parents, James Sullivan and Caroline (Sewall) Manley, were temporarily living. After going to the public schools of Augusta, he entered in 1853 the Abbott Family School for boys at Farmington, which he attended during four years. Since he never fully recovered from a severe illness he had at the age of five, he was compelled to give up the idea of going to college. In 1861 he began to study law in an office in Boston. In 1863 he was graduated from the law school at Albany, N. Y., and returned to Augusta, where he practised law with Hilton W. True for some years. Admitted to practice in the federal courts in 1865, he was appointed commissioner of the district court. He began his political career as a member of the Augusta city council in 1865 and the next year was president of that body. In 1869 he was a special agent for the federal government in the department of internal revenue, resigned in November 1876, and became agent of the Pennsylvania Railroad to adjust its claims with the Treasury Department. He gave up this work in the spring of 1878, when he purchased from Joseph H. Homan, formerly his father's partner, a half interest in the *Maine Farmer.* For several years he was in active charge of its editorial columns. President Garfield in May 1881 appointed him postmaster at Augusta, and President Harrison appointed him to the same office in 1889. He resigned in August 1892 to assume his duties during the presidential campaign as a member of the Republican national executive committee. He was a delegate to the Republican National Conventions of 1880, 1888, 1892, and 1900 and was chairman of the Republican national committee from 1896 to 1904. He was a member of the Republican committee of the state of Maine from 1881 to 1900 and its chairman from 1885 to 1900. He represented Augusta in the state legislature from 1887 to 1890 and again from 1899 to 1902. During the last session he was speaker. He was a member of the state Senate from 1903 to 1904.

He was James G. Blaine's closest political friend; of him the latter is reported to have said, "As a political organizer, and as an astute reader of political conditions and forecasts, I never met Mr. Manley's equal" (*Lewiston Evening Journal,* Me., Feb. 7, 1905). Where Blaine's political observations were general, his were specific. His detailed, acute, and accurate analyses were a great aid to Blaine in his political activities. After his defeat in the presidential campaign of 1884, Blaine personally asked Cleveland to keep Manley in office as postmaster at Augusta. Manley was in charge of Thomas B. Reed's interests at the Republican convention at Saint Louis in 1896. His honest though indiscreet and premature admission that McKinley's nomination was assured brought upon him the wrath of Reed's friends and supporting newspapers, who had planned to fight to the finish for Reed's nomination (S. W. McCall, *The Life of Thomas Brackett Reed,* 1914, p. 224). The opposition of the Reed forces, thus engendered, was much in evidence later when he sought to realize his life's ambition of being governor of Maine. A carefully planned campaign, whose preliminaries were carried on by mail for fifteen months, came to nought when he was forced to withdraw on account of ill-health. Nor could he accept President Theodore Roosevelt's offer of an appointment as first assistant postmaster general. He had numerous other business interests in addition to the *Maine Farmer.* He married on Oct. 4, 1866, Susan H. Cony of Augusta, the daughter of Governor Samuel Cony. They had four children.

[*Biog. Sketches of Representative Citizens of Me.* (1903); *Representative Men of Me.,* ed. by Henry Chase (1893); *Biog. Sketches of the Members of the Senate . . . of Me., . . . 1903,* comp. by Howard Owen (1903); *Geneal. and Family Hist. of the State of Me.,* ed. by G. T. Little (1909), vol. III; *Men of Progress,* ed. by P. W. McIntyre and W. F. Blanding (1897); *Biog. Encyc. of Me.,* ed. by H. C. Williams (1885); *Letters of Mrs. J. G. Blaine,* ed. by H. S. B. Beale (2 vols., 1898); *Daily Portland Press,* Feb. 8, 1905; *Lewiston Evening Jour.,* Feb. 7, 1905.] R. E. M.

MANLY, BASIL (Jan. 29, 1798–Dec. 21, 1868), Baptist clergyman, educator, was born near Pittsboro, Chatham County, N. C., second son of Basil and Elizabeth (Maultsby) Manly. The father was a farmer who had served with some distinction in the Revolution. Two other sons, Charles and Matthias, became men of local distinction, the former as governor of the state and the latter as a jurist. Basil, like his brothers, received his early education at Pittsboro and in the Bingham School. His father was a Catholic, but his mother became a Baptist, and Basil followed her into her church, being baptized Aug. 26, 1816. Soon afterwards he announced his desire to study for the Baptist ministry and, despite the opposition of his father, who refused to assist him toward further education, was licensed to preach by the Rocky Spring Church, Apr. 26, 1818. About this time Rev. W. T. Brantly, pastor of the Baptist church at Beaufort, S. C., and president of a small college located in that town, made a visit to this section of North Carolina. Impressed with the promise of young Manly, Brantly persuaded him to go to Beaufort and enter college there, where he could secure financial assistance.

After eighteen months of study in Beaufort, he entered the junior class of South Carolina College in December 1819, graduating as valedictorian and honor man of his class Dec. 3, 1821. During the later months of his college career, with the encouragement of Jonathan Maxcy [*q.v.*], president of the institution and an able and eloquent Baptist minister, he had begun to preach in the churches of the surrounding country. His ability was at once recognized and his services were much in demand. In January 1822 he settled in Edgefield, S. C., becoming pastor there and at Stevens Creek, a neighboring country church. He joined the Stevens Creek church, where he was ordained Mar. 10, 1822, by John Landrum and Enoch Breazeale. He was everywhere greatly loved as a pastor. His sermons were carefully prepared, packed with pungent thought, delivered with pathos and power.

His efforts soon reached beyond his own narrow field. He was elected secretary of the Baptist State Convention, and in 1823 was a member of the committee of five appointed to select a site, arrange courses of study, and complete all necessary details connected with the founding of Furman Academy and Theological Institution, the forerunner of Furman University. Throughout its early years of struggle he was the steadfast friend and ablest helper of this institution. On Dec. 23, 1824, he married Sarah Murray Rudulph of Edgefield, by whom he had five children. In

February 1826 he accepted a call to the pastorate of the First Baptist Church of Charleston, the oldest and at that time the wealthiest church of his denomination in the Southern states. Here he remained in a happy and prosperous pastorate for about twelve years. In 1835 he declined the presidency of South Carolina College, but in September 1837 accepted the presidency of the University of Alabama, a position which he held till 1855. He was also largely instrumental in founding the Alabama Historical Society and Judson, Howard, and Central colleges.

In 1853 he declined the presidency of Furman University, but two years later returned to South Carolina, to the pastorate of Wentworth Street Church, Charleston. He was an ardent promoter of the Southern Baptist Theological Seminary and president of the three conventions (1856, 1857, 1858) which established that institution. In 1859 he returned to Alabama as state evangelist and then became pastor in Montgomery. He gave whole-hearted support to the secession movement, and on Feb. 22, 1861, was chaplain at the inauguration of Jefferson Davis as president of the Confederacy, riding with the presidential party and delivering the prayer. In 1863 he returned once more to South Carolina. He was partially paralyzed in 1864, and died four years later in the home of his son Basil [*q.v.*], at Greenville.

[T. M. Owen, *Dr. Basil Manly, The Founder of the Ala. Hist. Soc.* (1904), repr. from *Trans. Ala. Hist. Soc.*, vol. IV (1904); Louise Manly, *The Manly Family* (1930); W. J. McGlothlin, *Baptist Beginnings in Education* (1926); B. F. Riley, *History of the Baptists in the Southern States East of the Mississippi* (1898); *Charleston Daily Courier*, Dec. 28, 1868.] W. J. M.

MANLY, BASIL (Dec. 19, 1825–Jan. 31, 1892), Baptist clergyman, educator, son of Basil [*q.v.*] and Sarah Murray (Rudulph) Manly, was born in Edgefield District, S. C. His early years were spent in Charleston, while his father was pastor of the First Baptist Church there, but in 1837 his father became president of the University of Alabama and Basil removed with the family to Tuscaloosa. He entered the University in 1839, at the age of fourteen, graduating four years later with first honors. On Oct. 19, 1840, he had united with the Baptist church of Tuscaloosa; he was licensed to preach May 13, 1844, and entered Newton Theological Institution, Newton Center, Mass., the same year. Increasing bitterness of feeling over slavery led to a split between Northern and Southern Baptists and the formation of the Southern Baptist Convention in May 1845, and this event rendered his position so uncomfortable at Newton that he withdrew and entered Princeton Theological Seminary, where he graduated in 1847. He was ordained by the Tuscaloosa church Jan. 30, 1848, having been called to the pastorate of the church at Providence, Ala. This position he held till Jan. 28, 1849, at the same time preaching at Sumterville, Ala., and in Noxubee County, Miss. He then became stated supply of the Tuscaloosa church, 1849–50, but on Sept. 1, 1850, went to the pastorate of the First Baptist Church of Richmond, Va. This important pastorate he held till Sept. 1, 1854, when he became president of the Richmond Female Institute, which he had assisted in founding. At the same time he supplied the Walnut Grove Baptist Church.

When the Southern Baptist Theological Seminary was being established, Manly was appointed to draw up the articles of faith which each professor is required to sign at his inauguration, and when it was opened at Greenville, S. C., in 1859, he was made professor of "Biblical Introduction" and "Old Testament Interpretation." In addition to his teaching, he preached for a time at the churches of Damascus, Siloam, and Clear Springs. The Seminary opened with bright prospects, but was soon closed by the Civil War, which left it in ruins. Manly returned with the others to the work of rehabilitation in 1865, but seems to have lost hope by 1871, in which year he became president of Georgetown College, Georgetown, Ky. In 1877, however, when the Seminary was removed to Louisville, he was reëlected to his old position, and the remainder of his life was given with singular devotion to the work of ministerial education.

He rendered other important services to his denomination, however. He was a great lover of sacred music and made important contributions to Christian hymnology. With his father he compiled and published *Baptist Psalmody* (1850), which was extensively used; later he prepared *Manly's Choice* (1891), a collection of the great old hymns. He wrote for the first Seminary Commencement an appropriate hymn which has been sung at every Commencement since. His most pretentious literary work, *The Bible Doctrine of Inspiration,* was published in 1888; he was also the author of numerous articles, addresses, and pamphlets. Under his leadership a Sunday School Board was established by Southern Baptists in 1863, of which he was president and John A. Broadus [*q.v.*] secretary. In 1866 they established the periodical *Kind Words,* which continued as an important Sunday-school publication for many years. Manly was singularly gentle, lovable, and versatile; an able scholar and an effective teacher. He was twice married: on Apr. 28, 1852, to Charlotte Elizabeth (Whitfield) Smith, who died in 1867; and on June 10, 1869, to Henrietta Summers Hair, who survived him. He died in Louisville, Ky., at the age of sixty-six.

[Louise Manly, *The Manly Family* (1930); *Necrological Report of Princeton Theological Seminary,* 1892; Minutes of the Southern Baptist Convention, the Baptist State Convention of S. C., and the Baptist Gen. Asso. of Ky.; *Seminary Mag.,* Mar. 1892; *Courier-Journal* (Louisville), Feb. 1, 1892.] W. J. M.

MANLY, CHARLES MATTHEWS (Apr. 24, 1876–Oct. 15, 1927), mechanical engineer, inventor, was born at Staunton, Va., the son of Charles and Mary Esther Hellen (Matthews) Manly. His father, a Baptist minister, was the son of Basil Manly, 1798–1869 [*q.v.*], and the brother of Basil, 1825–1892 [*q.v.*]. Mechanical aptitude was a common heritage in the Manly family, but rose to genius in Charles. Graduating at Furman University, Greenville, S. C., in 1896, he pursued graduate work at Cornell University, from which he received the degree of M.E. in 1898. On the recommendation of Prof. R. H. Thurston, he was engaged by Secretary Samuel P. Langley [*q.v.*] to have charge of the construction of a large aeroplane, then building at the Smithsonian Institution for the United States War Department. Langley had already flown (1896) 13-foot models with light steam engines in flights up to three-quarters of a mile, catapulting the models from a houseboat. The same launching method was to be followed with a large machine, though Manly suggested flying from wheels on land. In the final trials Oct. 7 and Dec. 8, 1903, disaster from the launching device occurred in both instances, and Manly, acting as pilot, narrowly escaped being drowned in the wreckage. His great contribution to Langley's work, and his permanent contribution to aviation, was his design and construction of a 5-cylinder water-cooled radial gasoline engine of fifty-two horsepower, weighing but 125 pounds. This engine performed in an exemplary manner, making continuous runs of ten hours in tests. Charles L. Lawrance, president of the Wright Aeronautical Corporation, speaking before the International Civil Aeronautics Conference at Washington, December 1928, said of it: "When we consider that the most popular type of airplane engine of today is almost identical in its general detail and arrangement with the one evolved by Charles Manly in 1902, we are lost in admiration for a man who, with no data at his disposal, no examples of similar art on which to roughly base his design . . . nevertheless, through the processes of a logical mind, the intelligent application of the science of mathematics, and the use of his surprising mechanical skill, succeeded in constructing [this] . . . engine [which] . . . may in fact be characterized as the first 'modern' aircraft engine in the world" (Lawrance, *post,* pp. 415–16).

While yet in Langley's employ, Manly invented and patented, Oct. 7, 1902, the Manly drive, a hydraulic device for transmitting power at variable speeds from a constant-speed motor. In essentials it comprised a radial multicylinder pump of constant speed delivering oil to a radial multicylinder motor. The throw of the pistons was continuously variable from zero to a maximum, thereby enabling a wide-ranged continuous change of speed of the driven element to be made at the pleasure of the operator. The firm of Manly & Veal, consulting engineers, and the Manly Drive Company developed this device in New York, applying it to heavy trucks and to battleship turrets. Manly was the owner of some fifty patents on automotive transportation and power generation and transmission.

He completed and edited the *Langley Memoir on Mechanical Flight,* published by the Smithsonian Institution in 1911, which was begun by Langley and gives in detail his experiments in aviation. He served as consulting aviation engineer to the British War Office, 1915; to the Curtis Aeroplane & Motor Corporation, 1915–19, of which from 1919 to 1920 he was assistant general manager; as a member of the United States commission to the International Aircraft Conference, London, 1918; and as consulting engineer to various corporations. He was a member and president (1919) of the Society of Automotive Engineers. In 1930 the Smithsonian Institution, in recognition of the permanent value of his pioneer work on the light radial internal combustion engine, awarded to him posthumously the Langley Gold Medal for Aerodromics. On June 9, 1904, he married Grace Agnes Wishart, who died May 15, 1921, leaving two sons.

[*Who's Who in America,* 1926–27; Louise Manly, *The Manly Family* (1930); unpublished records of the Smithsonian Institution; *Specifications and Drawings of Patents Issued from the U. S. Patent Office,* Oct. 1902, July 1904, Oct. 1905; *Ann. Report of the Commissioner of Patents,* 1913, ff.; C. L. Lawrance, "The Development of the Airplane Engine in the U. S.," in *International Civil Aeronautics Conference, 1928, Papers . . .* (1928); E. C. Vivian and W. L. Marsh, *A Hist. of Aeronautics* (1921); F. A. Magoun and E. Hodgins, *A Hist. of Aircraft* (1931); *Ann. Report of the Board of Regents of the Smithsonian Institution* (1930); *Jour. of the Soc. of Automotive Engineers,* Nov. 1927, Oct. 1928; *World* (N. Y.) and *N. Y. Herald Tribune,* Oct. 18, 1927.] C. G. A.

MANN, AMBROSE DUDLEY (Apr. 26, 1801–November 1889), diplomat, was born at Hanover Court House, Va. He was educated in the Virginia schools and at the United States Military Academy at West Point, whence he resigned just before graduation in order to avoid entering the military profession. He took up the legal profession and soon became interested in politics. In 1842 he was appointed United States consul at Bremen, Germany, and in 1846 he was given diplomatic powers as a special commissioner to the German states for the purpose of negotiating commercial treaties. He drew up commercial treaties with Hanover, Oldenburg, Mecklenburg-Schwerin, and with other German states. Acting on Mann's suggestion, Polk recognized the federal government of Germany at Frankfort in 1848. In 1849 Mann was appointed special agent of the United States to Kossuth's government in Hungary. He was virtually authorized to extend recognition if events seemed to warrant it. After the collapse of this project he was sent to Switzerland as special agent of the United States during the administration of Fillmore. In this capacity he negotiated and signed a general convention of friendship and reciprocal agreements. On his return to America he became assistant secretary of state and served from 1853 to 1856.

With the approach of the Civil War Mann was increasingly identified with the Southern Rights party. He was especially prominent in the advocacy of the economic independence of the South, which, because of his special knowledge of commerce and navigation, assumed the form of championship of a Southern merchant marine. He wrote pamphlets and articles for *DeBow's Review,* 1856–58, urging the establishment of a direct steamship line between the Southern states and Europe. He also advised building fast ships which would be specially fitted for Southern waters. Because of his representations to it, the Virginia legislature in 1858 incorporated a company for establishing the direct trade (*Acts of the General Assembly of Virginia,* 1857–58, ch. 187). The idea was very popular during this period when such men as Yancy, Hammond, DeBow, and others were attempting to convince the South of the necessity of casting off its vassalage to Northern industry and commerce. So when the South withdrew from the Union in 1861 the choice of Mann as joint commissioner with Yancy and Rost and as associate commissioner with Mason and Slidell was not entirely illogical.

But expert knowledge of trade and shipping and experience in arranging commercial treaties apparently constituted Mann's chief qualifications for a position which required diplomacy of the highest skill. He was credulous and lacking in penetration and seems never to have been aware of the real drift of affairs. His diplomatic correspondence is characterized by ponderous and bombastic phrases and sophomoric sentiments. He spent the first year of his mission in London and the last three years in Belgium where he wasted time cultivating the already friendly King Leopold, who it was hoped would exercise moving influence upon Napoleon and Queen Victoria. In two matters, however, he was not a complete failure: he managed to influence the press in both England and Belgium in 1861 at the time when the Confederacy had no regular propagandist agents in Europe; and in the winter of 1863–64 he went to the Vatican to obtain the aid of the Pope in checking the Federal recruiting in Europe of Catholic Irish and Germans. Altogether the Northern cause won large numbers of recruits from Europe, mostly in Ireland and Germany, and it would have been worth a whole series of successful campaigns to the Confederacy if this enlistment of foreigners could have been frustrated. The Pope expressed great indignation and horror when he learned to what extent his subjects were being utilized by the United States as cannon fodder and immediately attempted to put a check to their enlistment. But, while many were restrained by the Pope's objection, there was no appreciable decrease in the number of those who left Ireland and the other Catholic countries and entered the Federal armies to get the bounty. Mann remained in Europe after the overthrow of the Confederacy and lived in Paris until his death in 1889.

[The Pickett papers in the Manuscript Division of the Lib. of Cong. contain all of Mann's diplomatic correspondence during his mission to England and Belgium, 1861–65; James M. Mason's papers contain some private letters from Mann to Mason, 1861–65 (Manuscript Division of the Lib. of Cong.); his consular and diplomatic correspondence while in Germany and Switzerland, 1842–53, is in the Dept. of State. For his reports upon Hungary see *Senate Executive Doc. 43,* 31 Cong., 1 Sess., *Senate Doc. 279,* 61 Cong., 2 Sess., and *Senate Doc. 282,* 65 Cong., 2 Sess. For résumés of his diplomatic career by Lewis Cass, secretary of state, and by a congressional committee, see *House Executive Doc. 17* and *House Report 254,* 35 Cong., 2 Sess. Further sources include: Dunbar Rowland, *Jefferson Davis, Constitutionalist; His Letters, Papers and Speeches* (1923), vol. VII; H. M. Wriston, *Executive Agents in Am. Foreign Relations* (1929); *Journal des Débats* (Paris), Nov. 16, 1889; obituary reprinted from *Galignani's Messenger* (Paris) in the *N. Y. Tribune,* Dec. 1, 1889. Mann wrote the memoirs of his life but the whereabouts of this document is apparently unknown.]

F. L. O.

MANN, HORACE (May 4, 1796–Aug. 2, 1859), educator, one of five children of Thomas and Rebecca (Stanley) Mann, was born on the ancestral farm in the town of Franklin, Mass., a descendant of William Mann, an early settler of

Cambridge, Mass. From his father, who died of tuberculosis in 1809, Horace inherited a frail constitution and a susceptibility to this disease. His parents were people of meager education but of sterling character, and imparted to their children habits of industry and high ideals. Mann's childhood was an unhappy one passed in poverty, unremitting toil, repression, and fear. The studies and methods of the district school were stultifying, the school masters ignorant, and their discipline stern and terrifying. Still more terrifying were the Sunday sermons preached by the Rev. Nathaniel Emmons [*q.v.*], in which were pictured the eternal torments of those damned for the glory of God. Night after night the little lad, filled with grief and horror over the possible fate awaiting his loved ones, sobbed himself to sleep. Although Franklin possessed a town library, it brought little relief to the mind of the harrowed child, made up as it was chiefly of old histories and theological works. Undoubtedly, the immediate influence of school, church, and town library upon this highly sensitive boy were repressive, if not injurious; nevertheless, to the spirit of revolt engendered by their defects can be traced directly many of the most important reform efforts of his later life.

The superiority of Mann's mental gifts was revealed in connection with his preparation for college. Up to the time he was sixteen, he had never attended school more than eight or ten weeks in any one year, and he did not begin preparing for college until 1816. Then, in six months, under the direction of an eccentric but brilliant itinerant teacher named Barrett, he completed a course of study which enabled him to enter the sophomore class of Brown University. Here he made a brilliant record, graduating with high honors in 1819. He now entered a law office in Wrentham, Mass., but after a few months returned to Brown as a tutor in Latin and Greek. In 1821 he left Brown to enter the famous law school at Litchfield, Conn., and in 1823 was admitted to the bar of Norfolk County, Mass. For fourteen years, first at Dedham, Mass., and after 1833 at Boston, he practised with marked success. Meanwhile, he had begun his public career as a member of the Massachusetts state legislature, first serving in the House (1827–33), and then in the Senate (1833–37). During the last two years, he was president of the Senate, and as such signed the epoch-making education bill which became a law Apr. 20, 1837. This bill provided for a state board of education, to consist of the governor, lieutenant-governor, and eight citizens to be appointed by the governor. It empowered the board of education to appoint and employ a secretary at an annual salary of $1,000 (increased in 1838 to $1,500), and to make annual reports to the state legislature.

It had been expected that the board would choose as its first secretary James G. Carter [*q.v.*], the framer of the bill, a man whose services to education undoubtedly eclipsed those of any other citizen of the state up to that time. The selection of Mann, largely through the influence of Edmund Dwight [*q.v.*], was, however, a matter of no greater surprise than Mann's acceptance, involving, as it did, his abandonment of a lucrative legal practice and the prospect of an alluring political career; but his reasons for acceptance are not difficult to discover. Though exceedingly successful, he had never been ardently enthusiastic about his profession; from early childhood he had been possessed with a consuming desire to do something for the benefit of mankind; he saw in the secretaryship, moreover, a means of combating the grief and despair which had held him in clutch ever since the death of his wife, Charlotte Messer, daughter of President Asa Messer [*q.v.*] of Brown University, whom he had married Sept. 12, 1830, and who had died childless, Aug. 1, 1832.

The educational situation awaiting the new secretary offered ample scope for his many talents. The school-district system legalized in 1789 had brought with it a multitude of evils, including disastrous decentralization, a decline in public interest, and a decrease of financial support. Free schools, the one-time glory of colonial Massachusetts, were now regarded with contempt by the well-to-do classes, who more and more patronized private schools. The effects of this attitude were everywhere evident in short school terms, dilapidated and unsanitary schoolhouses, untrained and underpaid teachers, and irrational methods of teaching. To remedy these conditions as far and as soon as possible was the task awaiting Mann. Clothed with almost no authority except to collect and disseminate information, he brought to his new duties such a degree of courage, vision, and wisdom that during the brief period of twelve years in which he held office, the Massachusetts school system was almost completely transformed. His first task was to arouse and to educate public opinion with reference to the purpose, value, and needs of public education. With this end in view, he organized annual educational conventions in every county for the benefit of teachers, school officials, and the public. He not only addressed these meetings himself, but pressed into service distinguished clergymen, lawyers, and college professors. Realizing that there was little hope of any improvement in the schools apart from the improvement of the teaching profession, he rapidly consummated plans which led to the establishment of teachers' institutes and normal schools. During the second year of his office, Edmund Dwight, through Mann, anonymously offered $10,000 to the state of Massachusetts for improving the preparation of elementary teachers, provided the state would furnish a like amount. Dwight's gift and its conditions were accepted by the legislature, and within two years Massachusetts had established the first three state normal schools in the United States.

In 1838, with the avowed purpose of bringing about a better understanding of the problems of the public school, he started a semi-monthly magazine, the *Common School Journal,* which he edited for ten years. A far more important channel through which he disseminated a knowledge of existing conditions and needed reforms were the twelve annual reports which he prepared (1837–48) as secretary of the state board of education. Each contains not only the customary statistical data, but a presentation and discussion of school problems of crucial importance. The needs and remedies growing out of these problems are set forth with convincing clearness and with the fervor of a prophet and reformer.

The results of his labors were remarkable. When he became secretary, elementary men teachers were receiving an average annual wage of $185, and women, $65; one-sixth of the children of the state were being educated in private schools and academies, and approximately one-third were without any educational opportunities whatsoever. In multitudes of districts the school term did not extend beyond two or three months. Under Mann's influence, a minimum school year of six months was established by an act passed in 1839. More than $2,000,000 was spent in providing better schoolhouses and equipment. Appropriations for public education were more than doubled. The proportion of private school expenditure to that of public schools decreased from seventy-five to thirty-six per cent. of total school costs. Salaries of public school masters were increased to sixty-two per cent. and those of women, fifty-four per cent. The high-school law of 1827, largely a dead letter prior to his time, became effective, with the result that at least fifty new high schools were established during his secretaryship and opportunities for free public secondary education became widely distributed throughout the state. The professional training of teachers was placed on a firm basis, the elementary curriculum was enriched, and improved methods of instruction, including especially the Pestalozzian object methods and the word method of teaching reading, were introduced.

It was inevitable that Mann's aggressive efforts should sooner or later arouse bitter opposition. As a Unitarian, he contended that the Bible should be read in public schools, but without comment. He had scarcely entered upon his progressive educational program when one church after another began to charge him and the board of education with being responsible for creating a godless system of schools. With these charges came the demand that sectarian instruction, which had been excluded from the schools by an act of 1827, should be restored. Mann met these sectarian attacks with vigor, courage, and a final victory of great importance, not only to the schools of Massachusetts, but to the nation at large. Immediately after his marriage to his second wife, Mary Tyler (Peabody) Mann [*q.v.*], on May 1, 1843, he sailed for Europe with two purposes in mind: to recover his health, and to discover what America might learn from European schools. He spent five months studying educational conditions in England, Ireland, Scotland, Holland, Belgium, France, Germany, and Switzerland. His observations and conclusions, embodied in his seventh annual report, drew no comparison between the schools of the United States and those of European countries; nevertheless, his high commendation of German schools was interpreted by a considerable number of Boston school masters as implying a drastic criticism of their own professional preparation and practices. An acrimonious controversy ensued from which, however, Mann again came forth victorious.

In 1848 he resigned his secretaryship, having been elected to the United States House of Representatives as an anti-slavery Whig to succeed John Quincy Adams. Although allied with anti-slavery forces, Mann was not an abolitionist; nevertheless, he was eventually led into open conflict with Daniel Webster, whose friendship and political support he had enjoyed up to this time. In 1852 he met defeat as the candidate of the Free-Soilers for the governorship of Massachusetts. He then accepted the presidency of the recently established Antioch College at Yellow Springs, Ohio. Besides serving as president, he taught political economy, intellectual philosophy, moral philosophy, and natural theology. In 1859, owing to bad management, lack of funds, and internal dissensions, the college was sold for debt and reorganized. Following his delivery of the baccalaureate address of that year, Mann, exhausted and broken by the anxieties and persecution amid which he had labored, retired to his home, where he died within a few weeks. He was survived by his wife and their three sons.

Mann espoused many other causes beside that of the common schools, notably the establishment of state hospitals for the insane and the restriction of slavery, lotteries, and the liquor traffic. Essentially a Puritan without a theology, he denounced not only profanity and intemperance, but smoking and ballet dancing. His lasting place in American history rests, however, upon his services to public education. His influence in this field extended far beyond the boundaries of Massachusetts. Copies of his annual reports and other educational writings were widely disseminated throughout the United States with the result that one state after another sought and followed his advice. Owing to his efforts combined with those of other educational pioneers, there ensued a period so marked by educational progress and reform that it has ever since come to be known as the period of the common-school revival in the United States.

Among the many influences which played an important part in developing the character, philosophy, ideals, and aims of Horace Mann were the writings of Emerson and those of the Scotch philosopher and phrenologist, George Combe. Although Mann acquired from Combe a belief in phrenology, undoubtedly the greatest source of Combe's influence over him was the Scotch philosopher's unswerving faith in the unlimited improvability of the human race through education. The motivating principle of Mann's life was nowhere better or more clearly expressed than in the oft-quoted words with which he closed his last Commencement address at Antioch College: "Be ashamed to die until you have won some victory for humanity." In addition to his twelve annual reports which are included in abbreviated form in Mary Mann's *Life* (*post*, vol. III), and numerous articles in magazines, he published *Lectures on Education* (1845).

[Biographies and biographical sketches of Mann have been published in English, French, and Spanish. Of these the most important in English are: *Life and Works of Horace Mann*, ed. by Mary Tyler Peabody Mann (3 vols., 1865–68), enlarged and ed. by G. C. Mann (5 vols., 1891); B. A. Hinsdale, *Horace Mann and the Common School Revival in the U. S.* (1898); G. Compayré, *Horace Mann and the Public School in the U. S.* (tr. 1907); A. E. Winship, *Horace Mann the Educator* (1896). See also R. B. Culver, *Horace Mann and Religion in the Massachusetts Public Schools* (1929). For a genealogy of the Mann family, consult G. S. Mann, *Mann Memorial: A Record of the Mann Family in America* (1884). For bibliographies consult B. P. Mann, in *Report of the Commissioner of Education, 1895–96* (1897), vol. I, and B. A. Hinsdale, *supra*, pp. 311–19.] F. H. S.

MANN, JAMES (July 22, 1759–Nov. 7, 1832), army surgeon, was born in Wrentham, Mass., the son of David and Anna Mann and a descendant of William Mann, an early settler in Cambridge, Mass. He graduated from Harvard at the age of seventeen and then took up the study of medicine under Dr. Samuel Danforth. At the age of twenty he became surgeon of Col. William Shepard's 4th Massachusetts Regiment. In June of 1781 he was captured by the British and was imprisoned on Long Island during July and August. He left the army because of poor health on Apr. 14, 1782. He settled first at Wrentham but later moved to New York, where he practised until the outbreak of the War of 1812. Entering the army as a hospital surgeon, he was soon put in charge of the medical department on the northern frontier. Upon the establishment of peace in 1815 he apparently left the service, as his name is not in the next army register, but in August 1816 he is again shown as the senior hospital surgeon, on duty at Detroit. The reorganization of 1818, which established the medical corps and consolidated the hospital, garrison, and regimental surgeons on one list of post surgeons, ranked according to seniority, put him number twenty-four on that list. The reorganization of 1821, which reduced the number of surgeons to eight, left him an assistant surgeon. He served in that grade until his death, which occurred at Governor's Island on Nov. 7, 1832.

Mann was a scholarly person and an interesting writer. He published articles on the defeat of the Indians at Wrentham, and on diabetes, cholera infantum, pneumonia, amputations through joints, swelling of the inferior extremities of puerperal women, and on menorrhagia and leucorrhea and their treatment. But his fame rests principally upon his *Medical Sketches of the Campaigns of 1812, 13, 14, to which are added Surgical Cases, Observations on Military Hospitals; and Flying Hospitals Attached to a Moving Army, Also An Appendix . . .* (1816). The sketches, written in good English, reveal striking powers of observation. They describe not only the medical affairs of the Northern army but the country and the frontier villages of that day, when Buffalo, two miles above Black Rock, was a village of less than 200 houses, though rapidly increasing in population and trade. Mann's professional standing is witnessed by the fact that in 1819, while stationed in Boston, he was elected one of the eight consulting physicians of the Massachusetts General Hospital. He was also awarded an honorary degree of M.D. from Brown University in 1815. Unquestionably one of the most notable army surgeons of his day, he was, by an ironical fate, the individual victim of well-meant general legislation, which, though he had ranked next after the head of the department, left him an assistant surgeon at the time of his death at the age of seventy-three. Mann was married, Dec. 12, 1788, to Martha (or Mary) Tyler. They had five children.

[Army registers, 1815–32; G. S. Mann, *Mann Memorial: A Record of the Mann Family in America* (1884); W. I. T. Brigham, *The Tyler Geneal.* (1912), vol. I; *Mass. Hist. Soc. Colls.*, vol. X (1809); *Boston Medic. and Surgic. Jour.*, Nov. 14, 1918; N. I. Bowditch, *Hist. of the Mass. Gen. Hospital* (1881); *N. Y. American*, Nov. 8, 1832.] P. M. A.

MANN, JAMES ROBERT (Oct. 20, 1856–Nov. 30, 1922), lawyer, congressman, was born near Bloomington, Ill., the son of William Henry Mann, Illinois horticulturist, and Elizabeth Dabney (Abraham) Mann. He attended the University of Illinois, where he distinguished himself in student activities and athletics and graduated as valedictorian in 1876. He was also valedictorian of the class of 1881 at the Union College of Law (Chicago), and while a student, began to assist in the editing of certain United States court reports. On May 30, 1882, he was married to Emma Columbia of Champaign, Ill. His real-estate and legal connections with the nearby village of Hyde Park brought him a fortune which permitted him to indulge a taste for politics. He became attorney for the Hyde Park commissioners and the South Park commissioners of Chicago, and master in chancery of the superior court of Cook County. His aid in bringing the Columbian Exposition to the Hyde Park area sent him to the Chicago common council upon the incorporation of his village. Serving from 1892 to 1896, he became known as a hard fighter and a hater of "boodle," a not-unknown commodity in the council of that day. In 1897 his strongly Republican district sent him to Congress and kept him there until his death in 1922.

Mann was connected with much of the important legislation of his period. Seniority made him chairman of the commerce committee for a single congress before the Democratic landslide of 1912. Measures bearing his name or handiwork are: the Mann-Elkins act (railroad rate regulation, anti-rebate law), the pure food and drugs act (1906), the bureau of corporations act, the Mann act ("white slave" law), the wood-pulp tariff, isthmian canal legislation, the resolution providing for the woman-suffrage amendment, and numerous local matters. Cannon's choice of Mann as official "watchdog of legislation" in part explains his rise and his tendency to standpattism. Just at the time (1912) when his talents were coming to their peak the shift of parties threw him into the position of minority leader. Here he came into his own. A rather short, stocky, grizzly-bearded, beetle-browed individual, he made a formidable antagonist to anyone trying to put through loose, unwise, or Democratic legislation. Often on his feet, an able and willing filibuster, for six years he served his party by hectoring the Democratic majority.

After a short retirement in 1914 caused by illness Mann returned in 1915, seemingly with some notion of his own eligibility for the presidential nomination in 1916. Failing this, he lost the caucus nomination for the speakership in 1919, a defeat illustrating if not resulting from his own characteristics as minority leader. His devotion to the Cannonism which gave him his start made him unacceptable to the post-Progressive Republican party, and his very capabilities were a limitation. Better informed on legislation than his fellow Republicans, he tended to shoulder the entire burden, leading an exasperated colleague to accuse him of undertaking "not only to play Hamlet, but the fair Ophelia and the King and the Queen and first gravedigger" (*James R. Mann: Memorial Addresses*, *post*, p. 45). This hurt his larger usefulness while making him superficially even more valuable to the party. With his health and prestige weakened, he retired into a sort of emeritus position with the return of a Republican majority, ending his career as a sort of peppery oracle delivering opinions on the questions of the day. To his ability, industry, and keen insight into parliamentary intricacies friend and foe bore witness; the former with pride tempered by a somewhat smarting sense of Mann's self-imposed superiority, the latter with envy not untouched with humiliation at the flaws he had found in their legislative armor.

[See *Who's Who in America*, 1922–23; *Biog. Dir. Am. Cong.* (1928); *James R. Mann: Memorial Addresses Delivered in the House of Representatives . . . Jan. 14, 1923* (1924); *Chicago Tribune*, *Evening Star* (Washington), Dec. 1, 1922. The Mann papers (35 vols.) in the Lib. of Cong. contain a mass of newspaper material and a few letters. He destroyed his personal correspondence.] L. E. E.

MANN, LOUIS (Apr. 20, 1865–Feb. 15, 1931), actor and playwright, was born in New York City, the son of Daniel and Caroline (Hecht) Mann. His first stage appearance was at the Stadt Theatre on the Bowery, New York, at the age of three, when he impersonated a snowflake in a Christmas pantomime. But his parents had no thought of a stage career for him. In youth he worked for a time in a haberdasher's shop, and then was sent to the University of California. After some two years of study, he left the University surreptitiously to join a theatrical stock company in San Francisco. His parents at length traced him to central New York, where the company was playing *East Lynne, Ingomar,* and other old favorites. Unknown to him, the parents saw him perform, and deciding that he had talent, gave him $200 to further his dramatic education; but Louis turned it over to his manager to bolster the shaky finances of the company. For several years he played in support of Tommaso Salvini, Lewis Morrison, E. H. Sothern, Cyril Maude, and Daniel Bandmann. By 1890 he was making ventures at the head of small companies of his own in *Lady Audley's Secret* and other strenuous dramas. In 1892 he scored a hit in the part of Dick Winters in *Incog.* In the following year he again took a company of his own on tour in *The Laughing Girl.* His burlesque of Du Maurier's Svengali in *The Merry World* in 1895 was much praised. In 1897 in *The Girl from Paris* he shared honors with his wife, Clara Lipman, actress and playwright, whom he had married on Oct. 28, 1895.

Throughout the greater part of his career, Mann played dialect rôles—German, Jewish, French, and in *The Red Kloof* (1901) he assumed the part of a South African Boer farmer. In *The Telephone Girl* (1898), *The Girl in the Barracks* (1899), *All on Account of Eliza* (1900), and *Hoch the Consul* (1902) he continued playing these eccentric leading rôles, usually with his wife as co-star. In 1903 he appeared for a time with the Weber and Fields burlesque company. In 1904 he played Baron von Walden in *The Second Fiddle,* and in 1906–07 he appeared in New York and London in *Julie Bonbon,* written by Clara Lipman. *The White Hen* followed in 1907, and then *The New Generation,* later renamed *The Man Who Stood Still,* which continued from 1908 to 1910. In 1910 came his own play, *The Cheater,* and in 1911 *Elevating a Husband,* written by his wife (in collaboration with Samuel Shipman), and utilizing Mann's enthusiasm for baseball. *Children of To-Day* in 1913, *The Bubble* (1915), and *The Warriors* (1917) were not remarkable, but in 1918 he scored one of his greatest successes as co-star with Sam Bernard in *Friendly Enemies,* a war play. When it appeared in Washington, President Wilson sat in a box, and at Mann's invitation arose and spoke a few words in praise of the play—the first time in history that such an incident had occurred. This comedy ran for more than a year in New York and toured the country until late in 1920. In *The Unwritten Chapter,* Mann next appeared as Haym Salomon, Jewish financier of the American Revolution, in whose history the actor was deeply interested. Subsequent appearances were in *The Whirl of New York, Nature's Nobleman,* and *Give and Take.* Mann was a person of strong opinions and intense emotions, qualities which he injected into his stage characters. He was one of the organizers of the Actors' Fidelity League, which fought the Actors' Equity strike in 1919.

[*Who's Who in America,* 1930–31; John Parker, ed., *Who's Who in the Theatre* (1930); Felix Isman, *Weber and Fields* (1924), pp. 291–95; L. C. Strang, *Famous Actors of the Day in America* (1902), second series; the *Theatre,* Apr. 1905; obituaries in New York newspapers, Feb. 16, 1931; Robinson Locke Dramatic Collection, N. Y. Pub. Lib.]

A. F. H.

MANN, MARY TYLER PEABODY (Nov. 16, 1806–Feb. 11, 1887), educator, author, was born in Cambridge, Mass., the second of the seven children of Nathaniel and Elizabeth (Palmer) Peabody. The eldest child of the family was Elizabeth Palmer Peabody [*q.v.*], and the third was Sophia Amelia, who married Nathaniel Hawthorne in 1842. Their father, a graduate of Dartmouth College in the class of 1800, was a physician and dentist with varied cultural interests, and the mother conducted a school in which her own children received their excellent training.

In 1832 the Peabodys removed from Salem to Boston and opened a bookstore as a sort of family enterprise. They imported French and German books and periodicals, carried a stock of artists' supplies—chiefly for the personal convenience of Washington Allston—and made their shop one of the focal points of the Transcendental movement. About this time Mary first met Horace Mann [*q.v.*] in the Ashburton Place boarding house kept by the mother of James Freeman Clarke. They were alike in their intellectual ardor and in their devotion to educational and philanthropic work, and she was soon in love with him; but Mann was all but broken by grief for the death of his wife, and some nine years passed before he could bring himself to propose marriage to her. Meanwhile, Mary spent the years 1832–35 with Sophia in Cuba and on her return was Elizabeth's assistant in her school. On May 1, 1843, she and Horace Mann were married, and the marriage, contrary to his forebodings, proved singularly happy. Mrs. Mann was her husband's active collaborator and influenced his life and thought profoundly; she bore him three sons. After her husband's death at Yellow Springs, Ohio, Aug. 2, 1859, she returned to Massachusetts and made her home successively in Concord, Cambridge, and Jamaica Plain, where she died. She had already published a children's book, *The Flower People* (1838; rev. ed., 1875) and a cook book, *Christianity in the Kitchen: A Physiological Cook Book* (1857; 1858), based on the soundest scientific knowledge then available; she now devoted herself to writing her husband's life and editing his works, producing her *Life and Works of Horace Mann* (3 vols., 1865–68; extended edition in 5 vols., ed. by G. C. Mann, 1891). In the *Life* the only reference to herself is at the beginning of Chapter v: "On the 1st of May, 1843, Mr. Mann was again married, and sailed for Europe to visit European schools, especially in Germany, where he expected to derive most benefit." She wrote for various periodicals, made translations from the Spanish, supervised the education of her sons, interested herself actively in philanthropic work among Indians and negroes, and aided her sister Elizabeth in her kindergarten in Boston. Her essay, "Moral Culture of Infancy," was published in 1863 in a single small volume with Elizabeth Peabody's "Kindergarten Guide." *Juanita: A Romance of Real Life in Cuba Fifty Years Ago* (1887) appeared posthumously and exhibits both the limitations and the virtues of her remarkable mind, which kept its vigor to the end. A few hours before her death she called for the Boston *Evening Transcript* and listened with evident pleasure while a review of one of her sister's books was read aloud to her.

[S. H. Peabody and C. H. Pope, *Peabody Geneal.* (1909); Julian Hawthorne, *Nathaniel Hawthorne and His Wife* (1885); *Grandmother Tyler's Book: The Recollections of Mary Palmer Tyler* (1925), ed. by Frederick Tupper and H. T. Brown; G. A. Hubbell, *Horace Mann, Educator, Patriot and Reformer* (1910); Boston *Transcript*, Feb. 12, 15, 1887.] G. H. G.

MANN, NEWTON (Jan. 16, 1836–July 25, 1926), Unitarian clergyman, author, was descended through his father, Darwin H. Mann, from Richard Mann of Scituate, Mass., who emigrated from England about 1644; and through his mother, Cordelia Newton, from Richard Newton, who was a freeman of Marlboro, Mass., in 1645. Born in Cazenovia, N. Y., the first of five children, all surviving, and educated at Cazenovia Seminary, he was obliged to shorten his schooling at the death of his father in 1844 and take up the responsibilities of farming. So successfully, however, did he combine his duties with self-culture that at twenty he was acquainted with the best literature and philosophy of the day, notably Emerson, Renan, and Spencer, and had command of five languages. An inheritance of intellectual independence from his paternal grandfather, a physician, overcame the strongly sentimental orthodoxy of his Baptist mother and kinsfolk. His tendency toward heterodoxy was strengthened by a rebuff from the family minister, who told him that his doubts were a temptation of the devil. As a result Mann decided for "liberty,—liberty to choose, and to follow the good; deliverance from the dominating authority of what has been called the 'written Word'; . . . and the committal of the soul to the guidance of the free Spirit, out of which have come all bibles, all holiest thoughts, all highest things" (*Evolution of a Great Literature,* 1905, p. 371).

While on a visit to relatives in Wisconsin (1856–59) he came in contact with many Midwest Liberals and was engaged to supply the pulpit of the First Unitarian Church in Cincinnati (1859). A copy of Darwin's newly published *Origin of Species* came into his hands and prompted a sermon on "The Implication of Darwin's Philosophy," containing the first accurate forecast in the American pulpit of the effect of the hypothesis upon religious thought: "*The Origin of Species* marks a determining break in the whole history of thought. The theory of special creations, of man, of everything that falls within the realm of nature is from now on effectually disposed of. . . . Disposing of the special creation of Adam brings the fall of the doctrine of original sin. With the fall of the doctrine of original sin falls the Christian scheme of redemption and atonement." Such avowals made him an undesirable person even in the Unitarian pulpit of the day and he became principal of the school in Alton, Ill., whence, in 1861, he was called to be superintendent of the Western Sanitary Commission's soldiers' home at Vicksburg. Returning to the North and the ministry, he was ordained in 1865 as minister of the Unitarian Church in Kenosha, Wis., which he had organized. Three years later he became pastor of the Unitarian Society in Troy, N. Y., and in 1870 he was called to the Unitarian Church in Rochester, N. Y., where he remained until 1888. His years there were a period of great literary and scientific activity. He interpreted Kuenen in a series of lectures published in 1879 under the title, *A Rational View of the Bible*; he built an observatory on his lawn and computed the orbit of Sirius and its dark companion, the calculations and arguments appearing in *Popular Astronomy,* March 1897. In 1889 he became minister of the First Unitarian Church in Omaha, Nebr. Here he continued the cultural and scientific educational work he had begun in the Fortnightly Club of Rochester by founding Unity Club, the liberal and progressive programs of which exerted a profound influence upon the city. He also founded the Nebraska Humane Society and was its first president. During these years he published *The Evolution of a Great Literature* (1905, 1906), a lucid, scholarly presentation of modern Biblical criticism, and *The Import and Outlook of Socialism* (1910), in which he compared modern socialism with early Christianity, maintaining that "to perfect the great work and really bring peace among men, it needs that Christ come again, and with a more inclusive gospel, reaching to and moulding outward conditions as well as the inward spirit."

In addition to the published prose mentioned, Mann wrote many poems, usually upon religious or philosophic themes, which have never been collected, although his translation and adaptation of the Jewish hymn, "Praise to the Living God," is found in many hymnals. His death in Chicago at the age of ninety closed a life of remarkable mental vigor, independence, and originality. On Aug. 8, 1857, he married Eliza J. Smith, who died in 1908; by her he had four children. On Aug. 20, 1912, he married Rev. M. Rowena Morse of Chicago.

[G. S. Mann, *Mann Memorial: A Record of the Mann Family in America* (1884); *Meadville Theol. Sch. Quart. Bull.*, Oct. 1929; *Who's Who in America*, 1920–21; *Unitarian Yearbook*, 1927; *Christian Reg.*, Aug. 5, 19, 1926; *Chicago Tribune*, July 26, 1926.]

C. H. L—e.

MANN, WILLIAM JULIUS (May 29, 1819–June 20, 1892), Lutheran clergyman, author, was born in Stuttgart, Württemberg, the second son of Johann Georg Mann by his second wife, Auguste Friederike Gentner. His father, a merchant of good education and varied interests, was a founder and treasurer (1812–40) of the *Württemberger Bibelgesellschaft* and was city almoner (1845–58). Mann attended the *Lateinschule* at Blaubeuren (1827–33), the *Gymnasium Illustré* of his native city (1833–37), and the University of Tübingen (1837–41). As a theological student he was more influenced by Christian Friedrich Schmidt, an offspring of the old supranaturalistic school of Tübingen, than by either C. F. Baur or D. F. Strauss. After leaving the university Mann taught in a boys' school at Bönningheim, became assistant pastor there in February 1844, and in December of that year went to a similar position at Neuhausen, near Metzingen.

Meanwhile, in March, Philip Schaff [*q.v.*], whom Mann had first met in his gymnasial days, had gone to the United States and was soon urging his friend to join him at Mercersburg. Despite the sundering of family ties Mann was easily persuaded, for the thought of America had already fired his imagination. In 1843 he had written a children's story, *Die Ansiedler in Amerika* (Stuttgart, 1845), that indicates where his thoughts were wandering. He left Stuttgart Aug. 16, 1845, and arrived at Mercersburg Oct. 24. Having taught history and German at Mercersburg for a few months, he became assistant pastor in January 1846 of Salem German Reformed Church, Philadelphia, and was ordained May 17. In 1849 he married Margaretta Catherine, daughter of John Rommel of Philadelphia, who with a son and three daughters survived him. He did not feel at home outside the Lutheran Church and was happy when in 1850, without solicitation on his part, he was called to St. Michael's and Zion's congregation as assistant to Charles Rudolph Demme [*q.v.*].

In 1854 he succeeded Demme as chief pastor of the congregation, the largest of its denomination in America. He ministered to it with untiring fidelity and during the 1860's superintended its division into several independent congregations, himself retaining the pastorship of Zion's. When the Philadelphia Lutheran Theological Seminary was founded in 1864, he was elected to the German professorship, a post for which he was eminently qualified; but his parishioners would not accept his resignation, and for twenty laborious years he filled both offices. He taught Hebrew, ethics, symbolics, homiletics, and New Testament exegesis, and was housefather of the Seminary (1872–84). He took a prominent but dignified part in the controversy that led to the founding of the General Council of the Evangelical Lutheran Church in North America, publishing *A Plea for the Augsburg Confession in Answer to the Objections of the Definite Platform* (1856) and *Lutheranism in America* (1857), but after its organization he took little active interest in it. On the vexed question of pulpit and altar fellowship, and on several other matters of importance, he was in sharp disagreement with Charles Porterfield Krauth [*q.v.*] and other leaders of the General Council. He was president of the Ministerium of Pennsylvania from 1860 to 1862 and again in 1880 and active in all its work. He was a prolific writer in both German and English. He was co-editor, with Schaff, of the *Deutscher Kirchenfreund* from 1848 to 1859 and contributed voluminously, on a large variety of subjects, to ten other church papers. He edited an edition of Luther's *Small Catechism* (1863) in collaboration with G. F. Krotel and *Kohler's Familien-Bibel* (1865), published *Heilbotschaft* (1881), a volume of sermons, and several popular works in history and biography. During the last twelve years of his life he devoted much of his time to the early history of the Lutheran Church in America, producing his admirable *Life and Times of Henry Melchior Mühlenberg* (1887) and, in collaboration with Beale Melancthton Schmucker [*q.v.*], an annotated edition of the *Hallesche Nachrichten* (2 vols., 1886–95). Such work was possible only to a man whose mind and pen moved with equal rapidity, and who was habitually at his desk at four o'clock in the morning.

To his seventy-third year, in spite of not a little illness, he kept the freshness and energy of a young man. Unfatigued by the heavy duties of his profession, he was in his hours of leisure a poet, an artist, and a musician, a student of history and the sciences, a close observer of politics, and a delightful companion. Krotel's comparison of him to the man in the parable to whom the five talents were entrusted was best appreciated by those who knew him most intimately. On Oct. 28, 1891, he was prostrated by a heart attack and never recovered fully. He died the following June in a hotel in Boston and was buried in West Laurel Hill Cemetery, Philadelphia.

[Adolph Spaeth, "William Julius Mann, D.D., LL.D.," *Luth. Ch. Rev.*, Jan. 1893 (also separately printed), and *D. Wilhelm Julius Mann, Ein deutsch-amerikanischer Theologe* (Reading, Pa., 1895); *Memoir of the Life and Work of William Julius Mann* (privately printed, 1893), by his daughter, Emma T. Mann; D. S. Schaff, *The Life of Philip Schaff* (1897); T. W. Kretschmann, "William Julius Mann, D.D., LL.D.," *Luth. Ch. Rev.*, July 1917; G. W. Sandt, "Lutheran Leaders as I Knew Them," *Ibid.*, Oct. 1917; L. D. Reed, *The Phila. Sem. Biog. Record 1864–1923* (1923); *Public Ledger* (Phila.), June 21, 1892.] G. H. G.

MANNERS, JOHN HARTLEY (Aug. 10, 1870–Dec. 19, 1928), actor, dramatist, was one of the many successful writers for the stage who have served an apprenticeship as actors. He was born in London of Irish parentage, and going to Australia, began his career as an actor in Melbourne in 1898, his first rôle being Lord Chetland in *The Squire of Dames*, a once popular play anglicized by R. C. Carton from the younger Dumas's comedy, *L'Ami des Femmes*. Returning to London in the following year, he made his début there with George Alexander at the St. James's Theatre, Apr. 26, 1899, as Nat Brewster in Edward Rose's play, *In Days of Old*. He remained an actor in the London theatres for several years and was at one time a member of Sir Johnston Forbes-Robertson's company, playing Laertes to that star's Hamlet at the Imperial Theatre in 1902. During this period he began to attract attention as a writer of plays, and having completed *The Crossways* for Mrs. Langtry, he supervised its production in London in November 1902, himself playing the part of Lord Robert Scarlett. He came to the United States as a member of her company for its American tour, which began at the Garrick Theatre in New York, Dec. 29, 1902. Not long afterward he abandoned acting and thenceforth was a prolific playwright, the total number of plays that he wrote either alone or in collaboration being more than thirty. During the last twenty years of his life he was closely associated with the American stage, and marrying Laurette (Cooney) Taylor, the widow of Charles A. Taylor, in 1912, he made both her and himself prominent and popular with *Peg o' My Heart*, a simple play, that through the acting of his wife touched the hearts of multitudes of theatregoers. It was produced in 1912 and was acted more than six hundred times consecutively in New York, and for more than five hundred performances in London. Five companies or more were touring in it simultaneously through several seasons in the United States alone, and it even found favor in translation with audiences in France, Italy, and other European countries.

Manners was a playwright with aspirations for something more than mere popularity, but he never achieved it. The success of *Peg o' My Heart* unfortunately dimmed the reputation of his other work and made him scarcely more than a one-play dramatist. "I won't write 'situations' merely for the sake of 'situations,'" he said. "They . . . interest me only as they reveal character" (*Christian Science Monitor*, June 24, 1919). He also asserted that "reality is the curse of the modern theatre. Imagination is its boon!" (*New York Times*, Jan. 13, 1918). Others of his plays were *The House Next Door* (1909), *The Great John Ganton* (1909), *The Girl in Waiting* (1910), *Happiness* (1914), and last of all, *The National Anthem* (1922). He died in retirement in New York City after an illness of several months.

[Dixie Hines and H. P. Hanaford, *Who's Who in Music and Drama*, 1914; John Parker, *Who's Who in the Theatre*, 1925; *Who's Who in America*, 1926–27; article by John Corbin in the *N. Y. Times*, Jan. 13, 1918; interview in *Christian Science Monitor*, June 24, 1919; obituary in Boston *Transcript*, Dec. 20, 1928.] E. F. E.

MANNING, DANIEL (May 16, 1831–Dec. 24, 1887), secretary of the treasury under Cleveland, was born in Albany, N. Y., the second son of John and Eleanor Manning who were natives of Albany of Dutch, Irish, and English ancestry. When Daniel was six years old his father died and at eleven the boy was compelled to leave school to help support the family. In the winter of 1841 he was appointed a page in the state Assembly and held the position for two sessions.

At the end of the legislative session of 1842 he became a route carrier for the *Albany Atlas*. He soon advanced to the position of office boy and messenger, and at fifteen he went to the composing room where he learned the printer's trade. Economic necessity and the desire to better himself led him to study stenography and French; he also tried out as a reporter and on occasion was called upon by the *Atlas* to report proceedings of the legislature. In 1856 when the *Atlas* and the *Argus* combined, Manning was assigned a reporter's desk in the city department. This enabled him to come into contact with men of prominence in Albany County. In 1863 he was chosen by the Associated Press to report the proceedings of the state Assembly, and a few years later he became legislative correspondent of the *Brooklyn Eagle*. From 1858 to 1871 he reported the proceedings of the state Senate for the *Argus*. Meanwhile (1865) he became part owner and business manager of the Argus Company and in 1873 was elected to its presidency. As a newspaper man Manning gained the reputation of being a careful and accomplished writer.

His experience as a journalist proved to be good political training. A close friend and political lieutenant of Samuel J. Tilden, he virtually succeeded him in 1877 as the leader of the Democratic party of the state of New York. For ten years, 1874–84, he was a member of the state Democratic committee and of every state Democratic convention. From 1881 to 1884 he was chairman of the state committee. Like Tilden, he disliked Tammany and fought its repeated attempts to dominate New York state politics. As a delegate to the national Democratic conventions of 1876, 1880, and 1884, he worked indefatigably for the nomination of Tilden and Cleveland. Possibly Cleveland was indebted to Manning more than to any other person for his nomination as governor of New York and for his first nomination to the presidency.

Manning was not a speechmaker nor an office seeker for himself. He was a quiet man, and his power lay in his judgment of men and affairs, and in his abilities as a harmonizer and political manager. His appointment as secretary of the treasury by Cleveland in 1885, at the request of Tilden, elicited considerable surprise and some adverse criticism. During his two years in office, however, he proved to be not only an able treasury chief but a source of strength to the administration generally. His treasury reports are notable for their insight into fiscal affairs and for their recommendations concerning currency and taxation. He agreed with Cleveland that the further government purchase and compulsory coinage of silver should be suspended, and defeated the advocates of silver who made strenuous efforts to force the government to accept a silver basis. He vigorously condemned the proposals to reduce the treasury surplus by means of additional premiums to bondholders, extravagant appropriations, or treasury accumulations. In urging reduction of the tariff and retirement of the greenbacks he emphatically indorsed Cleveland's views. While ill health was a primary reason for his resignation from Cleveland's cabinet, the fact that Cleveland resented Tilden's desire to be "the power behind the throne" and, therefore, proscribed all of Tilden's friends, undoubtedly had much to do with Manning's withdrawal. Indeed, an evidently inspired editorial in *Leslie's Weekly* of Jan. 27, 1887, boldly asserted that Manning was "squeezed out" because of his independence of thought and action. After his resignation as secretary of the treasury he accepted the presidency of the Western National Bank of New York City. He was twice married. His first wife was Mary Little, who died in 1882. Two years after her death he was married to Mary Margaretta Fryer, daughter of William Fryer of Albany.

[Manning's reports as secretary of the treasury together with the detailed obituary in the Albany *Argus* of Dec. 25, 1887, are important. See also A. J. Parker, ed., *Landmarks of Albany County* (1897); Robert McElroy, *Grover Cleveland: the Man and the Statesman* (1923); G. F. Parker, *Recollections of Grover Cleveland* (1909); John Bigelow, *Letters and Lit. Memorials of Samuel J. Tilden* (1908); *Autobiog. of Andrew D. White* (1905); D. S. Alexander, *Four Famous New Yorkers: The Political Careers of Cleveland, Platt, Hill and Roosevelt* (1923); H. T. Peck, *Twenty Years of the Republic, 1885–1905* (1906); H. C. Thomas, *The Return of the Democratic Party to Power in 1884* (1919).]

H. J. C.

MANNING, JAMES (Oct. 22, 1738–July 29, 1791), Baptist clergyman, a founder and the first president of Rhode Island College (Brown University), was born in Piscataway, Middlesex County, N. J., son of James and Grace (Fitz-Randolph) Manning, and great-grandson of Jeffrey Manning, one of the earliest settlers in Piscataway township. His father was a prosperous farmer, and James had good educational advantages. At eighteen he became a pupil in the Latin Grammar School conducted by Rev. Isaac Eaton at Hopewell, N. J. In 1758 he entered the College of New Jersey, from which he graduated in 1762, second in a class of twenty-one. On Feb. 6, 1763, he was licensed to preach by the Scotch Plains Baptist Church, and on Mar. 23 of the same year he was married to Margaret, daughter of John Stites of Elizabethtown. He was ordained Apr. 19, 1763, and proceeded to travel through the colonies with a view to informing himself regarding religious conditions.

About this time the Philadelphia Association of Baptist Churches was discussing the advisability of establishing a college to be principally under the direction of the Baptists. It finally decided that it was practicable to found such an institution in Rhode Island, and Manning was put in charge of the project. Accordingly, in July 1763, on his way to Halifax, he stopped at Newport and laid the matter before a number of influential gentlemen, who gave it their active support. Manning prepared a rough plan for the constitution of the college, and, leaving it in the hands of a committee, who, with the assistance of Ezra Stiles [*q.v.*], were to draft a charter, went on his way. After considerable delay and friction, in March 1764 the Rhode Island Assembly granted a charter, which was signed and sealed by the governor and secretary Oct. 24, 1765. In the meantime, April 1764, Manning had settled in Warren, R. I., opened a Latin School, and become the first pastor of a Baptist church, organized in November 1764. In September 1765 he was elected president of the new college. He conducted both school and college in Warren until 1770, when they were moved to Providence, where the first college building, now known as University Hall, was soon erected.

That Manning should have been chosen by the Baptists when he was but twenty-five years old to lead their movement in behalf of higher education indicates that thus early he had impressive characteristics. They seem to have been both physical and mental. As a youth, we are told, "he was remarkable for his dexterity in athletic exercises, for the symmetry of his body, and gracefulness of his person" (Guild, *post*, p. 503). In his later years he was about three hundred pounds in weight. Among his principal diversions were mowing and laying stone walls. He was invariably cheerful and genial, and was a good conversationalist. His direction of the college through the first twenty-six years of its history reveals that he had administrative ability of a high order. All that had been accomplished previously was well-nigh destroyed by the Revolution, but at his death the institution was in a thriving condition. He was a good all-round scholar, but too busy to be a thorough student. In addition to his college duties, he assumed charge of the First Baptist Church, Providence, in connection with which for years he carried a heavy load of pastoral work.

Although Ezra Stiles, speaking from the Congregational point of view, called Manning a "bigotted Baptist," among Baptists themselves he was regarded as tolerant and broad-minded. He was one of their acknowledged leaders, and with Isaac Backus [*q.v.*] and others took a firm stand against the oppression suffered by Baptists under the "Standing Order" in Connecticut and Massachusetts. He was the moving spirit in the organization of the Warren Association, 1767, for the promotion of harmony and concerted effort among the New England Baptist churches. In 1774, at a conference with members of the Continental Congress, Philadelphia, he presented a memorial citing acts of oppression in Massachusetts and pleading for both civil and religious liberty. His influence in public affairs was considerable. Some apparently thought him not over-enthusiastic in his support of the Revolution. Stiles ill-naturedly accuses him of not praying for Congress or the success of the army until General Washington once attended his church in Providence; and remarks, "He was a Baptist Tory . . . an Enemy to the Revolution here, altho' afterw[ds] he trim'[d] about . . ." (*Literary Diary, post,* II, 23, III, 425). Though with Backus and others he fell under the charge of attempting to sow seeds of discord by presenting to the Continental Congress the previously mentioned memorial in behalf of religious liberty, his patriotism can hardly be questioned. He certainly deplored the war, and wished to have no part in it himself. Writing to an English friend under date of Nov. 13, 1776, he exclaims: "Oh horrid war! How contrary to the spirit of Jesus! . . . I desire to bless God, these scenes of carnage always appeared shocking to me, and I feel no disposition to destroy or injure my fellow-man." To another English friend, however, he wrote, Aug. 3, 1784: "Our blood indeed was wantonly shed. . . . I think I can say that I never in one instance doubted the justice of our cause, but I desire to bless God that I never thirsted for the blood of those who were shedding ours" (Guild, pp. 294, 379). In 1786 he represented Rhode Island in the Congress of the Confederation, and his letters contain strong arraignments of the states for not better supporting that body. He was chairman of a committee appointed by Providence in 1789 to draft a petition to Congress praying that since Rhode Island would probably soon join the Union, her ships be exempted from foreign tonnage and her goods from foreign duties. With Benjamin Bourne he went to New York to present the same. He strongly advocated the adoption of the Constitution. Interested in public education and long a member of the Providence school committee, in the summer of 1791 he drew up a report recommending the establishment of free public schools. This was one of the last acts of his career. While offering prayer in his home, Sunday morning, July 24, he suffered a stroke of apoplexy, and died five days later in his fifty-third year.

[R. A. Guild, *Early Hist. of Brown Univ., Including the Life, Times, and Correspondence of President Manning* (1897); F. B. Dexter, *The Literary Diary of Ezra Stiles* (3 vols., 1901); Morgan Edwards, "Materials for a History of the Baptists in R. I.," *R. I. Hist. Soc. Colls.*, vol. VI (1867); Isaac Backus, *A Hist. of New Eng. with Particular Reference to the Denomination of Christians Called Baptists* (3 vols., 1777–96); *Providence Gazette*, Aug. 6, 1791; Jonathan Maxcy, *A Funeral Sermon Occasioned by the Death of the Rev. James Manning* (1791); W. G. Goddard, "Memoir of the Rev. James Manning," *American Quart. Reg.*, May 1839; W. C. Bronson, *The Hist. of Brown University* (1914).]
H. E. S.

MANNING, RICHARD IRVINE (May 1, 1789–May 1, 1836), governor of South Carolina, was born in Camden district of that state. His father was Laurence Manning who emigrated from Ireland to Pennsylvania, served during the Revolution as lieutenant of the Continental legion commanded by "Light-Horse Harry" Lee, and after the war settled in South Carolina. His mother was Susannah Richardson, the daughter of Gen. Richard Richardson, a brigadier-general in the Revolution, who moved from Virginia to South Carolina and became the ancestor of six governors of the state. Richard Manning was graduated from South Carolina College in 1811, during the War of 1812 was captain of a militia company called to the defense of Charleston, and after the war became a planter in Sumter district. In 1814 he married his cousin Elizabeth Peyer Richardson, the daughter of Floride Bonneau (Peyre) and John Peter Richardson and the niece of Gov. James Burchill Richardson. They had five sons and four daughters of whom one son was John Laurence Manning, 1816–1889, who became a political leader and governor of the state, and another son was Richard Irvine Manning, the father of Richard Irvine Manning, 1859–1931 [*q.v.*]. In 1822 the Richard Manning of this sketch entered politics and became a member of the state House of Representatives. From 1824 to 1826 he was governor and when the Marquis de Lafayette made his second visit to America in 1825, it fell to him to entertain this distinguished guest during his stay in South Carolina.

When the question of Nullification divided the state into two well-defined groups, he attached himself to the Union party, which opposed the Nullification doctrines. In 1826 he was defeated as the Union candidate for Congress. In 1830 he was defeated for the governorship by James Hamilton [*q.v.*]. In the bitter struggle that ensued he was one of the leaders of the opposition to Nullification. He was one of the few Unionists elected to the state convention of 1832 and voted against the Nullification ordinance. He was one of the vice-presidents of the Union convention at Columbia in 1832, which adopted an official protest against Nullification as contrary to both state and national constitutions. When the state convention reassembled in March 1833, he was a member of the committee chosen to consider the mediation of Virginia's agent, Benjamin Watkins Leigh. After the death of James Blair in April 1834, Manning succeeded to his seat in the federal House of Representatives. In November 1834 he was reëlected for the full term. When Henry Laurens Pinckney introduced the gag resolution in 1836 he supported it by speech and by vote. He died in Philadelphia while attending Congress, and is buried in Trinity churchyard, Columbia, S. C.

[Information from his grandson, the late Richard I. Manning, Columbia, S. C.; *Journal of the Conventions of the People of S. C., . . . 1832 . . . 1833* (1833); T. D. Jervey, *Robert Y. Hayne* (1909); Yates Snowden, *Hist. of S. C.* (1920), vols. II, III; *Biog. Directory of the Am. Cong.* (1928); J. C. Hemphill, *Men of Mark in S. C.* (1907), vol. I.]
J. G. V–D.

MANNING, RICHARD IRVINE (Aug. 15, 1859–Sept. 11, 1931), governor of South Carolina, was the grandson of Richard Irvine Manning [*q.v.*] and the son of Elizabeth Allen (Sinkler) and Richard Irvine Manning, a Confederate colonel who died in service. He was born at Holmesley plantation, Sumter County, S. C. He went to school in the neighborhood, then in Amherst, Va., and entered the University of Virginia, where he was a student from 1877 to 1879, but was not graduated. He married on Feb. 10, 1881, Lelia Bernard Meredith, daughter of John A. Meredith, of Richmond, Va. Farming on poor land, living in a cottage, the husband could proudly give his wife a buggy only after the passage of several years. A capable manager, he prospered, bought plantations, invested in industries, and became president of a bank in the town of Sumter. In 1892 he was elected to the legislature and was one of the small minority opposed to the Democratic faction led by Gov. B. R. Tillman. A student, watchful of legislation, not active in debate, he was a progressive in politics. In 1894 when the Australian ballot was scarcely heard of in South Carolina he offered a bill for its adoption, which was, however, defeated, and he pressed for improvements in education and reforms in taxation. After three terms he was elected state senator in 1898 and served until 1906. As an author of a bill for the complete reform and rebuilding of the "state dispensary" or liquor-traffic system, he defended his plan in the campaign for the governorship in 1906, but he was defeated.

He spent the next years in caring for his interests as planter and business man, as well as for the affairs of the Protestant Episcopal diocese of South Carolina, in which he was perhaps the most prominent layman. In 1914 he ran for governor against eight candidates and was nominated by a large majority in the second primary, in a state where nomination was equivalent to election. He was not an adept politician but was a business man of quiet manner, tenacious purpose, and real courage. His administrations were the most notable in South Carolina since the régime of Wade Hampton after the Reconstruction period. He emphasized law enforcement and the suppression of lynching. He was especially concerned for the rehabilitation of the state hospital for the insane, which was accomplished at cost of more than a million dollars without increasing the state debt. A school for feeble-minded girls and a hospital for tuberculous patients were established, a tax commission, a board of welfare, and a board of labor conciliation were created. The last grew out of textile strikes in which his attitude toward labor cost him the support of some of the cotton-mill executives who had been his friends. A strenuous campaign by the former governor, Coleman L. Blease, was waged against him in 1916, but he was renominated by a decisive majority. During the World War he threw himself into the American cause and worked to administer the resources of the state as effectively as possible. His appointments were such as to make it an honor to serve on a county draft board under him. Six of his own sons, all but the youngest, served as soldiers. He moved from Sumter to Columbia shortly after his retirement as governor and died there, survived by his widow, six sons, and a daughter.

[Personal acquaintance; information from his son, Wyndham Manning, Columbia, S. C.; Yates Snowden, *Hist. of S. C.* (1920), vols. II, III; J. C. Hemphill, *Men of Mark in S. C.* (1907), vol. I; *N. Y. Times*, Sept. 9, 12, 1931; *News and Courier* (Charleston), Sept. 12, 1931.] W. W. B.

MANNING, ROBERT (July 18, 1784–Oct. 10, 1842), pomologist, was born at Salem, Mass., the son of Richard and Miriam (Lord) Manning. He was of English descent, his great-great-grandmother, Anstice Manning, widow of Richard Manning of Dartmouth, England, having come to Massachusetts with her children in 1679. He received his education in the common schools and as a young man opened a broker's office in Salem. When only twenty-four years of age he took charge of the family of his widowed sister, Elizabeth Manning Hawthorne, afterwards sending her son, Nathaniel Hawthorne [*q.v.*], to Bowdoin College. Later he took over the management of the extensive stage-coach lines with which his father and his uncle were connected. On Dec. 20, 1824, he was married to Rebecca Dodge Burnham.

In 1817 he began in a small way to collect choice varieties of fruits. In 1823 he branched out more widely and established a pomological garden, with the design of securing specimen trees of all the varieties of fruits which were hardy enough to withstand the climate of his section. Getting into touch with many noted fruit men of Europe, he received from them scions and trees of choice varieties. This interest in pomology involved the expenditure of much time and money, for, through the slowness of packet boats and from poor handling, much of the imported stock was ruined in transit. He also spared no pains to secure new varieties from fruit growers and nurserymen in America and even originated a few himself. Having tested all these, he established a nursery for the propagation and sale of the best of them, and, through his wide acquaintance with the fruit men of the country, his varieties were distributed far and wide. His interest and enthusiasm led him also to give away both scions and trees with a liberality that did more for the fruit interests of the country than for his own fortune. At the time of his death he possessed by far the finest collection of fruits in America and one of the best in the world, consisting of over one thousand varieties of pears alone, and nearly as many more of the other fruits combined. The practical importance which was attached to this collection by the men of his day is attested by the fact that when he died the officers of the Massachusetts Horticultural Society, of which Manning was one of the founders, fearing that the family might not be able to maintain the orchards, entered into an agreement by which the society was to contribute a certain amount of money each year for their upkeep, in return for which the family agreed to send to the society each year fruits for exhibition, and in particular to exhibit specimens of any new fruits as soon as they should begin to bear (*Transactions . . . for the Years 1843–4–5–6*, 1847).

Manning read widely and was for many years a regular contributor to various horticultural journals. While modest and unassuming, he was always delighted to give the best information he had regarding fruits to all comers. In 1838 he published the *Book of Fruits*—"Being a descriptive catalogue of the most valuable varieties of the Pear, Apple, Peach, Plum and Cherry for New England culture"; in 1844, two years after his death, a revised edition, *The New England Fruit Book,* was issued, with some additions by John M. Ives. To Manning, more than to any other man of his time, and perhaps more than to all others combined, the fruit growers were indebted for the introduction of new and choice fruits, for correcting the nomenclature of fruits —at that time in a state of great confusion—and for identifying varieties.

[W. H. Manning, *The Manning Families of New England* (1902); *Vital Records of Salem, Mass.* (1918), vol. II; Robert Manning [Jr.], *Hist. of the Mass. Horticultural Soc. 1829–1878* (1880); G. E. Woodberry, *Nathaniel Hawthorne* (1902); *New England Farmer,* Nov. 23, 1842; G. P. Lathrop, *A Study of Hawthorne* (1876); L. H. Bailey, *Cyc. of Am. Horticulture,* vol. II (1900); *Salem Register,* Oct. 13, 1842.] F. C. S.

MANNING, THOMAS COURTLAND (Sept. 14, 1825–Oct. 11, 1887), jurist, son of Joseph and Sarah (Houghton) Manning, was born in Edenton, N. C., where the Mannings, originally from Virginia, had settled. He was educated in the public schools of Edenton and at the University of North Carolina, which, although he did not graduate, conferred the honorary degree of LL.D. upon him in 1878. After leaving the university he taught school in Edenton, studied law, and on Jan. 18, 1848, married Mary Blair. About this time he was admitted to the North Carolina bar, and thereafter practised in his native town until 1855, when he removed to Louisiana, settling in Alexandria, Rapides Parish. He soon had a large and lucrative practice, and when the Civil War broke out he was the acknowledged leader of the bar in his section of the state.

From early manhood he had been a Democrat of the state-rights school, and he took an active part in the political life of Louisiana. In 1861 he was a member of the secession convention. Soon afterward he was made a lieutenant in the first Confederate military company raised in Rapides Parish, but shortly accepted the position of aide-de-camp on the staff of Gov. Thomas O. Moore [*q.v.*], which office he held until 1863, when he was appointed adjutant-general of Louisiana with the rank of brigadier-general. In 1864 he was appointed an associate justice of the state supreme court by Gov. Henry W. Allen [*q.v.*], serving in this capacity until the close of the war, when he returned to Alexandria and his law practice. In 1872 he was a delegate to the Democratic state convention, and presidential elector for the state at large. He was a delegate to the National Democratic Convention of 1876, where he supported Samuel J. Tilden for the presidential nomination. In 1877 he was appointed chief justice of the Louisiana supreme court, and held the office until 1880, when the new constitution of 1879 went into effect and ended his term by the formation of a new court. The following year he was again a presidential elector and was appointed by the Democratic governor to the seat in the United States Senate occupied by W. P. Kellogg [*q.v.*], but was not recognized by that body. In 1882 he was again appointed to the supreme bench of Louisiana, and served until 1886, when he was appointed United States minister to Mexico by President Cleveland. He held this office until his death in the Fifth Avenue Hotel, New York City, soon after his arrival to attend a meeting of the board of trustees of the Peabody Educational Fund, of which he was a member.

Manning was a man of imposing appearance and deportment, cultured, endowed with a large measure of self-esteem, self-reliant, reserved, and somewhat exclusive. He was a lawyer of extensive and varied acquirements and held a distinguished position at the bar of his state.

[Information as to certain facts from a grand-niece, Mary S. Manning of Chapel Hill, N. C.; *Alumni Hist. of the Univ. of N. C.* (2nd ed., 1924); 39 *La. Reports,* p. v; Percy Roberts, *Sketch of the Hon. Thomas Courtland Manning, LL.D., Chief-Justice of La.* (1880); Henry Rightor, *Standard Hist. of New Orleans, La.* (1900); *Green Bag,* Mar. 1891; *Daily Picayune* (New Orleans), Oct. 12, 19, Nov. 8, 1887.] M. J. W.

MANNING, VANNOY HARTROG (Dec. 15, 1861–July 13, 1932), second director of the United States Bureau of Mines, was born at Horn Lake Depot, Miss., the son of Vannoy Hartrog Manning and Mary Zilafro (Wallace). His father was a member of the national House of Representatives from 1877 to 1883. The son attended school at Holly Springs, Miss., and entered the University of Mississippi. Leaving at the end of his third year, he taught school at Holly Springs for a time and then went to Washington, D. C., toward the end of his father's second term in Congress. In 1885 he obtained a position with the United States Geological Survey as topographic aide, and for the next two years did topographic work in Massachusetts. From 1888 to 1894 he was in charge of topographic field parties in Wisconsin and North Dakota and was subsequently assistant to the supervisor of the survey of Indian Territory. In 1904 he became section chief in charge of the survey in Missouri and Arkansas, and in 1906 was placed in charge of the southern section of the eastern division. From 1907 to 1910 he was a member of the Geological Survey Business Committee. In 1908 he had charge of the Tallahatchie drainage work in Mississippi.

When, in 1910, part of the work done by the Geological Survey was transferred to the newly created Bureau of Mines, Manning was transferred to the new organization, with the title of chief clerk, to serve as its executive officer pending the appointment of a director. His title was later changed to assistant to the director, and in 1914 he was appointed assistant director. He was in effect the general manager of the Bureau's administrative work. On the death of Joseph Austin Holmes [*q.v.*], the first director of the Bureau, in 1915, Manning was appointed to succeed him and continued in office until 1920.

His vision and initiative led him to perceive that the special knowledge of the technical staff of his bureau should be utilized in preparing for the possible participation of the United States in the World War. The Secretary of the Interior, at his suggestion, in 1916 offered to aid the War Department in any capacity within his power, noting that the Bureau of Mines could aid in the study of methods and materials necessary for the manufacture of nitrogen products. Much work of this character was done by the Bureau with funds furnished by the War Department, various pilot plants were built, and eventually a $2,500-000 plant for the production of sodium cyanide, by the Bucher process, for gas warfare was constructed and turned over to the War Department in November 1918. Meanwhile the staff of the Bureau, experienced in such problems from its work in mine disasters, had begun work on gas masks. Financial support from the War Department was soon forthcoming and the work expanded into research on different types of poisonous and irritating gases and smokes, smoke screens, gas shells and gas bombs, flame throwers, trench projectors, signal lights, and gas bombs. In June 1918 the staff engaged in this work, including more than 700 chemists, was transferred to the War Department. Regulation of the use of explosives by the civilian population, promotion of the production of needed mineral substances formerly imported, and the study of airplane motor fuels were undertaken and successfully carried out by the Bureau; but the activity that has attracted most attention was the production of helium for use in lighter-than-air craft, which the Bureau initiated in 1917 and subsequently carried on with funds supplied by the Navy Department. The Bureau was one of the most important and efficient agencies in the conduct of the war, and there can be no doubt that its service in this regard was due in large measure to Manning's foresight, initiative, and administrative skill.

After the war, in 1920, the petroleum interests of the country organized the American Petroleum Institute, and he resigned his directorship of the Bureau of Mines to become director of research for the Institute. The industry never raised the necessary funds to initiate research in its own laboratories, however, and after organizing cooperative research with a number of universities and technical institutions, Manning resigned in 1924 to take up special work with the Pan-American Petroleum & Transport Company. In 1928 he became director of engineering and technical research for the Petroleum Research Corporation, which was affiliated with a large petroleum investment trust. The business depression which began at the end of 1929 seriously interfered with this activity and the following year he resigned. Ill health postponed his return to active work, and he died in 1932. In 1898 he was married at Denison, Tex., to Emily S. Stevens, of Washington, D. C. Two sons were born to them.

[*Who's Who in America,* 1930–31; U. S. Bureau of Mines, *Bull. 178* (4 parts, 1919), describing the war work of the Bureau; *Mining Cong. Jour.*, Sept. 1915; *Colliery Engineer,* Oct. 1915; *Hardware Age,* June 7, 1917; *Metallurgical and Chemical Engineering,* May 1, 1918; *Black Diamond,* May 8, 1920; *Engineering and Mining Jour.*, Feb. 21, 1920; *Science,* May 7, 1920; *Oil, Paint and Drug Reporter,* May 3, 1920; *Mining and Metallurgy,* Sept. 1932; *N. Y. Times,* July 14, 1932.]

T. T. R.

MANSELL, WILLIAM ALBERT (Mar. 30, 1864–Mar. 4, 1913), Methodist missionary, the son of Rev. Henry and Annie (Benshoff) Mansell, was born in Moradabad, India. At the age of six he could read the Bible in English, Urdu, and Hindi. At seven, he, along with his two sisters, was taken by his mother to America, where he remained for eighteen years. He made his home with his grandfather in Newark, Ohio, and there attended the public schools. He went to the "mourners' bench" at ten, and took an active interest in religion. Graduating from the Newark high school in 1880, he entered Ohio Wesleyan University in the fall of that year, and upon the completion of his college course in 1884, obtained a state teacher's certificate and was made principal for two years of the schools of Worthington, Ohio. In the fall of 1886 he entered the Boston University School of Theology and graduated therefrom three years later, being chosen one of two speakers representing his class at Commencement. During his senior year he was ordained deacon and applied for and received appointment to service in India under the Methodist Episcopal Church. After a summer's supply of the pulpit of the Methodist Church at Nahant, Mass., he sailed for India and arrived in Bombay on Nov. 19. He began work almost immediately as teacher of philosophy and English literature in Lucknow (later Reid) Christian College. For two years (1890–93) he acted as vice-principal, and was then made principal, serving until 1898. He served, also, as pastor of the local English Methodist church and as preacher on the Hindustani circuit, being ordained elder at Lucknow, Jan. 5, 1890, by Bishop Thoburn. In addition he edited *India's Young Folks.* On Mar. 17, 1894, he was married to Florence M. Perrine, daughter of Rev. W. H. Perrine, of Albion, Mich., who had come to Lucknow after her graduation from Albion College in 1888 to teach in the Isabella Thoburn College. In 1896 Mansell was one of the organizers of the Student Volunteer Movement in India.

In the following year he was appointed superintendent of the Oudh district of his Church, with headquarters in Lucknow, and in 1899 he acted as superintendent of the Sitapur district also. Early in 1900, with his wife, he left India on furlough, journeying to America by way of the Pacific and visiting Methodist conferences at Singapore, Shanghai, Kobe, and Osaka. After his return to Lucknow in March 1901, he served three years as superintendent of the Bijnor district, with headquarters in Bijnor town. During this time he prepared many "Helps" for the use of his associates, was chosen secretary of the India Epworth League, became editor of the mission vernacular periodical, *Kaukab-i-Hind* ("Star of India"), and during the last year acted as head of the Oudh district also.

From 1904 until his death, he was principal of his Church's theological seminary at Bareilly, and spent his unusual talents in the training of an Indian ministry. Having perfect control of Hindustani, he took occasion to visit widely throughout the Bareilly district in connection with ventures in religious education. For one year he acted as district superintendent. He continued to edit the *Kaukab-i-Hind,* and after 1908 was a member of the interdenominational United Council on Work among Young People. In 1909 he was superintendent of the Bijnor district again. In 1910 he was in charge of the open-air evangelism during the World's Christian Endeavor Convention in Agra. He then went to America on furlough, returning in two years to his work at Bareilly. Though in failing health for several years, he had persevered cheerfully in his chosen career, but in 1913 he died, in Bareilly, at the age of forty-nine. His associates had honored him with every important office in their gift save that of bishop—an office which would doubtless have come to him had he lived longer.

[L. A. Core, *The Life and Work of William Albert Mansell* (Madras, 1914); *Indian Witness,* Mar. 11, 25, 1913; *Missionary Review of the World,* May 1913; *Methodist,* Mar. 13, 1913; *Ann. Report of the Mission Stations of the North India Conference of the Meth. Episc. Ch.,* 1889–1907; alumni records of Ohio Wesleyan Univ. and Boston Univ. School of Theol.]

J. C. A.

MANSFIELD, EDWARD DEERING (Aug. 17, 1801–Oct. 27, 1880), author and editor, was the son of Jared [*q.v.*] and Elizabeth (Phipps) Mansfield. He was born in New Haven, Conn., and after spending his earlier boyhood, first at Marietta and later in Cincinnati, Ohio, attended a school in Connecticut and the Military Academy at West Point, where he graduated high in his class in 1819. Deciding to study law, he attended the College of New Jersey, graduating with the class of 1822, studied at the Litchfield Law School, 1823–25, and in 1825 was admitted to the bar in Connecticut. Returning to Cincinnati, he engaged in practice; but his interest lay chiefly in writing and publishing. In 1826, with Benjamin Drake [*q.v.*], he undertook a study of Cincinnati designed to stimulate immigration. To secure information for this work, each author made a house-to-house canvass of his allotted half of the city. Their booklet, *Cincinnati in 1826,* published the next year with the aid of a grant of seventy-five dollars from the city council, is a valuable study of the governmental organization and local economic and social conditions. It was republished in England and in Germany in translation, and undoubtedly greatly affected immigration to Cincinnati.

Mansfield began his editorial career with the *Cincinnati Chronicle* shortly after that paper was launched in 1826. In this enterprise he was again associated with Benjamin Drake. The *Chronicle* was merged with the *Mirror* in 1834, but later reëstablished under its old title. In 1849 it was consolidated with the *Atlas,* and ultimately with the *Cincinnati Daily Gazette.* Somewhat intermittently, Mansfield edited these papers. He was connected with the *Gazette* in one capacity or another from the time he assumed the editorship in 1857 until his death. A number of young writers who later became widely known, among them Harriet Beecher Stowe, first published their contributions in the *Gazette* and the *Atlas* under his editorship. He also edited the *Railroad Record* from 1853 to 1871. For some years, particularly during the Civil War, he was a vigorous writer for the *New York Times* over the signature, "Veteran Observer." His contributions to the *Gazette* over the initials "E. D.

M." were forcible and noteworthy. In politics, he was a strong Whig and later a Republican.

He was an industrious student and a prolific writer. His first book to appear after *Cincinnati in 1826* was *The Political Grammar,* which he published in 1834. This work, entitled *Political Manual* in later editions, was widely used as a textbook in the schools. Other volumes from his pen were: *The Utility of Mathematics* (1834); *The Legal Rights, Liabilities and Duties of Women* (1845); *The Life of General Winfield Scott* (1846); *The Mexican War* (1848); *American Education* (1850); *Memoirs of the Life and Services of Daniel Drake* (1855); and *A Popular and Authentic Life of Ulysses S. Grant* (1868). In 1879 he published his *Personal Memories, Social, Political, and Literary, with Sketches of Many Noted People 1803–1843,* a vivid picture of the times.

He was one of the early advocates of a railway connection from Cincinnati to the South, calling attention to the advantages of such a line in an article published in the *Western Monthly Magazine* in September 1836; and he was secretary of a committee under the leadership of William Henry Harrison which visited the South in the interests of the plan. He also prepared a pamphlet and map entitled *Railroad from the Banks of the Ohio River to the Tide Waters of the Carolinas and Georgia* (1835). He was for a time professor of constitutional law and history in Cincinnati College and was active in forming the College for Teachers. He held but one public office, that of commissioner of statistics for Ohio, 1858–68. He was married twice: first to Mary Wallace Peck of Litchfield, Conn., and second, Apr. 24, 1839, to Margaret Worthington, daughter of Thomas Worthington, a former governor of Ohio. There were two children of the first marriage and four of the second. Mansfield died at his country home near Morrow, Ohio.

[Mansfield's *Personal Memories* (1879); G. W. Cullum, *Biog. Reg. Officers and Grads. U. S. Mil. Acad.* (3rd ed., 1891); C. T. Greve, *Centennial Hist. of Cincinnati* (1904), vol. I; W. H. Venable, *Beginnings of Literary Culture in the Ohio Valley* (1891), ch. xiv; James Landy, *Cincinnati Past and Present* (1872); H. A. and K. B. Ford, *Hist. of Cincinnati, Ohio* (1881); Horace Mansfield, *The Descendants of Richard and Gillian Mansfield* (1885); *Cincinnati Daily Gazette,* Oct. 28, 1880.] S. G. L.

MANSFIELD, JARED (May 23, 1759–Feb. 3, 1830), teacher, investigator in the fields of mathematics and physics, United States surveyor general, was born in New Haven, Conn., the son of Stephen Mansfield, a sea captain, and Hannah (Beach) Mansfield. He was a descendant of Richard and Gillian Mansfield who settled in New Haven in 1639. Having entered Yale with the class of 1777 he was expelled in his senior year for various "discreditable escapades" (Dexter, *post*), but later regained the esteem of the college, receiving the degree of A.M. in 1787 and being enrolled with his class. In 1825 Yale conferred the honorary degree of LL.D. upon him. In 1786 he became rector of the Hopkins Grammar School, New Haven, resigning in April 1790 because of "brighter prospects" elsewhere. These did not materialize, however, and he soon returned to his former position, in which he remained until 1795. After teaching for a few months in the Friends' Academy, Philadelphia, he was connected with an advanced school for both sexes in New Haven until 1802. On Mar. 2, 1800, he married Elizabeth, daughter of David and Mary (English) Phipps.

While in the New Haven school he wrote his *Essays, Mathematical and Physical* (1801), which is considered to be the first book of original mathematical researches by a native American. The essays deal with problems in algebra, geometry, fluxions (calculus), and with nautical astronomy, giving practical methods of finding time, latitude, and longitude from observations at sea. A chapter on gunnery deals with fundamental problems of ballistics, and in it the importance of air resistance is pointed out, not only as a retarding force (which is considered in the light of our modern molecular theory of matter), but also in its effect on the projectile. That effect, he showed, is a deviation of the projectile from its due course—what is known today as the gyroscopic phenomenon. Prior to his book, projectiles were treated without consideration of the effect of the medium through which they passed.

The *Essays* brought him into prominence as a man of science and in 1802 President Jefferson appointed him captain of engineers in the United States army. From 1802 to 1803 he was acting professor of mathematics in the Military Academy, West Point, but in the latter year he was appointed surveyor general of the United States, with the rank of lieutenant-colonel, to survey Ohio and the Northwest Territory. Until he resigned his office he lived at Marietta (1803–05) and at Cincinnati (1805–12). Mansfield, Ohio, was named for him. While serving as surveyor general, he also made observations (with surveyor's instruments) of the comet of 1807 and calculated its orbit. In 1812 he was appointed professor of natural and experimental philosophy at West Point, but because of the war he was detailed to superintend fortifications at New

London and Stonington, Conn. In 1814 he resumed his teaching at West Point and continued there until 1828, when he resigned and went to live in Cincinnati. He died while on a visit to New Haven and was buried in Grove Street Cemetery. Edward Deering Mansfield [*q.v.*] was his son.

Among his published papers are: "A Calculation of the Orbit of the Comet which Lately Appeared," "On the Figure of the Earth," and "Observations on the Duplication of the Cube and the Trisection of an Angle," all of which were printed in *Memoirs of the Connecticut Academy of Arts and Sciences* (vol. I, pt. 1, 1810); and "On Vanishing Fractions," printed in the *Transactions of the American Philosophical Society* (vol. I, n.s., 1818).

[Horace Mansfield, *The Descendants of Richard and Gillian Mansfield* (1885); E. D. Mansfield, *Personal Memories, Social, Political, and Literary* (1879); L. W. Bacon, *An Hist. Discourse at the Two Hundredth Anniversary of the Founding of the Hopkins Grammar School* (1860); F. B. Dexter, *Biog. Sketches Grads. Yale Coll.*, vol. III (1903); *The Centennial of the U. S. Mil. Acad. at West Point, N. Y., 1802–1902* (2 vols., 1904); *Columbian Register* (New Haven), Feb. 6, 1830.]

A. F. K.

MANSFIELD, JOSEPH KING FENNO (Dec. 22, 1803–Sept. 18, 1862), military engineer, the son of Henry and Mary (Fenno) Mansfield, was born in New Haven, Conn. He was a lineal descendant of Richard Mansfield who came from Exeter, England, in 1639, and a nephew of Jared Mansfield [*q.v.*], professor at the United States Military Academy from 1812 to 1828, and a first cousin of Edward Deering Mansfield [*q.v.*]. Joseph Mansfield became a cadet at the Military Academy in 1817, and on graduation in 1822 was commissioned second lieutenant and assigned to the Corps of Engineers. Until the Mexican War he was engaged mainly in the construction of the coast defenses of the South Atlantic states and was specially charged with the construction of Fort Pulaski at the mouth of the Savannah River. He was promoted to first lieutenant in 1832 and captain in 1838.

During the Mexican War, he was chief engineer of the army under General Taylor and as such served with great distinction. At the beginning of operations he designed and constructed Fort Brown on the Rio Grande opposite Matamoras and took part in its defense. George Gordon Meade [*q.v.*], then a subaltern in this army, wrote in a letter that Mansfield "had gained for himself great credit for the design and execution of the work and still more for his energy and bravery in its defence" (*The Life and Letters of George Gordon Meade,* 1913, I, 76). At Monterey, he made the preliminary reconnaissance on which the plan of the battle was based and conducted one of the columns of attack. He was equally active in reconnoitering the ground and selecting the positions for the troops in the battle of Buena Vista. For gallant and distinguished services in the defense of Fort Brown he received the brevet of major, for gallant and meritorius conduct in the battles of Monterey and Buena Vista he received the brevets of lieutenant-colonel and colonel. After the war he was again engaged as a captain in the construction of coast defenses until 1853 when, upon the recommendation of Secretary of War Jefferson Davis, who had also served in Taylor's army, he received an unsolicited promotion to colonel and inspector-general of the army. Under his new commission he traveled extensively, inspecting frontier posts in Texas, New Mexico, California, and Oregon.

Shortly after the outbreak of the Civil War he was commissioned brigadier-general in the Regular Army and assigned to the command of the Department of Washington, which included the capital and surrounding territory. It was on his recommendation that the heights on the south bank of the Potomac opposite the city were promptly seized and fortified. When his department was merged into the Department of the Potomac under McClellan, he was assigned to command under General Wool at Fort Monroe and in 1862 took part in the occupation of Norfolk and Suffolk, Va., being commissioned major-general of volunteers in July. When McClellan reorganized the Army of the Potomac after the Manassas Campaign, Mansfield was recalled from Suffolk where he was in command, and assigned to the command of the XII Corps. He joined the army two days before the battle of Antietam and was mortally wounded in that battle, Sept. 17, 1862, while reconnoitering the enemy's position as his corps was coming into action. On Sept. 25, 1838, he had married Louisa Maria Mather, the daughter of Samuel and Catherine (Livingston) Mather. They had two daughters and two sons, one of whom, Samuel Mather Mansfield, became a brigadier-general in the Corps of Engineers.

[*Memorial of Gen. J. K. F. Mansfield* (1862); J. L. Dudley, *Discourse on the Death of Gen. Joseph K. F. Mansfield* (1862); J. M. Gould, *Joseph K. F. Mansfield* (1895); G. W. Cullum, *Biog. Reg. Officers and Grads. U. S. Mil. Acad.* (3rd ed., 1891), vol. I; Horace Mansfield, *The Descendants of Richard and Gillian Mansfield* (1885); *Battles and Leaders of the Civil War* (4 vols., 1887–88); *War of the Rebellion: Official Records (Army)*; *Hartford Daily Courant*, Sept. 22, 24, 1862.]

G. J. F.

MANSFIELD, RICHARD (Oct. 1, 1723–Apr. 12, 1820), Episcopal clergyman, was the son of Jonathan and Sarah (Alling) Mansfield, and great-grandson of Richard Mansfield who emigrated from Exeter in Devonshire, England, to New Haven in New England in 1639, where the younger Richard was born. He prepared for college at the Hopkins Grammar School in that town, entered Yale at the age of fourteen, and graduated with the class of 1741, receiving the Berkeley premium for his high standing in classics. He continued his studies at Yale for a year after his graduation and then served as rector of the Hopkins Grammar School for a period of five years. His father was a deacon of the Congregational Church and the son was brought up in the Congregational faith, but under the influence of Dr. Samuel Johnson of Stratford he accepted Anglicanism. An Anglican church had already been established at Derby, Conn., and in the absence of a clergyman, Mansfield read the services there. On Mar. 17, 1746/7, Johnson, in behalf of the Episcopal clergy of Connecticut, wrote to the Society for the Propagation of the Gospel in Foreign Parts, asking that Mansfield be permitted to go to England for holy orders and for his appointment as missionary to Derby (*Samuel Johnson, President of King's College, His Career and Writings,* 1929, edited by Herbert and Carol Schneider, III, 235). Permission was granted and Thomas Herring, Archbishop of Canterbury, ordained him a deacon Aug. 3, 1748, and a priest Aug. 7, 1748. Appointed missionary to Derby, West Haven, Waterbury, and Northbury, he returned to America, arriving at New York Oct. 23, 1748, and took up his residence at Derby. Here he served as rector of St. James Church for seventy-two years. On Oct. 10, 1751, he married Anna, the daughter of Joseph Hull of Derby, and by her had thirteen children, nine of whom lived to maturity. In 1755 the field of his labors was limited to Derby and Oxford.

At the outbreak of the American Revolution he preached subjection to the King, and under his influence 110 of the 130 families in his charge remained loyal to the Crown. He wrote to Governor Tryon in 1775 that several thousand men from the three western counties of Connecticut would join the King's troops sent to protect the Loyalists. When the contents of this letter became known he was forced to flee to Hempstead, Long Island, but soon returned to Derby. After the conclusion of peace, Mansfield and nine other Episcopal clergymen of Connecticut met at Woodbury to deliberate upon ecclesiastical affairs and organize for the future. He was chosen coadjutor to Bishop Seabury [*q.v.*] in a convention at Wallingford Feb. 27, 1787, but declined the office. In the fall of 1792 he served on a committee to revise the articles of religion in the Book of Common Prayer. He was the first Episcopalian to receive the degree of doctor of divinity from Yale (1792). About 1800 his voice failed and he ceased to preach but continued to hold the office of rector. He presided over a convention of clergy which met at New Haven June 2, 1819, to choose the third bishop of Connecticut. He died at Derby at the age of ninety-six.

[Horace Mansfield, *The Descendants of Richard and Gillian Mansfield Who Settled in New Haven, 1639* (1885); *Vital Records of New Haven, 1649–1850* (2 vols., 1917–24); F. B. Dexter, *Biog. Sketches Grads. Yale Coll.*, vol. I (1885); *Cat. of the Officers and Grads. of Yale Univ., 1701–1924* (1924); *Documentary Hist. of the P. E. Ch. in the U. S. of America* (2 vols., 1863–64), ed. by F. L. Hawks and Wm. S. Perry; E. E. Beardsley, *The Hist. of the Episcopal Ch. in Conn.* (2 vols., 1866–68); W. B. Sprague, *Annals Am. Pulpit,* vol. V (1859); Samuel Orcutt and Ambrose Beardsley, *The Hist. of the Old Town of Derby, Conn., 1642–1880* (1880); A. F. Sherwood, *Memories of Old Derby* (1924); *The One Hundred and Fiftieth Anniversary of the Founding of St. James's Parish, Birmingham, in the Town of Derby, Conn.* (1891); Lorenzo Sabine, *Biog. Sketches of Loyalists of the Am. Revolution* (1864), vol. II; *Columbian Register* (New Haven), Apr. 15, 1820.]

I. M. C.

MANSFIELD, RICHARD (May 24, 1854–Aug. 30, 1907), actor, one of the most vivid artists in the American theatre, was born in Berlin, Germany, while his mother was on an opera tour. His father, Maurice Mansfield, was a London wine merchant with musical proficiency; his mother, Erminia Rudersdorff, daughter of an Amsterdam violinist, was a noted opera singer. His father died in 1859, and Richard passed his boyhood in many places, both in England and on the Continent. He had a variety of schooling, and singing lessons from his mother. She wished him to go to Oxford, but he lacked sufficient scholastic application. In 1872, when Richard was eighteen, Madam Rudersdorff came to Boston, to sing at the Peace Jubilee, bringing her son with her, and she remained in Boston as a singing teacher, also buying a summer residence in Berlin, Mass. Young Richard passed the next few years either in Boston or Berlin (near Fitchburg), uncertain of what he wished to do, and often quarreling with his temperamental mother. For a time he was employed by Eben D. Jordan in the latter's great store in Boston. But trade did not appeal to him. He left his mother's house, took a room on Beacon Hill, and decided to become an artist. He also joined an amateur dramatic group, "The Buskin Club," and acted Beau Farintosh in *School,* Jan. 14, 1876. In June of the same year he gave a one-man entertainment at the Y. M. C. A. Hall on Boylston Street.

Feeling that he was getting nowhere with his painting in Boston, he returned to London in 1877 and there led a precarious existence for many months. To support himself he gave entertainments of song and mimetic skits in private houses, and when he could, in music halls. His painting brought him nothing. Finally he secured an engagement in a touring company of *Pinafore* to sing Sir Joseph Porter, at fifteen dollars a week, and kept the job till he asked for a raise—when D'Oyly Carte dropped him. But in December 1879 he was reëngaged for the part in a more important company and also sang in the copyright performance of the *Pirates of Penzance*. According to Paul Wilstach (*post*, pp. 74–75) the tune of "A Modern Major General" was improvised by Mansfield at the rehearsals, and retained by Sullivan. Until the spring of 1882 he eked out a poor existence playing small parts in London and the provinces, both in plays and operettas. His mother died in Boston in February 1882, and in April his old employer, Eben D. Jordan, found him lonely and discouraged, and persuaded him to return to America.

His first professional appearance in the United States was on Sept. 27, 1882, at the Standard Theatre, New York, as Dromez in the operetta *Les Manteaux Noirs*. He next sang both Nick Vedder and Nick's son in an operatic version of *Rip Van Winkle*, and then, in Baltimore, sang the Chancellor in *Iolanthe*. But a sprained ankle forced his resignation, and he returned to New York determined to break into the spoken drama. He was engaged by A. M. Palmer for the rôle of Baron Chevrial in *A Parisian Romance*, solely because J. H. Stoddart refused to play the part, and he spent hectic hours in lonely rehearsal. With a touch of arrogance that annoyed the older actors, he announced the day before the opening, "Tomorrow night I shall be famous." And he was! Few débuts of an unknown actor have been more sensational. The driveling death of this lecherous old baron was so vivid that the audience could watch nothing else, talk about nothing else. Mansfield toured with the Palmer company across the Continent till the fall of 1883 and then bought the play and with an access of ambition launched himself as an independent star. But he soon found that one success does not make a star. Very early in 1884 he had to disband his company in Cincinnati and borrow money to get back to New York. He at once joined the Madison Square Company, playing von Dornfeld in *Alpine Roses*, and remained there till summer. In January 1885 he was engaged for Wallack's stock company but remained only a month, going back for a time to operetta. In June he dashed to London and acted Louis XI for a single performance, but nothing came of it. In September 1885 he was back in New York supporting Minnie Maddern (later Mrs. Fiske) in *In Spite of All*. Then, in January 1886 he was reluctantly persuaded back into operetta by John Stetson of Boston, and sang Koko in *The Mikado* at the Hollis Street Theatre there—a most solemnly hilarious and perfectly Gilbertian performance it was, too. But his ambition knew no rest; he was determined to be a star in legitimate drama, or nothing, and on Apr. 5, 1886, he appeared at the Boston Museum as Prince Karl, in a play of that name by Archibald C. Gunter. This drama gave him the opportunity to display the romantic side of his art, and was very successful. He took it to New York May 3, where it ran all summer, and that run was followed by a tour of the East and Middle West which lasted until Apr. 25, 1887. He was finally established in the ranks where he had always declared he belonged, and thereafter, to the end of his life, was his own master and manager, whatever the burden and cost.

On May 9, 1887, at the Boston Museum, Mansfield first acted the rôle which was always the favorite with a large element of his public, and which was certainly his most spectacular performance—the dual rôle of Dr. Jekyll and Mr. Hyde in a play made by Thomas Russell Sullivan, from Stevenson's story. There was a considerable element of trickery in his transformations from one character to the other, in view of the audience, as well as considerable physical strain. But the changes were gruesomely spectacular, and the public never tired of staring at them. In August 1888 he took the play to London (Lyceum Theatre), and later acted Prince Karl and Chevrial. In March 1889, at the Globe, London, he made his Shakespearian début as Richard III, and in the autumn brought the production to America. It was always one of his most popular rôles thereafter. His next important production was *Beau Brummell*, by Clyde Fitch, after suggestions by William Winter (Winter, *post*, I, p. 128), at the Madison Square, New York, May 19, 1890. This added a vivid character rôle to his growing repertoire. In May 1891, at the Garden Theatre, New York, he produced *Don Juan*, written by himself. It was not successful, nor was *Nero*, by Thomas Sullivan, produced the next September. In September 1892, his next important production was made—a dramatization by Joseph Hatton of *The Scarlet Letter*. In 1893 he enriched his repertoire by adding Shylock, and now toured the country with at least half a dozen plays, alternately acted.

In 1894, Sept. 17, at the Herald Square Theatre, New York, he produced *Arms and the Man,* the first play by George Bernard Shaw ever seen in America. It considerably puzzled his audiences, accustomed to romantic drama. But when, in April 1895, he opened the Harrigan Theatre, on Thirty-fifth Street, New York (rechristened the Garrick), which he had rented and renovated, he chose the Shaw play for his first bill. The task of keeping open his own theatre was severe, and in midsummer he was stricken with typhoid and narrowly escaped death. He retained the management of the house only till the next December. On Oct. 1, 1897, at Albany, he produced *The Devil's Disciple,* the second Shaw play seen in America, and acted it, as the major item in his repertory, through the country, adding a production of *The First Violin* in the spring. In October 1898, at the Garden, New York, he produced, in an English version by Howard Thayer Kingsbury, Rostand's *Cyrano de Bergerac,* then the theatrical sensation of Europe. The same night, in Philadelphia, Augustin Daly's company produced another version. But Mansfield's Cyrano held the field and became so popular that he acted nothing else for a year. For romantic gusto and tragic pathos, it was a landmark of its era.

At the Garden Theatre, Oct. 3, 1900, he produced very elaborately *Henry V,* and acted it for a year. The care and expense of the company and production, especially on tour, was a severe drain, and the following October he produced Booth Tarkington's pleasant romance, *M. Beaucaire,* with enormous popular success, played it for a year, and recouped his fortunes. The next season—October 1902—found him again engaged in large undertakings—*Julius Cæsar,* with himself as Brutus. This, in 1903, was in turn followed by a light romance, *Old Heidelberg,* in which he gave an astonishing illusion of youth, and then in 1904 (Mar. 1), by another ample tragedy—Alexis Tolstoi's *Ivan the Terrible.* After a year in repertoire, he added (April 1905) Molière's *Alceste* to his rôles, and in October of the same year *Don Carlos,* in his own version of Schiller's play. His repertoire of parts on tour the following year consisted of Jekyll and Hyde, Shylock, Arthur Dimmesdale, Gloster, Alceste, Ivan the Terrible, and Baron Chevrial. In October 1906, he began his season in Chicago with the first American production of *Peer Gynt* —a difficult and baffling work into which he put every ounce of his strength and spirit. The play was warmly received in Chicago, and in February reached New York. Mansfield was warned that he was overtaxing his strength, but continued to act. On Mar. 23, he played Peer in the afternoon, and Chevrial in the evening—and that was his last appearance on the stage. He was taken ill the next day, when starting on a tour, and the tour was canceled. In May he was able to sail for England, but gained nothing by the change, and in July returned to his summer home in New London, Conn., where he died on Aug. 30, 1907. He had, almost literally, burned up his nervous energies.

The passing of Richard Mansfield was felt to be almost the passing of an era, because he had represented more brilliantly and persistently than any actor of his day in America the romantic tradition, the "grand style" in plays and playing, and the tradition, as well, of repertoire. In but few seasons had he devoted all his time to a single play; more often he acted a different part every night; and the plays included the works of Shakespeare, Molière, Rostand, and character rôles of striking picturesqueness or vivid appeal. On the other hand, while he thus represented the theatre of a grander past, he was the first to recognize the genius of Shaw, his performances in the Shaw plays were as mordantly modern as the comedies themselves, and his last work was a devoted production of Ibsen. If he was at the end of a great romantic era in acting, he also helped to usher in a new and different era. Had he lived, it is highly probable that he would have moved forward eagerly with the age. At any rate, the mounting costs of travel and production, and the changing tastes of the public, would have compelled him to abandon his tours with large companies and scenery for half a dozen plays. As it was, he practically killed himself at fifty-three, trying to carry the burden of his ambitious programs.

As actor, Mansfield was highly individual. A wag once said, "There are good actors, bad actors, and Richard Mansfield." He had a splendid voice, under perfect command, yet his inflections of speech were eccentric in the extreme. His listeners thought they were going to be annoying but instead they were curiously thrilling. His face was one of those comparatively rare masks which can, with little artificial aid, look like anybody, and his body was under unusual control. Hence, with his natural mimetic faculty, he was able to play a wide variety of character parts and give to each a superficial verisimilitude which pleased the crowd, though he never could, or tried to, conceal his own vivid personality behind the mask. What made his art unique was a certain electric quality; it gave off sparks, it was strangely exciting. He had no old timer's rant, nor did he follow the new cult of repression. His acting was not entirely naturalistic, even in modern plays. He never forgot the theatre, and in a sense foreshadowed the revolt from naturalism of a later generation. And when the play was poetic, as in Shakespeare or *Peer Gynt,* he could strike the chords of passionate music with sure hand. There was never a dull moment in his acting, least of all when whimsical or ironic or macabre humor was called for.

The story of Mansfield's life is largely confined to his professional career, because his driving and perhaps egocentric ambition kept him at his huge task of production and management. He was not a clubable man, which partly accounted for the acrimonious comments about him frequently made by other actors. And his temper, his outbursts of "temperament," became, before his death, a legend of the American stage. Without question he knew his capacities, and did not meekly minimize them; and, at the same time, he was driven by a deep, artistic urge to realize them fully in his art, and had small place in his mind for other matters. What often seemed arrogance was actually indifference. His temper, also, was really part of the same quality in the man. Highstrung, nervous, always carrying the whole weight of a production, and plunged in agony if anything went wrong, he was a hair trigger in the theatre, and his famous outbursts were not in the least a sign of unkindliness of disposition, but of sensibilities on edge. Actually he was a generous, gracious, and kindly man. In this paradox, he strongly resembled Macready. It is amusing to record that on one occasion, at least, he got a Roland for his Oliver. When he produced *The Devil's Disciple,* he converted Essie into a young girl. Shaw protested that this meant loss of heart interest. "Heart interest be damned," wrote Mansfield. "The same to you," Shaw cabled back. The wonder is that even in those early days, Shaw did not withdraw the play.

Mansfield's stature was below the normal height, a difficulty which he triumphantly overcame by pose and fire, as well as high heels. He always wore his scant hair cropped, displaying a broad and high forehead. His eyes were brown, his jaw aggressive, his neck large, his shoulders broad, and his whole figure athletic and sturdy. When playing young men, he kept his chin up, his face alert, and his heels almost off the ground, giving him a quality of expectation and vitality difficult to suggest, but very appealing. And he ranged from the young prince in *Old Heidelberg,* with his wistful renunciation of youth and happiness, to the horrible evil of Mr. Hyde, or the haunted, half-insane Brutus, after the murder of Cæsar (one of Mansfield's finest studies in psychology), making his face, his postures, even the very aspect of his body, conform to each rôle. It used to be his frequent custom, on the last night of an engagement, to present an act from five different plays, and these exhibitions of versatility were greatly enjoyed. His tastes were quiet, artistic, and fastidious, and centered largely, outside the theatre, about his estate at New London, Conn., and the playing and composition of music. Once, in 1891, in Washington, a concert of his songs was given during his engagement there. On Sept. 15, 1892, he was married in New York to Beatrice Cameron (Susan Hegeman) who had been for some time his leading lady. This marriage was an ideally happy one, and his domestic life absorbed most of his time when he was not professionally engaged. There was one child of the union, a son, who died in training camp when a member of the American Expeditionary Force in 1918.

[Wm. Winter, *Life and Art of Richard Mansfield* (2 vols., 1910); Paul Wilstach, *Richard Mansfield, the Man and the Actor* (1908), with bibliography; Mansfield Scrap Book, Locke Collection, N. Y. Pub. Lib.; Mansfield clippings, Shaw Collection, Harvard Univ. Lib.]

W. P. E.

MANSON, OTIS FREDERICK (Oct. 10, 1822–Jan. 25, 1888), physician, was born in Richmond, Va., the son of Otis Manson and Sarah Dews (Ferrill). His father, a skilled architect, came from a Massachusetts family which had emigrated from Glamis, Scotland. The son attended the public schools of his native city and was graduated in 1840 from the medical department of Hampden-Sidney College, later called the Medical College of Virginia. Shortly after his graduation he settled in Granville County, N. C., for the practice of his profession, and subsequently married Mary Ann Spottswood Burwell, the daughter of a prominent citizen of the county. In this rural community he resided for more than twenty years, building up a large practice and extending his reputation over the state.

The neighborhood was highly malarious and Manson was continually being faced with the problems of this disease. He early recognized the protean character of malaria and its importance as a causative agent and as a complication of other disease conditions. He perceived the relationship between malarial fever and pneumonia and is credited with being the first American writer to recognize puerperal malarial fever. He was an advocate of massive doses of quinine in malarial fever and of the treatment of pneumonia with the same drug. In 1857 he presented to the state society a paper on "Malarial Pneumonia" which aroused a controversy that filled the pages of the *North Carolina Medical Journal* for the two following years. Other notable works in this field, published much later, include *Remittent Fever* (1881), *Physiological and Therapeutic Action of Sulphate of Quinine* (1882), and *Malarial Hematuria* (1886). He was engaged upon an exhaustive "History of Fevers from the Earliest Times" at the time of his death, and left the most complete collection of the literature of malaria then in existence. The independent thought expressed in his writings, together with his aggressive advocacy of the revolutionary application of some of his ideas, brought down upon him the opposition of the leaders of his profession in the state. For years he was bitterly assailed and made to suffer all the trials of the reformer, but many of his bitterest opponents lived to see the complete vindication of his views and practices and to adopt them as their own.

Meanwhile, upon the request of Governor Vance of North Carolina, he went to Richmond in July 1862 to establish a hospital for disabled soldiers from that state. He secured a tobacco warehouse, naming it the Moore hospital, after the Surgeon General of the Confederate army. Though by choice an internist, in this position he showed himself a skilful operator. He held the grade of major in the medical service of the Confederacy until the end of the war. Its termination finding him in Richmond, he settled there to resume private practice. In 1869 he was appointed professor of pathology and physiology at the Medical College of Virginia, filling the position until 1882, when he became professor emeritus. In 1871–72 he was associate editor of the *Virginia Clinical Record*. His first wife died in 1872, and in 1881 he married Helen (Gray) Watson, daughter of William Gray, Esq., of Richmond. The stress of an arduous professional life brought on a nervous breakdown, followed by an apoplectic stroke from which he died, in Richmond.

Though positive in manner, Manson was kindly and gracious. Elegant in dress, he wrote in a florid style then not uncommon, but which has since disappeared from scientific writing. He early became a member of the Medical Society of North Carolina and was a member of the first State Board of Medical Examiners in 1859. He was a member of the Medical Society of Virginia from its origin in 1870, and of the Richmond Academy of Medicine. For several years he was president of the Richmond city council.

[S. S. Satchwell, *Memorial of Prof. Otis Frederick Manson* (1888) with portrait; T. F. Wood in *N. C. Medic. Jour.*, Mar. 1888; *Trans. Medic. Soc. N. C.*, vol. XXXV (1888); *Va. Medic. Monthly*, Mar. 1888; *The State* (Richmond), Jan. 25, 1888; family information.]

J. M. P.

MANTELL, ROBERT BRUCE (Feb. 7, 1854–June 27, 1928), actor, was of Scottish ancestry and birth, the son of James and Elizabeth Bruce Mantell. He was born in the Wheatsheaf Inn, at Irvine in Ayrshire, of which his father was the landlord, and was one of a family of four sons and four daughters. At the age of five he was taken to Belfast, where his father established himself as an inn-keeper, and there after receiving a brief schooling, he made his first tentative experiments in amateur theatricals. His début in a theatre, following appearances in halls, was in 1873 at the Theatre Royal, Belfast, as De Mauprat in *Richelieu*. The law was his first intended destiny, but it was given up soon in favor of an apprenticeship in the wholesale liquor business until he was nineteen, when he made up his mind, in spite of maternal objections, to become an actor. He called himself then, and he was known to the public for some time, as Robert Hudson. In May 1874 he worked his way to America as a steward on a steamship of which his brother was purser, and landing in Boston, he sought ineffectually for an engagement as an actor in the theatres of that city. Only ten days were sufficient to discourage him, and he returned to Belfast.

His career on the stage actually began Oct. 21, 1876, when he secured the small part of the Sergeant in Dion Boucicault's *Arrah-na-Pogue* with a stock company in Rochdale, England. Later he acted in support of Charles Mathews, Alice Marriott, Ellen Wallis, and other English stars, until, in October 1878, he set sail again for the United States under engagement to join Mme. Modjeska's company, making his début in America on Nov. 18, 1878, at Albany, N. Y., as Tybalt to the star's Juliet, playing then for the first time under his own name. At the end of the season he returned to England, where he passed several years of alternate hard work and lack of engagements. Coming back to the Unitd States, he acted variously and with little encouragement for about a year. Then, on Oct. 1, 1883, he played with exceptional acclaim the part of Loris Ipanoff to Fanny Davenport's Fedora in Sardou's play of that name at the Fourteenth Street Theatre in New York, and continued in it for the entire season. He went to Scotland for the summer, and returning in the autumn he was henceforth identified with the American stage for over forty years. In the spring of 1885 he acted the title rôle in Steele MacKaye's *Dakolar* during the opening weeks of the new Lyceum Theatre in New York. A contemporary reviewer said that his characterization, "although rough at present, is a very powerful sketch," and that "the young man's handsome presence, expressive face, fine voice, and physical vigor give him great advantages" (New York *Evening Post,* Apr. 7, 1885). Other engagements followed, including a return to the part of Loris Ipanoff with Fanny Davenport, but his desire to shine as a stellar attraction was soon foremost in his mind, and it did not subside until his ambition was realized. In 1886 he found himself at the head of his own company under the astute management of Augustus Pitou, playing in a romantic drama by John Kellar entitled *Tangled Lives.* The play itself was mediocre, but he gave it a wide popularity, and soon added *The Marble Heart, The Corsican Brothers, Monbars, The Face in the Moonlight,* and other melodramas new and old to his repertory, finally reaching the height of his ambition by devoting himself during his later years almost wholly to Shakespeare, with whose plays he had had abundant experience by acting secondary characters at intervals during many years. He first acted Romeo in 1887, Othello in 1888, Hamlet in 1890, Richard III in 1901, and so on through a Shakespearean repertory that also came to include Macbeth, Iago, Brutus, King John, Shylock, and King Lear. Because of marital difficulties, which involved the payment of alimony, he was little known in the New York theatres for a decade, although he found a warm welcome in other large cities.

In his younger days Mantell was handsome, graceful, and impassioned, his appeal being made more through the superficial phases of character interpretation dependent mainly upon force of action and vigor of voice than through intellectual subtlety. In his later days he became heavy, and he lacked the ability to carry the idea of inspiration and the illusion of reality across the footlights. His Shakespearean impersonations were studious, sturdy, and somewhat slow-moving. He was essentially a melodramatic and a romantic actor, and romance departed from him with the passing of his youth and his transition from middle to old age. In his last days on the stage he was hampered by lameness. He was first married to Marie Sheldon, from whom he was divorced in 1893, second to Charlotte Behrens, third to Marie Booth Russell, and fourth to Genevieve Hamper, who survived him. All were at one time or another actresses and members of his companies, usually playing leading feminine characters in his support. He died at his home in Atlantic Highlands, N. J.

[C. J. Bulliet, *Robert Mantell's Romance* (1918); J. B. Clapp and E. F. Edgett, *Players of the Present* (1900); *Who's Who in America,* 1922–23; John Parker, *Who's Who in the Theatre,* 1925; Francis Wilson, obituary in *The Players Year Book,* 1925–28; interview in *Christian Science Monitor,* Dec. 13, 1921; obituary in Boston *Transcript,* June 27, 1928; Walter Browne and E. De Roy Koch, *Who's Who on the Stage,* 1908.]

E. F. E.

MAPES, CHARLES VICTOR (July 4, 1836–Jan. 23, 1916), agricultural chemist, manufacturer, was the son of James Jay Mapes and the brother of Mary Mapes Dodge [*qq.v.*]. His mother was Sophia, *née* Furman. Born in New York City, where he spent his early boyhood, he moved with his family to a farm near Newark, N. J., in 1847. Possessing a versatile and brilliant mind with his family's characteristic taste for music, painting, and letters, he had also his father's bent toward practical science. He fitted up a laboratory in his own room and there laid the foundations for his future work. At twenty-one he was graduated from Harvard College with the class of 1857. He had intended to study medicine, but the state of his health and other circumstances caused him to abandon the plan and in 1858 he entered the counting room of a firm of wholesale grocers in New York. The following year, in partnership with one of his employers, B. M. Whitlock, who provided most of the capital, he established a factory near Newark and began to manufacture and sell agricultural implements and fertilizers. He also took over the publication of his father's paper, *The Working Farmer,* of which he had been assistant editor since January 1858.

Mapes's chief contribution to scientific agriculture was his pioneer work in developing fertilizers adapted to the peculiar needs of different crops and different soils. In 1874 he prepared a fertilizer especially for potatoes, the first special-crop manure produced in the United States. In 1877 he became vice-president and general manager of the Mapes Formula and Peruvian Guano Company, organized that year with offices in New York and factory at Newark. Becoming president later, he served in that capacity until his death. He was the first president of the New York Chemical and Fertilizer Exchange. He contributed "Some Rambling Notes on Agriculture and Manures" to the *Sixth Annual Report of the New Jersey State Board of Agriculture, 1878* (1879) and "The Effects of Fertilizers on Different Soils" to the *Seventh, . . . 1879–80* (1880), and wrote numerous articles for agricultural journals. For a while he was associated in soil tests with W. O. Atwater [*q.v.*], of the federal Department of Agriculture. He was a member of the American Association for the Advancement of Science, and of the Municipal Art Society. On June 25, 1863, he married Martha Meeker Halsted, and they had five sons.

[*Who's Who in America*, 1914–15; *Report of the Class of 1857 in Harvard College*, 1866, 1882, 1910; *Charles V. Mapes' Illus. Cat. (for 1861) of Plows, and Other Agricultural Implements and Machines* (1861); *N. Y. Times*, Jan. 24, 1916.] L. G.

MAPES, JAMES JAY (May 29, 1806–Jan. 10, 1866), agriculturist, was born in Maspeth, L. I., the son of Jonas and Elizabeth (Tylee) Mapes. His father, descended from Thomas Mapes who came from Norfolk, England, to Southhold, L. I., in 1649, served as major-general of the New York militia in the War of 1812 and for some years was senior partner in a New York firm of importers and merchant tailors. James was sent for a time to a classical school conducted by Timothy Clowes at Hempstead, L. I., but was in the main self-educated. A boy of precocious mind with a turn for the practical sciences, he began his career at the age of eight, when, after hearing a lecture on the subject, he produced illuminating gas with a clay pipe for a retort. In his teens he entered business as a clerk, but upon reaching his majority launched out for himself as a merchant. In this year (1827) he married Sophia Furman, of a Long Island family. About 1832 he invented a process of refining sugar. Acquiring a reputation as an analytical chemist, he abandoned his mercantile pursuits to open an office as consultant and was frequently called upon for expert testimony in patent cases. He made analyses of beer and wines for the New York Senate and temperance societies, and was the author of improvements in distilling, dyeing, and steel manufacture. An amateur miniature painter, he experimented with pigments, and between 1835 and 1838, as professor of chemistry and natural philosophy of colors in the National Academy of Design, New York, gave a course of lectures on the chemistry of colors which displayed both scholarship and a quiet, humorous humanitarianism. From 1840 to 1842 he edited the *American Repertory of Arts, Sciences, and Manufactures* in four volumes, and from January 1842 to June 1843 he was associate editor of the *Journal of the Franklin Institute*, Philadelphia. In January 1845 he became president of the Mechanics' Institute of the City of New York, delivering an *Inaugural Address*, published that year, in which he set forth the delights and advantages of a liberal education. He was also a member of the New York Lyceum of Natural History and in 1847, vice-president of the American Institute of the City of New York. In the latter connection he had a share in founding conversational schools and night schools that were the forerunners of such ventures as Cooper Institute. He was one of the organizers and second president of the Franklin Institute of Newark, N. J.

In 1847 he purchased a worn-out farm near Newark which he converted into productive acres by subsoil drainage, rotation of crops, and judicious fertilization, and there he demonstrated by precept and example the practical application of science to agriculture. His neighbors were invited to observe and benefit by the experiments conducted. Seeds were grown under controlled conditions to produce more hardy and profitable crops, and these were sold and given away with excellent advice for good measure. In February 1849 he founded, and edited until 1863, a journal called *The Working Farmer*, in which he published the results of his experimental farming, making it a point to explain the scientific principles underlying his practice. Through its columns he was an early advocate of a federal Department of Agriculture with a cabinet officer at its head. He took pupils in scientific agriculture on his farm, and advertised his services as consulting agricultural chemist. He invented a subsoil plow, and developed a formula for nitrogenized superphosphate which was probably the first complete plant food among artificial fertilizers used in the United States. This, after considerable litigation, he patented Nov. 22, 1859, and it was subsequently manufactured and sold by his son, Charles V. Mapes [*q.v.*]. Mapes's vigorous personality and winning conversational ability enhanced his influence among all classes and led many to adopt the measures which ahead of his time he advocated. His friend Horace Greeley, writing an editorial on his death, said of him, "American agriculture owes as much to him as to any man who lives or has ever lived" (*New York Daily Tribune*, Jan. 11, 1866). Mapes was for years an officer in the New York militia, and was honored by the presentation of a sword from his company. He died in New York City, at the age of fifty-nine, leaving his widow, three daughters, one of whom was Mary Mapes Dodge [*q.v.*], and his son Charles, who was also an agricultural chemist.

[C. R. Woodward, *The Development of Agriculture in N. J., 1640–1880* (1927); W. H. Shaw, *Hist. of Essex and Hudson Counties, N. J.* (1884), vol. I; *Newark News*, June 5, 1904; *The Family Record*, Jan., Mar., Sept., Oct. 1897; *Report of the Commissioner of Patents for the Year 1859* (1860); T. S. Cummings, *Hist. Annals Nat. Acad. of Design* (1865); N. Y. Directories; *Ann. Report Am. Inst. of the City of N. Y., 1865–66* (1866); *N. Y. Daily Tribune*, Jan. 11, 1866; *N. Y. Times*, Jan. 12, 1866.] L. G.

MAPPA, ADAM GERARD (Nov. 25, 1754–Apr. 15, 1828), soldier, typefounder, and land agent, was born of Dutch parents at Delft, Holland. When he was about twenty he was serving as an officer in the army, moving from post to post in the Netherlands and enjoying the rather stiff and formal society of the middle-class Dutch of that day. Then he fell in love with Anna Adriana Passpoort of Delft, whom, after some delay in obtaining parental consent, he married in 1780. His new responsibilities made army life irksome, and he therefore resigned his commission and became a typefounder, thanks to his father's purchase on his behalf of an established business in Rotterdam which he shortly moved to Delft. Since the management of this enterprise was not onerous, he had ample time to devote to politics. Liberal in political as in religious opinions, he took an active part in the Patriot movement which in that period of ferment aimed to recast the cumbersome and ultraconservative political institutions of the Netherlands. He had neither the social position, the intellectual gifts, nor the force of character to attain leadership in the movement. Thanks to his military training, however, he became colonel of one of the Patriots' volunteer militia regiments and took part in that revolution which evaporated so ingloriously in the summer of 1787 at the appearance of Prussian troops sent to restore the *stadhouder* to his ancient position.

Exiled with other Patriots, Mappa took refuge in France. He passed two dreary years near St. Omer; then, convinced that no military assistance could be expected from France, decided to begin life anew in America, the country of Patriot inspiration and the home now of several fellow exiles. With his wife and three children he reached New York on Dec. 1, 1789, and there set up the first type-foundry the city had known. His business did not prosper, however. For lack of type-casters he was forced himself to do the manual labor, and apparently lost orders because he was unable to fill them (Thomas Greenleaf's preface to his *Laws of the State of New York*, 2 vols., 1792). Hence he accepted with alacrity an agency with the Holland Land Company. By the spring of 1794 he was installed as assistant land agent at Olden Barneveld (now Trenton) in Oneida County, N. Y.

Life in the backwoods was not easy, but the early years at Barneveld were perhaps the happiest of Mappa's life. There were novelty and interest in the new work, relative prosperity with a good salary and a large farm which his employers had helped him to stock and develop, a prospect of future comfort—especially after his appointment in 1797 as agent in full charge of the settlement—above all, happiness in his family life and in the pleasant society of men of his own stamp. For there were soon nearly a score of Dutch in the little village, some his own relatives, some fellow exiles, among them the learned and kindly Francis Adrian Van der Kemp [*q.v.*], scholar and former clergyman of Leyden. To Mappa the New World at first offered ample compensations for the disappointments of the Old. Reverses were in store, however, which clouded his later years. He lacked the aggressive and energetic character necessary to the successful land agent. Sales were difficult and collections from not over-prosperous settlers still more so. His situation became increasingly embarrassing after 1818, when with a partner he bought the interests of his employers on credit. He fell behind in the payment of installments due on his contract; already his affairs were complicated by the failure of a textile mill which he had helped to finance and by the assumption of the debts of one of his sons. Gentle and kindly as he was, Mappa had little gaiety in his character; he became despondent under the weight of his burdens and died in 1828, feeling that his life had been a failure. He had, however, played a not unimportant part in settling his section of New York State.

[Helen L. Fairchild, *Francis Adrian Van der Kemp* (1903); Nina M. and Francis Tiffany, *Harm Jan Huidekoper* (1904); P. D. Evans, *The Holland Land Company* (1924), being Buffalo Hist. Soc. Pubs., vol. XXVIII; L. C. Wroth, *The Colonial Printer* (1931); *Ars Typographica*, July 1925; dates of birth and death from tombstone, Barneveld, N. Y.; Mappa's correspondence as land agent in the private archives of Van Eeghen & Company, Amsterdam.] P. D. E.

MARBLE, ALBERT PRESCOTT (May 21, 1836–Mar. 25, 1906), educator, author, was the son of John and Emeline Prescott Marble, descendants of old New England stock. He was born at Vassalboro, Me., where he spent most of his early life on the ancestral farm and developed a robust physique. By his own industry he accumulated enough money to send himself to academies at Yarmouth and Waterville and to enter, when past his twenty-first birthday, old Waterville College, now Colby. Here his abilities and maturity brought him distinction both from his classmates and from the faculty, and he graduated in 1861 with Phi Beta Kappa honors. In the same year he was married to Louise Wells Marston. The following year, 1862, Marble took his family to Beaver Dam, Wis., to accept the professorship of mathematics in Wayland University. While there he served as recruiting officer for the Northern army. His career as an educator had commenced even before he completed his undergraduate training; for he had taught in elementary and secondary schools and had been principal of a public school at Eastport, Me., and of a private school at Stockbridge, Mass.

From Wisconsin he returned to Maine for a short while and then (1866) accepted the principalship of Worcester Academy. In two years he raised the institution, then in a state of decline, to a position of success and eminence. The achievement of this feat brought him the superintendency of the public schools in Worcester, Mass., in 1868. Marble did much by personal example to make the city school superintendency a post of professional leadership rather than a pawn of political chieftains. His attention to the construction, sanitation, and equipment of school buildings not only made Worcester notable but through a secondary momentum gave Massachusetts a position of leadership in the nation. In the period when the public high school was wresting leadership from the academies in secondary education he gave it his special attention. He was never swept off his feet by the latest novelties in education, but he saw a place for the "English" high school in contrast to the classical and welcomed other progressive measures.

When the administration of New York City's public schools was reorganized in 1896 into a board of superintendents, Marble was brought from Omaha, Nebr., where he had been for the two years previous, and was put in charge of the city's first three high schools. When the charter of Greater New York was set in operation, he was retained in the same capacity on the new board of superintendents and held the position till his failing health demanded that he be relieved. He found time to take active part in professional associations, being three times president of the Massachusetts State Teachers Association and secretary and later president of the National Education Association. A prize speak er in college, he continued an engaging and fluent speaker in later life. He was also equally active and effective with his pen. His *Sanitary Conditions for School Houses* (1891) was published as a Circular of Information by the United States Bureau of Education. His interest in private education he continued as one of the board of visitors at Wellesley College.

[Clarence E. Meleney, memorial sketch in *Nat. Educ. Asso. Fiftieth Anniversary Vol., 1851–1906* (1907); *Proceedings* of the Nat. Educ. Asso. for the year 1906; Paul Monroe, *A Cyc. of Educ.*, vol. IV (1913); *Bulletin* of the High School Teachers Asso. (N. Y. City), Feb. 1932; *N. Y. Tribune*, Mar. 26, 1906; information as to certain facts from Marble's daughter, Katherine Marble Hodgkins.]

J. S. B.

MARBLE, DANFORTH (Apr. 27, 1810–May 13, 1849), actor of Yankee rôles, was born in East Windsor, Conn., the son of William and Mary Marble. At an early age and with only a very slight education he went to Hartford, where he remained for a number of years, first as errand boy in a dry-goods store and later as apprentice to a silversmith. His interest in the stage, which had been aroused by a company of actors visiting Hartford, prompted him to go to New York City. Thanks to the help of a friend, who was a silversmith, Marble was enabled to secure employment in his trade, and in the evenings gain admission behind stage at the Chatham Theatre. Before long under an assumed name he was playing minor rôles at the Chatham, and in addition became a member of a local Thespian Society of amateurs. Finally he abandoned his trade of silversmith, and on Apr. 11, 1831, made his first appearance under his own name—for which privilege he paid the sum of twenty dollars. In the following year while temporarily stranded in Newark, N. J., he first displayed his skill in Yankee dialect. In the hotel of the landlord for whom Marble was working there was a woman from Maine with an extreme Yankee accent, which the young actor took delight in mimicking. His skill attracted such attention that he was compared by his friends to George Handel Hill [*q.v.*].

During the course of the next four years, while he was on barnstorming tours in Virginia and in the smaller towns of upper New York state, he became increasingly proficient in his Yankee stories. But his reputation was not firmly established until in 1836 Dean and McKinney, enterprising Buffalo managers, presented him in *Sam Patch*, a Yankee play written especially for him by E. H. Thompson. The tremendous popularity of the rôle caused the managers to repeat it in Cleveland and in their newly opened theatre in Columbus, Ohio. During the remainder of his career Marble's most popular character was Sam Patch, and the scene in which the hero jumps from a height of forty feet into the swirling waters of Niagara, although trying to the actor, provided unfailing delight to audiences from Boston to New Orleans, from Savannah to St. Louis. In return for his performances in the Mississippi Valley theatrical centers alone Marble, over a period of ten years, received from the managers forty thousand dollars. "He was hailed with delight and enthusiasm whenever he appeared on the Mississippi," writes his biographer. "He was known to nearly every captain, clerk, and engineer, senator, and landlord from Pittsburg to New Orleans" (Kelly, *post*, p.

145). He was equally popular in the eastern theatres, especially at the Bowery, New York City. In September 1844 he was enthusiastically received at the Strand Theatre in London and afterward gave performances in Glasgow and Dublin. Marble's long list of Yankee rôles included, besides Sam Patch, those in *The Wool-Dealer, Jonathan in England, The People's Candidate, The People's Lawyer, Game Cock of the Wilderness, Down Easter, Home in the West, Next Steamer, Bushwhacker,* and in *Family Ties,* the prize-winning play in a competition sponsored by him. In general his types of characters were akin to those of the other Yankee comedians, but according to the testimony of his biographer he possessed complete individuality of dialect and accent. Marble died in Louisville, Ky., from an attack of cholera. His wife was Anne Warren, daughter of the distinguished Philadelphia actor and manager, William Warren.

[J. F. Kelly, *Dan. Marble* (1851); S. F. Smith *Theatrical Management in the South and West* (1868), pp. 220–21; N. M. Ludlow, *Dramatic Life as I Found It* (1880); J. N. Ireland, *Records of the N. Y. Stage* (2 vols., 1866–67); H. R. Stiles, *The Hist. and Geneals. of Ancient Windsor, Conn.*, vol. II (1892); O. S. Coad and Edwin Mims, Jr., *The Am. Stage* (1929).]

E. M., Jr.

MARBLE, MANTON MALONE (Nov. 15, 1835–July 24, 1917), newspaper editor and publisher, was born in Worcester, Mass., the son of Joel and Nancy Chapin (Coes) Marble. His early education was supervised by his father, and he was graduated from the Albany (N. Y.) Academy in 1853. After two years at the University of Rochester (B.A., 1855) he began newspaper work as a member of the staff of the *Boston Journal*. A year later (1856) he became an editor of the *Boston Traveler* and in 1858–60 was on the staff of the New York *Evening Post*. In 1860 he was made night editor of the New York *World* and in 1862 became editor and owner of that paper. His control of the *World* continued throughout the last two years of the Civil War and the period of reconstruction of the South. During the war he opposed many of the policies of the federal government, although he held that no course but war was open after the firing on Fort Sumter. He was against great extension of the federal power, a federal income tax, the issuing of greenbacks, negro suffrage, and the impeachment of President Johnson.

Early in 1864 the *World* was one of a few New York newspapers which were made the victims of a fraud in the publication of a forged call from President Lincoln for the addition of 400,000 men to the army by draft and enlistment, and appointing a day of national fasting and prayer. The President ordered the arrest of Marble and a military guard was put in charge of the *World* office. Three days later Marble succeeded in resuming publication of the paper and addressed an open letter to Lincoln declaring that the *World* had been imposed upon by methods which it had been impossible to detect. He protested against the President's action, declaring that "for the purpose of gratifying an ignoble partisan resentment you have struck down the rights of the press" (*World,* May 23, 1864, p. 6). The letter, which was long and couched in vigorous language, was reprinted (1867) in pamphlet form by a group of men who sympathized with Marble's stand. He supported the Geneva arbitration treaty and the *Alabama* awards, expressing the view that they constituted a beginning of a period of peaceful policies. In the attacks on the "Tweed ring" in New York he was active. He was credited with having written the New York state platform of the Democratic party in 1874 and the national platform of the party on which Samuel J. Tilden was nominated for president in 1876, as well as much of the national platform of 1884.

In 1876 Marble sold the *World* to a group of men headed by Thomas A. Scott, president of the Pennsylvania Railroad. He was sent abroad by President Cleveland in 1885 to sound European governments on bimetalism, and conferred with Gladstone, Bismarck, Freycinet, and other public men. After extensive investigation he reported to the President that the resumption of bimetallic coinage would not be carried out by any European government without the cooperation of Great Britain, which he saw no prospect of obtaining, since neither the British Conservative nor Liberal leaders were prepared for it. He advised Cleveland against further purchases of silver by the United States Treasury Department. The last years of his life were devoted to literary endeavors and leisure, and he spent much time in England, where he died. He was the author of a pamphlet entitled *A Secret Chapter of Political History; the Electoral Commission* (1878) and of a memoir of the Rev. Alexander G. Mercer, published in the latter's *Bible Characters* (1885). His name also appears as editor on the title page of *Memories of Familiar Books* (1876) by William B. Reed.

[Don C. Seitz, *Jos. Pulitzer: His Life and Letters* (1924); Frederic Hudson, *Journalism in the U. S. from 1690 to 1872* (1873); J. M. Lee, *Hist. of Am. Journalism* (1923); John L. Heaton, *The Story of a Page* (1913); Robt. McElroy, *Grover Cleveland: The Man and the Statesman* (1923), vol. I; *Who's Who in America*, 1916–17; *Worcester Births, Marriages, and Deaths* (1894), ed. by F. P. Rice; obituaries in the *World* and other N. Y. newspapers.]

A. S. W.

MARCH, ALDEN (Sept. 20, 1795–June 17, 1869), surgeon and anatomist, was born in Sutton, Worcester County, Mass., the son of Jacob and Eleanor (Moore) March, of old New England ancestry. His father, a poor farmer with a large family, had a hard struggle with the soil, and the son received little schooling. Upon the father's death in 1814 he took charge of the farm and family for a while. In 1817 he was in Hoosick, N. Y., teaching in a writing school and working in a stone and slate quarry. One year later he was influenced by an elder brother, David, then an army surgeon, to take up medicine, and during 1818–19 attended lectures on anatomy and surgery at Boston, at the same time making up for defects in his early education. In 1820 he graduated from the Medical Department of Brown University (later abolished). Before he was established, he performed an operation for harelip. He settled in Albany in 1820 as a general practitioner and at once opened a private school of anatomy with fourteen pupils. He taught by lectures and dissections, obtaining his first cadaver by freighting it overland from Boston. He also at once began a private collection of anatomical specimens. So much enterprise and originality on the part of a man of twenty-five antagonized the local representatives of his profession, and despite his efforts both practice and school failed to prosper. Sinking further and further into debt, he thought seriously of abandoning his practice in Albany and trying to find a more congenial location, but his landlord, one of his creditors, persuaded him to remain, and by 1824 his circumstances had changed for the better. In that year he married Joanna P. Armsby, and in the following year was made professor of anatomy and physiology in the Vermont Academy of Medicine at Castleton, Vt., with which he was connected until 1838, meanwhile continuing his practice and his school of anatomy. In 1830 he published *A Lecture on the Expedience of Establishing a Medical College and Hospital in the City of Albany,* thus incurring once more the hostility of the profession and notably that of the local Fairfield Medical College and the other medical schools of New York State. He went ahead with his project, however; the new institution was opened, and he served it as professor of anatomy and operative surgery. When the buildings were burned in 1834, however, he resumed his private venture, under the style of Practical School of Anatomy and Surgery. In 1839 the Albany Medical College was formally opened, and March, having resigned his chair at Castleton, became professor of surgery. His free surgical clinics on Saturdays, at which the students were enabled to watch all kinds of operations on a great variety of clinical material, made the College famous. The Fairfield Medical School soon agreed to merge with the new institution and eventually the Albany City Hospital was established. March was made professor of surgery in the consolidated college and retained the chair until his death. He had a farm near the city, and his only recreation was to visit it as often as possible and perform hard farm labor. His great surgical hobby was hip-joint disease. In 1853 he published a pamphlet entitled *Coxalgia or Hip Disease* and in the same year another on an ingenious forceps devised by him for harelip operation. He wrote a number of other papers, published chiefly in the *Transactions of the Medical Society of the State of New York.* In 1863 he was president of the American Medical Association. During the last year of his life he attended the meeting of the Association at New Orleans in apparent health, but his death revealed that for years he had suffered from prostatic obstruction. A controversy (see *New York Medical Journal,* October 1869, January, March 1870) was started after his death as to the correctness of the diagnosis and treatment.

[W. C. Wey, *The Late Alden March* (1869); *Trans. Medic. Soc. of the State of N. Y.,* 1870; *Trans. Medic. Soc. of the County of Albany,* 1870; J. L. Babcock, *Life and Character of Alden March, M.D.* (1871); *Tribute to the Memory of Alden March M.D.* (1870); *Cat. . . . of Castleton Medic. Coll. since 1818* (1854); *Albany Jour.,* June 17, 1869.]

E. P.

MARCH, FRANCIS ANDREW (Oct. 25, 1825–Sept. 9, 1911), philologist, was sixth in descent from Hugh March of Newbury, Mass., who emigrated from England in 1638, and his wife Judith. Their great-grandson Daniel settled by the Blackstone River in Sutton (now Millbury), Worcester County, Mass. Here was born Francis Andrew, the eldest child of Daniel's grandson Andrew Patch March (1798–1874) and Nancy (Parker) March (d. 1830). In 1828 Andrew March removed with his family to Worcester, Mass., and it was in this city that his son grew up. A precocious child, he was well taught in the excellent public schools of Worcester, and entered Amherst College in 1841. His four years at Amherst were among the most pregnant of his life. A brilliant student, he excelled likewise in public speaking and in athletics, and still found time to read philosophy and to ponder the history of his mother tongue. The latter interest, awakened by the lectures of Noah Webster [*q.v.*] and the instruction of Professor William C. Fowler, Webster's son-in-law, was destined to prove a decisive factor in his career.

March was graduated from Amherst in 1845, with first honors; in 1848 he was awarded the degree of M.A. by the same institution. From 1845 to 1849 he served as teacher in New Hampshire and Massachusetts, for two years as tutor at Amherst. During this period he made up his mind to become a lawyer, and devoted his spare time to legal studies, which he pursued under the direction of a Worcester attorney, Francis H. Dewey. In 1849 he became a student in the office of the legal firm of Barney & Butler in New York. The following year he was admitted to the New York bar, and, in partnership with Gordon L. Ford, opened a law office of his own. He had hardly been practising for two years when an ailment of the lungs developed which forced him to leave New York and seek health in a milder climate. In 1853 he secured a post as teacher in a private school of Fredericksburg, Va., and a teacher he remained for the rest of his days. In 1855 he was called to Lafayette College, at Easton, Pa., as tutor. The next year he was made adjunct professor and in 1857 he was appointed professor of the English language and comparative philology. This chair, the first of the kind to be established in any institution of learning in America or Europe, he held thenceforward until his retirement from active service forty-nine years later. On Aug. 12, 1860, he was married to Margaret Mildred Stone Conway (Jan. 25, 1837–Feb. 11, 1911), daughter of Walter P. Conway, of Falmouth, Stafford County, Va. The eldest of their nine children was Francis Andrew March, 1863–1928 [*q.v.*].

March's activities in Lafayette College were by no means confined to the teaching of English. During his earlier years at this institution he was called upon to conduct classes as well in French and German, Latin and Greek, the law, political economy, political science, philosophy, and even botany, and he continued to give courses in some of these subjects almost to the end of his career. His teaching program was so full, indeed, that he would have found time for nothing else had he not been gifted with an almost limitless supply of mental energy and the ability to toil interminably, and this in spite of the long precarious state of his health. His method as a teacher was exegetical, and he seems to have been the first to apply exegesis in all its scientific rigor to the classroom study of English literary monuments. In his hands the success of the method was nothing short of phenomenal. Through it he raised collegiate instruction in English to the dignity of a mental discipline, and gave to it the place which it has since occupied alongside the study of the classics. His influence on the teaching of English spread through his pupils, notably James W. Bright [*q.v.*] of the Johns Hopkins, from Lafayette to many another American seat of learning, and his method was adopted to admirable effect by many (notably George L. Kittredge of Harvard) who had not learned it directly from him. Since March's day the less rigorous method of the formal lecture has gained ground, largely because of its relative cheapness.

March's chief title to fame, however, rests on his researches in the field of English historical grammar. In agreement with the tastes and tendencies of his time, he specialized in the study of early medieval English, then called Anglo-Saxon, and published in 1870 an epoch-making work on the subject, the fruit of nearly ten years of exhaustive research, done under difficulties which would have proved insuperable to a lesser man. The title, *A Comparative Grammar of the Anglo-Saxon Language, in which its forms are illustrated by those of the Sanskrit, Greek, Latin, Gothic, Old Saxon, Old Friesic, Old Norse, and Old High German,* makes plain the nature of the work and indicates the importance of his achievement, which was no less than to show in detail the relationship of the English language to the other languages of the Indo-European group. March's *Comparative Grammar* won instant and general recognition, in America and Europe alike, as a piece of research of the first order. He had laid the foundation on which all future historical grammarians in the field of English were destined to build, and his fame will ever rest secure as in a very real sense the founder of a science. Besides his masterpiece he published *Introduction to Anglo-Saxon: An Anglo-Saxon Reader* (1870), for the classroom instruction of beginners, and numerous articles, addresses, and reviews by his hand appeared in encyclopedias, transactions of learned societies, and journals professional and popular.

In addition to his medieval studies, March did valuable work in English lexicography. He served for some years as director of the American workers for *The Oxford English Dictionary,* and was a guiding spirit in the preparation of the *Standard Dictionary* (2 vols., 1893–95), of which he was consulting editor. He was active in the movement for the reform of English orthography, and published an admirable pamphlet on the subject, *The Spelling Reform* (1881), which went through several editions. His methods of research and instruction alike are revealed with a luminous clarity in his earliest book, the *Method of Philological Study of the English Language* (1865), a work still of more than historical interest. He also found time to edit four volumes of Latin and Greek Christian classics: *Latin Hymns* (1874), *Eusebius* (1874), *The Select Work of Tertullian* (1875), and *Athenagoras* (1876). In sum, his labors were prodigious, varied, and of a uniformly high quality. His services to scholarship were recognized by numerous honorary degrees; by election to the presidency of the American Philological Association (1873–74 and 1895–96), the Spelling Reform Association (1876–1905), and the Modern Language Association of America (1891–93); and by a variety of other distinctions. He received several calls to chairs in other institutions of learning, but consistently refused to leave Lafayette College, loyalty to which was central in his professional career.

[*Addresses . . . in Honor of Prof. Francis A. March, . . . at Lafayette College, Oct. 24, 1895* (1895), containing list of writings to that time (little of importance was written by him thereafter); R. N. Hart, *Francis Andrew March, A Sketch* (Easton, Pa., 1907); D. B. Skillman, *The Biography of a College* (2 vols., 1932); J. W. Bright, in *Pubs. of the Modern Language Asso. of America,* March 1914; *Obit. Record of Grads. of Amherst Coll., for the Academic Year Ending June 26, 1912* (1912); *Who's Who in America,* 1910–11; family letters.]

K. M.

MARCH, FRANCIS ANDREW (Mar. 2, 1863–Feb. 28, 1928), lexicographer, was the eldest son of Francis Andrew March [*q.v.*] and Margaret Mildred Stone (Conway) March. He was born and brought up in Easton, Pa., and lived there all his days. His education was gained under the best possible auspices, since he was trained by his father, one of the most notable Anglicists of the day and professor of English in Lafayette College. Young March was graduated from Lafayette with the B.A. degree in 1881; later he received the degrees of M.A. and Ph.D. (1889) from the same institution. He began his professional career in 1882, when he was appointed tutor in his Alma Mater. In 1884 he was promoted to an adjunct professorship of modern languages, and in 1891 he was made professor of English literature, a chair which he exchanged in 1905 for that of professor of the English language. This professorship he held until his death. He was married on Sept. 4, 1889, to Alice Youngman, daughter of Robert B. Youngman, professor of Greek in Lafayette College. They had three children.

The younger like the elder March was first of all a faithful servant of Lafayette College. His loyalty expressed itself, not only in a lifetime of service as a teacher, but also in a lifetime of devotion to the athletic activities of the institution. Himself an outstanding athlete in his student days, March became in 1890 the member of the teaching staff entrusted with the supervision of the athletic side of student life, and his interest in these matters culminated in a study of the athletic history of the school, published in book form in 1926 under the title, *Athletics at Lafayette College.* March also took an interest in the local political scene, and served from 1905 to 1909 as mayor of Easton. But his chief contribution to American life was to be in the lexicographical field. He served his apprenticeship in this field as an assistant in the etymological department of *The Century Dictionary and Cyclopedia* (1 ed., 1889–91), the most ambitious lexicographical enterprise ever undertaken on American soil. When the staff of the *Standard Dictionary* (2 vols., 1893–95) was made up, March was invited to join it as editor in charge of the etymological department, and his services in this capacity had no little to do with making the dictionary standard in fact as well as in name. This task done, March undertook, in collaboration with his father, the editorship of a thesaurus dictionary. This work came out in 1902, under the title, *A Thesaurus Dictionary of the English Language,* and proved a great success; it has run to five editions. The connection of the elder March with this dictionary was little more than nominal, and to the younger must go the credit for its successful execution. March's interests, in his later years, seem to have shifted over to the historical field, for he wrote two books (popular rather than learned, it is true) about the World War: *History of the World War* (1918) and *America's Part in the World War* (1919), both in collaboration with R. J. Beamish.

[R. N. Hart, *Francis Andrew March, A Sketch* (1907); J. W. Bright, in *Pubs. of the Modern Language Asso. of America,* March 1914; D. B. Skillman, *The Biography of a College* (2 vols., 1932); *Who's Who in America,* 1926–27; (Philadelphia) *Public Ledger,* Feb. 29, 1928; family letters.]

K. M.

MARCHAND, JOHN BONNETT (Aug. 27, 1808–Apr. 13, 1875), naval officer, was born in Greensburg, Pa., the son of Dr. David and Catherine (Bonnett) Marchand. His father, a major-general of militia during the years 1812–14 and a member of Congress from 1817 to 1821, was descended from emigrants from Switzerland. Young Marchand entered the navy as a midshipman on May 1, 1828, and in the years 1829–32 saw his first sea service in the West Indies on the *Peacock* and *Porpoise.* After attending the Norfolk naval school and receiving in June 1834 a promotion to the rank of passed midshipman, he served from 1834 to 1837 with the Mediterranean Squadron, first on the *Potomac,* and later the *John Adams.* Attached to the *Porpoise* he engaged in the survey of the Savannah

River, and then again served in the West Indies. In 1840 he was promoted lieutenant and a year later, while in command of the *Van Buren,* he took part in the war against the Seminole Indians. From 1843 to 1845 he cruised in the East Indies on the *Brandywine.* In the Mexican War he served on the *Ohio* and participated in the bombardment of the castle of San Juan de Ulloa. After the war, a second cruise in the East Indies was followed by a second period of service in the Mediterranean. In 1855 he was advanced to the grade of commander and in 1858–59 he commanded the *Memphis* of the Paraguay expedition. At the outbreak of the Civil War, while acting as lighthouse inspector at Detroit, he was offered the command of a Michigan regiment but declined it, preferring service in the navy. On his application for active duty, he was on Aug. 31, 1861, placed in command of the *James Adger* and was employed in blockading the coast of South Carolina and searching for the Confederate steamer *Nashville.* Promoted captain from July 16, 1862, he was in the following October ordered to the *Lackawanna.* In February 1863 he reported to Admiral Farragut for blockade duty in the Gulf of Mexico. After capturing the *Neptune* and *Planter,* which ran the blockade at Mobile, he was placed in command of the third division of Farragut's squadron operating on the coast of Texas. He returned eastward in time to participate in the battle of Mobile Bay and in the capture of the ram *Tennessee.* In the latter part of 1864 he was detached from the *Lackawanna* and assigned to special duty. His last years of service were spent ashore on duty at Hartford and elsewhere and in command of the Philadelphia navy yard. He was promoted commodore from July 25, 1866, and was retired in that grade on Aug. 27, 1870. He died at his home in Carlisle, Pa. His wife, Margaret Donaldson Thornton, to whom he was married in 1856 or 1857, was the daughter of a naval paymaster.

[Record of Officers, Bureau of Navigation, 1825–78; G. D. Albert, *Hist. of the County of Westmoreland, Pa.* (1882), pp. 444–46; J. N. Boucher, *Hist. of Westmoreland County, Pa.* (1906), vol. III; *War of the Rebellion: Official Records (Navy)*, 1 ser. I, XIII, XIX–XXI; *Army and Navy Jour.*, Apr. 24, May 1, 1875.]

C. O. P.

MARCHANT, HENRY (April 1741–Aug. 30, 1796), Rhode Island jurist and delegate to the Continental Congress, was born on Martha's Vineyard, the son of Hexford Marchant, a sea-captain. His mother, whose maiden name was Butler, died when the boy was four, shortly after the family had removed to Newport. His father's later marriage to a daughter of Samuel Ward gave young Marchant a useful connection with a leading Rhode Island family. He studied at the College of Philadelphia (later the University of Pennsylvania) from 1756 to 1759, but did not graduate. In 1762, however, he received the degree of A.M. Meanwhile he was reading law with the greatest common lawyer and preceptor in New England, Edmund Trowbridge of Cambridge. This conservative judge hatched a numerous brood of young patriot barristers, among them Francis Dana, a fellow student of Marchant and his close friend.

After settling in Newport Marchant rose rapidly in his profession and in politics. He had stimulating contacts with the Redwood Library circle and was strongly influenced intellectually by his intimate friend and pastor, the erudite Dr. Ezra Stiles, whom he assisted in 1769 in observing the transit of Venus. An ardent Son of Liberty from Stamp Act days he was chosen attorney-general of Rhode Island in 1771 and each year thereafter through 1776. In 1771 when he went to England on private legal business before Privy Council he was designated joint colonial agent to press for compensation for the expenses of the 1756 campaign against Crown Point. He traveled widely in England and was Benjamin Franklin's companion on a visit to Scotland. Stiles noted with pride that his protégé "was personally acquainted with the Men of the first Eminence for Literature in Scotland and England" (*The Literary Diary of Ezra Stiles,* I, p. 304). He was also in close touch with the merchants, nonconformists, and radicals who made up the "friends of America" in Great Britain.

After his return in 1772 he fell under suspicion for accepting a retainer from the collector of customs, but he soon took his place in the leadership of the Revolutionary movement in the colony. In May 1773 he was named on the Rhode Island committee of correspondence, and in December 1774, on the committee to instruct the delegates to the first Continental Congress. At the outbreak of war he removed from Newport to his farm in South Kingstown. He was chosen delegate to Congress, 1777–79, and served on the standing committees on marine, appeals, treasury, and the southern department. He was elected again in 1780 and in 1783, but did not attend in either year, and in 1784 he resigned after reëlection.

From 1784 to 1790 he sat for Newport in the General Assembly and was a vigorous exponent of the commercial interests in those troubled times. He was associated with Varnum as counsel in *Trevett* vs. *Weeden.* In 1787 he signed the minority protest against Rhode Island's abstention from the Philadelphia Convention; in 1790 he introduced the bill for a ratifying convention. As a Newport member of the convention he took a leading part in the debates, and also in the maneuvers which finally brought Federalist success. He was promptly rewarded by President Washington with appointment as judge of the United States district court (July 2, 1790). He continued on the bench until his death at Newport six years later. Marchant married Rebecca Cooke, Jan. 8, 1765. His son, William, was graduated from Yale in 1792 when Marchant himself received the degree of LL.D. from his old mentor, President Stiles.

[See Edward Peterson, *Hist. of R. I.* (1853); W. R. Staples, *R. I. in the Continental Cong.* (1870); W. C. Ford, ed., *Jours. of the Continental Cong.*, vols. VII–XV (1907–09); E. C. Burnett, ed., *Letters of Members of the Continental Cong.*, vols. II–IV (1923–28); J. R. Bartlett, ed., *Records of the Colony of R. I.*, vols. VI–X (1861–65); J. N. Arnold, *Vital Record of R. I.*, vols. X (1898) and XII (1901); F. B. Dexter, ed., *The Lit. Diary of Ezra Stiles, D.D., LL.D.* (3 vols., 1901); and *Theodore Foster's Minutes of the Convention Held at South Kingstown, R. I., in Mar. 1790* (1929). Marchant's manuscript diary of his English journey and numerous letters are in family possession.]

V. W. C.

MARCOU, JULES (Apr. 20, 1824–Apr. 17, 1898), geologist, was born at Salins, France, and received his early education at the *Collège* there and at the *Lycée* of Besançon. He entered the College of St. Louis at Paris when eighteen years old but devoted himself so assiduously to mathematics that he undermined his health and was obliged to abandon his studies and return home in the spring of 1844. His interest and ability in the field of mathematics are demonstrated by the fact that he published three papers in the *Nouvelles Annales de Mathématiques* (vols. II, III, 1843–44) during those undergraduate days. On returning to Salins, he gave himself up to an out-of-door life and became interested in botany, but his family physician, who was an amateur collector of fossils, quickly turned his attention to the field of geology, where he found his life work. He soon became known as an authority on fossils and was visited by Louis Agassiz [*q.v.*], who encouraged him to publish his first geological work in 1845 ("Recherches Géologiques sur le Jura Salinois," *Mémoires de la Société d'Histoire Naturelle de Neuchâtel*).

He joined the faculty of the Sorbonne in 1846 as professor of mineralogy but within two years was made traveling geologist for the Museum in the Jardin des Plantes, and gave up teaching. North America was selected as the field for his first work, largely owing to the presence of Louis Agassiz here, and, coming to the United States in 1848, he accompanied Agassiz on his expedition to Lake Superior that summer. He left the party at Keweenaw Point, Mich., however, and devoted himself thereafter with extraordinary energy to collecting for the Paris Museum. In 1850 he resigned his connection with that institution, but in 1854 returned to Europe to live and in 1856 became professor of paleontology at the École Polytechnique in Zurich, where he remained four years. Returning to America in 1860, he finally settled in Cambridge, Mass., where he made his home until his death. He was at work as a geologist in the field more or less frequently until 1875, when he made his last long excursion, accompanying Lieut. George M. Wheeler's party on a surveying expedition to southern California. In 1862, he was appointed geologist in the Museum of Comparative Zoölogy at Harvard, but his official connection with the Museum seems to have ended two years later.

Marcou was a voluminous writer, 188 titles occurring in a bibliography which he himself compiled towards the close of his life. A large proportion of his publications were written in French and issued in Europe. His most important works, *Lettres sur les Roches du Jura* (1857–60), *Geology of North America* (1858), and *Geological Map of the World* (1862), were all published in Europe. During this brief period of five years Marcou seems to have reached "the acme of his career" (Hyatt, *post*, p. 654). In 1869, he published in Paris a volume, *De la Science en France,* which caused much comment because of its criticism of official methods. His *Life, Letters and Works of Louis Agassiz* (2 vols.), published in New York in 1895, also aroused interest and controversy by its unusual frankness. He was a great lover of books and his library was notable for the number of rare volumes which it contained. He was married in 1850 to Jane Belknap of Boston and had two sons. Throughout his life his health was unreliable and in spite of his extensive field work there were long periods when he was obliged to treat himself as an invalid. Nevertheless he was a man of striking personality, and in later years was a picturesque figure, tall and erect, with long, flowing beard. Energetic in his work, devoted to the truth as he saw it, he was apt to become very positive of the correctness of his own position and quite intolerant of opposition.

[Max Buchon, *Biographie Salinoise: Jules Marcou* (1865); Alpheus Hyatt, "Jules Marcou," in *Proc. Am. Acad. Arts and Sci.*, vol. XXXIV (1899); G. P. Merrill, *The First One Hundred Years of Am. Geology* (1924); bibliog. in *Bull. U. S. Nat. Museum,* no. 30

(1885); Boston *Transcript*, Apr. 19, 1898; information from a former colleague.] H. L. C.

MARCY, HENRY ORLANDO (June 23, 1837–Jan. 1, 1924), surgeon and gynecologist, was born in Otis, Mass., the son of Smith and Fanny (Gibbs) Marcy. He was descended on both sides from Puritan stock and his paternal grandfather, Thomas Marcy, was one of the first settlers of northern Ohio. Smith Marcy was a school-teacher and a veteran of the War of 1812. After attending Wilbraham Academy and Amherst College, Henry O. Marcy was graduated by the Harvard Medical School with the class of 1864. The year before his graduation, however, he entered the Massachusetts militia as a surgeon and served in various campaigns of the Civil War, especially at the siege of Charleston. In the last year of the war he was appointed medical director of Florida. His work was characterized by common sense, for he did much to prevent dysentery among the troops by supplying them with fresh and well-cooked food, and at Charleston his house-to-house cleaning, with a force of five hundred men, made a sanitary city out of one that was pest-ridden. Following the war, he returned to Boston, where he practised for a short time, being greatly influenced by Horatio R. Storer [*q.v.*], a pioneer surgeon in diseases of women. Feeling that his education was incomplete, Marcy spent two years in Europe studying pathology and surgery; in 1869 he was with Virchow, the pathologist, in Berlin; and the next year with the surgeons Paget and Spencer Wells, in London. Later he went to Edinburgh, where he became the first American pupil of Joseph Lister, the founder of antiseptic surgery.

On returning to Boston, he attempted to interest Henry J. Bigelow [*q.v.*] in Lister's methods, but, according to Marcy, Bigelow "declared that it was only another fad, unworthy of consideration" (*Transactions of the Southern Surgical Association* for 1920, p. 32). The younger man could make no headway against the powerful Bigelow, and accordingly retired to Cambridge, Mass., where in 1880 he established a private hospital for diseases of women. Through the use of the Lister methods and many innovations devised by himself, he attained considerable success in abdominal operations. He began to use catgut and other animal sutures, especially of the absorbable type which could be left in the wound, and was a pioneer in the use of antiseptic solutions and the disinfection of the surgeon's hands before operation, as well as in the use of rubber gloves. All these new methods were tested out carefully in Marcy's private hospital. Furthermore, he and his assistants were among the earliest bacteriologists in America.

Marcy was an ardent advocate of the American Medical Association, and year after year, over a long period of time, presented the results of his work before that body. Partly through his persistent efforts, Listerism was accepted in the United States and he should, undoubtedly, receive the credit for introducing the method of antiseptic wound treatment into America. His most important original contribution to American surgery, however, was the development of animal sutures. His publications include a long list of papers covering various aspects of surgery, especially the treatment of hernia, and a few on the history of surgery in America. Notable titles are: *The Radical Cure of Hernia by the Antiseptic Use of Carbolized Catgut Ligature* (1879); *The Best Methods of Treating Operative Wounds* (1882); *Recent Advances in Abdominal Surgery* (1887); *A Treatise on Hernia* (1889); and *The Scientific Rationale of Modern Wound Treatment* (1891). Historical papers that throw light on his own career include: "The Early History of Abdominal Surgery in America" (*Journal of the American Medical Association,* Feb. 19, 1910); "The Surgical Service of the Civil War Then and Now—the Progress of Fifty Years" (*Transactions of the Southern Surgical and Gynecological Association* for 1914, p. 138); and "The Semicentennial of the Introduction of Antiseptic Surgery in America" (*Ibid.* for 1920, p. 25). Never popular with his brother physicians in Boston, he held no hospital or teaching position of importance, but received a number of other honors, including the presidency of the American Medical Association in 1891.

Marcy was married to Sarah E. Wendell of Great Falls, N. H., in 1863. His only son became a physician and was associated for many years with his father. Marcy did much to develop Cambridge and was instrumental in building the Harvard Bridge, the Charles River Basin, with its Esplanade, and the Massachusetts Institute of Technology, of whose site he was chief owner.

[*Jour. Am. Medic. Editors' Asso.*, June 1925; *Am. Doctor,* May 1891; T. F. Harrington, *The Harvard Medic. School, A Hist.* (1905), III, 1513; *Jour. Am. Medic. Asso.*, Jan. 19, 1924; Boston *Transcript,* Jan. 2, 1924.] H. R. V.

MARCY, RANDOLPH BARNES (Apr. 9, 1812–Nov. 22, 1887), soldier, was born at Greenwich, Mass., the eldest son of Laban and Fanny (Howe) Marcy. He was descended from John Marcy, an Irish emigrant who was in Roxbury, Mass., as early as 1685 and died in Woodstock, Conn., in 1724. Marcy graduated at the Military Academy in 1832, as brevet second lieutenant in the 5th Infantry; reached the substantive rank of second lieutenant in 1835, first lieutenant in 1837, and captain in 1846. His service for some thirteen years was entirely on the Michigan and Wisconsin frontier, except for two short periods on recruiting duty in the East. In 1845 he went to Texas, and served there during the military occupation and in the battles of Palo Alto and Resaca de la Palma. He then went on recruiting duty again, but returned to Texas in 1847.

For the next twelve years he remained in the Southwest, much of the time in the field. In 1849 he escorted emigrants from Fort Smith to Santa Fé, reconnoitering and opening a new trail. In 1851 he commanded the escort of General Belknap, who traveled extensively in that region selecting sites for military posts. In 1852 he led an exploring expedition to the headwaters of the Red and Canadian rivers, and in 1854 he surveyed Indian reservations in northern and western Texas. His reports of the explorations of 1849, 1852, and 1854, were published as *Senate Executive Document No. 64* (31 Cong., 1 Sess.), *No. 54* (32 Cong., 2 Sess,), and *No. 60* (34 Cong., 1 Sess.). For a short time in 1857 he was engaged in the campaign against the Seminole Indians in Florida, but returned to the West in time to accompany Col. Albert Sidney Johnston's expedition against the Mormons in Utah. This expedition had to winter at Fort Bridger, under conditions of great hardship, its trains having been seriously crippled by Mormon raiders. Marcy, with a hundred men, made a winter march of nearly a thousand miles through trackless country and over the Rocky Mountains, to the military posts in New Mexico, to obtain animals and supplies; he reached Fort Bridger again in June 1858. Until this time his service had been entirely with his regiment. He was now detailed as acting inspector-general of the Department of Utah. After a few months on this duty he was ordered to New York to prepare a semi-official guidebook, called *The Prairie Traveler,* which was published in 1859 by authority of the War Department. It was an excellent compendium of practical hints for travelers, and included a remarkable collection of detailed road notes covering thirty-four important overland trails.

In August 1859 he was appointed major and paymaster, and served in the northwest until May 1861, when he became chief of staff of his son-in-law, Gen. George B. McClellan [*q.v.*]. In this capacity he served through the Peninsular and Antietam campaigns, holding the rank of colonel and inspector-general from Aug. 9, 1861, and the temporary rank of brigadier-general from Sept. 23, 1861, to Mar. 4, 1863. At the close of the war he received brevet commissions as brigadier- and major-general. From 1863 to 1878 he served as inspector in various departments and on Dec. 12, 1878, was appointed inspector-general of the army, with the rank of brigadier-general. He served in this capacity until his retirement from active service, Jan. 2, 1881. From his retirement to his death he resided at West Orange, N. J.

He was married in 1833 to Mary A. Mann, daughter of Gen. Jonas Mann of Syracuse, N. Y. She died in 1878. They had three children—a son who died in infancy; Mary Ellen, who married Gen. George B. McClellan; and Frances, who married Edward Clarke. Marcy was tall, broad-shouldered, and soldierly in bearing. He was essentially an out-of-doors man, and continued to make big-game hunting trips even after his retirement. At the same time he had some facility in writing and published two volumes of recollections of frontier service: *Thirty Years of Army Life on the Border* (1866), and *Border Reminiscences* (1872), besides the guidebook mentioned above.

[G. W. Cullum, *Biog. Reg. Officers and Grads. U. S. Mil. Acad.* (3rd ed., 1891); L. R. Hamersly, *Records of Living Officers of the U. S. Army* (1884); *Army and Navy Jour.*, Nov. 26, 1887; *N. Y. Times*, Nov. 23, 1887; *New-Eng. Hist. and Geneal. Reg.*, July 1875; *War of the Rebellion: Official Records (Army)*; Marcy's own books; personal and family notes furnished by Hon. George B. McClellan, his grandson.]

O. L. S., Jr.

MARCY, WILLIAM LEARNED (Dec. 12, 1786–July 4, 1857), lawyer and statesman, son of Jedediah and Ruth (Learned) Marcy, was born in Sturbridge (now Southbridge), Mass. He was descended on his father's side from John Marcy, whose name occurs under date of 1685 in the records of John Eliot's church at Roxbury, and on his mother's side from William Learned, who came to Massachusetts probably on one of the vessels of the Winthrop fleet in 1630 and joined the First Church at Charlestown in 1632. The boy's early education was obtained in the village school, in the academy at Leicester then under the preceptorship of Ebenezer Adams [*q.v.*], and—with an interval of teaching at Union, Conn.—at Woodstock Academy. In September 1805, he entered Brown University as a sophomore. Aiding himself during the winter of 1805–06 by conducting a private school in Newport, R. I., with his friend, Eleazer Trevett (*Newport Mercury,* Nov. 16, 1805, Mar. 29, 1806), he was graduated in September 1808, with a place on the Commencement program. After graduation he left Sturbridge, intending to seek his fortune in western New York, but stopped on the way at Troy, and remained there for the next fifteen years.

Quickly identifying himself with local interests, he won friends and the respect of his fellow townsmen. He read law and was admitted to the bar within three years. On Sept. 27, 1812, he married Dolly Newell of Sturbridge, Mass., who died in 1821, having borne him three children. He wrote for the *Northern Budget*, revealing a facility which served later to invigorate the columns of the *Albany Argus*, organ of the "Albany Regency." Interested while at Leicester Academy in Thomas Jefferson, he had developed since then convictions which led him into the Jeffersonian party. His *Oration on the Three Hundred and Eighteenth Anniversary of the Discovery of America*, delivered before the Tammany Society in 1809 and published that year—the first of his literary efforts to be printed—was a defense of the doctrines and policy of President Jefferson, and in view of the bitter attack upon Jefferson made by Stephen C. Carpenter (*Memoirs of the Hon. Thomas Jefferson*, 2 vols., 1809) was especially timely. As a member of the 155th Regiment, Marcy passed from the grade of ensign (May 20, 1812) by successive promotions to that of adjutant-general of the state (Feb. 12, 1821), and thereafter was often addressed as "General" Marcy. During the War of 1812 he took part as a minor officer in the capture of an Indian village at the mouth of the St. Regis River (Oct. 22–23, 1812), and in an engagement (Nov. 19–20) near Lacolle, in the province of Quebec. Afterward, for a time, he resumed his law practice, but returned to the army late in 1814. In April 1816 he was appointed first recorder of the newly organized city of Troy and for two periods (1816–18 and 1821–23) he served as a sort of vice-mayor with sundry judicial duties to perform. For five years (1818–23) he was associated with Jacob L. Lane in the firm of Marcy & Lane.

About 1818, deprived of his position as recorder through the machinations of Gov. De Witt Clinton, Marcy had won the friendly interest of Martin Van Buren, with whom he prepared a pamphlet, *Considerations in Favor of the Appointment of Rufus King to the Senate of the United States* (1819), which aided in securing King's return to the Senate in 1820. In 1821 Van Buren went to Washington as King's colleague, and Marcy was restored to the recordership of Troy. The political group which they had helped to organize came to include such local leaders as Benjamin F. Butler, Azariah C. Flagg, and Edwin Croswell [*qq.v.*], and later, Silas Wright, Jr., John A. Dix, Horatio Seymour, and Samuel J. Tilden. First popularly dubbed the "Holy Alliance," the combination was known for many years as the "Albany Regency." Democratic to the core, it influenced and directed state and federal appointments and as a powerful political machine became famous throughout the country. In 1823 Marcy accepted the state comptrollership of New York and moved from Troy to Albany, which was his home for the rest of his life. Here, about 1825, he married Cornelia, daughter of Benjamin Knower, one of his political associates. Three children were born to them.

In the capacity of comptroller (1823–29), aware that public indebtedness was increasing under the spell of a popular movement favoring canals and roads, Marcy exercised discerningly his power of restraint over the legislature. Late in 1827 (*Memoirs of John Quincy Adams*, VII, 1875, pp. 388, 404) he was considered for the governorship; early in 1829 Governor Van Buren appointed him associate justice of the state supreme court. For the court he delivered about 175 opinions (2–6 *Wendell's Reports, passim*). In several cases involving phases of the conspiracy in western New York to abduct William Morgan for his alleged revelations of the secrets of the Masonic order, Marcy displayed erudition and a high sense of justice. His task called for courage and clear thinking, for the popular furor aroused by Morgan's disappearance was so great as to result in the formation of a national Anti-Masonic party.

Resigning from the bench in 1831, he accepted reluctantly an election to the United States Senate. There he remained for a single long session (Dec. 5, 1831–July 17, 1832) and a month (December 1832) of the short session, serving on the finance committee and as chairman of the judiciary committee. On such subjects as the tariff and the bank he spoke briefly. His best effort was made in behalf of Van Buren, then minister in London on a recess commission. Twice (Jan. 17 and 25, 1832) Vice-President Calhoun, embittered toward President Jackson and jealous of Van Buren, used his casting vote in an evenly divided Senate to force the rejection of Van Buren's appointment (*Register of Debates*, 22 Cong., 1 Sess., 1309 ff.). Defending Van Buren against reflections on his alleged introduction into national affairs of the system of rewards and punishments ascribed to the "Albany Regency," Marcy declared that he could see "nothing wrong in the rule that to the victor belong the spoils of the enemy" (*Ibid.,* col. 1325), an expression that caught the attention of the public and gave the phrase "spoils system" to the language. In debate, however, Marcy made little impression against such experienced speakers as Clay, Webster, Benton, and Hayne. On Sept. 19, 1832, he was nominated for governor. Carrying the election, he resigned from the Senate in January 1833.

As governor for three terms (1833–38) Marcy left his mark upon the state. Aided by a gifted young secretary of state, John A. Dix [*q.v.*], he organized the first geological survey of New York's fifty-six counties. In the course of the survey the highest peak in the Adirondacks was given the name Mount Marcy in honor of the governor. He refused assent to the constitutional gloss by which in 1835 Governor Gayle of Alabama made requisition for Robert G. Williams, publishing agent of the American Anti-Slavery Society in New York, under an act of Congress concerning "fugitives from justice"—early evidence of his interest in extradition which later assumed international proportions. He reprobated activities of the Abolitionists (1836) as likely to destroy the Union, and even suggested that states might find it necessary to take action by penal laws against activities tending to promote insurrection in another state—sentiments which strengthened the hopes of Southerners in 1853 that as secretary of state he would uphold state's rights against federal interference with slavery. Under his régime the New York-New Jersey boundary dispute was settled.

From 1840 to 1842, as a member of the Mexican Claims Commission by appointment of President Van Buren, he exhibited skill at conciliation, and, with his colleagues, secured for the American claimants awards totaling nearly $2,400,000, leaving only a few cases unsolved (J. B. Moore, *History and Digest of the International Arbitrations to which the United States has been a Party,* 1898, II, 1209–44). In Washington he met the prominent leaders of the time; he attended public receptions, played whist (his favorite game) with Clay, and dined occasionally with Presidents Van Buren and Tyler at "the Palace." The Marcy Papers (*post,* V–IX, *passim*) show clearly that after 1840 he had set his mind on a high federal post. Early in 1844 Tyler considered him for the United States Supreme Court, and he received a few votes for the vice-presidency in the Baltimore convention of 1844 which selected Polk and Dallas. In November of that year, in a mood of watchful waiting, he declined Governor Bouck's offer of appointment to fill the unexpired term of Senator N. P. Tallmadge, resigned, because he wanted a place, preferably the Treasury, in Polk's cabinet. He accepted the secretaryship of war (*American Historical Review,* October 1924, pp. 76–83). With this position neither Van Buren nor the "Regency" (already losing power) had anything to do; it came to Marcy on his own merits. His acceptance of it marked a breach between him and the "Barnburner" faction of his party, with which Van Buren was now associated.

The war with Mexico involved Marcy in heavy duties. He was subjected to harsh criticism, especially from Gen. Winfield Scott in the field. An exchange of letters between Scott and the Secretary was given wide publicity ("Mexican War Correspondence," *House Executive Document No. 60,* 30 Cong., 1 Sess., pp. 1218–51). There were errors of judgment on both sides, and insubordination on the part of Scott, but when Marcy left the cabinet, he had added to his record of administrative competence. Among those near him able to appreciate his tasks, he had acquired rather than lost prestige. A friendship begun in the thirties between him and George Bancroft [*q.v.*], secretary of the navy, was firmly knit and lasted for the rest of Marcy's life. With Buchanan he kept up an intermittent correspondence—both men watchful of public opinion and eager alike for the presidency. To both, the results of the Baltimore convention of 1852 were disappointing. Neither could be ignored by President Pierce: he sent Buchanan as minister to England and made Marcy his secretary of state (*American Secretaries of State, post,* VI, 161–68, 177–79).

During the next four years Marcy was chiefly responsible for the negotiation of twenty-four treaties, the largest number ratified within an administration up to that time. Four are significant: the Gadsden Treaty with Mexico (Dec. 30, 1853) which added nearly 30,000 square miles to United States territory; the Reciprocity Treaty with Great Britain (June 5, 1854), relating to trade and the fisheries in Canada and the Maritime Provinces; a treaty with the Netherlands (Jan. 22, 1855) which first opened ports in the Dutch colonial possessions to American consuls; and the treaty with Denmark (Apr. 11, 1857) which, though ratified under Buchanan, was a result of Marcy's effort to abolish forever the Danish Sound dues. Eleven extradition treaties led the list numerically. Other treaties were made with the Argentine Confederation, Peru, Russia, Siam, and Persia. With treaties opening Japan (Mar. 31, 1854) and the Lew Choo Islands (July 11), the Pierce administration had nothing to do beyond ratification, since

Commodore Perry had sailed under instructions formulated in November 1852 by President Fillmore's acting secretary of state, but Marcy in 1855 sent to Japan Townsend Harris [*q.v.*], who laid the basis for notable accomplishments in the Far East.

Three cases involving the handling of delicate problems in international relations were settled during Marcy's term: the Koszta case with Austria (September 1853), the *Black Warrior* case with Spain (May 1855), and the Patrice Dillon case with France (August 1855). The "Dress Circular," containing instructions to United States agents abroad regarding dress to be worn on formal occasions, was issued in June 1856, and constitutes the substance of present-day usage as defined by statute Mar. 27, 1867. Marcy's two notes in explanation of the United States' refusal to join in the Declaration of Paris (Apr. 16, 1856) have become famous (Sir Francis Piggott, *The Declaration of Paris, 1856,* 1919, pp. 264–66, 393–404). Toward bringing Central American issues to a head Marcy made little progress, though he would have done so had the British government accepted the Dallas-Clarendon convention (Oct. 17, 1856) which was approved by both President Pierce and the Senate. A matter which created widespread sensation was the publication (March 1855) of the "Ostend Manifesto," a report made to the State Department on Oct. 18, 1854, recommending that the United States acquire Cuba by purchase or, that failing, by force. The document was chiefly composed by Buchanan, aided by Pierre Soulé and John Y. Mason [*qq.v.*], the American ministers to England, Spain, and France. For authorizing these men to advise him in regard to arranging differences of opinion with the Madrid authorities over Cuban relations hinging upon the *Black Warrior* affair, Marcy and the cabinet were at fault. Had Marcy not maintained a neutral attitude toward the rapidly developing issue over slavery, he might have avoided the error of putting trust in Soulé, an unsuitable appointee from Louisiana, who was bent on acquiring Cuba for Southern interests. The "Manifesto" came near to wrecking the solution of the *Black Warrior* case, which was, however, eventually settled to the satisfaction of the United States. Another sensational episode which was shrewdly if somewhat tardily handled (July 1856), was the dismissal of the British minister and three British consuls as the result of a controversy with Great Britain over attempts within the borders of the United States to enlist recruits for the Crimean War.

With the close of the Pierce administration (March 1857), Marcy's public life came to an end and on July 4 following he died, at Ballston, N. Y. He was buried in the Rural Cemetery five miles north of the city of Albany. At the time of his death he was reckoned "among the foremost men of the country" (Moore, *post,* 395), and he stands high on the list of American secretaries of state.

[Marcy Papers (1806–57), 76 vols., in MSS. Div., Lib. of Cong.; Instructions and Despatches (MSS.), 1853–57, Dept. of State; *State of N. Y.; Messages from the Govs.* (1909), vol. III; "Diary and Memoranda of Wm. L. Marcy," *Am. Hist. Rev.*, Apr.–July 1919; H. B. Learned, "The Sequence of Appointments to Polk's Original Cabinet," *Ibid.*, Oct. 1924; W. G. Rice, "The Appointment of Gov. Marcy as Sec. of State," *Mag. of Hist.*, Feb., Mar. 1912, Jan. 1913; J. B. Moore, "A Great Secretary of State: William L. Marcy," *Pol. Sci. Quart.*, Sept. 1915; Mrs. Calvin D. Paige, "The Marcy Family," *Quinabaug Hist. Soc. Leaflets,* no. 11 (n.d.), read 1902; H. B. Learned, in S. F. Bemis, *The Am. Secretaries of State and Their Diplomacy,* VI (1928), 145–294, 420–31, with portrait and bibliography; R. F. Nichols, *The Democratic Machine: 1850–1854* (1923); D. S. Alexander, *A Political Hist. of the State of N. Y.*, vols. I, II (1906); J. B. Brebner, in *Canadian Hist. Rev.*, Dec. 1930; A. A. Ettinger, *The Mission to Spain of Pierre Soulé* (1932); *N. Y. Times,* July 6, 1857; information as to certain facts from Johannes C. Westermann of Hilversum, The Netherlands.]

H. B. L—d.

MARDEN, CHARLES CARROLL (Dec. 21, 1867–May 11, 1932), philologist, son of Jesse and Anna Maria (Brice) Marden, was descended from old Colonial stock, Marylanders on his mother's side and New Englanders on his father's. He was born in Baltimore, his paternal grandfather having in 1829 removed to that city from New Hampshire. Receiving in 1889 his bachelor's degree from the Johns Hopkins University, he taught a year in Virginia at the Norfolk Academy, for another year was instructor in French at the University of Michigan, and then pursued graduate study under A. Marshall Elliott [*q.v.*] at the Johns Hopkins, completing his course in 1894 with a doctoral thesis on the Spanish dialect of Mexico city. While North America had early acquired an honorable name in Spanish studies with the publication in 1849 of George Ticknor's remarkable *History of Spanish Literature,* successors to Ticknor had been lacking, and Elliott, eager to see the interrupted tradition renewed, welcomed his pupil's desire to concentrate upon the domain in which he had made an auspicious beginning, and retained him as instructor at his alma mater, where Marden's work won him successive promotions through the intermediate ranks to the first American university professorship in Spanish, to which he was named in 1905 and which he retained until 1917. He was elected in 1916 to the newly established Emery L. Ford Chair of Spanish at Princeton, but for a year divided his time between the two universities. He also had an important part in another active center of Spanish studies, the University of Chicago, where between 1909 and 1928 he conducted graduate courses during seven of the summer quarters.

Marden's initial interest in Latin-American Spanish was never lost, and his last study in that field was dated 1925; but he early centered his attention on the language and literature of medieval Spain, and few were the years unmarked by some contribution from him in this domain. His text of the *Poema de Fernan Gonçalez,* issued in 1904, was the first critical edition ever issued of a medieval Spanish literary work. It won international commendation, and was followed by his election in 1907 as a corresponding member of the Spanish Academy. An edition of the *Libro de Apolonio* (2 vols., 1917–22) confirmed his standing as an accurate and penetrating interpreter of the early literature. In 1925 he discovered in Madrid a portion of the manuscript of the works of the first known Castilian poet, Gonzalo de Berceo—a priceless treasure which he generously presented to the Spanish Academy. While he was preparing this text for publication, his conviction grew that a systematic search within a circumscribed territory might bring to light other portions of the manuscript. When, in February 1928, he next went to Spain, and as soon as he had acquitted himself of his commission as Carnegie visiting professor to Spanish universities, he thoroughly combed the province of Logroño, and there, just on the eve of his departure, he found and acquired in a remote mountain village thirty-two of the missing folios, which he joined with those already in the Academy's possession. Upon the completion of his edition of the two parts of this manuscript (*Cuatro Poemas de Berceo,* 1928, and *Veintitrés Milagros,* 1929), he began what promised to be the crowning work of his career, an edition of the *Libro de Alexandre,* interrupted before its completion by his unexpected death.

While Marden's published work was limited to the field of Spanish, his influence had a wider reach. Many of his students who later became leaders in kindred subjects bear testimony to the contagiousness of his enthusiasm for scholarship and to the profit they derived from the sound principles which he unceasingly inculcated. Similarly, when after the death of Elliott, founder of *Modern Language Notes,* Marden was for several years managing editor of that journal (January 1911–December 1915), his adherence to those same principles was a stimulus and an example to a wide circle of contributors and readers. To his unbroken activity in research and the training of scholars he joined a live interest in the instruction of beginners in language, for whom he regularly conducted courses, and in *A First Spanish Grammar* (1926), collaborating with F. C. Tarr, he placed at the service of others his own clear and accurate analysis and exposition. He was also during some years chief examiner in Spanish for the College Entrance Examination Board. In addition to his corresponding membership in the Spanish Academy, he was Knight Commander in the Order of Isabel la Católica, fellow of the Medieval Academy and of the Hispanic Society, and at the time of his death, president of the Modern Language Association.

Honesty, clear thinking, and the capacity for taking pains lay at the basis of all Marden's accomplishment. He scrupulously controlled his material and as scrupulously made accessible the data behind his arguments. In analyzing the work of others he applied the same standards, and the reviews he wrote form no small element of his contribution to scholarship. Tender in his human sympathies, rather than voice a dissenting judgment he often kept silent; but if the word came, he was outspoken. Praise from him was highly prized, and the sincerity of his less favorable criticisms was never questioned. He was not effusive in his casual contacts but in company of kindred spirits became expansive and even jovial. Particularly happy in his family life, he was at his best in his home, and it was there by preference that he greeted his friends and that he carried on the work that made of him the leading American hispanist. He was survived by his wife, Mary Talbott Clark, daughter of John L. and Mary Corinne Clark of Howard County, Md., whom he had married on Dec. 2, 1897, and by their four children.

[*Who's Who in America,* 1932–33; H. Seris, in *Gaceta Literaria* (Madrid), Mar. 15, 1928; E. A. Peers, in *Bull. of Spanish Studies* (Liverpool), Apr. 1929; *N. Y. Times,* May 12, 1932; *Times* (London), May 28, 1932; *Princeton Alumni Weekly,* June 2, 1932; *Pubs. Mod. Lang. Asso. of America,* Sept. 1932; *Romanic Rev.,* July–Sept. 1932; *Mod. Philology,* Nov. 1932; sketch by H. C. Lancaster, with bibliography by F. C. Tarr, in *Mod. Lang. Notes,* Dec. 1932; *Hispanic Rev.,* Jan. 1933; G. A. Hanson, *Old Kent* (1876), under "John Brice"; J. D. Warfield, *The Founders of Anne Arundel and Howard Counties, Md.* (1905), under "Marden" and "Dr. Chas. Carroll."]
E. C. A.

MARDEN, ORISON SWETT (1850–Mar. 10, 1924), journalist, writer, the son of Louis and Martha (Cilley) Marden, was born near Thornton, N. H. At seven he was an orphan. As a boy he read Samuel Smiles's *Self Help* and determined that his career should be one of service to mankind. After graduating from New

Hampton Institute, N. H., in 1873, he attended Boston University (B.A., 1877) and then studied medicine at Harvard (M.D., 1882). At the same time he was working his way by catering and by hotel management with such success that on leaving college he had a capital of nearly $20,000. He then made an extensive continental tour through Italy, Austria, Germany, France, and the British Isles. His business career began with the purchase and enlargement of a hotel on Block Island, off Newport, R. I., a resort which Marden did much to develop through effective advertising and judicious investment in real estate. Until 1892 he was very fortunate in his ventures. Retaining his holdings on Block Island, he bought controlling interests in four or five hotels in the Northwest. Attracted by the Nebraska boom of the early nineties, he moved west and made himself proprietor of the Palmer House, Grand Island, and the Midway Hotel in Kearney, where as resident manager he soon became a leading citizen. The soubriquet of "Lucky" Marden seemed justified. But in 1892 he suffered financial reverses and in 1893, heavily in debt, he left Kearney for Chicago where he worked during the Columbian Exposition as manager of the Park Gate Hotel. He then closed his affairs in the West and returned to Boston where he went doggedly about making a fresh start. He devoted his energy toward framing the message of optimism which for so long he had felt it his mission to spread: namely, that the will to succeed is the most vital single factor in success. In 1894 he published his gospel in *Pushing to the Front*. The book was received with enthusiasm and began a phenomenal run of 250 editions. He then decided to found a magazine to be devoted to the teaching of his credo. Louis Klopsch, a New York publisher, agreed to float the venture, and in October 1879 the first issue of *Success* appeared. By 1900 Marden was able to maintain a permanent editorial office in New York City and under his guidance the magazine grew with extraordinary swiftness until 1910, when a somewhat quixotic editorial policy began seriously to impair its credit. In 1912 the venture failed, and Marden was again in financial straits. In May 1905 he had married Clare L. Evans of Louisville, Ky., and had bought a farm at Glen Cove, L. I. With his old tenacity he began at once to plan for the day when a new *Success* should appear. In 1917, in spite of war conditions, he felt that the world would welcome the message he had to offer. He found a financial backer in Frederick C. Lowrey of Chicago and by January 1918 was publishing the new *Success*. When on Mar. 10, 1924, Marden died, his magazine was well on the way to the record circulation he had predicted for that year. Typical of his works are: *Rising in the World* (1896); *He Can Who Thinks He Can* (1908); *Ambition and Success* (1919); and *Masterful Personality* (1921). Thirty of his books were translated into German, and over three million of them, variously translated into twenty-five languages, have been sold.

[Margaret Connolly, *The Life Story of Orison Swett Marden* (1925); R. M. Bayles, *Hist. of Newport County, R. I.* (1888); *Who's Who in America*, 1922–23; *Success*, May 1924; *N. Y. Times*, Mar. 11, 12, 1924.]

E. M. H.

MARÉCHAL, AMBROSE (Aug. 28, 1764–Jan. 29, 1828), Roman Catholic prelate, was born near Orléans, France, of a good family. On graduation from college, he studied law in accordance with parental instructions, although his pronounced inclination was for the ministry. In 1787, as a student in the Sulpician Seminary at Orléans, he received the tonsure and joined the community. Transferred on the eve of the Revolution to the Sulpician Seminary at Bordeaux, he was privately ordained in 1792 and immediately sent to America in company with Abbés Matignon [*q.v.*], Richard [*q.v.*], and Cicquard. Arriving in Baltimore June 24, 1792, he said his first mass on July 8 and was assigned to the Maryland missions. Later he taught at Georgetown College and at St. Mary's Seminary, where his exacting course won the approbation of Bishop John Carroll [*q.v.*]. Recalled by his superior general, who was engaged in reorganizing the French seminaries, he returned to France in 1803 and taught in the theological schools of his community at Saint-Flour, Lyons, Aix, and Marseilles. In 1810, Bishop Concanen of New York, with the approval of Archbishop Carroll, proposed Maréchal as his coadjutor with the right of succession, but nothing came of this plan, presumably because of Sulpician disinclination for an episcopal appointment. When Napoleon withdrew the seminaries from Sulpician control however, Maréchal accepted a reappointment to St. Mary's Seminary, Baltimore (1812). Four years later he was nominated to the See of Philadelphia, but his name was withdrawn at his request. Soon Archbishop Neale [*q.v.*] required a coadjutor and sought Cheverus [*q.v.*], who asked to remain in Boston and urged the selection of Maréchal. Neale acquiesced, and Rome named the Abbé a titular bishop and coadjutor of Baltimore (July 24, 1817). Archbishop Neale died before the papal briefs arrived, however, and Maréchal was elevated to the archbishopric. Consecrated by Bishop Cheverus and Bishop Connolly of New York (Dec.

14, 1817), he zealously undertook the management of his vast diocese.

A mild but firm man, he conducted himself well though confronted with innumerable difficulties: controversies over trusteeism in Norfolk, Charleston, and Philadelphia; a bitter conflict with the Jesuits, over their old manorial estates, which could not be compromised during his rule; malicious suspicions of some Irish-born priests that he favored the French and was intent on establishing a French hierarchy; annoying, though futile, clerical appeals to civil authorities quite in conflict with canonical regularities; and wretched ecclesiastical intrigues intended to discredit him with the Propaganda. While the Archbishop may have been anti-Irish and somewhat anti-Jesuit, he was thoroughly American in sympathy, as men like Jefferson and Carroll readily appreciated. Despite the insistence of Bishop England of Charleston [*q.v.*], a leader of the Irish element, he refused to summon a national synod, apparently feeling that such a move might aggravate rather than settle the racial afflictions of the Church. Assiduous in visiting the diocese, he gained the warm regard of his people, and with the aid of Rev. Enoch Fenwick, he was able to collect sufficient funds for the completion of the Cathedral (1821), then the finest church in the United States, with a great organ and paintings donated by Louis XVIII and French prelates. Soon after his return from an ecclesiastical mission to Canada in 1826, realizing that an incipient disease would soon end his working days, he applied for a coadjutor. Death came before the appointment of his vicar general, James Whitfield, was actually made. Though regarded as a man of superior talents and broad intellectual acquirements, Maréchal left no writings save some remarkable pastoral letters, and a few unpublished manuscripts, a fact explained by his own words to Bishop England in reply to a request for material for the *Catholic Miscellany:* "Such unfortunately have been the austere rules of criticism printed on my institutions in literature . . . that they actually are a torment to myself on a thousand occasions" (Guilday, *John England,* I, 468). It was as a teacher and as an administrator in trying times that he merited contemporary renown.

[R. H. Clarke, *Lives of the Deceased Bishops of the Cath. Ch. in the U. S.,* vol. I (1872); Peter Guilday, *The Life and Times of John Carroll* (1922), *The Life and Times of John England* (1927); J. G. Shea, *A Hist. of the Cath. Ch. in the U. S.,* vols. II, III (1888, 1890); Thos. Hughes, *Hist. of the Society of Jesus in North America* (1910); C. G. Herbermann, *The Sulpicians in the U. S.* (copr. 1916); *Am. Cath. Hist. Researches* (1884–1912), see index volumes and sketch in vol. XXVI (1909); M. J. Riordan, *Cathedral Records* (Baltimore, 1906); *Cath. Mag.,* Jan. 1845; *U. S. Cath. Almanac,* 1836; *Cath. Miscellany,* Feb. 16, 1828; "Diary of Archbishop Maréchal," in *Records Am. Cath. Hist. Soc.,* Dec. 1900.]

R. J. P.

MAREST, PIERRE GABRIEL (Oct. 14, 1662–Sept. 15, 1714), pioneer priest in Illinois, was a native of Laval, where he was baptized in the old Gothic cathedral, seat of the bishop's see. The family was a religious one and two sons entered the Jesuit order, Gabriel and Joseph, both to become missionaries in Canada. Gabriel entered his novitiate Oct. 1, 1681, at Paris, studied there and at Bourges, was instructor at Vannes, and in 1694, then thirty-two years old, was ordered to New France. When he arrived at Quebec, Iberville [*q.v.*] was just setting out on a buccaneering expedition to Hudson Bay and Marest was detailed as chaplain for the expedition, because, as he wrote, he knew no Indian language and could be better employed ministering to Canadians than to aborigines.

Marest has given a thrilling account of his experiences in Hudson Bay, of the cold and storms, of the attack on the English fort and its surrender, of the Indians who visited the post, of the death in his arms of the commander's young brother Chateauguay, and of the final departure of Iberville's fleet in September 1695, leaving Marest to minister to the men of the French garrison (*Jesuit Relations, post,* LXVI, 67–119). Not long after the vessels had gone, an English fleet swooped down on the post and carried the captured garrison off to England. There Marest experienced prison fare, but was shortly permitted to return to France, whence at the earliest opportunity he again set sail for Canada.

In 1698 he embarked on another long journey, this time to the interior of America, where Father Jacques Gravier [*q.v.*] needed reinforcement in the Illinois mission. Marest ministered to the Kaskaskia branch of the Illinois tribe, at first located on the upper Illinois River near the present Ottawa. In 1700 the Kaskaskia determined to remove to the Mississippi, having heard that a French colony had been founded near the mouth of that great river. Marest, learning that his old leader Iberville was the founder of the colony, did not discourage his neophytes' removal. They spent the first years on the west side of the stream at the Rivière des Pères, now a part of the city of St. Louis, then, in April 1703, they crossed to the east side and formed a village on a river called for them the Kaskaskia. At this mission Marest passed the remainder of his life, except for a journey to Mackinac to consult with his Jesuit brother Joseph, whom he opportunely met en route at the

St. Joseph mission. On his return he promised the Peoria to continue their mission; but his Kaskaskia converts and his colleagues would not consent to his removal. His mission was one of the most successful in North America; in 1707 he estimated that all the Kaskaskia, numbering over two thousand, were Christians. He is said to have been an accomplished Indian linguist, but none of his manuscripts has survived. His letters are well composed, artless, and sincere. He was buried in the chapel of his mission of the Immaculate Conception; but on Dec. 18, 1727, his remains were removed to the new church just finished at Kaskaskia.

[R. G. Thwaites, ed., *The Jesuit Relations and Allied Documents*, vols. LXIV, LXV, LXVI (1900), LXXI (1901); G. J. Garraghan, "Earliest Settlements of the Illinois Country," in *Cath. Hist. Rev.*, Jan. 1930; T. J. Campbell, *Pioneer Priests of North America*, vol. III (1911).] L. P. K.

MARETZEK, MAX (June 28, 1821–May 14, 1897), opera impresario, conductor, composer, was born in Brünn, Moravia. He studied music and composition in his youth with the Viennese composer, I. X. Seyfried, a piano pupil of Mozart and conductor at the An der Wien theatre. When he was twenty-one his three-act opera *Hamlet* was produced in Brünn. In the year following he gave up a theatrical conductorship in Agram, then the capital of Croatia, to go to Paris, where he dedicated a series of songs to the Duchess de Nemours and wrote ballet music for Grisi and Grahn. In 1844 he went to Her Majesty's Theatre in London as assistant conductor to Balfe, and in 1847 his ballet "Les Génies du Globe" opened the season at Drury Lane in conjunction with *Lucia di Lammermoor*. In 1848 he emigrated to New York as the conductor of the Italian Opera Company at the Astor Place Opera House, then under the management of Edward R. Fry. When the company failed in 1849, Maretzek reopened the same house as impresario-conductor. Thereafter, until 1879, he was active as an impresario and producer of Italian opera at the Astor Place and Grand opera houses and, notably, at the old Academy of Music, making occasional tours with his company through the United States and beyond. He opened the new Academy of Music in 1867 with Minnie Hauk in Gounod's *Romeo et Juliette*. In 1879 his three-act American opera, *Sleepy Hollow*, was given there.

Maretzek was the only impresario who, after others had failed, managed to establish Italian opera in New York as a permanent institution for a term of years. As he himself says (*Crotchets and Quavers*, p. iv): "During the first three years of my residence in New York, I carried out four regular seasons of Italian opera. This alone was more than anyone had done in this quarter of the world, since Christopher Columbus first discovered it." The first impresario in this country who conducted his own operatic performances, he gave grand opera at prices ranging from fifty cents to two dollars, and his career was marked by the production of many novelties and the introduction to the American public of many notable singers.

Maretzek, "the Magnificent." as he was familiarly known, retired from his managerial activities with the advent of James Henry Mapleson and devoted himself to teaching singing, coaching operatic aspirants, and contributing musical sketches to American, French, and German periodicals. A "golden jubilee concert" given in his honor at the Metropolitan Opera House (Feb. 12, 1889) testified to the esteem in which he was held by his associates. He died of heart disease at his home in Pleasant Plains, Staten Island, N. Y., in his seventy-sixth year. His two books of autobiographic reminiscences, *Crotchets and Quavers: or, Revelations of an Opera Manager in America* (1855), and *"Sharps and Flats": A Sequel to "Crotchets and Quavers"* (1890), a "serio-comic history of opera in America for the past forty years, with reminiscences and anecdotes," offer vivid pictures of operatic life in New York during the fifties, sixties, and seventies of the nineteenth century, and of the adventurous side of touring with an opera company in Cuba and Mexico in those days.

[Waldemar Rieck, "Max Maretzek, Impresario, Conductor and Composer," *Musical Courier*, June 22, 1922; Robt. Grau, article in the *Musical Leader*, Dec. 26, 1912; Clara Louise Kellogg, *Memoirs of an Am. Prima Donna* (1913); H. E. Krehbiel, *Chapters of Opera* (1908); *Music*, Sept. 1897; G. C. D. Odell, *Annals of the N. Y. Stage*, vols. V and VI (1931); *N. Y. Times*, May 15, 1897.] F. H. M.

MARGOLIS, MAX LEOPOLD (Oct. 15, 1866–Apr. 2, 1932), scholar, teacher, author, the son of Isaac and Hinde Bernstein Margolis, was born in Merech, Vilna, Russia. His father was a Rabbi and a descendant of the great Hebrew scholar, Lipmann Halevi Heller. Margolis was educated at Merech and Warsaw, 1873–83; graduated from the Leibnitz Gymnasium, Berlin, in 1889, in which year he came to America and entered Columbia University. He received the degrees of M.A. in 1890 and Ph.D. in 1891, and spent another year at Columbia in further postgraduate studies. He was essentially a philologian and devoted himself to the whole cycle of the Semitic languages. He also had a good knowledge of Latin and Greek. He began his teaching in 1892 at the Hebrew Union College,

Cincinnati, Ohio, where he was assistant professor of Hebrew and Biblical exegesis until 1897. He then was called to the University of California, where he was assistant professor of Semitic languages and literature from 1897 to 1898 and associate professor from 1898 to 1905. He returned to the Hebrew Union College, holding the professorship of Biblical exegesis from 1905 to 1907, and in 1909 was called to the chair of Biblical philology at the Dropsie College for Hebrew and Cognate Learning, retaining that position until his death. In 1924–25 he held the post of annual professor at the American School for Oriental Research in Jerusalem and also lectured at the Hebrew University in Jerusalem that year. In the various institutions in which he gave instruction, he was known as an exact and inspiring teacher and has left many devoted disciples in various parts of the world.

In 1908 Margolis was invited to become the secretary of a board of editors engaged in a Jewish translation into the English language of the Holy Scriptures and had added to this secretaryship the post of editor-in-chief. He labored with his colleagues from 1908 to 1914 and the translation was published in 1917. He was one of the editors of the *Journal of the American Oriental Society* from 1922 to 1932 and an editor of the *Journal of Biblical Literature* from 1914 to 1921. He began his production of scientific publications with two works, published in the early nineties, having to do with the study of the Talmud. Then he principally devoted himself to grammatical work in pure Hebrew and later took up studies in the Greek Old Testament. Some of the most useful and best known of his many works were his *Manual of the Aramaic Language of the Babylonian Talmud* (1910), of great use to students; *A History of the Jewish People* (1927), written in collaboration with Alexander Marx, a remarkably accurate study; *The Holy Scriptures with Commentary: Micah* (1908); *The Story of Bible Translations* (1917); and *The Hebrew Scriptures in the Making* (1922). For a long period of years he had set his heart on the study of the Greek text of the Book of Joshua. Toward this end he published many preliminary papers and before his death there appeared the first part of *The Book of Joshua in Greek* (1931), of which the Second Part followed. This was a most laborious undertaking and was called by Professor James A. Montgomery "the monument to the scholarship of Margolis." Margolis was short, rather solidly built, possessed of few recreations, a man of wide reading. When he wished to change the current in his thought in later years, he read astronomy. He was one of the very foremost Biblical scholars of his period—as a grammarian, as a textual critic, and as an exegete—and a teacher of the very first rank. He was married on June 20, 1906, to Evelyn Kate Aronson, by whom he had three children.

[David J. Galter, "Max L. Margolis—Distinguished Am. Scholar and Author," the *Jewish Exponent*, Apr. 8, 1932; *Who's Who in America*, 1930–31; *Jour. Am. Oriental Soc.*, June 1932; unpublished addresses delivered at a memorial meeting for Max Leopold Margolis by James A. Montgomery, Simon Greenberg, and Cyrus Adler, May 9, 1932; Alexander Marx, "Max Leopold Margolis—In Memoriam," *Proc. of the Rabbinical Assembly of the Jewish Theol. Sem. of America*, vol. IV, pp. 368–79.]

C. A.

MARIGNY, BERNARD (Oct. 28, 1785–Feb. 3, 1868), Louisiana planter, official and social leader, was born in New Orleans and was christened Bernard Xavier Philippe de Marigny de Mandeville. He was the son of Pierre Enguerrand Philippe de Mandeville, Écuyer Sieur de Marigny, Chevalier de St. Louis, whose grandfather, François Philippe de Marigny, the scion of a noble Norman house, was ordered to Canada as an infantry officer in 1709 and was later transferred to Louisiana as *"commandant des troupes,"* where he assisted Bienville in the founding of New Orleans. Bernard's mother was Jeanne Marie d'Estréhan, the daughter of a rich planter, who married Pierre Marigny when he was an officer in the Spanish colonial army in Louisiana. As the value of lands and slaves increased they became the richest family in the colony. Partly owing to Bernard's antipathy to study, and partly to his father's theory that a thorough training in fire arms, fencing, and horsemanship was the most important part of a gentleman's education, the boy did not have more than a common-school knowledge of the three R's.

In 1798 Louis Philippe, Duc d'Orléans, and his two brothers came to New Orleans and were royally entertained by Bernard's father. To prove his hospitality further he lent them a large sum of money on their departure. Two years later Bernard's father died, leaving him an orphan at sixteen. The boy was so wild that his kinsman and guardian, De Lino de Chalmette, finally sent him to England. Here he continued his dissipations, spending much time at Almack's playing "Hazard," a dice game then the rage at the coffee houses. When he returned he taught it to his Creole companions, and the Americans dubbed it the game of the "Johnny Crapauds," their nickname for Creoles. Soon this was shortened to "Crapauds," and finally "craps." Marigny became more and more fantastically extravagant until he was forced to subdivide and dispose of his plantation below New Orleans.

and when he opened up a roadway and sold off the lots on it to pay some pressing gambling debts, he named it Craps Street. Near it was "Rue de l'Amour" on which it was said he housed his mistresses in separate cottages; quite logically Good Children Street came next.

In 1803 when Louisiana was retroceded to France by Spain and later transferred to the United States, Marigny was present at both these historic ceremonies as an aide to the French envoy Pierre de Laussat, and then was appointed aide to General Wilkinson. His political career began with his election to the territorial legislature in 1810, and from then on until 1838 he served continuously in either the upper or lower house of the legislature of his state, and was in addition a member of the convention of 1812 which drafted its first constitution, and of the second one in 1845 which modified it. In 1815 when General Pakenham and his English forces marched on New Orleans, Marigny was chairman of the committee of defense of the House of Representatives and indirectly persuaded Gen. Andrew Jackson to enlist Jean Lafitte and his pirates in the city's defense.

After Louis Philippe had been on the throne of France for some few years, Bernard de Marigny, who had squandered most of his fortune, crossed the ocean to collect the money his father had lent the monarch when as the Duc d'Orléans he visited New Orleans. Louis Philippe received him cordially, made him a guest at the palace, and even asked his advice about the recognition of Texas by France, but he was deaf to every suggestion of repayment, and all Marigny got was the gift of a gold snuff-box and the promise of a cadetship at St. Cyr for his son Mandeville. Bitterly disappointed he returned to New Orleans and in the late forties his friends had him appointed registrar of conveyances to keep him from starving. He lost this position through politics in 1853. In order to make money he wrote a small history entitled *Thoughts upon the Foreign Policy of the United-States* (1854) and the House of Representatives passed a bill purchasing a thousand copies each of the French and English editions.

This remarkable old Creole, who had *"tutoyied"* a king of France and who had lived through the conflicting influences of the five changes in the flag flying over Louisiana, stubbed his toe on the foot-scraper of his humble cottage and, in falling, struck his head. He never regained consciousness and died on Feb. 3, 1868. In addition to his little history Marigny's published works include a few political pamphlets and his *Réflexions sur la Campagne du Général André Jackson en Louisiane* (1848). On May 28, 1804, Marigny was married to Mary Ann Jones, who died after four years, leaving two sons. Within a year he married again—Anne Mathilde, daughter of a former Spanish intendant of Louisiana, Juan Ventura Morales. Two sons and three daughters were the children of this marriage.

[E. L. Tinker, *Les Écrits de Langue Française en Louisiane au XIXe Siècle* (1932); *Bernard Marigny to his Fellow Citizens* (1853); Alcée Fortier, ed., *Louisiana* (1914), vol. II; W. H. Sparks, *The Memories of Fifty Years* (1870); Grace King, *Creole Families of New Orleans* (1921); J. S. Whitaker, *Sketches of Life and Character in La.* (1847); J. W. Cruzat, "Biog. and Geneal. Notes Concerning the Family of Philippe de Mandeville, Écuyer Sieur de Marigny," *La. Hist. Soc. Pubs.*, vol. V (1911); *La. Hist. Quart.*, July 1931; *New Orleans American*, Aug. 29, 1915.]   E. L. T.

MARION, FRANCIS (*c.* 1732–Feb. 26, 1795), Revolutionary general, was born probably in St. John's Parish, Berkeley County, S. C. The date of his birth is indicated only by the fact that he died in his sixty-third year. He was the grandson of Benjamin Marion, a Huguenot and a native of Poitou, who came to the province about 1690, and the fifth and youngest son of Gabriel, who married Esther Cordes. Francis spent his youth near Georgetown, his parents' modest property providing him with a country-school education and a small inheritance. About 1755 he returned to St. John's and in 1773 acquired Pond Bluff on the Santee, four miles below Eutaw Springs, where he established himself as a planter. In 1759 and 1761 he served in campaigns against the Cherokees. He was elected to the Provincial Congress of 1775 from his parish, and when that body provided for two regiments of troops, was made a captain in the 2nd Regiment. After five years of service in and near Charleston he commanded this regiment in the assault on Savannah, October 1779. He was then a lieutenant-colonel in the Continental service. A badly injured ankle saved him from capture with the garrison of Charleston seven months later, for with others unfit for duty he was ordered to the country before the surrender. At Camden he again escaped disaster, since the day before the battle he had been detailed by Gates to cut the British communications with Charleston, and, evidently, to take command of the militia between the Santee and Pedee.

The destruction of Gates's army put upon the militia for the second time the entire burden of the war in South Carolina, and for five months Marion could draw upon only the resources of his own district. He was thus placed in a position of peculiar perils and possibilities. In the center of his territory was the strongly Whig population of Williamsburg. From this base, attacks could be made upon Georgetown, or upon the main line of British communications where the road from Camden to Charleston crossed the Santee. On the other hand, there were strong British posts on three sides, and the Loyalists of the Pedee region on the fourth. The militia at times drove him to despair, for with the state's authority in eclipse they came and went at will; sometimes he gathered several hundred for an attack, again his force melted away to a handful. His patience, tact, and military skill, however, enabled him to use these troops as he could not have used regular soldiers. If the odds were favorable the British faced a formidable foe, if the situation changed they pursued a shadow. His first exploit was the release of a party of American prisoners taken at Camden, and a week later he dispersed a force of two hundred Tories on the Pedee. Twice in the next four months he was forced to retire from his district, twice he failed in attacks on Georgetown, but he won three important field assignments, and Tarleton could do no more than drive him to the swamps.

His work in disrupting the British communications and preventing the organization of the Loyalists joined with the battle of King's Mountain and other developments in the Piedmont to bring about the turn of the war in the South. In January 1781 Greene appeared, but retreated immediately, drawing Cornwallis after him. Behind them the reviving Whigs and alarmed British fought with redoubled vigor. Marion now had somewhat larger forces, but only by a masterly series of movements and three hard-fought engagements did he survive a determined attempt to destroy him made by several British detachments. He was in sore need of the rescue which Lee brought when Greene returned to the state. The recovery of South Carolina now began, and as brigadier-general of the militia Marion was brought out of his district into larger and more aggressive movements. Despite his jealousy of authority he was generally prompt and faithful in his cooperation, and his part in two important raids and in the capture of several posts further enhanced his reputation. He commanded the militia in the battle of Eutaw Springs, and from that time to the evacuation of Charleston was Greene's chief dependence for outpost duty.

The last year of Marion's army service was interrupted by a term in the state Senate, to which he was elected in 1781 and again in 1782 and 1784. The war left him little but his land, and in March 1784 the legislature, in gratitude for his "eminent services," provided him with the command of Fort Johnson, one of the harbor defenses, at a salary of £500 a year. After his marriage in 1786 to his cousin, Mary Esther Videau, a wealthy and elderly spinster, his salary was reduced to five shillings a day, but he continued his dual rôle of planter and commandant until 1790. He sat in the state constitutional convention of 1790, and the next year was elected to the state Senate to fill an unexpired term. He died at his home in St. John's in February 1795, and was buried at Belle Isle, St. Stephen's. The personal as well as the soldierly qualities of the plain little man endeared him to his contemporaries. Through a process begun by his friend and most trusted officer, Col. Peter Horry, who in his age aspired to turn author, he became an epic figure, and as the "Swamp Fox" has a distinctive place in Revolutionary legend.

[Horry apparently wrote his life of Marion without access to the General's papers, which were afterwards given to him (*S. C. Hist. and Geneal. Mag.*, Apr. 1924, p. 97). This biography appears to be the manuscript which he turned over to Mason L. Weems [*q.v.*]. The result was the *Life of Gen. Francis Marion* (Phila., Mathew Carey, 1809). Horry seems never to have recovered his manuscript. A memoir of his own career and the Marion papers formed the basis of the *Sketch of the Life of Brig. Gen. Francis Marion* (Charleston, 1821) by W. D. James, and *The Life of Francis Marion* (N. Y., 1844) by William Gilmore Simms [*q.v.*]. Comparison of these, together with Horry's indignant letters to Weems (P. L. Ford, *Mason Locke Weems*, a bibliography, ed. by E. E. F. Skeel, 3 vols., 1929), his manuscript diary for the years 1812–13, and his marginal notes on the first edition, leads to the conclusion that the manuscript which Horry turned over to Weems was a memoir full of anecdotes and interspersed with letters; that Weems omitted the letters, garbled a number of statements of fact, introduced imaginary speeches, and dressed up Horry's style—the process, however, leaving the authorship distinctly Horry's. Sources include the Marion letters, published in R. W. Gibbes, *Doc. Hist. of the Am. Revolution . . . in 1781 and 1782* (1853) and . . . *1776–1782* (1857). *The State Records of N. C.*, vols. XIV (1896) and XV (1898); and the manuscript Journals of the Senate of S. C. *The Southern and Western Monthly Mag. and Rev.* (Charleston), Mar.–Aug. 1845, has the only reliable data on Marion's family and youth. See also *S. C. Hist. and Geneal. Mag., passim.* Horry's diary and the annotated copy of the first edition of the Weems-Horry *Marion* are in possession of the Guignard family, "Still Hopes," Columbia, S. C. The inscription on Marion's tomb gives the day of his death as Feb. 27, but the *City Gazette, or Daily Advertiser* (Charleston), of Tuesday, Mar. 3, 1795, says he died on "Tuesday last," *i.e.* Feb. 26.]

R. L. M—r.

MARKHAM, CHARLES HENRY (May 22, 1861–Nov. 24, 1930), railway president, was the son of Daniel Markham, farmer, and Mary (Reddan), of County Clare, Ireland. His parents emigrated to the United States, living first in Clarksville, Tenn., where Charles was born, and subsequently in Addison, N. Y., where he attended the public schools until he was fourteen years old. He then left school to earn his own way. Three years later he started west, and in 1881 began his first railway work as a section laborer on the Atchison, Topeka, & Santa Fé at Dodge City, Kan. This was the beginning of a career which he was to follow, with a single interruption, until his death.

Leaving the Santa Fé after a few months, he went to work for the Southern Pacific at Deming, N. Mex., as a station helper, shoveling coal for locomotives. He stayed at Deming for six years, finally becoming baggage master. For the next ten years he served as agent for the Southern Pacific successively at Lordsburg, N. Mex.; Benson, Ariz.; Reno, Nev.; and Fresno, Cal. At Fresno he was also in charge of the solicitation of freight and passenger traffic for a district, and worked out an effective carloading plan which attracted the attention of Julius Kruttschnitt, then general manager of the road, who gave him other efficiency problems to solve. In 1897 he was sent to the Willamette Valley of Oregon as general freight and passenger agent of the Oregon lines of the Southern Pacific, charged particularly with promoting agricultural development. In 1901 he was transferred to San Francisco as assistant freight traffic manager, and three months later was elected vice-president of the Houston & Texas Central Railroad at Houston, in which position he was executive head of the Harriman lines in Texas. Early in 1904 he returned to San Francisco to become general manager of the Southern Pacific Company, and three months later was elected vice-president and general manager.

The rapidity of this series of promotions would have satisfied most men, yet Markham, toward the end of 1904, temporarily left railroading to accept the position of vice-president of the J. M. Guffey Petroleum Company at Beaumont, Tex., because this position offered him better opportunities than the railway business for the moment could afford. The change was one of executive responsibility only, since he had no financial interest in any oil property. In 1910 he became president of the Gulf Refining Company, the Gulf Pipe Line Company, and other properties embraced in the Mellon oil interests in Texas, Oklahoma, and Louisiana. In January 1911 he returned to railroad work as president of the Illinois Central Railroad Company; in February of the same year he was also elected president of the Central of Georgia Railway Company and the Ocean Steamship Company of Savannah, both subsidiaries of the Illinois Central; and in April 1914, he became chairman of the boards of directors of the two subsidiary companies. These positions he held until May 1918. Meanwhile, after the entrance of the United States into the World War, he entered the service of the federal Railroad Administration, and acted as regional director of the railroads comprising the Southern Region, with headquarters at Atlanta, Ga., from Jan. 1, 1918, to June 1, 1918, and as regional director of the railroads comprising the Allegheny Region, with headquarters at Philadelphia, from June 1, 1918, to Oct. 1, 1919. On completion of his war service he resumed the presidency of the Illinois Central and the chairmanship of the boards of the Central of Georgia and the Ocean Steamship Company, continuing in active service until Sept. 15, 1926, when illness compelled him to resign his office of president, accepting the less onerous position of chairman of the board of the Illinois Central. He died four years later at his winter home, Altadena, Cal. On Feb. 18, 1884, he had married Anna Eliza Smith, a native of Syracuse, N. Y. His wife died on Sept. 18, 1921. There were three children, of whom only one son survived him.

While Markham never attained great wealth, yet his rapid advance from the position of baggage master on the Southern Pacific in 1887 to that of president of the Illinois Central Railroad in 1911 is sufficient evidence that he possessed unusual executive ability. His record as president, moreover, bore out the promise of his earlier years. Upon his own system his administration was distinguished by a vigorous program of expansion and improvement, as well as by a determined effort to build up the territory in which the Illinois Central operated. The most spectacular part of this program, and perhaps that most generally associated with Markham's name, was the beginning of the electrification and modernization of his company's Chicago terminal, including the construction of a great classification and transfer yard south of Chicago and the first steps in the development of the valuable air rights over Illinois Central property in downtown Chicago. Outside of his activity in improving facilities and service upon his own system Markham was very generally known as a leader in developing improved relations between the railroad industry and the public. He devoted much time and thought to this aspect of the railroad problem, and is credited with successful pioneering work in a field now generally recognized to be important.

[*Who's Who in America*, 1930–31; *The Biog. Dir. of the Railway Officials of America* (1913); *Poor's Manual of the Railroads of the U. S.*, 1901–24; *Railway Age*, Nov. 29, 1930; *Chicago Daily Tribune*, Nov. 25, 1930; correspondence with Markham's family and friends.]

S. D.

MARKHAM, WILLIAM (*c.* 1635–June 12, 1704 o.s.), colonial governor of Pennsylvania and Delaware, was born in England about 1635.

His father was probably William Markham of Ollerton, Nottinghamshire, and his mother was a sister of Admiral Sir William Penn. Since he is called Captain or Colonel Markham in the provincial records, it is believed that he was at one time an officer in the English army. He received a commission as deputy governor of Pennsylvania from his cousin, William Penn, on Apr. 10, 1681, with instructions to assert the proprietor's authority over existing settlements, appoint a council, organize a judicial system, commission sheriffs and justices of the peace, and settle the question of the boundary between Pennsylvania and Maryland. Arriving at Upland (now Chester) in July 1681, he presided over the first provincial council on Aug. 3, reorganized the court, and joined Nathaniel Allen and John Bezar in selecting the site for the city of Philadelphia. He also conferred with Lord Baltimore about the boundary and, on July 15, 1682, purchased from the Indians the site of Pennsbury Manor on the Delaware River. He became an ordinary member of the council when Penn arrived in the province in October 1682, but was almost immediately sent to England to represent the proprietor's interests in the boundary dispute.

He returned to Pennsylvania shortly after Penn's departure (1684) and served as provincial secretary from May 1685 to March 1691, deputy governor of the lower counties (Delaware) from March 1691 to April 1693, and lieutenant-governor or governor of both the province and the lower counties from April 1693 to December 1699. During the latter part of this period, he came into conflict with Edward Randolph, His Majesty's surveyor general of the customs, and with Robert Quary, the judge of the court of vice-admiralty. As a result of their complaints that he harbored pirates and did not enforce the acts of trade and navigation, the Privy Council ordered his removal from office (Aug. 31, 1699). The dispute was finally settled in December 1699, when Penn returned to the province and superseded Markham as chief executive. At Penn's request, Markham was appointed register general of Pennsylvania in 1703, but his title was disputed by John Moore [*q.v.*], the former incumbent, and before the case was decided he died, in Philadelphia. He was survived by his wife, Johannah Markham, and by a daughter.

During the greater part of Markham's career in Pennsylvania, he was Penn's secretary and attended to his private business. He was not as learned or as able a man as James Logan [*q.v.*], who succeeded him as the representative of proprietary interests, but he was devoted to Penn and he worked hard to advance the welfare of the colony. The value of his services was not fully appreciated by the colonists, partly because he represented the prerogative influence in the government and partly because he was a member of the Church of England and could not accommodate himself to the Quaker point of view. His most influential opponents were Thomas and David Lloyd [*qq.v.*], the leaders of the democratic or anti-proprietary party. He opposed the Lloyds in their controversy with deputy-governor Blackwell in 1689 and he also had a dispute with David Lloyd and the Assembly over the question of constitutional reform, which was complicated by a demand for an appropriation to defend the frontiers of New York against the French. A compromise was finally reached in 1696: Markham's "Frame of Government" was adopted (Nov. 7, 1696) and money was voted "for food and raiment" for the Indian allies of New York who had suffered from the French attack. Although Markham was probably the chief author of the "Frame of Government," he does not deserve any special credit for its liberal character. On the other hand, he should not be blamed too severely for his failure to enforce the acts of trade and navigation, because the Quaker Assembly would not sanction the establishment of an adequate police force.

[Penn MSS., Hist. Soc. of Pa.; *Memoirs of the Hist. Soc. of Pa.*, vol. X (1872); *Minutes of the Provincial Council of Pa.*, vols. I, II (1852); "Papers of the Governors," *Pa. Archives*, 4 ser. I (1900); Samuel Hazard, *Annals of Pa. . . . 1609–1682* (1850); J. B. Linn, *Charter to William Penn and Laws of the Province of Pa.* (1879), Appendix B; Robert Proud, *The Hist. of Pa. 1681–1742* (2 vols., 1797–99); W. C. Armor, *Lives of the Governors of Pa.* (1872); W. R. Shepherd, *Hist. of Proprietary Govt. in Pa.* (1896); Isaac Sharpless, *A Quaker Experiment in Govt.* (1898); C. C. Hall, *Narratives of Early Md.* (1910); W. T. Root, *The Relations of Pa. with the British Govt., 1696–1765* (1912).]

W. R. S.

MARKOE, ABRAHAM (July 2, 1727–Aug. 28, 1806), capitalist, patriot, was born on the island of Santa Cruz (or St. Croix), one of the Virgin Islands, then subject to the Crown of Denmark. His grandfather, Pierre Marcou, a Huguenot, had accompanied Count Créqui from France to the Danish West Indies before the revocation of the Edict of Nantes. There he acquired one of the largest sugar plantations on the island of Santa Cruz, and became colonial governor of that settlement. His son Pierre, who seems to have been the first to change the family name to Markoe, married Elizabeth Farrell, and Abraham Markoe was their son. He inherited the rich plantations, traded with Europe and the American colonies, and in 1751 married a widow,

Elizabeth (Kenny) Rogers, who bore him two sons, Peter [*q.v.*], and Abraham. About the year 1770, his wife having died a few years before, he went to Philadelphia, where he established a residence. On Dec. 16, 1773, he was married in Christ Church to Elizabeth Baynton, daughter of John Baynton, a Philadelphia merchant. Seven children were born to this union.

Abraham Markoe became a prominent figure in the business and social life of Philadelphia. From the first rumblings of the Revolution he took the side of the Patriots, and was the founder of the first volunteer military association in what is now the United States. This was the Philadelphia Light Horse, now known as the First Troop, Philadelphia City Cavalry, which was organized Nov. 17, 1774. It was composed of gentlemen of fortune, who provided all their own equipment and paid for their own maintenance. The first active duty of the Troop, of which Markoe was the first captain, was to escort General Washington as far as New York, when, on June 21, 1775, he started for Cambridge to take command of the Continental Army. The standard of the Philadelphia Light Horse was presented to it by Markoe, and although there exists a bill from John Folwell for "drawing and designing the colours for the Light Horse," dated Sept. 16, 1775, Markoe is generally credited with having suggested the design. In the upper left-hand corner of the flag, in what is known as the canton, are thirteen stripes of alternate blue and silver, supposed to be the "earliest instance of the thirteen stripes being used upon an American banner" (Preble, *post,* p. 181). Markoe resigned his command early in the year 1776 because the government of Denmark, of which he was still a subject, had issued an edict of neutrality, and disobedience on his part would have imperilled his family and rendered his estates in Santa Cruz liable to confiscation. He never lost his interest in the cause of the colonies, however, and was present at the battle of Brandywine in October 1777. During the British occupation of Philadelphia he retired to Lancaster, Pa., but returned to the capital in time to witness the evacuation of that city by the King's troops. In 1782–83 he acquired by patents from the state of Pennsylvania a block of ground now bounded by Ninth, Tenth, Market, and Chestnut Streets, in Philadelphia. Upon this ground he erected a mansion, which was one of the wonders of the city being the first house to use marble lintels over its windows. He died in Philadelphia and was buried in Christ Church graveyard.

[C. W. Baird, *Hist. of the Huguenot Emigration to America* (1885), vol. I; *Book of the First Troop, Phila. City Cavalry* (1915), ed. by J. L. Wilson; *Extracts from the Diary of Christopher Marshall* (1877), ed. by William Duane; G. H. Preble, *Our Flag; Origin and Progress of the Flag of the U. S.* (1872); J. F. Watson, *Annals of Phila.* (3 vols., 1884); F. W. Leach, "Old Phila. Families—XVI: Markoe," *North American* (Phila.), Sept. 22, 1907; Joseph Jackson, *Market Street, Phila.* (1918); *Poulson's Am. Daily Advertiser,* Aug. 30, 1806.]

J. J.

MARKOE, PETER (*c.* 1752–Jan. 30, 1792), poet and dramatist, was the eldest son of Abraham Markoe [*q.v.*] by his first wife, Elizabeth Rogers (*née* Kenny). He was born on the island of Santa Cruz (or St. Croix) in the Danish West Indies, probably between Jan. 31 and Feb. 16, 1752, though at his matriculation at Pembroke College, Oxford, Feb. 17, 1767, his age was given as sixteen. The statement that he was educated at Trinity College, Dublin, appears to be without foundation. On May 29, 1775, he was admitted to Lincoln's Inn. It is usually said that he was in England during the period of the Revolution, but in 1775 he is listed as captain of Light Horse, 3rd Battalion, Philadelphia City Militia (*Pennsylvania Archives,* 6 ser. I, 183; 2 ser. XIII, 556). The Danish decree of neutrality (1775) which caused his father to resign from the Light Horse, may have prevented Peter Markoe's further participation in the war. It is possible that he returned to Santa Cruz, perhaps more than once, to transact business for his father after the latter settled in Philadelphia. (One of his brothers was drowned on such a trip.) Among his poems are "Verses Addressed to His Excellency General Van Roepstorf on his arrival in St. Croix, 1771" and "To Her Excellency Lady Clausen, of St. Croix, on Her Birth-Day, 1780." In 1784 he published in Philadelphia *The Patriot Chief,* a tragedy, the scene of which is laid in Lydia. It was offered to Lewis Hallam [*q.v.*], manager of the American Company, but rejected, and apparently was never produced. It called forth, however, an Epistle by Markoe's friend, Col. John Parke, "To Mr. Peter Markoe, on His Excellent Tragedy Called The Patriot Chief" (in Parke's *Horace,* 1786), in which the author urged Markoe to treat native themes and native heroes. On May 17, 1785, he received a lottery warrant for 500 acres of land in Northumberland County, Pa. His name appears in the muster roll of the Philadelphia militia from 1786 to 1789. In 1787 (May 28; cf. *Pennsylvania Packet and Daily Advertiser* of that date) he published by subscription a volume of *Miscellaneous Poems,* "many of them" according to the Preface, "written when I was very young." The following January (1788) he published *The Times,* a satirical poem full of allusions to local personages, only a few of whom can now be identified. Part of it had previously appeared "in one of the public papers" (Preface), and the whole was republished in July (printed for Prichard & Hall) with the addition of several hundred lines. A contemporary review of the poem in Noah Webster's *American Magazine* (September 1788) resents Markoe's criticism of Joel Barlow but adds: "It is but justice to Mr. Markoe to declare, that we think him one of the first poetic geniuses in America." In 1790 he published *The Reconciliation: or, the Triumph of Nature,* one of the earliest comic operas written in America. Charles Evans (*American Bibliography,* VI, 132, 213) attributes to Markoe *The Algerine Spy in Pennsylvania: or, Letters Written by a Native of Algiers on the Affairs of the United States in America, from the Close of the Year 1783 to the Meeting of the Convention* (1787) and *The Storm, a Poem: Descriptive of the Late Tempest, Which Raged with Such Fury Throughout the Southern Parts of North-America, in July, 1788,* issued with the Philadelphia edition of William Falconer's *The Shipwreck,* published in 1788.

Markoe died in Philadelphia, in his fortieth year according to family tradition, and was buried in the graveyard of Christ Church in that city. He seems to have had a reputation for conviviality not to be assumed from the sentiments expressed in his verse. He managed the couplet with ease but without distinction. That he was interested in other arts than literature is to be inferred from the design for a frontispiece which he contributed to Col. John Parke's volume, *The Lyrical Works of Horace Translated into English Verse; to Which Are Added a Number of Original Poems* (1786).

[*Pa. Archives,* esp. 6 ser.; register of Christ Church, Phila.; *Dunlap's Am. Daily Advertiser,* Jan. 31, 1792; Charles Evans, *Am. Bibliog.,* vols. VI, VII (1910–12), which confuses the two editions of *The Times*; F. W. Leach, "Old Philadelphia Families: XVI—Markoe," in *North American* (Phila.), Sept. 22, 1907; A. H. Quinn, *A Hist. of the Am. Drama, from the Beginning to the Civil War* (1923); family papers in the possession of Miss Emily Rivinus, Philadelphia, and Mr. Francis Hartman Markoe, New York.] A. C. B.

MARKS, AMASA ABRAHAM (Apr. 3, 1825–July 19, 1905), inventor, manufacturer, descended from Mordecai Marks, a native of London, England, who died in Derby, Conn., in 1771, was the son of Levi Merwin and Esther Tolles (Tuttle) Marks. He was born in Waterbury, Conn., where his father had established and operated a hauling business between Waterbury and New Haven. He attended the public schools in Waterbury until he was sixteen years old and then joined his father for a year or two, after which he went to farming. At the age of twenty, although he was without experience, he began a small wood-working business in New Haven. By some means he secured a large order for making hubs for carriages and wagons, then rented a mill, hired an expert wood-turner, and succeeded in filling the order with entire satisfaction. At the same time by close observation and practice he mastered the art of wood turning and for about six years carried on a fairly successful business. Shortly after his marriage on Aug. 22, 1850, to Lucy Ann Platt, a second cousin, he transferred his shop to New York.

Two years later he formed a partnership with his elder brother David, a dentist who had given considerable thought to improvements of artificial limbs. Upon the granting of a patent (No. 10,611) to David B. Marks on Mar. 7, 1854, the brothers began with enthusiasm to manufacture and introduce the new products. After several years during which they attained very little recognition, David withdrew from the partnership to resume the practice of his profession, but Amasa, with characteristic tenacity of purpose, carried on alone. He improved the mechanism of the artificial leg in 1856 by providing for knee articulation as well as ankle and toe movements, and further improved the ankle joint in 1858, but still the business made little progress. About 1861 he began to use rubber in the construction of artificial hands and feet, and after two years of active research, on Dec. 1, 1863, was granted Patent No. 40,763. The radical change in artificial limbs which this invention effected was the elimination of all mechanism from the calf of the leg down. Knee articulation was retained, but both ankle and toe movements were eliminated. In 1864 the Federal government awarded Marks a contract for furnishing artificial limbs to the disabled soldiers and sailors of the Civil War, and in a comparatively short time his products were used in practically every part of the world. He personally directed all phases of his rapidly expanding business during the next fifteen years and at the same time conducted experimental work looking toward the further improvement of his products. Eventually a rubber foot consisting of alternate layers of rubber and canvas was perfected which gave the toes greater resilience and forced the foot to return to its proper shape with more certainty. Shortly after securing Patent No. 234,596 (Nov. 16, 1880) for this improvement, Marks retired, leaving his business in the hands of his sons. He then took up his permanent residence in Sound Beach, Conn., where he had owned a country estate since 1872. Here he interested himself in local affairs, particularly in the improvement of schools. For his inventions he received awards in 1859, 1865, 1867, and 1870–78, from the American Institute, New York City. In 1889 he was the recipient, jointly with his son, George E. Marks, of the John Scott Legacy Premium and Medal awarded by the Franklin Institute of Philadelphia. He died at his home in Sound Beach at the age of eighty and was survived by three sons and one daughter.

[*Encyc. of Conn. Biog.* (1917), vol. IX; G. E. Marks, *A Treatise on Marks' Patent Artificial Limbs* (1888, 1894, 1896); E. J. Lines, *Marks-Platt Ancestry* (1902); *House Ex. Doc. 59*, 33 Cong., 2 Sess.; *House Ex. Doc. 60*, 38 Cong., 1 Sess.; *Specifications and Drawings of Patents Issued from the U. S. Patent Office*, Nov. 1880; *Jour. Franklin Inst.*, May 1889; *N. Y. Times* and *N. Y. Tribune*, July 20, 1905; National Museum correspondence with firm.] C. W. M.

MARKS, ELIAS (Dec. 2, 1790–June 22, 1886), physician, educator, founder of the South Carolina Female Collegiate Institute, was born in Charleston, S. C., the son of Humphrey and Frances Marks of Lancashire, who settled in Charleston in 1785. After preparatory training in Charleston, he completed his classical and medical education in New York City, graduating from the College of Physicians and Surgeons in 1815. His dissertation, *A Conjectural Inquiry into the Relative Influence of the Mind and Stomach* (1814), treats of the connection of moral faculties with bodily sense and the influence of mind on bodily functions. His *Aphorisms of Hippocrates from the Latin of Verhoofd* (1818), continues the classical and ethical interests observable in his first work. About 1817, he was married to Jane Barham, of Lincolnshire, a teacher. On account of her health he moved south and resumed practice in Columbia, S. C., where the two also conducted the Columbia Female Academy on Washington Street. After the death of his wife in June 1827, he continued a year longer with his school, in which he had both day scholars and boarders. In 1826 he had attempted to enlist the support of the legislature for what appears to have been a plan for the higher education of women. Failing that, he decided to establish a school of his own in the seclusion of the sandhills, at a place which he named Barhamville.

The prospectus of his South Carolina Female Institute appeared in 1828 as *Hints on Female Education.* The school was formally opened on Oct. 1, 1828. The few annual catalogues now remaining give evidence of systematic internal economy and increasing educational range and efficiency in accordance with Marks's theories. In 1833 he was married to Julia (Pierpont) Warne of Sparta, Ga., a friend and pupil of Emma Willard, who assumed the duties of directress of the Institute on Jan. 1, 1830. Through her influence, according to her daughter, the Institute became collegiate, and in 1835 the word "Collegiate" was added to the name. The reorganization of the school involved a modeling, in some measure, after "similar institutions in Prussia, Germany, and other parts of continental Europe."

The school gained wide popularity and reached an enrolment of 124 students. Marion Sims, writing in 1831, said: "Young ladies were sent there from all parts of the state to school, as it was the first and only school of its character at the South" (J. M. Sims, *The Story of My Life*, 1884, p. 102). Teachers were drawn from wherever talent offered, and the work was intensive and systematic. The curriculum offered four years of collegiate study beyond an academic year sometimes necessary for entrants. Resident graduates could pursue further studies, and the vacation period provided opportunity for private instruction in residence, possibly for making up deficiencies. From the first insistence was placed on thoroughness, thinking rather than memory, and regular reviews. Reliance was placed on the student's honor. Walks, entertainments, visits of approved troupes or singers, and May parties enlivened the routine. In 1855, six years before he gave over the school into other hands, Marks claimed nearly thirty-nine years of professional services during which time he had had in his charge over four thousand young women. Marks relinquished his connection with the Institute on June 15, 1861. He spent his declining years in Washington, cheered in his old age by expressions of love and respect of his former pupils. Throughout his life he had written occasional poems and in 1850 he published *Elfreide of Guldal, a Scandinavian Legend, and Other Poems.*

[J. W. Davidson, *The Living Writers of the South* (1869); Jean H. Witherspoon, "Dr. Marks and the Barhamville School," the *State* (Columbia, S. C.), Mar. 15, 1903; B. A. Elzas, *The Jews of S. C.* (1905).] H. C. D.

MARLING, JOHN LEAKE (Dec. 22, 1825–Oct. 16, 1856), journalist and diplomatist, was born in Nashville, Tenn., the son of Samuel and Charlotte Clara (Leake) Marling. Under the pen-name of "Clara" his mother wrote popular sentimental verses, and Marling inherited and to some extent practised his mother's gift. At seventeen he joined the Baptist church. Beginning his career in a printing office, Marling overcame his lack of a systematic education by reading in leisure moments, and though without wealth or family prestige won his way into public life by a precocious exercise of his talent for political writing. He studied law in the office of A. O. P. Nicholson and Russell Houston and was admitted to the bar, but did not practise. On May 16, 1850, he was married to Mary E. March of Nashville. In the following July he became editor and part-owner of the Nashville *Daily Gazette,* and thus, in the heat of the controversy over the territorial expansion of slavery, entered upon his short, but stormy and brilliant, journalistic career. On taking over the *Gazette* he announced that he would conduct it as an "independent" paper, avoiding partisan quarrels, but he speedily became embroiled in the excitement that attended upon the meetings of the Southern convention in Nashville in 1850. During the second session of the convention he uncompromisingly denounced the secessionist policies it expressed, to such effect that there was an attempt to exclude him from its sessions. In his editorial opposition he undoubtedly reflected a strong element of Tennessee opinion.

In September 1851, leaving the *Gazette,* Marling became part-owner and editor of the Nashville *Daily Union,* a prominent Democratic paper. The young editor soon was hotly involved in the presidential campaign of 1852, strongly advocating the candidacy of Pierce against a powerful Whig opposition, locally centered in the *Republican Banner,* edited by Felix K. Zollicoffer. On Aug. 20, 1852, at the height of the campaign, Marling topped a series of attacks on the *Banner* by openly charging its editor with misrepresentation of Pierce's Southern sympathies, and in effect giving Zollicoffer the lie. Zollicoffer's answer was to call Marling out for personal satisfaction, which Marling immediately tendered. That morning the two editors met on the street in front of the *Union* office and, with little preliminary, exchanged several shots. Marling was seriously wounded and was unable to resume his duties until the campaign was over. It was thought, even by Zollicoffer's friends, that the difficulty was less personal than political and that Marling, who was known as a brave man and a crack pistol shot, had been egged on by Democratic partisans who wished to put Zollicoffer, a strong political opponent, out of the way. At any rate the difficulty between the two was later composed. Marling continued his connection with the *Union* through its consolidation with the *American* in 1853. In 1854 he was rewarded by President Pierce with an appointment as United States minister resident to Guatemala. Less than two years later he became seriously ill and returned to Nashville, on leave, in May 1856, to die there of tuberculosis within a few months.

[John Wooldridge, ed., *Hist. of Nashville, Tenn.* (1890); Nashville *Daily Gazette,* July 30, 1850, Oct. 8–Nov. 19, 1850; Nashville *Daily Union,* Aug. 20, 21, 1850; *Republican Banner,* Aug. 24, 1850, and previous issues; obituaries in Nashville papers at the time of Marling's death; *Clara's Poems* (1861); private papers furnished by Octavia Zollicoffer Bond.] D. D.

MARMADUKE, JOHN SAPPINGTON (Mar. 14, 1833–Dec. 28, 1887), Confederate soldier, governor of Missouri, was born on a farm near Arrow Rock, Mo. His mother was Lavinia Sappington, a daughter of the well-known Dr. John Sappington of Saline County. His father was Meredith Miles Marmaduke, of Westmoreland County, Va. Upon the death of Gov. Thomas Reynolds, the elder Marmaduke, who was lieutenant-governor, served almost a year as governor of Missouri (1844). John S. Marmaduke was educated in the country schools of Saline County, in Masonic College at Lexington, Mo., at Yale (two years), and at Harvard. After attending Harvard less than a year, he left to accept a cadetship at West Point, from which he graduated in 1857. Thereupon commissioned second lieutenant, he was soon assigned to the 7th Regiment of United States Infantry and served in the Mormon War (1858–60) in Utah under Col. Albert Sidney Johnston. When secession began he was stationed in New Mexico.

At the opening of the Civil War Marmaduke came home on furlough and talked over the question of allegiance with his father, who favored the Union but told his son to make his own decision. The latter immediately resigned from the United States army and was made a colonel of state militia by Gov. Claiborne F. Jackson. Disappointed at the poor showing of the state forces at the battle of Boonville (June 17, 1861), Marmaduke resigned his colonelcy and rode to Richmond where he was commissioned a first lieutenant in the Confederate army. For a short time he was on duty in Arkansas and was there made a lieutenant-colonel. Shortly afterward he was placed in charge of the 3rd Regiment under his old commander, Albert Sidney Johnston, and fought so well at Shiloh that he was commissioned a brigadier-general (May 25, 1863, to rank from Nov. 15, 1862). After Shiloh he was sent to Arkansas again, where, although his forces were inadequate for ambitious offensive tactics, he nevertheless gave a good account of himself. Early in 1863 he made a raid into south central Missouri, but his attack on Springfield failed. In April of the same year he invaded southeast Missouri, but after a few minor victories he was forced to beat a hasty retreat back into Arkansas. For his faithful and often brilliant activities around Helena, Fayetteville, and Little Rock he was promoted to a major-generalship in March 1864. In charge of the cavalry in Price's raid (1864), Marmaduke had two horses shot under him at the battle of the Little Blue near Kansas City, and on the retreat a few days later he was captured while conducting a rear-guard action at the Marais des Cygnes River in western Missouri. He was a prisoner at Fort Warren (Mass.) until the summer of 1865.

For about five years after the war Marmaduke was engaged, with moderate success, in the commission and then in the insurance business in St. Louis. From 1871 to 1874 he was editor of the *St. Louis Journal of Agriculture,* and from 1880 to 1885 he served as a member of the newly created Missouri Railway Commission. Although defeated for the Democratic nomination for governor in 1880, he was easily nominated and elected to that office four years later. He died at Jefferson City a year before the expiration of his term. Prominent among the pressing public questions during his governorship was the problem of the regulation of railroads. The bill which he sponsored for that purpose was defeated in the first regular session of the legislature during his administration. Marmaduke immediately called the Assembly into special session, and, when the proponents of the railroads stood ready to adjourn without action, he threatened to continue calling special sessions until some such regulatory measure was passed. The threat was sufficient, and a law satisfactory to him was enacted. During his administration there occurred the first railway strike that seriously affected Missouri. For handling this problem so firmly that there was little loss of property and no loss of life, he was accorded much credit. Marmaduke never married. He was not a member of any religious denomination. He was more than six feet tall, and retained throughout life an erect military bearing.

[*Messages and Proclamations of the Govs. . . . of Mo.,* vol. VII (1926); J. F. Lee, "John Sappington Marmaduke," *Mo. Hist. Soc. Colls.,* July 1906; R. J. Rombauer, *The Union Cause in St. Louis in 1861* (1909); T. L. Snead, *The Fight for Mo.* (1886); W. B. Napton, *Past and Present of Saline County, Mo.* (1910); *Confed. Mil. Hist.* (1899), vol. IX; *Jefferson City Tribune,* July 20, 1883; Sept. 23, Oct. 29, 1884, Dec. 29, 1885, Jan. 13, Mar. 16, Nov. 7, 1886; *Boonville Weekly Advertiser,* Dec. 11, 1874, May 3, 1878, Aug. 4, 1882, July 13, 1883, Sept. 19, 1884, Jan. 16, July 24, Aug. 28, 1885, Dec. 30, 1887, Aug. 29, 1890, Nov. 30, Dec. 7, 1900.] H. E. N.

MARQUAND, ALLAN (Dec. 10, 1853–Sept. 24, 1924), university professor and art historian, was born in New York City, the son of Henry Gurdon Marquand [*q.v.*], a wealthy banker and patron of arts, and Elizabeth Love (Allen) Marquand, who was of old New England origin. Preparing at St. Paul's School, Allan graduated from Princeton in 1874, being Latin salutatorian and class president. As an undergraduate, he was stroke of the crew and a member of the Glee Club. For three years he studied theology, first at Princeton Theological Seminary and later at Union. He was licensed to preach by the New York Presbytery, but was never ordained; his interest had shifted to logic and philosophy. The year 1877–78 found him a student at the University of Berlin. Thence he passed to the new Johns Hopkins University, where he held a fellowship in philosophy and in 1880 received the degree of Ph.D. At Johns Hopkins, he invented an ingenious logic machine, which is preserved in the historical collections of Princeton University.

President McCosh called him to the College of New Jersey in 1881 as lecturer in logic and tutor in Latin, a position which he held for only two years. He was then made professor of history of art, the professorship being designated archaeology and history of art in 1890. That year he became, also, director of the Museum of Historic Art. In 1883, at Rome, he was stricken by a malignant fever, which left him much of a valetudinarian. The disadvantages of such a condition he overcame by a sensible regimen and by extraordinarily persistent and systematic habits of study. Although as a lecturer, because of his hesitant delivery he was at first mildly boring to the bulk of his undergraduate hearers, he made a personal impression through the charm and the kindliness of his manners, and always inspired a few elect students, among them, his later and brilliant colleague, Howard Crosby Butler [*q.v.*]. Quietly, he gained a national reputation through his patient and accurate scholarship. Living in a spacious way as a wealthy bachelor, he gathered personal disciples, entertaining them at his home and taking them on his travels. For a time Arthur L. Frothingham [*q.v.*], a most active and versatile scholar, was his associate. Together they edited and largely wrote the third volume (1887) of the *Iconographic Encyclopedia* (a translation and revision of Moritz Carrière's *Bilder Atlas*) and *A Textbook of the History of Sculpture* (1896). Marquand's willing drudgery on the *Encyclopedia* turned out to be the best possible training for his later work as a cataloguer.

From its beginning, Marquand deeply interested himself in the work of the Archaeological Institute of America, being an editorial contributor to its journal, the *American Journal of*

Archaeology, from the time it was started, in 1885, until his death. For over thirty years with characteristic secrecy he financed traveling fellowships of the Institute. On June 18, 1896, being forty-three years old, he married Eleanor Cross, by whom he had four children. She was much younger than himself, but already interested in his subjects and fitted for the ideal partnership which ensued. After their marriage they went to Rome, where he served as annual professor at the American School of Classical Studies.

Marquand came to what was to be his life work, the cataloguing of the sculpture of the Robbia family, almost accidentally. In 1882 his father bought a fine altar-piece by Andrea della Robbia. The son wrote an elaborate account of it for the *American Journal of Archaeology* (October–December 1891). His interest thus established in Robbia sculpture, he toured Italy for unstudied examples, and published his preliminary observations in the *American Journal of Archaeology* (January–March 1893) and in *Scribner's Magazine* (December 1893). The thoroughness of his methods may be inferred from the fact that it was nineteen years before the first of the Robbia catalogues appeared. Meantime, he wrote many journal articles, gave himself willingly to the drudgery of reviewing, fostered the interests of the Institute, and gradually built up a department of art and Archaeology for Princeton. Its essential apparatus of research was his own library and photograph collection, which he first lent and then gave to the University.

He was fifty-six years old when he published his first independent book, *Greek Architecture* (1909). He soon founded and financed the Princeton Monographs in Art and Archaeology, of which his own Robbia catalogues remain the most distinguished numbers. *Della Robbias in America* (1912) was an *hors d'œuvre* to the series, being an elaborate try-out of methods of classification. The World War brought some retardation of the work, for Marquand gave himself loyally to the drudgery of miscellaneous teaching in a militarized college with a depleted faculty. Since heraldry often meant chronology, he next dispatched that subject in *Robbia Heraldry* (1919). The breadth and wisdom of his long preparation was shown by the quickness with which the remaining volumes appeared: *Giovanni della Robbia* in 1920, *Benedetto and Santi Buglioni,* in 1921, and *Andrea della Robbia and His Atelier,* two volumes, in 1922. His never robust health was now beginning to break, but he left the last of the catalogues, *The Brothers of Giovanni della Robbia* (1928), so far advanced that it could readily be completed by his colleagues after his death. He died in a hospital in New York City.

Marquand was of middle stature and slight build, immaculate in person and dress. His manner was shy and hesitating, but his vivid blue eyes were friendly. His sagacity and his generosity, which he disliked to have mentioned, brought him widest influence. He was extraordinarily helpful to beginners in research. Profoundly the scholar, he was exquisitely the aristocrat and the gentleman.

[MS. material in possession of secretary of faculty and of the chairman of department of art and architecture, Princeton Univ.; C. R. Morey, *Art Studies,* vol. II (1924), preface; *Decennial Record of the Class of 1874 of Princeton Coll.* (1884); *Princeton Alumni Weekly,* Oct. 1, 1924; *Who's Who in America,* 1922–23; *N. Y. Tribune,* Sept. 25, 1924; *N. Y. Times,* Sept. 25, 26 (editorial), 1924.]

F. J. M., Jr.

MARQUAND, HENRY GURDON (Apr. 11, 1819–Feb. 26, 1902), capitalist, philanthropist, was born in New York City, the son of Isaac and Mehitable (Perry) Marquand. His father and his elder brother Frederick were connected with the firm of Marquand & Company, silversmiths. The boy received his education in New York and in Pittsfield, Mass. In 1839 Frederick Marquand withdrew from active association with the silversmith firm, and for twenty years thereafter Henry assisted him in managing large real-estate interests. During this time he acquired some knowledge of architecture and criticized the faulty design and poor construction of buildings then being erected in New York. Since he was not a professional architect, these criticisms were not at first kindly received, but ultimately many of his suggested improvements were adopted. From real estate he turned to banking, becoming prominent in Wall Street, and interested in railroad and other corporations. In 1874, with his brother Frederick and other capitalists, he purchased the St. Louis, Iron Mountain & Southern Railroad, serving as its vice-president from 1875 to 1881, and then for a year as its president. He was succeeded by Jay Gould, who had secured control of the road for his Missouri Pacific. Marquand remained a director of both roads for several years, however, and his interest in the company was such that his death occasioned a bear raid on the Missouri Pacific stock.

Retiring from the most of his business activities about 1881, he thereafter devoted much time to philanthropic and civic undertakings. He was one of the ablest and most generous supporters of the Metropolitan Museum of Art. Since the latter part of the eighteenth century there had been a more or less connected series of attempts to found such an institution. Finally, on Oct. 14, 1869, a meeting of the Union League was held to promote the project, after which the president of the League appointed a committee of fifty, of which Marquand was one, to perfect an organization and raise an endowment. From this time on Marquand was actively interested in the affairs of the Museum, serving as its treasurer from 1882 to 1889, and as its president from 1889 until his death. To him in large measure it owes its growth and distinction. Among his many gifts to it was $10,000, in 1886, which made possible the purchase of a collection of sculptural casts; and $30,000 for the endowment fund of the Museum art school. He purchased and presented to the Museum the collection of antique glass made by M. Charvet; the reproduction of many carvings exhibiting the medieval continuance of the art; the collection of Renaissance iron works; the Della Robbia altar-piece; the metallic reproductions of gold and silver objects in the Imperial Russian Museums; as well as a collection of paintings of the English School and old masters. Russell Sturgis said of Marquand, "He bought like an Italian Prince of the Renaissance" (Preface to Catalogue, *post*).

His benefactions were not limited to the Museum alone. He founded and endowed a free library at Little Rock, Ark. With his brother Frederick he gave to Bellevue Hospital the Marquand Pavilion; he gave Marquand Chapel to Princeton University and endowed the professorship of the history of art; with Robert A. Bonner, he also provided a gymnasium for Princeton. He was a member of the New York Historical Society, of the American Geographical Society, vice-president of the Municipal Art Society, and one of the board of managers of the Presbyterian Hospital. On May 20, 1851, he married Elizabeth Love Allen of Pittsfield, Mass. One of his four children was Allan Marquand [*q.v.*].

[*Am. Ancestry*, vol. IX (1894); F. B. Lee, *Geneal. and Personal Memorial of Mercer County, N. J.* (1907), vol. II; W. E. Howe, *Hist. of the Metropolitan Museum of Art* (1913); D. C. Preyer, *The Art of the Metropolitan Museum of N. Y.* (1899); *Bull. of the Metropolitan Museum*, Jan. 1911; Ernest Knaufft, "Henry G. Marquand as an American Art Patron," in *Rev. of Revs.* (N. Y.), Feb. 1903; T. E. Kirby, ed., *Illustrated Cat. of the Art and Literary Property Collected by the Late Henry G. Marquand* (copr. 1903); H. V. Poor, *Manual of the Railroads of the U. S.*, 1875, 1881, 1882, 1891; *Commercial and Financial Chronicle*, Mar. 1, 1902; *Who's Who in America*, 1901–02; *N. Y. Herald*, and *N. Y. Tribune*, Feb. 27, 1902.] K. S. E.

MARQUETT, TURNER MASTIN (July 9, 1829–Dec. 22, 1894), railway attorney, congressman for two days, was born on a farm in Clark County, Ohio, the son of John T. Marquette and Julia (Wright) Marquette, who had come as pioneers to Ohio from Virginia. His signature does not show the final *e* which was used by all other members of his family. He conceived an early ambition to become a lawyer and with that end in view attended successively the Springfield (Ohio) high school, Wittenberg College, and Ohio University, at Athens. After his graduation from the last-named institution in 1855 he went almost immediately to Plattsmouth, Nebraska Territory, where, to piece out his insignificant earnings as a lawyer, he found it necessary for a time to work in a store.

At the outset of his career young Marquett obviously had strong political aspirations. Beginning in 1857, he served in seven successive sessions of the territorial legislature, first in the House, then for the last four years in the Council. He was an ardent opponent of slavery, and he urged as early as the session of 1859 its definite prohibition within the boundaries of Nebraska. He took a prominent part in the movement for statehood, and in June 1866 was elected to represent Nebraska in the lower House of Congress, should admission be granted. When, on Mar. 2, 1867, Nebraska actually became a state, he took office; but only two days of the term for which he had been chosen remained. During this time, however, he voted on important reconstruction acts. In 1868 he was a candidate for the Republican nomination for Congress, but when this was denied him, his interest in a political career began to wane. Although he remained to the end of his life an ardent Republican, he never again held public office.

As a lawyer, meantime, Marquett's services were increasingly in demand, and when the Burlington Railroad began to build west of the Missouri River it selected him as the principal legal adviser of its corporation in Nebraska. It was in this capacity more than in any other that he distinguished himself. He became an expert on railroad and corporation law when experts in these fields were few, and he smoothed the way legally for the remarkable progress that the Burlington was soon able to make. His counsel was often sought by corporations other than his own, but he made it a point not to take more cases than he could fully master. His part in two cases, one at the beginning and one at the end of his career, won him much distinction. He appeared as counsel for the defense in the impeachment trial of Governor David Butler, and he represented the plaintiff in a suit brought by John Fitzgerald, a railway contractor, against the

Missouri Pacific Railroad, then dominated by Jay Gould. The impeachment case went against Butler, but in the Fitzgerald case Marquett won a notable victory for his client.

For the last twenty years of his life he resided in Lincoln, Nebr., an important western center of the Burlington. The high respect in which he was there held is attested by an unusual series of appreciations printed by court order in the introductory pages of the *Nebraska Reports* for 1894 (43 *Nebr.*, vii–xxix). He was twice married: first, in 1861, to Harriett Borders, who died in 1883, and by whom he had four children; second, in 1885, to Mrs. Aseneth Stetson, who survived him.

[There are useful sketches of T. M. Marquett and of his brother, Rev. David Marquette, a pioneer Methodist preacher, in J. Sterling Morton and Albert Watkins, *Illustrated Hist. of Nebr.* (3 vols., 1905–13), I, 353, II, 523; and in Andrew J. Sawyer (ed.), *Lincoln, the Capital City, and Lancaster County, Nebr.* (1916), II, 756. A good obituary notice appears in the *Nebraska State Journal* (Lincoln), Dec. 23, 1894. The history of the Fitzgerald case is reviewed in 41 *Nebr.*, 475, and in 160 *U. S.*, 556.]

J. D. H.

MARQUETTE, JACQUES (June 1, 1637–May 18, 1675), explorer and missionary, was a native of Laon, France, where his ancestors had been prominent from the fourteenth century. He was the sixth and youngest child of Nicolas and Rose (de la Salle) Marquette. The Marquettes were warriors and officials, but the La Salles were religiously inclined. From his early years Jacques was thoughtful and gentle, and when in 1654 at the age of seventeen he decided to become a Jesuit novice, he had the ready consent of his family. He passed his novitiate at Nancy; in 1656 he went to Pont-à-Mousson to study philosophy; then he taught for several years at Rheims, Charleville, Langres, and Pont-à-Mousson. All this time he cherished the hope that his ultimate calling would be that of a missionary overseas. He chose as his pattern the great Jesuit, Francis Xavier, and wished that it might be his fate to die in the wilderness. In 1666, designated by his superiors for service in New France, he set forth in the royal fleet of that year and on Sept. 20 landed at Quebec. He was not allowed to remain long at the capital, and on Oct. 10 left for Three Rivers, an outpost of the colony, where he became a pupil of a veteran missionary in the difficult Indian languages. He made such rapid progress that in 1668 he was appointed to the mission among the Ottawa Indians, kindred of those tribesmen whose language he had mastered.

The Ottawa mission had been begun in 1660 by Father Ménard [*q.v.*], who the next year was lost in the Wisconsin forests. In 1665 the work had been taken up again by Father Allouez [*q.v.*], who at Chequamegon Bay on the south shore of Lake Superior established the mission of La Pointe de St. Esprit. Here dwelt the fugitive Ottawa from the shores of Lake Huron, and in the vicinity a few refugee Hurons from Georgian Bay. Young Marquette was now ordered to this most difficult and dangerous mission of New France. He spent the first winter (1668–69) at Sault Ste. Marie in comparative comfort. The Indians of that region were friendly, and he baptized many children. Then on Sept. 13, 1669, he went to the mission at La Pointe, Father Allouez having left to visit Green Bay. During the eighteen months Marquette spent at Chequamegon he was visited by many tribesmen from far away, among others the Illinois, who had crossed a great river on their way. Marquette learned the rudiments of the Illinois language, and because these Indians were gentle and courteous he longed to establish a mission among them. The Hurons and Ottawa were less docile; nevertheless he endeavored to teach them by pictures and symbols, and he even sent a holy picture to the fierce Sioux, hoping to open a way to instruct them. His neophytes, the Hurons, had a quarrel with the Sioux, however, and finding themselves outnumbered abandoned their village at La Pointe and fled to Lake Michigan. Marquette accompanied them, and in the summer of 1671 founded the mission of St. Ignace on the north shore of the Straits of Mackinac.

It was at St. Ignace that Marquette's great opportunity came. While at the Sault in 1668 he had met a young Canadian explorer, Louis Jolliet [*q.v.*], then returning to New France. To St. Ignace came Jolliet on Dec. 8, 1672, with the tidings that the governor had commissioned him to find the great river of which the Illinois had spoken and that Marquette was to be his companion on the expedition. All through the winter they studied and planned, drew a map of the countries Jolliet and Marquette knew, gathered the personnel for the expedition, and prepared their simple supplies. It was mid-May before the straits were free of ice and the two explorers could slip their canoes into the waters of the lake. "Indian corn, with some smoked meat," wrote Marquette, "constituted all our provisions; with these we embarked—Monsieur Jollyet and myself, with five men—in two bark canoes, fully resolved to do and suffer everything for so glorious an undertaking" (Thwaites, *post*, LIX, 91). They went by way of Green Bay and Fox River. As far as the Mascouten village on the upper Fox the way was well known, and there they obtained guides to escort them to the portage: That crossed, "we left the waters flowing to Quebeq, four or five hundred leagues from here to float on those that would thenceforward take us through strange lands" (*Ibid.*, p. 107). On June 17, 1673, the two explorers shot out into the Mississippi and, turning their canoes southward, set forth to explore its waterway. In a month they reached the mouth of the Arkansas, where, learning that the river entered the Gulf of Mexico and that white men (Spaniards) were on the lower river, they turned back. They reached Lake Michigan by the Illinois River and the Chicago portage, coasted the lake shore, and came to rest at the mission of St. Francis Xavier at De Pere.

Since Marquette's strength was sadly depleted, he remained here for more than a year, recruiting his health and writing his journal. Then, in October 1674, he set forth to fulfil his long-cherished wish to found a mission among the Illinois. The weather was stormy, the lake rough, and Marquette and his two companions suffered such hardships that when they reached the mouth of the Chicago River the priest was seriously ill. Building a small hut, the three sheltered themselves as best they could from the elements. Parties of Illinois Indians frequently visited them, and by the end of March Marquette thought himself sufficiently recovered to proceed to their village on the Illinois River. There he spent Easter, preaching to a vast concourse; but his disease grew worse, and after a short stay he left for St. Ignace, hoping to reach that place before he died. His strength failed completely, however; he was carried ashore by his attendants, and at the mouth of the river now called the Père Marquette his life came to an end. Two years later some of his neophytes who were passing by carried his remains to the St. Ignace mission, where they were buried in the chapel. Two hundred years later (1877) vestiges of what were thought to be Marquette's bones were unearthed at St. Ignace, where they were reburied except for some fragments which were carried to Milwaukee and given to Marquette University.

Of all the Jesuit missionaries in the West, Marquette is the most renowned, partly because of his early death, partly because of his sweet and saintly nature, partly because he and Jolliet were the first to follow the course of the Mississippi River, a journey made known to the world by the journals, letters, and maps of the explorers. Cities, counties, a river, a university, and a railroad are named for Marquette, a statue of him is in the Capitol at Washington, but his best monument is the account he left of his Mississippi trip and of his last voyage on his way to death in the wilderness.

[The journal of the Mississippi voyage was first published in 1681 in Melchisédeck Thévenot's *Recueil de Voyages*; it was translated and published several times before it appeared, retranslated from the copy at Montreal, in vol. LIX (1900) of *The Jesuit Relations and Allied Documents*, ed. by R. G. Thwaites, which also includes Marquette's journal of his trip to the Illinois, first published by J. G. Shea in his *Discovery and Exploration of the Mississippi River* (1852), as well as Dablon's account of the Illinois mission and Marquette's death. The journal appears also in *Early Narratives of the Northwest* (1917), ed. by L. P. Kellogg. Biographies are R. G. Thwaites, *Father Marquette* (1902), Agnes Repplier, *Père Marquette* (1929). See also L. P. Kellogg, *The French Régime in Wisconsin and the Northwest* (1925), F. B. Steck, *The Jolliet-Marquette Expedition, 1673* (rev. ed., 1928).]

L. P. K.

MARQUIS, JOHN ABNER (Dec. 27, 1861–July 5, 1931), Presbyterian clergyman and college president, was born at Dinsmore, Pa. His father, James Taggert Marquis, lived on the farm which had belonged to his father and grandfather. The family, probably of Huguenot origin, settled in Washington County before the Revolution, and produced many Presbyterian clergymen. John's mother, Mary Campbell Bucher, also came of a line of Washington County farmers. Marquis graduated from Washington and Jefferson College in 1885, and after teaching in Blairsville College for Women (1885–87), studied in Western Theological Seminary, graduating in 1890. While serving as associate pastor of the First Presbyterian Church of Greensburg, Pa., he was ordained by the Presbytery of Blairsville on Jan. 2, 1891. Three Presbyterian pastorates followed, in Westminster Church, Greensburg, from 1892 to 1902, in Redlands, Cal., for three years, and in Beaver, Pa., for four years. Marquis was also associate editor of the *Presbyterian Banner* of Pittsburgh from 1899 to 1909. His original, thoughtful preaching and power of attaching people to himself brought to his churches substantial growth.

In 1909 he became president of Coe College at Cedar Rapids, Iowa. During his administration important advances were made in teaching, buildings, and endowment. His good sense, sincerity, sympathy, and humor gave him a standing with faculty and students which enriched the life of the college. His services to education and his growing reputation in the Presbyterian Church led to his election to be moderator of the General Assembly in 1916. This Assembly reflected some excitement in the church over an early manifestation of the fundamentalist controversy. Marquis' guidance of the meeting much increased his influence, and largely caused his election to be secretary of the Presbyterian Board of Home Missions in 1917. Coe College protested against his leaving, and he spent some time there until 1920. The board which he had undertaken to direct was then in trouble because of conservative opposition to some features of its policy and of disturbing changes in organization which had been imposed upon it. Marquis strengthened it in the confidence of the church, and overcame administrative difficulties by wisdom and friendliness in personal relations and by his gift for winning cooperation. Before long he met even graver problems through the combination of his board with others in the Presbyterian Board of National Missions. Of this he was chosen general secretary in 1923. Out of somewhat discordant elements he fashioned an effective organization, animated by his own high ideal of the board's function. Through these years he exercised a strong progressive leadership in the Presbyterian Church. In interdenominational relations also he was prominent, working energetically in the Home Missions Council of the American and Canadian churches and in the Federal Council of the Churches of Christ in America, of whose administrative committee he was chairman. He was a delegate of the Presbyterian Church at the Stockholm Conference of 1925 and the Lausanne Conference of 1927.

At Vienna, in September 1928, he suffered a stroke of paralysis, and after nearly three years of infirmity and suffering he died in New York City. He was married on Sept. 1, 1896, to Martha Miller Neilson of Greensburg, Pa., who with a son and two daughters survived him. Besides many articles in periodicals he published *Learning to Teach from the Master Teacher* (1913) and *The Christian Conception of Property* (1916).

[*Who's Who in America*, 1930–31; address by H. S. Coffin at memorial meeting Presbyt. Bd. Nat. Miss. (MS.); records of trustees of Coe Coll.; *Gen. Biog. Cat. Western Theol. Sem., 1827–1927* (n.d.); *N. Y. Times*, July 6, 1931; *Presbyterian Banner*, July 9, 1931; information from family.] R. H. N.

MARSH, CHARLES WESLEY (Mar. 22, 1834–Nov. 9, 1918), inventor, manufacturer, editor, was born on the old Marsh homestead near Trenton, Northumberland County, Ontario, Canada, on the north shore of the Bay of Quinte. He was the son of Samuel and Tamar (Richardson) Marsh and was descended from William Marsh of Kent County, England, who emigrated to Connecticut about the middle of the seventeenth century and whose grandson, born in Vermont, became a "United Empire Loyalist" and after the outbreak of the Revolution emigrated to Canada where he invested largely in lands. Marsh received his primary education at home and in the district school and helped in the farm labors after the age of six. When he was eleven his parents sold their farm and moved to Illinois. On the way, at Coburg, Canada, his father was converted to the Second Adventist teachings of William Miller with the result that the family migration was delayed for four years. During this period Marsh attended St. Andrews School for one and one-half years and then Victoria College in Coburg, winning prizes for scholarship in both institutions. When he was fifteen years old his family resumed its journey and after an overland trip by way of Chicago, took up late in 1849 a quarter section of government land near Shabbona and De Kalb in De Kalb County, Ill. During the succeeding decade he lived with his parents and experienced all that pioneer farming entailed, the building of a home, clearing and cultivating the land, and harvesting the crops.

In the course of time agricultural machinery was gradually added to the farm equipment including in 1856 a Mann reaping machine. With this Marsh and his younger brother William [*q.v.*] harvested grain for two consecutive years. The machine was of the side-delivery type with an endless belt which delivered the grain into a receptacle from which it was discharged in gavels onto the ground ready for binding into sheaves. In the course of working with the new machine the brothers were struck with the idea of binding the grain *on the machine,* and throughout the winter of 1857 and the following spring they conducted many experiments toward that end. In June 1858 they applied for a patent. Meantime they refitted their Mann reaper in accordance with their plan and successfully used it in the harvest of that year. Their patent for a "reaping machine" was granted on Aug. 17, 1858, No. 21,207. The machine was the first practical hand-binding harvester, furnishing the foundation for the modern harvesting machine in that it was the first and only machine to which self-binding devices could be successfully attached.

From 1858 to 1863 Marsh divided his attention between the farm and the harvester, refining the latter and taking steps toward its later manufacture. He unsuccessfully undertook the construction of twelve machines in 1860, but he built in 1861 a single machine which had all the qualities required for field work. In 1863, in connection with Lewis Steward, he established a manufactory for the harvester at Plano, Ill., and began building machines in a small way. Twenty-five were made and sold for the harvest of 1864. They performed so successfully that manufacturing licenses were applied for by others and within a few years Marsh harvesters were being made at two establishments in Illinois and at one in Ohio. The plant at Plano was enlarged from year to year and machines were manufactured under the firm name of Marsh, Steward & Company. In 1865 a financial interest in the establishment was secured by Gammon & Deering, which organization finally purchased the entire property. Then in 1869 Marsh established the Sycamore Marsh Harvester Manufacturing Company at Sycamore, Ill., and successfully operated that for seven years. In 1876 he sold a controlling interest in this enterprise to J. D. Easter & Company and retired the following year.

Easter & Company failed in 1877 and deeply involved the Harvester Manufacturing Company at Sycamore. Marsh, who still possessed a large financial interest there, endeavored to prevent a complete collapse of the business. In the course of the succeeding three years, however, matters went from bad to worse. In 1879 the original patents for the harvester expired as did also the manufacturing licenses, so that eventually in 1881 Marsh was compelled to close out the Marsh Company. He then founded the Marsh Binder Manufacturing Company, using the same plant and facilities at Sycamore, and endeavored to develop an automatic binding machine. Inventors were employed and inventions purchased for this purpose, but the attempt failed completely in 1884 and Marsh lost everything. In 1885 he became the editor of the newly formed trade journal *Farm Implement News,* the first number of which appeared in April 1885. The paper was successful from the start and became one of the leading farm machinery trade papers of the world. In the course of time Marsh was made president of the publishing company and continued to serve in this office, though retiring as editor at the age of seventy.

Marsh went abroad in 1870 and demonstrated the machine in Austria and Hungary. He participated in a number of competitive trials and in Hungary won the first prize. In 1868 he had served in the lower house of the Illinois legislature and two years later one term in the Senate. He also served for twenty years as a trustee of the Northern Illinois Hospital for the Insane. He was twice married: first, on Jan. 1, 1860, to Frances Wait, and after her death to Sue Rogers on Jan. 10, 1881. He was survived by his widow and by three children of the first marriage.

[C. W. Marsh, *Recollections, 1837–1910* (1910); *House Executive Doc. 105,* 35 Cong., 2 Sess.; *House Executive Doc. 51,* 38 Cong., 2 Sess.; *House Executive Doc. 52,* 39 Cong., 1 Sess.; *House Executive Doc. 96,* 40 Cong., 2 Sess.; *Specifications and Drawings of Patents Issued from the U. S. Patent Office,* June 18, 1872; *Decisions of the Commissioner of Patents for the Year 1872* (1873); L. M. Gross, *Past and Present of De Kalb County, Ill.* (1907), vol. II; E. W. Byrn, *The Progress of Invention in the Nineteenth Century* (1900); W. B. Kaempffert, *A Popular Hist. of Am. Invention* (2 vols., 1924); R. L. Ardrey, *Am. Agric. Implements* (1894); *Farm Implement News,* Nov. 14, 1918; *Farm Machinery-Farm Power,* Nov. 15, 1918; *Implement and Tractor Age,* Nov. 20, 1918; *Chicago Sunday Tribune,* Nov. 10, 1918.]

C. W. M.

MARSH, GEORGE PERKINS (Mar. 15, 1801–July 23, 1882), lawyer, diplomat, and scholar, a first cousin of James Marsh [*q.v.*], was born at Woodstock, Vt. His father, Charles Marsh, an eminent lawyer, was a descendant of John Marsh who settled at Hartford, Conn., in 1636, and the son of Joseph Marsh, a former lieutenant-governor of Vermont; his mother, Susan (*née* Perkins), at the time of her marriage to his father was the widow of Josias Lyndon Arnold. His ancestors on both sides belonged to the intellectual aristocracy of New England. Brought up in a family of Puritan restraint, George was a frail and serious child who played by preference with girls and almost ruined his eyesight when he was seven by too assiduous reading. Unable for long periods to use his eyes, he learned by listening to others read and entered Dartmouth College in 1816 having had only a few months of formal schooling. There he was recognized as the most brilliant scholar in his class. Studious almost to excess, he learned French, Spanish, Portuguese, Italian, and German in his spare time, yet a dry humor made him not unpopular with classmates. In 1820 he graduated with highest honors and immediately tried teaching, but finding it distasteful, studied law in his father's office. Admitted to the bar in 1825, he practised in Burlington, Vt., where he not only became prominent in his profession but also found time to familiarize himself with the Scandinavian languages. On Apr. 10, 1828, he married Harriet, daughter of Ozias Buell of Burlington, and her death in 1833, within a few days of that of the older of their two sons, was a crushing blow. Six years later he married Caroline, daughter of Benjamin Crane of Berkley, Mass. Meanwhile his ability as a lawyer, business man, and scholar had been recognized, and in 1835 he was appointed by the governor to the supreme executive council of the state. In 1834 he was elected to Congress as a Whig, and during two successive terms proved himself a cogent if dry speaker in support of high tariff and in opposition to slavery and the Mexican War.

In 1849 President Taylor appointed him minister to Turkey, and at Constantinople his encyclopedic knowledge of languages was most useful. He cooperated with Sir Stratford Canning in aiding many refugees from the central European revolutions of 1848 and arranged for the departure of Kossuth and fifty compatriots on an American frigate. In the summer of 1852 he was sent to Athens, where the United States had no regular diplomatic representative, to investigate the case of Jonas King [*q.v.*], an American missionary imprisoned by the local authorities. After careful study of the copious evidence in modern Greek, Marsh found him the victim of unscrupulous and bigoted persecution and returned the next spring to demand redress. While the Greek government procrastinated, the minister was recalled to Constantinople by an acrimonious dispute over Martin Koszta, a Hungarian revolutionist half-naturalized in the United States and illegally seized in Smyrna by an Austrian naval commander. Instructed by John Porter Brown [*q.v.*], the American chargé at Constantinople, Capt. Duncan N. Ingraham [*q.v.*] of the American sloop of war *St. Louis* had demanded the prisoner and cleared his ship for action to enforce compliance before the Austrian discreetly delivered him to the French consul. Marsh and the Austrian ambassador pointed out with equal correctness that both naval officers had flagrantly disregarded the sovereignty of Turkey, but the Porte did nothing, and excitement soon died down.

Recalled by a new administration in 1854, Marsh labored to mend his bankrupt fortunes, acted as railroad commissioner for the state of Vermont, and delivered at Columbia University and the Lowell Institute lectures on English philology and etymology which established his reputation as an outstanding authority in those fields. Having joined the Republican party in 1856, he was sent by President Lincoln as the first United States minister to the new kingdom of Italy in 1860. This post he held for the remaining twenty-one years of his life, gaining great prestige with the Italian government through his obvious honesty and sympathy with their aims, and building up a greater reputation as a scholar by his numerous reviews and encyclopedia articles. He died at Vallombrosa, near Florence, and was buried in the Protestant Cemetery at Rome.

A man of great personal dignity and reserve, Marsh was master of a punning humor and could turn a compliment prettily. With interests which ranged from comparative grammar to physiography and from the gathering of reptiles for the Smithsonian Institution to the collection of engravings, which were ultimately acquired by the Smithsonian, he was a sort of universal genius, a conscientious and erudite scholar in many fields. His early interest in Scandinavia resulted in the publication of *A Compendious Grammar of the Old-Northern or Icelandic Language* (1838), largely a compilation from the work of R. K. Rask; while another aspect of the same study showed itself in his preaching a gospel of old Teutonic simplicity and virtue, to which he attributed everything good in the English tradition (*The Goths in New-England,* 1843). His travels in the Near East inspired *The Camel, His Organization, Habits, and Uses, Considered with Reference to His Introduction into the United States* (1856). He was one of the early workers associated with the Oxford Dictionary (J. A. H. Murray, *A New English Dictionary,* vol. I, 1888, Preface, p. v). His *Lectures on the English Language* (1860) and *The Origin and History of the English Language* (1862) were excellent philological and etymological works for their day but have since become antiquated. His *Man and Nature, or Physical Geography as Modified by Human Action* (1864; revised edition of 1874 entitled *The Earth as Modified by Human Action*), embodying the fruit of many years' acute observation during his extensive travels, has been called "the fountainhead of the conservation movement" (Lewis Mumford, *The Brown Decades,* 1931, p. 78). It was a pioneer effort "to suggest the possibility and the importance of the restoration of disturbed harmonies and the material improvement of waste and exhausted regions" (Preface, quoted by Mumford, p. 75), and had a significant influence both at home and abroad.

[H. L. Koopman, *Bibliog. of George Perkins Marsh* (1892); Caroline Crane Marsh, *Life and Letters of G. P. Marsh* (1888), projected as a two-volume work, only one volume published; S. G. Brown, *A Discourse Commemorative of the Hon. George Perkins Marsh* (1883); D. W. Marsh, *Marsh Geneal.* (1895); H. L. Mencken, *The Am. Language* (1919), pp. 8, 144; *Proc. Am. Acad. Arts and Sci.*, vol. XVIII (1883); *Atti della R. Accademia dei Lincei . . . 1882–83* (3 ser. VII, 1883); the *Nation* (N. Y.), July 27, Aug. 3, Oct. 12, 1882; *N. Y. Times,* July 25, 1882.] W. L. W., Jr.

MARSH, GRANT PRINCE (May 11, 1834–Jan. 2, 1916), steamboat captain, pioneer, was born in Chautauqua County, N. Y., the son of John and Lydia (Dyer) Marsh. A few years later the family moved to Rochester, Pa., on the Ohio River. At the age of twelve young Marsh's schooling came to an end, and he became a cabin boy on a local steamboat plying from Pittsburgh. For more than sixty years thereafter, almost without interruption, he was connected with river transportation. In 1852, as a deckhand, he reached St. Louis, which for a long period was to be his home. As a watchman on the *A. B.*

Chambers, he narrowly escaped with his life in the great disaster of Feb. 27, 1856, when the breaking of an ice jam wrecked or sank some fifty vessels on the St. Louis waterfront. In the following year he became a mate, and in the winter of 1858–59 served with Mark Twain, with whom he formed a lifelong friendship. In 1861, at St. Louis, he married Katharine Reardon. He was the mate of the *John J. Roe* when that vessel, in March 1862, assisted in carrying Grant's army from Fort Donelson to Pittsburg Landing, and on the bloody Sunday of Apr. 6 aided in placing Buell's army on the left bank of the river. In 1864, in the service of transporting supplies for General Sully's army, operating against the Sioux, he had his first experience with the Indian country. He became a master in 1866, taking his vessel, the *Luella,* to Fort Benton, the head of navigation on the Missouri. He soon acquired an exceptional knowledge of the upper waters, and his skill as a pilot (for he always piloted his own vessels) caused him to be frequently employed by the military authorities during the Sioux wars. Early in 1873 he carried Gen. G. A. Forsyth's party of reconnaissance up the Yellowstone to a point near the mouth of the Powder, and on the voyage he gave names to many of the physical features of the valley. In the summer of that year he cooperated with the Stanley-Custer expedition along the Yellowstone, and two years later carried Gen. J. W. Forsyth's expedition nearly fifty miles above Pompey's Pillar. In 1876, in the historic *Far West,* he cooperated with the Custer-Terry expedition, forcing his boat up the tortuous channel of the Bighorn to the mouth of the Little Bighorn. From there he brought down the wounded from the Custer battlefield, and starting from Fort Pease, in the afternoon of July 3, took his vessel to Fort Abraham Lincoln, a distance of 710 miles, in the unparalleled time of fifty-four hours.

The close of the Sioux wars and the advent of railroads to the Upper Missouri had by 1882 paralyzed the steamboat industry in that region. For the next twenty-one years Marsh's service was on the Mississippi. A revival of steamboating on the Upper Missouri brought him again to the region in 1903, at first in the employ of Gen. W. D. Washburn and later of the Benton Packet Company. He made his home in Bismarck, N. Dak. In 1906 his wife died, and about 1910 he retired. He died at St. Alexius Hospital, Bismarck, and was buried, by his own request, on Wagonwheel Bluff, overlooking the Missouri River. Four children survived him.

Marsh was a man somewhat above medium height, of sinewy body and of great strength. He was keen-sighted, alert and quick of movement, and deliberate in speech. His manner was as a rule gentle, though at times he could be aroused to a high pitch of anger. His skill as a pilot and his fearlessness in time of danger were recognized by all. He was, wrote Gen. G. A. Forsyth, "the ideal man of his profession" (Hanson, *post,* p. 167); and Sherman, Sheridan, Custer Miles, Stanley, and others paid high tribute to his abilities and his character.

[J. M. Hanson, *The Conquest of the Missouri: Being the Story of the Life and Exploits of Captain Grant Marsh* (1909); *Bismarck Daily Tribune,* Jan. 4, 1916; information from Marsh's sister, Mrs. Lydia Gordon, Rochester, Pa.]

W. J. G.

MARSH, JAMES (July 19, 1794–July 3, 1842), philosopher and president of the University of Vermont, a first cousin of George Perkins Marsh [*q.v.*], was born on a farm at Hartford, Vt., the son of Daniel and Marion (Harper) Marsh, and the grandson of Joseph Marsh, first lieutenant-governor of the state. He was destined for the farm; but at the age of eighteen his circumstances changed, and after a brief preparation under William Nutting, a schoolmaster at Randolph, he entered Dartmouth College. Here he became an omnivorous reader, with a special devotion to the classics and to the Cambridge Platonists. In 1815 he was converted during a revival, and in 1817, upon graduation from Dartmouth, proceeded to Andover Theological Seminary. From 1818 to 1820 he was back at Dartmouth as a tutor; then returned to Andover until 1822. In his last year at Andover he contributed to the *North American Review* (July 1822) an article on "Ancient and Modern Poetry," and helped to translate J. J. Bellermann's *Geography of the Scriptures.* He was then out of employment for a year and even thought of settling down as a farmer. In 1823 he became a teacher at the college and theological school at Hampden-Sidney, Va., and in 1824 was appointed professor of Oriental languages there; in the same year he was ordained at Hanover, N. H., as a Congregational minister, and married Lucia Wheelock, niece of the president of Dartmouth. In 1826 he was chosen president of the University of Vermont.

Under Marsh's influence the institution became a leader in educational reform, both in New England and in the Middle West. His views on education are set forth in *An Address Delivered in Burlington upon the Inauguration of the Author to the Office of President of the University of Vermont, Nov. 28, 1826* (1827) and in *An Exposition of the Course of Instruction and Disci-*

pline in the University of Vermont (1829). He made the entrance qualifications less exclusive, allowed students greater freedom to follow their own interests, strengthened the personal contacts between teachers and undergraduates, and based discipline on personal influence rather than on obedience to rules. In 1829 he edited Coleridge's *Aids to Reflection,* with a preliminary essay, and the next year published *Selections from the Old English Writers on Practical Theology.* He also contributed to the *Vermont Chronicle* (Windsor, Vt.), beginning Jan. 16, 1829, a series of articles on popular education; and to the *Christian Spectator,* a review of Moses Stuart's two-volume *Commentary on the Epistle to the Hebrews* (1828–29), in which he defended German methods of Biblical criticism. Feeling that the University needed at its head a man of greater business ability, Marsh resigned the presidency in 1833 and became professor of philosophy. In the same year he published a translation of J. G. Herder's *The Spirit of Hebrew Poetry,* and in 1837, a translation of D. H. Hegewisch's *Introduction to Historical Chronology.* In 1836 during a religious revival in Vermont under one Burchard, who was making converts by arousing mob emotion, Marsh became a vigorous opponent of these "new measures."

He admired the poetry of the Romantic movement in England and Germany, which he considered a natural product of Christian influences; and his romanticism caused him to revolt against the philosophy of Locke and the Scotch school which then dominated New England. In his search for a modification of Calvinism which should "satisfy the heart as well as the head," he adopted the Coleridgean distinction between the reason and the understanding. His edition of *Aids to Reflection* created a ferment among young intellectuals, was read with enthusiasm by Emerson, and had a formative influence upon the transcendentalist movement. Though his voice and manner unfitted him for preaching to large audiences and he was stiff and diffident in society, he was a brilliant conversationalist, and his students found him a sympathetic and inspiring teacher. His wife having died in 1828, he married in 1833 her sister Laura, who died in 1838. He died at Burlington.

[Joseph Torrey, *The Remains of the Rev. James Marsh, . . . with a Memoir of his Life* (1843); John Wheeler, *A Discourse Delivered July 6, 1842 at the Funeral of James Marsh* (1842); G. B. Cheever, *Characteristics of the Christian Philosopher* (1843); W. B. Sprague, *Annals Am. Pulpit,* vol. II (1857); D. W. Marsh, *Marsh Geneal.* (1895); M. H. Nicolson, "James Marsh and the Vermont Transcendentalists," in *Philosophical Rev.,* Jan. 1925; *Vermont Chronicle* (Windsor), July 6, 1842.]

H. B. P.

MARSH, JOHN (Apr. 2, 1788–Aug. 4, 1868), Congregational clergyman, temperance reformer, a descendant of George Marsh who settled in Hingham, Mass., in 1635, was born in Wethersfield, Conn., where his father, Rev. John Marsh, was for many years pastor of the Congregational church. His mother was Ann, daughter of Capt. Ebenezer Grant of East Windsor, Conn. John grew up familiar with the hard drinking of a New England town, where even clerical hospitality was made perfect only by the aid of alcoholic stimulants. In his own home, during the winter seasons, flip was the antidote for the paralyzing chill of the meeting house. "Well do I remember," he says, "crying in meeting from the cold (there were then no stoves), and holding on to my chair after drinking the FLIP till my head became steady" (*Temperance Recollections,* p. 9). When he was ten years old he went to the school of Rev. Azel Backus [*q.v.*] at Bethlehem, Conn. Two years later he entered Yale College, from which he graduated in 1804, no longer able to say truthfully that he had not been drunk at least once in his life. After teaching school and studying theology with his father, in June 1809 he was licensed to preach by the Hartford South Association of Ministers. Having supplied several churches in the meantime, on Dec. 16, 1818, he was ordained to the ministry and installed as pastor of the Congregational church, Haddam, Conn.

The temperance movement, which was just then beginning to gain momentum in the United States, soon enlisted his vigorous support. His activities attracted increasing attention, and when the Connecticut Temperance Society was organized, May 1829, he was appointed secretary and general agent. On Oct. 21 of that year he delivered an address before the Windham County Temperance Society on *Putnam and the Wolf, or the Monster Destroyed,* more than 150,000 printed copies of which were sold. Securing three months' leave of absence from his parish in 1831, he accepted an invitation to promote the cause of temperance in Baltimore and Washington. In order to attract nation-wide attention to the movement he arranged for a congressional temperance meeting, which was held in the hall of the House of Representatives, and had the support of many prominent federal officials. His labors for the cause were now commanding so much of his time and interest that in the spring of 1833 he resigned his pastorate. He was a delegate to the first National Temperance Convention, held in Philadelphia, May 1833, and was one of its secretaries; and on Oct. 1, he began a three years' term of service as agent of the Pennsylvania State Temperance Society. In 1836 the executive committee of the reorganized American Temperance Union determined to establish a national press in Philadelphia, and Marsh was appointed editor, and corresponding secretary of the Union. A monthly publication, the *Journal of the American Temperance Union,* was begun, the first number of which appeared on Jan. 15, 1837; and in October 1839, the office now having been removed to New York, the *Youth's Temperance Advocate* was started. Not until 1865, when the American Temperance Union was superseded by a new organization, did Marsh's tireless editorial and promotional activities come to a close. At this time he had already suffered two attacks of partial paralysis; nevertheless he was engaged in raising money for a building for the Yale Divinity School when in 1868 the last and fatal attack came. His death occurred at his home in Brooklyn, N. Y., and he was buried in Wethersfield, Conn. During his last years he prepared *Temperance Recollections: Labors, Defeats, Triumphs. An Autobiography* (1866). He also published many pamphlets relating to temperance, and *An Epitome of General Ecclesiastical History from the Earliest Period to the Present Time* (1827), which went through numerous editions. His wife, whom he married Oct. 5, 1824, was Frances Fowler, daughter of John and Phebe Talmadge of Warren, Conn.

[In addition to *Temperance Recollections* cited above, consult F. B. Dexter, *Biog. Sketches Grads. Yale Coll.,* vol. V (1911), which lists Marsh's publications; E. J. Marsh, *Geneal. of the Family of George Marsh* (1887); *N. Y. Times,* Aug. 5, 1868; and *Congreg. Quart.,* Jan. 1869.] H. E. S.

MARSH, JOHN (June 5, 1799–Sept. 24, 1856), California pioneer, was the eldest of the seven children of John and Mary (Brown) Marsh and a descendant of John Marsh who emigrated from England to Salem, Mass., about 1633. Born and reared in South Danvers, Mass., he attended Franklin Academy in North Andover, Lancaster Academy, and was graduated from the Phillips Academy at Andover in 1819. Entering Harvard College he graduated with the class of 1823. He was appointed tutor to officers' children at Fort St. Anthony, now St. Paul, and arrived at this frontier post in October 1823. During his two years' service he studied medicine under Dr. Edward Purcell, the fort surgeon, and had almost completed the course mapped out, when his preceptor died. He mingled freely with the neighboring Indians and in 1824 and 1825 served as sub-agent to the Sioux at St. Peter. Here he fell in love with Marguerite Decouteaux, daughter of a French father and a Sioux mother. This romance profoundly influenced his life for it was, perhaps, the principal reason why he stayed in the wilderness instead of returning to the East. For seven years the couple lived together and raised an only son, who survived both parents. In 1826, with the help of Lewis Cass, then governor of Michigan Territory, Marsh was appointed sub-agent for Indian affairs at Prairie du Chien, and he served in that post and also as justice of the peace of Crawford County until the death of Marguerite. During these years he worked on a Sioux dictionary and wrote a brief grammar of the Sioux language, which were published in Caleb Atwater's *Remarks Made on a Tour to Prairie du Chien* (1831, pp. 149–72). His friendship with the Sioux indirectly led to the outbreak of the Black Hawk War of 1832, in which he organized and led a band of Sioux. Dispirited and melancholy over the death of Marguerite, he resigned as justice at the end of the war and had disposed of his fur-trade when he learned of the issuance of a warrant to arrest him on the charge of unlawfully selling arms and ammunition to the Indians. He fled down the Mississippi to St. Louis, located at Independence, Mo., and for two years was engaged in general merchandising. In 1835 he lost all his property and, still fearing arrest, departed secretly for Santa Fé, where he arrived only after escaping death at the hands of Indian captors.

In February 1836 he reached Los Angeles, where he soon received permission to practise as a physician, but in less than a year he had sold his practice and started north in search of a cattle range. In order to obtain a Mexican land title, he was baptized a Roman Catholic and became a naturalized Mexican citizen. Later he bought a rancho ten miles wide and twelve miles long in the San Joaquin Valley, near the site of the present city of Antioch. He resumed the practice of medicine and for many years was the only physician in the San Joaquin Valley. In return for his services he exacted heavy fees, usually in cattle, and soon became the owner of large herds. The discovery of gold drew him into the mines for a time and added greatly to his rapidly accumulating fortune. In June 1851 he married Abigail Smith Tuck of Chelmsford, Mass. She died in a few years, leaving him a daughter, who, with her half-brother, inherited the large estate. Impressed by the results of American infiltration into Texas, he became convinced that the story of Texas might be repeated in California and in Oregon. He wrote letters to friends in Missouri and to his former patron Senator Cass, urging immigration to California and begging for official encouragement of it.

Some of his letters were published in newspapers and seem to have been influential in starting the first American migration to California just before the discovery of gold. In person, he was tall, heavy, athletic, and commanding. He was fond of books and a linguist of no mean ability. As a business man he was adroit, exacting, and not over-scrupulous. Dissatisfied with their wages, three of his *vaqueros* waylaid, robbed, and murdered him not far from Martinez, Cal.

["Doctor John Marsh, Cal. Pioneer," an unpublished thesis by E. J. Ulsh at the University of Cal., with numerous letters from Marsh; G. D. Lyman, *John Marsh* (1930); *Hist. of Contra Costa County, Cal.* (1882); *The Hist. of Contra Costa County, Cal.*, ed. by F. J. Hulaniski (1917); L. B. Marsh, *The Geneal. of John Marsh of Salem* (1888); Joseph Palmer, *Necrology of Alumni of Harvard College, 1851–52 to 1862–63* (1864).]

P. O. R.

MARSH, OTHNIEL CHARLES (Oct. 29, 1831–Mar. 18, 1899), paleontologist, eldest son of Caleb and Mary Gaines (Peabody) Marsh, both of Danvers (now Peabody), Mass., was born in Lockport, N. Y. His father was a brother of John Marsh, 1799–1856 [*q.v.*], and a descendant of John Marsh who was established in Salem in 1637. After the death of his mother, when he was three years old, the boy lived for some two years with a maiden aunt whose interest in him thereafter seems to have had an important influence upon his future. His early education was acquired in the schools of Lockport and the Wilson Collegiate Institute. Graduating from Phillips Academy, Andover, Mass., in 1856, he entered Yale College, where he took a classical course and graduated with the degree of B.A. in 1860. In 1861–62 he pursued graduate studies in the Yale Scientific School and then spent three years in study at Berlin, Breslau, and Heidelberg, Germany. In 1866 he received an appointment to the chair of paleontology at Yale, the first chair of this nature to be established in America. This position he held for the rest of his life.

While but a youth, Marsh had shown more than passing interest in natural history and by the time he was nineteen the study was his dominant concern. His vacations from 1851 to 1862 were occupied with field trips throughout New York, the New England states, and Nova Scotia. In 1855 he found some fossil vertebrae in the coal-measures of the South Joggins, Nova Scotia, and the interest these aroused definitely turned him toward the subject that was to constitute his life work. Soon after his appointment at Yale, he went west over the newly constructed Union Pacific Railroad as far as Nebraska and Wyoming. Here, for the first time, he gained a realization of the almost boundless field to which he was henceforth to devote his major efforts. In 1870 he organized his first Yale Scientific Expedition, consisting of thirteen persons with a military escort to see them safely from post to post. This first year they explored the Pliocene deposits of Nebraska and the Miocene of northern Colorado, crossed over into the Bridger Basin of Wyoming, and pushed southward into the Uinta Basin and thence into California. During the following years similar expeditions were carried on, bringing to light an undreamed of wealth of material and placing Marsh—with the possible exception of Edward Drinker Cope [*q.v.*]—at the head of American vertebrate paleontologists. Until 1880, his expeditions were financed largely through his own private means, which had been augmented by his inheritance of a share of the fortune of his uncle, George Peabody [*q.v.*], who died in 1869. In 1882, following the reorganization of the various federal surveys, Marsh was appointed vertebrate paleontologist to the United States Geological Survey, incidentally, it may be added, much to the chagrin of Cope, who with the exception of Joseph Leidy [*q.v.*] was Marsh's only rival in his field. Between Marsh and Cope there was ever thereafter a warfare to the extreme limit possible to verbal combat.

Marsh's first great discovery was that already mentioned of *Eosaurus* remains in the coal-measures of Nova Scotia. From the beginning of his western trips in 1870 to the close of his active career, he accumulated materials more rapidly than he could study them, and his published bibliography is not as full nor as comprehensive as the opportunities he enjoyed seemed to warrant. Aside from numerous short papers in the *American Journal of Science*, his principal monographic works were *Odontornithes; a Monograph on the Extinct Toothed Birds of North America* (1880), and *Dinocerata; a Monograph of an Extinct Order of Gigantic Mammals* (1884). Several others which were projected were found after his death to be scarcely begun, so far as shown by written manuscript; and thus the expensive work of years of collection and preparation, while not wholly lost, did not yield its full measure of printed matter. His most masterly and comprehensive single paper, according to his biographer, Beecher, was his *Introduction and Succession of Vertebrate Life in America* (1877). He was the first to describe the remains of fossil serpents and flying reptiles in the western part of the American continent.

To Marsh must be given credit for putting the collection and preparation of vertebrate fossils upon a truly scientific basis. It is because of his influence and that of his able assistants that the exhibits of ancient vertebrate life in American museums are no longer limited to isolated fragments of bones, but often include entire skeletons as complete in every part as those of animals now living. It may be added that his interests as a collector were by no means limited to vertebrate fossils. He formed what was at the time of his death one of the most complete osteological collections in America. Minerals, invertebrate fossils, archeological and ethnological materials also came within his domain. "He not only had the means and the inclination, but entered every field of acquisition with the dominating ambition to obtain everything there was in it, and leave not a scrap behind" (Beecher).

Marsh was a man of fairly large frame, robust, and of about medium height. Throughout his youth he indulged freely in outdoor life, and until well past middle age could endure exposure and physical strain to a degree far beyond the ordinary. He was remarkably free from the petty annoyances of ill health, and through the beneficence of his uncle, George Peabody, was economically completely independent. As a man he was strongly self-reliant, inclined to be seclusive, but hospitable and kindly, and of pronounced esthetic tastes. He never married, but lived the life of a wealthy bachelor and patron of science in his fine house in New Haven. He died after a brief illness from pneumonia in his sixty-eighth year. Among the many honors he received were the presidency of the National Academy of Sciences (1883–95), the Bigsby medal from the Geological Society of London (1877), and the Cuvier prize from the French Academy (1898). He was connected with the United States Geological Survey from his appointment in 1882 until his death.

[C. E. Beecher, in *Am. Jour. Sci.*, June 1899, with bibliography; abridgments of the same sketch in *Bull. Geol. Soc. of America*, July 31, 1900, and *Am. Geologist*, Sept. 1899; G. B. Grinnell, in *Leading Am. Men of Sci.* (1910), ed. by D. S. Jordan; *Obit. Record Grads. Yale Univ.*, 1899; L. B. Marsh, *The Geneal. of John Marsh of Salem* (1888); *New Haven Evening Register*, Mar. 18, 1899.]

G. P. M.

MARSH, SYLVESTER (Sept. 30, 1803–Dec. 30, 1884), inventor, was born at Campton, N. H., in the sparsely settled Pemigewasset Valley. He was a descendant of Alexander Marsh who was in Braintree, Mass., as early as 1654, and the son of John and Mehitable (Percival) Marsh, who, toward the close of the eighteenth century, had emigrated from East Haddam, Conn., cleared a bit of forest, and begun farming. In this primitive environment (he was nine years old before he saw a wheeled vehicle) Marsh grew to manhood, working on the farm and attending the district school a few months each winter. At nineteen he left home and for the next three years worked about Boston as a farm hand, learned brickmaking, and tended a provision stall in Quincy Market, incidentally learning to cure and pack pork. Early in 1828, in company with a friend, he went to Ashtabula, Ohio, and there began a beef and pork packing business, shipping the products east by way of the Erie Canal. Five years later, in 1833, he moved on to Chicago and on the site of the present Court House established a beef-marketing business. Following the financial crash of 1837, in which he experienced the disastrous fate which overtook many other business men, he began all over again as a grain dealer. This enterprise was successful, and in the course of a quarter of a century, operating both in Chicago and in Davenport, Iowa, he built up a comfortable fortune. Much of his success was due to his inventions, patented between 1855 and 1865, for the mechanical handling of grain, for improvements in grain dryers, and for an improved process of manufacturing kiln-dried meal. This product was marketed as "Marsh's Caloric Dry Meal," the largest part of it being exported to the West Indies. During this period Marsh lived in several places. He moved from Chicago to Jamaica Plain, Mass., in 1855, and five years later returned to Chicago for four years. In 1864–65 he resided in Brooklyn, N. Y., managing his export business.

Some years earlier Marsh had conceived the idea of constructing a railroad up Mount Washington in New Hampshire, and as a first step obtained a charter from the state legislature in 1858. Before he could proceed to realize the project, however, the Civil War began and actual construction was not started until 1866. The road was completed in 1869 at a cost of $150,000. It is two and one-half miles long, the average grade being 1,300 feet to the mile, and one and one-half hours are required to make the ascent. Much of Marsh's mechanical ingenuity was called into play, not only in the construction of the roadway but also in the design of the steam locomotives. He patented an improvement in locomotive engines for ascending inclined planes (Sept. 10, 1861); apparatus for ascending gradients (Nov. 8, 1864); cog rail for railroads (Jan. 15, 1867); atmospheric brake for railway cars (Apr. 12, 1870). His central cog rail driving mechanism proved extremely successful, as did the braking system (there were six ways of stopping the train) and the plan was adopted subsequently in the construction of the railroad on Mount Rigi, Switzerland. The Mount Washington project was not a financial success, however, and up to the time that the Boston & Maine Railroad took over the property some time after Marsh's death, the officers of the company received no salaries. Marsh lived at Littleton, N. H., from 1865 to 1879, and spent the last five years of his life in Concord, N. H. He was married, first, Apr. 4, 1844, to Charlotte D. Bates of Monson, Mass., who died in 1850; and second, in March 1855, to Cornelia H. Hoyt of St. Albans, Vt. He was survived by his widow and four children.

[J. R. Jackson, *Hist. of Littleton, N. H.* (1905), vols. I, III; D. W. Marsh, *Marsh Geneal.* (1895), p. xxi; C. C. Coffin, "Sylvester Marsh," in *Bay State Monthly,* May 1885, repr. in *Granite Monthly,* May–June 1885; J. W. Merrill, "The Mt. Washington Railroad," *The Railway & Locomotive Hist. Soc. Bull.* no. 4, 1923; *Daily Monitor,* Concord, N. H., Dec. 31, 1884; Patent Office records.] C. W. M.

MARSH, WILLIAM WALLACE (Apr. 15, 1836–May 2, 1918), inventor, manufacturer, was the son of Samuel and Tamar (Richardson) Marsh and the younger brother of Charles Wesley Marsh [*q.v.*]. He was born on his father's farm near Trenton, Northumberland County, Canada, and was educated at home and in the district school near his home as well as in St. Andrews School and Victoria College at Coburg, Canada, where he was a student for three years. His schooling ceased when he was thirteen years old and he moved with his parents to De Kalb County, Ill. During the succeeding eight years he worked assiduously with his father and brother to improve the raw land and to make it produce profitable crops. In 1857, while working in the fields with their newly acquired Mann reaper, Marsh and his brother conceived the idea of binding the grain on the machine. Neither youth possessed much mechanical experience but by diligent effort they succeeded in carrying out their idea and patenting their implement on Aug. 17, 1858. The machine changed the farm system from "reaping" to "harvesting" and by this invention one man could do the work formerly required of two.

In the winter of 1860 Marsh built, in connection with a neighbor, a second machine which was ready for the harvest of 1861. He used it on the farm during the next three seasons and harvested over four hundred acres with it. He also staged public demonstrations and participated in public trials, one of which was held at De Kalb in 1863, when he won first prize by binding an acre of heavy grain in fifty-two minutes. While Charles looked after the business details of their venture, William Marsh devoted himself to the mechanical, and during the formative stage of the business he gave considerable study and thought to harvester improvements and details of its manufacture. In 1864 he took charge of the manufacturing plant which had been established at Plano, Ill., in 1863 and for the succeeding twenty years both there and at Sycamore, Ill., where the company established its second factory in 1869, he served in the general capacity of superintendent. Though this work consumed the greater part of his time, he devised a number of improvements on the machine. Patents on these were granted jointly to him and his brother on Jan. 5, 1864, Feb. 15, 1865, Nov. 12, 1867, and June 18, 1872. In addition he designed other farm machinery including a plow, cultivator, corn harvester, corn husker, wire stretcher, and windmill—a total of forty inventions. All of these products were manufactured in the Marsh factories.

After the failure of the Marsh brothers in 1884 with a combined loss in excess of $400,000, they had to separate, each to make his own way thereafter. William went to Lincoln, Neb., in 1887 to superintend a manufacturing plant, and five years later he was sent to Little Rock, Ark., to reorganize and redesign a stave and lumbering enterprise. In his halcyon days he had made purchases in these states of timber lands which after a few years yielded him sufficient income so that in 1895 he was able to retire to his home in Sycamore. He then became interested again in an agricultural machinery business and continued actively in its affairs until 1906. After his retirement he devoted his energies to the betterment of Sycamore. He had married on Jan. 8, 1871, Mary Jane Brown of Chicago. She died in 1891 and on Nov. 9, 1893, he was married to Emma L. Eldredge. At the time of his death in Sycamore he was survived by his widow and two children of his first marriage.

[C. W. Marsh, *Recollections, 1837–1910* (1910); L. M. Gross, *Past and Present of De Kalb County, Ill.* (1907), vol. II; R. L. Ardrey, *Am. Agric. Implements* (1894); *Ann. Reports of the Commissioner of Patents,* 1858 and years following, *Farm Implement News,* May 9, 1918; *Farm Machinery-Farm Power,* May 14, 1918.] C. W. M.

MARSHALL, BENJAMIN (1782–Dec. 2, 1858), merchant, manufacturer, was born in Huddersfield, in the West Riding of Yorkshire, England, the youngest of six brothers who were brought up to manufacturing pursuits. In 1798 he entered the cotton manufacture at Manchester. He brought an invoice of cotton goods to New York in 1803 and here became the friend of Isaac Wright, a Quaker merchant, and Francis Thompson, Wright's son-in-law, the New York representative of a West Riding firm of woollen-cloth manufacturers. He joined Thompson in the business of importing cotton goods and exporting cotton, and spent the winters in Georgia as a cotton buyer. In 1813, he married Niobe, daughter of Capt. John Stanton, commander of Wright & Thompson's fast-sailing transatlantic trading ship *Pacific.* In 1816, Benjamin Marshall, William Wright (Isaac Wright's son), and Jeremiah Thompson (Francis Thompson's nephew) acquired shares in the *Pacific,* and in a new ship, *Amity.* At this time, Benjamin Marshall and Jeremiah Thompson [*q.v.*] were doing business in the same premises at 273 Pearl St., New York. In the spring of 1817, the five partners placed another new ship, *Courier,* in transatlantic trade, and in October 1817 they announced the establishment of a line of American packets, to make regular monthly sailings from New York and Liverpool. This was the Black Ball Line, the first of the famous transatlantic packet lines of New York. The first sailing on a regular schedule was made Jan. 1, 1818. To complete the service a fourth ship, *James Monroe,* was purchased. The management of the line appears to have been principally entrusted to Jeremiah Thompson; there is no indication that Marshall did any special part of this work.

After the enactment of the tariff of 1824, Marshall turned from importing to manufacturing and printing cotton cloths. In partnership with Benjamin S. Walcott, Jr., who was already engaged in manufacturing at Whitestown, N. Y., he established the New York Mills on a waterpower a couple of miles to the west of Utica. In 1827 (or thereabouts), with his brother Joseph, he established the Hudson Print Works, near Hudson (later Stockport), N. Y., one of the earliest cotton-printing works in the United States. Benjamin seems to have left his brother in charge of the store in New York and to have withdrawn to Hudson to manage the enterprise there.

In 1833 he sold his share in the packet line to his brother. It had become by this time the leading shipping service of New York, with a fleet of eight first-class ships and regular sailings twice a month. Early in 1834, Joseph Marshall in turn sold the line to Jonathan Goodhue & Company. Later in that year, the two brothers divided their interests in the various factories they owned, Joseph taking the Hudson Print Works, and Benjamin their share in the New York Mills and some other factories at Troy, N. Y., and elsewhere. From this time onward he seems to have devoted himself principally to the development of the factories at Troy. The cottons produced by the New York Mills near Utica and the Mount Ida Mill at Troy appear to have been clearly the finest goods of their kind produced in the United States at this time. About 1840 Marshall developed the waterpower in the Poestenkill Creek at Troy by a series of tunnels and built a chain of mills down the creek. He became one of Troy's leading citizens, and was president of one of the banks of the city, of the Troy & Schenectady Railway, and of Mrs. Emma Willard's Female Seminary. In 1847 he sold his interest in the New York Mills to the Walcott family. His wife died in 1823, leaving him one son, who developed a mental disease about 1847 of which he died ten years later. To make provision for his and similar cases, in 1850 the father founded in Troy the Marshall Infirmary (now the Marshall Sanitarium), of which he was the first president. He died in Troy in December 1858.

[John Livingston, *Portraits of Eminent Americans,* vol. III (1854); Nathan Crosby, *Annual Obituary Notices . . . for 1858* (1859); C. C. Cutler, *Greyhounds of the Sea* (1930); W. R. Bagnall, *The Textile Industries of the U. S.* (1893), pp. 506–16; A. J. Weise, *Troy's One Hundred Years* (1891); C. P. Wright, "The Packet Ships of New York," unpublished thesis in Harvard Univ. Lib.; *Atlas & Argus* (Albany), Dec. 4, 1858.]

C. P. W.

MARSHALL, CHARLES HENRY (Apr. 8, 1792–Sept. 23, 1865), sea captain, shipping executive, was born on Nantucket Island, the third of the seven children of Charles and Hepzibah (Coffin) Marshall, and the descendant of generations of whaling skippers. With the island's industry ruined by the Revolution, the father abandoned whaling for farming, settling on a tract of virgin forest in the Saratoga Patent at Easton, N. Y. The hundred acres could not support so large a family and the five sons turned to the sea, where all became successful captains. Charles Henry started his career at fifteen on the Nantucket whaler *Lima,* and then made a voyage to England. He spent a winter in school at Johnstown, N. Y., and in 1810 sailed for Riga, being detained for a year in Denmark. During the War of 1812, he taught school for a time, served on the Hudson steamboat *Paragon,* and engaged in trade with his uncle at Sacketts Harbor. In 1815 he was at sea again, as mate in the *Mary* for Oporto, under Capt. Robert Waterman, later a well-known packet captain. By 1816, at the age of twenty-three, Marshall was a captain himself and drove his *Julius Cæsar* at top speed from Charleston to Liverpool to win a hotly contested race. His next voyage was to the East Indies, and in 1822 he married Fidelia Wellman of Piermont, N. H., a "rare beauty." That same year he was given command of a Black Ball packet, one of the most coveted maritime honors of that day.

The Black Ball or "Old Line" made the first successful attempt to provide regular transatlantic service under private auspices, as distinct from the official British mail packets. It was inaugurated in 1817 by Benjamin Marshall [*q.v.*], Isaac Wright, Francis Thompson, and Jeremiah Thompson, of New York, and its continued success was an important element in the rise of the port of New York. Its ships, run with the *élan* and discipline of East Indiamen, sailed from New York for Liverpool on the 1st and 16th of every month with passengers and select freight. It enjoyed a primacy among the various packet lines which developed, until eclipsed by the Cunard and Collins steamships; but even then its sailing vessels continued profitable until after the Civil War. Marshall commanded successively the line's *James Cropper, Britannia,* and *South America* for twelve years, making, altogether, ninety-four Atlantic crossings.

In 1834, he came ashore to make his home in New York as agent of the line for the remaining thirty-one years of his life. It had then passed from its original owners into new control, particularly that of Goodhue & Company, formerly its agents. Marshall soon bought out the company's share, becoming principal owner as well as active manager, with Baring Brothers as Liverpool consignees. He personally supervised the building of all the new ships for the line and raised the standard of sailing packets to a high degree. His principal venture in steam came about 1848 when, with William H. Webb [*q.v.*] and others, he built the *United States,* which was sold to Prussia for a steam frigate after two rather unprofitable years of running between New York and Southampton. Marshall also did some business as a general commission merchant. His wealth was estimated at $120,000 in 1845; $150,000 in 1847; and the same in 1855; but it was probably more by the time of his death. He was prominent in many of the activities of the port of New York, serving for years as a commissioner of pilots, as head of the Marine Society, and as a director of the Sailors' Snug Harbor. From 1851 to 1855, he was a commissioner of emigration. Strongly anti-slavery, he was first a Whig, and later a Republican. He was nominated for Congress in 1854 and defeated while absent in Europe. Early in 1861 he declined to cooperate with naval officials in the proposed relief of Fort Sumter, on the ground that it would precipitate a conflict. Once the war started, however, he was an active Union man, prominent on the local Union Defence Committee and in the Union League Club. In the name of the state Chamber of Commerce, he urged upon the navy a tightening of the blockade and energetic pursuit of the *Alabama,* suggesting privateers for that purpose. His picture shows a strong, square, rugged face with chin whiskers, tight lips, piercing eyes, and something of a permanent scowl. Even a eulogistic obituary states that he had "an air of sternness about him that was somewhat repulsive to strangers" (*New York Herald, post*), but he was a perfect gentleman and a delightful companion with his intimates. He was noted for his independence of spirit and fearless exposing of abuses.

[W. A. Butler, *Memorial of Charles H. Marshall* (1867), with portrait and autobiog. story of his first voyage; J. A. Scoville, *The Old Merchants of N. Y. City,* vols. I (1863), IV (1866); C. G. Davis, *Ships of the Past* (1929); C. C. Cutler, *Greyhounds of the Sea* (1930); *Vital Records of Nantucket, Mass.,* vols. II (1926), IV (1927); M. Y. Beach, *Wealth and Biography of the Wealthy Citizens of N. Y. City* (6th ed., 1845); *War of the Rebellion: Official Records (Navy),* 1 ser., I, 545, IV, 225, 246; *Confidential Correspondence of Gustavus Vasa Fox,* vol. I (1918), ed. by R. M. Thompson and Richard Wainwright; W. A. Butler, in *Portrait Gallery of the Chamber of Commerce of the State of N. Y.* (1890), compiled by George Wilson; *N. Y. Herald,* Sept. 24, 1865.]

R. G. A.

MARSHALL, CHRISTOPHER (Nov. 6, 1709–May 4, 1797), pharmacist, Revolutionary patriot, diarist, was born probably in Dublin, Ireland. He received a classical education in England, left his home in that country at the age of eighteen, and came to Philadelphia. There he became a noted pharmacist, conducting his business at the sign of the Golden Ball, one of the largest establishments of its kind in the city. By 1774 he had acquired considerable wealth and retired from active participation in his business, the control of which he transferred to his sons. From the beginning of the Revolution he heartily embraced the American cause, John Adams finding him, Sept. 20, 1775, "a fine, facetious old gentleman, an excellent Whig" (C. F. Adams, *The Works of John Adams,* vol. II, 1850, p. 425). As a member of the Philadelphia committee of inspection and observation he was active in enforcing the non-importation agreements, in collecting supplies for the army, in ferreting out inimical and suspected persons, and in other patriot undertakings. He was one of the managers of a factory established in 1775 for making woolens, linens, and cottons, and was a delegate to the provincial conference in Philadelphia (1776) which set the wheels in motion for a new state government. On Dec. 5, 1776, he was appointed by the Council of Safety to assist in procuring housing and other necessaries for sick and wounded soldiers returned to Philadelphia. In 1777, owing to ill health, and to escape the difficulties of imminent British invasion of Philadelphia, he moved to Lancaster. On Oct.

13, 1777, he was appointed to the Council of Safety, serving from Nov. 17 until Dec. 6 following. While in Lancaster he served as chairman of a price-fixing committee (1779), assisted in providing clothing for Pennsylvania troops, and in securing wheat and flour for the state. Although of a moderate temperament, he aligned himself with the Constitutional party which supported the state constitution of 1776.

Marshall is best known for the "Remembrancer," or diary, which he kept during the Revolution. One of the most valuable sources of the period, it contains, in addition to its observations on politics, illuminating data on food, crops, prices, customs, *et cetera.* It is the account of a conscientious Whig who in those troublous times was aware of only the serious side of life and constantly deplored seeing so many fellow Whigs engaged "in monopolizing, gaming, drinking, dancing" and other frivolities. To this ardent patriot, Howe's army was "that handful of banditti" or "a parcel of poltroons" and Howe, "that monster of rapine" (*Diary,* 1877 ed., pp. 152, 169). A comprehensive edition of the diary, containing matters of public interest, *Extracts from the Diary of Christopher Marshall, Kept in Philadelphia and Lancaster, during the American Revolution, 1774–1781,* was edited and published in 1877 by William Duane, who had previously issued *Passages from the Remembrancer of Christopher Marshall* (1839), covering the period 1774–76, and *Passages from the Diary of Christopher Marshall* (1849), covering the period 1774–77. A man of great moral courage, Marshall was thoroughly imbued with Quaker doctrine, and except in his support of the Revolution, for which he was read out of the Society of Friends, he adhered rigidly to its principles. He was married twice, his first wife dying prior to the Revolution, and his second, Abigail, in 1782. Three sons of his first marriage, two of whom survived him, followed his footsteps in business, Charles, the second, attaining considerable rank as a pharmacist. Marshall died in Philadelphia.

[Marshall's Letter Book and the six manuscript volumes of his "Remembrancer" are in the Hist. Soc. of Pa., Phila. See also *Minutes of the Supreme Exec. Council in Pa.,* XI (1852), 34, 325–53; *Pa. Mag. of Hist. and Biog.,* Oct. 1893, Jan. 1904; J. T. Scharf and Thompson Westcott, *Hist. of Phila.* (1884), vol. I; Henry Simpson, *The Lives of Eminent Philadelphians Now Deceased* (1859); Claypoole's *Am. Daily Advertiser,* May 6, 1797.] J. H. P—g.

MARSHALL, CLARA (*c.* 1848–Mar. 13, 1931), pioneer leader of women in medicine, was born in West Chester, Pa., of Quaker family, the daughter of Pennock and Mary (Phillips) Marshall. She attended the Woman's Medical College of Pennsylvania, graduating in the class of 1875. Although the college had been in existence since 1850, it was still small and had been able to achieve little standing in medical circles. Clara Marshall became identified with the faculty immediately after graduation and worked for the improvement of the college and the recognition of its graduates throughout a long career. It was largely through her efforts and those of the group with which she was associated that success was attained. Her entry in 1875 opened to women the doors of the Philadelphia School of Pharmacy and Science. She was so successful as a student that she was assigned the task of arranging the pharmaceutical display at the Centennial Exhibition in Philadelphia. During the year 1875–76, she served the Woman's Medical College as demonstrator of pharmacy. The following year she was made professor of materia medica and therapeutics, a post she held for thirty years. She acted as dean from 1888 till 1917, and continued at the college as emeritus professor until 1923.

In all her activities, she was noted for energy and enthusiasm. She was responsible for the addition of many new departments to the college, and at the beginning of the century, when it became necessary for a standard medical college to have its own hospital, she secured funds to add a hospital building to the Woman's Medical College. It is largely to her credit that the school received a rating of Grade A when the medical colleges of the country were inspected and classified in the years 1905–09. In addition to her teaching, she practised medicine in Philadelphia for many years. In 1882 she acted as obstetrician at the Philadelphia Hospital, and in 1886 she was appointed attending physician to the girls' department of the Philadelphia House of Refuge. In 1893 she was lecturer at the Nurses Training School of the Jefferson Hospital. She was the first woman to address the graduating classes of nurses at the St. Agnes Hospital and at Bryn Mawr Hospital. Because of her interest in politics she was asked to address a convention of women suffragists that met in Richmond in 1898. Her lecture, "Fifty Years in Medicine" (printed in the *Virginia Medical Semi-Monthly,* Jan. 27, 1899), bears upon the place of women in the profession and their contribution to the science. Well known as a writer on medical subjects, she contributed many short articles to professional journals and also prepared *The Woman's Medical College of Pennsylvania; An Historical Outline* (1897). She died in March 1931, at the age of eighty-three. A woman of decisive and energetic character, she made a choice of her career early in life and carried out her plans with thoroughness.

[*Who's Who in America*, 1910–11; *Woman's Who's Who of America*, 1914–15; *Evening Bull.* (Phila.), Mar. 14, 1931; *Pub. Ledger* (Phila.), Mar. 13, 14, 1931; *Bull. of Woman's Medic. Coll. of Pa.*, Apr. 1931; information from the registrar of the Woman's Medic. Coll.] F. E. W.

MARSHALL, DANIEL (1706–Nov. 2, 1784), one of the pioneer Baptist preachers of the South, was born in Windsor, Conn., the son of Thomas and Mary (Drake) Marshall and the grandson of Samuel Marshall who was settled at Woodbury in 1637. Converted at the age of twenty, he joined the Congregational Church. He took his religious duties with such seriousness that he was soon elected deacon, a position which he held for twenty years. He became a prosperous farmer, and on Nov. 11, 1742, married Hannah Drake, who died after she had given birth to one son. When Marshall was thirty-eight years of age he came into contact with George Whitefield [*q.v.*], under whose influence he was completely transformed and incited to spend the remainder of his life in religious work. Convinced that the second coming of the Lord was at hand, he left his comfortable farm and rushed off, with others, to preach the gospel to the Mohawk Indians located on the upper reaches of the Susquehanna. With him he took his second wife, Martha Stearns, whom he had married on June 23, 1747, and his three children. He remained in the Indian country for some eighteen months, but was finally driven out by strife among the Indians. After a short time spent elsewhere in Pennsylvania, he went southward into Virginia, settling near Winchester, where his brother-in-law, Shubael Stearns [*q.v.*], had preceded him. Stearns had been a Congregationalist, but as a result of Whitefield's influence he had become a "New Light," or "Separate," and finally a "Separate Baptist." Marshall and his wife, the latter a remarkable woman, full of energy, herself an excellent preacher or exhorter, now accepted Baptist views, and joined a Baptist church. Marshall was soon licensed to preach and henceforth devoted himself with consuming zeal to extensive evangelism.

There were already Baptists of the Philadelphia type, later known as "Regulars," in northern Virginia, but they were rigidly Calvinistic in theology, and dignified and orderly in their preaching and methods; consequently they were not altogether friendly to these newcomers from the North who were highly emotional, noisy, suspected of Arminianism, and disposed to allow women prominence in religious work not generally sanctioned. Accordingly, the "Separates" moved southward again to Guilford County, N. C., where in 1755 they established the Sandy Creek church. Marshall and his wife were among the constituent members. The former soon established Abbott's Creek church, some thirty miles distant, over which at the age of fifty-two he was ordained pastor by his brothers-in-law, Stearns and Ledbetter.

From this center the "Separate Baptists" spread with wonderful rapidity over much of Virginia, the two Carolinas, and Georgia. Marshall, who was but poorly educated and not highly endowed, made up for all other deficiencies by zeal and activity. Churches sprang up and men were called into the ministry wherever he went. In a few years he moved to South Carolina, settling a few miles north of Augusta, on Horse Creek, where he very quickly formed a church. His eyes were on Georgia, however, into which colony he extended his itinerating tours. On one of these trips he was arrested for preaching "in St. Paul's parish" contrary to a law of 1758. When haled into court at Augusta he defended himself with such meekness and firmness that both the constable and the magistrate were soon afterwards converted. In January 1771 he removed to Georgia and settled on Kiokee Creek about twenty miles northwest of Augusta, where he spent the remainder of his life. He soon founded the Kiokee church, the first Baptist church in the state, organized in 1772 and in 1789 formally incorporated as "The Anabaptist Church on Kioka." During the Revolution many of the preachers fled from the state, but Marshall remained with the people, sharing their hardships and dangers and affording the comforts and encouragements of the gospel. After the Revolution the Baptist cause flourished, and before his death Marshall saw six churches formed, and presided at the organization of the Georgia Association in 1784.

[H. R. Stiles, *The Hist. and Geneals. of Ancient Windsor, Conn., 1635–1891*, vol. II (1892); "Abraham Marshall," in *Ga. Analytical Repository* (1802); W. B. Sprague, *Annals of the Am. Pulpit*, vol. VI (1860); J. B. Taylor, *Lives of Va. Bapt. Ministers* (1837); A. H. Newman, *Hist. of the Bapt. Churches in the U. S.* (1915); B. F. Riley, *A Hist. of the Baptists in the Southern States East of the Mississippi* (1898); W. M. Gewehr, *The Great Awakening in Va., 1740–1790* (1930); W. J. Northen, *Men of Mark in Ga.*, vol. I (1907); J. H. Campbell, *Ga. Baptists: Hist. and Biog.* (1874).] W. J. M.

MARSHALL, HENRY RUTGERS (July 22, 1852–May 3, 1927), architect, psychologist, and writer, the son of Henry Perry and Cornelia (Conrad) Marshall, was born in New York City, a descendant of Edward Marshall who came thither from Barbados in the latter part of the seventeenth century, and of his son John, who married Elsie, daughter of the well-known brewer, Harman Rutgers 2nd. Henry Rutgers Marshall was therefore related to the famous Rutgers family of New York City and New Jersey. He was educated at private schools in New York, and then at Columbia College, where he received the degree of B.A. in 1873 and that of M.A. in 1876. After a year in business, he turned to architecture. His practice, begun in 1878, was widely scattered and included Rudyard Kipling's house in Brattleboro, Vt., the Storm King Club at Cornwall, N. Y., a Congregational church at Colorado Springs, Colo., and the old building (since destroyed) of the Brearley School in New York.

On May 18, 1881, he married Julia Robbins Gilman and after her premature death in 1888 his interest turned more and more toward psychology, philosophy, and aesthetics. He published "The Field of Aesthetics Psychologically Considered" (*Mind,* July, October 1892), *Pain, Pleasure, and Aesthetics* in 1894, and a year later, *Aesthetic Principles.* His aesthetic ideas were further clarified in *The Relation of Aesthetics to Psychology and Philosophy* (1905), and in *The Beautiful* (London, 1924). Marshall's aesthetic theory is mainly the result of the application of common sense to aesthetic speculation; he makes a sharp distinction between the aesthetic processes of the creator and those of the observer; and his psychological study led him to be suspicious of easy generalities like those of Bernard Bosanquet (see his review of Bosanquet's "Three Lectures on Aesthetic" in *The Nation,* July 29, 1915). He also lays great stress on the pleasure and pain factors of aesthetics. His philosophical interests widened continually. To academic psychology and philosophy he brought a refreshing and unconventional directness of speculation; *Instinct and Reason* (1898) and *Mind and Conduct* (1919) show the breadth and the basic simplicity of his approach. The more daring type of metaphysical speculation (yet governed by his typical persuasive common sense) is well illustrated in *Human and Other Types of Consciousness* (1905). Obviously humanistic in the broad sense, his philosophy led him to generally conservative ideals. He was an idealistic pacifist, and in *War and the Ideal of Peace* (1915) his hatred of war found expression. Yet, as the World War drew on his war-hatred gradually yielded to fear of German victory. When the United States finally entered the war, therefore, he, like so many other pacifists of his age and background, became enthusiastically patriotic, and in *The Atlantic Monthly* for May 1918, he published an article, "The Pacifist at War," which was perhaps the most forceful apologia for what was at best an illogical stand.

He was a member of the American Psychological Association and its president in 1907, and a member of the American Philosophical Association. He lectured an aesthetics at several universities and gave the principal address on aesthetics before the St. Louis International Congress of Arts and Sciences in 1904. With all his philosophic interests, Marshall never forgot his original profession. He was a fellow of the American Institute of Architects, and president of the New York Chapter from 1902 to 1904. He was also one of the committee of the Fine Arts Federation which elaborated the idea of a municipal art commission and procured its inclusion in the New York city charter. He was the architect member of that commission from 1902 to 1905, and from 1914 till his death he was its executive secretary, giving to it the greater part of his time and energy. During his later years he lived almost entirely at the Columbia University Club and at his summer home in Woodbury, Conn., spending his leisure hours at the Century Association, of which he was a much loved member. He was buried in Woodbury, Conn. His only child, a daughter, predeceased him.

[*N. Y. Times,* May 4, 1927; *The Nation* (N. Y.), May 18, 1927; *Who's Who in America,* 1926–27; *Am. Art Annual, 1927* (1928); William Cothren, *Hist. of Ancient Woodbury, Conn.* (2 vols., 1854, 1872); E. H. Crosby, "The Rutgers Family of New York," in *N. Y. Geneal. and Biog. Record,* Apr. 1886; J. M. Strong, *The Town and People, . . . Woodbury, Conn.* (1901), pp. 188–89.] T. F. H.

MARSHALL, HUMPHREY (1760–June 26, 1841), senator and historian of Kentucky, the son of John and Mary (Quisenberry) Marshall, was born in Fauquier County, Va. His father was a younger son in humble circumstances but was a member of a distinguished family. There is a tradition that the boy was sent to be educated at the home of his uncle, Thomas Marshall [*q.v.*], and that there in company with his first cousins he was instructed by members of the family and by their tutors. Among these cousins were John, Louis, and James Markham Marshall [*qq.v.*] and Mary (christened Anna Maria), to whom he was married on Sept. 18, 1784. In 1778 Humphrey Marshall enlisted in the Virginia forces, and in 1781 he was captain-lieutenant of the Virginia artillery. In 1782 he settled in Kentucky and became deputy surveyor of Fayette County in the office of his uncle Thomas Marshall. In December of that year he received from Virginia a warrant for 4,000 acres of land for his Revolutionary services, and before his death he had become one of the greatest landholders in Kentucky and one of its wealthiest citizens, according to tradition measuring his money by the peck. He studied law and attained a position of eminence as an attorney. Like most of the Marshalls he became a Federalist and doggedly remained so, in spirit, to the end of his days. In Kentucky, where Jeffersonians greatly predominated, such perversity was unforgivable. An additional provocation to his neighbors was his scorn for any revealed religion. He had an extreme amount of candor and very little tact. He did not believe in the rule of the masses and often publicly stated his contempt for them. He had a blistering tongue and a cutting pen, and though he spent all of his public life in the midst of bitter political warfare and personal contentions, he claimed never to have provoked them.

He first attracted public attention, when he began in 1786 to oppose the schemes of James Wilkinson to separate Kentucky from Virginia. He was elected a delegate from Fayette County to the Danville convention of 1787, where he came into collision with Wilkinson. The next year as a delegate to the Virginia convention he voted for ratification of the federal Constitution. In 1789 he was a delegate to the Danville convention that was attempting to advance Kentucky to statehood. Having moved to Woodford County he became surveyor there in 1790, and in 1793 and 1794 he was elected to the Kentucky legislature. Suspecting a plot he opposed the movement of George Rogers Clark [*q.v.*] to attack the Spaniards at New Orleans, under the direction of Genet, and he accused Governor Isaac Shelby of complicity. Jeffersonian Republicanism was so weakened by these Spanish and French schemes that the Kentucky legislature in 1795 elected Marshall to the United States Senate over John Breckinridge, 1760–1806 [*q.v.*]. By voting for the Jay Treaty in the Senate Marshall brought down upon himself in Kentucky hostility that did not stop short of mob violence. He was dragged to the Kentucky River and was only by a trick prevented from being ducked. He was actually stoned out of Frankfort. In 1806 he suspected Aaron Burr's motives and was instrumental in exposing him. At this time John Wood and Joseph M. Street [*q.v.*] set up their *Western World* and with Marshall's aid began to pry into the dealings of some prominent Kentuckians with Spain. Writing over the signature of "Observer" Marshall soon drove from the bench of the highest court in the state Benjamin Sebastian, and he began an onset upon Harry Innes [*q.v.*] that ran its course through lawsuits instituted by both parties and finally ended by both signing an agreement to cease attacking each other. Marshall was elected to the lower house of the legislature in 1807, 1808, and 1809. Already in conflict with Henry Clay in the Burr exposure, Marshall, in 1809, insulted him over a resolution that Clay had introduced calling for the wearing of homespun, and at Louisville the two crossed the Ohio into Indiana to fight a duel, in which both were slightly wounded.

Marshall has been remembered by subsequent generations largely for *The History of Kentucky,* which was first published in 1812 in one volume, and revised and republished in 1824 in two. It was the first formal history of the state. In it he vindicated himself and made havoc of his enemies. Notwithstanding the agreement he had signed, his second edition repeated the earlier attacks on Innes, who had died in 1816. He also wrote a large number of communications to the newspapers of Kentucky and now and then wrote verse. In 1810 he set up the only Federalist newspaper in the state, the *American Republic,* and as an act of defiance to his enemies, flew a rattlesnake from its masthead. He soon changed the name to the *Harbinger* and sold it in 1825. He had a daughter and two sons, Thomas Alexander [*q.v.*], and John Jay, who was the father of Humphrey Marshall, 1812–1872 [*q.v.*]. In his old age becoming paralyzed, he moved back to Lexington to live with his son Thomas Alexander Marshall and died there.

[A. C. Quisenberry, *The Life and Times of Hon. Humphrey Marshall* (1892); T. M. Green, *The Spanish Conspiracy* (1891); Lewis and R. H. Collins, *Hist. of Ky.,* revised ed. (2 vols., 1874); J. M. Brown, *The Political Beginnings of Ky.* (1889); Wm. Littell, *Political Transactions in and Concerning Ky.* (1806); R. M. McElroy, *Ky. in the Nation's Hist.* (1909); W. M. Paxton, *The Marshall Family* (1885); date of death accepted from *Louisville Daily Journal,* July 9, 1841, though date of July 3 officially reported to pension office, Quisenberry, *ante,* p. 13.]

E. M. C.

MARSHALL, HUMPHREY (Jan. 13, 1812–Mar. 28, 1872), soldier, minister to China and member of the United States Congress and of the Confederate Congress, was a son of John Jay and Anna Reed (Birney) Marshall. He was born in Frankfort, Ky. His father was a son of Humphrey Marshall (1760–1841), and his mother was a sister of James G. Birney [*qq.v.*]. At the age of sixteen he received an appointment to the Military Academy at West Point, where he was graduated in 1832, and he became lieutenant of the mounted rangers. On Jan. 23, 1833, he was married to Frances, the daughter of Charles McAllister of Franklin, Tenn., by whom he had six children. He resigned his commission in April 1833, studied law, and the same year began practice in Frankfort. In 1834 he moved to

Louisville, where he practised law until 1846. He developed political inclinations, served in the city council in 1836, and the following year was unsuccessful in the election for state representative. In 1836 he raised a company of Kentuckians and prepared to lead them to Texas, but on the arrival of news of Houston's victory at San Jacinto he disbanded the company. Taking an active part in the development of the state militia, from 1836 to 1846 he held successively the ranks of captain, major, and lieutenant-colonel. On the outbreak of war with Mexico in 1846 he raised the 1st Kentucky Cavalry and, on June 9, was commissioned its colonel. He took a prominent part in the battle of Buena Vista, in which he executed some brilliant cavalry charges. For a short period after the war he carried on farming operations in Henry County.

After a hard fight for election, in 1849 he entered Congress as a Whig and was reëlected two years later. Receiving a few votes for the speakership in the strenuous contest of 1849, he immediately took a position of prominence in the debates that developed around the many questions growing out of the Mexican War. He upheld the orthodox position of the Southern Whigs and spoke in favor of various points in Clay's compromise scheme. So prominent did he become in Whig affairs that in 1852, when a vacancy occurred in the Supreme Court, he was urged for the position. Since geographical considerations prevented his appointment, President Fillmore offered to appoint him minister resident to Central America, but he refused the honor. Thereupon Fillmore offered to send him to China. He accepted and resigning from Congress on Aug. 4, 1852, he arrived in China in January 1853, where he spent the next year in dealing with the details of American shipping in the free ports of China. He was also busied with the increasing Chinese emigration to the United States as well as with the delicate problems arising from China's unwillingness to be drawn into the maelstrom of western commercial and political relations. On his return to America early in 1854, finding the Whig party disrupted, he joined the Know-Nothings and became an important force in their national councils. Serving from 1855 to 1859 in Congress, he again took a prominent part in the proceedings. He tried to evade the slavery issue wherever possible, but he insisted on the rights of slave-holders and the South's right to equality in the Union. By 1859 he refused to run for Congress again; instead he settled down in Washington to practise law. In 1860 he supported Breckinridge for the presidency (*Speeches of Hon. Humphrey Marshall & Hon. B. F. Hallett . . . on the Nomination of Breckinridge and Lane,* 1860).

With the coming of war, he returned to Kentucky and sought to hold the border states to a peaceful course. Failing, he retired to Nashville, Tenn., in the fall of 1861 and, on receiving a commission as brigadier-general in the Confederate Army, set out for Eastern Kentucky. He was obsessed with the idea that he could swing Kentucky into line if he were given a free hand and proper support. During the winter of 1861–62 he fought a few engagements in the Big Sandy region and then retired into southwestern Virginia, where in May 1862 he surprised the Federals at Princeton, W. Va., and defeated them. He took part in Bragg's invasion of Kentucky in the autumn of 1862, after which he retired into southwest Virginia. He always wanted an independent command and never found conditions quite to his liking. In 1863 he resigned from the army, went to Richmond to practise law, and the next year was elected to the Second Confederate Congress in which he served to the end. When the war was over he fled to Texas and in November 1865 got permission to go to New Orleans. The next year he returned to Kentucky and practised law in Louisville until his death.

[Lewis and R. H. Collins, *Hist. of Ky.,* revised ed. (2 vols., 1874); J. S. Johnston, *Memorial Hist. of Louisville* (2 vols., 1896); *The Biog. Encyc. of Ky.* (1878); W. H. Perrin, J. H. Battle, and G. C. Kniffin, *Ky. A Hist. of the State* (1886); *Battles and Leaders of the Civil War,* ed. by R. N. Johnson and C. C. Buel, vols. I–III (1887–88); *War of the Rebellion: Official Records (Army),* esp. ser. 1, vols. IV, VII, XII, XVI (pt. 1), XX (pt. 1); *Sen. Doc. 234,* 58 Cong., 2 Sess. (1905), for service in Confederate Cong.; *House Exec. Doc. 123,* 33 Cong., 1 Sess. (1854), for dispatches from China.]

E. M. C.

MARSHALL, HUMPHRY (Oct. 10, 1722 o.s.–Nov. 5, 1801), botanist, was a cousin of John Bartram [*q.v.*] and belonged to a family of botanists. His father, Abraham Marshall, was born in Derbyshire, England, became a Friend, and about 1697 emigrated to Pennsylvania, where he settled near Darby and married Mary Hunt, the daughter of James Hunt, who had been a companion of William Penn. Soon after his marriage he moved to what is now Chester County, took up a large tract of land on the west branch of the Brandywine, and acquired a considerable fortune. Humphry was born there and after 1748 managed this farm. The eighth child in a family of nine, he is quoted as saying that "he never went to school a day after he was twelve years of age; and consequently, was instructed only in the rudiments of the plainest English education" (Darlington, *post,* p. 486). In the course of a long life he gave himself, however, an excellent education and became one of the best-read men of his times, specializing in all branches of natural history and astronomy. He was early apprenticed as a stone mason and followed the trade for a few years. On Sept. 16, 1748, he married Sarah Pennock of West Marlboro, Chester County. In 1764 he enlarged his father's house, doing all the work himself, even to making the bricks. He added a small conservatory for rare plants, probably the first conservatory in Chester County. In 1773 he built with his own hands the house at Marshallton, which is still standing, and not only included a hot-house but also a small observatory.

A considerable fortune left him by his father in 1767 enabled him to move to his own house at Marshallton in 1774. There he planned and laid out a botanic garden, which in time came to include not only many foreign specimens but also a noteworthy collection of native plants, shrubs, and trees and was only less celebrated than that of his cousin, John Bartram [*q.v.*]. Both men were correspondents of two enthusiastic English collectors, Peter Collinson and Dr. John Fothergill. Some time about 1767 Marshall began collecting and shipping to Fothergill in London plants, birds' nests and eggs, and other specimens of animal life. In return Fothergill sent him many books, a reflecting telescope, and, through the good offices of Benjamin Franklin, a microscope and a thermometer. In 1785 he published his "*Arbustrum Americanum, the American Grove,*" a list of native forest trees and shrubs. This is arranged in alphabetical order and the descriptions, which are still extraordinarily vivid, follow the Linnean system. It was according to his biographer "the first truly indigenous Botanical Essay published in the Western Hemisphers" (*Ibid.*, p. 489). He also wrote a a paper on agricultural botany in which he called attention to the instinct that animals show in choosing or rejecting different kinds of fodder as a subject worthy of study in animal husbandry (*Ibid.*, pp. 582–85). As early as 1772 he submitted to the American Philosophical Society a paper on his "Observations upon the spots on the Sun's Disk from Nov. 15, 1770 to Dec. 25, 1771," and was later elected to membership in that society.

After his first wife's death he married Margaret Minshall on Jan. 10, 1788. There were no children by either marriage, and in his later years the place of a son seems to have been taken by his nephew, Dr. Moses Marshall, the botanist, for whom J. C. D. Schreber, in his 1791 edition of the *Genera Plantarum* by Linnæus, named a genus of plants of the Compositae family, *Marshallia.* Toward the end of his life his eyesight was affected, though he never became totally blind. His interest in botany remained active, and his philanthropic zeal is evidenced by his activity in founding the Chester County alms house and the Westtown boarding school, one of the many educational foundations established by the Society of Friends.

[Wm. Darlington, *Memorials of John Bartram and Humphry Marshall* (1849); R. H. Fox, *Dr. John Fothergill and his Friends* (1919); J. W. Harshberger, *The Botanists of Philadelphia* (1899); *Hazard's Register of Pa.*, ed. by Samuel Hazard, vol. I (1828); *Early Proceedings of the Amer. Philosophical Soc.* (1884); *Bulletin of the Chester County Hist. Soc.*, Sept. 27, 1913.]

M. P. S.

MARSHALL, JAMES FOWLE BALDWIN (Aug. 8, 1818–May 6, 1891), merchant, diplomat, and educator, was born in Charlestown, Mass., son of Thomas, a prosperous banker, and Sophia (Kendal) Marshall. One grandfather, Christopher Marshall, had fought at Bunker Hill in a regiment commanded by his brother, while the other, Samuel Kendal, had been a noted preacher. James was sent to Harvard College in 1834, but during his sophomore year trouble with his eyes—a lifelong weakness —forced him to drop out. In 1838 he went to the Hawaiian Islands and engaged in business at Honolulu. When Lord George Paulet, commander of a British frigate, in February 1843 used the specious claims of an ambitious consul as grounds for provisional annexation of the islands, young Marshall was secretly appointed an envoy to put the Hawaiian case before the British government and the world. His instructions and commission as minister plenipotentiary to the Court of St. James's were made out on a coffin for a table in the royal tomb at Honolulu, where the native government was functioning in hiding, and signed by King Kamehameha III, who had taken refuge in mountain fastnesses.

The youth of twenty-four set out ostensibly as agent of the American firm from which Paulet had chartered a vessel—the only one permitted to sail—to carry his dispatches to England. Leaving Honolulu on Mar. 24, he traveled with the unsuspecting British messenger to San Blas and thence across Mexico to Vera Cruz, where the two parted company. Thence Marshall sailed to New Orleans, and on his journey from that place to Boston broadcast the news from Hawaii. In the interests of his mission he interviewed Daniel Webster, then secretary of state, who said: "We will await the result of your mission. If England does not then disavow the acts of Lord George Paulet and restore the group, *we'll make a fuss.*" (*Harper's Magazine,* September 1883, p. 516.) Hurrying to London, Marshall joined other Hawaiian envoys, with whose help he succeeded during the month of July in persuading Lord Aberdeen, the foreign secretary, to review the whole subject. An admission was finally obtained that the situation had been misrepresented to the British government and that justice would be done. Satisfied with this answer, which led eventually to joint recognition of Hawaiian independence by England and France in November, he sailed for America on Aug. 20, married Eunice S. Hooper in Charlestown, Nov. 9, 1843, and set out immediately for Honolulu. Reaching there in April 1844, he learned that at the very time when he was negotiating in London, Admiral Thomas, Paulet's superior officer, had restored the sovereignty of the islands to the native king. The incident has recently been explained as a move to prevent French occupation.

Marshall now returned to business and for a number of years was a partner in one of the largest trading firms of Honolulu. Deeply interested in public affairs, he was elected to the Hawaiian legislature, and there advocated the protection of native rights and the substitution of land-tenure in fee simple for the ancient feudal system. He was active also in encouraging agricultural improvements and temperance legislation. Shortly before 1860 he returned to Boston with a considerable fortune, and during the Civil War served as paymaster general of the Massachusetts troops and as agent of the state Sanitary Commission in charge of a hospital train. After the war he joined Gen. Samuel C. Armstrong [*q.v.*] at Hampton Institute (Va.), an industrial school for negroes and Indians, where from 1870 to 1884 he was resident trustee, assistant principal, treasurer, and instructor in bookkeeping. To his business reputation and able management of its finances the school owed much of its early growth in public confidence. Forced by failing eyesight to retire, he spent the last years of his life on his estate at Weston, Mass., where he died, only two days before the death of his second wife, Martha A. T. Johnson, daughter of John Johnson of Charlestown, Mass., whom he had married Oct. 4, 1848.

[Marshall's "Reminiscences," in *Twenty-Two Years' Work of the Hampton Normal and Agricultural Institute* (1893) and "An Unpublished Chapter of Hawaiian History," *Harper's Mag.*, Sept. 1883; portrait in *New Eng. Mag.*, June 1892; Josephine Sullivan, *A Hist. of C. Brewer and Company, Ltd.* (1926); *Town of Weston; Births, Deaths, Marriages 1707–1850* (1901); *Records of the Church in Brattle Square, Boston, 1699–1877* (1902); T. B. Wyman, *The Geneal. and Estates of Charlestown . . . Mass.* (1879); *Boston Daily Advertiser,* Nov. 11, 1843; Boston *Transcript,* Oct. 5, 1848; *Boston Post,* May 7, 9, 1891.] W. L. W., Jr.

MARSHALL, JAMES MARKHAM (Mar. 12, 1764–Apr. 26, 1848), land proprietor, was the fifth child of Mary Randolph (Keith) and Thomas Marshall [*q.v.*] and a brother of John and Louis Marshall [*qq.v.*]. He was born in Fauquier County, Va., and died there, though much of his life was spent elsewhere. He was educated at home by his parents, both of whom were of high intellectual attainments. When he was fifteen years of age, he joined the 1st Virginia Artillery, State Line, in which his father was colonel and in which he became captain. His father removed to Kentucky in 1785, but he did not follow until about three years later. When he arrived the district was in a state of excitement over problems of statehood and the unfolding schemes of Spanish plotters to join Kentucky to Louisiana. He became a strong partisan of the central government and joined the Federalist party as soon as it was crystallized. In 1790 he opposed John Brown, 1757–1837 [*q.v.*], for Kentucky's seat in Congress. He charged that Brown had plotted with Gardoqui, the Spanish minister, to deliver Kentucky to Spain, and as proof he cited a letter Brown had written Judge George Muter on July 10, 1788. Marshall forced the publication of the letter to substantiate his contention, but not before he had so embroiled himself with James Brown, a younger brother of John, that a duel was averted only through a trick by Humphrey Marshall, 1760–1841 [*q.v.*], his cousin and brother-in-law. He was defeated for Congress, but soon he was selected as a delegate to the ninth convention held by Kentucky in her quest for statehood. Here he drew up the memorial to the president of the United States and to Congress, declaring Kentucky's warm attachment to the federal government and reiterating her desire to enter the Union. He returned to Virginia, and he lived for a short time in Philadelphia, where he was married in April 1795 to Hester, the daughter of Robert Morris, who was considered one of the richest heiresses in America. In the meantime he had joined a group made up of his brother John Marshall, his brother-in-law Raleigh Colston, and General Henry Lee, 1756–1818 [*q.v.*], to buy up the large Fairfax estates in Virginia, and in January 1794 he had gone to England to negotiate the purchase from the Fairfax heirs. As the purchase price of £14,000 was much more money than his group could command at the time, at the instigation of his father-in-law, he was sent to Europe again in October 1795 in order to obtain the necessary loans. The money was finally borrowed and the Fairfax heirs were satisfied, but the situation in America had become considerably complicated with Virginia confiscation laws, squatters, and other disturbances. Finally an agreement with the Virginia legislature and the decision in the case of *Martin* vs. *Hunter's Lessee* (1 *Wheaton,* 304), resulted in clearing the title. About 180,000 acres were secured, confined to the Northern Neck, and through trading and purchase he personally acquired half of this estate. While in Europe he witnessed some of the excesses of the French Revolution, and, when Lafayette was arrested and thrown into prison in Berlin, he was appointed to bring about his release, which was obtained, however, before Marshall could act. When trouble developed with France in 1798, Marshall offered his services as aide-de-camp to Washington. Being in the good graces of John Adams, he was chosen by the president near the end of his term as assistant judge of the District of Columbia. Though he had been appointed before the judiciary act of 1801 had been passed, he went out with the "midnight judges." In Winchester, Va., he then took up the practice of law, which he had studied years before. He also gave time to the management of his estate. Long before his death he divided most of his great landholdings among his six children.

[There is considerable confusion as to the simple facts in the life of Marshall; the most reliable short sketch may be found in T. M. Green, *The Spanish Conspiracy* (1891), p. 175; for the Fairfax affairs see A. J. Beveridge, *The Life of John Marshall* (4 vols., 1919), E. P. Oberholtzer, *Robert Morris* (1903), L. C. Bell, "John Marshall: Albert J. Beveridge as a Biographer," *Va. Law Register,* Mar. 1927, for a critical view of the matter; see also W. M. Paxton, *The Marshall Family* (1885); J. M. Brown, *The Political Beginnings of Ky.* (1806); R. M. McElroy, *Ky. in the Nation's Hist.* (1909); A. C. Quisenberry, *The Life and Times of Hon. Humphrey Marshall* (1892).] E. M. C.

MARSHALL, JAMES WILSON (Oct. 8, 1810–Aug. 10, 1885), discoverer of gold in California, was born in Hunterdon County, N. J., the son of Philip and Sarah (Wilson) Marshall. His paternal grandmother was Rebecca Hart, the daughter of John Hart [*q.v.*]. In his boyhood Marshall received a fair education, learned to use a rifle, and learned from his father the trade of wheelwright. When of age he started west, seeking adventure and fortune. Stopping for brief periods in Indiana and Illinois, he settled for a longer time on the Platte Purchase, near Fort Leavenworth. Here he took up land, planted it in grain, and devoted two or three years to building up a homestead. But fever and ague attacked him, causing him great misery, and on the advice of his physician he decided to join an emigrant train for the Far West. The wagon train started across the Indian Country on May 1, 1844. Their route was along the Oregon Trail to Fort Hall on the Snake River, where they spent the winter of 1844–45. Although the main party continued toward California by way of the Humboldt River, Marshall and about forty others, without wagons, followed the Oregon Trail to the Willamette Valley. Here they joined a group traveling across the Klamath Mountains to California under the leadership of James Clyman [*q.v.*]. By this means Marshall arrived at Sutter's Fort, the site of the present city of Sacramento, early in July 1845.

John A. Sutter [*q.v.*] welcomed all immigrants to his establishment, and especially Marshall, who was a very useful man because of his technical skill. Soon Marshall acquired some live stock and enough means to purchase two square leagues of land in the Sacramento Valley in the present Butte County. When the Bear Flag war broke out in 1846 Marshall joined with the American settlers and afterward became a member of Frémont's California Battalion. He was a member of the party that marched to the relief of Kearny after the battle of San Pasqual in December of 1846. The next March he was mustered out of service, at San Diego, without pay. Making his way on foot, he reached Sutter's Fort again after an absence of about a year, only to find that his cattle had disappeared. In order to secure needed funds he was required to sell his ranch. Seeking to regain his meager fortune, he sought employment from Sutter and the two entered into a partnership for the construction and operation of a sawmill near Sutter's Fort. Sutter was to furnish the money, while Marshall agreed to superintend the construction and operation of the mill, the profits to be divided equally. In due course a site was selected on the South Fork of the American River at Coloma, Eldorado County. Early in 1848, when the mill was ready to begin operation, it was found necessary to deepen the tail race to enable the wheel to rotate freely. It was there, on Jan. 24, 1848, that gold was discovered during the excavation of the raceway. The discovery was kept quiet for a short time, but such important news could not be long suppressed. By May or June San Francisco and other California towns were deserted; by the end of the year settlers had poured in from Oregon and neighboring regions, and the gold rush of 1849 followed.

The discovery of gold by Marshall was an epoch-making event, but to Marshall himself it brought only misfortune. The sawmill venture failed for lack of laborers, since most able-bodied men were feverishly panning gold. The first comers paid a small fee for the right to dig gold, but later arrivals refused to pay and the claims of Sutter and Marshall were swept aside in the onrush of gold seekers. Marshall resented this treatment and became despondent and misanthropic, bringing to himself other misfortunes. In 1872 the California legislature voted him a pension, but this was discontinued in 1878. Marshall spent his later years as a gardener in the vicinity of Coloma, where he was buried in 1885. Near his cabin at Coloma, now preserved in a state park, a large monument with a bronze figure of Marshall was erected in his honor in 1890.

[P. B. Bekeart, "Jas. Wilson Marshall," *Quart. of the Soc. of Cal. Pioneers,* Sept. 1924; J. S. Hittell, "The Discovery of Gold in Cal.," *Century Mag.,* Feb. 1891; "The Discovery of Gold in Cal.," *Hutchings' Cal. Mag.,* Nov. 1857; G. F. Parsons, *The Life and Adventures of Jas. W. Marshall, the Discoverer of Gold in Cal.* (1870); H. H. Bancroft, *Hist. of Cal.,* vol. VI (1888); T. H. Hittell, *Hist. of Cal.,* vols. II and III (1885–97); C. C. Upton, *Pioneers of El Dorado* (1906); J. W. Revere, *A Tour of Duty in Cal.* (1849); O. C. Coy, *Gold Days* (1929); T. J. Schoonover, *Life and Times of Gen. John A. Sutter* (1907); M. A. Kelley, "Jas. W. Marshall, Life and Reminiscences of California's Gold Discoverer," *Grizzly Bear Mag.,* Jan.–May 1919; the *Morning Call* (San Francisco), Aug. 11, 1885.]

O. C. C.

MARSHALL, JOHN (Sept. 24, 1755–July 6, 1835), chief justice of the United States and principal founder of judicial review and of the American system of constitutional law, was born in a log-cabin in the wilderness on the Virginia frontier. His birthplace, near Germantown, Va., lay in the western part of Prince William County, which in 1759 became Fauquier County. About 1765 the Marshall family, increasing steadily in size and prosperity, removed thirty miles westward to a small inlet of the Blue Ridge called "the Hollow," and a second removal some miles eastward occurred in 1773. The frame dwelling erected on the latter site, commodious and even elegant for the time and place, still stands as a wing of "Oak Hill," the residence which was built many years later by Marshall's eldest son Thomas. Until his twentieth year, "John Marshall was never out of the simple, crude environment of the near frontier" for more than a year (Beveridge, *post,* I, 33; autobiographical letter to Story, *post*). The circumstance necessarily rendered parental influence and immediate home environment factors of inestimable importance in his development.

Marshall on his father's side was of humble origin. The first American Marshall of the line appears to have been a Welsh immigrant. His descendant John, a small farmer of Westmoreland County, married Elizabeth Markham and became the father of Thomas Marshall [*q.v.*] and the grandfather of the Chief Justice. Little more is known of the family. On the side of his mother, Mary Randolph (Keith), the story is a very different one. Of the famous William Randolph of "Turkey Island" [*q.v.*] and his wife Mary Isham, ancestors also of Thomas Jefferson, of Robert E. Lee, and of many noted Randolphs, John Marshall was the great-great-grandson. Both the Randolphs and the Ishams traced their descent from English county gentry, while the Keiths, descended from hereditary earls marischal of Scotland, supported even greater pretensions in the motherland. Marshall's grandfather William Keith, a clergyman of the Church of England, owed his residence in Virginia to a youthful indiscretion in taking sides with the Pretender, and when he wed Mary Isham Randolph, he was already well past middle life. Surprisingly enough, Marshall's early biographers make no reference to his more distinguished lineage on his mother's side. The explanation, it may be surmised, is to be found in the tradition that Mary Isham Randolph had been married, following an elopement, before she met Keith, that the husband had disappeared, having been—as it was believed—slain by her brothers, but that late in life she received a letter purporting to come from him (Paxton, *post,* pp. 25–26). From these circumstances the validity of Mary's marriage with Keith and so the legitimacy of Marshall's mother have been challenged. Unfortunately, an assured evaluation of the tradition seems today impossible. Even Beveridge, in apparent despair, consigns the story virtually without comment to a footnote.

A portrait survives of each of Marshall's parents—testimonial again to the fact that this was a rising family. That of the mother shows an intelligent and winsome face with much sweetness and humor about the eyes and lips. The countenance of the father is of sterner mold; it is an unusually long face, and the compressed lips show stubbornness and determination; friendliness nevertheless, as well as shrewdness, light the dark eyes and intellectual brow. If one can read these portraits aright, Marshall's temperament was a happy combination of his mother's amiability and his father's resoluteness of purpose. For the rest, John appears to have been distinctly a father's boy. From the first the relations between the two were those not merely of natural affection but of entire congeniality, and the Chief Justice's most cherished memory was of his father's superior ability and force of character. "It was," says Story, "a theme, on which he broke out with a spontaneous eloquence," attributing to his father "the solid foundation" of all his own success in life (Joseph Story, *post,* p. 9; autobiographical letter). Nor was his son peculiar in appreciating the virtues of Thomas Marshall. Between 1761 and 1776 at various times the latter represented Fauquier County in the House of Burgesses, exercised the lucrative office of sheriff of the county, became principal vestryman of his parish, and was made clerk of Dunmore (now Shenandoah) County. These offices brought him, and through him in due course his son, into touch with the great questions which were increasingly agitating the best minds of the colony and of America, a tremendous stimulation to a boyish mind. Another consequence of the elder Marshall's participation in public life was that he conceived an ever increasing admiration for his former neighbor and employer, George Washington, which he duly shared with his son. In young John's life this too was a formative influence of great importance.

Of the more usual tools of education there was, naturally, in the wilderness a considerable dearth. "The only book," says Beveridge, "which positively is known to have been a literary companion of John Marshall" in his early youth was a volume of Pope (Beveridge, I, 44); and, according to Story, he had "at the age of twelve . . . transcribed the whole of Pope's *Essay on Man,* and some of his moral essays; and had committed to memory many of the most interesting passages of that distinguished poet" (Joseph Story, p. 10; autobiographical letter). The effect of so early and intensive cultivation of a single author was unavoidable. Pope's optimistic outlook and his sententious style both affixed their hallmark on Marshall's mind. The *Essay on Man* depicts the universe as a species of constitutional monarchy which is governed "not by partial, but by gen'ral laws," and where, with reason to restrain it, "self-love" lies at the basis of all human institutions, the state, government, laws. Pope was, moreover, but the first of a succession of writers of similar outlook with whom Marshall would later become acquainted —Blackstone with his proprietarian legalism, Burke with his reasoned abhorrence of revolution, Adam Smith with his philosophy of *laissez faire.* For all these Pope's iambics had prepared receptive ground.

At the age of fourteen John was placed under the tuition of the Rev. Archibald Campbell of Westmoreland County, where he remained one year. The following year he was taught at home by a young Scotch clergyman, named Thompson, who during this period lived in the Marshall household. Under him, John "commenced reading Horace and Livy," studies which he later continued "with no other aid than my Dictionary" (autobiographical letter to Story). But his principal tutor was his father, who directed his reading in English literature, thus inculcating in him his most pronounced taste, the law aside, and one of his chief sources of pleasure in after life. Then in 1772 occurred the first American publication of Blackstone's *Commentaries,* one of the subscribers for which was "Captain Thomas Marshall, Clerk of Dunmore county, Virginia" (Beveridge, I, 56). As he had been "destined for the bar" from infancy ("Autobiography," Oster, *post,* p. 197), it is not unlikely that John now began his self-education in the law.

Though a child of the wilderness and reared amid its simple homespun conditions of life, Marshall was sheltered from the frontier's usual barbarism by parents who possessed uncommon gifts of character and entertained definite ideals for the advancement of their offspring. Frugality and helpfulness were watchwords of the small colony; for in time John's advent was followed by that of fourteen brothers and sisters, in whose daily upbringing he had a constant hand. All these children were reared to maturity and several of them attained distinction. From joyous youth spent largely out of doors Marshall derived that resiliency and health of body which he retained unimpaired till near the end of life itself, and a serenity of mind that never deserted him. To the same source are also to be traced his fondness for out-of-door relaxations, especially the primitive sport of tossing horseshoes, his love of wild nature, and his fondness for companionship—a much sought boon on the frontier. His "lax lounging manners," too, were not as Jefferson asserted, "affectations"; they were the habitual alertness at ease of the frontiersman which is stamped on all his portraits. Neither was his notorious carelessness of dress an artifice; it was due to the ingrained thrift of one of a family of seventeen most of whose apparel must have come from the family loom. With access to comparatively few books but living in a period of wide-flung and excited debate on the most profound topics of politics, he came naturally to fall into that category of mankind whose flow of mind is most readily started along the auditory nerve. His judicial opinions reveal this idiosyncrasy very strikingly. Marshall usually prepared these following hard upon the close of argument by counsel, sometimes even before it was concluded, and they betray the debater in every line, in the strength of their phrasing, in the sweep of their conclusions, and sometimes even in a point-by-point refutation of a rejected argument.

Further than this, Marshall was a leader of men. The group which he led was a small one, but its rôle in the country's government became of immense importance because of his leadership, and it was often exerted upon men of a divergent political faith, as well as upon men of professional attainments much surpassing his own. The raw stuff of leadership is, no doubt, a fact of nature rather than of nurture; yet nurture may give it shape. The distinctive feature of Marshall's leadership of the Supreme Court was its easy avoidance of anything suggestive of the strong hand. Its implement was not assertion but insinuation. In the words of a contemporary, John Marshall had the knack of "putting his own ideas into the minds of others, unconsciously to them" (George Gibbs, ed., *Memoirs of the Administrations of Washington and John Adams, . . .*, 1846, vol. II, p. 350). Any competent nursemaid has the same knack and Marshall had been nurse to a whole squadron of younger brothers and sisters. Marshall's political creed, which embraced nationalism and individualism as twin values, combined with distrust of the too-immediate democracy of the state legislature and its proclivity to interference with anything not within its own narrow experience and comprehension, is sufficiently explicable by his own participation in and observation of events during and following the Revolution, and by his personal interests. Yet it also drew sustenance from his early reading, from reverence for Washington, from the sense of superiority that a rising, well-disciplined family like the Marshalls must inevitably have felt for the generality of their frontier neighbors.

Young Marshall was propelled from the family nest by "the shot heard round the world." His politics were those of his father, which were those of Henry, the dominant voice in the Virginia revolutionary convention of the same year. The news of Lexington and Concord found the two Marshalls already self-instructed in the manual of arms, and they now began putting their neighbors through the prescribed evolutions. John's own active service began at Greatbridge, Va., in the autumn of 1775. He then went to the siege of Norfolk, as a member of the Culpeper Minute Men; and on July 30, 1776, he was mustered into the Continental service in the 3rd Virginia Regiment. Successively as lieutenant, captain-lieutenant, and captain, he fought at the Brandywine, Germantown, and Monmouth, shared with characteristic cheerfulness the rigors of Valley Forge, and participated in the capture of Stony Point. What the import of his experience was for his subsequent career was stated by himself years later: "I was confirmed in the habit of considering America as my country and Congress as my government" (Joseph Story, p. 20; autobiographical letter). Like his great leader, on whose outlook the French and Indian War had affixed a like impress, he became an American before he ever had time to become a Virginian. His regiment's term of enlistment running out in 1779, Marshall returned home to await a new command, and when this was not forthcoming he was mustered out of service in 1781. Meantime, in May–June 1780, he attended a course of lectures on the law given by Chancellor George Wythe [*q.v.*] at the College of William and Mary, on a foundation which his cousin Governor Jefferson had just created by converting to it funds which originally endowed a chair in theology. Altogether he must have spent at least a month under the learned Chancellor's tuition—his only institutional instruction of any sort; and during the same interval he contrived to fall in love with Mary Willis Ambler, the state treasurer's daughter. Nevertheless, on Aug. 28, 1780, he was admitted to the bar in Fauquier County.

In the autumn of 1782 Marshall was elected to the state Assembly from the family bailiwick, an event which transferred him to Richmond, Mary Ambler's home. On Jan. 3, 1783, they were married, and soon afterward he hung out his shingle in the new capital, thereby throwing down the gauntlet to the most brilliant bar in America. At the beginning things moved slowly, and during his first year he and Mary were glad to have his official salary. Perhaps his frontiersman's carelessness of attire hampered recognition fully as much as his exiguous professional equipment; to an even later period appears to belong the anecdote of an old farmer, who had at first engaged an empty-headed, showily powdered bigwig in preference to Marshall, but speedily repented his choice once he saw the two men in action (Beveridge, II, 166). At any rate, prosperity was not unduly delayed. Within two years, Marshall was recording considerable losses at whist and backgammon, generous contributions to churches, horse-races, festivals, card games, and balls, liberal purchases of wines and other drinkables, sundry entry fees to the Masons, "The Jockie Club," and "Farmicola's." He was also a frequent purchaser of books, though not often of law books; he bought an occasional slave, and in 1785 he made repeated purchases of "military certificates" which were redeemable in land. The same year he was presented with the Fauquier County estate by his father and was made city recorder (Beveridge, I, 148–99).

From this point Marshall's emergence both political and professional was swift. It is the latter which most demands explanation. One thing that greatly aided him in his struggle with his better-equipped competitors was the fact that following the Revolution English precedents were out of favor, while of American precedents there were as yet none. What was chiefly demanded of counsel was consequently not acquired learning, but just what Marshall had to a remarkable degree: a spider-like capacity, as it were, of rapidly absorbing material suited to the immediate occasion and then of spinning it out in his own silk—wrought, forsooth, into a web of argumentation which his opponents would find exceedingly baffling. Indeed, Marshall developed much ingenuity in making his daily practice in open court educate him in the law. As Beveridge has shown, he "preferred to close rather than open an argument," and so "informed himself from the knowledge displayed by his adversaries" (Beveridge, II, 177). He cited few authorities, thus anticipating a striking feature of his judicial opinions.

Marshall's emergence into political prominence proceeded with the crystallization of his political convictions. This was the period when governmental power was concentrated in the state legislatures; and they speedily forfeited the confidence of those elements of society whose views or interests transcended state lines, playing fast and loose with the treaty obligations of the Confederation, starting commercial wars among the states, and finally becoming in the majority of instances the abject tools of the numerous but bankrupt small-farmer class. To this course of policy in Virginia, Marshall himself, as a member of the Assembly and of the Executive Council from 1782 to 1784, was direct witness, and he did not hesitate to announce his disgust for it, as well as for the body responsible. The news from other states impelled him in the same direction, especially that of Shays's Rebellion, which he thought drew into question man's capacity to govern himself and so "cast a deep shade over that bright prospect which the Revolution in America and the establishment of our free governments had opened to the votaries of liberty throughout the globe" (to James Wilkinson, Jan. 5, 1787, *American Historical Review,* January 1907, p. 348). Accordingly, when Washington and Madison raised the banner of constitutional reform looking to a strengthened Union, they found in Marshall an eager recruit. In order to forward the ratification of the Constitution in Virginia, Marshall again entered the Assembly in the autumn of 1787, and it was through his skill that that document was submitted to the state-ratifying convention without hampering instructions with respect to amendments. Nor was his rôle in the ratifying convention, while comparatively inconspicuous, unimportant. Whether by accident or preference, he gave his chief attention in the debate to the judiciary article and in that connection championed the idea of judicial review. Should Congress, said he, "make a law not warranted by any of the powers enumerated . . . they [the judges] would declare it void" (Jonathan Elliott, *The Debates . . . on the Adoption of the Federal Constitution,* II, 1828, p. 404). But he also expressed the opinion that Bills of Rights were "merely recommendatory. Were it otherwise . . . many laws which are found convenient, would be unconstitutional" (*Ibid.,* p. 409).

A champion of Washington's administration and of Hamilton's financial measures from the first, Marshall gradually became the recognized leader of the Federalist interest in Virginia. In 1795 Washington offered him the attorney-generalship, which he declined. In 1795–96 he won more than a local reputation by his vigorous defense of the Jay Treaty, so that when, in the latter year, he appeared in Philadelphia to argue *Ware* vs. *Hylton* (3 *Dallas,* 199), his first and only case before the Supreme Court, his effort drew interested auditors from other states. One of these was Rufus King of Massachusetts, whom a year later we find declaring that "his head" was "one of the best organized of anyone that I have known" (C. R. King, *The Life and Correspondence of Rufus King,* II, 1895, p. 235). In 1796 he again refused appointment under the federal government, as minister to France; but in 1797 he was finally induced by President John Adams to become one of the famous X. Y. Z. mission to the same government. His immediate motive, it is to be suspected, was largely mercenary. In 1793 or 1794 he had become one of a syndicate to purchase the remnant of the great Fairfax estate in the "Northern Neck," and this investment, owing to an act of confiscation which had overhung it from the days of the Revolution and to the bankruptcy of Robert Morris, who had financed the deal, was now in desperate case. At any rate, from this single year's employment Marshall as commissioner obtained nearly $20,000, which, says his biographer, "over and above his expense," was nearly "three times his annual earnings at the bar" (Beveridge, II, 211). The Fairfax investment was thus saved from its creditors. The act of confiscation, however, still remained to be reckoned with.

In 1798 Marshall was offered James Wilson's place on the Supreme Court but declined. The following year, nevertheless, at Washington's warm insistence, he stood for Congress and was elected. Here his most conspicuous act was his successful defense of Adams against the charge of having usurped a judicial function in surrendering, under the Jay Treaty, an alleged fugitive from the justice of Great Britain. Adams, who had now split with the Hamiltonian elements of his party and cabinet, needed defenders outside of Congress too; and he soon concluded that John Marshall was his best reliance. On May 7, 1800, without consulting him, Adams nominated him secretary of war, to succeed James McHenry [*q.v.*], who had been forced to resign, and he promptly declined. Nothing daunted, the President a few days later asked him to become secretary of state (appointment May 12, 1800) in succession to Timothy Pickering [*q.v.*], who had just been dismissed. After a fortnight's pondering Marshall accepted, and by so doing won the harassed President's eternal gratitude.

The actual circumstances of Adams' nomination of Marshall to the chief justiceship on Jan. 20, 1801, are recounted by Marshall himself in the autobiographical sketch which he prepared for Story in 1827, and which has only recently been recovered (see bibliography). "On the resignation of Chief Justice Ellsworth," Marshall there wrote, "I recommended Judge Patterson [William Paterson] as his successor. The President objected to him, and assigned as his ground of objection that the feelings of Judge Cushing would be wounded by passing him and selecting a junior member of the bench. I never heard him assign any other objection to Judge Patterson, though it was afterwards suspected by many that he was believed to be connected with the party which opposed the second attempt at negotiation with France. The President himself mentioned Mr. Jay, and he was nominated to the Senate. When I waited on the President with Mr. Jay's letter declining the appointment he said thoughtfully 'who shall I nominate now?' I replied that I could not tell, as I supposed that his objection to Judge Patterson remained. He said in a decided tone, 'I shall not nominate him.' After a moment's hesitation he said 'I believe I must nominate you.' I had never before heard myself named for the office and had not even thought of it. I was pleased as well as surprised, and bowed in silence."

The nomination, as Beveridge, with pardonable litotes, remarks, "was not greeted with applause from any quarter" (Beveridge, II, 554–55). The Republicans bitterly resented Ellsworth's too-opportune resignation, which had snatched from their very grasp the highest of appointive offices, while the more rabid Federalists, resenting Marshall's practice of kicking over the party traces, wanted Paterson. The President, however, was adamant; on Jan. 27 the Senate gave its consent; and on Feb. 4, Marshall, with customary lack of haste, accepted and took his seat, thereby opening court for the first time in the new Capital on the Potomac. He continued as secretary of state till the end of the administration, though he did not draw the salary of that office. He was thus able to lend a helpful hand in the so-called "midnight appointments," one of which went to a certain William Marbury.

For all the lack of enthusiasm attending his elevation, the new Chief Justice possessed a personality to capture attention and then to captivate it. The contemporary pen of William Wirt pictures a man "tall, meagre, emaciated," loose-jointed, inelegant in "dress, attitudes, gesture," of swarthy complexion, and looking beyond his years, with a countenance "small in proportion to his height" but pervaded with "great good humour and hilarity; while his black eyes—that unerring index—possess an irradiating spirit, which proclaims the imperial powers of the mind that sits enthroned therein" (William Wirt, *The Letters of the British Spy,* 1803, p. 46). Marshall enjoyed, Wirt asserts, "one original, and, almost, supernatural faculty," that "of developing a subject by a single glance of his mind. . . . Nor does the exercise of it seem to cost him an effort." He determined immediately on which side a question was to be most advantageously assailed; and "his premises once admitted, the demonstration, however distant, follows as certainly, as cogently, as inevitably, as any demonstration in Euclid" (*Ibid.,* p. 47). In brief, he was a supreme debater. Another contemporary, Speaker Theodore Sedgwick, coming from the sterner atmosphere of Boston harbor, had previously been struck by his "very affectionate disposition," his "great simplicity of manners," his attachment to pleasures and "convivial habits strongly fixed." He was "indolent therefore" (King, *ante,* III, 1896, p. 237). The word is hardly the just one. Marshall led a leisurely life, but he did not permit his intellectual powers to corrode. On the contrary, the fresh energy of mind with which he usually met the larger occasions of his career is one of his most striking characteristics.

There being no causes to be heard in the February term of 1801, Marshall's first official duty as chief justice was to administer the presidential oath of office to Jefferson. In the August term, there was one case, *Talbot* vs. *Seeman* (1 *Cranch,* 1), and Marshall signalized the occasion to put into effect a significant reform. Hitherto the justices had frequently delivered *seriatim* opinions; henceforth for some years "the unanimous Court," or simply "the Court," was to speak generally through its Chief Justice. Of the reported opinions to the February 1805 term, Marshall delivered all except two, and those in causes over which he had presided on circuit. But one dissenting opinion was given, although the justices were not always agreed at other times. That the new procedure signified at this date Marshall's domination of his associates may be questioned; rather it betokened their appreciation of a common peril.

One of the last acts of the Federalists had been to enlarge the lower federal judicial establishment, and one of the early acts of the Jeffersonians was to abolish the new courts (Apr. 29, 1802). At the same time, in order to prevent a judicial test of the constitutionality of the repeal act, Congress postponed the next term of the Supreme Court to February 1803, by doing away permanently with all but the February term. Although Marshall was thus probably presented by his foes with several years of vigorous life, since in the warmer months Washington at this period was a malarial swamp, what he saw in their action was a dangerous challenge to the prestige of the Court, to the security of the lower federal judiciary, and to the principle, which had come to be generally accepted previous to the debate on the repealing act, that the Supreme Court was the final authoritative interpreter of the Constitution. It was, therefore, no wonder that he should make the most of the opportunity that soon offered to vindicate all these causes at one stroke. When the Court reconvened in February 1803, after its enforced vacation of fourteen months, the first case to claim its attention was that which appears in the *Reports* under the style of *Marbury* vs. *Madison* (1 *Cranch,* 137). Marbury and other "midnight appointees" to the office of justice of the peace in the District of Columbia were asking for a *mandamus* to the secretary of state, James Madison, to compel him to deliver their commissions, the basis of their application being section thirteen of the judiciary act of Sept. 24, 1789, which authorized the Court to issue this writ "to officers of the United States." Marshall, for "the unanimous Court," conceded that Marbury was entitled to the remedy he sought, but held that the Supreme Court could not award it, since to do so would be to assume original jurisdiction in a case not within the categories enumerated by the Constitution, and that section thirteen was unconstitutional and void.

A more cleverly contrived document for its purposes than Marshall's opinion in *Marbury* vs. *Madison* it would be impossible to imagine. By "backing into" the case, Marshall was able to read Jefferson a lecture on his legal duty, while by ultimately declining jurisdiction of it he avoided all danger of a direct clash with his antagonist. By holding the constitutional enumeration of cases in which the Supreme Court has original jurisdiction to be exclusive (wherein he had been anticipated by Ellsworth; 3 *Dallas,* 327), he put a spoke in Republican projects to abolish the lower federal judiciary and parcel out its jurisdiction between the Supreme Court and the state courts. Most important of all, by holding section thirteen unconstitutional, on the basis of an argument that Jefferson himself did not venture to traverse, he brought to the support of the Union, while the memory of the Virginia and Kentucky Resolutions was still green, the ineffably important proposition that the Constitution has one final interpreter, at the same time seizing for the Court its greatest prerogative. Nor is this to say that, considered as a judicial pronouncement, the opinion in *Marbury* vs. *Madison* is flawless. Section thirteen, by the logic of later cases, was not intended to increase the Court's original jurisdiction, but only to give it power to issue certain writs when it had jurisdiction; and in the recent case of *Myers* vs. *United States,* Jefferson's claim that he had removed Marbury, who was consequently not entitled to his commission, appears also to have been ratified by the Court. Besides, it was Marshall who had countersigned and sealed that commission, a circumstance which, by a nicer view of judicial propriety, should have disqualified him from sitting in the case at all.

The Federalist Court had drawn first blood in its feud with the Republican administration, but the decisive battle was still to be fought. Not all the justices shared their Chief's "wise as serpents, harmless as doves" disposition, least of all Justice Samuel Chase [*q.v.*]. Early in May 1803, Chase, to whom the Republicans had already succeeded in fastening something of the reputation of a "Bloody" Jeffries, had the unwisdom to assail "our late reformers" in a charge to a Baltimore grand jury, and on Mar. 12, 1804, the House voted articles of impeachment against him. What was even more alarming, the exponents of "judge-breaking" were now pressing the theory that impeachment was historically not a punitive process at all but "an inquest of office," talk which was at once interpreted by contemporaries as indicating that the entire bench of the Supreme Court was to be swept clean. For once in his life John Marshall was obviously perturbed. This was shown not only by his timid manner of testifying before the court of impeachment, ostensibly in Chase's behalf, but also by a letter to his brother James at this time in which he broached the remarkable suggestion that "the modern doctrine of impeachment should yield to an appellate jurisdiction in the legislature" (Beveridge, III, 177). In other words, if Congress would only leave John Marshall in office they might reverse such of his legal opinions as they "deemed unsound" to their heart's content, and thereby consign both judicial review and the principle of the separation of powers to the scrap-heap.

But Chase was not convicted, and in due course Marshall recovered his composure, so much so indeed that he was presently ready to tilt against the administration all by himself. The opportunity offered when Aaron Burr [*q.v.*] was brought, early in 1807, before his court at Richmond to be tried for treason. These proceedings began Mar. 30 and ended Sept. 15, and Marshall's conduct of them from start to finish was one prolonged baiting of the President, whose unholy zeal to see Burr hanged fairly exposed him to such treatment. In only one instance did Jefferson score, when he ignored a *sub poena duces tecum* which Marshall was incautious enough to send him. On the main point Marshall got his way: Burr's neck was saved, albeit in the process the whole common-law view of treason as a conspiracy, a view which the Constitution was undoubtedly intended to embody and which Marshall himself had accepted in the Bollman Case (4 *Cranch,* 75), was junked, with the "monstrous" result—as Wirt rightly urged—that it becomes impossible to convict the procurer of a treason who is canny enough to leave to his dupes the rest of the business—the "overt acts." Three years later Edward Livingston brought his famous "Batture Case" before Marshall at Richmond, in which he sued Jefferson for $100,000 damages on account of the latter's seizure when president of certain lands of Livingston in New Orleans. Fortunately a renewal of the vendetta between the two cousins was obviated when the case was dismissed on the point of jurisdiction (1 *Brockenbrough,* 203).

Meantime, Marshall had been busying himself for some years in hours off the bench with *The Life of George Washington* (5 vols., 1804–07). The work was doubly disappointing to its author. His hopes of large profits were blasted when Jefferson forbade the federal postmasters to take orders for it, and much of it was hastily written and badly proportioned. Yet it does not lack even to a present-day reader flashes of insight, especially in its treatment of the period immediately preceding the Convention of 1787. Furthermore, this part of the work stands in an important relation to Marshall's own later labors. Its preparation undoubtedly contributed not a little to that confidence which his famous constitutional opinions breathe of his knowledge of the intentions of the framers of the Constitution, as well as to his resolution that these should prevail. Indeed, the first half of his chief justiceship was largely a period of preparation for the greater achievement to follow. With the appointment of Duval and Story, in November 1811, the personnel of the Court became what it was to remain for twelve years and, with two changes, for eighteen years. As there was but one term of court annually and that, till 1827, rarely more than seven or eight weeks in length, none of the justices resided in Washington but they took lodgings, sometimes all in the same boarding-house, living, as Story wrote, "in the most frank and unaffected intimacy" (W. W. Story, *Life and Letters of Joseph Story,* 1851, I, 215). "Our social hours when undisturbed with the labors of law, are passed in gay and frank conversation, which at once enlivens and instructs" (*Ibid.,* p. 217). Circumstances could not have been better contrived to enable Marshall to bring to bear upon his associates, all of them except Washington Republican appointees and most of them his juniors, his charm of personality and his superiority in face-to-face discussion, or to win them with "the inevitability of gradualness" to his own constitutional faith. In the case of Story himself the process was not even gradual; he fell under the spell of "the Chief" at once. A uniquely fruitful friendship resulted. As Story testifies, Marshall's bias was "to general principles and comprehensive views, rather than to technical and recondite learning" (Joseph Story, *Discourse,* p. 70); while his own was that of the student and delver. The familiar legend that Marshall was accustomed to say to Story, "that, Story, is the law; now you find the precedents," is at least "well found." Nor should the Court under Marshall be thought of apart from the bar which practised before it. The membership of this body was almost as constant as that of the Court itself and included talent of the first order—William Pinkney, William Wirt, Luther Martin, Joseph Hopkinson, Daniel Webster, Jeremiah Mason, to mention only the most illustrious. Again Marshall's debt is discernible, even in the sphere in which he was supreme, although as regards Webster, this has been exaggerated. Indeed, one gains the impression that when it came to constitutional law, Marshall was often more grateful to counsel whose views he rejected than to their opponents, because of the stimulation they imparted to his own powers of analysis and statement.

His most important opinion during this early period, after that in *Marbury* vs. *Madison,* was in *Fletcher* vs. *Peck* (6 *Cranch,* 87), where he held that the "obligation of contracts" clause stood in the way of a state's rescinding a grant of public lands, although it had been induced by notorious bribery and corruption. The result is the more remarkable inasmuch as the "obligation" attributed to the fraudulent grant was manifestly not a legal but a moral one. The opinion indeed smacks of predetermination, and the case was probably a moot one. Could Marshall have been thinking of that act of confiscation which still overhung the Fairfax estate? Four years later this act too was before the Court (*Fairfax's Devisee* vs. *Hunter's Lessee,* 7 *Cranch,* 603). Quite properly Marshall declined to sit in the case, but his circumspection profited him little with his critics; if Story's opinion disallowing the measure was the voice of Esau, the hand that penned it was that of Jacob. Aside from those in *Marbury* vs. *Madison* and *Fletcher* vs. *Peck,* Marshall's foundational constitutional opinions are to be read in the following cases: *McCulloch* vs. *Maryland* (4 *Wheaton,* 316), *Sturges* vs. *Crowninshield* (17 *U. S.,* 122), and *Dartmouth College* vs. *Woodward* (17 *U. S.,* 518), all three delivered at the single term of 1819; *Cohens* vs. *Virginia* (6 *Wheaton,* 264), given in the 1821 term; *Gibbons* vs. *Ogden* (9 *Wheaton,* 1) and *Osborn* vs. *U. S. Bank* (22 *U. S.,* 738), rendered in 1825; *Brown* vs. *Maryland* (25 *U. S.,* 419) and *Ogden* vs. *Saunders* (25 *U. S.,* 213)—the latter Marshall's sole dissenting opinion in the constitutional field—rendered in 1827.

Herein is set forth a corpus of constitutional doctrine which possesses internal consistency to a notable extent, however open to attack some of its premises may have been on other grounds. The Constitution was the act of the people of the United States, although in bringing about its establishment they naturally made such use of existing governmental machinery as convenience dictated. It springs therefore from the ultimate source of authority in the country and possesses such characteristics as this authority chose to stamp upon it. By its own terms it is law and supreme law, wherefore its provisions control all governments and governmental agencies within the territory of the United States. Furthermore, being law, it is directly enforcible by courts in the decision of cases. Indeed, its clear intention is to designate the Supreme Court as the one final authoritative expositor of its terms; and while the Court has no will of its own apart from that of the law, it is none the less under obligation always to remember that "it is a constitution" which it is expounding, and that this Constitution was "intended to endure for ages to come" and hence to be "adapted to the various *crises* of human affairs." Especially should a narrow rendition of its terms be avoided when questions of the advancement of national unity and power or of the security of private, especially property rights, are involved. These were the interests which had suffered most acutely at the hands of the states during the period of the Confederation and concern for which had brought about the convention that framed the Constitution. By the same token must state power be sternly repressed whenever it entrenches upon the field of powers delegated by the Constitution to "the government of all" or when it menaces the principles on which public and private faith depends. The designated organ to effect these ends is the Supreme Court.

The immediate target, indeed, of all Marshall's great opinions following 1809 was furnished by the pretensions of the state legislature, the seat then as in 1787 of localizing and democratic tendencies. His system of constitutional doctrine thus becomes the vehicle to the present time both of his ingrained conservatism and of his love of the Union. But meantime a dilemma has arisen which, because of the then-particularistic outlook of democracy, Marshall did not have to face. Present-day American democracy is nationalistic, and at the same time it is more strongly inclined to regard government as an instrument of social betterment than ever before. By other preconceptions, too, his fellow citizens came to Marshall's assistance, even when perhaps they might have desired it otherwise. Natural science was still in its infancy, and intellectual method was deductive. Even the common law had not yet discovered that it was "inductive." Most intellectual enterprise set out accordingly from a safe base of agreed premises, and its chief weapon was the syllogism, of which Marshall was an acknowledged master. Furthermore, his age was willing to concede Marshall his three most vital premises. It acknowledged that the upright judge had no will of his own save that of the law. It acknowledged, too, that the meaning of the Constitution—like that of Scripture—was perfectly plain when the document was approached from the proper angle and with good intentions. Finally, it acknowledged that the proper angle in the case of the Constitution was furnished by the purposes of the framers.

Yet in the face of all this a constantly increasing consensus of his fellow countrymen found Marshall's reading of the Constitution less and less acceptable. The slogan of the day was "state rights" or "state sovereignty"—high-sounding phrases which not infrequently boiled down to a claim of right for some state legislature to foster "wild-cat" banking or to promote expedients of less than doubtful honesty for meeting public and private obligations. In Virginia, however, where the uprising started, it was based on grounds almost altogether personal and doctrinal. Here its spokesmen were Spencer Roane, chief judge of the court of appeals, and John Taylor of Caroline [*qq.v.*]. The latter's *Construction Construed, and Constitutions Vindicated* (1820) applies to some of Marshall's great opinions a dialectic worthy of the Chief Justice's best steel; and what Roane, who would have been chief justice if Jefferson had had the naming of Ellsworth's successor, lacked in subtlety he more than made up for in vehemence. Nor was Jefferson himself at all averse to shying a missile now and then from the leafy boscage of his voluminous correspondence at the "subtle corps of sappers and miners" which was "constantly working underground to undermine our confederated fabric" (P. L. Ford, Federal Edition, *The Works of Thomas Jefferson,* XII, 1905, p. 177). To the standard hoisted by Virginia soon repaired Ohio and Kentucky, whence the agitation spread to Congress. From 1821 on, hardly a congressional session intervened for some years which did not witness some proposal for weakening the Court or at least Marshall's weight on it; and by the act of Mar. 3, 1837, the Court was in fact enlarged by two additional justices. Marshall himself was now dead, but the measure guaranteed that the members who had survived him and whom he had presumably indoctrinated should be in a safe minority.

These proceedings did not leave Marshall altogether unmoved. Especially do his opinions in *Providence Bank* vs. *Billings* (4 *Peters,* 514) and in *Barron* vs. *Baltimore* (7 *Peters,* 243), in the latter of which he rejected a most persuasive invitation to make the Bill of Rights restrictive of state power, appear very like concessions to the spirit of the hour, and his announcement in 8 *Peters* that decisions setting aside state laws must be supported by a majority of the entire Court was unmistakably so. But to intellectual honesty there is, after all, a limit to concession, and in *Craig* vs. *Missouri* (4 *Peters,* 410) and *Worcester* vs. *Georgia* (6 *Peters,* 515) Marshall quite justly felt that this limit had been reached and passed. Never were state acts more palpably unconstitutional than those involved in these cases. Yet in the former the Chief Justice's opinion divided his associates three to three, and in the latter the Court's judgment was defied openly, while the word ran round that President Jackson had declared "John Marshall has made his decision, now let him enforce it" (Horace Greeley, *The American Conflict,* I, 1864, p. 106).

With these developments and the contemporary Nullification movement in South Carolina before him, Marshall saw the Union crumbling: it had been "prolonged thus far by miracles" (Oster, *post,* p. 143) and these could not continue. His hold upon the Court, too, was weakening; a new generation was rising with "new aspirations of power" and bent on finding "new versions of the Constitution" to meet these; his life's achievement was seemingly being engulfed before his eyes. One reassuring voice there was, however, for in 1833 Story published his *Commentaries on the Constitution of the United States* (1833). There Marshall saw his version of the Constitution systematized and given its historical setting, and in the dedication of the work to himself, he read: "Your expositions of constitutional law enjoy a rare and extraordinary authority. They constitute a monument of fame far beyond the ordinary memorials of political and military glory. They are destined to enlighten, instruct, and convince future generations; and can scarcely perish but with the memory of the constitution itself" (*Ibid.,* I, iii). That was it precisely—Marshall's fame was linked with that of the Constitution.

It has been observed that Marshall's judicial life was a somewhat leisurely one, although it became gradually less and less so. In his first three terms the Court decided, on the average, eight cases; in his last term of active service it decided sixty (8 *Peters,* 834). Meantime, beginning with 1827, the opening of Court had been moved up to the second Monday in January, with the result of lengthening the term from about nine weeks to twelve or thirteen. The Court's leisurely procedure, none the less, still continued, and in important cases counsel took their own time. In the argument of *Fletcher* vs. *Peck* the Court adjourned to enable Luther Martin to sober up; while on another occasion it permitted William Pinkney to go back and repeat part of an argument in order that some ladies who had just entered the courtroom might not miss some especially choice tropes. Marshall's own part in the labors of the Court were apparently considerably heavier than those of his associates. "Of a total of one thousand two hundred fifteen cases during that period [1801–1835], in ninety-four, no opinions were filed; in fifteen, the decision was by the Court; and in the remaining one thousand one hundred six cases, Marshall delivered the opinion in five hundred nineteen," of which thirty-six involved constitutional questions and eighty involved questions of international law or kindred questions (Warren, *post,* II, 273 note). The Chief Justice was free to lean on the learning of his associates, and doubtless often had their assistance in the preparation of opinions which he delivered, but the unmistakable *imprimatur* of his own style is on the opinions which support his fame.

In one respect Marshall had a distinct advantage over most of his brethren, in that he lived in his own circuit and near the seat of government. Altogether, his annual journeyings to and from court came to less than 900 miles, while the justice assigned to the seventh circuit had to travel more than 3,300 miles and over mountains. During the Burr trial Marshall was kept at Richmond continuously for nearly seven months, but usually his judicial labors on circuit both at Richmond and Raleigh could hardly have occupied more than three months. It thus appears that, except for opinion writing, Marshall had nearly half the year to devote to his duties and pleasures as householder, neighbor, and citizen. In all these capacities he appears in a singularly engaging light. For many years his wife was a nervous invalid, a fact which cut him off from society in the more formal sense, but far from repining he found in her conversation and their common fondness for good reading one of his chief satisfactions in life. When he eulogized to Story those qualities of womanhood which "make up the sum of human happiness and transform the domestic fireside into an elysium" (Oster, p. 125), he was voicing his own contentment. Bereavement, too, drew them together. Of the ten children born to them, four died early in life—"three of them," he informed Story, "bidding fairer for health and life than any that have survived them" (*Ibid.*, p. 135). Of the survivors five were sons—one of whom predeceased Marshall; his wife died Dec. 25, 1831. But with all his domesticity, Marshall never lost his intense delight in the companionship of men—in eating and drinking with them, frolicking with them, debating with them. A favorite resort of his when in Richmond was the famous Barbecue Club which had grounds just outside the city and was celebrated for its excellent repasts of roast pig and its generous supplies of choice drinks. The *raison d'être* of the organization, however, seems to have been furnished by the game of quoits, and more than one account remains of Marshall's boyish zest in this bucolic sport, in which he excelled. Besides the club, he had a farm nearby; while in summer he often retreated to his estate in the mountains out of the way of malaria—also, perhaps to refresh boyhood associations.

While official propriety forbade that Marshall should express himself publicly on political issues, in his correspondence he could be less reticent. A letter written in 1812 in criticism of the war with Great Britain suggests between the lines that he would not have regarded with aversion the Federalist nomination that year (Beveridge, IV, 35); and twenty years later he was hoping against hope for the election of Clay so that Jackson would not have the appointment of his successor, and when fate ruled otherwise, determining to stick it out to the end. Meanwhile, in 1829, he had accepted election, though with strong professions of reluctance, to the Virginia constitutional convention of that year. He at once took a leading rôle, and it was due in no small part to his and Madison's efforts that manhood suffrage was defeated and that the oligarchic system of county justices was fastened upon the state more tightly than ever.

Till his seventy-sixth year Marshall had scarcely known a day's illness. That year he underwent, at the hands of the celebrated Dr. Physick of Philadelphia, operation for stone. It proved successful and his health was restored. Three years later a more serious ailment appeared, an enlarged liver, and it was rendered critical by contusions received in a stage-coach upset. Again he went to Philadelphia, but this time surgery was impracticable. He died with his sons about him July 6, 1835, in the thirty-fifth year of his chief justiceship and the eightieth of life.

[A. J. Beveridge, *The Life of John Marshall* (4 vols., 1916–19), reproducing the notable portraits by Chester Harding and Inman; L. C. Bell, "John Marshall: Albert J. Beveridge as a Biographer," *Va. Law Register,* March 1927; Edward S. Corwin, *John Marshall and the Constitution* (1919); R. E. Cushman, "Marshall and the Constitution," *Minn. Law Review,* Dec. 1920; W. M. Paxton, *The Marshall Family* (1885); E. J. Lee, *Lee of Virginia 1642–1892* (1895); Joseph Story, *A Discourse upon the Life, Character and Services of the Honorable John Marshall, LL.D.* (1835), republished with eulogy by Horace Binney in J. F. Dillon, *John Marshall, Life, Character and Judicial Services* (3 vols., 1903); U. S. Supreme Court *Reports* from 1 *Cranch* to 9 *Peters,* inclusive; J. M. Dillon, ed., *John Marshall: Complete Constitutional Decisions* (1903); J. P. Cotton, ed., *The Constitutional Decisions of John Marshall* (2 vols., 1905); J. W. Brockenbrough, ed., *Reports of Cases Decided by the Honourable John Marshall . . . in the Circuit Court of the U. S., for the Dist. of Va. and N. C., from 1802 to 1833 Inclusive* (2 vols., 1837); *Reports of the Trials of Colonel Aaron Burr for Treason . . . and for a Misdemeanor,* by David Robertson, stenographer (2 vols., 1808); Charles Warren, *The Supreme Court in U. S. History* (3 vols., 1922). Most of Marshall's published letters, as well as his will and a brief autobiography which he evidently prepared for Delaplaine's *Repository* in 1818 will be found in John E. Oster's absurdly entitled and still more absurdly arranged *The Political and Economic Doctrines of John Marshall* (1914). The *Repository* was discontinued before the Marshall sketch could be published (see Oster, pp. 197–99). In 1931 William Wetmore Story's widow died in Rome, and among her papers was found the "letter written long afterwards to a friend" which is referred to in Joseph Story's *Discourse.* Actually the letter was written to Story himself, at his request, in 1827 and is the principal source of the portion of the *Discourse* covering Marshall's early life. It concludes with the passage quoted above about the circumstances of Marshall's appointment to the chief justiceship—circumstances regarding which the *Discourse* maintains a discreet silence. The letter has been acquired by the William L. Clements Lib., at the Univ. of Mich., and the writer of this sketch was permitted to see a photostatic copy of the document through the courtesy of Dr. Randolph G. Adams.]

E. S. C.

MARSHALL, LOUIS (Oct. 7, 1773–April 1866), physician and teacher, was the youngest of the fifteen children of Mary Randolph (Keith) and Thomas Marshall [*q.v.*]. He was a brother of John and of James Markham Marshall, a cousin of Humphrey Marshall, 1760–1841, and of the mother of Duff Green [*qq.v.*], and was related to many other distinguished men of Virginia and Kentucky. He was born on the family estate, "Oak Hill," in Fauquier County, Va. In 1785 he went with his family to Kentucky and settled at "Buckpond" in Woodford County. Here he was given his early educational training principally by his father and by Scotch tutors, among whom was Dr. Ebenezer Brooks. In 1793 he went to Philadelphia and spent a year with his brother, James Markham Marshall, and soon thereafter went abroad for study. After pursuing literary studies in Edinburgh he went to Paris, where he took courses in medicine and surgery. During the Revolution he was sent to prison and was in danger of execution when his brothers, John and James Markham Marshall, obtained his release. He returned to America, and in 1800 at Frankfort he married Agatha, the daughter of Francis Smith, a Virginian who had moved to Kentucky. They had five sons and one daughter. His father gave him the "Buckpond" estate, but, being by nature unsuited to the business of planting, he devoted his attention to the practice of medicine.

He was, however, much more interested in education than he had ever been in anything else, so he soon set up a classical school for boys at "Buckpond," which became celebrated not only for the fame afterwards attained by some of its graduates, but also for its rigid discipline and standards. Becoming president of Washington College (now Washington and Lee University) at Lexington, Va., in 1830, he entirely deserted the system of discipline and education he had employed at "Buckpond." According to his new methods there were no classes in groups unless a group so desired. Instead, individuals came at any time to the professor to recite or to obtain aid. Rules were discarded, and a state of nature was declared. His purpose was to develop an untrammeled individualism in the college, but he devastated the time and enthusiasm of the members of his faculty and raised up bitter opposition. The students, however, made of him a hero of the first magnitude. He played with them on the terms of the most complete familiarity; and in his class room, fitted up with a great arm-chair and a bed, pipe in mouth he received them as he lounged. Yet when his students began to take too many liberties, he began to meet them with sneers and sarcasm. Having lost the applause of his students and the support of his faculty, he set out for his Kentucky home in the summer of 1834 and never returned.

In Kentucky he began teaching boys again, and in 1838 Transylvania University elected him professor of languages and president *pro tempore* for two years. In 1844 his wife died, and thereafter he wandered among his kinsmen, spending a considerable part of his time in Covington, Ky., where he did some teaching. During the Civil War he was a Unionist with many reservations. He died at "Buckpond" and was at first buried there but was later removed to Frankfort. In France he had changed his name from Lewis to Louis, and had become an agnostic. On returning to America, however, he seems to have become genuinely religious and was long an elder in the Presbyterian Church. He expounded the Bible much to his students and gave especial attention to the prophecies. He actually set the date when the world would be destroyed. He was bitterly opposed to whiskey. He had an irregular temper, which got him into many duels in France, the scars from which he carried through life. In Kentucky he killed a person in a duel, and contemptuously refused to shoot at Gen. Thomas Bodley in another. He was eccentric in manners and speech, singular in his views, arbitrary and impatient of contradiction, yet a man of great intellectual attainment and force of character.

[Washington and Lee Univ., *Hist. Papers,* nos. 5, 6 (1895–1904); Louis and R. H. Collins, *Hist. of Ky.,* revised ed. (2 vols., 1874); Robert Peter, *Transylvania University* (1896); W. M. Paxton, *The Marshall Family* (1885).] E. M. C.

MARSHALL, LOUIS (Dec. 14, 1856–Sept. 11, 1929), lawyer, publicist, and civic and Jewish communal leader, was born in Syracuse, N. Y., the son of Jacob and Zilli Strauss Marshall, who emigrated from Germany to the United States in 1849 and 1853 respectively. They were of extremely modest means. Louis graduated from the Syracuse high school in 1874. His schooling had been interfered with even before he was in his teens, but his zest for knowledge was prodigious, and he acquired a knowledge of the leading modern languages, besides Latin, Greek, Hebrew, and Yiddish. After studying in a law office for a year, he took the two-year course at Columbia Law School in a single year (1876–77) and was admitted to the bar in January 1878. He was immediately made a junior member of the Syracuse law firm of which William C. Ruger, later chief judge of New York state, was the head. In February 1894 he moved to New York City to become a member of the law firm of Guggenheimer, Untermyer & Marshall, with which he was associated until his death.

Marshall is said to have argued no fewer than 150 cases in the New York court of appeals, before his removal to New York City, involving every branch of jurisprudence. It has also been said that he appeared in more cases in the United States Supreme Court than any one else, excepting the representatives of the government. Certainly no contemporary succeeded so frequently in striking down measures as violative of the federal or state constitutions. Among the leading cases in which he appeared were *People ex rel. Tyroler* vs. *Warden of Prison* (157 *N. Y.*, 116; 1898), in which the New York railroad ticket scalping act was adjudged unconstitutional, and in 1927 the Tyson case (273 *U. S.*, 418), in which the New York theatre ticket resale law was adjudged unconstitutional. His arguments were also sustained in the case of *Ives* vs. *South Buffalo Railway Company* (201 *N. Y.*, 271), in which the New York workmen's compensation act was held unconstitutional, before an express constitutional amendment authorized such measures. Similarly, he secured an adjudication (231 *N. Y.*, 465) invalidating New York's soldiers' bonus law. He was of successful counsel in *Pierce* vs. *Society of Sisters of the Holy Name* (268 *U. S.*, 510), adjudging the Oregon anti-parochial school law unconstitutional, and secured a favorable opinion in *Nixon* vs. *Herndon* (273 *U. S.*, 536), adjudging a state statute excluding negroes from political primaries unconstitutional. He also argued the Pacific Coast anti-Oriental land cases (263 *U. S.*, 225, 313, 326).

While he was unsuccessful in his efforts in the Leo Frank case (237 *U. S.*, 309) to secure a holding that a verdict in a capital case induced in the state courts by mob intimidation was a ground for reversal, under the Fourteenth Amendment, the dissenting opinion of Justice Holmes in that case was later adopted by the court in 261 *U. S.*, 86. In *Engel* vs. *O'Malley* (219 *U. S.*, 128), as counsel for the state of New York, he was upheld by the court when the New York private banking law which he had drafted was declared constitutional. He also argued in favor of the constitutionality of the migratory bird laws (252 *U. S.*, 416). He was of counsel successfully attacking the act enlarging the jurisdiction of the New York city court (207 *N. Y.*, 290), and was successful in the Onondaga County senatorial election case of 1891 (129 *N. Y.*, 395). He was of counsel in the case involving the constitutionality of the New York subway contracts (*Admiral Realty Company* vs. *City of New York,* 206 *N. Y.*, 110) and in the New York special franchise tax law case, as special counsel for New York state (199 *U. S.*, 1), in the Pennsylvania anthracite coal tax case (260 *U. S.*, 245), in the interstate commerce act railway valuation cases (252 *U. S.*, 178, leading up to the O'Fallon case, 279 *U. S.*, 461), and in the cases involving the right of municipal operation of buses in New York City under the home-rule amendment of the constitution (229 *N. Y.*, 570; 241 *N. Y.*, 96).

In cases involving aliens he secured holdings that naturalization is a judicial function, reviewable on appeal, and not merely administrative (*Tutun* vs. *United States,* 270 *U. S.*, 568), and that naturalized citizens enjoy rights equal to natural-born citizens (*Luria* vs. *United States,* 231 *U. S.*, 9). He also frustrated administrative efforts to prevent the naturalization of aliens whose families were still abroad (*American Jewish Year Book,* 1925–26, pp. 450–59, 1914–15, pp. 19–89, 1929–30, pp. 347–52). He was of counsel in the Sampson Simpson will case (133 *N. Y.*, 519), in the Gottlieb immigration case (265 *U. S.*, 310), in the case involving the constitutionality of the call for the New York constitutional convention of 1915 (212 *N. Y.*, 520), and in that involving the validity of the New York literacy test for voters (236 *N. Y.*, 437). He served as a member of the New York constitutional conventions of 1890, 1894, and 1915, and was a member (1903–22), and chairman after 1911, of the New York City Bar Association Committee on Amendment of the Law. In the constitutional convention of 1894 he was influential in the shaping of the judicial and charitable appropriations provisions and prepared the amendments to the judicial provisions of the civil and criminal codes thereby necessitated. He also drafted important amendments to the New York Civil Rights Law and was active in the revision of New York corporation laws.

In 1902 Marshall accepted Mayor Low's appointment as chairman of a committee to investigate the Rabbi Jacob Joseph funeral riot, and the committee report led to the checking of discrimination against Jewish and other immigrants on the part of the police and petty magistrates of New York City. In 1908 he became chairman of Governor Hughes's state immigration commission whose work culminated in a notable printed report recommending constructive measures for the benefit of the immigrants. He was active in the American Jewish Committee, and served as president from 1912 until his death. It was in this capacity that much of his best work after 1906 was rendered. The annual reports of the Committee from 1912 on were drafted mainly by him and displayed a comprehensive knowledge of Jewish and world affairs. On behalf of the American Jewish Committee he was a consistent and vigorous champion of liberal immigration laws. He argued before committees of Congress and drafted party platform planks, and it was largely due to his influence that adoption of a literacy test for immigrants was prevented until 1917, and that discriminatory measures were defeated.

As mediator in the New York cloak-makers' strike of 1910, involving seventy thousand people, Marshall effected a settlement, framing a protocol later used as a model in labor adjustments in several industries. In 1919 he was arbitrator in the clothing-workers' strike. He was one of the founders of the Jewish Welfare Board and was chairman of the American Jewish Relief Committee, which, in conjunction with two associated organizations, raised approximately sixty-five million dollars for the relief of Jews in the war zone. Soon after moving to New York he became a director of the Educational Alliance, and thereafter deeply influenced its work for the Americanization and improvement of the Jews on the East Side. He was also a founder of the Jewish Protectory, seeking to redeem youthful delinquents. He served as one of the reorganizers of the Jewish Theological Seminary of America and was chairman of its board of directors until his death. As a memorial to his wife, Florence Lowenstein, whom he married in 1895 and who died in 1916, he established a foundation to promote the religious education of Jewish girls. He served for many years and until his death as president of Temple Emanu-El of New York City. He was also for many years president of the New York State College of Forestry and at Governor Franklin D. Roosevelt's instance the building of the College at Syracuse University bears Marshall's name.

One of his most important achievements was his leadership of the movement for the abrogation of the Russian-American treaty of 1832, because of Russia's refusal to accord right to enter Russia to American Jews and American clergymen of certain other denominations. Marshall delivered an address demanding abrogation on Jan. 19, 1911, before the Union of American Hebrew Congregations, and subsequently when President Taft showed unwillingness to approve abrogation Marshall and his associates appealed to the American people. Mass-meetings were held all over the country. Marshall delivered masterly arguments before the House committee on foreign affairs on Feb. 15 and Dec. 11, 1911, and before the corresponding Senate committee on Dec. 13, 1911. Later in the month the abrogation of the treaty was effected.

Even more important was Marshall's championship of minority protective clauses at the Peace Conference of 1919. When he reached Paris on Mar. 2, 1919, he found that an unsatisfactory clause regarding Roumania's minorities had been approved by a committee for insertion in the peace treaties. Aided by Judge J. W. Mack he drafted a substitute in conjunction with the legal advisers of the United States. When this had been approved in principle by the "Big Four" of the Conference, it was referred to a newly constituted committee on new states, and Marshall cooperated with this body in drafting new clauses which were inserted into the treaties with Poland, Roumania, and other East-European states, primarily at the instance of the United States. Provisions forbidding all discriminations as to civil, religious, and political rights should, it was agreed by all these countries, be inserted in their constitutions, *ipso facto* nullifying all abridgments of minority rights, and infractions of these rights were made a "matter of international concern" and "placed under the guarantee of the League of Nations." Some of the most important decisions of the World Court have borne upon these provisions.

For years after the Balfour declaraton of 1917, Marshall worked to secure united Jewish support to establish a "national Jewish home" in Palestine for persecuted Jews. He attended a meeting in Zurich in August 1929 which adopted a constitution (largely drafted by him) of this enlarged "Jewish Agency." Practically all of world-Jewry united in the enlarged plans. Barely was this conference over when he was suddenly stricken down, and he died at Zurich Sept. 11, 1929. By his last will he left a tithe of his large personal estate to charitable organizations. In an interesting study published in the *New Yorker,* Sept. 21, 1929, many apparent anomalies in Marshall's character were described, such as his large philanthropies and his trifling personal economies, his refusal to accept assistance in the preparation of his numerous briefs, the contrast between his briefs and addresses and his sonnets and humorous dialect sketches, and his kindly, jovial nature, in contrast with his fearless and earnest denunciations. On the occasion of his seventieth birthday, an address of congratulation was presented to him, signed by more than eight thousand representatives of organizations throughout the world. On that occasion Benjamin N. Cardozo characterized Marshall as "a great lawyer; a great champion of ordered liberty; a great leader of his people; a great lover of mankind."

[*Louis Marshall: A Biog. Sketch by Cyrus Adler and Memorial Addresses by Cyrus Adler, Irving Lehman, Horace Stern* (1931), pub. by the Am. Jewish Committee; the *Am. Jewish Year Book,* 1929–30; *Jewish Tribune,* Dec. 10, 1926, Sept. 20, Oct. 4, 1929; *N. Y. Times,* Jan. 12, 1930; *Who's Who in America,* 1928–29; supplementary American chapters in Luigi Luzzatti, *God in Freedom* (1930), ed. by Max J. Kohler; Oscar I. Janowsky, *The Jews and Minority Rights (1898–1919),* (1933); personal acquaintance.]

M. J. K.

MARSHALL, THOMAS (Apr. 2, 1730–June 22, 1802), surveyor, legislator, soldier, was one of the ten children of John Marshall "of the forest," a small planter of Westmoreland County, Va., and his wife, Elizabeth Markham, daughter of Lewis Markham, one-time sheriff of Westmoreland County. Though heir to his father's acres, on his marriage in 1754 to Mary Randolph Keith, the sixteen-year-old daughter of an Episcopal clergyman, James Keith, and Mary Isham Randolph, a descendant of William Randolph of "Turkey Island," Thomas Marshall moved to Prince William County. He built a log-cabin near Germantown. Here John Marshall, eldest of their fifteen children and destined to be chief justice of the United States was born in the next year. There followed in steady succession, as the family constantly moved westward, the other fourteen sons and daughters, all of whom lived to reach maturity and position. Besides John, James Markham and Louis, 1773–1866 [*qq.v.*] attained special distinction. In later years, Chief Justice Marshall said of his father, "My father was a far abler man than any of his sons. To him I owe the solid foundation of all my own success" (J. F. Dillon, *John Marshall, Life, Character and Judicial Services,* 1903, III, p. 330).

Thomas Marshall was a man of great stature. He shared with his wife a deeply religious outlook and unusual hardihood. Although he was a frontiersman for most of his life, he had a liking for books, possessed some of his own, and followed intellectual interests. He became a land surveyor and was brought into close contact with his contemporary George Washington for whom he developed an intimate and lasting friendship. For a time he was engaged by Washington as assistant surveyor of the Fairfax estate. Like Washington he had close associations with Lord Fairfax. After some years at Germantown he moved farther westward and built in a valley in the Blue Ridge a more pretentious house of four rooms with a small stone meat house, a cabin for his two slaves, and a log stable. Here he lived for twelve years, moving in 1773 to seventeen hundred acres adjacent to North Cobler Mountain, a short distance from his earlier location. He built a seven-room house, "Oak Hill," which attested his steadily increasing property. His active service as an officer in Fauquier County began at the first court in that county in 1759 when he was sworn in as a justice of the peace, justice of the county court in chancery, and was given a commission as county surveyor. He was the leading citizen in Fauquier County in the succeeding years. He was a member of the House of Burgesses from 1761 to October 1767, when he became sheriff of Fauquier County. From 1769 to 1773 he again served as a Burgess from Fauquier and in the latter year was appointed clerk of Dunmore, later Shenandoah County. In 1775 he returned to the Burgesses. When Leeds Parish, embracing Fauquier County, was established in 1769 he was made the principal vestryman.

Marshall attended the Virginia Convention of 1775 and when Culpeper, Orange, and Fauquier counties raised regiments of minute men he was named their lieutenant in view of his prominence, his adherence to the Revolution, and his previous military experience as lieutenant and captain in the militia and a participant in the Indian wars. He fought with the Culpeper minute men at Great Bridge, the first battle of the Revolution in Virginia. While there he was appointed by the Virginia legislature major of the 3rd Virginia Regiment. With his son Lieut. John Marshall, he joined the Continental forces and had distinguished service at Trenton and at the Brandywine, where he had two horses shot under him. He had been promoted lieutenant-colonel on Aug. 13, 1776, and colonel on Feb. 21, 1777. The Virginia legislature rewarded him for his bravery at the Brandywine by electing him colonel of the Virginia State Regiment of Artillery. He served in this capacity until Feb. 16, 1781, when his men were discharged and he became a reduced officer. In 1780 he rode to Kentucky under special permit from the Virginia governor to locate land warrants. In November 1780 he was appointed surveyor for a part of Kentucky. The next year he was appointed on a commission to examine and settle the public accounts in the Western country. Though he had already acquired considerable property in Virginia, owning at least 2,000 acres in Fauquier and twenty-two negroes, he was embarrassed for lack of money at the close of the Revolution. He opened his surveyor's office in Kentucky and in 1783 moved his large family to their new home across the mountains. He acquired large tracts of land. In 1785 he gave his son John 824 acres of the best land in Fauquier County. He took prominent part in Kentucky affairs, represented the district of Kentucky in the Virginia legislature, and became "Surveyor of Revenue for the District of Ohio," resigning that office on June 30, 1797, because of age and infirmity. He had great faith in the Union and steadily opposed disaffection in Kentucky and feared foreign influence as the gravest danger to the young republic. Thomas Marshall died in 1802. His widow survived him until Sept. 19, 1809. He left in his will immense quantities of land to be divided among his children, including his home farm in Kentucky, "Buckpond."

[A. J. Beveridge, *The Life of John Marshall*, vols. I and II (1916), has the best material on Thos. Marshall. See also: Humphrey Marshall, *The Hist. of Ky.* (2 vols., 1924); "Thos. Marshall," *Bull. Fauquier Hist. Soc.*, July 1922, and "The Genesis of Fauquier," *Ibid.*; W. M. Paxton, *The Marshall Family* (1885); *Reg. of the Ky. State Hist. Soc.*, Jan. 1921, pp. 93–96.]

M. H. W.

MARSHALL, THOMAS ALEXANDER (Jan. 15, 1794–Apr. 17, 1871), jurist and congressman, was born in Kentucky, the son of Humphrey Marshall, 1760–1841 [*q.v.*], and of his wife Mary, who was a sister of John, Louis, and James Markham Marshall [*qq.v.*]. Thomas profited much from the position of influence and wealth of his father. He was sent to the celebrated school in Mercer County conducted by Joshua Fry and was there prepared for college. He was then sent to Yale College, where he received the B.A. degree in 1815. Returning to Kentucky, he read law and the next year established himself in Frankfort. On Nov. 26, 1816, he was married to Eliza Price, a sister-in-law of Henry Clay and a grand-daughter of Thomas Hart, one of the proprietors of Transylvania. Since Frankfort at this time had a full supply of able lawyers and was besides not particularly friendly to the Humphrey Marshall tradition, he removed to Paris, Bourbon County, in 1819. In 1827 he was elected to the lower branch of the legislature and served for two years. Finding that the Whig party came closest to the doctrines his father had advocated, he acted with it. He was elected to the Twenty-second and Twenty-third congresses, from 1831 to 1835, but was defeated for the Twenty-fourth. At Washington he attained a position of some influence. He served first on the committee on private land claims and then as chairman of the committee on Revolutionary claims. He spoke frequently and sometimes at great length, upholding the orthodox Whig position. He was active in the tariff debates of 1832 and often advocated rates higher than were obtained. He also spoke in favor of the United States Bank. He showed, perhaps, his greatest interest in the veterans of the Revolution who were seeking pensions or adjustments of claims.

He had a judicial turn of mind that could be better satisfied elsewhere than in the excitement of active politics. Following his defeat for a third term in Congress he was offered an appointment to the Kentucky court of appeals, which he readily accepted and was commissioned in March 1835. When his position became elective under the state's new constitution of 1850 he was elected and continued to serve until 1856. During his uninterrupted term of twenty-one years he was twice chief justice, once through appointment, 1847–51, and the second time through the operation of the provision in the constitution that provided each justice should serve his last two years as chief justice. Shortly after becoming a justice he accepted in addition a professorship of the law of pleadings, evidence, and contracts in Transylvania University, which he held from 1836 to 1849. On retiring from the court, he went to the rapidly developing city of Chicago, but, failing to be satisfied there, he soon returned to Kentucky. He settled in Louisville, where he spent the period of the Civil War. He became a Union man and took an inconspicuous part in the politics of the times by serving as a Louisville representative in the lower house of the legislature from 1863 to 1865. Eschewing the radicalism that gripped some of the Kentuckians after the war he joined the Conservatives. On Feb. 12, 1866, Gov. Thomas Bramlette appointed him chief justice of the court of appeals to fill the vacancy caused by the death of William Sampson. In the following August at the regular election he ran for the full term of six years, but his Unionism during the war was too much for Kentucky now turned Confederate so he was defeated. His active career ended with this reverse. He died at his home in Louisville, but his remains were buried in Lexington.

[Lewis and R. H. Collins, *Hist. of Ky.*, revised ed. (2 vols., 1874); *Green Bag*, Aug. 1900; F. B. Dexter, *Biog. Sketches of the Grads. of Yale College*, vol. VI (1912); W. M. Paxton, *The Marshall Family* (1885); Robert Peters, *Transylvania Univ.* (1896); *Cincinnati Commercial*, Apr. 19, 1871; *Courier-Journal* (Louisville), Apr. 17, 1871.] E. M. C.

MARSHALL, THOMAS RILEY (Mar. 14, 1854–June 1, 1925), governor of Indiana, vice-president of the United States, was born at North Manchester, Ind. His father, Daniel M. Marshall, was an old-fashioned country doctor, himself of Hoosier birth, but the son of a Virginia couple who had emigrated to Indiana when the state was still frontier. Thomas' mother, Martha (Patterson) Marshall, and his mother's parents, were natives of Pennsylvania. When Thomas was about two years old, he was taken by his parents to Illinois, remaining there long enough to acquire a distinct recollection of having attended the Freeport debate between Lincoln and Douglas. Soon the Marshall family went on to Kansas, but, finding the political situation there too tense for comfort, they moved again, first to La Grange, Mo., and later, back to Indiana.

After attending the public schools, young Marshall entered Wabash College, Crawfordsville, Ind., and was graduated in 1873 with Phi Beta Kappa honors. During his college years he made up his mind to study law, and, taking the advice of some lawyer friends, he read law in the office of Judge Walter Olds of Ft. Wayne. He was admitted to the bar on his twenty-first birthday at Columbia City, Ind., where he practised continuously for more than a third of a century, acquiring both a comfortable living and an enviable degree of contentment. Until well after his fortieth birthday he remained a bachelor, but on Oct. 2, 1895, Lois I. Kimsey of Angola, Ind., became his wife—a most felicitous marriage. As a typical "prominent citizen," Marshall was a member of the Presbyterian Church, taught a Sunday-school class, served on the local school board, and became a thirty-third degree Mason (*Review of Reviews*, August 1912, pp. 185–90).

"Democrats, like poets," said Marshall, "are born, not made." Like his father before him, Marshall was always a Democrat, and he served his party well. To his way of thinking, the fundamental principle of the Democratic creed was the right of every man to "his chance in life, unhampered and unaided by legislative enactment" (*Outlook*, Sept. 28, 1912, p. 221). For many years his interest in politics did not seem to extend to a desire to hold office; but once when he was importuned to run for Congress and refused on the ground that he "might be elected," he hinted that he would like to be governor. At length, in 1908, this nomination came to him, as he insisted, "through the inability of the leading candidates to obtain a majority of the votes of the convention" (*Recollections*, p. 161).

During this campaign the Republicans came out for county option on the licensing of saloons, and indeed actually put a county-option law on the statute books. The Democrats favored township option, a system by which cities would have the chance to vote their preference apart from the strongly dry rural population. The anti-saloon forces promptly denounced the Democratic stand as "wet," but in spite of this opposition Marshall won after a vigorous campaign, although the electoral vote of the state went to Taft. Not until 1911, however, were there enough Democrats in the legislature to make possible the enactment of a township-option law. Marshall himself believed that prohibition could be effective only when local sentiment was behind it, and that the substitution of township for county option was "of immense advantage to temperance" (*World's Work*, Oct. 1912, p. 633).

As governor for four years, Marshall also pushed to enactment an extensive program of labor and social legislation; and he attempted to secure in an unusual way the adoption of a much needed new constitution for the state. The "Tom Marshall Constitution," so-called because Marshall was credited with having written it himself, failed to materialize because of hostile action by the state supreme court (*Ellingham* vs. *Dye*, 178 *Ind.*, 336). While Marshall believed this judicial veto to be a "clear usurpation of authority," he yielded to it gracefully lest the respect properly due the court by the people should be diminished (*Recollections*, p. 213). It was Marshall's record as governor that led to the presentation of his name to the Democratic national convention of 1912 as Indiana's favorite son for president. When the nomination went to Wilson, Marshall was given second place with little opposition. His election followed, and four years later he was renominated and reëlected—the first vice-president in nearly a century to succeed himself.

As vice-president, Marshall was of greater consequence in the government than most of his predecessors. He made it his business to master the rules of the Senate, over which he presided with grace and tact. While scrupulously careful not to exceed his constitutional and legal powers, he exerted his personal influence most effectively on behalf of many administration measures. Nor did he deem it improper to speak his mind occasionally on public matters. Once, in 1913, his remarks on the subject of inheritances aroused much criticism in conservative circles (*Literary Digest,* May 3, 1913), but ordinarily what he had to say was well received. During his second term, when the President was for much of the time absent from the country or ill, Marshall often acted as ceremonial head of the nation, welcoming royal visitors to the United States, and discharging with democratic simplicity many other unwonted duties. Had he countenanced the idea, it is probable that he might have been declared president during the time that the stricken Wilson was incapable of carrying the full responsibilities of his office (*Outlook,* June 10, 1925).

Marshall was perhaps the most popular vice-president that the country ever had. His clear blue-gray eyes, his plentiful iron-gray hair, his genial smile, and his well-groomed appearance marked him out as a man of note, in spite of his instinctive modesty and his none too impressive physique. "Lovable, generous, kindly, keenly observant and always tolerant," he was above all else possessed of a never-failing sense of humor. Once during a tiresome debate in the Senate on the needs of the country, he let drop his most frequently quoted remark: "What this country needs is a really good five cent cigar." A devoted admirer of the original constitution, he payed his respects to some of the later changes by the observation that "it's got so it is as easy to amend the Constitution of the United States as it used to be to draw a cork" (*Literary Digest,* June 20, 1925, p. 45). Late in life he put much of his quaint humor and homely philosophy into a book of *Recollections,* "in the hope," so his foreword declared, "that the Tired Business Man, the Unsuccessful Golfer and the Lonely Husband whose wife is out reforming the world may find therein a half hour's surcease from sorrow." It may be that Marshall's love of fun led some undiscerning people to set too low an estimate on his ability. After leaving office in 1921, Marshall returned to Indiana, making his home in Indianapolis. He died four years later, in Washington, D. C., while on a business trip to the Capital.

[Marshall, as he said, "was never able to accumulate the note-making or the diary habit"; hence his book, *Recollections of Thos. R. Marshall, Vice-President and Hoosier Philosopher—A Hoosier Salad* (1925), is precisely what its title implies. Chas. Kettleborough, *Constitution Making in Ind.,* vol. II (1916), gives the history of the "Tom Marshall Constitution" and prints many documents, including the Constitution itself and the court decision which set it aside. Marshall's sketch of himself in the *Cong. Directory,* 63 Cong., 2 Sess., p. 3, is characteristically brief. Appreciative remarks on Marshall by John McSweeney of Ohio are in *Cong. Record,* 69 Cong., 1 Sess., p. 11548. Of the numerous periodical references to Marshall's career, the more important have already been cited.] J. D. H.

MARSHALL, WILLIAM EDGAR (June 30, 1837–Aug. 29, 1906), portrait painter, engraver, was born in New York City of Scotch parents. His father, Francis Marshall, coming to the United States a stone-mason, founded the contracting firm of Marshall, Bates & Company, builders. The son got his education at a public school in Varick Street. At seventeen he began his engraving in a watchcase factory. His free hours, he devoted to ambitious portrait ventures in line. He was encouraged by a friendly engraver, Cyrus Durand [*q.v.*], at whose suggestion the youth executed plates of both presidential candidates in the Buchanan-Frémont campaign. Submitted to the American Bank Note Company, these won Marshall, in 1858, a coveted chance to engrave portrait vignettes. He worked for this company several years and became one of its best engravers. Meanwhile, he published large portrait plates, two of which, Washington after Stuart, and Fenimore Cooper after Elliott, had wide circulation. He also tried his hand at painting original portraits. Finding that he had talent, he went to Paris about 1863 for study under Couture. Two of his student canvases won admission to the Salon. News of the assassination of Lincoln brought him home to paint, from photographs and descriptions, a portrait of the martyred President, which is now at Yale University. His engraving from this picture had an enormous sale. During a period spent in Boston, Emerson, Hawthorne, Longfellow, and Holmes sat for him.

About 1866 he returned to New York, taking up his permanent abode in Broadway, near Washington Square, where during the days when artists swarmed in that vicinity his studio became a rendezvous. He had an engaging, humorous personality and in conversation could draw from a wealth of entertaining anecdotes concerning his famous sitters, who, as the years went by, included Grant, whom he painted six times, Sherman, Blaine, Beecher, John Gilbert, Mark Hanna, Harrison, McKinley, and Roosevelt. He helped many a struggling painter, notably Albert P. Ryder [*q.v.*], whose talent he was among the first to recognize. When Clemenceau was in exile in America, he renewed a friendship with Marshall begun in the Latin Quarter, making the studio his headquarters.

About 1871, having engraved a head of Christ after Da Vinci, Marshall was fired with ambition to paint his own conception of the Galilean. To the project he devoted vast research, producing at length a colossal canvas depicting a dark-eyed, Greco-Arabian type, which he exhibited widely but refused to sell. During his later years he lived in retirement in his attic studio, 711 Broadway, keeping so aloof from currents of art life that many believed him dead, but happy with his engravings, his autograph letters, and the great head of Christ, which covered one whole wall. Here, cared for by a second wife, Florence Rogers Garrison, a widow whom he married in 1900, he died. From his first wife he had been divorced. Marshall is represented in the National Gallery of Art in Washington by his portrait of Longfellow, and one of himself painted at the age of twenty-three.

[Interview in Illus. Supp. to *N. Y. Tribune,* June 3, 1906; obituary articles in *N. Y. Tribune* and *N. Y. Times,* Aug. 30, 1906; D. M. Stauffer, *Am. Engravers upon Copper and Steel* (1907); Frank Weitenkampf, *Am. Graphic Art* (1924); W. S. Baker, *The Engraved Portraits of Washington* (1880), and *Am. Engravers and Their Works* (1875); F. J. Mather and others, *The Am. Spirit in Art* (1927); *Shields Mag. of Art,* Jan. 1908.]

M. B. H—t.

MARSHALL, WILLIAM LOUIS (June 11, 1846–July 2, 1920), soldier and engineer, was born in Washington, Ky., the son of Col. Charles A. and Phoebe A. (Paxton) Marshall. His grandfather, Thomas, was a brother of Chief Justice John Marshall [*q.v.*]. William attended the grammar school of Kenyon College, Ohio, from 1859 to 1860, and then entered the collegiate department. At the outbreak of the Civil War, however, he enlisted in the 10th Kentucky Cavalry, serving from Aug. 16, 1862, until Sept. 17, 1863, when ill health prevented further service. The following year he received an appointment as cadet at the United States Military Academy, from which he graduated in June 1868 and was assigned as second lieutenant to the corps of engineers.

His first important service was from 1872 to 1876, when he was engaged as assistant to Lieut. G. M. Wheeler [*q.v.*] in the exploration of the Rocky Mountain region of the West. It was during this period, 1873, that he discovered the Marshall Pass, now traversed by the Denver & Rio Grande Railroad, and, in 1875, the gold placers in the Marshall Basin of the San Miguel River, Colorado. From 1876 to 1884 he was assistant engineer on various river improvement projects in Alabama, Georgia, and Tennessee and in charge of a section of the Mississippi River. He was then placed in charge of river and harbor improvements in Wisconsin and Illinois, on which assignment he was engaged for fifteen years. Part of this time, 1890 to 1899, he was employed in constructing the Hennepin Canal, connecting the Illinois River at Lasalle with the Mississippi River at Rock Island, which was to be a part of an inland waterway from the Mississippi to Lake Michigan. This canal with its thirty locks has practically every type of structure employed in canal construction. "Begun in the early nineties before the art of concrete construction had become well known among engineers, all of its masonry is concrete. This courageous departure from the then existing practice was due entirely to . . . Marshall's sound judgment and bold initiative, and he then developed the details of methods which were subsequently adopted by the entire engineering profession and have continued in force practically unchanged to the present day" (Keller, *post,* p. 111). While constructing the canal, he patented several improvements connected with it, including a combined breakwater and beach, May 12, 1890; an automatic movable dam or sluiceway gate, Mar. 23, 1897; and an automatic dam, weir, or gate, Dec. 28, 1897, and Jan. 4, 1898. During this period, he also served on many important commissions and boards, among them a board to advise on the water supply of Washington, D. C., of which he was president; the Missouri River Commission; and the Lincoln Park Board, Chicago, for which he was consulting engineer.

In 1899 he was sent to New York City to take charge of both fortification and river and harbor work. Here he completed the Ambrose Channel, planned and completed the extension of Governor's Island, and displayed great originality in the construction of coast defenses. In the meantime he had been advanced through the various grades and on Aug. 27, 1907, commissioned colonel. In 1908, July 2, he was commissioned Chief of Engineers with the rank of brigadier-general, which position he held until his retirement from active service on June 11, 1910. In 1909, in addition to his other duties, he served on a board to report on the necessary defenses of the Panama Canal. Shortly after his retirement he was appointed by the President consulting engineer to the Secretary of the Interior, and as such served on various boards dealing with projects of the United States Reclamation Service and made reports on possible hydro-electric power development projects in different parts of the country. He held this position until his death, which occurred in Washington, D. C. On June 2, 1886, he married Elizabeth Hill Colquitt, daughter of Alfred H. Colquitt [*q.v.*], by whom he had one daughter.

[W. M. Paxton, *The Marshall Family* (1885); G. W. Cullum, *Biog. Reg. Officers and Grads. U. S. Mil. Acad.*, vols. III (1891), IV (1901), V (1910), VIa (1920); Charles Keller, in *Fifty-third Ann. Report Asso. Grads. U. S. Mil. Acad.* (1922); *The Official Gazette of the U. S. Patent Office*, May 12, 1891, Mar. 23, 1897, Dec. 28, 1897, Jan. 4, 1898; *Army and Navy Jour.*, July 10, 1920; *Who's Who in America*, 1918–19; *Evening Star* (Washington, D. C.), July 3, 1920.]

G. J. F.

MARSHALL, WILLIAM RAINEY (Oct. 17, 1825–Jan. 8, 1896), Union soldier, governor of Minnesota, was the son of Joseph and Abigail Black (Shaw) Marshall and the descendant of Joseph Marshall who emigrated from the north of Ireland about 1746 and settled near Carlisle, Pa. He was born in Boone County, Mo., and spent his boyhood in Quincy, Ill. For several years after 1841 he and his brother worked in lead mines of Illinois and Wisconsin, and during this time he obtained a practical knowledge of surveying. While living at St. Croix Falls in 1847 he went to the Falls of St. Anthony, where he staked out a claim, which he could not, however, make legal until 1849. In 1848 he was elected to the Wisconsin legislature but was disqualified because his residence was west of the St. Croix River. He was one of the leaders in the movement for the erection of Minnesota Territory and after 1849 was identified intimately with the development of Minnesota. He surveyed and plotted parts of the town at the Falls of St. Anthony (now part of Minneapolis), opened a hardware store, and was elected a member of the first territorial legislature. In 1851 he removed to St. Paul, where he plunged into a variety of activities, each of which seemed to him to promise greater possibilities than the last, for "his was the sanguine temperament in excess" (*Min. Hist. Soc. Colls.*, VIII, 510). He established and ran for a time a hardware store, was county surveyor, and in 1853 with his brother and Nathaniel P. Langford, whose sister, Abby, he married in 1854, set up a bank which prospered until the panic of 1857. He was chairman of the convention that founded the Republican party in Minnesota, sought unsuccessfully the office of delegate to Congress, and in 1861 started the *St. Paul Daily Press,* which soon absorbed the *Minnesotian.*

He soon sold his interest in the newspaper to his assistant editor, Joseph A. Wheelock, and entered upon that brief period of soldiering that probably brought him more satisfaction than any other experience. When the 7th Minnesota Infantry was recruited he was made lieutenant-colonel. He served with Sibley against the Sioux in the Minnesota Valley and participated in the punitive campaign of 1863. The 7th Infantry was then transferred to the South and attached to the XVI Army Corps. He was colonel in November 1863, and he campaigned in Arkansas, Missouri, Mississippi, and Tennessee. He was cited for distinguished skill and bravery in the fighting about Nashville in December 1864, and he was brevetted brigadier-general. Commanding his brigade at the siege of Mobile, he was wounded at the attack on Spanish Fort. The regiment was mustered out at Fort Snelling in August 1865, in time for him to capitalize his military prestige in the biennial gubernatorial campaign. He was nominated, elected by a narrow margin, and reëlected in 1867. No significant events marked his career as governor. He vetoed a bill to move the seat of government from St. Paul, and he vainly urged the legislature to redeem the credit of the state in the matter of the "Five Million Loan." A number of enterprises occupied him after his term as governor ended. He was one of the first railroad and warehouse commissioners in the state, holding the office from 1874 to 1882. Banking, farming, stock-raising, and other ventures engaged his attention but in none of them was he very successful, and he died poor. He was one of the founders and a life-long member of the Swedenborgian Church of St. Paul. He took an interest in the state historical society, being its president in 1868 and nominally its secretary from 1893 to 1895, but his health was failing and in 1894 he went to Pasadena, where he died.

[M. D. Shutter and J. S. McLain, *Progressive Men of Minn.* (1897); W. W. Folwell, *A Hist. of Minn.*, vols. II, III (1924–26); E. V. Smalley, *Hist. of the Republican Party* (1896); *Minn. Hist. Soc. Colls.*, vols. IV, VIII, IX, XII, XIII (1876–1908), esp. J. F. Williams, "Hist. of St. Paul" (vol. IV) and J. K. Baker, "Lives of the Governors of Minn." (vol. XIII); T. M. Newson, *Pen Pictures of St. Paul* (1886); *Daily Pioneer Press* (St. Paul), Jan. 10, 1896.]

L. B. S—e.

MARTIN, ALEXANDER (1740–Nov. 2, 1807), Revolutionary soldier, governor of North Carolina, United States senator, was the son of Hugh and Jane Martin of Hunterdon County, N. J. He received the degree of A.B. from the College of New Jersey in 1756 and soon thereafter moved to the village of Salisbury, N. C., where he was merchant, justice of the peace in 1764, deputy king's attorney in 1766, and judge in 1774–75. Incurring the hostility of the Regulators, he was severely whipped by them at the Hillsborough superior court in 1770 and was one of the signers of an agreement with them in Rowan County in 1771 to refund all fees taken illegally and to arbitrate all differences. He represented Guilford County, to which he had recently moved, in the North Carolina House of Commons (1773–74) and in the second and third provincial congresses (1775) as a supporter of the Patriot cause. Appointed lieutenant-colonel of the 2nd North Carolina Continental Regiment, Sept. 1, 1775, he participated in the "Snow Campaign" against the Loyalists in upper South Carolina late in the year; in the Moore's Creek campaign of February 1776; and, after promotion to a colonelcy, in the defense of Charleston in June. In 1777 he joined Washington's army in the North, but having been arrested for cowardice in the battle of Germantown, tried by court martial, and acquitted, he resigned his command on Nov. 22 and returned to North Carolina.

He represented Guilford County in the Senate, 1778–82, 1785, 1787–88, being speaker at every session except those of 1778–79; was a member in 1780–81 of the powerful Board of War and its successor, the Council Extraordinary; and acted as governor during the captivity of Governor Burke in the autumn and winter of 1781–82. The General Assembly elected him governor in 1782 over the conservative Samuel Johnston [*q.v.*], in 1783 over Richard Caswell [*q.v.*], and in 1784 without opposition. In December 1786 he was elected to the Continental Congress, but resigned the next year. He was the least strongly Federalistic and a relatively inconspicuous member of the North Carolina delegation to the Federal Convention of 1787. He left the Convention late in August and did not sign the completed Constitution. Nevertheless, his Federalism caused his defeat in the election of delegates to the Hillsborough Convention in 1788. He was again elected governor in 1789 and, by reëlections, completed in 1792 the constitutional limit of three consecutive terms.

Martin was not a public speaker or a man of remarkable ability. Suave, upright, moderate, faithful, an excellent parliamentarian, and a master of the art of conciliation, he courted with great success the favor of the powerful General Assembly by magnifying its ascendency over the governorship and drifting with the current of its opinion, in divining which he was an adept. In courteous gubernatorial messages he suggested clemency toward the Tories; encouragement of education; public support of ministers, regardless of denomination; greater power for the Continental Congress; stimulation of agriculture, commerce, and manufactures; and the construction of a system of internal improvements by convict labor. In public life he sought to placate both sides. A moderate Federalist before 1790, he inclined toward Republicanism thereafter. In 1792 the Republican legislature elected him to the United States Senate. Here his most conspicuous rôle was that of advocate of open legislative sessions. He voted for the Alien and Sedition acts, and probably for that reason failed of reëlection in December 1798. In 1799 he returned to his plantation, "Danbury," in Rockingham County, whither he had moved his residence prior to 1790, when he was reported as the owner of forty-seven slaves. He represented Rockingham County in the state Senate, 1804–05, serving as speaker during the session of 1805. He was a trustee of several academies and of the University of North Carolina, 1790–1807. He never married. On Nov. 2, 1807, he died at "Danbury," closing a public career unusual in length and popularity.

[*Colonial Records of N. C.* (10 vols., 1886–90); *State Records of N. C.* (16 vols., 1895–1905); Governors' Papers and Letter Books (MSS.), in N. C. Hist. Commission; *Journals of the House of Commons and Senate*, 1792, 1798; G. J. McRee, *Life and Correspondence of James Iredell* (2 vols., 1857–58); *Raleigh Register and N.-C. State Gazette*, Nov. 19, 1807; *The Papers of John Steele* (2 vols., 1924), ed. by H. M. Wagstaff; Francis Nash, *Governor Alexander Martin: An Address* (1908); R. M. Douglas, "Alexander Martin," in S. A. Ashe, *Biog. Hist. of N. C.*, vol. III (1905).]

A. R. N.

MARTIN, ARTEMAS (Aug. 3, 1835–Nov. 7, 1918), mathematician, was born on a farm in Steuben County, N. Y., the son of James Madison Martin and Orenda Knight (Bradley) Martin. During his early childhood the family moved to Venango County, Pa. His formal education consisted of three winters in the district school and a few months in the Franklin Academy when he was seventeen. As a boy he worked at farming and gardening in summer, and at woodchopping during the winter. Later he taught a district school for four winters, but for the most part, until he was fifty, he earned his living at farming, woodchopping, and oil-well drilling. His meager leisure he spent in the study of mathematics. Early in life he had begun to contribute mathematical problems and solutions to various journals, and in 1877, while making a bare living in market gardening on a small rented place in Erie County, Pa., he began to edit and publish the *Mathematical Visitor* (1877–94). In 1882 he began to publish the *Mathematical Magazine* (1882–1901). For financial reasons he found it necessary to do the typesetting as well as the editing, and he became an expert mathematical typesetter. His mathematical abilities received wide recognition: Yale conferred upon him the honorary degree of A.M. in 1877; Rutgers honored him with a Ph.D. degree in 1882; and in 1885 Hillsdale awarded him an LL.D. degree. Numerous learned societies in the United States and abroad honored him with membership.

In 1885 Martin joined the United States Coast and Geodetic Survey, first as librarian and later as computer. All of his spare time he still devoted to work in pure mathematics, to the editing of his mathematical journals, which did much to foster a love for mathematics on its less academic side, and to the preparation of papers which appeared in various journals at home and abroad. His writings dealt chiefly with the properties of numbers and of triangles, diophantine analysis, average, probability, elliptic integrals, and logarithms. He was an authority on early mathematical textbooks, of which he had a notable collection, and collaborated with J. M. Greenwood in the preparation of *American Text-Books on Arithmetic,* issued by the United States Bureau of Education in 1899.

Personally, Martin was a man of simple tastes but of prepossessing appearance. Although he exhibited some of the limitations imposed by pioneer life, he at the same time exemplified most of its robust virtues. He was fond of home life and of children, but he denied himself marriage that he might care for his parents and sisters. He died in Washington. His memory is perpetuated in the Artemas Martin Library of the American University. This library, consisting principally of mathematical works, was during Martin's lifetime considered one of the finest private mathematical collections in America. At the same university Martin also endowed an Artemas Martin Lectureship in mathematics and physics.

[The *Illustrated Buffalo Express,* Feb. 12, 1899; *Who's Who in America,* 1918–19; J. M. Cattell, *Am. Men of Sci.* (ed. 1910); *Science,* Nov. 22, 1918; the *Evening Star* (Wash., D. C.), Nov. 8, 1918; personal information.]

H. A. M.

MARTIN, FRANÇOIS-XAVIER (Mar. 17, 1762–Dec. 10, 1846), jurist and author, was born at Marseilles, France. He received an excellent education and was, it has been said, intended for the priesthood. At seventeen or eighteen, however, he joined an uncle in Martinique, and, after a short stay there, came to New Bern, N. C., seeking, so the story goes, a lost shipment of molasses. He is said, too, to have served a short time in the Continental Army, but the story is highly unlikely. In New Bern he taught French for a living and learned English. He secured a position in a printing office and, although he had never been in one before, held his place as a typesetter, finally becoming foreman of the shop and, ultimately, its owner. He began a publishing business which became extensive, handling school books, novels, and translations made by himself from the French. In the meantime he studied law and was admitted to the bar in 1789. Soon afterwards he wrote and published several volumes dealing with the duties of local officers, executors, and administrators, which had a wide sale. The legislature employed him to collect the Parliamentary statutes in force in the state—a task which he did very inaccurately (1792)—and later to collect the private laws of North Carolina (1794). Still later he was employed to make his well-known "Revisal" of the *Laws of the State of North Carolina.* Meanwhile he published reprints of North Carolina statutes, translations of *Latches Reports* (1793), Pothier, *A Treatise on Obligations* (1802), *Cases in the Court of King's Bench during the Reign of Charles I* (1793) and *Notes of a Few Decisions of the Superior Courts of the State of North Carolina* (1797). He served in 1806 as a borough member of the House of Commons, and was in active practice in the state for twenty years, during which time he acquired command of English, became a master of common and statute law, with a familiar acquaintance with Roman and French law, and laid by a comfortable estate.

Never a notable advocate, he was, nevertheless, admirably prepared for the career as a jurist into which he was ushered in 1809 when President Madison appointed him a federal judge for the Mississippi Territory. A year later he was transferred to the Territory of Orleans, then just moving toward statehood. His knowledge of French language and law was of immeasurable value here. He was the first attorney general of Louisiana (1813), and two years later, Jan. 31, 1815, he became a judge of the state supreme court. In 1836 he became chief justice. Retiring in 1846, when the new constitution abolished the court, he died a few months later.

When Martin came to the supreme court, Louisiana law was in apparently hopeless confusion, with both French and Spanish law in operation. The coming of English-American law only added difficulty. By act of Congress the common law was made the basis of criminal jurisprudence, and in 1808 a civil code had been adopted which did not repeal other law not in conflict with it. It was, therefore, necessary for the courts to study and compare Spanish and

French codes, to be familiar with Roman law and the essentials of the English common law. In other words, a jurisprudence had to be created, and Martin played a notable part in doing it, applying deep learning to the solution of the countless knotty problems with which the court was confronted, reconciling the conflicting systems, and bringing order out of chaos. Justly he won a great name in constructive jurisprudence, particularly for his skilful blending of the best principles of the English and Roman law. His numerous opinions run through fifty-one volumes of the *Louisiana Reports*. His first opinion, *Johnson* vs. *Duncan* (3 *Martin's Reports, Old Series,* 530), written during the War of 1812, is distinguished by its masterly and unanswerable argument sustaining the doctrine that neither the executive nor any subordinate had the power to suspend the regular operation of the laws or the writ of *habeas corpus,* holding such suspension a legislative power, and declaring that the legislative power could never be capable of impairing the obligation of private contracts.

Not alone as a judge did Martin acquire reputation. He began in 1811 to publish reports of cases decided by the courts, and continued them until 1830. He also published *A General Digest of the Acts of the Legislature of the Late Territory of Orleans and of the State of Louisiana and the Ordinances of the Governors under the Territorial Government* (1816). In 1827 his *History of Louisiana* appeared and two years later, his *History of North Carolina.* His total output amounted to thirty-four volumes, among which the *Reports* are much the most valuable. His histories, the result of tremendous research and labor, were poorly written, badly arranged, "as lifeless as the minutes and records of proceedings in a court of justice" (Gayarré, *post,* p. 246), and scarcely as valuable. At best they are collections of facts.

As a speaker Martin was neither eloquent nor pleasant, and was described as "dry as a hard-baked brickbat" (*Ibid.,* p. 245). Personally, before age and blindness made him hopelessly eccentric, he was a quiet, agreeable little man. His life was utterly cheerless, his French thrift combining with his recollection of poverty to make him a complete miser. "He lived, so to speak, on nothing, and heaped up his savings with compound interest" (Howe, in *History of Louisiana, post,* p. xxiv). He never married and left an estate of nearly half a million dollars to a younger brother. In 1838 he became quite blind, but continued his work easily and efficiently. In 1844 he visited France hoping for a cure, but met with failure. He died in New Orleans in December 1846.

[Memoirs by W. W. Howe, in Martin's *Hist. of La.* (2nd ed., 1882) and in W. D. Lewis, *Great Am. Lawyers,* vol. II (1907); sketch by H. A. Bullard in B. F. French, *Hist. Colls. of La.,* vol. II (1850); S. A. Ashe, *Biog. Hist. of N. C.,* vol. IV (1906); Charles Gayarré, *Fernando de Lemos* (1872); *State Records of N. C.* (16 vols., 1895–1905); *The Jeffersonian* (New Orleans), Dec. 12, 1846.]

J. G. deR. H.

MARTIN, FREDERICK TOWNSEND (Dec. 6, 1849–Mar. 8, 1914), author and philanthropist, the son of Henry Hull and Anne (Townsend) Martin, was born in Albany, N. Y. His father was a leading Albany lawyer and banker, and his mother was a woman well-established in the most fashionable Newport and New York society. From the first, therefore, young Martin had every material advantage. He was educated at the Albany academy and later the Albany Law School, where he studied law and in 1872 received the degree of LL.B. He was for eleven years active in the affairs of the Zouave Cadets, 10th Regiment of the New York state national guard. He traveled extensively and in the course of his world tours met an astonishing number of notables. At the same time he was a deeply interested observer of the conditions of labor and of poverty. He drew heavily upon his large fortune in helping the unfortunate both in the United States and abroad. He was particularly interested in the work of the Bowery mission in New York City, where each Christmastime he gave a dinner; and he was also well-known and well-loved by the poor of London's East End.

In time his observation led him to entertain theories that were considered radical in his own day. He became convinced that the age of great individual fortunes was passing and that, with it, the reign of the old social order was drawing to a close. These beliefs he stated very clearly in *The Passing of the Idle Rich* (1911) which appeared also in serial form in *Everybody's Magazine* (Feb.–Apr. 1911). In this book he set himself the task of illustrating the theory that decay always follows idleness and extravagance. His self-imposed mission was to call to the attention of other well-to-do members of society the dangerous foundation upon which their order rests. The work had an immense vogue and, being dramatized, appeared at the Garden Theatre in New York on May 1, 1913. In 1913 he published *Things I Remember,* and he wrote many magazine articles of a miscellaneous character. At the time of his death he was at work on another book, "Snobs." These books took the form of rather delightful descriptions of the earlier days of the Astor-McAllister dictatorship in New York society and of a variety of fashionable coteries in France and England, to which Martin, as a bachelor clubman and cosmopolitan society man, had *entrée*. Closely associated with his zest for travel was the hobby of Martin's latter days, his work as one of the founders and vice-president of the American Embassy Association. In 1909 he was struck by the fact that, with the exception of Constantinople, there were no permanent residences for American Ambassadors in the capitals of the world. With E. Clarence Jones, therefore, he toured the United States in an attempt to win public favor for an appropriation bill for embassy purchases. To further this aim and to manage the funds collected, they founded the association. His principal business connection was with the Metropolitan Trust Company of which he was a director. While in London arranging for the housing of an art bequest from his friend Henry Sands, he died of angina pectoris.

[*Who's Who in America*, 1912–13; *New York Times*, Mar. 9, 10, 21, 22, 1914; autobiographical references in published works.] E. M. H.

MARTIN, HENRY AUSTIN (July 23, 1824–Dec. 7, 1884), vaccinator and surgeon of Roxbury, Mass., the eldest son of Henry James Martin, was born in London. The Martins were descended from a distinguished Huguenot family, and his great-grandfather, Gen. James Agnew, was in command of the British troops in Boston at the outbreak of the American Revolution. Martin was also descended from the Earl of Eglintonn, and was a cousin of Lord Kinglake. He came to America when a boy and graduated from Harvard Medical School in 1845. Immediately after graduation he settled in Roxbury, Mass., where he enjoyed a large practice for nearly forty years. Although primarily a physician, he was skilful both as an accoucheur and surgeon. At the outbreak of the Civil War he was made staff surgeon at Fort Monroe and was subsequently transferred to Southeastern Missouri. Here he became ill and was forced to return to Norfolk, Va., where he served as medical director; later he was at Portsmouth in the same capacity, and finally at Newbern. Eventually he was appointed surgeon-in-chief of the 1st Division of the II Corps of the Army of the Potomac under General Miles. At the end of the war he was dismissed with the brevet rank of lieutenant-colonel, with special citation for his services. He then returned to Roxbury, where he practised until his death.

Martin's great service to American medicine arose from his energetic investigation of vaccination and the conditions essential for standardizing the procedure. After Jenner had convinced the world in 1798 that vaccinia (cowpox) gave permanent protection against smallpox, cases of spontaneous cowpox became rare, and many accidents had occurred through careless vaccination and the use of an attenuated humanized virus. On Apr. 26, 1866, a spontaneous case of cowpox occurred at Beaugençy, a town near Orléans, France. The strain was transmitted to a heifer and a strong virus was in this way produced. The heifer-transmitted Beaugençy virus was brought to America by Martin in 1870, and in a memorable report on animal vaccination in the *Transactions of the American Medical Association* (vol. XXVIII, 1877) Martin introduced the modern method of vaccination and of standardization of the vaccine virus. He was bitterly attacked both in the profession and out, as is evidenced by the following: "I gave them every aid in my power freely, frankly, and fully, and was repaid by ingratitude, slander, and an effort, as futile as it was earnest and persistent, to rob me of the scrap of professional honor and reputation I had worked so hard to win and deserve, in introducing and firmly establishing in America a system which has already conferred infinite though hardly fully appreciated blessings" (*Ibid.*, pp. 199–200). Martin was well known for his rubber bandage, used in treatment of ulcers of the leg ("Surgical Uses of the Strong Elastic Bandage other than Haemostatic," *Ibid.*, vol. XXVIII, 1877). He also advocated, and practised professionally, tracheotomy without tube (*Ibid.*, vol. XXIX, 1878).

Though a finished writer, Martin liked controversy, and few were more skilful in literary invective. He was a handsome, well-formed man—impatient, proud, quick to denounce, but loyal always to his friends. He collected books and works of art, and was widely read in the history of medicine. He died in Boston on Dec. 7, 1884, of diabetes. In 1848 he had married Frances Coffin Crosby, a daughter of Judge Nathan Crosby of Lowell, Mass. They had five children, two of whom, Stephen Crosby and Francis Coffin, became physicians.

[H. A. Kelly and W. L. Burrage, *Am. Medic. Biogs.* (1920); T. F. Harrington, *Harvard Medic. School* (1905), vol. III; *Boston Medic. and Surgic. Jour.*, Jan. 8, 1885; H. O. Marcy, article in *Jour. of the Am. Medic. Asso.*, Jan. 10, 1885; *N. Y. Medic. Jour.*, Dec. 13, 1884.] J. F. F.

MARTIN, HENRY NEWELL (July 1, 1848–Oct. 27, 1896), physiologist, was born in Newry, County Down, Ireland, the eldest of twelve children. His father was a Congregational minister and later a schoolmaster, and young Martin was not able to enjoy the advantages of school life, his early training being obtained mainly at home. When about sixteen years of age, he matriculated at the University of London, and attended the Medical School of University College, being at the same time apprenticed to a physician in the neighborhood. Later, in 1870, he went to Cambridge on a scholarship, becoming at the same time demonstrator to the prelector of physiology at Trinity College, Michael Foster. Both at London and Cambridge he made a brilliant record for scholarship in natural science, gaining eventually the degree of B.Sc. at Cambridge and the degree of M.B. at London. He was the first to take the degree of D.Sc. in physiology at Cambridge. He thus had the advantage of instruction under Foster in physiology and also under Huxley in biology, and in 1874 he served as assistant to Huxley in the latter's course in elementary biology. Under Huxley's supervision he prepared a textbook, bearing both names, entitled *A Course of Practical Instruction in Elementary Biology* (1875), which had wide use for many years.

In 1874 Martin was made fellow of Trinity College at Cambridge, and with his broad preparation in natural science was admirably fitted to carry on biological instruction and research at that University. His activities, however, were destined to be transferred to America, for on the founding of the Johns Hopkins University he was selected as the occupant of the chair of biology, and thus he came to Baltimore in 1876 as one of that small group of professors who were to give character to the new institution. Coming as he did at a time when biological problems were assuming large importance in the scientific world of Europe and Great Britain, Martin with his training was able to introduce at Baltimore the new conceptions of "the genetic relationships of living things," and to arouse a general and deep interest in the study of biology by the experimental method.

While Martin was primarily interested in physiology and his own research work lay in that field, during his seventeen years at the Johns Hopkins University he laid down broad foundations for instruction and research in the biological sciences, which brought distinction to the University and furnished inspiration to other institutions. In physiology, it is easy to trace the influence of Martin's work on the development of this branch of biology in the United States. He was in a sense a pioneer in the United States, helping to put physiology in its proper relation to the science and art of medicine. He held that physiology should be studied without regard to its applications to medicine; "that it should be cultivated as a pure science absolutely independent of any so-called practical affiliation" (Sewall, *post,* p. 328). At the same time he realized quite well that all knowledge of function must in time contribute to a fuller understanding of medicine. His own researches were mainly in the field of cardiac physiology, especially noteworthy being his discovery of a new method of studying the isolated mammalian heart, which paved the way many years later for extended researches by others on the functions of the heart, yielding results of great value to medicine. One of his researches, on the influence of temperature on the heart-beat, was the basis of the Croonian lecture of the Royal Society of London for 1883 ("The Direct Influence of Gradual Variations of Temperature upon the Rate of Beat of the Dog's Heart," *Philosophical Transactions of the Royal Society of London, for 1883,* pt. 2, 1883). The papers containing the results of his various researches were republished in 1895 by his friends and pupils in the form of a memorial volume entitled *Physiological Papers.*

Martin found time to write several textbooks which had wide use, notably *The Human Body* (1881), which became very popular and did much to arouse interest in physiology. He also founded and edited the *Johns Hopkins University Studies from the Biological Laboratory* (5 vols., 1877–93). The eminence attained by many of his pupils testifies to his ability as a teacher. He was endowed with a pleasing personality, always interested in the welfare of his pupils, sympathetic and with a joyous outlook on life that made him an interesting as well as a helpful companion. In 1878 he married Hetty (Cary) Pegram, the widow of an officer who served in the Confederate army. After the death of his wife, in 1892, his health, which during his later years was far from robust, broke down and he became unable to carry on his work. He resigned his position in 1893 and returned to England, hoping there to regain his health and the strength to continue his physiological investigations. This, however, was not to be and he died in 1896 at Burley-in-Wharfedale, Yorkshire.

[Henry Sewall, "Henry Newell Martin, Prof. of Biology in Johns Hopkins Univ., 1876–93," *Johns Hopkins Hospital Bull.,* Sept. 1911; *Proc. Royal Soc. of London,* vol. LX (1897); the *Johns Hopkins Univ. Circular,* May 1908; E. F. Cordell, *The Medic. Annals of Md.* (1903); the *Sun* (Baltimore), Nov. 2, 1896.]

R. H. C.

MARTIN, HOMER DODGE (Oct. 28, 1836–Feb. 12, 1897), landscape painter, was born in Albany, N. Y. His father Homer Martin, a carpenter, was of good plain New England stock; his mother, Sarah Dodge, was of an old Albany family and better educated. The desire to draw and make pictures manifested itself in his early boyhood. After a trial in his father's shop, and episodes as a clerk in a store and as a draftsman in an architect's office, young Martin, encouraged by the venerable sculptor Erastus D. Palmer, was allowed to follow his bent. Aside from a few weeks of instruction from the landscape painter James MacDougal Hart, Martin was self-schooled. At sixteen he was making a modest living from the sale of little landscapes of the lake and mountain scenery of New York and New England, pictures which were often garish in color and feebly slicked up, but already remarkably tasteful as compositions. He followed Thomas Cole's predilection for wild scenery and large spaces. For a matter of twenty years he tramped the Adirondacks, the Catskills, the Berkshires, and the White Mountains, bringing back sheaves of pencil sketches usually touched with white on tinted paper, very dry in method, but accurate in form and compositionally excellent. This constituted much of his apprenticeship, and after 1870 he sketched little.

In 1857, at twenty-one, he exhibited two Connecticut landscapes at the National Academy. On June 21, 1861, he married Elizabeth Gilbert Davis, a young woman of cultivation and ability, whose facile pen for years helped out the always scanty family budget. She was one of the early reviewers for the *Nation.* Martin was headed for a larger field, and after an essay in New York, in 1862 and 1863, as the studio mate of James Smillie, in 1865 he moved his family to the metropolis. He got ahead, had his passing mention in Tuckerman's *Book of the Artists* (1867) and the next year was elected an associate of the National Academy. In 1866 an election to the Century Club had made him free of the best literary and artistic society of the town, but his Bohemian and convivial tastes made him offish to those general social relations which were almost essential to any financial success.

Meanwhile his style had changed perturbingly. Under a closer study of nature and observation of good pictures the tight handling loosened up, instead of the conventional browns, recondite colors appeared, the compositions were simplified, with much elimination of needless detail. No American painter, with the exception of George Inness and John La Farge, was painting so well in landscape, but Martin's difference and distinction passed for eccentricity, and his patronage fell off. And the harmony of his home was at least qualified by his wife's conversion to Roman Catholicism, he himself being an agnostic. This is the period of the "Lake Sanford," in the Century Club, and the first pictures of the sand dunes on Lake Ontario, pictures grandly spacious and fraught with a noble melancholy. Within three years he made the firm friendship of John Richard Dennet of the *Evening Post,* and of William C. Brownell, the future critic. Among artists he saw few but Winslow Homer and John La Farge, whose studios were in the same building as his. And although the National Academy elected him to full membership in the seventies, he remained somewhat of an outsider —a position enhanced by his incorrigible, witty, and sometimes bitter tongue, as it was by his personal disfigurement in a permanently inflamed nose.

In 1876 a trip to England brought him the friendship of Whistler and the sight of fine pictures. The few pictures painted in the three or four following years, perhaps somewhat under Whistler's influence, are of great refinement in handling and tonality. "Andante, Fifth Symphony"—a forest brook opening gracefully into a pool—an eloquent record of Martin's musical enthusiasms, is perhaps the finest picture of this period, and the culmination of what may be called the American Martins. Practically none of the pictures of this period, which some prefer to the more popular canvases later painted in France, have found their way into museums. To eke out an always poor living, Martin had occasional recourse to illustration. It was paradoxically this gift that was to bring him the few years of tranquillity he ever enjoyed and the fulfilment of his genius. In *Scribner's Monthly* for February 1879 appeared certain illustrations made at Concord for Frank B. Sanborn's "The Homes and Haunts of Emerson." These with other cuts figured in *The Homes and Haunts of Our Elder Poets,* by Sanborn and others. The success of this venture incited the *Century* to send Martin to England to sketch in George Eliot's country. The immediate results of this expedition may be seen in Rose G. Kingsley's article in the *Century* for July 1885. The ulterior and unexpected results were an excursion to Normandy, in 1882, to visit an illustrator friend, William John Hennessy [*q.v.*].

By the winter of 1882 the Martins were settled at Villerville, on the estuary of the Seine, and there or at neighboring Honfleur they stayed for some four years. There were occasional trips to Paris, but generally the Martins let friends come to them. For the first time Martin caught the penetrating charm of a more intimate scenery, immemorially inhabited and cultivated. His scale is no longer panoramic but intimate. His method grows richer. There is more body of paint, more carefully adjusted flicks of tone to make the surface "twinkle." Possibly he was being influenced by that moderate impressionist, Boudin, who was painting in the same region. Some of Martin's most famous pictures were painted, or at least begun, in these years: "The Church at Criqueboeuf," "Mussel Gatherers," "Low Tide—Villerville," "Ontario Sand Dunes," and "Blossoming Trees." But the finest fruits of this experience were characteristically garnered in after years in America. With an eminently contemplative talent, he was at his best when working from remote and well-matured memories.

The Norman idyl closed with Mrs. Martin's decision to resume the struggle in America. By the new year of 1887 they were again in New York. At fifty Martin was already breaking. His eyesight, always defective, grew progressively worse. But he had nine amazing years before him still. His command of his mood and of his material was now complete. He drew at will from recent Norman memories or from American memories of his young manhood. To celebrate his return he finished "Sand Dunes, Lake Ontario," begun in France, painted "The Sun Worshippers," and that gravest of his American subjects, "Westchester Hills." Nothing much sold. The family moved uncomfortably from lodging to lodging.

To the early nineties belong such masterpieces as "Honfleur Light," "Criqueboeuf Church," the "Old Manor," and "View on the Seine." Still little sold except as groups of friends now and then bought a picture for a club or a museum. His eyesight grew so feeble that the contour had to be drawn for him on the canvas. His wife's nerves broke, and she took refuge late in 1892 with their eldest son Ralph at St. Paul. Within a few months he followed her. Then in an isolation he had never known he finished the "View on the Seine," the "Normandy Farm," and "Adirondack Scenery," perhaps his richest work. By the early days of 1896 it was clear that he had cancer of the throat. He lived on for a year, still worked, was cheered by the unexpected and favorable sale of a picture, and died in February 1897 in St. Paul. Within a few years of his dying deeply in debt his erstwhile unsalable masterpieces had become the sensation of the art market and he received the posthumous honor of being forged.

Martin was a painter of sentiment. He lacked the vigorous construction of Inness in his best estate and of Winslow Homer. Poet as much as painter, drawing from the contemplation of nature a gentle soothing and noble melancholy, Martin is the most distinguished American artist in that imaginative tradition of landscape panting which was splendidly inaugurated by Thomas Cole.

[In *Harper's Weekly* for Mar. 27, 1897, on the occasion of a memorial exhibition at the Century Club, Martin's friend Montgomery Schuyler published what remains one of the best personal appreciations. A valuable obituary, probably by S. G. Champlain, is in *Appletons' Ann. Cyc.*, 1897. To the *Art Interchange*, Oct. 1899, John J. A'Becket contributed an intimate appreciation. There is some suggestive but capricious criticism in Sadakichi Hartmann's *Hist. of Am. Art* (1902). The first elaborate critique is that of C. H. Caffin in *Am. Masters of Painting* (1902). Mrs. Martin's *Homer Martin, a Reminiscence* (1904) will remain classic as an interpretation, but offers relatively few biographical details. Samuel Isham's *Hist. of Am. Painting* (1905) gives an excellent technical analysis of Martin's two styles. Ann Nathan Meyer's article in the *Internat. Studio*, Oct. 1908, adds an anecdote and one or two genealogical details derived from correspondence from Martin's wife. The press reports of the Evans-Clausen trial (1907), in the matter of forgeries, gives the opinions of artists and critics cited as witnesses. See also: Frank Jewett Mather, Jr., *Homer Martin: Poet in Landscape* (1912).]

F. J. M., Jr.

MARTIN, JAMES GREEN (Feb. 14, 1819–Oct. 4, 1878), Confederate soldier, was the grandson of James Green Martin, a Methodist minister of Norfolk, Va., and the son of William Martin, a physician. The latter moved to Elizabeth City, N. C., where he became a prominent planter and shipbuilder, and was elected a member of the North Carolina General Assembly. He married Sophia Scott Daugé, a daughter of Gen. Peter Daugé of Camden County. Their eldest son, James Green, born in Elizabeth City, received his early education at St. Mary's in Raleigh, then a boys' school. He entered the United States Military Academy in 1836 and graduated in 1840, number fourteen in his class. Appointed second lieutenant of artillery, he did duty chiefly in Maine until 1846. At Newport, R. I., on July 12, 1844, he was married to Marian Murray Read, great-granddaughter of George Read [*q.v.*] of Delaware, a signer of the Declaration of Independence.

During the Mexican War, Martin commanded a battery which distinguished itself at the assault of Monterey and was later sent to reinforce Scott at Vera Cruz. He was promoted first lieutenant Feb. 16, 1847, and captain, Aug. 5. His battery participated in the severe fighting during the march on Mexico City. At Churubusco Martin's right arm was shattered by grape shot, necessitating amputation, and on Aug. 20 he was brevetted major for gallant and meritorious conduct here and at Contreras. After his discharge from hospital, he was stationed at Fortress Monroe, Va., at Schuylkill Arsenal, Pa., and at Nebraska City on the frontier. During this last assignment his wife died, leaving him with four young children. On Feb. 8, 1858, he was again married, to Hetty King, daughter of Charles King [*q.v.*], president of Columbia College. Soon afterwards he served as quartermaster under Albert Sidney Johnston [*q.v.*] in Johnston's Utah expedition.

When North Carolina seceded in May 1861, Martin was stationed at Fort Riley, Kan. He resigned his commission in June and went to Raleigh, where on Sept. 20 he was made adjutant-general of the ten regiments of state troops then being raised and on Sept. 28, was commissioned major-general of militia and given command of all the state forces and supervision of the entire defense of the state. He prepared all the North Carolina regiments for service; the militia laws were revised at his suggestion; instruction camps and powder, shoe, and clothing factories were established; horses were ordered from Kentucky, saddles and harness material from New Orleans; forts on the coast were erected and strengthened. At Martin's suggestion, blockade-running ships were first employed to bring supplies from Europe. He raised 12,000 more troops than the state's quota, which were of much service during McClellan's advance in 1862. It is chiefly for this brilliant administrative work that Martin will be remembered. North Carolina could with good reason claim that her troops were better trained and supplied than those of any other Confederate state.

When this task was done, Martin asked for active service and in May 1862 was promoted brigadier-general, Confederate States Army. On June 2, he was given command of the district of North Carolina, with headquarters at Kinston, and in the fall of 1863 he was commanded to organize a brigade for duty in the field. In the summer of 1864 his brigade was ordered to Petersburg, Va. After a gallant charge at Howlett's House, where he displayed conspicuous bravery, his men "carried him around on their shoulders, shouting: 'Three cheers for Old One Wing'" (Clark, *post,* IV, 531). Martin's health broke down under the strain of this campaign and he was transferred to the command of the district of Western North Carolina, where he served until the end of the war. He surrendered at Waynesville, May 10, 1865. After the war he took up the study of law, and practised in Asheville from 1866 until his death. During this period he was a prominent Episcopal layman, serving as a delegate to both Diocesan and General conventions of his Church.

[Walter Clark, *Memorial Address upon the Life of General James Green Martin* (delivered at Raleigh, 1916; privately printed), and *Hists. of the Several Regts. and Battalions from N. C. in the Great War* (1901); *Confed. Mil. Hist.* (1899), vol. IV; D. H. Hill, *N. C. in the War between the States* (2 vols., 1926); F. B. Heitman, *Hist. Reg. and Dict. U. S. Army* (1903), vol. II; *War of the Rebellion, Official Records (Army)*; G. W. Cullum, *Biog. Reg. Officers and Grads. U. S. Mil. Acad.* (3rd ed., 1891); *Morning Star* (Wilmington, N. C.), Oct. 9, 1878.] R. D. M.

MARTIN, JOHN ALEXANDER (Mar. 10, 1839–Oct. 2, 1889), journalist, Union military officer, and governor of Kansas, the son of James Martin and Jane Crawford, was born at Brownsville, Pa. He received his education in the common schools and in the printing office. Late in 1857 he went to Kansas and in February 1858, when he was not yet nineteen, he bought an Atchison newspaper, which he renamed *Freedom's Champion* (subsequently the *Champion* and still later the *Atchison Champion*). Within three years he was recognized as one of the political leaders of the younger generation in Kansas Territory, serving, among other positions of honor, as secretary of the Wyandotte constitutional convention and as state senator in the first state legislature. He resigned political office to become, Oct. 27, 1861, lieutenant-colonel of the 8th Volunteer Infantry. On Nov. 1 he was promoted to the rank of colonel, serving as provost-marshal of Nashville, Tenn., and later as brigade-commander during the Chattanooga campaigns. He was mustered out Nov. 17, 1864, and returned to the editorship of his newspaper. Martin had three ruling passions; the Old Soldier interest, the Republican party, and Kansas. During the period 1865–84 he was an active leader in the editorial organization of the state, and in the management of the affairs of the Republican party, local, state, and national. He was chairman of the Atchison county central committee, 1859–84, except during the war, a member of the state committee, beginning in 1870, and of the national committee almost continuously, beginning in 1868. He was secretary of the national committee during the early eighties and sponsored a plan for reapportioning representation in the national convention in order to recognize partially the growing Republican vote in the West.

Martin's major political ambition was the governorship of Kansas. He was elected in 1884 and reëlected in 1886. Among the chief issues of his administration was the enforcement of the prohibition law. He had been an opponent of prohibition at the time of the adoption of the constitutional amendment of 1880, but by 1883 he indorsed it and was nominated and elected on a platform containing a prohibition plank. He was convinced by the experience of the state and especially of his home town of Atchison that "the saloon-keepers, as a rule, were a lot of shameless ingrates, who were not only opposed to prohibition, but to any and all restraint on their dirty business" (Martin to Sol Miller, Dec. 4, 1885: Correspondence of the Governors of Kansas, Letterpress Books, personal, Vol. V, pp. 61–67). He felt that the only way to deal with them was to stand squarely on prohibition of the liquor traffic and thereby to eliminate its influence from politics. Prohibition under his administration became the settled policy of the Republican party in the state and of the state of Kansas. He advocated revision of legal procedure, the modification of the judicial system, both an enlargement and a reform in line with progressive practices adopted in some other states, and the codification of state law. He took great interest in penal reform, and was quite successful in dealing with railroad labor troubles, 1885–88. A state law providing for arbitration of labor disputes was enacted in 1886, and he urged the passage of a federal law in this field, as well as the federal licensing of locomotive engineers.

Martin's administration came in a period of unusual railroad building and of the settlement of the western part of the state. Local government units were induced by various means to issue excessive amounts of bonded indebtedness to finance railroad building. These practices were opposed by Martin, and he urged repeatedly, but without success, the adoption by both state and national governments of a program which might forestall the collapse of the boom in Kansas and elsewhere, and bring about a public control of big business. He advocated a comprehensive state corporation law designed to meet the abuses prevalent in the conduct of business, and attacked the monopoly question in its national aspect from the standpoint of the discriminative practices of the railroads: "They are monopolizing a dozen branches of business—the coal trade, the grain trade, the elevator business, the express business, etc." (Martin to Senator John J. Ingalls, Jan. 20, 1887: Correspondence of the Governors of Kansas, personal, Vol. IX, pp. 290–92). After four strenuous years as governor, he retired again to the editorship of his newspaper. He had married, on June 1, 1871, Ida Challiss, the daughter of Dr. W. L. and Mary (Harres) Challiss. In 1869 he published a *Military History of the Eighth Kansas Veteran Volunteer Infantry,* and in 1888 he printed, for private distribution, a volume of *Addresses.*

[The Wis. Hist. Soc. Lib. has the most complete file of the Atchison *Champion* for the period of Martin's editorship. This file includes the years 1865–89. The Kan. State Hist. Soc. Lib. has a file of the paper for 1858–63 and for 1876–89, together with some broken files for the middle years. The same library has his correspondence as governor, both the official and the confidential or personal files. This correspondence contains, in addition to state matters, information on such national matters as Indian defense, control of livestock diseases, quarantine for protection of public health, railroad labor strikes 1885, 1886, and 1888, national Republican party politics, press-association problems, and the National Soldiers' Homes. Except for the Civil War letters (in process of printing for private distribution) in possession of the family, all of Martin's correspondence prior to the governorship has been lost. Other sources include: D. W. Wilder, *The Annals of Kan.* (rev. ed., 1886); W. E. Connelley, *A Standard Hist. of Kan. and Kansans* (1918), vol. II; *Trans. Kan. State Hist. Soc.,* vol. IV (1890); the *Evening Standard* (Leavenworth), Oct. 2, 1889; the *Topeka Weekly Capital,* Oct. 3, 1889.] J. C. M.

MARTIN, JOHN HILL (Jan. 13, 1823–Apr. 7, 1906), lawyer and author, was born in Philadelphia, Pa., the son of William Martin, a lawyer and business man, and Sarah Ann (Smith) Martin. As a boy John lived with his grandmother on a farm in Chester County, Pa., but about 1836 he returned to his parents, then living in Chester, Pa., in order to attend school. On July 1, 1838, he entered the United States Military Academy at West Point, but he failed in his work and resigned in July 1841. He then studied law in the office of George L. Ashmead of Philadelphia and was a member of the Law Academy. On Nov. 13, 1844, he was admitted to the Philadelphia bar and for thirty-seven years he engaged in his profession. His practice was largely confined to cases in the Orphan's Court and to cases in Admiralty. He retired in 1881. He was always greatly interested in literary work and in June 1857 became the legal editor of the *Insurance Intelligencer,* later the *Philadelphia Intelligencer,* which post he held throughout his life. He spent his summers at Bethlehem, Pa., and in 1872 published his *Historical Sketch of Bethlehem in Pennsylvania, with Some Account of the Moravian Church,* which ran into two editions (Philadelphia, 1872 and 1873). In the same year, 1872, he wrote a series entitled "Sketches in the Lehigh Valley" which appeared in the Bethlehem *Daily Times.* In 1873 he edited and published a book by Rufus A. Grider: *Historical Notes on Music in Bethlehem, Pa.,* and also published *Martin's Bench and Bar of Philadelphia* which had appeared serially in the *Philadelphia Intelligencer* beginning in December 1876. In 1877 he published *Chester (and Its Vicinity) Delaware County, in Pennsylvania.* Besides these publications he compiled and edited many papers in history, genealogy, and marine insurance. In the spring of 1861 he was elected captain of an independent artillery company but saw no field service. He was a very active member of the Pennsylvania Historical Society and bequeathed a large collection of manuscripts of his books and other historical and genealogical data to that organization. He never married.

[J. W. Jordan, *Colonial and Revolutionary Families of Pa.*, vol. III (1911); *Reg. of the Officers and Cadets of the U. S. Mil. Acad.*, 1838–41; Martin's *Chester* and his manuscript autobiography in the possession of the Pa. Hist. Soc.; *Pub. Ledger* (Phila.), Apr. 9, 1906; the *Legal Intelligencer*, Apr. 20, 1906.]

J. H. F.

MARTIN, JOSIAH (1737–1786), colonial governor of North Carolina, was the son of Col. Samuel and Sarah (Wyke) Martin of Antigua, West Indies, and one of twenty-three children. He was an army officer from 1757 until ill health induced him to sell his lieutenant-colonelcy in 1769. In 1761 he married his cousin Elizabeth, daughter of Josiah Martin at whose country seat, "Rockhall," on Long Island he resided at various times. To this union were born eight children. Commissioned by the Crown as governor of North Carolina early in 1771, he sailed from Long Island in July and took the oath of office before the council at New Bern on Aug. 12.

Though reports of his amiable character preceded him, he soon became involved in protracted conflicts with the sensitive assembly, first, over the sinking-fund tax, whose discontinuance in 1771 he disallowed as illegal and violative of public faith; and, beginning in 1773, over the right of the courts to attach property in North Carolina for debts of non-residents to North Carolinians. The assembly, dominated by the eastern planters and merchants, would pass no new court law without the "foreign attachment clause"; and Martin, who was under positive instructions from the Crown, would not assent to a law containing the clause. Consequently, the judicial system of the colony collapsed in 1773, and the ensuing confusion and resentment was accentuated by the emergency creation by royal prerogative of criminal courts whose expenses the assembly in December refused to bear. The sinking-fund tax was not collected generally, and the province remained without courts for the trial of civil cases involving more than £20. The survey of the North Carolina-South Carolina boundary line in 1772, as decreed by the Crown, deprived the colony of much claimed territory and created dissatisfaction. In bold defiance of the governor, the Patriot leaders convened at New Bern in August 1774 a revolutionary provincial congress which elected delegates to the first Continental Congress and inaugurated a system of county committees of safety which gradually superseded the royal government as the source of authority. With his authority and influence gone and fearing personal violence from the local militia after the battle of Lexington, Martin fled from New Bern, arriving at Fort Johnston on June 2, 1775. In July he was driven aboard a British vessel in the Cape Fear River.

Though a military man without previous political experience, somewhat stubborn and insistent on prerogative, and unappreciative of the colonial position, Martin was accomplished, energetic, able, honest, faithful, as well as sincere and patient in his efforts to promote the public welfare and to conciliate the colony without violating his positive instructions and his conception of the duties of his office. He sought to become informed of conditions in the colony, to eliminate abuses in administration, and to pacify the Regulators, but he was not able to reconcile the tempers, aims, and political philosophies of colony and mother country. Aboard ship in the Cape Fear, he formulated a plan for the subjugation of the Southern colonies which was approved by the British government; but the Loyalist Scotch Highlanders, assembled under his direction, were defeated at Moore's Creek Bridge, Feb. 27, 1776, before the British reënforcements arrived off the Cape Fear. In May, Martin departed with the British for an attack on Charleston; he returned in the summer to "Rockhall," and in 1779 joined the Clinton expedition against South Carolina, serving with usefulness and credit as a volunteer with Cornwallis in the campaign of 1780–81 in the Carolinas.

Declining health caused him to leave Cornwallis at Wilmington in April 1781, and sail via Long Island for London, where he died in the spring of 1786. He drew his salary as governor until October 1783, and was granted compensation for his confiscated North Carolina property by the American Loyalist Claims Commission, before which he testified in behalf of the claims of many North Carolina Loyalists.

[*Colonial Records of N. C.* (10 vols., 1886–90); *State Records of N. C.* (16 vols., 1895–1905); *Journal of a Lady of Quality* (1921), ed. by E. W. Andrews; M. deL. Haywood and S. A. Ashe, "Josiah Martin," in S. A. Ashe, *Biog. Hist. of N. C.*, vol. III (1905); William Betham, *The Baronetage of England*, vol. IV (1804); transcripts of British records in N. C. Hist. Commission.]

A. R. N.

MARTIN, LUTHER (*c.* 1748–July 10, 1826), first attorney-general of the State of Maryland, member of the Continental Congress, member of the Federal Convention, and an eminent lawyer, was born near New Brunswick, N. J. The date of his birth is generally given as Feb. 9, and in some accounts is assigned to the year 1744. There is uncertainty also about the names of his parents, but it is probable that he was the third in a family of nine children of Benjamin Martin, a farmer, and his wife Hannah. His ancestors, who were of English stock, had been farmers in America for several generations. After attending the grammar school of the College of New Jersey (now Princeton University), he entered the college in 1762 and was graduated with honors in 1766. He went to Maryland to seek a position as teacher, and obtained a school at Queenstown, Queen Anne's County. Among his pupils were the children of Solomon Wright, a lawyer, in whose home he became a frequent visitor and whose library he was permitted to use. In 1769, after teaching nearly three years at Queenstown, Martin gave up his position and left for Somerset County, Md., to devote a year to the study of law with friends there. Shortly afterward, while making a brief visit in Queen Anne's County, he was served with five writs of attachment for debts; but Wright, acting as his attorney, succeeded in striking off the writs in the spring of 1770. In the summer of that year Martin left Somerset County to become superintendent of the grammar school at Onancock, Accomac County, Va. Here he served one year, continuing the study of law in the meantime. In 1771 he applied at Williamsburg for admission to the Virginia bar, was accepted, and in September qualified as an attorney in Accomac County. After practising a short time in Virginia, he decided to settle in Somerset County, Md., where his practice was lucrative until the outbreak of the Revolution.

In the fall of 1774 Martin was named on the patriot committee of Somerset County, and in December was a delegate to the convention of the Province of Maryland at Annapolis. In 1777 he published a reply to the appeal issued from the British fleet by Lord Howe; and his address, *To the Inhabitants of the Peninsula between the Delaware River and the Chesapeake to the Southward of the British Lines,* was circulated in handbills. On Feb. 11, 1778, Martin was appointed by Gov. Thomas Johnson, upon the recommendation of Samuel Chase, as attorney-general of Maryland; and qualifying on May 20 he took up his residence in Baltimore. During the remaining years of the war he prosecuted the Loyalists with great vigor. In 1785 he was a delegate to the Continental Congress. He was also a delegate to the Federal Convention at Philadelphia, where he opposed the plan of a strong central government. Before the convention was over, he walked out with John Francis Mercer [*q.v.*] and returned home without signing the Constitution. He assailed the proposed form of government before the Maryland House of Delegates in 1787 in a speech which attracted wide attention. In 1788, as a member of the Maryland convention, he made a futile effort to prevent the ratification of the federal Constitution.

On Dec. 25, 1783, Martin married Maria (sometimes referred to as Mary) Cresap, eldest daughter of Capt. Michael Cresap [*q.v.*], Maryland frontiersman. Cresap was charged with the murder of the family of the Indian chief, Logan; and Thomas Jefferson, in his *Notes on the State of Virginia,* quoted Logan's speech. To defend Cresap's character, Martin published letters (1797–98) in the Baltimore newspapers in reply to Jefferson (John J. Jacob, *A Biographical Sketch of the Life of the Late Capt. Michael Cresap,* 1826). Jefferson refused to make any reply in the newspapers, holding that Martin's object was to gratify party passions (P. L. Ford, *The Writings of Thomas Jefferson,* vol. VII, 1896, p. 137). Martin's domestic life was unhappy. His wife died young, leaving two daughters. He courted a wealthy client, the widow of Jonathan Hager, of Washington County, Md., but she married another man. (The letters of entreaty written by him to Mrs. Hager in 1800 and 1801 are in J. T. Scharf, *History of Western Maryland,* 1882, vol. II, pp. 1013–15.) Martin's daughters married when very young, against his will, and both of the marriages ended tragically. Maria married Lawrence Keene, a naval officer, but soon separated from him and died insane. Eleonora eloped with Richard R. Keene (unrelated to Lawrence), son of a Queen Anne's County farmer, who had entered Martin's office in 1799 and became a member of the bar in 1801. Martin condemned Keene in a series of five pamphlets entitled *Modern Gratitude,* printed in 1801 and 1802. The son-in-law replied in a pamphlet of fifty printed pages, *A Letter from Richard Raynal Keene to Luther Martin, Esq.* (1802). Martin later became infatuated with the beautiful Theodosia Burr [*q.v.*], who was already married; his "idolatrous admiration" for her doubtless served to blind him to the faults of her father's character (W. H. Safford, *The Blennerhassett Papers,* 1861, p. 469).

Martin, now allied with the Federalist party because of his hatred of Jefferson, went to the aid of Justice Samuel Chase [*q.v.*] in the impeachment trial before the United States Senate in 1804. In 1805, after twenty-seven years of service, he resigned as attorney-general of Maryland. In 1807 he was one of the lawyers who came to the rescue of Aaron Burr at his trial for treason in Richmond, where he attacked the Administration with so much bitterness that President Jefferson in a letter dated June 19, 1807, wrote to George Hay, United States district attorney for Virginia: "Shall we move to commit L[uther] M[artin], as *particeps criminis* with Burr? Graybell will fix upon his misprision of treason at least. And at any rate, his evidence will put down this unprincipled & impudent federal bull-dog, and add another proof that the most clamorous defenders of Burr are all his accomplices" (P. L. Ford, *The Writings of Thomas Jefferson,* vol. IX, 1898, p. 58). After the trial, Burr, and Harman Blennerhassett were entertained by Martin in Baltimore; a mob threatened to do violence; but Martin's house was guarded by the police, and the mob spent the force of its indignation on the hanging of effigies (*American Law Review,* January 1867, p. 278). In 1813 Martin became chief judge of the court of oyer and terminer for the City and County of Baltimore and served in this office until the tribunal was abolished in 1816. In February 1818, forty years after the date of his first appointment, he was reappointed attorney-general of the state. His last important case was *McCulloch* vs. *State of Maryland* (4 *Wheaton,* 316), wherein as attorney-general of Maryland in 1819 he opposed Daniel Webster, William Pinkney, and William Wirt on the question of state rights, and Chief Justice Marshall held that a state tax on the Bank of the United States was unconstitutional. In 1820 Martin was incapacitated for active service by a stroke of paralysis, and although an assistant attorney-general was appointed he was obliged to resign in 1822. Always of a convivial disposition, he had become increasingly addicted to the use of intoxicants; his brilliant faculties had decayed and he now faced the world broken in health, worn out in mind, and financially destitute. His plight led the legislature to pass a resolution compelling every practitioner of law in the state to pay an annual license fee of five dollars to be turned over to trustees for the use of Martin (*Acts of Maryland,* December Sess., 1821, Resolution No. 60). During the time the resolution was in effect only one protest was made against it; and it was repealed in 1823 before its constitutionality could be tested (*Ibid.,* December Sess., 1822, Resolution No. 16). Martin, wrecked by misfortunes, drunkenness, extravagance, and illness, was now welcomed into Burr's home in New York, where he was permitted to remain until the time of his death. He was buried in the Trinity Churchyard in New York.

Martin's chief faults were his intemperance and his improvidence in financial affairs. He was a stanch opponent of slavery, and was known for his generosity and his loyalty to his friends. While not a polished orator, he became a leader of the American bar because of his thoroughness and extraordinary memory. Blennerhassett, following Mercer, called him the "Thersites of the law." Chief Justice Taney said that Martin was "strong in his attachments, and ready to make any sacrifice for his friends" (Samuel Tyler, *Memoir of Roger Brooke Taney,* 1872, p. 68). He has been described as "the rollicking, witty, audacious Attorney-General of Maryland; . . . drunken, generous, slovenly, grand; bull-dog of federalism, . . . the notorious reprobate genius" (Henry Adams, *John Randolph,* 1882, p. 141). At the time of the Chase impeachment trial, Martin was "of medium height, broad-shouldered, near-sighted, absent-minded, shabbily attired, harsh of voice . . . with a face crimsoned by the brandy which he continually imbibed" (A. J. Beveridge, *The Life of John Marshall,* vol. III, 1919, p. 186).

[No definite biography of Luther Martin has been written. An autobiographical sketch of his early life is included in the last pamphlet of his *Modern Gratitude* (1802), in which he states that he was eighteen years old in 1766. On the other hand, an obituary in the N. Y. *Evening Post,* July 11, 1826, states that he died in his eighty-second year. An early sketch of his life, in *The Nat. Portrait Gallery of Distinguished Americans,* vol. IV (1839), pp. 167–74, was followed by a sketch in *Am. Law Review,* Jan. 1867, pp. 273–81; an article in *Biog. Cyc. of Representative Men of Md. and D. C.* (1879); "Luther Martin: The 'Federal Bull-Dog,'" by H. P. Goddard, published by the Md. Hist. Soc. in *Fund-Publication No. 24* (1887); and "Luther Martin," by E. L. Didier, in *The Green Bag,* Apr. 1891. Later sketches include those by A. M. Gould, in W. D. Lewis, ed., *Great American Lawyers,* vol. II (1907); H. H. Hagan, *Eight Great American Lawyers* (1923); T. C. Waters, in *Am. Bar Asso. Jour.,* Nov., Dec. 1928; and J. F. Essary, in *Md. in Nat. Politics* (1915), pp. 59–78. An article, "The Influence of Luther Martin in the Making of the Constitution of the United States," by E. D. Obrecht, appeared in the *Md. Hist. Mag.,* Sept.–Dec. 1932.

Martin's address, *The Genuine Information, Delivered to the Legislature of the State of Maryland, Relative to the Proceedings of the General Convention, Lately Held at Philadelphia,* published in 1788, is included in *American Eloquence,* edited by Frank Moore (1859), vol. I, 373–400; and in Jonathan Elliot, *The Debates . . . on the Adoption of the Federal Constitution* (2 ed., 1836); a different draft of the speech, from a MS. in the Lib. of Cong., appeared in the *Md. Hist. Mag.,* June 1910, pp. 139–50. Charles Warren, *The Making of the Constitution* (1928), p. 792, refers to newspaper letters of Martin. See also Max Farrand, *The Records of the Federal Convention* (3 vols., 1911); E. S. Delaplaine, *The Life of Thomas Johnson* (1927).]

E. S. D.

MARTIN, THOMAS COMMERFORD (July 22, 1856–May 17, 1924), author, editor, was born in London, England, the son of Thomas and Catherine (Commerford) Martin. He attended an academical school at Gravesend, England, continued his early education under private tutors, and then became a student in divinity at the Countess of Huntingdon Theological College. Being of a naturally active and adventuresome nature, and intensely interested in physics, although not a trained physicist, he left England at the age of twenty-one and came to the United States with letters to men of prominence here. At that time America offered splendid opportunities for the advancement of a young man interested in scientific research. Alexander Graham Bell, Charles J. Brush, Elihu Thomson, Thomas A. Edison, and others were converting electrical energy from a school-room curiosity into the channels of industrial application in many fields. Martin entered the Edison laboratory at Menlo Park in 1877 and remained there until 1879. Some of the experimental work on which he was engaged during this period had to do with the early phonograph, the electric pen, printing and embossing telegraphs, and the carbon telephone transmitter.

He soon developed special aptitude for clear and concise description of mechanical and scientific subjects. In 1878 he began to contribute articles to various New York papers, pointing out in graphic and dramatic style the interesting developments which were taking place or anticipated in the Edison laboratory. Soon this reportorial work became of greater interest to him, or as he put it, he found it "more agreeable than laboratory work with Wheatstone's Bridge, grimy carbon telephone buttons, inky electric pens and rebellious tinfoil." Late in the year 1879 he received an invitation to act as editor of a daily newspaper in Kingston, Jamaica, W. I., and being in ill health by reason of his combined experimental and journalistic labors, he eagerly accepted the opportunity, and served on the *Daily Gleaner* from 1880 until the end of 1882. While in Jamaica he married Elizabeth Gould of Kingston.

In 1882 Martin returned to the United States and after serving for a time as editor of the *Operator,* in 1883 became editor of the *Electrical World.* In 1890 he became editor of the *Electrical Engineer,* which in 1899 merged with the *Electrical World.* From that date until 1909 Martin and W. D. Weaver were joint editors of the journal. During this time the publication became the largest and best known magazine in the electrical field. In the year 1919 he became secretary of the National Electric Light Association, composed of practically all the public service corporations in the country, and continued in active service with that organization until 1921, and in an advisory way until his death. During the years from 1900 to 1915, he acted as special agent for the United States Census Bureau, writing an exhaustive report covering the electrical industries of the United States, published in 1902, and during his career he contributed special electrical articles to the *Encyclopædia Britannica, Chambers's Encyclopedia,* and *The Encyclopedia Americana.* Besides these activities, he prepared numerous articles, principally upon electrical subjects, for the *North American Review, Century,* and other publications.

Among the books of which he was author or co-author are: *The Electric Motor and Its Applications* (1887); *The Inventions, Researches and Writings of Nikola Tesla* (1894); *Edison, His Life and Inventions* (2 vols., 1910); *The Story of Electricity* (2 vols., 1919–22); and *Forty Years of Edison Service, 1882–1922* (1922). He was a frequent lecturer before electrical and engineering societies, including the Royal Institution of Engineers, Great Britain, and the Société Internationale des Électriciens, France, as well as various American Colleges and Universities. During the Great War he took an active part on behalf of the allied nations and frequently spoke before and assisted in organizing societies for the successful prosecution of that tragic enterprise. In this special work he became chairman of the Marconi Fund for Italian War Relief, and secretary of the Florence Nightingale Hospital for the training of nurses in France. He was a founder of the American Institute of Electrical Engineers (president, 1887–88), a member of other scientific, commercial, and charitable societies, and a trustee of the engineering college of George Washington University. He died at the House of Mercy Hospital in Pittsfield, Mass., survived by his second wife, Carmelita Beckwith, whom he had married in 1910.

[*Jour. Am. Inst. Electrical Engineers,* May, June, 1924; *Electrical World,* May 24, 1924; *Who's Who in America,* 1924–25; *N. Y. Times,* May 18, 1924; letters and memoranda from Edison employees; Martin's autobiographical notes.]

F. L. D.

MARTIN, THOMAS STAPLES (July 29, 1847–Nov. 12, 1919), senator from Virginia, was born in Scottsville, Va., the son of John Samuel Martin, a merchant and manufacturer, and Martha Ann (Staples) Martin. He entered the Virginia Military Institute at Lexington on Mar. 1, 1864, and served for a year in the Confederate army with the famous New Market Corps of cadets. He then attended the University of Virginia from 1865 until 1867. In 1869 he was admitted to the bar and began the practice of law in Albemarle County, Va. Before many years had passed, he had built up a large clientele.

His first important political activity came as a Democratic leader during the heated contests of the eighties, when Gen. William Mahone [*q.v.*], a "Readjuster," took advantage of the problems presented by the state debt to make himself a power with the aid of the negro vote. Then in 1893, although he was comparatively unknown, Martin announced his candidacy for the United States Senate. It was the first time he had ever run for public office, and many believed that he stood little or no chance of success. His opponent was the popular and magnetic Fitzhugh Lee [*q.v.*], nephew of Gen. Robert E. Lee, who had served as major-general of cavalry in the war and had been governor of Virginia. To the surprise of thousands, Martin was elected by the General Assembly. He took his seat in the Senate on Mar. 4, 1895.

This was the beginning of a service in that body which lasted without interruption until his death in 1919. Martin was never a fluent or polished speaker, and he made few addresses while in Congress, but those who predicted that he would be a failure in politics found that they had misjudged their man. He soon revealed unusual political astuteness, and shortly after the turn of the century, he came to be regarded as the leader of the Democratic "machine" in Virginia, which leadership he retained for the remainder of his life. At the same time his influence in the Senate increased steadily, and he was majority floor leader for the two years beginning in March 1917. He also served as chairman of the committee on appropriations during the war period, when billions were spent by the government.

Martin was what is known as a "business senator." He was notable for his industry, common sense, and knowledge of men, and for his willingness to go to almost unlimited trouble to accommodate a constituent. He belonged to the school of thought which believes in always "standing by your friends," and in that ancient Jacksonian principle, "to the victor belong the spoils." During the last ten years that he was boss of the Democratic "machine" in Virginia he was in alliance with the Anti-Saloon League. This combination was generally unbeatable. Unfortunately, Martin was a conservative, and the state made comparatively little progress under his régime. On the other hand, he rendered conspicuous services to his country during the World War, when as majority floor leader of the Senate and chairman of the appropriations committee he had charge of much of the important war legislation. Warned many times that he was working to excess, he refused to spare himself, and his life is believed to have been shortened as a result. His absolute personal honesty is attested by the fact that despite the vast sums which he handled, he died a poor man.

On Oct. 10, 1894, he married Lucy Chambliss Day, of Smithfield, Va. They had two children, a daughter and a son.

[Sketch in *Biog. Directory of the Am. Congress, 1774–1927* (1928); in *Men of Mark in Va.*, vol. I (1906); *Register of Former Cadets, Va. Mil. Institute* (1927); obituaries in Richmond *Evening Journal*, Nov. 12, 1919, in *Richmond Times-Dispatch*, Richmond *Virginian* and *N. Y. Times*, Nov. 13, 1919; editorial in Richmond *News Leader*, Nov. 13, 1919.] V. D.

MARTIN, VICTORIA CLAFLIN WOODHULL [See WOODHULL, VICTORIA CLAFLIN, 1838–1927].

MARTIN, WILLIAM ALEXANDER PARSONS (Apr. 10, 1827–Dec. 17, 1916), missionary, educator, and author, was born in Livonia, Ind., the son of William Wilson Martin and Susan Depew, both of frontier Scotch-Irish stock. His father was a Presbyterian minister, and all of the three sons were named for foreign missionaries. Given such an environment, it is not strange that he early decided to devote his own life to the missionary enterprise. He was graduated from Indiana University in 1846 and for three years thereafter studied theology in the Presbyterian seminary at New Albany, Ind. In 1849, the year of his graduation, he married Jane Vansant (who died in 1893) and was ordained to the ministry by the Presbytery of Salem, Ind. As a boy he had had his attention drawn to China by the first war between that country and Great Britain (1839–42), and now, his preparation completed, he sought appointment under the foreign mission board of his church to one of the ports which that struggle had opened to foreign residents. In the spring of 1850 he and his brother Samuel Newall and their wives arrived in China. He was assigned to Ningpo and early proved himself both energetic and able. Before he had been six years in China he had worked out, through public lectures and discussions before Chinese audiences, a series of studies on evidences of Christianity which sought to present the Christian gospel convincingly to Chinese. These he put into the literary language and had published. They became very popular, and went into many editions in both China and Japan.

Martin learned not only the local dialect and

the literary language, but Mandarin, and it was his knowledge of the latter colloquial which helped to open to him the opportunity which led him away from Ningpo and into the region where the major part of his life was to be spent. During the second war between Great Britain and China, he was appointed, on his own application, as an interpreter to William B. Reed [*q.v.*], who obtained for the United States the treaty of 1858 with China. Martin had a share in the negotiations and the following year went north again, this time to Peking, to assist in the exchange of ratifications of the treaty. After a well-earned furlough in America, in 1862 he returned to China and for a short time was connected with the Presbyterian Mission Press in Shanghai. While there he translated into Chinese Wheaton's *Elements of International Law*. The following year he removed to Peking, founding in that city a mission of his denomination which later grew to large proportions.

In Peking his contact with officials, begun during the negotiation of the Treaty of Tientsin, continued, and his interest increased in the diplomatic relations with Western powers into which China was so reluctantly and awkwardly entering. In 1868, accordingly, he accepted a position as teacher of international law in the T'ungwên Kuan, a school which had recently been formed by the government to train in Western languages and learning Chinese youths who were to serve in intercourse with foreign countries. After spending a few months in America in further preparation for his new work, in 1869 he assumed his duties, not only as teacher, but as head of this institution. In these positions he continued until 1894, and through his translations and original works in Chinese, his contacts with officials, and his teaching, he had a significant part in introducing Western learning to China. In 1898 he was made president of the imperial university which the reform movement of that year had brought into existence. The Boxer outbreak (1900) caught him in Peking, and, although then past seventy years of age, he was active in the defense of the legations. After the raising of the siege he was in the United States for a time, lecturing on China, and then, at the invitation of the Viceroy Chang Chih-tung, he once more returned and lectured on international law in an institution which that dignitary was attempting to establish in Wuchang. With the transfer of Chang Chih-tung to Nanking, Martin deemed it advisable to withdraw. Most of the remainder of his life was spent in Peking. Here he taught individual Chinese students, wrote, and, about 1911, rejoined the staff of the Presbyterian mission, serving on it until his death.

Martin's literary output was voluminous. It included many works in Chinese on international law, natural science, and Christianity, and a number of works on China in English, among them *Hanlin Papers* (two series, Shanghai, 1880, 1894); *The Chinese* (1881), a reprint of the first series of *Hanlin Papers*; *A Cycle of Cathay* (New York, 1896); *The Lore of Cathay* (1901); and *The Awakening of China* (1907). He received many honors, both in China and in the United States.

[Martin's book, *A Cycle of Cathay* (1896); *Gen. Cat. Presbyt. Theol. Sem., Chicago* (1928); *Who's Who in America*, 1914–15; *Chinese Recorder*, Feb. 1917; *Reports of the Board of Foreign Missions of the Presbyt. Ch. in the U. S. A.*, 1911–17.] K. S. L.

MARTIN, WILLIAM THOMPSON (Mar. 25, 1823–Mar. 16, 1910), Confederate soldier, railroad builder, was the eldest son of John Henderson and Emily Monroe (Kerr) Martin. Born at Glasgow, Ky., he graduated from Centre College in 1840, shortly after the family had moved to Vicksburg, Miss. Following the death of the father he moved to Natchez in 1842 and was there admitted to the bar as soon as he reached his majority. As district attorney, he made an enviable reputation as a vigorous prosecutor and as an eloquent and forceful speaker. On Jan. 5, 1854, he married Margaret Dunlop Conner, whose mother lived near Natchez. He was a man of moral as well as physical courage, and he did not hesitate to take unpopular stands in following his own best judgment. He was a Whig and opposed secession in 1851 and again in 1860, when he was accused of unfaithfulness to the South and of untrustworthiness. Though a Unionist he prepared for the conflict, after becoming convinced that it was inevitable, by organizing in the spring of 1861 the Adams County troop of cavalry, of which he was elected captain. After the firing on Fort Sumter he led his men to Richmond. He proved himself a resourceful and daring cavalry leader, was soon given command of the Jeff Davis Legion, and participated in all the battles against McClellan in the Peninsular campaign. When J. E. B. Stuart made his famous raid around McClellan's army, Martin commanded the rear third of the detachment. Upon the battlefield at Sharpsburg (Antietam) he acted as personal aide to Robert E. Lee. In December 1862 he was made brigadier-general and in November 1863 major-general. After the failure of Lee's Maryland campaign, Martin was ordered to the West. He was in the battle of Chickamauga and a number of other important engagements, commanding a division of Wheeler's cavalry during the Atlanta campaign. Toward the close of 1864 he was transferred to northwest Mississippi and ordered to protect that region from lawless bands.

After the war he took an active interest in politics, education, and railroad building. He was a delegate to the state constitutional convention of 1865. In the Mississippi constitutional convention of 1890, he was one of three members who did not sign that document. He followed this course because the constitution contained a provision forbidding the legislature to pay principal or interest of the Union Bank bonds and the Planters' Bank bonds. Before the war he had opposed repudiation and had advocated the payment of these bonds. He was a delegate to Democratic national conventions between 1868 and 1880, and was a member of the state Senate from 1882 to 1894. In 1884, under his sole presidency a railroad line between Natchez and Jackson, known as the Natchez, Jackson & Columbus Railroad, was completed. For twelve years he was a trustee of the University of Mississippi, and for a time was president of the board of trustees of Jefferson College, Washington, Miss. He was survived by his wife, four sons, and five daughters.

[Manuscript sketch by his son, W. C. Martin, Natchez; *Who's Who in America,* 1906–07; C. A. Evans, *Confederate Military Hist.* (1899), vols. III, VII; *War of the Rebellion: Official Records (Army)*, esp. ser. I, vols. V, XI, XXX (1881–90); Douglas Walworth's sketch of military career prepared for J. F. H. Claiborne's second volume of the history of Mississippi, in *Daily Democrat* (Natchez), June 8, 1908; *Ibid.*, Mar. 17, 1910.] C. S. S.

MARTINDALE, JOHN HENRY (Mar. 20, 1815–Dec. 13, 1881), lawyer, soldier, was born at Hudson Falls (formerly Sandy Hill), N. Y., the son of Henry C. Martindale. His father was a prominent member of the community and served several terms in Congress as a Whig. Martindale entered West Point in July 1831 and upon graduation in 1835 was commissioned a brevet second lieutenant of Dragoons, to his great disappointment, for he had hoped to become an engineer. While on leave of absence, he had the opportunity of joining the engineering staff of the Saratoga & Washington Railroad of New York, and he resigned his commission (Mar. 10, 1836) without ever having served with troops. He soon turned to the study of law, was admitted to the bar of New York in 1838, and launched on the career that was to bring him prominence. Establishing a residence in Batavia, he practised there until 1851, meanwhile serving as district attorney of Genesee County for two terms. He continued his law practice in Rochester during the decade preceding the Civil War.

When war between the North and South became a certainty, Martindale took an active part in organizing volunteer regiments. He believed that by utilizing officers of the regular army as instructors, the volunteer organizations would be greatly improved and the military strength of the North brought to bear on the South more quickly. In addition, he proposed to the War Department that the first and second classes at West Point be graduated immediately and sent to their respective homes to drill and aid the people. With considerable vision, he wrote to the secretary of war on Apr. 25, 1861: "We can have a long and exhausting war, or we can conquer a peace before the end of another winter if we will only organize and use our power promptly" (*War of the Rebellion: Official Records, Army,* 3 ser. I, p. 111). He was commissioned a brigadier-general of volunteers in August 1861 and was stationed in the defenses of Washington during the following winter. Commanding a brigade in the Army of the Potomac, he was in the field from March until July 1862, taking part in the engagements at Yorktown, Hanover Court-House, Mechanicsville, Gaines's Mill, Malvern Hill, and Harrison's Landing.

While convalescing from an attack of typhoid fever, he was the subject of an investigation by a court of inquiry looking into charges preferred by Maj.-Gen. Fitz John Porter to the effect that Martindale had influenced men to surrender at Malvern Hill. He was exonerated by the court and restored to duty as military governor of the District of Columbia. This position required tact, firmness, and legal ability, involving as it did the control of a large civilian population as well as the masses of troops in Washington. Martindale distinguished himself in the performance of this duty, but again desiring a field command, he was given a division in the Army of the James in 1864 and took part in the battle of Bermuda Hundred and in the operations south of Richmond. Transferred to the Army of the Potomac, he led his division in the Cold Harbor and Petersburg campaigns. In the latter, he commanded the XVIII Corps for a short time. Again overtaken by sickness, he resigned from the army because of ill health in the fall of 1864. On Mar. 13 of the following year he was brevetted a major-general of volunteers for gallant and distinguished service at the battle of Malvern Hill.

Martindale returned to his law practice at Rochester, N. Y. He was an interesting figure of the bar of New York and gained prominence especially in his handling of cases against the New York Central Railroad involving personal damages. He was elected attorney-general of the state of New York for the term of 1866–68. From 1868 to 1879 he was vice-president of the board of managers of the National Asylum for Disabled Volunteer Soldiers. He died in 1881 at Nice, France, where he had gone for his health. He had married on June 16, 1840, Emeline M. Holden at Batavia, N. Y. They had two sons and three daughters.

[G. W. Cullum, *Biog. Reg. . . . U. S. Mil. Acad.*, vol. I (1891); *War of the Rebellion: Official Records (Army)*, 1 ser. V, XI, pts. 1, 2, and 3, XIX, pt. 2, XXI, XXXIII, XXXVI, pts. 1, 2, and 3, XL, pt. 1, and LI, pt. 1; War Dept. records, *Thirteenth Ann. Reunion, Asso. Grads. U. S. Mil. Acad.*, 1882; F. W. Beers, *Gazetteer and Biog. Record of Genesee County, N. Y.* (1890); *Army and Navy Jour.*, Dec. 17, 1881; information as to certain facts from Martindale's daughter, Mrs. James B. Perkins.]

J. R. V.

MARTINY, PHILIP (May 19, 1858–June 25, 1927), sculptor, son of Philip and Kathrine (Blacke) Martiny, was born in Strasbourg, Alsace, France, and as a boy often hid in the cellars during the Franco-Prussian War. He claimed lineal descent from the Sienese painter Simone Martini, who died in Avignon, France, in 1344. Whether or not this claim is just, much of what the critic J. Addington Symonds wrote of the Italian painter is strikingly true of the American sculptor: "full of delicate inventiveness, and gifted with a rare feeling for grace," an "ingenious and delightful master" (*Renaissance in Italy, The Fine Arts*, 1877, p. 218). Foreign sources state that Martiny was a pupil of Eugen Dock, who was born in Strasbourg in 1827, who studied at the Beaux-Arts in Paris, and who became in 1860 the foremost decorative sculptor in his native town. American accounts state that as a boy Philip worked as a carver with his father, and that he studied in various French ateliers. Certain it is that he came to New York as a young man thoroughly well grounded in old-world technique and tradition.

In the early eighties, Augustus Saint-Gaudens was superintending the wood-carving in the important scheme of decoration he had planned for the Vanderbilt house. "I had noticed," he wrote in his *Reminiscences* (vol. II, pp. 5–6) "that one of my carvers reproduced models with an artistic felicity so markedly superior to any of the others that I asked him to come and help me in my studio. This was Philip Martiny," who during his first period of a year or so in the Saint-Gaudens studio, worked on the figure of the "Puritan." Saint-Gaudens often recalled Martiny's boundless skill and inventiveness, then displayed with a fervor which the master was no doubt obliged to curb, in order to keep the integrity of his own design. At this period Martiny came into contact with Saint-Gaudens' close friends, McKim, Mead, and White. The young Frenchman's instinct for the decorative aspect of sculptural form met appreciation from this famous firm, and indeed from other architects, with the result that when he started out for himself, he had plenty of work. For the Chicago world's fair of 1893, in which McKim, Mead, and White were actively interested, Martiny received a fifty-thousand-dollar contract to execute an ambitious scheme of sculptural decoration for McKim's Agricultural Building. The design was to include figures of eighty-three great angels, forty towering eagles, and sixteen large groups. No wonder that in 1891, McKim wrote to Saint-Gaudens, in the whimsical vein customary between the two, "Martiny is 'clean bust' as usual, and if you can come down and . . . make an estimate of what is due him, you will save him from the poorhouse and McK., M. & W. from the lunatic asylum" (Charles Moore, *The Life and Times of Charles Follen McKim*, 1929, note p. 119).

This first large commission of Martiny's was typical of others to follow. It called for exuberant imagination, a consummate understanding of sculptural light and shadow, a power of quick decision, and an ability to make the best use of assistants. Deities, angels, men, women, infants, oxen, horses, goats, fruits, flowers—all were stuff for his undaunted designs. In the roof decorations for McKim's building, with their "Groups" and "Seasons," he triumphed as the foremost decorative sculptor of the day. His impassioned improvisations of *putti* and *frutti*, of trumpery trumpets and papery drapery supplied every demand of the sculptural pageantry. He juggled with his plaster, apparently creating a figure by assembling parts once belonging to another. It would seem that in some such manner he put together the study for the central motive of his "Fountain of Abundance" for the Pan-American Exposition at Buffalo in 1901—a garlanded figure surrounded by dancing cherubs. The method was dubious, the result delightful. For the St. Louis world's fair of 1904 he made the group of "Apollo and the Muses," crowning the main entrance to Festival Hall, and two massive quadrigae, "Progress of Art" and "Progress of Commerce," flanking the dome of the New York State Building. Apparently no subject baffled his imagination or exceeded his capacity.

Martiny's technique was suitable for world's fairs, but at times unpleasing traces of this facility appear in his more lasting productions—

perhaps in his bronze "Lampbearers" on the newel-posts of the famous double staircase in the entrance hall of the Library of Congress, but not in his idyllic high-relief marble carvings of the balustrade. Only a pedant could find fault with those twenty-six panels, in which babes astride garlands disport themselves at various genial trades, such as the "Hunter with a Rabbit," and the "Vintager with Grapes." Other works by Martiny in this building are cartouche and tablet figures for ceiling and dome. Adequate to their purpose, they display that "papery drapery" in which he was at times all too skilful, for monumental ends. To the same period, yet in different vein, belongs one of the most impressive productions of his career, the Soldiers and Sailors' Monument in Jersey City, N. J., 1899. A seated female figure, draped and helmeted, holding a sword in her left hand, an olive branch in her right, surmounts a high pedestal of beautiful design. The ensemble is monumental rather than decorative. Both monumental and decorative, as well as perfectly adapted to its architectural purpose, is Martiny's south pair of bronze doors, with limestone frieze and marble tympanum, for Saint Bartholomew's Church, New York City. The frieze of the "Road to Calvary" is fine, the marble tympanum less so. As a whole, his contribution to the St. Bartholomew façade is notable for actual richness of surface rather than for suggested depth of religious feeling.

Between 1903 and 1908, an enormous volume of architectural sculpture in granite, and of heroic size, was executed in the Martiny studio for the New York City Hall of Records. The list includes eight cornice statues of New York worthies, from the seventeenth century onward; sixteen symbolic cornice statues; two seated entrance figures, "Justice" and "Authority"; two entrance groups of three figures each, "New York in its Infancy," and "New York in Revolutionary Times." Of earlier date are his two groups for the New York Chamber of Commerce, with their central figures of John Jay and Alexander Hamilton, and his marble statue of Confucius for the appellate court (1899). He made sculpture for the residences of Senator Clark and Charles T. Yerkes, New York City; for the Carnegie Library, Washington, D. C.; for the Courthouse at Elizabeth, N. J.; for the Kunhardt Memorial, Moravian Cemetery, Staten Island; for a tympanum over the doors of the Shepherd memorial chapel, Scarboro-on-the-Hudson; for the Cullum Memorial at West Point. His statue of Vice-President Hobart, erected in Paterson, N. J., in 1902, is considered excellent. His McKinley monument at Springfield, Mass., with its familiar French motive of a draped female figure of Fame, reaching upward to adorn with a palm branch a portrait bust on a lofty pedestal, has dignity and beauty, yet on the whole is decorative rather than monumental. In 1919, for New York's celebration of the return of American troops from overseas, his vigorous staff group, "Our Allies," had a prominent place on the Flatiron Building. His last public works of importance were two World-War memorials for New York City. The monument to the soldiers from Greenwich Village is on a high pedestal in Abingdon Square, and shows a single bronze figure of an American soldier defending the flag. The tribute to the soldiers from the Chelsea district is in Chelsea Park. Here a lofty, well-designed stele of granite is used as a background for a bronze figure in a resolute attitude. Both these memorials are simple, dignified, eloquent, though their monumentality is slightly impaired by Martiny's characteristic "papery" rendering of flag and uniform.

In view of his amazing fecundity, his list of portrait busts is not long. He was no solitary worker; from boyhood he had the habit of gregarious endeavor. He spent little time in soul-searching, either of himself or others, and so has left behind none of those vivid records of contemporary personalities, such as Grafly's portraits of his artist friends, or Saint-Gaudens' bust of Sherman. Of the countless heads his nimble fingers shaped, all decorative, all somehow suited to his purpose of the moment, few or none awake in the beholder a new and poignant sense of human beauty or of human greatness. Yet both as to inner meaning and outward expression, he brought a new note into American sculpture. In his creations it is vain to seek for what he never set out to disclose, a feeling for the profounder issues of life. It would be equally wrong to call his contribution to our art a superficial one. On the contrary, his spontaneous grace of color and rhythm, supported by unlimited technical resources, indicated to American sculptors at least one way to avoid a Puritanic drabness in expression. His work might set a standard for the wise as well as a snare for the foolish.

Martiny's temperament was jovial. In the words of one of his assistants, he earned largely, and spent everything twice—once before he had it, and once after. He was twice married, first to Hermine Horning, a German, afterward to a young French woman, Yvonne E. Flouret. His closing years were clouded by illness; a stroke incapacitated him. He died in New York, of paralysis, leaving a widow as well as four children of the first marriage and eight of the second.

[U. Thieme and F. Becker, *Allgemeines Lexikon der Bildenden Künstler,* vol. XXIV (1930); *The Reminiscences of Augustus Saint-Gaudens* (2 vols., 1913), ed. by Homer Saint-Gaudens; Lorado Taft, *The Hist. of Am. Sculpture* (1930); C. H. Caffin, *Am. Masters of Sculpture* (1903); C. R. Reynolds, *Washington Standard Guide* (1924); Sadakichi Hartmann, *A Hist. of Am. Art* (1932), vol. II; *Cat. of the Works of Art Belonging to the City of N. Y.* (1909); *Who's Who in America,* 1926–27; *Architectural Record,* Apr. 1904; *Am. Architect,* Feb. 5, 12, 1898; the *Art Digest,* July 1927; *Am. Art Annual,* 1927; *N. Y. Times,* June 27, 1927; private information.] A. A.

MARTY, MARTIN (Jan. 12, 1834–Sept. 19, 1896), prelate and Indian missionary, the son of Jacob Alois Marty, a shoemaker and church sexton, and of Elizabeth (Reichlin) Marty, was born and baptized as Aloysius at Schwyz in Switzerland. He attended a local preparatory college until the Jesuit fathers were banished in an anti-clerical campaign. In 1848 he transferred to the Benedictine college of Einsiedeln, where he translated into German a French edition of the "Annals of the Propagation of the Faith," thus acquiring a youthful zeal for missionary labors. In 1854 he pronounced his monastic vows as Brother Martin, O.S.B., and on Sept. 14, 1856, was ordained priest together with a life-long friend, Frowin Conrad, later abbot at Conception, Mo. He continued at Einsiedeln as a teacher and wrote an essay on the manner of teaching in monastic institutions a thousand years ago, which won commendation from the University of Berlin. In 1860 he volunteered for American service and joined the monastery at St. Meinrad, Ind., which had been established by a colony of monks from Einsiedeln in 1854. In 1866 he became prior, and, when St. Meinrad's monastery was made an abbey by Pope Pius IX four years later, he was chosen its first mitred abbot. In answer to appeals for Indian missionaries, about 1873 he led a group of Benedictines to the Standing Rock agency of the Sioux. His activities extended over the Dakotas, where he soon acquired a wide acquaintance with the natives and pioneers who trusted him as a counsellor. He became proficient enough in the Siouan tongues to translate hymns and prayers. In recognition of his influence with the Indians, he was appointed a member of the Indian commission established by the plenary council at Baltimore.

In 1879 when the territory of Dakota was created into a vicariate, as titular bishop of Tiberias, he was named vicar apostolic with headquarters at Yankton. Consecrated by Bishop Francis Silas Chatard on Feb. 1, 1880, he became an ideal frontier bishop, traversing the vast region in a wagon or on horseback, fighting the cause of temperance in wigwam and camp, and often rolling himself up in furs to spend the night on the snow-covered prairie. Not unmerited was his title of "Angel of the West." In 1884 he was an active participant in the council of Baltimore and thereafter he went to Europe in the interest of his vicariate. As the region grew he saw his priests increase from twelve to ninety, his churches from twenty to about 130, and the Catholic population from 14,000 to about 80,000. When the vicariate was divided he was selected as first bishop of Sioux Falls. He had built, or at least fostered, a score of schools, ten industrial institutes for boys and girls, and three academies. He introduced the Jesuits into the diocese and several communities of nuns, who managed academies and hospitals at Fargo, Grand Forks, Yankton, and Deadwood, as well as Indian schools at the various agencies. While at Sioux Falls for only five years, his success was marked especially in the creation of mission schools. He found time to write a life of the first bishop of Milwaukee, *Dr. Johann Martin Henni* (1888), and in 1890 he published his revision of *Katolik Wocekiye,* the ritual in the Siouan language composed by Father Augustin Ravoux. In 1895 he was transferred to the quiet diocese of St. Cloud, Minn., where he died among his Benedictine brethren of the St. John's University.

[Marty's papers and letters were burned by a family in ignorance of their value; material supplied by Ignatius Forster, O. S. B., of Yankton, S. D., who is planning to write a biography; a careful, detailed biography is in *Paradies-Früchte,* Dec. 1914–Oct. 1916. See also *Acta et Dicta,* July 1917; Hoffmans' *Catholic Directory,* 1897, p. xxxi; J. H. O'Donnell, "The Catholic Hierarchy," *The Catholic University of America Studies in Am. Church Hist.,* vol. IV (1922); J. G. Shea, *The Hierarchy of the Catholic Church* (1886), p. 396; *Dakota Catholic,* 1889–90.] R. J. P.

MARTYN, SARAH TOWNE SMITH (Aug. 15, 1805–Nov. 22, 1879), author, was born in Hopkinton, N. H., the daughter of the Rev. Ethan and Bathsheba (Sanford) Smith, both descendants of seventeenth-century settlers in New England. Her early education was directed by her father, a scholarly clergyman, who, as a youth, had served in the Revolution, and afterward graduated from Dartmouth College. Under his tutelage she studied Greek and Hebrew and learned to translate readily from modern languages. She spent a brief period at a school for young ladies in New York City, where her considerable talent for music received some training. As she grew older she shared with her father his ardent interest in the temperance and anti-slavery movements. She was warmly sympathetic with Oberlin College in its early efforts and was invited to act as one of the first principals of its "female department." This honor she declined, feeling that her work lay in another direction. She was active in the Female Moral Reform Society of New York after 1836 and assisted in editing its journal, the *Advocate of Moral Reform,* until 1845, when dissension within the society caused her to secede from it with the disaffected minority. In March 1841 she married her brother-in-law, Job H. Martyn, a clergyman in New York City. She lived in New York until 1868, with the exception of three years (1850–53) spent in Waukesha, Wis., while her husband was in charge of a church in that place. Three sons and a daughter were born of this marriage, the eldest, William Carlos, becoming a well-known minister and writer.

After her marriage Mrs. Martyn continued her devotion to religious and reform movements. In 1842 she acted as editor for a few weeks of the *Olive Plant and Ladies' Temperance Advocate.* Following her separation from the *Advocate of Moral Reform* she was connected for a short time with a rival, the *True Advocate.* In April 1846 she began the publication of the *White Banner,* an undertaking that gave place the following month to the *Ladies' Wreath,* "a magazine devoted to literature, industry, and religion." This periodical she edited from 1846 to 1850, writing a large part of its decorous contents herself. In addition to these editorial ventures she wrote for the American Tract Society many unpretentious volumes designed for juvenile readers and a number of more ambitious works dealing with historical subjects. Among these are *Margaret, the Pearl of Navarre* (1867), *The English Exile, or William Tyndale at Home and Abroad* (1867), *Daughters of the Cross* (1868), and *Women of the Bible* (1868). She was known among the literati of New York as a gracious hostess in whose home well-known writers and reformers frequently assembled. After the death of her husband in 1868, she divided her time between New York and Connecticut, living with her children and sharing their interests. She died in New York City and was buried in Cheshire, Conn.

[*New-Eng. Hist. and Geneal. Reg.,* Apr. 1847; J. Q. Bittinger, *Hist. of Haverhill, N. H.* (1888); files of the *Ladies' Wreath* and of the *Advocate of Moral Reform*; obituary notices and personal information in possession of family; John S. Hart, *A Manual of Am. Lit.* (1874).] B. M. S.

MARVEL, IK [See MITCHELL, DONALD GRANT, 1822–1908].

MARVIN, DUDLEY (May 29, 1786–June 25, 1852), congressman, the son of Elisha and Elizabeth (Selden) Marvin, was born in Lyme, Conn., where his ancestor, Reinold Marvin who emigrated from Essex County, England, before 1638, finally settled and died. He attended the Colchester Academy in Connecticut and then followed the path of New England pioneers westward into New York and settled in Ontario County at Canandaigua. With a general education such as was afforded by a small New England academy of that time he studied law and was admitted to the bar, probably in 1811. At the outbreak of war with Great Britain the following year he took active military duty with the state militia and served as lieutenant. After peace had been declared he continued to take a prominent part in the militia, rising eventually to the rank of major-general. He was married on Jan. 31, 1818, to Mary Jepson Whalley, the daughter of Joseph and Hannah (Saltonstall) Whalley of Canandaigua. They had one child.

Marvin practised law successfully and was recognized as one of the ablest barristers in the western counties of the state. In 1822 he was elected to Congress, as an Adams Democrat, and was reëlected in 1824 and in 1826. He came under the influence of Henry Clay's leadership and espoused the Whig cause. In Congress he advocated with distinction the dominant interests of the rising industrial power of the North, a protective tariff and the limitation of slavery. During his first term he became a member of the committee on manufactures and was an ardent advocate of a protective tariff. In the debate over the celebrated tariff of 1824 he defended against Southern opposition the cause of the Northern manufacturing interests, then slowly developing. He maintained that the tax that falls in the first instance upon the cotton planters "is paid back again by all other States, in the various proportions in which they are consumers of cotton" (*Annals of Cong.,* 18 Cong., 1 Sess., col. 1527). The fact that two-thirds of the cotton crop was consumed abroad did not in his mind disturb the logic of the Northern position. After completing his third term in Congress, he went to Maryland and to Virginia for a time and then removed to New York City to practise law there and in Brooklyn. About 1843 he again removed to the outlying districts of the state and settled in Ripley, Chautauqua County. In 1847 he returned to Congress as a Whig and served for one term. The stirring controversy over slavery in the territory newly acquired from Mexico brought him once more into the sectional debate. "It will not be denied," he asserted, "that the introduction of slavery equally excludes from a participation in the enjoyment of these acquisitions the free laboring men of the North" (*Congressional Globe,* 30 Cong., 1 Sess., App., p. 1211). The right of the federal government to exclude slavery from the territories he declared to be derived from the sovereign rights of the nation, the territories having been acquired in the first place "by the act of war—an act of sovereignty in which the respective sovereign States in the Union neither were nor could be known" (*Ibid.,* p. 1209). The remainder of his life was spent in Ripley. He interested himself in community affairs, was active in the temperance movement, and in the Presbyterian Church.

[A. W. Young, *Hist. of Chautauqua County* (1875); *Biog. Dir. Am. Cong.* (1928); G. F. and W. T. R. Marvin, *Descendants of Reinold and Matthew Marvin* (1904) as authority for dates of birth and death.]
G. L. R.

MARVIN, ENOCH MATHER (June 12, 1823–Nov. 26, 1877), bishop of the Methodist Episcopal Church, South, was a descendant of Reinold Marvin, born in Great Bentley, England, who emigrated to America about 1637 and settled in Hartford, Conn. In 1817 Wells Marvin married Mary Davis, of Welsh ancestry, in Pittsfield, Mass. The young couple immediately set out for the West, and established themselves near Peruque Creek, in what is now Warren County, Mo. There in a log-cabin Enoch Mather Marvin was born. Until he was twelve years old he was taught in a school conducted by his mother for her own and her neighbors' children. So far as is known, he attended school only six months thereafter; yet, as time went on, he acquired a good knowledge of history, an acquaintance with the scientific lore of his day, and enough Latin and Greek for his professional needs.

His father had little concern for religion, but his mother was a Baptist. In Missouri, however, the Baptists were so thoroughly Antinomian that she was never a member of a church there. Methodist circuit-riders came early to the Peruque Creek community, and Enoch was converted under their preaching when he was seventeen. A year later he was licensed to preach and admitted on trial in the Missouri Conference. At this time he was so homely and awkward that, dressed in ill-fitting homespun, he attracted no little attention. His first circuit covered three hundred miles along the Missouri-Iowa border, and his salary for the year was fifteen dollars. He soon demonstrated that he was a preacher of unusual power, especially among the common people, by whom he was always beloved. In 1854–55 he served as financial agent for St. Charles College, in which capacity he raised an endowment for that institution. From 1855 to 1862 he was pastor of some of the larger Methodist congregations in Missouri. During the Civil War he was chaplain in the Confederate army, serving with forces operating in Arkansas and the West. Some of the greatest preaching of his career is said to have been his sermons to soldiers in the camps. Hundreds were converted as a result of his appeals. He was also successful in organizing religious activities among the men. Following his term as chaplain he was transferred to Texas and stationed at Marshall. Though he was not a delegate, and not even present until after his election, the General Conference of 1866 chose him as one of the bishops of the Methodist Episcopal Church, South. "He was too rudely dressed to enter the church where he was to be received as bishop-elect, so several ministers . . . insisted on presenting to him a clerical suit becoming the occasion. He was the first man of his church who had been elected to the episcopacy with a full suit of beard" (*Frank Leslie's Sunday Magazine,* April 1878, p. 506).

Two achievements mark his eleven years in the episcopacy: upon his own responsibility he secured a sum of $5,000 for want of which, apparently, the whole work of the Methodists in the Indian Territory would have failed; and during the year preceding his death, he undertook a visitation to the East, during which he made a careful survey of all the foreign mission work carried on by the denomination, presenting the result of his observation in a series of articles in the church papers. He was author of *Errors of the Papacy* (1860); *The Work of Christ* (1867); *Life of William Goff Caples* (1870); *Sermons* (1876); *The Doctrinal Integrity of Methodism* (1878); *To the East by Way of the West* (1878). In 1845 he was married to Harriet Brotherton Clark, who with five children survived him.

[G. F. and W. T. R. Marvin, *Descendants of Reinold and Matthew Marvin* (1904); T. M. Finney, *Life and Labors of Enoch Mather Marvin* (1880); D. R. McAnally, *The Life and Labors of Rev. E. M. Marvin* (1878); *The Centennial Vol. of Mo. Methodism* (1907); *Cyc. of Methodism* (1882), ed. by Matthew Simpson; *Meth. Rev.* (Nashville), Nov.–Dec. 1895; *St. Louis Globe-Democrat,* Nov. 28, 1877; *To the East by Way of the West,* Appendix.]
R. W. G.

MARWEDEL, EMMA JACOBINA CHRISTIANA (Feb. 27, 1818–Nov. 17, 1893), apostle of Froebelianism and the kindergarten movement in Germany and the United States, particularly on the Pacific Coast, was born in Münden, near Göttingen, Germany. Little is known of her education; whether or not she was a pupil of Froebel, of his widow, or whether her training as a kindergartner was entirely self-acquired are still mooted questions. She was one of five children born to Captain Heinrich Ludwig Marwedel and his wife Jacobina Carolina Christiana Maria (Brokmann) Marwedel. The death of her mother placed a large share of the household work and the care of her brothers and sisters upon her shoulders. It may be that this early experience laid the foundation of her life-long interest in the welfare of little children and in the training of mothers. On the death of her father, left without sufficient means, she was obliged to go to work, thus breaking with the traditions of the social class to which by birth she belonged, but at the same time acquiring an interest which continued throughout her life in the welfare and education of working women.

At this time educational facilities for women were meager in Germany and it is certain that what she became was due largely to self-instruction. It was even more difficult for a woman to gain public recognition. Yet in 1864 she was elected to the board of directors of an association for the promotion of public education in Leipzig, and in 1865 she became a member of the first German association for the advancement of women. In 1867–68 she was directress of the Girls' Industrial School in Hamburg during the first year of its existence. At the same time she conducted a kindergarten of which Elizabeth Palmer Peabody wrote, "It was Miss Marwedel who, in 1867, first introduced me to Froebel's genuine Kindergarten in the city of Hamburg, and inspired me with the courage to make the main object of the remainder of my life to extend the Kindergarten over my own country" (Marwedel, *The Missing Link, the Continuation of the Three-fold Development of the Child from the Kindergarten to the Manual-Labor School,* p. 37). While in Hamburg Emma Marwedel spent over a year visiting female industrial schools in France, Belgium, and England, an account of which she published in 1868 under the title, *Warum bedürfen wir weibliche Gewerbeschulen? und wie sollen sie angelegt sein?* (reviewed by E. P. Peabody, *Harper's New Monthly Magazine,* May 1870). Soon after this, at the earnest request of Miss Peabody, she emigrated to America. Failing to find the opportunity she had expected for kindergarten work, she established in 1870 near Brentwood, Long Island, a women's cooperative industrial training school. Following the speedy failure of this institution, she went to Washington, D. C., where for four years she conducted with great success a school of industrial arts, a German-American kindergarten, and a Froebelian training school.

Under the combined auspices of the Froebel Union of New England, the United States Bureau of Education, and Caroline Seymour Severance [*q.v.*] she moved to Los Angeles in 1876 and established there a kindergarten and the first kindergarten normal class conducted in California. Her normal class, which numbered only three pupils, included Katherine Douglas Smith (Kate Douglas Wiggin), Mary Hoyt, and Nettie Stewart. At the end of two years, dissatisfied because of the lack of interest her work had aroused in Los Angeles, she moved her schools to Oakland in 1878, to Berkeley in 1879, and to San Francisco in 1880. She played an important part in the establishment in 1878 of the Silver Street Kindergarten of San Francisco, and in 1879 organized and became the first president of the California Kindergarten Union. In connection with her Pacific Kindergarten Normal School she conducted a primary department and a model kindergarten. After her retirement from active teaching about 1886 until the close of her life, she devoted herself to writing, lecturing, and the improvement of her system of kindergarten materials. In her latter years she suffered increasing financial difficulties and declining health. She died at the German Hospital (later the Franklin Hospital) in San Francisco and was buried in the Mountain View Cemetery, Oakland, Cal.

Emma Marwedel represents the traditional, sense-training type of Froebelianism. Her life was animated by the belief that through the kindergarten and the extension of Froebelian principles to the home and to the higher levels of education, particularly through the industrial arts, lay the path to the prevention of crime and the regeneration of human society. These ideas she embodied not only in her teaching activities but in numerous writings, most notably in *Conscious Motherhood, or the Earliest Unfolding of the Child in the Cradle, Nursery and Kindergarten* (1887) and in *The Connecting Link, to Continue the Three-Fold Development of the Child from the Cradle to the Manual-Labor School* (1891). The recognition which California early gained as one of the foremost leaders of the kindergarten movement was largely the result of her work. By her educational writings and by addresses delivered throughout the United States she promulgated the ideas not only of Froebel but of Seguin, Preyer, and other educational philosophers and psychologists of her day, and thus became one of the most important leaders in education. Her writings, in addition to those mentioned, include *An Appeal for Justice to Childhood* (n.d.), and *Games and*

Studies in Life Forms and Colors of Nature for Home and School (n.d.).

[The data in the present account concerning Emma Marwedel's birth and parentage have been taken directly from the birth and baptismal register of the church of St. Blasius, Münden. See Earl Barnes, "Emma Marwedel," in *Pioneers of the Kindergarten in America* (1924); "Kindergarten Work in Cal.," *Barnard's Am. Jour. of Educ.*, Sept. 1880; W. S. Monroe, "Emma Marwedel and the Kindergarten," *Education*, Feb. 1894; E. P. Peabody, "Industrial Schools for Women," *Harper's New Monthly Mag.*, May 1870; and F. H. Swift, *Emma Marwedel, Pioneer of the Kindergarten in Cal.* (1931), Univ. of Cal. Pubs. in Educ., vol. VI, no. 2, in which attention is called to inaccuracies in previous accounts. Important papers, filed in the matter of the estate of Emma Marwedel, are in the superior court for Alameda County, Cal.] F. H. S.

MARZO, EDUARDO (Nov. 29, 1852–June 7, 1929), composer, organist, and teacher, was born in Naples, Italy, the son of Carlo Marzo, a journalist and author, and Angiola Bertolè-Viale. After studying in his native city with Guglielmo Nacciarone and Giorgio Miceli he came to New York in 1867 as a boy pianist but soon returned to Italy to complete his studies in composition with Salvator Pappalardo. In 1869 he came to the United States to stay. For several years he toured the country as a musical director of opera troupes and concert companies and was the accompanist of many of the great solo artists then appearing in America, among them Carlotta Patti, Giuseppe Mario, Tom Karle, Giorgio Ronconi, Ernest de Munck, Gaetano Braga, Louise Carey, Émile Sauret, and Pablo Sarasate. In 1878 he definitely established himself in New York where in 1882 he married Clara L. Philbin, daughter of Eugene A. Philbin. He devoted himself to composition, voice teaching, and his work as a church organist. The constructive value of his work in music was recognized in Italy as well as in the United States, and he was made knight of the Crown of Italy (1884); member of the Royal Academy of St. Cecilia (1892), and knight of the Order of St. Sylvester (1914)—an honor conferred by Pope Benedict XV.

Marzo's secular compositions include songs, duets, operettas, piano pieces, some fugues for stringed quartet, and orchestral preludes. His sacred music, which is considerably more important, includes fifteen masses, four vespers, and over forty songs for Catholic services, as well as anthems and songs for the Protestant church. He also compiled various collections: *Songs of Italy* (1904); *Neapolitan Songs* (1905); *Dance Songs of the Nations* (1908); *Fifty Christmas Carols of all Nations* (1923); *Children's Carols* (1925); and *Sixty Carols of all Nations* (1928); and arranged a series of voice studies in *The Art of Vocalization* (18 vols., 1906), and *Preparatory Course to the Art of Vocalization* (1908). His *Collected Works* were published in twenty volumes (1870–1917).

Marzo filled a number of organ positions in New York, at the churches of St. Agnes, All Saints', St. Vincent Ferrer, and Church of the Holy Name. At the time of his death he was the organist of the Church of the Holy Spirit in the Bronx. He was one of the founders of the American Guild of Organists. During his long and successful career as a voice teacher he numbered among his pupils members of well-known New York families. In various articles contributed to musical magazines he gave interesting pictures of musical life in New York in the seventies and eighties of the nineteenth century. On Nov. 7, 1917, a number of the composer's friends tendered him a banquet at the Waldorf-Astoria Hotel in commemoration of his completion of fifty years of musical activity in the United States.

[Marzo's "Memoirs" and a "Sketch of Eduardo Marzo" by Otto Kinkeldey are in the N. Y. Pub. Lib. For printed sources see: *Musical America*, Dec. 15, 1917, July 13, 1918; *Who's Who in America*, 1928–29; *Il Carroccio* (N. Y.), Nov. 1917; the *Cath. Choirmaster*, July–Aug.–Sept. 1929; the *Am. Organist*, July 1929; *N. Y. Herald Tribune* and *N. Y. Times*, June 8, 1929.] F. H. M.

MASCHKE, HEINRICH (Oct. 24, 1853–Mar. 1, 1908), mathematician, was born in Breslau, Germany, where his father was owner of the Raths-Apotheke and had a position of considerable importance in the medical profession. As a student Heinrich showed marked ability in the Gymnasium of that city, and in 1872 he entered the University of Heidelberg, where he came under the influence of Königsberger. After serving his required term of one year in the army, he went to Berlin and here studied under Weierstrass, Kummer, and Kronecker. Proceeding to Göttingen, he received his doctor's degree there in 1880. After teaching for a few years in the Luisenstädtische Gymnasium in Berlin, he returned to Göttingen for a year's work (1886–87) under the direction of Prof. Felix Klein. He then resumed his position in Berlin, also taking up the study of electrotechnics at the Polytechnicum in Charlottenburg. In 1890, however, he resigned his position in the Gymnasium in order to do practical work in the Berliner Allgemeine Electricitätsgesellschaft. The following year he completed his technical training in the Polytechnicum at Darmstadt, under Professor Kittler.

Feeling at this time that there were greater opportunities for him in America, he came to the United States in the spring of 1891, did some work for a year with the Western Electrical Instrument Company, Newark, N. J., and in 1892 was called to the University of Chicago as assistant professor of mathematics. He devoted the remainder of his life to the training of mathematicians and to assisting in building up and maintaining a strong department in that university. He was a teacher of great ability and his courses were made more valuable by his all-round culture, by his originality of thought, and by his personal interest in the large numbers of young mathematicians who attended his lectures. Among those of foreign birth who have contributed notably to the advance of mathematics in the United States, he holds high rank.

Maschke's original work in pure mathematics may be said to have begun with his memoir *Ueber die quaternäre endliche, lineare Substitutionsgruppe der Borchardtschen Moduln* (1887), developed under the inspiration of Klein's courses in Göttingen. This carried him extensively into the theory of finite groups of linear substitutions, a subject already attracting attention in this country through the translation of Eugene Netto's work on the theory of substitutions by Frank Nelson Cole [*q.v.*] and the latter's work at Ann Arbor and Columbia. His second line of major activity lay in the theory of quadratic differential quantics and led to the development of a symbolic method for the treatment of differential quantics, a study which occupied his attention during his later years. His wife, Theresa, survived him; they had no children.

[Oskar Bolza, "Heinrich Maschke: His Life and Work," in *Bull. Am. Mathematical Soc.*, Nov. 1908; *The Univ. Record* (Chicago), Apr. 1908; *Chicago Tribune*, Mar. 2, 1908.] D. E. S.

MASON, CHARLES (Oct. 24, 1804–Feb. 25, 1882), jurist, was born in Pompey, Onondaga County, N. Y., the son of Chauncey and Esther (Dodge) Mason. He entered the United States Military Academy at West Point in 1825 and was graduated in 1829 at the head of his class, with Joseph E. Johnston and Robert E. Lee as classmates. For the next two years he was assistant professor of engineering at West Point. His interest in law, already manifest at West Point, led him to devote his whole time to its study. He read law in New York City, was admitted to the bar in June 1832, and began practice at Newburgh, N. Y. Within two years he returned to New York City, where he contributed to the *Evening Post* and during the temporary absence of its regular editor, William Cullen Bryant, served for a short period as acting editor. In 1836 he went West on a tour of observation and, in April 1837, was appointed by Gov. Henry Dodge as an aide and as public prosecutor of Des Moines County in Wisconsin Territory. On Aug. 1, he was married to Angelica Gear, of Berkshire, Mass., the aunt of John Henry Gear [*q.v.*], and in November he established himself in Burlington.

When the new Territory of Iowa was organized in 1838, he was appointed chief justice of the supreme court. He was twice reappointed to this position and retained his seat for several months after the organization of the state of Iowa in December 1846. Among his notable decisions was the one relating to the legal status of the negro, Ralph (1 *Iowa Reports,* 1). His view in this case was that a slave going into a free territory by the consent of his master was thereafter to be treated not as a fugitive and chattel but as a free man—a theory in conflict with a later pronouncement of the Supreme Court of the United States in the case of Dred Scott. In 1847 he was attorney for Iowa in the Iowa-Missouri dispute that was submitted to the Supreme Court of the United States and decided in favor of Iowa (*Annals of Iowa,* Oct. 1866–Jan. 1867). As a member of the commission to draft the first code of the state, *The Code of Iowa . . . 1851* (1851), he exercised a marked influence on the laws of the state and subsequently on the codes of other states. In the interval between his work on the Iowa code commission and his election, in 1851, to the position of county judge of Des Moines County, he was in law partnership with Samuel R. Curtis and John W. Rankin at Keokuk. Appointed federal commissioner of patents in 1853, he laid down certain precedents that are followed by the agriculture department to the present time. He resigned this office in 1857 and became a member of the first Iowa state board of education. Two years thereafter he was legal adviser to Munn & Company in their patent agency, effecting, among other things, the extension of the Morse telegraph patent in the face of vigorous opposition.

Later he went to Washington, D. C., where he engaged in the practice of patent law. He was active in efforts to provide for the city of Washington a more efficient system of drainage and was able to draw upon his own knowledge of engineering for the plans. He declined the Democratic nomination for the governorship of Iowa in 1861, was defeated in 1863 for a position on the supreme court of Iowa, and in 1867 was defeated for the governorship. In 1864 he was chairman of the national central committee of his party and was a delegate to the nominating conventions of 1868 and 1872. He wrote various pamphlets on financial subjects, drainage, and sanitation. Among these were: *Articles on the Currency* (1858), *A Plan for Specie Resumption* (1874), and *What Shall Be Done with the Surplus Funds of the Patent Office?* (1870). The last years of his life were spent partly in Washington and partly in Iowa, where he continued his connections with the financial and industrial interests of the community. One of his three daughters, the wife of George Collier Remey [*q.v.*], survived him.

[Diaries in the possession of the historical department of Iowa; information from his grandson, Charles Mason Remey, Washington, D. C.; letter from Mason in E. H. Stiles, *Recollections and Sketches of Notable Lawyers* (1916); *Iowa Hist. Record,* Oct. 1893; *Annals of Iowa,* July–Oct. 1864, July–Oct. 1895, Oct. 1896, Jan. 1901, Jan. 1902, Apr., Oct. 1926, Apr. 1929; J. C. Parish, *Robert Lucas* (1907); Walter Geer, *The Geer Geneal.* (1923); *Iowa Jour. of Hist. and Politics,* Jan. 1914.] B. F. S.

MASON, CLAIBOURNE RICE (Nov. 28, 1800–Jan. 12, 1885), builder of bridges and railroads, the son of Rev. Peter Mason, a Baptist minister, was born in Chesterfield County, Va. (Waddell, *post*), but spent at least part of his early boyhood in Richmond. His ancestors had removed on account of religious persecution from the south of England to Holland and from there came to America. His mother, Elizabeth, died when the lad was very young, and at the age of eight he ran away from home and made his living for a time doing chores on a farm in Pennsylvania. Later he carried mail in Maryland, and at the age of sixteen or seventeen worked in Washington as apprentice to a ship's carpenter. In 1829 he began his career as a contractor in connection with the construction of the Midlothian Railway of Virginia, one of the earliest in the country. In 1836 he began the Louisa Railroad, the oldest part of the line that later became the Chesapeake & Ohio, and for a time he acted as its superintendent. An interesting feature in the operation of this railroad was the stable car containing four horses which were used for the purpose of helping the engine pull the train up hill. He was also a contractor, perhaps the largest, on the Virginia Central Railroad.

At the outbreak of the Civil War, though he was past sixty years of age, he raised a company of Confederate volunteers, mainly at his own expense, and was chosen captain. He saw his chief service under "Stonewall" Jackson, and in the army came to be known as "Jackson's bridge builder." Jackson's brilliant successes were unquestionably due in part to the short cuts made possible by Mason's resourcefulness. Not an engineer by training, he possessed many of the attributes of the engineer. He had an uncanny mathematical ability, and it was said of him that he could look at a hill and declare immediately how many cubic yards of material it contained. His special talent lay in his ability to plan and execute jointly. A story is told that once when Jackson needed a bridge quickly in order to cross the Shenandoah River he instructed his engineers to prepare plans for Mason, but before the plans were finished the bridge was built.

After the war Mason returned to railroad contracting. In 1872, when the Chesapeake & Ohio Railway completed its line from Richmond to Huntington, he drove the last spike at Hawks' Nest, thirty-six years after he had turned the first shovelful of earth for the old Louisa Railroad at Doswell. Among his notable achievements on the Chesapeake & Ohio were the construction of Jerry's Run Fill, 575 feet high, and the Lewis Tunnel. He had contracts also on the Valley Railroad of Virginia, the Baltimore & Ohio, the Cincinnati Southern, the Kentucky Central, the Richmond, Fredericksburg & Potomac, the Richmond & Allegheny, the Richmond & Mecklenburg, the Kentucky Union, and the Virginia & North Carolina Extension. The last large contract executed under his personal supervision was for the Southern Pennsylvania Railroad.

Mason was a man of mild deportment, good physique, and tireless energy. Believing in the policy of a protective livelihood other than contracting, some time before the Civil War he bought a farm at Swope's Station, Augusta County, Va., which was his home thereafter until his death. Here he cared for his horses and mules during off seasons and stored his surplus contracting equipment. On Mar. 13, 1838, he married Drucilla W. Boxley, who bore him eleven children, three of whom died young. Through the Mason Syndicate and the Mason & Hanger Company, Inc., of New York, of which he is considered the founder, two of his sons and their sons and grandsons were carrying on construction activity a hundred years after Mason took his first contract. He died at his home in 1885.

[Dixon Merritt, *Sons of Martha* (1928); a history of the Mason & Hanger Company; *War of the Rebellion: Official Records (Army),* 1 ser. V, XII, XXXVII, LI, 2 ser. 1; J. A. Waddell, *Annals of Augusta County, Va.* (1902); J. P. Nelson, *The Chesapeake and Ohio Railway* (1927); *Richmond Dispatch,* Jan. 13, 1885; information as to certain facts from the Mason & Hanger Company, Inc.] W. T. L.

MASON, FRANCIS (Apr. 2, 1799–Mar. 3, 1874), Baptist missionary, was born in York, England. His father, Thomas Mason, was a cobbler by trade, a radical in politics, and a lay preacher of a local Baptist society; his mother's maiden name was Hay. The son acquired a rudimentary education at the parish school (for the children of workers) and served as errand-boy in a shoe-factory. Too poor to pay the apprentice's fee in the factory, he finally went to work with his father. Because of a strike in York, the family moved to Hull, where the boy became interested in geography and mathematics, and studied Euclid in a night school conducted by a retired naval officer. From Hull the family moved to Leeds, the mother's native city.

In 1818 at the age of nineteen, Francis emigrated to the United States, his passage money being provided by a maternal uncle already in America. He landed in Philadelphia and worked his way as a journeyman shoe-maker to Pittsburgh, thence went by boat down the Ohio and the Mississippi rivers to Cincinnati, St. Louis, and New Orleans, and finally by sea to Boston, where he arrived in 1824. Soon thereafter he settled at Randolph, Mass., boarding at the home of the Baptist minister, Rev. Benjamin Putnam, working at his trade, and teaching school. In 1825 he married Lucinda Gill (died 1828), daughter of a farmer living in Canton, Mass., to which place Mason now removed and opened a shoe shop of his own. Influenced by his wife and by the reading of Butler's *Analogy,* he professed conversion and joined the Canton Baptist Church. By this church, on Oct. 1, 1827, he was licensed to preach, and in the following November he entered Newton Theological Institution to prepare for the ministry. He had previously begun privately the study of Hebrew and Greek, and had read widely in literature, science, and theology. During his senior year at Newton, Dec. 7, 1829, he received appointment from the Baptist missionary society to service in Burma. On May 23, 1830, he was ordained to the ministry, and on the same day was married to Helen Maria Griggs (died 1846). Three days afterward he and his bride sailed from Boston for Calcutta, arriving in October, and passing on to Maulmain in the following month. Stationed in Tavoy for work among the Karens, he began his duties in January 1831, and spent in all twenty-two years there. He was superintendent of the station several years; conducted a training school for mission workers, which was later moved to Maulmain and finally to Rangoon; engaged in extensive evangelism; and made translations, especially of the Christian Scriptures, into the Sgau and Pgho Karen dialects. He published at Tavoy in 1837 a Karen version of the Gospel of Matthew—on a press established that year, which was removed to Rangoon in 1853. In 1843 his Sgau Karen New Testament appeared and also, in English, *The Karen Apostle, or Memoir of Ko Thah-byu,* edited by H. J. Ripley. These were followed by *Synopsis of a Grammar of the Karen Language* (1846), *The Natural Productions of Burmah, or Notes on the Fauna, Flora, and Minerals of the Tenasserim Provinces of the Burman Empire* (1850), a memoir of his second wife, Helen Griggs, entitled *A Cenotaph to a Woman of the Burman Mission* (1851), and his Karen Bible issued in 1853.

In 1847 he was married to Mrs. Ellen Huntly Bullard, widow of the Rev. E. B. Bullard, formerly of Maulmain. On the completion of the Karen Bible, he turned for a time to evangelism, taking up residence in Toungoo, where he established a new station. His health was failing, however, and in January 1854 he set out for the United States, journeying by way of India, South Africa, Europe, and the British Isles, where he visited his aged mother in Leeds. He sailed again for Burma on July 2, 1856, and reached Toungoo on Jan. 2, 1857. In 1860 he published in Rangoon his valuable *Burmah, its Peoples and Natural Productions.* For this and other researches and literary works he was admitted to membership in the Royal Asiatic Society and the American Oriental Society. There was a time (Apr. 25, 1865, to July 11, 1871) when both Mason and the mission suffered much from the effects of a form of dementia which afflicted his wife and led to the temporary establishment of a cult. She claimed to have found in the Karen women's dresses and in various objects connected with Buddhist worship, the language in which God spoke to Adam, and believed that she had the key by which she could read it. Mason was asked to sever his connection with the mission for a time, and during that period he published a Pali grammar (Toungoo, 1868), and an autobiography, *The Story of a Working Man's Life* (New York, 1870). He was later reinstated and died a member of the mission which he had served so conspicuously. He was buried in Rangoon.

[In addition to Mason's autobiography, see article on "Burmah" in Harvey Newcomb, *Cyc. of Missions* (2nd ed., 1856); *Baptist Missionary Mag.,* June 1874; S. F. Smith, *Missionary Sketches* (6th ed., 1879); William Cathcart, *Baptist Encyc.* (1881); *Encyc. of Missions* (1904).]

J. C. A.

MASON, FRANK STUART (Oct. 21, 1883–Oct. 25, 1929), musician, was a son of Frank Hale and Lucretia Augusta (Chipman) Mason, of Weymouth, Mass. He was of Pilgrim and Puritan lineage. Early disclosing musical talent, Stuart, as he was always called, was sent, after his graduation from the Weymouth schools, to the New England Conservatory of Music in Boston, where he had as his principal instructor J. Albert Jeffery. While still a music student he made many public appearances of local note. Graduated in 1907 at the head of his class, he continued his professional education at Paris where he studied the pianoforte with Isidor Philipp, Raoul Pugno, and André Wormser, and composition with André Gedalge. He began at this time researches in old French music which he pursued throughout his career with scholarly thoroughness and an artist's enthusiasm.

Mason returned to Boston singularly well equipped for professional success. His training had been of the best. He possessed remarkable physical energy and mental buoyancy. No struggle was needed to establish him in a city where he was already well known. A place was at once offered him on the Conservatory faculty, with a full teaching schedule. Because of his reputation and the charm of his personality pupils were eager to attend his classes in pianoforte, harmony, harmonic analysis, canon, fugue, composition, and instrumentation. When Louis C. Elson [*q.v.*] died Mason took over his celebrated course in the history of music and maintained its popularity. While teaching long hours at the Conservatory he multiplied his contacts in the community. His début as a pianist with the Boston Orchestral Club in 1910 was followed by many engagements. In 1919 he was invited by Emil Mollenauer, conductor, to be assistant conductor of the newly organized People's Symphony Orchestra of Boston, of which he himself later became conductor, showing marked ability in arranging unusual programs and in inspiring a band containing both professional and amateur players. As a composer he made a most auspicious start toward eminence with his "Rhapsody on a Persian Air" and the orchestral suite, "Bergerie," both which were produced by several symphony orchestras. His published work also included pianoforte and chamber music compositions and several songs. He continued to give programs of ancient French music at frequent intervals, and accounts of them, sent to his friends in France, led to his being twice decorated by the French government. He was invited in 1923 to be guest conductor of the Boston Symphony Orchestra, an unusual honor for a resident musician.

Mason meantime lectured on the history and appreciation of music throughout the state under the university extension division of the Massachusetts department of education. He gave courses in the summer school of Boston University, ranking as assistant professor. He wrote music criticism for the *Christian Science Monitor,* "always," according to a contemporary, "with admirable clarity, discrimination and avoidance of meaningless eulogy and puff." He was married on Dec. 25, 1925, to Margaret C. Mason, formerly of Clarinda, Iowa, who like himself was a high-honor graduate of the New England Conservatory and a member of its faculty. Mason was often warned by friends that he was doing too much, but his reply was always that of a vigorous and genial man who took his responsibilities seriously, himself not at all so. A breakdown occured in October 1929, from which he appeared to be recovering when he was fatally stricken in his classroom.

[Obituary in the *New Eng. Conservatory of Music Bull.,* Nov. 1929; tribute by Philip Hale, *Boston Sunday Herald,* Nov. 3, 1929; notes on Mason as conductor of the People's Symphony Orchestra, *Musical Courier,* Dec. 4, 1924; biographical sketch in the program notes in *Boston Symphony Orchestra: Forty-Third Season: Ninth Programme,* Dec. 21, 22, 1923.] F. W. C.

MASON, GEORGE (*c.* 1629–*c.* 1686), colonist, progenitor of the fourth George Mason [*q.v.*], author of the Virginia Declaration of Rights, was traditionally one of the cavalier emigrants to Virginia during the rule of Cromwell. The first known mention of him in the colonial records is in a patent of March 1655 for land in Westmoreland County, headrights for eighteen persons brought into Virginia. In 1664 and again in 1669 he secured large tracts of adjacent lands on Potomac Creek at the mouth of Accoceek, where he had his dwelling. In a deposition dated Aug. 20, 1658, he declared his age to be twenty-nine, thus establishing approximately the date of his birth. From another record of Westmoreland (1655) his wife is known to have been named Mary. His son, George, was active in Stafford County affairs. A will of the date of 1686, known to have been on file in Stafford before 1840, is assumed to be that of the first George Mason, and it is therefore inferred that his death occurred in that year.

In 1667 Mason was active on the Northern Neck committee charged with the defense and local government of that region, and a member of the committee representing the counties of Westmoreland, Northumberland, and Stafford to carry out an act of the Assembly providing for the erection of a fort on Yeocomico River. He was sheriff of Stafford County in 1669, clerk of the court in 1673, and was sent as a burgess to the Assembly of 1676, which passed the measures known as "Bacon's Laws," democratic in tone and designed to correct certain abuses of the administration. He held the office of county lieutenant, and, doughty and daring, he and his aggressive neighbors often took the law in their own hands in defense of northern Virginia against the Indians. In 1661–62, with Col. Gerard Fowke, Capt. Giles Brent, and John Lord, he was subjected to disciplinary measures imposed by the Assembly for what it considered unjust treatment of Wahanganoche, king of the Potomac Indians. Mason was ordered to pay damages to the Indian king and to the public treasury for contempt of the Governor's warrant and was suspended from all civil and military power until he could clear himself of Wahanganoche's charges. He and his recalcitrant neighbors, however, formed the governing group in northern Virginia, and they were returned to official favor.

It is as an Indian fighter and precipitator of events culminating in Bacon's Rebellion that Mason is chiefly remembered. When, in 1675, a band of Doegs made raids in his community and finally killed a neighbor, Mason and Col. Giles Brent gathered about thirty men and pursued the murderers into Maryland. There Brent attacked the Doegs, who had taken refuge in a cabin among the Susquehannocks, and Mason with his men pursued the Indians who fled from a neighboring cabin. When he discovered the Indians were the friendly Susquehannocks, Mason cried out, "for the Lords sake shoot no more, these are our friends the Susquehanoughs." Unwittingly, however, he had set loose a chain of circumstances that provoked the Susquehannocks to take the war path and resulted in Bacon's Rebellion. Mason agreed to fight under Bacon's command against the Indians, but he had no sympathy with the young radical's democratic program. When, therefore, it was clear that Bacon's leadership meant opposition to the established government, Mason took no part in the campaigns. It is significant that the troops from Stafford were loyal to Berkeley and helped to put down the young rebel's forces. With his neighbors of position and power, among them Col. William Ball and Col. John Washington, Mason served in 1677 on the committee ordered by the Assembly to lay a levy in the Northern Neck for the costs of suppressing "ye late rebellion." In his later years he continued to be a successful landholder and official, carving out an inheritance for his heirs and giving dignity to the family name.

[Peter Force, *Tracts and Other Papers, Relating Principally to the Origin, Settlement, and Progress of the Colonies in North America,* vol. I (1836); W. W. Hening, *The Statutes at Large; Being a Collection of All the Laws of Virginia,* vol. II (1823); H. R. McIlwaine, *Executive Jours. of the Council of Colonial Va.,* vol. I (1925); H. R. McIlwaine, *Jours. of the House of Burgesses of Va., 1659/60 . . . 1693* (1914), p. 14 (suspension), and *passim*; *Va. Mag. of Hist. and Biog.,* July 1893, Oct. 1896, Jan. 1898, Oct. 1904, Oct. 1909, Jan. 1915; *William and Mary College Quart. Hist. Papers,* July 1893; *William and Mary College Quart. Hist. Mag.,* July 1895, Apr. 1901, Jan. 1905; Kate Mason Rowland, *The Life of George Mason 1725–1792* (2 vols., 1892); Fairfax Harrison, *Landmarks of Old Prince William* (2 vols., 1924); T. J. Wertenbaker, *Va. under the Stuarts, 1607–1688* (1914); E. D. Neill, *Va. Carolorum* (1886).] M. H. W.

MASON, GEORGE (1725–Oct. 7, 1792), planter, Revolutionary statesman, constitutionalist, was the fourth of his name and line in Virginia. The first American George Mason [*q.v.*], who probably emigrated from England soon after the battle of Worcester, settled in the Northern Neck on 900 acres near Pasbytanzy; he and his descendants added to this original grant so that when the fourth George Mason came of age and settled at Dogue's Neck, on the Potomac below Alexandria, he controlled some 5,000 acres in the region. Because of the death of his father, the third George Mason, when he was ten, the boy grew up under the guardianship of his mother, Ann (Thomson) Mason, and his uncle by marriage, John Mercer of "Marlborough," an exceptionally able lawyer. Mrs. Mason's account books show payments to private tutors during the years 1736–39, but Mason found his education in Mercer's library. It numbered upwards of 1,500 volumes, a third of them on law, and at the time of his guardianship Mercer was at work among them. This association accounts for the fact that while Mason was never licensed as an attorney he was called in as a notably competent counsel on questions of public law throughout his later life. On Apr. 4, 1750, he married Anne Eilbeck of "Mattawoman," Charles County, Md.; soon afterward, their portraits were painted by John Hesselius. In 1758 their new home, "Gunston Hall," begun in 1755, was completed; its architect was William Buckland, a skilled craftsman from Oxford whom Mason's younger brother Thomson brought back with him under indenture in 1754. In the course of the twenty years after their marriage, five sons and four daughters were born.

Mason persisted in regarding himself as a private gentleman, even during his most intensive periods of public service. Without the aid of a steward, he personally managed his large and practically self-sufficient plantation. He served as trustee of the recently founded town of Alexandria from 1754 until its incorporation in 1779; Alexandria was also the seat of Fairfax County, and he was one of the gentlemen justices of the county court from his early manhood until his resignation in 1789. Parallel to the jurisdiction of the county ran that of the parish, which under the Establishment was vested with governmental duties in respect of the moral and charitable obligations of the community; Mason was a vestryman of Truro Parish from 1748 until 1785, serving as one of the overseers of the poor after relief became a lay function. As the executor of Daniel French, the original contractor, he supervised the building of Pohick Church, some of whose details repeat the carvings at "Gunston." This triple experience in local government formed an important part of his political apprenticeship.

Complementary to Mason's familiarity with the tidewater section of the colony was his association with the problems of the West. He became a member of the Ohio Company in 1752, and served as its treasurer until 1773. His initial interest in it was merely as a speculation, but as the company changed from a private economic venture into the lever which upset the political balance, first between French and British forces in the New World, and then, after the Peace of Paris, between Crown and Colony across the Alleghanies, the constitutional aspect of Virginia's claims to the Northwest Territory engaged his attention; when the Crown, in 1773, abrogated the Ohio Company's rights and regranted the area they covered to the Grand Company organized by a group of Pennsylvanians, Mason produced his first major state paper, *Extracts from the Virginia Charters, with Some Remarks upon Them* (1773, reprinted in Rowland, I, 393–414).

Prior to midsummer, 1775, Mason's part in the Revolution was in the wings of the public stage. Various reasons have been adduced for his reluctance to accept office; on the one hand his chronic ill-health, on the other the death of his wife early in 1773, leaving him, as he wrote in 1775, with a sense of "the duty I owe to a poor little helpless family of orphans to whom I must now act the part of Father and Mother both" (*Ibid.,* I, 198). It is true that after his marriage, on Apr. 11, 1780, to Sarah Brent he accepted a seat in the Federal Convention in Philadelphia (1787), but by far the most probable cause of his persistent refusals to serve was the low rating which he put upon human nature in committee. In 1759 he and Washington had served together in the House of Burgesses; at the end of his first term he withdrew with an opinion of that body which did not change when he went to take the place of the newly-elected Commander-in-chief in the July convention of 1775. Writing Washington on Oct. 14, 1775, in regard to the session he said: "I never was in so disagreeable a situation and almost despaired of a cause which I saw so ill conducted. . . . Mere vexation and disgust threw me into such an ill state of health, that before the Convention rose, I was sometimes near fainting in the House. . . . However, after some weeks the babblers were pretty well silenced, a few weighty members began to take the lead, several wholesome regulations were made" (*Ibid.,* I, 210–11). Off-stage, however, Mason had played a highly important part ever since 1765, when, at the instance of Washington and G. W. Fairfax, he contrived a method of replevying goods under distress for rent without the use of stamped paper. His open letter of June 6, 1766, to a committee of London merchants (*Ibid.,* I, 381–89) tersely summarized the mood of the colonists in its balanced profession of loyalty and independence: they were ready wholeheartedly to welcome the repeal of the Stamp Act as an act of justice; that repeal was a favor they would never admit. When the Townshend duties revived the trade dispute, Mason prepared the resolutions which Washington presented to the dissolved House of Burgesses and which, adopted by them as a non-importation association, were passed on for subsequent approval by the Continental Congress. After the Boston Port Act brought matters to a head, he wrote the Fairfax Resolves of July 18, 1774 (*Ibid.,* I, 418–27), stating a version of the constitutional position of the colonies *vis-à-vis* the Crown which was successively accepted by the county court in Fairfax, the Virginia convention in Williamsburg, and the Continental Congress in Philadelphia; some weeks later his plan for the organization of troops led to the creation of the Fairfax Independent Company of volunteers.

During the period in which he was writing these important papers, Mason was exerting a parallel influence on the consolidation of public opinion by word of mouth. Philip Mazzei, in his memoirs, and Edmund Randolph, in his manuscript history of Virginia, both emphasize this aspect of his effectiveness. Randolph said: "Among the numbers who in their small circles were propagating with activity the American doctrines, was George Mason in the shade of retirement. He extended their grasp upon the opinions and affections of those with whom he conversed. . . . He was behind none of the sons of Virginia in knowledge of her history and interest. At a glance he saw to the bottom of every proposition which affected her" (Quoted, *Ibid.,* I, 178). Washington's diary bears witness to the frequency of his collaboration with Mason in the years before his departure to lead the army, and the letters of the three younger colleagues who succeeded him as the Virginia dynasty all testify specifically to the influence upon them of conversations at "Gunston Hall."

In 1775 Mason emerged from retirement as a member of the July convention, and served on the committee of safety which took over the executive powers vacated by the flight of Governor Dunmore. In 1776, as a member of the May convention, he achieved his outstanding contribution as a constitutionalist by framing the Declaration of Rights (reprint of original draft, *Ibid.*, I, 433–36) and the major part of the constitution of Virginia. The former was drawn upon by Jefferson in the first part of the Declaration of Independence, was widely copied in the other colonies, became the basis for the first ten amendments to the Constitution of the United States, and had a considerable influence in France at the time of the French Revolution. The latter was notable as a pioneer, written "constitution," prepared with a view to permanence, and used by a commonwealth over a period of years. The years 1776–80 were occupied in implementing the various provisions of the two documents, with Mason in the forefront of legislative activity, closely collaborating with such men as Jefferson, Henry, and Wythe. He was a member of the committee of five entrusted with the revision of the laws, and while he resigned after the general plan had been agreed on, he continued to contribute his share of the new drafts, particularly those relating to the western lands. He was among the liberal churchmen who effected disestablishment. He was active in the organization of military affairs, particularly in the West. Mason's connection with the Northwest Territory is worthy of special note. His relation to George Rogers Clark was as close as that of father to son; he was one of Governor Henry's secret committee that authorized Clark's conquest, and it was to him that Clark sent his full account of the campaign. Since it was his *Extracts from the Virginia Charters* that had convinced Virginians of the western extent of their sovereignty, he was in some measure responsible for the fixing of the British-American boundary, in the treaty of 1783, at the Great Lakes rather than the Ohio, and it was he who sketched the plan out of which grew the cession by Virginia of her western lands to the United States, and Jefferson's ordinance for their government (Letter to Joseph Jones, July 27, 1780, Rowland, I, 360–67).

During the early eighties Mason was among those whom disgust at the conduct of public affairs drove into retirement; not until 1786 could he be again prevailed upon to go to the Assembly. His return to active life was motivated by his desire to prevent Virginia from indulging in a further orgy of inflation, and his growing conviction, in spite of his lifelong attachment to doctrine of state rights, that the Articles of Confederation were an inadequate basis for the central government. He was an active member of the Virginia delegation at the Mount Vernon meeting of 1785; he was appointed to but did not attend the Annapolis meeting of 1786 which grew out of it; in the debates at Philadelphia he was one of the five most frequent speakers. An examination of Madison's notes on the Federal Convention shows the extent of the constructive influence which Mason exerted on the Constitution. His decision not to sign the document was made during the last two weeks; until the final days of the convention he struggled for the inclusion of certain clauses and the exclusion of others which he regarded as respectively essential and iniquitous. In several instances his "Objections to the Federal Constitution" (reprinted in P. L. Ford, *Pamphlets on the Constitution,* 1888), on the basis of which he conducted his campaign against ratification in the Virginia convention of 1788, though negative in their immediate application, proved in the long run to have been well-founded. In two cases, his justification is written into the Constitution. His insistence on the necessity of a Bill of Rights bore fruit in the first ten amendments. The eleventh amendment, in 1798, testified to the correctness of his strictures on one part of the judiciary article, when his prophecy that suits would be brought against states was ridiculed by a young lawyer named John Marshall. In a third case his justification is written into general American history. Mason's outstanding reason for refusing to sign the Constitution was that it incorporated the compromise between the New England states and those of the extreme South on the tariff and the slave trade. His opposition to the institution of slavery was perhaps the most consistent feature of his public career. His first political paper opens with a paragraph on the advantage of settling land with free as contrasted with slave labor; his final speeches in the Richmond convention reiterate his opinion that "such a trade [in slaves] is diabolical in itself and disgraceful to mankind."

Mason's constructive proposals for the situation in which a century and a half of slave-owning had left his community, proposals which run curiously parallel to the solution of the problem effected by the British Parliament in 1833, can be taken as illustrative of his general philosophical attitude. More than perhaps any other

American statesman of the period, he represented the rationalist spirit, the Enlightenment in its American manifestation. He believed in the existence of a rule of right reason, and in the possibility of giving it concretion in terms of the problem at hand. He believed life, liberty, and the use of property to be central human rights. Applying those criteria to slavery, he favored manumission, so that one man's life should not be at the mercy of another, preceded by education, so that liberty might be given a positive content; at the same time he desired recognition of the property rights of the owner, so that the termination of an undesirable economy might take place without the confiscation of a large part of the community's capital. His conclusions were thorough, impersonal, convinced. They may stand as indicative of the mental fiber of Mason the gentleman, the representative of the Enlightenment, and the statesman.

[MS. materials include the George Mason Papers and other collections, and the Truro Parish Book in the Lib. of Cong.; Mason letters in the Emmet Collection, N. Y. Pub. Lib.; Minute Book of the Alexandria Trustees, City Hall, Alexandria, Va.; Fairfax court records, Courthouse, Fairfax, Va. K. M. Rowland, *The Life of George Mason, 1725–1792* (2 vols., 1892), reprints valuable correspondence, writings, and speeches. See also H. B. Grigsby, *The Va. Convention of 1776* (1855), and *The Hist. of the Va. Federal Convention of 1788* (2 vols., 1890–91); James Madison, reporter, *The Debates in the Federal Convention of 1787* (1920), ed. by Gaillard Hunt and J. B. Scott; H. R. Connor, *Gunston Hall, Fairfax County, Va.* (1930), the Monograph Series, No. 3, vol. XVI; R. W. Moore, "George Mason, the Statesman," *William and Mary Coll. Quart.*, Jan. 1933. Other items in Virginia publications may be located through the checklist prepared by E. G. Swem. A biography by Helen Hill is in manuscript.]
H. H.

MASON, HENRY (Oct. 10, 1831–May 15, 1890), piano manufacturer, fourth son of Lowell Mason [*q.v.*] and Abigail (Gregory) Mason, was born in Brookline, Mass., and educated in the Boston public schools. Like his brother William [*q.v.*] he completed his education abroad, studying at the universities of Göttingen, Paris, and Prague. On his return to America he entered the music store of Sylvanus B. Pond in New York and at the same time served as a church organist. In 1854 he left New York for Boston and with Emmons Hamlin [*q.v.*], founded the Mason & Hamlin Organ Company, though he continued for a time as a church organist in Cambridge and was active as a music critic for various Boston newspapers. Mason's partner, who had an inventive mind, was very successful in improving the reed quality and tone-color of their instruments. In 1855 the firm brought out an Organ-Harmonium, an improvement on the existing reed-organ. It was provided with double bellows, making possible a greater volume of sound and the production of a continuous tone. With further improvements the instrument became the American Cabinet Organ, introduced in 1861, and under that name it became widely known. In 1882 the firm branched from organ construction to piano manufacturing, reorganizing as the Mason & Hamlin Organ and Piano Company. Insisting upon the maintenance of high standards of workmanship, the firm produced a piano of excellent quality. In the illustrious musical family of which he was a member, Henry Mason represented the creator of musical values in the mechanical and commercial fields, as his brother William did in those of concert pianism and pedagogy. He died in his home in Boston at the age of fifty-nine. In 1857 he had married Helen Augusta Palmer. One of his sons, Henry Lowell Mason, became the head of the firm of Mason & Hamlin in 1906.

[H. L. Mason, *The Hist. and Development of the Am. Cabinet Organ* (n.d.), reprinted from *Presto*, June 4, 1903; Alfred Dolge, *Pianos and Their Makers* (2 vols., 1911–13); the *Folio*, June 1890; Boston *Evening Transcript*, May 15, 1890.]
F. H. M.

MASON, JAMES MURRAY (Nov. 3, 1798–Apr. 28, 1871), representative, senator, Confederate diplomatic commissioner to Europe, was born in Georgetown, D. C. A grandson of George Mason [*q.v.*] of Revolutionary fame, and the son of Gen. John Mason and Anna Maria Murray, he had five brothers and four sisters all of whom lived to manhood. His early education was obtained in the schools of Georgetown and the neighborhood, and he graduated from the University of Pennsylvania in 1818 after four years of study. He then studied law at the College of William and Mary. After spending a short time in the office of Benjamin Watkins Leigh of Richmond, he did an unusual thing for a Tidewater aristocrat by moving to the Valley and establishing a practice at Winchester (1820). On July 25, 1822, he was married to Elizabeth Margaretta Chew, daughter of Benjamin Chew, Mason's devoted friend and counselor during his college days in Philadelphia and until Chew's death.

Just on the outskirts of the town of Winchester the young couple bought a modest home which they called "Selma." Here their eight children were reared. Devoted to his family, Mason was destined to spend a great part of his life away from them. Except for the term of 1827–28, he represented his county in the state legislature from 1826 to 1831. In 1829, as a delegate to the Virginia constitutional convention, he proved himself once again unorthodox, from the point of view of the Tidewater, by favoring the white basis of representation, as advocated by the back country. It was good politics for him to champion the interests of his constituents, but there is evidence that he followed convictions of long standing. In 1832 he was an elector on the Jackson-Van Buren ticket, a fact which is rather interesting in view of his later friendship with Calhoun. In 1837 he was elected to Congress and represented his district one term. In 1847 he was sent to the United States Senate to fill the unexpired term of Senator Pennybacker. Reëlected in 1849 and 1855, he was in the Senate when Virginia seceded.

At Washington, Mason was intimately associated with the most prominent Southern-Rights Democrats. Calhoun and R. M. T. Hunter were for years his mess mates during the session of Congress and he fell especially under Calhoun's influence. It is not surprising, therefore, that he drafted the famous fugitive-slave law of 1850 and that it was he who read the speech of John C. Calhoun to the Senate on the proposed compromise measures. When Lincoln was elected, Mason, unlike many border state leaders, believed that compromise was not possible and that the South must withdraw from the Union or be submerged and exploited by the North. To him, as to Calhoun, the "irrepressible conflict" was between two social and economic systems, or civilizations, one of which was agrarian and the other industrial. Slavery while strongly upheld by Mason was only one of the elements of the Southern system.

With his clear stand upon Southern rights, his restrained and conciliatory demeanor, his high social connections, his ten years as chairman of the Senate's foreign relations committee, and his friendship with Davis, Mason was well qualified to go to England as Confederate diplomatic commissioner and a colleague of John Slidell who was dispatched to France in the same capacity. The seizure of Mason and Slidell while on board the *Trent* by Captain Wilkes of the United States navy nearly caused a war between Great Britain and the United States and helped create an atmosphere favorable to the Confederacy. The prisoners were held at Fort Warren, Boston Harbor, until Jan. 1, 1862. Upon arriving in England Mason was received as one born of the manor. He shared the universal conviction of the South that Great Britain would recognize the Confederacy or actually intervene in its behalf in order to obtain cotton. The hostility to a strong American Union and the prospect of practically free trade with the South he thought would likewise be inducements for British intervention. He probably did all that could have been done. He cultivated the friendship of the leading members of the Lords and Commons, of the great merchants and manufacturers, and of the newspaper men. He acted as central agent for the various naval and military purchasing agents of the Confederacy, and cooperated with the Confederate propagandists. He aided in the raising of money and the sale of Confederate bonds and entered into communication, chiefly written, with members of the British government over such matters as recognition, the Federal blockade, and the Confederate iron-clads. But the British government never received him officially and refused with two or three exceptions to hold interviews with him as a private citizen. The government was friendly enough to the Confederacy, but there was a two-year surplus of cotton in the country out of which great profit was realized. Profits in munitions, linen, and woolens, and the great expansion of the merchant marine made Great Britain prosperous as a result of war. As for her desire to see the United States divided, the dread of a war with the possible loss of her merchant marine and her war profits counteracted any inclination to intervene.

In April 1866 Mason repaired to Canada where he remained nearly three years because of his fear of being arrested by the federal government as an important Confederate official. After Johnson's second proclamation of amnesty in 1868 he returned to Virginia, though not to his old home, "Selma," for that had been burned by Sheridan during the war. On Apr. 28, 1871, he died at "Clarens" near Alexandria, Va.

[See Virginia Mason, *The Pub. Life and Diplomatic Correspondence of Jas. M. Mason, with some Personal Hist. by his Daughter* (1903); R. K. Crallé, ed., The *Works of John C. Calhoun* (6 vols., 1854–60); Dunbar Rowland, ed., *Jefferson Davis, Constitutionalist: His Letters, Papers and Speeches* (10 vols., 1923); F. L. Owsley, *King Cotton Diplomacy* (1931); *Evening Star* (Washington), Apr. 29, 1871. The Pickett Papers, Manuscript Division, Lib. of Cong., contain all of Mason's diplomatic correspondence, most of which has been published in *War of the Rebellion: Official Records (Navy)*, 2 ser. III. The Mason Papers, Manuscript Division, Lib. of Cong., contain unofficial papers, for the most part written while Mason was commissioner. His private papers were burned with his house.] F. L. O.

MASON, JEREMIAH (Apr. 27, 1768–Oct. 14, 1848), lawyer, United States senator, was born in Lebanon, Conn., the sixth of nine children of Col. Jeremiah Mason and his wife, Elizabeth (Fitch) Mason, and fifth in direct descent from Maj. John Mason, 1600–1672 [*q.v.*], the famous Indian fighter and conqueror of the Pequots. His father, except for some years in the Revolutionary army, was a farmer, occupying land originally deeded to his family by Uncas, the Mohican chief. The boy, after two years of preparation under Nathan Tisdale, entered Yale College in 1784, graduating with distinction in 1788. A year of legal study with Simeon Baldwin [*q.v.*], in New Haven, was followed by two years in the office of Stephen Row Bradley [*q.v.*], in Westminster, Vt. After several years of practice in small towns in Vermont and New Hampshire, he moved in 1797 to Portsmouth, N. H., then the largest city in the state. In November 1799 he married Mary Means, daughter of Col. Robert Means of Amherst, N. H. Five sons and three daughters were born to them.

Within a brief period, Mason became one of the acknowledged leaders of the New Hampshire bar. It has been said that, from 1805 to 1808, the number of original entries made by him at any court session was larger than that of all the other attorneys in Portsmouth together. With the arrival of Daniel Webster [*q.v.*] in Portsmouth in 1807, Mason had keener competition, and the two men were soon retained on opposite sides in nearly every important case in Rockingham County. Webster, who was inclined to be rhetorical and grandiloquent, learned much from Mason, who was direct, colloquial, and economical of speech. Furthermore, Mason, through his thoroughness and earnestness, compelled Webster to exert himself to the utmost. The latter often testified to his indebtedness to Mason for what he had learned from him in courtroom pleadings, and more than once expressed the opinion that he was the greatest lawyer he had known.

Although Mason, like Rufus Choate [*q.v.*], really preferred law to public life, he was drawn inevitably into political affairs. In 1802 he was appointed attorney-general of New Hampshire, serving acceptably in that capacity till 1805. Elected in 1813 to the United States Senate by the Federalist party, he joined with Webster—who was then in the House of Representatives—in opposing the War of 1812 and criticizing the policies of the administration. A conservative by temperament, he disliked Jefferson's theories of government and found congenial friends in such senatorial colleagues as Rufus King [*q.v.*] and Christopher Gore. He resigned his seat in June 1817, disgusted with the hopeless decline of his party and unwilling to be longer separated from his family. For several terms (1820, 1821, 1824) he sat in the New Hampshire legislature, where he assisted in revising the legal code of that state. In 1824 he was again a candidate for the United States Senate, but was defeated in the legislature. He declined several important positions on the bench, including that of chief justice of the highest court of New Hampshire (1816), choosing instead the more active life of the courts.

Mason was associated with Webster and Jeremiah Smith [*q.v.*] in the earlier stages of the so-called Dartmouth College Case, and his arguments were used freely by Webster before the United States Supreme Court in 1819 (Fuess, *Webster, post,* I, 221–24). During the summer of 1828, he reluctantly accepted the presidency of the Portsmouth Branch of the United States Bank. Some of his policies aroused the antagonism of certain strong adherents of President Andrew Jackson, notably Isaac Hill [*q.v.*], then assistant comptroller of the treasury through a recess appointment, and a movement for Mason's dismissal was initiated; but President Nicholas Biddle [*q.v.*] of the Bank refused to listen to the partisan protests of the Jacksonians and reappointed Mason.

He removed in 1832 to Boston, where he practised actively for six years, accumulating a considerable fortune. He retired at the age of seventy. Mason was of unusual stature, being six feet, six inches in height. His stooped shoulders, awkward manner, and slow movements made him appear sluggish, and his handsome face, except for his piercing and vigilant eyes, was not immediately impressive. In the courtroom, however, he was transformed. His homely phrases and provincial pronunciation, to a large extent deliberately adopted, caught the attention of the jury, and he held them by the clearness and sincerity of his arguments. He had a gift for cross-examination, and was a master of sarcasm. It has been said of him that "no other man ever tried so many cases and lost so few, in proportion to the whole number that he tried" (Hillard, *post,* 1917 ed., p. 368). The testimony of Webster, Choate, and Joseph Story [*q.v.*] bears evidence to the energy and sagacity of his mind and places him among the greatest lawyers of his time. In character he was generous, high-minded, scrupulously honest, and deeply religious. Retaining his intellectual powers almost to the last, he died in his eighty-first year and was buried in Mount Auburn Cemetery. His wife survived him by almost ten years.

[*Memoir, Autobiography and Correspondence of Jeremiah Mason* (1873), ed. by G. S. Hillard, repr. in 1917, with notes and additions by G. J. Clark; J. C. Gray, in W. D. Lewis, *Great Am. Lawyers,* vol. III (1907); C. H. Hill, in *Am. Law Rev.,* Jan. 1878; A. P. Stokes, *Memorials of Eminent Yale Men* (2 vols., 1914); F. B. Dexter, *Biog. Sketches Grads. Yale Coll.,* vol. IV (1907); *Boston Transcript,* Oct. 16, 1848; references to Mason in biographies of Webster and Choate, esp. J. B. McMaster, *Daniel Webster* (1902); C. M. Fuess, *Daniel Webster* (2 vols., 1930); Joseph Neilson, *Memories of Rufus Choate* (1884); C. M. Fuess, *Rufus Choate* (1928).]

C. M. F.

MASON, JOHN (*c.* 1600–Jan. 30, 1672), colonial soldier and magistrate, was born in England and saw service in the Low Countries. Coming to Massachusetts before July 2, 1633, he was soon made captain of militia for Dorchester (*Records of the Governor and Company of the Massachusetts Bay Colony,* vol. I, 1853, pp. 106, 110), and was one of the leaders in the migration thence in 1635 to found Windsor on the Connecticut (*Massachusetts Historical Society Collections,* 2 ser. IX, 154 and note; 4 ser. VII, 411).

In the ensuing Indian troubles Mason won his chief claim to distinction. The powerful Pequots had been latently hostile to the colonists for some time when, in the autumn of 1636, open strife was precipitated by a fruitless expedition sent against them by Massachusetts. Their outrages then became so flagrant that in May 1637 the Connecticut authorities were obliged to take the offensive (Orr, *post,* p. 19). Mason was dispatched with eighty white men and one hundred Indian auxiliaries led by Uncas [*q.v.*] to invade the heart of Sassacus' domain. At Saybrook Fort, Capt. John Underhill [*q.v.*] joined him with nineteen Massachusetts men, who relieved twenty of the original company for home defense (*Ibid.,* p. 20). According to his commission Mason was to proceed by water to Pequot River (now the Thames) and begin operations directly. Disregarding these instructions, he boldly decided upon the more strategic course of going first to Narragansett Bay and then marching overland to strike where he would be less expected. This plan was followed with great success. After a brief delay among the Narragansetts, who provided a large addition to his native cohorts, he advanced toward the enemy's stronghold near the Mystic River. By a combination of good judgment and good fortune he took the Pequots completely by surprise. Attacking their fort before dawn, his soldiers effected an entrance from two sides almost unopposed. The slaughter began with musket and sword; but Mason, to bring a more speedy termination to the battle, fired the wigwams and gave orders to encircle the place and cut down any who tried to escape. The number killed, including women and children, was probably six or seven hundred (*Ibid.,* pp. 21–31). The power of the Pequots was broken. All that remained was to accept the submission of those who yielded and to hunt down the few that fled. In this work Mason cooperated with the Massachusetts troops under Capt. Israel Stoughton (*Ibid.,* pp. 34–40).

After the war Mason was promoted to the rank of major. On Oct. 2, 1656, at a meeting of the General Court, he was requested to write a history of the Pequot War. It was printed without the preface in *A Relation of the Troubles that Have Hapned in New England . . .* (1677), by Increase Mather, who was apparently unaware that Mason was the author, and was reprinted with an introductory sketch of Mason's life by Rev. Thomas Prince, under the title *A Brief History of the Pequot War,* in 1736. For over thirty years after 1637 Mason took a prominent part in Connecticut affairs. He served as deputy, 1637–42; magistrate, 1642–60; deputy governor, 1660–69; and assistant, 1669–72. During most of the period he was chief military officer of the colony, and handled Indian relations both for it and for the New England Confederation. In 1660 he was one of the founders of Norwich, where he spent the last twelve years of his life. His first wife died in Windsor, prior to Mar. 16, 1638, leaving a daughter, and in July 1639 he married Anne Peck. He left seven children by his second wife.

[The four classical contemporary histories of the Pequot War are Mason's, John Underhill's *Nevves from America* (1638), Philip Vincent's *A True Relation of the Late Battell Fought in New-England Between the English and the Pequet Salvages* (1638), and "Leift Lion Gardener his Relation of the Pequot Warres," first printed in *Mass. Hist. Soc. Colls.,* 3 ser. III; these have been collected in a single volume by Charles Orr under the title, *Hist. of the Pequot War* (1897). An important variant of Mason's account appears in William Hubbard's *A Narrative of the Troubles with the Indians in New England . . .* (1677). See also *Records of the Colony of New Plymouth in New England,* vols. IX, X (1859), ed. by D. Pulsifer; William Bradford, *Hist. of Plymouth Plantation* (2 vols., 1912), ed. by W. C. Ford; *Winthrop's Journal* (2 vols., 1908), ed. by J. K. Hosmer; "Winthrop Papers," in *Mass. Hist. Soc. Colls.,* 4 ser. VI, VII (1863–65), 5 ser. I, VIII (1871, 1882); biog. of Mason by George Ellis in Jared Sparks, *Library of Am. Biog.,* 2 ser. III (1844); H. R. Stiles, *The Hist. and Geneals. of Ancient Windsor, Conn.,* vol. II (1894); F. M. Caulkins, *Hist. of Norwich, Conn.* (1845); *Pub. Records of the Col. of Conn.,* vols. I, II (1850–52); information as to certain facts from L. B. Mason, Esq., New York City.]

G. P. B.

MASON, JOHN (Oct. 28, 1858–Jan. 12, 1919), actor, was born in Orange, N. J., the son of Daniel Gregory and Susan W. (Belcher) Mason, and grandson of Lowell Mason [*q.v.*], the musician and teacher. His full name was John Hill Belcher Mason. He lived and studied for a time during his youth in Germany, and upon his return to the United States attended Columbia University (1876–77) but did not graduate. His beginnings on the stage were in the acting of small parts in Philadelphia, New York, and other cities, including a tour as a singing actor with Maggie Mitchell, but his first distinctive engagement was at the Boston Museum, where he made his début as a member of its stock company in the rôle of Careless in *The School for*

Scandal on Aug. 25, 1879. He remained there, with a few intermissions, for more than ten years and gradually rose from general utility parts to the position of leading man, succeeding to many of the principal old comedy rôles and other characters that had been acted by Charles Barron. He appeared in many new plays, including *The English Rose, Sweet Lavender, Harbor Lights,* and *Held by the Enemy,* and in such familiar rôles as Eliot Grey in *Rosedale,* Captain Absolute in *The Rivals,* Young Marlow in *She Stoops to Conquer,* Charles Surface in *The School for Scandal,* Dazzle in *London Assurance,* Littleton Coke in *Old Heads and Young Hearts,* Zekiel Homespun in *The Heir at Law,* and Harry Dornton in *The Road to Ruin.* During the interruptions to these seasons at the Boston Museum, he played the Duc de Villafour in Steele MacKaye's *Dakolar* on the opening night at the Lyceum Theatre in New York in April 1885, and for a time he acted in support of Nat Goodwin.

After his engagement at the Boston Museum had ended, Mason went to London and in February 1891 he played the American character of Simeon Strong in *The Idler* with George Alexander at the St. James's Theatre. He starred for a time in comic opera and in plays with Marion Manola, and in a later London engagement in 1895 he played Colonel Moberly in E. S. Willard's production of Augustus Thomas' *Alabama.* He became in his middle age an extremely accomplished and finished actor, his skill at impersonation increasing notably with the passing years. He won wide-spread praise for his acting of Horatio Drake in *The Christian,* following that with a series of important characters in Daniel Frohman's Lyceum Theatre company, and later appearing successively in support of Elsie DeWolfe, Annie Russell, and Mrs. Fiske. He won new laurels for his acting with Mrs. Fiske as Rawdon Crawley in *Becky Sharp,* Eilert Lovborg in *Hedda Gabler,* John Karslake in *The New York Idea,* and Paul Sylvaine in *Leah Kleschna.* Beginning in 1907, he acted Jack Brookfield in Augustus Thomas' drama, *The Witching Hour,* more than a thousand times, and he had no less success some years later as Dr. Seelig in the same playwright's *As a Man Thinks.* Among the plays in which he appeared during his final years on the stage were *Liberty Hall, The Attack,* and *Big Jim Garrity.* After the first performance of *The Woman in Room 13* he was stricken suddenly and died at Stamford, Conn. Mason was an actor of exceptional native and acquired ability, with an assurance and a poise that were especially effective in their realization of men of distinction. He was, says Augustus Thomas, "one of the best actors that America has ever produced. . . . His power lay in his great self possession and a wonderful sense of time. . . . His voice was deep and resonant, modulated and trained. . . . He never showed a consciousness of his audience" (*The Print of My Remembrance,* pp. 444–45). His first wife was Marion Manola, from whom he was divorced. His second wife was Katharine Grey, who survived him.

[Augustus Thomas, *The Print of My Remembrance* (1922); J. B. Clapp and E. F. Edgett, *Players of the Present* (1900); Kate Ryan, *Old Boston Museum Days* (1915); Dixie Hines and H. P. Hanaford, *Who's Who in Music and Drama,* 1914; *Who's Who in America,* 1918–19; Wm. L. Mason, *A Record of the Descendants of Robt. Mason* (1891); interview in *N. Y. Dramatic Mirror,* Apr. 16, 1898; *Boston Herald,* Mar. 10, 1912; obituary in the *Morning Telegraph* (N. Y.), Jan. 13, 1919; *Boston Globe,* Jan. 19, 1919; Walter Browne and E. De Roy Koch, *Who's Who on the Stage,* 1908.]

E. F. E.

MASON, JOHN MITCHELL (Mar. 19, 1770–Dec. 26, 1829), clergyman and educator, was born in New York City, the second child of Rev. John Mason and Catharine (Van Wyck) Mason. In 1761 his father had been sent by the Associate Synod of Scotland to be pastor of the Scotch Presbyterian church on Cedar Street. He was a man of vigorous mind and notable scholarship, and he gave his son most of the boy's earlier education. At Columbia College, from which the younger John graduated in 1789, he revealed a versatile and profound mind. His theological training was received from his father and at the University of Edinburgh, from which he graduated in 1792. A tribute to his nascent reputation was the call he received to become successor to his father shortly after the latter's death in that same year. He was licensed to preach on Oct. 18 and in April 1793 was ordained and installed as pastor. Five years later he published *Letters on Frequent Communion,* a successful appeal to his denomination, the Associate Reformed Church of North America, to observe the Lord's Supper oftener and more simply. Early feeling the need for elevating the educational standards of the American ministry, after some years' thought he outlined a plan for establishing a theological seminary. In 1804 it was opened in New York with Mason as its first professor. It was the forerunner of Union Theological Seminary. To obtain a library for it he had spent more than a year in Great Britain, where he gathered about 3,000 volumes. The intellectual quality of his addresses abroad made a deep impression on the British public. Several printings were required to meet the demand for his sermons, *Living Faith* (1801) and *Messiah's Throne* (n.d.).

In 1806 he founded *The Christian's Magazine,* and for several years he wrote much of its contents, which were mainly polemic. One of his most notable publications was the indirect result of a change in pastorates. In 1810 he resigned his first charge for the purpose of forming a new congregation, which in 1812, as Murray Street Church, occupied its new edifice. In the interim his people had worshipped in the Cedar Street Presbyterian Church, and had joined with its congregation in the communion service. Though the General Synod declined to censure him for this departure from denominational regularity, criticism was general and severe. He responded in 1816 with *A Plea for Sacramental Communion on Catholic Principles,* a book which produced keen interest in America and abroad.

From 1795 until 1811, and from 1812 to 1824, he was a trustee of Columbia College. In 1809 he became a member of a committee on raising the standards for college admission, and spent much time on the problems involved. The trustees in 1811 adopted a final report, providing for a new curriculum. The same year the office of provost was created, and Mason was elected thereto. His duties were to exercise "the like general superintendence with the president" (*An Historical Sketch of Columbia College,* 1876, p. 54), to occupy the president's position in the latter's absence, and to teach classics to the senior class. The office evidently was created specially for his occupancy. His work on the committee and as provost definitely enhanced the reputation of the college.

Ill health caused his resignation as provost on July 11, 1816; even his strong physique could not long endure the strain of his many duties in college, seminary, church, and public affairs. Despite several rest periods, during one of which he spent four months in Europe, his vigor was so evidently impaired that in 1821 he resigned his other positions in New York and, hoping that change of climate and responsibilities would benefit him, accepted the presidency of Dickinson College, Carlisle, Pa. His health failed to rally, however, and in 1824 he returned to New York, where, in moderate physical health, he remained until his death. While at Carlisle, in 1822, he left the Associate Reformed Church and became a member of the Presbyterian Presbytery of New York. At his best period he had no superior in America as a preacher (C. F. Himes, *A Sketch of Dickinson College,* 1879, p. 52), and in all the English-speaking world he was "one of the greatest pulpit orators of a period which produced Robert Hall and Thomas Chalmers" (John DeWitt, "The Intellectual Life of Samuel Miller," *Princeton Theological Review,* April 1906, p. 175). He was handsome, with patrician features, graceful gestures and carriage, and had a manner attractive and sympathetic. His quick perceptions, power of rapid analysis, extensive vocabulary, and forceful, original speech gave him command of his hearers both in conversation and in public address. His wife was Ann, only child of Abraham Lefferts of New York, whom he married May 13, 1793. He had five sons and two daughters. *The Complete Works of John M. Mason, D.D.,* edited by his son Ebenezer, was published in four volumes in 1832.

[Jacob Van Vechten, *Memoirs of John M. Mason, D.D., S.T.D.* (1856); W. B. Sprague, *Annals of the Am. Pulpit,* vol. IV (1859); W. D. Snodgrass, *The Victorious Christian Awaiting His Crown* (1830), a memorial sermon; *N. Y. Mercury,* Dec. 30, 1829.]

P. P. F.

MASON, JOHN YOUNG (Apr. 18, 1799–Oct. 3, 1859), congressman, jurist, diplomat, son of Edmunds Mason and Frances Ann (Young) Mason, and grandson of Capt. James Mason of the 15th Virginia line, was a native of Greensville County, Va. Educated at the University of North Carolina (A.B., 1816) and at the law school at Litchfield, Conn., he was admitted to the Virginia bar in 1819 and began the practice of law at Hicksford (Greensville County), but removed to Southampton County in 1822. From 1823 to 1831, he was a member of the General Assembly; in 1830, he represented a Tidewater district in the constitutional convention. In this distinguished assembly, Mason did not participate in the discussions but was an opponent of the extension of the suffrage and of the establishment of the white basis of representation. He served in Congress from Mar. 4, 1831, to Jan. 11, 1837, and during his congressional career was a supporter of the Jacksonian measures, with the exception of the "force bill." He refused to vote for the rechartering of the National Bank, even at the request of the Virginia General Assembly. As chairman of the House committee of foreign affairs, he advocated naval preparedness in the face of France's dilatory attitude over the spoliation claims, and introduced the bill recognizing the independence of Texas. Resigning from Congress, he held a federal judgeship until his appointment, Mar. 14, 1844, by Tyler as secretary of the navy. He was the only member of Tyler's cabinet retained by Polk, who made him attorney-general. He served from Mar. 4, 1845, to Sept. 9, 1846, when he succeeded Bancroft as secretary of the navy. Under him the naval affairs in the Mexican War were conducted. Though an expansionist, Mason opposed in the cabinet the incorporation of Mexico into the United States and advocated the acceptance of the treaty signed by Nicholas P. Trist with Mexico.

After his retirement from the cabinet, he resumed the practice of law in Richmond. At the same time, he became president of the James River & Kanawha Company, being elected in May 1849. He realized the economic and political importance of a transportation system connecting eastern and western Virginia and urged the rapid extension of the canal to the Ohio. In the meantime, in 1850, he was elected without his solicitation to represent his old constituency in the constitutional convention of 1850–51 and was chosen unanimously by this body as its presiding officer. The *Richmond Whig* for Nov. 6, 1850, said of him: "Fat, ruddy, and fifty-five [*sic*], comes the President of the Convention, a fair, pleasant speaking man, with one of those voices Shakespeare so much commends in women. . . . He has the habit of success. . . . Judge Mason is a very influential man. He is a great Democrat, a transcendental Democrat, passionately fond of the people, but votes against the free basis." Although he voted against the final engrossment of the constitution, after its adoption by the convention, he expressed the hope that the new constitution would allay sectional strife and promote a cordial feeling among the people. He was a member of the Democratic state central committee in the presidential contest of 1852 and urged the South "to cherish and defend Northern men like Pierce who had risked so much for the maintenance of Southern rights and honor" (*Richmond Enquirer,* Oct. 9, 1852). From Oct. 24, 1853, until his sudden death from apoplexy in 1859 he was envoy extraordinary and minister plenipotentiary to France. His career as a diplomat was inglorious, though with Buchanan and Soulé he signed on Oct. 18, 1854, the Ostend Manifesto. Courteous, generous, and popular, Mason was a loyal Virginian, devoted to the institutions and to the social and political ideas of the state. He married Mary Anne Fort, Aug. 9, 1821, and was the father of eight children.

[S. F. Bemis, *The Am. Secretaries of State and Their Diplomacy,* vols. V and VI (1928); Kemp P. Battle, *Hist. of the Univ. of N. C.,* vol. I (1907); *Jour., Acts and Proc. of a Gen. Convention, of the State of Va.* (1850); E. I. McCormac, *James K. Polk, A Pol. Biog.* (1922); *Proc. and Debates of the Va. State Convention of 1829–30* (1830); annual reports of the James River and Kanawha Company, 1850–54; *Richmond Enquirer,* Oct. 9, 1852, Mar. 30, 1853, Oct. 17, 18, 1859; Justin H. Smith, *The War with Mexico* (2 vols., 1919); L. G. Tyler, *Letters and Times of the Tylers,* vol. II (1884); A. A. Ettinger, *The Mission to Spain of Pierre Soulé, 1853–55* (1932); M. B. Field, *Memories of Many Men* (1874); information as to certain facts from Mason's grand-daughter, Miss Mary Mason Heath, Washington, D. C.]

W. G. B.

MASON, JONATHAN (Sept. 12, 1756–Nov. 1, 1831), United States senator from Massachusetts, was born at Boston, Mass., the son of Jonathan and Miriam (Clark) Mason. His father was a prominent merchant, a Son of Liberty, a deacon of the Old South Church, a selectman of the town of Boston (1769–71), and one of the witnesses of the Boston Massacre. Mason attended the South Grammar or Latin School, but unlike most of his schoolmates he went to the College of New Jersey (now Princeton) instead of to Harvard for his higher education. He received the degree of A.B. in 1774 and then read law with John Adams and in the office of Josiah Quincy. On Dec. 3, 1779, he was admitted to the bar of Suffolk County, and in 1780 he delivered the annual oration to commemorate the Boston Massacre. From 1786 to 1796 he was a member of the Massachusetts House of Representatives; in 1797 and 1798, a member of the Executive Council; and in 1799 and 1800, state senator. When Benjamin Goodhue [*q.v.*], United States senator from Massachusetts, resigned from office in 1800, Mason was chosen to fill his place and served in that capacity from Nov. 14, 1800, until March 1803. Though not a member of the Essex Junto, he was a strong Federalist; his career as senator was notable chiefly because of the part he took in the debates on the repeal of the Judiciary Act of 1801. Returning to Boston in 1803 he resumed the practice of the law, was elected to the state Senate for the year 1803–04 and to the Massachusetts House of Representatives 1805–08. At a special town meeting at Boston, Aug. 9, 1808, he moved that President Jefferson be requested to remove the Embargo, and the motion was carried.

After this time he "refused every office of every kind" and rarely even talked politics (Letter to Wilson C. Nicholas, Nov. 26, 1814, in *Massachusetts Historical Society Collections,* 7 ser. I, 1900, p. 214). Nevertheless he was elected to the Fifteenth and Sixteenth congresses, serving from March 1817 until his resignation in May 1820. Like all orthodox Federalists of his time he took a very gloomy view of the political situation, and in the letter cited above he predicted: "We shall not be destroyed today or tomorrow, but it will come, and the end of these measures will be disunion and disgrace" (p. 220).

Besides his law practice, Mason was interested to a considerable extent in Boston real estate. He and Harrison Gray Otis, Joseph Woodward [*qq.v.*], and Charles Ward Apthorp formed the syndicate which bought the southwestern slope of Beacon Hill in 1795 and turned it into the fashionable residential district of the town. A later venture, probably not so successful, was the development of Dorchester by the South Boston Association, of which Mason was a prominent member. He was also a director of the Boston branch of the United States Bank. In 1779 he married Susannah, daughter of William Powell of Boston. They had two sons and four daughters, one of whom married the elder John Collins Warren [*q.v.*]. Mason died at Boston and was buried in Mount Auburn Cemetery, Cambridge. A portrait of him painted by Gilbert Stuart in 1805 shows a face of striking intelligence and good breeding.

[Biographical sketches have often confused Mason with his father, who bore the same name. For date of birth see *A Report of the Record Commissioners of Boston*, 1894, p. 289, and *Columbian Centinel*, Nov. 5, 1831. There are frequent glimpses of him in S. E. Morison, *The Life and Letters of Harrison Gray Otis, Federalist* (1913). His diary of a journey to Savannah in 1804–05 is printed in *Proc. Mass. Hist. Soc.*, 2 ser. II (1886); his Boston Massacre oration is in *Orations Delivered . . . to Commemorate the Evening of the Fifth of March, 1770* (1785). See also J. S. Loring, *The Hundred Boston Orators* (2nd ed., 1853); C. F. Adams, *Works of John Adams*, IX (1854), 422, 432; *Proc. Mass. Hist. Soc.*, 1 ser. XIX (1882), 152–57, 161–64; H. A. Hill, *Hist. of the Old South Church* (1890), vol. II, *passim*; *New-Eng. Hist. and Geneal. Reg.*, Apr. 1884, pp. 235, 236; Lawrence Park, *Gilbert Stuart* (1926), II, 512, and IV, 321.] L. S. M.

MASON, LOWELL (Jan. 8, 1792–Aug. 11, 1872), musical educator and hymnwriter, was born in Medfield, Mass., the son of Johnson and Catharine (Hartshorn) Mason and a descendant of Robert Mason who emigrated to Salem in 1630. He described himself as "a wayward, unpromising boy" (Seward, *post*, p. 4). His father, besides being a manufacturer of straw goods and a member of the state legislature, was a good 'cellist, and his son, beginning at an early age, learned to play on "all manner of musical instruments that came within his reach" (Thayer, in *Dwight's Journal*, Nov. 22, 1879). At twenty he went as a bank clerk to Savannah, Ga. He had already been leading a church choir in his native town, and in Savannah he taught singing and played a church organ. With F. L. Abel, a teacher of harmony, he made a collection of psalm tunes based upon William Gardiner's *Sacred Melodies*. The Handel and Haydn Society of Boston sponsored the publication of the work and at Mason's request, because he did not wish to be known as a musician, issued it as the work of the Society. It was published in 1822 under the title: *The Boston Handel and Haydn Society's Collection of Church Music*. Republished in many later editions, it proved astonishingly profitable both to Mason and to the Society.

Mason remained in Savannah until 1827, when he was invited to take charge of the music for six months, successively, at three Boston churches. He did not carry out the original plan, but he became definitely connected with the musical life of Boston. After serving for five years (1827–32) as president of the Handel and Haydn Society he organized in 1833 the Boston Academy of Music which established a music school and promoted the introduction of music instruction in the public schools. The Academy's normal class for teachers was the origin of the musical "convention," an institution which, under the leadership of Mason and George J. Webb, spread from Boston to New England and farther west. At these gatherings, which offered a variety of musical activity, musical and pedagogical training was offered to adults.

In developing a system of instruction for children, used at the Academy, Mason had taken up a study of Pestalozzian methods and developed his system in accordance with its principles. Thus his *Manual of Instruction* (1834) emphasized the teaching of singing prior to the teaching of symbols—"the thing before the sign." He was aided in his efforts to introduce music training into the public schools by Samuel Atkins Eliot [*q.v.*], first president of the Academy and a member of the Boston School committee. In 1837, after Mason had visited Pestalozzi in Zurich and had made a study of teaching methods abroad, he was permitted to teach music in one of the Boston schools, but he was obliged to conduct his classes without pay and to supply his own materials. His efforts met with the approval of the school authorities and in 1838 he was appointed to teach in all of the Boston schools. This work he continued until 1841, when he left to devote himself to music conventions. In 1851 he moved to New York City. After 1854 he lived in Orange, N. J., where he died in 1872. He had married, in 1817, Abigail Gregory of Westboro, Mass. They had four sons: William and Henry [*qq.v.*], pianist and piano manufacturer, respectively, and Daniel Gregory and Lowell Mason, Jr., music publishers. In the last years of his life Mason continued his musical activities and devoted himself to the enlargement of his library, the nucleus of which was the musical library of Johann Rinck, the German organist, which Mason had purchased in 1852. In its entirety Mason's collection comprised over eight thousand printed works and several hundred manuscripts. It included some seven hundred volumes in hymnology and valuable sixteenth and seventeenth century works in theory, some of which were rare first editions. After Mason's death the library was presented to Yale College.

Mason was not a great composer. Many of his tunes were adaptations of melodies from Händel, Haydn, and Mozart, and from earlier church music, but they came to replace the "fugue tune" of the earlier nineteenth century and gained great popularity throughout the United States. Beginning with the Handel and Haydn collection, Mason published more than fifty books of tunes, sacred and secular. His chief works, aside from the first collection, are: *The Juvenile Psalmist* (1829); *The Juvenile Lyre* (1830); *Lyra Sacra* (1832); *Boston Academy's Collection of Church Music* (1835); *Sabbath-School Songs* (1836); *Boston Anthem Book* (1839); *The Psaltery* (1845); *Cantica Laudis* (1850); *The New Carmina Sacra* (1850); and *The Song Garden* (3 parts, 1864–65). Among his best-known tunes are the "Missionary Hymn" ("From Greenland's Icy Mountains"); "Olivet" ("My Faith Looks up to Thee"); and "Bethany" ("Nearer, My God, to Thee"). It has been well said (C. A. and M. R. Beard, *The Rise of American Civilization,* 1927, I, p. 801): "A compiler of church music, an organizer of choral societies . . . and an originator of conventions for the training of music instructors in the public schools, Mason impressed himself indelibly on the democracy of his times."

[T. F. Seward, *The Educ. Work of Dr. Lowell Mason* (n.d.), with bibliography of Mason's works; F. J. Metcalf, *Am. Writers and Compilers of Sacred Music* (1925); Wm. Mason, *Memories of a Musical Life* (1901), especially App., pt. 1; C. C. Perkins and J. S. Dwight, *Hist. of the Handel and Haydn Soc. of Boston, Mass.,* vol. I (1883); Wm. L. Mason, *A Record of the Descendants of Robt. Mason* (1891); *Dwight's Jour. of Music,* Nov. 22, Dec. 6, 1879; *Music,* Feb. 1892, Sept. 1893, and Feb., Apr. 1896; *New Music Rev.,* Nov., Dec. 1910, Jan. 1911, Jan. 1927; *Musician,* Nov. 1911; *Etude,* Mar. 1910; "The Rise and Fall of the Fugue-Tune in America." *Musical Quart.,* Apr. 1930; the *N. Y. Times,* Aug. 13, 1872.] F. H. M.

MASON, LUTHER WHITING (Apr. 3, 1828–July 14, 1896), musical educator and teacher, was born in Turner, Me., the son of Willard and Mary (Whiting) Mason. His father died in 1834 and the boy was apprenticed to his step-brother to learn the trade of last-making. At the same time he studied Greek, Latin, and music. He gave up his plan of becoming a missionary in favor of a career as a musician. He was practically self-taught in music, having acquired his knowledge, in part, by teaching his pupils. His talent as an instructor was such, however, that at the age of twenty-five he was superintendent of music in the Louisville, Ky., schools. Some years later, in Cincinnati, where he filled the same office, he prepared the "National System" of music-charts and books, the success of which established his fame in the school-music field. Called to Boston in 1865, he settled there and, as supervisor of music, improved musical instruction in the primary schools of the city.

In the late seventies, when experts in education were invited by the Japanese government to bring Western ideas into Japan, Mason was asked to organize music education in the Japanese schools. He went to Japan and introduced a modification of his music system in the public schools, as well as establishing a school of music with an orchestra that played both Japanese and European music. As governmental music supervisor he procured the introduction of the diatonic scale, and was so successful in his educational efforts that Western school music in general in Japan came to bear his name. He also gave piano lessons in the homes of the Japanese nobility, and taught singing to Kalakaua, King of Hawaii, who was visiting in Japan at the time. When Mason left Japan in 1882 after three years, the University of Tokyo, which had opened its doors in 1877, bestowed its first doctor's degree to be awarded a musician upon him. Returning to Boston with the increased reputation gained by his successful educational adventure in the Far East he compiled, in collaboration with George A. Veazie, Jr., *The National Music Course* (4 vols., 1887–97). His studies in Germany made in connection with this work, led him, with the approval of the faculty of the University of Leipzig, to issue it in a German version. Mason died in Buckfield, Me., at the age of sixty-eight.

[W. S. B. Mathews, "Luther W. Mason and School Music," *Music,* Sept. 1892; *The Mason Testimonial: Addresses at the Reception of Luther Whiting Mason, Dec. 3, 1879*; *Lewiston Evening Jour.* (Lewiston, Me.), July 15, 1896.] F. H. M.

MASON, OTIS TUFTON (Apr. 10, 1838–Nov. 5, 1908), ethnologist, was born in Eastport, Me. At the time of his birth his parents, John and Rachel Thompson (Lincoln) Mason, were affected by business reverses, and for a while could give few opportunities for education to their children. During Otis' boyhood they moved to Philadelphia, then to Haddonfield, N. J. Here the boy, with able teachers, laid the foundation for his future activities. Removing again, to Woodlawn, Va., in 1851, Mason in his later teens had the opportunity to enter Columbian College (now George Washington University), where he graduated in 1861. In the next year he became principal of its preparatory school, and taught there for more than twenty years. Meantime he became interested in ethnology and in 1872 was appointed collaborator in ethnology in the Smithsonian Institution. In 1884 he gave up his teaching to become curator of ethnology in the Smithsonian, and from that time, for the rest of his life, he devoted his attention to the classification and regulation of the newly founded National Museum. He was one of the leaders in American museum science, his disciplined mind and gospel of hard work carrying him far. In 1902 he became head curator of anthropology.

His proficiency in all branches of anthropological science is evident in his publications, which cover a great variety of subjects. The history of human culture—especially the technological aspect, concerned with the tangible evidence of man's progress—was his specialty, and the elucidation of aboriginal technology is regarded as his most valuable contribution to his science. Noteworthy papers in this field include: "Basket-work of the North American Aborigines," *Report of the United States National Museum, 1884* (1885), greatly elaborated in "Aboriginal American Basketry: Studies in a Textile Art without Machinery," *Ibid., 1902* (1904); "Cradles of the North American Aborigines," *Ibid., 1887* (1889); "Aboriginal Skin Dressing," *Ibid., 1889* (1891); "The Ulu, or Woman's Knife, of the Eskimo," *Ibid., 1890* (1891); "The Man's Knife Among the North American Indians," *Ibid., 1897* (1899); "Aboriginal American Harpoons," *Ibid., 1900* (1902); and "North American Bows, Arrows, and Quivers," *Annual Report of the . . . Smithsonian Institution . . . 1893* (1894). Always with the idea of instructing in the background, his papers conveyed a message in an intelligible, even a literary form, thus reaching a wide audience. Papers of broader scope are: "What is Anthropology?," in *The Saturday Lectures Delivered in the Lecture Room of the United States National Museum* (1882); "Resemblances in Arts Widely Separated," *American Naturalist* (March 1886); "The Birth of Invention," *Annual Report of the . . . Smithsonian Institution . . . 1892* (1893); "Technogeography, or the Relation of the Earth to the Industries of Mankind," *American Anthropologist* (April 1894); "Mind and Matter in Culture," *Ibid.,* (April–June 1908). Mason was also the author of two books of popular science: *Woman's Share in Primitive Culture* (1894) and *The Origin of Inventions* (London, 1895). In 1879 he was one of the founders of the Anthropological Society of Washington and for years contributed to its organ, the *American Anthropologist.* For many years he was anthropological editor of the *American Naturalist* and the *Standard Dictionary.* His knowledge of American Indian nomenclature gave him a place on the United States Board of Geographic Names, in which connection he served for eighteen years. Mason had pleasant features and a most attractive manner, which inspired confidence. In 1862 he married Sarah E. Henderson. He died in Washington, D. C.

[Walter Hough in *Am. Anthropologist,* Oct.–Dec. 1908; Aleš Hrdlička, in *Science,* Nov. 27, 1908; *Popular Science Mo.,* Jan. 1909; *Who's Who in America,* 1908–09; *Evening Star* (Washington), Nov. 5, 1908.]

W. H.

MASON, RICHARD BARNES (Jan. 16, 1797–July 25, 1850), soldier, first military and civil governor of California, was born in Fairfax County, Va., in the environs of Mt. Vernon. He was the son of George Mason VI by his second wife, Eleanor Patton, and a great-grandson of George Mason [*q.v.*] of "Gunston Hall." The boy was carefully educated, principally by tutor. On Sept. 2, 1817, he was commissioned a second lieutenant in the 8th Infantry of the regular army. Owing to the temporarily rapid promotion in that branch of the service, he was immediately advanced to the grade of first lieutenant, and on July 31, 1819, was made a captain of the 1st Infantry, which participated in the Black Hawk War. In the same regiment with Zachary Taylor, he took part in the successful battle of the Bad Axe, Aug. 2, 1832. Two days after Congress created the First Dragoons on Mar. 2, 1833, he was elected as its major, a distinction heightened by the fact that the unit later became the first regiment of Cavalry in the United States army. He rose to be its lieutenant-colonel on July 4, 1836, and its colonel on June 30, 1846. When Gen. Stephen Watts Kearny, who had just commanded the regiment, went on his memorable conquest of New Mexico and California at the outset of the War with Mexico, he took Mason and some of the dragoons with him. They reached and occupied Los Angeles in January 1847. Shortly thereafter, when Kearny was called to other fields, Mason again relieved him and became the military commander of that region, authorized to establish temporary civil government in California.

Although Mason understood the supreme power of the province to be vested in himself, he assumed a conservative attitude and continued the alcalde. In view of the situation, he decided that it would be unwise to establish a government on the old Mexican basis. Accordingly he and his staff prepared a code of laws "for the better government of California." But on the news that Mexico had ceded the territory to the United States, Mason felt that the responsibility for its government had shifted to Congress and withheld the distribution of the code. Meanwhile, lacking a uniform and understood law, the settlers chafed and became restless. The discovery of gold in 1848, with its consequent influx of "forty-niners," made the situation more tense. Mason delayed in providing standard laws in the faith that Congress would act, but in neither the session of 1848 nor that of 1849 was any measure taken. As a consequence the citizens began to take the initiative to the extent of forming the Legislative Assembly of San Francisco. At this juncture Brig.-Gen. Persifor F. Smith relieved Mason as military commander, and in April 1849, Brig.-Gen. Bennet Riley relieved him as acting-governor of California.

Though Mason had given painstaking attention to the civil affairs of the territory, he had allowed technical impediments to outweigh emergency needs. Altogether his command, though negative, was constructive. He was brevetted a brigadier-general, May 30, 1848, for meritorious conduct. During his tour of duty he visited with Lieutenant (afterward General) W. T. Sherman the initial operations of the gold collectors in the El Dorado. His report at Monterey, Aug. 17, 1848 (copy in Revere, *post*), remains today the most authentic and descriptive story of the discovery of the gold deposits in California, especially at Sutter's Fort. It was copied in all parts of the world, published everywhere in the newspapers, and distributed in thousands of pamphlets. After his relief in California, Mason returned to the headquarters of the First Dragoons at Jefferson Barracks, Mo., where he died. He was survived by his wife and two daughters.

[R. D. Hunt, *Cal. and Californians* (1926), vol. II; *Ann. Report of the Secretary of War*, Dec. 1, 1848; J. W. Revere, *A Tour of Duty in Cal.* (1849); H. E. Hayden, *Va. Geneals.* (1891); F. E. Stevens, *The Black Hawk War* (1903); W. A. Ganoe, *The Hist. of the U. S. Army* (1924); *Daily Mo. Republican* (St. Louis), July 27, 1850; Old Files Section, Adj.-General's Office, War Department.]

W. A. G.

MASON, SAMUEL (*c.* 1750–July 1803), desperado and river pirate, was born in Virginia and is believed to have been a member of the distinguished Mason family. By one chronicler he is said to have "grown up bad." He served with distinction, however, as a captain in the Ohio County (Va.) militia during the Revolutionary War. Letters and receipts written by him show that he had obtained some schooling. He seems to have married at an early age. After the war he moved with his family to Washington County, in eastern Tennessee, but was soon driven out for petty thieving. He next appeared in Russellville and later in Henderson, Ky., where several acts of outlawry compelled another exodus. During most of the year 1797 he made his home in the once famous Cave-in-Rock, on the Illinois side of the Ohio, and with his two older sons and several other outlaws preyed upon passing boatmen.

About the end of the year he disappeared. He and his band are next heard of as robbers of travelers along the Natchez Trace and of boatmen on the lower Mississippi. Daring and shrewd, he was almost uniformly successful. The fame of his depredations spread throughout the western country, and many efforts were made to capture him. In January 1803, near New Madrid in the present Missouri, Mason, his four sons, a man variously known as Setton, Taylor, or Wells, and the wife and three children of one of the sons were arrested by the Spanish authorities. Examined at length before the local commandant, they were sent under guard to the governor general at New Orleans. Convinced that none of the crimes was committed west of the Mississippi, that official ordered the outlaws turned over to the American officials at Natchez. On the way, Mar. 26, Mason shot the commander of the boat and with the remainder of the party made his escape. In July he was waylaid and killed by Setton and a companion, James May. Bringing in his head in expectation of a reward, they at once came under suspicion. May was identified as a former member of the band and Setton as the notorious Wiley (Little) Harpe, former accomplice and reputed brother of Micajah (Big) Harpe, perhaps the bloodiest ruffian in frontier annals, who in August 1799, after a series of murders in Kentucky and Tennessee, had been killed and decapitated. The hanging of these two outlaws, Feb. 8, 1804, at Old Greenville, Miss., marked the end of Mason's band.

Mason was a large man, described as "fine looking." His manner was agreeable, and his favorite pose was that of an injured innocent diligently seeking the men guilty of the crimes falsely attributed to himself. Unlike Harpe, he was primarily a robber; and he killed only when killing was thought to be essential for safety.

[Otto A. Rothert, *The Outlaws of Cave-in-Rock* (1924), contains an extensive bibliography on Mason, the Harpes, and other desperadoes of the region and period.]

W. J. G.

MASON, STEVENS THOMSON (Dec. 29, 1760–May 10, 1803), United States senator from Virginia, was a member of one of the most distinguished of Colonial families. His original American ancestor, George Mason [*q.v.*], emigrated to Virginia in the seventeenth century. The family established itself in the Northern Neck, acquired considerable property, and named the county of Stafford in memory of the English shire of its origin. Stevens Thomson Mason was a lineal descendant of this emigrant. The son of Thomson Mason [*q.v.*] and his first wife, Mary King Barnes, he was born at "Chippawamsic," Stafford County, was educated at the College of William and Mary, and prepared himself in Virginia for the practice of law. His first real contact with life came when his father, who had reared him with strictness, sent him, during the Yorktown campaign, to General Washington with a tender of his services. He was now little more than twenty years of age, but the General made him an aide on his staff (Kate Mason Rowland, *The Life of George Mason,* 1892, II, pp. 20, 39).

Returning home after this experience, the young man began to take an active interest in politics, and in 1783 served his first term in the House of Delegates, sitting with his father, who was serving his last. After this service in the lower house of the Assembly, he was, in 1787, elected to the state Senate. In 1788 he was a member of the Virginia ratification convention and there sided with his more famous uncle against the adoption of the Constitution. Later in the Assembly he opposed the amendments proposed by Congress on the ground that they were inadequate. In 1794 he was elected to the United States Senate to succeed James Monroe, and at the commencement of his career in that body achieved notoriety by publishing an abstract of the articles of Jay's treaty when its fate was still in the balance. The rules of the Senate forbade such a violation of its secrecy, and the proponents of the treaty were loud in condemnation. Its opponents applauded, as did the Virginia Assembly. There can be no doubt but that Mason's motives were honorable. The strength of his partisan feeling was manifest by the aid and comfort he gave to Thomas Cooper (Dumas Malone, *The Public Life of Thomas Cooper,* 1926, p. 133), James Thomson Callender (*The Writings of Thomas Jefferson,* Monticello Edition, X, 1904, pp. 330–33), and Matthew Lyon (J. B. McMaster, *A History of the People of the United States,* II, 1885, p. 401) when they were prosecuted under the Sedition Act. From this beginning he became a consistent opponent of Federalism and a steady friend of Jefferson and his cause (*The Writings of Thomas Jefferson,* X, 1904, p. 61).

Mason was an able jurist, and his last speech in the Senate, delivered in support of the bill to repeal the Judiciary Act of 1801, shows that he was a debater of no mean powers. He married Mary Elizabeth Armistead of Louisa County and lived at "Raspberry Plain," the country seat in Loudoun County which had been left him by his father (Robert A. Lancaster, *Historic Virginia Homes and Churches,* 1915, pp. 377–78). His two sons, Armistead Thomson and John Thomson, won distinction in public life, the former becoming a United States senator, and the latter secretary of Michigan Territory. His grandson, Stevens Thomson Mason [*q.v.*], was the first governor of the state of Michigan. Mason died in Philadelphia while still a member of the Senate. There is an account of his funeral in that city in the *Aurora* for May 14, 1803. His remains were later reinterred at "Raspberry Plain."

[There are brief sketches of Mason in the *Biog. Dir. Am. Cong.* (1928) and in L. T. Hemans, *Life and Times of Stevens Thomson Mason,* 1920, pp. 13–15. There is a more detailed account in H. B. Grigsby, "Hist. of the Va. Fed. Convention of 1788," *Va. Hist. Soc. Colls.,* n. s. X (1891).] T. P. A.

MASON, STEVENS THOMSON (Oct. 27, 1811–Jan. 4, 1843), first governor of the state of Michigan, was born in Loudoun County, Va., probably at Leesburg, where his father was practising law, the second of the eight children of John Thomson and Elizabeth (Moir) Mason, and a grandson of Stevens Thomson Mason [*q.v.*]. In 1812 the family migrated to Kentucky, settling first at Lexington and later at Owingsville and Mt. Sterling. At one time they were tenants of Henry Clay's "Ashland." John Mason was a brother-in-law of William Taylor Barry and counted Andrew Jackson and Richard Mentor Johnson among his friends. In 1828 Stevens —or Tom, as he was usually called—left Transylvania University and became a grocer's helper, for his father was in financial straits. Two years later President Jackson rescued the sinking fortunes of the family by appointing John Mason secretary of Michigan Territory. Father and son arrived at Detroit together July 18, 1830, but a year later the Secretary resigned and set out for Texas and Mexico, ostensibly on private business but conjecturally on a mission for the President, who promptly named Stevens Thomson Mason to the vacant secretariat. The appointment excited general indignation and protest, for Mason was only nineteen years old. Ignoring the furore, he took the oath of office July 25, 1831, and conducted himself so discreetly that he gained acceptance. He was modest, courteous, and affable, spoke and wrote intelligently, and was precocious in his political sagacity.

During most of the next five years he was acting governor *ex officio.* He seized the leadership of the movement for statehood and vigorously prosecuted the boundary dispute with Ohio, calling out the militia to guard the disputed area. According to the Ordinance of 1787, the northern boundary of Ohio, Indiana, and Illinois should have been a line running east and west from the southern bend of Lake Michigan, but in carving these states out of the Northwest Territory, this stipulation of the Ordinance had been disregarded. Mason's insistence on Michigan's right to the "Toledo strip" was a serious embarrassment to President Jackson and the Democratic party. Congress refused to admit Michigan as a state until the dispute was settled in Ohio's favor, but as compensation the Upper Peninsula was added to the state of Michigan. Mason was elected the first governor of Michigan in 1836 and served two terms. He appointed an able superintendent of public instruction, used his veto to protect the university lands, and proved himself a friend of education. He opposed imprisonment for debt and solitary confinement in the penitentiary, advocated a geological survey, and in general showed an enlightened attitude toward public problems. Unfortunately, he was too inexperienced to perceive the danger lurking in the banking law of 1837 or to negotiate successfully with Eastern bankers for the flotation of $5,200,000 of state bonds. In consequence the state suffered severely from the financial stringency that set in in 1837, and Mason was held accountable for much of the trouble. Declining to run again for governor, he retired in January 1840. At the invitation of his successor, a Whig, he wrote a farewell message to the legislature, which refused to receive it.

Mason had been married Nov. 1, 1838, to Julia Elizabeth Phelps of New York, who with three children survived him. In 1841 he removed to New York, where he practised law until his death in 1843 after a short illness. As the "boy governor" he became a romantic hero in Michigan, and in 1905 his body was reinterred, with fitting ceremony, in Capitol Square, Detroit.

[Mason's private letters 1833–42, his executive correspondence and documents 1831–40, and his father's family correspondence 1831–49 are in the Burton Hist. Coll., Detroit Pub. Lib. L. T. Hemans, *Life and Times of Stevens Thomson Mason* (1920) is the standard work; see the review, *Am. Hist. Rev.*, July 1921. See also: J. V. Campbell, *Outlines of the Political Hist. of Mich.* (1876); "Letters of Hon. S. T. Mason to his father, John T. Mason," *Wm. and Mary Quart.*, July 1908; L. T. Hemans, "Michigan's Debt to Stevens T. Mason" and D. E. Heineman, "The Portraits of Gov. Mason," *Mich. Pioneer and Hist. Soc. Colls.*, vol. XXXV (1907); numerous minor references in same series (see index vols.).]

G. H. G.

MASON, THOMSON (1733–Feb. 26, 1785), Revolutionary patriot, legislator, was born in Prince William County, Va., the third and youngest child of Col. George and Ann (Thomson) Mason. He was eight years younger than his famous brother, George Mason [*q.v.*] of "Gunston Hall." The father met his death by drowning when Thomson was two years old, and George eventually assumed a measure of guardianship over him, helping defray part of the cost of his education. After some preparation under private tutors, Thomson went to England and was admitted to the Middle Temple in 1751. On his return from London he began the practice of law in his native state. He represented Stafford County in the Virginia Assembly from 1758 to 1761 and from 1765 to 1772; Loudoun County, from 1772 to 1774, and from 1777 to 1778. In the last named year he was elected one of the five judges of the general court, but in 1779 he was again in the Assembly as representative from Elizabeth City County. He resigned his seat that year, but his resignation was not accepted. He vacated it, however, by accepting a coroner's commission.

His vigorous defense of American liberties came to a climax in the nine letters of a "British American," which he wrote in the summer of 1774. In the concluding paragraph of the last letter he disclosed his identity. The theme of the letters was that Parliamentary Acts after 1607 were not binding on Virginia, a theme he developed by a copious use of references to English legal and constitutional documents. He suggested that the first Continental Congress be held in a Virginia or Maryland frontier town, where the members would be amply protected by the excellent marksmanship of the frontier riflemen. Throughout all of the letters he cautioned against rash moves and radical tendencies. America was to save England from the madness of her Parliament. Mason's best contribution to the reorganized Virginia government was his leadership in the move to conserve the work of George Rogers Clark [*q.v.*], in the Northwest Campaign. In this connection he was the author and champion of the bill through which the Virginia Assembly organized the Northwest as the County of Illinois.

During the Revolutionary period Virginia claimed the services of an array of lawyers unique in American annals. From the standpoint of legal knowledge and sheer ability, Mason was probably the chief among them. His independence and fearlessness and his unwillingness to sponsor measures merely on the basis of their popularity undoubtedly stood in the way of his political advancement. In 1783 he was again a member of the General Assembly. He advocated the exclusion of Loyalists from citizenship, and sought to regulate the payment of foreign and domestic debts, by canceling interest during the war and allowing for depreciation of the currency. He also opposed granting a permanent fund to Congress, but was willing to grant funds collected by state officers. Any inclination to assume that he benefited from the prestige and echoed the sentiments of his more famous elder brother is dispelled by the poignant appraisal of Jefferson, "T. Mason is a meteor whose path cannot be calculated" (P. L. Ford, *The Writings of Thomas Jefferson,* vol. III, 1894, p. 318). A hint of his political and social philosophy may be derived from a peculiar but emphatic provision in his will for the rearing of his minor children under such conditions that they would not "imbibe more exalted notions of their own importance than I could wish any child of mine to possess."

Mason died when only a few years beyond middle age. He was twice married, first, in 1758 or 1759, to Mary King Barnes; and second, to Elizabeth (Westwood) Wallace. From the earlier of these unions there was born Stevens Thomson Mason [*q.v.*] who achieved greater distinction than his father, though he was probably no more able. It is perhaps worthy of note in view of Thomson Mason's interest in the Northwest, that the grandson of Stevens, also named Stevens Thomson Mason [*q.v.*], was the "boy governor" of Michigan Territory, in its critical years, and the first governor of the state.

[The best account of Mason is to be gathered from the frequent references to him in K. M. Rowland's *Life of George Mason, 1725–1792* (2 vols., 1892); his "British American" letters, IV–IX, are in Peter Force, *Am. Archives,* 4 ser., vol. I (1837); information as to his political activities must be gleaned from *Jours. of the House of Burgesses of Va., 1758–1776* (5 vols., 1905–08); *Jour. of the House of Delegates,* 1777–83, and H. R. McIlwaine, *Legislative Jours. of the Council of Colonial Va.,* vol. III (1919); see also, H. B. Grigsby, *The Hist. of the Va. Federal Convention of 1788,* vol. II (1891); E. A. Jones, *Am. Members of the Inns of Court* (1924).] F. H. H.

MASON, WILLIAM (Sept. 2, 1808–May 21, 1883), inventor, manufacturer, was the son of Amos and Mary (Holdredge) Mason. He was born at Mystic, Conn., but when he was six years old his parents moved to Stonington, where his father cultivated a small farm and worked as a blacksmith. William spent his boyhood helping in his father's shop and going to school occasionally in the winter time. When he was thirteen he began an apprenticeship in the spinning room of a cotton factory at Canterbury, Conn., but three years later entered a cotton-thread factory in Lisbon, Conn. He was here only a year, but in that time he won a reputation as a skilled mechanic by repairing complicated machinery, and, though he was but seventeen years old, his services were requested to start the machinery in a new mill at East Haddam. This mission accomplished, he returned to his first employer, whose machine shop he now entered, and finished his apprenticeship at twenty.

During the succeeding four years, from 1828 to 1832, he engaged in various occupations. Going to New Hartford, near Utica, N. Y., he went to work for a company that failed a few months later. While there, however, he turned his attention to machinery for making diaper cloth, and after going back to Canterbury he designed and built the first power loom in the United States for the manufacture of this material. He next constructed an ingenious loom for weaving damask table cloths. Thereafter, as he told a friend, "I was fooling about for some time painting portraits, making fiddles, and one thing and another" (*Railroad Gazette, post,* p. 341). In 1832 he was surprised to receive an order for some diaper looms, which he proceeded to fill by renting space in a shop in Willimantic, Conn., and having the frames made there. The making of these looms brought him a handsome profit. In 1833 his services were requested in Killingly, Conn., to work on a new device for spinning cotton since known as the ring frame. The device had been patented in 1828 but had ruined the manufacturer who tried to make it of practical use. Mason remodeled and perfected it within two years and brought about its extensive use in the textile industry.

In 1835 he went to Taunton, Mass., to operate the shop of Crocker & Richmond, taking his ring frame machinery with him. The company failed in 1837, but Mason continued as foreman for Leach & Keith, the firm that succeeded it, and concentrated his attention on improvements in cotton machinery. He patented a speeder for cotton roving machines on May 4, 1838, and on Oct. 8, 1840, secured the patent for his greatest invention, the "self-acting mule," for spinning cotton and other fibrous materials. Two years later Leach & Keith failed and Mason purchased the establishment with the aid of a cotton machinery commission house of Boston. The prosperous times which succeeded the tariff of 1842 were favorable to Mason and his business grew rapidly, so that in 1845 he was able to build a new plant. Competition called for improvements on the self-acting mule, and on Oct. 3, 1846, he received a second patent on this device. Gradually he added to the products of his plant and besides cotton and woolen machinery he made tools, cupola furnaces, blowers, gears, shafting, and Campbell printing presses, the methods of manufacture and the machinery used being chiefly of his own invention. In 1852 he began the building of locomotives, the first of which was completed Oct. 11, 1853, and the seven-hundreth, just a week after his death. The Mason locomotives were recognized the world over for their beauty and symmetry of design and for the excellence of their workmanship; they exerted a great influence on locomotive construction in the United States, especially with respect to harmony of the visible outlines. As an outgrowth of locomotive building, Mason began the manufacture of car wheels with tubular spokes, in contradistinction to the "plate" or "disc" wheel generally used. During the Civil War he produced a large quantity of Springfield rifles. Ten years before he died he reorganized his company as the Mason Machine Works and, with the assistance of his sons, directed its affairs until his death. At that time the plant covered ten acres of land; a thousand people were employed; and the firm did more than a million dollars' worth of business annually.

Mason was a founder and first president (1847–57) of the Machinists' National Bank of Taunton, and a director of the Taunton Gas Company. He was interested in art, and found recreation in portrait work and playing the violin. On June 10, 1844, he married Harriet Augusta Metcalf of Cambridge, Mass., and was survived by two sons and a daughter.

[*Railroad Gazette,* June 1, 1883; J. L. Bishop, *A Hist. of Am. Manufactures from 1608 to 1860* (1868), vol. III; *Railway and Locomotive Hist. Soc. Bull.,* no. 15, Nov. 1927; Angus Sinclair, *Development of the Locomotive Engine* (1907); *Taunton and the Machinists' National Bank* (1928); J. D. Van Slyck, *Representatives of New England: Manufacturers* (1879); S. H. Emery, *Hist. of Taunton, Mass.* (1893); Edward Hungerford, *The Story of the Baltimore and Ohio Railroad, 1827–1927* (1928), vol. II; *Report of the Commissioner of Patents,* 1828, 1838, 1840, 1846; *Boston Daily Advertiser,* May 22, 1883; date of birth from tombstone.] C. W. M.

MASON, WILLIAM (Jan. 24, 1829–July 14, 1908), pianist, teacher, and composer, was born in Boston, Mass., the third son of Lowell Mason [*q.v.*] and his wife Abigail Gregory. He evinced his inherited musical talent at an early age. He studied the piano with Henry Schmidt in Boston and made his début as a boy of seventeen at a concert at the Boston Academy of Music on Mar. 7, 1846. In 1849 he went to Germany to complete his studies. In Leipzig he was the pupil of Ignaz Moscheles, Moritz Hauptmann, and Ernst Friedrich Richter; in Prague he took piano lessons of Alexander Dreyschock, and in Weimar (1853–54) he studied with Franz Liszt. It was Liszt who probably exerted the greatest influence on his development, and from whom he largely derived the rich tone-color and variety in expression that marked his playing. While at Weimar Mason associated with Rubinstein, Von Bülow, Klindworth, Pruckner, and other music students, appeared as a concert-pianist in Weimar, Prague, Frankfurt, and London, and returned to America with the prestige attaching to a brilliant young disciple of Liszt.

Upon his return in 1854, he toured the country as a concert-pianist, playing with success in various cities from Boston to Chicago. He then (1855) established himself permanently in New York City where, besides teaching, he devoted much time to public performance, and was the first pianist to introduce the "Hungarian Rhapsodies" and other Liszt compositions to American audiences. He was possibly the first pianist to tour the United States giving piano recitals exclusively; Gottschalk and others always toured with a singer or another instrumentalist. During the winter of 1855–56, with Theodore Thomas, Carl Bergmann, Joseph Mosenthal, and George Matzka, he founded the Mason-Thomas Soirées of Chamber-Music, a series of concerts of high quality which were continued until 1868. At these concerts many notable works, including compositions by Schumann and Brahms, were performed for the first time before American audiences.

After 1868 Mason devoted himself principally to teaching, at which he was very successful. In collaboration with E. S. Hoadly he wrote *A Method for the Pianoforte* (1867) and *A System for Beginners in the Art of Playing Upon the Pianoforte* (1871), and with W. S. B. Mathews he compiled *A System of Technical Exercises for the Pianoforte* (1878). His most widely popular piano textbook, however, was his *Touch and Technic* (*opus* 44), the sum of his more than forty years experience, which Paderewski pronounced the best piano method known to him. It undoubtedly played an important part in stabilizing the piano technique of his day.

Mason wrote about forty pieces for the piano, refined in style and poetically imaginative, among them "Silver Spring" (*opus* 6); the mazurka-caprice "Spring Dawn" (*opus* 20); "Rêverie Poétique" (*opus* 24); "Serenata" (*opus* 39); and "Capriccio Fantastico" (*opus* 50). But his chief importance lies in his work as a teacher. Liszt had praised him for rising above mere finger virtuosity; this higher outlook upon piano playing he sedulously inculcated in his pupils. He was generous in his sympathy and encouragement to young composers, and always a gentleman. He died in his home in New York at the age of seventy-nine. He had married, on Mar. 12, 1857, Mary Isabella Webb, by whom he had three children.

[The principal source of information is Mason's autobiographical *Memories of a Musical Life* (1901). See also: H. C. Lahee, *Famous Pianists of To-Day and Yesterday* (1901); L. C. Elson, *The Hist. of Am. Music* (1925); *Dwight's Jour. of Music,* Sept. 30, 1854; the *N. Y. Musical Gazette,* July 1873; the *Musician,* Sept. 1908; *Musical Observer,* Dec. 1928; *Etude,* Sept. 1908, Nov. 1914; *Musical Courier,* July 22, 1908.]

F. H. M.

MASON, WILLIAM ERNEST (July 7, 1850–June 16, 1921), representative and senator from Illinois, the son of Lewis J. and Nancy (Winslow) Mason, was born at Franklinville, N. Y. When he was eight years old his family took him to Bentonsport, Iowa, where he attended school. Four years of teaching led him to the study of the law, and in 1872 he was admitted to the Illinois bar from Chicago. A relatively short residence in his adopted state gave him some local prominence, and he obtained a seat in the state House of Representatives in 1879 and in the Senate from 1881 to 1885. He served in the Fiftieth and Fifty-first federal congresses from 1887 to 1891. His reputation as a stump speaker was enhanced by a stirring campaign against Bryan in 1896, which resulted in his election to the Senate, where he served from 1897 to 1903, as an avowed opponent of the Lorimer machine that had been dominant in Chicago politics for some time. Sympathy with the downtrodden, possibly inherited from a father who was an ardent abolitionist, led him to champion the Cuban revolt against Spain. It also led him into conflict with the administration, at the moment in a temporizing mood (*Congressional Record,* 55 Cong., 1 Sess., pp. 1130–35). His resolution of Feb. 9, 1898, requested the president to declare and maintain peace in Cuba and was designed to force McKinley into action (*Ibid.,* 2 Sess., pp. 1578–85, 3294–95, 4035). His supporting speech came on the same day that de Lome, the Spanish minister, admitted writing derogatory statements about the president and caused a sensation that placed Mason among the insurgents who flayed executive inaction. With these he demanded intervention coupled with recognition of Cuban independence. Early in 1899 he proposed a resolution "that the Government of the United States of America will not attempt to govern the people of any other country in the world without the consent of the people themselves, or subject them by force to our dominion against their will" (*Ibid.,* 55 Cong., 3 Sess., p. 528). This might be taken as the text of his many speeches and occasional filibusters against the increasingly evident imperialistic trend of the administration and of the country at large. His efforts to prevent the acquisition of the Philippines failed, and, after voting at his constituents' instance for the treaty provisions concerning the islands, he turned his efforts toward obtaining self-government there.

This double defiance of the administration and of the party sent him into retirement. During those years he practised law in Chicago and in 1910 published a religious novel, *John, the Unafraid,* which was an expression of his own faith in the power of revealed religion. In 1917, although he lacked both an organization and money, he was returned to Washington as congressman-at-large. Here he rounded out his career, serving until his death. Again it was his convictions that forced him to oppose American entry into the World War and the selective draft (*Ibid.,* 65 Cong., 1 Sess., pp. 326–28, 1190–93, 3850–55). So bitter was his hostility that he was at one time made the object of a proposed investigation by Senator Heflin (*Ibid.,* pp. 5756–57, 7711–15; *Chicago Tribune,* Sept. 28, Oct. 4, 7, 1917). Cessation of hostilities found him, for once, with his own party, in fighting the League of Nations, but he championed one more lost cause by pleading for the recognition of the Irish republic. On June 11, 1873, he was married to Edith Julia White of Des Moines. At his death one of their daughters was chosen to serve the rest of his unexpired term in the Senate.

[*Wm. E. Mason, Memorial Addresses Delivered in the House of Representatives* (1924); *Who's Who in America,* 1920–21; *Biog. Dir. of Amer. Cong.* (1928); *Chicago Tribune,* July 11, 1886, Jan. 20, 21, 1897, June 17, 1921.]

L. E. E.

MASQUERIER, LEWIS (b. Mar. 14, 1802), pioneer in phonetic spelling and reformer, was born in Paris, Ky. His father, Lewis Masquerier, a son of French Huguenot parents, and a brother of John James Masquerier, the English painter, was educated in England, emigrated to Java, and during the French revolution returned to England and later went to Haiti. Narrowly escaping a general massacre of whites at Santo Domingo, he took ship for Philadelphia and about 1800 emigrated to Kentucky, where he married Sarah Hicklin. Their son, Lewis, received the meager schooling of a frontier community, read the few books in his father's house, and worked on the farm. As a boy he was more fond of spending his Sundays in the forest than in learning Old Testament stories, which even then shocked his moral sense and his ideas of human rights. After his father died, his mother married again, and in 1818 the family moved to the Boonslick settlement on the Missouri River. Lewis soon returned to Paris, Ky., where he went to work in a printing shop. Ambition to be an orator led him to study law. He was licensed and began practice in Quincy, Ill., but there he discovered that he was too shy to succeed as a trial lawyer and that office work bored him. Neglecting his practice, he indulged a "thirst for promiscuous learning" (*Appendix, post,* p. 29). Meanwhile he made a living by land speculation. Among the subjects that aroused his mental curiosity was phonetic spelling. In 1830 he invented a new alphabet of eleven vowels and twenty-two consonants, and in 1834 he published in St. Louis a pamphlet on the subject. He went to New York to obtain better facilities for popularizing his phonetic system. A special font of letters was cast and specimens of a small dictionary were published, which included a treatise on scientific orthography. In 1867, he published *The Phonotypic Spelling and Reading Manual.* In this field Masquerier was a pioneer, preceding by more than twenty years Smalley in the United States and Ellis in England.

In New York Masquerier's attention was soon diverted by schemes for general social reform. He became one of the first disciples of George Henry Evans [*q.v.*] and, with characteristic disregard of practical considerations, pushed Evans' doctrines of individualism to their logical conclusion, which was anarchism. In lectures, delivered in New York and Boston, and in pamphlets he developed the outlines of an agrarian Utopia. The entire surface of the earth was to be divided into townships six miles square with villages in the geometric centers. The townships were to be subdivided into homesteads of forty acres each. Thus landlordism, rent-paying, and the wage system were to be abolished. Although his ideas attracted no important following, he lived to see the adoption of one principle of agrarianism, the distribution of the public domain to actual settlers, in the Homestead Act of 1862. In his passion for individualism he would have abolished not only organized government but also organized religion, which he regarded as an additional means of enslaving humanity. In 1877 his writings, comprising newspaper articles, pamphlets and poems on phonetics, land reform, and theology, were collected in a volume entitled *Sociology, or the Reconstruction of Society, Government, and Property. An Appendix to Sociology* was published in 1884. About 1840 he married Anna Taber of Bradford, Vt. The date of his death has not been found.

[J. R. Commons, *Hist. of Labor* (1918), vol. I; autobiog. material in *Sociology* (1877), esp. pp. 132–36 and in *Appendix to Sociology* (1884); G. L. Randall, *Taber Geneal.* (copr. 1924), p. 35.] P. W. B.

MASSASSOIT (d. 1661), "great chief," or more properly Ousamequin, "yellow feather," has appeared under many names with great variance in spelling. He was chief of the Wampanoags, making his main home at Pokanoket, or Mount Hope, near Bristol in Rhode Island. Even the approximate date of his birth is unknown but in 1621 he was described as a "very lusty man, in his best years, an able body, grave of countenance, and spare of speech" (Drake, *post,* book II, p. 22). His sway is said to have extended over Cape Cod and all of Massachusetts and Rhode Island between Massachusetts and Narragansett Bays, with somewhat indefinite boundaries westward. Just before the Pilgrims arrived at Plymouth, however, his tribes had been almost decimated by some illness and their strength greatly reduced.

He had already become acquainted with white men. It is likely that he was the "king of the country" whom John Smith met when cruising the New England coast, and Capt. Thomas Dermer was in communication with him in 1619, recovering from him two Frenchmen who had been cast away. On Mar. 22, 1621, Massassoit and his brother Quadequina, with sixty warriors, accompanied Samoset and Squanto to Plymouth and there met the Pilgrims. After the proper preliminaries, and a drink of whiskey that "made him sweat all the while after" (Young, *post,* p. 191), the chief negotiated a treaty of peace and amity with the whites, which he never broke. The following July Edward Winslow and Stephen Hopkins paid him a visit at Pokanoket to forward the relations and spy out his position and strength. They found many skeletons of his followers still lying on the ground, the dead having been so many in the "great sickness" that the living could not bury them. The same year, when John Billington was lost, Massassoit located him with some Indians and returned him to Plymouth. In 1623 he sent word to his new friends that he was very ill if not dying, and Winslow and others went to see him. Owing to their treatment he recovered and disclosed to them the facts of an Indian conspiracy to destroy Weston's plantation (Bradford, *post,* I, 292).

In 1632 the Narragansetts tried to capture him and he fled to Plymouth for protection. Winslow went to see him in 1634 and Massassoit returned to Plymouth with him. He had frightened the Pilgrims by sending word that Winslow was dead and when they both arrived, he explained his act by saying it was an Indian custom to make them more glad of his arrival when he came safely (*Winthrop's Journal,* I, 131). The next year Roger Williams made peace between Massassoit and Canonicus in order to have quiet in Rhode Island. In 1638 Massassoit went to

Boston with eighteen beaver skins, saying he understood the English were provoked with him, and sued for peace. Apparently he had no cause for his anxiety. He again visited Boston in July 1642 with many men and some sagamores and was entertained by Winthrop. Seven years later he sold the site of Duxbury to the English. Some of the earlier histories state that he died in 1656 but it is known from the New Plymouth Colony records that he was alive in or shortly before May 1661 when he complained of an attack by other Indians; a letter of Roger Williams, Dec. 13, 1661, refers to him as deceased (*Publications of the Narragansett Club,* vol. VI, 1874, p. 316). His son Metacomet became famous as King Philip. Always inclined to peace, even among his own race, Massassoit remained a faithful friend to the English throughout his entire life.

[F. W. Hodge, *Handbook of American Indians,* pt. I (1907); S. G. Drake, *The Book of the Indians* (8th ed., 1841); *Winthrop's Journal* (2 vols., 1908), ed. by J. K. Hosmer; William Bradford, *Hist. of Plymouth Plantation, 1620–1647* (2 vols., 1912), ed. by W. C. Ford; Alexander Young, *Chronicles of the Pilgrim Fathers* (1841); David Pulsifer, *Records of the Colony of New Plymouth . . . Acts of the Commissioners of the United Colonies of New England,* II (1859), 268–69.]

J. T. A.

MASSEY, GEORGE BETTON (Nov. 15, 1856–Mar. 29, 1927), physician, born near the village of Massey, Kent County, Md., was the son of Benjamin Hemsley Clinton Massey and a descendant of James Massey who came from Guernsey, Channel Islands, in 1644, to settle in Maryland. Under the instruction of his intellectually gifted mother, Bersheba (Betton) Massey of Tallahassee, Fla., the boy developed a taste for scientific studies, especially physics. After the Civil War he attended an academy at Galena, Md., and later taught school for a year. In 1873 he began his preliminary medical studies at Tallahassee, under the guidance of his maternal uncle, Dr. George W. Betton. He attended the Medical College of South Carolina in 1874, receiving a prize for proficiency in chemistry, and in 1876, before he was twenty years of age, graduated with the degree of M.D. from the University of Pennsylvania, submitting a thesis entitled "Salicylic Acid."

His first experience in private practice was in Tallahassee; but he was soon called to the position of assistant physician in the State Hospital for the Insane at Danville, Pa., where he served for some two years, resigning in 1879 to enter private practice in Philadelphia. For a time he was assistant to Dr. William Goodell of the University of Pennsylvania. Meantime, he continued his studies of nervous disorders in the Orthopedic Hospital and Infirmary for Nervous Diseases, where he became associated with Dr. S. Weir Mitchell [*q.v.*] and his staff. For seven years he was electrical assistant to Mitchell, who was one of the first specialists to advocate the use of electrotherapy, and from 1881 to 1887 he was electrotherapist in the institution, a position created for him. Resigning from the Infirmary in 1887, he was appointed attending physician to the department of diseases of the mind and nervous system in Howard Hospital, but the next year was transferred to the gynecological clinic of that hospital, where he demonstrated electrotherapeutics in the diseases of women until 1898.

When the International Electrical Exposition of the Franklin Institute was held in Philadelphia, in 1884, Massey served on the board of judges. He participated in the affairs of numerous local, state, and national medical societies and of the Pan-American Medical Congress, and represented the United States at the Third International Physiotherapeutic Congress held in Paris in 1910. The American Electro-Therapeutic Association, the first national association of its kind, owed its establishment largely to the stimulus which Massey gave it as a founder and as president in 1891. His zeal for the advancement of electrotherapeutics was further shown by his share in founding the American Oncologic Hospital, in Philadelphia, for the treatment of cancerous affections, with which institution he was connected as attending surgeon from 1904 to 1912. His writings on medical subjects were voluminous; his work as one of the pioneers in the field of electrotherapeutics and his reports and clinical observations therein placed him in the front rank as an investigator and gave him an international reputation. He was one of the editors of *An International System of Electrotherapeutics* (2nd ed., 1901), collaborator in the *American Journal of Electrotherapeutics and Radiology* from 1917, and the author of *Electricity in the Diseases of Women* (1888; 2nd ed. 1890), *Conservative Gynecology and Electrotherapeutics* (1898, 6th ed. 1909), *Ionic Surgery in the Treatment of Cancer* (1910), *Practical Electrotherapeutics and Diathermy* (1924), and joint author with Frederick H. Morse of *Galvanic Currents and Low Voltage Wave Currents in Physical Therapy* (1927). Massey was married, Mar. 25, 1885, to Harriet Louise Stairs of Philadelphia, who with three children survived him. He died in his seventy-first year.

[*A Sketch of the Life of George Betton Massey, M.D.* (4 pp., n.d.), and other family papers in the possession of Massey's daughter, Mrs. George L. Winslow, Pittsburgh, Pa.; records of the School of Medicine, Univ. of Pa.; *Index.-Cat. of the Lib. of the Surgeon-General's Office,* 2 ser. X (1905), 3 ser. VII (1928); *Who's Who in America,* 1926–27; *Jour. Am. Medic. Asso.,* Apr. 16, 1927; *Evening Bulletin* (Phila.), Mar. 30, 1927.]

R. L. B.

MASSEY, JOHN EDWARD (Apr. 2, 1819–Apr. 24, 1901), Baptist clergyman, politician, was born in Spotsylvania County, Va., son of Benjamin and Elizabeth (Chewning) Massey. In 1836, from the old-field school near his home, with his belongings packed in a pillowcase, he journeyed on foot the sixty miles to the Virginia Baptist Seminary, now University of Richmond, for a year's study. Further work in private schools and another year at the Seminary followed, after which he read law while working in his father's shop to pay for his lawbooks. In 1843 he was admitted to the bar. The youngest in a very religious household, however, he had from infancy successfully "exhorted" at revivals, and now men said that he ought to be a preacher. Accordingly, the next year he was licensed, and for eight years thereafter as the Virginia Baptist Association's missionary he energetically carried his message to the people of the heterogeneous Valley region from Winchester to Lexington, meeting considerable success and learning much about the psychology of plain men and the arts of dialectic and side-stepping. He was a pastor in Albemarle and Nelson counties from 1854 to 1862; and then, alleging ill health, he purchased the "Ash Lawn" farm in Albemarle and thither retired with Margaret Ann Kable, his wife since 1847.

He had originally been a Whig, but a trip through New England about 1854 made him a Democrat; by 1860 he was an ardent and argumentative secessionist; and during the Civil War he raised "grain and provender" for the army and bought Confederate bonds. During Reconstruction he was resentful but quiet. Then, after he had passed his fiftieth birthday, he began a career of thirty years as a "champion of the people." Asserting that, through the corrupt collusion of Carpet-baggers, bankers, and brokers, taxes and interest rates had become excessive while the state's schools and charities were neglected and farming languished he declared that the recent "funding act" ought to be undone and the state's enormous debt "readjusted" to the state's diminished capacity to pay. Accordingly, notwithstanding his opposition to ministers' participating in politics, since other capable and trustworthy men were lackng because of the penalties of Reconstruction, he announced himself as a candidate for the legislature. Elected to the House in 1873 and 1875 and to the Senate in 1877, he was ere long dubbed "Father of the Readjuster Movement," through which the various elements of discontent eventually compelled a definite settlement of the debt issue. The movement was strongly disapproved by the "best people," however, and when Massey found his gubernatorial aspirations thwarted and his group being led into the Republican party by William Mahone [*q.v.*], he revolted and aided powerfully in the restoration of a liberalized Democratic régime. His unsuccessful campaign for the place of congressman at large (1882), his election as lieutenant-governor (1885), and his election as superintendent of public instruction (1889) were incidents in this "redemption" of the state. As state auditor under the Readjusters (1879–81), he had rendered important service, though not without an eye to politics; as superintendent he desired that schools for negroes should receive only such taxes as had been paid by negroes for that purpose. Always a temperance advocate, he distinctly aided the local-option movement but vigorously opposed any identification of the anti-liquor agitation with a party. There were many stories reflecting upon his personal financial integrity, but most of these he disproved to the satisfaction of a jury in 1895; and shortly before his death he was elected to the constitutional convention of 1901–02.

Massey's strength lay in the common man's conviction of his honesty and sympathy and in his remarkable skill as a rough-and-tumble debater. Thoroughly understanding the shallower aspects of finance and the deep needs of his people, he was so full of anecdote and Scriptural quotation, so ready at repartee, so self-confident and poised, that few public men could boast of a successful encounter with him. In 1890 he married Mattie E. McCreary of Alabama.

[E. H. Hancock, *Autobiog. of John E. Massey* (1909); Ida B. Patterson, "John E. Massey" (1929), unpublished master's thesis, Univ. of Va.; C. C. Pearson, *The Readjuster Movement in Va.* (1917); *Richmond Dispatch*, Apr. 25, 1901; *Times* (Richmond), Apr. 25, 1901.]

C. C. P.

MAST, PHINEAS PRICE (Jan. 3, 1825–Nov. 20, 1898), inventor, manufacturer, was born in Lancaster County, Pa., the son of John and Elizabeth (Trego) Mast. His father, also born in eastern Pennsylvania, was a farmer and school teacher. When young Mast was five years old his parents moved to Ohio and established themselves on a farm near Urbana, where the boy grew to manhood. He helped in the farm work, attended the public schools, and with the assistance of his father prepared for college. When he was twenty years old he entered Ohio Wesleyan University and graduated in 1849, having given especial attention to scientific and Biblical studies. He then returned to his home where he remained for a number of years, teaching school in the neighborhood, assisting his father in the farm work, and devoting his spare time to the grain and stock business. On Jan. 4, 1850, he married Anna M. Kirkpatrick and six years later moved to Springfield, Ohio, where, with capital given him by his wife, he formed a partnership with John H. Thomas, bought the patent rights to the cider-mill invention of T. J. Kindelberger, and began its manufacture.

Within a short time the partners undertook the manufacture of farm implements, their first products being a Buckeye grain drill and a corn plow. Seeing many opportunities for improvements in agricultural machinery, they began developing ideas of their own and within two years began making implements of their own invention, the first one being a seed planter, patented July 27, 1858. This was followed by other inventions, twelve in all, including improved seeding machines, cultivators, and fertilizer distributors. In 1871 Thomas retired from the firm, Mast purchasing his interest and organizing the corporation, P. P. Mast & Company, of which he was president throughout his life. He associated with him men of inventive minds and carried forward his development work. Between 1872 and 1880 a number of patents were issued to him as a co-patentee, and assigned to his company. Most of these were for improvements in grain drills, and all were incorporated in the machines manufactured by his company. About 1880 he became interested in the improvement of lawn mowers and windmills and organized Mast, Foos & Company for the manufacture of these devices with novel features of his own invention. Still later, he purchased the Driscoll Carriage Company and reorganized it as the Mast Buggy Company. At the time of his death he was the directing head of all three concerns.

Mast was also financially interested in the publishing business. In 1879 he organized the firm of Mast, Crowell & Kirkpatrick and began the publication of *Farm and Fireside,* one of the most extensively circulated agricultural journals in the United States; the firm also published the *Woman's Home Companion.* Mast was president of the Springfield National Bank, established Mar. 31, 1882, and took an active part in the municipal affairs of Springfield, serving on the city council for twenty-two years. In 1895 he was mayor of the city. In addition to his manufacturing interests, he had large holdings of real-estate in Ohio, Kansas, California, and Georgia. At the time of his death in Springfield he was survived by three adopted daughters who were the children of his deceased brother.

[C. Z. Mast, *A Brief Hist. of Bishop Jacob Mast and other Mast Pioneers* (1911); W. M. Rockel, *20th Century Hist. of Springfield and Clark County, Ohio, and Representative Citizens* (1908); *Farm Implement News,* Nov. 24, 1898; *Farm Machinery,* Nov. 22, 1898; *Implement Age,* Dec. 1, 1898; *Report of the Commissioner of Patents,* 1858, 1862, 1865, 1866, 1868, 1869, 1870, 1871; *Ohio State Jour.* (Columbus), Nov. 21, 1898.]

C. W. M.

MASTERSON, WILLIAM BARCLAY (Nov. 24, 1853–Oct. 25, 1921), frontier peace officer, sports writer, familiarly known as "Bat" Masterson, was the son of Thomas and Catherine McGurk Masterson and was born in Iroquois County, Ill. Little is recorded of his youth. In 1871 the family moved to a farm near Wichita, Kan., and in the following fall young Masterson and his brother Edward joined a party of buffalo hunters which set out from Fort Dodge. With a partner, in the summer of 1872, he undertook a grading contract on the Atchison, Topeka & Santa Fé railroad. Two years later he was again with a party of buffalo hunters, and on June 27, 1874, in the desperate battle with Indians at Adobe Walls, won distinction for coolness and bravery. For a time he was a scout under General Miles. In the spring of 1876 he served as a deputy-marshal of Dodge City, but in July he resigned and joined in the gold rush to Deadwood. He returned in the fall and in November 1877 was elected sheriff of Ford County. Early in 1878 he won an added distinction by surprising and capturing the noted outlaw, Dave Rudabaugh, and on Apr. 9, when his brother Edward, then the acting marshal of Dodge City, was shot down by two gunmen, he arrived on the scene in time to kill one and mortally wound the other.

At some time in 1880 he went to Tombstone, then considered the most lawless town in the world, and on several occasions assisted Wyatt Earp in his duties as a federal marshal. He left Tombstone in 1881, was for some months in Trinidad, Col., and was apparently back in Dodge City in 1883. By 1885 he seems to have established himself in Denver, where on Nov. 21, 1891, he married Emma Walters. In the main his occupation was gambling, a mode of livelihood which in those days on the frontier was generally deemed quite as reputable as any other gainful employment. He became deeply interested in athletics, especially pugilism. In May 1902 he moved to New York City, and within a year became a sports writer on the *Morning Telegraph.* President Roosevelt, by whom he was greatly admired, appointed him a federal deputy-marshal early in 1905, but finding the intermittent calls to duty in conflict with his newspaper work he resigned the post within two years. At the time of his death he was the sports editor of the *Morning Telegraph* and the secretary of the company. He died suddenly, while working at his desk. His funeral, on Oct. 27, 1921, was largely attended, and the interment was at Woodlawn Cemetery. He was survived by his wife.

Masterson usually dressed well and was something of a dandy. He was genial and easy of approach, had many friends, and was highly respected. As a frontier peace officer he ranks with Earp, Hickok, and Tilghman, a fearless company of whom it has been strikingly said that they "shot their way to heaven" by subduing the lawless, protecting the weak, and establishing peace and order.

[Robert M. Wright, *Dodge City, the Cowboy Capital* (1913); Olive K. Dixon, *Life of Billy Dixon* (revised ed., 1927); Fred E. Sutton and A. B. Macdonald, *Hands Up!* (1927); N. Y. *Morning Telegraph, Times, World,* and *Tribune,* Oct. 26, 1921; information from Kirke Mechem, Topeka, Kan., Thomas Masterson, Wichita, Kan., and Mrs. Emma Masterson, New York.]

W. J. G.

MASTIN, CLAUDIUS HENRY (June 4, 1826–Oct. 3, 1898), surgeon, was born at Huntsville, Ala., to Francis Turner Mastin and Ann Elizabeth Caroline (Levert). His paternal grandfather had emigrated from Wales to Maryland; his maternal grandfather was chief surgeon of Rochambeau's fleet. Mastin attended Greenville Academy at Huntsville and later the University of Virginia. Returning to Huntsville, he began the study of medicine under Dr. John Y. Bassett, an accomplished physician and anatomist. He received the degree of M.D. in 1849 from the University of Pennsylvania. After brief periods of practice at Huntsville, and Nashville, Tenn., he went to Europe where he attended lectures at the University of Edinburgh, the Royal College of Surgeons, London, and the University of France in Paris. In 1854 he settled for practice in Mobile, Ala., in association with an uncle, Dr. Levert. From the first he devoted himself to surgery and in time became the leading operator of his section. Although a general surgeon, he was particularly interested in genito-urinary surgery, for which purpose he devised a number of instruments. He was a pioneer in the employment of metallic sutures and is credited with being the first to use silver wire for ligating the external iliac artery for aneurism of the femoral artery. This operation was performed in June 1866. About the same time he employed silver wire for the closure of a vesico-vaginal fistula. From 1854 to 1857 he was employed by the United States Marine Hospital Service in Mobile and in 1855 he was appointed surgeon to the Mobile City Hospital. In 1861, at the outbreak of the Civil War, he was commissioned as a surgeon in the Confederate army and served as medical director, first on the staff of Gen. Leonidas Polk and later with Gen. Braxton Bragg and Gen. G. T. Beauregard. He was the chief medical officer at the battle of Shiloh. Returning to Mobile after the war, he resided there until his death.

Mastin was an organizer of the Congress of American Physicians and Surgeons, which held its first meeting in 1888 (*Transactions . . . First Triennial Session, 1888,* 1889). He was an original fellow of the American Surgical Association and its president in 1890–91, and was a member of the Southern Surgical and Gynecological Association. One of the organizers of the American Genito-Urinary Association, he was president in 1895–96. He was active in the affairs of the alumni association of the medical department of the University of Pennsylvania and in 1874 delivered the annual address. To him is largely due the credit for the erection of the monument to Dr. Gross in Philadelphia. He made a notable address upon the unveiling in 1895. His writings are mainly journal articles published in the transactions of the societies to which he belonged. Among the more notable are: *Inguinal Aneurism: Successful Ligation of External Iliac Artery by Means of Silver Wire* (1866), *Internal Urethrotomy as a Cure for Urethral Stricture* (1871), *Chronic Urethral Discharges* (1872), *New Method of Treating Strictures of the Urethra* (1873), *Causes and Geographical Distribution of Calculous Diseases* (1877), and *Hernia, a Comparison of the Various Methods Employed for its Cure* (1889).

Mastin was a scholarly man, a facile writer, and an effective public speaker. Physically he was tall, slight, and erect. He was married Sept. 20, 1848, to Mary Eliza, daughter of William McDowell of Huntsville. Two sons followed him in the practice of medicine.

[*Ala. Medic. and Surgic. Age,* Apr. 1896, portr.; *Trans. Am. Surgic. Asso.,* vol. XVIII (1900); *Trans. So. Surgic. and Gynecol. Asso.,* vol. XV (1903); portr.; H. A. Kelly and W. L. Burrage, *Am. Medic. Biogs.* (1920); *Memorial Record of Ala.* (1893), vol. II; J. H. McDowell, *Hist. of the McDowells and Connections* (1918); *Medic. Record* (N. Y.), Oct. 8, 1898; *Daily Register* (Mobile, Ala.), Oct. 5, 1898.]

J. M. P.

MASURY, JOHN WESLEY (Jan. 1, 1820–May 14, 1895), manufacturer, inventor, was born in Salem, Mass., the son of John and Priscilla (Carroll) Masury and a descendant of the French Huguenot family of Le Mesuriers. After receiving a good secondary education he worked in various capacities in Salem until 1842, when he went to Brooklyn, N. Y., which was his home for upwards of forty years. Here he became a clerk in the retail paint store of John D. Prince. A few years later, at the suggestion of Masury, Prince established a factory for the making of ground dry colors under the firm name of John D. Prince & Company, with Masury as partner.

The business was imediately successful and in a short time a third partner, to serve as salesman, was admitted and the company name changed to Prince, Masury & Weeks. Subsequently, Masury and Weeks bought out Prince and the two partners continued the business until the death of the latter in 1857. In order to buy his deceased partner's holdings Masury secured as a partner Frederick L. Whiton, and the firm was known as Masury & Whiton. On the death of Whiton in 1871, Masury took his son-in-law, F. L. Miller, into the business, changing the name of the concern to John W. Masury & Son.

A short time after Prince and Masury began the manufacture of dry colors, the latter conceived the idea of making ready-mixed paints as well. The greatest problem involved was that of securing a suitable metal container, and Masury began experimenting with this object in view. As early as 1857, Apr. 28, he patented a "metallic paint canister," and on July 5, 1859, he secured a second patent for an "improved paint can"; but it was not until 1873 that he perfected a paint can with a top so thin that it could be cut with a pocket knife. The use of this type of can as a container for ready-mixed paints marked the beginning of a very successful business for Masury, since his company enjoyed a monopoly of the invention for twenty-one years. Another important invention of Masury was an improved paint mill, patented Oct. 4, 1870, for grinding colors to an impalpable fineness in quick-drying varnish. Such grinding required that the millstones be held in close contact, and in the ordinary mill the frictional heat developed was sufficient to spoil the thinning material. Masury, however, devised a method by which a stream of cold water was passed over the outer surfaces of both the upper and lower millstones, thus preventing a destructive temperature. This invention alone permitted the manufacture of the so-called coach colors, which, prior to this time, had been made wholly in individual shops. Within two years after he began making coach colors, ground in Japan, with his improved mill, the demand for them called for more than three hundred tons a year per color.

Masury wrote a number of books and pamphlets on paints and painting, the best known of which is *House-Painting, Carriage-Painting and Graining,* published in 1881. He was twice married: first, Oct. 15, 1844, to Laura A. Carlton of Salem, and, second, to Grace Harkins of Brooklyn. He died at his residence in New York and was buried at Center Moriches, L. I.

[*Vital Records of Salem, Mass.,* vol. IV (1924); *Report of the Commissioner of Patents,* 1857, 1859, 1870–73; Henry Hall, *America's Successful Men of Affairs* (1895), vol. I; *N. Y. Tribune,* May 15, 1895, *Salem Daily Gazette,* May 16, 1895.] C. W. M.

MATEER, CALVIN WILSON (Jan. 9, 1836–Sept. 28, 1908), Presbyterian missionary to China, was born in Cumberland County, Pa., a few miles west of Harrisburg. His parents, John Mateer and Mary Nelson (Diven), were both of Scotch-Irish stock, and, true to that tradition, reared their family on the Bible and the Shorter Cathechism. His mother, especially, instilled in the children a love of education and an admiration for missionaries. Mateer made his way through country school, academy (at Hunterstown and then at Menittstown), and Jefferson College (later Washington and Jefferson), taking his bachelor's degree in 1857 with one of the two highest scholastic averages of his class. For two years after graduation he taught school with marked success, and then, having decided to enter the ministry, went to Allegheny (Western) Theological Seminary, graduating in 1861. While in seminary, he determined to be a missionary, but since the mission board at first lacked funds to send him, for two years he held a pastorate at Delaware, Ohio. In 1863, however, he was appointed to the mission in the recently opened port at Tengchow, in the province of Shantung, China, and there he spent most of his life.

Quiet, persevering, indefatigable, scholarly, with an aptitude for and an interest in mechanics amounting almost to genius, unyielding in his religious convictions, but possessing beneath his reserved exterior a tender heart for children and his students, he had a versatile and rather noteworthy career. He traveled extensively through the rural districts of Shantung, preaching, distributing literature, and helping to found churches, often in the face of persecution and personal danger. Early he established a school for boys, and under his patient and skilful management in time it became a college, one of the institutions that were eventually merged into what was later Shantung Christian and then Cheeloo University. He was president of the college until 1895 and retained his connection with it until 1907. He emphasized teaching in Chinese rather than in English. Largely with his own hands he built laboratory equipment for the college and examples of Western mechanical appliances which he collected into a museum for the purpose of educating the Chinese in Occidental science. In 1871–72 he was in charge of the Presbyterian Mission Press in Shanghai. He achieved a noteworthy mastery of the Chinese language and engaged in extensive literary activity in that medium. His voluminous *Mandarin Lessons* (first edition, 1892) was for many years the standard text for introducing Protestant missionaries to the various forms of Mandarin. He prepared many textbooks in Chinese and served as chairman of a committee on textbooks appointed by the Missionary Conference (of Protestant missionaries in China) of 1890. That conference also appointed him on committees for the revision of the translations of the Bible into Mandarin and the literary language. He labored on these for many years, especially on the Mandarin version of the New Testament. He also wrote numerous articles and brochures in English. He died at Tsingtao, whither he had gone for medical care. He was married twice: on Dec. 27, 1862, to Julia A. Brown, who died Feb. 16, 1898; and on Sept. 25, 1900, to Ada Haven, who for years had been a missionary in China under the American Board of Commissioners for Foreign Missions.

[D. W. Fisher, *Calvin Wilson Mateer, Forty-five Years a Missionary in Shantung, China* (1911); R. M. Mateer, *Character Building in China: The Life Story of Julia Brown Mateer* (1912); *Who's Who in America*, 1908–09; F. W. Baller, in *Chinese Recorder*, Nov. 1908; W. A. P. Martin, in *Ibid.*, Dec. 1908; *Ann. Reports of the Board of Foreign Missions of the Presbyt. Ch. in the U. S. A.*, 1863–1908.] K. S. L.

MATHER, COTTON (Feb. 12, 1662/63–Feb. 13, 1727/28), Puritan clergyman, scholar, and author, was the eldest son of Increase [*q.v.*] and Maria (Cotton) Mather, and the grandson of Richard Mather and John Cotton [*qq.v.*]. His schooling he received partly at home and partly at the Boston Latin School, but the greatest influence in his early years was that of his family. He came to see himself as by birth appointed to carry on its tradition of leadership in the church and of championship of Congregational ideals. Sensitive and self-conscious as a boy, and given to fits of melancholy, he felt increasingly that he was predestined to a kind of priesthood. By the time he was twelve and entered Harvard as the youngest student who had ever been admitted there, he had already tried his hand at correcting his less pious comrades. At college he was at first "hazed," and, justifiably enough, apparently, regarded by some as a prig. More popular with his tutors than with his classmates, he showed a definite interest in science. After his graduation in 1678 he was so handicapped by stammering that he feared he could not enter the pulpit, and undertook the study of medicine. By 1680, however, he was able to preach, and soon began to assist his father at the Second Church in Boston. He took the degree of M.A. at Harvard in 1681, and refused a call to a church in New Haven. In 1685 he was finally ordained at the Second Church, where he held office for the rest of his life, serving as his father's colleague until 1723. Once regularly settled in Boston he became an Overseer at Harvard.

In 1686 he married Abigail Phillips, daughter of John Phillips, a prosperous citizen of Charlestown. Two years later his father's departure for England in order to plead for the restoration of the Massachusetts charter left to Cotton Mather the whole responsibility of conducting the Second Church as well as the task of working at home, as his father was working abroad, in the interests of what many colonists believed were their rights in opposition to the will of James II, expressed in Massachusetts through the royal governor, Sir Edmund Andros [*q.v.*]. When open rebellion against Andros broke out, Mather was a ringleader, and wrote *The Declaration of the Gentlemen, Merchants, and Inhabitants of Boston,* published in 1689 (W. H. Whitmore, *The Andros Tracts,* vol. I, 1868, pp. 11–20), which served as the manifesto of the insurgents. This increased his reputation, which his ability as a preacher and his skill as a writer, evidenced thus far in about a dozen printed works, had already made great. By 1690, when he was elected a fellow of Harvard, he was recognized, in spite of his youth, as one of the most eminent divines in New England. When his father came home in 1692, bringing a new royal charter for Massachusetts and accompanied by the new governor, Sir William Phips [*q.v.*], whom he had nominated, Cotton Mather rejoiced at the chance for political influence which was now offered him. Phips was a disciple of the Mathers and had been baptized by Cotton Mather not long before. He wrote much to defend both the charter and Phips's acts as governor. Two works of this character are his "Political Fables," circulated in manuscript in 1693 (*Andros Tracts,* vol. II, 1869, pp. 324–32), and his *Pietas in Patriam* (1697), a life of Phips.

One of Sir William's first official acts was the appointment of a court to try certain suspected witches who had been arrested at Salem Village. This was the beginning of the famous Massachusetts witchcraft prosecution of 1692. Cotton Mather's connection with the affair has provoked much debate, but the facts, so far as they can now be ascertained, are easily summarized. Very early Mather adopted the theory that persons molested by the Devil might best be treated by fasting and prayer, and he seems to have decided that it was his duty to study cases of supposed diabolical possession in order to combat Satan's wiles. His fervent introspection, coupled with his taste for scientific investigation, led him not only to scrutinize everything which might tend to demonstrate the reality of the world of spirits but also to exaggerate the importance of his observations. In 1688 he took into his house a child believed to be a victim of witchcraft, in order that he might study her case. He published the result of his observation in his *Memorable Providences, Relating to Witchcrafts and Possessions* (1689). In 1690 and 1691 he printed in at least two other works his views on witchcraft. Just before the Salem witch court began its work he warned one of the judges against putting on so-called "spectral evidence," unfavorable to the accused, as much emphasis as had been usual in many earlier trials in England, and suggested that punishments milder than execution might be imposed (*Massachusetts Historical Society Collections,* 4 ser. VIII, 397 ff.). He then wrote a statement of advice to the judges, signed and issued by him and other leading ministers, in which he repeated the same warning, though he urged careful examination of the accused and vigorous prosecution of those safely to be suspected of guilt. In 1693 he published *Wonders of the Invisible World,* a narrative of a few of the Salem trials, written at the request of the judges. In this work he argued for the justice of the verdicts in the trials he described, since in each there was evidence enough, by contemporary standards, English and American, to convict a witch. He attended no one of the trials, but appeared at one execution and there publicly defended the sentence of the court. Throughout the summer of 1692 the judges did not heed his advice and that of the other ministers, and put to death many persons who by Mather's tests were not proved guilty. During the trials, however, Mather, like the others who doubted the justice of what was being done, uttered no public protest. In 1693, after the last execution, he eagerly investigated the case of a girl whom he believed to be bewitched, but made no attempt to start a new prosecution. He wrote an account of the affair, and entered into controversy with Robert Calef [*q.v.*], a man unusual in his time for his scepticism about witchcraft. Much recrimination resulted—Calef endeavoring to show that the Mathers, especially Cotton, were in some ill-defined way responsible for the injustice done at Salem. He published his views in *More Wonders of the Invisible World* (1700), including in the volume, apparently without permission of its author, Mather's narrative of the "bewitched girl" of 1693, hitherto unprinted. The publication of Calef's book was sponsored by those who opposed Mather's influence in the church and in politics and saw that by 1700, when it was generally admitted that wrong had been done at the Salem trials, even vague insinuations against Cotton Mather as an agent in the execution of the accused might undermine his power. When the book appeared, however, Mather had already declared his belief that the methods of the court had been unfair, and had sent to press his *Magnalia Christi Americana* (published in London in 1702), in which he quoted with approval John Hale's view of the trials, which went as far as Calef in asserting that innocent persons had been condemned. Although it may be said that he helped, through his talking and writing of the reality of witchcraft, to make possible the tragedy at Salem and to keep alive the excitement out of which it came, there is no evidence that he sought to accomplish what came to pass. The only cases of witchcraft with which he was directly concerned he endeavored to treat not by legal action but by fasting and prayer, and like many of his brethren he advocated principles in respect to evidence, which, if the court had accepted them, would have prevented most of the executions.

After 1692 his popularity waned somewhat, partly because of his identification with Phips's policies and the new charter, both of which had critics, partly because of his aggressiveness in controversy and his too frequent arrogance of tone, and, especially, because changed conditions had lessened religious ardor in Massachusetts and had weakened the old Puritan ideal of the dominance of the clergy. His hot temper made matters worse. He was not a skilful politician, and when Joseph Dudley [*q.v.*] became governor in 1702, Mather, who had urged his appointment, found that he could not hope to influence political action as he had done during Phips's régime. His efforts by correspondence with English friends and by pamphleteering to oust Dudley were unavailing; his zeal in keeping the loyalty of Massachusetts nonconformists before the eyes of English royalty bore little fruit, and after 1706, when he finally broke with Dudley, he must have seen that his dream of holding power in the state as well as the church could not come true.

He met defeat at Harvard also. His father was forced to give up its presidency in 1701, and Cotton Mather, mourning that the college was in the hands of the less orthodox, longed to be president himself. His name was considered at least twice, but he was not chosen. In 1703 the House of Representatives did appoint him president of Harvard, but their action was overruled. In the same year he gave up his fellowship. He soon came to look upon Yale, not Harvard, as the hope of the Congregational education in which he believed. He virtually committed the founders of the Connecticut College to naming it after Elihu Yale, thereby securing benefactions from him, and in other ways did what he could for the new seat of learning. In 1721 he was invited to become its president (*Colonial Society of Massachusetts Publications,* XXVI, 388–401).

In spite of frustrated ambitions, failure in politics, and the loss of some of the popularity which he once had, he remained a leader in the church, and his fame steadily increased. He projected societies for various "good causes," the maintenance of peace, the building of churches in poor communities, the relief of needy ministers, the distribution of tracts, Indian missions, and the like, imitating in part the many reform societies springing up in England. He worked much with children, and seems to have been popular with them. He set up and supported a school for the education of the slaves, and to others of the poor and afflicted he gave generously both of his time and money. His tireless activity as a writer won him unique eminence among his countrymen, and many of his works extended his reputation abroad, where also his learning, his scientific communications to the Royal Society (to which he was elected in 1713), and his correspondence with such men as Lord Chancellor King, William Whiston, John Desaguliers, Sir Richard Blackmore, Dr. Woodward, and August Hermann Francke made his name more familiar than those of other Americans. When smallpox broke out in Boston in 1721, he interested Dr. Zabdiel Boylston [*q.v.*] in inoculation, of which he had learned some years before, and—opposed by other physicians, by the people generally, and by some of the clergy—he defended ably in print what seemed to him a beneficent medical practice and by his zeal made possible its successful use in Boston.

There was much tragedy in Mather's life. His first wife died in 1702; his second, Elizabeth (Clark) Hubbard, mother of his son Samuel [*q.v.*], in 1713, and his third, Lydia (Lee) George, became mentally unbalanced. Of his fifteen children all but six died young, and only two lived until his death. One of his sons was a scapegrace. Three widowed sisters became largely dependent on him. He was himself far from robust nervously; he was a prey to a morbid love of introspection and, perhaps, the victim of hallucinations. It is impossible now to estimate finally either his character or the quality of his accomplishment. Some of his faults, his vanity, his instability, his occasional intemperance in speech, and his too great acerbity in debate, may have been produced by his craving to realize an ideal too great for him, which led him by indefatigable industry to overtax nerves always irritable and made more so by disappointments and bereavements. His honesty in money matters and even his sexual morality have been questioned, but no such charges have been substantiated. It is difficult, however, to acquit him of self-seeking, though it is fair to remember that his ambition for power and rank may have been determined at least in part by his desire to preserve orthodoxy and piety as he conceived of them, as well as by love of worldly position for its own sake. Essentially a conservative, he was always torn between allegiance to inherited ideals and realization that a newer day demanded new standards. He was often bitter in his denunciation of other sects, but he was consistently more tolerant in deed than in word, and his tolerance grew as he aged. By 1726 he boasted in print that he had seen admitted to communion in his own church not only Anglicans but Baptists, Presbyterians, and Lutherans, and urged upon candidates for the ministry certain highly tolerant principles (*Manductio ad Ministerium,* pp. 116–121, 126–127). Though bred in Calvinism he expounded in his *Christian Philosopher* (1721) doctrines which represent a step toward deism. Neither a thorough-going reactionary nor a thorough-going liberal, he reflected in his life much of the conflict of a period in which ideas were changing rapidly and the colonists' attitude toward this world and the next was being radically modified. Much in his nature seems repellent; his religious transports appear too often to be deliberate efforts to imitate saints of whom he had read rather than genuine expressions of his own emotion; his erudition sometimes carried him over the line into pedantry; his missionary zeal misled him into something perilously like dishonest casuistry, and his constant efforts to derive religious meaning from every experience, however small, savor today of artificiality. But, however unlovable he may appear, he commands a measure of respect for his studiousness, his industry, and for the self-forgetfulness in his work for what he believed were the best means of serving his generation.

Of his numerous books—more than 450 in all —the most were published after 1692. They reveal Mather as an able editor and compiler, a historian, a well-bred amateur of many fields of knowledge, and a *prosateur* with a definite theory of style. This theory, as he explained (*Manductio ad Ministerium,* 1726, pp. 44–46) was that of a lover of allusions and quotations and of prose made ornate by them, and that of a man who set richness of content above mere elegance of expression. Much that he wrote is dull; some of it is too hastily written to succeed, but the most, probably, however far from literary greatness in the narrow sense and however out of accord with modern conventions, is artistically more worthy than the bulk of American literature prior to 1728. Of his books, those having the greatest interest for today are, first, the *Magnalia Christi Americana: or the Ecclesiastical History of New England from its First Planting* (1702), a more considerable literary achievement than any previously produced in Massachusetts, and then, in addition to the others previously mentioned: *A Poem to the Memory of . . . Mr. Urian Oakes* (1682); *The Present State of New England* (1690); *Eleutheria: Or an Idea of the Reformation in England: And a History of Non-Conformity* (1698); *Pastoral Letter to the English Captives in Africa* (1698); *A Family Well-Ordered* (1699); *La Fe del Christiano* (1699), an effort in Spanish; *Reasonable Religion* (1700); *Some Few Remarks upon A Scandalous Book . . . By one Robert Calef* (1701); *Le Vrai Patron des Saines Paroles* (1704); *A Faithful Man . . . Michael Wigglesworth* (1705); *The Negro Christianized* (1706); *Corderius Americanus . . . The Good Education of Children* (1708); *Bonifacius* (1710), which under its later title of *Essays to do Good* had great popularity and was praised by Franklin; *Fair Dealing between Debtor and Creditor* (1716); *Brethren Dwelling together in Unity* (1718), a sermon preached at a Baptist ordination; *Psalterium Americanum* (1718), a translation of the Psalms for use in singing; *The Accomplished Singer* (1721), a tract to aid the movement for better congregational singing; *Sentiments on the Small Pox Inoculated* (1721); *An Account . . . of Inoculating the Small-Pox* (1722); *The Angel of Bethesda* (1722), the same title having been used for another book by Mather preserved in manuscript at the American Antiquarian Society; *Parentator* (1724), a biography of his father, and *Ratio Disciplinae* (1726), still a valuable exposition of Congregational polity. His *Biblia Americana,* a work which the author considered his greatest, is in manuscript at the Massachusetts Historical Society.

[The best biography is Barrett Wendell's *Cotton Mather* (1891, 1926). A. P. Marvin, *The Life and Times of Cotton Mather* (1892) is fuller but less valuable as a character study. The most recent biography is R. and L. Boas's *Cotton Mather* (1928). Mather's diary so far as it is preserved has been printed, ed. by W. C. Ford, in *Mass. Hist. Soc. Colls.*, 7 ser. VII, VIII (1921–22). Of the other biographical works the following are useful: Benjamin Colman, *The Holy Walk* (1728); Samuel Mather, *The Life of the Very Reverend and Learned Cotton Mather* (1729); K. B. Murdock, "Introduction," in *Selections from Cotton Mather* (1926), and chapter on Cotton Mather in A. B. Hart, ed., *Commonwealth Hist. of Mass.*, vol. II (1928); W. B. O. Peabody, in Jared Sparks, *Lib. of Am. Biog.*, vol. VI (1836); A. H. Quint, "Cotton Mather," in *Congreg. Quart.*, July 1859; Chandler Robbins, *A Hist. of the Second Church . . . in Boston* (1852); and J. L. Sibley, *Biog. Sketches of Grads. of Harvard*, vol. III (1885), which contains the most nearly complete bibliography. *The Cambridge Hist. of Am. Lit.*, I (1917), 407–23, contains a check-list of brief titles which adds many items to Sibley's list. For notable treatments of special phases of Mather's life and work, see esp. Robert Calef, *More Wonders of the Invisible World* (1700), the basis of later attacks upon Mather's attitude toward the witch trials; S. G. Drake, introduction and notes in *The Witchcraft Delusion* (3 vols., 1866); Kuno Francke, "The Beginning of Cotton Mather's Correspondence with August Hermann Francke," in *Philological Quart.*, July 1926, and two articles on this correspondence in *Studies and Notes in Philology and Literature,* V (1896), 57–67, and *Americana Germanica,* vol. I, no. 4 (1897), pp. 31–66; C. N. Greenough, "A Letter Relating to the Publication of Cotton Mather's Magnalia," in *Col. Soc. Mass. Pubs.*, vol. XXVI (1927); T. J. Holmes, "Cotton Mather and His Writings on Witchcraft," in *Papers of the Bibliog. Soc. of America,* XVIII (1924), 30–59, and "The Surreptitious Printing of One of Cotton Mather's Manuscripts," in *Bibliog. Essays: A Tribute to Wilberforce Eames* (1924); G. L. Kittredge, "Cotton Mather's Election into the Royal Society," in *Col. Soc. Mass. Pubs.*, XIV (1913), 81–114, "Further Notes on Cotton Mather and the Royal Society," *Ibid.*, 28–92, "Introduction," in the Cleveland, 1921, reprint of Increase Mather's *Several Reasons*, "Cotton Mather's Scientific Communications to the Royal Society," in *Proc. Am. Antiq. Soc.*, n.s., XXVI (1916), "Notes on Witchcraft," *Ibid.*, n.s., XVIII (1907), 148–212, and "Some Lost Works of Cotton Mather," in *Proc. Mass. Hist. Soc.*, XLV (1912), 418–79; K. B. Murdock, "Cotton Mather and the Rectorship of Yale College," in *Col. Soc. Mass. Pubs.*, XXVI (1927), 388–401; W. F. Poole, *Cotton Mather and Salem Witchcraft* (1869); I. W. Riley, *Am. Philosophy, The Early Schools* (1907); C. W. Upham, *Salem Witchcraft* (2 vols., 1867); "Salem Witchcraft and Cotton Mather," in *Hist. Mag.*, Sept. 1869. See also T. J. Holmes, *The Mather Literature* (1927); H. E. Mather, *Lineage of Rev. Richard Mather* (1890); "The Mather Papers," in *Mass. Hist. Soc. Colls.*, 4 ser. VIII (1868); Albert Matthews, introduction and notes to the early Harvard records printed in *Col. Soc. Mass. Pubs.*, vols. XV, XVI (1925); K. B. Murdock, *Increase Mather* (1925); Josiah Quincy, *The Hist. of Harvard Univ.* (1840); J. H. Tuttle, "The Libraries of the Mathers," in *Proc. Am. Antiq. Soc.*, n.s., XX (1910), 269–356; M. C. Tyler, *A Hist. of Am. Lit. . . .* (1878), vol. II; Williston Walker, "The Services of the Mathers," in *Papers of the Am. Soc. of Ch. Hist.*, V (1893), 61–85. The Am. Antiq. Soc. owns two paintings of Cotton Mather, both by Peter Pelham, who also did a mezzotint of Mather in 1727.]

K. B. M.

MATHER, FRED (Aug. 2, 1833–Feb. 14, 1900), pisciculturist, writer on outdoor life, was born in Greenbush, now Rensselaer, N. Y. His parents were Joseph and Chianna (Brockway) Mather of Lyme, Conn., and he was a descendant of Rev. Richard Mather [*q.v.*] of Toxteth, England, who came to Massachusetts in 1635 and settled in Dorchester. After the removal of his family to Albany in 1850, Mather studied at the Classical Institute of Prof. Charles Anthony. In 1854 he married Elizabeth McDonald. During boyhood he had exhibited a strong interest in outdoor pursuits, particularly hunting and fishing, and it was probably this that impelled him, soon after his marriage, to join the great Western migration. He located temporarily in Wisconsin, where he was interested in lead mines at Potosi, also engaging in hunting and trapping. He participated in the government surveys in Minnesota and passed some time in Kansas prior to the Civil War. In 1862 he enlisted in the 113th New York Volunteers and served with credit throughout the Civil War, being discharged with the rank of captain in the 7th New York Artillery.

What led him to adopt fish culture as a life work is not clear, but he may have been influenced by the activities of Seth Green [*q.v.*] and other pioneers in this field between 1860 and 1870. In any case, he experimented with the hatching of perch eggs in the rooms of the State Geological Survey at Albany in 1867. The following year he established himself at Honeoye Falls, Monroe County, N. Y., initiating the more extensive piscicultural work in which he rapidly gained distinction. With the establishment of the United States Fish Commission in 1872 he was called upon for various services, being entrusted with the shipment of live shad to Europe in 1874. He repeated the trip in 1877, carrying eggs of the California salmon in a case of his own designing, and bringing back a few European sole for planting in American waters. In 1874 and 1875 he experimented with the hatching of Michigan grayling and made some efforts to propagate the sea bass. His first wife had died in 1861 and in 1877 he married Adelaide Fairchild. He supervised the American representation at the International Fisheries Exhibition at Berlin in 1880, and gained European recognition. In 1883 he was placed in charge of the state hatchery at Cold Spring Harbor, N. Y., holding the position until 1895. During this period he conducted many of the experiments which were the basis of his numerous technical reports and articles on fish culture. Here he developed methods for the propagation of cod, lobsters, smelt, and other marine forms. The Mather hatching cone, a device for suspending fish eggs in a current of water, in the originating of which he was assisted by Charles Bell was one of his earlier inventions (1875), and embodied a new principle in fish culture.

In his literary activities he was prominently identified with *Forest and Stream,* serving as a member of its editorial staff and furnishing frequent contributions. His work also appeared in *Rod and Gun and American Sportsman,* and in the *Chicago Field* now the *American Field,* the fishing department of which he edited from March 1878 to April 1880. The latter periodical alone published over three score short articles from his pen. A compilation of his writings shows over seventy titles of a technical nature in addition to the foregoing. As a prominent member of the American Fish Cultural Association and its successor the American Fisheries Society he wrote extensively for their annual *Transactions.* Other works, such as *Men I have Fished With* (1897), *In the Louisiana Lowlands* (1900), and *My Angling Friends* (1901), consisted largely of anecdotes and reminiscences of his experience during his travels and numerous field investigations. He was author of *Memoranda Relating to Adirondack Fishes* (1886) of some scientific value, and a technical handbook, *Modern Fish Culture* (1901). His contributions as a developer as well as originator of technical methods in fish culture were of marked value. He died near Lake Nebagomain, Wis.

[Mather's writings constitute the most prolific source of information regarding his activities as a pisciculturist; see also *Bull. of the U. S. Fish Commission,* vols. III (1883), IV (1884); *Report of the U. S. Commissioner of Fisheries,* 1882–87 inclusive; *Report of the Am. Fish Cultural Asso.,* 1879, 1881; *Trans. Am. Fisheries Soc.,* 1890, index; *Am. Field,* Mar. 3, 1900; *Forest and Stream,* Feb. 24, 1900; *Albany Evening Jour.,* Feb. 15, 1900; *Who's Who in America,* 1899–1900; H. E. Mather, *Lineage of Rev. Richard Mather* (1890).]

M. C. J.

MATHER, INCREASE (June 21, 1639–Aug. 23, 1723), Puritan clergyman, politician, author, was the youngest son of Richard [*q.v.*] and Katherine (Holt) Mather. He was born in Dorchester, Mass., and was brought up there in the strict Puritanism of his father's household. His early education he received at home and in a free school in Boston. In 1651 he entered Harvard, but during most of his course he lived in Ipswich or in Boston, studying under the tutorship of the Rev. John Norton. In 1656 he graduated with the degree of A.B. On June 21, 1657, he preached his first sermon. A few weeks later he went to England and thence to Ireland, where he entered Trinity College, Dublin, and received the degree of M.A. in 1658. The Irish climate disagreed with him, and, refusing an academic post at Trinity, he returned to England. There John Howe, one of Cromwell's chaplains and one of the most famous English Puritans, delegated the young Bostonian to preach in his stead at Great Torrington, Devonshire. In 1659 Howe came back to his own flock, and Mather went as chaplain to the garrison at Guernsey. Thence he was called to Gloucester, where he would have been content to stay, but the signs of the impending Restoration led him once more to leave England for Guernsey. He arrived there in April 1660, and on the last day of May Charles II was proclaimed king. Mather refused to rejoice or to express confidence in the Stuarts. His attitude was not tolerated, and, early in 1661, he went to Weymouth and Dorchester, in Dorset, where he worked to establish Congregational churches. But, although he found England more to his taste than Massachusetts, he saw that unless he accepted Anglicanism, to which he was tempted by substantial offers, his only opportunity as a minister lay in the land of his birth.

He arrived in Boston in September 1661. At once half a dozen churches called him, but he stayed in Dorchester with his father. In March 1662 he married Maria Cotton, his step-sister, the daughter of the Rev. John Cotton [*q.v.*]. Later in the same year he made his first important public appearance as a delegate from Dorchester to an ecclesiastical synod. In its councils he opposed his father and most of the clergy by arguing against the Half-Way Covenant, which, he believed, weakened the pristine strength of Congregationalism by relaxing the tests for admission to church membership. Practical experience soon convinced him, however, that the churches could not prosper unless their standards made possible the obtaining of new members; and he became an advocate of the Half-Way Covenant. In 1675 he published two books defending it.

He became teacher of the Second Church in Boston in 1664; in 1674 he was appointed one of the licensers of the press, and fellow of Harvard College. Seven years later he was elected president of that institution, but, adhering to a principle from which he never deviated, he put his duty to his church before all else, and declined the offer from Cambridge because his Boston congregation was not willing to release him. By 1683 he had published more than twenty-five books, which, together with his skill as a preacher, brought him recognition as one of the foremost divines of the time and place. He organized in Boston a society for the discussion of scientific matters, and his interest in such topics is displayed also in his *Essay for the Recording of Illustrious Providences* (1684). Superficially the book is like many other collections of pious tales of God's intervention in human affairs, but it differs from them in its more scientific method, and in the devotion of some space to the exploding of superstition and the treatment of purely scientific subjects.

The crisis produced late in 1683 by the *quo warranto* against the Massachusetts charter drew him into politics. He exhorted the citizens of Boston not to submit to the king's behests, and his words had great influence. In 1685 he was appointed acting president of Harvard, and, a year afterwards, definitely took charge with the title of Rector. Without relaxing his care of his church, he managed to guide the college through troublous days. He encouraged the study of science and showed willingness to make the institution something more than a ministerial training school, but at the same time resisted successfully all efforts to undermine its Congregationalism. He won the enmity of advocates of the royal policy in Massachusetts, but when, in 1688, it seemed desirable to try to regain the charter by an appeal to James II, Mather was chosen to take to the king petitions from the Congregational churches in the colony. Naturally Edward Randolph [*q.v.*] and the royal officials in Boston opposed his going. They had charges brought against him, based on a libelous letter which he was said to have written. The letter was a forgery, and he was acquitted, but Randolph again threatened him with arrest, so that in April 1688, when he set out for England, he was forced to steal away in disguise.

In London he enlisted in his cause many of the nonconformists who had for the moment political influence. He gained a hearing with Sir Nicholas Butler, Lord Culpeper, the Earl of Sunderland, William Penn, Lord Bellasis, Powis the attorney-general, and others of the powerful at court. He was aided, too, by the Countess of Anglesey and Mrs. Blathwayt, whose husband, the clerk of the privy council, was by no means well disposed toward Mather's cause. The first stage of his quest ended with the fall of James II, who had no time to carry out the large promises he had made. Mather had had five interviews with him, and William III was hardly in London before the colonial emissary obtained an audience. His assurances of New England's loyalty to the new king and his censure of Governor Andros [*q.v.*] were heeded, and when a royal order confirmed in power most of the colonial governors—an order which would have made Andros' position impregnable—Massachusetts was expressly excepted. Later in 1689 Boston citizens revolted against the royal governor, and Mather explained this action to the king not as disloyalty to English authority but simply as defiance of James II, the tyrant. Until 1690 Mather was not an official representative of the colonial government, but he was then appointed one of four agents from Massachusetts. His colleagues were two Bostonians, Elisha Cooke [*q.v.*] and Thomas Oakes, and Sir Henry Ashurst of London. Plans for restoring the charter by parliamentary act came to nothing, and in spite of the agents' exertions it became evident that a new charter would be issued. Mather and his fellow agents had to decide whether by refusing to accept a new charter framed by William III they should escape blame for any of its clauses which might prove unpopular at home, or whether they should meet the king half way in order to try to win concessions for their countrymen. Cooke chose the former course; Mather and Ashurst, the latter.

The wisdom of Mather's policy was proved by its results. Although the new charter took away the colonists' right to elect their own governors, his entreaties helped to preserve most of the power of the representative assembly elected by the voters. Instead of objecting to the provision —which he may well have regretted—removing the old restriction of the franchise to church-members, he argued for more power for the people's representatives and against the king's authority to veto their acts. Knowing that by accepting the new charter he gave up what was dear to the narrower Congregationalists and in other ways ran the risk of popular hostility, he knew also that even if the old charter could have been regained many of the "rights" once enjoyed under it could no longer be exercised, and that William III's plan had the merit of giving for the first time legal sanction to certain "liberties" dear to the colonists. Mather was accorded by the king the privilege of nominating the governor, who was to rule during the royal pleasure, and also all the other officers to be appointed for the first year of the new government. The slate he drew up was accepted and he was thus given unique influence in Massachusetts politics.

During his agency his inexperience and one or two unfortunate outbursts of temper were largely atoned for by some diplomatic skill and much personal persuasiveness. Anthony Wood, the antiquarian, who hated Puritans, remarked that among them Mather alone was unfailingly courteous to him—a comment which helps to explain the colonial agent's success. He knew no law, but he took the advice of eminent English lawyers; the pamphlets he wrote and published in London showed adroitness in political debate. Political negotiation, however, was not his only interest. He made friends of Robert Boyle, the scientist, and Richard Baxter, the famous Puritan. The latter dedicated his *Glorious Kingdom of Christ* (1691) to Mather, testifying to his respect for the New Englander's learning. For Harvard he did much, persuading several Englishmen to make bequests and planting the seed which eventually bore fruit in Thomas Hollis' generosity to the college. In nonconformist circles he was welcomed and respected, and he had a large share in the plan for union of Presbyterians and Congregationalists, drawn up in 1691. Furthermore, he took advantage of opportunity by buying in London many books, of which a considerable number dealt with science and with politics.

He came back to Boston in May 1692, with Sir William Phips [*q.v.*], the royal governor whom he had nominated. Officially they were well received, and Mather's work in England was praised. But Cooke and the others who regarded the old charter as the foundation of Massachusetts liberties, together with those who resented the political influence of Mather and other orthodox Congregationalists, soon mustered a considerable party which was eager to discredit him. His policy was to defend the new charter, and, now that the government was no longer solely in the hands of church-members, to educate the voters to elect only the pious. As rector of Harvard he tried also to bring up colonial youths to revere the old standards. In order to safeguard its Congregationalism and to provide for its stability he tried to secure a charter for Harvard, and wished to go to London again to plead for one from the king. His enemies prevented this maneuver, and centered their attack in an attempt to oust him from office at the college. In spite of them he held the rectorship until 1701, and even then had he been willing to compromise by neglecting what he believed was the prior claim of his church, he might have held his post.

The outbreak of suspected witchcraft at Salem Village occurred while Mather was in England, and when he landed in Boston many reputed agents of the devil were under arrest. A court appointed by Phips to try them gave to "spectral evidence," damaging to the prisoners, more weight than Mather and most of the other ministers believed to be just. Except for signing the ministers' statement of advice to the court, written by his son, Cotton [*q.v.*], and issued in June, Increase Mather made no public protest against the trials until autumn. During the summer, however, Thomas Brattle [*q.v.*], also an opponent of the judges' methods, expressed his views in a private letter and listed Mather as one of those who agreed with him. In October the ministers put out an explicit statement of their opinion. This was written by Mather, and published as *Cases of Conscience Concerning Evil Spirits*. The printed version is dated 1693, but the manuscript was circulated and perhaps even printed before the end of 1692. The book was definite in its disapproval of the emphasis put on "spectral evidence" during the Salem trials. Cotton Mather maintains that it ended the executions for witchcraft in Massachusetts. Phips reported to England that Increase Mather's opinion led him to stop the carrying out of sentences imposed on the convicted "witches." Both statements are true, at least in part. *Cases of Conscience* was the most outspoken, and almost certainly the earliest, public utterance issued in New England in opposition to the practice of the court.

More cautious than his son, Increase Mather, though he never questioned the reality of witchcraft, wrote and preached on the subject comparatively rarely and during the trials did nothing to increase the excitement. He summed up his attitude when he said that he felt that it was better for a guilty witch to escape than for an innocent person to die. Robert Calef [*q.v.*], in his *More Wonders of the Invisible World* (1700), accusing Cotton Mather of responsibility for the death of innocent victims at Salem, also attacked Increase Mather, but criticized him chiefly for his political course as representative of the colony in England.

Mather's political prestige, like his son's, declined after 1692, and for the same reasons. He was committed to the new charter, which he had helped to obtain, and a supporter of Governor Phips, whom he had nominated. Wherever the charter and the governor were unpopular, Mather was censured; his opposition to the polity proposed by the founders of the Brattle Street Church also won him their enmity and that of their friends. His opponents succeeded by 1701 in making it impossible for him to continue as president of Harvard unless he neglected his church and lived in Cambridge, and he chose to give up his office. Thenceforth he mingled less in politics, though he partook in his son's unsuccessful campaign against Governor Dudley. He continued to write, of course, and to pursue his ministry. He interested himself in Yale, which he hoped might remain a stronghold of orthodoxy, and in the councils of Massachusetts Congregationalism he was to the end a leader. In 1721 his lifelong openmindedness toward scientific progress bore fruit in his championship of the highly unpopular cause of inoculation for smallpox.

Two years later he died, and the extent of the mourning and the tributes paid to him then prove that he had lost neither his fame nor the approbation of his people. One of his former enemies said: "He was the patriarch and prophet among us, if any one might be so called" (Benjamin Colman, *The Prophet's Death*, 1723, p. 32), and the comments of his contemporaries and of later historians agree in picturing him as unequaled in reputation and power by any native-born American Puritan of his generation. His hot temper, his confidence in his own wisdom and in his right to lead others, and his liking for power, all tend to estrange sympathy. As the spokesman of Massachusetts Congregationalism and, during a short period, of a political party, he was often embroiled in controversy; but with few exceptions he managed his debating with less personal virulence than did his adversaries. What seems like ambition in him may have been in part the product of his belief that only in places of authority could he make his voice heard in defense of the ideals which he sincerely felt were for the public good. He was by no means implacable toward those who disagreed with him: he preached at a meeting of reconciliation between the orthodox Boston congregations and the Brattle Street Church; in 1718 he helped to ordain a Baptist minister. He leaned away from the democracy of the original Independents toward a somewhat Presbyterianized ecclesiastical system, and seems always to have preferred an oligarchy dominated by the most learned and devout, yet in civil affairs he argued for the preservation of democratic institutions. He gave much to charity, and the young Bostonian who saw his last appearance in the pulpit and declared that the old preacher's face was to his audience "the face of an angel" no doubt voiced an affection shared by others of the townsfolk (*Colonial Society of Massachusetts Publications*, vol. XXVI, 1927, p. 390).

As an author he mastered a style strong in its simplicity and directness though usually without brilliance; and the number and variety of his publications—there are about one hundred and thirty books or pamphlets and some sixty-five prefaces or contributions to books by others—made him deservedly renowned. The most interesting of them today are his political tracts, written in connection with his agency; his two histories, *A Brief History of the Warr with the Indians* (1676) and *A Relation of the Troubles Which Have Hapned in New-England by Reason of the Indians There* (1677); his *Life and Death of that Reverend Man of God, Mr. Richard Mather* (1670), and two sermons, *The Great Blessing, of Primitive Counsellours* (1693) and *The Surest Way to the Greatest Honour* (1699), which outline his political position after 1692.

By his first wife he had three sons and seven daughters. Of these one died young. His eldest son, Cotton, became famous in his turn and was always his father's close ally. The third son, Samuel, also became a minister, spending most of his active life in England, preaching at Witney, Oxfordshire; and a daughter, Elizabeth, became the mother of the Rev. Mather Byles [*q.v.*]. In 1714 the first Mrs. Mather died, and in the next year her husband married Ann (Lake) Cotton, his nephew's widow.

[T. J. Holmes, *Increase Mather; a Bibliog. of His Works* (2 vols., 1931), with intro. by G. P. Winship and supplementary material by K. B. Murdock and G. F. Dow, is complete. K. B. Murdock, *Increase Mather* (1925), the only detailed biography, contains a full list of sources. Mather's manuscript autobiography and diaries covering many years are in the Am. Antiq. Soc. Another diary is in the Mass. Hist. Soc., and some of Mather's entries for 1674–87 are printed in the Society's *Proceedings*, 2 ser. XIII (1900), 339–74, 397–411. Cotton Mather's *Parentator* (1724) is a life of his father. An abridgment of it, *Memoirs of the Life of the Late Rev. Increase Mather* (1725), was made by Samuel Mather of Witney, and contains an introduction by Edmund Calamy. The best brief sketches are those by J. L. Sibley in his *Biog. Sketches of Grads. of Harvard*, vol. I (1873) and by Williston Walker, in *Ten New England Leaders* (1901). See also Samuel Palmer's edition of Edmund Calamy's *Nonconformist's Memorial* (1802), II, 245–49; Enoch Pond, *The Lives of Increase Mather and Sir Wm. Phipps* (1870); H. E. Mather, *Lineage of Richard Mather* (1890); Chandler Robbins, *A Hist. of the Second Ch., or Old North, in Boston* (1852); and Barrett Wendell's *Cotton Mather* (1891, 1926). The *Calendar of State Papers, Colonial Series, America and West Indies*; W. H. Whitmore, *The Andros Tracts* (3 vols., 1868–74), and R. N. Toppan and A. T. S. Goodrick, *Edward Randolph* (7 vols., 1898–1909), are valuable authorities on Mather's political activities. For his connection with Harvard see especially the early records of the college, printed with an invaluable introduction by Albert Matthews, in *Colonial Soc. of Mass. Pubs.*, vols. XV and XVI (1925). The best study of the inoculation episode is G. L. Kittredge's Introduction to the Cleveland, 1921, reprint of I. Mather's *Several Reasons.* On other special topics consult St. J. D. Seymour, *The Puritans in Ireland* (1921), and R. H. Murray, *Dublin Univ. and the New World* (1921). K. B. Murdock, *The Portraits of Increase Mather* (1924), reproduces and discusses all the known pictures which have any claim to be considered authentic likenesses of Mather.] K. B. M.

MATHER, RICHARD (1596–Apr. 22, 1669), Puritan clergyman, author, was born at Lowton, in Lancashire, the son of Thomas and Margaret (Abrams?) Mather (*New-England Historical and Genealogical Register*, July 1900, pp. 348–49). During his boyhood he lived in Lowton, attending school at Winwick, a few miles away. At fifteen he was ready for the University, but his parents were poor and he went instead to Toxteth Park, now part of Liverpool, as master of a grammar school. He lived in the household of Edward Aspinwall, whose influence and that of various preachers brought about Mather's "conversion" in 1614. In May 1618, he was admitted to Brasenose College, Oxford, but in November was called back to occupy the pulpit at the Toxteth Park Chapel. He was ordained by Bishop Morton of Chester, but his Puritan tendencies developed rapidly, so that when he wooed Katherine Holt (or Hoult) of Bury, her father, one of the local gentry, "not being affected towards Non-conformable Puritans," opposed his suit (Increase Mather, *post*, ed. of 1850, p. 51). In 1624, however, Richard Mather and Katherine Holt were married, and went to live in Much Woolton. He continued to preach at Toxteth, and occasionally at Prescot, Liverpool, and other Lancashire towns. As his influence widened, his Puritanism attracted attention from the ecclesiastical authorities, and in 1633 he was suspended from his ministry. Friends had the sentence revoked after three months, but in the next year visitors from Archbishop Neile of York haled Mather before them, and once more he was forbidden to preach.

He drew up a series of arguments for emigration, which, together with what he had heard from John Cotton and Thomas Hooker [*qq.v.*], who were already in the colonies, led him to sail with his family from Bristol in May 1635. After a narrow escape from shipwreck, he landed at Boston on Aug. 17. Invited to preside over several of the churches in Massachusetts, he chose to go to Dorchester, whence most of the original congregation had moved to Connecticut. On Aug. 23, 1636, the church in Dorchester was formally reorganized with Mather as teacher. His ministry there continued till his death.

From the first he was a leader of Massachusetts Congregationalism, and to it he devoted his energies as writer and preacher. His *Church-Government and Church-Covenant Discussed* (1643) was "the first elaborate defense and exposition of the New England theory of the Church and its administration to be put forth in print" (Walker, *post*, p. 115). It was printed without his name, as was his *Apologie of the Churches in New-England for Church Covenant* (1643), an argument for the Congregational principle as to the basis of the church in a covenant of members; but both works are surely his. With the Rev. William Tompson he collaborated in *A Modest & Brotherly Answer to Mr. Charles Herle* (1644) and *An Heart-Melting Exhortation* (1650). The former was another defense of the Congregational scheme, as was Mather's *Reply to Mr. Rutherfurd* (1647). With the Rev. John Eliot and the Rev. Thomas Welde he translated the Psalms in meters adapted for singing in the meeting-houses, the result being *The Whole Booke of Psalmes* (1640), better known as the "Bay Psalm Book." Mather, in his preface, shows that he was in no doubt as to the book's literary shortcomings, declaring that its object was "Conscience rather then Elegance, fidelity rather than poetry." But the most important of Mather's works was the original draft of the famous "Cambridge Platform," which, amended and adopted by a synod at Cambridge in 1646 and printed as *A Platform of Church Discipline* (1649), was for many years the basic document of New England Congregationalism.

He took an active part in all the church controversies of his day, especially that concerning admission to membership in Congregational churches. Originally only those who could offer evidence of sincere faith and genuine conviction were admitted, but a question soon arose about the status of such of their children as had not experienced "conversion." Might they be members of a church, and might their children in turn be baptized? A compromise was proposed: the Half-Way Covenant, which provided that those who had been granted baptism by virtue of their parents' church-membership might enter into covenant relations with the church and have their children baptized, but could not sit at the Lord's table or vote in the business meetings of the church. In 1657 a ministerial convention at Boston advocated the Half-Way Covenant, and its conclusions were drawn up by Mather. Five years later a synod approved the decision of the convention, and in its debates he championed the cause which prevailed.

It is as an expositor of Congregational doctrine and organizer of Congregational polity that Mather is important. He wrote forcefully, though without literary distinction, and his contemporaries must have relied principally upon his works for authoritative statements of the New England ecclesiastical system. He was a practical teacher and minister rather than a theorist, and the reasons for his advocacy of the Half-Way Covenant show his fundamental attitude. To him, a system which denied to many of the younger members of the community any connection with the church seemed impracticable; he believed that in them lay the only hope for the continued development of Congregationalism, and he saw the Half-Way Covenant as a means of causing "the Rising Generation in this Country" to be "brought under the Government of Christ in his Church" (I. Mather, p. 79). Similarly certain Presbyterian elements in the system which he favored were probably recommended to him by the chance that they might strengthen the organization of the colonial church and lessen the differences between some of the more powerful English Puritans and their brethren in Massachusetts.

A portrait owned by the American Antiquarian Society and reproduced in a woodcut by John Foster in 1670 shows Mather to have been bearded, and apparently florid in complexion. It suggests also that he was of moderate stature. More vivid is the impression to be derived from Hooker's statement, "My brother Mather is a mighty man" and from his grandson's comment on his preaching: "His voice was loud and big, and uttered with a deliberate vehemency, it procured unto his ministry an awful and very taking majesty; nevertheless, the substantial and rational matter delivered by him, caused his ministry to take yet more" (C. Mather, *Magnalia,* 1702, Bk. III, pt. 2, ch. xx, §14). For the rest we know of his personal characteristics only through the eulogies of his descendants, who emphasize his diligence, his patience, and his zeal for learning. By his first wife he had six sons, one of whom died in childhood. Of the others all but one became ministers. The two eldest, Samuel and Nathaniel, returned to England after graduating from Harvard; the others, Eleazar and Increase [*q.v.*], occupied Massachusetts pulpits. Shortly after the death of his first wife in 1655, Mather married Sarah (Hankridge or Hawkridge) Cotton, widow of the Rev. John Cotton.

In addition to the works already mentioned, Mather is known to have published the following books: *A Catechism* (1650); *An Answer to Two Questions* (1712); *A Defence of the Answer . . . of the Synod* (1664), with Jonathan Mitchell; *A Disputation Concerning Church-Members* (1659); *A Farewel-Exhortation* (1657), an Election Sermon (1660); *The Summe of Certain Sermons* (1652), and a few shorter pieces printed in books by others.

[The best authority is Increase Mather, *The Life and Death of that Reverend Man of God, Mr. Richard Mather* (1670), reprinted with Mather's journal of his voyage to America in *Dorchester Antiq. and Hist. Soc. Colls.,* no. 3 (1850). Other early biographies based on Increase Mather's book are by Cotton Mather, in his *Magnalia Christi Americana* (1702), Bk. III, Pt. 2, ch. xx; and by Samuel Clarke, in *The Lives of Sundry Eminent Persons* (1683). The best modern study is in Williston Walker, *Ten New Eng. Leaders* (1901). See also K. B. Murdock, "Richard Mather," in *Old-Time New Eng.,* Oct. 1924; H. E. Mather, *Lineage of Richard Mather* (1890); *Records of the First Ch. at Dorchester* (1891); William Beamont, *Winwick* (n.d.); Benjamin Brook, *The Lives of the Puritans* (1813), III, 440–45; V. D. Davis, *Some Account of the Ancient Chapel of Toxteth Park* (1884); S. A. Green, *Ten Fac-simile Reproductions Relating to Various Subjects* (1903); *Hist. of the Town of Dorchester* (1859); T. J. Holmes, "Notes on Richard Mather's 'Church Government,'" in *Proc. Am. Antiq. Soc.,* n.s., XXXIII (1924), 291–96; W. B. Sprague, *Annals Am. Pulpit,* vol. I (1857); John Winthrop, *Hist. of New Eng.* (2 vols., 1853), ed. by James Savage; and Anthony Wood, *Athenae Oxonienses,* vol. II (1692).]

K. B. M.

MATHER, SAMUEL (Oct. 30, 1706–June 27, 1785), Congregational clergyman, author, son of Cotton Mather [*q.v.*] and his second wife, Elizabeth (Clark), was born in Boston, attended the North Grammar School, and received the degree of A.B. from Harvard in 1723. During his college course he was granted financial aid from the gifts of Nathaniel Hulton and Thomas Hollis, which his grandfather had helped to obtain for the college. In August 1724 he began preaching at Castle William, where he remained chaplain till 1732. In October 1724 he delivered a sermon at the Second Church of Boston, where his father was minister. He became an assistant to the Rev. Joshua Gee at the Second Church in 1731 and on Jan. 28, 1732, was chosen pastor by sixty-nine out of one hundred and twelve votes. On Aug. 23, 1733, he married Hannah Hutchinson, sister of Thomas [*q.v.*], later royal governor of Massachusetts. By 1741 some of Mather's flock challenged his doctrines and accused him of improper conduct. An ecclesiastical council called to investigate the charges failed to effect a reconciliation, and on Dec. 12, 1741, the church dismissed Mather with one year's salary. Ninety-three of his congregation withdrew with him and established a new church, where he ministered until his death. The charges against him do not seem to have seriously damaged his reputation in the community, and are not precisely defined. An enemy in 1773 wrote of "the fair Daughters of Liberty on whose account you have already suffered a dire flogging at an ecclesiastical council," but this is insecure evidence, even if it refers to the affair of 1741 (Timothy Prout?, *Diana's Shrines Turned into Ready Money,* 1773, p. 7).

Mather published about twenty books or pamphlets and some contributions to books by others, which display erudition rather than distinction in style or marked intellectual strength. His *Life of the Very Reverend and Learned Cotton Mather* (1729) is a useful though unsatisfactory biography. His *Attempt to Shew That America Must Be Known to the Ancients* (1773) reflects his patriotic views. He wrote verse, and his poem, *The Sacred Minister,* was printed by itself in 1773.

His eldest son, Samuel, became a Loyalist and left Boston; Thomas, the second son, died in 1782; and Increase, a third, was lost at sea. Samuel Mather was, therefore, the last of the "Mather dynasty" in the Boston pulpit. Respected, apparently, as a scholar, minister, and owner of a great library of books and manuscripts, he had neither wide public influence nor as great power as his ancestors or many of his contemporaries. He was not a successful preacher, and late in life he is said to have had "an audience of not more than twenty or thirty." A contemporary says that, "though a treasury of valuable historical anecdotes," he was "as weak a man as I ever knew" (*Proceedings of the Massachusetts Historical Society,* vol. XXXVII, 1903, p. 335). His enemies twitted him with "an itch of writing" and ambition to be president of Harvard (*Diana's Shrines,* p. 7). Against this must be weighed the recognition of his talents shown in an honorary degree of D.D. from Harvard in 1773, of M.A. from Glasgow in 1731, and of D.D. from Aberdeen in 1762. In his will he asked that there be no "funeral encomiums" for him, and that only one bell be tolled for five minutes, lest, as he said, "sick and infirm persons should be disturbed . . . at the carrying of the body of my humiliation to the silent grave."

[Most of the library which Mather inherited or accumulated was given to the Am. Antiq. Soc. by his daughter, Hannah Mather Crocker [*q.v.*]. Albert Matthews, "Samuel Mather (H. C. 1723) His Honorary Degrees and Works," in *Col. Soc. Mass. Pubs.,* vol. XVIII (1917), contains biog. data and a bibliog. of Mather's writings. See also records (MSS.) of the Second Church, Boston, and some MSS. by Mather at the Am. Antiq. Soc., the Mass. Hist. Soc., and the Boston Public Library; W. B. Sprague, *Annals Am. Pulpit,* vol. I (1857); H. E. Mather, *Lineage of Richard Mather* (1890); Chandler Robbins, *A Hist. of the Second Church, or Old North, in Boston* (1852); "Diary of Cotton Mather, 1681–1700," *Mass. Hist. Soc. Colls.,* 7 ser. VII, VIII (1911–12); J. H. Tuttle, "The Libraries of the Mathers," in *Proc. Am. Antiq. Soc.,* n.s. XX (1910); *Col. Soc. Mass. Pubs.,* vol. XVI (1925).]

K. B. M.

MATHER, SAMUEL (July 13, 1851–Oct. 18, 1931), iron merchant, financier, and philanthropist, was born in Cleveland, Ohio, the eldest son of Samuel Livingston Mather [*q.v.*] and Georgiana Pomeroy (Woolson) Mather. His mother was a grandniece of James Fenimore Cooper (Clare Benedict, *Voices Out of the Past: Five Generations, 1785–1923,* 1930, p. 71); his father was descended from the Rev. Richard Mather [*q.v.*]. Samuel attended the Cleveland high school and Saint Mark's School, Southboro, Mass., and intended to enter Harvard College in 1869. During the summer of that year he was time-keeper and payroll clerk in his father's business, the Cleveland Iron Mining Company, at Ishpeming, Mich. Seriously injured in an explosion at the company's mines, July 14, he was an invalid for nearly two years, an experience which probably prepared the way for many of his charitable interests. He then traveled in Europe for a year and a half, slowly recovering his health and acquiring an intimate knowledge of European culture.

On his return to the United States late in 1873, he entered the employ of the Cleveland Iron Mining Company, to learn the business his father had made extraordinarily successful. Following his marriage, Oct. 19, 1881, to Flora

Amelia Stone, youngest daughter of Amasa Stone and only sister of Mrs. John Hay, he spent another period in extensive travel abroad. In 1883, with Col. James Pickands and Jay C. Morse, he organized Pickands, Mather & Company, dealers in iron ore, coal, and pig iron. On the death of Pickands in 1896 Mather became senior partner, and the business grew enormously under his guidance. The company became one of the two or three largest shippers of iron ore from the Lake Superior ranges, operated coal mines in Pennsylvania and West Virginia, blast furnaces at Chicago, Toledo, Duluth, and Erie, and a large fleet of freight carriers on the Great Lakes. Through stock ownership in the Lackawanna Steel, the Youngstown Sheet and Tube, and United States Steel concerns, the partners in Pickands, Mather & Company were assured of a market for their products. Mather's brother, William G. Mather, became president of the Cleveland Cliffs Iron Company in 1890, the successor of the old family property, the Cleveland Iron Mining Company, and Samuel was a director in this organization and also in the United States Steel. The industrial history of Northern Ohio, and to a considerable extent of the United States, is the record of the achievements of the Mathers in the iron and steel business.

Mather amassed a large fortune, and gave of it liberally and discriminatingly in varied ways. A list of his charities, like one of his corporation directorships and institutional trusteeships, would be very long. His most notable benefactions were his gifts to Kenyon College and to Western Reserve University and its affiliated hospitals; his most notable public service was his share in the establishment of the Cleveland Community Fund. The latter grew out of the Cleveland Red Cross War Council, of which Mather became chairman in 1917. Of the Community Fund he was honorary chairman from its origin (1920) until his death, eleven years later, and its largest contributor. His will provided for the continuation of his support of this fund and of some fifty-six other annual subscriptions to as many educational or charitable institutions. For forty-five years he gave invaluable service as a trustee and, from 1914, as vice-president of Western Reserve University. In 1920 the government of Serbia honored him with the Cross of Mercy for his generous gifts to its people during the Great War; France, in 1922, awarded him the Cross of the Legion of Honor for similar benefactions. In 1924 he became the first recipient of the Cleveland Chamber of Commerce medal for conspicuous service in his own community. In the view of Mather's closest friends his first interest was his church, the Protestant Episcopal. He was senior warden of Trinity Cathedral, Cleveland, an active officer in the diocese of Ohio, an annual delegate to the diocesan convention, and regularly a deputy to the General Convention. He was also a member of the National Council of the Episcopal Church. His vigorous, dominating personality impressed all who were associated with him. He grasped the details of complex situations whether in business, charitable, or educational affairs; remembered these details when others thought them forgotten; and reached decisions with promptness and finality. His wife, who was actively interested in all his charities, died in 1909; three of their four children survived him.

[H. E. Mather, *Lineage of Rev. Richard Mather* (1890); *Who's Who in America*, 1928–29; *Who's Who in Finance*, 1911; E. M. Avery, *A Hist. of Cleveland and Its Environs* (1918), vol. III; *Cleveland Plain Dealer, Cleveland News*, and *Cleveland Press*, Oct. 19, 1931; notes collected for use in a biography by T. J. Holmes, librarian of the W. G. Mather Library, Cleveland.]

E. J. B.

MATHER, SAMUEL HOLMES (Mar. 20, 1813–Jan. 14, 1894), lawyer, banker, the second of the two sons of Dr. Ozias and Harriet (Brainard) Mather, was born in Washington, N. H. His father was the son of Dr. Augustus Mather of Lyme, Conn., and a descendant of Rev. Richard Mather [*q.v.*] of Dorchester, Mass.; his mother, the daughter of Jabez Brainard of Washington and Lempster, N. H., was also a member of an old New England family of English ancestry. Ozias Mather died the same year Samuel was born. The boy attended the academy of his native town, and Kimball Union Academy, Meriden, N. H. He graduated with high honors from Dartmouth College in the class of 1834. For fifteen months after graduation he studied in a law office in Geneva, N. Y. Attracted to Cleveland, Ohio, in December 1835, by reports friends gave him of the opportunities in that growing city, he continued his study of law there and was admitted to the bar in 1836.

In 1849 he joined with others who had formerly lived in New England in establishing the Society for Savings, modeled after an organization then popular in New England, the name being suggested by that of a similar society in Hartford, Conn. Mather was from the first its secretary and chief officer, and soon began to devote practically all his time to the institution. In 1884 he became its president, an office he held until his death, Myron T. Herrick [*q.v.*] succeeding him. Mather described the Cleveland Society for Savings as "a benevolent institution, without capital, managed by trustees without salary, in the interest of the depositors only, to whom profits are paid, or for whose benefit they are accumulated and reserved." Under Mather's direction it came to be a powerful, conservative banking house. Its policies, and particularly the high rate of interest it could pay on time savings deposits, benefited savings accounts in all the Cleveland banks. At the time of his death, one in six of the population of Cleveland was a depositor in the Society for Savings, and the total deposits amounted to $23,000,000.

Mather's record as a business man was above reproach. Fairness and trustworthiness won him the confidence of his community. From 1854 to 1857 inclusive he was a member of the board of education, and for the first three years secretary, or acting business manager, of the schools. In the latter capacity he was charged with much of the detail work which fell to the board, the selection of teachers, and the supervision of the construction of buildings. On May 9, 1842, he married Emily W. Gregory, daughter of Uriah M. Gregory of Sand Lake, N. Y. His interests, aside from his business, were centered in the Second Presbyterian Church, of which he was an elder. He was survived by two children.

[H. E. Mather, *Lineage of Rev. Richard Mather* (1890); L. A. Brainard, *The Geneal. of the Brainerd-Brainard Family in America* (1908); G. T. Chapman, *Sketches of the Alumni of Dartmouth Coll.* (1867); obituary in *Cleveland Leader*, Jan. 14, 1894, reprinted in the *Annals of the Early Settlers Asso. of Cuyahoga County, Ohio* (1894); *Cleveland Weekly Leader*, Jan. 20, 1894; *Three Score Years and Ten: The Story of the Rise of the Society for Savings* (1919); *The Banker's Mag.*, Feb. 1894.] E. J. B.

MATHER, SAMUEL LIVINGSTON (July 1, 1817–Oct. 8, 1890), capitalist, was born in Middletown, Conn. His father, Samuel, was descended from the Rev. Richard Mather [*q.v.*] of Dorchester, Mass.; his mother, Catherine (Livingston), was a daughter of Abram Livingston of Stillwater, N. Y. Samuel Livingston Mather's grandfather, Samuel, was a lawyer of Middletown, and a stockholder in the Connecticut Land Company which purchased the Western Reserve Tract along the south shore of Lake Erie. His son, Samuel Mather, Jr., graduated from Yale College in 1792 and went into the commission business in Albany, N. Y. Samuel Livingston graduated from Wesleyan University, Middletown, in 1835. He was in his father's employ for a time and later, until 1843, was in the commission business in New York City on his own account. During these years he twice visited Europe. He was subsequently sent to Cleveland to dispose of the family's Western Reserve holdings and to act as agent for other eastern interests with land in Ohio. Soon after his settlement in Cleveland he was admitted to the bar, but never practised law.

The discovery of iron ore in the Lake Superior region determined his life interest. About 1850 several Cleveland business men, of whom he was one, organized the Cleveland Iron Mining Company to conduct exploration for iron ore and to purchase ore lands. In 1853 Mather became secretary-treasurer, and the driving force in the organization. Within a year the company began shipping ore. For a short time the ore was hauled by wagons to the lake shore, transferred to small wooden sailing vessels, unloaded for portage at "The Soo," loaded again for lake passage to Cleveland, and there transferred to canal and railroads for distribution to the furnaces of Ohio and Pennsylvania. Under Mather's guidance the Cleveland Iron Mining Company, later known as the Cleveland Cliffs Company, steadily improved the means of shipping iron ore, building railroad lines and larger ore boats. The construction of the canal at Sault Sainte Marie greatly facilitated the company's ore trade. The foresight and business ability of Mather and a few others revolutionized the iron industry in the United States; gave it a bountiful supply of raw material; and drew it toward northern Ohio, and the lake ports. The beginning of Cleveland's industrial prominence may be attributed to the Cleveland Iron Mining Company more than to any other single enterprise. In 1869 Mather became president and treasurer of the company, offices which he held until his death. As the iron industry developed he extended his personal activities and investments into allied fields. He was secretary and manager of the Marquette Iron Company, a director of the Bancroft Iron Company, president of the Cleveland Boiler Plate Company, of the American Iron Mining Company, and of the McComber Iron Company. After his death his sons, Samuel, 1851–1931 [*q.v.*], and William G. Mather, carried on and developed further their father's manifold iron interests.

On Sept. 24, 1850, Mather married Georgiana Pomeroy Woolson, who died Nov. 2, 1853; on June 11, 1856, he married Elizabeth Lucy Gwin. He gave liberally of his abundant means to charitable and religious objects.

[H. E. Mather, *Lineage of Rev. Richard Mather* (1890); *Alumni Record of Wesleyan Univ.* (1883); *Cleveland Leader* and *Cleveland Plain Dealer*, Oct. 9, 1890; E. M. Avery, *A Hist. of Cleveland and Its Environs* (1918), vol. III; *The Cleveland Cliffs Iron Company, An Hist. Rev.* (*c.* 1920); MSS. in the W. G. Mather Library, Cleveland.] E. J. B.

MATHER, STEPHEN TYNG (July 4, 1867–Jan. 22, 1930), organizer and director of the

National Park Service of the Interior Department, was a descendant of Rev. Richard Mather [*q.v.*], who became teacher of the church at Dorchester, Mass., in 1636. The son of Joseph Wakeman Mather of Connecticut and Bertha Jemima (Walker), he was born in San Francisco and graduated from the University of California in 1887. After graduation, he was a successful reporter on the New York *Sun* until 1893, when he went into the New York office of the Pacific Coast Borax Company, of which his father was manager. In 1894 he planned and established the company's distribution center at Chicago, and became its manager. In 1903, he helped organize the Thorkildsen-Mather Borax Company of Chicago in competition for the business of the continent, and about 1920 became president of its successor, the Sterling Borax Company. He was also president of the Brighton Chemical Company of Pennsylvania.

It was not, however, as a business man that he achieved nation-wide repute, but as organizer and upbuilder of the system of national parks. In order to bring the fourteen national parks into cooperation under a bureau to be created for the purpose, he accepted in 1915 Franklin K. Lane's invitation to become assistant to the secretary of the interior, and upon Lane's insistence, two years later, he became first director of the new National Park Service. During his twelve years' administration of this office, he brought the national park system into a high degree of development, differentiated it from land systems of lesser scenic standard, and made it celebrated over the world.

Since Congress had never verbally defined national parks to distinguish them in kind and use from state parks and others, Mather at the very outset of his administration sought warrant for his idealistic views in the national parks already created by Congress. A study of these authorized their official defining as areas of unmodified primitive condition, scenically the finest—each of its kind—in the country, preserved forever from industrial use. This view, agreed to by the Interior Department and accepted in Congressional practice, became his measure for park selections. The fourteen national parks in unrelated existence at the time he assumed office had become twenty-one closely related cooperating units of a highly developed system when failing health forced his resignation in 1929. Several had been eliminated, while those added under his promotion included Rocky Mountain, Hawaii, Lassen Volcanic, Mount McKinley, Grand Canyon, Zion, Bryce Canyon, Grand Teton, and Great Smoky Mountains. His opposition in Congress to many local bills for proposed national parks of lesser scenic importance performed excellent service in educating both Congress and the people in national park ideals. His establishment and maintenance of the national park standards were the greater achievement because during the period of his administration long-distance motor touring spread over the country a mesh of surfaced highways and filled the parks to overflowing with motoring explorers. For a decade, recreation became the nation's fetish to the exclusion from public recognition of the parks' major uses of education and inspiration.

Mather probably owed his popularity as much to his personality as to the dignity and sincerity of his public service. Modest, simple, and friendly in manner and speech, he was fearless and untiring in the prosecution of what he conceived to be a high mission of civilization. A profound lover of beauty in nature in its simplest as well as its sublime manifestations and an uncompromising defender of wild life, he nevertheless saw all in terms of human enjoyment and inspiration. He was a constant traveler and a ready and frequent speaker on national park policies, but though he was an able writer made little use of his pen, even in private life preferring the telegraph or long-distance telephone. His bibliography consists of signed reports of park progress and planning from 1915 to 1930 inclusive, together with articles and letters to be found in the files of the National Park Service. Those who were closely associated with him during his public career found him devoid of political and personal ambition of any kind. His defender, he used to say, would always be his record, and the story of the National Parks in the process of organization is his biography.

Mather was married, Oct. 12, 1893, to Jane Thacker Floy of Elizabeth, N. J. They had one child, a daughter. Mather's residence from the time of his connection with the National Park Service was in Washington, D. C., but the old Mather place at Darien, Conn., was his summer home for many years. He died in Brookline, Mass.

[*Who's Who in America*, 1928–29; H. E. Mather, *Lineage of Rev. Richard Mather* (1890); *Survey*, July 1930; *Saturday Evening Post*, Feb. 23, 1929; *Nature Mag.*, Mar. 1930; *Playground*, Mar. 1930; *Science*, Feb. 26, 1932; *N. Y. Times*, Jan. 23, and editorial, Jan. 24, 1930; files of the Nat. Park Service; information as to certain facts from Mrs. Mather; personal acquaintance.]

R. S. Y.

MATHER, WILLIAM WILLIAMS (May 24, 1804–Feb. 26, 1859), geologist, son of Eleazar and Fanny (Williams) Mather, was born in Brooklyn, Windham County, Conn. His father was of English descent, through Timothy, son of Richard Mather [*q.v.*], who came to Massachusetts in 1635 and settled in Dorchester the following year. It is said that William was at first inclined toward the medical profession and went to Providence, R. I., to study; but in 1823, when not quite nineteen years of age, he sought and secured admission to the United States Military Academy at West Point, and was graduated and brevetted second lieutenant of the 7th Regiment of Infantry in 1828.

He early showed a bent toward the sciences. During his West Point career he made experiments to determine the temperature at the bottom of an ice-coated stream and is said to have aided in the preparation of Webster's textbook of chemistry (Austin, *post*), and in the year of his graduation (1828) he published in the *American Journal of Science* an article, "On the Non-conducting Power of Water in Relation to Heat." After a brief service on the Louisiana frontier, he was acting professor of chemistry and mineralogy in the Military Academy, 1829–35, and meantime, with permission of the Secretary of War, acted during 1833 as professor of chemistry, mineralogy, and geology in Wesleyan University, Middletown, Conn. In this year he published *Elements of Geology for the Use of Schools,* which seems to have been fairly well received. Promoted first lieutenant in 1834, he served as a topographical engineer with G. W. Featherstonhaugh in a geological survey from Green Bay, Wis., to the Coteau de Prairie, June–December 1835, and was then assigned to frontier duty in Indian Territory. On Aug. 31, 1836, he resigned his commission to enter upon the profession of geology.

For a short while he was professor of chemistry at the University of Louisiana (Cullum, *post,* p. 412). From 1836 to 1844 he served as geologist of the first district in the geological survey of New York; during 1837 and 1838 he served also as director of the geological survey of Ohio, and in 1838–39 as state geologist of Kentucky. Of his work with the several state surveys, that in New York was most important. His report (*Geology of New York,* Pt. I, 1843), comprising 639 quarto pages with forty-five plates and a geological map, was the most voluminous of the series, but while highly creditable was not the most valuable. His views on causes of folding, uplift, and depression of portions of the earth's crust seem to have excited little interest, and he assigned the glacial drift to ice-laden currents from the north, a not uncommon explanation at that period. In general, he made too large an appeal to oceanic currents to account for sundry effects possibly ascribable to other causes. His work with the contemporaneous Ohio and Kentucky surveys was necessarily limited in large degree to administration. The Ohio survey lasted but two years and yielded two annual reports, both bearing the date of 1838. His personal contribution had to do mainly with economic questions. He estimated that there were within the state limits coal resources "not only sufficient for domestic use for any reasonable time, but to supply the country around the lakes, and throughout the valleys of the Ohio and Mississippi, for as long a time as it is proper to calculate" (*Second Annual Report of the Geological Survey of the State of Ohio,* p. 8). His work in Kentucky was purely in the nature of reconnaissance and yielded no direct results (*Report on the Geological Reconnoissance of Kentucky Made in 1838,* 1839).

From 1842 to 1845 he was professor of natural science in Ohio University at Athens, and after 1847 vice-president and acting president of the same institution. He was at various times elected to scientific and literary organizations, and for fifteen years was a trustee of Granville College, Ohio. He died in Columbus, quite unexpectedly, in his fifty-fifth year.

Mather was a man of powerful frame and robust health, with resolute will and enthusiastic devotion to his chosen calling. He was twice married, first to his cousin, Emily Maria Baker, who died in November 1850, leaving six children, and second, in August 1857, to Mrs. Mary Curtis (*née* Harry), by whom he had one child, a son.

[I. J. Austin, in *Memorial Biogs. of the New-Eng. Hist. Geneal. Soc.,* vol. III (1883); W. J. Youmans, *Pioneers of Science in America* (1896); *Am. Jour. Sci.,* May 1859; G. W. Cullum, *Biog. Reg. Officers and Grads. U. S. Mil. Acad.* (3rd ed., 1891); H. E. Mather, *Lineage of Rev. Richard Mather* (1890); *Ohio Statesman* (Columbus), Mar. 1, 1859.]
G. P. M.

MATHESON, WILLIAM JOHN (Sept. 15, 1856–May 15, 1930), chemist, financier, and philanthropist, was born in Elkhorn, Wis., the son of Finlay and Anna Meigs (Lighthall) Matheson. After a boyhood in British Guinea, he was educated at St. Andrews, Scotland. His interest in chemistry began during his school days, and when twenty years old he opened a laboratory in New York City. Little was then known in America regarding the production of synthetic colors, and in the development of the processes of dyeing he found his greatest opportunity. He secured, first, an appointment as representative of A. Porrier, Paris, but by 1880 he had joined Leopold Cassella & Company, beginning an association which covered a period of forty years. Though in time he organized his own companies, among them the W. J. Matheson Company, Ltd., the Matheson Lead Company, and the Hamolin Company, it was the Cassella Color Company, distributors of synthetic hydro-carbons, to which in later years he gave almost his entire attention. At the outbreak of the World War, he devoted his energies to stabilizing the dye industry, and when the entry of the United States into that conflict cut off the American importation of German dyes, he used his experience and ability in meeting his country's needs. As president and chairman of the board of the National Aniline & Chemical Company, he was a leader in the development of the practical as well as the scientific aspects of the dye industry. He was also instrumental in organizing the Allied Chemical & Dye Corporation, usually regarded as the climax of his business career of fifty years, covering almost the entire history of American synthetic dyes. In 1920 St. Andrews University, Scotland, bestowed upon him the degree of LL.D. in recognition of his achievements.

His interests were by no means confined to his chosen profession. He was a pioneer in real-estate projects in Florida, where he made his winter home for twenty-five years, beginning operations there in 1904. To the Long Island Biological Association, which he served as president from 1905 to 1923, he gave freely of his time and resources. One of his important achievements, it is said, was the extermination of mosquitoes from the north shore of Long Island. Occasionally he turned antiquarian, and in 1918 published *An Historical Sketch of Fort Hill, Lloyd Neck, Long Island.*

Though many philanthropic enterprises gained his attention from time to time, perhaps his greatest service to mankind was the establishment of a fund, in 1927, for an international study of epidemic encephalitis, popularly known as "sleeping sickness." A committee of eminent physicians representing the laboratory, clinical, and epidemiological viewpoints was appointed for the purpose of collecting and tabulating the work being done throughout the world on this subject. The first report of the Matheson Commission, *Epidemic Encephalitis,* was published in 1929. The commission was deprived of his personal assistance by his sudden death on board his yacht, the *Seaforth,* while returning from a cruise in the Bahama Islands, but the continuance of its work was assured by the terms of his will, which established a fund of two million dollars for the organization and maintenance of the William J. Matheson Foundation for charitable and educational purposes, its first work to be in encephalitis research. In 1881 Matheson married Harriet Torrey, and to them two sons and one daughter were born.

[*N. Y. Times,* June 5, 1927, Nov. 17, 1929, May 16, 27, 29, 1930; *Miami Herald,* May 16, 1930; *Chemical Markets,* June 1930; *Textile Colorist,* June 1930; *Who's Who in America,* 1930–31; *Who's Who in Finance, Banking, and Insurance,* 1929–30; preface to *Epidemic Encephalitis* (1929).]

I. V–F.

MATHEWS, ALBERT (Sept. 8, 1820–Sept. 9, 1903), author, the son of Oliver and Mary (Field) Mathews, was born of a well-to-do family in New York City and there received his early education. Entering Yale College he graduated in 1842 and devoted the next three years to the study of law, first at the Harvard Law School and later in New York. In 1845 he was admitted to the bar and immediately went into partnership with Augustus L. Brown. The new firm of Brown & Mathews became attorneys for the sheriff, and Mathews found himself launched almost at once into a lucrative practice. He was married twice, first on Dec. 12, 1849, to Louise Mott Strong, who lived only a few years, and, on Mar. 20, 1861, to Mrs. Cettie (Moore) Gwynne, who died in 1884. All through his early years as a practising lawyer, he had contributed essays and articles to the periodical press, but not until a few months before his second marriage, and perhaps in connection with his courtship, did he begin to take authorship very seriously. In 1860 he published his first book, *Walter Ashwood, A Love Story.* This novel is altogether a very wooden performance having a faintly Byronesque hero and the approved sentimental flavor of the day. As his *nom de plume* he continued to use Paul Siogvolk, the same name under which his earlier essays and legends had been written and which he used for all subsequent writing of a non-legal character. His essays and legends are the best of the work he has left and are of creditable literary quality, though, of course, outmoded as regards technique and style. In the main their tone is rather grave than gay, and their appeal was limited to the thoughtful and reflective few. He figured prominently in the foundation of the New York City bar association. In 1879 he became a member of the bar association of the state of New York. In the same year he brought out a collection of essays under the title *A Bundle of Papers.* Other writings of a mixed character followed in rapid succession: *Thoughts on Codification of the Common Law* (1881); *Memorial of Bernard Roelker* (1889); *Ruminations* (1893); *A Few Verses* (1896). By 1897 both his partners A. L. Brown and G. W. Blunt were dead, and he, himself, had virtually retired. To his friends he was known as an amiable and genial character, and among them he acquired a degree of celebrity by the enticing way in which he was able to word legal forms of a content intrinsically grim. Though nicknamed after the Prince Consort because of his stately bearing, he could unbend when occasion demanded and beam very winningly through his antique gold spectacles upon judges and juries who failed to respond to impersonal logic. In a purely professional way, he was distinctively a court lawyer and dealt for the greater part in the trial of causes and the arguing of appeals. As he specialized closely in no single branch of the law, he has left no work of a permanently valuable character. In the proceedings of the bar associations of the city and of the state he was active to the end of his life and to the city association he left a generous legacy when he died. His death occurred at Lake Mohonk, N. Y.

[*Who's Who in America*, 1903–05; *Biog. Record of the Class of 1842 of Yale College* (1878); *Green Bag*, Jan. 1897; *Asso. of the Bar of the City of N. Y. Reports . . . 1904* (1905); *N. Y. State Bar Asso. Reports*, vol. V (1882); *N. Y. Times*, Sept. 10, 12, 1903.]

E. M. H.

MATHEWS, CORNELIUS (Oct. 28, 1817–Mar. 25, 1889), author, was born in Port Chester, N. Y., the second son of Abijah and Catherine (Van Cott) Mathews. He was descended from Annanias Mathews an early settler in Long Island. During the years 1830–32 he was enrolled in Columbia College, but in the fall of 1832 he matriculated at the University of the City of New York (now New York University), which had just opened for instruction, and in July 1834 he received his A.B. degree at the first Commencement of the new university, delivering an oration on "Females of the American Revolution." He was, apparently, related to the first chancellor of the University, Rev. James M. Mathews; this relationship may have had some connection with his transfer from Columbia to the new university. His membership in the college literary society, the *Adelphic*, which published a magazine (under the inspiration of Professor Henry B. Tappan, afterward chancellor of the University of Michigan), may possibly have affected his later career. To please his father he studied law and in 1837 was admitted to the New York bar, but he soon abandoned this profession and turned to literary production and editorial work.

He had since 1836 contributed regularly to the *American Monthly Magazine*, the *New York Review*, and the *Knickerbocker Magazine* articles in both prose and verse, mostly humorous in character. In 1839 appeared his first romance, *Behemoth: a Legend of the Mound Builders*, an imaginative story of which it can at least be said that the plot is original. In 1840, with his friend Evert A. Duyckinck [*q.v.*], he founded and edited a monthly magazine, *Arcturus, a Journal of Books and Opinion*, of which three volumes appeared, and in which Mathews wrote numerous articles, mostly critical, but including a novel, "The Career of Puffer Hopkins" (June 1841–May 1842) on the theme of New York politics. He had already turned to the drama, and in 1840 brought out *The Politicians*, a comedy on New York electioneering life, which had no success. In 1846 his tragedy, *Witchcraft, or the Martyrs of Salem*, met with unusual success, and was even translated into French. Its blank verse is often excellent, and it possesses considerable dramatic power. Two other plays, *Jacob Leisler* (1848), a tragedy, and *False Pretences* (1855), a satire on social parvenus, met a less popular response.

His *Poems on Man in His Various Aspects under the American Republic*, published in 1843, was favorably received by critics, especially by James Russell Lowell, whose remarks upon them in the *Fable for Critics*

> "(which contain many verses as fine, by the bye
> As any that lately came under my eye)"

give Mathews today perhaps his chief claim to fame. Lowell, be it added, has several other less complimentary references to Mathews in the *Fable for Critics*, particularly with regard to the copyright issue and in association with E. A. Duyckinck. Perhaps the reader of today will best sympathize with Lowell's caustic judgment of *Yankee Doodle*, a comic magazine edited by Mathews in 1846–47:

> "That American Punch, like the English, no doubt,
> Just the sugar and lemons and spirit left out."

Mathews in his earlier years, at any rate, was a vigorous nationalist in his literary ideals and insisted that the United States needed a literature which should not be imitative of Europe, but original and American in its essence. At the same time he was always an enthusiastic champion of international copyright, and welcomed the occasion of speaking on that topic at the dinner given to Charles Dickens in 1842. Elizabeth Barrett Browning, also, found his friendship of assistance in first securing American attention to her verse.

After 1855 he published little. The *Indian Fairy Book*, which was compiled by Mathews from material supplied by Henry R. Schoolcraft, is the only book to bear his name. It was issued first in 1856 and was republished in later editions, in 1877 as *The Enchanted Moccassins*. Mathews appears, however, to have continued his association with the world of journalism and after 1882 was regularly until his death a contributing editor of the *New York Dramatic Mirror.* He never married.

[E. A. and G. L. Duyckinck, *Cyc. of Am. Lit.* (2 vols., 1875); C. Mathews, "Temple Court," in the *Manhattan,* July 1883; *N. Y. Dramatic Mirror,* Apr. 6, 1889; *N. Y. Times,* Mar. 27, 1889; A. H. Quinn, *A Hist. of the Am. Drama from the Beginning to the Civil War* (1923); manuscript records of N. Y. Univ., manuscript recollections of Mathews' niece, Frances A. Mathews.] T. F. J.

MATHEWS, GEORGE (Aug. 30, 1739–Aug. 30, 1812), Revolutionary soldier, congressman, and governor, son of John Mathews, a recent Irish immigrant, was born in Augusta County, Va., and fought the Indians at Point Pleasant (Oct. 10, 1774). During the Revolution he took part in the campaigns around Philadelphia, spent some months in a British prison ship, and later served with distinction as colonel of Virginia troops in Greene's Carolina campaigns. Removing to Georgia in 1785, he became brigadier-general in the militia of that state, governor in 1787, and its representative in Congress, 1789–91. As governor of the state again, 1793–96, he opposed the filibustering operations of Elijah Clarke [*q.v.*] and his associates and signed the notorious Yazoo Act. In 1798 President Adams nominated him as first governor of Mississippi Territory, but within a month was obliged to withdraw his name because of his dubious land speculations and suspected connection with the Blount Conspiracy (Cox, "Border Missions," *post,* p. 309). Mathews journeyed to Philadelphia, according to reports, to chastise the President, but desisted from his purpose when his son was given a federal appointment (Gilmer, *post,* pp. 73–82). He appears to have been married three times; his first wife, *née* Woods, was of Albemarle County, Va.; his second, Mrs. Reed of Staunton, whom he divorced; and his third, Mrs. Flowers of Mississippi. He had four sons and two daughters.

In the fall of 1810 he was employed, evidently on the initiative of William H. Crawford [*q.v.*], to sound Vizente Folch, the Spanish executive of West Florida, on the question of delivering that province to the United States. In this he failed (Cox, *op. cit.,* pp. 310–12), but his observations around Mobile and St. Augustine convinced him that both Floridas should at once be brought under the control of the United States. During the following winter he was at Washington when the administration received from Folch a belated but conditional offer to deliver his province. Congress having authorized its acceptance and also, in certain contingencies, the occupation of East Florida, Mathews and John McKee, the bearer of Folch's offer, were authorized to take the necessary steps in the transfer. When, however, the commissioners interviewed Folch at Mobile in March 1811, that executive refused to make the proffered delivery (*Ibid.,* 312–17).

This refusal evidently convinced Mathews that in respect to East Florida, where he believed his instructions empowered him to continue irregular activities, he must employ more direct if dubious methods. He had already (1810–11) sought to stir up insurrection there and by an interview with Crawford in October 1811 was further confirmed in his tortuous course, although the administration left him without further instructions. His method of procedure was to organize the English-speaking Spanish subjects of East Florida, draft recruits in nearby Georgia, and when these irregular contingents were ready, secure "volunteers" from among the American regulars. Thus he hoped to bring about the surprise and capture of St. Augustine. This plan failed through the opposition of the American military commander, but the "insurgents" declared independence of Spain and on Mar. 17, 1812, aided by recruits from Georgia and by the intervention of the American gunboats on the St. Marys, forced the surrender of Fernandina. On the following day Mathews took formal possession of that smuggling center in the name of the United States. Following this initial success the "insurgents" successively occupied outlying portions of the province and then turned each over to Mathews, who, with his regulars, followed them closely. In this piecemeal fashion the two contingents, early in June, came within sight of St. Augustine. Here Mathews was halted by Secretary Monroe's tardy but complete disavowal of his course. The Secretary in a private letter praised his agent's zeal, but regretted that he had not used more "restrained" methods.

For some weeks the repudiated commissioner preserved silence; then, the rôle of silent martyr becoming unbearable, the impulsive old man started northward, fell ill at Augusta, and fulfilled Crawford's presentiment that he would "die of mortification and resentment" (Pratt, *post,* p. 114) over his repudiation. By his demise the authorities at Washington escaped the consequences of his threat that he'd "be dam'd if he didn't blow them all up" (*Ibid.,* p. 115), and he carried to the grave much evidence that might explain his debatable conduct.

[The foregoing account is largely based on manuscript material found in *Papeles procedentes de la Isla de Cuba,* Archivo General, Seville; in the Pickering Papers at the Mass. Hist. Soc.; and in the various collections of the Division of Publications, Dept. of State, and of the Lib. of Cong. Consult I. J. Cox, "The Border Missions of General George Mathews," in *Miss. Valley Hist. Rev.*, Dec. 1925; J. W. Pratt, *Expansionists of 1812* (1925); and I. J. Cox, *The West Fla. Controversy* (1918). An article based on printed material is R. K. Wyllys, "The East Florida Revolution of 1812–1814," in *Hispanic Hist. Rev.*, Nov. 1929. Some details of Mathews' early life are found in *Cyc. of Ga.* (1906), vol. II, and in G. R. Gilmer, *Sketches of Some of the First Settlers of Upper Ga.* (1855). An obituary notice appeared in the *Republican and Savannah Evening Ledger*, Sept. 3, 1812.] I. J. C.

MATHEWS, HENRY MASON (Mar. 29, 1834–Apr. 28, 1884), governor of West Virginia, the eldest son of Mason and Eliza Shore (Reynolds) Mathews, was born in Greenbrier County, Va., now W. Va. His mother was a sister of Alexander Welch Reynolds [*q.v.*]. The elder Mathews was a successful merchant and was able to give his son good opportunities for schooling. Young Mathews was prepared for college at the Lewisburg academy and in his eighteenth year entered the University of Virginia. He was a student there from 1852 to 1856 and received the A.B. degree in 1855 and the A.M. degree in 1856. After leaving the university he studied law for one year in the school conducted by Judge John W. Brockenbrough, of Lexington, Va. In 1857 he began the practice of the law at Lewisburg, the county seat of Greenbrier County, and on Nov. 24 of that year he married Lucy Clayton Fry, the daughter of Judge Joseph L. Fry, of Wheeling. They had two daughters and a son. For a short period before the Civil War he added to his duties as an attorney the teaching of modern languages and history in Allegheny College, a school for boys at Blue Sulphur Springs. When hostilities broke out he enlisted in the Confederate service and by the end of the war had attained the rank of major.

At the close of the war he returned to Lewisburg, but for a while was debarred from the practice of his profession by the proscriptive laws against former Confederates. In like manner he was also excluded from the state Senate, although he had been elected by an overwhelming majority. In 1872 he was a member of the state convention that framed the present constitution of West Virginia. He was in this same year also elected attorney-general of the state. Four years later, in 1876, he was nominated by the Democratic party for governor and was elected by a very large majority. He became governor at a time when passions born of civil war and reconstruction ran high. He was well qualified by temperament, education, and experience for the task of allaying strife and of mediating between the opposing parties. His genial disposition and gentle demeanor enabled him to make contacts with his political opponents with a minimum of friction. The keynote of his inaugural address was harmony, and the policy of his administration was characterized by the same spirit. He appointed representatives of both parties on all important governmental boards, a practice that was unusual for that period. The most dramatic event of his four-year term was the great railroad strike, which was caused by a ten per cent. reduction in the wages of employees of the Baltimore & Ohio Railroad. It started at Martinsburg in July 1877 and soon spread to other points in West Virginia and to other states, since the same reduction in wages had been made by other railroad systems. The mob violence that attended the strike at Martinsburg was beyond the control of the police authorities, and at other places outbreaks were threatening. He insisted that grievances, however great, must be redressed through legal means alone, and so he promptly ordered out the state militia, but the force at his command was too small to cope with the riot. Thereupon he called upon the president for federal troops. This request was complied with, and order was promptly restored. Mathews showed the same firmness in dealing with the coal strike that broke out along the Chesapeake and Ohio Railway three years later, in January 1880. The strikers, who were threatening injury to persons and the destruction of property, were moving toward the Ansted mines in Fayette County to compel the miners there to cease work. At the request of the sheriff of the county he promptly sent a battalion of infantry and all disorder was quickly put down. The last few years of his life were spent at Lewisburg in the practice of his profession.

[Information from his daughter, L. Josephine Mathews, and from the registrar of the University of Virginia; Phil Conley, *The W. Va. Encyc.* (1929); R. E. Fast and Hu Maxwell, *The Hist. and Government of W. Va.* (1901); G. W. Atkinson and A. F. Gibbens, *Prominent Men of W. Va.* (1890); *Jour. of the House of Delegates of . . . W. Va.*, 1879, pp. 32–34, 1881, pp. 23–24; *Wheeling Daily Intelligencer*, Mar. 6, 7, July 17–21, 1877, Jan. 12–17, 1880; *Wheeling Register*, Apr. 30, 1884.] O. P. C.

MATHEWS, JOHN (1744–Oct. 26, 1802), delegate to the Continental Congress, governor of South Carolina, was born at Charlestown (now Charleston), S. C., the son of John and Sarah (Gibbes) Mathews. In 1760 he was ensign and then lieutenant in the expedition against the Cherokee. On Oct. 27, 1764, he was admitted to the Middle Temple in London to study law and on Sept. 22, 1766, was admitted to the bar of South Carolina. In December of that year he was married to Mary Wragg, the daughter of William Wragg and the half-sister of Charlotte

Wragg who married William Loughton Smith [*q.v.*]. In the quarrel between Great Britain and the colonies he early took the colonial side, served in the first and second provincial congresses from St. George's, Dorchester, was elected as associate justice of the court of general sessions in 1776, and became speaker of the General Assembly under the temporary constitution of 1776 and the first speaker of the House of Representatives under the constitution of 1778. From 1778 to 1782 he represented South Carolina in the Continental Congress, where he voted against the motion privately to instruct the minister to Spain that he might recede from the claim to free navigation of the Mississippi River, bitterly opposed Samuel Huntington of Connecticut, the president of Congress, bent his whole efforts to defeating the proposal to make a separate peace between Great Britain and the other colonies at the price of abandoning the Carolinas and Georgia, and signed the Articles of Confederation. On the committee at headquarters in 1780 he was most active in his efforts to strengthen Washington's authority and greatly injured the Congress' sense of its own dignity by his outspoken expression of impatience at its failure to act. In 1782 he was elected governor by the Jonesborough Assembly. Through the next year of the war, he transacted the business of his office from various places, part of the time from his plantation of "Uxbridge" on the Ashley River, which had been a part of the Ashley barony. He negotiated with the British on the difficult questions of sequestration, confiscation, and destruction of property, struggled with the conflicting interests of the inhabitants and the army that had been impressing the foodstuffs of which it stood in urgent need, and, when at last the British troops sailed out of Charlestown harbor, took possession of his own capital city. He has been accused of the abuse of men and property left behind by the British evacuation and even of permitting the hanging of several Tories, but a recent examination of the evidence seems to indicate that such charges were unfounded (J. W. Barnwell, "Evacuation of Charleston by the British," *South Carolina Historical and Genealogical Magazine,* January 1910).

When the court of chancery was established on Mar. 21, 1784, he was appointed by the legislature as chancellor and, after the organization of the courts of law and equity in 1791, continued to serve as a judge of the court of equity. His decisions show his legal capacity and learning as well as his grasp of the principles of fundamental justice (1 *S. C. Equity Reports,* especially the case of *Deveaux* vs. *Executors of Barnwell,* pp. 497–98). He resigned in November 1797. He was one of the original trustees of the College of Charleston and he helped found the St. George's Club of St. George's Parish, Dorchester, for the encouragement of the breeding of good horses. After the death of his first wife he married, on May 5, 1799, Sarah, the sister of John and Edward Rutledge [*qq.v.*]. No children survived him.

[A few MSS. in the Lib. of Cong.; R. W. Gibbes, *Documentary Hist. of the Am. Revolution,* vols. II (1857), III (1853); E. C. Burnett, *Letters of Members of the Continental Cong.,* vols. IV–V (1928–31); Wm. Moultrie, *Memoirs of the Am. Revolution* (1802), vol. II, esp. pp. 330–36, 343–51, 359; J. B. O'Neall, *Biog. Sketches of the Bench and Bar of S. C.* (1859), vol. I; Edward McCrady, *The Hist. of S. C. under the Royal Government* (1899) and *The Hist. of S. C. in the Revolution* (1901); David Ramsay, *The Hist. of S. C.* (1809), I, pp. 468, 471–75, II, pp. 135, 146–47, 155, 384; E. A. Jones, *Am. Members of the Inns of Court* (1924); *S. C. Hist. and Geneal. Mag.,* Oct. 1902, Apr. 1906, Jan., Apr. 1907, Apr. 1910, Jan. 1916, Oct. 1917, July 1919, July 1924, Oct. 1925, Jan., Apr. 1926; *Carolina Gazette,* Nov. 4, 1802.]

K. E. C.

MATHEWS, SAMUEL (*c.* 1600–January 1660), colonial planter and last governor of Virginia under the Commonwealth, was born in England, coming to Virginia in 1622 and forthwith engaging actively in the colony's affairs. The next year, after serving in the Assembly and commanding an expedition against the seat of the Pamunkeys, he became a member of the council, in which body he served intermittently until his election as governor. In 1624 he was one of the four commissioners—"certayne obscure persons," Sandys acrimoniously designated them later—appointed by the Privy Council to investigate conditions in the colony. Industrious and forceful, he rapidly acquired a fortune through planting and trading, and added to his standing as well as his acreage by his marriage in 1629 to Frances, daughter of Sir Thomas Hinton, and widow successively of Capt. Nathaniel West and of the wealthy Abraham Piersey. With William Claiborne he built the palisade between the York and James rivers for protection against Indian attack, and he contracted alone to rebuild the fort at Point Comfort but expended so liberally of his own resources in this enterprise that Governor Harvey sought his favor by recommending him to King Charles for special privileges in compensation. Mathews, however, was not to be bought; "a man of a bold spiritt, turbulent and strong" (C. C. Hall, ed., *Narratives of Early Maryland,* 1910, p. 59), he was soon alienated by the executive's usurpations and abuses of power, and led the council in the revolt which culminated in Harvey's deposition. When Harvey was returned to office by the King, he sent the chief rebels to England under accusation of treason and seized their estates.

The leaders of this first American uprising in defense of popular rights were never called to trial, but so rancorous was Harvey that he despoiled and ransacked Mathews' property and delayed obeying the Privy Council's order to make complete restitution to him (T. J. Wertenbaker, *Virginia under the Stuarts,* 1914, ch. iii). Mathews regained his seat in the council in 1642 and again busied himself in the contention with Baltimore over the Maryland territory. Himself a Puritan and an early convert to the Parliamentary cause—although named by John Hammond the chief persecutor of the 'Independents' in Virginia—from 1652 to 1657 he was in England as agent to recover Maryland to Virginia; but before returning from his unsuccessful mission, he signed, November 1657, an agreement with Baltimore settling the differences between the two colonies. On Mar. 13, 1658, he succeeded Digges as governor, and shortly became involved in a controversy with the Assembly. When the burgesses, disregarding precedent, refused the governor and council seats in the House, Mathews declared the body dissolved. The burgesses refused to disperse, claiming supremacy as representatives of the people; whereupon the Governor offered certain concessions. These the Assembly rejected and deposed Mathews and his councilors, but upon their recognizing the authority of the House reëlected them as responsible to it alone. The remainder of his term, until his death in office, was uneventful; but he governed with efficiency, honesty, and liberality, and under him Virginia prospered. Posterity has overlooked both the passionate striving for justice and the sturdy independence of this "most deserving Common-wealth's-man," who, according to a contemporary, kept a good house, lived bravely, and was a true lover of Virginia (Peter Force, *Tracts and Other Papers,* II, 1838, pp. 14–15); but for a time he was perhaps the leading and most influential citizen of the colony, distinguished little less for his extensive holdings of land and his comfortable, self-sufficing plantation at Blunt Point than for his unquestioned ability and character.

[See P. A. Bruce, *Econ. Hist. of Va. in the Seventeenth Century* (2 vols., 1895); J. H. Claiborne, *Wm. Claiborne of Va.* (1917); E. D. Neill, *Va. Carolorum* (1886); W. W. Hening, *The Statutes at Large,* vol. I (1823); *Va. Mag. of Hist. and Biog.,* July, Oct. 1893, Apr. 1894, Apr. 1906. Mathews' name is variously spelled. His signature, given in the *Va. Mag. of Hist. and Biog.,* Apr. 1894, gives the form adopted in this sketch.]

A. C. G., Jr.

MATHEWS, WILLIAM (July 28, 1818–Feb. 14, 1909), journalist, teacher, and author, was born in Waterville, Me., the eldest son of Simeon and Clymena (Esty) Mathews. After preparation in various academies in Maine, he was ready at the age of thirteen to enter Waterville (now Colby) College. He received the A.B. degree in 1835. He then studied law in the office of the Hon. Timothy Boutelle of Waterville and in the Harvard Law School. In 1838 he was admitted to the bar of Kennebec County and in 1839 received the degree of LL.B. from Harvard. He taught school for a time and in 1841 began the practice of law in Waterville. He also launched in May 1841 a literary and family weekly known as the *Watervillonian,* devoted to "Literature, Morals, Agriculture, News, Etc." Within two years the newspaper enterprise required all of his time, and he abandoned the practice of law, moved the paper to Gardiner, Me., and changed its name to the *Yankee Blade.* In 1847 the *Blade* was moved to Boston, where in 1856 Mathews sold the enterprise to the *Boston Mercantile Journal.* It was then merged with an existing periodical published by the owners of the *Journal* under the title of the *Portfolio.*

Freed from editorial responsibilities, Mathews moved in 1856 to Chicago, where for three years he edited a financial weekly, conducted a department in the *Daily Tribune,* and gave public lectures. In 1859 he was made librarian of the Chicago Y.M.C.A. and continued to contribute to various periodicals. From 1862 to 1875 he was professor of rhetoric and English in the University of Chicago. A series of articles which he wrote for the *Tribune* in the early part of 1871 on the general subject of success in life proved so popular that he revised and issued the essays in 1873 in a volume entitled *Getting on in the World.* The book was well received, reaching a sale of 70,000 copies. It was followed in 1874 by *The Great Conversers and Other Essays.* The success of these two ventures encouraged Mathews to give up his professorship and devote his time to literary work, and in 1876 he published *Words: Their Use and Abuse,* of which 25,000 copies were sold. A volume of literary essays, *Hours With Men and Books,* appeared in 1877, and in the same year he published a translation of Sainte-Beuve's *Causeries du Lundi* under the title *Monday Chats. Oratory and Orators* followed in 1879.

In 1880 Mathews returned to New England and for the rest of his life made his home in Boston, devoting himself to the writing of essays, to lecturing, and to prolonged travel abroad. His later works include: *Literary Style and Other Essays* (1881); *Men, Places, and Things* (1887); *Wit and Humor: Their Use and Abuse*

(1888); *Nugae Litterariae* (1896); and *Conquering Success* (1903). In 1896 he supplied critical notes and introductions for an elaborate edition of Bulwer-Lytton. He also contributed largely to Appletons' *Cyclopædia of American Biography*. Mathews was thrice married; in 1845 to Mary Elizabeth Dingley, of Winslow, Me.; in 1850 to Isabel I. Marshall, of China, Me., and in 1865 to Harriet M. Griggs of Chicago. In 1907 he was injured by a fall and confined to his bed for two years, but he continued his literary work by dictation. He died in the Emerson Hospital at Forest Hills.

[E. C. Whittemore, *The Centennial Hist. of Waterville, Kennebec County, Me.* (1902); "Senior Colby Graduate," *Boston Sunday Globe*, Jan. 24, 1909; the *Colby Echo*, Jan. 27, 1909; *Who's Who in America*, 1908–09; obituary in the *Boston Herald*, Feb. 15, 1909.]

J. C. F.

MATHEWS, WILLIAM SMYTHE BABCOCK (May 8, 1837–Apr. 1, 1912), teacher, musician, and writer on musical subjects, was born in Loudon, N. H., the son of Samuel S. Mathews, a Methodist minister, and Elizabeth Stanton Babcock. His mother encouraged the development of his musical talent from an early age. After studying piano with local teachers, he attended the Lowell, N. H., Conference Seminary, and then continued his studies in Boston. At the age of fifteen he was already a teacher of music at the Appleton Academy, Mount Vernon, N. H. From 1857 to 1860 he was professor of music at the Wesleyan Female College of Macon, Ga. Later he taught piano in Greensboro, N. C., and in Marion, Ala., but he left the South for Chicago where, from 1867 to 1893, he was organist of the Centenary Methodist Episcopal Church. During this period also he wrote most of his books on music. In 1866 he had become a contributor to *Dwight's Journal of Music*, and he continued to write for the journal until its discontinuance in 1881. From 1869 to 1871 he edited Lyon and Healy's *Musical Independent*, and at various times he acted as music critic for the *Chicago Record, Times*, and *Daily Tribune*. On Nov. 1, 1891, he issued the first number of the magazine *Music*, which he edited until it merged with the *Philharmonic* in 1902.

Mathews' books on music, popular and educational in character, include: *An Outline of Musical Form* (1868), with William Mason [*q.v.*]; *Emerson Organ Method* (1870), in collaboration with L. O. Emerson; *A System of Technical Exercises for the Pianoforte* (1878), with William Mason; *How to Understand Music* (2 vols., 1880–88); *One Hundred Years of Music in America* (1889); *A Popular History of the Art of Music* (1890); *Pronouncing and Defining Dictionary of Music* (1896), with Emil Liebling [*q.v.*]; *Music, Its Ideals and Methods* (1897); *The Masters and Their Music* (1898); and *The Great in Music* (3 vols., 1900–03), each volume designed to cover a year's work in study and appreciation for music-student extension clubs. He also published various compilations of instructive technical studies for the piano, notably the *Studies in Phrasing* (2 vols., 1883–88); *Standard Graded Course of Studies for the Pianoforte* (1893) in ten grades; and the supplementary eight volumes of *Graded Materials for Piano Teaching* (1895).

Mathews did much to raise the general level of music education in the West. He was a zealous advocate of the cultural value of music in the community and continually preached the need of organization among teachers and musicians. In 1910 he removed from Chicago to Denver where he died two years later. Just before his death he spent several months in Dallas, Tex., revising the correspondence courses of the Columbian Conservatory of Music. Mathews' first wife was Flora E. Swain, of Nunda, N. Y., to whom he was married in 1857. His second wife was Blanche Dingley, whom he married in 1902.

[See *Who's Who* in America, 1912–13; the *Musician*, May, June 1912; the *Etude*, May, June 1912; *Musical America*, Apr. 6, 1912; *Musical Courier*, Apr. 10, 1912; *Rocky Mountain News* (Denver), Apr. 2, 1912. In a letter to the Lib. of Cong., relative to the spelling of his name, Mathews spelled his second name as it is given in this sketch.]

F. H. M.

MATHEWSON, CHRISTOPHER (Aug. 12, 1880–Oct. 7, 1925), baseball player, son of Gilbert B. Mathewson and Minerva J. (Capwell) Mathewson, was born at Factoryville, Pa. His father was a gentleman farmer. At the age of fourteen Christopher entered Keystone Academy, graduated in 1898, and having won a scholarship at Bucknell College, Lewisburg, Pa., entered that institution. To pay his living expenses, he did the catering for the student eating club. He had played baseball from childhood and at Bucknell became the star pitcher of the college nine. He was interested, also, in student activities in general and was popular with his fellows.

The lure of professional baseball drew him from college, however, before he had completed his course. He had played professionally during summer vacations, being with the Taunton team of the New England League in 1899, and with the Norfolk team of the Virginia League until midsummer of 1900, when he was sold to the New York Giants. With them he remained for sixteen years, becoming one of the greatest pitchers that baseball has ever known, and setting numerous records, some of which have stood down to the present time. He aided his team in winning many pennants and in capturing World's Series championships. In the World's Series of 1905 he pitched three winning games against the Philadelphia Athletics without allowing the opposing team a single run. During his career in the National League he won 511 games, and was famous for his "fade-away" delivery, a ball that dropped deceptively and on the "inside" for a right-handed batter.

In 1916, after his long and honorable career with the Giants, he became manager of the Cincinnati Reds, a position he held until he enlisted in the United States Army in 1918 and became a captain in the gas and flame division of the American Expeditionary Force in France. On his return from the war, he joined his old team, the Giants, as a coach, and remained in that capacity until 1920. Symptoms of pulmonary tuberculosis were apparent in his later years with the Giants and he spent many rest periods at Saranac, N. Y. His precarious state of health brought an end to his coaching career but there was a popular interest in keeping such a famous figure in baseball, and in 1923 he was asked to accept the presidency of the Boston Braves, with the understanding that he would give that club as much attention as his health permitted. For two years he did what he could, spending part of the time in baseball work and part at Saranac. It was a vain fight and he died at Saranac during the playing of the World's Series of 1925 at Pittsburgh. His death cast a gloom over the series and, with many baseball officials attending, he was buried in Lewisburg, Pa., the town in which he had gone to college and which for many years he considered his home. His grave is in the cemetery below the Bucknell Stadium, the entrance to which is the Mathewson Memorial Gateway. There is also a bronze memorial tablet to him on the outfield wall of the Polo Grounds in New York, and a memorial building at Saranac, commemorating his sports career and his war service. He was survived by his wife Jane (Stoughton) Mathewson and their only child, Christopher Mathewson, Jr.

"In addition to physical ability, Mathewson had the perfect temperament for a great ball player. Always he sought to learn something new, and he never forgot what he had learned in the past. He had everything—strength, intelligence, courage and willingness" (John J. McGraw, *post,* p. 221). It was the character as much as his accomplishments of Mathewson, known all over the country as "Matty," "Christy," and "Big Six," that brought him lasting fame and wide recognition. A college man, a gentleman, a soldier, and an outstanding athlete, he was an inspiration to the younger lads of the country, a sportsman that educators could point to as a model for college athletes to emulate. He had scholarly interests as well, and during his days at Saranac he took up the study of natural history and became acquainted with all the birds, trees, and flowers of that region. Because of a promise made to his mother, he never played baseball on Sunday through his whole career. He was much in demand as a speaker before boys' clubs and college gatherings. By his example and his success, he became the leader of the "college element" in big-league baseball and did much to improve the tone of the game.

[F. C. Richter, *Richter's Hist. and Records of Baseball* (1914); J. B. Foster, *Spalding's Official Baseball Guide* (1926); J. J. McGraw, *My Thirty Years in Baseball* (copr. 1923); C. H. Claudy, *The Battle of Baseball* (1912); *Baseball Mag.*, Dec. 1925; *Literary Digest*, Oct. 24, Dec. 26, 1925; *Collier's Weekly*, Apr. 11, 1925; *N. Y. Times*, Oct. 8, 9 (editorial), 10, 11, 1925; family records.]

J. K.

MATIGNON, FRANCIS ANTHONY (Nov. 10, 1753–Sept. 19, 1818), Catholic priest, was born in Paris of a good family. Early in life he displayed talents of a high order and was prepared for the Seminary of Saint Sulpice, from which he received the bachelorate in divinity. As a Sulpician, he was ordained (Sept. 19, 1778), and on the completion of four years as a curate, he entered the Sorbonne, from which he received a doctor's degree in theology (1785). Assigned to the chair of theology in the College of Navarre, he continued teaching until 1789, when, through Cardinal de Brienne, he obtained an annuity from Louis XVI. As a royalist, he was compelled to flee the wrath of the Revolutionists and sought refuge in England. Returning later to Paris, he set out from there in 1792 for Baltimore with three distinguished Sulpicians, Abbés Richard, Maréchal [*qq.v.*], and Francis Cicquard. Bishop Carroll assigned him to the small Catholic church in School Street, Boston, where the over-zealous convert, John Thayer [*q.v.*], had aroused rather than allayed Puritan hostility.

A scholar and a gentleman, the French abbé with kindness, humility, and quiet demeanor disarmed even the most captious critics. In 1795 he invited another French refugee, John Louis Ann Magdalen Lefebre de Cheverus [*q.v.*], then in England, to be his assistant, and with him he worked in perfect harmony and brotherly friendship. The epidemic of the year 1798 gave Matignon a wider opportunity for service. In 1799, since the old church was outgrown, he commenced the collection of funds for Holy Trinity Church in Franklin Square. Fully a fifth of the amount was subscribed by Protestant friends, including President Adams; Charles Bulfinch [*q.v.*] donated his services as architect. Recognizing the epochal character of the occasion in New England, Bishop Carroll accepted Father Matignon's invitation and consecrated the edifice (1803). Renewing their efforts, the inseparable priests gathered a congregation of about a thousand communicants. Bishop Carroll petitioned Rome to have Boston made a see with Matignon as bishop, and when the latter learned of the fact he offered strong protest, even threatening to leave for France, and urged that Father Cheverus be named. Appointed bishop in 1808, Cheverus retained Matignon as pastor and served as his curate when not on missions. In 1813, while on his way to New York, Matignon was forced by a Sunday anti-traveling law to remain in Hartford, where he experienced the unusual courtesy of being permitted the use of the First Church of Christ, Congregationalist, of which Dr. Nathan Strong was pastor, for Catholic services. On his death, Boston thronged to pay respect to the humble priest, over whose funeral services Bishop Cheverus presided, and to follow his remains to the Granary burial ground, from which they were soon removed to the new St. Augustine's Cemetery in South Boston.

[J. G. Shea, *Hist. of the Cath. Ch. in the U. S.*, vol. II (1888); Peter Guilday, *The Life and Times of John Carroll* (1922); Jas. Fitton, *Sketches of the Establishment of the Church in New England* (1872); W. Byrne and others, *Hist. of the Cath. Church in the New England States* (2 vols., 1899); W. F. Kenny, *Centenary of the See of Boston* (1909); *Memorial Volume, One Hundredth Anniversary Celebration of the Dedication of the Church of the Holy Cross, Boston* (1904); *Am. Cath. Hist. Researches*, 1884–1912, index vol.; *U. S. Cath. Hist. Mag.*, Apr. 1890; *Cath. Encyc.*, II (1907), 704; *Records of the Am. Cath. Hist. Soc.*, Mar. 1904; C. A. Place, *Charles Bulfinch, Architect and Citizen* (1925); *Boston Monthly Mag.*, June 1825; *Columbian Centinel* (Boston), Sept. 23, 1818.]

R. J. P.

MATLACK, TIMOTHY (d. Apr. 14, 1829), Revolutionary patriot, state official, was the son of Timothy and Martha (Burr) Matlack, members of the Society of Friends, who in 1745 or 1746 removed from Haddonfield, N. J., to Philadelphia, where Timothy followed in his father's footsteps as a merchant. Varying dates are given for his birth: a family record (Stackhouse, *post*, p. 4) says it occurred "At Haddonfield, . . . the 28th day of 3rd month [May] 1736 O.S."; his tombstone gives Apr. 26, 1734 (*Publications of the Genealogical Society of Pennsylvania,* May 1902); but in the notice of his death (*National Gazette,* Philadelphia, Apr. 15, 1829) his age was given as ninety-nine years. He early found irksome the restraints which the Quaker discipline imposed, being fond of convivial company and interested in horse racing, cock fighting, and other sports of the day. He was married, Oct. 5, 1758, to Ellen, daughter of Mordecai Yarnall, a leading Quaker preacher, but was disowned by the Quakers in 1765 for "frequenting company in such manner as to neglect business whereby he contracted debts, failed and was unable to satisfy the claims of his creditors" (quoted by Stackhouse, p. 6).

In May 1775, shortly after the news of the battle of Lexington reached Philadelphia, he joined the Philadelphia Associators, and in the same month was employed as an assistant to Charles Thomson, secretary of the Continental Congress. A few of the minutes of Congress are in Matlack's handwriting and he wrote the commission for Washington as commander in chief (May 20, 1775). The following year, it is probable, he was employed to engross the Declaration of Independence. Congress appointed him a storekeeper for military supplies. He was elected colonel of a battalion of Associators raised early in 1776 and in the same year was a member of the constitutional convention for Pennsylvania, in which he served on the committee to prepare the draft. On July 24, 1776, he became a member of the Council of Safety and on the adoption of the new state constitution, when the executive functions were assumed by the Supreme Executive Council, he was made its secretary (Mar. 6, 1777), which office he filled with great zeal until the end of the war. In the military operations around Trenton and Princeton, he took the field with other Pennsylvania militia as colonel of a rifle battalion. Returning from this campaign he devoted himself to the various offices of secretary of the council, keeper of the great seal, and keeper of the register of persons attainted.

In 1779, he was designated a trustee of the newly created University of the State of Pennsylvania. In 1780, he was elected a member of the Continental Congress, in which he was active and influential, serving for two years. On the formation of the Bank of North America by Robert Morris in 1781, he was one of the first members on the board of directors. A member of the American Philosophical Society from about 1780 until his death, he was one of its secretaries, and delivered numerous addresses before that body. In 1782, he was removed as secretary of the Supreme Executive Council on charges of irregularities in his accounts. Judgment was obtained against him and for a time he was imprisoned for debt. He vigorously resented these charges and in 1783 the Council of Safety of Philadelphia, as a mark of confidence, presented him with a silver urn for the many valuable services he had rendered the cause of Independence. After a brief residence in New York in 1784 he returned to Philadelphia. He was one of the commissioners appointed under the act of Sept. 28, 1789, "to view the navigable waters" of Pennsylvania, being assigned with two others to the Delaware River. Later he resided in Lancaster, Pa., as a minor official of the state government, serving as clerk of the Senate and master of the rolls. After the death of his wife, he married on Aug. 17, 1797, Elizabeth, sister of David Claypoole the printer and widow of Norris Copper. He was appointed prothonotary of the United States district court at Philadelphia, Mar. 14, 1817. In 1813 he had been elected an alderman of the city, and served till 1818, when he retired from public life. He was active in forming, in 1781, the Society of Free Quakers, composed of those who had been disowned, or who had resigned from the Society of Friends on account of their wartime activities. Of this society he was a member for the rest of his life, and on his death he was buried in the Free Quaker burying ground in Philadelphia, the bodies from which were later removed to Matson's Ford across the Schuylkill River from Valley Forge. By his first marriage he had five children; through the three daughters and one son who lived to maturity, he left numerous descendants.

[A. M. Stackhouse, *Col. Timothy Matlack* (privately printed, 1910), contains footnote references to sources. See also Lincoln Cartledge, "Timothy Matlack—Penman of the Declaration of Independence," *Papers Read Before the Hist. Soc. of Frankford*, vol. II (1922); J. H. Martin, *Martin's Bench and Bar of Phila.* (1883); J. T. Scharf and Thompson Westcott, *Hist. of Phila.* (1884); Charles Wetherill, *Hist. of the Religious Soc. of Friends Called by Some Free Quakers in the City of Phila.* (printed for the society, 1894). Charles Wilson Peale's portrait of Matlack painted in 1826 hangs in Independence Hall. Peale made two earlier portraits, one of which is now in the Clark Collection of American portraits.] C. F. J.

MATTESON, JOEL ALDRICH (Aug. 2, 1808–Jan. 31, 1873), governor of Illinois, the son of Elnathan and Eunice (Aldrich) Matteson, was born in Watertown, N. Y., where he worked as a boy on his father's farm and attended the local schools. He then worked in a store in Prescott, Ontario, taught school and engaged in business in Brownsville, N. Y., and in 1831 went South and worked as foreman on the first railroad in South Carolina. At the age of twenty-five he established himself on a farm in Kendall County, Ill. During the speculative boom of 1836 he sold his land and moved to Joliet, where he went into business. The period was one of rapid development and of great enthusiasm for internal improvements, the legislature authorizing some 1,300 miles of railroad, the construction of canals, and the distribution of a cash bonus to those counties which did not share in the improvements. Matteson secured large contracts for work on the Illinois and Michigan canal in 1838, which he executed with great ability.

In 1842 he was elected to the state Senate on the Democratic ticket and was reëlected in 1844 and 1846. In his private affairs and as chairman of the Senate committee on finance he showed himself a practical business man and, although he lacked the art of public speaking, was put forward by his party on account of his executive ability. In 1852 he was elected governor of Illinois, serving from 1853 to 1857. He favored internal improvements and liberal banking laws, and belonged to the moderate anti-slavery group. During his administration he did much to restore the credit of the state, which had been sadly strained by the excesses of the internal-improvement era, and to liquidate its debt. For the fiscal years 1853–54 principal and interest to the amount of $3,950,037 were paid on the state debt, and in four years the payments aggregated $11,129,236. The system of free schools was first introduced into Illinois during Matteson's administration, and the cause of education in general received impetus. While in office (1855) he was a candidate on the Democratic side for the United States Senate against Abraham Lincoln, the Whig candidate, and others. A deadlock ensued and Lincoln withdrew in favor of Lyman Trumbull, who was elected. Upon the conclusion of his term Matteson retired to private life a popular and respected man.

The following year, however, a grave scandal developed in connection with the theft and refunding of certain canal scrip, in which Matteson was unfortunately implicated. In 1839 a large number of ninety-day warrants had been issued by the canal commissioners, payable at the Chicago branch of the State Bank; these had been paid and the vouchers had been packed in a box without being cancelled or destroyed. In the same box were the original check books of the canal commissioners, in which a number of blank checks had been signed but never used. Governor Matteson had ordered the box containing these papers conveyed to his office, and later presented $107,450 of the old canal scrip and $10,100 of the unused checks, properly filled out, to the canal commissioners, receiving in return state bonds as provided for by an act of 1847. He testified that he bought the warrants at sundry times and of sundry persons, but could not tell who they were or where they lived. The evidence of Matteson's guilt seemed conclusive, but he was permitted to turn over to the state for its indemnification property to the value of nearly $250,000, which was practically the amount of the stolen securities together with the accumulated interest paid on them.

Matteson had become interested in the railroad construction then rapidly going on and in 1847 had been associated with H. N. Ridgley and James Dunlap of Springfield in the purchase of the Northern Cross Railroad. He was for many years a lessee and president of the Chicago & Alton Railroad, and had a controlling interest in several Illinois banks. During his later years his home was in Chicago, where he died. On Oct. 7, 1832, he married Mary, daughter of Calvin Bacon and Clarissa (Sterling) Fish. They had three sons and four daughters.

[A. M. Sterling, *The Sterling Geneal.* (1909); Newton Bateman and Paul Selby, *Hist. Encyc. of Ill.* (1900); John Moses, *Ill.: Hist. and Statistical,* vol. II (1892); D. W. Lusk, *Politics and Politicians* (1884); A. C. Cole, *The Era of the Civil War, 1848–1870* (1919); *The Diary of Orville Hickman Browning, . . . 1850–1864* (1925), ed. by T. C. Pease and J. G. Randall; *Memoirs of Gustave Koerner, 1809–1896* (2 vols., 1909), ed. by T. J. McCormack; *Governors' Letter-Books, 1840–1853* (1911), ed. by E. B. Greene and C. M. Thompson; *The Governors of Ill. 1818–1918* (1918); *Chicago Daily Tribune,* Feb. 1, 1873.]

E. L. B.

MATTESON, TOMPKINS HARRISON May 9, 1813–Feb. 2, 1884), historical and genre painter, born at Peterboro, N. Y., is remembered chiefly for his popular patriotic pictures, which were widely known through reproductions. His father, an astute Democratic politician, named him for Governor Tompkins of New York, and having been appointed deputy sheriff for Madison County, he permitted his son to take his first lessons in art from a clever Indian prisoner in the Morrisville jail, who was awaiting trial on a charge of murder. Several other incidents showing the boy's zeal in the pursuit of knowledge are recorded. He copied prints, cut out silhouettes, obtained a paint-box, and experimented assiduously in the intervals of work in a pharmacy and a tailor's shop. He ran away from home and started for Albany, hoping to be able to support himself on the way by making crayon likenesses. With an occasional lift on a canal-boat, he finally reached his destination, but his cash and courage were exhausted and he was forced to return home. Then he wandered for a while, making portraits in Manlius, Cazenovia, Hamilton, and other towns near his birthplace. In 1834 he found his way to Sherburne, making his first appearance there as Othello in a company of strolling players whose star performer had been prostrated by sickness in Hamilton. Soon after this he went to New York. He drew from the antique in the National Academy school, opened a studio, and in 1839 went back to Sherburne, where he was married to Elizabeth Merrill.

After a move to Geneva, N. Y., in 1841 Matteson made his second invasion of the metropolis. This time he was prosperous, and much of his best work was done in this period. His "Spirit of Seventy-six" was received with enthusiasm and was bought by the Art Union. Among his other works were "Signing the Compact on the Mayflower," "The First Sabbath of the Pilgrims," "Perils of the Early Colonists," "Washington's Inaugural," and "Eliot Preaching to the Indians." He was made an associate of the National Academy and exhibited frequently up to 1869. In 1850 he retired to Sherburne, and the rest of his life was passed there. He had a large family. Elihu Vedder, who was one of his pupils, says: "his good wife . . . presented him with the yearly child,—one, no more, no less." He was a useful and respected citizen, serving in various public offices—as a member of the legislature, as president of an agricultural society, as president of the school board, as foreman of the fire department, and in other capacities. He was always busy; he painted many portraits; had a group of students; and conducted drawing classes in the schools. After his death at Sherburne in 1884, the National Academy paid a tribute to his character and talents. The Sherburne Public Library owns his "King Lear" and "Washington Crossing the Delaware." His "Trial of George Jacobs for Witchcraft" belongs to the Essex Institute, Salem, Mass. Matteson's drawing is more spirited than accurate. He had a knack of suggesting action, however. His color is rather dry. His most successful motives were drawn in black and white for reproduction.

[H. T. Tuckerman, *Book of the Artists* (1867); Elihu Vedder, *The Digressions of V.* (1910); F. J. Mather, Jr., and others, *The Am. Spirit in Art* (1927); *Sherburne Illustrated* (1896); the *Sherburne News,* Dec. 6, 1866, Apr. 2, 1868, May 24, July 26, 1873, Dec. 5, 1874, Mar. 27, 1880, Feb. 9, 1884.] W. H. D.

MATTHEW, WILLIAM DILLER (Feb. 19, 1871–Sept. 24, 1930), vertebrate paleontologist, was born at St. John, New Brunswick, the son of George Frederic and Katherine Mary (Diller) Matthew. His father, who was connected with the Canadian Customs, was an amateur geologist and invertebrate paleontologist of high rank, and to his tutelage Matthew's interest in the earth sciences can be attributed. His education began in the public schools of St. John; later he entered the University of New Brunswick, where he received the degree of A.B. in

1889; and then, going to New York, he enrolled in the School of Mines at Columbia University. Here he received the degree of Ph.B. in 1893, the master's degree in 1894, and the following year, the degree of Ph.D.

At Columbia he came under the influence of Prof. James F. Kemp [*q.v.*], the head of the department of geology, and for a time Matthew's interests were in that science, nearly all of his earliest published studies being on geologic or petrogeographic subjects. His inspiration for vertebrate paleontology came during his last year at Columbia. Prof. Henry F. Osborn had just established, in the department of biology, a course on the evolution of the vertebrates and Matthew, with his geological knowledge as a background, became a deeply interested and brilliant student in this field. After Matthew had finished his work at Columbia, Osborn, who had also just founded the department of vertebrate paleontology at the American Museum of Natural History, appointed him an assistant there. His rise in the department was gradual; in 1911 Osborn relinquished the curatorship to him; and eleven years later he became curator-in-chief of the division which embraced paleontology and geology, a position which he held until his resignation in 1927. During the thirty-two years of his association with the American Museum he published about two hundred and forty papers, nearly all of which deal directly or indirectly with his chosen science. While the majority of these papers are highly technical, he had a facility for popularizing a difficult subject and the pages of *Natural History* contain many of his articles on extinct creatures written in an entertaining and instructive style. Probably no one knew the fossil vertebrate faunas of the world so well as did Matthew. He was familiar with the great American collections, and several trips to Europe and one around the world gave him an excellent acquaintance with foreign collections. Arising out of this extensive knowledge, coupled with his early geologic training, came his greatest work, "Climate and Evolution" (*Annals of the New York Academy of Sciences,* vol. XXIV, 1915), in which he argued for the relative permanency of the great ocean basins and the continental masses, and against the existence of former land bridges across what are now abyssal depths. The population by terrestrial mammals of such islands as Cuba he attributed to transportation by means of natural rafts. One of the main theses of this important contribution to science was that the majority of the orders and families of mammals had their origin in the Northern Hemisphere, subsequently spreading to southern areas, and that long isolation in the more remote southern areas, such as Australia, accounted for the extraordinary primitive faunas found there. Other important publications were "The Evolution of the Horse" (*Quarterly Review of Biology,* April 1926) and "Evolution of the Mammals in the Eocene" (*Proceedings of the Zoological Society of London,* 1927).

In 1905 Matthew married Kate Lee of Brooklyn who with two daughters and one son survived him. His home for over twenty years after his marriage was at Hastings-on-Hudson. In 1927 he accepted the professorship of paleontology in the University of California. He was brilliantly successful there and in the three years before his death he had established himself as a most popular instructor of large and enthusiastic classes of undergraduates, and had gathered about him a group of promising advanced students. By previous arrangement he returned to the American Museum for two months each summer to complete important studies which he had under way at the time of his resignation. It was while he was putting the finishing touches on the first and most important of these memoirs, "The Paleocene Faunas of New Mexico," that he was stricken, in the summer of 1930, with his final illness. He was taken immediately to the Pacific Coast and died in San Francisco three months later.

[H. F. Osborn, "Memorial to William Diller Matthew," in *Bull. Geol. Soc. of America,* Mar. 1931; A. S. Woodward in *Nature,* Oct. 11, 1930; W. K. Gregory in *Natural Hist.,* Nov.–Dec. 1930, and *Science,* Dec. 26, 1930; *Am. Museum Novitates,* May 14, 1931; Walter Granger, in *Jour. of Mammalogy,* Aug. 1931; *Who's Who in America,* 1930–31; *San Francisco Examiner* and *N. Y. Times,* Sept. 25, 1930.] W. G.

MATTHEWS, BRANDER [See MATTHEWS, JAMES BRANDER, 1852–1929].

MATTHEWS, CLAUDE (Dec. 14, 1845–Aug. 28, 1898), stock-breeder, governor of Indiana, was born at Bethel, Ky., the son of Thomas and Eliza Ann (Fletcher) Matthews. His maternal grandfather was Thomas Fletcher, who represented a Kentucky district in Congress, 1816–17. Matthews graduated from Centre College, Danville, Ky., in 1867, and the following year, Jan. 1, married Martha Renwick Whitcomb, daughter of Senator James Whitcomb [*q.v.*], a former governor of Indiana. Leaving Kentucky shortly after his graduation, he settled on a farm near Clinton, Ind., where he became intensely interested in the breeding of fine live-stock, and soon attracted much attention by his success with shorthorn and Jersey cattle, and with trotting horses. He was largely instrumental, also, in the formation of the National Association of Breeders of Short Horn Cattle in the United States and Canada. Acutely conscious of the difficulties that confronted the rural classes in the United States, he became an active member of the Farmers' Mutual Benefit Association.

Matthews was a stockman rather than a politician, but he spoke well in public, and sometimes campaigned for Democratic candidates. In 1876 he was elected to the Indiana legislature from a strongly Republican district, and thereafter was much in demand for political speeches. In 1882 he stood for election to the state Senate, but was defeated. In 1890, however, when the influence of the Farmers' Alliance demands was being felt throughout the country, he was nominated for secretary of state on the Democratic ticket, and was elected. His long interest in farming made him an available candidate for governor in 1892, and with him at the head of their state ticket the Democrats won a notable victory.

His term of office, from January 1893 to January 1897, coinciding as it did with one of the worst periods of depression the nation had known, was far from tranquil. The election of a Republican legislature in 1894 increased his difficulties. From April to June 1894, a coal-miners' strike occasioned much disorder in the vicinity of Terre Haute, Fontenet, and Farmersburg. Militia had to be used freely to insure the passage of coal trains. The coal strike was scarcely settled when the Pullman railroad strike spread into Indiana. At Hammond the disorders were so serious that Federal troops were sent from Chicago to maintain order until the state militia should arrive on the scene. Matthews promptly called out eight companies of militia, including a section of artillery, later relieved by eight more, and in a short time had the situation in complete control. When the state auditor, on advice of the attorney-general, held that there was no state money available to pay these troops, the Governor promptly borrowed the necessary sum, $40,962, on his own personal credit. A later legislature voted payment of the bill. His vigorous handling of the Indiana situation contrasted sharply with the methods used by Gov. John P. Altgeld [*q.v.*] in Illinois. Matthews' administration was also notable for his contest with a corporation that carried on winter races, prize-fighting, and similar amusements at Roby, Lake County, Ind. Claiming that the law was being deliberately evaded, the Governor asked the courts for an injunction against the Roby gamesters, which he finally secured. Less spectacular, but probably more important, was the enactment of amendments to the tax law during his administration. Matthews' prominence as governor of Indiana, together with his adherence to free-silver views, led to the presentation of his name for the Democratic presidential nomination at the Chicago convention in 1896. He received the vote of his own state on several ballots, in spite of the strong Bryan sentiment that finally overcame the convention. He did not long survive his term of office as governor.

[Matthews' career as governor can be traced in the volumes of *Appletons' Ann. Cyc.*, 1893–96, inclusive, under the caption, "Indiana"; there is a brief sketch of his life in *Ibid.*, 1898, pp. 557–58. See also, J. P. Dunn, *Indiana and Indianans* (1919), vol. II; Charlotte Whitcomb, *The Whitcomb Family in America* (1904); *Indianapolis Sentinel*, Aug. 29, 30, 31, Sept. 1, 1898.] J. D. H.

MATTHEWS, FRANKLIN (May 14, 1858–Nov. 26, 1917), the son of J. H. and Mary (Force) Matthews, was born in St. Joseph, Mich. He was named Albert Franklin Matthews but dropped the first name in his adult life. After receiving his secondary education in the local schools he matriculated in 1879 at Cornell University. In 1883 he received the degree of B.A. and after a year of graduate work joined the staff of J. B. Pond's lyceum bureau. During his two years with the bureau he traveled as lecture agent for many notables, one of whom was Clara Louise Kellogg [*q.v.*], whose cousin, Mary Crosby of New Haven, he married in 1886. In this year he met Talcott Williams, the managing editor of the Philadelphia *Press*, who employed him as a reporter. With his wife, he settled in Philadelphia, and by 1890 he was editor of the *Press*. After a short service with the New York *World* he began to write for the *Sun*. With this paper for twenty-two years, he worked variously as reporter, copy reader, telegraphic editor, city editor, and special correspondent. Through his association with Charles A. Dana and S. Merrill Clarke he gained an unrivaled knowledge of practical newspaper technique. He traveled widely as correspondent for the *Sun* and for *Harper's Weekly* and in a series of articles having the title "Bright Skies in the West" described the return of prosperity to the drought-ridden western states. At the time of the American occupation of Cuba, he was sent by the *Weekly* to report conditions at Havana and Santiago de Cuba. In 1899 these dispatches were collected and issued in book form as *The New-Born Cuba*. About the same time he brought out a popular naval history, *Our Navy in Time of War* (1899). The continued popularity of this book justified its revision fifteen years later (1915). With the outbreak of the Russo-Japanese War he sailed for the Orient and followed the southward drive of the Japanese down the Liaotung peninsula toward Port Arthur, assisting Dr. Louis M. Seaman in gathering material for his medical history of the war. His last and most memorable experience as a correspondent came in 1907 when he accompanied the Atlantic fleet on its cruise round the world, as special correspondent for the *Sun*. *With the Battle Fleet* (1908) is the literary log of the first half of the cruise, enlivened with a wealth of seagoing anecdote. *Back to Hampton Roads* (1909) deals in a similar way with the return cruise from San Francisco through Australasia, the Suez Canal, and the Mediterranean, and home again across the Atlantic. After his return he lectured extensively upon his war experiences and on the navy, contributing articles on the same subjects to the *Century*, the *Atlantic Magazine*, and to Frank Leslie's periodicals. In 1912 he joined the staff of the *New York Times* as Sunday editor and the next year was night city editor. In 1912, at the invitation of Talcott Williams, he had accepted a teaching post in the Pulitzer school of journalism at Columbia University, and in 1914 he was made associate professor. He was serving in this position at the time of his death.

[*Who's Who in America*, 1916–17; *Cornell Alumni News*, Nov. 29, 1917; *Columbia Alumni News*, Nov. 30, 1917, Jan. 11, 1918; *Sun* (N. Y.), Nov. 27–28, 1917; *New York Times*, Nov. 27, 29, Dec. 12, 22, 1917.]

E. M. H.

MATTHEWS, JAMES BRANDER (Feb. 21, 1852–Mar. 31, 1929), university professor and man of letters, was born in New Orleans, La. His father, Edward Matthews, of a family which had, since the seventeenth century, lived on Cape Cod, could, on the maternal side, claim descent from William Brewster, leader of the Pilgrims on their voyage to New England, as well as from Thomas Prince, twice governor of the Plymouth colony. His mother, Virginia Brander, was daughter of James S. Brander, a Scotsman who settled in America and married Harriet McGraw of Chesterfield County, Va. Thus, Brander Matthews came of American stock that might be rated as of the sturdiest and the best. Though born in New Orleans he became a devoted citizen and lover of New York City.

Since the business ventures of the elder Matthews carried him north and south, east and west, the first years of Brander Matthews' life found him in various cities of the United States, and once on a long trip abroad. The father's wealth and fine taste allowed him to surround his children with luxuries and with beautiful objects of art. Brander Matthews passed a happy boyhood, among refined home influences, at school, in attending plays, and in wandering about the city that he grew to love. From the windows of his father's home in lower Fifth Avenue he saw the torchlight parade of Lincoln's supporters, and, shortly thereafter, regiment after regiment marching to the war.

In 1866 the family again went to Europe and for a year and a half the growing boy saw at close range exciting affairs in France and viewed the art of Italy. In those lands he met notable persons, leaders in all walks of life. On his return to New York in 1867, he prepared for entrance to Columbia College and in 1868 was admitted to the sophomore class, graduating in 1871. His best training for literary and professional pursuits was gained outside of college walls. After graduation he entered, at the age of nineteen, the Columbia Law School, attaining the degree of LL.B. in 1873. On May 10, 1873, before commencement, he married Ada S. Smith, an English actress well known under the stage name of Ada Harland. In consequence of the financial panic of 1873, the father's fortune dwindled, and in 1887 was found to be almost without assets. From the mid-seventies Brander Matthews devoted himself to literature, contributing to such periodicals as the *Galaxy*, the *Nation*, the *Critic*, *Appletons' Journal*, *Puck*, and others. A bibliography of those early, fugitive pieces would fill many pages. An early success was an article on "Actors and Actresses of New York," in *Scribner's Monthly*, April 1879. Thereafter he published stories in that and other magazines, soon dropping from his name the baptismal James. But he was chiefly experimenting in playwriting, then the object of his ambition.

During the decade of the eighties, he was prominent among the literary men and the artists of New York. He was of the group which, in 1882, founded the Authors' Club. Almost as an outcome of this was organized in 1883 the American Copyright League, known later as the Authors' League, in the activities of which he was prominently associated. With Laurence Hutton and others he founded in 1885 the Dunlap Society, devoted to printing important works relating to the theatre. The Kinsmen, a social club of international membership, with affiliations in London, was started in 1882, with E. A. Abbey, Lawrence Barrett, Laurence Hutton, W. M. Laffan, Frank D. Millet, and Brander Matthews as earliest members; W. D. Howells, Thomas Bailey Aldrich, Joseph Jefferson, and Charles Dudley Warner were elected later. Matthews was, in 1889, one of the fifteen founders of The Players, that royal gift of Edwin Booth to his fellow actors. His London associates were also notable. His first intimate acquaintance in that city was Austin Dobson, through whom he met Andrew Lang, Edmund Gosse, and Frederick Locker-Lampson. He became a member of the Savile Club and The Athenæum. Fleeming Jenkin, Thomas Hardy, William Black, W. E. Henley, and, somewhat later, Rudyard Kipling came, in greater or less terms of intimacy, among those he met in his London visits. In September 1883, Walter Pollock invited him to become a contributor to the *Saturday Review,* for which thereafter he wrote frequently.

In this same decade, 1880–90, his interest in the theatre definitely shaped his writings. A volume on *The Theatres of Paris* (1880), since treasured by collectors, and another on *French Dramatists of the 19th Century* (1881), were followed in 1885 by his edition of *The Rivals* and *The School for Scandal,* the introduction to which threw light on several problems, hitherto unsolved, in the life of Sheridan. In 1884, his comedy, *Margery's Lovers,* was played in London, and three years later it was presented at a special matinée in New York, followed by subsequent performances in Chicago. With Laurence Hutton he edited in 1886 five volumes of essays, *Actors and Actresses of Great Britain and the United States.* In collaboration with George H. Jessop he wrote the comedy *A Gold Mine,* produced in 1887 by John T. Raymond in Memphis, and in 1889 by Nat C. Goodwin, in New York. In 1889, also, William H. Crane staged Jessop and Matthews' farce, *On Probation.* Both of these plays were successful, as were the one-act comedies of the same period by Matthews—*The Silent System,* adapted from the French for Coquelin and Agnes Booth, and *The Decision of the Court* (1893), also played by the accomplished Mrs. Booth. Meanwhile, in the eighties, Matthews had written in conjunction with H. C. Bunner some short stories, collected under the title *In Partnership.* To *St. Nicholas* (November 1891–October 1892) he contributed a serial story for boys, "Tom Paulding," published in book form in 1892. These are only the more striking of his writings of that time.

When Thomas R. Price, professor of English at Columbia College, spent the academic year of 1891–92 in Europe, he arranged to have Matthews, as a man of letters, lecture to the students during his absence. Matthews undertook the work with some hesitation but was so successful that he was appointed, in 1892, professor of literature in Columbia, a position he held till 1900, when he was created professor of dramatic literature, the first man, he always proudly asserted, to hold a chair of that title in an American university. His account in *These Many Years* (1917) of his earliest experiences in teaching shows him demanding from his classes more reading than they could perhaps digest, but he felt that "if they were exposed to the contagion of literature, some of them might catch it." His success is shown by the large number of playwrights, critics, and novelists, once his students, who proclaim the inspiration of his lectures and his personality. Trained for his professorship by constant intercourse with many of the most stimulating minds of Europe and the United States, he brought to the classroom a wealth of personal experience, of anecdotes of great men, that was nothing short of a revelation to his listeners.

Thenceforward Matthews' books were, to a great extent, by-products of his courses at Columbia. He wrote, to be sure, several volumes of fiction, all founded on life in the New York that he knew and loved: *Vignettes of Manhattan* (1894); *His Father's Son, a Novel of New York* (1895); *Outlines in Local Color* (1897); *A Confident To-Morrow* (1899); *The Action and the Word* (1900); and *Vistas of New York* (1912). But his major interests—in subjects relating to the theatre (especially to dramaturgy) and to questions of English language and literature—bore fruit in *Americanisms and Briticisms* (1892); *Studies of the Stage* (1894); *Bookbindings Old and New* (1895); *Aspects of Fiction* (1896); *An Introduction to the Study of American Literature* (1896); *Parts of Speech* (1901); *The Historical Novel* (1901); *The Development of the Drama* (1903); *Inquiries and Opinions* (1907); *A Study of the Drama* (1910); *Molière: His Life and His Works* (1910); *A Study of Versification* (1911); *Gateways to Literature* (1912); *Shakspere as a Playwright* (1913); and *A Book about the Theater* (1916). He inspired and directed the volume of *Shaksperian Studies* produced by the members of the department of English at Columbia University, in 1916, the tercentenary of Shakespeare's death. His autobiography, a striking gallery of pictures of life, here and abroad, among professional men and artists of the last half of the nineteenth century, appeared in 1917. Remaining volumes were compilations of mellow essays that he had contributed to various periodicals: *The Principles of Playmaking* (1919); *Essays on English* (1921); *Playwrights on Playmaking* (1923), and *Rip Van Winkle Goes to the Play* (1926)—the last his final production, and one of those most widely discussed. In it he treats of the theatre of that day, to which, after an enforced abstention, he returned with zest and enjoyment in 1924. Unlike most praisers of past times, he found that much of the new was better than the old, and he won young actors by sympathetic understanding of their aims and their accomplishment.

Honorary degrees came fast during the later years of his academic life. In 1902 he delivered before the Brooklyn Institute of Arts and Sciences seven of his lectures on the development of the drama; three of these he repeated in the same year at the Royal Institution in Albemarle Street, London. In 1908 he gave before the Lowell Institute, Boston, six lectures on Molière. In 1907 he received from France the decoration of the Legion of Honor, in recognition of his services in making French literature known more widely in the United States. In 1910 he served as president of the Modern Language Association of America. In this same period he was actively writing, lecturing, and administering as chairman of the Simplified Spelling Board—a cause which he took deeply to heart. He was one of the original members, in 1898, of the National Institute of Arts and Letters (president, 1913–14); in 1904, a central group from that organization was formed as the American Academy of Arts and Letters, a select body to which he was, in time, elected. From 1922 to 1924 he was chancellor of the Academy, and in 1922 officer of the French Legion of Honor. Ill health forced his resignation from his prized professorship at Columbia; he resigned, formally, on the anniversary of his birth, Feb. 21, 1924, less than a month, as it happened, after the death of his wife. Their only child, Mrs. Nelson Macy, had died a few years previously.

In his last years he found great pleasure in attending the dinners of The Round Table, a group of notable men who met and dined and talked, at intervals, during the winter. At the very end, before his last protracted illness, his keenest delight was in meeting kindred spirits at this club, or at The Century, or at The Players, or in his own home, or in the offices and in the Faculty Club of his beloved Columbia. To all these gatherings he brought an ardent friendship, an unwearied intellect, and a wit that had suffered no diminution with the passing of time. He died on Mar. 31, 1929, an unforgettable figure in American life and letters.

Brander Matthews was perhaps the last of the gentlemanly school of critics and essayists that distinguished American literature in the last half of the nineteenth century. His style is exact, fastidious, and founded on close study of French and English masters, yet easy and apparently spontaneous. His influence was felt most in the drama. His oft-repeated dictum that a play "is something written to be acted before an audience in a theatre" implied, of course, that playwriting is an art with rules of its own adapted to the medium in which it works. His best years coincided with the rise and acceptance of the "well-made" play as exemplified in the works of the Jones-Pinero school in England; of the theories and principles of that school he was a chief expounder for America. A comparison of the loosely constructed plays produced in this country before 1890 with the well-knit plays of subsequent years will show what he and his disciples largely helped to effect. He was a great personality, intolerant of affectation or pretense, but stimulating and helpful to all who aimed at genuine literary or artistic expression. His genius for friendship has seldom been equaled; a choice spirit, a wit, master, and inspirer of brilliant talk, he has become a tradition.

[This essay is founded upon Matthews' autobiography, *These Many Years,* and on an intimate personal and professional friendship of nearly forty years. There are, as yet, no trustworthy biographies and but few trustworthy critical estimates of Matthews. A lengthy unpublished bibliography of his works is at Columbia Univ.]

G. C. D. O.

MATTHEWS, JOHN (1808–Jan. 12, 1870), inventor, manufacturer, was born in London, England. He is said to have been christened John Henry, but apparently never used the middle name. After gaining a common-school education he became an indentured apprentice in the machine shops and manufactory founded in London by the distinguished engineer Joseph Bramah. After completing his apprenticeship and working as a machinist for a few years in the Bramah establishment, he emigrated to the United States at the age of twenty-four. Settling in New York, he immediately opened a modest shop and began general machine repairing. In England he had gained a thorough knowledge of the Bramah system of manufacturing soda water and of the apparatus with which to make it. Within a year after coming to New York he began to manufacture these products. At the time soda water was commonly made by individual druggists in copper fountains. One of Matthews' first improvements was to construct his fountains of cast iron and line them with tin. At first he had considerable difficulty in marketing his apparatus because of the druggists' prejudice, but by manufacturing soda water for use in his fountains and peddling them, filled, about the city, he gradually built up a prosperous business, and at the time of his death, soda water manufactured by him was sold at more than five hundred places in New York alone.

Matthews, however, was much more interested in improving the manufacturing and dispensing machinery. Leaving the fountain peddling to others, he devoted his whole time and a large portion of his income to experimental work looking toward the improvement of the apparatus, though he never patented any of his inventions. In his generators, which were made of cast iron lined with lead, the carbonic acid was produced from marble dust and oil of vitriol. After being purified by passing through water in a purifying chamber it was conducted to the fountain where it was combined with water by means of a revolving agitator. The dispensing apparatus was a simple draft-tube projecting up from the counter, beneath which the fountain lay incased in ice. The flavorings were kept in glass bottles on the counter. Matthews' manufacturing business grew by leaps and bounds, his products were used all over the world, and in 1865 when he retired and turned over the business to his sons, his plant at First Avenue between Twenty-sixth and Twenty-seventh streets was of immense proportions. He had married in 1830, before coming to the United States, Elizabeth Chester of Bristol, England, and at the time of his death was survived by his widow and two sons. He was buried in Brooklyn, N. Y.

[Henry Hall, *America's Successful Men of Affairs,* vol. I (1895); C. M. Depew, ed. *One Hundred Years of Am. Commerce* (1900), vol. II; *Am. Artisan,* Jan. 26, 1870; *N. Y. Times,* Jan. 14, 1870.] C. W. M.

MATTHEWS, JOSEPH MERRITT (June 9, 1874–Oct. 11, 1931), chemist, textile expert, was born in Philadelphia, Pa., the son of Joseph Merritt and Blanche (Fowler) Matthews. He attended the University of Pennsylvania, receiving the degrees of B.S. in 1895 and Ph.D. in 1898. Appointed professor of chemistry and dyeing in the Philadelphia Textile School in 1898, he became interested in textile chemistry and dyestuff application and during the next few years he combined with teaching intensive study and writing. In 1904 he published *The Textile Fibres, Their Physical, Microscopical and Chemical Properties,* which, enlarged and republished in later editions, was a standard work of reference. In 1907 he resigned his position at the Philadelphia Textile School and for three years was manager of the dyeing department of the New England Cotton Yarn Company. In 1910 he entered a broader field, establishing himself as a consulting expert to the textile and dyestuff industries. He was regularly retained by a number of prominent textile and dyestuff interests and through this consulting practice, which involved a vast amount of industrial research, he gained recognized standing in his profession. In 1916 he became interested in the publication of the *Color Trade Journal,* an interest which he maintained first as editor and later as publisher. An extended development of his *Laboratory Manual of Dyeing and Textile Chemistry* (1909) appeared in 1920 under the title *Application of Dyestuffs to Textiles, Paper, Leather and Other Materials,* and in 1921 he published *Bleaching and Related Processes.*

Matthews possessed a mild and genial disposition. Of a retiring nature, he did not have many close friends, but he had innumerable friendly acquaintances. His services were almost without exception sought rather than offered. He was a member of the Chemist's Club in New York and for many years maintained a research laboratory and office in their building. He was also an active member of many technical and scientific societies, among them the American Chemical Society, the Society of Chemical Industry, the Society of Dyers and Colourists of England, a charter member of the American Association of Textile Chemists and Colorists, and a fellow of the American Association for the Advancement of Science. As a hobby he made a study of Japanese prints and of these he had a notable collection. During his later years he was greatly handicapped by failing health and in 1925 he found it necessary to retire from all active work. The remaining years of his life were spent on the French Riviera, in Bermuda, and finally in San Diego, Cal., where he died. His wife was Augusta Spalding Gould, to whom he was married on May 15, 1903.

[J. M. and Jaques Cattell, *Am. Men of Sci.* (1927); *Who's Who in America,* 1930–31; *Am. Dyestuff Reporter,* Oct. 26, 1931; *N. Y. Times,* Oct. 13, 1931; information from Matthews' associates; personal acquaintance.] L. A. O.

MATTHEWS, NATHAN (Mar. 28, 1854–Dec. 11, 1927), municipal official and reformer, was born in Boston, lived in Boston practically all his life, served his city actively for over forty years, and died there. He came from an old New England family that, ever since the English immigrant, James Matthews, settled there probably as early as 1638, had had a record of public service in the little town of Yarmouth on Cape Cod. His father, Nathan Matthews, moved to Boston at the age of nineteen. His mother, Albertine (Bunker) Matthews, is credited with giving to her son much of his cultural interest and devotion to ideals. The father's fortunes fluctuated between the extremes of wealth and bankruptcy; but, although the son saw his father fail three times, he also saw him each time resolutely turn to the task of paying back every cent of his debts. The impression made by such an attitude must have been very deep, for instances show that the son throughout his life "leaned backward" in the honesty of his dealings. The young man's education was of a varied character, somewhat unusual for the times. From Epes Sargent Dixwell's Boston school he entered Harvard College at eighteen. He was graduated from the college in 1875 and from the law school in 1893 as of the class of 1880. During the years from 1875 to 1877 he traveled and studied in Europe, chiefly at the University of Leipzig. His chief interests there, as always, were in political economy and jurisprudence, but he found time also to indulge in numerous canoe trips. His love of forests, stream, and garden never left him, and, joined with an antiquarian tinge, made him a devotee of the New England country side and its old homesteads. He was admitted to the bar in 1880 and practised law in Boston. On Apr. 5, 1883, he married Ellen Bacon Sargent. They had two children.

His public life dates from his activity in the Cleveland-Blaine campaign of 1884. In 1888, with others, he helped to form the Young Men's Democratic Club of Massachusetts, and by 1889 this group was in control of the state Democratic party, with Matthews as the president of the state convention. The next year he was chairman of the state executive committee and under his leadership the Democrats elected William E. Russell as governor. Up to this time his interests had been largely in the realm of state and national politics. Because of his eminent services to his party he became the logical candidate for mayor of Boston and was elected without difficulty. He served four terms and retired voluntarily in 1895. Choosing the municipal field as he did, his public life, on the surface, does not appear to be as important as that of many of his contemporaries who have probably left much less permanent imprint. Together with Seth Low [*q.v.*] he must be credited with revealing to students of municipal government the practical possibilities of the strong mayor type of municipal character and with thus indicating the course of municipal reform for many years. Before this time the council had been the center of power if not of prestige. The 1885 Boston charter had nominally given the chief power to the mayor, but not until his vigorous administration had that power received effective use. As early as the 90's he advocated the small, unicameral council, election at large, consolidation of city departments, longer terms of office, and nonpartisan civil service. During his later life he continued these interests. From 1907 to 1909 he was chairman of the city finance commission, which resulted in a remodeling of the Boston charter, and he served on other commissions later. From 1909 to 1917 he lectured on municipal government at Harvard. His published works include *The City Government of Boston* (1895) and *Municipal Charters* (1914) in addition to a number of articles and addresses. He was ever an indefatigable worker, outspoken, almost brutal at first, but developing a tenderness with the years, a man of strong will and courage who "had no boss but himself."

[Letter from his brother, Albert Matthews, Boston; *Harvard College Class of 1875 Secretary's Rept.*, nos. IV, VI, VII, X (1884–1925); *Harvard Graduates' Mag.*, Mar. 1928; New England Hist. and Geneal. Register, July 1928; *Proc. Mass. Hist. Soc.*, vol. LXI (1928); *Proc. in the Supreme Judicial Court at Boston in Memory of Hon. Nathan Matthews, Oct. 26, 1929* (1929); *Boston Herald* and Boston *Evening Transcript*, Dec. 12, 1927.] E. S. G.

MATTHEWS, STANLEY (July 21, 1824–Mar. 22, 1889), jurist, was born in Cincinnati, Ohio, the eldest child of Thomas Johnson Matthews and his second wife, Isabella Brown. He was named Thomas Stanley, but dropped the name Thomas in early manhood. His father, a native of Leesburg, Va., spent his youth in Alexandria, Va., and in Philadelphia, and emigrated with his family to Cincinnati in 1818. His mother was a daughter of William Brown, a pioneer of the Miami country, who settled in Columbia, Hamilton County, Ohio, in 1788. Thomas Johnson Matthews was for several years Morrison professor of mathematics and natural philosophy at Transylvania University, Lexington, Ky., but he returned to Cincinnati as president of Woodward College, later Woodward High School, which his son attended. Stanley Matthews entered Kenyon College as a junior, graduating in the summer of 1840. After two years spent in the study of law in Cincinnati, he went in 1842 to Maury County, Tenn., to assist the Rev. John Hudson in the conduct of Union Seminary. In the same year he was admitted to the Tennessee bar, commenced the practice of law at Columbia, and in February 1843 was married to Mary Ann, daughter of James Black. He edited a weekly political paper, the *Tennessee Democrat,* in the interests of James K. Polk. In 1844 he returned to Cincinnati to practise law and soon came before the public through his appointment as assistant prosecuting attorney, and as editor, for about a year, of the *Cincinnati Morning Herald,* an anti-slavery paper. The latter activity resulted in his election as clerk of the Ohio House of Representatives for the session of 1848–49.

Upon the adoption of the constitution of 1851 in Ohio, Matthews was elected one of the three judges of the court of common pleas for Hamilton County, but soon resigned the position because of the inadequacy of the salary and resumed the practice of law. He served one term in the Ohio Senate and was appointed by President Buchanan in 1858 United States attorney for the southern district of Ohio, a position which he resigned after the inauguration of President Lincoln. While United States attorney, he prosecuted a reporter, W. B. Connelly, under the Fugitive-Slave Law for assisting two negro slaves who were trying to escape. Connelly was convicted, but the feeling ran high against Matthews and this incident contributed to his defeat as a candidate for Congress in 1876 in a very close election, and was used later in opposing his confirmation as justice of the Supreme Court.

During the war Matthews served as lieutenant-colonel in the 23rd Ohio Infantry and later as colonel of the 51st Ohio Volunteers. While in camp in 1863, he was elected to serve with Bellamy Storer and George Hoadly [*qq.v.*] on the superior court of Cincinnati. He resigned from the army to take his place on the bench, and two years later resigned from the bench for the more lucrative practice of the law. By this time he had reached a position of eminence as a lawyer. He attracted national attention in 1877 as one of the counsel before the electoral commission that passed upon the disputed returns in the Hayes-Tilden contest for the presidency. He made the opening argument in the Florida contest and the principal argument in the Oregon case. The decision of the commission in the Florida case followed the line of argument which Matthews advanced, namely, that Congress should not go behind the returns of the state electors, but that the action of the duly constituted state authorities should be final. Matthews later joined Congressman Charles Foster of Ohio in a letter to Senator John Brown Gordon of Georgia and Congressman John Young Brown of Kentucky, leading Southern Democrats, which was of great importance in alleviating fears of a continuation of federal interference in South Carolina and Louisiana.

In March 1877 the Ohio legislature elected Matthews to the United States Senate to fill the vacancy caused by the appointment of John Sherman as secretary of the treasury. His short term of two years was marked chiefly by the passage on Jan. 25, 1878, of the "Matthews resolution" for the payment of the principal and interest of the United States bonds in silver and making silver legal tender. Upon the resignation of Justice Noah W. Swayne, President Hayes submitted the name of Matthews as his successor. Hayes had known Matthews first as a student at Kenyon College, then as a fellow lawyer in Cincinnati, and as a fellow officer in his regiment during the war. Matthews had campaigned actively for Hayes and had made the most important arguments in his behalf before the electoral commission. Matthews' name had been considered by President Grant before he nominated Morrison R. Waite to succeed Chief Justice Chase. But the Senate refused to confirm the appointment of Matthews, and there was criticism of Hayes for submitting the name as a reward, it was alleged, for Matthews' earlier support.

The vacancy on the bench was still unfilled when Garfield became president, and Matthews' name was again submitted to the Senate. The opposition to the confirmation of the appointment continued. It was partly political and partly due to the belief that, as a former attorney for railroads and large corporate interests, he might favor them in suits before the court. The Senate's committee on judiciary, with the single exception of Senator Lamar, opposed confirmation, but the Senate approved the nomination by a majority of one. The doubts regarding Matthews' ability and fairness as a judge proved unfounded. He was a member of the Supreme Court from May 12, 1881, until his death in 1889. It was a period in which the powers of the federal government were greatly extended by a liberal interpretation of the constitution, particularly the commerce clause and the clause empowering Congress to borrow money. Matthews wrote the majority opinion in the Virginia Coupon Cases (114 *U. S.*, 269) in which it was held that when a state had issued bonds the passage of a subsequent statute forbidding the acceptance of coupons of these bonds for taxes was void as impairing the obligations of contract, and delivered the opinion of the court in the case of *National Bank* vs. *Insurance Company* (104 *U. S.*, 54), in which he laid down the rule that money deposited by one in a fiduciary capacity is not subject to a banker's lien for debts the depositor owes the bank. In *Bowman* vs. *Chicago and North Western Railway Company* (125 *U. S.*, 465) he declared that a state statute prohibiting the carrying of intoxicating liquor into the state by common carriers amounted to a regulation of interstate commerce and was repugnant to the constitution of the United States. In *Yick Wo* vs. *Hopkins* (118 *U. S.*, 356) he held that a law though fair on its face and impartial in appearance, was nevertheless a denial of the equal justice the Fourteenth Amendment guarantees if administered in such a way as to make unjust discriminations.

Politically, the career of Stanley Matthews showed independence and courage. He was a Douglas Democrat before the war but took a leading part in the abolitionist movement. His actions in the Connelly case showed his willingness to prosecute the violation of the unpopular Fugitive-Slave Law, as required by his oath of office, even at personal sacrifice. A Republican after 1863 and a presidential elector on the Lincoln and Johnson ticket in 1864, and on the Grant and Colfax ticket in 1868, he joined the Liberal-Republican movement in 1872, and as temporary chairman of the convention declared that since the war was over, so should military rule end. He did not support Greeley, however, the nominee of the convention for president. Matthews' first wife died in 1885, and in 1887 he married Mrs. Mary Theaker of Washington. He had eight children by his first marriage, five of whom survived him.

[C. T. Greve, "Stanley Matthews, 1824–1889," in *Great Am. Lawyers*, vol. VII (1909), ed. by W. D. Lewis; C. R. Williams, *The Life of Rutherford Birchard Hayes* (2 vols., 1914) and *Diary and Letters of Rutherford Birchard Hayes* (5 vols., 1922–26), ed. by C. R. Williams; Charles Warren, *The Supreme Court in U. S. Hist.* (1922), vol. III; James Landy, *Cincinnati Past and Present* (1872); the *Green Bag*, May 1889; *Cincinnati Enquirer*, Mar. 23, 26, 1889.]
S. G. L.

MATTHEWS, WASHINGTON (July 17, 1843–Apr. 29, 1905), ethnologist, the son of Dr. Nicholas Blayney and Anna (Burke) Matthews, was born in Killiney, County Dublin, Ireland, and was named Washington as an American appreciation. While the child was still an infant, his mother died and his father brought him to America, settling in Wisconsin. Later the elder Matthews moved to Dubuque, Iowa, where Washington was brought up. After a common-school education, he began the study of medicine with his father, took a course of lectures in the University of Iowa, and received the degree of M.D. in 1864. Immediately he volunteered in the United States army and was assigned to the post at Rock Island, Ill., as acting assistant surgeon. Mustered out in 1865, he was appointed post surgeon at Fort Union, Mont. His many assignments in the West acquainted him with various tribes of Indians and incited him to investigate their languages and mythology. Few of the old army had more extended opportunities to become acquainted with the Indians and few knew better how to handle the Indian. Especially at Fort Berthold, where he remained six years in contact with the Hidatsa, was his work productive, yielding three important studies: *Grammar and Dictionary of the Hidatsa (Minnetarees, Grosventres of the Missouri)*, in Shea's American Linguistics (ser. II, no. 1, 1873); *Hidatsa (Minnetaree) English Dictionary,* in the same series (ser. II, no. 2, 1874); and *Ethnography and Philology of the Hidatsa Indians* (United States Geological and Geographical Survey, Miscellaneous Publications, no. 7, 1877).

Following his transfer to the Southwest Matthews wrote several papers on the Navaho. Of these Indians he was the first and foremost student. "Navajo Silversmiths" in the second (1883) and "Navajo Weavers" in the third (1884) annual report of the Bureau of American Ethnology were the initial papers on these Indians. In 1887 "The Mountain Chant: a Navajo Ceremony" appeared in the fifth annual report. His book entitled *Navaho Legends* was issued as a memoir of the American Folk-Lore Society (vol. V, Boston, 1897). "The Night Chant," his last important work, was published in the *Memoirs of the American Museum of Natural History* (vol. VI, 1902). This monograph shows Matthews' insight into Navaho mythology.

In 1885 Matthews took up the study of physical anthropology, then a comparatively new science, and designed apparatus for making measurements. His chief paper on the subject was "Human Bones of the Hemenway Collection in the United States Army Medical Museum" (*Memoirs of the National Academy of Science,* vol. VI, 1893). He published in all fifty-eight papers, each of which required careful research. He was a member and presiding officer of a number of learned societies. Outside of his profession he was interested in botany, mathematics, poetry, and art. He died in Washington, D. C. He had married, in 1877, Caroline Wotherspoon. Because of his scientific methods of work, his results are regarded as of permanent value in the study of the American Indian.

[Jas. Mooney, "Washington Matthews," *Am. Anthropologist,* July–Sept. 1905; *Who's Who in America,* 1903–05; I. A. Watson, *Physicians and Surgeons of America* (1896); *Jour. of Am. Folk-lore,* July–Sept. 1905; personal recollections.]
W. H.

MATTHEWS, WILLIAM (Mar. 29, 1822–Apr. 15, 1896), bookbinder, writer on bookbinding, was born at Aberdeen, Scotland. Before the child was a year old his father died, and when he was seven his mother took him to London, where he was sent to school and later apprenticed to a bookbinder. Employed in one of the largest binderies at the time of the great strike of 1841, young Matthews remained faithful to his employers and advanced rapidly to a responsible position and a broad and thorough knowledge of the business. In 1843 he emigrated to New York, where his ability was promptly recognized. Three years later he established a bindery of his own, at 74 Fulton Street, winning the highest award given for binding for his exhibit at the International Crystal Palace Exhibition in Reservoir Park in 1853. This attracted the attention of the firm of D. Appleton & Company, and the following year he became the head of their bindery, retiring in 1890, when he was succeeded by his son, Alfred. Among the large editions issued by the firm was an annual output of one million copies of Webster's spelling book. Matthews was preëminent in his art, his name becoming a synonym for good workmanship, while his advice and his bindings were alike eagerly sought by fellow-workers and by collectors. While thoroughness was to him the highest essential, he added a scholarly knowledge of the history of his craft, and the taste that is necessary to elevate it to the status of an art. For special work he could use to advantage all the resources at his command, but he denounced the "story-telling cover of commerce," holding to restrained decoration for commercial binding. The forwarding of a book was always, to him, as important as the finishing. He regarded Francis Bedford as the greatest modern English binder.

Matthews' winning personality, admirable qualities, and public spirit made him an active force in the charitable, religious, social, and commercial life of the city, and his hospitable home in the Flatbush section of Brooklyn was a center for the friends who sought his well-filled library and listened to his talk of the books and the bindings which he loved. Aside from his bookbinding interests, he was president of the Flatbush Water Works Company. In 1895 he moved to Brooklyn Heights, where his death at the age of seventy-five resulted from the shock of being run down by a bicycle. He left a widow (*née* Marle), two sons, both bookbinders, and three daughters. Interested in many and varied associations, he was an active member of the Grolier Club and a cherished friend of that group of book-lovers of the eighties and nineties who worked so effectively to stimulate and improve all phases of bookmaking. In 1885 he delivered before the Club a lecture, "Modern Bookbinding Practically Considered," which was published in 1899 as the Club's tenth publication. He was also the author of the article upon bookbinding in Appletons' *American Cyclopædia* and of professional contributions to magazines. He collaborated with William Loring Andrews in *A Short Historical Sketch of the Art of Bookbinding* (1895) and contributed "Suggestions how to Bind our Books" to *The Book-Lover's Almanac for 1895.* His memories of James Lenox, in the form of a letter to Samuel P. Avery, appeared in *Harper's Weekly* on Aug. 1, 1896. When Matthews' library was sold at auction on Feb. 10 and 11, 1897, the catalogue described many books bound by him.

[S. P. Avery, tribute in *The Book-Lovers Almanac for 1897*; Brander Matthews, *Bookbindings Old and New* (1895); the *Critic*, Apr. 1896; J. C. Derby, *Fifty Years Among Authors, Books, and Publishers* (1884); *N. Y. Times*, *N. Y. Tribune*, and *Evening Post* (N. Y.), Apr. 16, 1896; reminiscences of Thomas M. Moore, a pupil of Matthews.] R. S. G.

MATTHIESSEN, FREDERICK WILLIAM (Mar. 5, 1835–Feb. 11, 1918), metallurgist, manufacturer, philanthropist, was one of the pioneers who developed the zinc industry in the United States. He was born at Altona, in Schleswig-Holstein, Germany. A graduate of the Bergakadamie (school of mines) at Freiberg, Saxony, he came to the United States in 1857 in company with E. C. Hegeler, who was afterward his partner in their joint enterprises. Landing in Boston, they went to New York, where they were engaged by Joseph Wharton, to design for him a zinc-smelting plant to treat the zinc ore mined at Friedensville, near Bethelehem, Pa. The project was abandoned, partly through Wharton's failure to agree with the designers and partly for financial reasons. Matthiessen and Hegeler then went West to build a plant to smelt the zinc ores from the Platteville district of Wisconsin, locating it at La Salle, Ill., because of the coal there. Work was started Dec. 24, 1858, and the plant was running successfully (the first commercial production of zinc in the United States) when the outbreak of the Civil War caused a temporary shutdown for lack of market. In 1862 a lively demand developed for zinc to be used in making the brass for cartridges. Together Matthiessen and Hegeler, though the latter was the chief technical man of the partnership and invented most of the improvements, built the first zinc rolling-mill in America at La Salle in 1866 and it has been continuously in operation, ever since, though many times redesigned and rebuilt. They began mining their own coal in 1874 and in 1881 Matthiessen started a sulphuric acid manufacturing plant.

In 1864 he married Fannie Clara Moeller, of Mineral Point, Wis. There were five children. Matthiessen's contact with the public has a broad, though generally unrecognized phase, since he started at La Salle the Western Clock Manufacturing Company, which produces the widely-known "Big Ben" alarm clock. The growth of its business to large proportions from small beginnings was the more remarkable because the manufacture of brass clocks had for so long been practically monopolized by Connecticut. Matthiessen had many other technical and business interests, among them the La Salle Short Railway and the La Salle Machine & Tool Company.

In his later years his contributions to education and philanthropy made his name well known. As a gift to the cities of La Salle, Peru, and Oglesby, Ill., he endowed the Tri-City Hygienic Institute, which maintains a staff of health officers and facilities which include an isolation hospital, an infant-welfare station, and a free dental clinic as well as a milk station, a bacteriological laboratory, and a medical library. He made the La Salle-Peru township high school a model for secondary education in the United States, and he converted Deer Park into a model scenic resort, turning over the profits from its operation to the charities of La Salle. He was three times elected mayor of La Salle and contributed to the welfare and development of the city in many ways in addition to those already mentioned. His death occurred in February 1918, toward the close of his eighty-third year.

[*Bull. Am. Inst. Mining Engineers,* Apr. 1918; *Trans. Am. Inst. Mining and Metallurgical Engineers,* vol. LXI (1920); *Engineering and Mining Jour.,* Feb. 23, 1918.] T. T. R.

MATTICE, ASA MARTINES (Aug. 1, 1853–Apr. 19, 1925), mechanical engineer, naval officer, the son of Frederick Martines Mattice and Melissa (Driggs) Mattice, was born in Buffalo, N. Y., and received his preliminary education in the public schools of that city. Graduating in 1874, at the head of his class, from the separate course for engineers at the United States Naval Academy, he was assigned to sea service as cadet engineer and assistant engineer (Feb. 26, 1875) on the *Brooklyn, Vandalia,* and *Trenton* until 1879. He was then instructor in engineering at the Naval Academy, 1879–82, and with John C. Kafer [*q.v.*] developed a course in mechanical drawing which was one of the best in the country. Sea service (1882–85) on the *Miantonomoh* and the *Juniata* followed. While on the *Juniata* he was engaged in relief work (August 1883) following the eruption of Krakatoa in the Strait of Sunda. Assigned then to the Bureau of Steam Engineering, he performed special duty with Chief Engineer George W. Melville [*q.v.*] in designing machinery for new vessels. When Melville became engineer in chief of the Navy, Mattice was made chief designer, in which capacity he was responsible for some excellent work, including the machinery of the original *Maine,* blown up in Havana Harbor in 1898. The specifications for this machinery were the most complete ever prepared up to that time and served as a model for many years. Granted leave of absence in 1889, he became principal assistant to E. D. Leavitt [*q.v.*], a prominent consulting engineer, and on June 30, 1890, resigned from the Navy.

During the next ten years he designed engines and other machinery for the Calumet & Hecla Mining Company, the Bethlehem Steel Company, Pope Tube Company, and various other concerns. The machinery for the Calumet & Hecla Mining Company has received especial commendation from competent judges. After leaving Leavitt, Mattice conducted an office of his own for about a year and then became chief engineer of the Westinghouse Electric and Manufacturing Company, and three years later, of the Westinghouse Machine Company. At the invitation of B. H. Warren, an old friend and classmate, who had become president of the Allis-Chalmers Company, he joined that concern in 1904 as chief engineer and manager of manufacturing. In 1906, he formed a partnership for consulting practice with John C. Kafer and Warren; but after the death of both partners that same year he closed the office and became works manager of the Walworth Manufacturing Company of Boston. In 1911 he resigned this position to retire from active business. Purchasing a farm in Lockport, N. Y., he began to raise poultry and fruit. At the Westinghouse and Allis-Chalmers plants, however, he had formed a warm friendship with Charles C. Tyler who later became vice-president of the Remington Arms Company, and with the great expansion of that organization during the World War, Tyler persuaded Mattice to resume active work as its advisory engineer. He took up the new duties in 1915 and continued with the Remington company until his death, which occurred at the Engineers' Club, New York, ten years later.

Mattice's mind worked with great quickness and accuracy; his information was encyclopedic as to scope and readiness. With all his ability he was very modest and willing to receive suggestions. He was also very practical, and it was his habit, with important designs, to have the work of the drawing office examined and criticized by the shop foremen who would later be responsible for the actual work of construction.

This practice resulted often in suggestions for changes which would expedite and reduce the cost of the work. Mattice was inclined to be retiring, especially in his last years, but was by nature affectionate and devoted to his intimate friends. His naval service came before the era of good feeling, when there was strife between the line and the staff. His prominence in the engineer corps made him active in this controversy, but he was universally respected and had many warm friends in the line. He was never married.

[*Jour. Am. Soc. Naval Engineers,* Aug. 1925; *Army and Navy Jour.,* Apr. 25, 1925; *N. Y. Times,* Apr. 21, 1925; Navy Registers; personal acquaintance; information as to certain facts from the family.]
W. M. M.

MATTISON, HIRAM (Feb. 8, 1811–Nov. 24, 1868), Methodist Episcopal clergyman and reformer, was born at Norway, Herkimer County, N. Y., one of the twelve children of Solomon and Lydia W. Mattison. His parents, natives of New England, were poor, high-minded, and devoted Methodists. In his infancy the family removed to a wilderness farm near the site of Oswego, N. Y. The boy's education was derived chiefly from his mother. He was of a serious and reflective temperament and displayed much mechanical ingenuity. At the age of twenty-four, after a transforming religious experience, he left the farm to become a Methodist minister in the Black River Conference (1836), although the weakness of his lungs several times interrupted his pastoral work. In 1840–41 he represented the American Bible Society in New Jersey, showing notable gifts as a preacher, but soon returned to northern New York, where he preached and edited an outspoken paper, the *Primitive Christian* (at first called *Tracts for the Times,* and later *The Conservative*). From 1846 to 1852 he was again disabled, but found congenial occupation in the study of astronomy, writing lectures and a school textbook, *Elementary Astronomy* (1847), revised as *A High-School Astronomy* (1853), which achieved wide popularity. In 1850–51 he taught the subject in Falley Seminary, Fulton, N. Y. From 1852 to 1858 he served New York City churches (John Street and Trinity) as a supply pastor.

As a member of the General Conference in 1848, 1852, and 1856, he displayed power in debate. In the General Conference of 1856 he ardently but unsuccessfully advocated the exclusion of slave-holders from church membership. Transferring to a pastorate in Adams and Syracuse, N. Y., he continued to agitate the question of slave-holding, and, though defeated for membership in the General Conference of 1860, bombarded that body with petitions signed by 100,000 Methodists of Central New York and Great Britain praying the church to sever all connection with slavery. When that prayer was disregarded, he lost hope for his denomination, resigned from the Conference, and founded St. John's Independent Methodist Church in New York City. This body was denounced as a nest of abolitionists; his house was ransacked and his life threatened by the draft rioters in 1863. In 1864, however, when the Methodist Episcopal Church tardily took the action for which he had fought, he was welcomed back to its ministry, entering as a local preacher in August 1865 and being assigned to a Jersey City pastorate. Later he was admitted to Newark Conference. In Jersey City he became involved in a vigorous controversy with one Father Smarius, a Jesuit missioner, which led to his employment by the American and Foreign Christian Union (1868), to which he devoted the last of his failing energy, speaking, writing, and printing against "Romanism." His endeavor to rescue Mary Ann Smith, a convert alleged to have been abducted by Catholics to save her from Protestantism, used up his strength, and he died of pneumonia in Jersey City at the age of fifty-seven.

Mattison was by nature controversial, and he fought slavery, intemperance, and pernicious amusements as fiercely as he did "Romish superstitions and idolatries" and doctrines which he believed to be erroneous or heretical. He was twice married. His first wife, Melinda Griswold, died young, leaving four children. By his second wife, Elizabeth S. Morrison, who survived him, he had five children. Throughout his career he wrote much for publication in books, pamphlets, and church periodicals. Among his works were *A Scriptural Defence of the Doctrine of the Trinity; or A Check to Modern Arianism* (1846); *Spirit Rappings Unveiled* (1853); *The Resurrection of the Dead* (1864); *Popular Amusements* (1867); *The Abduction of Mary Ann Smith* (1868).

[Nicholas Vansant, *Work Here, Rest Hereafter; or the Life and Character of Rev. Hiram Mattison* (1870); *Minutes of Ann. Conferences of the Meth. Episc. Ch.,* 1869; *Christian Advocate* (N. Y.), May 1856, May 1860, Dec. 3, 1868; I. S. Bingham, "History of Black River Conference," in *Minutes of Northern N. Y. Ann. Conf. of the Meth. Episc. Ch.,* 1878; L. C. Matlack, *Anti-Slavery Struggle and Triumph in the Meth. Episc. Ch.* (1881); *Daily Evening Times* (Jersey City), Nov. 25, 1868.]
J. R. J.

MATTOCKS, JOHN (Mar. 4, 1777–Aug. 14, 1847), congressman and governor, was born in Hartford, Conn., the youngest son of Samuel Mattocks. Originally a farmer, the father moved in 1778 to Tinmouth, Vt., where he served in the state legislature, became a judge and chief justice of the Rutland county court, and was long state treasurer (1786–1801). At the age of fifteen, his son went to live with a married sister, Rebecca Miller, in Middlebury. Largely self-educated, he studied law first with Samuel Miller and later at Fairfield, with Judge Bates Turner, and was admitted to the bar in February 1797. In the same year, he opened an office at Danville, Caledonia County, Vt., but moved three years later to Peacham, in the same county, where he was soon engrossed in politics.

In 1807 he was sent to the legislature, where, in all, he sat five terms—1807, 1815, 1816, 1823, and 1824. In 1820, he was elected to the national House of Representatives, and later served for two other terms—in 1825–27 and 1841–43. He was a vigorous opponent of negro slavery, and his most noteworthy appearance in debate was in a speech on the presentation of a petition for abolishing slavery in the District of Columbia. He was chosen in 1832 as judge of the supreme court of Vermont, but resigned within a year. In 1843, running as a Whig, he was elected governor of Vermont, but declined a reëlection. He was proud of the fact that he was never defeated for any office for which he was a candidate. While governor, he made an unsuccessful effort to establish Thanksgiving on Dec. 25. The people at large objected to having New England Thanksgiving "disgraced by . . . Popish nonsense," and Churchmen objected to Christmas being merged into a "Pumpkin pie Holiday" (Chandler, *post,* p. 37).

In 1806 he was made a director of the Vermont State Bank. During the War of 1812 he was a brigadier-general in the Vermont militia. He married, Sept. 4, 1810, Esther Newell, of Peacham, who died, July 21, 1844, leaving three sons and one daughter. Of the sons, one became a clergyman, one an attorney, and one a physician.

Mattocks was perhaps best known as a lawyer. During nearly fifty years of practice, he became the most important figure at the Vermont bar. It was said that he was frequently engaged in every jury trial at a session of the county court and won every case. He adopted an easy, conversational manner, with no rhetorical flourishes, making his appeal mainly on the basis of common sense. He was a large and robust man, somewhat inclined to corpulency, and of a sanguine temperament. To his younger colleagues at the bar he was exceedingly kind and helpful. In his own time he was notorious, like Rufus Choate, for his crabbed and illegible handwriting. His witty stories and clever repartee were frequently quoted. He was an orthodox Congregationalist, of firm religious principles.

[W. H. Crockett, *Vermont* (1921), vol. III; A. M. Hemenway, *The Vt. Hist. Gazetteer,* vol. I (1868); J. G. Ullery, *Men of Vermont* (1894); O. P. Chandler, in *Vt. Bar Asso. Constitution, Proceedings, Papers, and Addresses, 1886,* vol. II (1887); *Vt. Patriot* (Montpelier), Aug. 26, 1847.]

C. M. F.

MATTOON, STEPHEN (May 5, 1816–Aug. 15, 1889), Presbyterian clergyman, was, with his co-worker Samuel Reynolds House [*q.v.*], the founder of the Presbyterian mission in Siam. He was born at Champion, Jefferson County, N. Y., the son of Gershom Mattoon and Anna Nancy (Sayre). With his parents he removed to Geneva, N. Y., where he obtained his early schooling. Deciding to enter the ministry, he set about acquiring the necessary education, earning his way by teaching. At the age of twenty-two he entered Union College, and graduated in 1842. After a year as principal of the academy and minister of the Presbyterian church at Sandy Hill (now Hudson Falls), N. Y., he went to Princeton Theological Seminary, where he graduated in 1846. In February of that year he was ordained by the Presbytery of Troy, and on June 3 married Mary, daughter of Hon. George Lowrie of Coila, Washington County, N. Y.

Very soon, with his wife and his associate, Dr. House, he sailed for Siam, reaching Bangkok in March 1847. At once he gave himself to the study of Siamese and eventually gained a thorough mastery of the structure and difficult pronunciation of the language. It fell to his lot to supervise nearly all the building operations during his term of service. When in 1851 King Maha Mongkut (Rama IV) provided the mission with a permanent location, Mattoon designed and superintended the erection of the buildings, although in order to erect a permanent brick house he had not only to learn the principles of architecture but also to teach his workmen new trades. In ecclesiastical affairs he was the leader. In 1849 he became the pastor of the first Presbyterian church organized in Bangkok. He baptized the first convert in 1851. When in 1858 the first Presbytery was organized, since he was about to sail for the United States, he was chosen the first commissioner to represent the Presbytery in the General Assembly. Because of his proficiency in both the native and the Bible languages he was assigned the task of making a new translation of the New Testament. Excellent as was the previous version of Rev. John Taylor Jones [*q.v.*], the growth in the understanding of Siamese idiom on the part of the Americans made a new translation desirable.

Mattoon gave nearly fifteen years to the task, his version being published in 1865.

His mastery of both the written and spoken language brought two appointments of honor. When Sir John Bowring, the British ambassador, reached Siam in 1855 to accomplish the revision of a treaty, the King desired to appoint Mattoon and House as official interpreters "because of his express confidence in their integrity," and when the ambassador objected on account of their American citizenship, circumvented the objection by having them serve privately. In the following year an American embassy, headed by Townsend Harris [*q.v.*], also came seeking a treaty revision. Mattoon was appointed official interpreter for the embassy, and by his knowledge of the language and of the British negotiations was an invaluable aid to the Americans.

Upon completion of the treaty, Harris appointed Mattoon the first United States consul at Bangkok. Concerning this appointment Dr. W. M. Wood, surgeon-general of the East India squadron, who accompanied Harris to Siam, said in his book *Fankwei* (1859): "It was very evident that much of the apprehension they felt in taking upon themselves the responsibilities of a treaty with us would be diminished if they could have Rev. Mr. Mattoon as the first United States Consul to set the treaty in motion" (p. 194). How well he discharged the delicate duties is indicated by the testimonial which was tendered him when he resigned from the consulship in 1859 before taking a furlough in America. The King and high officials gave him distinguished marks of their esteem; the English and American residents extended public honors to him, and the Americans presented him with a purse for the purchase of a silver table service to be inscribed with a laudatory legend prepared by the committee.

Resigning from the mission in 1865, Mattoon returned to the United States in 1866, was pastor of the Presbyterian Church at Ballston Spa, N. Y., for nearly three years, and then served as president (1870–85) of Biddle Institute (now J. C. Johnson University) at Charlotte, N. C. After resigning from the presidency he continued as professor in the theological department until his death. He died at the home of a daughter in Marion, Ohio.

[Biographical sketch (MS.) by Mattoon's daughter, in archives of Presbyt. Bd. Foreign Missions, N. Y.; G. B. McFarland, *Hist. Sketch of Protestant Missions in Siam* (1928); G. H. Feltus, *Samuel Reynolds House of Siam* (copr. 1924); *Siam and Laos as Seen by Our American Missionaries* (copr. 1884); *Necrological Report . . . Princeton Theol. Sem.*, 1890; *Morning Star* (Wilmington, N. C.), Aug. 20, 1889.] G. H. F.

MATTSON, HANS (Dec. 23, 1832–Mar. 5, 1893), Swedish pioneer in Minnesota, publisher, emigration agent, was born in Önnestad parish, Skåne, Sweden, the son of Matts and Elna (Larson) Mattson. His father was a well-to-do land-owning farmer and gave his studious and ambitious son the advantages of an education above the average for that time. After two years in the Latin school of Kristianstad, Mattson became an artillery cadet in 1849, but at the age of eighteen abandoned the life of a soldier and emigrated to America, landing in June 1851 at Boston. His experiences in Boston, Buffalo, Albany, New York, and Contoocook, N. H., and as a ship's boy, belong rather to the pages of fiction than to the sober pages of history. In the summer of 1852 the young immigrant was joined by his father and brother, and the party made their way to the West, where they won a living by engaging in the drudgery that usually fell to the lot of immigrants. Among the Swedes in Moline, Ill., Mattson found a number who were agitating the establishment of a settlement where land could be acquired on liberal terms. Since he was the only one among them who spoke English, he was appointed the leader of a party that took passage on a Mississippi River steamboat to find a location in Minnesota Territory in the summer of 1853. About twelve miles from the present Red Wing Mattson and two companions established claims by writing names on trees. This was the beginning of the Vasa settlement, for a long time known as "Mattson's settlement," which gained publicity through the leader's letters in *Hemlandet* describing the attractions of the new country.

Mattson soon found the life of a pioneer farmer somewhat cramped and fell victim to the fever of speculation that preceded the panic of 1857. In consequence, he and his young wife were compelled to start life anew. He was admitted to the bar and held several local political offices; but with the outbreak of the Civil War he recruited a company of his countrymen, served for the period of the war, and was mustered out with the rank of colonel. With the prestige of a military title and endowed with the qualities of a leader and organizer, he remained to the end of his life a power among the Swedish-Americans. He was a mediocre speaker and had no literary style, but these shortcomings were more than balanced by his imposing appearance, kindliness, generosity, honesty, and interest in the welfare of the plain people. In 1866 he was appointed special emigration agent by the governor of Minnesota and the following year a member of the state board of immigration, a position he retained *ex-officio* in his capacity as secretary of state, 1870–72. In the sixties and seventies he resided for some time in Sweden as agent for the Northern Pacific Railroad, land companies, and the Canadian government. He was one of the few emigration agents to win the good will of the newspapers in Sweden in spite of his outspoken criticism of the bureaucracy and class distinctions of his native land. As a newspaper editor and publisher he cast his lot with the more liberal element, although he always remained within the Republican fold. From 1866 to 1867 he was editor of *Svenska Amerikanaren* (Chicago); in 1877 he established *Minnesota Stats Tidning* in Minneapolis, which he edited until 1881; during the same period he was business manager of *Svenska Tribunen* (Chicago), dividing his time between Chicago and Minneapolis. He served as United States consul general in India from 1881 to 1883 and again as secretary of state in Minnesota, 1887–91. On Nov. 23, 1855, he married Cherstin Peterson. Toward the end of his life he wrote an autobiography, published in Swedish as *Minnen af Öfverste H. Mattson* (Lund, 1890, 1891) and in English as *Reminiscences: the Story of an Emigrant* (1891).

[A number of Mattson's letters, pertaining chiefly to the Civil War, are in the manuscript collection of the Minn. Hist. Soc.; a few are printed in the *Year-Book of the Swedish Hist. Soc. of America*, 1923–24. An account of the settlement of Vasa by Carl Roos, which appeared originally in *Minnesota Stats Tidning*, Feb. 1, 1877, is printed in translation in the *Year-Book*, 1924–25. Mattson's work as emigration agent is explained in T. C. Blegen, "Minnesota's Campaign for Immigrants," *Ibid.*, 1926. See also Mattson's letters and advertisements in *Svenska Amerikanaren, Kristianstads Bladet, Nya Verlden* (Gothenburg), and *Swerige och Amerika* (Jönköping), 1867, 1868, 1871–73. For brief sketches see C. F. Peterson, in *Valkyrian* (New York), Sept. 1897; Luth Jaeger in A. E. Strand, *A Hist. of the Swedish-Americans of Minn.* (1910), I, 80–89; and Malte Persson, *Överste Mattson* (Kristianstad, 1932). An obituary appears in *Minneapolis Tribune*, Mar. 6, 1893.] G. M. S.

MATZELIGER, JAN ERNST (1852–1889), inventor, was born in Dutch Guiana. His father was a Dutch engineer engaged in important government work in the colony; his mother, a native black woman. At the age of ten, Matzeliger was put to work in the government machine shop, where, in the course of a long apprenticeship, he developed a keen interest in mechanics and showed a natural aptitude for machine work. When about twenty years old, he emigrated to the United States and for five years worked at the machinist's trade in various places.

In 1877 he went to Lynn, Mass., and there secured employment in the shoe factory of Harney Brothers, operating a McKay stitching machine for turned shoes and a burnishing machine. While thus occupied, he directed his attention to possible improvement which he might make in these machines, and decided to attempt the perfection of a complete turned-shoe sewing machine. While considering this project, however, he overheard, with considerable disgust, the hand lasters at the factory boasting that no one would ever devise a machine to supersede hand lasting of shoes. Matzeliger thereupon forgot his earlier idea and closely observed the lasters' motions with a view to imitating them by machinery. He rented a room over the old West Lynn Mission and with pieces of wood, old cigar boxes, and similar material, worked alone and at night for six months on a model of a machine incorporating his ideas. This, when completed in September 1880, indicated to Matzeliger that he was on the right track and he then proceeded with the construction of a full size working machine. Though roughly made, it proved capable of pleating the leather around the toe. His efforts became known and, in spite of the fact that he was extremely poor, he refused an offer of $1,500 for the toe pleating device and with renewed energy went to work on a third machine. This he completed and patented in 1883, receiving patent No. 274,207 on Mar. 20, two-thirds interest being assigned to M. S. Nichols and C. H. Delnow. Shortly afterward, the Consolidated Hand Method Lasting Machine Company was formed by the several Lynn men who had helped Matzeliger financially, and he began the construction of a fourth machine. When completed this could simultaneously and in a minute's time hold the last in place to receive the leather; move it forward step by step so that the other coaching parts might draw the leather over the heel; properly punch and grip the upper and draw it down over the last; lay the leather properly at the heel and toe; feed the nails and hold them in position for driving; and then discharge the completed shoe from the machine.

Unfortunately Matzeliger developed tuberculosis, and his plans for the further improvement of his machine and for the development of his company were frustrated. After a lingering illness he died at the age of thirty-seven years. His patent and the stock of his company were exchanged for stock of the United Shoe Machinery Company and the Matzeliger laster eventually completed the series of machines now required for making shoes. Some years before his death Matzeliger became a member of the North Congregational Church at Lynn and he bequeathed to this society a block of the stock of his original company. By 1904 these shares had more than doubled in price and enabled the church to pay off a mortgage.

[M. N. Work, *Negro Year Book,* 1921–22; D. W. Culp, *Twentieth Century Negro Literature* (1902); *Pamphlet of Consolidated Hand-Method Lasting Machine Company,* Boston, Mass., privately printed; Patent Office records; Waldemar Kaempffert, *A Popular Hist. of Am. Invention* (1924); information as to certain facts from the pastor of North Church, Lynn, Mass.] C. W. M.

MAURY, DABNEY HERNDON (May 21, 1822–Jan. 11, 1900), Confederate soldier, was born in Fredericksburg, Va., the son of Capt. John Minor Maury of the United States Navy, and Eliza (Maury) Maury. His parents were first cousins, descendants of Jean de la Fontaine, Huguenot, said to have been burned at the stake by French Catholics, whose great grand-daughter married in Dublin Matthew Maury, also of Huguenot descent, and came with him to America in 1718. From this stock sprang all the Virginia Maurys, including Dabney, his paternal uncle, Matthew Fontaine Maury [*q.v.*], and his great-grandfather, the Rev. James Maury, whom Patrick Henry [*q.v.*] opposed in the "Parson's Cause."

Maury received the degree of A.B. from the University of Virginia in 1842 and studied law there and at Fredericksburg. Disliking the law, he obtained an appointment to the United States Military Academy, where he was graduated in 1846. As second lieutenant of the Mounted Rifles, later the 3rd Cavalry, he went to Mexico, was mentioned in general orders for gallantry at the siege of Vera Cruz, and was brevetted first lieutenant for bravery at Cerro Gordo. From 1847 to 1850 he was assistant professor of geography, history, and ethics and from 1850 to 1852 assistant instructor of infantry tactics at West Point. He then served four adventurous years on the Texas frontier, hunting buffalo and deer, and chasing Indians. In 1856 he married Nannie Mason of King George County, and was appointed superintendent of the cavalry school at Carlisle, Pa. Here he remained until 1860, when he was promoted captain and appointed assistant adjutant-general of the Department of New Mexico. In 1859 he published a standard manual, *Skirmish Drill for Mounted Troops.*

At Santa Fé, in May 1861, telegrams forwarded by mail brought the news of the fall of Fort Sumter and of the secession of Virginia. Maury immediately resigned his commission, bade a sorrowful farewell to his brother officers, and went to Richmond, where he was appointed captain of cavalry in the Confederate States Army. Early in 1862 he was promoted colonel and made assistant adjutant-general and chief of staff to General Van Dorn, commander of the Trans-Mississippi Department. For his conduct at Pea Ridge, Ark., Mar. 7–8, 1862, he was promoted brigadier-general. This was after Van Dorn had highly praised his courage and patriotism, and his readiness "either with his sword or his pen" (*Official Records,* 1 ser. VIII, 286). Later Maury fought with the Army of the West at Iuka, Corinth, and Hatchie Bridge; at Corinth he commanded the center, driving the enemy through the town and fighting doggedly in the subsequent retreat. In November 1862 he was promoted major-general, and, after brief service in East Tennessee, in July 1863 was made commander of the district of the Gulf with headquarters at Mobile. In this capacity he served for the rest of the war, losing the harbor defenses to Farragut in August 1864 and in the following year, with about 9,200 effectives, defending the city against Farragut's fleet and Canby's army of 45,000 from Mar. 27 to Apr. 12, when after heavy loss he retired to Meridian, Miss.

The end of the war found him penniless and unfitted by training and temperament for a business career. After teaching at Fredericksburg, Va., and holding various positions in Louisiana, he made his home in Richmond. There he is remembered as a small, spare man, socially, and, at least in his younger days, even convivially inclined, but with a sense of duty and honor worthy of the best of the traditional Virginia gentleman officers. When old and impoverished, he declined to be a supervisor of drawings for the Louisiana Lottery at a yearly salary of $30,000, and once he gave up his business in order to serve as a volunteer nurse in a New Orleans yellow-fever epidemic. In 1868 he organized the Southern Historical Society, opening its records to the United States war records office in return for free access by former Confederates to records of the latter. He was chairman of the executive committee of the Society until 1886 and contributed a number of articles to its *Papers.* He was also the author of *A Young People's History of Virginia and Virginians* (1896; 2nd ed., 1904) and the entertaining *Recollections of A Virginian* (1894). In 1873 he assisted in organizing the Westmoreland Club of Richmond. During the critical year of 1876 he started the movement for the improvement of the United States volunteer troops, and served as a member of the executive committee of the National Guard Association until 1890. From 1885 to 1889 he was United States minister to Colombia. He died at the home of his son, in Peoria, Ill.

[Maury's *Recollections* (1894); *Battles and Leaders of the Civil War* (1887–88), vols. II–IV; C. A. Evans, *Confed. Mil. Hist.* (1899), vol. III; *Richmond Dispatch,*

Jan. 12, 14, 1900; *So. Hist. Soc. Papers,* vol. XXVII (1899); *War of the Rebellion: Official Records (Army)*; G. W. Cullum, *Biog. Reg. Officers and Grads. U. S. Mil. Acad.* (3rd ed., 1891); *Thirty-first Ann. Reunion Asso. Grads. U. S. Mil. Acad.* (1900); James Fontaine, *Memoirs of a Huguenot Family* (1853); R. A. Brock, *Docs. Rel. to the Huguenot Emigration to Va.* (1886); information as to certain facts from Dabney H. Maury, Jr., Chevy Chase, Md.] R. D. M.

MAURY, FRANCIS FONTAINE (Aug. 9, 1840–June 4, 1879), surgeon, was born near Danville, Boyle County, Ky., and spent his boyhood days on the farm which was the scene of the research of Dr. Ephraim McDowell [*q.v.*], who gave to surgery the operation of ovariotomy. Maury's parents were Matthew Fontaine Maury, an Episcopal clergyman, and Eliza (Chipman) Maury, of Middlebury, Vt. His grandfather, for whom he was named, was a first cousin of the distinguished naval officer, Matthew Fontaine Maury [*q.v.*].

Maury received the degree of bachelor of arts from Centre College on June 28, 1860, and entered the medical department of the University of Virginia the same year. He continued his medical studies at Jefferson Medical College, graduating Mar. 8, 1862. In that year he was appointed to an unexpired term as resident interne to the Philadelphia Hospital (now Philadelphia General Hospital). Here he proved himself possessed of abundant energy, acuity of observation, a retentive memory, and astuteness in evaluating a patient's ability to withstand surgery. On Apr. 1, 1863, he was commissioned acting assistant surgeon in the United States Army, with duties at the South Street General Hospital, which position he occupied until Apr. 15, 1865. In October 1863 he was elected clinical assistant to Prof. S. D. Gross [*q.v.*] in the department of surgery at Jefferson Medical College, and here conducted private teaching until 1864, when he became chief of the surgical clinic at Jefferson Medical College. On Nov. 27, 1865, he was appointed chief surgeon to the Philadelphia Hospital. His private practice in surgery grew with unusual rapidity. He became a member of the American Dermatological Association and Pathological Society of Philadelphia in 1865; of the College of Physicians in 1866, the Academy of Natural Sciences in 1868, and the Philadelphia County Medical Society in 1877.

Among his notable feats in surgery were ligation of the common carotid and subclavian arteries for aortic aneurism; gastrotomy for relief of syphilitic stricture of the esophagus (he was the first to perform this operation in America; see *American Journal of the Medical Sciences,* April 1870); resection of a portion of the brachial plexus to relieve the pain in neuroma of the skin of the upper extremity (*Ibid.,* July 1874; the first operation of this nature on record); the removal of cystic goiters; and his special plastic operation for exstrophy of the bladder, using the flap from the perineum and scrotum. He had the first recovery following amputation of the hip joint, in America; and was dexterous at lithotomy and lithotrity. He edited conjointly with Dr. Duhring, the *Photographic Review of Medicine and Surgery* (1870–72). His last literary contribution was a paper written in collaboration with C. W. Dulles on "Tattooing as a Means of Communicating Syphilis" (*American Journal of the Medical Sciences,* January 1878). Dr. Samuel W. Gross, in a memoir of Maury (*post*) read before the College of Physicians, characterized him as a cool, dextrous, cautious surgeon, of sound judgment.

[Memoirs by S. W. Gross in *Trans. Medic. Soc. of the State of Pa.,* vol. XIII, pt. I (1881), and repr. in J. W. Croskey, *Hist. of Blockley* (1929); J. H. Adams, *Hist. of the Life of D. Hayes Agnew* (1892); H. A. Kelly and W. L. Burrage, *Am. Medic. Biogs.* (1920); *Phila. Medic. Times,* June 21, 1879; *N. Y. Medic. Jour.,* Aug. 1879; *Boston Medic. and Surgic. Jour.,* June 13, 1879; *Public Ledger* (Phila.), June 5, 1879.] L. N. B.

MAURY, MATTHEW FONTAINE (Jan. 14, 1806–Feb. 1, 1873), naval officer, oceanographer, the fourth son in a family of five sons and four daughters of Richard Maury and Diana (Minor) Maury, came of Huguenot, Dutch, and English stock long settled in Virginia. [See sketch of Dabney Herndon Maury for ancestry.] He was born near Fredericksburg, Va., but in his fifth year the family emigrated to Tennessee, settling on a farm near the frontier village of Franklin. The country schools of the region furnished his schooling to the age of twelve, when he entered Harpeth Academy, near Franklin. Since an elder brother had become a naval officer, Maury looked forward to a career in the navy. In 1825 he secured a midshipman's warrant and in the following nine years made three extended cruises. The first was to Europe on the war vessel that took Lafayette back to France after his memorable visit to the United States; the next, around the world in the *Vincennes*; and the third, to the Pacific coast of South America. Returning in 1834 he applied for leave of absence, and on July 15 was married to Ann Hull Herndon of Fredericksburg, Va. Establishing his residence there, he used his leisure in the publication of a work on navigation which he had begun during the last part of his recent tour of sea duty. This appeared in 1836 under the title *A New Theoretical and Practical Treatise on Navigation* and met with immediate favor.

Promoted to the rank of lieutenant in 1836, he was attached the following year, as astronomer, to the Exploring Expedition to the South Seas which was being organized by the navy. Objecting to what he thought an exhibition of favoritism in the final selection of the commanding officer, Maury asked to be detached from the expedition, and was then assigned to surveying duty in the harbors of the southeastern states. Meanwhile, under the pseudonym of Harry Bluff, U. S. Navy, he published five articles in the *Richmond Whig and Public Advertiser* in which he criticized the former Secretary of the Navy for inefficiency and called upon his successor to restore the navy to its earlier prestige. These appeared in the summer of 1838; and in December of that year he followed them up with seven more articles in the same paper, inscribed "From Will Hatch to his old messmate Harry Bluff." In these he went into further detail regarding inefficiency in the administration of the navy and suggested specific reforms. In the fall of 1839, while returning from a visit to his parents in Tennessee, Maury sustained a severe injury to his right knee in a stage-coach accident, which resulted in permanent lameness. He made use of the enforced leisure in writing a series of articles under the title "Our Navy: Scraps from the Lucky Bag," published in the *Southern Literary Messenger* during the years 1840 and 1841. These articles also dealt with the need of reform in the conduct of naval affairs, and were written under his former pseudonym, Harry Bluff, but in July 1841 a sketch of Maury appeared in the *Messenger* which connected him with the authorship of the series.

In the following year he was appointed superintendent of the Depot of Charts and Instruments of the Navy Department at Washington, succeeding J. M. Gilliss [*q.v.*]. The post included the superintendency of the new Naval Observatory and in 1854 the institution was officially designated United States Naval Observatory and Hydrographical Office. Maury, however, gave little attention to the astronomical part of the work, being much more interested in its hydrographic and meteorological aspects (G. A. Weber, *The Naval Observatory, Its History, Activities, and Organization,* 1926, p. 17). Soon after his appointment he began his researches on winds and currents, and in 1847 issued his *Wind and Current Chart of the North Atlantic,* which was followed in the next year by explanatory sailing directions under the title *Abstract Log for the Use of American Navigators,* issued in subsequent editions as *Notice to Mariners* (1850) and *Explanations and Sailing Directions to Accompany the Wind and Current Charts* (1851). So confident was he of the practical utility of his charts and sailing directions that he predicted a saving of from ten to fifteen days in the passage from New York to Rio de Janeiro by their use. The fulfillment of his prediction created great interest in the new charts on the part of mariners, and Maury turned this interest to account by securing the cooperation of the mariner in noting the winds and currents encountered in various regions. The success of these cooperative oceanographic observations made Maury conceive of extending the system universally. As a result of his labors an international congress was held at Brussels in the fall of 1853; Maury was the United States representative and leading spirit; and the uniform system of recording oceanographic data he advocated was adopted for the naval vessels and merchant marine of the whole world.

Back again in Washington, he threw himself into his oceanographic work with renewed enthusiasm. On the bases of the data now coming in from all quarters of the earth, he revised his wind and current charts of the Atlantic and Pacific oceans and drew one up also for the Indian Ocean. The gold rush to California which had begun several years before made the sailing time between the Atlantic ports of the United States and San Francisco a most important matter. Prior to the use of Maury's charts the passage from New York to San Francisco averaged 180 days; but by 1855 this time had been reduced to 133 days. Other passages were shortened in like measure, resulting in savings amounting to millions of dollars annually. During this period, also, Maury was busily engaged in lecturing and writing on scientific subjects connected with the sea, and in 1855 he published *The Physical Geography of the Sea,* now recognized as the first textbook of modern oceanography. The sea, for the first time, was here viewed as the subject matter of a distinct branch of science with problems of its own. The importance of these problems Maury discussed in engaging and stimulating fashion. The book went through numerous editions and was translated into half a dozen different languages. In the early fifties the idea of a trans-Atlantic cable was being actively discussed, and aroused Maury's interest. He prepared a chart representing in profile the bottom of the Atlantic between Europe and America, calling attention to the existence of what he termed "the telegraphic plateau," and stated definitely that in so far as oceanographic conditions were concerned "the practicability of a submarine telegraph across the Atlantic is proved" (Corbin, *post,* p. 100). His wide knowledge of the sea was called upon in selecting the most advantageous time for undertaking the laying of the cable; Cyrus Field [*q.v.*] consulted him frequently and publicly expressed his indebtedness to Maury.

His attainments now received wide recognition. Foreign governments vied with one another in bestowing honors and medals upon him; several universities awarded him honorary degrees; and he was elected to membership in various learned societies at home and abroad. In 1853 the merchants and underwriters of New York presented him with a fine silver service and a purse of $5,000 in recognition of the benefits he had conferred on the commerce of that port. With his scientific reputation secure, however, he was placed in a humiliating position by a board of naval officers convened by act of Congress in 1855 to "promote the efficiency of the navy." Meeting in secret, the board recommended that certain officers be dropped from the navy, others be placed on furlough, and still others on leave of absence. Maury's name was included in the third list, ostensibly because the injury to his leg unfitted him for sea duty. It is not improbable, however, that his fame, gained on shore, did not endear him to many officers who found themselves assigned to less pleasant service afloat. Maury appealed to his friends to help him secure justice; several newspapers took up his cause; resolutions in favor of his restoration to active service were passed by the legislatures of seven states; and in 1858 the president restored him to active service, promoting him at the same time to the rank of commander, retroactive to the date when he was placed on leave of absence.

While engaged in his oceanographic pursuits, he was also deeply interested in the development of Southern commerce. He cherished as a favorite project the opening of the Amazon Valley to free trade, hoping that one effect of such a measure would be to draw the slaves from the United States to Brazil. He was keenly interested in the Amazon expedition of his brother-in-law, W. L. Herndon [*q.v.*], and used material from Herndon's report to support his own arguments (see Maury's articles in *De Bow's Southern and Western Review,* February 1852, May–June 1853, and *The Amazon and the Atlantic Slopes of South America,* 1853, a collection of letters originally contributed to the *National Intelligencer and Union*). In the growing antagonism between North and South, his sympathies were naturally with his section, but in regard to the questions at issue he favored conference and conciliation. On the day of Lincoln's inauguration he wrote: "The line of duty, therefore, is to me clear—each one to follow his own State, if his own State goes to war; if not, he may remain to help on the work of reunion" (Corbin, p. 186). On Apr. 20, 1861, three days after the secession of Virginia, he tendered his resignation and proceeded to Richmond, where he soon was commissioned a commander in the Confederate States Navy.

Assigned to harbor defense, he began experimenting with electric mines, but in the fall of 1862 was sent to England as special agent of the Confederate government. Here his world-wide reputation made him an effective spokesman for the Southern cause. He was instrumental in securing ships of war for the Confederacy and he also continued his experiments with electric mines. With the purpose of making use of these mines in the war, he set out for America in the spring of 1865, but when he reached the West Indies the Confederacy had collapsed, and he found himself in a precarious situation; for the representatives of the Confederacy abroad were excluded from the pardon of the amnesty proclamations that were issued upon the close of the war.

Maury now offered his services to the Emperor of Mexico, laying before him a scheme for the colonization of former Confederates and their families, and in August 1865 he was appointed imperial commissioner of immigration. Some progress in colonization was made, but the troubled political conditions in Mexico, coupled with the failure of a large exodus from the Southern states to materialize, caused the scheme to be abandoned the following year: Maury meanwhile returned to England, where for the next two years he busied himself with his electric mines and with writing a series of geographies for school use, at the request of a New York publishing house. His *First Lessons in Geography* (1868), *The World We Live In* (1868), and *Manual of Geography* (1870) went through many editions, under varying titles. During this time he was presented with a purse of 3,000 guineas raised by popular subscription in appreciation of his services to the maritime world, and Cambridge University honored him with the degree of LL.D.

Urged now by his friends at home to return to the United States, he left England in 1868 to accept the professorship of meteorology in the Virginia Military Institute at Lexington. Here he spent the last four years of his life. He undertook a survey of the state, publishing a preliminary report, *Physical Survey of Virginia,*

No. I, in 1868. Even before the war he had stressed the importance of a system of telegraphic meteorological observations in the interests of agriculture; and now he took this subject up again in a number of addresses delivered before various organizations. While on such a lecture tour in the fall of 1872 he fell ill, dying four months later. After temporary interment at Lexington he was finally laid to rest in Hollywood Cemetery at Richmond, between the tombs of Presidents Monroe and Tyler.

Maury's name is commemorated in a long list of memorials. The Pilot Charts of the oceans, published monthly by the Hydrographic Office of the United States Navy, bear a caption stating that they are founded upon Maury's researches. At the Naval Academy, Annapolis, there are Maury Hall and the annual Maury Prize. In 1916 the State Board of Education designated Jan. 14—the day of his birth—as Maury Day in the schools of Virginia, and in 1923 the State of Virginia placed a bronze tablet in his honor at Goshen Pass on the North Anna River. A monument erected through the efforts of the Maury Memorial Association was unveiled in Richmond in 1929. There are minor memorials in various places, both at home and abroad.

Personally, Maury is described as a stout man about five feet six inches in height, with a fresh and ruddy complexion; and, despite the many honors showered on him, of a modest and reserved nature. He was happy in his family life, devoting considerable time to the teaching of his five daughters and three sons. Himself largely self-educated, he had definite ideas regarding education. As against Latin and Greek he urged mathematics and the sciences. West Point he is said to have considered "the only tolerable institution in the United States because of the absence there of the humbuggery of the Learned Languages" (Lewis, *post,* p. 131). He thought little of female seminaries, regarding them as "downright cheats" because of the superficiality of the knowledge taught there. An indefatigable worker himself, he stressed the importance of industry, declaring: "It's the talent of industry that makes a man" (Corbin, p. 161).

[Diana Fontaine Maury Corbin, *A Life of Matthew Fontaine Maury* (1888); J. A. Caskie, *Life and Letters of Matthew Fontaine Maury* (1928); C. L. Lewis, *Matthew Fontaine Maury: The Pathfinder of the Seas* (1927); J. W. Wayland, *The Pathfinder of the Seas: the Life of Matthew Fontaine Maury* (1930); R. M. Brown, "Bibliography of Commander Matthew Fontaine Maury," *Bull. Va. Polytechnic Inst.,* vol. XXIV, no. 2 (Dec. 1930); W. H. Beehler, "The Origin and Work of the Division of Marine Meteorology, Hydrographic Office," *Proc. U. S. Naval Inst.,* vol. XIX (1893); R. L. Maury, *A Brief Sketch of the Work of Matthew Fontaine Maury During the War, 1861–65* (1915); *Richmond Daily Dispatch,* Feb. 3, 1873; *Richmond Times-Dispatch,* Nov. 12, 1929.]

H. A. M.

MAUS, MARION PERRY (Aug. 25, 1850–Feb. 9, 1930), soldier, was the son of Isaac Rhodes and Mary Malvina (Greer) Maus, and was born at Burnt Mills, Montgomery County, Md. His maternal grandfather, James Greer, was a Presbyterian minister, born in Scotland, who settled in Georgetown, D. C., probably about 1800. On the paternal side, his first ancestor in America was Frederick Maus, an Alsatian, who arrived in early colonial times. A great-uncle, Philip Maus, sacrificed his fortune in aiding the Revolutionary cause and also served as a soldier; another relative, Matthew Maus, was a surgeon in the ill-fated Montgomery expedition to Quebec (1775–76). Young Maus attended the local public schools and later Charlotte Hall Academy. In 1870, through the influence of Montgomery Blair, he was appointed a cadet at West Point. Graduating in 1874, he was assigned to the 1st Infantry, at Fort Randall, in the present South Dakota, and for the next two years took part in a series of actions against bandits and Indians and in the work of expelling prospectors from the Black Hills. He served under Gen. Nelson A. Miles [*q.v.*] in the winter campaign (1876–77) against Lame Deer's band; in the following autumn, as commander of the white and Indian scouts, in the Nez Percé campaign ending in the surrender of Chief Joseph, he won a silver citation for gallantry in action.

In 1880, a first lieutenant (Sept. 29, 1879), he was transferred to Texas, and in May 1882, to Arizona, where for several years he rendered notable service against the Apaches. In the fall of 1885 he succeeded Britton Davis as commander of the Apache scouts, and for his conduct in an attack on Geronimo's band and a defensive action against a body of Chihuahua troops (Jan. 10–11, 1886), near the Aros River, Mexico, was awarded the Congressional medal of honor. Further frontier service took him to Colorado and to the theatre of the Ghost Dance troubles which culminated in the battle of Wounded Knee, S. Dak., Dec. 29, 1890. In November of that year he became a captain. In 1897, as aide-de-camp to Miles, he witnessed some of the operations of the war between Greece and Turkey, and in the following year, in the same capacity, took part in the Cuban and Porto Rican campaigns of the Spanish-American War. He was promoted major, June 16, 1899. In July of that year he was appointed inspector-general of the department of California and the Columbia. Three years later he accompanied Miles in an official tour of the island possessions of the United States. On June 28, 1902, he was made lieutenant-colonel. From 1903 to March 1906, he was on active duty in the Philippines. His next station was Monterey, Cal., and from there, on receipt of the news of the earthquake and fire of Apr. 18, 1906, he was transferred to San Francisco to take command of the troops guarding the financial district. He had become a colonel Jan. 24, 1904, and in 1909 he attained the rank of brigadier-general and was assigned to the command of the department of the Columbia. On Aug. 20, 1913, he retired. He died at New Windsor, Md., and was buried, with full military honors, at Arlington.

At Skaneateles, N. Y., on June 28, 1899, Maus was married to Lindsay, the daughter of Charles H. Poor, who survived him. His long career of exceptionally varied duties was marked by efficient performance, and in his frontier campaigns he displayed a courage, resourcefulness, and endurance that rank him among the most noted of the Indian fighters.

[G. W. Cullum, *Biog. Reg. Officers and Grads. U. S. Mil. Acad.* (1891), vol. III, and succeeding supplements; *Sixty-First Ann. Report Asso. Grads. U. S. Mil. Acad.* (1930); N. A. Miles, *Personal Recollections and Observations,* chs. XX–XXI (1896); Britton Davis, *The Truth About Geronimo* (1929); *Who's Who in America,* 1920–21; the *Evening Star* (Washington), Feb. 10, 1930; information as to certain facts from Mrs. M. P. Maus and Capt. R. G. Carter.] W. J. G.

MAVERICK, PETER (Oct. 22, 1780–June 7, 1831), engraver, was born in New York City, the son of Peter Rushton and Anne (Reynolds) Maverick. He was the grandson of Andrew Maverick, a painter, born in Boston in 1728/29 and admitted a freeman in New York in 1753, and a descendant of Elias, brother of Samuel Maverick [*q.v.*]. Peter was a pupil of his father in copper-plate engraving and began to engrave at an early age. The frontispiece of the *Holy Bible Abridged* (New York, 1790) is signed "P. Maverick sct. Æ 9 years." For some time he was occupied in New York City but later he went to Newark, N. J., where Asher B. Durand [*q.v.*] served an apprenticeship (1812–17) and then went into partnership with him. "The preference which Trumbull gave to Durand," says Sumner (*post,* p. 175) "by employing him to the exclusion of Maverick, broke up the business connection." Maverick returned to New York, where he established himself as a general engraver and copper-plate printer; he eventually added lithographic printing, as did more than one other engraver. This "general graphic business" covered "bank-notes engraved on copper or steel, with all the variety of die work and machine facilities now in use" (Weitenkampf, *post,* p. 80). He engraved a number of portraits in line and in stipple, notably that of Cadwallader D. Colden, after Waldo and Jewett, signed "Peter Maverick & Durand & Co.," as well as views, historical scenes, many book illustrations after British designers, and also bookplates, cards, college commencement tickets, and similar objects. One of his lithographs was "Daughter of Charles B. Calmody," after Lawrence (1829); among the lithographs he printed was a view of Wall Street, as rare as it is artless.

Maverick was one of the founders of the National Academy of Design, which had a number of engraver members in the early days. He died in New York City. Stauffer reports that his portrait was painted by John Neagle, though it did not figure in the exhibition of portraits by Neagle held by the Pennsylvania Academy of the Fine Arts in 1925; Sumner names Jarvis as the painter of a portrait. Maverick's son Peter, Jr., is listed in the New York directories (1832–45) as "engraver and lithographer," which appears to be all that is known of him. Augustus, the son of his second wife, Matilda Brown, whom he married in 1828, became an assistant editor on the staff of the *New York Times.* His brothers Samuel and Andrew were engravers and plate-makers; his daughters Maria and Emily are likewise said to have engraved.

[The chief sources of information are D. M. Stauffer, *Am. Engravers upon Copper and Steel* (2 vols., 1907) and Mantle Fielding's supplement to the same (1917); Wm. Dunlap, *A Hist. of the Rise and Progress of the Arts of Design in the U. S.* (ed. 1918), vol. II, p. 370; Frank Weitenkampf, *Am. Graphic Art* (1912); W. H. Sumner, *A Hist. of East Boston* (1858), pp. 173–75; *New-Eng. Hist. and Geneal. Reg.,* Apr. 1894; and *Names of Persons for Whom Marriage Licenses were Issued by the Secretary of the Province of N. Y. Previous to 1784* (1860). The *Evening Post* of June 8, 1831, and the *Morning Courier & N. Y. Enquirer* of June 9 carry death notices, but no obituaries.] F. W.

MAVERICK, SAMUEL (*c.* 1602–*c.* 1676), colonist, came of a Devonshire family which gave a number of clergymen to the Church of England. His father, Rev. John Maverick, later teacher of the church at Dorchester, Mass. (1630–36), was the son of Peter, vicar of Awliscombe, Devon, and the nephew of Radford Maverick, rector of Islington, where John was married in 1600 to Mary Gye and may have served for a time as his uncle's curate. Samuel apparently received a good education and became a man of culture and gentle manners. About 1624 he came to America, settling on Boston Bay. He seems to have been connected with the Gorges plans for colonizing, owned lands in Maine, and about 1628 married Amias (Cole), widow of David Thompson, one of the settlers sent out by Gorges in 1623, who later established himself on an island in Boston Harbor. About 1625 Maverick built a fortified house at Winnisimmet (Chelsea), where he was living in 1630 when Winthrop and his party arrived. To the newcomers he was generous and courteous. He took the oath as freeman of the colony of Massachusetts Bay in October 1632. An entry in Governor Winthrop's journal in December of the following year (*post,* I, 115), speaks of his kindness to the Indians during an epidemic of smallpox: "Among others, Mr. Maverick of Winesemett is worthy of a perpetual remembrance. Himself, his wife, and servants went daily to them, ministered to their necessities, and buried their dead, and took home many of their children." He engaged in commerce and had several vessels on the coast. In 1635–36 he spent about a year in Virginia, returning "with two pinnaces," bringing "some fourteen heifers, and about eighty goats" (*Ibid.,* p. 185). He had negro slaves (Sumner, *post,* pp. 90–91) as well as other servants and was noted for his hospitality. At his house on Noddle's Island he entertained Henry Vane and Lord Ley at dinner, during the controversy of 1637, and John Josselyn [*q.v.*], who visited him in 1638, later characterized him as "the only hospitable man in all the Country" (*An Account of Two Voyages to New England,* Veazie reprint, 1865, p. 13).

Although himself a freeman of the colony and apparently held in considerable respect, Maverick came into conflict with the Puritan authorities over the matter of civil and religious rights for settlers who were not of the Congregational fold. In 1646 he was one of those who signed the petition of Dr. Robert Child which described the Massachusetts government as an "ill compacted vessel" and prayed for admission to full civil rights or exemption from taxation and military service, for permission to maintain a church and minister of their own, since they were not admitted to baptism and the sacrament of the Lord's supper in the New England churches, and for the establishment of the body of English law as the law of the colony. As a result of his connection with this petition and the subsequent controversy in 1647, Maverick was fined £150 (later reduced by half). He professed himself willing to pay, but not an excessive amount, and deeded Noddle's Island to his son to prevent its confiscation. He seems to have left Massachusetts about 1650. After the restoration of the Stuarts he returned to England, where he pressed a plan for a more rigid supervision of the colonies. While here he wrote (1660) "A Briefe Discription of New England and the Severall Townes Therein," probably for the use of Clarendon in regulating the New England government. In 1664 he returned to Massachusetts as one of four royal commissioners sent out to hear and determine complaints. His duties took him to New York and for his services there he was granted a house on Broadway by the Duke of York in 1669. Maverick had two sons and a daughter. His death occurred between 1670 and 1676.

[Maverick's "Briefe Discription" in *New Eng. Hist. and Geneal. Reg.,* Jan. 1885, and in *Proc. Mass. Hist. Soc.,* 2 ser. I (1885), 231; letters to the Winthrops in *Mass. Hist. Soc. Colls.,* 4 ser. VII (1865), and to the Earl of Clarendon in *N. Y. Hist. Soc. Colls. . . . 1869* (1876), being Pub. Fund Ser., vol. II; C. F. Adams, *Three Episodes of Mass. Hist.* (1892), I, 328–35; W. H. Sumner, *A Hist. of East Boston* (1858); *New Eng. Hist. and Geneal. Reg.,* Apr. 1894, Apr. 1915; *Proc. Mass. Hist. Soc.,* 2 ser. I, 366; *Winthrop's Journal* (2 vols., 1908), ed. by J. K. Hosmer; *Records of the Governor and Company of the Mass. Bay,* vols. I–IV (1853–54).]

J. T. A.

MAXCY, JONATHAN (Sept. 2, 1768–June 4, 1820), college president, was born in Attleborough, Mass., son of Levi and Ruth (Newell) Maxcy, and a descendant of Alexander Maxcy who moved to Attleborough from Gloucester, in 1721. Virgil [*q.v.*] was a younger brother of Jonathan. The latter prepared for college at Wrentham Academy under William Williams, who was a member of the first class that graduated at Rhode Island College (now Brown University), which institution Maxcy entered in 1783. After his graduation in 1787 he remained at the college as tutor, acting also as librarian. He was licensed to preach Apr. 1, 1790, and succeeded James Manning [*q.v.*], president of the college, as pastor of the First Baptist Church of Providence, being ordained Sept. 8, 1791. While in charge of the church he also served the college as its first professor of divinity, and as a trustee. President Manning died suddenly in 1791, and Maxcy succeeded him in the presidency, resigning his pastorate and being elected president *pro tempore* in September 1792. It indicates the esteem in which he was held that at this time he had just passed his twenty-fourth birthday. In September 1797 he was chosen president. The college "flourished under his administration, and his fame was extended over every section of the Union" (Elton, *post,* p. 14). His chief service to the institution was his teaching of oratory and belles-lettres, and the widening of its fame by his personal reputation as an orator and divine (Bronson, *post,* p. 132). Naturally, in the state of Roger Williams and in a college the charter of which required that the trustees be of several denominations, Maxcy developed breadth of sympathy and a catholicity of view in religion.

After having served Brown for fifteen years as tutor, professor, and president, he resigned in 1802 to become president of Union College, Schenectady, N. Y. Here he was remarkable for diligent and persevering labor. As a result, his health became impaired, and, wishing to live in a milder climate, he was glad to accept, in 1804, a call to become the first president of the University of South Carolina (then South Carolina College). Richard Furman [*q.v.*], a strong advocate of education in South Carolina, recommended him for the position, since through his students he had become favorably known in the South. Both Furman and Maxcy were Federalists. The college opened in January 1805 with Maxcy and one professor as faculty. The former taught belles-lettres, criticism, and metaphysics.

While it is clear from the "rules and regulations," which he no doubt drew up, that the college he launched was of the ordinary classical type, it is significant that in the year 1811 a chair of chemistry was established, paving the way for a succession of eminent scientists on the faculty. Maxcy also recommended the establishment of chairs of law and political economy. Mineralogy was added to the department of chemistry, and natural philosophy was joined to mathematics. Some provision was made for students who did not wish to take Latin and Greek. In 1813, probably as a result of student uprisings due to lax discipline, Maxcy was censured by the trustees and asked to show cause why he should not be removed from office. The matter was ultimately dropped, however.

While the extant sermons and orations of Maxcy have little interest for our more practical and scientific age, Robert Henry records that he seems to have had no superior in his time as an orator. His sermon, *The Existence of God Demonstrated from the Works of Creation* (1795), delivered at Providence, "produced the most lively and striking effect on the audience," and was frequently spoken of at the end of half a century. The power of his personality is to be judged from the reverence in which he was held by such of his students as James L. Petigru and George McDuffie [*qq.v.*]. He was a man of medium stature, but "had a peculiar majesty in his walk." "His features . . ., when they were exercised in conversation or public speaking, were strongly expressive, and exhibited the energy of the soul that animated them" (Elton, p. 21). A central principle of his life was religious freedom. "I am not . . . disposed," he said, "to be so rigidly tenacious of my own sentiments, as to imagine I may not be in an error. All men have full liberty of opinion, and ought to enjoy it without subjecting themselves to the imputation of heresy" (*Ibid.*, p. 149). In his funeral sermon for Dr. Manning he coupled the "great theological champions" Edwards and Hopkins, with Priestley and Price, "preeminent in virtue," and asked if the former were to engross heaven while the latter sank to regions of darkness and pain (*Ibid.*, p. 151).

On Aug. 22, 1791, he married Susan Hopkins, daughter of Commodore Esek Hopkins [*q.v.*], of Providence, R. I. Of this union there were born four sons and several daughters. He died in Columbia, S. C. A monument to his memory stands upon the campus of the University of South Carolina, erected by the Clariosophic Literary Society, of which he was an honorary member.

[Romeo Elton, *The Lit. Remains of the Rev. Jonathan Maxcy, D.D. . . . with a Memoir of His Life* (1844); J. C. Hungerpiller, "A Sketch of the Life and Character of Jonatnan Maxcy, D.D.," with bibliography, *Bull. of the Univ. of S. C.*, July 1917; Robert Henry, *Eulogy on Jonathan Maxcy* (1822); W. B. Sprague, *Annals Am. Pulpit*, vol. VI (1860); W. C. Bronson, *The Hist. of Brown Univ.* (1914); E. L. Green, *A Hist. of the Univ. of S. C.* (1916); Maximilian LaBorde, *Hist. of the S. C. College* (2nd ed., 1874); John Daggett, *A Sketch of the Hist. of Attleborough* (1894); *City Gazette* (Charleston) and *Charleston Courier*, June 10, 1820.] S. C. M.

MAXCY, VIRGIL (May 5, 1785–Feb. 28, 1844), lawyer, legislator, diplomat, was born in that part of Attleborough, Mass., which was later annexed to Wrentham. He was the son of Levi and Ruth (Newell) Maxcy, and a younger brother of Jonathan Maxcy [*q.v.*]. The boy grew up in a home of the best New England tradition, and matriculated at Brown University two years before his brother Jonathan resigned as president of that institution to become head of Union College, Schenectady, N. Y. At nineteen Virgil graduated from Brown with the degrees of A.B. and A.M. After an interlude as tutor in the home of a Southern family, he studied law in Baltimore under Robert Goodloe Harper [*q.v.*], and was admitted to the Maryland bar. He married Mary Galloway, the grand-daughter of Chief Justice Benjamin Chew [*q.v.*] of Philadelphia. Samuel Galloway, her paternal grandfather, had built an estate at "Tulip Hill," near Annapolis, and this became the home of the Maxcys.

An able scholar, a persuasive speaker, and a fluent writer, Maxcy was not long in establishing a reputation for himself as a lawyer in Anne Arundel County. In 1811 he published in three volumes *The Laws of Maryland, with the Charter, the Bill of Rights, the Constitution of the State and Its Alterations . . . 1692–1809*. Politics, however, claimed his chief interest. He was chosen a member of the Maryland executive council in 1815, and afterward served as a member of the state Senate and of the House of Delegates, where he vigorously supported the interests of the rural districts. He campaigned actively for Andrew Jackson for president, speaking tirelessly and writing innumerable newspaper articles and pamphlets. He took a leading part in the calling and transactions of the state Jackson convention early in 1827, the first to be held in the United States. When Jackson was elected Maxcy vainly hoped for an appointment as First Comptroller of the treasury, but on May 29, 1830, the office of solicitor of the treasury was created by act of Congress as recommended by President Jackson in his first annual message, and Maxcy, nominated May 29, 1830, had the distinction of becoming the first solicitor. He held office until 1837. On June 16 of that year he was appointed by President Van Buren American chargé d'affaires at Brussels, capital of the new Kingdom of Belgium, and the appointment was confirmed Sept. 18.

The political situation in Belgium, following its secession from the Kingdom of the Netherlands in 1830, was much unsettled. Maxcy, the second representative of the United States at Brussels, witnessed the critical period accompanying the negotiation and signing of the "Twenty-four Articles" and the Treaty of London. During his term of service he tried to accomplish two things. One was to negotiate a treaty of commerce between Belgium and the United States; the other, to bring to a settlement the claims of American merchants whose goods were destroyed when the *Entrepôt Royal de libre re-exportation,* a government warehouse at Antwerp, was burned during the revolution in 1830. In neither endeavor was he successful, but in both he made material progress. He was a conscientious representative of the United States and the interests of its citizens. He made careful and frequent reports on political and economic conditions, the first of which was written at Liverpool, en route to his station, scarcely two hours after he had landed. He resigned his post on June 17, 1842, and later returned to Maryland, where he again took up his private law practice. On Feb. 28, 1844, while he was a guest of President Tyler on the *Princeton,* a gun (called the "Peacemaker") exploded, killing him instantly, with several others. He was buried at "Tulip Hill."

[*Vital Records of Wrentham, Mass., to the Year 1850* (1910), vol. I; Romeo Elton, *Am. Eloquence; . . . Being the Literary Remains of Rev. Jonathan Maxcy, D.D., with a Memoir of His Life* (1845); John Daggett, *A Sketch of the Hist. of Attleborough from Its Settlement to the Division* (1894); a long letter from Maxcy to Calhoun, reviewing his political activities in support of Jackson, in "Correspondence of John C. Calhoun," ed. by J. F. Jameson, *Ann. Report of the Am. Hist. Asso. for the Year 1899,* vol. II (1900); U. S. Dept. of State Archives: Belgium, Diplomatic Correspondence, vol. I; *Baltimore Clipper,* Mar. 2, 1844.]

I. L. T.

MAXEY, SAMUEL BELL (Mar. 30, 1825–Aug. 16, 1895), Confederate general and senator from Texas, was born at Tompkinsville, Monroe County, Ky. His father, Rice Maxey, came of a Virginia family of Huguenot extraction, and his mother was the daughter of Samuel Bell of Albemarle County, Va. In 1846 he was graduated from the United States Military Academy at West Point and was immediately assigned to the 7th Infantry as second lieutenant. He served during the Mexican War, was brevetted first lieutenant for gallant conduct in the battles of Contreras and Churubusco, and was present at the capture of the City of Mexico. When the war was over he soon wearied of the monotony of garrison life and in 1849 resigned his commission. His father was a lawyer and within a year the young man had learned enough law to begin practice at Albany, Clinton County, Ky. On July 19, 1853, he was married to Marilda Cassa Denton. Four years later the Maxeys, father and son, removed to Texas, where they practised at Paris until the outbreak of the Civil War. Originally a Whig, Maxey became a Democrat, voted for Breckinridge, and advocated secession. In 1861 he declined election to the Texas legislature in order to join the forces of the South.

Organizing the 9th Texas Infantry, he entered the war as a colonel but was soon made a brigadier-general and later a major-general. He was actively engaged in the campaigns of 1862 and 1863 in Tennessee and Mississippi, and on Dec. 11, 1863, received his most important assignment as commander in the Indian territory. For the next year he was responsible for the security of this western outpost of the Confederacy. Finding the prospects of the South at a low ebb he used tact and energy in organizing three brigades of Indians, respecting fully the tribal loyalties of the Creek, Cherokee, and Choctaw. His ability as an orator, for which he was already well known, served him in good stead. He also established a printing-press in order to reach a larger audience. Both at the council-fire and through printed propaganda he persuaded the Indians that victory for the South was essential to their safety. He had soon gained their almost pathetic good will as no other Texan had done since the days of Sam Houston. A recent writer sums up the account of his activities,

"Behind all this virility was General Maxey. Without him, it is safe to say, the war for the Indians would have ended in the preceding winter" (Abel, *post*, p. 329).

The war over, he practised law for ten years. In 1873 he declined the appointment as federal judge of the 8th district of Texas. In 1875, at the end of Reconstruction, he was sent to the United States Senate, where he served for twelve years. In the Senate he was not unlike other members of the group known as the "Confederate Brigadiers." He advocated economy but did not fail to obtain appropriations for Texas rivers, harbors, and postroads. His most notable speeches, and he made many, were on Indian relations. Maxey was among the first to favor individual farms as the ultimate solution of the Indian question. On constitutional grounds he was opposed to the prevailing policy of protective tariffs. Defeated for reëlection he retired to practise law in Paris. He died at Eureka Springs, Ark.

[*The Encyc. of the New West*, ed. by W. S. Speer and J. H. Brown (1881); J. H. Brown, *Indian Wars and Pioneers of Texas* (189?); *Biog. Directory Am. Cong.* (1928); *Confederate Military Hist.*, ed. by C. A. Evans (1899), vol. XI; A. H. Abel, *The Slaveholding Indians*, vol. II (1919); *War of the Rebellion: Official Records (Army)*, 1 ser., vols. X, pt. 2, XVI, pt. 1, XXII, pt. 2, XXXIV, pts. 1–4 (1884–1902); *Galveston Daily News*, Aug. 17, 1895.] R. G. C—l.

MAXIM, HIRAM STEVENS (Feb 5, 1840–Nov. 24, 1916), inventor, engineer, was the eldest of the eight children of Isaac Weston and Harriet Boston (Stevens) Maxim and was born at Brockway's Mills, near Sangerville, Piscataquis County, Me. The region was still sparsely settled: bears outnumbered the men; money and the common comforts were scarce; and survival depended on strength, endurance, frugality, and resourcefulness in making a few devices serve many ends. The Maxims, however, were fitted to survive. According to family tradition they were of Huguenot origin and had been domiciled at Canterbury before coming to America, but from Isaac the direct line could be traced back only four generations to a Samuel Maxim of Rochester, Mass. The father was a farmer and wood-turner with a taste for philosophic speculation and a talent for invention. Among the ideas that he tinkered with were an automatic gun and a flying machine. Hiram, because of his precocious strength of body and application to business, early became the paragon of the household. At the age of fourteen he was bound out to a carriage-maker, Daniel Sweat, at East Corinth. He studied whatever scientific books came in his way, and with a faculty for drawing and painting and an uncanny facility in handling tools quickly became an adept at several trades. Deciding, on the advice of a friendly physician, not to waste any time on pugilism or the Civil War, he went to Montreal and thence to several towns on either side of the international boundary—Malone, N. Y.; St. Jean Chrysostome, Que.; Brasher Falls, N. Y.—where he worked as carriage-painter, cabinet-maker, and mechanic; discovered, but utilized for only a few days, some profitable innovations in the art of bar-tending; and won renown as a practical joker and tamer of bullies. Having satisfied his *Wanderlust* in the North, he returned home and secured employment in the engineering works of his uncle, Levi Stevens, at Fitchburg, Mass. During the next few years he studied hard and was deeply influenced by Oliver P. Drake, a scientific instrument maker of Boston. His genius for invention, nurtured from childhood by his environment, now came to fruition. In 1866 he took out his first patent, an improvement in irons for curling hair, although he already had several useful inventions to his credit. For the next few years he lived in New York and occupied himself chiefly with machines for generating illuminating gas, but also invented a locomotive headlight. In 1878 he was appointed chief engineer of the United States Electric Lighting Company, the first enterprise of its kind in the country. He therefore turned his attention to the incandescent carbon lamp and devised the method of "flashing" the filaments in a hydrocarbon atmosphere so as to even them up by a deposit of carbon on the thinner places. This invention was of fundamental importance to the electric lighting industry, but through a combination of accident and machination it became public property both in England and the United States.

In 1881 he went to the Paris Exposition to exhibit an electric pressure regulator that brought him the decoration of the Légion d'Honneur. A little later he set up a laboratory in Hatton Garden, London, and though at first disgusted with the ways of English workingmen he soon came to like the country and remained there permanently. He formed the Maxim Gun Company in 1884 and effected a merger in 1888 with the Nordenfeldt Company, and in 1896 the firm was absorbed into Vickers Sons and Maxim, of which Maxim was a director. On his retirement in 1911 the name was shortened to Vickers, Ltd. He became a British subject in 1900 and was knighted by Queen Victoria in 1901. He received numerous decorations from other governments.

Maxim was the equal of any mechanician of

his day. His knowledge of physics and chemistry and his ingenuity in tool-making were always available to him: he could use no machine or process without seeking to improve it. In all he took out 122 patents in the United States and 149 in Great Britain. His range of invention included an improved mouse-trap, automatic gas-generating plants, automatic sprinkling apparatus for extinguishing fires, automatic steam pumping-engines for supplying houses with water, feed-water heaters, steam and vacuum pumps, engine governors, gas motors, and an inhaling apparatus for medicating the throat. His international fame was gained by his invention of the Maxim gun, which completely changed the technique of modern warfare, and by his experiments with flying machines. Though it had been preceded by the Gatling gun (1862), the mitrailleuse (1867), and the Nordenfeldt (1877), his automatic gun of 1883 was the first efficient weapon of its class. It fired eleven shots a second from a single barrel, the loading, firing, extracting, and ejecting of the cartridges being effected automatically by utilizing the recoil of the barrel as each shot was fired. Subsequently he made various improvements in it, some of which were suggested by Lord Wolseley, who also pointed out the necessity of using a smokeless powder. Maxim himself discovered a smokeless powder of the cordite type and made numerous other contributions to gunnery.

His interest in flying began about 1889, when he reached the conclusion that "if a domestic goose can fly, so can a man." His experiments culminated in 1894 with the trial at Bexley, Kent, of a machine that was technically successful, since it actually lifted itself from the ground. Unfortunately, as Maxim himself expressed it, he had no time to invent an internal combustion engine and therefore had to make use of steam. His two compound steam engines and the water-tube boiler were marvels of lightness, weighing about six pounds per horse-power, but the weight of the fuel and water made the machine impracticable.

Maxim was twice married: first, to Louisa Jane Budden, by whom he had a son, Hiram Percy Maxim, inventor of the Maxim silencer, and two daughters; and second, to Sarah Haynes of Boston, who survived him. He was about six feet tall and well built, with fluffy hair and beard, jet black in early life, and snow white in his later years. Unlike so many inventors, he was fastidious about his appearance. A philosophic nihilist and a citizen of the world, he retained to the last many of the traits of the Maine Yankee and of the successful self-made man. Lawyers and labor leaders—classes with which he had had much experience—were his special abominations. Despite an active sense of humor he was distinctly vain and jealous of other inventors, especially of Thomas A. Edison, his rival in electric lighting, and of his own brother, Hudson Maxim [*q.v.*], his rival in ammunition making. But his boastfulness was happily accompanied by a personal charm totally disarming. He died at his home at Streatham after a short illness, having kept his vigor and his scientific interests to the end.

[H. S. Maxim, *My Life* (1915); P. F. Mottelay, *The Life and Work of Sir Hiram Maxim* (1920); Clifton Johnson, *Hudson Maxim: Reminiscences and Comments* (1924); Brysson Cunningham, article in *Dict. Nat. Biog. 1912–21* (1927); London *Times*, Nov. 25, 1916; J. F. Sprague, "Sir Hiram Maxim," *Sprague's Jour. of Me. Hist.*, Apr. 1917.] G. H. G.

MAXIM, HUDSON (Feb. 3, 1853–May 6, 1927), inventor and expert in explosives, was born in Orneville, Piscataquis County, Me., and was the sixth child of Isaac Weston and Harriet Boston (Stevens) Maxim. He was named for his father but disliked the name so much that he dropped it when eighteen years old and took that of Hudson. His father was a wood-turner, millwright, and miller, impoverished in worldly goods but a philosopher, lover of poetry and history, a gifted story teller, and the source of abounding inspiration to his children. Maxim's early life, accordingly, was a difficult but happy one. He rarely had decent clothing and obtained his first pair of shoes when thirteen, but he developed into an unusually strong and healthy boy, full of ambition and determination to amount to something. He attended the district schools occasionally between the ages of nine and seventeen and then worked for a year for his brother Hiram [*q.v.*], the machine-gun inventor, in New York. During the next seven years he alternately worked a few months and attended Maine Wesleyan Seminary, Kent's Hill, Me., completing there the course in chemistry and the natural sciences.

For the next decade he was engaged in job printing and book publishing with a schoolmate, Alden Knowles, who was an expert ornamental penman. The first part of this period was spent in the vicinity of Columbus, Ohio, where the partners enjoyed considerable success canvassing with their chart of writing styles and their colored ink powders; but in Pittsfield, Mass., where they later established themselves and began publishing their own book, *Real Pen-Work Self-Instructor in Penmanship* (copr. 1881), their success was phenomenal. In five years, through canvassers and mail orders, over a half-million copies of the book were sold. It was followed by a family record book, the sale of which reached more than a million copies. With the advent of the fountain pen and the typewriter, however, their business stopped.

Maxim then hired a number of mechanics for his brother Hiram, and went with them to England to work in the latter's gun factory. There Hudson had his first opportunity to examine some smokeless powder of French manufacture, and after a few simple experiments he determined its composition. This work proved fascinating, and upon returning to Pittsfield, Mass., in December 1888, as the American representative of the Maxim-Nordenfeldt Guns and Ammunition Company, Limited, he began the serious study of explosives. Although he had a two-years' contract with his brother's company, business difficulties soon arose and Hudson felt bound to look to his own future. He continued his studies, began experimenting, and occasionally contributed articles to the newspapers on his favorite subject. He secured a patent on the production of high explosives, Sept. 17, 1889, and another for a detachable gas check for projectiles, May 20, 1890. Early in 1891 the contract between the Maxims expired, and shortly thereafter Hudson, known chiefly through his newspaper writings, became chief engineer of the Columbia Powder Manufacturing Company, makers of dynamite at Squankum, N. J. He thereupon moved to New York and for a year or more worked on the problem of making a safer dynamite. He assigned two patents, issued May 10 and Aug. 2, 1892, to the company; and when it failed in 1893, he organized the Maxim Powder Company and took over the plant at Squankum. He then began serious work on smokeless powder and secured a number of patents between 1893 and 1895. He was unsuccessful in selling these to his brother in England but in 1897 sold them, together with his plant, to E. I. du Pont de Nemours & Company of Wilmington, Del. He now became a consultant for this company, which position he held throughout his life. From 1895 to 1900 Maxim worked on the perfection of a shock-proof high explosive for guns of large caliber and finally produced an explosive, which he named "Maximite," that could propel a projectile through the heaviest armor plate and was fifty per cent. more powerful than dynamite. For this invention Maxim received $50,000 from the United States government in 1901. That year the Du Pont Company established an experimental laboratory for him at Lake Hopatcong, N. J., and from that time until his death he worked there. He invented "stabillite," a smokeless powder that could be used as soon as produced and gave much better ballistic results. He also devised the machinery to manufacture smokeless powder and invented a number of gun cartridges as well as the United States service projectiles. He was a consultant for E. W. Bliss Company of Brooklyn, N. Y., manufacturers of torpedoes for submarines and destroyers, and secured a number of patents for torpedo-boat improvements; for "motorite," an explosive compound for driving torpedoes; and for apparatus for propelling torpedoes. Interspersed with his inventions in the explosive field, Maxim invented an automobile in England as early as 1895; a process of manufacturing calcium carbide, patented Oct. 8, 1901; and a game of skill in 1912, patented June 25. During the World War he served as chairman of the committee on ordnance and explosives on the Naval Consulting Board in Washington.

He was a fluent public speaker, a frequent contributor to newspapers and periodicals on current topics, and the author of *The Science of Poetry and the Philosophy of Language* (1910). A man of decisive opinions, he was no respecter of persons or reputations and voiced his likes and dislikes with great freedom and emphasis. In 1915 he published *Defenseless America*, a vitriolic denunciation of pacifism; in 1916, *Leading Opinions Both for and Against National Defense*; and *Dynamite Stories*. He was greatly interested in aviation and became president of the Aeronautical Society of New York. He was also a member of the Navy League and the Chemists Club of New York. He was married, first, in 1888, to Jane Morrow of Pittsfield, Mass., from whom he was soon afterwards divorced; second, on Mar. 26, 1896, to Lilian Durban, of London, England. No religious services were held at his death and his body was cremated. He was survived by his widow and a son by his first wife.

[Clifton Johnson, *Hudson Maxim: Reminiscences and Comments* (1924); *Who's Who in America*, 1926–27; *N. Y. Times*, May 7, 8, 1927; Pat. Office records.]

C. W. M.

MAXWELL, AUGUSTUS EMMETT (Sept. 21, 1820–May 5, 1903), United States representative, Confederate senator, Florida jurist, was born at Elberton, Ga., the son of Simeon and Elizabeth (Fortson) Maxwell. His parents were natives of Georgia, but the family came from Virginia. In 1822 the Maxwells removed to Greene County, Ala., and there the boy received his elementary education. He attended the University of Virginia from 1837 to 1840. Returning to Alabama he was admitted to the bar in 1843 and began the practice of law at Eutaw, but in 1845 he removed to Tallahassee, Fla. Aided by the influence of his brother-in-law, William H. Brockenbrough, he entered into the political life of the new state and began a public career that lasted almost until the time of his death. He was a member of the state legislature in 1847, was attorney-general in 1846 and 1847, secretary of state from April 1848 to July 1849, and state senator from 1849 to 1850. In the latter capacity it is evident that he exerted considerable influence, holding the chairmanship of both the judiciary and the federal relations committees as well as being a member of the committees on schools and colleges and on amendments and revisions of the constitution. His election to the federal House of Representatives seemed to promise him a national career, but his two terms, from 1853 to 1857, evidently did not add much to his reputation. He seems to have taken little part in legislation except to forward the passing of local bills. He retired from Congress at the end of his second term and took up the practice of law at Pensacola. Appointed navy agent at Pensacola in 1857 he held the position until Florida seceded in 1861. He was elected to the Confederate Senate and served throughout the war.

Although he had been educated in law and had a reputation as a lawyer of ability, his public career had been chiefly in legislative positions, but after the war he devoted himself more closely to the law and made a second career for himself as a jurist. Immediately after the war he was appointed associate justice of the Florida supreme court, but, finding it impossible to go on with his work under the Carpet-bag rule, he resigned in 1866 and resumed the practice of law at Pensacola in partnership with Stephen R. Mallory [*q.v.*], the former secretary of the navy in the Confederacy. When the Democrats regained control of Florida in 1877 he was appointed judge of the 1st judicial circuit. He held this position until his resignation in 1885. In 1887 he was appointed chief justice of the supreme court of Florida. The new constitution of 1885 provided that the chief justiceship should be filled by lot from the justices, and as a result of this arrangement, in 1889, he became associate justice and served until 1891. Retiring to Pensacola he practised law in partnership with his son until the latter was appointed circuit judge in 1896. At this time he gave up his law practice and retired from active life after a public career of over half a century. In 1896 he was a candidate for elector on the Palmer and Buckner ticket but was defeated. He was married twice. His first wife was Sarah Roane Brockenbrough, whom he married at Charlottesville, Va., in 1843. After her death he married, in 1853, Julia Hawks Anderson of Pensacola, the daughter of Walker Anderson, the chief justice of the state supreme court. In 1902 he removed to Chipley, where he died. He was buried from the Christ Episcopal Church of Pensacola of which he had long been a member. He was survived by two of the three children of his first marriage and three of the five children of the second.

[Information from his son, E. C. Maxwell, Pensacola; Journal of the General Assembly of Florida, 5 Sess.; H. C. Armstrong, *Hist. of Escambia County* (1930); R. H. Rerick, *Memoirs of Florida* (1902), vol. I; *Who's Who in America*, 1901–02; *Pensacola Daily News*, May 6, 7, 1903.] R. S. C.

MAXWELL, DAVID HERVEY (Sept. 17, 1786–May 24, 1854), physician, legislator, born in Garrard County, Ky., the son of Bazaleel and Margaret (Anderson) Maxwell, came of the Scotch-Irish Presbyterian stock which figured conspicuously in the making of early Indiana. Reared in a pioneer environment, he had meager opportunities for early schooling, but at the age of eighteen he went to Danville, Ky., an educational center, where he became proficient in mathematics and well read in English. He then studied medicine at Danville under Ephraim McDowell [*q.v.*], a noted surgeon of the day. In 1809 he married Mary E. Dunn of Danville, and settled down to the practice of his chosen profession. Emigrating a year later to Indiana, then a new and promising country, he settled in Jefferson County about the time the town of Madison was founded. There he practised medicine for nine years, serving for part of the time as military surgeon during the War of 1812.

In 1816 Indiana became a state, and at this time Maxwell first appeared in a public capacity, as a delegate to the convention which framed the state constitution. A dynamic member of that convention, he introduced the clause prohibiting slavery in the state, and though not a member of the "committee relative to education," was probably a supporter of the clause which provided for "a general system of education, ascending in a regular gradation, from township schools to a state university, wherein tuition shall be gratis and equally open to all" (Art. IX, sec. 2). This theoretical system was so far in advance of what was possible at that time and place that more than thirty-five years elapsed before it actually existed.

From the time of his activity in the constitutional convention, Maxwell was concerned in educational affairs, his chief interest being in the establishment of a state university. In the federal enabling act which paved the way for statehood, a township of land had been donated for the benefit of a "seminary of learning," the exact tract to be designated by the president of the United States. The land chosen chanced to be in Monroe County, on what was then the state's frontier, and to Maxwell's mind this was the logical place for the state university provided for by the constitution. In 1818 the little backwoods town of Bloomington, Monroe County, was in its first struggle for existence, and thither he moved to lay his plans for a school campaign. The legislative assembly of 1819–20 found him on hand as a lobbyist for a bill to establish a state seminary at Bloomington, and so effective was his influence that the law was passed Jan. 20, 1820, with Maxwell as one of six members of a board of trustees. He proved to be the leading member and for many years was the president of that board. To further his influence in promoting the welfare of the university and of education generally he several times sought election to the state legislature, serving in the House during the sixth, eighth, and ninth sessions (1821, 1823–25), and in the Senate during the years 1826–29. In the eighth session he was speaker of the House. Throughout his legislative service he was recognized as a champion of education, and his name is repeatedly found on educational committees. An unexpected honor that fell upon him in 1836 was his nomination by Governor Noble to the State Board of Internal Improvements and his unanimous election to the presidency of that board. He was also twice postmaster at Bloomington. It is for his long and unflagging interest in higher education, however, that he is chiefly remembered. Indiana University's memorial to him is Maxwell Hall, named for him and his son, Dr. James Darwin Maxwell. Maxwell died in Bloomington, in his sixty-eighth year.

[Sketch by Louise Maxwell in *Ind. Quart. Mag. of Hist.*, Sept. 1912; J. A. Woodburn, in *Ind. Univ. Alumni Quarterly*, July 1916, p. 355; Logan Esarey, "Internal Improvements in Early Indiana," *Ind. Hist. Soc. Pubs.*, vol. V (1912); "Ann. Reports of the State Board of Internal Improvements" in *Documentary Jours. of Ind.*, 1836; *Jour. of the Conv. of the Indiana Territory* (1816); Charles Kettleborough, *Constitution Making in Ind.*, vol I (1916); *Ind. Univ. 1820–1920 Centennial Memorial Vol.* (copr. 1921); F. W. Houston and others, *Maxwell Hist. and Geneal.* (copr. 1916).] G. S. C.

MAXWELL, GEORGE TROUP (Aug. 6, 1827–Sept. 2, 1897), physician and legislator, was born in Bryan County, Ga. His father, John Jackson Maxwell, was a planter who served a number of terms in the state Senate; his mother was a daughter of Col. John Baker, an officer in the Revolutionary War. After obtaining his preliminary education at Chatham Academy, Savannah, he entered the medical department of the University of the City of New York, from which he obtained the degree of M.D. in 1848. He settled in Tallahassee, Fla., for practice and remained there until 1857, when he was appointed surgeon to the Marine Hospital at Key West. In 1860 he was appointed professor of obstetrics and diseases of women and children in Oglethorpe Medical College, and moved to Savannah. At the outbreak of the Civil War he enlisted as a private in the 1st Florida Cavalry. He was later commissioned major of cavalry, and colonel in 1862. In that grade he commanded a brigade of Florida troops in the Army of the Tennessee under General Bragg, until he was captured at the battle of Missionary Ridge. His capture prevented his acceptance of a commission as brigadier-general which was on the way to him. He was a prisoner until March 1865, when he returned to Tallahassee. Shortly thereafter, as a representative of Leon County, he took an active part in the proceedings of the convention held under the proclamation of President Johnson for the purpose of rewriting the constitution and reorganizing the state government of Florida. The next winter he was elected a member of the state legislature. In 1866 he moved to Jacksonville, where he practised his profession until 1871. In that year he went to New Castle, Del., where he conducted a daily paper in addition to the practice of medicine. Here he was prominent in Democratic politics and in Masonic activities. He was vice-president of the Delaware Medical Society in 1874 and secretary in 1875–76. From Delaware he moved to Atlanta where he practised for a brief time, after which he accepted a professorship at the State Agricultural College, Lake City, Fla. In 1888 an outbreak of yellow fever took him to Jacksonville, where he remained during the epidemic and afterward until his death, which resulted from a stroke of apoplexy.

Maxwell was always a prolific contributor to medical periodicals. While in Delaware he wrote "An Exposition on the Liability of the Negro Race to Yellow Fever," "A Demonstration of the Non-digestive Powers of the Large Intestine" and "The Laryngoscope, an American Invention." The last-named paper, published in the *Medical Record*, New York, Jan. 1, 1873, described an instrument which Maxwell had perfected in 1869. Though the credit for the first laryngoscope goes to Manuel Garcia, the Spanish music teacher, Maxwell's instrument showed originality, and he is credited with being the first American physician to see the vocal cords of a living subject. After his return to Jacksonville he published pamphlets on *Malarial Hæmoglobinuria* (1892), *Municipal Hygiene* (1894), and a paper on "Hygiene in Florida" (*Proceedings of the . . . Florida Medical Association*, 1896). The Florida Medical Association, of which he had been president, adopted resolutions upon his death which not only reviewed his career but made note of his exceptional social qualities and conversational powers. He married Augusta Jones of Tallahassee shortly after his graduation in medicine. She died of yellow fever while he was serving at the Marine Hospital in Key West.

[*Twenty-fifth Ann. Session Fla. Medic. Asso.* (1898); R. F. Stone, *Biog. of Eminent Am. Physicians and Surgeons* (1894); W. B. Atkinson, *Biog. Dict. of Contemporary Am. Physicians and Surgeons* (1880); H. A. Kelly and W. L. Burrage, *Am. Medic. Biogs.* (1920); *Florida Times-Union* (Jacksonville), Sept. 3, 1897.] J. M. P.

MAXWELL, HUGH (1787–Mar. 31, 1873), lawyer, was born in Paisley, Scotland. About 1790 the family emigrated to New York where his father, William Maxwell, operated a distillery and a tallow chandlery. Hugh was educated at Columbia College, graduating in 1808, nineteenth in a class of twenty-one members. Owing to his participation in the "riotous commencement" of 1811, the A.M. degree in course which he was to have received at that time was withheld until 1816. Maxwell, at the commencement of 1811 held in Trinity Church, took the part of one of the candidates who had been refused his degree, and addressed the audience on behalf of the student. Gulian C. Verplanck, a distinguished alumnus, supported Maxwell and moved a vote of thanks. Faculty supporters intervened and the ceremonies were adjourned in disorder. Both Maxwell and Verplanck were indicted by a grand jury, arraigned before Mayor Clinton, and fined. As a consequence, Maxwell joined Verplanck in his attacks upon Clinton.

In 1814 Maxwell was appointed assistant judge-advocate-general of the United States army. In 1817 he was appointed district attorney for the twelfth district (New York County). After the passage of the law of 1818, under which an attorney was named for each county, he was appointed district attorney for New York County, serving from 1821 to 1829. In 1826 he conducted the prosecution of Jacob Barker [*q.v.*] and others on charges of fraud and conspiracy, following the failure of the Life and Fire Insurance Company. Barker fought the indictment bitterly and Fitz-Greene Halleck, who had been in Barker's employ, attacked Maxwell as "Billingsgate McSwell" in a privately circulated poem.

Maxwell was active in the Whig party, largely in the capacity of a party manager, in association with Thurlow Weed. From 1849 to 1853 he held the post of collector of the port of New York. At the age of seventy he gave up his successful law practice and retired from business and politics. His death occurred in 1873. He had married Agnes Stevenson, by whom he had four children.

["The Riotous Commencement of 1811," *Columbia Univ. Quart.*, June, Sept. 1901; *The Trial of Gulian C. Verplanck, Hugh Maxwell and Others for a Riot in Trinity Church* (1821); W. M. MacBean, *Biog. Reg. of St. Andrew's Soc. . . . of N. Y.* (2 vols., 1922–25); E. A. Werner, *Civil List and Constitutional Hist. . . . of N. Y.* (1889); David McAdam, *Hist. of the Bench and Bar of N. Y.*, vol. I (1897); D. R. Fox, *The Decline of Aristocracy in the Pol. of N. Y.* (1918); J. G. Wilson, *The Life and Letters of Fitz-Greene Halleck* (1869), pp. 313–19; I. S. Clason, *Horace in N. Y.* (1826), pp. 31–34, *The Conspiracy Trials of 1826 and 1827* (1864) with an introduction by R. D. Turner; *N. Y. Tribune*, Apr. 1, 1873.] P. W. B.

MAXWELL, LUCIEN BONAPARTE (Sept. 14, 1818–July 25, 1875), frontiersman, rancher, was one of the twelve children of Hugh B. and Marie Odille (Menard) Maxwell and was born in Kaskaskia, Ill. The mother was a daughter of the noted Pierre Menard [*q.v.*], the first lieutenant-governor of Illinois. The son seems to have had a fair degree of schooling. Probably before he was twenty he accompanied a trading caravan or a trapping party to Taos, N. Mex. Here he met Kit Carson, with whom he formed a close friendship that lasted until death separated them. For a time, about 1840–41, he was employed at Fort St. Vrain, on the South Platte. He was the hunter for Frémont's first expedition (1842), of which Carson was the guide. In the same year, at Taos, he married Luz, the daughter of Charles Beaubien, one of the two owners of the vast Beaubien-Miranda tract granted by the Mexican government. With Carson he joined Frémont's third expedition, which left Bent's Fort in August 1845 and arrived at Sutter's Fort on Dec. 9, and he was an active and valuable member of the Pathfinder's force in the events culminating in the conquest of California. He was one of the party of fifteen, led by Carson, that started from Los Angeles in September 1846 to carry dispatches to Washington; and on Oct. 6, near Socorro, N. Mex., where they met Kearny's expedition, westward bound, rendered a notable service by persuading the angry Carson not to ruin his career by defying Kearny's order that he give up his dispatches and return as guide to the army.

He now settled down to the management of

his father-in-law's estate. Beaubien had become the sole owner of the grant, a tract of 1,714,764 acres, the largest single holding in the United States, and Maxwell energetically applied himself to its development. Under the American rule the products of his fields found a ready market with the government purchasing agents, and he prospered. At the town of Cimarron, in the present Colfax County, N. Mex., he built a large dwelling, with an encircling veranda and a central patio, where he entertained with princely hospitality. In the spring of 1853 he and Carson set out from the Cimarron for California with two large herds of sheep, some 12,000 head. By way of the Oregon Trail and the Humboldt River they reached Sacramento in September. Selling their animals at a good profit, they returned by the southern route and on Christmas eve were again in Taos.

Beaubien died in 1864, and Maxwell, by purchasing the holdings of the other heirs, became the sole owner of what has ever since been known as the Maxwell Grant—a tract that in later years was to be the subject of much litigation and the scene of occasional settlers' wars. In 1870 he founded the First National Bank of New Mexico, but soon tiring of his plaything disposed of it. In 1871 he sold his entire estate to a Colorado syndicate headed by Jerome B. Chaffee [*q.v.*]. A series of reverses followed. For a time he engaged in mining, and he was one of the founders of Silver City, N. Mex. His last days were spent at Fort Sumner, and he was buried there in the government cemetery. He was survived by his wife and several of his nine children. As a trapper, hunter, and Indian fighter Maxwell was brave and self-reliant. He was improvident, and he seems to have had more than his share of eccentricities; but he was a kindly, generous, and dependable man, who was universally liked and whose friends were devotedly attached to him.

[R. E. Twitchell, *The Leading Facts in New Mexican Hist.*, vol. II (1912); E. L. Sabin, *Kit Carson Days* (1914); C. L. Camp, "Kit Carson in California," *Quart. Cal. Hist. Soc.*, Oct. 1922, also pub. separately; *Daily New Mexican* (Santa Fé), July 29, 1875; information from the Rev. G. J. Garraghan of St. Louis Univ., and from Maxwell's daughter, Mrs. Odila Abreü, Fort Sumner, N. Mex.]

W. J. G.

MAXWELL, SAMUEL (May 20, 1825–Feb. 11, 1901), Nebraska jurist, congressman, author of legal treatises, was born in Lodi, N. Y., the son of Robert Maxwell, a well-to-do farmer, and Margaret (Crosby) Maxwell, a woman of education and refinement. During his boyhood, financial reverses caused the family to move to Michigan, and here young Maxwell, following a well-worn western formula, worked on a farm, taught school, and studied law. In 1856 he pushed farther west, to Plattsmouth, Nebr., where he took and improved a "claim." Within two years, however, he returned to Michigan, read law in a brother's office at Bay City, and was admitted to the bar. The year 1859 found him once again in Nebraska.

His political career was early under way. He was a member of the territorial legislatures of 1859–60, 1865, and 1866, of the first state legislature, June 1866, and of the constitutional conventions of 1864, 1871, and 1875. The first of these conventions was opposed to statehood, and refused to draw a constitution. In the others Maxwell, thanks to his knowledge of legal fundamentals and his skill as a debater, took a prominent part. In 1870 he was an unsuccessful candidate for the Republican nomination for governor. In 1872 he was elected justice of the state supreme court, and by successive reëlections was a member of the court continuously from 1873 to 1894, serving much of the time as chief justice. His influence over the court during this formative period was tremendous. He served longer than any other judge who sat with him, and he wrote far more than his share of the court's opinions. One of his outstanding characteristics was an impatience of legal technicalities. If substantial justice could be done, he was content, and as "Substantial Justice" Maxwell he was generally known. This pleased the public, but lawyers who saw well established rules of law treated with little respect did not always approve. Moreover, Maxwell was never an ardent party man, and some of his decisions failed to find favor with the Republican machine. His renominations, therefore, were conceded somewhat grudgingly, and finally in 1893 a Republican convention rejected him. This defeat undoubtedly was meant as a rebuke to the Chief Justice for his attitude in two important cases. In one, an election contest with the governorship of the state at stake, he had held against the majority of the court that the Democratic candidate was entitled to the office (31 *Nebr.*, 682). In the other, which involved the impeachment of some faithless Republican state officials, he had again deserted his colleagues and had written a blistering dissenting opinion (37 *Nebr.*, 96 and 38 *Nebr.*, 584).

Maxwell now went over to the Populists, in whose doctrines he had come to believe. He was their unsuccessful candidate for the supreme court in 1895, and as a fusionist won a seat in Congress by the election of 1896. Here he did his share towards carrying on the losing fight for free silver, but he failed of renomination, and in 1899 retired to private life. He died at Fremont, Nebr., and was buried at Plattsmouth. Three times married: first to Amelia A. Lawrence of Michigan, second to Jenette M. McCord of Cass County, Nebr., third to Elizabeth A. Adams, also of Cass County, he was the father of eleven children, nine of whom survived infancy. He was in comfortable financial circumstances at the time of his death in 1901, and left a small legacy to his family.

Maxwell's best-known book is *A Treatise on Pleading, Practice, Procedure, and Precedents in Actions at Law and Suits in Equity* (1880). He also wrote or compiled *Digest of the Decisions of the Supreme Court of the State of Nebraska* (1877), *A Treatise on the Powers and Duties of Justices of the Peace, Sheriffs, and Constables* (1879), *A Practical Treatise on Criminal Procedure with Directions and Forms* (1887), and *A Treatise on the Law of Pleading under the Code of Civil Procedure, Designed for All the Code States* (1892). Most of these books are handy manuals of great value to the practising lawyer. They have gone through many editions and have continued in use through much of the Middle West.

[Maxwell correspondence, 1853–1901, in State Hist. Soc. of Nebr.; J. M. Klotsche, "The Political Career of Samuel Maxwell," in *Nebr. Law Bull.*, May 1928; R. D. Rowley, "The Judicial Career of Samuel Maxwell," manuscript thesis in Univ. of Nebr. Lib.; J. S. Morton and Albert Watkins, *Illus. Hist. of Nebr.* (3 vols., 1905–13); *Biog. Dir. Am. Cong.* (1928); *Nebr. State Jour.* (Lincoln), Feb. 12, 1901.] J. D. H.

MAXWELL, WILLIAM (*c.* 1733–Nov. 4, 1796), Revolutionary soldier, was born of Scotch-Irish ancestry near Newtown Stewart, County Tyrone, Ireland. His parents, John and Ann Maxwell, with four children, of whom William was the eldest, came to America about 1747, settling in Greenwich township, Sussex (now Warren) County, N. J. William was brought up as a farmer's son, with only ordinary educational advantages. When twenty-one he entered military service in a British regiment to take part in the French and Indian War, and was with General Braddock at the battle of Fort Duquesne in 1755. Later he became an ensign in Col. John Johnston's New Jersey regiment, and, later still, lieutenant in Col. Peter Schuyler's New Jersey regiment. In 1758 he was in the army under General Abercromby [*q.v.*] in the expedition against Fort Ticonderoga, and he is believed to have fought under Wolfe at the capture of Quebec in September 1759. Toward the close of the French and Indian War, he became attached to the British commissary department at Mackinac, with the rank of colonel. He was there until 1774, when, learning that New Jersey was nearly ripe for a revolution against Great Britain, he returned to his home in Sussex County, N. J.

He was a member of the Provincial Congress at Trenton, which met in May 1775. In August he was chairman of the Committee of Safety of his county, and in October, when again a member of the Provincial Congress, was recommended by that body to the Continental Congress for appointment as colonel of the Western Battalion of New Jersey Continental troops, and elected to that office Nov. 7, 1775 (*Journals of the Continental Congress*). He at once raised what became the 2nd Battalion, 1st Establishment, of the troops named, and in February 1776, with five full companies, started on the expedition against Canada, under the command of Gen. John Sullivan. He was at the battle of Three Rivers, June 8, 1776. Because of his bravery in this campaign the Continental Congress commissioned him brigadier-general, Oct. 23, 1776, and he was placed by Washington in command of four battalions in the 2nd Establishment of New Jersey Continental troops. From Dec. 2, 1776, to the summer of 1777, he harassed the enemy in New Jersey at Elizabethtown, Rahway, and Springfield; on Sept. 11, 1777, he fought in the battle of Brandywine, Pa.; then in the battle of Germantown, Oct. 4. He spent the winter and spring, 1777–78, at Valley Forge. On June 28, 1778, his brigade took an active part in the battle of Monmouth, and during the rest of that year and the following winter was stationed chiefly near Elizabethtown, N. J., again harassing the enemy, interfering with foraging parties from New York and Staten Island. When the Sullivan expedition left Easton, Pa., June 18, 1779, to proceed against the Six Nations in Western Pennsylvania and New York, Maxwell's brigade was with it, and continued with it until the return in October, when the brigade went into winter quarters near Scotch Plains, N. J. In June 1780, Maxwell fought at the battle of Springfield and the skirmish at Connecticut Farms. This ended his army service, since he resigned his commission in July. Washington, in forwarding the resignation to Congress, spoke of him as "an honest man, a warm friend to this country, and firmly attached to her interests" (to Samuel Huntington, July 20, 1780, Washington Papers, Library of Congress).

In 1783 Maxwell was elected to the New Jersey Assembly. He died in November 1796 while on a visit to an army friend at Lansdown, N. J. He was buried in the graveyard of the old Stone Church (Presbyterian) near his home, where a monument, describing his virtues, marks his grave. He never married. Maxwell is said to have been a "tall, stalwart man" with a "florid complexion." Because of his Scotch accent his soldiers, by whom he was greatly beloved, called him "Scotch Willie." The state of New Jersey has always considered him one of its foremost soldiers.

[H. D. Maxwell, *The Maxwell Family* (1895); *Archives of the State of N. J.*, 1 ser. IX (1885); *Selections from the Corresp. of the Executive of N. J., 1776–86* (1848); J. H. Griffith, "William Maxwell of New Jersey," *Proc. N. J. Hist. Soc.*, 2 ser. XIII, no. 2 (June 1897); W. S. Stryker, *Official Reg. of the Officers and Men of N. J., in the Revolutionary War* (1872), and *Gen. Maxwell's Brigade of the N. J. Continental Line in the Expedition against the Indians in the year 1779* (1885); B. J. Lossing, *The Pictorial Field-book of the Revolution*, vol. II (1852); *The First Sussex Centenary* (1853); Sullivan's Orderly Book (1779), in the possession of the N. J. Hist. Soc.; Wm. Nelson, *N. J. Biog. and Geneal. Notes* (1916).]

A. V–D. H.

MAXWELL, WILLIAM (*c.* 1755–1809), pioneer publisher, born in New York or New Jersey, was the son of William Maxwell, an emigrant from Scotland. In 1792 he started for the West, and before the close of that year was engaged in the printing business in Lexington, Ky. In this enterprise he evidently had partners. The title page of *A Process in the Transilvania Presbytery*, by Adam Rankin, bears the imprint: "Lexington: Printed by Maxwell & Cooch. At the sign of the Buffalo, Main-Street." The copyright date of this pamphlet is Jan. 1, 1793. Another pamphlet, *A Narrative of Mr. Rankin's Trial*, bears the imprint: "Lexington: Printed by W. Maxwell & Co. M,DCC,XCIII."

Later in 1793 he arrived in Cincinnati, where, on Nov. 9, 1793, he issued the first number of *The Centinel of the North-Western Territory*. It was published at the corner of Front and Sycamore streets. A four-page, three-column sheet, it was a brief chronicler of the times and contained little local news. In it, however, were discussed from its beginning questions that were claiming the attention of the small frontier village in which it was published. In the first issue appeared an account of an attack by the Indians near Fort St. Clair and a contribution on local taxation filling a column and a half. The paper was issued regularly on Saturday of each week through practically all the years of its existence. In the summer of 1796 its founder, who had been appointed postmaster of Cincinnati, sold the *Centinel* to Edmund Freeman who changed the name to *Freeman's Journal*. Before Maxwell disposed of his printing office, however, he published a compilation, *Laws of the Territory of the United States, Northwest of the Ohio*, which has since been known as the "Maxwell Code." It bears the date of 1796 and was the first book published in the Northwest Territory. In 1799, he moved to Dayton and later in the same year to a tract on the Little Miami River in what is now Beaver Creek Township, Greene County, but was then a part of Hamilton County.

He was elected to the House of Representatives of the first General Assembly of Ohio which convened in Chillicothe, Mar. 1, 1803. At its first session the Assembly passed a law for the erection of Greene County and elected Maxwell as one of its first associate judges. On Dec. 7, 1803, he was chosen sheriff of Greene County, and through reëlection served till 1807. He was also active in the organization of the state militia; was commissioned captain, June 19, 1804, and lieutenant-colonel, Jan. 1, 1806, and was thereafter generally addressed as Colonel Maxwell. After his arrival in Cincinnati he met and married Nancy Robins, and of this union were born eight children. Maxwell died and was buried on his farm in Greene County in 1809. His widow, who later married John White, died Nov. 9, 1868, in the 108th year of her age.

[Files of the *Centinel of the North-Western Territory* still exist; the only known copy of the first issue is in the Library of the Ohio State Archaeol. and Hist. Soc., Columbus. Sources include Maxwell's Salutatory in the *Centinel*, Nov. 9, 1793; interview with Mrs. Nancy Maxwell White, former wife of William Maxwell, reprinted in the *Xenia Gazette*, Jan. 26, 1869; manuscript records from the office of the Governor of Ohio, 1803–06; manuscript journal of the legislature of the Northwest Territory, 1795; C. B. Galbreath, "The First Newspaper of the Northwest Territory," *Ohio Archaeol. and Hist. Quart.*, July 1904; "Legislature of the Northwestern Territory, 1795," *Ibid.*, Jan. 1921; *The Ohio Newspaper*, vol. X, no. 4, pp. 9–10; D. C. McMurtrie, "Antecedent Experience in Kentucky of William Maxwell, Ohio's First Printer," *The Filson Club Hist. Quart.*, July 1931; R. G. Thwaites, "The Ohio Valley Press Before the War of 1812–15," *Proc. Am. Antiq. Soc.*, n.s., XIX (1908); W. H. Venable, *Beginnings of Literary Culture in the Ohio Valley* (1891).]

C. B. G.

MAXWELL, WILLIAM (Feb. 27, 1784–Jan. 10, 1857), lawyer, college president, was born in Norfolk, Va., the son of James and Helen (Calvert) Maxwell, natives of Scotland. The father was "general superintendent" of the Virginia fleet. William prepared for college chiefly under the tutorship of Rev. Israel B. Woodward of Wolcott, Conn., and graduated from Yale in 1802 at the age of eighteen. He studied law in Richmond, Va., and in 1808 was admitted to practice at the Norfolk bar. His brilliant talents soon gave him a leading position among the attorneys of Virginia and a reputation beyond the borders of the state. He was noted also for his keen wit and oratorical abilities. His readiness was remarkable; his addresses were never written; and if he was "knocked up at midnight and requested to speak, he would make a finer speech than anyone else could have done after deliberate preparation" (Grigsby, *post,* p. 39). Having literary tendencies, he published in 1812 a small volume entitled *Poems.* Although attributed to Maxwell, *Letters from Virginia,* a translation from the French issued anonymously in 1816, was probably the work of George Tucker. In 1827 Maxwell was elected editor of the *New York Journal of Commerce,* but he retained his home in Norfolk, and held the position for only about a year. In 1828 he presented to his native town a lyceum for lectures and scientific experiments.

From 1830 to 1832 he was a member of the Virginia House of Delegates. Elected to the state Senate for an unexpired term, he was returned for the following term, serving in all from 1832 to 1838. During this period, 1835, he published his most ambitious library work, *A Memoir of Rev. John H. Rice, D.D.,* valuable not only as a biography but also as a sidelight on Presbyterian history. In 1836 Hampden-Sidney College conferred on him the degree of LL.D., the third it had awarded in a period of more than sixty years. He was at the same time elected a trustee and in 1838, president of the college, a position which he held until 1844. While president he married Mary Robertson.

Upon his resignation he removed to Richmond where he practised and taught law. He was an active member of the Virginia Colonization Society and of the Virginia Bible Society. With others he reëstablished the Virginia Historical Society, and from 1848 to 1853 was editor of the *Virginia Historical Register.* Of his many addresses, only one was published, *An Oration on the Improvement of the People,* a plea for better education in Virginia, delivered at the anniversary of the Literary and Philosophical Society of Hampden-Sidney, September 1826. An unpublished manuscript of his, now in the Virginia State Library, Richmond, "My Mother's Memoirs," which records events of Revolutionary days, is of historical value. He died near Williamsburg, Va., and was buried in Hollywood Cemetery, Richmond.

[F. B. Dexter, *Biog. Sketches Grads. Yale Coll.,* vol. V (1911); H. B. Grigsby, in *Bull. of Hampden-Sidney Coll.,* Jan. 1913; W. H. T. Squires, *William Maxwell, A Virginian of Ante-Bellum Days* (n.d.), and article in *Union Seminary Rev.,* Oct. 1918, supplemented and corrected by J. D. Eggleston, *Ibid.,* Jan. 1919; *Southern Argus* (Norfolk), Jan. 15, 1857; *Richmond Enquirer,* Jan. 16, 1857.] J. D. E.

MAXWELL, WILLIAM HENRY (Mar. 5, 1852–May 3, 1920), educator, was the son of John and Maria (Jackson) Maxwell and a descendant of John Knox, the great Scotch reformer. The second of three children, he was born at Brigh Manse, Stewartstown, County Tyrone, Ireland. His father, a Presbyterian clergyman of more than parochial reputation, tutored him in the classics after the local national schools had grounded him in the common branches. Later the Rev. George MacCloskie taught him mathematics and modern languages, ultimately sending him to the Royal Academical Institution at Belfast. Thence he proceeded to Queen's College, Galway, where he took his bachelor's and master's degrees with honors (1872 and 1874), especially distinguishing himself in metaphysics and English and classical literature. His last two years he supported himself by teaching, being concurrently sub-master in the Royal Academical Institution and lecturer in the Ladies Collegiate Institute. Originally he planned to read law, but when he failed by a single vote of the secretaryship of the "Liberal Association" with its annual stipend and when no further financial assistance from his family was in sight, he decided to seek his fortune in the United States.

Arriving in America (1874) armed only with a letter to President McCosh [*q.v.*] of Princeton, Maxwell found entrance into the public schools barred because he lacked the patronage of a ward boss. This initial discouragement and a letter of introduction to Whitelaw Reid [*q.v.*] led him to try journalism. Work as reporter for the *New York Tribune* and the *New York Herald* and as associate editor of the *Metropolitan Weekly* was followed by five years spent as managing editor of the *Brooklyn Times.* From this vantage-point he returned to his interest in education with a series of powerful articles on the needs and future development of the public-school system. He succeeded in gaining an appointment as teacher and lecturer in the evening schools of Brooklyn; in 1882 was appointed associate superintendent of schools; and in 1887, superintendent. To this office he was thrice reëlected. When the greater city of New York was chartered, Manhattan desired Andrew S. Draper [*q.v.*] for the new joint superintendency of schools, while Brooklyn demanded Maxwell. On Draper's recommendation Maxwell was chosen (1898). Here in three stormy terms he achieved his greatest successes. Once on motion of the opposition his salary was raised. When his health failed in 1917 the city charter was amended so that he could retire as superintendent emeritus with full pay.

Few professional educators have been so frequently criticized or so consistently vindicated as was Maxwell. Among other struggles, he contended for vocational education and the enrichment of the elementary-school curriculum in social content, but insisted always upon a curriculum hacked and hewed down to fundamentals. He aided in the diversification of the educational ladder to permit of kindergartens, summer, and continuation schools, and schools for the atypical. He helped to organize the public high-school system and even conducted some early experiments in intermediate schools. Overcrowding of school buildings with consequent part-time attendance presented a problem which he never quite solved. Playgrounds, free meals and eyeglasses for poor children were all part of his program. To gain all these he had to spend the public's money generously. Fought by the board of estimate and apportionment, he became an advocate of financial independence for city boards of education. He placed the city's teaching personnel on a high plane by securing the passage of a law requiring high and normal school preparation for all teachers of the city's schools. The achievement in which he took the greatest personal pride, however, was his placing the appointment and promotion of teachers on a merit basis, beyond the reach of politicians.

His leadership, later demanded in regional, state, and national educational associations, was finally crowned with the presidency of the National Education Association in 1905. An anniversary collection of excerpts from his more important educational pronouncements was published in 1912 under the title, *A Quarter Century of Public School Development*. On his death the *Educational Review*, of which he was a founder and editor, rated him, together with William T. Harris and Andrew S. Draper, as among the three greatest American educators since the time of Horace Mann. Although he was not the equal of Harris as an educational philosopher, he was unsurpassed in the skill with which he managed lay boards and politicians. Though both his lay and professional enemies charged him with autocratic tactics, the courage and fierceness with which he fought for his high standards was an inspiration to those despairing of efficient public service in American democracy. Over six feet in height and of vigorous frame, he made an impressive appearance. In 1877 he married Marie A. Folk. A son and a daughter were born to them.

[Extensive obituary notices appeared in *N. Y. Evening Journal*, May 3, 1920; *N. Y. Times*, *N. Y. Tribune*, *Sun*, *N. Y. Herald*, and *Brooklyn Eagle*, May 4, 1920; the *Sun* and *Times* included editorials on May 4 and 5 respectively. A pamphlet, *The Election of William H. Maxwell as City Supt. of Schools Emeritus* (1918), sketches his career, while the *Educ. Rev.*, June 1920, and *School and Society*, May 15, June 26, 1920, contain estimates of his life. M. I. MacDonald, "Dr. Maxwell as Educator," unpublished doctor's dissertation at N. Y. Univ., is a mediocre evaluation of his educational labors but contains a nearly complete catalogue of his writings. A letter, July 26, 1930, from his sister, Mrs. A. M. Browne, a resident of Ireland, gives a full account of the Irish setting of his life.]

J. S. B.

MAY, EDWARD HARRISON (1824–May 17, 1887), historical and portrait painter, was born in Croydon, England. He was brought to the United States as a boy of ten by his father, the Rev. Edward Harrison May, a Reformed Dutch clergyman, who had been called to a pastorate in New York. The May family was one of culture and talent. Edward himself had unusual ability as a draftsman, a mathematician, and civil engineer, but he abandoned engineering for the art of painting and took up training under Daniel Huntington. His early work met with some success in New York. Aided by other young painters, he made a panorama of "The Pilgrim's Progress," which was exhibited in several cities and proved profitable. He soon left for Europe, and thereafter most of his life was spent abroad.

In 1851 he was working in Thomas Couture's studio in Paris. Later he made several trips to Italy to study the work of the old masters. He also made several visits to England, where he painted a number of portraits. In Paris he made exceptionally good copies of some of the old Italian works in the Louvre, including Titian's "Entombment" and Murillo's Madonna. As early as 1855 he began to exhibit pictures at the Salon. His "Death of a Brigand," which received a medal, is now the property of the Pennsylvania Academy of the Fine Arts. Couture thought highly of his "Cardinal Mazarin Taking Leave of his Pictures in the Louvre," and Théophile Gautier warmly praised his "Francis I Lamenting the Death of his Son." These typical Salon canvases, with a score or more of other elaborate historical compositions, were hung in the Salon between 1855 and 1885. Notable examples were the "Last Days of Christopher Columbus" (1861) and "Milton Dictating to his Daughters" (1883). The French critics were more than merely respectful in their comments on his work. The *Annales Historiques* alluded to the exactitude and firmness of his drawing, the harmony and depth of his color, and his striking veracity of expression.

Among May's many portraits were those of Gen. John Meredith Read, United States consul-general in Paris, Edouard de Laboulaye, the historian, Anson Burlingame, United States minister to China, Jerome Bonaparte, Count A. E. de Gasparin, William Lewis Dayton, United States minister to France, and other personages of the time. His large picture of Lady Jane

Grey taking leave of the constable of the Tower as she went to her execution was acquired by Joseph Harrison, Jr., of Philadelphia. Other important historical and genre pieces came to the United States. "Mary Magdalen" and "The Brigand" are in the permanent collection of the Metropolitan Museum, New York.

May's pictures were unquestionably academic, and they had the excellences and defects of the type. Like Hunt, he mastered the method of work taught by Couture, but, unlike Hunt, he continued to use it throughout his career. He was a first-rate draftsman, and his compositions are very well organized in the conventional manner of the old painters. Isham remarks that there is no intensity of personal emotion in his work; on the other hand they make no appeal to the gallery by excess of sentiment. During the Franco-Prussian War of 1870 May served as captain of an American ambulance corps at the front, for which he was awarded a medal by the French government. He died at Paris in his sixty-fourth year.

[Samuel Isham, *The Hist. of Am. Painting* (1905); H. T. Tuckerman, *Book of the Artists* (1867); *Illustrated Cat.: Paintings in the Metropolitan Museum of Art* (1905); *Galignani's Messenger* (Paris), May 19, 1887.]

W. H. D.

MAY, SAMUEL JOSEPH (Sept. 12, 1797–July 1, 1871), Unitarian clergyman and reformer, was born at Boston, Mass., the son of Col. Joseph May and Dorothy (Sewall) May, and brother of Abigail May who became the wife of Amos Bronson Alcott [*q.v.*]. His father was descended from John May of Mayfield, Sussex, who was admitted a freeman of Roxbury, Mass., in 1641; his mother was a descendant of Judge Samuel Sewall [*q.v.*]. Their home was a place where cheerful and practical piety was much in evidence. The father stanchly supported the rational teachings of Dr. James Freeman of King's Chapel, and May himself never felt anything but horror for "the heart-withering theology of . . . Calvin" (*Brief Account*, p. 6). After graduating from Harvard in 1817 and teaching in small schools, he read divinity under Norton and Ware in Cambridge, gladly adopting the liberal doctrines now known as Unitarian. For some months he assisted Dr. William Ellery Channing at his Boston church. In 1822 he was ordained, and three years later, June 1, 1825, he married Lucretia Flagge Coffin.

May's energetic life was spent in pastoral duties and in humanitarian services. As a pastor, he served churches at Brooklyn, Conn., 1822–36; South Scituate, Mass., 1836–42; and Syracuse, N. Y., 1845–67. He had small interest in expounding systematic theology, but an unflagging ambition to convert men to the life of personal righteousness, marked by "the spirit of true goodness, active benevolence, stern integrity, moral courage." His gentle and cheerful nature did much to disarm the hostility of his orthodox critics. As a humanitarian, he worked ardently in the service of many reforming causes. He was a disciple of the venerable Noah Worcester in the movement for universal peace, writing and speaking much in its favor. He organized the Windham County (Conn.) Peace Society in 1826, and twelve years later called the convention of the American Peace Society which gave birth to the New England Non-Resistance Society. This association was too extreme for May to support, however, although he was always a friend of peace. When the Civil War began, he modified his views somewhat, but could not bring himself to urge men to enlist. As an advocate of temperance, he persuaded many retailers to cease selling liquor, converted scores of persons to abstinence, drilled youngsters in a Cold Water Army, and preached effectively on the theme for a generation. But he preferred the pledge system and individual self-control to prohibitory laws. In vigorous fashion, he championed equal rights for women, and wrote and spoke much in defense of his position. He cooperated heartily with Lucretia Mott [*q.v.*] and gave the public sentiment of the times a rude shock by inviting Angelina Grimké to occupy his pulpit and address his congregation on abolitionism. In his widely circulated sermon-pamphlet, *The Rights and Condition of Women* (1846), he asserted that "if the people have the right of self-government, then I am unable to see why a half of the people have a right to govern the whole." He played a part in promoting the cause of efficient popular education and while at Brooklyn called a convention (May 1827) to discuss the improvement of the common-schools in Connecticut; later, at Horace Mann's earnest request, he served from 1842 till 1844 as principal of the Normal School at Lexington, Mass. At all times he did much to soften the asperities of American educational practice. May took great pride in his service as an abolitionist. He knew Garrison well, attended the Philadelphia Convention of 1833, acted as general agent and secretary of the Massachusetts Anti-Slavery Society for more than a year, gave substantial aid to Prudence Crandall [*q.v.*] in her time of need, counseled resistance to the Fugitive-slave Law, and in 1851 took part in the public rescue of a slave. He helped negroes to reach Canada, his house being a station on the Underground Railroad. Kindly and brave, with a rich fund of sympathy, he gave of himself without stint to so many humanitarian tasks, great and small, that he thoroughly earned Bronson Alcott's epithet: "the Lord's chore boy."

[May gave his collection of anti-slavery material to Cornell University. His literary remains consist of sermons, addresses, reports, etc., on humanitarian themes. Of special interest are his autobiographical discourse, *A Brief Account of His Ministry* (1867); and *Some Recollections of Our Anti-slavery Conflict* (1869). See also *Samuel Joseph May* (1871); *Memoir of Samuel Joseph May* (1873), prepared by G. B. Emerson, S. May, and T. J. Mumford; *New-Eng. Hist. and Geneal. Reg.*, Apr. 1873; *Autobiog. of Andrew Dickson White* (2 vols., 1905); *Christian Register*, July 8, 15, 1871; *N. Y. Times*, July 3, 1871.] F. M.

MAY, SOPHIE [See Clarke, Rebecca Sophia, 1833–1906].

MAYER, ALFRED GOLDSBOROUGH [See Mayor, Alfred Goldsborough, 1868–1922].

MAYER, ALFRED MARSHALL (Nov. 13, 1836–July 13, 1897), physicist, nephew of Brantz Mayer [*q.v.*], was born in Baltimore, Md. His parents were Charles F. Mayer, a distinguished member of the Baltimore bar, and his second wife, Eliza Blackwell. The father, expecting his son to follow the law, sent him for schooling in the classics to St. Mary's College, Baltimore, but the boy early showed that his bent was toward science, and at sixteen became a machinist in the shop of a Baltimore engineer. Here and in the drafting-room he worked for some two years, then began to acquire a small practice as analytical chemist, and before he was nineteen published his first scientific paper, on a new apparatus for the determination of carbonic acid (*American Journal of Science*, no. 57, 1855). This early work won the approval of Joseph Henry [*q.v.*], through whose influence Mayer was appointed assistant professor of physics and chemistry in the University of Maryland at the age of twenty, and two years later, to a similar position at Westminster College, Fulton, Mo. From 1863 to 1865 he studied physics, mathematics, and physiology at the University of Paris, being a pupil of the distinguished physicist Regnault. In 1865 he became professor of physical sciences in Pennsylvania College, Gettysburg, and two years later was called to the chair of physics and astronomy at Lehigh University. Here he designed and equipped the astronomical observatory given to the university by Robert H. Sayre [*q.v.*]. Chosen to accompany the expedition sent out by the office of the United States Nautical Almanac to make observations of the solar eclipse of Aug. 7, 1869, he directed the taking of some forty photographs with results accounted as remarkable in those early days of photography (*Journal of the Franklin Institute*, October 1869; *Proceedings of the American Philosophical Society*, vol. XI, 1871). He published observations of Jupiter (*Journal of the Franklin Institute*, August 1870) and a number of papers on electricity, heat, and magnetism.

In 1871 he was invited to the newly founded Stevens Institute of Technology to organize and conduct the department of physics, and was identified with that institution thenceforth until his death. The exceptional instrumental equipment provided for him, together with proximity to New York, afforded him intellectual stimulus, and he began here the series of experiments on acoustics, reported in the *American Journal of Science*, 1872–96, which made him "decidedly the leading authority on this subject in America" (Stevens, *post*, p. 263). During his quarter-century at Stevens he published, in a dozen or more of the leading scientific magazines in America and Europe, fifty-four papers embodying the results of original research on subjects dealing mostly with sound, heat and light, gravity, and electricity. In addition he devised a number of measuring instruments; wrote three books of a popular character: *The Earth a Great Magnet* (1872), *Light* (1877), with Charles Barnard, and *Sound* (1878); and prepared several articles for cyclopedias and technical journals.

Between 1881 and 1889 he achieved a reputation as an amateur of outdoor sports. In 1884 he won first prize at the amateur Minnow-Casting Tournament of the National Rod and Reel Association with a rod of his own invention; he contributed a number of articles on sporting subjects to the *Century Magazine*, and edited *Sport with Gun and Rod in American Woods and Waters* (1883). In 1890, moving from his country place near Maplewood, N. J., into the city, he resumed his activity in science and published some sixteen or seventeen papers before his death. He was married in 1865 to Katherine Duckett Goldsborough, by whom he had one son, Alfred Goldsborough Mayor [*q.v.*], who changed the spelling of the family name. After the death of his wife he was married, in 1869, to Louisa Snowden. Two sons were born of the second marriage. Among the honors accorded Mayer for his scientific work were the degree of Ph.D. granted by Pennsylvania College in 1866—his only academic degree—and election to the National Academy of Sciences.

[A. G. Mayer and R. S. Woodward, in *Nat. Acad. Sci. Biog. Memoirs*, vol. VIII (1919), with biblog.; W. Le Conte Stevens, in *Science*, Aug. 20, 1879; *Morton Memorial: A Hist. of the Stevens Inst. of Technology* (1905), ed. by F. DeR. Furman; *N. Y. Times*, July 14, 1897.] F. DeR. F.

MAYER, BRANTZ (Sept. 27, 1809–Feb. 23, 1879), lawyer, author, was born in Baltimore, Md. His father, Christian Mayer, a native of Ulm, Württemberg, came to Maryland in 1784 and became a trader—later president of a local insurance company and consul-general of Württemberg in the United States. He married Anna Katerina Baum of Kutztown, Pa. Their son, named for Lewis Brantz, his father's partner, was educated partly in the Baltimore schools and at St. Mary's College (Sulpician), but largely by a private tutor. At eighteen he traveled to China and India, studying law by the way. He completed his law course at the University of Maryland, and, on admission to the bar in 1832, visited Europe, stopping for a while at Ulm. After his return he practised law until 1841, when he went to Mexico as secretary of the United States legation.

Evidently his mind turned to history, for in 1844 on his return to Baltimore he was instrumental in founding the Maryland Historical Society, of which he subsequently became president (1867–71). In this year he published *Mexico as It Was and as It Is* (1844), which ran through three editions. It was well-timed, for the United States was on the verge of the Mexican War. Though the book was on the whole a scholarly work, its references to the Catholic Church caused heated controversy. In 1845 Mayer edited, for the Historical Society, the *Journal of Charles Carroll of Carrollton, during His Visit to Canada in 1776,* a valuable record which was republished by the Society in 1876. As president of the Library Company of Baltimore, he directed the erection of the Atheneum Building in 1846. In 1851 he published *Tah-Gah-Jute: or Logan and Captain Michael Cresap* (rev. and enl., 1867), defending Cresap [*q.v.*] from the charge of murdering the family of the Indian, James Logan [*q.v.*]. This was followed by *Mexico, Aztec, Spanish and Republican* (2 vols., 1851) and *Calvert and Penn* (1852). In 1854, he edited and published *Captain Canot; or Twenty Years of an African Slaver,* illustrated by his nephew, Frank Blackwell Mayer. It was a highly colored account, though evidently based on fact; seventeen thousand copies were sold, and it was republished in London and Paris, with a New York edition as late as 1928.

In 1851 and again in 1855 Mayer was called to Louisiana as executor of the will of John McDonogh [*q.v.*], and in this capacity drew the plan and charter of the McDonogh School near Baltimore. Retiring from practice in 1855, he continued to interest himself in writing, contributing articles to the *Baltimore American,* of which he was an editor. Other works of his include: "Observations on Mexican History and Archaeology," in *Smithsonian Contributions to Knowledge,* vol. IX (1857); *Outlines of Mexican Antiquities* (1858); *Memoir of Jared Sparks* (1867); *Baltimore: Past and Present* (1871); and *Memoir and Genealogy of the Maryland and Pennsylvania Family of Mayer Which Originated in the Free Imperial City of Ulm, Wurtemberg, 1495–1878* (1878). In 1866 he urged the state to create an archive commission and depository, and eventually the state records were placed with the Historical Society under whose auspices publication of the *Archives of Maryland* has been carried on ever since, fifty volumes of this important series having appeared by 1933.

On the outbreak of the Civil War Mayer was elected chairman of the Maryland Union Central Committee, where his spirit of conciliation was valuable. He was appointed in 1862 a brigadier-general of Maryland volunteers, was active in recruiting troops, and in 1863 was appointed an additional paymaster. On Jan. 17, 1865, he was made a major and paymaster in the regular army, and the following year was brevetted lieutenant-colonel, to date from Nov. 24, 1865, for his services during the war. He continued in the pay department of the army until 1875, the last five years in California, and then retired with the rank of colonel.

He was an untiring student and an able writer; his work on local history is still considered authoritative. His writings on Mexico, still referred to, contain numerous errors, due, no doubt, to the vast extent of his subject, and the unreliable government statistics of the time, but he was a pioneer in encouraging the study of local material, especially on social history. By his first wife, Mary Griswold, whom he married Sept. 27, 1835, at St. Mary's, Ga., he had five daughters. She died Oct. 30, 1845, and on Nov. 15, 1848, at Baltimore, he married Cornelia Poor. Three daughters were born to this union. He was a member of the Unitarian Church.

[B. C. Steiner, "Brantz Mayer," in *Md. Hist. Mag.*, Mar. 1910, with many references; Mayer's *Baltimore: Past and Present* (1871), and *Genealogy*; John Bigelow, *Retrospections of an Active Life,* I (1909), 300–14; *Army and Navy Jour.*, Mar. 1, 1879; *Baltimore American*, Feb. 24, 1879.] J. L. W.

MAYER, CONSTANT (Oct. 3, 1829–May 12, 1911), genre and portrait painter, was born at Besançon, Doubs, France. His father, Salomon Mayer, merchant, was a native of Durmenach, Haut Rhin, and his mother, Joséphine Mayer, was born at Verdun, Meuse. He was educated in the schools of Besançon and at an early age went to Paris and entered the École des Beaux-

Arts. He also studied under Léon Cogniet, an able instructor, whose school was celebrated. Mayer lived and worked in Paris until 1857, when he came to the United States, opened a studio in New York, became a naturalized citizen, was elected an associate of the National Academy of Design, and met with considerable success. His genre pictures, usually rather large canvases, with life-size figures, were exhibited in the Academy; many of them were reproduced in black-and-white; and they made a strong appeal to the popular taste. His "Maud Muller" was exhibited in New York in 1867 and at the Paris Salon of 1870. The remark of a critic of 1867 to the effect that the girl's whole story was told by her eyes explains the painter's ability to catch facial expression as well as his shrewdness in capitalizing Whittier's sentiment. In 1869 the artist received the cross of the Legion of Honor from the French government. He was *hors concours* in the Salon, where he was a frequent exhibitor during his several visits to his native land.

In his "Song of the Shirt" and "Evangeline," Mayer showed his predilection for pathetic or mildly melancholy subjects, which, illustrating Hood's and Longfellow's familiar ballads, supplied perfect pictorial equivalents of the original poetic images, and thus made an easy conquest of the public. Less obviously sentimental were such scenes from everyday life as "The Organ Grinder," "Street Melodies," "The Knitting Lesson," and "The Vagabonds," but in "Love's Melancholy," shown at the Centennial exposition in 1876, he reverted to his most romantic vein. "A thoroughly competent painter," wrote Isham, "with a tendency to commonplaceness." The verdict is not unjust. His "Orphan's Morning Hymn," first exhibited in 1875, made a favorable impression on several subsequent occasions, especially at the first exhibition of American pictures held by the Art Institute of Chicago in 1888. The *Art Journal* (May 1875, p. 158) spoke of his work as being "invested with an expression of sentiment which reflects the highest credit upon his genius" and added that it showed no evidence of sentimentalism. "The First Communion," painted in 1886, was reproduced in an etching by Thomas Hovenden. "The Knitting Lesson" was prominent in the Prize Fund exhibition held in New York in 1885. "Dimanche," a young Quakeress with a Bible on her lap, was exhibited at the National Academy of 1883, and at the Paris Salon of 1897. In the field of portraiture Mayer met with a fair degree of success. Among his best-known sitters were Generals U. S. Grant and Philip H. Sheridan. About 1895 Mayer returned to France, and the remaining years of his life were spent in Paris, where he died in the spring of 1911. One of his pictures, "Femme iroquoise de l'Amérique du Nord," is in the art museum of his native city of Besançon. It was shown in the Paris Salon of 1869.

[C. M. Kurtz, *Am. Acad. Notes*, 1881, 1883, 1885; *Aldine*, Nov. 1875; Samuel Isham, *The Hist. of Am. Painting* (1905); *La Chronique des Arts et de la Curiosité*, May 29, 1911; *Am. Art News*, June 17, 1911; *Boston Transcript*, May 16, 1911; Bulletin de Naissance de la Ville de Besançon; information from the *conservateur* of the public library of Besançon.]

W. H. D.

MAYER, EMIL (May 23, 1854–Oct. 20, 1931), laryngologist, was born in New York City, the son of David Mayer, a native of Prussia, and of Henrietta (Rosenbaum), of Bavaria. After receiving his preliminary education in the public schools and the College of the City of New York, he graduated in 1873 from the College of Pharmacy of the City and County of New York. He then took up the study of medicine and graduated from the Medical Department of the University of the City of New York in 1877. After serving as an interne at the hospital on Blackwell's Island he began the practice of medicine in New York City. From the outset he devoted himself particularly to diseases of the nose and throat, working after 1880 with Dr. Morris J. Asch [*q.v.*] at the New York Eye and Ear Infirmary. From 1893 to 1904 he was chief surgeon to the clinic for diseases of the throat in that institution, and then became attending laryngologist at the Mount Sinai Hospital. In 1919 he was appointed consulting laryngologist at the Mount Sinai Hospital.

Mayer was a pioneer in the performance of the operation of submucous resection of the nasal septum. In the *New York Medical Journal*, June 13, 1896, he described his method in this operation, and the instruments devised by him for the purpose. During the World War he served in the medical intelligence bureau of the American Red Cross. He was chairman of the section of laryngology of the American Medical Association in 1920; from 1915 to 1918 he was abstract editor of the American Laryngological Association, and was president of the Association in 1922. He also served as chairman of the section of laryngology of the New York Academy of Medicine and as president of the Academy of Ophthalmology and Oto-Laryngology. The Laryngological Society of Berlin elected him a corresponding fellow, and he was American correspondent of the *Centralblätt für Laryngologie*. When the Therapeutic Research Committee on Pharmacy and Chemistry of the American Medical Association undertook to investigate the advantages and dangers of local anesthetics, Mayer was chosen as chairman and as such submitted the report presented by the committee to the American Medical Association (*Local Anesthesia in Otolaryngology and Rhinology by James Joseph King . . . with Supplement on the Toxic Effects of Local Anesthetics . . . edited by Emil Mayer, M.D., Chairman, Research Committee on Local Anesthesia,* 1926). This report constitutes a most valuable contribution to the subject. Mayer was a frequent contributor to the periodical literature of his specialty. The papers which he read before the various societies of which he was a member were remarkable for their originality and for facility of expression.

In 1884 he married Louise Blume, who died several years before his decease. They had no children. Mayer suffered in his later life from organic heart disease and had retired from active practice some years before his death, which occurred at his home in New York City in October 1931. His genial disposition, kindness—especially toward the younger men—and wide erudition won him well-deserved popularity and respect among his professional colleagues.

[D. B. Delavan, in *Trans. . . . Am. Laryngological Asso.,* 1932; *Laryngoscope,* Nov. 1931; *Jour. Am. Medic. Asso.,* Oct. 31, 1931; bibliography of Mayer's writings in *Annals of Otology, Rhinology, and Laryngology,* Dec. 1931; *N. Y. Times,* Oct. 21, 1931; information from Dr. Delavan and Dr. M. C. Myerson, of New York; personal acquaintance.] F. R. P.

MAYER, LEWIS (Mar. 26, 1783–Aug. 25, 1849), German Reformed clergyman, was born at Lancaster, Pa., the third of the seven children of George Ludwig Mayer, a prosperous, well-educated tradesman, by his second wife, Maria Barbara Haller, and the seventh in descent from Melchior Mayer, who was made *Stadthauptmann* of the Free Imperial City of Ulm in 1550. Lewis' father had emigrated with his parents from Ulm to Frederick, Md., in 1751–52 and settled later in Lancaster. His death in 1793 interfered seriously with his son's education. At Frederick, Md., where Lewis was employed for a time, he attended an academy and was converted to the Reformed faith by the Rev. Daniel Wagner, who prepared him for the ministry. He was licensed in 1807 and ordained in 1808 by the Synod of the United States, and was pastor at Shepherdstown, Martinsburg, and Smithfield, Va. (now W. Va.), 1808–21, and at York, Pa., 1821–25. On Nov. 5, 1809, he married Catharine Line of Shepherdstown, who bore him a son and three daughters and died in 1820. Later he married Mary (Gonder) Smith of York, who survived him for almost sixteen years. In 1818, despite threats of violence, he preached the first English sermon ever delivered in the Second Street Reformed Church of Baltimore.

He was by this time one of the leaders of his denomination and especially prominent in the movement to secure an official theological seminary. In 1824 the Synod authorized the establishment of a seminary, which was to be affiliated with Dickinson College. Neither Philip Milledoler [*q.v.*] nor Samuel Helffenstein would accept the professorship; money and moral support were almost entirely lacking; and the prospect that the seminary would ever open was dark until Mayer himself agreed to undertake the work. His qualifications as a teacher of theology were probably as adequate as those of any other German Reformed minister of the time. He had a very respectable command of Greek and Latin, had mastered Dutch, and could read French and Hebrew; he was an excellent preacher in both German and English; and he was more than merely well-read in Reformed theology. To his courage and unselfishness at a critical juncture his denomination owes much.

After visiting the seminaries at Princeton and New Brunswick to obtain information about books and courses of study, he opened the seminary at Carlisle, Pa., to five students in the spring of 1825. The seminary failed to attract many students, partly because of opposition to it among the conservative German congregations and partly because of its location in a region chiefly Scotch-Irish. In 1829 Mayer, acting on his own initiative, moved it to York, where it began to prosper. Daniel Young was called in to assist him, and a preparatory school was started with the brilliant Frederick Augustus Rauch [*q.v.*] as principal. In 1835 the school was moved to Mercersburg and was reorganized as Marshall College; when the seminary was also removed there in 1837 Mayer resigned. Since no one was available to take his place, he resumed his professorship in 1838. His doctrinal position had by this time become somewhat low-church; he found himself in sharp disagreement with the high-church Rauch, who was preparing the way for the "Mercersburg theology," and in 1839 he resigned again. He spent the rest of his life in York, where he died. He was the author of *Expository Lectures, or Discourses on Scriptural Subjects* (1845), *The Sin against the Holy Ghost* (1867), and *History of the German Reformed Church* (1851), which brings the story of the Swiss Reformation down to the close of the year 1525. He was editor of the *Magazine of the German Reformed Church* from its first publication in 1827 until 1835. He accumulated much material relating to the German Reformed Church in Pennsylvania, and also published some sermons.

[Elias Heiner, "Life of the Rev. Lewis Mayer, D.D.," *Mercersburg Rev.*, May 1851, and prefixed to Mayer's *Hist. of the German Ref. Ch.* (1851); Henry Harbaugh, *The Fathers of the German Ref. Ch.*, vol. III (1872); Brantz Mayer, *Memoir and Geneal. of the Md. and Pa. Family of Mayer* (1878) and H. H. Maÿer, *The Maÿer Family* (1911); J. H. Dubbs, "The Ref. Ch. in Pa.," *Proc. Pa. Ger. Soc.*, vol. XI (1902); J. I. Good, *Hist. of the Ref. Ch. in the U. S. in the 19th Century* (1911).]

G. H. G.

MAYER, PHILIP FREDERICK (Apr. 1, 1781–Apr. 16, 1858), Lutheran clergyman, was born in New York, the son of George Frederick and Mary Magdalene (Kammerdiener) Mayer. His father was a Swabian, his mother a native of New York State. Mayer graduated from Columbia College with first honors in 1799 and studied for the ministry under John Christopher Kunze [*q.v.*], teaching meanwhile to support himself. The habit of early rising and morning study, formed in these years, remained with him through life and assisted his vigor of body and mind. One of his most treasured books was a Cruden's *Concordance*, inscribed in Latin, which Kunze presented to him on Trinity Sunday, 1801, to commemorate the preaching of his first sermon. He was licensed Sept. 1, 1802, by the New York Ministerium. On May 24, 1804, he married Lucy W., daughter of Daniel Rodman of New York, who with six of their eight children survived him. After serving the Lutheran congregation at Loonenburg (Athens), N. Y., 1803–06, he accepted a call to the newly organized St. John's Church in Philadelphia, the second strictly English Lutheran congregation in the country. Of this large and influential church he was pastor for fifty-two years. Although at this time his denomination was generally committed to parochial schools, he was an earnest advocate of public education. He was one of the founders of the Pennsylvania Bible Society, a trustee of the University of Pennsylvania, and the president of the Philadelphia Dispensary and of the Pennsylvania Institution for the Deaf and Dumb. In 1814 he declined the degree of D.D. from Harvard College on the ground that he was too young to receive such a distinction; later he accepted it from Columbia and from the University of Pennsylvania. He was indefatigable in visiting the sick and the afflicted of his immense congregation, refused to have an assistant, and took only a brief yearly vacation, when he would visit his mother and attend the meetings of the New York Ministerium. He was a close student of Biblical criticism and laid the exegetical foundation of his sermons with scholarly care. His reputation as a preacher was great and lasting, but like his German contemporary, Charles Rudolph Demme [*q.v.*], he would not allow his sermons to be published. With his master, Kunze, and his step-father, Frederick Henry Quitman [*q.v.*], he edited *Dr. Martin Luther's Catechism Translated from the German* (Hudson, N. Y., 1804); in 1806 he prepared another edition, with numerous changes, for his own congregation; and his final version of Luther's Short Catechism, with even greater revision, formed the chief part of his *Instruction in the Principles and Duties of the Christian Religion for Children and Youth* (1816; last edition, 1846). "It is doubtful whether any Lutheran pastor has surpassed him in purity and elegance of style in English writing. In literary culture he was thoroughly competent for the task. . . . Nine-tenths of this translation remains to-day as the accepted and enduring version; not more than one-tenth has been superseded in later revisions." (B. M. Schmucker, *post,* p. 105.) The dignity for which he was noted was not incompatible with his sallying forth to market every morning with a capacious basket under his arm. He conversed easily in Latin and German. His death occurred after an illness of several months. His daughter Mary became the wife of Robert Montgomery Bird and the mother of Frederick Mayer Bird [*qq.v.*]. His successor at Old St. John's was Joseph Augustus Seiss [*q.v.*].

[M. L. Stoever, *Memorial of Rev. Philip F. Mayer, D.D.* (1859), also in *Evangelical Rev.*, Oct. 1858; J. G. Morris, *Fifty Years in the Lutheran Ministry* (1878); B. M. Schmucker, "Luther's Small Catechism," *Luth. Ch. Rev.*, Apr., July 1886; *Press* (Phila.), Apr. 19, 1858.]

G. H. G.

MAYES, EDWARD (Dec. 15, 1846–Aug. 9, 1917), chancellor of the University of Mississippi, author, was born at "Montverde," near Jackson, Miss. His parents, Daniel and Elizabeth (Rigg) Humphreys Mayes, both natives of Virginia and the former a descendant of the Reverend William Mayes (or Mease) who had emigrated to America in 1611, moved from Kentucky to Mississippi in the late 1830's. In Kentucky Daniel Mayes had attained distinction in the state legislature, on the bench, and as professor of law in Transylvania University. The beginning of the Civil War found Edward at Bethany College, located in what is now West Virginia. He at once returned to Jackson and, though very young, assumed charge of a clothing store. In April 1864 he volunteered for service, became a private in the 4th Mississippi Cavalry, and served until the end of the war. When the University of Mississippi again opened its doors to students in October 1865, he was one of the youthful veterans in the freshman class. He received the liberal arts degree in 1868 and the law degree probably in 1870. On May 11, 1869, he was married to Frances Eliza Lamar, the daughter of L. Q. C. Lamar, and the granddaughter of Augustus Baldwin Longstreet [*qq.v.*]. He remained one year at the university as tutor in English and then practised law for several years, first at Coffeeville and then at Oxford.

From 1877 through 1891 he was professor of law in the University. From 1886 to 1889 he was chairman of the faculty, acting virtually as chancellor, and then filled the office of chancellor from its reëstablishment in 1889 until his resignation on Jan. 1, 1892. During his administration there were a number of material improvements and a reorganization of the curriculum. His legal training stood the university in good stead when he defeated J. Z. George [*q.v.*] in a controversy over the endowment act of 1880. As a result of his success the state continued to pay to the university the interest on the endowment lent the state. In the Mississippi constitutional convention of 1890 he was chairman of the committee on bill of rights and general provisions, and he was particularly noted for having originated the plan to aid in the maintenance of white supremacy by electing the officers of the state by the county electoral votes. The active practice of law in Jackson, including the district attorneyship for the Illinois Central Railroad, engaged his attention after he retired from the university, though he found time also to perform the duties of professor of law and dean of the law school in Millsaps College at Jackson. His prominence in religious affairs is indicated by the fact that in 1891 and in 1901 he was a delegate to the ecumenical conference of the Methodist Episcopal Church, South. He was an able and scholarly writer. He was the first president of the Mississippi Historical Society and contributed to the *Publications of the Mississippi Historical Society* (esp. vols. VI, XI, 1902–10). His chief writings were *Lucius Q. C. Lamar: his Life, Times and Speeches* (1896) and the *History of Education in Mississippi* (1899). He also prepared a short outline of legal study for the use of law students entitled, *Ribs of the Law* (1909), and *Genealogical Notes on a Branch of the Family of Mayes* (1928?).

[Biog. material in Edward Mayes, *Geneal. Notes on a Branch of the Family of Mayes* (1928?), p. 42, b–112, c–56; *Biog. and Hist. Memoirs of Miss.* (1891); *Report of the . . . Miss. State Bar Asso. . . . 1918* (1918); Dunbar Rowland, *Miss.* (1907), vol. III; *Who's Who in America*, 1916–17; *Who's Who in Miss.* (1914); *Hist. Cat. of the Univ. of Miss.* (1910); *Vicksburg Herald*, Aug. 10, 1917.] C. S. S.

MAYES, JOEL BRYAN (Oct. 2, 1833–Dec. 14, 1891), Cherokee chief, son of Samuel and Nancy (Adair) Mayes, was born in the old Cherokee Nation near what is now Cartersville, Ga. His father was a white man and his mother a Cherokee who was the daughter of Walter Adair and the grand-daughter of John Adair. Young Joel went to that part of Indian Territory which is now Oklahoma with his family in 1838, when the Cherokee were driven westward from Georgia. He attended the Cherokee public schools and in 1851 entered the seminary near Tahlequah, where he graduated in 1855. From 1855 to 1857 he taught school and then left the school room to engage in live-stock raising until the outbreak of the Civil War. Enlisting as a private in the 1st Confederate Indian Brigade, he was soon promoted to the office of paymaster and later to that of quartermaster, which he retained until the close of the war. He returned to his home in 1865 and resumed the business of farming and stock raising. He was appointed clerk of the district court and was elected judge of the northwestern circuit of the Cherokee Nation. During the next four years he was successively clerk of the commissioners court, clerk of the national council, associate justice, and chief justice of the Cherokee supreme court. In 1887 he was elected principal chief to succeed Dennis Wolf Bushyhead and was reëlected in 1891, but soon afterward he was stricken with influenza and died. He was married in 1857 to Martha J. Candy. Upon her death a few years later he married Martha M. McNair. She also died after some years, and he married Mary Vann. He was a Methodist, a Royal Arch Mason, and a man of highest character. For nearly forty years he worked hard for the educational and material advancement of the Cherokee people and few men have contributed more to their welfare.

[Letters and papers of Mayes in Cherokee Archives, Charles Eldred Papers, manuscript hist. of Mayes Family by J. M. Mayes, all in the Univ. of Okla. Manuscript Coll.; Emmet Starr, *Hist. of the Cherokee Indians* (1921), esp. pp. 184, 232, 263, 284, 293; J. B. Thoburn and M. H. Wright, *A Hist. of Okla.* (1929), vol. II.] E. E. D.

MAYHEW, EXPERIENCE (Feb. 5, 1673 N.S.–Nov. 29, 1758), missionary, translator, author, was the eldest son of John and Elizabeth (Hilliard) Mayhew, the grandson of Thomas Mayhew, Jr. [*q.v.*], and the great-grandson of Gov. Thomas Mayhew [*q.v.*], patentee of Martha's Vineyard. John Mayhew was minister to the churches of Tisbury and Chilmark, Martha's Vineyard, and also preached to the Indians. Experience was born at Chilmark (*Vital Rec-*

ords of Chilmark, Mass., 1904). Of the five Mayhews who engaged in missionary work he was preëminent. As a boy he became a master of the Indian tongue of the Vineyard and later studied other dialects (Letter to Paul Dudley, Mar. 20, 1721/22, published as *Observations on the Indian Language,* 1884, ed. by J. S. H. Fogg). In March 1693/94 he began preaching to the Indians and in October of that year was asked to be "teacher" of the English church in Tisbury. It is not known whether or not he accepted (Banks, *post,* I, 249). From this time until his death he was employed by the Society for the Propagation of the Gospel in New England (*Ibid.,* p. 253). Cotton Mather said of him that "in the evangelical service among the Indians, there is no man that exceeds that Mr. Mayhew, if there be any that equals him" (*Magnalia,* 1853 ed., II, 665, note). A lecture by Cotton Mather, *The Day Which the Lord Hath Made,* was translated into the Indian tongue by Mayhew in 1707. The Society employed him to make a new Indian version of the Psalms of David and the Gospel of St. John, which he did in the *Massachusee Psalter* (1709). Of this work J. H. Trumbull says: "Next to Eliot's Indian Bible, this is the most important monument of the Massachuset Language. His version has some of the peculiarities of the dialects of Martha's Vineyard, . . . but in literal accuracy and its observance of the requirements of Indian grammar, it perhaps surpasses even Eliot's" (*Proceedings of the American Antiquarian Society,* October 1873, pp. 60–61). An account of his visit to the Indians on the mainland, authorized by the Society, is preserved in "A Brief Journal of My Visitation to the Pequot and Mohegin Indians, 1713–1714." In 1720 Harvard College conferred upon him the honorary degree of A.M. It is probable that the *Indiane Primer* of 1720 was revised by Mayhew (J. C. Pilling, *Bibliography of the Algonquian Languages,* 1891, p. 252). He wrote *Indian Converts* (1727), probably the best known of his writings, to show that the Indian work was not in vain. His theological writings, of which *Grace Defended* (1744) was the most important, show him to have been a moderate Calvinist who deviated, as he himself realized, from the strictly orthodox. He seems to have spoken for a measure of free will against the doctrine of total depravity, and it has been said that he wrote in opposition to Jonathan Dickinson and Whitefield (Alden Bradford, *Memoir of . . . Jonathan Mayhew,* 1838, pp. 14–15). He was twice married: first, in 1695, to Thankful Hinckley, daughter of Governor Thomas and Mary Hinckley of Barnstable; and second, in 1711, to Remember Bourne, daughter of Shearjashub and Bathsheba Bourne of Sandwich. He preached until the last week of his life and died of apoplexy in 1758. Jonathan Mayhew [*q.v.*] was a son of his second marriage.

[There is an account of Mayhew in C. E. Banks, *The Hist. of Martha's Vineyard* (3 vols., 1911–25), I, 249–54, with genealogy, III, 305; and one by Thomas Prince, in *Indian Converts,* pp. 306–07. A number of MSS. are in the possession of the Mass. Hist. Soc., including a letter to Cotton Mather, 1723; Sermons in Indian and English, 1714–28; and the following papers: "Key to the Indian Language," "Of the Trinity," "Covenant of Grace," and "A Discourse on Human Liberty" (1752). Inserted in a copy of *Indian Converts* in the Boston Public Library is a manuscript by Zachariah, son of Experience, which contains a few facts about the father.]

R. F. F. T.

MAYHEW, JONATHAN (Oct. 8, 1720–July 9, 1766), clergyman, was born at Chilmark, Martha's Vineyard, the son of Experience [*q.v.*] and Remember (Bourne) Mayhew. After graduating with honors from Harvard in 1744, he was called to the pastorate of the West Church, Boston, in 1747, and there remained till his death. A volume of sermons published in 1749 won him favor abroad and soon procured him the degree of D.D. from Aberdeen. A vigorous thinker and ready writer, he was theologically in advance of his time; years afterward James Freeman [*q.v.*] of King's Chapel declared that Mayhew had anticipated him in all his theological conclusions. He preached a rational and practical Christianity based on the Scriptures and not on Calvin; he defended the right of private judgment, rejected the Trinitarian view as early as 1755, and affirmed the doctrine of free will (Eliot, *post*). With the American followers of Whitefield he had small patience. A true Puritan, he detested prelatical institutions and worked and wrote vigorously against them. As Dudleian Lecturer at Harvard in 1765 he delivered a sermon on *Popish Idolatry.* He roundly condemned the Society for the Propagation of the Gospel in Foreign Parts for its policy of sending Anglican missionaries into the settled parts of New England, and censured in strong terms the much-discussed scheme of introducing an American episcopate. He composed three controversial discourses in support of his position, one of them being a reply to a pamphlet by Archbishop Secker (A. L. Cross, *The Anglican Episcopate and the American Colonies,* 1902, ch. vi). When aspects of his theology were attacked by a neighboring minister, he replied with *A Letter of Reproof to Mr. John Cleaveland* (1764), in tone so disdainful and caustic that after a century and a half its pages still sting.

He was a stanch upholder of civil liberty against arbitrary rule; his mind fed upon Milton, Locke, Sidney, and the Bible, and from these writings derived liberal theories in government. His *Discourse Concerning Unlimited Submission and Non-Resistance to the Higher Powers* (1750) defended popular disobedience in cases where commands contrary to God's laws were enjoined (Baldwin, *post,* 44–45). After the repeal of the Stamp Act, he preached a sermon, *The Snare Broken* (1766), in which he counseled the people to observe the laws, but at the same time to have a watchful care for their rights. Though the sermon bore a dedication to William Pitt, Mayhew did not scruple to write: "I will not meddle with the thorny question, whether, or how far, it may be justifiable for private men, at certain extraordinary conjunctures, to take the administration of government in some respects into their own hands. Self-preservation being a great and primary law of nature . . . the right of so doing, in some circumstances, cannot well be denied" (p. 42). Ten years afterward that "extraordinary conjuncture" which he had envisaged occurred, and he was not the least of those whose preparatory labors had helped to bring about the event. In June 1766 he had proposed that the Massachusetts lower house send out circular letters to draw the colonies closer so that they might the more effectively defend their liberties.

Mayhew's friendship was sought by Thomas Hollis of London, and by other distinguished Englishmen, and he was the intimate of such provincial leaders as Otis, Quincy, and Samuel Adams. John Adams had a high regard for him, said he was a "transcendent genius," and that "To draw the character of Mayhew, would be to transcribe a dozen volumes" (*The Works of John Adams,* vol. X, 1856, p. 288). He had great learning and boundless industry. His enemies charged him with vanity and harshness and there is no doubt that he had a good deal of severity in his character, but since he was championing great causes, his friends largely glossed over these faults, and he was accounted a social and gracious person by those who knew him well. Worn out by heavy labors, he died at Boston in his forty-sixth year, survived by two daughters and his widow, Elizabeth (Clarke) Mayhew, whom he had married Sept. 2, 1756.

[Hollis Papers 1759–1771, and Belknap Papers, in the Mass. Hist. Soc. library; Francis Blackburne, *Memoirs of Thomas Hollis* (2 vols., 1780), with many letters and an engraved portrait of Mayhew; *Mass. Hist. Soc. Colls.,* vol. LXXIV (1918); William Tudor, *The Life of James Otis* (1823); J. W. Thornton, *The Pulpit of the Am. Rev.* (1860); A. M. Baldwin, *The New England Clergy and the Am. Rev.* (1928); F. H. Foster, *A Genetic Hist. of the New England Theology* (1907); Alden Bradford, *Memoir of the Life and Writings of Rev. Jonathan Mayhew, D.D.* (1838), eulogistic, poorly arranged, but containing much excellent source material; S. A. Eliot, *Heralds of a Liberal Faith* (1910), vol. I; C. E. Banks, *The Hist. of Martha's Vineyard,* vol. III (1911–25).]

F. M.

MAYHEW, THOMAS (1593–Mar. 25, 1682), patentee and first governor of Martha's Vineyard, missionary to the Indians, was baptized at Tisbury, Wiltshire, England, Apr. 1, 1593. His parents were Matthew and Alice (Barter) Mayhew. After apprenticeship, he became a mercer in Southampton (Banks *post,* I, 108, 110; III, 300). Before 1632 he settled in Medford, Mass., as factor for Matthew Cradock, London merchant, for whom he built a mill at Watertown, later acquiring and operating it himself. On May 14, 1634, he was admitted a freeman of the Bay Colony. He engaged rather unsuccessfully in mercantile ventures, acting also as agent for Cradock who, becoming dissatisfied, ended this relationship about 1637. From the first, Mayhew served on responsible committees appointed by the General Court. He was deputy from Medford in 1636, and between 1637 and 1644 from Watertown, where he served locally as selectman and commissioner and built a bridge across the Charles River.

In September 1641 he purchased, under Lord Stirling's patent, Martha's Vineyard, Nantucket, and the Elizabeth Islands, also securing under the Gorges patent a more valid title to the Vineyard, where his son Thomas [*q.v.*] settled with others about 1642 (Dukes County Deeds, VIII, 83; Experience Mayhew, *post,* p. 80; see also R. C. Winthrop, *Life and Letters of John Winthrop,* vol. II, 1867, p. 152). Thomas the elder followed about 1646, and thereafter acted as magistrate. The younger Thomas converted the Indian Hiacoomes [*q.v.*] to Christianity in 1643, and developed the work of Christianizing the natives until his death at sea in 1657. Thereafter his father continued and extended it throughout his own life. All the Vineyard, and many Nantucket, Indians became professed Christians, acknowledging Mayhew's rule. Their first church was organized in 1670, Mayhew refusing the pastorate because of his age and his magisterial duties. He governed first as magistrate in the Massachusetts manner, but a later tendency to govern as patentee through himself and his family was confirmed in 1671, when Lovelace, governor under the Duke of York, proprietary successor to Stirling and Gorges, commissioned him governor for life (New York Colonial MSS.; Deeds, III, 70). In 1673–74, when the Dutch again held New York, Mayhew's paternal rule was challenged by the Vineyard settlers, but not overthrown. His commission was afterward confirmed by Andros. During King Philip's War the Vineyard Indians, then the most fully civilized and Christianized in New England, remained entirely loyal to the English. Mayhew formed and armed an Indian guard, to which the common safety was entrusted. He died (1682) just short of eighty-nine years of age (Banks, I, 109, 247 note), active to the last as governor and father to the Indians, the first of five generations of Mayhews who were Indian missionaries. He was succeeded as missionary and chief magistrate respectively by his grandsons John and Matthew. Thomas Mayhew was married first, in England, to the mother of his son Thomas Jr., and second, about 1635, to Jane (Gallion?), widow of Thomas Paine, a London merchant. Four daughters were born of this second marriage.

[N. B. Shurtleff, ed., *Records of the Governor and Company of the Mass. Bay in New England* (1853), vols. I, II; account by Thomas Prince in Experience Mayhew, *Indian Converts* (1727); "Winthrop Papers," *Mass. Hist. Soc. Colls.*, 4 ser. VII (1865), 30–43; letters from Thomas Mayhew, Jr., on the Indian work in four of the "Eliot Tracts," *Mass. Hist. Soc. Colls.*, 3 ser. IV (1834), 69–260; Cotton Mather, *Magnalia Christi Americana* (1702); Matthew Mayhew, *A Brief Narrative*, etc. (1694), dealing with Vineyard politics; W. B. Sprague, *Annals Am. Pulpit*, vol. I (1857); C. E. Banks, *The Hist. of Martha's Vineyard* (3 vols., 1911–25), vol. I; L. C. M. Hare, *Thomas Mayhew, Patriarch to the Indians, 1593–1682* (1932).]

J. G. K., Jr.

MAYHEW, THOMAS (*c.* 1621–1657), Congregational clergyman, first English missionary to the Indians of New England, was the only son of Gov. Thomas Mayhew [*q.v.*] of Martha's Vineyard. The name of his mother is not known and few of the details of his early life are recorded. He was born in England and it is supposed that he came to America with his father in 1631 and that his boyhood days were spent at Medford and Watertown in the Massachusetts colony. With his father he was in 1641 granted the ownership and government of Martha's Vineyard, Nantucket, and the Elizabeth Islands. A settlement was planted on Martha's Vineyard in 1642 by a group of colonists under the leadership of the younger Thomas, at what is now Edgartown. A church society was early formed and the plantation's youthful leader, who had shortly before attained his majority, was called to its pastoral office.

His pity was aroused by the poverty and ignorance of the Indian inhabitants of the Vineyard and the islands adjacent. Acquiring a knowledge of their language, in which he became a recognized proficient, he undertook to convert them to Christianity. His first convert was Hiacoomes [*q.v.*], who accepted the white man's faith in 1643, three years before missionary work was begun on the mainland by John Eliot. Mayhew trained Hiacoomes and another Indian to preach to their fellows on Sundays, and himself conducted fortnightly services, spending more time in "familiar reasoning" than in the sermon itself (Prince, *post*, p. 286). In 1652 he opened a school to teach the Indian children to read. His labors progressed in spite of the early enmity of powwows and sagamores, who were generally against the new way. In time Indian priests and noblemen alike were converted.

The expenses of the mission were for many years borne by Mayhew out of his private purse. Devoting almost his entire time to the Indian service, he neglected his personal estate, which in consequence became so seriously impaired that " 'twas bare with him for food & rayment" (Thomas Mayhew, Sr., to John Winthrop, Jr., *Massachusetts Historical Society Collections*, 4 ser. VII, 1865, p. 35). The Indian mission at Martha's Vineyard was one of the first Protestant missions in the world to have more than ephemeral existence. Shortly before the founder's death the work came under the financial patronage of the Society for the Propagation of the Gospel in New England, an organization of philanthropists in London incorporated by Parliament to support the work of Mayhew and Eliot.

Mayhew sailed for England in 1657, accompanied by an Indian convert, with the double purpose of stimulating interest in missionary work and attending to matters of business connected with the patrimony of his wife, whose father had died seized of estates in Northamptonshire. The ship in which he took passage was lost at sea and the missionary was never heard of again. By his wife, Jane Paine, daughter of Thomas Paine, a London merchant, and Jane (Gallion?) Paine who married as her second husband the elder Thomas Mayhew, Thomas the younger had three sons, one of whom, John, became minister at Tisbury and Chilmark, Martha's Vineyard, and was the father of Experience Mayhew [*q.v.*]. In conjunction with John Eliot, Thomas Mayhew, Jr., was the author of a number of Indian tracts published in London. These included *The Glorious Progress of the Gospel* (1649) and *Tears of Repentance* (1653).

[Matthew Mayhew, *A Brief Narrative*, etc. (1694); Cotton Mather, *Magnalia Christi Americana* (1702); Daniel Gookin, "Historical Collections of the Indians in New England," *Mass. Hist. Soc. Colls.*, vol. I (1792); C. E. Banks, *The Hist. of Martha's Vineyard* (3 vols., 1911–1925); biography by Thomas Prince in Experience Mayhew, *Indian Converts* (1727); Mayhew's writings and other material in *Mass. Hist. Soc. Colls.*, 3 ser. IV (1834); L. C. M. Hare, *Thomas Mayhew, Patriarch to the Indians, 1593–1682* (1932).]

L. C. M. H.

MAYNARD, CHARLES JOHNSON (May 6, 1845–Oct. 15, 1929), taxidermist and naturalist, was born in West Newton, Mass., the son of Samuel and Emeline (Sanger) Maynard and a descendant of John Maynard who emigrated from England about 1638 and settled in Sudbury, Mass. When Charles was but twelve years of age his father died and the boy was forced within a few years to leave school and work on his mother's farm. Later he engaged in watchmaking, but from early youth he had been deeply interested in natural history, especially ornithology, and having learned something of taxidermy he soon turned his attention to this more congenial occupation.

As early as 1866 he did work for the Boston Society of Natural History, thus becoming acquainted with T. M. Brewer [*q.v.*], Henry Bryant, Alpheus Packard, and F. W. Putnam, and the association with these leaders in science undoubtedly brought him much inspiration and valuable knowledge. He was also employed by E. A. Samuels to secure natural history specimens for the Massachusetts state collection while he likewise furnished bird skins to such leading ornithologists as J. A. Allen, William Brewster, and Henry W. Henshaw [*qq.v.*], with whom he became well acquainted. In 1881 he moved his taxidermy shop and the natural-history establishment which he had developed to Boston, where it remained for many years. During all this time he was making collecting trips to various parts of the country. He made nine expeditions to Florida and five to the Bahamas, as well as visits to Grand Manan and the Magdalen Islands. All told his field work covered a period of fifty years.

He was a keen observer and did not hesitate to publish his observations. His first note, which appeared in the *American Naturalist* for December 1869, described the occurrence of the Baird's Sparrow at Ipswich, Mass., and commented on sexual differences in the painted turtle, the latter remarks being cited in Darwin's *Descent of Man* (1871; II, 28). The sparrow proved to be in reality a new species, the Ipswich Sparrow, which he subsequently described and named. These first papers were followed shortly by *Naturalist's Guide* (1870), a work that went through several editions and served as a first textbook for many a budding naturalist. Maynard published "A Catalogue of the Birds of Coos Co., N. H., and Oxford Co., Me.," with notes by William Brewster, in the *Proceedings of the Boston Society of Natural History*, vol. XIV (1872), and various notes in other standard journals, but most of his literary work consisted of books published by himself, even to the setting of the type and the making of the woodcuts which served as illustrations, as well as the tools with which they were cut. His most important works were *The Birds of Florida* (6 parts, 1872–78); *The Birds of Eastern North America* (16 parts, 1872–81; rev. ed., 1881); *Eggs of North American Birds* (1888), a monograph of the genus *Strophia*, in his *Contributions to Science* (three volumes covering a wide range of subjects, issued in parts, 1889–96); *Manual of North American Butterflies* (1891); *Handbook of Sparrows, Finches, etc. of New England* (1896); *The Warblers of New England* (1905); *Methods in Moss Study* (1905). There are also twelve volumes entitled *Walks and Talks with Nature*, published between 1908 and 1921.

While Maynard's observations were voluminous, often original, and covered a wide field, his lack of early scientific training was frequently evident in his publications and he fell short of the accomplishments that might have been his had he had a thorough foundation in science. Nevertheless, as one of his biographers has said, "It is possible this would have spoiled his independence and originality, and made a narrow specialist of him" (Townsend, *post*, p. 7). In addition to his business activities and his publications he conducted bird and nature walks which became very popular and served to stimulate the young people who made up his classes, as well as the adults, to a real interest in nature. He also prepared comprehensive school collections, gathering and preparing the specimens himself and constructing models of the more minute or perishable forms of life. He was an early member of the Nuttall Ornithological Club, its vice-president in 1876, and one of the editors of the first number of its *Bulletin*. In 1912 he became an associate member of the American Ornithologists' Union and was president of the Newton (Mass.) Natural History Society. He was married at Somerville, Mass., in 1883, to Elizabeth B. Cotter, by whom he had one daughter, who survived him. His death occurred at West Newton, in his eighty-fifth year.

[C. W. Townsend, in *Bull. Boston Soc. Nat. Hist.*, Jan. 1930; *Who's Who in America*, 1928–29; *Vital Records of Newton, Mass.* (1905); *Am. Ancestry*, vol. IX (1894); *Boston Transcript*, Oct. 15, 1929; slight personal acquaintance.]

W. S.

MAYNARD, EDWARD (Apr. 26, 1813–May 4, 1891), dental surgeon, inventor, was the son of Moses and Chloe (Butler) Maynard, both of English descent. He was born at Madison, N. Y., where his father, a farmer, was county sheriff and in later life a member of the New York legislature. After taking a preparatory course at

Hamilton Academy, Maynard entered the United States Military Academy at West Point when he was eighteen years old, but frail health caused him to resign during his first year there. He then began the study of dentistry, completing the course in 1835, and in 1836 settled in Washington, D. C., where he practised his profession, except for short intervals, for the rest of his life. From the very beginning of his career he was a profound research student and as early as 1836 announced the existence of dental fevers. This discovery was much discussed by the American Society of Dental Surgeons and was subsequently proven correct by the aid of microscope. He was the first to fill teeth with gold foil (1838), filling also the nerve canals in molars and bicuspid teeth, and he introducd the practice into Europe in 1845. He invented many improvements in dental instruments. From 1843 to 1846 he was co-editor of the *American Journal of Dental Science.* In 1846 he announced before the faculty of the Baltimore College of Dental Surgery the great diversity of situation, form, and capacity of the large cavities of the superior maxillaries, a discovery which proved of great importance in the treatment of these cavities. From 1857 until his death he held the chair of theory and practice in the Baltimore College of Dental Surgery and from 1887 to 1891 a like position in the National University, Washington.

In spite of his notable work in dentistry, however, Maynard is probably best known for his improvements in firearms. In 1845 he patented a system of priming consisting of a coiled, tape-like paper strip containing fifty fulminate caps spaced at equal distances apart, and a mechanism which automatically fed the tape, a cap at a time, from the recess of the gun in which it was protected, into position for firing. The Maynard tape primer, as it was called, was adopted by the federal government and generally used by the governments of Europe. In 1851 he patented an improvement in breech-loading rifles which, with subsequent improvements made by him in the succeeding fourteen years, brought about the general adoption of the Maynard rifle by governments and sportsmen throughout the world. Prior to 1886 he patented also a number of minor improvements in firearms, including a method of converting muzzle-loaders into breech-loaders; a method of joining two rifle or shotgun barrels to permit longitudinal expansion or contraction; and a device to indicate the number of cartridges in a magazine of a repeating firearm. For his work in the advancement of the science of dentistry and for his inventions in firearms he received many honors: he was designated court dentist to Emperor Nicholas I of Russia, was made a chevalier of the military order of the Red Eagle by the King of Prussia, and received from the King of Sweden a gold medal of merit. He held several honorary degrees and was an honorary member of the American Academy of Dental Sciences and the European Society of American Dentists, and a member of the International Medical Congress. He was twice married: in 1839 to Ellen Sophia Doty at Sherburne, N. Y., and in 1869 to Nellie Long of Savannah, Ga. At the time of his death in Washington he was survived by eight children, one of whom was George Willoughby Maynard [*q.v.*].

[E. W. Byrn, *Progress of Invention in the Nineteenth Century* (1900); Patent Office records; *A Coll. of Ann. Reports and Other Important Papers Relating to the Ordnance Dept.*, vol. II (1880); *The Maynard Rifle* (Mass. Arms Co., Chicopee Falls, Mass., 1886); V. D. Stockbridge, *Digest of Patents of Breech-loading and Magazine Small Arms* (1875); C. B. Norton, *Am. Inventions in Breech-loading Small Arms* (1880); obituaries in many dental journals, notably: *Dental Cosmos*, June 1891, *Am. Jour. Dental Sci.*, May 1891, *Archives of Dentistry,* July 1891; *Forest and Stream*, May 7, 1891; *Evening Star* (Washington), May 5, 1891; correspondence with family.] C. W. M.

MAYNARD, GEORGE WILLIAM (June 12, 1839–Feb. 12, 1913), mining engineer, was born in Brooklyn, N. Y., and in 1855 became a student in Columbia College, registering under the name of George William Toy. Before he reached his majority, however, his name had been changed to Maynard, and the names of his parents, as given in *Who's Who in America* (1910–1913), are George Washington and Caroline Augusta (Eaton) Maynard. He graduated from Columbia in 1859, having earned a large part of his expenses. In the following year he was employed as assistant by the professor of chemistry, and in 1860 he went abroad to study at Göttingen, where he specialized in chemistry, physics, and mineralogy, under Wöhler and other distinguished teachers. Later he went to the school of mines at Clausthal to study mining and mineralogy. His first professional engagement (1863–64) was to devise a suitable process for the treatment of pyritic ores at Wicklow, Ireland. This he successfully accomplished. Returning to the United States, he opened an engineering office and chemical laboratory under the firm name of Maynard & Tiemann. In 1864 he received the degree of A.M. from Columbia College. Being sent to Colorado the same year to examine a gold mine, he was so much impressed with prospects there that he established an engineering and assay office in Gilpin County which he maintained some three years. On June 12, 1865, he married Fannie Atkin of New York City.

Returning to the East in 1867, he took charge of a small plant for manufacturing sulphuric acid, on Staten Island, but in 1868 accepted the professorship of metallurgy and practical mining at Rensselaer Polytechnic Institute, Troy, N. Y. Four years later, since the Institute was without the means to establish an adequate school of mines, he returned to New York, and on his retirement the course was discontinued. In 1873 he went to England to endeavor to negotiate the sale of an iron property in the Southern states, and, to occupy himself in the intervals of the protracted negotiations, opened an office in London, becoming consulting engineer for sundry steel works in England and Wales. Sidney Gilchrist Thomas was then developing his modification of the Bessemer steel-making process which permits steel to be made from pig iron that is too high in phosphorus to be used in the ordinary or "acid" Bessemer. Maynard directed the first test in England, on a large scale, of the Thomas process. He remained abroad for six years, part of the time in Russia, where he erected a copper smelting plant at Vosskressensk for a British company.

During this time he had maintained his friendship with Thomas, and on returning to the United States in 1879 he succeeded in selling the American rights to the Thomas process, which never proved of any importance in this country, although it became the principal basis of the German iron industry, making available for use the extensive ore deposits of Alsace-Lorraine. Maynard wrote a careful historical account of the development of this process which was published in the *Transactions of the American Institute of Mining Engineers* (vol. XLI, 1911). The remainder of his life was spent in practice as consulting engineer with offices in New York, although his work took him to Nova Scotia, Newfoundland, British Columbia, the Yukon, Mexico, and Cuba. He was active in the development of technology, and in addition to being for two years a vice-president of the American Institute of Mining Engineers, he contributed to its *Transactions* a half-dozen technical papers, most of them dealing with iron and steel, and was a frequent contributor to other technical journals. He was interested in art and natural history and was active in organizations in those fields. Attacked during a professional journey with the disease of which he died, he was taken to the home of his daughter in Boston and died in that city in his seventy-fourth year. The notices of his death quite generally referred to him as "the dean of American mining engineers."

[*Bull. Am. Inst. Mining Engineers*, Apr. 1913; *Engineering and Mining Jour.*, Feb. 22, 1913; *Who's Who in America*, 1912–13; *Boston Transcript*, Feb. 13, 1913.]

T. T. R.

MAYNARD, GEORGE WILLOUGHBY (Mar. 5, 1843–Apr. 5, 1923), portrait, figure, and mural painter, born at Washington, D. C., was the son of Edward [*q.v.*] and Ellen Sophia (Doty) Maynard. At the age of twenty-three he began to study drawing and modeling under Henry K. Brown, the sculptor, and a year later he entered the school of the National Academy of Design, New York. Soon after this he became the pupil of Edwin White, historical painter, with whom he went to Florence in 1869. He subsequently visited Rome and thence found his way to Antwerp, where he continued his studies under J. H. F. Van Lerius at the Royal Academy of Art in that city. In 1873, in company with his friend Francis D. Millet, he went on a long journey through southeastern Europe. After an absence of five years he returned to New York in the spring of 1874. He exhibited a picture, "The Angelus," at the National Academy of Design in 1875, and thenceforth became a regular exhibitor of portraits and figure pieces. Among his subjects were "The Strange Gods," the "Ancient Mariner," and the "Bachelor's Breakfast." He was elected associate of the National Academy in 1882, and academician in 1885.

In 1876 Maynard sent to the Centennial exposition in Philadelphia "Vespers in Antwerp" and "1776." "In Strange Seas," a group of mermaids at play, was shown at the Paris exposition of 1900 and later hung in the Metropolitan Museum of Art, New York. "Sirens" and "A Sea Witch," similar motives, appeared at the Chicago exposition of 1893, and a composition entitled "Mermaids and Marines" was in the National Academy exhibition of 1890. At the St. Louis exposition of 1904 he exhibited "Surf" and "Sport." For a time he taught drawing classes at the Cooper Institute and at the National Academy. Among his portraits were those of William M. Evarts, Francis D. Millet, Kate Field, Chester Chapin, Judge Addison Brown, and C. C. Beaman. His numerous honors included the award of the Temple gold medal of the Pennsylvania Academy, 1884; a gold medal at the prize fund exhibition in New York, 1886; the Evans prize of the American Water-color Society, 1889; the Shaw prize of the Society of American Artists, 1897; and a special medal for decoration at the Chicago exposition, 1893.

Maynard made his first essay in mural painting as one of the assistants of John La Farge in the decoration of Trinity Church, Boston, in 1876. At the close of this undertaking, having become deeply interested in this branch of the art, he went abroad in 1877 and made a special study of the most important mural decorations in Italy, France, and England. He then took a studio in Paris (1878) but returned to New York before the end of that year, to find his services in great demand for decorative work in public and private buildings. His productions in this field include two panels in St. James' Church, Jamaica Plain, Mass.; figures on each side of the proscenium in the Metropolitan Opera House in New York—"The Chorus" and "The Ballet"; a large part of the interior decoration of the Ponce de Leon Hotel at St. Augustine, Fla.; parts of the entrance hall of the Boston Public Library; decorations in Keith's Theatre, Boston, in the houses of Whitelaw Reid and William Rockefeller at Tarrytown, N. Y.; in Sherry's ball-room and in the Waldorf-Astoria, the Manhattan, the Plaza, the Savoy, and the Imperial hotels, New York. His most important commission was that for the exterior decoration of the Agricultural Building at the World's Columbian exposition at Chicago, 1893. This, like many of his other decorations, was in the Pompeian style. According to Samuel Isham it was probably the most effective of any on the grounds, and it was for this work that he was awarded the special medal before-mentioned. Especially fine were the classic themes of the great main portico, with the figures of "Abundance" and "Fertility," the Greek frieze, and the side panels showing Cybele, the mother of all the gods, seated in a golden chariot drawn by lions, and King Triptolemus, sent forth in Demeter's car with its team of winged dragons, to instruct all the nations of the earth in farming. This was his *magnum opus*.

Less impressive though still felicitous are his Pompeian panels in the north and south corridors of the second floor of the Library of Congress, Washington. Here he chose for his designs eight floating female figures typifying "The Virtues"—clad in classic drapery and relieved against the rich red background of the wall. In his decorations of the southwest pavilion he was given four tympanums and the disc in a domed ceiling, and selected for his subjects in the tympanums "Adventure," "Discovery," "Conquest," and "Civilization" and for the disc appropriate qualities—"Courage," "Valor," "Fortitude," and "Achievement." The ingenuity of the conceptions and the excellent workmanship are in a measure nullified by the awkward shape of the spaces, especially in the tympanums. In his adaptations of the Pompeian style and color scheme he was eminently successful; moreover he manifested intelligent realization of the principles governing mural work. His decorations are rich in classical ideas treated with dignity and distinction and in pertinent historical allusions, though it is true that his symbolism is at times of a stereotyped order. Maynard was married on Dec. 26, 1907, to Louise Brownell of Brooklyn, N. Y. He died in New York City.

[W. A. Coffin, "The Artist Maynard," *Century Mag.*, Dec. 1890; Pauline King, *Am. Mural Painting* (1902); Herbert Small, *Handbook of the Lib. of Cong.*; *Who's Who in America*, 1922–23; Mich. State Lib., *Biog. Sketches of Am. Artists* (1916); *Cat. of Paintings in the Metropolitan Museum of Art* (1905); *N. Y. Times*, Apr. 7, 1923.]

W. H. D.

MAYNARD, HORACE (Aug. 30, 1814–May 3, 1882), congressman and Unionist, was the son of Ephraim and Diana Harriet (Cogswell) Maynard. Born in Westboro, Mass., he was prepared for college at Millbury Academy and was graduated with high honors at Amherst College in 1838. He went immediately to Knoxville, Tenn., where he had been appointed tutor in the preparatory department of East Tennessee College (now the University of Tennessee), and where he made his home for the remainder of his life. He was soon advanced to a professorship of mathematics. On Aug. 30, 1840, he was married to Laura Ann Washburn, the daughter of Azel Washburn of Royalton, Vt. They had seven children. In 1844 he deserted teaching for the practice of law and entered political life as a Whig. More than six feet tall, thin, straight, with a swarthy complexion, dark and piercing eyes, and long, black hair that fell to his shoulders, he was popularly supposed to have Indian blood in his veins and was commonly referred to as "the Narragansett." In his political campaigns he displayed oratorical powers and made effective use of invective and sarcasm. He was able and successful, but he never was an idol of the people. One explanation for this can perhaps be found in the fact that as a university professor he wrote an article in which he characterized the masses as "the common herd," with whom he desired "no fellowship" (Temple, *post*, p. 147). Certainly this was used to defeat him in his first campaign for a seat in Congress in 1853. Four years later, however, he was elected as a candidate of the Whig and American parties and two years later was reëlected.

In 1860 he campaigned for the Bell and Everett ticket in Massachusetts and in Tennessee. In the following year, when secession threatened, he joined forces with Andrew Johnson, Thomas A. R. Nelson, Oliver P. Temple, and William G.

Brownlow to fight bitterly against the withdrawal of Tennessee from the Union. His section of the state, the eastern, remained loyal to the Union, however, and he was returned in the August election to a third term in the federal Congress. In Washington he was an ardent but unsuccessful advocate of immediately sending a federal army to the relief of the Unionists of East Tennessee. In 1863 he became attorney-general of Tennessee under the military governorship of Andrew Johnson and held this office, much to the dislike of conservative Unionists, until the reëstablishment of civil rule under Governor Brownlow. He was then reëlected to Congress and took his seat in the House, on July 24, 1866, when Tennessee was readmitted to representation in that body. Here he broke with his fellow Unionist of Civil War days, President Johnson, and aligned himself with the radical Republicans. Consequently, he was thoroughly hated by the conservatives of his state, who took advantage of the first opportunity to gerrymander his district. He refused to retire to private life, however, and as a candidate for Congress from the state at large in 1872 defeated his two Democratic opponents, Andrew Johnson and Benjamin F. Cheatham [*qq.v.*]. Two years later he was the Republican party's unsuccessful candidate for the governorship. In 1875 his long and able services to his party were rewarded by President Grant, who appointed him minister to Turkey. After five years in Constantinople he returned to the United States to succeed David M. Key as postmaster-general in the cabinet of President Hayes. In the following year he retired to private life.

[*Vital Records of Westborough, Mass.* (1903); James Park, *Life and Services of Horace Maynard* (1903); *Report of the Proc. of the Numismatic and Antiquarian Soc. of Philadelphia . . . 1882* (1883); O. P. Temple, *Notable Men of Tennessee* (1912); *Amherst College Biog. Record of the Grads. and Non-Grads.* (1927); *War of the Rebellion: Official Records (Army)*, ser. 1, vols. VII, XVI (pt. 2), XX (pt. 2), ser. 2, vols. I, IV (1882–99); *Knoxville Daily Chronicle*, May 4–6, 1882.] P. M. H.

MAYO, AMORY DWIGHT (Jan. 31, 1823–Apr. 8, 1907), Unitarian clergyman, educator, was born in Warwick, Franklin County, Mass., the son of Amory and Sophronia (Cobb) Mayo, and a descendant of John Mayo of Roxbury who emigrated to Massachusetts with his mother and her second husband in 1632. Educated in a district school and the Deerfield Academy, he entered Amherst College at the age of twenty but because of ill health was unable to complete the freshman year. For a time he taught school and then studied theology with Hosea Ballou, 1796–1861 [*q.v.*]. He was ordained in 1846 and settled over the Universalist church in Gloucester, where he remained until 1854. There followed pastoral service in each of the following churches: Independent Christian Church, Cleveland, Ohio, 1854–56; Division Street Unitarian Church, Albany, N. Y., 1856–63; Church of the Redeemer, Cincinnati, Ohio, 1863–72; Church of the Unity, Springfield, Mass., 1872–80. Appointed in 1863 as non-resident professor of church polity and administration in Meadville Theological Seminary, he served this institution for thirty-five years, delivering usually a course of twelve or fifteen lectures on the principal denominations in the United States, at first annually and after 1883, triennially. During the year 1897–98 he also delivered lectures on the Ballou Foundation entitled "The New Education."

His interest in education, which began when he lived in Albany, developed strongly during his life in Cincinnati and Springfield. He was an active and able member of the school board in each of these cities. He was a leader of the "Christian Amendment Movement," which had for its purpose the incorporation in the federal Constitution of a provision guaranteeing the right to teach the Bible in public schools. When he moved to Boston in 1880 his greater ministry of education began. From 1880 to 1885 he was associate editor of the *Journal of Education.* From 1880 to 1900 he devoted himself as a private citizen to the development of education in the Southern states. During these twenty years he traveled two hundred thousand miles, visiting schools in the South and conferring personally with school committees and state legislatures. He gave freely his lectures, sermons, and counsel, his expenses being cared for by a few friends interested in education and by an annual grant, for some years, from the American Unitarian Association. Everywhere he was received with great cordiality and there was general recognition that he had contributed largely to the building up of the public-school systems of the South.

During his career as a clergyman he published *The Balance; or, Moral Arguments for Universalism* (1847); *Graces and Powers of the Christian Life* (1853); *Selections from the Writings of Mrs. Sarah C. Edgarton Mayo: With a Memoir by her Husband* (1849); *Symbols of the Capital or Civilization in New York* (1859). Educational publications include *Religon in the Common Schools* (1869); *The Bible in the Public Schools* (1870), with Thomas Vickers; *Talks with Teachers* (1881); and *Industrial Education in the South* (1888). From 1900, at the instance of the United States Commissioner of Education, Dr. William T. Harris, he devoted himself to writing a history of the American common-school. Many chapters had been published in the annual reports of the commissioner of education from 1893 on, but the work was not completed at the time of his death. Besides this series, he also published in both reports and Circulars of Information many articles on education, especially in the South.

Mayo's first wife, whom he married July 28, 1846, was Sarah Carter (Edgarton) Mayo [*q.v.*] of Shirley, Mass. She died July 9, 1848; on June 7, 1853, he married Lucy Caroline Clarke of New Brighton, Pa. His death occurred in Washington, D. C.

[C. G. Mayo, "The Mayo Family in the U. S." (1927), 2 vols., typewritten, in Library of Congress; *Jour. of Education,* Mar. 14, 28, Apr. 18, 1907; *Unitarian Year Book,* July 1, 1907; *Christian Reg.,* Apr. 18, 1907; *Evening Star* (Washington), Apr. 9, 1907; memoranda furnished by son, W. S. Mayo, Washington, D. C.]

D. A. R—n.

MAYO, FRANK (Apr. 18, 1839–June 8, 1896), actor, was born on Essex Street, Boston, and at the age of fourteen went to California with his parents by way of Cape Horn. When he became an actor he discarded his family name, McGuire. His first speaking part was the waiter in *Raising the Wind,* at the Adelphi Theatre, San Francisco, July 29, 1856. He lost his next job, at Maguire's Opera House, when as a super in *Pizarro,* he ruined a scene by mistaking a cue and cheering Rolla too soon. Junius Brutus Booth, Jr., the Rolla of the production, was so enraged that he insisted on Mayo's dismissal. Then Mayo acted for five weeks in George Chapman's company at Sacramento, but quit when no pay was forthcoming, went the rounds of the towns and mining camps with Charles Wheatleigh's troupe, and fell in with Edwin Booth, for whom he played De Mauprat in *Richelieu.* Finally, in 1863, he returned to Maguire's as leading man in the same company from which he had been so ignominiously expelled. He finished his San Francisco engagement June 14, 1865, sailed for New York by the Panama route, and made his Eastern début Aug. 8, 1865, as Badger in *The Streets of New York,* a part that he had originated on the Coast. Theatre-goers were astonished and delighted by the artistry with which he transformed Boucicault's crude sketch into something theatrically fine, and from then till his death Mayo was one of the most popular actors on the American stage.

His first New York appearance was as Ferdinand in *The Tempest,* at the Grand Opera House, Mar. 31, 1869. He appeared often, and with much satisfaction, in the leading rôles in Münch-Bellinghausen's *Ingomar,* Sheridan Knowles's *Virginius,* Bulwer Lytton's *Richelieu,* and other favorites of that class, of which his own *Nordeck* (1883), written in collaboration with John G. Wilson, was a characteristic example. *Hamlet* and *Macbeth* were in his regular repertory, and he was also an excellent Iago and Richard III. He was most popular, however, and was probably at his best, in American character parts. Two of these are inseparably associated with his interpretation of them. *Davy Crockett,* which was written for him by Frank Hitchcock Murdoch [*q.v.*], was first put on Sept. 23, 1872, at the Opera House, Rochester, N. Y., of which Mayo was the manager (*Rochester Democrat and Chronicle,* Sept. 23, 1872). It was then hardly a success, but Mayo tried it again from time to time, and after a few years it became extremely popular. On June 9, 1879, he began an English tour with it at the Alexandra Theatre, Liverpool. After its 2,000th performance Mayo lost track of the number of times he appeared in it. In its final form the play may have been as much his work as it was Murdoch's. Mayo was the author, also, of the stage version of Mark Twain's *Puddin'head Wilson,* which was first played at Proctor's Opera House, Hartford, Apr. 8, 1895. His interpretation of the title rôle was a masterpiece of restrained humor and mellow realism. He gave his last performance of the play at the Broadway Theatre, Denver, June 6, 1896. Two days later he died of heart disease on a train near Grand Island, Nebr. He was buried in West Laurel Hill Cemetery, Philadelphia. His wife and three children survived him.

[A. H. Quinn, *A Hist. of the Am. Drama from the Civil War to the Present Day* (1927), vol. I; Katherine Goodale, *Behind the Scenes with Edwin Booth* (1931); *Harper's Weekly,* June 22, 1895; *Phila. Inquirer,* June 9, 10, 13, 1896; *Public Ledger* (Phila.), *N. Y. Daily Tribune, Boston Herald, Boston Daily Advertiser,* and *Boston Transcript,* June 9, 1896; *N. Y. Clipper,* June 13, 1896; John Drew, *My Years on the Stage* (1922), pp. 98–99.]

G. H. G.

MAYO, MARY ANNE BRYANT (May 24, 1845–Apr. 21, 1903), pioneer Grange and Farmers' Institute worker, was born in Convis Township, Calhoun County, Mich., near Battle Creek. She was the eldest child of James Bryant and Ann (Atmore) Bryant. Her mother was born near Norwich, England, and came to America in 1840. Her father's family came originally from New England and New York. She was tutored while very young in a private school taught by two maiden aunts from New England. Later she graduated from the Battle Creek High School and began to teach a district school at seventeen. On Apr. 14, 1865, she was married to Perry Mayo, soon after his return from service in the Union army. He and his young wife purchased a farm and began their home-making in a log house in Marshall Township. As the years went by they continued their education through home study and Mrs. Mayo completed the four years' course of the Chautauqua Reading Circle. They were active in their home neighborhood organizations, and early in their married life they identified themselves with the Grange movement. They became officers in the county Grange and were early sent as delegates to the state Grange. In the latter Mrs. Mayo acted first as lecturer, and for twelve years as chaplain, holding this office at the time of her death.

Seeing what was being done for city and town women through social and study clubs, Mrs. Mayo believed that the Grange and kindred organizations offered corresponding opportunities to isolated farm women. She visited nearly every township in the state, talking at farmers' picnics, institutes, and other gatherings. As chairman of the woman's work committee of the State Grange, she introduced the "Fresh Air" feature by which many children of the poor in the cities were sent into the homes of the Grange for a few weeks' enjoyment of country life. She was also responsible for the origin and development of children's day in the Grange. In the activities of the Farmers' Institute she was a pioneer in holding separate women's sections at the meetings, a feature that later became permanent and accomplished much good. She was the leader and champion from the farm for a woman's department at the Michigan State Agricultural College. Her labors in this direction covered a period of from ten to fifteen years and culminated in the introduction, in 1897, of a course for women and in the erection in 1900 of a woman's building. In recognition of her services the Michigan state board of agriculture on Sept. 11, 1931, named the new dormitory for women at the Michigan State College the Mary Mayo Hall. She was closely identified with many charitable and reformatory organizations in her state, particularly with the Michigan State Industrial Home for Girls at Adrian, which she served for several years as a member of the Board of Control. As a public speaker she was a general favorite wherever she went. Her writings were principally articles contributed to the *Michigan Patron* and the *Michigan Farmer*. At the time of her death probably no woman was more widely known and loved throughout her state, particularly among farm women. She was survived by her husband and two children.

[Jennie Buell, *One Woman's Work for Farm Women, the Story of Mary A. Mayo's Part in Rural Social Movements* (1908); articles in the *Michigan Farmer*, May 2 and 9, 1903; a manuscript "Hist. of the Mayo Family," written by Mrs. Mayo's son, Nelson Slater Mayo of Highland Park, Ill.; a manuscript letter by Dr. F. C. Kedzie, dated Jan. 6, 1931, and addressed to the dean of women, Mich. State Coll.] C. R. B.

MAYO, SARAH CARTER EDGARTON (Mar. 17, 1819–July 9, 1848), author, daughter of Joseph Edgarton and his second wife, Mehitable (Whitcomb), was born in Shirley, Mass., and spent there all but two of her brief twenty-nine years. She was a descendant of Dennis Edgarton who lived in Bridgewater, Mass., and died in 1734. Her grandfather, John Edgarton, had marched from Shirley on Apr. 19, 1775, to serve his country, and had returned to become a prominent man in local politics. Her father played an important part in the industrial development of the village. She grew up in a pleasant home, one of a large family, assisting with domestic duties and reading eagerly whatever books the neighborhood afforded. Her limited educational advantages were supplied by the district school and by fourteen weeks at the academy of Westford. With an intense desire for self-improvement, however, she taught herself several languages and read widely in history, fiction, and poetry. "I do believe," she wrote in 1840, "that there is nothing in life so beautiful and elevating as the cultivation and improvement of the intellect in connection with moral sentiments" (A. D. Mayo, *post*, p. 42).

When she was about seventeen she began to write for publication, moved by a desire to contribute to the family income, then much reduced by reverses in her father's business. An ardent Universalist, she sent her first offerings to a periodical which had been devoted to the improvement and instruction of the women of her denomination since 1833—*The Universalist and Ladies' Repository* of Boston. She promptly became identified with this paper, supplying it regularly with sketches, poems, and short tales. From 1839 to 1842 she acted as its associate editor, and continued to write for it after withdrawing from this connection. By 1842 she had published two little books for children—*The Palfreys* and *Ellen Clifford*, and two volumes made up of her magazine articles—*Spring Flowers* and *The Poetry of Woman*. Her best work, both in prose and verse, appeared in the ten volumes of a Universalist annual called *The Rose of Sharon: A Religious Souvenir*, which she edited from 1840 until her death. In addition to this she published *Poems, by Mrs. Julia H. Scott, Together with a Brief Memoir* (1843), *The Flower Vase* (1843), *Fables of Flora* (1844), and *The Floral Fortune Teller* (1846).

On July 28, 1846, she married the Rev. Amory Dwight Mayo [*q.v.*] and accompanied him to his parish in Gloucester, Mass., where she spent the last two years of her life. The illness of her husband and the death of a talented younger brother with whom she had planned further literary ventures saddened these years, although the serenity of her religious faith enabled her to write of life even at this time, "I see no mysteries, and hear no discords" (Mayo, p. 116). After the birth of a daughter in September 1847, her health failed rapidly, and she died the following July.

[Seth Chandler, *Hist. of the Town of Shirley, Mass.* (1883); E. S. Bolton, *Shirley Uplands and Intervales* (1914); A. D. Mayo, *Selections from the Writings of Mrs. Sarah C. Edgarton Mayo: With a Memoir* (1849); Mrs. E. R. Hanson, *Our Women Workers* (1882); Phoebe A. C. Hanaford, *Daughters of America; or, Women of the Century* (1882); R. W. Griswold, *The Female Poets of America* (1849); *The Rose of Sharon: A Religious Souvenir for 1849*; *Boston Transcript*, July 13, 1848.] B. M. S.

MAYO, WILLIAM (*c.* 1684–1744), surveyor, son of Joseph and Elizabeth (Hooper) Mayo, was christened at Poulshot, Wiltshire, England, Nov. 4, 1684. Prior to 1712 he went to Barbados, and made a survey of that island which appears to have been accepted as standard. William Byrd, 1674–1744 [*q.v.*], attests its accuracy, and in April 1722 the board of trade ordered its secretary to subscribe "for the use of the Board, for one of the maps of Barbados, which Mr. Mayo is about to publish" (*Journal of the Commissioners for Trade and Plantations . . . 1718 . . . 1722,* 1925, p. 348). He married in Barbados Frances Gould, and about 1723 removed with his family to Virginia.

When Goochland County was erected in 1728 he was appointed justice of the peace and county surveyor. In 1728, also, he helped to run the boundary line between Virginia and North Carolina. The task was not easy. At the Great Dismal Swamp the other surveyor "was excus'd from the Fatigue, in complement to his Lungs," but Mayo won through. William Byrd, one of the Virginia commissioners, was impressed by his skill, and wrote of him: he "endured the same Hardships and underwent the Same Fatigue that the forwardest of the Men did, and that with so much Cheerfulness as if Pain had been his Pleasure, and Difficulty his real Diversion" (*post,* p. 253). One of the rivers encountered was named in his honor. Byrd's high opinion of Mayo, who was appointed major of militia in 1730, led to their being associated in later enterprises. An expedition in 1731 was prevented by Byrd's illness, but Mayo was not idle, the council directing him to run the boundary between Goochland and Hanover counties. His first wife having died, he now (August 1731) wrote to induce Anne, daughter of John Perratt of Barbados, to come to Virginia as his bride; and she consented. In 1733 Mayo accompanied Byrd on his "Journey to the Land of Eden," and with him "laid the foundation of two large Citys. One at Shacco's, to be called Richmond, and the other at the Point of Appamattuck River, to be nam'd Petersburgh. These Major Mayo offered to lay out into Lots without Fee or Reward" (*Ibid.,* p. 292). Both sites were shrewdly located at the falls line. Within four years Mayo laid out the city of Richmond in a rectangle eight squares long and four wide. Each square was divided into four lots, which were advertised for sale in the *Virginia Gazette,* and each lot brought seven pounds Virginia currency. Meanwhile, in 1732, Byrd had been appointed a commissioner for the crown to determine the southern boundary of Lord Fairfax's proprietary, the Northern Neck. Mayo was selected chief engineer, and when the surveyors had completed their work he combined their plats into a general map "in a Masterly Manner," a comparison with modern surveys demonstrating the almost uncanny accuracy of his work. The duties of the surveyor of Goochland having perhaps grown too onerous for a man of advancing years, in 1739 the council permitted Mayo to employ Ambrose Smith as assistant. Time had prospered him, and his surveys included many broad acres of his own. His will was proved Nov. 20, 1744, and he is said to have died Oct. 20, preceding (*Virginia Magazine of History and Biography,* January 1924, pp. 55–57). He had eight children, four by each marriage.

[J. S. Bassett, ed., *The Writings of "Colonel William Byrd, of Westover in Virginia Esqr"* (1901); M. N. Stanard, *Richmond, Its People and Its Story* (1923); *William and Mary Coll. Quart. Hist. Mag.,* Jan. 1924; Alexander Brown, *The Cabells and Their Kin* (1895); E. G. Swem, "Maps Relating to Va.," in *Va. State Lib. Bull.,* vol. VII (1914), no. 263.] L. D.

MAYO, WILLIAM KENNON (May 29, 1829–Apr. 9, 1900), naval officer, was born at Drummondtown (or Accomac), Va., son of Peter Poythress and Leah Custis (Upshur) Mayo, and a descendant of William Mayo [*q.v.*], an English civil engineer who came to Virginia about 1723. His mother was a sister of Abel P. Upshur [*q.v.*], secretary of the navy and secretary of state under Tyler. Appointed midshipman from Virginia Oct. 18, 1841, Mayo made his first cruise in the frigate *United States* of the Pacific Squadron, and was in charge of the boats of the landing party at the temporary occupation of Monterey, Cal., October 1842. The following year he was transferred to the *Cyane*. In the sloop *St. Mary's* he saw active duty throughout the Mexican War, including the blockades of Tampico and Vera Cruz and service of the naval battery during the attack on the latter port. He attained the grade of passed midshipman, Aug. 10, 1847, and after study at the newly established Naval Academy, 1847–48, he was for several years engaged in survey and scientific work, returning to Annapolis in 1854 as instructor in seamanship and gunnery. While on this duty he prepared a manuscript, "System of Naval Tactics and Fleet Sailing," used for the instruction of midshipmen. Promoted to lieutenant Sept. 15, 1855, he was on the Asiatic station in the *Minnesota,* 1857–59; instructor in ethics and English at the Naval Academy, 1859–60; and in the *St. Mary's,* Pacific Squadron, from December 1860 to January 1862. Service on this remote station doubtless facilitated his decision to remain loyal to the Union in the Civil War. He was the only member of his family to do so; his younger half-brother Wyndham Mayo joined the Confederate navy.

Early in 1862 he was transferred to the East Coast and became executive of the *Housatonic* off Charleston. After promotion to lieutenant commander, July 16, 1862, he commanded the *Kanawha* of the West Gulf Squadron from November 1862 to November 1863, capturing six blockade-runners and receiving commendation from Commodore H. K. Thatcher [*q.v.*] for gallantry in a sharp action, Oct. 12, 1863, with Fort Morgan (*Annual Report of the Secretary of the Navy,* 1864, pp. 478–79). He commanded the monitor *Nahant* off Charleston from July 1864 until the evacuation of Charleston in February 1865, and then until the close of the war was ordnance officer of the South Atlantic Blockading Squadron, retaining his command of the Bay Point Depot until May 1866. Commissioned commander July 25, 1866, he was engaged during the next three years in technical navigation work at Boston, during which time he designed a new type of navy binnacle. Subsequently, he commanded the *Tuscarora* and the *Congress* of the North Atlantic Squadron, 1870–71; the *Omaha* in the Pacific, 1872–74; and the *Hartford* in the South Atlantic, 1877–79; and was commandant of the Norfolk Navy Yard, 1882–85. He was promoted to captain Dec. 12, 1873, and to commodore July 2, 1882, but failed of promotion to rear admiral owing, it is said, to "infirmity of temper," and retired voluntarily May 18, 1886. His home thereafter was in Washington, D. C., where his death occurred after a brief illness. He was twice married, first to Virginia Kendall of Hartford, Conn., and second to Nannie Glover, who survived him. There were no children by either marriage.

[L. R. Hamersley, *The Records of Living Officers of the U. S. Navy* (6th ed., 1898); *Army and Navy Journal,* Apr. 14, 1900; *Washington Post,* Apr. 11, 1900; *Who's Who in America,* 1899–1900; information from family sources.] A. W.

MAYO, WILLIAM STARBUCK (Apr. 15, 1811–Nov. 22, 1895), physician and author, son of Obed and Elizabeth (Starbuck) Mayo, was descended in the seventh generation from the Rev. John Mayo, first regular minister (1655–72) of the North Church in Boston, and, on his mother's side, from the Starbucks of Nantucket, whalers and merchantmen. His father, it is said, went to sea first as a stowaway, but very soon earned for himself a position on a merchantman. At the instigation of his wife, however, who had an aversion to the sea, he abandoned the calling, settled in Ogdensburg, N. Y., and became a builder of lake and river boats. In that town William Starbuck Mayo was born. Eight years after his birth his father died, and about three years later the boy was sent to the academy in Potsdam. From there he turned to the study of medicine. After studying under two local physicians, he attended the College of Physicians and Surgeons in New York and graduated in 1832. He practised for a few years in Ogdensburg; then he was forced by ill health to travel. His subsequent tour of Spain and the Barbary States left upon him an indelible impression which colored his novels. Upon his return he settled in New York City and resumed medical practice. In 1851 he married Helen Stuyvesant, daughter of Nicholas Warren Stuyvesant. He began writing with minor contributions to a number of periodicals, but it was his fiction which brought him prominence.

The success of his first novel or tale was astonishing, even to the author. *Kaloolah, or Journeyings to the Djébel Kumri* (1849), purporting to be an autobiography of Jonathan Romer edited by W. S. Mayo, M.D., went through not less than nine editions, of which the latest bears the date 1900. Critical notices classed the novel with Melville's *Typee,* a relationship which Mayo disavowed, affirming in the Preface to the fourth edition (1850) that *Kaloolah* was written before *Typee* issued from the press. It is a rollicking tale of Yankee prowess, cunning, and self-reliance in love and adventure on the high seas and in Africa. Its prolonged popularity may be explained by the author's extraordinary versatility in ranging without discrimination from improbable heroism and delicately romantic love, through satire and common sense to practical joking and buffoonery. Only slightly less popular was his novel *The Berber; or, the Mountaineer of the Atlas* (1850, 1873, 1883). In it Mayo set himself to tell an agreeable story which should provide an illustration of Moorish manners, customs, history, and geography—and an exemplification of Moorish life as it actually was in Barbary in that day. Unlike *Kaloolah, The Berber* has a plot, complicated but well controlled, and although its incidents are romantic, the character types, the manners, and the settings are clearly the result of study and first-hand observation.

Mayo's last novel carries out the promise of a portion of *Kaloolah* by returning to the American scene. *Never Again* (1873) pits a Yankee somewhat less impetuous than Jonathan Romer but just as shrewd and self-reliant, against the moneyed society of New York. In addition to the novels mentioned Mayo wrote *Romance Dust from the Historic Placer* (1851), republished in 1855 under the title *Flood and Field,* a collection of short tales not essentially different in type from the novels. He has also been credited with scientific interests, indicated by his *Illustrations of Natural Philosophy* (1850), and by a letter, *To the Hon. Gideon Welles* (1862), on the construction and design of warships. With his generous background of catholic reading, his independent observation, his penetration of character and sanity of view he might, had he written with more singleness of purpose and control, have achieved a much less temporary distinction. He died in New York City.

[C. G. Mayo, "The Mayo Family in the U. S." (1927), vol. II, a manuscript genealogy of which there is a copy in the Lib. of Cong.; obituary in *Report . . . of the Century Asso. for the Year 1895* (1896); the *Internat. Mag. of Lit., Art and Sci.,* July 1851; *Blackwood's Edinburgh Mag.,* Aug. 1849; the *British Quart. Rev.,* Feb. 1851; *N. Y. Tribune,* Nov. 23, 1895.]

A. L. B.

MAYO, WILLIAM WORRELL (May 31, 1819–Mar. 6, 1911), physician, surgeon, was born in Manchester, England, of well-to-do parents, in a family many of whom had been physicians. He attended Owens College, Manchester, where he studied physics with John Dalton. Coming to America when twenty-six years of age, he taught physics and chemistry in New York for some two years. In 1847 he took up the study of medicine with Dr. Eleazer Deming of Lafayette, Ind., and two years later entered the Medical School of the University of Missouri in St. Louis, where he gave instruction in chemistry while completing his medical course. Here, in 1851, he married Louise Abigail Wright, who had been born Dec. 23, 1825, in New York. After receiving his medical degree from the University of Missouri in 1854, he returned to La Porte, Ind., and began the practice of medicine.

In the spring of 1855 Mayo removed with his family, consisting of his wife and two daughters, to St. Paul, Minn., then on the extreme frontier of civilization. His experiences in the next ten years were typical of those of the pioneer physicians of the period. The habit he acquired during this time of failing to collect his professional accounts became fixed for the rest of his life. Besides treating the sick he took part in the further organization of the territory, serving as chairman of the first board of county commissioners of St. Louis County. He located the county seat at a point where the city of Duluth is now built. He took the census of 1855 in St. Louis County. In 1856 he settled on a farm near Le Sueur, Minn., and a year later became a resident of Le Sueur. During this year and the next he also engaged in steamboating on the Minnesota River with James J. Hill.

In 1862 Mayo served as a surgeon with a relief force sent to quell the Sioux Indian outbreak in the vicinity of New Ulm, and in the spring of the following year was appointed provost surgeon for southern Minnesota with headquarters in Rochester, where he soon became the leading physician and surgeon of Olmstead County. In 1871 he took a postgraduate course in medicine at Bellevue Hospital in New York. When in 1883 a cyclone killed twenty-two persons and injured many others in the town of Rochester, Mayo was placed in charge of an emergency hospital for the injured and was assisted by the sisters of the Order of St. Francis. Two years later this Order began the erection of a forty-bed hospital on the edge of town. This original building is still the central nucleus of an institution (St. Mary's) now grown to a capacity of more than eight hundred beds.

Mayo was an untiring practitioner of medicine at a time when country practice in Minnesota was a very laborious task. His fierce struggle to wrest a precarious living from adverse nature in the wilderness developed a rugged manhood which formed a stable setting for, without burying, his scholarly and professional training. He was one of the earliest physicians in the West to use the microscope for diagnostic work. He was a surgeon as well as a physician of keen observation and professional skill. In 1871 he performed his first of thirty-one laparotomies for ovarian tumor. One of the founders of the Minnesota State Medical Society in 1868, he was its president in 1873, and contributed numerous technical articles to its *Transactions* (1871–87). He organized the Olmstead County Medical Society in 1882 and was a member of the American Medical Association for nearly fifty years. From the time they were twelve years of age, his two sons, William James Mayo and Charles Horace Mayo, were his companions and assistants whenever possible.

Mayo took an active interest in politics, serving as mayor of Rochester several times and as state senator twice, in spite of the fact that he was a liberal Democrat living in a Republican state and community. He died in Rochester in his ninety-second year, after an illness which was the result of an accident.

[*Sketch of the Hist. of the Mayo Clinic and Mayo Foundation* (1926); L. B. Wilson, "Wm. Worrell Mayo: A Pioneer Surgeon of the Northwest," *Surg., Gynecol., and Obstetrics*, May 1927; *The Jour. Minn. State Medic. Asso. and the Northwestern Lancet*, Mar. 15, 1911; *Minneapolis Morning Tribune*, Mar. 7, 1911; personal acquaintance.] L. B. W.

MAYO-SMITH, RICHMOND (Feb. 9, 1854–Nov. 11, 1901), statistician and economist, was born in Troy, Ohio, the third child of Preserved and Lucy Richards (Mayo) Smith. He was a direct descendant in the ninth generation of a distinguished Puritan family of clergymen established in America in 1641 when the Rev. Henry Smith, who had come from England some years earlier, became the first settled pastor in Wethersfield, Conn. His mother was the daughter of Seth Mayo of Medford, Mass., also of old New England stock. Preserved Smith emigrated to Ohio in 1839 where he became a successful railroad man and car manufacturer. The family moved from Troy to Dayton in 1856, and there Richmond spent an uneventful childhood. He was graduated from a Dayton high school in 1871 and the same year entered Amherst College. During his college course, under the influence of Prof. John W. Burgess, he became interested in economics and allied subjects. He was graduated in 1875 and went to Europe for further study at the suggestion of Burgess, who offered him a chair in economics and statistics in the new faculty of political science at Columbia, contingent upon his study abroad. After two years of study at the universities of Berlin and Heidelberg, Mayo-Smith returned to the United States in 1877 as an instructor in history and political science at Columbia, beginning a connection with the university that terminated only with his death. From 1878 to 1883 he was assistant and adjunct professor of political economy and social science; in 1883 he became a full professor. In 1880 he was named as one of the five original instructors in the graduate School of Political Science, simultaneously carrying on his teaching of undergraduates. At the reorganization of the university in 1890 he was selected as a member of the council and was continued as such until the year of his death. He had marked success as a teacher in both graduate and undergraduate departments. His course in statistics, said to be the first given in an American university, attracted numbers of able graduate students, many of whom subsequently became distinguished statisticians.

His most significant contributions to American thought and scholarship were in the kindred subjects of economics and statistics in which he became a recognized authority. Desiring to place statistics on an adequate scientific basis, he published many scholarly papers which gained him immediate and gratifying recognition from official statisticians as well as from his academic colleagues. In 1889 he assisted in the revival of the then dormant American Statistical Association and became one of its vice-presidents, a position he retained until his death. In 1890 he was made a member of the National Academy of Sciences, an honor hitherto usually reserved for pursuivants of the pure and natural sciences. He was one of the most active American members of the International Statistical Institute, to which he was elected in 1889; contributed to its bulletins; and attended several meetings (Vienna, 1891; Chicago, 1893; St. Petersburg, 1897; and Christiania, 1899). In 1890 he was elected honorary fellow of the Royal Statistical Society. His best-known writing on statistics is the two-volume work, *Science of Statistics.* Volume I, *Statistics and Sociology,* appeared in 1895 and contained one of the first systematic applications of statistics to social problems; Volume II, *Statistics and Economics,* published in 1899, was designed to show what economic problems could be treated by statistical inquiry. The author was well aware of the limits of the then new science and made no extraordinary claims in its behalf. Both volumes were used as standard texts for years and still remain sources of the first importance.

Though subordinated to his statistical investigations, his study of economics was no less vigorous and sound. His writings in the economic journals cover a range of subjects, but his only book in this field was *Emigration and Immigration* (1890), a treatise largely devoted to the effects of population movements on the ethnical and ethical standards of communities. This book is perhaps the least significant of the three, since he argues from the *a priori* assumption that American political ideals may be treated as a standard. He was one of the founders of the American Economic Association in 1885 and a member of its council, contributing freely to its meetings and publications. When the *Political Science Quarterly* was founded in 1886, he was a member of the original editorial board and supported the publication with indefatigable zeal by his frequent articles, reviews, and skilful editing. In 1895 he read a paper before the American Economic Association on the "Desirability of a Permanent Census Bureau." As a result of his constructive opinion, the Association, conjointly with the Statistical Association, prepared memorials and reports for Congress, and after the joint committee was disbanded, the Economic Association on its own responsibility appointed him chairman of a committee to report on various ways of improving census work. This committee presented a five-hundred-page octavo volume, *The Federal Census, Critical Essays by Members of the American Economic Association,* which was published in March 1899.

Mayo-Smith married Mabel Percy Ford of Brooklyn in June 1884, and had four children. Following a boating accident, he suffered a nervous collapse, and died suddenly in New York City a few months later as the result of a four-story fall.

[E. R. Seligman, in *Memoirs Nat. Acad. Sci.,* vol. XVII (1924), with portrait and bibliography, also in *Columbia Univ. Quart.,* Dec. 1901; W. F. Willcox, "The Development of the American Census Office since 1890," *Pol. Sci. Quart.,* Sept. 1914; *N. Y. Times,* Nov. 12, 1901.] W. R. L.

MAYOR, ALFRED GOLDSBOROUGH (Apr. 16, 1868–June 24, 1922), biologist, the son of Alfred Marshall Mayer [*q.v.*] and his wife, Katherine Duckett (Goldsborough), was born near Frederick, Md., at the home of his grandfather, Dr. Charles H. Goldsborough, a beloved and self-sacrificing physician. Alfred G. Mayor (whose name was legally changed in August 1918 from Mayer) studied engineering at Stevens Institute of Technology, where his father was professor of physics, took the degree of M.E. in 1889, was assistant to Prof. A. A. Michelson [*q.v.*] at Clark University, 1889–90, and then to Prof. L. I. Blake at the University of Kansas, 1890–92. He was strongly attracted toward zoology, however, and in 1892 left Kansas abruptly to study at Harvard. Here his artistic capacity attracted the attention of Alexander Agassiz [*q.v.*], whom he thereafter accompanied on marine voyages to the Atlantic and Pacific, making colored drawings of jellyfish, on which organism he later published several beautifully illustrated volumes. From 1895 to 1900 he was assistant in charge of radiates at the Museum of Comparative Zoology, Harvard, and in 1897 received the degree of D.Sc. In 1900 he became curator of natural science in the new Museum of the Brooklyn Institute of Arts and Sciences, and, in 1904, curator-in-chief.

As an experimental naturalist he found museum work too static, however, and, accordingly, accepted the appointment of the Carnegie Institution of Washington to organize and direct their proposed marine laboratory at Dry Tortugas, Florida Keys. For eighteen years he conducted this laboratory and he edited the fifteen large volumes of researches that issued from it during his lifetime (*Papers from the Tortugas Laboratory of the Carnegie Institution,* vols. I–VI, 1908–14; *Papers from the Department of Marine Biology of the Carnegie Institution,* vols. VII–XV, 1915–22). His own researches included studies of the development, function, and significance of coloration of the wing and wing scales of butterflies; the reactions of butterflies both in larval and imaginal stages; the physical nature and chemical basis of muscular contraction, especially rhythmical pulsation as seen in jellyfishes; the method of formation of coral reefs, based on analytical studies in Torres Straits and American Samoa, in which latter studies he showed that Darwin's theory of coral-reef formation does not apply universally. With those associated with him at Tortugas and elsewhere, he made many additions to scientific knowledge relating to the growth of corals, the formation of limestone deposits through bacterial action, the nature of phosphorescent light, and the significance of the diversity of island faunas.

Mayor's achievements were the outgrowth of a remarkable personality. Like his father he had the fondness of a physicist for precise experimentation. He used a wide range of physical instruments in the study of heat, light, and friction in relation to organisms; and he made extensive use of mathematical analysis. He utilized his facility in mathematics during the World War when he wrote a book on navigation (*Navigation, Illustrated by Diagrams,* 1918) and taught this subject to naval recruits, being commissioned as captain. His interest in the sea was a trait which appeared in several of the Goldsboroughs—notably Charles and Louis M. [*qq.v.*], naval officers—as well as in the merchantmen among the early Mayers. Mayor was slightly below average stature, of athletic build, and with deep-set, blue eyes capable of the liveliest expression. His traits of generosity, companionableness, love of conversation, and sense of humor made him generally adaptable to the drawing room, to marine usage, or to the hut of Papuans. He had the concern for the well-being of his associates that characterized his grandfather, the rural physician. Mayor seemed to have a wiry constitution, but a hereditary weakness in the ciliary muscles of the eyes prevented too close application to the microscope; and when, following influenza, tuberculosis of the lungs became active in 1920, despite a sojourn in Tucson during the winters, he grew rapidly worse while conducting the laboratory at Tortugas and died there at the scientific workshop he had created.

On Aug. 27, 1900, Mayor married Harriet Randolph Hyatt, a sculptor, the daughter of Prof. Alpheus Hyatt [*q.v.*], paleontologist. Artistic talent reappeared in all their four children. Mayor was president of the American Society of Zoologists, and a member of the National Academy of Sciences and other scientific organizations. His published technical works include seventy-five scientific papers, four volumes, *Medusae of the World* (3 vols., 1910) and *Ctenophores of the Atlantic Coast of North America* (1912), also eighteen reports as director of the Tortugas Laboratory, and numerous popular papers.

[C. B. Davenport in *Memoirs Nat. Acad. Sci.*, vol. XXI (1926); *Science*, July 21, Aug. 4, 18, 1922; *Papers from the Dept. of Marine Biol., Carnegie Inst. of Washington*, vol. XIX (1924), containing posthumous papers by Mayor and a bibliography; *Carnegie Inst. of Washington: Year Book No. 21* (1923); *Brooklyn Museum Quart.*, Oct. 1922; Brantz Mayer, *Memoir and Geneal. of the Md. and Pa. Family of Mayer* (1878); supplemented by H. H. Maÿer, *The Maÿer Family* (1911).] C. B. D.

MAZUREAU, ÉTIENNE (1777–May 25, 1849), lawyer and state official, was born in France in 1777. He began school at the age of nine and after his father died, four years later, entered a lawyer's office. When war was declared in 1793 he enlisted in the navy and saw service on *L'Entreprenant* and *Le Formidable.* The latter ship was captured at the battle of Groces off the coast of Ireland during the winter of 1794 and Mazureau was taken prisoner. He was exchanged after four months' incarceration in England and accompanied Delatouche on a legal mission for the French government to Spain, where he remained long enough to acquire a thorough knowledge of the language and law of the country—most useful to him in later years.

After various adventures he found himself at the age of twenty-two inspector of agriculture of French Guiana, but he returned to Paris when the Directorate fell. One evening he was told that Napoleon was about to crown himself Emperor of France, and indiscreetly replied that although he greatly admired Napoleon, he would regard him in that position as the usurper of the throne of the Bourbons. The remark was reported to the authorities and brought about his imprisonment. As soon as he was released he sailed for New York, and after fifteen months spent in New Jersey, in March 1804 went to New Orleans and was soon after admitted to the bar. His industry and his familiarity with both French and English were of great assistance to him in this bilingual city where most of the jurors and witnesses spoke only one of these languages, and where the law required an interpreter to be present in every court room.

For a time he was a partner of the well-known attorney, Edward Livingston [*q.v.*], and in 1815 was appointed attorney-general of Louisiana, a position he repeatedly occupied later. He also served two terms in the state legislature. In his day, he appeared on one side or the other in every important case tried. The best known were the famous Batture Case, in which he argued against his former partner, Edward Livingston, who was conducting a long-drawn-out litigation to obtain possession of a valuable piece of ground formed by accretions from the river; and the case of *The State* vs. *Hyppolite Truette* in which the defendant was charged, under a new law prohibiting duelling, with the murder of Paulin Prué. Mazureau was the prosecutor and his attack upon the *code duello* aroused a great furore in a day when gentlemen considered this method the only one by which a personal disagreement could be settled. Mazureau was short and stout, with a head much too large for his body. As an orator he was fiery, adroit, convincing, and eloquent. His knowledge of the law was encyclopedic, and the income from his practice was great, but his generosity and extravagance were greater, and he died in New Orleans in 1849, a very poor man.

[Edward L. Tinker, *Les Écrits de Langue Française en Louisiane au XIXe Siècle* (1932); E. Mazureau, *Aux Électeurs de l'État de Louisiane* (1827); H. S. Foote, *The Bench and Bar of the South and Southwest* (1876); W. H. Sparks, *The Memories of Fifty Years* (1870); Alcée Fortier, ed., *Louisiana* (1914), vol. II; Chas. Gayarré, "The New Orleans Bench and Bar in 1823," *Harper's New Monthly Mag.*, Nov. 1888; *L'Abeille de la Nouvelle-Orleans*, May 26, 1849.] E. L. T.

MAZZEI, PHILIP (Dec. 25, 1730–Mar. 19, 1816), physician, merchant, horticulturist, agent of Virginia in Europe during the American Revolution, author, was born at Poggio-a-Caiano, Italy, the fourth child of Domenico and Elisabetta Mazzei. Having received there and in Prato an elementary education, he studied surgery at Santa Maria Nuova in Florence. In 1752 he accompanied a Dr. Salinas to Smyrna to practise medicine. Three years later he went to London, where he was a wine merchant for about eighteen years. In 1773 he sailed for Virginia to introduce the culture of grapes, olives, and such other fruits as might be expected to flourish there. Early in 1774 he married Marie (Hautefeuille) Martin.

Mazzei's agricultural experiment was carried on at "Colle," a few miles east of Charlottesville, adjoining "Monticello." It was not a success, mainly on account of the American Revolution, to which Mazzei devoted most of his time and energy. He was an ardent supporter of both religious and political freedom in Virginia. In June 1779, Gov. Patrick Henry sent Mazzei abroad to borrow money from the Grand Duke of Tuscany for the Commonwealth of Virginia. He, his wife, and his step-daughter were captured by the British and imprisoned for about three months on Long Island. To destroy evidence against him, Mazzei had thrown overboard his instructions and commission from the Governor, so when he finally arrived in Europe he found himself without the authority to act. Benjamin Franklin, believing that the federal government alone should make foreign debts, blocked at every turn Mazzei's attempt to borrow for the individual state of Virginia. So Mazzei busied himself gathering useful political and military information which he sent to Governor Jefferson. For his services the State of Virginia paid him six hundred luigi a year from Jan. 8, 1779, to Apr. 8, 1784. Late in 1783 Mazzei returned to America in quest of a consulate, but he was disappointed.

On June 16, 1785, Mazzei sailed from New York for Europe, never to return to America. He published in Paris his *Recherches historiques et politiques sur les États-Unis de l'Amérique septentrionale* (4 vols., 1788). Based in part on materials furnished by Jefferson, this was the most accurate work on America that had appeared in French, but, because of its very lack of extravagance, it failed to gain popularity (Bernard Faÿ, *L'Ésprit Révolutionnaire en France et aux États-Unis,* 1925, p. 136). He had previously written several pamphlets on America. In 1788 he was appointed "Intelligencer to the King of Poland," with a salary of 8,000 livres annually. In 1792 Mazzei went to Warsaw, where he was private adviser to Stanislas II, until the second division of Poland forced his retirement.

His first wife having died in Virginia in 1788, Mazzei remarried in Pisa about 1796, and in 1798 had a daughter, Elisabetta. In 1802 the Emperor of Russia began paying him the pension of 1,200 rubles a year, which the Polish government had granted him on his retirement. This pension continued until his death. In 1813 he completed his *Memorie della Vita e delle Peregrinazioni del Fiorentino Filippo Mazzei.* He died in Pisa and is there buried. This extraordinarily versatile man lived in twenty-odd cities of importance in the old and new worlds, was a naturalized citizen of Virginia, and later a naturalized Pole. He carried on an active correspondence with Madison, Jefferson, Thomas Adams, and other Virginians. A letter to him from Jefferson, written on Apr. 24, 1796 (see article on Jefferson, and P. L. Ford, *Writings of Thomas Jefferson,* VII, 72–78), became famous in the history of American political controversy.

[Filippo Mazzei, *Memorie della Vita e delle Peregrinazioni del Fiorentino Filippo Mazzei* (2 vols., 1845–46); *William and Mary Coll. Quart.,* July, Oct. 1929, Jan. 1930; R. C. Garlick, Jr., *Philip Mazzei, Friend of Jefferson; His Life and Letters* (in press) and article on Mazzei in *Italy and the Italians in Washington's Time* (1933); MSS. in archives of Va. State Lib., and in Va. Hist. Soc., Richmond, and in Dept. of State, Washington, D. C.; P. L. Ford, *The Writings of Thomas Jefferson* (10 vols., 1892–99).] R. C. G., Jr.

MAZZUCHELLI, SAMUEL CHARLES (Nov. 4, 1806–Feb. 23, 1864), Roman Catholic missioner, architect, and schoolman, was born in Milan, Italy, to Luigi Mazzuchelli and Rachele Merlini. The father was a member of an affluent family of bankers long prominent in the financial circles of the Lombard capital. Educated first by tutors at Milan, Samuel then studied at Faenza and at Rome, and in the former city became a novice of the Dominican order in 1823. He left for the American missions in 1828, going first to Bardstown, Ky., and then to Ohio, where on Sept. 5, 1830, he was ordained to the priesthood in the Cincinnati Cathedral by the Dominican bishop, Edward Fenwick.

He departed immediately for the island of Mackinac to commence his missionary endeavors, but three years later made Green Bay his headquarters. From these points he made frequent visits to Arbre Croche, St. Ignace, Sault Sainte Marie, and Fort Winnebago, and also labored a short while in Detroit. He worked among the French Canadians and half-breeds, but principally among the Indians—the Menominee, Ottawa, Chippewa, and Winnebago. He mastered their languages with facility; numerous conversions crowned his efforts; and in 1833 he printed a prayerbook and catechism in the difficult Winnebago tongue. Though accustomed to the polished society of Old-World capitals, he lived cheerfully amid the squalid savages and primitive pioneers of the rough Northwest.

Early in 1835 he crossed the snows on his second journey to Prairie du Chien and commenced the first church for that entire area. He then visited the fast growing villages of Galena and Dubuque and hastened down the valley to St. Louis to make a report of his missions. That same spring, by steamboat, coach, horseback, and foot he traveled seven hundred miles to visit his Dominican superiors in Ohio, and thirteen hundred more to return to Galena and Dubuque. Here he found himself for several years the only priest among Indians and whites for a distance of hundreds of miles in some directions and thousands of miles in others. His *Memoirs* recount his experiences among the rough, hard-drinking, but sincere pioneers. When Dubuque was created a diocese in 1837, he was the sole representative of Bishop Loras [*q.v.*] until the latter's arrival and then for several years acted as his vicar general and missioner extraordinary. Among his daring excursions was a visit in February 1843 to Nauvoo, where he interviewed Joseph Smith [*q.v.*], the Mormon leader, and attempted to convert him. In that year he participated in the Fifth Provincial Council of Baltimore, acting as the theologian of Bishop Loras. He visited his native land, finished his *Memoirs,* written in Italian, and had them printed in Milan in 1844.

Returning to America, he commenced in 1845 the erection of Sinsinawa Mound College for the education of young men, at Sinsinawa, Wis. Of this institution he was the first president and chief teacher. Later he confided its direction to his fellow Dominicans from Ohio, while he devoted himself, after 1847, to the founding of a congregation of teaching sisters, the Dominican Congregation of the Most Holy Rosary. He was chaplain of the first territorial legislature of Wisconsin. He persuaded the first Senate of the Iowa Territory to hold its sessions in his yet undedicated church in Burlington. He was the architect of the county courthouse at Galena; he built the bishop's residence in Dubuque; and he designed the first capitol of Iowa at Iowa City. While acting as pastor of the church at Benton, as chaplain of the sisterhood, and as director of the Benton Academy which he had founded, Father Mazzuchelli died from exposure to a severe blizzard while on a sick-call to a dying parishioner.

[Mazzuchelli's memoirs are available in English translation as *Memoirs Historical and Edifying of a Missionary Apostolic of the Order of St. Dominic among the Various Indian Tribes and among the Catholics and Protestants in the U. S. A.* (1915). See also Rosemary Crepeau, *Le Père Samuel-Charles-Gâetan Mazzuchelli* (Paris, 1932); *Freeman's Jour.* (N. Y.), June 10, 1876; *Golden Bells in Convent Towers, the Story of Father Samuel and St. Clara* (1904); J. D. Butler, "Father Samuel Mazzuchelli," *Wis. Hist. Soc. Colls.,* vol. XIV (1898); "Who Designed Iowa's Old Capitol?," *The Witness* (Dubuque), June 21, 1928; letters and documents in the St. Louis Archdiocesan archives, and in St. Clara Convent, Sinsinawa, Wis.]

M. M. H.

MEAD, CHARLES MARSH (Jan. 28, 1836–Feb. 15, 1911), Congregational clergyman, biblical scholar, was born in Cornwall, Vt., youngest of the nine children of Rufus and Anna (Janes) Mead. His father, a descendant of John Mead who came from England and settled in Greenwich, Conn, about 1650, was a farmer who placed high value on mental training. Charles completed his preparation for college under his brother Hiram in Flushing Institute, New York, and entered Middlebury College, graduating as valedictorian in 1856. He taught in the classical department of Phillips Academy, Andover, Mass., 1856–58, then entered Andover Theological Seminary. He was tutor in Middlebury College, 1859–60, and graduated at Andover Seminary in 1862. He studied in Germany, 1863–66, mainly in Halle and Berlin, taking the degree of doctor of philosophy at Tübingen in 1866. While in Germany he was appointed in 1865 to the Hitchcock professorship of Hebrew in Andover Seminary.

Returning to America in 1866, he was ordained to the Congregational ministry, Aug. 10, at Cornwall, Vt., and in the autumn was inaugurated at Andover. On Aug. 2, 1867, he married Caroline, daughter of Joseph H. and Martha S. Thayer of Boston. In 1871–72 they spent sixteen months in Europe and the Near East, and made a study of Palestine. Shortly after their return, Mead began serving as a member of the American committee cooperating with the English committee in Bible revision, an undertaking in which he was engaged for nearly thirty years. He resigned the Andover professorship in 1882, and the following ten years were spent abroad with his wife, mainly in studies at Bonn and Berlin. In 1889 he was temporarily in America, lecturing in Princeton Theological Seminary. From 1892 to 1898 he was Riley Professor of Christian Theology in the Hartford (Conn.) Theological Seminary. For several years thereafter he gave his entire time to Biblical revision. The American committee did not disband, as the English committee had done when their revision was published in 1885, but continued to work on the projected American revision. Mead was the youngest of the American revisers, and an increasingly large share of the labor devolved upon him. He was deputed to go through the Old

Testament, making notes and suggestions to be sent to the other members for their votes. He prepared the topical page-headings, a large part of the Scripture references, the preface, and an appendix for the first edition; he also revised the paragraph divisions of the English revision. The reading of the proof of the Old Testament fell to him, an exacting labor by which his health was impaired for several years. His work of Biblical revision, for which he had exceptional equipment, stands probably as his most distinctive service in Christian scholarship.

Mead was of slender physique, with quiet, kindly manner. His learning was extensive, his thought well-balanced, his expression clear, often trenchant, with a vein of subtle humor. He translated from the German the volume on Exodus (1876) in the J. P. Lange *Commentary on the Holy Scriptures,* and, in part, I. A. Dorner's *System of Christian Ethics* (1887). He was the author of *The Soul Here and Hereafter* (1879); *Supernatural Revelation* (1889); *Romans Dissected* (1891)—employing an ironic use of conjecture in Biblical criticism; *Christ and Criticism* (1893); *Irenic Theology* (1905). Besides various addresses and lectures he wrote many articles, some of which were reprinted separately.

[G. N. Boardman, "Tribute to Charles Marsh Mead by His Friends," in *Bibliotheca,* Apr. 1912, with bibliography of Mead's writings; *Congregationalist,* Feb. 25, 1911; *Congregational Year-Book* (1912); *Hartford Times,* Feb. 16, 1911; personal recollections of the writer; letters from Prof. Arthur L. Gillett of Hartford Seminary and others.] E. D. E.

MEAD, LARKIN GOLDSMITH (Jan. 3, 1835–Oct. 15, 1910), sculptor, son of Larkin Goldsmith and Mary Jane (Noyes) Mead, was born at Chesterfield, N. H., and was of distinguished colonial stock. He was brought up in Brattleboro, Vt., where his father was a prosperous lawyer. His mother was a sister of John Humphrey Noyes [*q.v.*], founder of the Oneida community. Brattleboro had unusual cultural advantages. Partly because of a water cure established there by Dr. Wesselhoeft, a German political refugee, it was visited by famous persons. The Mead home was a scene of intellectual and artistic activity, and several of the nine children were skilful in drawing and painting. Larkin's sister Elinor was an artist, and became the wife of William Dean Howells. A younger brother, William Rutherford Mead [*q.v.*], was long the central partner in the firm of McKim, Mead & White, architects.

From 1853 to 1855 Mead received excellent training in the studio of Henry Kirke Brown, who was at that time working on his equestrian statue of Washington. In 1856 he established himself in Brattleboro, and on the evening of Dec. 31, built up at a crossroads in Brattleboro a colossal snow figure called "The Recording Angel," which astonished the townsfolk, and later was celebrated in James Russell Lowell's poem, "A Good Word for Winter." This picturesque exploit came to the attention of Nicholas Longworth, of Cincinnati, Ohio, who encouraged him by giving him his first order. In 1857 he completed a nineteen-foot figure, "Vermont," for the dome of the capitol at Montpelier, and in 1861 a marble statue, "Ethan Allen," for the interior of the same building. For six weeks during 1861 he was at the battle front and sent to *Harper's Weekly* graphic sketches of camp life. In 1862 came the long-desired voyage to Italy for study. On the way he escorted his sister Elinor to Paris and gave her in marriage to Howells, then United States consul at Venice. Encouraged by Hiram Powers, the young sculptor established himself in Florence, occasionally going to Venice, there to act as vice-consul in the absence of Howells. On Feb. 26, 1866, he married a beautiful Venetian girl of impoverished noble family, Marietta di Benvenuti. The courtship had begun before she could speak English, or he Italian. Their married life was spent in Florence, where later he became honorary professor of sculpture in the school where Michelangelo had taught.

At about the time of his marriage he had returned to New York, where he showed four popular pieces in marble, "Echo," "La Contadinella," "Thought of Freedom," and "The Returned Soldier, or the Battle Story," a life-size statue representing a soldier and a listening child. What was more important, he brought also a plaster study in competition for the proposed Lincoln monument for Springfield, Ill., the most extensive undertaking of the kind then known in the United States and destined to cost over $200,000. His elaborate design had a professional look and was chosen. It included a bronze figure of Lincoln, with four great groups. To execute the whole in plaster Mead returned to Florence. The bronze casting was done at Chicopee, Mass. The work at Springfield dragged. Foundations were begun in 1869; the statue of Lincoln was dedicated in 1874; the infantry and navy groups were placed in 1877; the artillery group came in 1882, and the cavalry group in 1883, completing a conscientious design, doubtless the best to be had at the time. But from 1865 to 1884, American sculpture experienced a profound change. Younger sculptors, disdaining pseudo-classicism, were seeking inspiration from France instead of from Italy. Mead kept his old allegiance and did his work in Florence, returning home at times for business reasons. In 1876 his large marble statue of Ethan Allen, a vigorous, carefully carved work of its generation, sent by the state of Vermont, was placed in Statuary Hall in the Capitol at Washington, D. C. His "Triumph of Ceres," a pedimental group for McKim's Agricultural Building at the Columbian Exposition of 1893, was carried forward with enthusiasm in his Florence studio, and had many beautiful passages. Its chief lack was what the occasion demanded, a striking decorative effect; he was already listed as "sculptor of the old school." His last important public work was a heroic reclining marble figure, "The Father of Waters," which after many vicissitudes, found a place in Minneapolis, Minn.

Mead died in Florence, leaving a widow but no children. One of the last of the American expatriates, he was not only a "sculptor of the old school." He was a kindly, cultivated gentleman, honorably displaying in a foreign land some of the finest traits of the American character.

[Lorado Taft, *The Hist. of Am. Sculpture* (1930); H. T. Tuckerman, *Book of the Artists* (1867); Chas. Moore, *The Life and Times of Chas. Follen McKim* (1929); *Life in Letters of Wm. Dean Howells* (2 vols., 1928), ed. by Mildred Howells; Mary R. Cabot, *Annals of Brattleboro, 1681–1895* (2 vols., 1921–22); Chas. E. Fairman, *Art and Artists of the Capitol of the U. S. of America* (1927); *Am. Art News*, Oct. 22, 1910; *N. Y. Times*, Oct. 16, 1910.] A. A.

MEAD, WILLIAM RUTHERFORD (Aug. 20, 1846–June 20, 1928), architect, was born in Brattleboro, Vt., the son of Larkin Goldsmith and Mary Jane (Noyes) Mead. He spent two years at Norwich University, Northfield, Vt., and graduated from Amherst College in 1867. Having been influenced toward architecture by his admiration for the classical Capitol of Vermont at Montpelier, he spent a year in an engineer's office, and, in July 1868, entered the office of Russell Sturgis, architect, in New York as a paid student. There he was under the guidance of George Fletcher Babb, who afterwards became a formative influence in the firm of McKim, Mead & White, and a life-long friend of the three partners. In 1871 Mead went to Florence for a year and a half, living with his brother, Larkin G. Mead [*q.v.*], the sculptor, and continuing his studies in the Academia de Belle Arte, where his interest in Renaissance architecture developed. Returning in the autumn of 1872, Mead fell in with C. F. McKim [*q.v.*]. For five years they shared an office at 57 Broadway and helped each other. In 1878 they formed a partnership under the name of McKim, Mead & Bigelow; in 1879, Stanford White [*q.v.*] took the place of William B. Bigelow. In the firm of McKim, Mead & White, Mead managed the office, often conceived the basic scheme of the plan (as in the Capitol at Providence), and acted efficiently as critic of the designs of both his creative partners, who were bent primarily on producing works of art. The association was a companionship both in and out of business hours and Mead's influence was potent. He was especially helpful to the multitude of young men who got their early training in that office.

On the death of McKim in 1909, Mead took up his partner's work as president of the American Academy in Rome, an institution founded after the World's Columbian Exposition (Chicago, 1893) to give to American students of the fine arts opportunity to become familiar, under competent direction, with the masterpieces of all time, and thus to prepare them to solve the problems their own practice would present, and especially to train their appreciation of beauty as the fundamental requirement in works of dignity and permanence. For eighteen years, Mead was the stabilizing influence in this fast-growing and expanding institution for the training of architects, painters, sculptors, landscape architects, and musicians.

A loyal alumnus of Amherst, he had a large part in replanning and rebuilding the college along the lines of effective amenity; he left a considerable fund to foster the artistic side of education. On Nov. 13, 1884, he married, at Budapest, Olga Kilyeni, whom he had known in New York. They had no children. Mead died in Paris and his body was placed with his brother Larkin's in the American Cemetery in Florence.

[M. R. Cabot, *Annals of Brattleboro 1681–1895*, vol. II (1922); *Amherst Grads.' Quart.*, Nov. 1928; L. G. White, *Sketches and Designs by Stanford White* (1920); Charles Moore, *Life and Times of Charles Follen McKim* (1929); C. C. Baldwin, *Stanford White* (1931); *A Monograph of the Work of McKim, Mead & White 1879–1915* (n.d.); *Who's Who in America*, 1928–29; *Jour. Am. Inst. of Architects*, July 1928; *N. Y. Herald Tribune*, June 21, 22, 1928.] C. M.

MEADE, GEORGE (Feb. 27, 1741–Nov. 9, 1808), merchant, was born in Philadelphia, Pa., the son of Robert and Mary (Stretch) Meade. His father, who was probably born in Ireland, went to Philadelphia about 1732 from Barbados and was a shipping and commission merchant with extensive interests in the West Indies. The son was educated under the supervision of his uncle, George Stretch, in Barbados, and at an early age was captain of a vessel trading between the island and Philadelphia. He then established a firm with his brother in Philadelphia under the name of Garrett and George Meade, engaging in importing, freighting, and shipping. They built up an extensive business, became prominent merchants of Philadelphia, and were among the signers of the Non-Importation Resolutions of 1765. Upon the retirement of Garrett Meade the firm became George Meade & Company, with Thomas FitzSimins, Meade's brother-in-law, as a partner. This connection lasted for some years until FitzSimins' public duties forced his retirement. Meade was an ardent patriot and contributed large sums from his private fortune toward the cause of the colonies. During the Revolution he was a member of the 3rd Philadelphia Battalion (1775–76) but did not take part in any military engagements. He served, however, on various relief, correspondence, and other committees and was a member of the Public Defence Association. In 1780 his firm subscribed a large sum toward organizing the Pennsylvania Bank, which was to supply Washington's army with food and clothing.

Meade was a prominent citizen though he was not drawn to public office. He was, however, a member of the common council of Philadelphia in the years 1789–91 and in 1792 was chairman of the board of management of Philadelphia prisons. He was a stanch Roman Catholic and was instrumental in the building of Saint Mary's Church, one of the oldest Catholic churches in Philadelphia. He was also one of the original members of the Society of the Friendly Sons of St. Patrick, established about 1771, and one of the incorporators of the Hibernian Society in 1792. About 1795 he invested largely in undeveloped land in various parts of the country, but he failed in the financial crisis of 1796. He continued to manage his affairs until he was forced in 1801, because of his increasing age and declining health, to go into bankruptcy. His son Richard Worsam Meade, 1778–1828 [*q.v.*], was appointed as his assignee. He had married Henrietta Constantia Worsam, the daughter of Richard Worsam of His Majesty's council, Barbados, on May 5, 1768, and they had ten children. He died in Philadelphia.

[Meade family manuscript in possession of the Pa. Hist. Soc.; R. W. Meade, "Geo. Meade: A Patriot of the Revolutionary Era," *Records of the Am. Cath. Hist. Soc. of Phila.*, vol. III (1891); Geo. Meade, *The Life and Letters of Geo. Gordon Meade* (1913), vol. I; R. M. Bache, *Life of Gen. George Gordon Meade* (1897); *Poulson's Am. Daily Advertiser*, Nov. 11, 1808.]

J. H. F.

MEADE, GEORGE GORDON (Dec. 31, 1815–Nov. 6, 1872), soldier, the victor of Gettysburg, was born in Cadiz, Spain, where his father Richard Worsam Meade, 1778–1828 [*q.v.*], was naval agent for the United States. His mother, Margaret Coates (Butler) Meade, was the daughter of Anthony Butler, of Perth Amboy, N. J. His grandfather, George Meade [*q.v.*], a merchant of Philadelphia, contributed generously to the American cause in the Revolution. His father, after having lived in affluence in Spain, died in Washington, D. C., in poverty, through the failure of the government to pay a just debt. Because of this financial loss, young Meade had to be withdrawn from Mt. Airy School near Philadelphia and sent to one conducted by Salmon P. Chase in Washington. Afterward he attended a Mt. Hope school in Baltimore. Though his tastes pointed toward a collegiate education, lack of funds turned his attention toward West Point, where he became a cadet, Sept. 1, 1831, having received an appointment upon his second application. While at the Academy he was not a particular admirer of the course, and determined to resign from the military service as soon as he could properly do so. He was graduated number nineteen among the fifty-six members of the class of 1835. During his graduation leave he helped with the survey of the Long Island Railroad. As brevet second lieutenant of the 3rd Artillery, he was ordered to Florida. Though he was advised not to go to that climate because of the weakness of his health, he arrived at the outbreak of the Seminole War. After serving a year in southern Florida, where he was stricken with fever which rendered him unfit for duty, he was ordered to Watertown Arsenal, Mass., on ordnance work. There he resigned from the army, Oct. 26, 1836, along with many others who foresaw little promotion in the service. He at once became assistant engineer of the Alabama, Florida, & Georgia Railroad. In 1839 he acted as principal assistant engineer on a survey of the mouths of the Mississippi. In 1840 he was one of the assistants to the joint commission for establishing the boundary between the United States and Texas. During the same year he returned to Washington, where he was married on his twenty-fifth birthday to Margaretta Sergeant, daughter of John Sergeant.

At work now as one of the civil assistants of the survey of the northeastern boundary, he determined with the new responsibilities of matrimony to apply for reinstatement in the army. Accordingly, on May 19, 1842, he was appointed a second lieutenant of Topographical Engineers, his classmates already having attained the rank of captain. As a military engineer he was continued on the northeastern boundary survey until the end of 1843, when he was transferred to Philadelphia in the work of designing and constructing lighthouses in the Delaware Bay. He was on this duty when, in August 1845, he was ordered to Aransay Bay, Tex., with Taylor's army of occupation. He arrived at Corpus Christi

Sept. 14, 1845, a young man in robust health, tall, gaunt, with a hatchet face and prominent aquiline nose. During the Mexican War he was engaged in the battles of Palo Alto and Resaca de la Palma, and was brevetted a first lieutenant (Sept. 23, 1846) at Monterey for performing daring reconnaissances. He was then transferred to Scott's column, participating in the siege of Vera Cruz, whence, because of the superfluity of topographical engineers and the lack of opportunity for further active service, he was returned to Philadelphia. There he was presented by a body of citizens with a sword for his services in the war. From 1847 to 1849 he was employed in the construction of lighthouses in Delaware Bay and in making surveys and maps of the Florida reefs. In 1849 and 1850 he was in Florida in active service against the Seminoles. In 1850 and 1851 he was again in the Delaware Bay at work upon lighthouses and the Delaware breakwater. On Aug. 4, 1851, he was promoted a first lieutenant of Topographical Engineers. In 1851 and 1852 he was in Florida at work upon the Iron Screw Pile Lighthouse on Corysfort Reef; and from 1852 to 1856 at Sand Key. He was promoted a captain of Topographical Engineers, May 17, 1856. He was then ordered to Detroit, Mich., on the geodetic survey of the Great Lakes, his report of which was of such value as to place him in charge of the Northern Lake Surveys from 1857 to 1861.

When the Civil War broke out, Meade, through the efforts of Gov. Andrew G. Curtin of Pennsylvania, was made a brigadier-general of volunteers, Aug. 31, 1861, and given one of the three Pennsylvania brigades with Reynolds and Ord. It was at this time that the close friendship between Reynolds and Meade began, to end only when Reynolds was killed early in the battle of Gettysburg. Meade's first active service in command of his brigade was in the defenses of Washington, D. C., where he assisted in the construction of Fort Pennsylvania, near Tennallytown. In March 1862, he was transferred with his command to McDowell's army, and after the evacuation of Manassas went into the Department of the Shenandoah. In June 1862 he was ordered to the Peninsula under McClellan, when (June 18) he was promoted to major in the Topographical Engineers of the regular army. His brigade took part in the battles of Mechanicsville, Gaines's Mill, and Glendale. At Glendale he received the wound which was to trouble him the remainder of his career and which was to be the indirect cause of his death. The ball entered just above the hip joint, indented his liver, and passed out near his spine. Simultaneously another ball hit his arm. In spite of these wounds he stuck to his horse, directed his subordinates in the action, and was forced to quit the field only through loss of blood. Though afterward his hat was riddled with bullets, his mounts were killed, and his leg was numbed by a shell, he was never again actually wounded. Before he was fully recovered at Philadelphia, he rejoined his command and participated in the Second Bull Run, Aug. 29–30, 1862. When Reynolds' division at South Mountain, Sept. 14, 1862, was without its leader, Meade was placed in temporary command. His successful and skilful advance elicited written praise from his superiors. At Antietam, on Sept. 16–17, he again pressed forward with intrepidity until the ammunition of his troops was exhausted. When Hooker was carried off the field, Meade was placed in temporary command of the I Corps, which he led for the remainder of the battle. He was then engaged under McClellan in the pursuit of Lee to Falmouth, Va., in October and November 1862, during which time he was given the old division of Reynolds, who succeeded by rank to the command of Hooker's Corps. On Nov. 29 Meade was made a major-general of volunteers, and on Dec. 25 was given the regular command of the V Corps, after the disastrous battle of Fredericksburg. On Jan. 26, 1863, he was placed in command of the Center Grand Division, composed of the III and VI Corps. On Feb. 5, when Hooker abolished the grand divisions, Meade reverted to the command of the V Corps, which in the battle of Chancellorsville, May 24, 1863, gave an excellent account of itself in so far as Hooker used it.

It was because of Meade's insight and advice in this battle that Couch and Reynolds both recommended him to Washington as the next commander of the Army of the Potomac, though this act may not have affected the appointment. While leading his corps northward paralleling Lee, he was awakened in the early morning of June 28 by a messenger from the President, who delivered a letter placing him in command of the Army of the Potomac. Thoroughly surprised and displeased, he protested against his selection. Nevertheless, even with his handicaps and his unfamiliarity with Hooker's plans, he quickly adjusted himself to his new office and began at once to carry out his sudden and complicated mission. He at once issued orders for taking up a position on the line, Emmitsburg-Hanover, for the protection of Baltimore and Washington, thus concentrating his forces but making no attempt to destroy Lee's army. The Gettysburg position was an accident induced by a meeting engagement of advance elements. Though Meade generally handled his troops well, he has been criticized for not strengthening his flanks, for holding out no reserve, and for failure on July 2–3 to counter-attack and to pursue in exploitation of his success. His was no Napoleonic victory, nor did he display—doubtless because of the same heckling that had beset all early commanders of the Army of the Potomac—the aggressiveness that he had urged at Chancellorsville. But it must be remembered he had been given the command only five days before, that his troops were exhausted, and that the topography of the country favored an orderly retirement by the master soldier, Lee. On Jan. 28, 1864, he received the thanks of Congress "for the skill and heroic valor which, at Gettysburg, repelled, defeated and drove back, broken and dispirited, beyond the Rappahanock, the veteran army of the Rebellion"; and after the battle he was promoted a brigadier-general in the regular army to rank from July 3, 1863. He was continued in sole command of the Army of the Potomac through the Rapidan campaign and the Mine Run operations. However, when Grant who had been made a lieutenant-general in command of all the Union forces, Mar. 12, 1864, decided to accompany the main army in Virginia, Meade's powers were mechanically curtailed. It was an anomalous situation for both Grant and Meade, which, even with the deference Grant displayed, relegated Meade's work to the tactical rather than the strategical realm. But notwithstanding tense moments, when Meade's high-strung, scholarly nature grew irascible and petulant, he was unswervingly loyal to his superior and carried out the orders given him with skill and fidelity. He was retained in command of the Army of the Potomac continuously from Gettysburg to Appomattox, during which time he was promoted a major-general in the regular army, Aug. 18, 1864.

At the close of the war he was placed successively in command of the Military Division of the Atlantic, and the Department of the East with headquarters at Philadelphia. On Jan. 2, 1868, he was transferred to Atlanta, Ga., in command of the third military district of the Department of the South, comprising the states of Georgia, Alabama, and Florida. He served there until Mar. 12, 1869, when he was transferred to the command of the Military Division of the Atlantic with headquarters in Philadelphia. His work in the South was unusually trying and responsible, because of the almost impossible task of administering the unjust reconstruction laws. His uncompromising attitude and sense of fairness were able to make tolerable a most difficult situation (C. M. Thompson, *Reconstruction in Georgia,* 1915, pp. 179–85). From 1866 until his death he acted as commissioner of Fairmount Park, Philadelphia, the plan and beautification of which are ascribed to his energies more than to those of any other. On Oct. 31, 1872, while taking his daily walk from his office with his wife, he was attacked with a violent pain on the side of his old wound. It was the second time since the war that pneumonia had overtaken him. He died Nov. 6, 1872. There had been six children from his marriage, four sons and two daughters.

Meade's outstanding qualities were soundness and steadfastness. His mind was scientific, and his convictions were deep-seated. These traits, coupled with an intense honesty and unswerving adherence to what he believed to be the truth, often brought him into heated contentions with inferiors and superiors, regardless of person or place. He was not a popular type, but in the field of efficiency his rugged, lofty character outweighed any possible defects of tact.

[George Meade, *The Life and Letters of George Gordon Meade* (2 vols., 1913); R. M. Bache, *Life of Gen. George Gordon Meade* (1897); I. R. Pennypacker, *General Meade* (1901); G. W. Cullum, *Biog. Reg. of the Officers and Grads. of the U. S. Mil. Academy,* vol. I (1891); *War of the Rebellion: Official Records (Army)*; *Battles and Leaders of the Civil War* (4 vols., 1887–88); Civil War Pamphlets, War College Library, Washington, D. C.; obituary in Philadelphia *Press,* Nov. 7, 1872.]

W. A. G.

MEADE, RICHARD KIDDER (July 14, 1746–Feb. 9, 1805), Revolutionary soldier, was born in Nansemond County, Va., the son of David Meade and his wife Susannah, daughter of Gov. Richard Everard of North Carolina. He was educated in England at Harrow, and later in a small private school. One of his masters declared that while he would never make a learned scholar, he would make what was far better, *vir probus.* His subsequent career justified the prediction. He threw himself zealously into the struggle between England and the colonies, and was chosen (May 8, 1775) member of a "committee of intelligence" in Prince George, the function of which was "to convey any alarm as speedily as possible to the adjacent counties." On June 24, 1775, he helped to remove certain arms from Governor Dunmore's palace at Williamsburg. In the battle of Great Bridge, Dec. 9, 1775, he served as captain of a company under Colonel Woodford. Writing shortly afterward to his friend Theodorick Bland [*q.v.*], he vowed that he would see the controversy with England through to the end or die in the attempt.

He at once sold his estate at Coggins' Point,

Prince George and tendered his services to the patriot cause. He was appointed (Jan. 12, 1777) aide-de-camp to Washington, with the rank of lieutenant-colonel. Highly esteemed by the General, he thenceforth accompanied him on all his campaigns. Being an excellent horseman and possessed of a rugged physique, he was especially useful in carrying orders and reconnoitering; his fine black mare was a sight familiar to both British and American armies. At Monmouth he narrowly escaped capture. He assisted in making the arrangements for the execution of Major André, although confessing that he could not contemplate the event "without a tear" (letter to Bland, *Bland Papers,* II, 34). At the close of the war, Washington counseled him: "Friend Dick, you must go to a plantation in Virginia; you will make a good farmer and an honest foreman of the grand jury of the county where you live" (William Meade, *post,* I, 295).

With part of the proceeds from the sale of his former estate, he acquired a thousand acres of land in Frederick County, then a wild, backwoods region. The enterprise proved so successful that the estate became known as "Lucky Hit." As often as his health would permit, he served as foreman of the grand jury. In 1798 Washington, whom he sometimes visited at Mount Vernon, consulted him regarding the choice of officers for the army it was proposed to raise in view of possible war with France. Meade was twice married. In 1765 he espoused Jane Randolph of "Curles," aunt of John Randolph of Roanoke. In 1780, after her death, he married Mary Fitzhugh (Grymes), widow of William Randolph of "Chatsworth." In a time of great need she had contributed handsomely to the patriot cause. He died "at the seat of Matthew Page, Esq., in Frederick County," of gout aggravated by the hardships of military life. Of his eight children, four were sons and four, daughters. One of the sons, William [*q.v.*], became eminent as the third Protestant Episcopal bishop of Virginia.

[*The Bland Papers* (2 vols., 1840–43), edited by C. Campbell; William Meade, *Old Churches, Ministers, and Families of Va.* (2 vols., 1857); Charles Campbell, *Hist. of the Colony and Ancient Dominion of Va.* (1860); John Johns, *A Memoir of the Life of the Rt. Rev. William Meade* (1867); "Meade Family History: Autobiography of David Meade," *Wm. and Mary Coll. Quart., Hist. Mag.,* July–Oct. 1904; W. C. Ford, *The Writings of George Washington,* vol. XIV (1893); P. H. Baskervill, *Andrew Meade of Ireland and Va.; His Ancestors and Some of His Descendants* (1921).]

E. E. C.

MEADE, RICHARD WORSAM (June 23, 1778–June 25, 1828), merchant, was born in Chester County, Pa., where his parents, George [*q.v.*] and Henrietta (Worsam) Meade were residing during the British occupation of Philadelphia. He attended private schools in Philadelphia and then entered his father's business and while so employed made several voyages to the West Indies. In 1795, as supercargo on board one of his father's vessels, he went to Europe and subsequently toured through England and France, returning in 1796. He then went to the island of Santo Domingo in the West Indies and established a business on his own account. At the end of three years he had accumulated a considerable fortune. After his return to Philadelphia he was married in 1801 to Margaret Coates Butler and went into business, at the same time taking charge of his father's affairs which had become seriously complicated. While on a visit to Spain he decided to establish a commercial house in Cadiz, and in 1804 his family took up residence there. Two years later he was appointed naval agent for the United States at the port of Cadiz, a position which he held until 1816. He resided in Spain for seventeen years, living luxuriously and occupying a favored social position. He gathered a choice collection of pictures and statuary which later formed the basis for one of the first private collections in America. He also took an active interest in the exportation of merino sheep to the United States.

Meade was in Spain during the Peninsular War. At the time of the French invasion he entered into many contracts with the Spanish government involving quantities of supplies of all kinds. In one year alone his vessels brought some 250,000 barrels of flour to Cadiz. In this way he contributed materially to the support of the Spanish cause and Spain became greatly indebted to him for funds and merchandise. In recognition of his services he was offered, but declined, full citizenship of the country. In the confusion which followed the return of Ferdinand VII to the throne, he was greatly embarrassed and delayed in obtaining a settlement of his claims. He also became involved in legal difficulties arising out of his efforts to settle the affairs of an insolvent English mercantile firm doing business in Cadiz of which he had been appointed assignee. He was ultimately arrested and imprisoned in May 1816 in the fort of Santa Catalina at Cadiz. After nearly two years he was released by a royal order, demanded by the United States minister to Spain. In the meantime he had sent his family to America and immediately upon his release moved to Madrid to continue his efforts to obtain payment of the amounts due him. On May 9, 1820, a special tribunal appointed by the Spanish government awarded him a certificate of debt amounting to $491,153.62. Under the Treaty of Florida, signed in 1819, all just claims of American citizens then existing against Spain, to the amount of five million dollars, were assumed by the United States. Meade returned to Philadelphia and later moved to Washington in order to prosecute his claim more vigorously. In 1822 the claims commission refused to consider the certificate of debt which he had received from the Spanish government, demanding original vouchers. Before these could be presented the session of the commission terminated and the fund which had been provided was exhausted. Meade retained some of the most famous lawyers in the country in an effort to obtain a rehearing of the claim and the passage of a bill for its payment by Congress, but was unsuccessful, as were his heirs in later attempts to prosecute the claim. Meade's disappointment undermined his health and he died in Washington, D. C., at a comparatively early age. Richard Worsam, 1807–1870, and George Gordon Meade [*qq.v.*] were his sons.

[Meade family manuscript in the possession of the Pa. Hist. Soc.; R. W. Meade, "Geo. Meade: A Patriot of the Revolutionary Era," *Records of the Am. Cath. Hist. Soc. of Phila.*, vol. III (1891); Geo. Meade, *The Life and Letters of Geo. Gordon Meade* (1913), vol. I; *The Case of Richard W. Meade, . . . Imprisoned 2nd of May, 1816, by the Govt. of Spain, and Still Detained* (1817); *The Claim of Richard W. Meade upon the U. S. . . . with all the Documents . . . Connected with It* (1825); *Daily Nat. Intelligencer* (Wash., D. C.), June 26, 1828.]

J. H. F.

MEADE, RICHARD WORSAM (Mar. 21, 1807–Apr. 16, 1870), naval officer, was born at Cadiz, Spain, son of Richard Worsam Meade [*q.v.*], United States naval agent at that place, and Margaret Coates (Butler) Meade. He was a brother of George Gordon Meade [*q.v.*]. Returning with his mother to Philadelphia in his tenth year, Richard received a good education at Constant's School, Philadelphia, and at St. Mary's College, Baltimore. He was appointed midshipman Apr. 1, 1826, made his first cruise in the *Brandywine* in the Pacific, 1827–30, served in the *St. Louis* in the West Indies, 1833–35, and was promoted to lieutenant Dec. 20, 1837. After varied service afloat and ashore, including active duty during the Mexican War in the *Scorpion* and *Potomac* and a Pacific cruise as commander of the *Massachusetts*, 1853–55, he was still lieutenant when the selection board of 1855 made a drastic overhauling of officer personnel. Meade was dropped, but in 1857 secured reinstatement with the rank of commander as of Sept. 14, 1855. The testimony in his appeal (*Defense of Richard W. Meade before the Court of Inquiry*, 1857) indicates a man of chivalrous spirit, high character, great abilities and energy, but also of an intractable temper which involved him in difficulties with superiors and subordinates. Despite his reinstatement, sea assignments went to others, and for the first three years of the Civil War he was kept chafing as commander of the receiving ship *North Carolina* in New York. At last, in his own words, he "floored all his enemies" (*Army and Navy Journal*, Apr. 23, 1870, p. 566), gained his captain's rank (dating from July 16, 1862), and sailed in May 1864, commanding the *San Jacinto* of the East Gulf Squadron. Misfortune followed him. On Jan. 1, 1865, his ship grounded on No Name Key, Bahama Islands. Though all lives and stores were saved, largely through the commander's exertions, the ship was abandoned. Meade suffered a severe attack of brain fever. In May following he was suspended for three years, and a second trial in February 1866, after appeal to the President, confirmed the suspension. On Dec. 11, 1867, he was retired for physical disability. From his illness, the strain of the litigation preceding, and a paralytic stroke, his mind became clouded, and for a short time in the autumn of 1868 he was under confinement. Secretary of the Navy Welles (*Diary, post*) complained of the powerful influence exerted in Meade's behalf and of Meade's alleged threats of violence. The claims of his father's estate, of which he was executor, were also under litigation at this time, and his death from apoplexy was hastened by an adverse judgment of the Supreme Court two weeks before. Meade was married, Dec. 5, 1836, to Clara Forsyth, daughter of Congressman Henry Meigs of New York and grand-daughter of Josiah Meigs [*q.v.*]. He was survived by two daughters and three sons—Richard Worsam [*q.v.*], Henry Meigs, a naval paymaster; and Robert Leamy [*q.v.*], who rose to the rank of brigadier-general in the Marine Corps.

[H. B. Meigs, *Record of the Descendants of Vincent Meigs* (1901); L. R. Hamersly, *The Records of Living Officers of the U. S. Navy and Marine Corps* (1st ed., 1870); *Defence of Capt. Richard W. Meade, Tried for the Loss of the U. S. Str. San Jacinto on the Bahama Banks, Jan. 1, 1865* (1866); *War of the Rebellion: Official Records (Navy)*; *Diary of Gideon Welles* (1911), vols. II, III; George Meade, *The Life and Letters of Geo. Gordon Meade* (1913), vol. I; *Army and Navy Jour.*, Apr. 23, 1870; Rebecca P. Meade, *Life of Hiram Paulding* (1910), pp. 259–64; *N. Y. Tribune*, Apr. 18, 1870; information from family sources.]

A. W.

MEADE, RICHARD WORSAM (Oct. 9, 1837–May 4, 1897), naval officer, son of Capt. Richard Worsam Meade, 1807–1870 [*q.v.*], and Clara Forsyth (Meigs), was born at his maternal grandfather's home, Fourth and Perry streets, New York. Following study at Fordham School and Worcester Academy, he entered the Naval Academy at thirteen, and after six years' training, four of them at sea, graduated fifth in the class of 1856. Two years later, Jan. 23, 1858, he was promoted to lieutenant. In 1860 he was court-martialed and reprimanded for calling Lieut. Thomas Field of the Marine Corps "a liar and a coward." In the Pacific Squadron at the opening of the Civil War, he was invalided home with fever, August 1861; served as ordnance instructor in the receiving ship *Ohio* at Boston; and after brief assignments in the *Dacotah* and *Conemaugh,* and promotion to lieutenant commander (July 14, 1862), was in command of the *Louisville* on the Mississippi, September–December 1862. Detailed to ordnance work in New York after a recurrence of illness, he had charge of the naval battalion which preserved order in the lower section of New York during the Draft Riots, July 13, 1863. He next commanded the *Marblehead,* September 1863–May 1864, on the Charleston blockade. Admiral John A. B. Dahlgren [*q.v.*] commended him in general orders following his action with shore batteries while supporting the flank of Gen. Quincy A. Gillmore [*q.v.*] in Stono Inlet, Dec. 25, 1863, during which his ship was hulled thirty times in a two-hour bombardment. Afterward, until the end of the war, he commanded the *Chocura* in the Gulf, capturing seven prizes, and on Jan. 22, 1865, cutting out and destroying the blockade runner *Delphina* in the Calcasieu River, Louisiana. He was head of the seamanship department, Naval Academy, 1865–68 (promoted to commander Sept. 20, 1868), and prepared for midshipmen's use *Manual of the Boat Exercise at the U. S. Naval Academy* (1868) and *A Treatise on Naval Architecture* (1868). Subsequently, he also published several translations of French naval articles, and wrote frequently on professional subjects. The famous yacht *America,* used as a training ship at the Academy after war service, was under his command, though he did not actually sail her, in the second America's Cup race off New York, Aug. 8, 1870, in which there were eighteen entries; she finished fourth, and the British yacht, tenth. The year before he had commanded the *Saginaw* on an Alaskan cruise. Admiral Seaton Schroeder [*q.v.*], then under him, describes him as a "well-known, daring, and skillful seaman," naturally kind of heart, but "disconcertingly frank in both look and spoken expression" (*A Half Century of Naval Service,* 1922, p. 15). He had indeed great energy, emotional temperament, aggressiveness, and also combativeness. In 1871–73 he took the *Narragansett* on an extraordinary Pacific cruise —60,000 miles, chiefly under sail, in 431 days—during which he protected American interests in innumerable places, made the first treaty with Samoa (see *Report of the Secretary of the Navy . . . 1872,* pp. 14–15), and according to the Secretary of the Navy (Hamersly, *post,* p. 82), "accomplished more professional work than any other ship afloat for the past two years." After ordnance duty in Brooklyn, he commanded the *Vandalia,* North Atlantic Squadron, 1879–82, Admiral Robert H. Wyman [*q.v.*] declaring that "as a commanding officer he has no superior" (*A Tribute, post,* p. 28). With the rank of captain (Mar. 13, 1880), he was commandant of the Washington Navy Yard, 1887–90; as commodore (May 5, 1892), was naval representative at the World's Columbian Exposition, Chicago; and as rear admiral (Aug. 1, 1894) was selected to command the North Atlantic Squadron. After a very active cruise in the West Indies, during which he was thanked by the British government for the services of the fleet in preventing the destruction by fire of Port of Spain, Trinidad, Meade became dissatisfied with his relations with the Navy Department under Secretary Hilary A. Herbert [*q.v.*], resigned his command, and voluntarily retired, May 7, 1895. Thereafter, he lived at Germantown, Pa. His death from appendicitis occurred in Washington, and he was buried at Arlington. In appearance he was strikingly handsome. He was married, June 6, 1865, to Rebecca, daughter of Admiral Hiram Paulding [*q.v.*], and had a son and four daughters.

[L. R. Hamersly, *Records of Living Officers of the U. S. Navy* (4th ed., 1890); *Army and Navy Jour.,* May 8, 1897; W. F. Brown, *A Tribute of Respect by Lafayette Post No. 140 . . . Grand Army of the Republic in Memory of Commander Richard Worsam Meade* (1898); *Evening Star* (Washington), May 4, 1897; information from family sources.] A. W.

MEADE, ROBERT LEAMY (Dec. 26, 1841–Feb. 11, 1910), officer of the United States marine corps, was born at Washington, D. C., the son of Richard Worsam Meade, 1807–1870 [*q.v.*], of the United States navy, and Clara Forsyth (Meigs) Meade. Gen. George Gordon Meade [*q.v.*], commander of the Union forces at Gettysburg, was his uncle, and Richard Worsam Meade, 1837–1897 [*q.v.*], a rear-admiral in the United States navy, was his brother. He received his early education at Mt. Saint Mary's College, Emmitsburg, Md., and was graduated from the United States Naval Academy on Sept. 30, 1856, with the rank of acting midshipman. Some months later he resigned his commission in the navy and until the outbreak of the Civil

War served as watch-officer on the United States coast survey steamer, *Bibb*. Seeking active war service, he was on June 4, 1862, appointed a second lieutenant, United States marine corps, from the state of Tennessee, and in July of the following year commanded a company of marines engaged in quelling the New York draft riots. In August he accompanied the Federal expedition of combined land and naval forces against the forts guarding the city of Charleston, S. C., and volunteered his services for the unsuccessful night attack upon Fort Sumter, Sept. 8, 1863, in which he, with a number of others, was taken prisoner by the Confederates (D. D. Porter, *The Naval History of the Civil War,* 1886, pp. 447–49). As a prisoner of war, Meade remained in Charleston for some fifteen months, suffering the hardships of prison life until exchanged. For gallant and meritorious services in storming the forts, he received the brevet of first lieutenant. His regular promotion to that grade followed on Apr. 2, 1864.

The Civil War ended, Meade served on board the *Shenandoah* during an extended cruise to the Orient (1865–69), visiting India, China, Japan, and Korea in the interest of better international relations. During this cruise he surveyed some 2,100 square miles of Korean territory, surveys later utilized by Admiral John Rodgers and his naval command in the occupation of the Korean capital (*Boston Transcript,* Feb. 11, 1910). He was promoted captain, Jan. 22, 1876, and served at Brooklyn and Philadelphia, on lake duty attached to the *Michigan,* as fleet marine officer on board the *Hartford,* at Boston, and at Pensacola, Fla. In April 1885 he accompanied the naval expedition to the Isthmus of Panama, having for its object the protection of the lives and property of American citizens endangered by the revolution. He commanded the marine barracks, Washington, D. C., 1890–92, and on Sept. 6, 1892, was promoted major. His lieutenant-colonelcy followed, Aug. 10, 1898.

During the Spanish-American War Meade served as fleet marine officer, on board the *New York* of Admiral Sampson's North Atlantic Squadron, and participated in the battle of Santiago-de-Cuba. Later he commanded a prison camp at Camp Long. He became a colonel, Mar. 3, 1899, and the year following took part in the China Relief Expedition for the relief of the allied legations at Peking at the time of the Boxer Rebellion. For gallant conduct at the battle of Tientsin, China, he received the brevet of brigadier-general. He was retired from active service with the rank of brigadier-general, Dec. 26, 1903, and died at his home, Lexington, Mass., some years later, after a prolonged illness. He was married in New York City, Feb. 6, 1865, to Mary, the daughter of Admiral Hiram Paulding, who with two sons and two daughters survived him. Interment was at Huntington, Long Island.

[*War of the Rebellion: Official Records* (*Navy*), 1 ser., XIV; R. S. Collum, *Hist. of the U. S. Marine Corps* (1890); *Army and Navy Jour.*, Feb. 19, 1910; *Boston Post* and *N. Y. Times,* Feb. 12, 1910; personal records on file in the Historical Section, Headquarters Marine Corps, Washington, D. C.] C. D. R.

MEADE, WILLIAM (Nov. 11, 1789–Mar. 14, 1862), third bishop of the Protestant Episcopal Church in the Diocese of Virginia, was born in Frederick (later Clarke) County, Va., the son of Col. Richard Kidder Meade [*q.v.*], aide on Washington's staff during the Revolution, and his wife, Mary Fitzhugh (Grymes), widow of William Randolph. The father was a descendant of Andrew Meade who emigrated from County Cork, Ireland, about 1685, lived in New York for some five years, where he married Mary Latham, a Quakeress, and finally settled in Nansemond County, Va. William attended a private school and entered the junior class of the College of New Jersey in 1806, graduating in 1808 as valedictorian. In preparation for the ministry of the Episcopal Church he studied under Rev. Walter Addison of Maryland, was ordained deacon by Bishop James Madison of Virginia in 1811; and priest, by Bishop Claggett of Maryland in 1814.

The situation of the Episcopal Church in Virginia was then wellnigh hopeless. In spite of the notable devotion of both clergy and people to the American cause in the Revolution the Church had been unable, because of inadequate organization and intense opposition, to meet the changed conditions and had steadily declined, until at the General Convention in 1811 the fear was expressed that the Church in Virginia was dead. Meade entered the ministry expecting to serve in his own community while supporting his family by manual labor on his farm; but the movement of events and his innate ability soon made him a leader in the little group still loyal to the church of their fathers. He was largely influential in securing as second bishop of Virginia, in 1814, Richard Channing Moore [*q.v.*], of New York, to whom is chiefly due the beginning of the revival of the Episcopal Church in Virginia. Recognized as a strong and notable preacher, Meade was such a leader as Virginia needed. Widespread infidelity fostered by the French Revolution and paralysis of the Church for many years had produced a condition of godlessness and license for more than a generation. Meade's character and leadership made him a power for good throughout not only the Episcopal Church but the entire state.

In 1829 he was unanimously elected assistant bishop of Virginia, and from 1841 until his death in 1862 he was bishop of the diocese, which included the present states of Virginia and West Virginia. The revival of the Church begun under Bishop Moore had extended in 1829 to about half of the former colonial parishes; under Bishop Meade it extended throughout the state. Meade was intensely interested in the spiritual condition of the negroes, preaching to them constantly and seeking to arouse interest in their welfare. Early in his ministry he liberated his slaves, although afterwards he believed that this was a mistaken kindness. The American Colonization Society and the establishment of Liberia owed much to him. One of the most influential men in the House of Bishops, he was regarded as a leader of the Evangelicals in the contest between the High Church and Low Church parties. Like many leading Virginians he was strongly opposed to secession, but went with his state when the die was cast. As senior bishop he was the presiding officer of the convention in Columbia, S. C., Oct. 16, 1861, which formulated the constitution of the General Council of the Protestant Episcopal Church in the Confederate States, of which he became presiding bishop. In March 1862, although ill, he was a consecrator of Rev. Richard H. Wilmer [*q.v.*], elected at that General Council as Bishop of Alabama. Meade died eight days later; his body is buried at the Theological Seminary in Alexandria, Va., which he helped to establish in 1823 and to guide throughout his lifetime.

He published many addresses, tracts, charges to the clergy, and sermons delivered upon special occasions. Of more extended works his *Family Prayers Collected from the Sacred Scriptures, the Book of Common Prayer, and the Works of Bishop Wilson* (1834), had a wide circulation. In 1846 he published *Companion to the Font and the Pulpit,* and three years later, *Conversations on the Catechism.* His *Lectures upon the Pastoral Office* (1849), a series of lectures delivered annually for several years to students at the Virginia Theological Seminary, was long in use as a textbook upon pastoral theology; another of his publications is *The Bible and the Classics* (1861). By far the best known of his writings, however, is his *Old Churches, Ministers, and Families of Virginia* (2 vols., 1857). In spite of numerous slight errors and a too sweeping characterization of the unworthiness of the colonial ministers, denied by later students of Virginia history, this book remains an indispensable storehouse of information about the ecclesiastical history of Virginia during the colonial period. He was twice married, first, Jan. 31, 1810, to Mary, daughter of Philip and Sarah Burwell Nelson of Clarke County, who died in 1817; and second, Dec. 2, 1820, to Thomasia, daughter of Thomas and Frances Page Nelson of Yorktown, both grand-daughters of Gov. Thomas Nelson, signer of the Declaration of Independence and major-general of Virginia militia at the siege of Yorktown.

[P. H. Baskervill, *Andrew Meade of Ireland and Va.* (1921); John Johns, *A Memoir of the Life of the Rt. Rev. Wm. Meade, D.D., etc.* (1867); E. L. Goodwin, *The Colonial Church in Va.* (1927); W. A. R. Goodwin, *Hist. of the Theol. Sem. in Va. and its Historical Background* (2 vols., 1923–24); *Addresses and Hist. Papers Before the Centennial Council of the Protestant Episcopal Church in the Diocese of Va.* (1885); Philip Slaughter, *Memoir of the Life of the Rt. Rev. William Meade, D.D.* (1885); Robert Nelson, *Reminiscences of the Rt. Rev. William Meade* (1873); *Richmond Enquirer,* Mar. 15, 1862.]

G. M. B.

MEAGHER, THOMAS FRANCIS (Aug. 23, 1823–July 1, 1867), politician, laywer, soldier, was born in Waterford, Ireland, the son of Thomas Meagher, a wealthy merchant in the Newfoundland trade, who for a time represented his district in Parliament. His mother, of the well-known family of Quan, died while Thomas Francis was yet an infant. He attended the Jesuit college of Clongowes-Wood, Kildare (1833–39), and the English college of Stonyhurst, near Preston, Lancashire (1839–43). He joined the Young Ireland party in the year 1845 and in 1846 made his first appearance as a public speaker at the great national meeting at Kilkenny, over which Daniel O'Connell presided. In the following year he became one of the founders of the Irish Confederation and a member of the so-called "War Directory," and in April 1848 went to France in its interest, bringing back to the city of Dublin an Irish tri-color. Meagher made presentation of the flag the occasion for an incendiary speech, and was arrested July 11, 1848, charged with sedition. In October he was tried for high treason at Clonmel and condemned to death. The sentence of the court was commuted and in July 1849 he was banished to Tasmania, where on Feb. 22, 1851, he was married to a Miss Bennett, daughter of a farmer. Escaping in January 1852, he arrived in the United States in the following May, took out citizenship papers in August, and became the virtual leader of the Irish element in New York City. He lectured throughout the East with considerable success, studied law and was admitted to the bar in 1855, became editor of the *Irish News* in 1856, and practised law from 1856 to 1861. His first wife had died in Ireland in

1854, and on Nov. 14, 1855, he was married to Elizabeth Townsend of Southfield, N. J.

With the outbreak of the Civil War, Meagher organized in 1861 a company of Zouaves which became part of the 69th Volunteers. With his regiment he took part in the first battle of Bull Run, where he had a horse shot under him while acting as a field-officer. In the winter of 1861–62 he organized in New York City the Irish Brigade, and became its commander, Feb. 3, 1862, participating in the battles of the Peninsular Campaign, Second Bull Run, Antietam, Fredericksburg, and Chancellorsville. When his brigade was so decimated as to be non-effective, Meagher resigned his commission and returned to New York City where, June 25, 1863, he was banqueted by a number of leading citizens and presented with a gold medal. Early in 1864 he was reappointed a brigadier-general and in November took over command of the district of Etowah. In the following January he joined General Sherman's army at Savannah, where he was mustered out of the service with the coming of peace. Later in 1865 he was appointed territorial secretary of Montana, and after his arrival in October served for a year as temporary governor in the absence of Gov. Sidney Edgerton. He encountered many obstacles in the administration of his office. In July 1867, while engaged in a reconnoissance on the Missouri River near Fort Benton, he fell from the deck of a steamer and was drowned. Meagher published *Speeches on the Legislative Independence of Ireland* (1853), *The Last Days of the 69th in Virginia* (1861), and other letters and papers.

[Michael Cavanagh, *Memoirs of Gen. Thos. Francis Meagher* (1892); W. F. Lyons, *Brig.-Gen. Thos. F. Meagher* (1870); C. G. Bowers, *The Irish Orators* (1916); J. C. O'Meagher, *Some Hist. Notes of the O'Meaghers of Ikerrin* (1893); *N. Y. Times,* July 8, 1867.] C. D. R.

MEARNS, EDGAR ALEXANDER (Sept. 11, 1856–Nov. 1, 1916), naturalist, army surgeon, was born at Highland Falls, Orange County, N. Y., the son of Alexander and Nancy (Carswell) Mearns. His family was of Scotch descent on the side of the father and of New England descent on the side of the mother. At a very early age he began to take interest in birds and other animals, and this interest, intelligently directed by his parents, was destined to dominate his entire career. He received his formal education at Donald Highland Institute, Highland Falls, and at the College of Physicians and Surgeons, New York City, graduating from the latter in 1881. Having passed the examinations for entrance into the medical department of the United States army, in December 1883 he received his commission as assistant surgeon, with the rank of first lieutenant. Among the several stations that were open for his choice, he selected the arid and desolate Fort Verde in Central Arizona as the one that offered the greatest interest to the naturalist. After remaining nearly four years in Arizona he went to Fort Snelling, Minn., where he served for about three years.

Late in the year 1891 Mearns (now captain) was appointed medical officer of the Mexican-United States International Boundary Commission. Through cooperation between the authorities of the commission and those of the United States National Museum and the American Museum of Natural History, he was enabled by September 1894 personally to explore the entire boundary line, from El Paso, Tex., to the Pacific Coast, and he brought together not less than 30,000 specimens representative of the animal and plant life of the region. During the next eight years he collected in the Catskills, at Fort Clark, Tex., at Fort Adams, R. I., in Florida, and in the Yellowstone National Park. He received his advancement to surgeon, with the rank of major, in 1901. Two terms of service in the Philippines, 1903–04 and 1905–07, gave him an opportunity to become acquainted with tropical life. With the cooperation of many associates and in particular of Gen. Leonard Wood, he was enabled to make important collections, especially of mammals, birds, and plants. At considerable personal risk he ascended all three of the highest peaks in the Philippines, something that no naturalist had previously done.

In 1908 Mearns, with two assistants, Edmund Heller and J. Alden Loring, was selected to act as naturalist for the Smithsonian African Expedition. He retired from the army with the rank of lieutenant-colonel on Jan. 1, 1909, and immediately reported for duty on the expedition. He was in the field with the explorers nearly a year, traversing parts of British East Africa (now Kenya), Uganda, and Lado Enclave, returning by way of the White Nile and Egypt. In 1911 he again successfully visited Africa, this time as the guest of Childs Frick. The objective was Abyssinia and some of the less-known parts of eastern Africa. Mearns finally returned in September 1912 and began to prepare a report on the birds obtained by the two expeditions. But the disease, diabetes, from which he had known he was suffering since 1907, so sapped his strength that the task could not be completed. He died in Washington, leaving a widow, Ella Wittich Mearns, whom he had married in 1881, and a daughter. Diphtheria had already taken his son, Louis DeZeraga Mearns, a gifted young astronomer, in April 1912. His busy life as an army surgeon and his extraordinary activity as a collector prevented him from making any large contribution to scientific literature, but he printed more than a hundred articles in technical journals and in publications of the National Museum. His most important study, *The Mammals of the Mexican Boundary of the United States,* Part 1, was published as a bulletin of the Museum (no. 56, 1907). As a gatherer of material for the use of specialists in systematic zoölogy and botany, Mearns made his great contribution to the advance of learning, and unquestionably outdid every other American in his particular field of activity. His zoölogical additions to the national collections number approximately: mammals, 7,000; birds, 20,000; reptiles, 5,000; fishes, 5,000. Other important material that he gathered went to the American Museum of Natural History in New York City. At the time of his death his contributions to the National Herbarium were greater than those made by any other one man.

[Notice in *Report on the Progress and Condition of the U. S. Nat. Museum for the Year Ending June 30, 1917* (1918), pp. 92–94; C. W. Richmond, "In Memoriam: Edgar Alexander Mearns," the *Auk*, Jan. 1918; *Who's Who in America,* 1916–17; *Evening Star* (Washington, D. C.), Nov. 3, 1916.] G. S. M.

MEARS, DAVID OTIS (Feb. 22, 1842–Apr. 29, 1915), Congregational and Presbyterian clergyman, eldest son of David and Abigail (Burnham) Mears, was born in Essex, Mass., a town of shipbuilding fame. His father was a manufacturer of cotton line for the rigging of ships, a quiet man of sterling integrity and business shrewdness. The mother, well-educated for that day, was deeply religious and a fine singer. In 1858 David entered Phillips Academy, Andover, of which the famous "Uncle Sam" Taylor was then principal. Graduating in 1861, he entered Amherst College and received the degree of A.B. in 1865. His years of preparation for the ministry were spent as the special personal student of Dr. Edward N. Kirk [*q.v.*], a noted Boston pastor. On Oct. 2, 1867, he was ordained pastor of the North Avenue Congregational Church, Cambridge, Mass. During the following nearly ten years the church had marked growth and the pastorate was distinguished by outspoken Sunday-evening addresses on the duties of citizens and on social questions, as well as by the effective interest of the pastor in the improvement of church music. He was a founder of the "Monday Club" of ministers in Boston and vicinity. In 1877 he became pastor of the Piedmont Congregational Church, Worcester, Mass. During the first years of this pastorate he led the successful effort to clear off the heavy debt with which the house of worship was encumbered. His advocacy of moral reform was continued. In 1886 a No-license League was formed in the church, and the movement spread to other churches and cities, until a Massachusetts Anti-Saloon League was organized in 1892, of which Mears was the first president. In 1888 he made an extended journey in England and on the Continent.

In 1893 he accepted an invitation to the Calvary Presbyterian Church of Cleveland, Ohio, notwithstanding the determined opposition of his Worcester people. The Cleveland pastorate was marked by activities and results similar to those characterizing his preceding pastorate. In 1893 the Anti-Saloon League of Ohio was organized and Mears, who was one of the founders, became its first president. He accepted in 1895 a call to the historic Fourth Presbyterian Church of Albany, New York. Here for fourteen years, while devoted to the upbuilding of the church, he actively participated in the movement to secure temperance instruction in the schools, in the effort to amend the Raines law in the interest of temperance, and in the sound-money campaign of 1896. After the close of his active ministry he lived at "Orchard Home" on the ancestral estate in Essex, Mass.

Mears was of medium height, of vigorous physique and had a resonant voice. For one of such strong convictions he had unusual ability to recognize the sincerity and appreciate the views of those differing with him. His power of effective speech, his musical gifts, deep pastoral feeling, and capacity for lasting friendships were elements of his strength. He married, Sept. 11, 1867, Frances J. Bentley of Amherst, Mass., who died Mar. 26, 1879; on Sept. 6, 1882, he married Mary Chapin Grinnell, daughter of Hon. Josiah B. Grinnell [*q.v.*], of Grinnell, Iowa. Besides single addresses, articles, and sermons, he published *Life of Edward Norris Kirk* (1877); *The Deathless Book* (1888); *Oberlin Lectures of 1892; The Pulpit and the Pews* (1892); *Inspired Through Suffering* (1895).

[*David Otis Mears, D.D. An Autobiog.* (copr. 1920), with memoir and notes by H. A. Davidson; *Biog. Record of the Alumni of Amherst Coll. 1821–1871* (1883); *Who's Who in America,* 1912–13; *Albany Evening Jour.*, May 1, 1915, editorial; *Albany Argus,* Apr. 30, 1915; *Congregationalist and Christian World,* May 13, 1915; *Continent* (New York), June 24, 1915.] E. D. E.

MEARS, HELEN FARNSWORTH (Dec. 21, 1876–Feb. 17, 1916), sculptor, third daughter and youngest child of John Hall Mears and Mary Elizabeth (Farnsworth) Mears, was born in Oshkosh, Wis., of Scottish ancestry on both sides. Her father was a native of Hawkesbury, Ontario, and her mother, of Groton, Mass. Both parents were well endowed mentally; the mother had attained modest fame as a writer. In early childhood, Helen shaped figures in any plastic stuff she could find—mud, dough, putty, tar—until her father gave her clay. Later he guided her attempts, and since he had studied to be a surgeon, taught her something of anatomy. At the age of nine, she exhibited at the county fair a clay head of Apollo, baked in her mother's oven. When she was sixteen, photographs of her kneeling figure called "Repentance" were shown to Ward and to Saint-Gaudens, both of whom expressed interest by inviting her to their workshops.

During a few weeks of study under Lorado Taft at the Chicago Art Institute, she received an order for a nine-foot statue, "The Genius of Wisconsin," to represent that state at the World's Columbian Exposition in Chicago (1893). This work, cut in marble, was later placed in the rotunda of the Capitol at Madison, Wis., and won from the Milwaukee Women's Club a prize of $500. With her prize money Helen Mears went to New York for study at the Art Students' League. Here her modeling met approval from Saint-Gaudens, who accepted her as assistant in his private studio. Under this uncompromising but friendly master, her progress was real. Aided by a wealthy woman, she went to Paris and broadened her horizon by seeing museums and monuments, as well as by studying under the painters Raphael Collin and Luc Olivier Merson, and the sculptors Alexandre Charpentier and Denys Puech. While Saint-Gaudens was in Paris, engaged on his Sherman equestrian group and other undertakings, she again acted as one of his assistants. She exhibited in the Salon, and visited Italy.

In 1898, she received in competition the commission for the marble statue of Frances E. Willard, gift of the State of Illinois to the national Capitol at Washington, D. C. Both the first and second blocks of marble revealed bad faults after much work had been spent on them, and were discarded for a third. The statue was unveiled in Statuary Hall in 1905. At the St. Louis Exposition of 1904, her monumental three-paneled wall fountain, "The Fountain of Life" (a work in which it was her good fortune to have the collaboration of Henry Bacon, architect of the Lincoln Memorial), received praise from distinguished critics and won a silver medal. It was the most ambitious project of her lifetime. Saint-Gaudens' faith in her ability appears in the thoughtful letters of counsel he wrote to her about these two efforts, the Frances Willard statue and the fountain, her main endeavor during five years. In 1907, she became a member of the National Sculpture Society.

Among her works are bronze busts, "General George Rogers Clark" in the Milwaukee Public Library, and "Dr. William T. G. Morton," pioneer in anaesthesia, in the Smithsonian Institution. Her bronze bas-relief portraits include those of her mother, Mary Elizabeth Mears, in the possession of the Madison Art Association; her master, Augustus Saint-Gaudens, at Peabody Institute, Baltimore; the composer Edward MacDowell, in the Metropolitan Museum. She created many imaginative figures and groups, mainly in private ownership. Her command of the monumental is shown in the "Adin Randall Fountain," erected in Eau Claire, Wis., 1914. Although competent criticism had already pointed her out as a figure of unusual promise, it is recorded that privation hastened her end. She died suddenly in her studio in Washington Square, New York, surrounded by a quantity of good work in many stages, bearing witness to her spiritual outlook, her intellectual grasp, and her tireless self-dedication. Memorial exhibitions of her works were held in Milwaukee, 1917, in Baltimore, 1918, and at the Brooklyn Museum, 1920.

[*The Reminiscences of Augustus Saint-Gaudens* (1913), II, 29, 30, 185; *Wisconsin History Bulletin*, Mar. 1927; *Am. Art Annual*, vol. XIII (1916); *Catalogue, International Exhibition of Contemporary Medals* (Am. Numismatic Soc., 1911); Catalogue, *Helen Farnsworth Mears Memorial Exhibition* (Milwaukee Art Inst., 1917); C. E. Fairman, *Art and Artists of the Capitol of the U. S. of A.* (1927); P. V. Lawson, "Mary Elizabeth Mears," in *Proc. Wis. Hist. Soc.*, 1916; *Art Rev.*, Mar. 1908; *Biog. Sketches of Am. Artists* (1924), pub. by Mich. State Lib.; *N. Y. Times*, Feb. 18, 19, 1916; *N. Y. Herald*, June 4, 1916. The year of birth is variously given as 1872, 1874, 1876, and 1878, but the weight of evidence seems to rest with 1876.]

A. A.

MEARS, JOHN WILLIAM (Aug. 10, 1825–Nov. 10, 1881), Presbyterian clergyman, educator, author, son of Henry Haller Mears and his wife, Ann Barbara (Birkinbine) of Reading, Pa., was a descendant in the fifth generation from William Mears, who emigrated from Everton, England, about 1735, and settled in Georgia. John Mears, son of the emigrant, settled in Philadelphia about 1754. Although identified with the Society of Friends, he was during the Revolutionary War one of the "fighting Quakers." Later he removed to Reading, and then, possessed of the pioneer spirit, pushed on over the mountains and laid out and built the road connecting the valleys of the Schuylkill and Susquehanna rivers, founding the town of Catawissa. His grandson, Henry Haller Mears, was a successful business man in Philadelphia and an elder in the Prebyterian Church. John William Mears was born in Reading, and graduated from Delaware College in 1844, studied at the Yale Scientific School, 1846–48, and in the Divinity School, 1848–49. Three years later, on Apr. 15, 1852, he was ordained to the Presbyterian ministry. On Sept. 2, of the same year, he married Phebe A. H. Tatem. He was pastor at Camden, N. J., 1852–53; at Elkton, Md., 1854–57; and at Milford, Del., 1857–60. As a representative of the views of the "new school" of the Presbyterian Church he was one of the editors of the *American Presbyterian* of Philadelphia from 1860 to 1865, and thereafter was editor and publisher until 1870, when the periodical was merged with the *New York Evangelist.*

On Mar. 6, 1871, he was appointed to the Albert Barnes Professorship of Intellectual and Moral Philosophy at Hamilton College, Clinton, N. Y., in which connection he continued until his death, at Clinton, ten years later. His inaugural address (*American Presbyterian Review,* October 1871) reveals his attitude as that of an idealist, in opposition to materialistic types of philosophy. He was recognized by his colleagues and students as "a thorough scholar, possessed of a mind that was inquisitive and keenly analytical." On the platform and with the pen he was master of a vigorous style. He was successful in securing important accessions to the college library, of which he had charge for a time. He also gave instruction in German and French. Out of his classroom instruction in the philosophy of Kant came the plan of celebrating the centennial of the publication of the Critique of Pure Reason. On that occasion he delivered an address at Saratoga, N. Y., July 6, 1881, which was later given before the Concord School of Philosophy and printed in the *Journal of Speculative Philosophy* (January, July 1881). He was interested in public questions and identified himself with the Prohibition party, standing as their candidate for Congress in 1878, and for governor of New York in 1879. Through his active efforts the sentiment that existed in central New York against the institution of "complex marriage" as practised at the Oneida Community found effective expression, with the result that in 1879 that feature of the Community system was voluntarily abandoned. In 1878 he was president of the New York State Teachers' Association.

His earliest published work, *The Bible in the Workshop* (1857), dealt with the relation of Christianity to labor. Later works, published by the Presbyterian Board, were: *The Martyrs of France* (1860); *The Beggars of Holland and the Grandees of Spain* (1867); *The Story of Madagascar* (1873); *Heroes of Bohemia* (1874); *From Exile to Overthrow* (1881). His address, "The Presbyterian Element in our National Life and History," delivered before the Synod of Central New York in 1876, was published in the second part of P. H. Fowler's *Historical Sketch of Presbyterianism within the Bounds of the Synod of Central New York* (1877). In 1879 his *Brief English-French Compend of the Grammar of the French Language* appeared.

[*Notice of Henry Haller Mears, with a Geneal. of the Mears Family* (1873); H. C. Kirk, *A Hist. of the N. Y. State Teachers' Asso.* (1883); *Am. Socialist,* Aug. 28, Sept. 4, 1879; *Utica Herald,* Feb. 15, Aug. 30, Sept. 1, 1879, Nov. 11, 14, 1881.] E. F.

MEARS, OTTO (May 3, 1840–June 24, 1931), Colorado pioneer and roadbuilder, was born in Courland, Russia, of mixed English and Hebrew stock. Orphaned at the age of two, he was taken into the family of an uncle who had thirteen children. When ten years old, he emigrated to California, where he was to have met an uncle, but failed to find him. In a strange land, unable to speak English, the boy was thrown upon his own resources. He began selling newspapers and later took odd jobs of various kinds. At the outbreak of the Civil War he enlisted in Company H of the 1st California Volunteers and saw service in the New Mexico region. When his term expired he became a store clerk in Santa Fé, then he began business for himself at Conejos, Colo., in 1865. With a partner he established a pioneer sawmill and a gristmill, and to increase the grists of the flourmill, he began to grow wheat. He brought the first mower, reaper, and threshing machine into the region, much to the astonishment of his Mexican neighbors.

Mears found a demand for flour in the mountain mining camps to the north, but there was no wagon road to this market. He therefore built a road over Poncho Pass. This incidental project inaugurated the great road-building projects that were to become his chief contribution to the development of Colorado. When rich mines were discovered in the inaccessible San Juan Mountains, he organized a company and built a toll road to the region. To aid in promoting the district he published newspapers at Saguache and Lake City. He extended his system of toll roads until they embraced 300 miles of road. After the Meeker massacre of 1879, Mears assisted in rescuing the women captives. He then accompanied an Indian delegation to Washington where a treaty was negotiated, further reducing the Indian reservation. The Utes at home refused at first to accept the treaty, but Mears secured their acceptance by privately paying each Indian two dollars. Charges of bribery were preferred against him, but were dismissed by the secretary of the interior, who reimbursed him for the $2,800 he had paid the Indians.

Mears continued his toll-road building and operated freighting outfits and pack trains. Then he began railroad construction, building the Rio Grande Southern and the Silverton Northern railroads in southwestern Colorado. He also acquired an interest in certain mining and smelter properties in the district. In 1884 he was elected to the Colorado legislature and continued for many years thereafter as an important influence in the Republican party of the state. He accumulated a fair-sized fortune, much of which was lost in the panic of 1893. His last railroad venture was the building of the Chesapeake Beach Railroad in Maryland. He spent his last years in California where he developed ranch and hotel property. In 1870 he had married Mary Kampfschulte, by whom he had two daughters. His portrait appears in one of the stained-glass windows of the Colorado Capitol and a historical tablet is set in the granite wall of the mountain beside one of his picturesque pioneer roads in the San Juan Mountains near the present town of Ouray, Colo. He died at Pasadena, Cal.

[Sidney Jocknick, *Early Days on the Western Slope of Colo. and Campfire Chats with Otto Mears, the Pathfinder* (1913); *The Colo. Blue Book*, 1891; *Ann. Report of the Commissioner of Indian Affairs . . . for the Year 1881*; W. F. Stone, *Hist. of Colo.*, vol. IV (1919); J. C. Smiley, *Hist. of Denver* (1901); J. H. Baker and L. R. Hafen, *Hist. of Colo.* (1927), vol. V; *Daily Press* (Montrose, Colo.), Aug. 30, 1926; *Denver Post*, June 24, 1931; *Rocky Mountain News*, June 25, 1931; information as to certain facts from Mears's daughter, Mrs. J. R. Pitcher, and from his associates.]

L. R. H.

MEASE, JAMES (Aug. 11, 1771–May 14, 1846), physician, scientist, and author, the son of John and Esther (Miller) Mease, was born in Philadelphia, Pa. His father was a wealthy shipping merchant and a Revolutionary patriot. James entered the University of Pennsylvania in 1784 and after graduating in the College in 1787, began a course in the medical school of the same institution, receiving the degree of M.D. in 1792. In August 1790, while he was still a student, he published an article on hydrophobia in the *American Magazine*. When he prepared his thesis for his medical degree, he enlarged the same subject in his *Inaugural Dissertation on the Disease Produced by the Bite of a Mad Dog or Other Rabid Animal* (1792). The essay was dedicated to Benjamin Rush, who had been one of his professors. In 1808 he published in the *Philadelphia Medical Museum* (vol. V, no. 1) a paper revealing the quackery practised in connection with diseases produced by the bites of snakes and mad dogs. During the War of 1812 he served as a hospital surgeon (Sept. 2, 1814–June 15, 1815). He became identified with many of the organizations of Philadelphia. He was one of the managers of the "Company for the Improvement of the Vine," in connection with which he developed a vineyard, and he was a leader in the organization of the Pennsylvania Horticultural Society. Many of his papers were read before the American Philosophical Society to which he was elected in 1802 and which he served from 1824 to 1830 as curator and from 1832 to 1836 as councilor. He was one of the founders and first vice-president of the Philadelphia Athenæum.

Mease wrote, edited, or compiled several medical works, although he is principally remembered for his contributions to literature unidentified with his profession. Of his printed works, his *Picture of Philadelphia* (1811) is best known, but his *Geological Account of the United States* (1807), a physical and commercial geography, was a valuable compilation and a pioneer work in its field. He edited *The Surgical Works of the Late John Jones, M.D.* (1795); the first American edition of *The Domestic Encyclopædia* of A. F. M. Willich (1803–04); and *Archives of Useful Knowledge* (2 vols., 1811–12). In addition, he wrote *An Address on the Progress of Agriculture* (1817); *Address on the Subject of Establishing a Pattern Farm in the Vicinity of Philadelphia* (1818); "Description of Some of the Medals Struck in Relation to Important Events in North America," published in the *Collections of the New York Historical Society* (vol. III, 1821); *Observations on the Penitentiary System and Penal Code of Pennsylvania* (1828); *On the Utility of Public Loan Offices and Savings Funds by City Authorities* (1836); and *Thermometrical Observations as Connected with Navigation* (1841). He married Sarah, daughter of Pierce Butler [*q.v.*], United States senator from South Carolina in the First Congress, July 3, 1800, and their two sons, in order to secure an inheritance, later had their names changed to Butler. One of these, Pierce Butler, married Frances Anne Kemble [*q.v.*], actress and poetess. Mease died in Philadelphia and lies buried in the ground of the Third Presbyterian Church in that city.

[J. T. Scharf and Thompson Westcott, *Hist. of Phila.* (1884), vols. I and II; H. A. Kelly and W. L. Burrage, *Am. Medic. Biogs.* (1920); Henry Simpson, *The Lives of Eminent Philadelphians* (1859); *Univ. of Pa.: Biog. Cat. of the Matriculates of the Coll., 1749–1893* (1894); *The Athenæum of Phila.* (1884); *Poulson's Am. Daily Advertiser*, July 7, 1800; *North American* (Phila.), May 15, 1846.]

J. J.

MEASON, ISAAC (1742–Jan. 23, 1818), pioneer ironmaster west of the Alleghanies, came from Virginia before 1771 and settled upon a 323-acre tract of land called "Mount Pleasant," in what is now Fayette County, Pa. In some records his name appears as Mason, and he was probably a member of a well-to-do family of that name in Sussex County, Va. He took steps to secure his land in southwestern Pennsylvania within one year after purchase of the land from the proprietors had become legal. Since a definite boundary line between Pennsylvania and Virginia was not determined until October 1786, for a number of years the uncertainty of allegiance caused legal confusion in the Western country. Although Isaac Meason had bought his land from Pennsylvania, he was recommended in 1775 as a proper person to be added to the commission of the peace for Augusta County, Va. There is reason to believe that in 1776 he served in the Continental Army under Col. Anthony Wayne (*Pennsylvania Archives,* 5 ser., II, 1906, p. 150). On Apr. 28, 1778, Thomas Gist swore that, being a magistrate, in April 1772 he had "solemnized the wrights of Matrimony between Isaac Meason and Catharine Harrison," whose father was Lawrence Harrison (Yohogania County Court Records, quoted by Crumrine, *post,* p. 217; Ellis, *post,* p. 527). Other witnesses said that at the time all parties, including Catharine, were required by Isaac Meason to swear "not to divulge said marriage." Isaac and Catharine became the parents of two sons and two daughters. In October 1779, Meason was elected to the Pennsylvania Assembly from Westmoreland County. During the Revolution he was among those who wrote to the state government of the dangers threatening western settlements; in 1782 his brother-in-law, William Harrison, was captured, burned, and cut in pieces by the savages. In October 1783, Meason was elected by Westmoreland County to the Supreme Executive Council of Pennsylvania.

The first recorded reference to iron ore in this section of Pennsylvania occurred in 1780 when Col. William Crawford, one of Meason's neighbors, surveyed a farm on the Monongahela "to include a bank of iron ore" (Ellis, p. 233). By 1791 Meason had established Union Furnace on Dunbar Creek, the first successful iron works west of the Alleghany Mountains. Two years later he formed a partnership with Moses Dillon and John Gibson as Meason, Dillon & Company, and built a larger furnace. Here were manufactured in great numbers the "castings, stoves, pots, sugar kettles, salt kettles and other articles" needed by the thousands of immigrants who at that time began to flock over the mountain and down the Ohio River to the country further West. The trade brought Meason such wealth that in 1803 he erected a splendid Georgian mansion of limestone at Mount Braddock.

In 1816, despite those who urged him "not to impose upon the old gentleman," one Thomas C. Lewis, a Welshman, persuaded Meason to finance a mill for puddling and rolling bar iron. Lewis, who had learned the process in Wales, had tried without avail for more than a year to convince Eastern iron masters that iron could be rolled into bars. Meason, by financing Lewis's project, contributed one more step to the development of the Western Pennsylvania iron and coal industry in which he had been the first to achieve success. When he died he left to his heirs over 20,000 acres of the best coal land in Western Pennsylvania, in addition to Middleton Iron Works, Dunbar Furnace, Mount Vernon Furnace, Union Furnace, Maria Forge and Union Forge, toll ferries and bridges, gristmills, rolling-mills, salt works, the town of New Haven, and lands in other parts of Pennsylvania and Kentucky.

[Account books of Union Ironworks, Mount Vernon Forge, etc., in the Uniontown, Pa., Public Library; *The Jour. of the Rev. Francis Asbury* (3 vols., 1821); court records, deeds, wills, etc., of Fayette County, Pa.; *Pa. Archives,* 1 ser. IX (1854), 5 ser. II (1906); gravestone inscriptions; Boyd Crumrine, *Hist. of Washington County, Pa.* (1882); Franklin Ellis, *Hist. of Fayette County, Pa.* (1882), esp. pp. 502–03.] E. A.

MECHEM, FLOYD RUSSELL (May 9, 1858–Dec. 11, 1928), lawyer, teacher, author, was born at Nunda, N. Y., the son of Isaac J. and Celestia (Russell) Mechem. He attended the public schools at Battle Creek, Mich., and Titusville, Pa. While he was still a boy, his father died leaving him to assume part of the responsibility of supporting the family. Deprived of opportunity to attend college, he completed his education outside. At the age of twenty-one he was admitted to the Michigan bar and for the following few years devoted himself to the practice of law, first in Battle Creek (1879–87), then in Detroit (1887–93). In 1891–92 he held a professorship at the Detroit College of Law and from that time on devoted the greater part of his time to legal education. In 1892 he became a member of the faculty of the University of Michigan and remained there, teaching and writing, until 1903 when he moved to Chicago to assume a professorship in the newly organized law school of the University of Chicago. He remained in this position until his death. He was married to Jessie Collier, Dec. 4, 1884, and they had two sons. He was president for several years of the University of Chicago Settlement; a member of the district appeal board, number 1, northern district of Illinois; and a member of the summer-session law faculty of Columbia University (1919, 1920), the University of Colorado (1922), and Stanford University (1923).

Mechem was internationally known as an authority on agency, partnership, sales, and corporations, and his published treatises and his numerous articles in law reviews illustrate the precision of his writing and his broad conception of legal problems. Any writing to him included the labored exhaustion of all the contributory subject matter, and his citations were strengthened by his intimate knowledge of the allied cases. The portion of the world of knowledge he had made his own lay in his mind in orderly array. One of his outstanding characteristics was his complete independence of thought, his habit of reëxamining for himself opinions however confidently they might be entertained even by those whose judgment he most respected. He was wont to say that although almost everybody's believing a thing may not create a presumption of its being false, it certainly does not prevent its being so. His basic political outlook was occasionally reflected in his teaching to the great advantage of his students, who were coming to maturity during a period when contemporary thought was submerging the individual for the "social good" without pointing out that this, like everything else, costs something. His conviction that the more important ultimate values were individual, not social, served to warn students of the half-truth of contemporary thought which all but completely lost sight of the individual. Nor was his view on this matter the result of an uninformed conservatism; it was a thoughtfully developed philosophy.

Mechem's most notable work was his *Treatise on the Law of Agency* (1889), revised and republished in 1914, which more than any other single work shaped the law of agency in the United States. Next in importance was his *Treatise on the Law of Sale of Personal Property* (2 vols., 1901), an exhaustive study, which has been widely cited by the courts. His other works, *A Treatise on the Law of Public Offices and Officers* (1890); his edition (1891) of Robert Hutchinson's *Treatise on the Law of Carriers*; and his *Elements of the Law of Partnership* (1896), as well as his case books in agency, partnership, and damages, exerted a strong influence in shaping contemporary legal education. In November 1923 he undertook the task of directing the "Restatement of the Law of Agency" for the American Law Institute. Without neglecting his heavy teaching program, he worked continuously on this project. It was a gigantic undertaking and he had hoped to be able to complete it, but he was taken suddenly ill and died of influenza before the work was finished.

[H. A. Bigelow, memoir in *Am. Bar Asso. Jour.*, Mar. 1929; *Ill. Law Rev.*, Feb. 1929; *Ann. Report of the Ill. State Bar Asso.*, 1929, pp. 403–04; *Who's Who in America*, 1928–29; *Chicago Daily Tribune*, Dec. 12, 1928.] H. O.

MECOM, BENJAMIN (b. Dec. 29, 1732), printer, born at Boston, Mass., was the third of the twelve children of Edward Mecom and Jane, youngest sister of Benjamin Franklin. He was apprenticed to James Parker of New York City, whose business had been established by Franklin in 1742 as a copartnership. Franklin also established the first printing office in Antigua with a manager, in 1748, who died in midsummer of 1752; whereupon Franklin appointed his nephew as his new manager on shares. Mecom sailed from Philadelphia on Aug. 20, 1752, and at St. John found an equipped printery, the only one in the Leeward Islands, with an established, though sometime suspended, newspaper, the *Antigua Gazette,* which he revived, with a new serial numbering, in November. It was a weekly until January 1755 and thereafter came out thrice a week, until June 26, 1756, or later. Franklin had planned to give this business to his nephew, but in view of his youth, and to steady him, held him under strict terms, which irked Mecom because he wished to be independent. Mecom made the fact known and was offended when his uncle long delayed an answer, and notified him of his decision to quit Antigua. The printing outfit was shipped to Franklin, with whom he later settled all accounts honorably, thereby becoming its owner. He sent it to Boston and there set himself up as a printer and bookseller at Cornhill, before June 1757.

Mecom printed editions of *The New-England Primer Enlarged* (1757) and *The New-England Psalter* (1758) for the Boston booksellers on terms so low as to be unprofitable. Among a variety of pieces printed during his Boston career, the most interesting were the first separate collection of Franklin's Poor Richard proverbs, brought out in 1758 as *Father Abraham's Speech* (2nd ed., 1760), and the *New-England Magazine,* which in three numbers ran from August 1758 to March 1759. His business career at "The New Printing-Office" at Boston ended in 1762, probably because he was a very poor business manager. Thomas (*post,* I, pp. 32, 260) credits him, so far as he knew, with being "the first person in this country . . . who attempted stereotype printing." Mecom moved his outfit to New York early in 1763, and there established the "Modern Printing-Office on Rotten-Row." He attempted to issue a newspaper, the *New-York Pacquet,* with a zero trial number appearing on July 11, 1763. The only other extant issue is Number 6, for Aug. 22, 1763.

He failed in New York. Among his creditors was Parker, with whom, by Franklin's consent, the book stock and old Antigua printing outfit were stored as security. Mecom rented Parker's New Haven printery, which was really Franklin's property, and arrived at New Haven early in 1765 to print books and pamphlets, and also to serve as Parker's deputy in the post-office. On July 5, 1765, he revived the *Connecticut Gazette,* which he carried on till Feb. 19, 1768. Failure in liquidating debts and paying rent to Parker forced his resignation from the postal service in February 1767. But as the press was his uncle's property, he continued to use it until he took it to Philadelphia in 1768 to start anew. Here, in January 1769, he began the *Penny Post,* a diminutive news sheet, issued thrice a week, which died after only nine issues. In September 1770 he petitioned for a license to sell spirituous liquors in Philadelphia, in order "to support a Number of young growing Children." However, instead of becoming a rum seller, he got work at his trade with William Goddard, and when the latter removed to Baltimore in 1774, Mecom took his family to Burlington, N. J., where he was employed by Isaac Collins. A sad last notice remains of him in a letter from William Smith of Burlington to Franklin, on July 19, 1776, saying that Mecom was often *non compos mentis* and dangerous, and bidding that he be put in a hospital or incarcerated.

[The best source is Wilberforce Eames, "The Antigua Press and Benj. Mecom, 1748–65," in *Proc. Am. Antiquarian Soc.,* n.s., vol. XXXVIII (1929), and separately reprinted (1929). See also: Isaiah Thomas, *The Hist. of Printing in America* (2nd ed., 2 vols., 1874); C. S. Brigham, "Bibliog. of Am. Newspapers," *Proc. Am. Antiquarian Soc.,* n.s., vol. XXIII (1913); vol. XXX (1921); C. R. Hildeburn, *Sketches of Printers and Printing in Colonial N. Y.* (1895); H. S. Hall, article in the *New England Mag.,* Jan. 1906; Parker's letters to Franklin in *Proc. Mass. Hist. Soc.,* 2 ser., vol. XVI (1903).]

V. H. P.

MEDARY, MILTON BENNETT (Feb. 6, 1874–Aug. 7, 1929), architect and architectural consultant, was born in Philadelphia of parents native to that city, Milton Bennett and Mary Emma (Cregar) Medary. Trained at the University of Pennsylvania, where he graduated (B.A.) in 1894, he was steeped in Philadelphia traditions, which he broadened but did not transcend. A year of travel in Europe preceded his architectural apprenticeship in the office of Frank Miles Day [*q.v.*], whose example of public service the pupil ever followed. For ten years (1895–1905) he was a member of the firm of Field & Medary; for five years he practised alone; in 1910 he entered the firm of Zantzinger, Borie & Medary, in which association he continued until his death. On Dec. 27, 1900, he married Hannah Leech Stadelman, of Bala, a suburb of Philadelphia, where they made their home and reared a family.

Gothic architecture appealed to his nature. Infinite detail within clearly defined structural form delighted his sensitive soul. In his art, as in his life, he sought first the pattern and, that determined, he filled it with richness and beauty. Endowed with the faculty of clear thinking and direct, forceful, and picturesque expression, he became a leader among his fellows and a convincing and persuasive advocate with clients in national as well as in private enterprises.

Early in his practice he undertook the Washington Memorial Chapel at Valley Forge, carrying on the work through the years as money came, and putting into the design the evidences of his own expanding and ripening thought. There, where as nowhere else the soul of the Revolution revealed itself and where today the natural scenery imposes a sense of tragic solemnity, the intricately wrought Gothic chapel wins a response which a structure historically more appropriate might fail to evoke. The Divinity School, Philadelphia, the Foulke and Henry dormitories at Princeton, the Penn Athletic Club, and hospitals in Philadelphia and Bryn Mawr are distinctly his conceptions. All show the influence of his Gothic predilections. His preliminary sketches for Penn Charter School in Germantown, however, give abundant evidence of a fine feeling for the colonial type of architecture with its good proportions, flexibility, simple straightforwardness, and economy of construction—traits for which he himself was conspicuous, and which he repeatedly expressed in city-planning problems. The culminating work of his career is the carillon tower designed for Edward A. Bok at Mountain Lake, Fla., on which he spent infinite time and patience. He had the collaboration and sympathetic cooperation of Frederick Law Olmsted in the landscape setting. The resulting structure, so individual in conception, in service, and in isolation, will stand apart during the generations as a memorial to the donor and to the designers. If the completed work, which endeavored to incorporate the ideas of another, did not altogether satisfy Medary's fastidious sense, he but experienced the fate common to architects, as expressed in the epitaph of Framinio Vacca in the Pantheon: "He never did anything which completely satisfied him."

The intensely practical, common-sense portion of his nature found expression during the World War in the government buildings on Neville Island, Pittsburgh, hastily constructed but thoroughly planned for effective administration. He was vice-president and predestined president of the American Institute of Architects when the National Commission of Fine Arts recommended to President Harding the appointment of Medary as one of the three architectural members of that body. The first problem to engage attention after his appointment (1922) was the disputed location of the Arlington Memorial Bridge, and to the resulting satisfactory solution his contribution was significant. After the expiration of his term (1926), he continued his work on the development of the National Capital as a member of the National Capital Park and Planning Commission, by successive appointments of President Coolidge and President Hoover; and then the Secretary of the Treasury made him one of the architectural consultants on the so-called Triangle group of public buildings (1927), assigning to his firm the designing of the Department of Justice building. On this work he was engaged at the time of his sudden death, which occurred in Philadelphia.

He was president of the American Institute of Architects in 1926–28, and the bestowal upon him of the gold medal of that body in 1929 marked the culmination of a career of widespread public usefulness cut short at the time of his greatest power in stimulating and directing public taste. The last works of his pencil were three studies for dormitories at the University of Chicago, dated by him four days before he died.

[*The Year Book of the Ann. Arch. Exhibition, Phila.*, 1929, dedicated to M. B. Medary, contains reproductions of his sketches and photographs of his work, with a sketch of his life by J. I. Bright, and a portrait. See also *Proc. of the Ann. Conventions of the Am. Inst. of Architects*, 1926–29; *Who's Who in America*, 1928–29; *N. Y. Times*, and *Public Ledger* (Phila.), Aug. 8, 1929.] C. M.

MEDARY, SAMUEL (Feb. 25, 1801–Nov. 7, 1864), editor, was born of Quaker parentage in Montgomery County, Pa., where he spent his youth. He attended the academy at Norristown, though he never graduated, and taught school in Montgomery County to earn money to pay for his education. At the age of sixteen he was contributing prose and poetry to the *Norristown Herald and Weekly Advertiser.* In 1820 he went with his father and mother to Montgomery County, Md., in 1823 to Georgetown, D. C., and in 1825 he moved to Batavia, Ohio, where he became a co-worker with Thomas Morris in the Democratic party. Two years later he was a school trustee, county surveyor, and soon afterward, auditor of Clermont County. A born agitator, he with Morris established the *Ohio Sun* at Bethel in 1828 to support Andrew Jackson for president. The people of Clermont County sent him three times to the state legislature and in 1837 his party elected him supervisor of public printing, a post which he held for a decade while he ran the Democratic organ entitled the *Ohio Statesman.* In 1844 he was chairman of the Ohio Democratic delegation to the Baltimore convention. It was in the capacity of editor of a party paper that he became almost a party dictator in Ohio. He ardently supported the movement for the annexation of Texas, the reoccupation of Oregon, and the Mexican War. He also supported the popular cry of "Fifty-four Forty or Fight," but the generally accepted belief that he originated it is without substantiation. His interests were not limited to politics of a local and national character. He advocated sanitation, helped to organize and promote the Ohio Horticultural Society, became an incorporator and director of four railroads, aided Louis Kossuth in his attempt to raise money in America, sympathized with the Cuban revolutionists in 1851, and did more than any other man to cause the adoption of the new constitution of Ohio in 1851. Believing that a constitution should be changed when the people willed it, he devoted his time and energy in 1849 to the publication of a newspaper which he headed with the caption, *The New Constitution.*

Medary supported the Kansas-Nebraska Act and at the National Democratic Convention of 1856, where he served as temporary chairman, he worked for the nomination of Douglas. President Buchanan appointed him to serve as governor of the Minnesota Territory (1857–58), and of the Kansas Territory (1858–60), and he held a brief appointment as deputy postmaster of Columbus, Ohio, from February to December 1858. He assisted in the formation of the state constitution of Minnesota, and he favored the Lecompton Constitution for Kansas. While in Kansas he made a futile attempt to capture John Brown, begged the citizens of Kansas to be peaceable, contributed to the *National Democrat* of Lecompton, Kan., and vetoed a bill to prohibit slavery. He returned to Columbus in 1860 where he founded and edited the *Crisis* (first number, Jan. 31, 1861). As a "Peace Democrat," a supporter of Clement Laird Vallandigham, and of Gen. George B. McClellan for president in 1864, he was one of the most hated men in Ohio by the loyal supporters of the Lincoln administration. He opposed war from the beginning because he believed it might cause the dissolution of the Union and leave the people in debt and misery. He believed that influential editors could have prevented the war, and that no power outside of the individual states of the united confederacy could legally abolish slavery. He made himself so obnoxious to the Unionists that his paper was officially denied circulation in some places, and his press was wrecked by an infuriated mob in 1863. He died the following year in Columbus, Ohio. His wife was Eliza Scott, a Quakeress; they had twelve children.

[C. B. Galbreath, *Hist. of Ohio* (1925), vols. II and III; G. H. Porter, *Ohio Politics during the Civil War Period* (1911); O. C. Hooper, *The Crisis and the Man* (1929); *Proc. of the Democratic State Convention* (Columbus, 1862); R. C. McGrane, *Wm. Allen: A Study in Western Democracy* (1925); E. O. Randall and D. J. Ryan, *Hist. of Ohio* (1912), vol. IV; the *Ohio Statesman*, 1837–57; *Crisis*, 1861–64; *Cincinnati Daily Enquirer*, Nov. 9, 1864; Medary papers in the library of the Ohio Archæol. Soc. at Columbus; scattering letters in the Van Buren and Jackson papers at the Lib. of Cong.; and the Wm. Allen papers at Chillicothe, Ohio.] W. E. S.

MEDILL, JOSEPH (Apr. 6, 1823–Mar. 16, 1899), journalist, was born in a village near St. John in the province of New Brunswick, Canada. He was of Scotch-Irish stock, and for generations his ancestors had been shipbuilders in Belfast. His father, William Medill, emigrated to America in 1819 and settled in an area that was later awarded to Canada by the Webster-Ashburton treaty of 1842. When he was nine his parents moved to Stark County, Ohio, and there he worked on the farm and received such education as the district schools and an academy in Massillon afforded. Upon reaching the age of twenty-one, he determined to enter a law office and after several years of study was admitted to the bar in 1846; but as law practice was at best uncertain, he turned to journalism. With three younger brothers he purchased the *Coshocton Whig* in 1849 and immediately renamed it the *Republican*. Within two years he moved to Cleveland and established the *Daily Forest City*. A year later he consolidated it with a Free-Soil journal and established the *Cleveland Leader*. Accepting the election of 1852 as foreshadowing the end of the Whig party, he labored diligently for the organization of a new party to be called Republican. In March 1854 a secret meeting was held in the office of the *Cleveland Leader* and plans adopted for the new anti-slavery party. There is evidence to show that he was the first man to advocate the name Republican even before the Kansas-Nebraska bill was passed (A. J. Turner, "Genesis of the Republican Party," *Wisconsin State Register*, Mar. 1898; Cleveland, *post*, p. 85).

In the winter of 1854–55 he visited Chicago and with Dr. Charles Ray bought an interest in the *Chicago Tribune*, which was experiencing financial difficulties. He was at that time thirty-two years of age and fired with enthusiasm for the Republican party and the cause of freedom. In the campaign of 1856 he played an important part in the welding of discontented political groups into a compact Republican party and during the Lincoln-Douglas debates threw the resources of his paper behind the Republican candidate. He was a close friend of Abraham Lincoln, and more than once Lincoln conferred with him in the office of the *Tribune*. Although at first in favor of Salmon P. Chase, he soon arrived at the conclusion that Lincoln was the most available candidate and urged him on that ground. He always told with pleasure how he urged Carter of Ohio to change several votes to Lincoln in the Chicago convention, with the result that a landslide was started in favor of the Illinois candidate (Cleveland, *post*, p. 85). At the outbreak of the Civil War, he was opposed to any compromise with the South and at all times demanded an active prosecution of the war. Taking his stand in favor of emancipation and confiscation of southern property, he continually urged the administration to adopt a more radical course of action. He was among the first to advocate the arming of the slaves and insisted from the beginning of the conflict that the soldier in the field should not lose his right to vote. It was largely due to his efforts that several states in the Northwest passed laws to that effect in 1864 (*Chicago Tribune*, Jan. 8, 21, Feb. 4, 1864; *Graphic*, Dec. 19, 1891; Andreas, *post*, vol. II, p. 51). He was also one of the organizers of the powerful and influential Union defense committee, which became the mainstay of the government during the uncertain days of civil strife. In the reconstruction of the South following the war, he supported Congress and was heartily in favor of the radical policies of the Republican party.

He was elected to the Illinois constitutional assembly in 1869, and was the chairman of the committee on electoral and representative reform that wrote the minority-representation clause (*Debates and Proceedings of the Con-*

stitutional Convention . . . Ill. . . . 1869, 1870, vol. I, pp. 560–61). He served as one of the first civil-service commissioners under President Grant. Following the great fire which swept over Chicago in 1871, he was elected mayor and during his term of office labored diligently to remove the municipal government from politics. He greatly enhanced the appointive and removal power of the city administration. In 1874 he bought a majority of the stock of the *Tribune* company and during the remainder of his life controlled the policy of his paper. He had able colleagues, but it was he who gave the paper its impetus and direction. Until the day of his death he was actively in charge of the paper. While in San Antonio, Tex., he was taken ill with heart disease and died at the age of seventy-six. The day before his death he had written a short editorial, which appeared in the same issue of the *Tribune* that carried the news of his death. His last words were, "What is the news?" (*Chicago Tribune,* Mar. 17, 1899). He was married on Sept. 2, 1852, to Katharine Patrick, the daughter of James Patrick of New Philadelphia, Ohio. During the Civil War she took part in the labors of the sanitary commission and was active in all phases of war work. There were three children.

[Lyman Trumbull MSS. in Lib. of Cong.; miscellaneous MSS. in Chicago Hist. Soc. Lib.; manuscript biography written in 1907 by M. Dodge in the office of the *Chicago Tribune*; H. I. Cleveland, "A Talk with . . . the Late Joseph Medill," *Saturday Evening Post,* Aug. 5, 1899; *The W. G. N.; a Handbook of Newspaper Administration* (1922); *Pictured Encyc. of the World's Greatest Newspaper* (copr. 1928); W. J. Abbot, "Chicago Newspapers," *Review of Reviews,* June 1895; A. T. Andreas, *Hist. of Chicago,* 3 vols., 1884–86; *Chicago Times-Herald,* Mar. 17, 1899, *Chicago Tribune,* Mar. 17, 1899.] T. E. S.

MEEHAN, THOMAS (Mar. 21, 1826–Nov. 19, 1901), botanist, horticulturist, author, was born in England, the son of Edward and Sarah (Denham) Meehan. He spent his boyhood on the Isle of Wight and learned gardening from his father, who was an expert gardener. He made experiments on his own initiative and while still young was elected to membership in the Royal Wernerian Society of Edinburgh. After several employments as gardener and nurseryman, including two years at Kew Gardens, he emigrated to America in 1848 and was hired by Robert Buist of Philadelphia. He was in Buist's employ for about a year, then he was made superintendent of Bartram's Garden, at that time owned by Andrew M. Eastwick. In 1852 he took charge of the grounds and conservatories of Caleb Cope, near Holmesburg, Pa. Here he gave special attention to raising the *Victoria regia* from seed which Cope had received from Kew Gardens, and he succeeded in producing blossoms. He was married in 1852 to Catherine Colflesh, daughter of a farmer and florist in Kingsessing. While with Eastwick, he had made a catalogue of the trees growing in Bartram's Garden. He was persuaded by William Darlington [*q.v.*] to enlarge the scope of the work and in 1853 published *The American Handbook of Ornamental Trees.* At about the same time he established his own nurseries in Upper Germantown which grew to large proportions and were successful as a business venture.

From 1859 to December 1887 Meehan was editor of the *Gardner's Monthly.* In 1891 he established *Meehan's Monthly,* which was continued after his death by his sons. For many years he was agricultural editor of *Forney's Weekly Press* and at one time or another he was editor or contributor to various magazines and papers. After his election in 1860 to the Academy of Natural Sciences of Philadelphia he took great interest in its herbarium and spent much time in studying its dried plants from various parts of the world. He published in the *Proceedings* of the Academy a series of "Contributions to the Life History of Plants" (March 1900) in which he blended his botanical observations with philosophic speculation and thought, and shortly before his death he presented a paper, "Bending of Mature Wood in Trees," which was the result of years of observation. In 1868 he was made a member of the American Association for the Advancement of Science (fellow, 1875), and in 1871 he was made a member of the American Philosophical Society. In 1877 he was appointed by Governor Hartranft botanist on the state board of agriculture and held the position until his death. His *magnum opus, The Native Flowers and Ferns of the United States,* a series of descriptions of plants, with colored plates, appeared in four volumes (1878–80).

In 1882 Meehan was elected a member of the Philadelphia Common Council. He fostered the movement for small parks and as a result the City Parks Association was formed. Mainly through his efforts twenty-eight small parks were added to the city, one of which was Bartram Park.

[See *Meehan's Monthly,* Jan. 1902; John W. Harshberger, *The Botanists of Phila. and Their Work* (1899); the *Gardeners' Chronicle* (London), May 11, 1901; "Gardens and Gardeners of Germantown" in *Germantown Hist.* (1915); *Who's Who in America,* 1901–02; *Country Life in America,* Feb. 1902; and obituaries in the Philadelphia newspapers at the time of his death. For details of his publications on flowers and flower pollination see *Handbook of Flower Pol-*

lination (3 vols., 1906–09), I, 307, translated by J. R. A. Davis from the German of Paul E. O. W. Knuth.]
J. W. H.

MEEK, ALEXANDER BEAUFORT (July 17, 1814–Nov. 1, 1865), author, the son of Anna (McDowell) and Samuel Mills Meek, a physician and Methodist minister, was born in Columbia, S. C. The family removed to Tuscaloosa, Ala., when he was about five years old. He had the advantages of a cultured home and apparently received the best educational opportunities available. In 1833 he was graduated from the University of Alabama. He was admitted to the bar in 1835 and began practice in Tuscaloosa. In 1836 he served as a non-commissioned officer in the Indian war in Florida and, later in the year, was appointed by Governor Clay attorney-general of the state to fill a vacancy. In 1841 he published *A Supplement to Aiken's Digest of the Laws of Ala.* He was appointed in 1842 to fill out a term as probate judge of Tuscaloosa County, but he was defeated in the election to succeed himself. He supported Polk for the presidency and obtained an appointment in the federal treasury department. Later he was appointed federal attorney for the southern district of Alabama. This appointment carried him to Mobile, where he lived for many years in a congenial literary atmosphere. After the end of Polk's term he became associate editor of the Mobile *Daily Register,* contributing poetry and essays as well as editorials to this notable paper.

In literature and service to education he won his right to recognition in Alabama history. His literary efforts covered the fields of journalism, oratory, history, essays, and poetry. He was a frequent contributor to newspapers and to magazines, and he was for a short time on the editorial staff of the *Flag of the Union* at Tuscaloosa and on that of the *Southron.* Some thought he was superior in oratory to either William L. Yancey or Henry W. Hilliard. A pioneer worker in Alabama history, he contributed *The Southwest* (1840) and *Romantic Passages in Southwestern History* (1857). He wrote numerous lyrics, the best of which he published in *Songs and Poems of the South* (1857). He is best known for "The Red Eagle" and "Balaklava." The latter, an imitation of the "Charge of the Light Brigade," met with popular acclaim in America and in England. His leadership in the founding of Alabama's public-school system is his most distinguished service. Distressed by Alabama's backwardness in public school legislation, he entered the legislature in 1853 determined to make the Mobile system of public schools statewide. As chairman of the committee on education he reported a bill to establish a public-school system for the state, and the voluminous and compelling report on education which he drew up helped him succeed where others had failed. His bill became law and became the basis for future development.

In 1859 he returned to the legislature and was made speaker of the House. He was a delegate to the Charleston convention in 1860. As a conservative Democrat he joined the secession movement with a good deal of unwillingness. During the war he served from 1862 to 1864, as trustee of the University of Alabama and wrote occasional lyrics. In 1856 he was married to Mrs. Emma (Donaldson) Slatter, who died in 1863. In 1864 he was married to Mrs. Eliza Jane Cannon, the widow of William R. Cannon. He had no children.

[T. M. Owen, *Hist. of Ala. and Dict. of Ala. Biog.* (1921), vol. IV; Wm. Garrett, *Reminiscences of Public Men in Ala.* (1872); Wm. R. Smith, *Reminiscences* (copr. 1889); *Trans. Ala. Hist. Soc.,* vol. V (1906); *Library of Southern Literature,* ed. by E. A. Alderman and others, vol. VIII (copr. 1907); W. Brewer, *Ala.* (1872); B. F. Riley, *Makers and Romance of Ala. Hist.* (1915); *Flag of the Union,* Sept. 5, 1835, May 21, 1836; *Advertiser and State Gazette* (Montgomery), Mar. 25, 1852; H. C. Nixon, *A. B. Meek* (1910).]
A. B. M.

MEEK, FIELDING BRADFORD (Dec. 10, 1817–Dec. 21, 1876), paleontologist, was born in Madison, Ind. His father, a lawyer, had migrated thither from Hamilton County, Ohio, where his parents, Irish Presbyterians who came to America about 1768, had settled prior to his birth. When Fielding was but three years of age his father died. The boy was educated in the public schools of Madison, but was greatly hampered by ill health, which handicapped him throughout his life. During this early period, however, he began to show an inclination toward the sciences. As soon as he was grown he undertook a mercantile venture which proved a failure and was followed by a second, equally unsuccessful. For several years thereafter he struggled with poverty, gaining a meager livelihood by accepting any employment that was offered. He had already conceived an interest in the invertebrate fossils which abounded in the rocks of his vicinity, and throughout this period of hardship persistently seized every opportunity to further his studies of the subject. His first public recognition was from David Dale Owen [*q.v.*], who employed him during 1848 and 1849 as one of his assistants in the United States Geological Survey of Iowa, Wisconsin, and Minnesota. In 1852 Meek entered the employ of the distinguished paleontologist James Hall [*q.v.*] and moved to Albany, N. Y., where he remained until 1858, though absenting himself for three summers: one, that of 1853, spent in the Bad Lands of Nebraska in association with F. V. Hayden [*q.v.*], also employed by Hall, and two, 1854, 1855, spent in work with the Geological Survey of Missouri.

In 1858 Meek took up his residence in Washington, having rooms in the Smithsonian building, where he remained for the rest of his life. The association first formed with Hayden in 1853 was renewed and continued for the most part until Meek's death, though in the meanwhile he accepted occasional employment with other organizations. The names Meek and Hayden became inseparably linked through their joint labors during the existence of the Hayden Survey. Perhaps their most notable publication was *Paleontology of the Upper Missouri* (Smithsonian Contributions, vol. XIV, no. 172, 1865). Meek was a skilled, careful, and conscientious worker and became recognized as one of America's leading paleontologists. Had he possessed the robust frame and mental vigor of some of his fellows he might have outranked them all, but he was never in robust health, he was modest and retiring to a marked degree, and asked in return for his labors only a sum barely sufficient for the most meager and commonplace existence. His first scientific publication was an important memoir on the Cretaceous fossils of Nebraska published in *Memoirs of the American Academy of Arts and Sciences* (new series, vol. V, pt. II, 1855). This was prepared in collaboration with James Hall. Meek's complete bibliography runs to 106 titles, including works of which he was sole author as well as the results of collaboration with Hayden, Worthen, and others. His most important publication was his "Report on the Invertebrate Cretaceous and Tertiary Fossils of the Upper Missouri Country," comprising 629 quarto pages and forty-five full-page plates, published in 1876 as one of the monographs of the Hayden survey (*Report of the United States Geological Survey of the Territories,* vol. IX).

Meek was of tall and slender build, his height being at times somewhat exaggerated by the tall black silk hat he persistently wore. He was naturally diffident, and a growing deafness which began in early manhood gradually cut him off from all associations but those with personal and scientific friends. "Gentleness and candor were apparent in every lineament of his face and in every word he uttered; yet he was eminently self-reliant and rigorously circumspect in all his actions" (White, "Memoir," *post,* p. 80). He never married and died of tuberculosis, with no near relatives, in his room in the Smithsonian.

[C. A. White, "Memoir of Fielding Bradford Meek," *Nat. Acad. Sci. Biog. Memoirs,* vol. IV (1902) and "In Memoriam: Fielding Bradford Meek," *Am. Jour. Sci.,* Mar. 1877; J. B. Marcou, "Bibliographies of American Naturalists, III: Bibliography of Publications Relating to the Collection of Fossil Invertebrates in the United States National Museum," *Bull. U. S. Nat. Museum,* no. 30 (1885); *Ann. Report . . . of the Smithsonian Inst. . . . 1877* (1878); *Evening Star* (Washington), Dec. 21, 1876; *Nat. Republican* (Washington), Dec. 22, 1876; reminiscences of personal friends.]

G. P. M.

MEEK, JOSEPH L. (1810–June 20, 1875), trapper, pioneer settler, was born in Washington County, Va. In after years he spoke of his father as a slaveholding planter and claimed relationship to President Polk. As a boy he was headstrong and lazy, refusing either to work or to learn, and at sixteen he could not read; but he had an inexhaustible fund of animal spirits, and he loved field sports. At eighteen, a strong and athletic youth, he started for the West. He reached St. Louis in the fall, and on Mar. 17, 1829, set out with W. L. Sublette's expedition for the mountains. For eleven years, at various times in company with Bridger, Carson, Fitzpatrick, Milton Sublette, and other noted mountain men, he was employed as a trapper, and in his many wanderings he traversed almost every part of the West. Though adventurous and brave to the degree of foolhardiness, he was best known as a wag and practical joker, whose bubbling humor never left him even in times of extreme peril.

In 1840 he and his friend Robert Newell, convinced that the trapping era was over, journeyed to Oregon and settled as farmers on the Tualatin plains on the Willamette, where later the town of Hillsboro grew up. He was an active spirit in the Americanization movement and a dominating influence in the Champoeg convention of May 2, 1843. On the completion of the provisional government, July 5, he was made sheriff of the territory, and in 1846 and again in 1847 elected to the legislature. After the Whitman massacre he was elected a special messenger to Washington to ask for protection for the colony. Setting out on Jan. 4, 1848, he reached Washington in May. Fond of notoriety, he had loudly announced himself on the way as "envoy extraordinary and minister plenipotentiary from the Republic of Oregon to the Court of the United States," and though "ragged, dirty and lousy" on his arrival, acted his rôle with a spectacular impressiveness. He was warmly welcomed and by popular voice was dubbed "Colonel"—a title that ever afterward clung to him. Congress, on the last day of the session, Aug. 14, passed the Oregon bill, and Polk on the same day appointed Gen. Joseph Lane governor and

Meek United States marshal. One of the acts of his marshalship was the hanging of the five chiefs convicted of the Whitman murders. He lost his office when the Pierce administration came in, and though he served as a major in the Indian war of 1855–56 his remaining days were mostly spent as an indifferent farmer on his Hillsboro tract, where he died. He was thrice married, each time to an Indian woman.

Meek was six feet two in height, well-formed, with a round, jovial, and well-bearded face and twinkling dark eyes. His voice was melodious and well modulated. As a story-teller he had few equals, though in his speech he never overcame the backwoods dialect of his youth. He was a natural leader, and with a better education and something less in his make-up of the wag and the showman he might have attained high office. His autobiography, written from his dictation by Mrs. F. F. Victor and published as *The River of the West* (1870), is a fascinating story, a blend in about equal parts of fact and fiction.

[Mrs. F. F. Victor, *The River of the West* (1870) and "Col. Joseph L. Meek," *Trans. . . . Ore. Pioneer Asso.* for 1875 (1876); J. C. Alter, *James Bridger* (1925); H. W. Scott, *Hist. of the Ore. Country* (1924), vols. I, II; L. A. Long, "Joe Meek, Oregon's Pioneer Politician," *Morning Oregonian* (Portland), Sept. 17, 1905; Osborne Russell, *Jour. of a Trapper . . . 1834–43* (2nd ed., 1921); W. F. Wagner, *Leonard's Narrative: Adventures of Zenas Leonard* (1904); G. W. Ebbert, in *Ore. Hist. Soc. Quart.*, Sept. 1918; *Morning Oregonian* (Portland), June 22, 23, 1875.]

W. J. G.

MEEKER, EZRA (Dec. 29, 1830–Dec. 3, 1928), Oregon and Washington pioneer, was born near Huntsville, Butler County, Ohio, the son of Jacob Redding and Phoebe (Baker) Meeker. His father's ancestors came from England in 1637, and his mother was of mingled English, Welsh, and German blood. In 1837 the father moved his family to Covington, Ind., and later to the outskirts of Indianapolis, where he found employment as a miller. The boy had a few months at school but, disliking its restraint, went to work at an early age. A gift from his mother's father in 1845 enabled the parents to buy a small farm, which for several years the youth operated, the father remaining at his trade. On May 13, 1851, Meeker married a neighbor's daughter, Eliza Jane Sumner, and in October of that year the young couple set out in an ox-drawn covered wagon for Iowa. Near the present Council Bluffs, the following spring, with his wife and infant child, he joined the emigrants for Oregon, and on Oct. 1 reached Portland. Early the following year, in company with his brother Oliver, he journeyed to the north of the Columbia in search of a site for a home. He settled on McNeil's Island, in Puget Sound, later removing to the site of Puyallup, where he built the first cabin. For the greater part of fifty-three years he remained in this region as a farmer and hop-grower, though he spent four winters in London and made several prospecting trips to the Yukon.

Well versed in the history of the Pacific Northwest and deeply impressed with the significance of the emigration movement, he resolved, in his seventy-fifth year, to devote the rest of his life to the commemorative marking of the Oregon Trail. On Jan. 29, 1906, with an ox-team drawing a covered wagon, he started from Puyallup, following such parts of the Trail as were still open, painting inscriptions on various landmarks and urging the citizens of the various settlements to set up inscribed stones and monuments. From the end of the Trail he continued on a tour of the East, everywhere attracting great attention. In 1910 he repeated this performance; in 1915 he traveled over a considerable part of the Trail in an automobile, and in 1924, at the age of ninety-three, he followed its course for 1300 miles in an airplane. Two years later he founded the Oregon Trail Memorial Association, Inc., with headquarters in New York City. From the Atlantic Coast, in the summer of 1928, he started in an automobile to follow the Trail again; but on the way he was taken ill, and after remaining for a time in a Detroit hospital, was conveyed to Seattle, where, two months later, he died.

Below medium height, of somewhat slender build, his head and face framed in a luxuriant snowy shock of hair and bushy beard, Meeker became, in his later years, a familiar figure throughout a great part of the country. He also became widely known as an author. In 1870 he published a descriptive pamphlet, *Washington Territory West of the Cascade Mountains,* which was followed during the next thirty-five years by a number of minor writings. In 1905 he published *Pioneer Reminiscences of Puget Sound*; in 1906, *The Ox-Team; or the Old Oregon Trail, 1852–1896* (revised and reissued in 1922 as *Ox-Team Days on the Oregon Trail*); in 1909, *Ventures and Adventures of Ezra Meeker, or Sixty Years of Frontier Life* (revised and reissued in 1916 as *The Busy Life of Eighty-Five Years of Ezra Meeker*); in 1915, *Story of the Lost Trail to Oregon* (pamphlet); in 1921, *Seventy Years of Progress in Washington*; and in 1926, *Kate Mulhall, a Romance of the Oregon Trail.* During his last years he was engaged on a revision of his autobiographical writings, but the work was not finished. Despite his loose and disconnected style and his carelessness with dates and incidents, his work will remain valuable as a picture of the migration and settlement period. His persistent efforts, in spite of many discouragements, to popularize the study of pioneer history have borne fruit, and to him more than to any other person is due the credit for the nation-wide celebration of 1930 of the first use of wagons on the Oregon Trail.

[In addition to Meeker's writings, see C. B. Galbreath, "Ezra Meeker, Ohio's Illustrious Pioneer," in *Ohio Archaeol. and Hist. Quart.*, Jan. 1927; *Who's Who in America*, 1926–27; *Seattle Daily Times*, *Post-Intelligencer* (Seattle), Dec. 3–4, 1928.] W. J. G.

MEEKER, JOTHAM (Nov. 8, 1804–Jan. 12, 1855), missionary and printer, was born in Hamilton County, Ohio, trained in youth as a printer in Cincinnati, and became a Baptist missionary to the Indians in 1825, serving as teacher and preacher among the Potawatomi, the Ottawa, and later the Chippewa or Ojibway, at missions in what is now Michigan. He mastered the closely related languages of the three tribes and, while at a mission at Sault Sainte Marie in 1832, began his experiments in using the characters of the English alphabet to create an orthography for writing the Indian languages. In 1833 he was ordered to remove to the newly created Indian Territory and to take printing equipment with him. In October 1833 he arrived at the new Shawnee Mission, just beyond the western boundary of Missouri and near the present Kansas City, Kan. On Mar. 8, 1834, he did the first printing in what is now Kansas, in the form of a leaflet containing the text of a hymn in Shawnee. The first book printed in the territory, a twenty-four-page primer in the Delaware language, he completed on Mar. 21. In all, he printed some 65 works, in ten Indian languages, including a Shawnee "newspaper," using his orthographic system, and also in English. Most of the works printed were of a religious character.

In May 1837 he moved to a mission of his own, among his old charges, the Ottawa, near the present city of Ottawa, Kan. There for eighteen years he devoted himself to the temporal and spiritual welfare of his Indians, upholding and guiding them in drought, flood, fire, pestilence, and famine, and helping them to become, before his death, a fairly well organized and self-respecting agricultural community. He was their preacher, teacher, physician, banker, broker, and attorney, their model and instructor in farming, building, and other basic industries of frontier life, and, above all, their friend in whom they learned to have unshakable confidence. In 1849 he took the mission printing plant to Ottawa and for a time resumed printing, producing among a few other things a code of the Ottawa tribal laws in the native language and in English. He died at the Ottawa mission. The diary that he kept reveals him as a practical person not given to expressions of sentiment, devout in his earlier years but toward the close of his life much more a man of practical interests than a missionary, an earnest, honest, sincere man, devoted to his work, with tenacious will advancing in the face of discouragements and reverses and in spite of the handicap of a slight physique and recurring illness. In September 1830 he married Eleanor Richardson, a fellow teacher at the Ottawa Indian mission on Grand River. They had three children.

[Journal in possession of Kan. State Hist. Soc.; D. C. McMurtrie and A. H. Allen, *Jotham Meeker* (1930), for biography, bibliography, and extracts from journal; Isaac McCoy, *Hist. of Baptist Indian Missions* (1840); *Missionary Mag.*, Apr., July 1855.] D. C. M.

MEEKER, MOSES (June 17, 1790–July 7, 1865), pioneer lead-miner, physician, was born in Newark, N. J., and educated in his native state. In 1817, following the migration westward, he settled in Cincinnati, Ohio, and engaged with success in manufacturing white lead. The following year he married Mary R. Henry. In 1822, while in St. Louis in search of a supply of raw material, he learned that lead was to be found in great abundance in northwestern Illinois, near the present city of Galena. Returning to Cincinnati, he closed out his business, and in the fall of 1822 made a trip by boat and on horseback to the Fevre River region. His inspection convinced him of the value of the lead deposits there, and he returned to Cincinnati to secure the necessary concession from the federal government. After correspondence with John C. Calhoun, secretary of war, and upon the execution of the ten-thousand dollar bond offered by Meeker in accordance with the law, he was given authority "to build furnaces, operate mines, and make other improvements, with no interference until some action on the part of Congress should determine the procedure for the lead-mining region." He thereupon loaded a seven-thousand dollar outfit onto a keelboat, and with a party of forty-two other persons, including women and children, made the eighty-nine day trip down the Ohio and up the Mississippi to the Fevre River. Here he engaged in lead mining, to his great profit, the first year's output of smelted ore from the region amounting to 425,000 pounds. He went back to Cincinnati in 1824, returning to the lead mines with his family and a year's supply of provisions.

In the Black Hawk War (1832) he became a captain and at the close of the conflict removed to Iowa County, Wis., also a lead-mining region, where in 1837 he began the erection of one of the first smelting furnaces in the territory of Wisconsin—a four-blast furnace, the largest thereabout, which cost him $25,000. In this year, his first wife having died in 1829, he married Eliza P. Shakelton. In 1842 he was elected from Iowa County to serve in the territorial legislature, and was reëlected in 1843. In 1846 he moved to Mineral Point, in the same county, and was there chosen a delegate to the constitutional convention of that year. While living in Cincinnati he had undertaken the study of medicine, although he had not regularly practised, and because of the lack of doctors in the whole lead-mining region, his services were often commandeered, and he became known far and wide as "Dr." Meeker. In 1854 he removed to a farm near Benton, Lafayette County, Wis. Having retired from active life, he became a corresponding member of the State Historical Society, and wrote in 1857 an entertaining and valuable account of the early settlement of the Illinois and Wisconsin lead region as he knew it—an account which is a source for the years (1822–25) which it covers. He was an active Freemason and for several years an officer of the Grand Lodge of Wisconsin. He died at Shullsburg, Lafayette County, in July 1865, a few months after taking up his residence there, and was buried at Galena, Ill. He was the father of five sons and three daughters.

[Moses Meeker, "Early History of the Lead Region of Wisconsin," with brief sketch of Meeker by L. C. Draper, in *Report and Colls. State Hist. Soc. of Wis.*, vol. VI (1872; repr. 1908); M. M. Quaife, "The Convention of 1846," *Wis. Hist. Soc. Colls.*, vol. XXVII (1919); Joseph Schafer, *The Wisconsin Lead Region* (1932); *The U. S. Biog. Dict. and Portrait Gallery of Eminent and Self-Made Men: Wis. Vol.* (1877); H. A. Tenney and David Atwood, *Memorial Record of the Fathers of Wis.* (1880); C. W. Butterfield, *Hist. of LaFayette County, Wis.* (1881).] L. K. M. R.

MEEKER, NATHAN COOK (July 12, 1817–Sept. 29, 1879), newspaper writer and Indian agent, founder of the Union Colony of Colorado at Greeley, was born in Euclid, near Cleveland, Ohio, the son of Enoch and Lurana (Hulbert) Meeker. He attended school in Oberlin and in Hudson. From his seventeenth year to 1870 he was a wanderer, changing his home and vocation so rapidly that even his wife could not remember accurately, after his death, when and why the changes had taken place. We read of newspaper work in New Orleans, of teaching in Euclid, of literary labors in New York, of teaching at Allentown, Pa., in 1842, and at Orange, N. J., in 1843, and of a small business store at Euclid in 1844. At this time he married Arvilla Delight Smith who accompanied him on his later wanderings and survived him. While in Euclid, he became interested in the teachings of François Marie Charles Fourier and began to lecture on the subject. Because of this interest he joined the Trumbull phalanx at Braceville, Ohio, where Fourierism was being practised. He worked on a farm, lectured, taught school, prospered, and, as he said later, "learned how much co-operation people would bear" (Boyd, *post*, p. 15). Three years' experience sufficed him, and in 1849 he reëntered the business world in Euclid. Early in the fifties he was invited to open a store in Hiram, where a group of Campbellites were preparing to start a college. While there he wrote a novel, "The Adventures of Captain Armstrong," which was an interesting commentary upon the final phase of his own life, for the captain, wrecked on an island in the South Seas, tried to educate the savages in the ways of civilized life (*Ibid.*, pp. 15–16). The panic of 1857 brought this Hiram venture to a close. He opened a store in southern Illinois, became a newspaper correspondent, and about 1865 joined the staff of the *New York Tribune*. As agricultural editor of Greeley's paper he became a well-known man. More and more interested in cooperation as one means of economic deliverance, his series of articles on the Oneida Community attracted wide attention. A book, *Life in the West* (1868), though largely a collection of stories about the people of the Mississippi Valley, shows where his heart lay. In 1869 he was sent west to survey the work of the Mormons. While he did not reach Utah he learned much about their cooperative plans and still more about the conditions in the Territory of Colorado. Out of this trip grew his plan to organize an agricultural colony in the West.

With the support of Horace Greeley and of the *Tribune* he launched the Union Colony in December 1869. Early the next year he set out, with two others, to choose a suitable site for the colony and, on Apr. 5, selected a site on the Platte River, north of Denver and on the Denver Pacific Railway. His call for settlers proved successful and his earlier wish, to form a community of the people whose interests were in moral and intellectual development, was about to be realized. He returned for a time to New York in order to arrange for the transportation of settlers at reduced fares and to attend to many necessary details. By early May about 12,000 acres of land had been bought from the railroad and from individuals, while agreements had been made with the railroad and with the government to obtain 111,000 acres more. The colony was cooperative, a new type of organization in Colorado. Yet the little settlement was eager to have it understood that it was not a community in the sense of the Oneida Community. Instead it recognized private ownership of land and individual control of activity (*First Report, post,* p. 6). No saloons and no billiard halls were tolerated. A school was opened at once, a library started, and a lyceum founded. The inhabitants of Colorado looked upon the colonists as cranks and as led by a chief crank, Meeker, the president of the colony, tall, awkward, slow of speech, and tactless. On Nov. 16, 1870, he published the first issue of his paper the *Greeley Tribune,* in which his editorials were wise and idealist admonitions to the people who lived in the little town of Greeley set in the center of their irrigated fields. Even though it must have been hard for such a wanderer, he remained in Greeley for eight years. In 1878, however, he accepted the appointment as Indian agent at the White River reservation and proceeded to attempt to carry out his ideas of the proper method of managing Indians. Like the Captain Armstrong of his novel he believed in the civilizing effect of work. He thought to induce the Utes to live in log houses, to plow the fields, to raise crops, and to support themselves. His lack of tactful understanding led him into difficulties. The Utes, hostile to his plans, rose and killed him with all the rest of the white men in the agency.

[Manuscript sketch of life from his wife's dictation in the Bancroft Lib.; articles by his son, Ralph Meeker, in *Tribune-Republican* (Greeley) in the year 1910; *First Ann. Report of the Union Colony of Col.* (1871); J. F. Willard, *The Union Colony at Greeley* (1918); David Boyd, *A Hist.: Greeley and the Union Colony* (1890); T. F. Dawson and F. J. V. Skiff, *The Ute War* (1879).]

J. F. W.

MEERSCHAERT, THÉOPHILE (Aug. 24, 1847–Feb. 21, 1924), Catholic missionary and prelate, was the eighth of ten children born of sturdy parents in Russignies, Belgium. On the mother's death, the family was reared by an elder sister who set aside her religious vocation. Educated in the village school, at the College of Renaix (1859–64), and at the College of Audenarde, from which he was graduated in 1868, Meerschaert, under the inspiration of a clerical professor, Charles Van Quekelberghe, who had labored in the Mississippi Valley, determined to prepare himself for the American missions. With this objective, he continued his theological studies at the American College, Louvain, until his ordination (Dec. 23, 1871), and then spent several months perfecting his knowledge of English. He then sailed for New York and reported to Bishop Elder of Natchez (October 1872), who assigned him to missionary work in Hancock and Harrison counties, Miss., where the scattered Catholics faced some hostility and post-war poverty. As pastor at Ocean Springs, he broke down prejudices by a self-sacrificing service in the yellow-fever epidemic of 1875, until his own life was despaired of. For such ministrations he was well qualified by his collegiate experiences as a St. Vincent de Paul agent among the lowly. In 1878 when he learned that his people were confronted with another epidemic, he immediately returned from Europe whither he had gone to enlist missionaries. Since six priests out of twenty-six in the diocese had succumbed to the fever, Father Meerschaert assumed additional parochial duties in Biloxi and Pascagoula. A year later, he was transferred to Bay St. Louis and in 1880 to the rectorship of St. Mary's Cathedral, Natchez. Here as vicar general (1887), he was Bishop Janssens' main reliance, and on the latter's translation to New Orleans, he was named administrator by the Holy See (1888), serving as such until the appointment of Bishop Thomas Heslin, who reappointed Meerschaert to the vicar generalship.

On June 2, 1891, he was elevated to the titular see of Sidyma as vicar apostolic of Indian Territory. Consecrated at Natchez by Archbishop Janssens on Sept. 8, he set out for Guthrie, where he learned that his territory had only 6,000 white Catholics and sixteen priests of whom about one half were stationed at the Indian school of Sacred Heart. A good pioneer, the bishop won popularity among Indians and settlers as he journeyed in a wagon from station to station and accepted gratefully the humble accommodations of the region. As the territory developed rapidly, Oklahoma was erected into a diocese (1905) with Meerschaert as first bishop. Rome again rewarded him with an appointment as assistant at the pontifical throne in 1916. Five years later, he celebrated his golden anniversary as a priest, which was made the occasion of an elaborate religious function attended by a score of prelates, two hundred priests, and a large body of citizens who honored him as a state-builder as much as a churchman. At the time of his death the diocese had over a hundred priests, including Benedictines and Carmelites, 150 churches and fully as many missions, 60,000 communicants, hospitals at Oklahoma City, Tulsa, and McAlester, an orphanage at Oklahoma City, and several academies and junior colleges.

[J. B. Thoburn, *A Standard Hist. of Okla.* (1916), vol. V; annual Catholic directories; *Who's Who in America,* 1922–23; *Daily Am. Tribune* (Dubuque),

Oct. 11, 1921; *Catholic Advance* (Wichita), Oct. 1, 15, 1921; *Tulsa World*, Feb. 22, 1924; *Nat. Cath. Welfare Conference News Service*, Feb. 25, 1924.] R. J. P.

MEES, ARTHUR (Feb. 13, 1850–Apr. 26, 1923), choral and orchestral conductor, organist, teacher, was born in Columbus, Ohio, the second of three sons of a Lutheran minister, the Rev. Konrad Mees and Elise (Adam) Mees. The family showed an unusual literary tendency and the sons were educated both in America and in Europe and were chosen for high places in the field of education. The eldest, Theophilus Martin Konrad, an ordained Lutheran minister, was professor of Latin, Hebrew, and of mental and moral philosophy in Capital University, Columbus, Ohio; the youngest, Carl Leo, became president of Ohio University at Athens, Ohio. Little is known of Arthur's early training in music except that he began playing the organ in his father's church when very young and that when he later took up instrumental study, he also tried to write anthems. In 1870 he was graduated from Concordia College, Fort Wayne, Ind., with the degree of A.B. He had evidently decided early to make music his life work, for after his graduation he accepted a position in Wesleyan Female College, Cincinnati, Ohio, as teacher of piano and theory. He was also organist of various Cincinnati churches and conductor of singing societies. In 1873 his work as choral accompanist attracted the attention of Theodore Thomas, who appointed him accompanist of the first Cincinnati May Festival. During the same year he went to Berlin, and upon the advice of Rubinstein he studied piano with Theodore Kullak, theory with Carl Friedrich Weitzmann, and score-reading with Heinrich Dorn. He remained in Europe for several years, the last of which he spent at the Leipzig Conservatory.

In 1880 Mees returned to Cincinnati as teacher of harmony and composition at the College of Music, continuing as organist of the May Festivals and trainer of the chorus. In 1886 Thomas called him to New York to become assistant conductor of the chorus of the National Opera Company. This company was short-lived, and when it disbanded, Mees became director of the Orpheus Society of New York, the Albany Festival Chorus, and of the Orange (New Jersey) Mendelssohn Union and numerous smaller organizations. From 1896 to 1898 he was in Chicago as assistant conductor of the Theodore Thomas Orchestra and conductor of an auxiliary choral organization, and from 1898 to 1904 he was conductor of the New York Mendelssohn Glee Club. In 1913 he conducted the Bridgeport (Connecticut) Oratorio Society and in 1918 the Worcester (Massachusetts) festivals and the Cecilia Society of Boston. From 1900 to 1916 he was assistant conductor to Richmond Peck Paine in the Norfolk (Connecticut) festivals, succeeding the latter as conductor in 1916. He became an experienced and gifted director of choral and orchestral organizations but notwithstanding his strenuous work as a conductor he found time to write *Daily Studies for the Piano* (1877) and *Choirs and Choral Music* (1901), the latter a valuable work. He also edited the program books of the New York Philharmonic Society, 1877–96, and of the Chicago Symphony Orchestra, 1896–98. He introduced many novelties to American audiences, such as Granville Bantock's *Omar Khayyám*, Gabriel Pierné's *St. Francis of Assisi*, and Percy Grainger's *Marching Song of Democracy*. He was married on Jan. 28, 1897, to Susan Marguerite Howell of Alfred, N. Y., but they had no children. He died at his home in New York City after a long illness.

["Arthur Mees' Work for Music in America," *Musical Courier*, Oct. 30, 1907; *Who's Who in America*, 1922–23; *Internat. Who's Who in Music* (1918); *Musical Digest*, May 1, 1923; *N. Y. Times*, Apr. 27, 1923.] F. L. G. C.

MEGAPOLENSIS, JOHANNES (1603–1670), Reformed Dutch clergyman, first minister of the church at Rensselaerswyck, in New Netherland, was the son of Catholic parents and adhered to their faith until he was twenty-three years of age. "When I relinquished Popery," he wrote late in life, "I was thrust out at once from my inherited estate" (*Ecclesiastical Records State of New York*, I, 602). He became a minister of the gospel, serving in a couple of parishes in Holland from 1634 to 1642. In the latter year he signed a contract with Kiliaen van Rensselaer by which he bound himself for a period of six years to minister to the patroon's colony at Rensselaerswyck at an annual salary of 1,000 florins for the first three years and of 1,200 for the remainder. He sailed with his wife Machtelt, daughter of Willem Steengen, and four children from The Texel on June 14, 1642, and arrived at New Amsterdam on Aug. 4. Thirteen days later, he preached his first sermon in the *packhuys*, the patroon's storehouse, to an audience of about one hundred. In the following year he began to preach to the Indians, with whose language he had somewhat familiarized himself at great pains. Letters that he wrote to correspondents in Holland about the Mohawk Indians, their country, language, religion, and government, were printed there without his consent. The University Library of Ghent, Belgium, possesses the only extant copy known of this pamphlet (*Een Kort Ontwerp van de Mahakvase*

Indiaenen . . .), which was published at Alkmaar in 1644. Megapolensis, in this booklet, shows himself entirely free from that haughty scorn for the ignorant Indians that Jonas Michaelius [*q.v.*] expressed in his letters. He lived with them on friendly terms, he let them come to his services, which sometimes ten or twelve would attend, each smoking a long tobacco pipe, and had, at one time, "eight at once lying and sleeping upon the floor near my bed." He frankly admitted his failure to convert them; they never would be converted, he said, "until they are subdued . . . and reduced to some sort of civilization; and also unless our people set them a better example" (*Ecclesiastical Records,* I, 398). He found fault with his Catholic fellow missionaries for baptizing the Indians in their ignorance of what baptism meant, and his refusal to follow their example may account for the confidence that the Indians showed him; for they looked upon the christening ceremony as a form of magic that would do them harm. Thanks to these good relations with the Indians, Megapolensis was able, in 1642, to rescue Father Isaac Jogues [*q.v.*], of the Society of Jesus, from their hands. When his six years' term had expired, he arranged, in 1649, for his return to Holland, but Governor Stuyvesant and his Council persuaded him to accept a call to New Amsterdam as successor of the Rev. J. C. Backer. Here he maintained his reputation as a humane Christian, though he was far from being a tolerant man. He requested the authorities in Holland to put a stop to the immigration of Jews; yet he took pity on the twenty-three who, in 1654, arrived at New Amsterdam from Brazil and had his consistory appropriate a few hundred guilders for their immediate needs. He also opposed and prevented the establishment of a Lutheran church at New Amsterdam. In 1657 he received a visit from the Jesuit missionary Simon le Moyne; a sequel to this call was a Latin treatise which the latter sent to Megapolensis urging him to return to the Mother Church. Le Moyne's plea is lost, but its contents may be guessed from the domine's acrimonious Latin reply, which has been published with English translation in *Reply of Rev. Johannes Megapolensis . . . to a Letter of Father Simon Le Moyne* (1907). On Aug. 29, 1664, Megapolensis and his son Samuel, with two of the city magistrates, acted as messengers between Stuyvesant and Col. R. Nicholls, but their names do not appear in the "Remonstrance," signed by ninety-three citizens, urging capitulation. On Oct. 2, however, he swore the oath of allegiance to the King of England, and he continued to minister to his congregation until his death. His attitude at the time of the surrender was evidently criticized in Holland, for on Aug. 27, 1668, Peter Stuyvesant and three members of his former Council signed a certificate in which they declared that Megapolensis had acted no otherwise "than it was the duty of a faithful subject, and as was proper for a godly and pious preacher to act on such an occasion" (*Ibid.,* I, 593).

[*Ecclesiastical Records State of New York,* vol. I (1901); *New York State Lib. Van Rensselaer Bowier Manuscripts* (1908), translated and ed. by A. J. F. van Laer; *Narratives of New Netherland 1609–1664* (1909), ed. by J. F. Jameson; Albert Eekhof, *De Hervormde Kerk in Noord-Amerika 1624–1664* (2 vols., 1913); I. N. Phelps Stokes, *The Iconography of Manhattan Island,* vols. II (1916), IV (1922), VI (1928); W. B. Sprague, *Annals Am. Pulpit,* vol. IX (1869).]

A. J. B.

MEGRUE, ROI COOPER (June 12, 1883–Feb. 27, 1927), dramatist, was born in New York City, the son of Frank Newton and Stella Georgiana (Cooper) Megrue. He studied at Columbia University, from which he was graduated in 1903, and his first contacts with the professional stage were made in a clerical position in the play-brokerage offices of Elizabeth Marbury. His first play to be acted, after many discouragements and disheartening delays, was *White Magic,* which he completed from an unfinished dramatization of David Graham Phillips' novel of that title. It was produced at the Criterion Theatre in New York on Jan. 24, 1912, with Gertrude Elliott as the star, and although it met with but little popularity, it was really the starting point of his brief career. His first successful play was *Under Cover,* a sensational drama involving a smuggled necklace, a mysterious secret-service quest, and New York Custom-House graft. It was first acted in Boston in 1913, and was followed in succession by *It Pays to Advertise* (1914), written in collaboration with Walter Hackett; *Under Fire* (1915), one of the first plays dealing with the World War, and having for its crucial scene the German troops entering a German city; *Potash and Perlmutter in Society,* first called *Abe and Mawruss* (1915), written in collaboration with Montague Glass; *Seven Chances* (1916); *Under Sentence* (1916), written in collaboration with Irvin S. Cobb; *Where Poppies Bloom* (1918), from the French; and *Tea for Three* (1918), taken from a play by Carl Slaboda. Several of these plays were acted in London, but they attracted little notice there.

Megrue was a typical playwright who wrote always with his finger on the public pulse, with his eye on the footlights, and with his mind on events as they were recorded on the first page of the daily newspaper. After passing through some five years of popularity, he was unable to keep up with the demands of those play-goers who had grown enthusiastic about *Under Cover.* He found that he had exhausted his vein, and that he could not attract the public indefinitely by means of ephemeral sensation. His view of the dramatist's technique was unblushingly revealed by him in an interview in which he declared that the only kind of art he knew was the ability to get his plays over the footlights. For some years prior to his death he was little heard of by the play-going public except through an occasional stock-company revival of one or two of his best-known plays. He never married.

[Dixie Hines and H. P. Hanaford, *Who's Who in Music and Drama,* 1914; John Parker, *Who's Who in the Theatre,* 1925; *Who's Who in America,* 1926–27; interviews in the *Sun* (N. Y.), Dec. 1, 1918 and Apr. 20, 1919; Burns Mantle and G. P. Sherwood, *The Best Plays of 1900–11* (1933); *The Nineteen Hundred and Three Class Book: A Record of the Senior Class of Columbia Coll.* (1903); *N. Y. Times,* Feb. 28, 1927.]

E. F. E.

MEIGGS, HENRY (July 7, 1811–Sept. 29, 1877), builder of South American railroads, was born in Catskill, N. Y., the second son in a family of nine children. Elisha and Fanny (Williams) Meiggs, his parents, were both of old New England stock, the father descended from Vincent Meigs who settled in New Haven, Conn., about 1644. After receiving a common-school education, Henry worked at the lumber trade in Catskill, Boston, and New York. In 1837 he opened his own yard in Williamsburg, N. Y., and the confidence which he usually inspired is shown in his soon being elected a member, and then president, of the village board of trustees. Yet he was insolvent in 1842 and his fortunes continued uncertain until 1848, when news of the gold discovery led him to load a vessel with lumber and sail by Cape Horn to San Francisco. Arriving when the town was booming he sold at a large profit. He invested heavily in lumbering, erecting the largest sawmill in the territory and sending hundreds of men into the woods to cut timber. He donated to the city an imposing music hall, was elected to the board of aldermen, and interested himself in many civic improvements. His success and confidence impressed every one and he had no difficulty borrowing capital. When the boom slowed down, however, he found he had over-reached himself. In a frenzied effort to cover his loans he was tempted to forge warrants purloined from the office of the city treasurer. When discovery became inevitable he placed his family and personal property on board the barque *America,* and, under cover of darkness, Oct. 5, 1854, sailed out into the Pacific, leaving behind him obligations of over $800,000.

During the whole of his subsequent career Meiggs was a fugitive from justice. Landing in Chile, he had, by 1861, gained a reputation by his record as construction superintendent of certain stretches of the Santiago al Sur Railroad. The Chilean government then contracted with him to complete for $12,000,000 the Valparaiso and Santiago line which had already ruined several contractors. Allowed four years, he finished it in less than two years and made a profit of $1,320,000. He built a $500,000 home in Santiago, had surveys made for a road across the Andes, planned railroads in Bolivia, dealt extensively in Bolivian guano, and founded a bank in La Paz. His chief theatre of action, however, was furnished by the Peruvian government, which was planning an extensive system of railways to be financed from its nitrate and guano monopolies. Beginning in 1868 with the contract for a line from Mollendo to Arequipa, Meiggs in the next five years, by a system of bribery which paralyzed all opposition, secured contracts totaling at least $120,000,000 for some 1,015 miles of standard gauge road. Completion of the Arequipa line in 1870 was celebrated by an entertainment attended by the Peruvian president and 2,000 other guests, which lasted two weeks and cost $200,000—a typical Meiggs gesture. He continued the Arequipa road to Puno on Lake Titicaca, crossing the Andes at 14,665 feet, and he also built a branch to Cuzco, the old Inca capital. His executive genius was best shown, however, in his construction of the famous Callao, Lima & Oroya railroad, the highest in the world, which, tunneling under Mount Meiggs at 15,658 feet, "broke the backbone of the Andes." This line, with its dizzy viaducts and its sixty-seven tunnels, built in the face of incredible difficulties, remains one of the engineering wonders of the world. Before it was complete Peru was bankrupt, and Meiggs, having sunk his fortune in the construction of the road, looked about desperately for the means to extricate himself. He persuaded the government to give him a new contract to complete the line, with the right also to drain and operate the famous Cerro de Pasco silver mines. He issued new notes on this contract, the workers were recalled, and confidence again reigned until it was found the notes were returned from England unhonored. A succession of paralytic strokes carried Meiggs to his death, and with elaborate ceremonies he was buried on his hacienda at the side of the Oroya railroad, his grave looking out to the Pacific.

A man of commanding presence, admirable tact, and untiring activity, Meiggs was also vain, impetuous, and an incurable prodigal. He repaid most of his San Francisco debts, and did much to improve the environs of Lima with parks and boulevards. In 1874 he secured the passage of a law by the California legislature, over the governor's veto, making it illegal for a grand jury to indict him for offenses committed before 1855 (Hittell, *post,* III, 441, citing *California Statutes,* 1873–74). He was married Apr. 9, 1832, to Gertrude Burns of Catskill, who died in 1833, and in 1837 to Caroline Doyle of Ulster County, N. Y., who died in 1861. Two sons and a daughter survived him.

[H. B. Meigs, *Record of the Descendants of Vincent Meigs* (copr. 1901); T. H. Hittell, *Hist. of Cal.,* III (1897), 434–41; Samuel Nuñez Olaechea, *Los Ferrocarriles del Estado* (Santiago, 1910); Federico Costa y Laurent, *Reseña Historica de los Ferrocarriles del Perú* (Lima, 1908); F. M. Halsey, *Railway Expansion in Latin America* (1916); E. W. Middendorf, *Peru* (3 vols., 1893–95); *Collección de Leyes, Decretos, Contratos y Demes Documentos Relativas a los Ferrocarriles de Perú* (1871), collected by Meiggs's order; articles in *The Pioneer* (San Francisco), Nov. 1854, p. 297, Jan. 1855, pp. 16–22; *Overland Monthly,* Aug. 1871; *Scribner's Monthly,* Aug. 1877; and *Engineering News,* Oct. 20, 1877; *N. Y. Tribune,* Oct. 11, 1877; *San Francisco Chronicle, Daily Morning Call* (San Francisco), and *N. Y. Times,* Oct. 12, 1877.]

O. W. H.

MEIGS, ARTHUR VINCENT (Nov. 1, 1850–Jan. 1, 1912), physician, author, was born in Philadelphia, a grandson of Charles Delucena Meigs [*q.v.*] and a son of John Forsyth Meigs [*q.v.*] and Ann Wilcocks (Ingersoll), his father being thirty-two years old. William Montgomery Meigs [*q.v.*] was a younger brother. When Arthur was six years of age he had the misfortune to lose his mother, but he received the affectionate care of his father's mother, and spent much of his time in childhood at his grandfather's beautiful country place at Hamanassett. As a boy he attended the Classical Institute of J. W. Faires, from which he entered the Academic Department of the University of Pennsylvania in 1866. His father was so anxious to have him begin his medical studies, however, that he took him from college at the end of his second year and entered him in the Medical Department, from which he was graduated in the spring of 1871. Since he was not yet twenty-one years of age, he did not receive his diploma until some months later. After spending parts of the year 1871–72 abroad, chiefly in Vienna, he returned to become a resident physician in the Pennsylvania Hospital. Here he remained until 1874, when he began the practice of medicine which he continued to the time of his death. His success was assured on account of his excellent preparation, distinguished ancestry, and social position. In 1878 he married Mary Roberts Browning. Their family consisted of three sons, one of whom became the fourth physician in the direct line of family descent.

Arthur Vincent Meigs was made a visiting physician to the Pennsylvania Hospital, to succeed his father, in 1881. He also became a visiting physician to the Children's Hospital and to the Sheltering Arms (a home for foundlings). He was an active fellow of the College of Physicians and its president from 1904 to 1907. He was also much interested in the Philadelphia Pathological Society, of which he was president in 1891–92. He was for a time a consulting physician to the Eastern Penitentiary and to the Pennsylvania Institute for the Instruction of the Blind, and in 1899 he was elected a member of the American Philosophical Society. He was also for a time a trustee of the University of Pennsylvania and of the Wistar Institute.

He represented the most conservative type of medical practitioner, by whom ideas not their own are always regarded with caution, yet who cling tenaciously to any they themselves have originated. Meigs was not lacking in originality. He conceived it strange that infants should thrive upon their mothers' milk, but often pine and die when fed upon cow's milk, and believed that it was the result of chemical difference in the composition of the foods. This idea was scouted by his contemporaries, to whom milk was milk. Nevertheless, he spent much time in analyzing milks both human and bovine and succeeded in "modifying" the cow's milk so as to make it practically as wholesome for babies as their mothers'. This was his most important contribution to medical science, and it is the one for which he should be remembered. In his own eyes, however, it was probably of less value than his belief that he had demonstrated that the capillary blood-vessels of the heart actually penetrate into the muscle cells. His chief writings are: *Proof that Human Milk Contains Only about One Per Cent of Casein; with Remarks upon Infant Feeding* (1883); *A Study of the Arteries and Veins in Bright's Disease* (1888); *The Artificial Feeding of Infants* (1889); *The Microscopic Anatomy of the Human Heart, Showing the Existence of Capillaries within the Muscular Fibres* (1891); *The Origin of Disease, etc.* (1897); *Analysis of Human Milk the Basis of the Artificial Feeding of Infants* (1902).

Meigs was a thorough gentleman, good to look at, pleasant to talk to, well-groomed, cultured and refined to the highest degree. He was very sensitive and so extremely sympathetic with pain that he could scarcely endure seeing it in others. He was so highly conscientious that he was continually telling his patients that they could help themselves more than he could help them. He was fond of the open air, and especially of horses and boats. His death occurred at his home in Philadelphia, in his sixty-third year.

["Memoir of Arthur Vincent Meigs, M.D.," by his son Edward B. Meigs, in *Trans. Coll. Phys. of Phila.*, 3 ser. XXXVI (1914); H. B. Meigs, *Record of the Descendants of Vincent Meigs* (1901); T. G. Morton and Frank Woodbury, *The Hist. of the Pa. Hospital* (1895); *Public Ledger* (Phila.), Jan. 2, 1912.]

J. M.

MEIGS, CHARLES DELUCENA (Feb. 19, 1792–June 22, 1869), physician, author, son of Josiah Meigs [*q.v.*] and Clara (Benjamin) Meigs, the fifth of ten children, was born at St. George, Bermuda, and there passed the first four years of his life. The next four years were spent in New Haven, Conn., where his father was professor of mathematics in Yale College. These years probably had great influence in the formation of his moral and mental character, and it may have been then that "honesty, honor, love of country, inflexible uprightness, liberality of mind and love of knowledge were there implanted in him" (J. F. Meigs, in *Quarterly Summary, post*, p. 421). Later his father became president of the University of Georgia, at Athens, whither the family moved in 1801. Here the boy made the intimate acquaintance of an intelligent and cultivated *émigré*, M. Petit de Clairvière, and from him learned the French language and also perhaps the gentle and courteous manners that characterized his long professional career. He was graduated from the University of Georgia in 1809, at seventeen years of age, and immediately began to read medicine with Dr. Thomas Hanson Marshall Fendall, to whom he became apprenticed and under whose roof he lived for three years. In 1812–13 he pursued a course of medicine at the University of Pennsylvania, then, as he wrote later, "went home to set up for myself, and practice on that stock in trade" (*Ibid.*, p. 426). In 1814–15 he returned to Philadelphia to study for another year. He was graduated from the University of Pennsylvania, apparently *in absentia*, in 1817, and the subject of his thesis was *Prolapsus uteri*.

In Philadelphia, in 1814–15, he met Mary Montgomery, whom he married Mar. 15, 1815, and took with him to Georgia, where he set up practice in Augusta. But since Mrs. Meigs was made unhappy by slavery as she saw it in the South, and the doctor suffered repeated attacks of the "bilious fever," they left Georgia after a couple of years and took up their residence in Philadelphia. Meigs worked hard at his profession and soon became intimate with a number of the best physicians of the city. On the death of his wife's mother, the family moved to the Montgomery home on Arch Street above Sixth Street, after which his practice grew and success began to arrive. His family also grew; there were ten children, among whom were John Forsyth and Montgomery Cunningham Meigs [*qq.v.*]. In 1826 Meigs became one of the editors of a new periodical, the *North American Medical and Surgical Journal*, and continued in this capacity as long as the publication continued, which was until 1831.

In 1830 he began to lecture in midwifery in what was called the "School of Medicine." This probably led him into a more careful study of the subject, for in that same year he made a translation from the French A. A. L. M. Velpeau, which appeared the next year under the title, *Elementary Treatise on Midwifery* (1831). In 1838 he published his first independent work in the form of an octavo volume of 370 pages, entitled *The Philadelphia Practice of Midwifery*. It at once became popular, and a second edition in 1842 was increased to 408 pages. His practice grew and became more remunerative, and consequently, in 1835, he moved to Chestnut Street above Tenth Street, where he continued to live until 1850. With his success in practice and in authorship his reputation also grew, and in 1841 he was elected professor of obstetrics and diseases of women in the Jefferson Medical College, which position he filled with great satisfaction to both faculty and student body until 1861, when he voluntarily retired.

After retiring from his professorship he ceased to be any longer interested in medical subjects, and spent his remaining years enjoying life in the country at Hamanassett, where he died at the age of seventy-six. He was, perhaps, not an original thinker, his one important contribution being to call attention to cardiac thrombosis as a cause of sudden death in childbirth. His only invention was a form of ring pessary. He strenuously opposed the probability of puerperal fever being an infectious disease. As a lecturer, however, he was eloquent, polished, and entertaining, presenting his subject clearly and forcibly. With his superb education and high sense of morality, he influenced his students profoundly. He was far in advance of his times in believing that the standards of medical education should be raised, and that "a young man, destined to the study of medicine, should begin by obtaining a knowledge of Latin and Greek, the French, German and Italian languages" (J. F. Meigs, *op. cit.*, p. 439). He brought his sons and grandsons up to a knowledge of the family history and a sense of "the rigid duty incumbent upon them, to do whatever might be in their power to promote its honorableness" (*Ibid.*, p. 6). Besides the books already noted he wrote *Woman, Her Diseases and Remedies* (1847), *Obstetrics; the Science and Art* (1849), *Treatise on Acute and Chronic Diseases of the Neck of the Uterus* (1850), *Childbed Fevers* (1854), and published *A Treatise on the Diseases and Special Hygiene of Females* (1845), translated from the French of Marc Colombat de l'Isère.

[J. F. Meigs, *Memoir of Charles D. Meigs, M.D.* (1876), published also in *Quart. Summary of the Trans. of the Coll. of Phys. of Phila., 1872* (1873); John Bell, in *Proc. Am. Phil. Soc.*, vol. XIII (1873); *Boston Medic. and Surgic. Jour.*, May 23, 30, 1849; H. B. Meigs, *Record of the Descendants of Vincent Meigs* (1901); *Public Ledger* (Phila.), June 23, 1869.]

J. M.

MEIGS, JAMES AITKEN (July 31, 1829–Nov. 9, 1879), physician, teacher, and anthropologist, was born in Philadelphia, the son of John G. and Mary A. Meigs. His parents were of English, Scotch, and German descent; his father, known as "Honest John," was a shoe merchant. After preparation at the Mount Vernon Grammar School and at the Boys' Central High School, James entered Jefferson Medical College, from which he graduated with high honors in 1851. He then began general practice and became especially noted for work in obstetrics. From 1854 to 1862, he served as professor of climatology and physiology in the Franklin Institute and, from 1856 to 1859, as librarian of the Academy of Natural Sciences of Philadelphia. During these years, most of his papers on medical and scientific data appeared. His interests seem to have touched a wide range of subjects; in 1855 he contributed a paper entitled, "Relation of Atomic Heat to Crystalline Form," to the *Proceedings of the Academy of Natural Sciences;* and to the *North American Medical and Chirurgical Review* for 1859, "Some Remarks on the Methods of Studying and Teaching Physiology." Outside of the medical profession, he is perhaps best known for his anthropological work, which reached its climax in the "Catalogue of Human Crania in the Collection of the Academy of Natural Sciences of Philadelphia"; this formed a special supplement of 103 pages to the *Proceedings* for 1856. He also contributed an article on "The Cranial Characteristics of the Races of Men" to J. C. Nott and G. R. Gliddon, *Indigenous Races of the Earth* (1856), and edited the American edition of W. S. Kirkes's *Manual of Physiology* (1857). Papers by him were also published in the *Medical Examiner* and in the *American Journal of Medical Sciences.*

After several years' assistantship to the professor of physiology at the Philadelphia College of Medicine, he was appointed in 1857 to the chair of Institutes of Medicine in that school. In 1859, he transferred to a professorship on the same subject at Pennsylvania Medical College and was appointed physician and clinical lecturer in the Philadelphia Hospital at Blockley, but resigned his teaching position at the outbreak of the Civil War. For thirteen years, beginning in 1855, he was also physician in the department of pulmonary diseases at Howard Hospital and Infirmary for Incurables. In 1868 he became professor of the Institutes of Medicine and Medical Jurisprudence at Jefferson Medical College, and appears to have been especially successful in physiological demonstrations and in lectures on the eye and ear. The same year, he was chosen as physician to the Pennsylvania Hospital. In 1871, he was elected president of the Philadelphia County Medical Society, in which he had successively acted as secretary and vice-president. He also served several years on the board of trustees of the Polytechnic College of the State of Pennsylvania. During the latter years of his life, his duties as a teacher and practitioner occupied the most of his attention. He never married but lived with his aged father, and, after a short sickness which was diagnosed as malaria, died of blood poisoning.

[George Hamilton, "James Aitken Meigs, M.D., 1829–1879," in *Trans. of the Medic. Soc. of the State of Pa.*, vol. XIII, pt. 1 (1880); H. C. Chapman, "Memoir of James Aitken Meigs, M.D.," in *Trans. Coll. of Physicians of Phila.*, 3 ser., vol. V (1881); E. J. Nolan, "Report of Librarian," *Proc. Acad. Nat. Sci. Phila., 1895*, vol. XLVII (1896); *Phila. Medic. Times*, Nov. 22, 1879; *Medic. and Surgic. Reporter*, Nov. 15, 1879; *Boston Medic. and Surgic. Jour.*, Nov. 20, 1879; *Medic. Record* (N. Y.), Nov. 22, 1879; *Phila. Times* and *Phila. Record*, Nov. 11, 1879.]

H. B. B.

MEIGS, JOHN (Aug. 31, 1852–Nov. 6, 1911), educator, son of Rev. Matthew K. Meigs and Mary Morton (Gould), both of New England ancestry, was descended from Vincent Meigs who settled in New Haven about 1644. His father served as a Presbyterian pastor in Michigan and Virginia and later was president of Delaware College. Determining on account of his health to retire from his college position, he bought an old stone house on a hill near Pottstown, Pa., and in it established a small day school where he planned to train his own boys. In this house John Meigs, the fifth child and fourth son, was born. He entered Lafayette College at fourteen, but upon the death of a brother in December, was taken from college and spent the rest of the year in Europe, returning to Lafayette in the fall of 1867. Graduating in 1871 with honors, he began to teach under his father, but in 1872 became tutor in Latin and Greek at Lafayette, and in 1875, adjunct professor of modern languages. He was awarded the degree of doctor of philosophy in 1876.

In the fall of that year, in response to his mother's urging, he reluctantly went home to take charge of the school, from which his father wished to withdraw. With The Hill School he was identified for the rest of his life. He found the institution established in extemporized quarters with meager and primitive equipment, a faculty of three teachers, and an enrollment of sixty boys. Giving evidence at once of his extraordinary energy and tenacity, he assumed the responsibility of direction and at the same time conducted as many recitations as any one of the other teachers—about twenty-five a week. In addition, he kept the accounts; wrote all the letters with his own hand, saw to all matters of discipline; kept the general records; and received all the visitors. The school had no endowment, nor any wealthy friends. By his management, he provided the funds with which to improve and enlarge the buildings according to the rapidly rising standards which he partly created for himself and partly accepted from the general progress of educational ideas. Three disastrous fires, one in 1884, the second in 1890, and the third in 1901, though entailing great immediate loss, became in each case the occasion for bolder plans. Year by year he put back into the school whatever profit there had been from the year before, and by the time of his death the institution was one of the most extensive and completely equipped schools in America.

Of his qualities as a man and as a schoolmaster, most notable were his own extraordinary capacity for work, and his ability to require and to gain the utmost energy of those who worked with him. He set and exacted high standards of industry and thoroughness both for masters and for boys. Vehement and impetuous and quick to anger, he was quick also to tenderness and able to inspire loyalty. He reflected Thomas Arnold of Rugby in his passionate moral purpose and Edward Thring of Uppingham in his emphasis upon beauty and dignity in equipment and surroundings, and in his concern not only for the brilliant but for the ordinary boy.

Like his mother before him, John Meigs was instinctively and strongly religious. In 1882 he married Marion Butler of New York, and as "Mrs. John" her influence was linked with his in creating the general tone of the school and in developing the religious interest of individual boys. Although an Evangelical in spirit, John Meigs stood among the theological liberals in his beliefs and sympathies. As a member of the Presbyterian General Assembly which in 1893 conducted the ecclesiastical trial of Charles Augustus Briggs [*q.v.*] he did his utmost to prevent Briggs's condemnation for heresy. An epidemic of typhoid fever of which nearly one hundred, boys and masters, fell ill in the early summer of 1902, laid John Meigs under such a strain physically and emotionally that in the following years his great vitality began to wane. In 1906 it was evident that he had serious heart-trouble. With intervals of seeming improvement, this grew worse in the next five years; and in 1911 he died of a heart attack at The Hill School, in the house in which he was born.

[H. B. Meigs, *Record of the Descendants of Vincent Meigs* (1901); W. R. Bowie, *The Master of The Hill, A Biography of John Meigs* (1917); *Outlook*, Nov. 18, 1911; *Who's Who in America*, 1910–11; S. J. Coffin, *Record of the Men of Lafayette* (1879); *Public Ledger* (Phila.), Nov. 8, 1911.] W. R. B.

MEIGS, JOHN FORSYTH (Oct. 3, 1818–Dec. 16, 1882), physician, pediatrician, author, brother of Montgomery C. Meigs [*q.v.*], was the son of Charles Delucena Meigs [*q.v.*] and Mary (Montgomery) Meigs, and the third of ten children. He was born in Philadelphia, soon after his father, aged twenty-six, had arrived in that city to start upon the practice of medicine. Being by nature quiet and sober-minded, and having before him the example of his cultured and industrious father, from early childhood he desired to become a physician and never departed from this purpose, which was early recognized and accepted in the family. He first attended a "dame's school" in Cherry Street, and later went to the Classical Institute of Mr. Samuel Crawford, a notoriously harsh and cruel man who is said to have used his rattan unmercifully. Since his father was impatient to have him begin his medical studies, he was taken from school before he was sixteen and began attending lectures "upon two of the elementary branches at the University of Pennsylvania, and at the same time studying music and having a tutor who gave him some further instruction" (A. V. Meigs, *post*, p. lxxiv). He was graduated at the University of Pennsylvania in 1838, when less than twenty years of age, and almost immediately became a resident physician to the Pennsylvania Hospital, a position to which he had been appointed before graduation.

With the completion of his service, in 1840, he sailed for Europe to spend some six or seven months in Paris, where he enjoyed the lectures and clinics of Velpeau and Louis. In 1841 he began to practice medicine in his father's house on Chestnut Street, in his native city, with the latter's great reputation and large clientele to aid him. Success came at once. Following his father's example he began, in 1843, to teach obstetrics and later the practice of medicine and diseases of children, in the Philadelphia Association for Medical Instruction—an enterprise whose function was to provide supplementary courses for medical students in the spring and autumn. He continued to teach here until 1854, when his practice absorbed too much of his time.

On Oct. 17, 1844, he married Ann Wilcocks Ingersoll, daughter of Charles Jared Ingersoll [*q.v.*], by whom he had eight children, six of whom survived. The union was terminated by his wife's death after about twelve years, and he never remarried. At the age of thirty, in 1848, he completed his book, *A Practical Treatise on the Diseases of Children,* published as a volume of the Medical Practitioner's and Student's Library. It was an immediate success and became a standard work upon the subject in all English-speaking countries. Other editions were soon called for, but as he reaped justified rewards for his labors in an ever increasing practice, he found himself too busy to prepare the fourth edition. He, therefore sought a worthy young associate to collaborate with him, finally selecting Dr. William Pepper, to whom he gave one-half the rights of ownership. Under the names of Meigs and Pepper appeared the fourth, fifth, sixth, and seventh editions (1870–86).

In 1859 Meigs was elected one of the physicians to the Pennsylvania Hospital, which position he held until 1881, when he resigned. He was also at various times a visiting physician to the Children's Hospital, a consulting physician to the Women's Hospital and to the Blind Asylum, a fellow of the College of Physicians, and a member of the American Philosophical Society. He is described as gentlemanly, modest, and correct in all things; a keen observer, an accurate medical diagnostician, and a physician loved and revered by patients and friends. His life was so simple as to have been almost austere. He lived for his family and his work, dying in December 1882 after a short illness from pneumonia, at the age of sixty-four years. One of his sons, Arthur Vincent Meigs [*q.v.*], carrying on the family tradition of medical distinction, was his father's successor as physician to the Pennsylvania Hospital; another, William Montgomery Meigs [*q.v.*], was noted for his scholarly biographies and studies in constitutional law.

[A. V. Meigs, "Memoir of J. Forsyth Meigs, M.D.," *Trans. Coll. of Phys. of Phila.,* 3 ser. VII (1884); Wm. Pepper, "Obituary of John Forsyth Meigs, M.D.," *Proc. Am. Phil. Soc.,* vol. XXI (1884); T. G. Morton and Frank Woodbury, *The Hist. of the Pa. Hospital* (1895); H. B. Meigs, *Record of the Descendants of Vincent Meigs* (1901); *Medic. News* (Phila.), Dec. 23, 1882; *Public Ledger* (Phila.), Dec. 18, 1882.]

J. M.

MEIGS, JOSIAH (Aug. 21, 1757–Sept. 4, 1822), lawyer, editor, educator, and public official, was a native of Middletown, Conn., the thirteenth child of Return Meigs, a hatter, and Elizabeth (Hamlin) Meigs. He was a descendant of Vincent Meigs, or Meggs, who came from England and finally settled in New Haven about 1644. One of Josiah's brothers, Return Jonathan, 1740–1823 [*q.v.*], rendered distinguished service in the War of the Revolution, and his son, Return Jonathan, 1764–1824 [*q.v.*], had a notable political career. Josiah graduated from Yale in 1778. Among his classmates were Joel Barlow, Noah Webster, Zephaniah Swift, and Oliver Wolcott [*qq.v.*]. He was teaching at Claverack, N. Y., when, in 1781, he was elected tutor in Yale College. That year he delivered an oration at the New Haven celebration of the victory over Cornwallis, which was published in 1782. On Jan. 21, 1782, he married Clara, daughter of Col. John Benjamin of Stratford, Conn. He was admitted to the bar in April 1783, and in February 1784, at the first election following the establishment of city government, was chosen city clerk of New Haven. After resigning as tutor in 1784, with Daniel Bowen and Eleutheros Dana he opened a printing office and established *The New Haven Gazette,* a weekly newspaper, the first number of which was issued May 13, 1784. In February 1786 Bowen retired, and the name of the publication was changed to *The New Haven Gazette and the Connecticut Magazine.* After Aug. 2, 1787, Meigs was sole proprietor until its discontinuance at the close of 1788. It supported the adoption of the Federal Constitution, and among the literary contributions which appeared in its columns was "The Anarchiad," written by Joel Barlow, John Trumbull, David Humphreys, and Lemuel Hopkins [*qq.v.*]. Keenly interested in scientific subjects, in 1787 Meigs delivered lectures at Yale on natural philosophy and astronomy.

He retained his position as city clerk until 1789, and at the Fourth of July celebration of that year delivered an oration which was described as "replete with benevolence and Federal ideas" (*Connecticut Journal,* July 15, 1789, quoted by Meigs, *post,* p. 26). A few months later he left New Haven for St. George, in the Bermuda Islands, to care for the interests of Connecticut clients. During the latter part of his sojourn there, which lasted until 1794, he advocated the causes of American claimants of captured property in the Court of Vice-admiralty so successfully as to incur the enmity of those who were directly or indirectly engaged in privateering. Furthermore, he was a man of hot temper and occasional recklessness of speech. As a result of his unpopularity and unguarded statements, he was arrested on the charge of treason, and was acquitted and released only through the exertions of Gov. Henry Hamilton.

After his return to the United States, he was appointed, Oct. 8, 1794, professor of mathematics and natural philosophy in Yale College, of which his friend Ezra Stiles [*q.v.*] was then president. He had by this time become an ardent Jeffersonian. In a Federalist stronghold, and with the inexorable Federalist Timothy Dwight [*q.v.*] as president of Yale—Stiles had died shortly after Meigs's appointment—it was inevitable that he should get into trouble. Consequently, after several years of friction, in December 1800 he resigned to accept a professorship in the University of Georgia—"exiled" from his native state "to the backwoods of Georgia only twelve miles from the Cherokee Indians," his wife declared with bitterness years later, "for no earthly reason but his stern democracy" (Meigs, *post,* pp. 42–43).

Chartered in 1785, this institution was as yet unestablished. Abraham Baldwin [*q.v.*] was its titular president, and it was at his instigation that Meigs had been called there. Baldwin now resigned and Meigs was elected in his place. He gathered students out of the academies of the state, and instructed them under the trees, in a tavern, and in his own dwelling, until a temporary log building was erected. In 1806 Franklin College, a substantial, three-story brick structure, was ready for occupancy. There were now some seventy students and the institution had acquired reputation throughout the state. Meigs's political pronouncements, however, his ill-concealed contempt for Georgians, whom he considered rude and uncivilized, and his frankness of speech soon made him enemies. The number of students decreased; his salary was reduced; and in August 1810 he resigned the presidency. He continued as professor for a year, and at the end of that time was charged with gross criticism of the trustees, and was dismissed. He published *A Statement of the Causes of the Removal* . . . (1811).

In November 1812 the President appointed him surveyor-general of the United States, and he took up his residence in Cincinnati. Two years later, October 1814, he was made commissioner of the General Land Office of the United States, at Washington. In this city he lived pleasantly for the remainder of his life. From 1819 until his death he was president of the Columbian Institute. He was one of the original corporators and trustees of Columbian College (now George Washington University), and professor of experimental philosophy there. His daughter Clara married John Forsyth [*q.v.*], later secretary of state under Jackson and Van Buren; Charles Delucena Meigs [*q.v.*] was his son; Montgomery C. Meigs and John Forsyth Meigs [*qq.v.*], were his grandsons.

[Wm. M. Meigs, *Life of Josiah Meigs* (1887) contains many references to source material. See also H. B. Meigs, *Record of the Descendants of Vincent Meigs* (copr. 1901); F. B. Dexter, *Biog. Sketches Grads. Yale Coll.,* vol. IV (1907); E. M. Coulter, *College Life in the Old South* (1928); A. L. Hull, *A Hist. Sketch of the Univ. of Ga.* (1894); C. E. Jones, *Education in Ga.* (1889); *Daily National Intelligencer* (Washington, D. C.), Sept. 5, 1822.]

H. E. S.

MEIGS, MONTGOMERY CUNNINGHAM (May 3, 1816–Jan. 2, 1892), soldier, engineer, was born in Augusta, Ga., the son of Dr. Charles Delucena Meigs [*q.v.*] and of Mary (Montgomery) Meigs of Philadelphia. He was an elder brother of John Forsyth Meigs [*q.v.*]. During his childhood the family moved from Georgia to Philadelphia, where he matriculated at the University of Pennsylvania in 1831. He later entered the United States Military Academy, graduating in 1836, fifth in his class. After temporary assignment to the artillery, he was transferred to the engineer corps of the Army, and thereafter, for a quarter of a century, his conspicuous ability was devoted to many important engineering projects. Of these, his favorite was the Washington Aqueduct, carrying a large part of the water supply from the Great Falls of the Potomac to the city of Washington. This work, of which he was in charge from November 1852 to September 1860, involved not only the devising of ingenious methods of controlling the flow and distribution of the water, but also the design of the monumental bridge across Cabin John Branch which for some fifty years remained unsurpassed as the longest masonry arch in the world. To this task was added from 1853 to 1859 the supervision of the building of the wings and dome of the national Capitol, and from 1855 to 1859, of the extension of the General Post Office building, as well as the direction of many minor works of construction. In the fall of 1860, as a result of a disagreement over certain contracts, Meigs "incurred the ill will of the Secretary of War, John B. Floyd," and was "banished to Tortugas in the Gulf of Mexico to construct fortifications at that place and at Key West" (Abbot, *post,* p. 317). Upon the resignation of Floyd a few months later, however, he was recalled to his work on the aqueduct at Washington.

Here, in the critical days preceding the actual outbreak of the Civil War, Meigs and Lieut.-Col. E. D. Keyes were quietly charged by President Lincoln and Secretary Seward with drawing up a plan for the relief of Fort Pickens, Fla., by means of a secret expedition; and in April 1861, together with Lieut. D. D. Porter of the Navy, they carried out the expedition, embarking under orders from the President without the knowledge of either the Secretary of the Navy or the Secretary of War. On May 14, 1861, Meigs was appointed colonel, 11th Infantry, and on the following day, promoted to brigadier-general, he became quartermaster-general of the Army, in which capacity he served throughout the war. Of his work in this office James G. Blaine remarked: "Montgomery C. Meigs, one of the ablest graduates of the Military Academy, was kept from the command of troops by the inestimably important services he performed as Quartermaster-General. . . . Perhaps in the military history of the world there was never so large an amount of money disbursed upon the order of a single man. . . . The aggregate sum could not have been less during the war than fifteen hundred millions of dollars, accurately vouched and accounted for to the last cent." (*Twenty Years in Congress,* vol. II, 1886, p. 30.) William H. Seward's estimate was "that without the services of this eminent soldier the national cause must have been lost or deeply imperilled" (letter, May 28, 1867, from the Secretary of State, asking the good offices of diplomatic officers for General Meigs during a tour of Europe; in possession of the family). His brilliant services during the hostilities included command of Grant's base of supplies at Fredericksburg and Belle Plain (1864), command of a division of War Department employes in the defenses of Washington at the time of Early's raid (July 11–14, 1864), personally supervising the refitting and supplying of Sherman's army at Savannah (Jan. 5–29, 1865), and at Goldsboro and Raleigh, N. C., reopening Sherman's lines of supply (March–April 1865). He was brevetted major-general July 5, 1864.

As quartermaster-general after the Civil War, Meigs supervised plans for the new War Department building (1866–67), the National Museum (1876), the extension of the Washington Aqueduct (1876), and for a hall of records (1878). In 1867–68, to recuperate from the strain of his war service, he visited Europe, and in 1875–76 made another visit to study the government of European armies. After his retirement on Feb. 6, 1882, he became architect of the Pension Office building. He was a regent of the Smithsonian Institution, a member of the American Philosophical Society, and one of the earliest members of the National Academy of Sciences. In 1888, although he "was not a literary person and had no taste for writing except of official reports of work done," at the request of the editors of *Battles and Leaders of the Civil War* he submitted an article on the relations of Lincoln and Seward to the military commanders during the war which was apparently intended as a reply to some of the statements in *McClellan's Own Story* (1887). It was not printed, however, until long after the author's death, when it appeared as a "document" in the *American Historical Review* (January 1921).

Meigs died in Washington after a short illness and his body was interred with high military honors in the National Cemetery at Arlington. The General Orders (Jan. 4, 1892) issued at the time of his death declared that "the Army has rarely possessed an officer . . . who was entrusted by the government with a greater variety of weighty responsibilities, or who proved himself more worthy of confidence." In 1841 he had married Louisa Rodgers, daughter of Commodore John Rodgers, 1773–1838 [*q.v.*]. Four of their seven children lived to maturity, but one of these, John Rodgers Meigs, a lieutenant of engineers, was killed in action during the Civil War.

[G. W. Cullum, in *Asso. Grads. U. S. Mil. Acad. Ann. Reunion,* 1892; H. L. Abbot, in *Nat. Acad. Sci. Biog. Memoirs,* vol. III (1895); the *Times* (London), Jan. 4, 1892; H. B. Meigs, *Record of the Descendants of Vincent Meigs* (1901); G. W. Cullum, *Biog. Reg. Officers and Grads. U. S. Mil. Acad.* (3rd ed., 1891); *Battles and Leaders of the Civil War* (4 vols., 1887–88); *War of the Rebellion: Official Records (Army)*; J. G. Nicolay and John Hay, *Abraham Lincoln: a History* (1890), esp. vols. III, IV; *Am. Hist. Rev.,* Jan. 1921, containing many other references; *Washington Post,* Jan. 3, 1892; information as to certain facts from Meigs's grandson, Col. J. R. M. Taylor.]

C. D. R.

MEIGS, RETURN JONATHAN (Dec. 17, 1740–Jan. 28, 1823), soldier and pioneer, was born at Middletown, Conn., the son of Return and Elizabeth (Hamlin) Meigs and the descendant of Vincent Meigs, who emigrated from Dorsetshire, England, about 1635. His brother was Josiah Meigs [*q.v.*]. His father, a hatter, was a member of the Connecticut General Assembly. In Feb. 14, 1764, he married Joanna Winborn, who died in 1773. She was the mother of his son, Return Jonathan Meigs, 1764–1824, and the grandmother of Return Jonathan Meigs, 1801–1891 [*qq.v.*]. On Dec. 22, 1774, he married Grace Starr, who died in Tennessee in 1807. In 1772 he was commissioned by Governor

Trumbull of the Connecticut colony as lieutenant in the 6th Connecticut Regiment. Two years later he was made captain. After the battle of Lexington he swiftly assembled his company and marched to the aid of Boston. He was commissioned major and, in September, with his command joined Arnold's ill-fated expedition to Quebec, during which he kept a diary, written with ink made by mixing powder and water in his palm, which was afterward published ("Journal," *Massachusetts Historical Society Collections,* ser. 2, vol. II, 1814, and privately printed 1864). At the assault of the city he was one of those who scaled the walls and was made prisoner of war. He was paroled and the following January was exchanged. He reëntered the Continental service and was commissioned lieutenant-colonel. In 1777 he led the brilliant Sag Harbor expedition in reprisal for Tryon's Danbury raid. Taking about 160 men from General Parson's forces, in thirteen whaleboats he crossed Long Island Sound under convoy of two armed sloops, not forgetting to take an extra sloop in which to bring back the prisoners. Landing on Long Island he marched across to Sag Harbor, surprised the garrison, burned eleven or twelve vessels, destroyed a large quantity of military stores, killed several of the enemy, and took about ninety prisoners, without losing a man. For this exploit he was voted a sword by Congress. Soon afterward he became colonel and reported at Peekskill with his 6th Connecticut Infantry, "the Leather-Cap Regiment." During the summer and fall he took part in all the principal engagements along the Hudson. At the storming of Stonypoint under Gen. Anthony Wayne, which did so much to raise the morale of the American army, he led a regiment and was one of the first to storm the fort. In May 1780 he received a personal note of thanks from Washington for his prompt action in suppressing a mutiny among the Connecticut troops. Upon the discovery of Arnold's treason in September his regiment was one of those sent to West Point to meet any consequent attack by the British. When the Connecticut regiments were reorganized in 1781 he was retired.

Becoming interested in the organization of the Ohio Company, he was appointed one of its surveyors, and in April 1788, he landed at the mouth of the Muskingum with the small group of other settlers from New England. He drew up a code of rules, which were adopted by the colony, and posted them on a big oak tree. In 1801 he was appointed Indian agent to the Cherokee, who named him "The White Path." He was commissioner to negotiate treaties in 1804, 1805, and 1807, and in 1808 he was given authority to negotiate a convention between the state of Tennessee and the Cherokee. When he was eighty-two years old, having given up his quarters to an elderly visiting Indian chief and moved into a tent, he contracted pneumonia and died. He was buried at the Cherokee agency in Tennessee.

[MSS. in Lib. of Cong.; H. B. Meigs, *Record of the Descendants of Vincent Meigs* (1901) with facsimiles of Revolutionary documents; S. P. Hildreth, *Biog. and Hist. Memoirs* (1852), pp. 195–96, 258–78; *Am. Archives,* ed. by Peter Force, ser. 5, vol. I (1848); *The Record of Conn. Men in the Military and Naval Service during the . . . Revolution,* ed. by H. P. Johnston (1889); *Am. State Papers: Indian Affairs* (2 vols., 1832–34); G. H. Hollister, *The Hist. of Conn.* (1855); T. J. Summers, *Hist. of Marietta* (1903).] I. L. T.

MEIGS, RETURN JONATHAN (Nov. 17, 1764–Mar. 29, 1824), governor of Ohio, senator, and postmaster-general, was the son of Joanna (Winborn) and Return Jonathan Meigs, 1740–1823 [*q.v.*], and the uncle of Return Jonathan Meigs, 1801–1891 [*q.v.*]. He was born in Middletown, Conn., graduated from Yale College in 1785, studied law, and was admitted to the Connecticut bar. In 1788 he married Sophia Wright. The same year he moved to Marietta, Ohio, a settlement so near the frontier that he, along with other settlers, narrowly escaped death at the hands of Indians. In 1798 he was appointed one of the judges of the territorial government. With the organization of the territorial legislature in 1799 he was elected to represent the Marietta region. He supported the cause of statehood in 1801 and, upon the creation of the new state, was appointed chief justice of the supreme court. In October 1804 he resigned this position to accept an appointment as commandant of United States troops and militia in the St. Charles district of Louisiana. In 1805 he was appointed a judge in Louisiana Territory. He returned to Ohio in 1806 and was called to Richmond, Va., on business relating to Burr's trial. He was transferred to serve as a judge in Michigan Territory but resigned for he became a candidate for governor of Ohio in opposition to Nathaniel Massie. He won the election by a considerable majority but was declared to be constitutionally ineligible because of his prolonged absence from the state. He was elected to the federal Senate to fill the vacancy created by the resignation of John Smith, who was alleged to have been an accomplice of Burr. He was reëlected the next election and sat in the Senate from Dec. 12, 1808, to May 1, 1810. In 1810 he ran again for governor with Thomas Worthington as his opponent. Worthington represented the ardently democratic Scioto settlements, while Meigs, on account of his conservatism and New England connections, gained the support of the conservative Republicans and of the Federalist minority. He was elected by the strength of this combination.

Although the governors under the first constitution were almost powerless, the imminence of war with Great Britain gave him an opportunity for real leadership. Largely through his efforts 1,200 state militiamen were recruited and equipped in time for Hull's rendezvous at Dayton in 1812. The war spirit in Ohio was dampened by Hull's defeat, however, and for a time Meigs suffered severe criticism. Nevertheless he was again elected in 1812, and in the following year again was active in raising men and supplies for the war. In March 1814 he resigned as governor to accept the position of postmaster-general, an appointment that was a recognition of his vigorous support of the war. During his administration of the post office department the number of post offices increased from approximately 3,000 to 5,200 and the mileage of post-roads from about 41,000 to 85,000. Consequently he experienced difficulty in maintaining the department on a self-supporting basis. Occasional deficits and alleged irregularities in the awarding of mail-contracts led to an investigation of the affairs of the department by Congress in 1816 and again in 1821. Neither investigation resulted in more than a charge of inefficiency against him. He resigned from office in June 1823 because of ill health and returned to Marietta, where he died. His wife and their only child, Mary, who married John George Jackson [*q.v.*], survived him.

[MSS. in the Lib. of Cong. and in the Ohio State Lib. at Columbus; F. B. Dexter, *Biog. Sketches of the Grads. of Yale College*, vol. IV (1907); *Biog. Sketches with other Literary Remains of the late John W. Campbell* (1838); for reports of post office *Am. State Papers: Post Office Department* (1834), pp. 46–113; H. B. Meigs, *Record of the Descendants of Vincent Meigs* (copr. 1901); *Green Bag*, Mar. 1893.] W. T. U.

MEIGS, RETURN JONATHAN (Apr. 14, 1801–Oct. 19, 1891), lawyer, the son of John and Parthenia Clendinen Meigs, was born near Winchester in Clark county, Ky. He was the grandson of Return Jonathan Meigs, 1740–1823, the nephew of Return Jonathan Meigs, 1764–1824, and was related by marriage to John George Jackson [*qq.v.*]. After his father died in 1807 he lived part of the time with his uncle, James Lemme, in Bourbon County. In the schools of the community he acquired the fundamentals of a classical education. He studied law and was admitted to the bar in Frankfort in 1822. He moved to Tennessee where, on Nov. 1, 1825, he married Sally Keys Love. For some ten years or more he practised law in Athens, Tenn. On account of popular prejudice against lawyers he was defeated in 1834 for a seat in Tennessee's constitutional convention. Soon he moved to Nashville, the capital of the state, where for a quarter of a century he was a distinguished and highly respected member of the bar. In 1838 and 1839 he was attorney-general of the state and reporter of its supreme-court decisions (19 *Tenn. Reports,* 1839). In 1841 he was appointed United States attorney for the Middle Tennessee district. In 1848–50 he published a two-volume *Digest of all the Decisions of the Former Superior Courts of Law and Equity, and of the Present Supreme Court of Errors and Appeals in the State of Tennessee.* In 1858 he and William F. Cooper published their compilation of the *Code of Tennessee,* the only one legally adopted by the legislature until 1931. As a Whig he served one term in the state Senate from 1847 to 1848. In this body he sponsored a free banking bill, based upon New York's banking laws, that was defeated at this time but subsequently enacted. He was also an advocate of public education and state and local aid to internal improvements. As early as 1831 he had supported proposals for the building of railroads to connect Tennessee with the Atlantic seaboard. He took a prominent part in the encouragement of the educational, cultural, and humanitarian development of his adopted state. He was the first president of the Tennessee society for the diffusion of knowledge, a corresponding secretary of the Tennessee historical society, a member of the Nashville board of education, a trustee of the University of Nashville and of the state school for the education of the blind, and an incorporator of the Tennessee society for the colonization of free negroes. He was a patron of public lectures, the theatre, and music. He was said to have declined a position on the state's supreme court because the salary, $1,800, was too small, but in 1856 he accepted appointment as state librarian at a salary of $500. He was one of the few prominent inhabitants of Middle Tennessee who remained loyal to the Union after the Civil War began. In 1861, severely censured by his neighbors for his Unionism and in danger of mob violence, he resigned the office of librarian and went to New York. When Andrew Johnson became military governor of Tennessee, he gave him legal advice regarding the government of the state. He is said to have declined election to the United States Senate in 1865 and an offer of appointment to the United States Supreme Court (statement of son in *Record of Descendants, post,* p. 250; see *Star, post*). In 1863 he was appointed clerk of the supreme court of the District of Columbia. He continued in the active discharge of the duties of this office until almost the day of his death at the age of ninety. He was survived by his five sons.

[J. T. Moore, *Tenn.* (1923), vol. II; J. W. Caldwell, *Sketches of the Bench and Bar of Tenn.* (1898); H. S. Foote, *The Bench and Bar of the South and Southwest* (1876); H. B. Meigs, *Record of the Descendants of Vincent Meigs* (copr. 1901); *Evening Star* (Washington), Oct. 20, 1891.] P. M. H.

MEIGS, WILLIAM MONTGOMERY (Aug. 12, 1852–Dec. 30, 1929), lawyer and historian, was one of the eight children of Dr. John Forsyth Meigs [*q.v.*] and Ann Wilcocks (Ingersoll) Meigs. Arthur Vincent Meigs [*q.v.*] was his brother; their progenitors included Chief Justice Benjamin Chew [*q.v.*] of Pennsylvania, Professor Josiah Meigs [*q.v.*] of Yale and the University of Georgia, and Charles Jared Ingersoll [*q.v.*], historian, playwright, and member of Congress. After the death of their mother, the children were cared for in part by their paternal grandmother, while their grandfather, Charles Delucena Meigs [*q.v.*], taught them the family history and the "duty incumbent upon them . . . to promote its honorableness." William attended John W. Faires's Classical Institute (1862–68) and the University of Pennsylvania (A.B., 1872; A.M. and M.D., 1875), read law in the office of George W. Biddle, and in 1879 was admitted to the Philadelphia bar. Unhappily, after this preparation for several sorts of useful citizenship, he remained handicapped by persistent ill health; but by adjusting his activities to his limitations he achieved a life of singular unity. Selecting two fields of historical interest, he explored them in parallel lines thenceforward: legal problems of the relationship between constitutions and courts; biographical problems of certain men whose lives spanned the septennial of 1780–1850.

American legal origins and practice, concerning the powers of federal and state courts, were the objects of careful study, which he summarized in numerous articles contributed to the *Southern Law Review, American Law Review, American Law Register,* and *Constitutional Review* (see *Index to Legal Periodicals*). When federal courts were called upon to determine questions arising from state laws, Meigs concluded, they should, generally, follow the laws of the states and the decisions of state courts thereon. But the power of supreme courts to declare laws unconstitutional and to refuse to enforce them was sound and eminently beneficial, if not abused. Contrary arguments, that this power was in itself "a great usurpation," aroused his amazement. He edited Brinton Coxe's *Essay on Judicial Power and Unconstitutional Legislation* (1893); and produced his own topical summary of the debates waged in the Constitutional Convention and the action finally taken in *The Growth of the Constitution in the Federal Convention of 1787* (1900; reprinted in W. M. Meigs and T. H. Calvert, *The Constitution and the Courts,* 3 vols., 1924).

In biography, the semi-invalid found "an occupation that could be taken up or dropped at will." In the course of his travels in search of health he searched for distant source materials. Sick or well, he kept to the rigorous standards of his first book in this field, *Life of Josiah Meigs* (1887). "I have made every effort," he wrote in the preface, "to be accurate and to avoid writing a sentence . . . which would not be easily capable of proof . . . while not hesitating at the same time to speak in plain language" (p. vii). He then turned to a study of "Pennsylvania Politics Early in this Century," published in the *Pennsylvania Magazine of History and Biography,* December 1893. Next, another ancestral biography, *The Life of Charles Jared Ingersoll* (1897), developed the thesis that the men who agitated against slavery, with disregard for the Union, were not necessarily right. Thereafter for some time Meigs concentrated his efforts upon *The Life of Thomas Hart Benton* (1904), producing an able and scholarly biography of a character in whom he had long been interested. Years of industrious examination of sources next were devoted to *The Life of John Caldwell Calhoun* (2 vols., 1917), a work accepted by J. S. Bassett as "the long-desired complete and impartial life of the Great Nullifier" (*American Political Science Review,* February 1918, p. 139). Its breadth of treatment and sense of proportion, its discussion of economic causes behind nullification, were especially commendable. Southerners found in it an indication of Northerners' improved understanding of the South's predicament (*Virginia Law Review,* October 1919, pp. 73–75), and although W. E. Dodd thought that it had certain defects as history, he commended it as biography unsurpassed for thoroughness of research (*American Historical Review,* July 1918, pp. 872–74). Meigs never married. Despite his frail health he lived to a ripe age, dying four months after the completion of his seventy-seventh year.

[*Who's Who in America,* 1928–29; H. B. Meigs, *Record of the Descendants of Vincent Meigs* (1901); C. J. Cohen, *Memoir of Rev. John Wiley Faires* (1926); *Phila. Inquirer, Public Ledger, N. Y. Times,* Dec. 31, 1929; information as to certain facts from Miss A. I. Meigs.] J. P. N.

MELCHERS, GARI (Aug. 11, 1860–Nov. 30, 1932), painter, probably received the germ of his proficiency by transmission from his father, Julius Theodore Melchers, a Westphalian who had a Franco-Dutch mother. The elder Melchers was himself a sculptor and decorator, who had studied under Carpeaux and Étex in Paris. On coming to America—and marrying Marie Bangetor—he made his home in Detroit, where the son, named Julius Gari, was born. From the start there seems to have been complete sympathy on the father's part for his son's gravitation toward an artistic career. The boy was only seventeen when he was permitted to go abroad to study painting, not amid the beguilements of Paris, to be sure, but in either Munich or Düsseldorf, as he chose. Melchers selected Düsseldorf and entered the Royal Art Academy there under Professor Von Gebhardt. His sojourn was indicative of future contacts. He was always to have ties with the artistic side of Germany. But in his youth the lure of Paris was not to be withstood. He visited the great exposition there in 1878. Returning to Düsseldorf he remained for three years but at the end of that period he entered the École des Beaux-Arts, where he received instruction and criticism from Boulanger and Lefebvre. It was the turning point in his career. Paris completed what Düsseldorf had begun and he had a picture accepted for the Salon of 1882.

A brief period of work in Italy followed and after that a visit to his home, but in 1884 he was in Europe again, with studios in Paris and at Egmond, in Holland. Thenceforth he was active on both sides of the Atlantic down to the time of his death. He achieved an international repute through the solidity of his gift and through the wide range covered in its exercise. Religious as well as secular motives came within his scope. He was skilled alike in portraiture and in the painting of landscape and flowers, and his works in the Library of Congress at Washington and elsewhere testify to his aptitude in mural decoration. He was in a rare degree the thoughtful practitioner, working in all the categories and functioning therein with a full-rounded equipment of both mind and hand. In 1903 he married Corinne Lawton Mackall, of Savannah, Ga., and in 1916 they established themselves on a delightful estate above the Rappahannock at Falmouth, near Fredericksburg, Va. It was there that he died, childless, very soon after the American Academy of Arts and Letters, of which he was a member, had opened a retrospective exhibition of his works and the National Institute of Arts and Letters had awarded him its gold medal. He was president of the Century Association in New York at the time. He died literally "full of years and honors." All his life fortune had smiled upon him, appreciation had met him upon every side. It was as a distinguished artist that he was in 1909 invited by the Grand Duke of Saxe-Weimar to occupy one of the park pavilions at Weimar. His colleagues in America and in Europe recognized his powers. He was a member of the Royal Academy of Berlin, the International Society of Sculptors, Painters, and Gravers in England, the Société-Nationale des Beaux-Arts in Paris, the Institute of France, the Royal Society of Austrian Painters, and the National Academy of Design in his own land. He was an officer of the Legion of Honor and was the recipient of more than one European Order. The enumeration of these honors has no merely conventional significance. It points rather to the character of his art.

His early training had much to do with the felicity of his painting, for it grounded him in habits of fine draftsmanship and sound design which he never lost. The retrospective exhibition mentioned above made this last circumstance impressively manifest, illustrating as it did with equal brilliance the diverse aspects of a long career. In his early manhood at Egmond he inscribed over the door of his studio the Dutch words "Waar en Klaar," and he pursued those qualities with unremitting ardor and astonishingly even success. His art was, indeed, true and clear, true to nature, and invested with the clarity only attainable by an expert technician. Nothing offers better evidence of his poise than the unforced nature of that quality in his work to which the word "picturesque" must be applied. He long had a keen interest in the humble life of Holland, the milkmaids in the fields, the peasant girl dressed for Communion, the villagers at worship, and he loved both the distinctive dress they wore, and the background against which they moved. But his most ambitious design was never the set "costume piece." On the contrary it was a page from life, singularly direct and sincere. So when he chose "The Last Supper" for a theme he treated it imaginatively, tenderly, but above all things humanly.

Melchers was a forthright, candid man, pungent in speech, frank in action, and of altogether generous and genuine traits. His character, as lovable as it was virile, passed into his work. There is nothing fumbling or uncertain about his stroke. The drawing in a picture of his is firm and flowing, the touch of the brush forceful, the color pure, strong, and charming. As a colorist, indeed, he was exceptionally dowered, making a note of white, or green, or violet, or orange, sing with equal plangency and beauty. He had deep feeling. It comes out in the earnest countenances of the men and women assembled in one or another of his Dutch church interiors. It is perceptible in his "Last Supper," a composition of noble dignity and warm emotional content. His insight is disclosed by his portraits, which are vivid characterizations. His rank is determined by these imponderables and by his ability as a painter pure and simple, a master of his craft who was devoted to the integrity of art.

[*Gari Melchers: Painter* (1928) is a book of plates containing a Foreword by Henriette Lewis-Hind. See also: *Who's Who in America*, 1932–33; *Am. Art Annual*, 1931; Christian Brinton, *Modern Artists* (1908); *Biog. Sketches of Am. Artists* (1924), pub. by the Mich. State Lib.; *Internat. Studio*, Mar. 1907, Dec. 1912; *World's Work*, Apr. 1908; *Mag. of Art*, Feb. 1900; obituaries in *N. Y. Herald-Tribune, N. Y. Times, Boston Transcript*, and other papers. This spelling of Melchers' mother's name is correct, although the form Bangertor appears in *Who's Who in America*.] R. C.

MELISH, JOHN (June 13, 1771–Dec. 30, 1822), geographer, traveler, merchant, was born in Methven, Perthshire, Scotland, where he spent his early years and attended the parish school. He was apprenticed to a wealthy cotton factor in Glasgow who permitted him to take the examinations at Glasgow University with his own son, and in time he became a member of his employer's firm. In 1798 he voyaged to the West Indies and on the trip began to study geography and navigation. In 1806 he sailed to Savannah, Ga., and there established a mercantile house of his own through which passed manufactured goods from abroad and raw cotton from the South. He traveled extensively through the cotton states, taking numerous notes as he went with the intention of publishing later a work on the geographical, social, and political character of the United States. In 1807 he returned to Scotland, but in 1808 his business suffered from the effects of the Orders in Council and the Non-Intercourse acts, and in 1809 he again sailed to the United States to look after his affairs, bringing his family with him. For a time he was in New York, engaged in the importing business, then he resumed his travels in America, this time through Upper Canada and the West.

In 1811 he settled in Philadelphia, which was thereafter his home. He decided to write the narrative of his travels in America, hoping that it would encourage British subjects to emigrate to the United States, and in 1812 he published in two volumes *Travels in the United States of America, in the Years 1806 & 1807, and 1809, 1810 & 1811.* The work was republished, with a slight variation in title, in 1815 and 1818. Melish displayed his talent for draftsmanship in the eight maps which illustrated the work. "Here is a kind of phenomenon," said a reviewer in the *Port Folio* (February 1813, pp. 114, 132), "two whole volumes of travels in America; without any material errors; with no palpable falsehoods; no malignant abuse of individuals; no paltry calumnies on the institutions of the U. S. . . . A singular example of the good temper, the sound sense, and the candid feelings which a sensible foreigner has brought to the examination of our country."

While Melish was engaged in drawing the maps for his first work, it was suggested to him that a map of the seat of the War of 1812 would be useful, and from his own and two British army maps he compiled *A Military and Topographical Atlas of the United States, Including the British Possessions & Florida* (1813), which was republished in enlarged form in 1815. Melish was listed in the Philadelphia directory in 1813 as a merchant, in 1814 as a map and print seller, in 1816 as a map publisher, and in 1818, in association with Samuel Harrison, as a geographer, engraver, and map publisher. He built up an establishment which at one time employed thirty persons. He continued to publish his own works. His most notable undertaking was *The State Map of Pennsylvania* (1822) for which the state legislature made provision in 1816. Much of the data for the chart was collected by Melish. Some geological data was supplied by William Maclure [*q.v.*]. His other works include: *A Statistical Account of the United States* (1813); *A Description of East and West Florida and the Bahama Islands* (1813), with map; *A Description of the Roads in the United States* (1814); *The Sine Qua Non: A Map of the United States, Shewing the Boundary Proposed by the British Commissioners at Ghent* (1814); *A Geographical Description of the United States with the Contiguous British and Spanish Possessions* (1816), to accompany a map; *A Geographical Description of the World* (1818), to accompany a map of the world; *The Necessity of Protecting and Encouraging the Manufactures of the United States* (1818); *Information and Advice to Emigrants to the United States* (1819); and *Views on Political Economy* (1822). Melish died in Philadelphia and, although he was not a Quaker, was buried in the ground of the Free Quakers. He had married, in Scotland, Isabella Moncrieff.

[There is some autobiographical information in Melish's *Travels*. Other sources include: R. B. Beath, *Hist. Cat. of the St. Andrew's Soc. of Phila.*, vol. II (1913); *A Cat. of Maps and Geog. Works Published and for Sale by John Melish* (1822); W. H. Egle, *Notes and Queries*, I (1894), 361; *Poulson's Am. Daily Ad-*

vertiser, Jan. 1, 1823; manuscript register of the Philadelphia board of health.] J. J.

MELL, PATRICK HUES (July 19, 1814–Jan. 26, 1888), Baptist clergyman, teacher, author, born in Walthourville, Liberty County, Ga., was the eldest surviving son in a family of eight children. His father was Benjamin Mell, whose ancestors were among the early settlers of Charleston, S. C., and his mother, Cynthia Sumner, a descendant of New England Puritans who went to Georgia in the migration of 1754. When Patrick was still in his teens, both his parents died. The estate having been lost on a surety bond, Mell was obliged to provide for the family. Having received some educational training before the death of his father, he continued his schooling at the academies of Walthourville and of Darien, teaching in the primary department to pay his tuition. His industry attracted the attention of George Walthour, who provided funds for his education at Amherst College, and Mell enrolled there in 1833. His independent disposition caused him to accept this financial aid with reluctance, and disagreement over his expenses together with a distaste for some of his instructors caused him to leave college in 1835. He immediately found a teaching position in a West Springfield school and in 1836 became associate principal of the high school in East Hartford, Conn. In 1837 he returned to Georgia and was thereafter identified with that state.

For two years he taught successively at Perry's Mill in Tatnall County and at Ryall's in Montgomery County. From 1839 to 1841 he was the principal of a classical and English school at Oxford. He had joined the Baptist Church in 1832, abandoning an inclination to study law, and in October 1839 he received a license to preach. He now began preaching to the destitute congregations in the countryside. In 1841 he was elected professor of ancient languages at Mercer College, an institution which the Baptists had established a few years previously at Penfield, and he continued in this position for fourteen years. Following a rather common practice of teaching and preaching at the same time, he was ordained Nov. 19, 1842, and took charge of the Baptist congregation at Greensboro. After serving this congregation for ten years, he accepted calls from two churches, one at Bairdstown and the other at Antioch, continuing his ministry to the latter for twenty-six years. At Mercer College a conflict developed between him and the president on the question of the respective rights and duties of each, which resulted in his forced resignation. Much bitterness resulted which a faction of the Baptists long kept alive.

By this time Mell's influence had become so widespread that he was offered various pastorates in the state and the presidency of several Baptist colleges. In 1856 he accepted the professorship of ancient languages at the University of Georgia, Athens, and when in 1860, the University was reorganized with a chancellor and vice-chancellor at its head, he accepted the latter position. At the same time he was transferred to the professorship of ethics and metaphysics. He remained vice-chancellor until 1872 when the office was abolished, but retained his professorship for the rest of his life. At the outbreak of the Civil War he was made captain of a company known as the Mell Rifles. Because of the death of his wife on July 6 following, he resigned; but in 1863, when the state was in danger of invasion from the Tennessee border, he raised a regiment, made up in part of students and professors of the university, and became its colonel. He remained in the service until the end of the war.

His strenuous work as teacher and preacher broke down his health in 1871 and it was not fully restored until after a trip to Europe two years later. In 1878 he was elected chancellor of the university, which position he held until his death. He was an able educator and a strict disciplinarian, erect in figure, austere in manner, independent in disposition, reserved and distant generally, though courteous and punctilious. As a preacher he was powerful though not eloquent, and as a parliamentarian he was unequaled in the state. He was moderator of the Georgia Baptist Association for twenty-nine years, president of the Georgia Convention for twenty-five years, and of the Southern Baptist Convention for fifteen years. The best known of his numerous writings are *Baptism in Its Modes and Subjects* (1852); *Manual on Corrective Church Discipline* (1860); *A Manual of Parliamentary Practice* (1868); and *Church Polity* (1878). He was married twice: first, June 29, 1840, to Lurene Howard Cooper of Montgomery County, who died July 6, 1861, and by whom there were eight children, one of whom was Patrick Hues Mell, 1850–1890 [*q.v.*]; second, Dec. 24, 1861, to Eliza Elizabeth Cooper of Scriven County, who bore him six children.

[The most satisfactory and complete account is P. H. Mell, Jr., *Life of Patrick Hues Mell* (1895). His record as chancellor of the University of Georgia may be found in the Minutes of the trustees and of the faculty, in the University Library. See also Dr. and Mrs. P. H. Mell, *The Geneal. of the Mell Family in the Southern States* (1897); *Amherst Coll. Biog. Record of the Grads. and Non-Grads.* (1927), ed. by R. S. Fletcher and M. O. Young; A. L. Hull, *A Hist. Sketch of the Univ. of Ga.* (1894), and *Annals of Athens, Ga., 1801–1901* (1906); E. M. Coulter, *College Life in the*

Old South (1928); *Proc. Thirty-third Session of the Southern Bapt. Convention* (1888); B. D. Ragsdale, *Story of Ga. Baptists* (copr. 1932); *Atlanta Constitution,* Jan. 27, 1888; W. J. Northen, *Men of Mark in Ga.* (1911), vol. III.] E. M. C.

MELL, PATRICK HUES (May 24, 1850–Oct. 12, 1918), scientist, educator, was born in Penfield, Ga., the son of Patrick Hues Mell [*q.v.*] and Lurene Howard (Cooper). He was reared in an atmosphere of discipline, scholarship, and culture, which left its stamp upon him. Entering the University of Georgia in 1866, he received the degree of A.B. in 1871 and that of M.E. in 1872; eight years later he was awarded the degree of Ph.D. In 1874, he became chemist for the Georgia Department of Agriculture. Resigning in 1877 because of ill health, he tramped and rode through the mountains of Alabama, Georgia, and North Carolina collecting specimens of clays and other minerals. These and magazine articles which he wrote attracted attention, and in 1878 he was elected professor of natural history in the State Agricultural and Mechanical College (Alabama Polytechnic Institute) at Auburn, Ala.; later his title was changed to professor of geology and botany. In 1884, in addition to his teaching, he had charge of the state weather service for Georgia, Florida, and Alabama, and when separate bureaus were formed in these states he became director of the Alabama weather service. In the latter work, which he carried on until 1893, he originated the system of weather signals long in use by the United States Weather Bureau (*Who's Who in America,* 1918–19). From 1888 to 1902 he was also connected with the Alabama Agricultural Experiment Station, serving as botanist and meteorologist and from 1898 as director. He declined the presidency of Mercer University, Georgia, in 1893, and of the North Georgia Agricultural College in 1897, but in 1902, accepted the presidency of the Clemson Agricultural College, South Carolina. The institution was then only nine years old, and Mell's experience was most valuable in directing its affairs, his enthusiasm and ability as a teacher of science making themselves distinctly felt. Resigning in 1910, he made his home thereafter in Atlanta, and gave his time to the work of treasurer of the board of missions of the Southern Baptist Convention.

Mell was a pioneer in several lines of science. His collections of fossils was one of the best in the South; his work in hybridizing cotton was extensive for his day and of suggestive value to plant breeders; and his work on the climatology of Alabama was of permanent value. Among his publications were "Auriferous Slate Deposits of the Southern Mining Region" (*Transactions of the American Institute of Mining Engineers,* vol. IX, 1881), "The Southern Soapstones, Kaolin, and Fireclays and Their Uses" (*Ibid.,* vol. X, 1882); *Wild Grasses of Alabama* (1886), issued by the Alabama Department of Natural History and Geology; *Climatology of Alabama* (1890), *A Microscopic Study of the Cotton Plant* (1890), *Experiments in Crossing for the Purpose of Improving the Cotton Fiber* (1894), all bulletins of the Alabama Agricultural Experiment Station; and *Report on the Climatology of the Cotton Plant* (1893), a bulletin of the United States Department of Agriculture Weather Bureau. He also contributed extensively to periodicals, revised several works by others, and published a biography of his father, *Life of Patrick Hues Mell* (1895).

Probably his most distinctive contribution, however, was his service as a teacher. The agricultural and mechanical colleges of the South were in their infancy when he went to Alabama, and in the development of two of these he was an important agent. "He was a very modest man and an extremely courteous one, but his influence was not to be resisted. In this he was a fine type of the Southern professor of the old days. He was not a specialist; he was a scientist with broad sympathies and attractive personality" (Calhoun, *post,* p. 45). On June 15, 1875, he married Annie R. White of Athens, Ga. He died in Fredericksburg, Va., while visiting a brother-in-law.

[Dr. and Mrs. P. H. Mell, *The Geneal. of the Mell Family in the Southern States* (1897); F. H. H. Calhoun, "Memorial of Patrick Hues Mell," in *Bull. Geol. Soc. of America,* Mar. 1919; *Bulls. of Ala. Agric. Experiment Station,* 1888–1902; P. H. Mell, *Life of Patrick Hues Mell* (1895); *Reports* of the board of trustees of Clemson Coll., S. C., 1906–11; *Science,* Nov. 22, 1918; *Who's Who in America,* 1918–19; *Atlanta Constitution,* Oct. 15, 1918; information from associates; date of death from a brother.] E. W. S.

MELLEN, CHARLES SANGER (Aug. 16, 1851–Nov. 17, 1927), railroad executive, son of George K. and Hannah M. (Sanger) Mellen, was born at Lowell, Mass. He was educated in the public schools of Concord, N. H., graduating from the high school in 1867. He began his career in the cashier's office of the Northern New Hampshire Railroad (1869), and then rose in his profession through successive positions on the Central Vermont (1872–73), Northern New Hampshire (1873–80), and the Boston & Lowell (1880–88). He became general purchasing agent for the Union Pacific in 1888 (*Railroad Gazette,* Aug. 31, 1888, p. 580), and was later advanced to general traffic manager. In 1892 he was made general manager of the New York & New England Railroad and then second vice-president of the New York, New Haven & Hartford. During this period he was married twice: first, to Marion Beardsley Foster of St. Albans, Vt., on Sept. 23, 1875; and second, to Katharine Lloyd Livingston of Brooklyn, N. Y., on Nov. 15, 1893.

Mellen's advance from 1892 on, was due largely to the influence of J. P. Morgan, who was instrumental in obtaining for him in 1897 the presidency of the Northern Pacific. Mellen's term of office was during a significant period in the history of the Northern Pacific, but he had little to do with the financial affairs of the company. He acquired feeders, improved the road, and produced a favorable operating ratio. His competition with the Great Northern was objectionable to James J. Hill [*q.v.*], and as Hill's power increased, a change became inevitable. In 1903 Mellen returned to the New York, New Haven & Hartford Railroad as president. By this time he had a national reputation. In 1904 he was a delegate to the Republican National Convention. During the same year President Roosevelt consulted him about railroad affairs and quoted him extensively in the annual message to Congress (See *Congressional Record,* 58 Cong., 3 Sess., p. 12).

Mellen's policy with the New Haven was similar to that which he had followed with the Northern Pacific. Leaving the financial affairs largely in the hands of the road's directors and bankers, he improved the rolling stock, added new track, built stations, beautified the yards, installed safety devices, electrified the entrance to New York City, and joined the Pennsylvania Railroad in constructing the Hell Gate route. He nearly succeeded in monopolizing the transportational system of New England by buying trolley lines, steamships, and railroads (he was president of both the Boston & Maine and the Maine Central from 1910), and by preventing the Grand Trunk from entering Providence. Mellen was a hard worker and had a driving personality, but he tended to be glacial in his human contacts, dictatorial to his subordinates, and subservient to his superiors. Furthermore, he had marital troubles during the years 1912–13. A series of very serious train accidents in these same years brought to a climax the growing resentment against a virtual monopoly of New England transportation. The Interstate Commerce Commission, after an investigation, called the Mellen management "one of the most glaring instances of maladministration revealed in all the history of American railroading" (31 *Interstate Commerce Commission Reports,* 33). Most of the charges against Mellen can be read in this report. The bad financial practices were probably only slightly his fault, but as president he had to assume the responsibility. The failure to maintain proper equipment and service must be laid at his door, although he had made some improvements and was handicapped by a conservative board of directors. No matter where the fault lay, the popular outcry plus a long series of governmental investigations finally caused his resignation in 1913. After rumors of other possible positions, he retired from practically all his business interests to live at his home at Stockbridge, Mass. Later he returned to Concord, N. H., where he died.

[Newspapers and magazines, particularly during the years 1912–13, contained a great amount of material about Mellen; among the magazine articles may be mentioned E. P. Lyle, Jr., "C. S. Mellen, Master of Traffic," *World's Work,* May 1905; G. W. Batson, "Charles S. Mellen: Railroad Organizer," *Rev. of Revs.* (N. Y.), Aug. 1907; B. J. Hendrick, "Bottling Up New England," *McClure's Mag.,* Sept. 1912; Garet Garrett, "Things That Were Mellen's and Things That Were Cæsar's," *Everybody's Mag.,* July 1914. The best adverse analysis of the Mellen régime is L. D. Brandeis, *Financial Condition of the New York, New Haven & Hartford . . .* (1907), and the most extensive defense is J. F. Moors, "Betraying New England!" in *New Eng. Mag.,* Mar. and Apr. 1913. Mellen's testimony before the Interstate Commerce Commission was reprinted as a pamphlet, *Official Stenographer's Report of the Testimony of Charles S. Mellen . . . at Boston, Mass., May 2, 1913*; see also *Sen. Doc. 543,* 63 Cong., 2 Sess. Among Mellen's public utterances may be mentioned *Letter of C. S. Mellen . . . to the Public on Dec. 20, 1912* (n.d.) and an interview by F. C. Leupp in the *Outlook,* Feb. 3, 1912. For biographical details see *Who's Who in America,* 1924–25; and obituary in *N. Y. Times,* Nov. 18, 1927.]

R. E. R.

MELLEN, GRENVILLE (June 19, 1799–Sept. 5, 1841), author, the son of Prentiss Mellen [*q.v.*] and Sarah (Hudson) Mellen, was born at Biddeford, now in the state of Maine, before his father's removal to Portland. He attended Portland Academy and entered Harvard in 1814. In college he cultivated his interests in poetry and oratory and was class poet at graduation in 1818. He next attended the newly established Harvard Law School until 1820, spent another year in his father's law office, was admitted to the Maine bar, and practised his first year at Thomaston. In the autumn of 1823 he settled at North Yarmouth, Me., where he was married, Sept. 9, 1824, to Mary King Southgate, and lived happily, much in demand as a local orator and poet. The first of many occasional poems, his "Ode" for the two-hundredth anniversary of the landing at Plymouth, Dec. 22, 1820, was followed by another for the dedication of the Bunker Hill Monument in June 1825. Together with his fellow townsman, Henry W. Longfellow, he contributed poems, prose sketches, and tales to the *United States Literary Gazette* and to the annuals, the *Atlantic Souvenir* and the *Legendary.* His volume of *Sad Tales and Glad Tales,* by "Reginald Reverie," published at Boston in 1828, is interesting chiefly as pioneer work leading up to the short story as later developed by Hawthorne and Poe. His tales show the influence of Irving, but are more diffuse, sentimental, and mystifying.

The deaths of Mellen's infant daughter in September 1828, and of his wife in the following May were blows from which he never recovered. His own health was undermined; he lived an unsettled life at North Yarmouth, Portland, and Boston; tried vainly for a diplomatic post in the Netherlands; and for a few months in 1829 acted as editor of the *Portland Advertiser.* At Boston he delivered in 1830 the Harvard Phi Beta Kappa poem, "The Age of Print," and in September 1833 published a volume of verse, *The Martyr's Triumph; Buried Valley; and Other Poems.* His poetry, largely influenced by Byron, has at its best a delicacy of which Byron was seldom capable. Unfortunately however, John Neal, his friend, was justified in saying: "He dealt too much in mystery—the mystery of language, not of thought" ("The Unforgotten Dead," in *Brother Jonathan,* Jan. 1, 1842, p. 25). After 1836, Mellen lived mostly at New York, in the household of Samuel Colman, for whom he acted as co-editor of the *Monthly Miscellany* in 1839. He also delivered the Yale Phi Beta Kappa poem for that year. He devoted his last days to historical and statistical compilations, *A Book of the United States* (1838), and "General View of the American Continent," left in manuscript at his death. A voyage to Havana in the winter of 1839–40 failed to benefit his health, and he died at Colman's home late in the following summer.

[The authoritative account of Mellen is Joy L. Nevens' "Grenville Mellen, a Study of his Life and Works" (1925), University of Maine master's thesis, with bibliography. His works in manuscript, carefully edited by himself, with a notebook "Bibliography" containing valuable information regarding the composition and reception of his productions, are preserved in the Maine Hist. Soc. Lib. An unfinished autobiography in Byronic stanzas called "Something" sheds much light upon his early years. For printed sources see L. B. Chapman, *Monograph on the Southgate Family of Scarborough, Me.* (1907); E. A. and G. L. Duyckinck, *Cyc. of Am. Lit.* (1875), vol. II; *N. Y. Tribune,* Sept. 6, 1841.]

M. E.

MELLEN, PRENTISS (Oct. 11, 1764–Dec. 31, 1840), senator, chief justice of Maine, eighth of the nine children of the Rev. John and Rebecca (Prentiss) Mellen, was born in Sterling, Mass. His father, a graduate of Harvard in the class of 1741, prepared his sons Henry and Prentiss for his own college, which they entered in 1780, graduating in 1784. Prentiss then spent a year as tutor in the family of Joseph Otis of Barnstable, later studying law with the eccentric lawyer, Shearjashub Bourne, of that place. In after years Mellen used to refer semi-humorously to the inadequacy of his professional preparation. Admitted to the bar in Taunton in October 1788, he practised for about eight months in Sterling, then he removed to Bridgewater. Not being as successful here as he had hoped, he left in November 1791 and spent the winter with his brother Henry who was practising law in Dover, N. H. Upon the advice of his friend, George Thacher, a lawyer and at that time a representative in Congress from the District of Maine, he removed to the nearby town of Biddeford, now in the state of Maine. Here with a meager law library, but with an unbounded ambition, he opened his humble law office in Squire Hooper's tavern. By 1806 his law practice in the adjoining county, Cumberland, had grown so extensive that he moved to Portland, where he became a leader in what was commonly considered to be the ablest bar in the commonwealth of Massachusetts. In 1808, 1809, and 1817 he was a member of the executive council of Massachusetts. In 1818 he was chosen senator from Massachusetts, thus becoming a colleague of Harrison Gray Otis. In 1820, when Maine became a state, he left the Senate to accept appointment as chief justice of the supreme court of Maine, an office which he held until October 1834, when, having reached the age of seventy, he was required by law to retire.

As chief justice Mellen wrote a majority of the court's decisions and thus left an indelible impress upon the law of his state. Tall and imposing, fervid and impassioned in speech, he was an effective lawyer. Perhaps the most famous case in which he appeared was that in 1809 when he, with Samuel S. Wilde, successfully defended seven men accused of the murder at Malta, Me., of Paul Chadwick, who was engaged in surveying land (*Trial of David Lynn ... for the Murder of Paul Chadwick,* 1810). As a judge, Mellen was conscientious, and his opinions are careful and pointed. His long service was crowned, Jan. 1, 1840, when he with two colleagues appointed by the governor in July 1838 submitted their report containing the revision and codification of the statutes of Maine (*Revised Statutes of the State of Maine,* 1841). Mellen died at Portland, Me. He had married, on May 5, 1795, Sarah Hudson of Hartford, Conn., by whom he had six children. His son, Grenville [*q.v.*], after studying law, deserted that profession for literature. In this he may well have been influenced by his father's lifelong interest in and practice of the composition of verses.

[Simon Greenleaf, "Memoir of the Life and Character of the Late Chief Justice Mellen," in 17 *Maine Reports,* 467; Wm. Willis, *A Hist. of the Law, the Courts, and the Lawyers of Maine* (1863); H. C. Williams, ed., *Biog. Encyc. of Me. of the Nineteenth Century* (1885); *Biog. Dir. Am. Cong.* (1928); "Presentation of Portrait of Prentiss Mellen to the Town of Sterling . . . Nov. third 1911," typed MS. in the Lib. of Cong.; Willis Papers, Me. Hist. Soc. Lib., Book Y; *Eastern Argus* (Portland), Jan. 1, 1841; and *Portland Advertiser,* Jan. 5, 1841.] R. E. M.

MELLETTE, ARTHUR CALVIN (June 23, 1842–May 25, 1896), first governor of South Dakota, born in Henry County, Ind., is said to have been descended from Jean de Mellet, a sub-lieutenant in the Régiment de Bourbonnais, a French military organization that sailed for America in 1780 and at the close of the Revolution returned to France. De Mellet is said to have emigrated to Virginia with his family after resigning his commission. Charles Mellette, father of Arthur Calvin, was born in Monongalia County, Va. (now W. Va.), and removed in 1830 to Henry County, Ind., where he spent the remainder of his life and where he was married on Apr. 14, 1836, to Mary Moore; she bore him five children. Arthur spent his youth as a farmer lad with an insatiable desire for education, and in his elementary learning he was almost self-taught. He attended Marion Academy and entered the sophomore class of Indiana University, where he received the A.B. degree in 1864. After graduation he served as a private until the end of the Civil War. He returned to the university and completed his law studies in 1866, received the LL.B. degree, and was admitted to the bar. He was married, on May 29, 1866, to Margaret, the daughter of Theophilus Adam Wylie, long associated with Indiana University. He settled in practice at Muncie but was soon diverted from the law by journalism. He conducted the *Muncie Times* with success and acquired influence in politics. He was a member of the state House of Representatives from Delaware County in the session of 1872 and 1873 and was largely responsible for the development of the Indiana township school system, which has become the model system for many states.

In 1879, when his wife's health failed and a change of climate was imperative, he removed to Dakota Territory, where influence from Indiana soon obtained for him an appointment as register of the United States land office, then located at Springfield but soon removed to Watertown, where he lived for the remainder of his life. When he retired from the land office in 1882 he resumed the practice of law, but having acquired a competence his attention was chiefly devoted to his personal affairs. He was a member of the first constitutional convention of 1883 and was chiefly responsible for the provisions in the constitution placing a limit on the legal indebtedness of the state and on tax levies for state purposes, fixing salaries of state officers at a very low figure, and providing that the state should engage in no work of internal improvement. These limitations were carried over to the second and to the third constitution, under which South Dakota was admitted to statehood. In 1885 he was chosen provisional governor of the "State of Dakota," to which admission was denied. He was the original advocate in the Northwest of Harrison's nomination for president, in 1888 was successful in obtaining for him the support of Dakota and some adjacent states, and was made national committeeman of the Republican party for Dakota. Among the first appointments made by President Harrison, was that of Mellette to be governor of Dakota Territory, and at the election of 1889 he was elected the first governor of the state of South Dakota. As the first governor he took infinite pains to establish precedents of simplicity and economy. He was himself philanthropic by nature, and he spent himself and his fortune in benevolence. When he left the governorship, in January 1893, his health was seriously impaired, and he was never again strong. The tragic death of his eldest son and the loss of his fortune through the treachery of a friend added to the burden of his declining years. It was characteristic that, upon the defalcation of the state treasurer for whom he had become surety, he immediately turned over to the state all of his possessions. He was hoping to devote himself to experimentation in the field of physics when broken health and broken fortune brought his useful years to a close. He died at Pittsburg, Kan., and was buried at Watertown, S. D.

[Doane Robinson, *South Dakota* (1930), vol. I; *S. D. Hist. Colls.,* vols. I, X (1902–20); *Les Combattants Français de la Guerre Américaine* (1903); T. A. Wylie, *Indiana University* (1890), esp. pp. 107, 236.] D. R.

MELSHEIMER, FRIEDRICH VALENTIN (Sept. 25, 1749–June 30, 1814), Lutheran clergyman, entomologist, was born at Negenborn, near Holzminden, Duchy of Brunswick, the son of Joachim Sebastian and Clara Margaretha Melsheimer. His father was superintendent of the ducal forests. Melsheimer attended school at Holzminden, matriculated in 1769 at the University of Helmstedt, and in 1776 was appointed chaplain of the Dragoon Regiment of Brunswick Auxiliaries commanded by Major-General Friedrich Augustus Riedesel, which was hired by the British Crown to help subdue the rebellious colonies in America. His journal for the period Feb. 22–Sept. 21, 1776, published in that year, displays an admirable talent for topographical writing (*Tagebuch von der Reise der Braunschweigischen Auxiliär Truppen von Wolfenbüttel nach Quebec,* Minden, 1776, including an *Erste Fortsetzung*; another edition with identical pagination, Frankfurt and Leipzig, 1776; translated by William Wood and W. L. Stone in *Transactions of the Literary and Historical Society of Quebec,* no. 20, 1891, pp. 133–78). He was wounded in the arm at the battle of Bennington, Aug. 16, 1777, and was taken prisoner (*Letters from America 1776–1779,* translated by R. W. Pettengill, 1924, p. 96). He was one of a party of captured German officers who arrived at Bethlehem, Pa., Jan. 26, 1779, and were quartered there pending their exchange.

While his friends were enlivening the village with their musical serenades, Melsheimer fell in love with Mary Agnes Mau, daughter of Samuel Mau, a former redemptioner. He meanwhile was exchanged for W. Cardelle, chaplain of the 11th Virginia Regiment, received permission to travel (U. S. R. Miscellaneous Papers, Jan. 18, 1779, Library of Congress), was married to Agnes Mau on May 10, 1779 (J. M. Levering, *A History of Bethlehem, Pennsylvania,* 1903, pp. 492–93), and applied unsuccessfully for the pastorate at Lebanon, which had been left vacant by the death of John Caspar Stoever, Jr. (T. E. Schmauk, *Old Salem in Lebanon,* 1898, pp. 111–12). Presumably he never intended to rejoin his regiment. That autumn he assumed the pastorship of five small Lutheran congregations in Dauphin County and attended the Tulpehocken convention of the Ministerium of Pennsylvania, into which, however, he was not received as a member until 1785. Later he served for three years as secretary of the Ministerium, was officially designated as an instructor in theology, and was chairman of the committee on English congregations. He was pastor at Manheim, Lancaster County, 1784–86; at New Holland, 1786–87; professor of Greek, Latin, and German in Franklin College, 1787–89, working manfully to keep the college alive; and finally pastor of St. Matthew's, Hanover, York County, from 1789 until his death.

Besides being a faithful pastor he was an enthusiastic friend of education and a careful student of natural history, his *Catalogue of Insects of Pennsylvania, Part First* (Hanover, 1806) being the first volume published on the entomology of North America. It lists 1,363 species of beetles, of which over four hundred have been identified. He was not a mere collector but paid considerable attention to food habits and mode of occurrence; his notes are few and brief but occasionally telling, as the description of the rose-bug—*"Habitat praecique in rosarum floribus qui misere destruit."* Until the year of his death he maintained a correspondence with his school friend, August Wilhelm Knoch, who mentions him in his *Neue Beyträge zur Insectenkunde, Erster Theil* (Leipzig, 1801), and sent him hundreds of specimens of American insects. He is said to have contributed a description of Pennsylvania to the *Schleswig'sche Journal* of 1792 and geographical essays to the same periodical in 1794. Some notes of his *"Über bisher Unbekannte Käfer"* appeared in Oken's *Isis* (vol. XXII, 1830, cols. 608–10). He was also the author of *Gespräche zwischen einem Protestanten und Römischen Priester* (Hanover, 1797) and *Wahrheit der Christlichen Religion für Unstudirte* (Frederick, Md., 1811). He was elected to membership in the American Philosophical Society in 1795. Melsheimer was short in stature and frail of body, suffered for many years from a disease of the lungs, but remained active till shortly before his death. He died at Hanover and was buried in the yard of his church. Two of his sons, Johan Friedrich and Ernst Friedrich, were Lutheran ministers and carried on his studies in entomology.

[*Evangelisches Magazin,* IV (1817), 62–63; J. H. C. Schierenbeck, *Lebensbeschreibungen von Lutherischen Predigern in Amerika* (Selingsgrove, Pa., *c.* 1864); *Doc. Hist. Ev. Luth. Ministerium of Pa., 1748–1821* (1898); J. H. Dubbs, *Hist. of Franklin and Marshall Coll.* (1903); J. G. Morris, "American Zoology, No. 1," *Lit. Record and Jour. Linnaean Asso. of Pa. Coll.* (Gettysburg), Aug. 1845, and "Contributions toward a History of Entomology in the U. S.," *Am. Jour. Sci.,* Jan. 1846; G. R. Prowell "F. V. Melsheimer," *Proc. Hist. Soc. York County, Pa.,* vol. I (1903), reprinted in *Pa.-Ger.,* May 1908; H. A. Hagen, "The Melsheimer Family and the Melsheimer Collection," *Canadian Entomologist,* Oct. 1884; E. A. Schwarz, "Some Notes on Melsheimer's Catalogue of the Coleoptera of Pennsylvania," with a note by C. V. Riley, *Proc. Entomol. Soc. Wash.,* III (1895), 134–38; H. B. Weiss, "First Book on Insects in America and its Author," *Am. Collector,* Oct. 1927.] G. H. G.

MELTZER, SAMUEL JAMES (Mar. 22, 1851–Nov. 7, 1920), physician, physiologist, was born in Ponevyezh, Courland, Russia, the son of Simon Meltzer, of Hebrew ancestry. He received his early training at Königsberg, Prussia, going from there in 1875 to the University of Berlin, where he devoted himself to the study of philosophy and medicine, receiving the degree of M.D. in 1882. The following year he came to the United States, defraying his expenses by serving as ship's surgeon. He engaged in his profession in New York, gradually building up a practice sufficient to support himself and his family; but his chief interest was in the advancement of clinical medicine through knowledge of physiology. To this end he worked early and late, whenever he could find time from his medical practice, carrying on experimental work in physiology with such success that he soon gained for himself wide recognition in the field of scientific medicine and became ultimately, in 1906, the head of the department of physiology and pharmacology of the Rockefeller Institute for Medical Research. Having attained that position, he was able to devote all his time and energies to research work in physiology and kindred fields, although by so doing he was compelled to relinquish the larger income derived from his medical practice. This sacrifice, however, was for Meltzer a small matter compared with the wider opportunity of enlarging the boundaries of knowledge in physiology and medicine. Endowed with a clear mind, tireless energy, and a devotion to high ideals, he became one of the leading American physiologists of his generation.

Meltzer's career as a research worker in the field of physiology was determined while he was still a student in Berlin, through his association with Professor Hugo Kronecker. Under the latter's supervision, he carried on a series of experiments to determine the mechanism of swallowing, from which came the Kronecker-Meltzer theory of deglutition, published prior to Meltzer's graduation and constituting his first contribution to medical science ("Ueber die Vorgänge beim Schlucken," in *Archiv für Anatomie und Physiologie,* 1880, pts. IV, V). The extent of his productive work is indicated by a list of nearly two hundred and fifty scientific papers covering a wide range of physiological and medical research on such subjects as excitation and inhibition, theory of shock, the action of adrenalin, the anaesthetic effects of magnesium salts, and artificial respiration through intratracheal insufflation. He founded and was the first president of the Society for Experimental Biology and Medicine, and its vigorous growth and wide influence constitute a testimonal of his ability to arouse interest in research, and justify his vision of the part experimental study and investigation were destined to play in the development of scientific medicine. During the latter years of his life he was troubled by a disease that curtailed his activities somewhat, but he pursued his research work to the very end, his active mind constantly suggesting new problems for solution. His life was one of service, devoted to the progress of the art and science of medicine, through experimental methods; and his work made an indelible impression upon American physiology. When twenty years old he married, in Russia, Olga T. Levitt, by whom he had two children.

[W. H. Howell, "Biog. Memoir, Samuel James Meltzer, 1851–1920," in *Memoirs Nat. Acad. Sci.*, vol. XXI (1927); *Memorial Number for Samuel James Meltzer, Founder and First President of the Soc. for Experimental Biology and Medicine* (1921); *Science*, Feb. 4, 1921; *Lancet* (London), Sept. 17, 1921; *Medic. Record* (N. Y.), Mar. 12, 1921; *Who's Who in America,* 1920–21; *N. Y. Times,* Nov. 8, 1920.]

R. H. C.

MELVILLE, DAVID (Mar. 21, 1773–Sept. 3, 1856), pewterer, inventor, son of David and Elizabeth (Thurston) Melville, was born in Newport, R. I. He was descended from David Melville who came to Boston, Mass., from Scotland during the last decade of the seventeenth century and later married Elizabeth, daughter of Rev. Samuel Willard, 1640–1707 [*q.v.*], pastor of South Church and vice-president of Harvard College. While little is known of Melville's environment, it is believed that he was of a family of metal craftsmen and that after securing a common-school education he learned this trade. By the time he was thirty years old he was established in Newport as a pewterer, maker of household utensils, and the proprietor of a hardware store, as indicated by his advertisement in the *Rhode Island Republican* of June 4, 1803.

About this time there was considerable interest in France and England in public demonstrations of illuminating gas. It is probable that Melville took note of these but was not aware of the processes involved. He was an ingenious individual, however, and having his curiosity aroused, he began experimenting and in 1806 succeeded in lighting his house on Pelham Street in Newport with coal gas. Encouraged by the public interest, he continued experimenting for upwards of seven years, constantly improving the process, and on Mar. 18, 1813, obtained the first United States patent for apparatus for making coal gas. He then formed a partnership with Winslow Lewis [*q.v.*] of Boston and advertised in the newspapers for business in the lighting of "manufactories, mines, mills, streets, theatres, lighthouses and other buildings" by gas. During the year he succeeded in lighting a cotton factory at Watertown, Mass., and a factory of the Wenscott Manufacturing Company near Providence, R. I. The cost of installation and operation was almost prohibitive, however, and he soon realized that the opportunities for general gas lighting were extremely limited. With the help of his partner, therefore, he concentrated his attention on interesting the government in using gas for lighthouses and in 1817 obtained a contract to install his gas light in the Beaver Tail Lighthouse at Newport and demonstrate it for a year. Melville fulfilled the terms of his contract, but the government declined to adopt gas lights, owing chiefly to opposition by persons who had contracted to furnish oil, including his own partner, and by those engaged in whale fisheries. Wholly discouraged, he abandoned his project and for the balance of his life gave his attention to his trade and to the hardware business. The defection of his partner and the latter's attempt to deprive him of his patent rights were a bitter disappointment to him. To clarify his position he published in 1819 the whole story of his relationship with Lewis under the title *An Exposé of Facts Respectfully Submitted to the Government of the U. S. Relating to the Conduct of Winslow Lewis.* He married Patience S. Sherman of Newport on Mar. 4, 1812, and was the father of seven children. He was buried in Newport.

[E. M. Tilley, "David Melville and his Early Experiments with Gas in Newport," *Bull. Newport Hist. Soc.*, no. 60, Jan. 1927; R. M. Bayles, *Hist. of Newport County, R. I.* (1888); Waldemar Kaempffert, *A Pop. Hist. of Am. Invention* (1924), vol. I; J. N. Arnold, *Vital Record of R. I., 1636–1850*, vol. IV (1893); Am. Gas Institute, *Lectures on the Centenary of the Introduction of Gas as an Illuminant* (1912); *Newport Advertiser*, Sept. 10, 1856; *Newport Mercury*, Sept. 13, 1856.]

C. W. M.

MELVILLE, GEORGE WALLACE (Jan. 10, 1841–Mar. 17, 1912), naval officer, was born in New York City, the son of Alexander and Sarah Douther (Wallace) Melville, and the grandson of James Melville of Stirling, Scotland, who emigrated to America in 1804. Manifesting a taste for mechanics, young Melville went from the public schools to the Brooklyn Collegiate and Polytechnic Institute, and from there to the engineering works of James Binns of East Brooklyn. On July 29, 1861, he entered the Engineer Corps of the navy as third assistant engineer and served on various vessels throughout the war. He was on board the *Wachusett* at Bahia, Brazil, when she captured the *Florida.* Previous to the engagement he attempted to board the *Florida* in broad daylight in civilian clothes for the purpose of obtaining information respecting her fighting strength, thus taking the risks of a spy. At the capture of Fort Fisher he served on torpedo boat *No. 6* in Admiral Porter's fleet. In October 1863 he was promoted second assistant engineer; 1865, first assistant engineer; and 1881, chief engineer. After the Civil War he served in various positions at sea and at the navy yards and shore stations. In 1867 he was on board the *Tacony* during the French evacuation of Mexico; from 1869 to 1871 on the *Lancaster,* the flagship of the South Atlantic Squadron; and from 1875 to 1878 on the *Tennessee,* the flagship of the Asiatic Squadron. For his successful performance of the routine duties of his profession he was often commended by his superior officers. Thus it was said officially that he exhibited as an officer of the *Lancaster* an "amount of mechanical ability, energy, and engineering skill rarely found" (Cathcart, *post,* p. 466).

Ambitious and enterprising, Melville was not content to rest on the laurels that might be won in ordinary naval occupations. In the spring of 1873, when the *Tigress* was chartered for the rescue of the missing members of the crew of the *Polaris,* originally commanded by Capt. Charles F. Hall [*q.v.*], Melville volunteered to serve as her chief engineer. At the end of the search he was strongly commended for his "great fertility of resource, combined with thorough practical knowledge" (Cathcart, *post,* p. 466). Fascinated by polar exploration, six years later he again volunteered for Arctic service, this time as the chief engineer of the *Jeannette,* Lieut. George W. De Long [*q.v.*]. Held in the ice almost two years as she drifted in the Arctic Ocean westward of Alaska, the *Jeannette* was kept afloat largely by reason of the energy and skill of Melville. His taking possession of Henrietta Island in behalf of the United States was described by De Long as a "brave and meritorious action." After the *Jeannette* sank, for many days he led the working force on its fearful march to Bennett Island. He commanded one of the three boats upon which the expedition embarked when it came to the open sea. His boat was one of the two that reached Siberia, and he was the only boat commander to survive and bring his crew to safety. After a few weeks of rest, although still feeble, he again turned northward and led a fruitless expedition in search of De Long. A few months later he was once more in the field and finally found his dead shipmates and gave them a respectable burial. Recognition by the government of his extraordinary efforts was tardy and inadequate, owing to jealousies largely within the navy. In 1882 his friends introduced a resolution in the Senate tendering him the thanks of Congress, advancing him forty numbers, and giving him a pecuniary reward. Eight years later (Sept. 3, 1890) a law was passed omitting the "thanks," advancing him fifteen numbers, and giving him a medal. In the meantime, in 1884, as the chief engineer of the *Thetis* in the Greely Relief Expedition, he had brought to a close his Arctic services, being among the first to reach the dying explorers at Cape Sabine.

On Aug. 9, 1887, Melville was appointed by President Cleveland, over forty-four senior officers, chief of the Bureau of Steam Engineering. He remained in that office sixteen and a half years, an epoch-making period in the construction of the new navy. He superintended the designing of the machinery of 120 ships. Among the innovations that he introduced, often in opposition to conservative opinion, are the water-tube boiler, the triple-screw system, vertical engines, the repair ship, and the "distilling ship." He designed the machinery of the *Columbia* and *Minneapolis,* two vessels that held the record for speed among warships for almost a decade. He was influential in obtaining the amalgamation of the Engineer Corps with the Line and the establishment of a post-graduate school in naval engineering. On Mar. 3, 1899, he was made a captain with the rank of rear admiral, and on Jan. 10, 1903, was retired in the latter grade. He received many honors from governments, scientific societies, and universities, and in 1899 served as president of the American Society of Mechanical Engineers. He wrote many technical articles and one book, *In the Lena Delta* (1885), which contains accounts of some of his Arctic experiences. Sometimes gruff and irascible, he possessed a dauntless and masterful spirit, which suited his massive frame, leonine head, and great dome-like forehead. Melville was divorced from his first wife. On Oct. 18, 1907, he was married in New York City to his second wife, Estella Smith Polis. He died in Philadelphia.

[Record of Officers, Bureau of Navigation, 1859–88. *Who's Who in America,* 1912–13; F. M. Bennett, *The Steam Navy of the U. S.* (1896); W. L. Cathcart, "Geo. Wallace Melville," *Cassier's Mag.,* Apr. 1897; Emma De Long, ed., *The Voyage of the Jeannette* (2 vols., 1883); *Army and Navy Jour.,* Mar. 23, 1912; *Pub. Ledger* (Phila.), Mar. 18, 1912.] C. O. P.

MELVILLE, HERMAN (Aug. 1, 1819–Sept. 28, 1891), author, was born at No. 6 Pearl Street, New York City, the second son and third of the eight children of Allan Melville, a merchant, and Maria Gansevoort, daughter of General Peter Gansevoort [*q.v.*] of Albany. His ancestry was distinguished on both sides, for his father's father was Major Thomas Melville of Boston, celebrated by Oliver Wendell Holmes in "The Last Leaf," one of the "Indians" in the Boston Tea Party, and a direct descendant of John Melville, Lord of Raith in Fifeshire, who was beheaded during the reign of Mary, Queen of Scots, "becaus," as an old record stated, "he was known to be one that unfainedlie favoured the truthe," and of a numerous race of Scottish worthies of whom the earliest known was one Sir Richard de Melvill, who flourished in the reign of Alexander III and was compelled in 1296 to swear allegiance to King Edward I of England when the latter overran Scotland. Both of Melville's grandfathers served with distinction in the Revolutionary War, General Peter Gansevoort having been in command of Fort Stanwix, for his gallant defence of which he received a vote of thanks from Congress; and both families were among the earliest and most aristocratic settlers of the country. Harmen Harmense Van Gansevoort was well known as a brewer in Beverwyck in 1660 and his descendants intermarried during the following generations with the Van Rensselaers, the Van Schaicks, and most of the other leading colonial Dutch families.

Melville himself took a great and natural pride in the stock from which he sprang and which had left its traces in the magnificent bearing and physique and the high adventurous courage that characterized him. His family, however, was falling on evil days at the time of his birth. His father, a widely traveled and cultivated man, underwent many financial ups and downs, finally went into bankruptcy, and died when Herman was twelve years old, leaving his wife and eight children virtually destitute. Herman was thus left in the care of his mother, a cold, "haughty" woman, whose portrait he is said to have drawn in Mrs. Glendinning in *Pierre,* and whose unsympathetic attitude towards her son may have had something to do with his leaving home at the age of seventeen, "driven out an infant Ishmael into the desert, with no maternal Hagar to accompany and comfort him" (*Pierre,* 1930, p. 101). Of her he is said to have remarked years later: "She hated me." He was described by his father as "very backward in speech" in his early boyhood, and "somewhat slow in comprehension," though "docile and amiable" (Weaver, *post,* pp. 62, 66). His only schooling he received at the Albany Academy, where he is said to have been a favorite pupil, distinguished especially for his writing, but he received no formal education after the age of fifteen. In 1834 he became a clerk in the New York State Bank. There were, however, certain compensations in his childhood: the fine library which his father had left and in which he browsed to the good effect revealed in his later style, the vacations passed at his uncle's farm, "Broadhall," near Pittsfield, the summers spent at the country home of the Gansevoorts in Saratoga County, N. Y., which he describes so poetically in *Pierre* under the name of "Saddle-Meadows."

In 1837, at the age of seventeen, Melville, after experimenting with his clerkship, with a small post in his brother's fur and cap store, with farming, and even school-teaching, suddenly decided to go to sea and shipped as cabin-boy on the *Highlander,* bound for Liverpool, on the voyage described in *Redburn.* After a month on the sea, which left in his mind experiences and characters that he was never to forget, he spent six weeks in Liverpool, returning to New York, with a taste for the sea that was never to leave him, to engage in various activities, school-teaching again, at Pittsfield and East Albany, and writing with the passionate zest he describes in *Pierre,* taking ship again at Fairhaven (opposite New Bedford) on his famous voyage on the whaler *Acushnet,* on Jan. 3, 1841, for the South Seas. This was the beginning of the great adventure of his life. On the *Acushnet* he spent the eighteen months which he recreated imaginatively years later in *Moby Dick,* escaping finally (July 9, 1842), when he could no longer endure the hardships of a whaleman's existence, at the Marquesas Islands, where, in company with his shipmate, Toby (Richard Tobias Greene), he experienced the adventures described in *Typee.* They struggled for five days through the jungle, reaching at length the valley of Typee, which Melville remembered ever afterwards as an earthly paradise. There he dwelt among the friendly cannibals, with the lovely Fayaway as his constant companion, chatting and smoking with the bachelors of the Ti, or men's club, an idyllic existence of which recollected traces are to be found in *Mardi.* Then, finding the savage life irksome, he escaped by a clever ruse from the warriors who were holding him captive and succeeded in getting aboard an Australian whaler, the *Lucy Ann* (called by Melville the *Julia*), where he slowly regained his health and formed the famous friendship with Doctor Long Ghost, celebrated in *Omoo.* He was very glad to escape again when the *Juila* sailed into the harbor of Papeete (Sept. 9, 1842). At Tahiti he hired himself out for a time as a field-laborer, studied the island life with all the charmed and amused interest that is reflected in the pages of *Omoo,* and enlisted Aug. 17, 1843, as an ordinary seaman on the frigate *United States.* Here he spent the year pictured in *White-Jacket, or The World in a Man-of-War,* from which he was discharged Oct. 14, 1844, on the vessel's return to Boston. He had passed nearly four years wandering and accumulating memories that were to furnish material for the whole of his literary life.

He came home, a romantic figure indeed, "the man who had lived among the cannibals," and immediately set to work writing out his experiences. *Typee* (1846) was finished and the manuscript bought by John Murray within scarcely more than a year after his return. *Omoo* (1847) followed a year later. Melville found himself immediately both famous and notorious, for his attacks on the missionaries had stirred up a hornet's-nest of criticism. Meanwhile, on Aug. 4, 1847, he had married Elizabeth, the only daughter of Lemuel Shaw [*q.v.*], Chief Justice of Massachusetts, an old friend of his family, and had established a household at 103 Fourth Avenue, New York, where he continued industriously writing, preparing *Mardi* (1849), *Redburn* (1849), and *White-Jacket* (1850) for the press. His first child was born in February 1849; and in October of that year he sailed for England to interview his publishers and try to make better terms with them. He visited Paris also at this time, gathering impressions that served him well later in the composition of *Israel Potter*; then, returning home, he moved with his family to Pittsfield, where he bought the farm "Arrowhead," which became his home for the next thirteen years. It was there that he formed his intimate friendship with Hawthorne, who was living close by at Lenox and writing *The House of the Seven Gables.* Melville finished and published *Moby Dick* in 1851, dedicating it to his friend, and immediately followed this with the composition of *Pierre: or the Ambiguities* (1852), which revealed the strain and torment through which he had passed and marked the decline of his powers, for his great book, as he put it, had been "broiled in hell-fire." Thereafter his talent passed slowly into a sort of eclipse that was never, however, to result in actual extinction. Broken with overwork, he set out in 1856 for a tour to the Holy Land, visiting Hawthorne on the way at the latter's consulate in Liverpool and remarking that he had "pretty much made up his mind to be annihilated" (Weaver, *post,* p. 331). He was in search of he knew not what, the philosopher's stone, some secret of religious faith; and on his return he tried to describe his quest in the long metaphysical-narrative poem *Clarel,* published many years later in 1876. Fortune had turned against him. His great book, *Moby Dick,* was a complete practical failure, misunderstood by the critics and ignored by the public; and in 1853 the Harpers' fire destroyed the plates of all his books and most of the copies remaining in stock. After failing to obtain a consulship for which he had applied he continued to write as well as he could out of a depleted imagination. He published in 1855 *Israel Potter,* a story of the American Revolution, remarkable for its portraits of John Paul Jones and Benjamin Franklin. *The Piazza Tales* followed in 1856, containing among other stories the sombre narrative of "Benito

Cereno"; and in 1857 appeared *The Confidence Man,* the first volume of an abortive satire, as we may assume, though the precise significance of the work is not clear, on the over-developed commercial smartness of the period. Thereafter Melville wrote no more prose except *Billy Budd,* completed during the last year of his life and only published in 1924, a story based on the character of Jack Chase, the "handsome sailor" who appears in *White-Jacket.* He turned to the composition of poetry, and published, besides *Clarel,* three volumes, *Battle-Pieces and Aspects of the War* (1866), *John Marr and Other Sailors* (1888) and *Timoleon* (1891), the two latter privately printed, most of this verse being undistinguished. He tried lecturing as a mode of supplementing his income, going as far west as San Francisco, his subjects being the South Seas and "Statuary in Rome." In 1861 he was introduced to Lincoln at Washington, where he was again applying unsuccessfully for a consulship. His literary life had died of inanition, overstrain, and excessive subjectivity, as well as of neglect on the part of the reading public.

Melville's later life was marked by a complete withdrawal from society. In 1863 he moved with his family to New York, and in 1866 he received an appointment as out-door customs inspector on the wharf at the foot of Gansevoort Street, which he held for nineteen years; but he had passed so entirely out of public notice that Robert Buchanan wrote in 1885: "I sought everywhere for this Triton, who is still living somewhere in New York. No one seemed to know anything of the one great writer fit to stand shoulder to shoulder with Whitman on that continent" (*Academy,* Aug. 15, 1885, p. 103). But amid the obscurity there are evidences of a certain surviving geniality in the old writer. He carried on a friendly correspondence with W. Clark Russell, who wrote to him in gratitude for his "delightful books" and informed him of the high regard in which his work was still held in England (New York *World,* Oct. 11, 1891; see also *North American Review,* Feb. 1892). He devoted his leisure hours to reading and study, and continued to write poetry at intervals, returning in memory to his early experiences on the sea. He completed the manuscript of *Billy Budd* three months before his death. He died at his home 104 East Twenty-sixth Street, and was buried in Woodlawn Cemetery.

As Clark Russell said, Melville's fame never passed into obscurity in England. But he was virtually ignored in the literary histories of his own country until about 1920, when his greatness came to be recognized for the first time, largely as an indirect result of the sudden vogue of books dealing with the South Seas. *Typee* and *Omoo,* which had enjoyed a brief romantic reputation on their first appearance, came back into popular favor, but are overshadowed now by the mighty bulk of *Moby Dick* and with close rivals in *White-Jacket* and *Redburn.* Even *Pierre* and *Mardi* came in for a measure of popular interest. During the years immediately following, a sumptuous complete edition of Melville's works was published, and it was generally recognized that at his highest moments Melville is one of the great masters of English prose and one of the two or three supreme writers of America. Allowing for certain excesses of enthusiasm due to so sudden a re-discovery, this position which Melville has assumed will probably never again be challenged, for it is based on certain substantial realities of thought, and especially of style and feeling.

Undoubtedly *Moby Dick* will continue to be regarded as Melville's masterpiece; but all of his books published before his thirty-third year are sterling contributions to literature, notable for their clear, firm, classical style, their gusto, their vivid portraiture and their wealth of keen-eyed and well-organized observations. *Typee* and *Omoo* are models of romantic narrative, written with all the exuberance of the young man who could have contrived such unsuual adventures, adventures that were almost unprecedented at the time, for Melville was among the first white men to explore certain parts of the South Sea Islands and the very first literary artist to do so. He may be considered in some respects, in these books, a disciple of Rousseau, for no one has ever glorified more than he the virtues of the natural man, the primitive man, as against such specimens of the civilized man as found their way to those parts, the missionaries whose narrow Protestantism was destroying all joy of life in the islanders, and the visiting sailors who brought with them only the vices of their countrymen. And certainly no other author has celebrated with a greater charm and exuberance the engaging natural features of the islands and the pagan ways of the islanders, an exuberance that led Stevenson to characterize Melville as a "howling cheese." His portrait of Fayaway, in various attitudes and scenes, swimming, smoking, floating in a canoe or, as on one occasion, standing upright in the bow of the canoe with arms upraised and her tappa robe stretched out like a sail, is one of the best-known of its kind in modern literature. Memorable also are the figures of Kory-Kory and his mother, among the natives; and, among the white men, those of

Toby, that "strange, wayward being, moody, fitful and melancholy," and especially Doctor Long Ghost, the ship's doctor of the *Julia,* who quoted Virgil and repeated "Hudibras" by the canto and in company with whom Melville hired himself out as a farmer-laborer on the island of Imeeo.

These two books will probably always remain the most popular, aside from *Moby Dick,* that Melville wrote. *Redburn, the Sailor-Boy Confessions and Reminiscences of the Son-of-a-Gentleman,* deserves a place beside them for its youthful high spirits, for the swiftness of its narrative and the vividness of its portraits. Although the book was written twelve years after the adventure took place, Melville seems to have forgotten none of the details, perhaps because, as he says, he loved ships as he loved men, and the bizarre characters whom he describes do not seem to be fictitious: rather we may suppose that he had a gift for encountering types that were never seen before on sea or land. As he was only seventeen at the time, everything that passed before him was etched on his memory as with acid, the miseries of the forecastle, the phosphorescent corpse of the dead sailor, the demoniacal figure of Jackson, as well as the dismal sights of Liverpool, all of which he describes with biting realism. *Redburn* may survive most properly perhaps as a boys' book, but it must always hold a distinguished if minor place in the literature of the sea.

White-Jacket is more ambitious, though not so lively as a composition. Its purpose was to "give some idea of the interior life in a man-of-war," and it must always remain as a standard document illustrating a phase of American naval history. Here we find also several powerful bits of writing, such as the macabre account of the amputation of the seaman's leg, and the splendid figure of "noble Jack Chase," the ideal sailor, the frank and charming Jack, idol of his fellows, who could speak five languages and was indeed "better than a hundred common mortals," a character as vivid in its virtue, its manifestation of all the manly virtues, as Jackson's is vivid in its viciousness. The atmosphere of the book fairly shines with the fresh and jubilant spirit of the days when American shipping ruled the seas.

Mardi and *Pierre* retain certain powerful features, energetic passages of writing and, above all, traces of deep feeling. In *Pierre,* especially, Melville has given us much of himself: the book is plainly autobiographical, especially in the account of the author's childhood, of his forbidding mother and the aristocratic traditions of the Glendinning family, the beautiful, idyllic life at "Saddle-Meadows," Pierre's preparation for authorship and especially the composition of the "great work," that "Inferno," composed in the midst of "clamourous pennilessness," which is evidently no other than *Moby Dick.* If the love-story is fantastic and improbable to a degree, the pages dealing with the struggles of the writer's soul have a splendid passion and veracity, equal to those of *Moby Dick* itself. And there are many chapters of *Mardi* of an ethereal beauty, many pages of profound speculation, and the book contains two or three characters, such as Anatoo and Jarl, that are highly successful as grotesque portraits. In its general scheme it is reminiscent of Rabelais, being a voyage in search of happiness, in this case represented by the girl Yillah instead of the oracle of the Bottle, conducted by the narrator and his three companions, Mohy the chronicler, Babbalanja the antiquary, and Yoomy the minstrel, who set out in their three canoes for a tour of the isles, here of course the South Sea Islands which had left such glorious impressions in Melville's memory; and we can find in the "ontological heroics" that formed the substance of their conversation direct reminiscences not only of the talk that must have passed between Melville and Hawthorne in the Berkshires but more especially of the cheerful confabulations during the Feast of Calabashes at the Ti, in the valley of Typee. And the thatched huts, the verdurous arbors, the luxuriant glens that form the local color of the book are all those of the Marquesas. The whole composition is a curious compound of Rabelais, the earlier Melville, and Thomas Moore, for there is a certain faint Oriental aroma lingering over the scene that distinctly recalls *Lalla Rookh.*

Nothing that Melville wrote is wholly without quality, though *The Confidence Man* virtually touches the absolute of incomprehensibility. *Israel Potter,* a minor work, contains, besides the portraits of Franklin and John Paul Jones, a remarkable picture of a naval engagement, for Melville seldom fails completely when he touches the sea. In *The Piazza Tales* one finds "Benito Cereno," the most successful of his shorter pieces, and "The Encantadas," a grim and powerful sketch of certain deserted volcanic islands that Melville had visited in his voyages. *Clarel,* his longest poem, is extremely involved and obscure; he described it himself as "a metrical affair, a pilgrimage or what not, of several thousand lines, eminently adapted for unpopularity," but Frank Jewett Mather had reason for saying that it was "about all America has to show for the poetical stirrings of the deeper theological waters which marked the age of Matthew Arnold, Clough, Tennyson and Browning" (*The Review,* Aug. 16, 1919, p. 300). But Melville's permanent fame must always rest on the great prose epic of *Moby Dick,* a book that has no equal in American literature for variety and splendor of style and for depth of feeling. No doubt the story would flow with more consistency if many of the sections dealing with whaling were omitted, for Melville's sense of form was very defective; but there is not a page of the book that is not richly rewarding. The heroic figures of Captain Ahab and Father Maple, the fantastic figures of Queequeg, Tashtego and the gigantic Negro, Daggoo, are almost of Homeric proportions. "Give me a condor's wing!" exclaims Melville in the midst of his inspiration. "Give me Vesuvius' crater for an inkstand!" And he is justified in his enthusiasm; for the mighty rhythm of the book recalls that of the great Scandinavian sagas.

[R. M. Weaver, *Herman Melville, Mariner and Mystic* (1921), and Lewis Mumford, *Herman Melville* (1929), are full biographical studies; the only complete edition of Melville's writings was published by Constable, London, 1922–24. Among the biographical and critical studies the most useful are: "Notes on Herman Melville," in Van Wyck Brooks, *Emerson and Others* (1927); Lincoln Colcord, "Notes on Moby Dick," *Freeman,* Aug. 23, 30, 1922; Carl Van Doren, "Lucifer from Nantucket," *Century Mag.,* Aug. 1925; H. H. Scudder, "Melville's Benito Cereno and Capt. Delano's Voyages," *Mod. Lang. Asso. Pubs.,* XLIII (1928), 502–32; Russell Thomas, "Melville's Use of Some Sources in the Encantadas," *Am. Lit.,* Jan. 1932; W. S. Gleim, "A Theory of Moby Dick," *New England Quarterly,* July 1929; Michael Sadleir, *Excursions in Victorian Bibliog.* (1922); D. H. Lawrence, *Studies in Classic Am. Lit.* (1922); V. S. Parrington, *The Romantic Revolution in America 1800–60* (1927); John Freeman, *Herman Melville* (1926); R. M. Weaver, intro. to *Shorter Novels of Herman Melville* (1928); R. S. Forsythe, intro. to *Pierre, or The Ambiguities* (1930); Henry Chapin, ed., Melville's *The Apple-Tree Table and Other Sketches* (1922) and *John Marr and Other Poems* (1922); Meade Minnigerode, *Some Personal Letters of Herman Melville and a Bibliog.* (1922). See notes by A. H. Starke and R. S. Forsythe, *Am. Lit.,* Nov. 1929 and 1930; "Family Correspondence of Herman Melville," *N. Y. Pub. Lib. Bull.,* July and Aug. 1929; O. W. Riegel, "The Anatomy of Melville's Fame," *Am. Lit.,* May 1931; J. N. Reynolds, *Mocha Dick or the White Whale of the Pacific* (1932), with intro. by L. L. Balcom (reprinted from *Knickerbocker Mag.,* May 1839). Robert S. Forsythe and John H. Birss have in preparation a bibliography of Melville, including all imprints of his works, a calendar of letters pub. and unpub., a description of existing manuscripts, a list of portraits, catalogue of books that Melville is known to have possessed, and a list of biog. and critical articles on him.]

V. W. B.

MEMBRÉ, ZENOBIUS (1645–1687?), Recollect missionary, was born of good family in Bapaume, department of Pas-de-Calais, France. He was a cousin of Chrétien le Clercq, who was the historian of the Recollects in New France. It is supposed that the name Zenobius was taken by Membré upon entering the Recollect convent at Artois, where he was the first novice in the newly created Franciscan department of St. Anthony. In 1675 Le Clercq and Membré were sent to Canada, where the latter tarried two or more years at the Recollect convent at Quebec.

In 1678 he was ordered to Fort Frontenac on the north shore of Lake Ontario, whence he accompanied La Salle's men to their shipyard on Niagara River near Buffalo. Membré ministered to the shipwrights and the men preparing the *Griffon,* and in the summer of 1679 he sailed around the Great Lakes to Green Bay. There the *Griffon* was loaded with peltry and sent back, while Membré accompanied La Salle's party in small boats around Lake Michigan to St. Joseph River. The party tarried at Milwaukee River, the name of which first appears in Membré's account. Late in the year, La Salle's party reached its destination on the Illinois River, built Fort Crêvecoeur, and laid the keel of a small vessel. La Salle was called back to Fort Frontenac, because of the loss of the *Griffon*; Tonty was left in charge with the two priests, Membré and La Ribourde. Before La Salle's return a party of Iroquois attacked the Illinois Indians; Tonty, the two priests, and three other men made a retreat through the woods to Lake Michigan. In this flight Father de la Ribourde was killed; Membré and the others, after suffering great hardships, finally reached the mission at De Pere (L. P. Kellogg, "A Wisconsin Anabasis," in *Wisconsin Magazine of History,* March 1924). Membré met La Salle at Mackinac in the summer of 1681 and again accompanied him to the Illinois. Thence, late in December, they set forth to explore the Mississippi and descended to its mouth, where, Apr. 9, 1682, La Salle took possession for France of the Mississippi Valley and named it Louisiana. Father Zenobius signed the act of taking possession (*Collections of the State Historical Society of Wisconsin,* vol. XI, 1888, pp. 33–35). When on the return journey La Salle was taken ill, the Recollect priest cared for him tenderly and on his recovery accompanied him to Canada and finally, at his request, to France.

Arrived in the Old World, Membré was sent to the convent of the Recollects at Bapaume, his birthplace, where he was warden for several months. Thence he was summoned by La Salle to join a new expedition for the founding of a colony at the mouth of the Mississippi and was made superior of the group of Recollect missionaries that La Salle took with him. Missing the mouth of the Mississippi, the expedition landed in Texas, where a settlement was made on the Garcitas River in Lavaca Bay. There, at the colony named St. Louis, Membré and his companions passed two years. At one time a mission was attempted for the Cenis Indians, but because of threatened hostilities Membré and Maximus le Clercq retreated to Fort St. Louis. There La Salle left them in 1687, and subsequently the entire colony perished; how or why is not known.

Membré was a voluminous writer and his journals of his expedition were embodied in the history of his order in the New World, compiled by his cousin Chrétien le Clercq, under the title *Premier Établissement de la Foy dans la Nouvelle France* (Paris, 1691). His style is plain and simple, not that of a learned man. He had great physical hardihood and seems to have been adaptable to his surroundings and on good terms with his companions. His writings give certain details of La Salle's expedition not found elsewhere.

[J. G. Shea translated and edited Le Clercq as *First Establishment of the Faith in New France* (2 vols., 1881); I. J. Cox, in *The Journeys of Réné Robert Cavelier Sieur de La Salle* (2 vols., 1905) includes Membré's narrative and a brief biography of him; for the site of La Salle's colony in Texas see H. E. Bolton, in *Miss. Valley Hist. Rev.*, Sept. 1915; *Early Narratives of the Northwest* (1917), edited by L. P. Kellogg, p. 292, gives a note on Membré.] L. P. K.

MEMMINGER, CHRISTOPHER GUSTAVUS (Jan. 9, 1803–Mar. 7, 1888), South Carolina legislator and secretary of the treasury of the Confederacy, the son of Christopher Godfrey and Eberhardina (Kohler) Memminger, was born in Nayhingen, in the Duchy of Württemberg, Germany. His grandfather, Johann Friedrich Memminger, was an official of the University of Babenhausen. Soon after the child's birth his father, an officer in the army of the duke, was killed, and the mother, with her parents, emigrated to Charleston, S. C. She died there, and the boy, four years of age, was placed in the Charleston Orphan House. At the age of eleven he was taken into the home of Thomas Bennett, later governor of the state. A year or so later he was sent to the South Carolina College, where he graduated in 1819. Returning to Charleston, he studied law, acquired a license, and began to rise in his profession. He opposed nullification and wrote a satirical booklet in biblical style, called *The Book of Nullification* (1830) against the leaders of that movement. In 1836 he became a member of the state house of representatives and soon afterward, as chairman of the committee on finance, began a long struggle to disassociate the state from banking corporations and to force the banks to maintain specie payments on pain of forfeiture of their charters. In these contests he won considerable reputation as a sound financier (but see F. H. Elmore, *Defense of the Bank of . . . S. C.*, n.d.). In 1855 he became a commissioner of schools for Charleston, a position he held for more than thirty years, and began constructive work on the public-school system of the city. He also served for thirty-two years on the board of the South Carolina College. Although he was fully convinced of the righteousness of slavery and was apprehensive of the designs of the northern anti-slavery element, he acted with the conservative Democrats of South Carolina. During the period from 1850 to 1852 he opposed separate action on the part of his state as dangerous and fruitless, although he was himself dissatisfied with the compromise measures of 1850. In January 1860, in consequence of the John Brown raid, he was sent as commissioner to address the Virginia legislature on the necessity for joint defensive measures (*Address . . . before the Assembled Authorities of . . . Va., . . . Jan. 19, 1860,* 1860). By December he was won over wholly to secession. He was an active member of the secession convention of South Carolina and was one of the delegates to the southern convention at Montgomery, where he was chairman of the committee that drafted the provisional constitution of the Confederate States.

Put forward by his delegation for the office of secretary of the treasury and appointed by Jefferson Davis, he faced a difficult and, as it proved, a hopeless task. He seems to have hoped to use treasury notes sparingly, for he was well aware of the danger in them, but the new bonds issued for the absorption of the notes were taken slowly, while the obligations of the government for the support of the war accumulated rapidly. There was no means of meeting requisitions except by issuing more treasury notes. Hoping to stimulate the sale of bonds, he advised a "produce loan," by which the cotton and tobacco planters would exchange the proceeds of their crop sales for bonds, but the result was disappointing. The first effort at a direct tax was unsuccessful, for most of the states assumed the burden and paid in their own notes, thereby swelling the flood of paper. Congress passed no comprehensive tax law until April 1863, when it was too late. Meanwhile, military reverses and redundant notes had caused rapid depreciation of the currency. Prices rose alarmingly, increasing governmental expenditures that could be met only by more treasury notes. Bonds were taken sparingly. His various funding schemes failed, partly because of business conditions and partly because of the tinkering of Congress. The blockade prevented the exportation of cotton, the only resource that could command cash. That he was fully aware of the causes of the derangement of the finances is clear from his reports and correspondence, but it is equally clear that he saw no way to remedy the situation. In 1863 he recommended a stringent reduction of the volume of the currency through compulsory funding in bonds, and Congress responded with the famous funding act of February 1864, which varied materially from his recommendations and was unquestionably a worse measure than the one he had proposed. When the credit of the government collapsed completely he was generally held responsible for the disaster. Most students of the subject have severely criticized his handling of the treasury and have attributed his failure to lack of constructive imagination. There is some ground for the criticism, but it is hard to see how even a gifted financier could have coped successfully with the difficulties that beset him. On June 15, 1864, he resigned and retired to his country home at Flat Rock, N. C., where he remained until after the war. In 1867 he received presidential pardon, returned to Charleston, and began once more the practice of law. In 1868 he organized a company for the manufacture of sulphuric acid and super-phosphates. His chief public service in the post-war years was in behalf of the public schools for both races. He was married in 1832 to Mary Wilkinson, a daughter of Willis Wilkinson. After her death he was married, in 1878, to her sister, Sarah A. Wilkinson. Eight children survived him.

[H. D. Capers, *The Life and Times of C. G. Memminger* (1893); M. C. Kneece, "The Contributions of C. G. Memminger to the Cause of Education," *Bulletin of the University of South Carolina*, No. 177 (1926). Ernest A. Smith, *The History of the Confederate Treasury* (1901), and J. C. Schwab, *The Confederate States of America* (1901). *News and Courier* (Charleston), Mar. 1, 8, 10, 1888.] C. W. R.

MENARD, MICHEL BRANAMOUR (Dec. 5, 1805–Sept. 2, 1856), Indian trader and founder of Galveston, Tex., was born at Laprairie, Lower Canada, the son of Michel B. and Marguerite (deNoyer) Menard. When he left home at about the age of fourteen he had received little, if any, formal education, but during the next four years, while in the service of a fur company with headquarters probably at Detroit, he gained a mastery of woodcraft, the technique of the Indian trade, and an insight into Indian psychology that was to make possible his career. In 1823 he arrived at Kaskaskia, Ill., to take employment under his uncle, Pierre Menard [*q.v.*], as a trader among the Delaware and Shawnee in the vicinity of Sainte Genevieve, Mo. Humiliated by the contrast between his own untutored state and the comparative elegance of his cousins, he applied himself diligently to study and in three months he learned not only to speak but to read English. It was his custom thereafter to read while on trading expeditions, and eventually he passed as a well-informed man. He lived among the Shawnee on the White River in the Arkansas territory, by whom he was adopted and elected a chief. Years later he is reported to have said that he almost succeeded in uniting the northwestern tribes into an Indian nation, making himself their king, and moving them to California and Utah. However that may be, he moved southward with the Shawnee and in 1826 was in the vicinity of Shreveport.

When the Indians pushed into the region between the Trinity and Red rivers in Texas, he received permission from the Mexican officials to settle at Nacogdoches, where he traded with Mexicans as well as Indians and became prominent as a land operator. In 1833, with Thomas F. McKinney and Samuel M. Williams, he established a sawmill on Menard Creek, forty miles above Liberty on the Trinity River. There he also maintained a trading-post and continued to acquire lands in various parts of Texas. As a representative of the municipality of Liberty in the consultation at Washington-on-the-Brazos, he signed the Texas Declaration of Independence on Mar. 2, 1836, and was a member of the committee that drafted the constitution of the Republic. President Burnet selected him to make sure the neutrality of the Shawnee and other Indians in northwest Texas during the struggle with Mexico. After two missions to the Indians with A. J. Yates he tried unsuccessfully, as Texas commissioner, to negotiate a five-million-dollar loan for Texas in the United States.

The First Congress of Texas validated, for $50,000, Menard's claim to a league and a labor of land, about six square miles, which he had located in 1834 on the east end of Galveston Island (*Laws of the Republic of Texas,* 1838, I, pp. 70–72). In 1838 he organized and became president of the Galveston City Company, which issued one thousand shares of stock at a book value of $1,000 each. Generous terms were offered to attract settlers and donations of land were liberally made for public and charitable purposes. Shares, which at one time sold for ten cents on the dollar, were at par at the time of his death and fourteen years later were worth $10,000. He was also president of the wharf company and actively engaged in various commercial enterprises. He lived to see the population of the city he founded approach 7,000. He represented Galveston county in the Fifth Congress of Texas from 1840 to 1842 and was considered one of the best authorities in that body on the vexed question of Texas land titles. He also advocated the scheme of public finance known as the "exchequer system," which was adopted after he retired from Congress. He held no other political office. In the 40's he erected, on a ten-acre lot in Galveston, a large residence, where he dispensed a lavish hospitality to his white and Indian friends. He was four times married: first, in 1832, at Sainte Genevieve, Mo., to Marie Anne (Diane) Leclere, who died the next year; second to Adeline Maxwell, of Kaskaskia, his second cousin, who did not long survive; third to Mary Jane Riddle, of St. Louis, who died in 1845; and fourth to Mrs. Rebecca Mary Bass, of Georgia, who, after Menard's death, married Colonel J. S. Thrasher. Menard was a useful, though not a spectacular figure in the development of Texas. He was primarily a business man and the success that attended his commercial ventures attests his practical sagacity. He was a man of powerful physique and was counted a delightful raconteur. After his death, which resulted from a carbuncle, his body was buried in the old Catholic Cemetery at Galveston. A county, created in 1858, was named in his honor.

[MSS. in Rosenberg Lib. of Galveston; information from the archives of Mo. Hist. Soc. through the courtesy of Stella M. Drumm; *Galveston Directory, 1866–67* (1866), pp. 42–45; Joseph Tasse, *Les Canadiens de L'Ouest* (1878), vol. II; *Galveston Daily News*, Dec. 9, 1906; *Hist. of Texas, together with a Biog. Hist. of the Cities of Houston and Galveston* (1895); S. C. Griffin, *Hist. of Galveston* (1931); F. W. Johnson, *A Hist. of Texas* (1914) ed. by E. C. Barker, vol. II; his Christian names were sometimes spelled Michael Brindamour.] H. P. G.

MENARD, PIERRE (Oct. 7, 1766–June 13, 1844), fur-trader, merchant, and statesman, was born at St. Antoine, Quebec, the son of Jean Baptiste and Marie Françoise (Cirée) Menard. His father, a native of Languedoc, France, sided with the colonists in the Revolution and is said to have served under Montgomery at Quebec. His mother, a woman of superior intelligence and education, was a Canadian. The youth, according to Gov. John Reynolds (*post*, p. 242) received a "common, plain education." About 1787 he moved to Vincennes, Ind., where he was employed by the Indian trader, Col. François Vigo [*q.v.*]. In 1789 he accompanied Vigo to Carlisle, Pa., to consult Washington regarding the protection of the frontier. Two years later he moved to Kaskaskia and with Toussaint DuBois as a partner opened a store. He was married, June 13, 1792, to Thérèse Godin. On the organization of Randolph County he was appointed by Gov. Arthur St. Clair (Oct. 7, 1795) major of the county's first regiment of militia, and was recommissioned five years later. In February 1801, Gov. William Henry Harrison appointed him a judge of the county court of common pleas, a position he retained for ten years. In 1803 he was elected a delegate to the Indiana legislature (serving until the separation of Illinois in 1809) and in 1806 he was appointed lieutenant-colonel commanding the county militia.

His wife died in 1804, and on Sept. 22, 1806, he married Angélique Saucier, whose sister was the wife of Jean Pierre Chouteau [*q.v.*]. He was one of the organizing partners (Mar. 7, 1809) of the St. Louis Missouri Fur Company, and, as a captain of infantry on special service, commissioned by Gov. Meriwether Lewis, he accompanied its first expedition, which restored the Mandan chief, Big White, to his people. From Fort Mandan, the trading-post established by the company, he and Andrew Henry [*q.v.*] led the first organized invasion of trappers to the Three Forks of the Missouri, where they arrived Apr. 3, 1810; but on being driven out by the Blackfeet he returned to his home in Kaskaskia. At the beginning of 1811 he resigned his judgeship. He was elected in 1812 to the first Illinois senate (legislative council), of which he was made the first president, continuing to serve until statehood was attained. Until 1816 he had held his various offices without having been formally naturalized. In 1818 he was the general choice for the state's first lieutenant-governor; and the constitutional convention, in order to permit his election, altered the requisite period of citizenship, which it had placed at thirty years, making eligible for office a citizen who had resided in the state two years preceding the election. Elected by acclamation, he served with ability. At the end of his term he retired to his home, a place famous throughout the West for its hospitality. In 1828, on the appointment of President John Quincy Adams, he served with Lewis Cass on a commission to treat with the Winnebagos at Prairie du Chien; and in the following year, reappointed by President Jackson, he served with Caleb Atwater and Gen. John McNeil on a like commission to treat with other tribes of the region. No further public duty seems to have called him from his retirement. His later days were spent quietly in the care of his many business interests, in the dispensing of aid to the needy, and in the companionship of his family. He had four children by his first wife, and six by his second, who died in 1839. He died at his home.

Menard won the high esteem of all with whom he came in contact. Gov. Reynolds praised him in unstinted terms. "An honorable, high minded gentleman," is the tribute of Gen. Thomas James, who heartily detested the other officials of the St. Louis Missouri Fur Company whom he knew. An Illinois county, organized in 1839, is named for him, and a statue of him, presented by Charles P. Choutou and unveiled on Jan. 10, 1888, stands in the capitol grounds at Springfield.

[John Reynolds, *The Pioneer Hist. of Ill.* (1852); *Chicago Hist. Soc. Colls.*, vol. IV (1890); "The Governors' Letter-books 1818–1834," ed. by E. B. Greene and C. W. Alvord, *Colls. of the Ill. State Hist. Lib.*, vol. IV (1909); Thomas James, *Three Years Among the Indians and Mexicans* (1916), ed. by W. B. Douglas.]
W. J. G.

MÉNARD, RENÉ (Sept. 7, 1605–August 1661), the first Jesuit missionary in the upper Great Lakes region, was Parisian born and entered the Jesuit order as a novice, at Paris, Nov. 7, 1624. He completed his novitiate after studying in Paris, La Flèche, Bourges, and Rouen. Subsequently he was an instructor at Orléans (1629–32) and at Moulins (1636–39). He had long cherished a desire to enter the missionary field and was ordered in 1640 to reinforce the Jesuits in Canada, where he arrived about the last of June.

The new missionary was detailed to learn the Algonquian language and was registered at Sillery for the first year. In 1641 he accompanied co-workers to Huronia, where he was expected to evangelize the outlying tribes of Algonquian stock. In April 1642 Pijart and Ménard opened a mission for the Nipissing, north of the lake of that name. Because of this tribe's wandering habits, the mission was abandoned eighteen months later and Ménard ministered among the Huron until 1649, when he withdrew to Canada. For several years he was stationed at Three Rivers, acting for a time as superior at that center. In 1656 he was one of the Jesuits chosen for the hazardous experiment of founding a French colony among the Iroquois. During the somewhat less than two years of this mission he suffered the indignities and torture heaped upon the emissaries of the gospel by this fierce race. When, in March 1658, the entire colony fled to Canada and Ménard "was compelled to forsake that fair harvest it was like tearing his heart out of his bosom" (*Jesuit Relations,* XVIII, 141).

In 1660 the first mission to the Ottawa country was undertaken. Bishop Laval wrote to the pope that he was sending Father Ménard thither. Ménard himself knew it was his death warrant; but frail and worn as he was in body, his spirit was indomitable. He gloried in the opportunity, like St. Francis Xavier, to seek the wilderness alone. The Indians who promised to care for the missionary broke their promise; he was forced to paddle and portage with the strongest of them; he was nearly starved; and finally on the shore of Lake Superior a tree fell upon and crushed his canoe. At last, on Ste. Thérèse's day (Oct. 15), he reached a village in a cove now called L'Anse. The chief was brutal and turned him out of his hut; he then dwelt in a hut made by himself of fir branches. Fortunately, the winter was mild; wine did not congeal until February. In March some traders came for him and escorted him to the main Ottawa village on Chequamegon Bay. There he learned that some fugitive Hurons were starving in the interior, and against the advice of his trader friends, he insisted on visiting them. With one helper he set forth and somewhere en route was lost in the forest. Older historians, ignoring his visit to Chequamegon Bay, placed the site of his death on the upper Wisconsin River. It is now thought that it took place on a tributary of the Chippewa in Taylor County, Wisconsin, even yet a region of dense woodlands. His companion endeavored to persuade the Hurons to go in search of the father, but they refused. Since he had some provisions with him, it was thought he might have kept alive until the day of the Assumption of the Virgin, Aug. 15. His effects were reported to have been seen in an Indian cabin, but the rumor was not verified. An old, frail man he no doubt became confused in the forest paths and died from exhaustion. His saintly character, his high courage, and earnest zeal were extolled by his superior and have given him a place in the history of the Northwest.

[R. G. Thwaites, ed., *The Jesuit Relations and Allied Documents* (73 vols., 1896–1901), esp. vols. XVIII, XLIII–XLIX, LXXI; T. J. Campbell, *Pioneer Priests of North America,* vol. I (1908); L. P. Kellogg, *The French Régime in Wis.* (1925).]
L. P. K.

MENDENHALL, THOMAS CORWIN (Oct. 4, 1841–Mar. 22, 1924), physicist, administrator, educator, was born on a farm near Hanoverton, Ohio, the youngest of five children of Stephen Mendenhall and Mary (Thomas) Mendenhall. Of Quaker stock, he grew up in a community intensely anti-slavery in sympathy during a period when grave public questions were matters of wide and earnest discussion. He was largely self-educated, his formal education being limited to the local public schools and to a short period in the Southwest Normal School at Lebanon, Ohio, from which he graduated in 1861.

Following his graduation he taught mathematics and science in various high schools of his native state, meanwhile studying physics and higher mathematics privately. Possessed of the power of lucid presentation and imbued with enthusiasm for experimentation, he met with such success as a teacher that he was elected in 1873 to the chair of physics and mechanics in the newly founded Ohio Agricultural and Mechanical College (later Ohio State University) at Columbus. In addition to his teaching, he was active in popularizing science through the organization of scientific societies and through popular lectures. At this time, scientific education in the Middle West was in its infancy, and by his ability as a teacher, his interest in research, and his charm as a lecturer he was instrumental in furthering to a marked extent the spread of science.

In 1878 he was called to the chair of physics at the Imperial University at Tokyo, Japan. Here he remained three years, during which time he established a physical laboratory and a meteorological observatory. He was also influential in organizing a seismological society and in inaugurating a system of popular lectures. While in Japan he measured the absolute force of gravity at Tokyo and the relative force of gravity between Tokyo and Fujiyama. From these measurements he determined the mean density of the earth, his result representing the best value obtained by this method at that time.

Returning to the United States in 1881, he again occupied the chair of physics in the Ohio State University until 1884, at the same time organizing and directing the State Weather Bureau. In the next two years he served as professor of electrical science in the United States Signal Corps at Washington, in which connection he organized and equipped a physical laboratory, made systematic observations on atmospheric electricity, and established the systematic collection of data relating to earthquakes. In 1886 he left Washington to assume the office of president of Rose Polytechnic Institute at Terre Haute, Ind., remaining there three years, during which time his book *A Century of Electricity* (1887) was published.

In 1889 President Harrison appointed him superintendent of the United States Coast and Geodetic Survey, in which position he made his influence felt both as scientist and as administrator. As scientist he was responsible for the development of an improved portable apparatus for the measurement of gravity, which permitted the determination of the relative force of gravity with greater facility and accuracy, and under his plans a transcontinental series of gravity measurements were made. He was the first to propose the use of the ring pendulum for the measurement of the absolute force of gravity, a method which is now receiving considerable attention. As administrator he was responsible for inaugurating and maintaining high standards of scholastic attainment as a prerequisite to entrance into the technical force of the Coast Survey, and this at a time when the ideals of civil service were not yet firmly established. During this period he was also an active member of various important boards and commissions such as the United States Lighthouse Board, the United States Board of Geographic Names, the first Bering Sea commission, and the Alaska boundary commission.

After five years as head of the Coast and Geodetic Survey, he left in 1894 to accept the presidency of Worcester Polytechnic Institute. In 1901 ill health compelled his resignation and he went to Italy to recuperate, remaining eleven years in Europe. Returning to the United States in 1912, he settled in Ravenna, Ohio, where he died in 1924 in the eighty-third year of his age. On July 12, 1870, he had married Susan Allen Marple of Columbus, Ohio. Happy in their family life for forty-six years until the death of Mrs. Mendenhall, they had the further happiness of seeing their only son become a distinguished physicist.

Mendenhall's principal scientific contributions were to the subjects of electricity, gravity, seismology, and atmospheric electricity, but his labors covered a much wider field, evidenced by numerous monographs, reports, and papers. His scientific attainments received wide recognition. Although not a college graduate, he was awarded honorary degrees by many American universities. He was elected to the National Academy of Sciences (1887), and to the presidency of the American Association for the Advancement of Science (1889); and various other scientific societies honored him with membership. In 1901 he was awarded the Cullum Geographical Medal by the American Geographical Society; in 1911 the National Educational Society of Japan bestowed a gold medal on him; and in 1918 the Franklin Institute awarded him a Franklin Medal at the same time that a similar medal was awarded Marconi. In the High School at Salem, Ohio, in which he taught early in his career, a bronze tablet has been erected to his memory, and at the Ohio State University the physics building has been named the Mendenhall Laboratory of Physics in his honor.

[*Who's Who in America*, 1922–23; *Science*, July 11, 1924; *Jour. of the Franklin Inst.*, July 1918; *Ohio State Jour.*, Mar. 23, 1924; W. H. Siebert, *Thomas Corwin Mendenhall: Teacher, Scientist, Administrator* (pamphlet, repr. from History, Columbus High School, 1847–1910); *Hist. of the Ohio Sate Univ.* (3 vols., 1920–26), ed. by T. C. Mendenhall.] H. A. M.

MENDES, FREDERIC DE SOLA (July 8, 1850–Oct. 26, 1927), rabbi, son of the Rev. Abraham Pereira and Eliza (de Sola) Mendes, was born in Montego Bay, Jamaica, British West Indies, where his father was minister. He was a descendant of David Pereira Mendes, who, after fleeing from Spain to Bayonne, settled in Jamaica in 1768. His mother's mother, Rica Meldola, traced her ancestry to Isaiah Meldola of Toledo, who was born in 1282. When Frederic was a year old, his family went to England, and spent the next seven years in Birmingham. From there they moved, in 1858, to London, and young Mendes received his education at his father's private school, at University College School, London, and at London University (B.A. 1869). Proceeding to Germany, he studied at the University of Breslau, receiving the degree of Ph.D. at the University of Jena in 1871. At the same time, he obtained his rabbinic training in the Jewish Theological Seminary, Breslau, 1870–73. Returning to England, he was licensed to preach in 1873 by the Sephardic Chief Rabbi, Benjamin Artom. After serving as preacher for a few months in the New Synagogue, London, in December 1873 he accepted the call to become assistant to Rev. Samuel M. Isaacs [*q.v.*], minister of Congregation Shaaray Tefila in New York, taking office on Jan. 1, 1874. Isaacs, who had served the congregation since its organization in 1845, retired in 1874, whereupon, Mendes was elected preacher, and after the death of Isaacs, on May 19, 1878, he became the rabbi of the congregation, a position which he held until elected rabbi emeritus on Oct. 1, 1920. On Feb. 14, 1877, he married Isabel, daughter of Aaron N. and Isabel Frances Cohen, who bore him two sons and four daughters. His death in New Rochelle, N. Y., closed a career of almost fifty-four years with the one congregation.

Mendes belonged to the generation of scholarly rabbis who came to America from Europe in the last third of the nineteenth century. He inherited from his father, and from his maternal ancestors in the learned De Sola and Meldola families a tradition of scholarship which influenced him towards a literary rabbinate. In 1876 he helped to found and conduct the *Independent Hebrew,* a magazine which lived for only three months. He took the lead in establishing the *American Hebrew* in 1879, and was its editor from 1879 to 1885. He edited two volumes of *The Menorah Monthly,* 1901–02; he was revising editor of the *Jewish Encyclopedia* and chief of its translation bureau until September 1902; and was a contributor to *Johnson's Encyclopedia* and the *Encyclopedia Americana.* Among his other writings may be mentioned *The Child's First Bible* (1877; 4th ed., 1887); *Defence, not Defiance, a Hebrew's Reply to the Missionaries* (1876); *Jewish Family Papers; Letters of a Missionary* (1875), a translation from the German of Gustav Meinhardt (Wilhelm Herzberg); *The Life of Menasseh ben Israel* (London, 1877), a translation from the German of Meyer Kayserling; and *Outlines of Jewish History* (1886).

Mendes took part in the development of the Jewish community of New York in its critical years of prodigious growth at the end of the nineteenth and beginning of the twentieth centuries. After the massacres of Jews in Russia in 1881 and the promulgation of the May Laws in 1882, Russian Jewish refugees began to find their way in large numbers to the United States. Mendes was actively interested in trying to keep them out of the cities, and gave much time to the founding and the administration of the agricultural village alliance near Vineland, N. J. He was also one of the founders and a president of the New York Board of Jewish Ministers, and one of the founders of the Young Men's Hebrew Association in New York.

In the weekly magazine, the *American Hebrew,* which for decades was devoted to the conservation of historical Jewish tradition, Mendes expressed his religious views. Though in later years he reluctantly moved with his congregation more towards reform Judaism, he always remained a conservative Jew. He was strongly opposed to the radical reform Judaism of his day, and was one of those who in 1885 uncompromisingly denounced the Pittsburgh Program of Reform Judaism. His interests were broad, including such subjects as chemistry, poetry, anatomy, music, Semitic languages, scientific farming and gardening. He was small in stature, but his geniality, tolerance, culture, and humane scholarship gave him an unvarying dignity, and commanded general respect.

[*The Jewish Encyc.*; *Am. Hebrew,* Apr. 10, 1914, Oct. 28, 1927; Nathan Stern in *Yearbook: Central Conf. Am. Rabbis,* vol. XXXVIII (1928); *Who's Who in America,* 1926–27; *N. Y. Times,* Oct. 27, 1927.]

D. deS. P.

MENEELY, ANDREW (May 19, 1802–Oct. 14, 1851), bell-founder, was the son of Andrew Meneely and Eleanor Cobb. His father came to the United States from the north of Ireland in 1795 and settled in West Troy (now Watervliet), N. Y., where the younger Andrew was born. At the age of seventeen, after an elementary education, Meneely was apprenticed to Julius Hanks, who, with his brother Oscar, was engaged in making bells, clocks, and scientific instruments. Their father, Benjamin Hanks, had come to West

Troy from Mansfield, Conn., and had established his foundry there in 1808. He was one of the first founders in the country to cast church bells and brass cannon, and he is said to have made the first tower clock and surveying instruments produced in this country. In 1826 Meneely established in West Troy a bell foundry of his own, and at about the same time he married Philena, daughter of Rodney Hanks, the brother of his employer. Bell-making had been only one of several enterprises in which the Hanks family had engaged. Meneely, on the other hand, devoted himself to this work, and by constant experimentation he greatly improved upon the methods used by his former employers. He was, after a few years, able to predict with accuracy the weight and tone of each bell he cast. Such precision had not previously been attained in America, and it had been common, both in the United States and abroad, to secure the desired tone by chiseling off portions of the bells after they were cast.

As Meneely was one of comparatively few foundrymen specializing in bell-metal bells, that is, bells made of copper and tin, usually in the proportion of four to one, and inasmuch as his preëminence was easily established, his foundry was soon sending bells not only throughout the United States but also throughout the world. His chimes were particularly sought after and won many prizes at fairs and expositions. The business grew rapidly, and Meneely came to be regarded, in the words of a contemporary newspaper, as "one of those who have done most for the general advancement of the industrial arts in all their branches." Though he devoted himself unsparingly to his business, even to the detriment of his health, he took an interest in his community and was twice, in 1839 and again in 1843, president of the village of West Troy. His chief interest, however, was the local Reformed Dutch Church of which he was a ruling elder. To this church he gave generously both of time and money, contributing also to the support of other religious institutions. After his death the business was carried on by his sons, who further improved the technique of bell-making, and still later by his descendants.

[Sources include: O. H. Gregory, *Memoir of Andrew Meneely, Esq., a Ruling Elder in the Reformed Dutch Church of West Troy, N. Y.* (1852); J. T. Myers, *Hist. of the City of Watervliet, N. Y., 1670–1910* (n.d.); J. L. Bishop, *A Hist. of Am. Manufactures from 1608–1860*, vol. II (1864); and information as to certain facts from the Meneely family. The date of Meneely's birth was taken from the family Bible in the possession of his great-grand-daughter.] G. H.

MENÉNDEZ DE AVILÉS, PEDRO (Feb. 15, 1519–Sept. 17, 1574), Spanish naval officer, founder of St. Augustine, was a member of a noble but somewhat impoverished Asturian family. At an early age he sought his fortune at sea. All the rest of his life he followed the sea, seldom finding opportunities to return to his wife, Ana María de Solís, and his children. At thirty he distinguished himself fighting pirates off the French coast, and at thirty-five he was appointed by Charles V captain-general of the Indies fleet. Between 1555 and 1563 he made three voyages to the New World and served Philip II ably in Flanders and in England; during these years he demonstrated his honesty, his seamanship, and his capacity for vigorous and intelligent action. Early in 1565 the king selected him to resist the encroachments of the French in Florida. By contract of Mar. 20, 1565 (translated in Connor, *Pedro Menéndez de Avilés*, pp. 259–70) he was given the title of *adelantado* of Florida, and in return for various privileges undertook at his own expense to explore and colonize the Florida coast; and he was ordered to drive out by any means he saw fit any "settlers who are corsairs, or of any other nations not subject to Us" (p. 261).

He sailed with his fleet from Cadiz in June; late in August he found Jean Ribaut's fleet at anchor off the St. John's River whither it had come to reinforce the French port of Fort Caroline. He scattered it with a bold night attack, and then took his fleet south to the harbor of St. Augustine, where on Sept. 6th a fort was started. Five days later Ribaut's fleet, about to attack the new fort, was driven south by a violent storm. Menéndez seized the chance for an overland attack on Fort Caroline. Leading a force of 500, he surprised and took the badly guarded French fort, killed or captured three-quarters of the 240 occupants, and, leaving a garrison, returned at once to St. Augustine. Ribaut's fleet had been wrecked. Twice in the next three weeks Menéndez faced the problem of dealing with large parties of Frenchmen, trapped at Matanzas Inlet in their attempt to win their way back to Fort Caroline. On each occasion, after a parley in which Menéndez promised no mercy and forced an unconditional surrender, those who accepted his terms were disarmed, ferried across the inlet in small groups, and slaughtered behind the sand dunes. Over 200 Frenchmen, including Ribaut himself, were thus put to the knife. Menéndez wrote the king that such treatment of heretic interlopers was "necessary for the service of God Our Lord and of Your Majesty" (Ruidíaz, *post*, II, p. 103). Perhaps doubts as to his ability to feed and guard so many captives played a part in his decision. But in his letter to the king (Oct.

15, 1565) he did not disguise his satisfaction that the able Ribaut had been put out of the way.

The later capture (on a promise of mercy, which he kept) of the few Frenchmen who had not surrendered at Matanzas, ended the French danger. Menéndez now proceeded with his plans for posts on both coasts of Florida, at Port Royal and in Chesapeake Bay, and searched for a water route from the Gulf of Mexico through the peninsula. (See map in Lowery, *post,* p. 210, for location of settlements.) In all his explorations he dealt honorably with the Indians, tried to pacify them and to save them from exploitation, and worked, though handicapped by a scarcity of missionaries, to implant the rudiments of Christianity. In May 1567, unable to get sufficient support in the West Indies, he returned to Spain to seek help from the king, but Philip's response was disappointingly small. Menéndez made his fifth voyage to the west in 1568–69 and may have visited Florida. In 1570 he was at sea protecting Spanish commerce from pirates; not till 1571 could he return to St. Augustine. Conditions in Florida were deplorable. Only a handful of discouraged colonists and mutinous soldiers in the three posts of St. Augustine, San Mateo, and Santa Elena was the result of his efforts over the past six years. Leaving such aid as he could, he sailed again for Spain in April 1572. In 1573 he asked permission to wage war on the Florida Indians and to export as slaves any who should be taken alive (Connor, *Colonial Records of Spanish Florida,* I, pp. 30–81). Later he asked to be allowed to take his two daughters and sons-in-laws and fifty settlers with their households to Florida. But while in command of a large fleet at Santander he died, Sept. 17, 1574. In 1591 his body was taken for final burial to his native city of Avilés.

Menéndez was a man of honor and of strong religious feeling, an expert seaman and a bold and resourceful leader. His early dealings with the Indians, before he not unnaturally lost patience, are a refreshing contrast to the conduct of many early explorers. Like most adventurers in colonization, he overestimated the results to be expected and underestimated the difficulties; his plans were too large for his resources; he scattered his forces too widely, perhaps because of the scanty food supply. Nevertheless he did succeed in establishing Spanish power in Florida. He will be chiefly remembered, however, as the author of the slaughters of Matanzas; these can be explained but never excused.

[Andrés Gonzáles Barcia, *Ensayo Cronologico para la Hist. General de la Fla.* (1723); J. T. Connor, ed., *Pedro Menéndez de Avilés* (1923), a translation of the biography by Solís de Merás, Menéndez' brother-in-law, which is no. 3 of the Publications of the Fla. State Hist. Soc.; J. T. Connor, ed., *Colonial Records of Spanish Fla.,* vol. I (1925), which is no. 5 of the Publications of the Fla. State Hist. Soc.; Genaro García, *Dos Antiguas Relaciones de la Fla.* (1902), containing a biography of Menéndez by Bartolomé Barrientos; C. M. Vigil, *Noticias Biográfico-genealógicas de Pedro Menéndez de Avilés* (1892); Woodbury Lowery, *The Spanish Settlements within the Present Limits of the U. S., 1562–74* (1905); translation of letters of Menéndez to the King in 1565 in *Proc. Mass. Hist. Soc.,* 2 ser., vol. VIII (1894); Eugenio Ruidíaz y Caravia, *La Fla., Su Conquista y Colonización por Pedro Menéndez de Avilés* (2 vols., 1893–94), containing the biography by Solís de Merás, many letters written by Menéndez, and documents relating to his life.]

F. P.

MENETREY, JOSEPH (Nov. 28, 1812–Apr. 27, 1891), educator and missionary, was born in the Swiss canton of Freiburg, where he probably attended the University. On Sept. 29, 1836, he entered the Society of Jesus and passed through the regular Jesuit training prior to ordination late in 1846. As a volunteer for the American missions, he sailed on a ten months' voyage via Cape Horn for Oregon, where he arrived Aug. 13, 1847, and set about learning the Indian dialects in which he ultimately gained fluency. From St. Paul's, Ore., he passed to other mission stations in Idaho, Montana, and Washington, working among the Kalispel, Blackfeet, Flathead, Spokane, Coutenais, and Coeur d'Alène tribesmen. Monuments to the activity of "Pel Leméné," as he was known to the natives, were found everywhere. In 1854, along with Adrian Hoecken, S. J., he founded the model mission of St. Ignatius with a church, barracks, shops, and farms, in the heart of the Pend d'Oreilles country in the Siniélemen Valley. This, as a center on occasions of feasts, attracted the various tribesmen for two hundred miles around. In 1874 a printing press was brought from St. Louis and religious tracts and an Indian dictionary (*A Dictionary of the Kalispel or Flat-head Indian Language,* 2 vols., 1877–79), were printed. For a time, Menetrey was located at the Sacred Heart Mission among the Pointed Hearts Indians (*c.* 1859). Later he was the first pastor of Frenchtown, from which he ministered to scattered white and half-breed Catholics in Hell's Gate Valley and visited the gold gulches of a wide area.

In 1874, he was sent to Last Chance Gulch or Helena, where he built a church and attended stations as far-flung as Crow Creek, Gallatin Valley, Boulder, and the Missouri River settlements. Transferred to Missoula in 1877, he established a flourishing congregation and built St. Patrick's Hospital and St. Francis Xavier Church. In 1888, broken in health, he retired to St. Ignatius Mission, where, three years later, he died on the feast of St. Peter Canisius whom he especially revered. His funeral services were attended by a concourse of Indians of various tribes, of whom 1,000 are said to have received communion for the repose of his soul. Few missionaries were more widely known or labored more successfully for the conversion of the Indians.

[Annual Catholic directories; L. B. Palladino, *Indian and White in the Northwest* (1894); S. J. Sullivan, *The Golden Jubilee of St. Joseph's Church, Canton, Mont.* (1926); H. M. Chittenden and A. T. Richardson, *Life, Letters, and Travels of Father Pierre-Jean De Smet, S. J.* (1905); *Helena Herald*, Apr. 29, 1891.]

R. J. P.

MENEWA (fl. 1814–1835), Creek chief, was born probably about 1766 with white and Indian blood in his veins. He was called Hothlepoya, "the crazy war hunter," in his younger days, when he was famous for the skill and effrontery of his plundering expeditions across the Tennessee border. His notoriety was so great that there grew up around his name a body of frontier tradition comparable to the stories told of such figures as Robin Hood and Rob Roy. As he grew older he adapted himself to the more lucrative economic system of the white man, kept large herds of cattle, and traded with the Indians for furs and skins. He sent to Pensacola heavily laden trains of horses, perhaps fifty to a hundred at a trip. By the time Tecumseh [*q.v.*] went south to preach confederation, he had risen to the rank of second chieftain of the Oakfuskee villages in what is now Alabama and was known as Menewa, "the great warrior." He had scant sympathy with Georgia's efforts to possess the lands of the Indians, was the bitter enemy of William McIntosh [*q.v.*], and led the warriors of his villages into the Creek War. Superstitious faith in the advice of the first chief of his people, a medicine man, betrayed him into placing his troops in a vulnerable position at the battle of Horseshoe Bend in 1814. When he saw his defenses attacked by Andrew Jackson he realized his terrible mistake, for vengeance killed the false prophet, and rushed into hopeless battle. Wounded and left for dead, after the battle he saved himself only by incredible exertions. Although stripped of his wealth by the war, he assumed again the leadership of what remained of his band of warriors, who chose him in 1825 to execute their death sentence on McIntosh for ceding tribal lands against tribal law. The next year he was one of the delegation to Washington to protest against the treaty signed by McIntosh. There he smoked the pipe of peace and had his portrait made for the gallery of the War Department. Ten years later when the Creeks joined the Seminoles in war he served with the Alabama troops and for his services was promised the privilege of remaining to die in his native land. The promise was broken, however, and he was transported with the rest of his tribe across the Mississippi.

[T. L. McKenney and James Hall, *Hist. of the Indian Tribes of North America*, vol. I (1836); F. W. Hodge, *Handbook of Am. Indians*, vol. I (1907); James Pickett, *Hist. of Ala.* (1851), II, 343–44.]

K. E. C.

MENGARINI, GREGORY (July 21, 1811–Sept. 23, 1886), Catholic missionary and educator, was born in Rome of a distinguished family. He entered the novitiate of the Society of Jesus, Oct. 28, 1828; and on completion of his philosophical training, he taught in Jesuit colleges in Rome, Modena, and Reggio. In 1839, while in the Jesuit seminary in Rome, he was much affected by the public reading of a letter from Bishop Joseph Rosati of St. Louis, which appealed for missionaries to the Flathead Indians, who were petitioning for a "black robe." Ordained a priest in March 1840, he volunteered for the Indian missions and sailed in July from Leghorn to Philadelphia. After spending a few months at Georgetown College, he went to St. Louis, from which he accompanied Fathers Pierre de Smet, Nicholas Point, and three Alsatian and Belgian lay brothers to Fort Hall, Idaho (Aug. 15, 1841). Escorted by a party of Flatheads, the missionaries went to St. Mary's Mission in the Bitter Root Valley. Here in a log-cabin with windows of thin beaten skin, Mengarini, despite suffering from bitter cold to which he was unacclimated, served the Indians, composed hymns in various dialects, trained a native choir, and compiled a *Selish or Flat-head Grammar; Grammatica Linguae Selicae*, which was published from his third manuscript, in 1861, as the second volume of J. G. Shea's Library of American Linguistics. It is said that he became so fluent in the Selish or Kalispel dialect that in speech he could pass for a tribesman. About this time he wrote a Kalispel Indian-English dictionary, which was ultimately published with an English-Indian supplement by the Indians and missionaries of the St. Ignatius Mission in Montana (*A Dictionary of the Kalispel or Flat-head Indian Language*, 2 vols., 1877–79).

In spite of Mengarini's entreaties to his superiors at St. Paul, Ore., St. Mary's Mission was ordered closed because of trouble with the Blackfeet tribesmen in 1850. Two years later, the repentant Blackfeet appealed for his return. Their petition was not granted, but the Jesuits reëstablished the St. Ignatius Mission. In the meantime, Mengarini had been ordered to the Santa Clara mission in California, where he assisted in the foundation of the College of Santa Clara, the first collegiate institution on the Pacific slope. Here serving as director of studies, as professor of modern languages, as treasurer, or as vice-rector, he continued his work until stricken by apoplexy. He had not only a deep affection for the Indians but a scientific interest in their language and customs. He furnished vocabularies of the Colville, Coeur d'Alène, Flathead, and Santa Clara dialects in John Wesley Powell's *Contributions to American Ethnology* (vols. I, III, 1877). Toward the end of his life, he dictated personal reminiscences which appeared in the *Woodstock Letters* (1888).

[*Cath. Encyc.*, X, 189; annual Catholic directories; *Woodstock Letters* (1887); *Jour. of the Anthropological Institute of N. Y.*, vol. I (1871–72); *Records of the Am. Cath. Hist. Soc.*, II (1889), 174 f.; H. M. Chittenden and A. T. Richardson, *Life, Letters, and Travels of Father Pierre-Jean De Smet, S. J.* (1905); L. B. Palladino, *Indian and White in the Northwest* (1894); *Morning Call* (San Francisco), Sept. 25, 1886.] R. J. P.

MENKEN, ADAH ISAACS (June 15, 1835?–Aug. 10, 1868), actress and poet, was born probably in Milneburg, a suburb of New Orleans, La. Accounts of her birth and early life, most of which are based on her own statements, are conflicting. These declarations, naming her father variously as Josiah Campbell, James McCord, Richard Irving Spenser, and Ricardo Los Fiertes, are fabrications and were made for purposes of publicity. It is true, however, that she was born a Jewess, and that her given name was Adah Bertha. Her father (whose surname was probably Theodore), died when she was about two years old, and her mother married again. Of this union, two children were born. Adah studied the classics, knew French, Hebrew, German, and Spanish, could ride, sing, and dance, and in later years became an amateur painter and sculptor. About 1853 the stepfather (probably named Josephs) died, leaving the family in straitened circumstances.

In 1856, she is said (probably incorrectly) to have privately printed a volume of verse entitled *Memories,* under the pseudonym "Indigena." In Livingston, Tex., on Apr. 3 of that year, she married Alexander Isaac Menken, son of a Cincinnati dry-goods merchant. In March 1857 she appeared at James Charles' theatre in Shreveport, La., as Pauline in *The Lady of Lyons*; on Aug. 29 she made her début in New Orleans, at Crisp's Gaiety as Bianca in *Fazio.* On Sept. 25 she published a poem in the Cincinnati *Israelite,* and subsequently contributed regularly to this paper until Apr. 22, 1859.

With her husband as her manager, she appeared in the principal Southern and Western cities during the next year, meeting with moderate success. On Mar. 1, 1859, she made her New York début at Purdy's National Theatre as Widow Cheerly in *The Soldier's Daughter.* In July, she left Alexander Menken, and believing herself to have been divorced by him, married John Carmel Heenan [*q.v.*] in New York on Sept. 3 (Heenan divorce bill presented before the circuit court, McHenry County, Ill., October 1861, by Adah Isaacs Menken). At Pfaff's, New York's Bohemian rendezvous, she met Ada Clare, Walt Whitman, Fitz-James O'Brien, and other American writers and critics. In January 1860 the news of her marriage to Heenan became public. Subsequently a scandal arose when Alexander Menken announced that he had never divorced his wife but that he would now proceed to do so. In the summer of that year, Adah Menken bore Heenan a son who died within a short time. Heenan, returning from England in July after his fight with Tom Sayers, repudiated his wife. To add to her unhappiness, she received word in September from her half-sister, Annie Campbell Josephs, telling of her mother's death in New Orleans. Her poems written in this year, twelve of which were later included in *Infelicia,* reflect her depression of spirit.

With the new year, however, she resumed her theatrical activities, meeting especial success in Milwaukee and Pittsburgh. On June 3, 1861, she made her first appearance as Mazeppa at the Green Street Theatre, Albany, before the largest audience in the history of that theatre. In April of the following year she received her divorce from Heenan, and on Sept. 24, married Robert Henry Newell [*q.v.*]. In November, an amazing success in Baltimore was accompanied by a gift of diamonds worth $1,500. She declared herself a secessionist and was promptly arrested and brought before Provost-Marshal Fish, who released her on parole. On July 13, 1863, she sailed for San Francisco with her husband, appearing at Tom Maguire's Opera House on Aug. 24. To the literary group including Mark Twain, Bret Harte, Artemus Ward, Joaquin Miller, and others that met in Joe Lawrence's *Golden Era* office, she was a strange, beautiful goddess.

On Apr. 23, 1864, she sailed for England. Newell, who accompanied her as far as the Isthmus, returned to New York. Opening in *Mazeppa* at Astley's, London, on Oct. 3, she created a tremendous sensation. At her salon in the Westminster Palace Hotel such men as Dickens,

Reade, Swinburne, Rossetti, Burne-Jones, Purnell, and Charles Fechter were among her guests. On Aug. 24, 1865, she arrived in New York, but her stay was short, and on Oct. 9, she opened at Astley's in *Child of the Sun* by John Brougham [*q.v.*]. The play was withdrawn after six weeks and *Mazeppa* revived. In March 1866 she returned to New York, where on Apr. 30, at Wood's Broadway Theatre, she played before a house jammed to suffocation. She had divorced Newell in 1865, and after a triumphal tour of the larger cities, she was married, on Aug. 19, 1866, to James Barkley by Alderman John Brice at her home, 458 Seventh Avenue. Three days later she sailed alone for Europe. Barkley later went to California, where he died in 1878.

In Paris, "la Menken" went into retirement until the birth early in November of her son, who was christened, in honor of George Sand, his godmother, Louis Dudevant Victor Emanuel Barkley. On Dec. 30, she opened in *Les Pirates de la Savane* at the Théatre de la Gaité to the greatest triumph that had ever been accorded an American actress. Her apartment at the Hôtel de Suez was crowded with admirers, including Gautier and Dumas *père*. After a short engagement in Vienna, she returned to Paris. Astley's recalled her to London in the fall. At Sadler's Wells Theatre, on May 30, 1868, she gave her last performance. On July 9, in Paris, while rehearsing a new version of *Les Pirates,* she collapsed; on Aug. 10, she died and was buried in the Jewish sector of Père Lachaise. Edwin James removed the body, Apr. 21, 1869, to Montparnasse, where a marble monument bearing the inscription "Thou Knowest" (from Swinburne's *Ilicet*) had been erected. A collection of her poems, *Infelicia,* edited by John Thomson, Swinburne's secretary, and dedicated to Charles Dickens, was published in London, Aug. 18, 1868. Twenty-five of these poems had appeared in the New York *Sunday Mercury* in 1860 and 1861, and one in the *Israelite* of Sept. 3, 1858.

"The Royal Menken" was probably not a great dramatic figure, but her acting was as free from the platitude of the stage as her poetry was from its language. Swinburne, in his extravagant manner, wrote across a copy of *Infelicia,* "Lo, this is she that was the world's delight." Volatile, fearless, and uninhibited, she scandalized the staid Victorians of her day by her unconventional conduct, and, after her death, biographers accepted as fact her rumored immoralities. She possessed a keen intellect that recognized the genius of Walt Whitman as early as 1860. Under his stimulus she developed her own technique in the "rolling rhythms" of her poems. Dante Gabriel Rossetti called them "really remarkable." Driven by an insatiable ambition, and aided by her vivid personality and strange beauty, she climaxed a meteoric career with the fame she so ardently desired.

[Collection belonging to Alfred F. Goldsmith of New York City; Album of Adah Isaacs Menken (MS.), owned by Richard Gimble; H. S. Gorman, *The Incredible Marquis: Alexandre Dumas* (1929); Edmund Gosse, *The Life of Algernon Charles Swinburne* (1917); Harvard College Library Theatre Collection; Edwin James, *Biog. of Adah Isaacs Menken* (1881?); marriage records, N. Y. City Board of Health; "Ada Isaacs Menken, the Wife of John C. Heenan," *N. Y. Illustrated News,* Mar. 17–Apr. 14, 1860; Richard Northcott, *Adah Isaacs Menken* (1921), unreliable; *Dante Gabriel Rossetti: His Family-Letters* (1895), ed. by W. M. Rossetti; Constance Rourke, *Troupers of the Gold Coast* (1928); highly colored "autobiographical" fragment, ed. by Augustin Daly, in *N. Y. Times,* Sept. 6, 1868; C. W. Stoddard, "La Belle Menken," *Nat. Mag.,* Feb. 1905; T. E. Welby, *A Study of Swinburne* (1926); obituaries in *N. Y. Tribune, N. Y. Times,* Aug. 12, 1868; A. F. Lesser, "The Romantic Vagabond: Adah Isaacs Menken," dissertation in preparation at N. Y. Univ.]

A. F. L.

MENOCAL, ANICETO GARCIA (Sept. 1, 1836–July 20, 1908), civil engineer, was born in Cuba, the son of Gabriel Garcia Menocal, a wealthy planter, and his wife, Carmen Martin Monte Rey. He came to the United States to attend Rensselaer Polytechnic Institute, where he graduated in 1862 with the degree of C.E. Almost immediately he became assistant engineer and later chief engineer in charge of construction at the waterworks of Havana. On June 16, 1866, he married Elvira Martin, who survived him. They had four children.

In 1870 Menocal left Cuba, returning to the United States. After two years in the Department of Public Works of New York City, he entered the service of the United States Navy Department, being commissioned chief engineer in the navy on July 15, 1874. During his connection with the Navy Department, he was chief engineer of all the surveys made at Panama and Nicaragua, with a view to the construction of an interoceanic canal, but he is chiefly remembered as an early and persistent advocate of the Nicaraguan route. This he mapped in 1872–74; and in 1874–75 he pointed out the impracticability of a sea-level canal at the Isthmus. Convinced of the merits of his first proposals, he induced General Grant and others to organize the Provisional Interoceanic Canal Society (1880), which was later (1887) merged in the Maritime Canal Company of Nicaragua. Although, as chief engineer, he secured the necessary concessions, the project came to nothing because Grant's failure led to that of the Company. Unable to obtain further support in the United States, Menocal turned to the government of

Nicaragua, under whose auspices he carried out improvements at Grey Town, on the Rio San Juan, and at Lake Managua. He also investigated conditions at Panama. At length, in 1887, he became chief engineer of the newly organized Maritime Canal Company of Nicaragua and again secured concessions from Nicaragua, as well as from Costa Rica. Although work, beginning propitiously, continued until 1890, he was once more thwarted by a financial panic; and, in spite of his efforts to obtain capital in Europe or to secure government aid for the undertaking, it ended in disastrous failure. Nevertheless, his activities were not without fruit. Through his reports he kept the advisability of a canal before important groups; and through his papers read at the International Conference at Paris (1879), before the American Association for the Advancement of Science, at the Fourth International Conference on Inland Waterways at Manchester, England (1890), and at the World's Columbian Water Commerce Congress (1893), he appealed to a wider audience. His efforts helped to awaken the public interest which eventually made possible the construction of the interoceanic canal, though the route adopted, through Panama, was not that he had favored.

In 1881 as consulting engineer for the bureau of yards and docks he had designed the naval gun plant at Washington. After his retirement from the navy, Sept. 1, 1898, with the rank of commander, he continued to be called upon for assistance. He served on the board appointed to take charge of the properties surrendered in Cuba; he went to the Philippines to aid in the establishment of a naval base; and, in 1902, he investigated the sites available for a coaling station in Liberia. He was also retained by the government of Cuba and in the last two years of his life developed an irrigation system for the northern provinces of that country. He died in New York City.

[Menocal's activities are reflected in his reports and papers, especially in those contributed to the *Proceedings* of the United States Naval Institute and the *Transactions* of the American Society of Civil Engineers. See also memoir in *Trans. Am. Soc. Civil Engineers,* vol. LXXXIV (1921); H. B. Nason, *Biog. Record Officers and Grads. Rensselaer Polytechnic Inst.* (1887); R. P. Baker, *A Chapter in Am. Educ.: Rensselaer Polytechnic Inst.* (1924); *Who's Who in America,* 1908–09; *Army and Navy Jour.,* July 25, 1908; *N. Y. Times,* July 21, 1908; Navy Registers.]

R. P. B—r.

MENOHER, CHARLES THOMAS (Mar. 20, 1862–Aug. 11, 1930), soldier, came of Scotch-Irish colonial stock. His parents, Samuel and Sarah Jane (Young) Menoher, moved from Ohio to Johnstown, Pa., where Charles was born while his father was a soldier in the Civil War. He attended the borough schools, was interested as a boy in local literary and musical organizations, taught school for a while, and in the year 1882 was selected from among fifteen applicants to enter the United States Military Academy. Upon graduation in 1886, he was assigned to the artillery, and rose through all intermediate grades to become colonel, July 1, 1916. Meanwhile, he had graduated from the Artillery School (1894) and the Army War College (1907), and had been selected for the original General Staff Corps.

With the advent of the World War, he was appointed brigadier-general, National Army, Aug. 5, 1917; and while in command of the School of Instruction for Field Artillery at Saumur, France, was advanced to the grade of major-general, National Army, Nov. 28, 1917. His assignment to the 42nd (Rainbow) Division followed, with service in the Lunéville and Baccarat sectors; in repelling the critical German Champagne-Marne offensive; in the Allied offensive across the Ourcq River; in the attack on the St. Mihiel salient; and in the Meuse-Argonne offensive. His brilliant services were recognized, Nov. 7, by appointment as brigadier-general, Regular Army, and his assignment, Nov. 10, 1918, to command the VI Army Corps. For his conspicuous record in the World War, he was awarded the Distinguished-Service Medal, the citation stating in part that "The reputation as a fighting unit of the Forty-Second Division is in no small measure due to the soldierly qualities and the military leadership of this officer." He received also many foreign decorations, and was entitled to wear the American Victory Medal with five clasps.

With the signing of the Armistice, Menoher was appointed by the president to be director of the Air Service at Washington, Jan. 2, 1919, and was commissioned major-general, chief of Air Service, the next year, July 3, 1920. His successful administration of this office was impaired by friction with his principal assistant, Col. William Mitchell, over questions affecting the adequacy and conduct of the Air Service, and although upheld in the main by the Secretary of War, Menoher finally requested and received duty with troops. He commanded the Hawaiian Division, 1922–24, and then the Hawaiian Department until February 1925, after which he was in command of the IX Corps Area at San Francisco until the date of his retirement by operation of law, Mar. 20, 1926.

An officer of sterling character, high professional attainments, and strong sense of duty, Menoher was characterized by Secretary of

War Weeks as "a man of fine fighting record in France, a man of good judgment and level head, and a very capable executive" (*New York Times,* Aug. 12, 1930). He was married early in life to Nannie Wilhelmina Pearson, daughter of Maj. William H. Pearson, U. S. A. She died in 1919, and on Jan. 17, 1923, at Honolulu, he married Elizabeth Painter, who survived him, as did three sons by his former marriage, all of whom entered the military service.

[G. W. Cullum, *Biog. Register Officers and Grads., U. S. Mil. Acad.,* vol. III (3rd ed., 1891), and supplements; *Who's Who in America,* 1930–31; ; *Ann. Report, Asso. Grads. U. S. Mil. Acad.,* 1931; *N. Y. Times,* Aug. 12, 1930; *Army and Navy Jour.,* Sept. 28, 1918, July 24, 1920, Feb. 17, 1923; Mar. 27, 1926, and Aug. 16, 1930; information furnished by the Secretary, Asso. Grads. U. S. Mil. Acad., and by a son, Maj. Pearson Menoher, U. S. A.] C. D. R.

MERCER, CHARLES FENTON (June 16, 1778–May 4, 1858), congressman from Virginia, was born at Fredericksburg, Va., the youngest son of Eleanor (Dick) and James Mercer [*q.v.*]. His mother died when he was two years old and thirteen years later his father died leaving heavy debts, which the son later undertook to pay. The boy entered the College of New Jersey (Princeton) in 1795 and graduated in 1797 at the head of his class. In college he began his lifelong friendship with John Henry Hobart [*q.v.*] and became a devout Episcopalian. From 1797 until 1802 he read law at Princeton and at Richmond, Va. When war with France threatened in 1798 he volunteered and was twice offered a commission in the army, but since the threat of war had already passed he declined. In 1802 he was licensed to practise law. Soon afterward he went to England on business and also visited France. On his return he settled at Aldie, Loudoun County, Va., and began the practice of his profession. He became a member of the House of Delegates of Virginia in 1810 and served until he resigned in 1817 to enter Congress. While a member of the legislature he took a leading part in efforts to increase the banking capital of Virginia, to found a new bank, to promote the colonization in Africa of free negroes from the United States, and to build roads and canals. He offered a bill to provide for a complete system of public education, from common-school to state university, which was defeated in the Senate in the spring of 1817 after having passed the House (see his *Discourse on Popular Education: Delivered in . . . Princeton . . . Sept. 26, 1826,* 1826). He was also the author of the act by which a sword and pension were given to George Rogers Clark. During the War of 1812 he served with the Virginia troops, rising to the rank of brigadier-general.

His enthusiasm for internal improvements, the suppression of the slave trade, and the colonization of free negroes gave direction to his efforts when he became a member of the federal House of Representatives in 1817. He was chairman of the committees on roads and canals and on the District of Columbia. Though a member of the Federalist party until its dissolution and then a Whig, he was never an ardent party man. He enjoyed the friendship of Monroe and of John Quincy Adams. He disliked Jackson and Van Buren and on Jan. 26, 1819, delivered an address in Congress in which he assailed Jackson's course in the Seminole War (*Annals of Congress,* 15 Cong., 2 Sess., cols. 797–831). He was a strong Unionist but was alarmed at the rapidly increasing power of the president and was opposed to the executive's control over federal patronage. He was active in the movement that resulted in the building of the Chesapeake and Ohio Canal and was for five years, from 1828 to 1833, president of the company. He was a leader in the Virginia constitutional convention of 1829–30, in which he advocated manhood suffrage, equal representation, and the popular election of important officers with the whole power of his distinguished oratorical ability.

Resigning from Congress on Dec. 26, 1839, he became cashier of a bank in Tallahassee, Fla. He was original grantee, partner, and agent of the Texas association, a company which obtained a contract to settle colonists in Texas and to receive pay from the Republic in land. When the convention in 1845 declared colonization contracts unconstitutional he and his associates brought suit to force payment, but the case was decided against them in the United States courts. In 1845 he published *An Exposition of the Weakness and Inefficiency of the Government of the United States.* In 1847 he built a house near Carrollton, Ky., which he made his home until 1853, when he disposed of his property there. For three years he traveled in Europe, working in the interest of the abolition of the slave trade. Ill with cancer of the lip, he returned to Fairfax County, Virginia, where he was nursed by relatives until his death. He was never married.

[J. M. Garnett, *Biog. Sketches of Hon. Charles Fenton Mercer* (1911); W. F. Dunaway, "Charles Fenton Mercer," manuscript thesis in the lib. of Univ. of Chicago; *Wm. and Mary College Quart.,* Jan. 1909, p. 210; *The Correspondence of John Henry Hobart,* esp. vol. III (1912); John McVicar, *The Early Life and Professional Years of Bishop Hobart* (1838); *Memoirs of John Quincy Adams,* ed. by C. F. Adams, vols. IV–X (1875–76), esp. X, p. 360, for Adams' explanation of Mercer's becoming a bank cashier at Tallahassee.] C. F. A.

MERCER, HENRY CHAPMAN (June 24, 1856–Mar. 9, 1930), archeologist, antiquarian, inventor, was born at Doylestown, Pa., and was the son of William Robert and Mary Rebecca (Chapman) Mercer. He attended the Tennent School near Hartsville, Pa., and Harvard College, receiving the degree of A.B. in 1879. He then read law in Philadelphia and was admitted to the bar in 1881, but his rapidly developing enthusiasm for archeology outweighed his interest in law, and after a few years he gave up the legal profession. As early as 1885 he published a monograph on *The Lenape Stone,* in recognition of which Spain later conferred a decoration upon him. He was an honorary member of the United States Archeological Commission at Madrid in 1893 and that same year became editor for anthropology in the *American Naturalist.* In 1894 he was made curator of American and prehistoric archeology for the University of Pennsylvania and filled that position until 1897. During this time he explored many caves and Indian mounds in the United States and Mexico. In the caves he identified the remains of several extinct animals, some of them hitherto unknown, including the prehistoric tapir, mylodon, peccary, and sloth. He explored the caves and ruins of Yucatan, fixing a geological date for the latter, and published his *Hill Caves of Yucatan* in 1896. He studied aboriginal remains in the Delaware, Ohio, and Tennessee valleys, discovering Indian stone-blade quarries and workshops along the Delaware, and giving much time to a study of technical comparison of these stone blades with the supposed geologically ancient human implements found in America (in drift gravels in New Jersey, for example) and with those of the Pleistocene Age in Europe, particularly around Abbeville and in the Dordogne Valley, France, and in Spain and Belgium, where he did much work in drift gravels and flint quarries. His study of human remains in the American river valleys aided in tracing the lines of early migrations. His *Researches upon the Antiquity of Man in the Delaware Valley and the Eastern United States* appeared in 1897.

The possession of ample private means enabled Mercer to drop his curatorship and editorial connection with the *American Naturalist* in 1897 and pursue his favorite studies at will. From that time until his death he made his headquarters at Doylestown, his birthplace. He was never married. He had been one of the founders of the Bucks County Historical Society at Doylestown in 1880, and it was with that society that he began depositing his growing collection of utensils and implements illustrating the colonial history of the United States. He published a monograph on the subject entitled *Tools of the Nation Maker* in 1897, and that name came in time to be applied to the collection itself. He was president of the society from 1911 until his death. In 1916 he built and endowed with his own funds a large concrete building to serve as museum for the collection and as a home for the society. Here, each in its own compartment, are complete sets of tools of varied metal, wood, clay, and textile working industries, as carried on by American pioneers, and other unusual yet kindred exhibits, as for example, an original Conestoga wagon, a "Democrat" wagon and a Norse gristmill, brought from a North Carolina mountain glen, but of an ancient type found in the northern Scottish isles and Scandinavia. Here also is a collection of the remarkable stove plates of the Pennsylvania Germans, regarding which Mercer wrote his monograph, *The Bible in Iron,* in 1914. He likewise studied the other artistic remains of the early German settlers, developing their processes of making and decorating pottery, until he finally invented in 1899 a new method of making mural decorative tiles, and in 1902 a new process for mosaics. He established a factory for the production of these tiles and designed many of them himself, taking his subjects from the Bible, history, literature, and mythology. In 1904 he invented a process for printing large designs in color on fabrics and paper, and was awarded a grand prize on it at the Louisiana Purchase Exposition in St. Louis that year.

He made a number of other excursions in pursuit of his researches, meanwhile writing numerous articles on scientific and antiquarian subjects, and for several years prior to his death men under his guidance were employed in various parts of the world, such as China, southern Europe, and the near East, mostly in search of ancient implements, from which he was tracing the descent of modern tools. In this field he published *Ancient Carpenters' Tools* in 1929. He had made an intensive study of old houses and was often able to determine the age of a building by examining the door hardware, nails, screws, lath, and shaping of timbers. During the years 1906–08 he erected his own residence, "Fonthill," a unique monolithic structure of sixty-six rooms near Doylestown, portions of it embellished with his own tiles, other rooms illustrating American colonial interiors. This, by his will, was endowed and bequeathed to the public as a museum, the ground around it to be an arboretum and bird sanctuary. He also left $100,000 to finance an expedition to the Far East to collect tools and utensils used in the daily life of those countries. He was a fellow or member of a number of learned societies.

[*Who's Who in America*, 1928–29, and articles in the *Doylestown* (Pa.) *Intelligencer* of Mar. 10 and 14, 1930, furnish notices of Mercer's life and his will. A partial idea of the scope of his work may be gained from his articles and books. The papers of the Bucks County Historical Society from 1917 to 1930 contain numerous articles by him which show his interest in antiquarian subjects. Information for this sketch was also gained through Mercer's associates and by the author's acquaintance with the archeologist.]

A. F. H.

MERCER, HUGH (*c.* 1725–Jan. 12, 1777), Revolutionary soldier, was born in Aberdeenshire, Scotland, the son of the Rev. William Mercer and his wife, Anna Munro. Educated as a physician at Marischal College, University of Aberdeen (1740–44), he joined the army of Prince Charles Edward as a surgeon's mate, and was present at the battle of Culloden. The collapse of the Pretender's cause led him to emigrate to America, and after a brief sojourn in Philadelphia, where he landed in 1746 or 1747, he settled near the present site of Mercersburg, Pa.

For about ten years he practised his profession in the Conococheague settlement, winning the esteem of the frontier community by his skill and courage. At the outbreak of the French and Indian War, he abandoned the lancet for the sword, becoming an officer of the Pennsylvania Regiment, a provincial corps. After having ranked as captain, major, and lieutenant-colonel, he was commissioned colonel of the third battalion, Apr. 23, 1759. Many daring escapes from the Indians are ascribed to him. It is said that he took part in Braddock's expedition in 1755 and was wounded in the action of July 9. He participated in the attack upon the Indian village of Kittanning in September 1756, and for gallantry was awarded a vote of thanks and a medal by the corporation of the city of Philadelphia. He accompanied the expedition of General Forbes to Fort Duquesne in 1758, and on its successful termination was appointed commandant at Fort Pitt, where in the following year he conducted important negotiations for peace with chiefs and warriors of the Six Nations and other tribes. During the course of the war he made the acquaintance of Washington, and at his suggestion, it is said, removed from Pennsylvania to Fredericksburg, Va., where he took up once more the practice of medicine and also conducted an apothecary shop. He attended the same Masonic lodge as Washington, and was an occasional visitor at Mount Vernon. He married Isabella Gordon of Fredericksburg, and had four sons and a daughter.

When the colonies rebelled against Great Britain, Mercer again deserted the medical for the military profession. On Sept. 12, 1775, he was elected colonel of minute men for the counties of Caroline, Stafford, King George, and Spotsylvania. He presently relinquished this position for the colonelcy of the 3rd Virginia Regiment, to which he was elected by the Virginia Convention on Jan. 11, 1776. Previously he had been nominated for the colonelcy of the 1st Regiment, but had been defeated in a close contest by Patrick Henry.

At Williamsburg he set about organizing and drilling his battalion. On June 5, he was elected brigadier-general by the Continental Congress. Washington directed him to repair to Paulus Hook, and placed him in charge of the Flying Camp, comprising militia from Pennsylvania, Delaware, Maryland, and New Jersey. Its function was to hover between Howe's forces and Philadelphia, at the same time protecting northern New Jersey against attack by the British troops on Staten Island. Mercer experienced difficulty in holding his command together. Despite his patriotic appeals, scores of his men went home on the expiration of their enlistments, or deserted outright. He accompanied the army in its retreat across New Jersey, and was employed for a time in guarding the ferries of the Delaware against passage by the British. If he did not exclusively originate the plan of recrossing the river and surprising the Hessians at Trenton, he helped to execute it. His brigade was assigned to the left wing under General Greene, and was one of the first corps to enter Trenton on the morning of Dec. 26, 1776.

The claim that he suggested to Washington the stroke which resulted in the subsequent victory at Princeton has been challenged, but there is no doubt as to his part in the battle. On the morning of Jan. 3, 1777, in accordance with the orders of the commander-in-chief, he attempted to seize the bridge over Stony Brook on the American left, but his men were driven back in disorder and his horse was shot from under him. As he was attempting to rally his brigade on foot, he was surrounded by redcoats, clubbed on the head with the breech of a musket, forced to the ground despite his efforts to defend himself with his sword, and bayonetted in seven places. After the battle he was carried by his aide to a neighboring farmhouse, where he died. His remains were buried with civic and military honors in Christ Churchyard, Philadelphia, and in 1840 were transferred to Laurel Hill Cemetery. The Continental Congress voted to erect a monument in his honor (not accomplished, however, until 1902), and to educate his youngest son.

Washington, who repeatedly lauded his judgment and experience, in a letter to the President of Congress, Jan. 5, 1777, characterized him as "the brave and worthy Gen'l Mercer."

[J. T. Goolrick, *The Life of Gen. Hugh Mercer* (1906) is invaluable. See also Peter Force, *Am. Archives*, 4 ser. (1837–46); I. D. Rupp, *Early Hist. of Western Pa.* (1846); W. S. Stryker, *The Battles of Trenton and Princeton* (1898); J. S. Keene, "Hugh Mercer," in *The John P. Branch Hist. Papers of Randolph-Macon Coll.*, vol. II (1908); W. E. McCulloch, *Viri Illustres Universitatum Abredonensium* (1923); *Va. County Records*, I (1905), 31; *The Writings of George Washington* (1932), ed. by J. C. Fitzpatrick; *Journals of the Continental Congress*, 1775–77; W. B. Blanton, *Medicine in Va. in the Eighteenth Century* (1931); *Pa. Evening Post*, Jan. 18, 1777.] E. E. C.

MERCER, JAMES (Feb. 26, 1736–Oct. 31, 1793), Revolutionary patriot, member of the Continental Congress, was one of the foremost men of his day in Virginia. His father, John Mercer, emigrated from Dublin, Ireland, in 1720, settled at "Marlborough," Stafford County, Va., acquired a considerable fortune as a successful lawyer and business man, and was secretary of the Ohio Company, in the affairs of which his two sons, James and George, were also active. By his first wife, Catherine Mason, the aunt of George Mason, *c.* 1629–*c.* 1686 [*q.v.*], he was the father of James, and by his second wife was the father of John Francis Mercer [*q.v.*]. James Mercer was educated at the College of William and Mary. He served in the French and Indian War and was in command, with the rank of captain, of Fort Loudoun at Winchester, Va. In 1762 he was elected to represent the nearby county of Hampshire, now in West Virginia, in the Virginia House of Burgesses. He continued to serve this county, not only in that position, but also as a member of the Revolutionary conventions of 1774, 1775, and 1776.

He joined with his neighbors at Fredericksburg in drafting resolutions against the oppressive acts of the British government and was appointed, on June 1, 1774, a member of the committee of correspondence. He was active in bringing about the first Virginia Revolutionary convention of August 1774 and was elected by the convention on Aug. 17, 1775, to the first Committee of Safety, which governed Virginia until the state government was inaugurated in 1776. Reëlected to the committee upon its reorganization on Dec. 16, 1775, he aligned himself with the progressive group. As a member of the committee of the convention of 1776 that was appointed to draft a declaration of rights and a new plan of government for Virginia he was very active; he was considered one of the best speakers of the period. On June 18, 1779, he was elected by the General Assembly to the Continental Congress and took his seat on Sept. 9, 1779.

In 1779 he was appointed to the General Court and served also as a member of the first court of appeals. On Nov. 18, 1789, he was elected one of the five judges of the state's highest court, the reorganized court of appeals, to succeed John Blair, who resigned. He died in Richmond, while attending a session of the court, and was buried in St. John's church yard. A brief sketch in *Call's Reports* (IV, p. xx) thus describes him: "He possessed a sound understanding; was an honest man, a learned lawyer, and an impartial and upright judge." He was married on June 4, 1772, to Eleanor, the daughter of Charles Dick of Fredericksburg, Va., commissary in the French and Indian War and associated with Fielding Lewis in manufacturing arms and ammunition for the Revolutionary army. The youngest of their two sons was Charles Fenton Mercer [*q.v.*] and their only daughter was Mary Eleanor Dick Mercer, who married James Mercer Garnett, 1770–1843 [*q.v.*], her first cousin.

[Account of destruction of Mercer papers by Federal troops in *Wm. and Mary College Hist. Quart.*, Apr. 1893; J. M. Garnett, "James Mercer," *Ibid.*, Oct. 1908, Jan. 1909; *Ibid.*, July 1898, Oct. 1909, Jan. 1912, Oct. 1918; *Calendar of Va. State Papers*, vols. V, VI, VIII (1885–90); sketch of Mercer family, *Va. Mag. of Hist.*, Jan. 1907.] R. L. M—n.

MERCER, JESSE (Dec. 16, 1769–Sept. 6, 1841), Georgia pioneer preacher and philanthropist, was born in Halifax County, N. C., the great-grandson of a Scotch emigrant who settled in Virginia about the end of the seventeenth century. His father Silas Mercer was reared a devout Episcopalian, but shortly after his removal from North Carolina to Wilkes County, Ga., about 1775, he became a Baptist and later a minister, the founder and pastor of several prominent churches of the original Georgia Association, constituted probably in 1784. Jesse, the eldest of eight children, was brought up on the frontier with scant opportunity for an education in books, but after he began to preach he was able to go back to school from time to time. After passing through a depressing religious struggle of some twelve years, he was baptized in 1787 by his father. In 1789 he was ordained a Baptist minister in Phillips' Mill Church. A tall, slender youth, rather unprepossessing in appearance, mainly on account of his oddly shaped head with an unusually high crown and slanting forehead, he went the next year to be pastor at Sardis in Wilkes County and, on his father's death in 1796, succeeded to his place as pastor of the churches at Phillips' Mill in Wilkes County, at Bethesda in Greene County, at Powelton in Hancock County, and later he became pastor at Eatonton in Putnam County. On his marriage to his second wife he removed to Washington, Ga., to minister to a newly organized church there. He purchased the *Christian Index* and, having transferred it from Philadelphia, Pa., to Washington, was its editor from 1833 to 1840, when he resigned and donated it to the Baptist State Convention.

He was an important figure in the councils of the Baptists of America. In Georgia he was a kind of bishop, without the prerogatives of that office, over a body that by 1840 had grown to number 30,000 members. For almost the whole period from 1795 to 1816 he was clerk of the Georgia Baptist Association, and, becoming moderator of the body in 1816, he served in the office until 1839. In 1838 he published *A History of the Georgia Baptist Association.* He was for eleven years a member of the board of managers of the Baptist general convention for missionary purposes, a national body organized in 1814. When, in 1822, a general state association was formed as the General Baptist Association of the State of Georgia, later the Baptist Convention of the State of Georgia, he became the first moderator and served until 1841. His leadership was owing to his frank democracy, modesty, and devotion to the support of benevolent enterprises, especially foreign missions and higher education. In meeting dissension in churches and associations he practised conciliation and tact. He was reluctant to participate in politics unless what he considered the fundamental Christian principles lying at the base of the government were threatened. As a delegate to the state constitutional convention of 1798, he was instrumental in defeating a motion to make ministers ineligible to the legislature, though he advised against their taking part in "every-day politics of the country" (*Memoirs, post,* p. 102). He was not a scholar, but his writings show simple strength and beauty. He was exceptionally cogent in expounding matters of church discipline and doctrine.

His own efforts to obtain an education lasted throughout his lifetime, and he contributed largely to making possible an education for others. Very early in his life he began to give his time to teaching, in his own home, young men too poor to afford other means of advancing their education. In his honor the Baptist school near Greensboro was named Mercer Institute, when it was opened in 1833 to combine a classical and theological training with agricultural labor and study. He devoted great effort to the project for founding a Baptist college at Washington, Ga., but, when the plan was given up in spite of his earnest advice, he lent his aid to obtaining the transfer of most of the subscriptions and himself subscribed $5,000 to the enlargement of Mercer Institute, which was renamed Mercer University in 1837. In later years and by his will he gave to the university a sum of more than $40,000. On Jan. 31, 1788, he was married to Sabrina Chivers, a member of the church in which he was ordained. She bore him two daughters and died in 1826. On Dec. 11, 1827, he was married to Nancy Simonds, a wealthy widow of Washington, Ga., formerly Nancy Mills of Virginia. It was through the wise management of her properties that he was able to give generously to benevolent causes. He died in Butts County, Ga.

[C. D. Mallary, *Memoirs of Elder Jesse Mercer* (1844); *Hist. of the Baptist Denomination of Ga.* (1881); S. G. Hillyer, *Reminiscences of Ga. Baptists* (1902); J. H. Campbell, *Ga. Baptists,* 2nd ed. (1874).]
W. J. B.

MERCER, JOHN FRANCIS (May 17, 1759–Aug. 30, 1821), soldier, congressman, and governor of Maryland, belonged to the distinguished Mercer family of Virginia. His father, John Mercer, its founder, came of a family which originated in Chester, England. Born in Ireland, he emigrated in 1720 to Virginia, where he became known as an able lawyer and wealthy man of affairs. By his first wife, Catherine Mason, he had ten children, one of whom was James Mercer [*q.v.*]. His second wife, the mother of John Francis, was Ann Roy of Essex County, Va. The son, fifth of her nine children, was born at "Marlborough," his father's estate in Stafford County, Va., and received his higher education at the College of William and Mary. Since war with England seemed inevitable, early in 1776 he enlisted as lieutenant in the 3rd Virginia Regiment. He was promoted to a captaincy Sept. 11, 1777, and in the following year became aide-de-camp to Gen. Charles Lee [*q.v.*]. When, after the battle of Monmouth, the latter was court-martialed and disgraced, Mercer resigned his commission (October 1779) and returned to Virginia. In the fall of 1780 he reëntered the war as lieutenant-colonel of infantry under General Lawson; and the following May he recruited a small group of cavalry to aid Lafayette, under whom he served for a short time. He then raised a corps of militia grenadiers, whom he commanded, with the rank of lieutenant-colonel, at the surrender of Cornwallis at Yorktown.

During the first interval in his military service (1779–80) Mercer studied law for a year at Williamsburg under the direction of Thomas

Jefferson, then governor of Virginia; and between his service under Lawson and that under Lafayette he practised law at Fredericksburg. This appears to have been the extent of his experience as an active practitioner. Subsequently, he devoted most of his time to politics. He was a member of the Virginia House of Delegates in 1782 and in 1785–86. In December 1782, he was elected member of Congress from Virginia, to succeed Edmund Randolph who had resigned; and the following year he was reëlected. Early in 1785 he married Sophia Sprigg of Maryland, and soon thereafter took up his residence at "Cedar Park," an estate in Anne Arundel County inherited by his wife from her father. He was a member from Maryland of the Federal Convention of 1787, and was so strongly opposed to the centralizing character of the document drawn up that he left before the gathering finished its work. As a delegate to the Maryland ratification convention, he spoke and voted against the Constitution; and after it was adopted, aligned himself with the Republicans. He was a member of the Maryland House of Delegates in 1788–89 and 1791–92. Elected in 1791 to the federal House of Representatives to take the place of William Pinkney, resigned, he was reëlected, but resigned his seat in April 1794 and retired to "Cedar Park." This terminated his career in national office.

He was again a member of the state House of Delegates in 1800–01, and in November 1801 was chosen Republican governor of Maryland by the state Assembly. The term of governorship was one year, and in the following autumn he was reëlected. During his incumbency a constitutional amendment providing for manhood suffrage and vote by ballot was adopted, but Mercer appears to have had no special part in bringing this action about. His second term as governor ended, he served in the House of Delegates, 1803–06. When the trouble with England began in Jefferson's administration, he broke with the Republicans, virtually allied himself with the Federalists, and worked hard to avert war. During his last few years, because of poor health, he lived quietly at "Cedar Park." Death came to him in Philadelphia, where he was seeking medical aid. Margaret Mercer [*q.v.*] was his daughter.

[The biographical sketch in H. E. Buchholz's *Governors of Maryland* (1908) contains many errors, but the article by James Mercer Garnett in *Md. Hist. Mag.*, Sept. 1907, is dependable and quotes some rare documents. See also, in addition to the *Annals of Cong.* and Md. legislative journals: J. M. Garnett, *Geneal. of the Mercer-Garnett Family of Essex County,, Va.* (1910); W. C. Ford, *The Writings of George Washington*, vols. XI, XII (1891); *The Writings of Thomas Jefferson* (Memorial Ed.), vols. VIII, IX, XI (1903–04); Gaillard Hunt, *The Writings of James Madison* (9 vols., 1900–10); S. M. Hamilton, *The Writings of James Monroe* (7 vols., 1898–1903); Max Farrand, *The Records of the Federal Convention of 1787* (3 vols., 1911) · E. G. Swem and J. W. Williams, *A Reg. of the Gen. Assembly of Va.* (1918); F. B. Heitman, *Hist. Reg. of Officers of the Continental Army* (1893); *Baltimore Patriot and Mercantile Advertiser*, Sept. 8, 1821.]

M. W. W.

MERCER, LEWIS PYLE (June 27, 1847–July 6, 1906), Swedenborgian clergyman, was born at Kennett Square, Chester County, Pa., the son of Pennock and Ann (Pyle) Mercer, both Quakers. He was educated in the common-schools of Chester County, in the Normal School, and at Taylor's Scientific and Classical Academy, Wilmington, Del., where he also taught. At Wilmington, in 1865, he became interested in the teachings of Swedenborg, and after hearing lectures on the subject by the Rev. Abiel Silver, he sought out the lecturer and began with him a study of Swedenborg's doctrines. With the New Church ministry in mind he continued his studies with the Rev. Willard H. Hinkley and the Rev. Nathan C. Burnham, going finally for a term to the New Church Theological School, Waltham, Mass. In 1868 he married Sarah Taylor Pennock of Chester County, Pa., by whom he had six children.

In this year he went West to teach at East Rockport near Cleveland. Here he found an opportunity to preach and in 1870 was licensed, taking charge of the New Church society there and also later for a short time of the society in Cleveland. In 1872 he accepted a call to Detroit and was ordained to the ministry of the General Convention of the New Jerusalem in the United States of America. In Detroit he quickly attained popularity, with the result that in 1877 he was called to Chicago. Here a difficult task awaited him. After a prosperous beginning, the society had been weakened by the great fire of 1871 and the panic of 1873. The wide extent of the city and internal friction had led to dissatisfaction and division. The result was the formation of a separate body, the Union Swedenborgian Church, to the pastorate of which Mercer was called. Under his leadership the new society was immediately successful. His sermons were published regularly in the newspapers and helped spread the teachings to which he was devoted. It was his conviction that these doctrines were divinely provided to meet the needs of the age, and he preached them as such, but he did not believe that assent to elaborate doctrinal definition should be a basis for organization. In 1881 the Union Swedenborgian Church united with the original Chicago society under Mercer's leadership. From a membership of 175 in 1880 the society had grown to 484 in 1900, and in 1894 had been organized into four strong parishes. In 1884 Mercer became president of the Illinois Association of the New Church and in 1895, general pastor, resigning his Chicago charge in 1900 to devote his whole time to this wider field. In 1901, however, he accepted a call to Cincinnati, where he continued in active service till his death. In 1903 he was consecrated as the general pastor of the Ohio Association.

While still in Chicago he had been instrumental in organizing the Western New Church Union (1886), for missionary, educational, and publication purposes in the West. He also took an active part in the organization of the World's Parliament of Religions in connection with the Columbian Exposition, was editor of *The New Jerusalem in the World's Religious Congresses of 1893* (1894), and author of *Review of the World's Religious Congress* (1893). He possessed considerable literary talent, and wrote *The Bible, Its True Character and Spiritual Meaning* (1879) and other expositions of New Church Doctrine which at the time were highly valued. He edited the shortlived *New-Church Review,* 1882–84, and in 1893 founded *The Sower,* the first New Church Sunday-school paper. Always interested in science, he became a member of the Swedenborg Scientific Association, organized for the study and publication of Swedenborg's scientific works, and when this body adopted as its organ *The New Philosophy,* he became the managing editor, serving from July 1900 to April 1902. In 1905 he was chosen president of Urbana University, Urbana, Ohio, a New Church college. He began the raising of an endowment fund which has grown to considerable proportions.

Mercer was of a very devout nature, sanguine, generous, capable of evoking deep friendship and enthusiastic cooperation. On these qualities rather than on his considerable intellectual gifts depended his success. He was a man of strong convictions, yet never anxious to force them on others. His willingness to work with anyone who would work with him held him aloof from party strife. His greatest contribution to the New Church was his talent as organizer and administrator.

[*The New Church and Chicago* (Western New Church Union, Chicago, 1906); *New-Church Messenger,* July 11, 18, 1906; *Jour. of the Eighty-Seventh Ann. Sess. General Convention of the New Jerusalem in the U. S. A.* (1907); E. C. Silver, *Sketches of the New Church in America* (*c.* 1920); *New Church Life,* Aug. 1906; *Cincinnati Enquirer,* July 7, 1906.]

F. R. C.

MERCER, MARGARET (July 1, 1791–Sept. 17, 1846), anti-slavery worker and educator, was born in Annapolis, Md., the daughter of John Francis Mercer [*q.v.*] and his wife, Sophia Sprigg. Most of her childhood was spent in Annapolis, while her father filled various public offices, or at "Cedar Park," the estate of her maternal grandfather in Anne Arundel County, Md., which was the country home of the Mercer family for many years. She had a superior mind and a strong scholarly bent, and her education, carefully supervised by her father, was exceptional for a woman of her period.

From a religious motive, she began in her early youth to devote herself energetically to altruistic service. To Sunday schools—which then offered elementary education to the poor, as well as religious instruction—she gave time and money, working in connection with her church, the Protestant Episcopal. For the Greeks, then struggling for independence from Turkey, she also helped raise funds. Through many years, however, her chief interest was probably the anti-slavery cause as represented by the activities of the American Colonization Society, which aimed, through the removal of free negroes to Liberia, to encourage manumission and thereby ultimately to eliminate slavery from the United States. She urged emancipation upon others and after her father's death set an example by freeing her share of the family slaves and sending to Liberia those who were willing to go. She also raised money to purchase the freedom of other slaves, and for educational work in Liberia.

Much of the later part of her life was given to teaching. Cedar Park Institute, her first school, was conducted in her home; but later she moved her school to Franklin, near Baltimore; and, finally, settled at Belmont, near Leesburg, Va., where, on a run-down farm, she started a new boarding-school for girls which soon became noted for its high academic standards and strong religious and moral influence. In the interest of spiritual and ethical training, she wrote two books: *Studies for Bible Classes,* published some time before 1841, and *Popular Lectures on Ethics or Moral Obligation for the Use of Schools* (1837). The Belmont school soon developed into what was virtually a social settlement, including a little church built from money she had raised. The humble inhabitants of the region brought their problems to the leaders of the school, and sent their children to the free classes which it offered in primary subjects and agriculture. During most of Margaret Mercer's busy life she was handicapped by frail health, due to a tendency to tuberculosis; and from this disease she died in the home which she had developed in Virginia.

[Caspar Morris, *Memoir of Miss Margaret Mercer* (1848), which is a eulogy rather than a biography, contains many of her letters, and is the fullest account of her life; her *Popular Lectures on Ethics,* referred to above, throws light upon her ideals and intellectual ability; obituaries appeared in the *Md. Colonization Journal,* Nov. 1846, and the *Daily National Intelligencer* (Washington, D. C.), Sept. 22, 1846. See also J. M. Garnett, *Geneal. of the Mercer-Garnett Family of Essex County, Va.* (1910).] M. W. W.

MERCIER, CHARLES ALFRED (June 3, 1816–May 12, 1894), Creole author, was born in McDonogh, a surburb of New Orleans, the son of Jean Mercier, a native of Louisiana, and Éloise Le Duc, a Canadian. Intended for the law, he was sent to France at fourteen to study at the Collège Louis-le-Grand, where he read extensively both the classical and romantic writers. Not finding law to his taste, he turned to literature. In 1838 he returned to Louisiana for a short stay; then went to Boston to perfect his English; but soon crossed to Paris again, where he published *La Rose de Smyrne; L'Ermite du Niagara; Erato Labitte* (1840). The first is an Oriental tale in verse; the second a mystery play, telling the story of an Indian girl and her white lover; the third, a series of short poems redolent of Louisiana. After the appearance of this volume Mercier traveled far and wide in Europe. In Paris he composed a drama, *Hénoch Jédésias,* which was lost during the Revolution of 1848. A novel of the same name written at this time, a gruesome tale of miserliness, he later rewrote and published in New Orleans (*Comptes Rendus de l'Athénée Louisianais,* March 1892–November 1893). In 1848 he published in Paris *Biographie de Pierre Soulé,* a study of the career of his brother-in-law [*q.v.*]. On May 10, 1849, he married Virginie Vezian.

His interest in literature yielded somewhat to medicine, and in 1855 his dissertation appeared in Paris under the title, *De la fièvre typhoide dans ses rapports avec la phtisie aiguë.* He returned to New Orleans to practise his profession but in 1859 was again in Paris, then sojourned in Normandy for several years. Although he disapproved of slavery, when he saw in the American Civil War the approaching triumph of what he called Anglo-Saxon civilization, he broke his silence in *Du Pan-Latinisme—Nécessité d'une Alliance entre la France et la Confédération du Sud* (n.d.). After the war he returned to New Orleans to seek a livelihood in medicine. The rest of his life was divided between the arduous duties of a family physician and the profitless pursuit of literature. In 1873, *Le Fou de Palerme* was issued, with its gypsies and daggers. On Jan. 12, 1876, he founded the Athénée Louisianais, an organization devoted to the perpetuation of the French language in Louisiana, in whose *Comptes Rendus* he created a vehicle for his prose and verse. The following year he published *La Fille du Prêtre,* a novel in three parts attacking the celibacy of the priesthood. Of his numerous poems found in the *Comptes Rendus,* the best are "Tawanta" (November 1887) and "*Les Soleils*" (March 1889); of his travelogues, "*Excursion dans les Pyrénées*" (July–September 1889) is typical. Along scientific lines, "*Sommeil, Rêves, Somnambulisme*" (March 1889) best represents his thought; in philology, "*Étude sur la Langue Créole en Louisiane*" (July 1880). His best novelettes are *Lidia* (1887), a Parisian and Sicilian idyll, and *Émile des Ormiers* (1891), the pathetic tale of a Parisian painter. Mercier also wrote a long drama, *Fortunia* (published in *Comptes Rendus,* November 1888), whose purpose was to teach that fate rules the world. A long philosophical poem entitled *Réditus et Ascalaphos* (1890) described the efforts of the hero to attain studious solitude. A novel, *L'Habitation Saint-Ybars* (1881), was written to show that Louisiana masters were not all cruel; its local color is heightened by its French negro dialect. A second novel, *Johnelle* (1891), was a condemnation of infanticide. The French government rewarded the author's efforts with its *Palmes académiques* in 1885.

Mercier belonged to that generation of French Creoles of Louisiana who wished to be primarily Louisianians; to be identified as Latins rather than Anglo-Saxons, but as Americans in France. His was a cultivated mind. His talent was best at narration in prose; his style was clear and elegant; but he was too much inclined toward romanticism and he was prone to preach. He remains perhaps the leading French Creole writer of Louisiana; and the Athénée Louisianais, his proudest creation, is a monument to him. After a long illness, bravely borne, he died of cancer in 1894, survived by his widow and three children. Services were held in the Catholic church of Ste. Rose de Lima and interment was in Metairie Cemetery, New Orleans.

[Eulogy by Alcée Fortier, in *Comptes Rendus de l'Athénée Louisianais,* July 1894, offers a good pen picture. In *Louisiana Studies* (1894), Fortier reviewed thoroughly Mercier's literary effort. E. J. Fortier in *Mémoires, Premier Congrès de la Langue Française au Canada* (1914) summarized his father's appreciation. See also R. A. Caulfeild, *The French Literature of La.* (1929); E. L. Tinker, *Les Écrits de Langue Française en Louisiane au XIXe Siècle* (1932); Cyprien Dufour, *Esquisses Locales* (1847), the article on Mercier being translated in *La. Hist. Quart.,* Apr. 1932; Charles Testut, in *Portraits Littéraires de la Nouvelle-Orléans* (1850); Bussière Rouen, "*Les Poètes Louisianais,*" in *Comptes Rendus de l'Athénée Louisianais,* Apr. 1921; *The Louisiana Book* (1894), ed. by Thomas M'Caleb; *Lib. of Southern Lit.,* vol. VIII (1909); obituaries in

the *Times-Democrat* and *l'Abeille,* of New Orleans, May 13, 1894, and in the *Daily Picayune* the next day.]
L. C. D.

MERCUR, ULYSSES (Aug. 12, 1818–June 6, 1887), congressman, jurist, a son of Henry and Mary (Watts) Mercur, was of Austrian ancestry. His father, who was educated abroad, returned to America and settled in 1809 at Towanda, Bradford County, Pa., where Ulysses was born. His early life was spent on a farm and in the common-schools of the vicinity. When sixteen years old he became a clerk in his brother's country store. His father intended to establish him as a farmer, but because of the boy's desire to go to college, he sold his farm in order to finance his son's schooling. Ulysses entered Jefferson College at Canonsburg, Pa. (later merged with Washington College at Washington, Pa., to form Washington and Jefferson College), and graduated in 1842. He read law with Judge William McKennan and in 1843 began his career as a lawyer at Towanda. On Jan. 12, 1850, he married Sarah Simpson Davis. In 1856 he was a delegate to the Republican National Convention in Philadelphia. He had been a Democrat, but he favored free-soil doctrines and opposed the repeal of the Missouri Compromise. In 1860 he went so far as to serve as a presidential elector on the Lincoln and Hamlin ticket. He was associated with the group which was led by Galusha A. Grow and David Wilmot, and upon the election of Wilmot to the Senate in 1860 was appointed to fill his place as presiding judge of the thirteenth judicial district of Pennsylvania. At the election for the next full term as judge, he was chosen without opposition, and he served in this position till Mar. 4, 1865.

Mercur was elected to Congress in 1864 and served continuously as a member of the lower house from Mar. 4, 1865, to Dec. 2, 1872. In Congress he was particularly active as an advocate of the extreme measures in dealing with the Southern States, and as an opponent of luxury taxes, especially the taxes on tea and coffee. In connection with Reconstruction, he once said that if the Southern states "will not respect the stars they must feel the stripes of our glorious flag" (Heverly, *post,* II, p. 123). He resigned as a member of Congress to become associate justice of the supreme court of Pennsylvania. He held this position from 1872 till 1883, and from 1883 till his death in 1887 he was chief justice of the court. He died at Wallingford, Pa., and was buried at Towanda. Just as the distinctive policy of his group in Congress in connection with Reconstruction was reversed and discredited, so his conception of the judiciary was soon regarded as antiquated. As a judge, he was described by an associate as "conservative and cautious, looking to the old landmarks" (116 *Pa.,* xxiii). By the end of his career the old landmarks were rapidly being destroyed by the necessity of adjusting government and law to conditions alien to his generation.

[Sources include: *Biog. Dir. Am. Cong.* (1928); 116 *Pa. Reports,* xix-xxxi; *Legal Intelligencer* (Phila.), June 10, 17, 1887; *Pittsburgh Legal Jour.,* June 8, 15, 1887; H. C. Bradsby, *Hist. of Bradford County, Pa.* (1891); C. F. Heverly, *Pioneer and Patriot Families of Bradford County, Pa.,* vol. II (1915); the *Press* (Phila.), June 7, 1887. Mercur's judicial opinions are in 73–116 *Pa. Reports.*]
W. B—n.

MEREDITH, EDWIN THOMAS (Dec. 23, 1876–June 17, 1928), journalist, publisher, secretary of agriculture, was born on a farm near Avoca, Iowa, the son of Thomas Oliver and Minnie Minerva (Marsh) Meredith, who were of English and Welsh ancestry. He attended the country schools until he was sixteen years of age when he entered the business school of Highland Park College (later Des Moines University) at Des Moines, Iowa, meanwhile assisting his grandfather, "Uncle Tommy" Meredith, on the *Farmers' Tribune* which was a weekly county farm paper devoted to the cause of Populism. During the next two years he devoted all of his time to the paper, serving in the capacity of bookkeeper, conducting the correspondence, and selling advertising. On Jan. 8, 1896, when he was nineteen years of age, he was married to Edna C. Elliott of English and Irish ancestry. His grandfather gave him as a wedding present the *Farmers' Tribune* which he transformed into a non-partisan farm paper with a state-wide circulation. Tobacco and liquor advertisements were refused. Profiting in this venture, in 1902 he embarked upon a greater project, founding *Successful Farming,* and two years later he sold the *Farmers' Tribune* in order that he might devote his entire time and attention to the new publication. In 1922 he purchased the *Dairy Farmer,* and in the same year he founded *Fruit, Garden and Home,* which in August 1924 became *Better Homes and Gardens.* Meanwhile the publishing plant was greatly enlarged and the circulation of his periodicals increased.

Meredith created an innovation in the publication of farm papers which was generally adopted by other editors. In the first number of *Successful Farming* he announced that he would make good any loss to paid subscribers sustained by trusting any deliberate swindler advertising in his columns and that any such swindler would be publicly exposed. Soon afterward he made this guarantee more effective by the promise that if the purchaser of any article advertised in *Successful Farming* found it to be otherwise than represented, his money would be returned. In the days when patent medicine was the backbone of most advertising revenues, he closed the advertising columns of *Successful Farming* to it, thus making a noteworthy contribution to the cause of "truth in advertising." He devoted his publications to farming in the Middle West, and to better homes in all parts of the country.

Meredith first voted as a Republican but early became affiliated with the Democratic party. He was the party's candidate for United States senator in 1914 and for governor in 1916 but was defeated in both contests. In January 1920 he was appointed secretary of agriculture by President Wilson, succeeding David F. Houston and serving with distinction until the end of the Wilson administration. His name was mentioned as a possible presidential nominee of the Democratic party in the campaigns of 1924 and 1928. He was an ardent prohibitionist, a champion of "farm relief," tariff reform, adequate military preparedness, tax reform, and the World Court and the League of Nations. He held a number of positions on various boards and commissions. He was a member of the Board of Excess Profit Advisors appointed by Secretary McAdoo in 1917, a member of the Labor Commission to the British Isles appointed by President Wilson in 1918, a director of the Chicago Federal Reserve Bank from 1918 to 1920, and a director of the United States Chamber of Commerce from 1915 to 1919 and from 1923 to his death. He was interested in the boys' and girls' club movements and was an active and enthusiastic supporter of the 4-H Club. Independent, resourceful, and public-spirited, he was a born leader.

[*Who's Who in America*, 1928–29; *Ann. Report of the U. S. Dept. of Agric.*, 1920, and the *Yearbook* for the same year; *Better Homes and Gardens*, Aug. 1928; *Dairy Farmer*, Aug. 7, 1928; *Successful Farming*, Aug. 1928; *Independent*, Mar. 10, 1928; *Des Moines Reg.*, June 18, 1928; manuscript materials prepared by Edwin T. Meredith, Jr., and Peter Ainsworth.]

L. B. S—t.

MEREDITH, SAMUEL (1741–Feb. 10, 1817), financier, was born in Philadelphia, Pa., the son of Reese Meredith, a merchant, and Martha (Carpenter) Meredith. He attended private schools in Philadelphia and Chester, Pa., then entered his father's business. He took an active part in ante-Revolutionary affairs, was one of the signers of the non-importation resolutions adopted in Philadelphia on Nov. 7, 1765, and attended, as a deputy from Philadelphia, the Provincial Convention held in that city from the 23rd to the 28th of January, 1775. During the war he served as a major and then as lieutenant-colonel of the 3rd Battalion of Associators, known as the Silk Stocking Company. He distinguished himself in the battles of Trenton and Princeton and on Apr. 5, 1777, was promoted to brigadier-general of Pennsylvania militia for gallant services in the battles of Brandywine and Germantown. He resigned from the army Jan. 9, 1778, and resumed his business connections. He served three terms in the Pennsylvania Colonial Assembly (1778–79, 1781–83) and on Nov. 26, 1786, was elected to the Congress of the Confederation, serving until 1788. In August of the following year he was appointed surveyor of the Port of Philadelphia. He resigned this post to accept an appointment, urged upon him by George Washington, as treasurer of the United States, the first appointed under the Constitution.

Meredith entered upon his new duties Sept. 11, 1789, at a time when the treasury needed conservative management. He lent the government more than a hundred thousand dollars which it was unable to repay upon his retirement from office. He remained in office until Oct. 31, 1801, when, owing to the state of his health and finances, he retired. With his brother-in-law, George Clymer [*q.v.*], he had purchased large amounts of wild lands in western Virginia, eastern Kentucky, Delaware and Sullivan counties, N. Y., and in all the northeastern counties of Pennsylvania. In 1796 he began to make improvements at a place in the township of Mount Pleasant, Pa., which he afterward named Belmont. In 1802 he moved to this place and devoted the last years of his life to the management of his land, dying in the manor house of the estate. He had married, on May 19, 1772, Margaret Cadwalader of Philadelphia, daughter of Dr. Thomas Cadwalader [*q.v.*]. They had seven children.

[*Biog. Dir. Am. Cong.* (1928); Chas. Lanman, *Biog. Annals of the Civil Gov't. of the U. S., During its First Century* (1876); C. P. Keith, *Provincial Councillors of Pa.* (1883); S. M. M. Graham, *A Short Hist. of the Three Merediths* (n.d.); Wharton Dickenson, "Brig.-Gen. Samuel Meredith," *Mag. of Am. Hist.*, Sept. 1879; F. W. Leach, "Old Phila. Families," the *North American* (Phila.), Feb. 4, 1912; Samuel Whaley, *Hist. of the Township of Mount Pleasant, Wayne County, Pa.* (1856); *Poulson's Am. Daily Advertiser*, Feb. 22, 1817.]

J. H. F.

MEREDITH, WILLIAM MORRIS (June 8, 1799–Aug. 17, 1873), Pennsylvania lawyer and official, secretary of the treasury, was born in Philadelphia, Pa., the son of William Meredith and Gertrude Gouverneur Ogden and the grandson of Jonathan Meredith who emigrated from Wales about 1755. His father was a prominent lawyer and bank president who so educated his precocious son that he was able to graduate from the University of Pennsylvania at the age of thirteen. Five years later, in December 1817, he was admitted to the bar and then was forced to pay the penalty of his rapid advance. He had to wait a long time for a successful practice. Finally he became associated with John Sergeant and Horace Binney [*qq.v.*] in the famous Girard will case and thereafter his fame grew until he became one of the leaders of the Philadlphia bar. While waiting for legal opportunity, he entered politics. He served in the legislature, 1824–28, and from 1834 to 1849 was president of the select council of Philadelphia. When the Whig party was formed he became a member and allied himself with the faction opposed to Thaddeus Stevens and to the anti-Masonic element. In the state constitutional convention of 1837 he attracted considerable attention by a vigorous attack upon Stevens. On June 17, 1834, he married Catherine, daughter of Michael Keppele.

When the Whigs triumphed in 1840, Harrison appointed Meredith (Mar. 15, 1841), United States attorney for the eastern district of Pennsylvania, an office which he held only a year. In 1849 he was defeated for the United States Senate by a fellow Whig, James Cooper, but shortly thereafter his greatest honor came to him. President-Elect Taylor wished a Pennsylvanian for his cabinet, a wish complicated by a factional war in the party. In March 1849 he chose Meredith, a moderate Whig, for his secretary of the treasury, in spite of the fact that the Whig congressmen recommended Andrew Stewart. In this office Meredith's principal achievement was his annual report in which he set forth an elaborate argument for a protective tariff (*Senate Executive Document 2,* 31 Cong., 1 Sess.). He shared Taylor's disapproval of the compromise measures of 1850 and when the President died joined his colleagues in retiring (July 1850).

When the opponents of the Democratic organization in Pennsylvania formed the Opposition or People's party in the days before the Civil War, Meredith joined the new group. He acted as a delegate to the Peace Convention of 1861 and Governor Curtin made him attorney-general of the state, 1861–67. When the Union League Club formed in Philadelphia, he became its first president. He was appointed one of the counsel of the United States in the *Alabama* claims case, but, after aiding in the preparation of the briefs, retired, not wishing to go to Geneva. His last service was as president of the state constitutional convention (November 1872–June 1873) when, in spite of ill health, he remained in this trying position till a few weeks before his death. He died in Philadelphia.

[The available materials on Meredith's life are meager. A sketch of himself and his family by Frank W. Leach in his series on "Old Philadelphia Families" appeared in the Philadelphia *North American,* Feb. 4, 1912. An obituary notice and the proceedings of the Philadelphia bar are found in *Ibid.,* Aug. 18, 21, 1873. See also: J. T. Scharf and Thompson Westcott, *Hist. of Philadelphia* (1884), vols. I and II; *Proc. and Debates of the Convention of . . . Pa. to Propose Amendments to the Const. . . . 1837,* vol. II (1837), pp. 76 ff.; *Proc. of the Const. Convention and Obit. Addresses on the Occasion of the Death of Hon. Wm. M. Meredith* (1873); and H. R. Mueller, *The Whig Party in Pa.* (1922). A few of Meredith's letters are in the collections of the Historical Society of Pennsylvania.]

R. F. N.

MERGENTHALER, OTTMAR (May 11, 1854–Oct. 28, 1899), inventor of the linotype, was born in Hachtel, Germany, the son of Johann George and Rosina (Ackermann) Mergenthaler. He came from a family of teachers and it was expected that he would follow the family calling. After an ordinary grade-school education, however, he showed a decided leaning toward mechanics and accordingly, at the age of fourteen, began an apprenticeship in watch and clock-making under the brother of his stepmother at Bietigheim, Württemberg. Here he applied himself diligently for four years, meanwhile attending night and Sunday schools. Upon the completion of his apprenticeship he sailed for the United States to avoid being drafted into the army. Landing in Baltimore, Oct. 26, 1872, he proceeded to Washington, D. C., where he began work immediately in the scientific instrument shop of August Hahl, son of his former master.

For the next four years Mergenthaler was wholly engrossed in the interesting work of instrument making, especially for the United States Signal Service. His ingenuity, skill, and ability to grasp quickly an inventor's ideas were soon recognized, and his services were much sought after. When Hahl transferred his business to Baltimore in 1876 Mergenthaler went with him and shortly thereafter they were called upon to correct defects in the model of a newly devised writing machine made by Charles Moore of West Virginia. The purpose of the machine was to produce print by typewriting and to multiply the work by the lithographic process. Mergenthaler soon corrected the defects, whereupon James O. Clephane of Washington, who was the originator of the idea, ordered the construction of a full-sized machine. This was completed in 1877 but could never be made to yield satisfactory results. Mergenthaler, however, now definitely launched upon the devising of a machine to eliminate type-setting, enthusiastically took hold of Clephane's next suggestion: a machine which would substitute stereotyping for lithography. Such a machine, incorporating the rotary stereotypic system, was completed late in 1878, but again many troubles were experienced, particularly in obtaining clean type from the papier-maché. After working during most of the year 1879 to correct the difficulties, Mergenthaler and Hahl abandoned the project.

During the next four years they continued with general instrument making, Mergenthaler becoming a partner in the establishment in 1880 and taking up permament residence in Baltimore. He never fully dismissed the idea of a type-setting machine, however, and in spare moments devised a plan calling for an invariable spacing between the lines and the use of regular type as a means of getting perfect impressions into the matrix. Shortly after opening his own shop in Baltimore on Jan. 1, 1883, he communicated this new idea to Clephane and his associates and received an order to proceed with the construction of a machine possessing these features. It was completed in the fall of 1883 and was satisfactory except for the paper matrix. Shortly afterward Mergenthaler hit upon the plan of stamping matrices into type bars and casting type metal into them in the same machine. From this idea the linotype was developed. By July 1884 the first direct-casting linotype was completed. It worked with entire success, but had no provision for automatic justification of the line. On Aug. 26, 1884, Mergenthaler received his first patent on the new machine and shortly thereafter Clephane and his associates organized the National Typographic Company of West Virginia for its manufacture. Not content with his product, Mergenthaler proceeded in his enthusiastic way to improve that which seemed already perfect, and by February 1885 a second machine with automatic justification was completed. On July 3, 1886, the first of twelve machines made by the company for the *New York Tribune* was used to compose a part of that day's issue of the paper. Before all the machines had been delivered, Mergenthaler had devised nine patented improvements, including the single or independent matrix, all of which were incorporated in the last of the twelve. Meanwhile the control of the National Typographic Company and its subsidiary Mergenthaler Printing Company, organized in 1885, passed into the hands of a group of newspaper owners and an entire change in policy for the conduct of the business was put into effect. This caused a break between the board of directors and Mergenthaler, resulting in his resignation in 1888. His pride and passion was the linotype, however, and notwithstanding the rupture with the company he continued to add to its value by devising more than fifty patented improvements. Constant application and never ending anxiety undermined his health, and he succumbed to tuberculosis after a desperate fight of five years. Some years before his death he was awarded a medal by Cooper Union, New York, for his great invention, and the Franklin Institute, Philadelphia, awarded him the John Scott medal and the Elliott Cresson medal. He commenced an autobiography which he was unable to complete because of failing health. Mergenthaler was naturalized in Baltimore, Oct. 9, 1878, and was married there on Sept. 11, 1881, to Emma Frederica Lachenmayer. At the time of his death, in Baltimore, he was survived by his widow and four children.

[*Biog. of Ottmar Mergenthaler and Hist. of the Linotype* (1898); Waldemar Kaempffert, *A Popular Hist. of Am. Invention* (1924); George Iles, *Leading Am. Inventors* (1912); E. W. Byrn, *The Progress of Invention in the Nineteenth Century* (1900); *Ottmar Mergenthaler, 1854–1929, Der Moderne Buchdrucker* (Berlin, 1929); *The Big Scheme of Simple Operation* (Mergenthaler Linotype Co., Brooklyn, N. Y., 1923); the *Sun* (Baltimore), Oct. 16, 30, 1899; Patent Office records; correspondence with family.]
C. W. M.

MERGLER, MARIE JOSEPHA (May 18, 1851–May 17, 1901), physician, was born in Mainstockheim, Bavaria, youngest of the three children of Dr. Francis R. and Henriette (von Ritterhausen) Mergler. Her father brought his family to America when Marie was two years of age, settling in Illinois, where he practised until his death. At the age of seventeen Marie graduated from Cook County Normal School and three years later from the State Normal School at Oswego, N. Y., having completed a classical course. For four years she taught in Englewood High School, and then entered the Woman's Medical College at Chicago, graduating as valedictorian of her class in 1879. She took the examinations for interne in Cook County Hospital and stood second, but was barred from service on grounds of sex. Feeling the need of further experience, she studied for a year (1880) in Zurich, Switzerland, specializing in pathology and clinical medicine. In 1881 she took up the practice of medicine in Chicago. She was immediately made adjunct professor of gynecology in the Woman's Medical College under Prof. William Heath Byford [*q.v.*] and served in that capacity until 1890, when she was made professor of gynecology to fill the vacancy left by his death. She acted as secretary of the faculty of the Woman's Medical College from 1881 to 1892, when it became the Northwestern University Woman's Medical School, then continued as secretary until 1899, when she was made dean. This position she held until her death two years later. In 1882 she was appointed attending physician on the staff of the Cook County Hospital, being the second woman to receive such an appointment; in 1886 she became attending surgeon to the Woman's Hospital of Chicago, in 1890 attending gynecologist to Wesley Memorial Hospital, and in 1895–97 she was head physician and surgeon at the Women's and Children's Hospital of Chicago. From 1895 to 1901 she was also professor of gynecology in the Post-Graduate Medical School of Northwestern University. Her activities during the last year of her life were greatly curtailed on account of her suffering from pernicious anemia, of which she died in Los Angeles, Cal., at the age of fifty.

Marie J. Mergler's professional life of only a score of years was of an intense and highly specialized character. Few medical men or women attained such proficiency or occupied positions of such responsibility and importance as early in life as did she. She was notable among women operators for her success in abdominal surgery; she contributed a number of papers to medical journals, wrote a student's classbook: *A Guide to the Study of Gynecology* (1891), and was joint author with Charles W. Earle of "Diseases of the New Born" in *An American Textbook of Obstetrics* (1895), by J. C. Cameron and others. An earnest and able teacher, she left a distinct impression upon her pupils. By her will she bequeathed a generous sum to the Woman's Hospital and founded a medical scholarship in the University of Chicago.

[H. A. Kelly and W. L. Burrage, *Am. Medic. Biogs.* (1920), in which, strangely, the name is misspelled Meigler throughout the article; *Northwestern Univ., A Hist., 1855–1905* (1905), vol. IV; *Woman's Medical School Northwestern Univ.* (*Woman's Medical Coll. of Chicago*), *the Institution and Its Founders* (1896); *Jour. Am. Medic. Asso.*, May 25, 1901; *Chicago Medic. Recorder*, July 1901; *Revue de Chirurgie* (Paris), July 1901; *Woman's Jour.* (Boston), June 15, 1901; *Chicago Tribune*, May 22, 1901; *N. Y. Tribune*, June 13, 1901.]

B. V–H.

MERRIAM, AUGUSTUS CHAPMAN (May 30, 1843–Jan. 19, 1895), philologist and archeologist, the youngest of thirteen children of Ela and Lydia (Sheldon) Merriam, was born at "Locust Grove," in Leyden, Lewis County, N. Y. His ancestor, Joseph Merriam, had come to Massachusetts from Kent, England, in 1638, settling near Concord; his grandfather, Judge Nathaniel Merriam, had moved from Meriden, Conn., to Leyden, N. Y., shortly after 1800. The boy was prepared for college at the Columbia Grammar School, and both there and in Columbia College, to which he was admitted in 1862, had the advantage of the stimulating teaching of Dr. Charles Anthon [*q.v.*]. He was graduated at the head of his class in 1866, and after some months spent in Topeka, Kan., returned to New York City to teach in the Columbia Grammar School. In 1868 he was appointed tutor of Greek and Latin in Columbia College, and for eight years gave instruction in both languages. Beginning with 1876, however, he was able to devote all his energies to Greek, and in 1880 was advanced to the post of adjunct professor of the Greek language and literature. His notable edition of *The Phaeacian Episode of the Odyssey,* published in that year, revealed at once his insight into Homer, the rare charm of his style, and his appreciation of the illuminating contribution to the enjoyment of great poetry which can be made by art and archeology. In fact, from this time on he was more and more captivated by research in archeology and epigraphy, and his published work was such as to gain for him before his death a high international reputation in these fields.

In 1883 he wrote a masterly monograph, *The Greek and Latin Inscriptions on the Obelisk-Crab in the Metropolitan Museum, N. Y.* (published 1884), in which, by establishing a new date, he succeeded in bringing for the first time every detail of the inscriptions into accord with already known history. He was then drawn on, by his inability to accept Mommsen's ascription of the temple in front of which this obelisk had formerly stood, to write a brilliant paper on "The Caesareum and the Worship of Augustus at Alexandria" (*Transactions of the American Philological Association 1883,* vol. XIV, 1884, pp. 5–35). The presence of solid scholarship and the absence from his demeanor of everything that could suggest self-adulation greatly endeared him to his associates and helped to make him president of the American Philological Association for the year 1886–87. His presidential address dealt with the inscriptions published during that year from Naucratis, Crete, Epidaurus, Athens, and Peiraieus (*American Journal of Archaeology,* July–December 1887, pp. 303–21), but he was unable to read it in person, having already sailed for Greece (accompanied by his wife, Louise Oley, whom he had married July 23, 1869) to assume the directorship of the American School of Classical Studies at Athens. There, during the year 1887–88, he conducted successful excavations at Sicyon and at Dionyso, definitely proving the latter place to be the site of the deme Icaria, the birthplace of Thespis, founder of Greek tragedy (*Seventh Annual Report of the Managing Committee of the American School of Classical Studies at Athens, 1887–88,* 1889, pp. 39–98). His distinctive power had by this time been so strikingly shown that in 1890 he was appointed to the newly created chair of Greek archeology and epigraphy at Columbia. From 1888 to 1894 he was chairman of the committee on publication of the School at Athens, and from 1891 to 1894 was president of the New York Society of the Archaeological Institute of America.

Merriam was by nature a productive scholar. In addition to the titles already cited the following works of his deserve especial mention: "A Greek Tunnel of the Sixth Century B.C." (*School of Mines Quarterly,* March 1885); *The Sixth and Seventh Books of Herodotus* (1885), an admirable textbook; "Aesculapia as Revealed by Inscriptions" (*Gaillard's Medical Journal,* May 1885), a most interesting description of the sanctuaries of Aesculapius at Athens and Epidaurus and of the cures believed to have been wrought there by the god; "Law Code of the Kretan Gortyna; Text, Translation, Commentary" (*American Journal of Archaeology,* October 1885, January–March 1886), an interpretation of permanent value, written shortly after the discovery in 1884 by Halbherr and Fabricius of that remarkably humane code; "Telegraphing among the Ancients" (*Papers of the Archaeological Institute of America, Classical Series,* vol. III, no. 1, 1890). His last articles were three papers contributed to *Classical Studies in Honour of Henry Drisler* (1894). In his classroom, through the play of a constructive and delightful imagination, the past lived again, and the beauty and music inherent in great poetry and prose were engagingly made clear. Death came to him in the fulness of his powers, while he was in Athens on sabbatical leave. A severe cold developed into pneumonia, and the end came swiftly. He was buried in his beloved "City of the Violet Crown," where a beautiful monument marks his grave.

[For partial lists of Merriam's writings consult the Index to *Am. Jour. Archaeol.,* vols. I–XI, 1885–96, and to *Trans. and Proc. Am. Philological Asso.,* vols. I–XX, 1869–89. For his life and character consult the account of the memorial meeting at Columbia in the *Univ. Bull.,* Mar. 1895; also the obituary by Dr. C. H. Young, a favorite pupil, in *Am. Jour. Archaeol.,* Apr.–June 1895. See also C. H. Pope, *Merriam Geneal. in England and America* (1906); *N. Y. Tribune,* Jan. 21, 1895. Some additional details are on file in the Columbiana Collection at the University.]

N. G. M.

MERRIAM, CHARLES (Nov. 31, 1806–July 9, 1887), publisher, descended from Joseph Merriam who came to America in 1638, settling near Concord, Mass., was born at West Brookfield, Mass., the second of nine children of Dan and Thirza (Clapp) Merriam. In 1797 his father and uncle founded a newspaper in that village and under the firm name of E. Merriam & Company continued until 1823 to do miscellaneous printing and publishing. Among their books were several editions of William Perry's *Royal Standard English Dictionary* (1801, 1806, 1809), and thus the Merriam name was associated with the publication of dictionaries from an early date. During his boyhood Charles attended district school and worked on his father's farm. At the age of fourteen he was apprenticed to a printer in Hartford, Conn., where he remained until the death of his father in 1823. After completing his apprenticeship in the shop now conducted by his uncle and his elder brother, George (Jan. 19, 1803–June 22, 1880), he spent a year in the academies at Monson and Hadley, taught school through the next winter, worked in Philadelphia for a few months, and then for several years in Boston as journeyman and foreman in the well-known printing shop of T. R. Marvin. On the recepit of an invitation from Rev. Samuel Osgood to come to Springfield and start a newspaper, he left Boston, and with his brother George went to Springfield to look over the prospects. The time did not seem to be propitious for a newspaper, but the two brothers with another relative established a printing house and bookshop in 1831, which in 1832 became G. & C. Merriam. A third brother, Homer, became a member of the firm in 1856.

Although all three brothers connected with the firm as partners were exceptionally capable, Charles appears to have had the greatest literary bent. In the early days he was in charge of the bookstore, and in later years concerned himself with the publishing end of the work, even trying his hand at writing verse. The firm was successful from the start, but its great fortune came after the death of Noah Webster [*q.v.*] in 1843, when it purchased from J. S. & C. Adams of Amherst the unsold copies of Webster's two-volume *American Dictionary of the English Language* and the right to publish it in the future. Securing the editorial services of Dr. Chauncey Allen Goodrich [*q.v.*] of Yale, Webster's son-in-law, the Merriams had the book revised along more conservative lines, printed it in one volume, and reduced the price to six dollars. Extensive advertising and large sales of the Unabridged helped promote the sales of the various abridged editions and the firm quickly bought up the rights of these also. Charles Merriam himself read the complete proof of one edition. The firm also published school books, law books, Bibles, and other volumes, but the business connected with the dictionary became so great that they eventually withdrew from their bookstore and general printing. Charles retired from active participation in the firm at the age of seventy and sold his interest in the business in 1877. Although his main interest was in the publishing venture, he was also a director of the Springfield Fire and Marine Insurance Company and of the old Springfield Bank. He was a man of intense and unremitting industry, of unassuming demeanor, and of simple and scholarly tastes. An ardent and strictly orthodox Congregationalist, he taught a Bible class for many years and was one of the founders in 1842 of the South Church of Springfield. He gave liberally to the church and church institutions, particularly to home and foreign missions. For his native town of West Brookfield he built a public library and endowed it; in the Springfield library he took a lively interest, serving as one of the first members of the association and using his best efforts to establish a free system. When the government of the city of Springfield was organized in 1852, he was a member of the Common Council. He was married twice: on Aug. 11, 1835, to Sophia Eleanor Warriner, who died Apr. 26, 1858; and on May 8, 1860, at Detroit, Mich., to Rachel White (Capen) Gray, a widow. By his first marriage he had three daughters and two sons, one of whom died in infancy; by his second marriage he had one daughter.

[*Springfield Republican*, Nov. 13, 1880, July 10, 1887; *Springfield Daily Union*, July 9, 1887; material on the Merriams in the Conn. Valley Hist. Soc. library at Springfield, particularly a ninety-page manuscript, "Memorial of Charles Merriam" (1892), by Mrs. Rachel Merriam; *Vital Records of Brookfield, Mass.* (1909); C. H. Pope, *Merriam Geneal.* (1906); J. C. Derby, *Fifty Years Among Authors, Books, and Publishers* (1884); *100th Anniversary of the Establishment of G. and C. Merriam Company, Springfield, Mass., 1831–1931* (n.d.); *Biog. Review . . . of Hampden County, Mass.* (1895); Moses King, *King's Handbook of Springfield, Mass.* (1884).] H. U. F.

MERRIAM, HENRY CLAY (Nov. 13, 1837–Nov. 18, 1912), soldier, was a descendant of Joseph Merriam of Kent, England, who came to Concord, Mass., in 1638. He was born at Houlton, Me., the son of Lewis and Mary Ann (Foss) Merriam, and received his early education at Houlton Academy and Colby College, where his law studies were interrupted by the outbreak of the Civil War. Colby College granted him the degree of B.A. in 1864, however, and that of M.A. in 1867.

He left college in 1862 to become captain in the 20th Maine Volunteers, and participated in the battle of Antietam, where he was brevetted lieutenant-colonel for gallantry, and in the battles of Shepherdstown and Fredericksburg. As captain in the 80th United States Colored Infantry, he led in the assault on Port Hudson, La., May 27, 1863, and was promoted lieutenant-colonel. At Fort Blakely, Apr. 9, 1865, he again led in the assault on the enemy's works, an attack resulting in the capture of some 6,000 prisoners. For this achievement, he was awarded the Congressional Medal of Honor and the brevet of colonel in both the Regular and Volunteer services. Mustered out of the military service Oct. 24, 1865, he resumed the study of law until recommissioned a major in the Regular Army, July 28, 1866. Subsequently, he commanded Fort McIntosh, Tex., during prolonged border troubles. On Apr. 10, 1876, he assumed responsibility for firing upon Mexican federal forces in reprisal for outrages committed against American citizens; and on Aug. 22, crossing the Rio Grande, he rescued the American commercial agent, held prisoner by revolutionists. He was promoted lieutenant-colonel, 2nd Infantry, June 10, 1876, and took part in the Nez Percé Indian campaign of the year following, receiving high commendation from Generals Oliver O. Howard and Nelson A. Miles [*qq.v.*] and from the territorial authorities of Idaho and Washington. He was promoted colonel, 7th Infantry, July 10, 1885. During the Sioux Indian War of 1890–91, he was instrumental in disarming some three hundred of Sitting Bull's followers. He was promoted brigadier-general, Regular Army, on June 30, 1897. Appointed major-general of volunteers May 4, 1898, after the outbreak of the war with Spain, he had charge of organizing and equipping the Philippines Expeditionary Force. The following year, while in command of the Department of Colorado, he was in charge of the troops sent at the request of the Idaho authorities to help suppress the labor riots at the Coeur d'Alène lead mines. Here he acted with vigor and good judgment; martial law was declared and order was restored. A subsequent investigation, ordered by the president to satisfy public opinion aroused by the labor agitators, resulted in Merriam's conduct being officially approved.

On Nov. 13, 1901, he was placed on the retired list by reason of age, but by Act of Congress in February 1903 he was advanced to the grade of major-general. He died at his home in Portland, Me., after an illness of nearly two years, and was interred at Arlington with high military honors. He was the inventor of a successful pack for infantry soldiers which bore his name, and for which he was awarded a gold medal by the French Academy of Inventors. He was twice married: on Jan. 16, 1866, to Lucy J. Getchell, who was drowned with an infant daughter, in a cloudburst at Staked Plains, Tex., Apr. 24, 1870; and on June 4, 1874, to Una Macpherson-Macneil of Kingston, Jamaica, who survived him, together with three sons and two daughters.

[*Official Army Register*, 1903; F. B. Heitman, *Hist. Reg. and Dict., U. S. Army* (1903), vol. I; *Army and Navy Jour.*, Nov. 23, 1912; *N. Y. Herald, N. Y. Times*, Nov. 19, 1912; *Report to the Gov. of Idaho on the Insurrection in Shoshone County, Idaho, by Samuel H. Hayes, Atty. Gen.*, June 30, 1900; *Sen. Doc. No. 142*, 56 Cong., 1 Sess.; C. H. Pope, *Merriam Geneal.* (1906); information as to certain facts from a son, Col. Henry M. Merriam, U. S. A., retired.] C. D. R.

MERRIAM, WILLIAM RUSH (July 26, 1849–Feb. 18, 1931), banker, politician, and director of the Twelfth Census, was born at Wadham's Mills, N. Y., the son of John Lafayette and Mahala Kimpton (De Lano) Merriam. His father was descended from Joseph Merriam who came to Massachusetts in 1638 and settled near Concord. In 1861 the family moved to St. Paul, Minn., where the elder Merriam became prominent in the business and civic life of the frontier city and of the state. Young Merriam was sent, at the age of fifteen, to Racine College, Wisconsin, where he remained until 1871, completing both preparatory and college courses and becoming valedictorian of his class.

After an apprenticeship as clerk in the First National Bank of St. Paul, in 1871 he was made cashier of the newly organized Merchants' National Bank, and subsequently became vice-president (1880) and president (1884). Banking and other business activities, and even a rather lively participation in various civic and community enterprises, did not satisfy him, however; he cherished definite political ambitions. In 1883 he was elected as a Republican to the state legislature and had a considerable part in bringing about the defeat of the veteran Senator Windom for reëlection and the selection of Dwight M. Sabin for his place. In 1886 he was again elected from his district and was made speaker of the House, where his "good-nature, gracious manners and attractive personality" (Folwell, *post*, III, 184) stood him in good stead and made him especially *persona grata* to the rural members of the legislature. This fact contributed to his election as vice-president (1887) and president (1888) of the State Agricultural Society, honors which in turn had a bearing on his later political career.

In 1888 Merriam sought the gubernatorial nomination from the Republican convention and secured it despite the unwritten rule that an incumbent had an almost vested right to renomination. Gov. A R. McGill's stand for high license and the fear of some Republicans that a strong Democratic candidate with the backing of liquor interests stood a chance of winning the election undoubtedly contributed to Merriam's choice. But the episode caused resentment which had after results. The election gave Merriam a substantial majority. In 1890 he was renominated practically without opposition and was elected by a small plurality over Democratic and Farmers' Alliance candidates. Issues of paramount significance were lacking during his governorship, although it was then that Minnesota adopted the Australian ballot, refunded the state debt, and made provision for leasing iron-ore lands which formed a part of the school fund.

As his term drew to an end Merriam aspired to the United States Senate. His friends worked up a sentiment which was calculated to throw the nomination by the Republican caucus to him instead of to Cushman K. Davis [*q.v.*], the incumbent; their zeal diminished, however, and Davis was nominated, although subsequent investigation showed that, if they had stood firm, they probably would have carried their plan through (C. B. Cheney in *Minneapolis Journal*, Aug. 13, 1922). Davis was elected by a majority of one vote in the legislature; he evidently looked upon Merriam as the principal cause of opposition and his resentment was probably responsible later for McKinley's failure to designate Merriam to a diplomatic post, a reward that might have been expected from Merriam's part in the campaign of 1896, both as a delegate to the Republican National Convention and as a worker in the state canvass.

Davis' animosity did not, however, block McKinley's selection of Merriam as director of the Twelfth Census in 1899. To this new position Merriam took the organizing ability, and the willingness to delegate authority to competent persons which had served him in his business career. According to S. N. D. North, his successor as director, the Twelfth Census "was not only the best census ever compiled in the United States, from the point of view of accuracy and comprehensiveness, but it was also the most economical, tested on the per capita basis, and what is even more important, the most expeditious in publication of the results" (Baker, *post*, p. 319). North also gave Merriam credit for securing the establishment of the permanent Bureau of the Census (*Ibid.*, p. 320).

In 1903 Merriam resigned his position as director and from then to the end of his life sought no further political preferment. He continued to reside in Washington, being active in business; for some years he was president of the Shenandoah Coal and Iron Company and of the Liberty Furnace Company; later he was president of the Tabulating Machine Company. The last years of his life were spent in retirement and he died at Fort Sewall, Fla. On Oct. 2, 1873, he married Laura E. Hancock, niece of Gen. Winfield Scott Hancock [*q.v.*], and to them were born five children.

[J. H. Baker, "Lives of the Governors of Minnesota," *Minn. Hist. Soc. Colls.*, vol. XIII (1908); W. W. Folwell, *A Hist. of Minn.*, vol. III (1926); *N. Y. Times*, Feb. 19, 1931; *St. Paul Pioneer-Press*, Feb. 19, 1931; *Minneapolis Jour.*, Aug. 13, 1922; *Western Mag.*, Sept. 1919; *Who's Who in America*, 1918–19; C. H. Pope, *Merriam Geneal. in England and America* (1906).] L. B. S—e.

MERRICK, EDWIN THOMAS (July 9, 1808–Jan. 12, 1897), jurist, was born in Wilbraham, Mass., the eldest son of Thomas and Ann (Brewer) Merrick and a descendant of Thomas Merrick who emigrated from Wales in 1636 and settled later in Springfield. On his mother's side he was of English descent. Left fatherless while yet a mere boy, he was brought up by his uncle, Samuel Brewer of Springfield, Mass. At the age of nineteen he entered Wesleyan Academy at Wilbraham and graduated in 1832. While in the academy he began the study of law in the office of William Knight, and after his graduation he went to New Lisbon, Ohio, where he completed his law studies in the office of his uncle, Alonzo L. Brewer. He was admitted to the bar of Ohio in 1833 and began to practise at Carrollton. A year later he took charge of his uncle's business at New Lisbon and formed a partnership with William E. Russell. In 1838 he formed a partnership with James H. Muse to practise law in Louisiana and opened an office in Clinton under the firm name of Muse & Merrick. Inasmuch as the civil law instead of common law was the basis of Louisiana jurisprudence, Merrick was obliged to make special preparation for admission to the bar. He is said to have passed a very brilliant examination and was admitted to the bar in 1839. With his knowledge of both categories of the law he soon acquired a large practice at Clinton and was retained in nearly all the important litigation in that part of the state. In 1854 he was elected judge of the seventh judicial district of Louisiana which included East and West Feliciana parishes. He was frequently called upon to act in adjoining districts. In 1855 he was elected chief justice of Louisiana for a term of eight years on the Whig ticket. One of his most famous decisions (1856) was that in *Succession of Daniel Clark* (11 *Louisiana Reports*, 124), involving the legitimacy of Myra Clark Gaines, the plaintiff.

When Louisiana withdrew from the Union, although Merrick was opposed to secession, he remained loyal to her cause. After the capture of New Orleans by the Federals in 1862, he moved to the western part of the state and held court at Opelousas and Shreveport. He was reelected chief justice in 1863 but was removed from office at the close of the war under the Reconstruction régime. He returned to New Orleans, but as he declined to take the "iron-clad oath," he was debarred from the practice of law. He was finally pardoned for giving aid and comfort to the Confederacy and was allowed to resume the practice of law and also to recover his home in New Orleans and his plantation in West Feliciana which had been taken from him during the war. He was active in carrying appeals to the United States Supreme Court from Louisiana in cases arising out of the system of administration in the state during the Reconstruction period, and was very successful in these appeals. In later years he associated his second son Edwin Thomas Merrick, Jr., with him, under the name of Merrick & Merrick. He had married, Dec. 3, 1840, Caroline E. Thomas, of Jackson, La. He died at his home in New Orleans. He was the author of several legal treatises, notably *The Laws of Louisiana and their Sources* (1871).

[Alcée Fortier, *Louisiana* (1909), vol. II; G. B. Merrick, *Geneal. of the Merrick-Mirick-Myrick Family of Mass., 1636–1902* (1902); biographical sketch and editorial in the *Times-Democrat* (New Orleans), Jan. 13, 1897; information as to certain facts from Edwin Thomas Merrick, Jr., New Orleans, La.]

E. M. V.

MERRICK, FREDERICK (Jan. 29, 1810–Mar. 5, 1894), Methodist Episcopal clergyman and educator, was born on the ancestral farm in Wilbraham, Mass. His father, Noah, a first cousin of Pliny Merrick [*q.v.*] was in the fifth generation from Thomas Merrick who came to Massachusetts from Wales in 1636, settling first in Roxbury and then in Springfield; his mother was Statira Hays, of Hartford, Conn. His parents were pious Congregationalists, his grandfather having been a minister of that communion, but the novelty and vitality of the Methodist meetings attracted the boy, who was of an introspective turn. From his fifteenth year he worked as a clerk in a store in Springfield, Mass., becoming a partner before he was twenty. In 1829, after a joyous and transforming spiritual experience he joined the Methodist Society. Feeling called to be a minister, he attended the Wesleyan Academy in Wilbraham, and entered Wesleyan University at Middletown, Conn. He left college (1834) to teach in Amenia Seminary (N. Y.), a Methodist secondary school of which he was principal until 1838, when he was elected professor of natural science in Ohio University at Athens. While in college he had been licensed as an exhorter and local preacher, and at Amenia he had married, in 1836, Sarah Fidelia Griswold of Suffolk, Conn.

At Athens he achieved marked influence and popularity and was much sought as a teacher by the Methodist colleges springing up in what was then the West. In 1841 he joined Ohio Conference on trial and in 1842–43 was pastor at Marietta. He was ordained elder in 1843. The churches of the state had embarked on the ambitious enterprise of founding a college at Delaware, and in that year Merrick became one of its financial agents. The Ohio Wesleyan University then consisted of a sulphur spring and the buildings and grounds of a bankrupt sanitarium, without faculty, students, or endowment. From that year until his death he was identified with the school, coming to be venerated as one of its "Great Five" founders. The college opened its doors in 1844 and in 1845 he began to teach natural science there, later (1851) transferring to the chair of moral philosophy. For a brief period he was acting president, and for forty years he was auditor, financial watchdog, and emergency man in several crises. Chapel, library, laboratories, museums, endowments, were largely the fruit of his personal influence and untiring zeal. Merrick Hall was named for him. From 1860 to 1873 he was president, continuing as lecturer on natural and revealed religion after ill health compelled him to relinquish the executive office. At his death, leaving no issue, he willed his small property to the institution to found the Merrick Lectureship on experimental and practical religion.

Merrick's diary reveals him as a man of intense devotion, who sought divine guidance through prayer for every action, great or small. One of his critical decisions was called for in 1845 when he was asked to lead a Methodist Mission in China, an offer which he did not decline without a struggle. Although he was zealous to build up the University in buildings and funds, his first care was the character and religious life of its students, and his precept and example made the school a prolific mother of ministers and missionaries. He was a vigorous advocate of total abstinence and a militant foe of the liquor traffic. He opposed slavery and helped to operate the "underground railway." In 1860, 1864, and 1876 he was a delegate to the General Conference of his denomination, and at the centennial conference at Baltimore in 1884, which commemorated the founding of the Methodist Episcopal Church, he gave the closing message. Though he preached on many occasions, he lacked the greater gifts of pulpit eloquence. He lectured frequently and his only published volume, *Formalism in Religion* (1865), is a series of lectures. He had a singularly serene and steady habit of mind, based on a supreme faith in a loving and wise providence, and in his later years he came to enjoy in the college community a unique reputation for saintliness. He died at Delaware, Ohio, at the age of eighty-four.

[W. G. Williams, "Frederick Merrick," *Meth. Rev.*, May-June 1895 (also reprinted separately); J. W. Bashford, "Frederick Merrick," *Ann. Report of President to Trustees of Ohio Wesleyan Univ.*, 1894; *Fifty Years of Hist. of the Ohio Wesleyan Univ.* (1895), ed. by E. T. Nelson; Isaac Crook, *The Great Five: The First Faculty of the Ohio Wesleyan Univ.* (1908); Diary of Frederick Merrick, 1843–88 (MS.), in Library of Ohio Wesleyan University ("mostly personal experiences relating to my religious life. F.M."); G. B. Merrick, *Geneal. of the Merrick-Mirick-Myrick Family of Mass., 1636–1902* (1902); *Cincinnati Commercial Gazette*, Mar. 6, 1894.] J. R. J.

MERRICK, PLINY (Aug. 2, 1794–Jan. 31, 1867), Massachusetts jurist, counsel for Prof. John White Webster in his trial for the murder of Dr. George Parkman, was descended from Thomas Merrick who emigrated to America in 1636 and later settled in Springfield. His parents, Pliny and Ruth (Cutler) Merrick lived at Brookfield where the father, a Harvard graduate, was a respected lawyer and public servant. The son attended Leicester Academy and Harvard, graduating in 1814. He read law at Worcester in the office of Levi Lincoln [*q.v.*], son of Jefferson's attorney-general. His preceptor was a distinguished lawyer and judge and subsequently governor. After three years Merrick was admitted to the bar. Now heavily in debt, the young lawyer cast about for a practice without immediate success. He had an office in Worcester, then at Charlton and at Swansea in Bristol County, then at Taunton where for a while he was a partner of Marcus Morton. In 1824 he returned to Worcester, where he was appointed district attorney for Worcester and Norfolk counties and served from 1832 until his appointment to the court of common pleas in 1843. While his service as a prosecuting officer made him a master of the criminal law, his civil practice increased until it sometimes happened that he was retained as senior counsel in every case to be tried at a term of court.

In these earlier years Merrick was active in politics. Like Caleb Cushing, whom he succeeded on the supreme court, he was somewhat inconstant in party affiliations. In 1834 he appears to have favored a National Republican-Antimasonic alliance in Massachusetts to oppose the Jackson administration; yet on Jackson's death he pronounced his eulogy at Faneuil Hall. (Speech in J. S. Loring, *The Hundred Boston Orators,* 1852, pp. 635–38.) As a leader of the minority party, he received few of the rewards of office: four years a selectman of Worcester, in 1827 a representative in the legislature; in 1850 a senator. He was active in local affairs and for a time he edited the Worcester *National Aegis.* In 1848, after five years of service on the common pleas bench he became president of the Worcester & Nashua Railroad, then in a precarious situation financially. When Merrick relinquished the presidency in 1850 the road was operating on a sound financial basis.

At this time he became engaged in one of the *causes célèbres* of American criminal law. Professor Webster of Harvard Medical School, becoming hopelessly indebted to Dr. Parkman, had killed his creditor but was detected before he had completed the destruction of the body. He was indicted, convicted before the supreme court, and hanged on Aug. 30, 1850. So erratic was the accused toward the line of defense to be pursued that Rufus Choate declined to take the case (Joseph Neilson, *Memories of Rufus Choate,* 1884, pp. 15–21), and Merrick was retained as senior counsel. The evidence was overwhelming and the accused an untrustworthy client, yet the defense was conducted with ability and eloquence. In 1851 Merrick was reappointed to the court of common pleas, and in 1853, when Caleb Cushing resigned from the supreme judicial court to become attorney-general in Pierce's cabinet, he was promoted to fill the vacancy. Two years later he moved to Boston. In the spring of 1864 he was stricken with paralysis and was forced to give up his work, resigning on Aug. 15 following. A subsequent stroke caused his death. In character and style his opinions showed a marked improvement during his years of service. On the bench he was "kind, courteous, and dignified; and if his quickness at any time outran the slower development of the cause before him, thereby sometimes disturbing the sensitiveness of counsel, no one ever doubted that his convictions were unbiased, though to the losing party they sometimes may have seemed to have been hastily formed" (*American Law Review,* April 1867, p. 585). Merrick had married, on May 23, 1821, Mary Rebecca Thomas, whose brother Benjamin became one of his associates on the supreme court. She died childless in 1859. On his death the judge left bequests to the public library at Brookfield and to the orphanage at Worcester.

[*Am. Law Rev.,* Apr. 1867; Wm. Lincoln, *Hist. of Worcester, Mass.* (1837); D. H. Hurd, *Hist. of Worcester County, Mass.* (1889), vol. I; G. B. Merrick, *Geneal. of the Merrick-Mirick-Myrick Family of Mass., 1636–1902* (1902); A. B. Darling, *Pol. Changes in Mass., 1824–48* (1925); Geo. Bemis, *Report of the Case of John W. Webster* (1850); Geo. Dilnot, *The Trial of Prof. John White Webster* (1928); Pliny Merrick, *A Letter on Speculative Free Masonry* (1929), and the rejoinder, by an anonymous author, *Strictures on Seceding Masons* (1830); *Boston Evening Transcript,* Feb. 2, 1867.] C.F.

MERRICK, SAMUEL VAUGHAN (May 4, 1801–Aug. 18, 1870), manufacturer and railroad executive, was born in Hallowell, Me., the son of John and Rebecca (Vaughan) Merrick. His father, an emigrant from England in 1798, had been educated as a Unitarian minister but spent most of his life as a student and writer (D. R. Goodwin, *Memoir of John Merrick, Esq.,* 1862). The boy attended the schools of his native town and in 1816 entered the employ of his uncle, John Vaughan, a wine merchant of Philadelphia, Pa. In 1820 he left his uncle and joined John Agnew in the firm of Merrick & Agnew, to manufacture an improved type of fire-engine. His knowledge of mechanical engineering was slight at this time but through constant study he gained a good practical knowledge of engineering and developed an innate talent for mechanics. On Christmas day 1823 he was married to Sarah Thomas, by whom he had six children. In 1836, with John H. Towne [*q.v.*] as junior partner, he established the Southwark Foundry for the manufacture of heavy machinery and boilers. Upon Towne's retirement in 1849, Merrick took his son, J. Vaughan Merrick, into partnership. As Merrick & Son, and after 1852 as Merrick & Sons, the firm continued until the retirement of the senior partner in 1860. Among their notable achievements were the construction of the engines of a number of naval vessels, notably those for the steam frigate *Mississippi.* They also built the iron lighthouses along the coast of Florida and the *New Ironsides,* a pioneer armor-clad vessel.

Merrick was an early advocate of the use of gas for street lighting in Philadelphia, and in order to bring about its adoption ran for and was elected to the City Council. He was appointed chairman of the committee to investigate the matter and was sent abroad to study European methods of gas manufacture. Upon his return in 1834 he was given charge, as chief engineer, of building the gas works and distributing the gas throughout the city. This work was completed on Feb. 8, 1836, and on Feb. 8, 1837, he resigned his official position in order to devote himself to his private business.

Realizing the importance to Philadelphia of a railroad connection with the interior, he was an early promoter of the Pennsylvania Railroad Company, which was organized, Apr. 13, 1846; and on Mar. 31, 1847, he became its first president. While not possessing technical training, he was well fitted to manage and inspire confidence in the enterprise. He held this position until Sept. 1, 1849, when, with the construction of the road progressing satisfactorily, and the prospect that sufficient capital would be raised for its completion, he tendered his resignation. He remained as a director, however, until Feb. 2, 1852. In 1856 he was prevailed upon to accept the presidency of the Sunbury & Erie Railroad, then on the verge of bankruptcy, and held this post until December 1857, when he resigned because of ill health. During this time he saved the road from failure by advancing large sums from his private funds. He was also a director of the Catawissa Railroad and was connected in various official capacities with other corporations. A founder of the Franklin Institute of Pennsylvania in 1824, he was its president from 1842 to 1854. In 1833 he was elected to the American Philosophical Society. After the Civil War he became interested in the problems of education in the South and made large gifts toward the maintenance of schools in that section. He was also a liberal giver to other agencies, particularly the Episcopal Hospital in Philadelphia. He died in Philadelphia.

[J. T. Scharf and Thompson Westcott, *Hist. of Phila.* (1884), vols. I, III; E. P. Oberholtzer, *Phila.—A Hist. of the City and Its People* (n.d.), vol. II; H. W. Schotter, *The Growth and Development of the Pa. Railroad Company* (1927); W. B. Wilson, *Hist. of the Pa. Railroad Company* (2 vols., 1899); D. R. Goodwin, in *Proc. Am. Philosophical Soc.*, vol. XI (1871); Ellwood Hendrick, *Modern Views of Physical Science; Being a Record of the Proc. of the Centenary Meeting of the Franklin Inst. at Phila., Sept. 17, 18, and 19, 1924* (1925); E. T. Freedley, *Phila. and Its Manufactures . . . in 1857* (1858); *Public Ledger* (Phila.), Aug. 19, 1870; name of wife and date of marriage from a descendant, J. Hartley, Esq.]

J. H. F.

MERRILL, DANIEL (Mar. 18, 1765–June 3, 1833), Baptist clergyman, was the son of Thomas and Sarah (Friend) Merrill of Rowley, Mass., and a descendant of Nathaniel Merrill, who emigrated to America in 1635. At fifteen he enlisted in the 3rd Massachusetts Infantry and served until the end of the Revolution. He decided to become a Congregational minister and entered Dartmouth College, from which he graduated in 1789. After studying theology, probably with Dr. Spring of Newburyport, he was licensed to preach in 1791. He went to Sedgwick, Me., where his first sermon started a revival in which nearly one hundred were converted. He preached at Sedgwick for five months, then after an absence of eighteen months, when he was preaching elsewhere, he returned to Sedgwick and was ordained pastor of a new Congregational church on Sept. 17, 1793. He led revivals in 1798 and 1801, and by 1805 his church had one hundred and eighty-nine members and was the largest in Maine.

In 1803 part of his congregation began to have doubts about the efficacy of infant baptism. Merrill studied to confute them, but was himself converted to their opinion. In February 1805 a majority of the church agreed to become Baptists, and in May Merrill and eighty-seven of his congregation were baptized by three ministers from southern New England in the tide-waters of Benjamin's River. The next day he was re-ordained as a Baptist. In the same year he published seven sermons under the title *The Mode and Subjects of Baptism Examined* (1805) in which he argued that the Baptists had been the uninterrupted church of Christ from the days of the apostles, whereas all other Protestant churches sprang from the Church of Rome.

The Baptist ministers in Maine were for the most part uneducated farmers, and in 1810 the Bowdoinham Association elected a committee, of which Merrill was one, to consider the foundation of a college. Merrill, chiefly in order that he might help the cause of education, had been elected to the General Assembly of Massachusetts, and in 1813 he took the lead in securing a charter and a grant of land for the "Maine Literary and Theological Association," and was named one of the twenty-one trustees. The institution was established at Waterville and its name afterward changed to Waterville College (now Colby College). In 1814 Merrill moved to Nottingham West (now Hudson), N. H. Seven years later he returned to Sedgwick, of which church he remained pastor until his death. In 1805 he published *Eight Letters on Open Communion*, in 1807 *Letters Occasioned by the Rev. Samuel Worcester's Two Discourses*, and in 1815 a Thanksgiving sermon entitled *Balaam*

Disappointed. He was twice married: on Aug. 14, 1793, to Joanna Colby of Sandown, N. H., who died in three months; and on Oct. 14, 1794, to Susanna Gale, of Salisbury, N. H., by whom he had thirteen children. In appearance Merrill was short and stout. He was an old-fashioned puritan, simple, straightforward, and outspoken, who worshiped the Bible and drew a very distinct line between the saved and the damned.

[G. T. Chapman, *Sketches of the Alumni of Dartmouth Coll.* (1867); Samuel Merrill, "A Merrill Memorial" (1917–28), 2 vols., mimeographed, in Lib. of Cong.; H. S. Burrage, "The Beginnings of Waterville Coll.," *Colls. and Proc. of the Me. Hist. Soc.,* 2 ser., IV (1893); E. C. Whittemore, *Colby Coll., 1820–1925* (1927); W. B. Sprague, *Annals Am. Pulpit,* vol. VI (1860); Joshua Millet, *A Hist. of the Baptists in Me.* (1845).] H. B. P.

MERRILL, GEORGE EDMANDS (Dec. 19, 1846–June 11, 1908), Baptist clergyman, president of Colgate University, was born in Charlestown, Mass., the son of Nathan and Amelia (Edmands) Merrill and a descendant of Nathaniel Merrill, an early emigrant to Massachusetts. His father had been a successful teacher in Portsmouth, Charlestown, and Boston. His mother had a brilliant mind and a keen sense of humor which seem to have been transmitted to her three sons. His father died when George was about ten years of age. An elder half-brother, J. Warren Merrill, of Cambridge, Mass., cared for him and his younger brother, supplying them a home and education. George was graduated from the Cambridge High School in 1865 and from Harvard College in 1869. He was elected to Phi Beta Kappa and was class poet. He spent the next three years in Newton Theological Seminary and was ordained on Oct. 3, 1872. He was pastor of the First Baptist Church in Springfield, Mass. (1872–77), and of the First Baptist Church in Salem, Mass. (1877–85). Failing health demanded rest for an over-worked body, and he spent the summer of 1885 in Europe. In the following November he was compelled to leave the East to regain his broken health and spent five years in Colorado, during which time he steadily recovered. For two years he was pastor of the First Baptist Church in Colorado Springs. He returned to New England in 1890 to become pastor of the Immanuel Baptist Church of Newton, Mass. From there he was called to the presidency of Colgate University at Hamilton, N. Y., in 1901. Here he achieved honor and rendered a notable service. He gave his life to the work, dying in office there on June 11, 1908.

Merrill was a man of wide interests and varied avocations. He was fond of carpentry and was proficient as an architect. Besides his sermons he wrote many poems, stories, and essays. Among his published books were *The Story of the Manuscripts* (1881); *Crusaders and Captives* (1890); *The Reasonable Christ* (1893); and *The Parchments of the Faith* (1894). He had a keen appreciation and understanding of music and art. In all his pastorates he was successful, but his outstanding achievement was his contribution as president of Colgate University. His plans for that institution included the renovation and remodeling of old buildings, the erection of new buildings, better equipment, a broader curriculum, a larger faculty, a beautified campus, and the organization of a strong body of alumni who should be influential in forming the future policies of the university. He lived long enough to see all of these features of his vision well under way. Merrill was married three times. Florence A. Whittemore accompanied him as a bride to his first pastorate in Springfield. Her early death left him with a baby daughter. On Apr. 5, 1877, he married Carrie A. Beebe, who died during his pastorate in Salem. On Sept. 19, 1882, he married Emma M. Bateman of Springfield, who with his daughter Elinor survived him.

[*Who's Who in America,* 1908–09; *The Inauguration of the Rev. Geo. Edmands Merrill, D.D., as President of Colgate Univ.* (1901); *The Colgate Univ. Centennial Celebration, 1819–1919* (1920); Samuel Merrill, "A Merrill Memorial" (1917–28), 2 vols., mimeographed, in Lib. of Cong.; *Tenth Report of the Class of 1869 of Harvard Coll.* (1908); article in *N. Y. Educ.,* May 1899; the *Utica Observer,* June 12, 1908; the *Watchman* (Boston), June 18, 1908; information as to certain facts from Miss Elinor Merrill.] F. H. A.

MERRILL, GEORGE PERKINS (May 31, 1854–Aug. 15, 1929), geologist, was born at Auburn, Me., one of seven children, and died there suddenly at the age of seventy-five while on his way to collect beryl crystals. His father, Lucius Merrill, a carpenter and cabinet maker, was a descendant of Nathaniel Merrill, a settler of old Newbury, Mass., in 1635, who traced his ancestry to the Huguenot, De Merles, driven out of France after the massacre of St. Bartholomew's Day; his mother, Elizabeth Anne (Jones), was the daughter of the Rev. Elijah Jones, of the First Congregational Church at Minot, Me., and it was this grandfather who influenced Merrill toward science. Prepared in the schools of Auburn, he worked his way through the University of Maine, graduating in 1879 with the degree of B.S. He was married in November 1883 to Sarah Farrington of Portland, Me., to whom were born one son and three daughters. She died in 1894, and in 1900 he married Katherine L. Yancey, of Virginia, who became the mother of one daughter.

As a small boy and as a student Merrill collected natural-history specimens. At college he specialized in chemistry, and after graduating was assistant to Prof. W. O. Atwater [*q.v.*] at Wesleyan University (1879–80). Meeting here America's greatest pioneer in museum administration, G. Brown Goode [*q.v.*], then in charge of the United States National Museum, he was later (1881) given a position on the staff of that Museum, where he remained the rest of his life. He was at first assistant to George W. Hawes, in charge of geology, and was influenced by him to become a geologist. He soon rose to the rank of curator (1887) and finally to that of head curator (1897). Under his care the department of geology and paleontology grew from insignificant size to include one of the great collections of the world.

Aside from this work of organization, Merrill was a pioneer in research along three lines: on building stones and the processes of rock-weathering, on meteorites, and on the history of American physical geology. His most widely known book, *Stones for Building and Decoration* (1891, with subsequent editions, 1897, 1903), treats of the building stones of the United States, their physical and chemical properties and weathering qualities. The volume that gave him an international reputation was, however, *A Treatise on Rocks, Rock-weathering and Soils* (1897). The first book of its kind, it is the source from which American textbooks on soils have drawn their materials, and its contribution to scientific agriculture is beyond estimate. A third book, *Non-metallic Minerals* (1904, 2nd ed., 1910), is a classic in its field.

In later life, his chief interest lay in meteorites, "the chips of other worlds." He built up at Washington the sixth most important collection of these celestial bodies, and described the microstructure of forty new falls. Meteorites, he concluded, are a result of explosive activity. The stony meteorites he was at first inclined to regard as the solidified molten drops of a "fiery rain" or world-making mist, but later he gave up this idea and held that they were originally tuffaceous or volcanic in character and that they owe their crystalline condition, where such exists, to "heat and pressure in a non-oxidizing or even reducing atmosphere" ("On Chondrules and Chondritic Structure in Meteorites," *Proceedings of the National Academy of Sciences,* 1920, vol. VI). Detailed by the Smithsonian Institution in 1906 to study the so-called Coon Butte or Meteor Crater in Arizona, a crater-like hole 4,000 feet in diameter and 600 feet deep, about the origin of which there were conflicting opinions, Merrill concluded that it was formed by the impact of a huge meteorite, which plowed deeply into the underlying water-bearing Coconino sandstone and converted its moisture into steam, with a resulting explosion which might well have disrupted the meteor and built up the crater rim.

As pioneer historian of American physical geology, Merrill published three books that portray the rise of this science in North America up to the close of the nineteenth century. These are "Contributions to the History of American Geology" in *Annual Report of the Board of Regents of the Smithsonian Institution: Report of the United States National Museum, 1904,* published in 1906; *Contributions to a History of American State Geological and Natural History Surveys* (Bulletin 109, United States National Museum, 1920), and *The First One Hundred Years of American Geology* (1924). He was the author of numerous encyclopedia articles and wrote many of the sketches of geologists for the *Dictionary of American Biography,* to which he also contributed invaluable counsel. His complete bibliography includes more than two hundred titles. From 1893 to 1916 he was professor of geology and mineralogy at George Washington University. He was elected to the National Academy of Sciences in 1922, and in that same year received its J. Lawrence Smith gold medal.

Physically, Merrill was tall and sturdy, with sandy hair and keen blue eyes. Alert and active, he was always occupied, possessing, in addition to his scientific bent, a love for poetry and music. Always critical and reserved, he was nevertheless fond of humor and apt quotation. In science he was rarely speculative, preferring, as he said in James Dwight Dana's words, to be "always afloat in regard to opinions in geology."

[Samuel Merrill, "A Merrill Memorial" (1917–28), 2 vols., mimeographed, in Lib. of Cong.; Marcus Benjamin, "George Perkins Merrill," *Am. Jour. Sci.,* Oct. 1929; J. H. Benn, in *Science,* Aug. 2, 1929; O. C. Farrington, "Tribute," in *Bull. Geol. Soc. of America,* Mar. 1930; Charles Schuchert, "George Perkins Merrill," *Ann. Report . . . Smithsonian Inst. . . . 1930* (1931); *Bull. Geol. Soc. of America,* Mar. 1931, with complete bibliography; *Portland Press Herald,* Aug. 16, 1929.] C. S.

MERRILL, JAMES CUSHING (Mar. 26, 1853–Oct. 27, 1902), army surgeon and ornithologist, was born in Cambridge, Mass., the son of James Cushing and Jane (Hammond) Merrill and a descendant of Nathaniel Merrill, an early settler in Massachusetts. Following preliminary studies in his native town he spent some time in Dresden and other German schools. His medical education was obtained at the University of Pennsylvania where he graduated in 1874. His graduation thesis was entitled *Anomalies of Human Osteology*. In 1875 he was appointed assistant surgeon in the United States army and for the following twenty years he served in posts in the West and Southwest. During this period he developed into one of the best-known naturalists of the country. He made extensive studies of the fauna of Texas, Oregon, Idaho, and what is now Oklahoma. He was primarily interested in birds, but he made collections of insects, mammals, and fishes, most of which he contributed to the collections of the National Museum. He was an active member of the American Ornithologists' Union, attended its first Congress in 1883, and for twenty years he was one of the leading American contributors to the literature of ornithology. His "Notes on the Ornithology of Southern Texas," published in the *Proceedings of the United States National Museum* (vols. I and II, 1879–80), was the result of two years' observation of birds in and around Fort Brown, Tex. "Notes on the Birds of Fort Klamath, Oregon," was published in the *Auk* (April, July, October 1888), and "Notes on the Birds of Fort Sherman, Idaho," in the same journal (October 1897, January 1898). He made many interesting contributions to *Forest and Stream* and other publications of a popular nature. He also wrote an article, "On the Habits of the Rocky Mountain Goat," for the *Proceedings* of the National Museum for 1879 (vol. II, 1880).

In the meantime Merrill had reached the grade of major and in 1897 he was named to succeed Col. David L. Huntington as librarian of the Library of the Surgeon-General in Washington. He occupied this position for five years, giving to medical bibliography the same enthusiasm that he had spent on nature study. He edited volumes III to VII of the second series of the *Index Catalogue of the Library of the Surgeon-General's Office*. Merrill was singularly well fitted for his work as librarian. He read thirteen languages and was adding Russian at the time of his death. During this time, however, his health gradually broke down and he was a semi-invalid for a year or more before his death at his home in Washington. He was tall and slender, alert and active in movement, and always scrupulously well dressed. To a distinguished appearance he added an attractive personality which gave him a host of friends. In his western days he developed into an ardent hunter of big game. In this connection he formed a friendship with President Theodore Roosevelt, who speaks of Merrill's prowess in his *Hunting the Grisly and Other Sketches* (1900). While in Washington he found diversion in duck shooting at the Dedlo Island Hunting Club.

[Sources include: *The Alumni Reg., Univ. of Pa.*, Feb. 1903; H. A. Kelly and W. L. Burrage, *Am. Medic. Biogs.* (1920); Samuel Merrill, "A Merrill Memorial" (1917–28), 2 vols., mimeographed, in Lib. of Cong.; *Proc. of the Washington Acad. of Sci.*, vol. V (1903–04); the *Auk*, Jan. 1903; *Boston Medic. and Surgic. Jour.*, Jan. 22, 1903; the *Evening Star* (Washington, D. C.), Oct. 28, 1902.] J. M. P.

MERRILL, JAMES GRISWOLD (Aug. 20, 1840–Dec. 22, 1920), pastor and educator, was born in Montague, Mass., the son of the Rev. James Hervey and Lucia (Griswold) Merrill and a descendant of Nathaniel Merrill, an early emigrant to Massachusetts. In 1863 he received the degree of A.B. from Amherst, then studied for a year in Princeton Theological Seminary, then transferred to Andover Theological Seminary, where he graduated in 1866. On Oct. 11, 1866, he married Louisa W. Boutwell of Andover, Mass. In January 1867 he was ordained a minister of the Congregational Church and was accepted for service by the Congregational Home Mission Society. His first assignment was at Mound City, Kan., where he continued for two years (1866–68). He then went to Topeka, Kan. (1868–69), and for the following three years he was the superintendent of home missions in the state of Kansas. Following this period of service he was in the regular Congregational pastorate for some twenty-two years. From 1872 to 1882 he was at Davenport, Iowa, and during this time he published two volumes of children's sermons. For seven years (1882–89) he was pastor of the First Congregational Church in St. Louis, and for five years (1889–94) of the Payson Memorial Church at Portland, Me.

In 1874 Merrill left the pulpit to become the editor of the *Christian Mirror*, which was subsequently absorbed in the *Congregationalist*. He left editorial work to accept in 1898 the chair of logic and ethics at Fisk University and also became dean of the institution. In 1899, owing to the failing health of Erastus Milo Cravath [*q.v.*], the first president of Fisk, Merrill was named acting president. On the death of Cravath, Merrill was elected president of the university and served in that capacity for seven years (1901–08). Three features characterize his service in that institution. He put the finances of the university on a more substantial basis by raising a building and endowment fund; he confirmed the policy of the institution in having a bi-racial faculty, a policy which has been an important contributing factor in the growth of the University, and he was instrumental in helping to create a very wide-spread interest in the work of the "Fisk Jubilee Singers." He contributed the chapter on Fisk University to a volume entitled *From Servitude to Service* (1905). He was honored by the National Congregational Council (1907) at Cleveland, Ohio, by being elected first assistant moderator of that body. Primarily owing to the failing health of his wife, in 1908 he resigned as president of Fisk University but continued his active interest in the University by service on the board of trustees during the remainder of his life. On leaving Fisk, for three years (1909–12) he was pastor at Somerset, Mass., and following that for five years (1912–17) was pastor at Lake Helen, Fla. In 1917 he retired from active work and spent the remaining three years of his life at Winter Park, Fla., Andover, Mass., and Mountain Lakes, N. J. He died at Mountain Lakes, in his eighty-first year and was buried at Andover, Mass.

[Sources include: W. L. Montague, ed., *Biog. Record of the Alumni of Amherst Coll. . . . 1821–71* (1883); Samuel Merrill, "A Merrill Memorial" (1917–28), 2 vols., mimeographed, in Lib. of Cong.; *Who's Who in America*, 1920–21; files of the *Christian Mirror* and the *Congregationalist*, especially the latter for Jan. 6, 1921; files of the *Nashville Banner*, especially June 10, 1901; files of the *Nashville Tennessean*, especially June 10, 1908; *Fisk University Herald*, vol. VIII, p. 1, vol. XIX, pp. 6–11; catalogues of Fisk University, 1901–08.] O. E. B.

MERRILL, JOSHUA (Oct. 6, 1820–Jan. 15, 1904), chemist and pioneer oil refiner, was born at Duxbury, Mass., the sixth child and fourth son of Abraham Dow Merrill and his first wife, Nancy (Morrison) Merrill. On his father's side he was descended in the eighth generation from Nathaniel Merrill who settled in Newbury, Mass., in 1635, and on his mother's from John Morrison who emigrated from Scotland to Londonderry, N. H., around 1720. His grandfather, Joshua Merrill, served in the War of 1812, and his father was a successful Methodist minister, who served charges in Massachusetts, Rhode Island, and Vermont. Merrill's formal education, which he received in the grammar school at Lowell, was short, for he left school at the age of fifteen to work for an elder brother who was engaged in Boston in the manufacture of paper hangings. During the next few years he was employed by both Luther Atwood and Samuel Downer [*q.v.*], oil merchants, who were to become pioneers in the development of mineral oils. In 1852 the first coal-oil made for sale in the United States was produced by Luther Atwood and manufactured as a lubricant by the United States Chemical Company at Waltham. This product was known as "Coup Oil," and Merrill was engaged in 1853 to introduce it to the market. He continued in this capacity after Downer secured control of the company in 1854. In 1856 George Miller & Company of Glasgow, Scotland, appealed to Downer for assistance in the manufacture of coal tar, and Luther Atwood and Joshua Merrill were sent to aid in the erection of a factory. While in Scotland they discovered new methods of obtaining oil from coal and succeeded in purifying it of its offensive odor. This opened up the possibility of hydro-carbon oils for illumination, and Atwood and Merrill, who had gone to Scotland to manufacture lubricating oil, returned to manufacture illuminants. In the years following 1856 Merrill carried on ceaseless experiments in the production of both lubricants and illuminants from a hydro-carbon base, manufacturing them from Trinidad asphaltum, Cuban chapapote bitumin, and particularly, in the years 1857 and 1858, from albertite, a bituminous coal obtained from Albert County, New Brunswick.

While Merrill and his associates were in the midst of their experiments with albertite, turning out large quantities of various kinds of hydro-carbon oils, and rapidly developing the business into a position where it was endangering the prestige of whale and sperm oil, there came the news of the discovery of petroleum in Pennsylvania. Downer reorganized his business into the Downer Kerosene Company and set out for the oil regions to insure a supply of raw materials, while Merrill and his assistants turned their talents to the problem of refining the new product. After the trying experiences which he had encountered with albertite and other bituminous products, he found the problems of refining petroleum relatively easy, especially after Luther Atwood's process of distillation, known as "cracking," was successfully applied to the new material. Many of the most important technological processes and discoveries in the early days of the oil business were worked out in the laboratories of the Downer Kerosene Oil Company. Among these should be particularly noted Merrill's invention in 1869 of a method of distilling by steam at so low a temperature that the partial decomposition, which usually takes place in oil distillation at high temperature, might be avoided, thereby producing less odorous paraffine lubricating oils (patent no. 90,284, May 18, 1869). In 1869 also Joshua patented a rosin oil and in 1870 Rufus S. Merrill received a patent (no. 100,915) which was assigned to his brothers, Joshua and William, for a process and burner for "the production of light from heavy hydro-carbons." So important was the work carried on in the Downer company that a reliable expert said in 1872 that he found it "generally acknowledged" that to Merrill "more than to any one else, belongs the honor of bringing this manufacture to its present advanced state" and that "an account of his labors and discoveries in this connection would provide a nearly complete history of the art" (Hayes, *post*, p. 7). When Downer disposed of much of his interest in the company in 1871, Merrill and his three brothers took over the management and Joshua became president. He was also senior partner in the firm of Joshua Merrill & Son, dealers in petroleum. For almost half a century Merrill was a generous benefactor of the Tremont Street Methodist Episcopal Church, and one of the most prominent Methodist laymen of Boston, serving for many years as president of the Boston Wesleyan Association and as trustee of Boston University. He married on June 13, 1849, Amelia S. Grigg, who with three daughters and one son survived him.

[For biographical and genealogical details see: Samuel Merrill, "A Merrill Memorial" (1917–28), 2 vols., mimeographed, in Lib. of Cong.; *Biog. Encyc. of Mass. of the Nineteenth Century*, II (1883), 442–47; *Boston Transcript*, Jan. 15, 1904. On his contributions to the oil industry see: S. D. Hayes, *On the Hist. and Manuf. of Petroleum Products: A Memoir, Communicated to the Soc. of Arts, Mass. Inst. of Technol., Mar. 14, 1872*; Merrill's account of his work in *The Derrick's Hand-Book of Petroleum: A Complete Chronological and Statistical Rev. of Petroleum Developments from 1859 to 1898* (1898), pp. 880–90; *Ann. Report of the Commissioner of Patents*, 1869–71.] H. U. F.

MERRILL, SAMUEL (Oct. 29, 1792–Aug. 24, 1855), Indiana official, was the second of nine sons of Jesse and Priscilla (Kimball) Merrill of Peacham, Vt. His first American ancestor, Nathaniel Merrill, settled at Newbury, Mass., in 1635. Samuel Merrill attended an academy at Peacham and studied for a year, 1812–13, as a sophomore at Dartmouth College. He then taught school and studied law for three years at York, Pa. In 1816 he settled at Vevay, Switzerland County, Ind., in the next year was admitted to the bar, and soon took his place as an active member of the community. Appointed tax assessor, he made the round of the county on foot for necessary economy; he was a contractor in the erection of a stone jail; superintendent of a town Sunday school started as early as 1817; and a representative of the county in the General Assemblies of 1819–20, 1820–21, and 1821–22. The General Assembly elected him state treasurer on Dec. 14, 1822, and he held the office for four terms, till 1834. In 1824 he moved the state offices from Corydon to Indianapolis, one wagon sufficing for all the records and money. It took eleven or twelve days to cover the distance (125 miles by present highways); the road through the wilderness was impassable in some places, and a new way had to be cut through the woods.

He lived henceforth at the capital. In the absence of teachers, he personally conducted a school; he acted for a time as captain of the first military company, served as a commissioner for the erection of the state capitol building, which was finished in 1835, was an early president of the Temperance Society, a manager of the State Colonization Society, a trustee of Wabash College, and the second president of the Indiana Historical Society, 1835–48. He was active in the organization of the Second Presbyterian Church (New School) and an intimate friend of Henry Ward Beecher during his pastorate. On Jan. 30, 1834, the General Assembly elected him president of the State Bank of Indiana. In this capacity he personally examined each of the thirteen branches twice a year. An excellent law and the efficient service of such officers as Merrill, Hugh McCulloch, and J. F. D. Lanier [*qq.v.*] combined to develop one of the best of all the state banks. After two terms in the office, Merrill was replaced by the choice of a Democratic legislature. From 1844 to 1848 he was president of the Madison & Indianapolis Railroad, during which time it was completed to Indianapolis. He spent the next two years compiling a third edition of the *Indiana Gazetteer* and in 1850 he bought Hood and Noble's bookstore, which later, under the name of the Merrill Company, undertook some publishing and eventually entered into the Bowen-Merrill (now the Bobbs-Merrill) publishing company. He also, with others, constructed a mill on Fall Creek.

On Apr. 12, 1818, Merrill married Lydia Jane Anderson of Vevay, daughter of Capt. Robert and Catherine (Dumont) Anderson. Ten children were born to them. After his wife's death in 1847, he was married, second, to Elizabeth Douglas Young, of Madison, Ind. Throughout his life he was the personification of traditional New England Puritanism: conscientious, industrious, and devout. He is said to have read the entire Bible every year after he reached the age of twelve. The square-cut features, tightly-closed lips, and clean-shaven face shown in most of his portraits reveal a sober, straightforward, uncompromising character. A bitter, twenty-four-page pamphlet which he published in 1827 attacking Gov. James Brown Ray illustrates the thoroughness with which he performed "an unpleasant task." During the existence of the Whig party, he adhered to it—with a strong anti-slavery leaning—and was an active party worker. He died in Indianapolis and was buried in Greenlawn Cemetery, though his remains were subsequently removed to Crown Hill Cemetery.

[Unpublished memoirs of Mrs. John L. (Jane Merrill) Ketcham; Samuel Merrill, "A Merrill Memorial" (1917–28), 2 vols., mimeographed, in Lib. of Cong.; *Ind. Mag. of Hist.*, Mar. 1916; Perret Dufour, *The Swiss Settlement of Switzerland County, Ind.* (1925); G. I. Read, *Encyc. of Biog. of Ind.* (1899); J. H. B. Nowland, *Early Reminiscences of Indianapolis* (1870); J. P. Dunn, *Ind. and Indianans*, vol. I (1919).]

C. B. C.

MERRILL, SELAH (May 2, 1837–Jan. 22, 1909), Congregational clergyman, archeologist, consul, was born at Canton Center, Hartford County, Conn. His parents, Daniel Merrill and Lydia (Richards), sprang from old New England stock; an ancestor, Nathaniel Merrill (or Merrell, as the name was then spelled), is known to have been at Newbury, Mass., in 1635. After preparing for college at Westfield, Mass., as well as at Williston Seminary, Easthampton, Merrill entered Yale with the class of 1863, but left college before graduation to study at the Yale Divinity School. In 1864 he was ordained as a Congregational minister, and was appointed chaplain of the 49th United States Infantry, a colored regiment, with which he served at Vicksburg, 1864–65. After the war he preached in Le Roy, N. Y., 1866–67, San Francisco, 1867–68, and Salmon Falls, N. H., 1870–72.

Though he received the honorary degree of A.M. from Yale "for special services in Biblical learning," and spent two years (1868–70) at the University of Berlin, his lack of an adequate academic training was later to affect the value of his work very seriously. His interest in the Holy Land was whetted by an extended tour through Egypt, Palestine, and Syria, in 1869, but it was not until 1874 that his archeological career began. Before it was well under way he had been thrice married: first, Mar. 15, 1866, to Fanny Lucinda Cooke, who died the following year; then, Sept. 16, 1868, to Phila (Wilkins) Fargo, who died in 1870; and on Apr. 27, 1875, to Adelaide Brewster Taylor, a direct descendant of Elder Brewster of the *Mayflower*.

In 1870 a large group of American scholars launched the American Palestine Exploration Society, formally organized the following year. In 1873 an expedition was sent to Palestine to carry out a geographical and archeological survey of Eastern Palestine (Transjordan), parallel to the Survey of Western Palestine which had just been begun by the English Palestine Exploration Fund, but the expedition was a total failure, both from the standpoint of cartography and from that of archeology. In 1874–75 a new expedition was organized, with Col. J. C. Lane as leader and Merrill as archeologist. After an initial trip into Eastern Palestine Lane saw that the task was too difficult for the limited resources of the society, and resigned, whereupon it was decided to give up any attempt to make a complete survey and to restrict the work to archeological exploration. Merrill was placed in charge of the expedition, and in three extended trips (1876–77) collected a mass of archeological, topographical, and ethnographical data. His most important results were published in popular form in his *East of the Jordan* (London, 1881). Such success as he had was undoubtedly due, in large measure, to his practical ability and his skill in dealing with the natives. He possessed a respectable knowledge of the documentary and philological material, and indeed surpassed his English colleagues of the Palestine Exploration Fund in this respect. Had he been able to follow in the footsteps of Edward Robinson, the founder of the scientific study of Palestinian geography, and to combine a sound European philological and critical training with his New England endurance and practicality, his work might easily have been epoch-making.

After two years as teacher of Hebrew in the Andover Theological Seminary, he secured appointment as American consul at Jerusalem, a position which he occupied during all the Republican administrations from 1882 to 1907, his tenure being interrupted only by Cleveland's two terms. He took his duties very seriously, and administered his post efficiently, as might be expected from a man of his practical bent. Being, however, a man of strong prejudices, he became involved in a most unfortunate feud with the American religious community founded by Spafford and generally called "The American Colony." He was also drawn into an attack on the authenticity of the Holy Sepulchre, in which he took a narrow Puritan attitude, as may be seen from his big book, *Ancient Jerusalem* (copyright 1908), a work almost entirely devoted to the problem of the ancient northern walls of the city and their relation to the site of the Holy Sepulchre. Aside from his prejudiced approach and the lack of critical training which the book manifests, it was a most useful production, anticipating some much more recent discoveries and conclusions. While consul in Jerusalem, he aided greatly in the establishment and later success of the American School of Oriental Research, founded in 1900. After retiring from his post at Jerusalem, he was appointed consul at Georgetown, British Guiana (1907–08), and only two years later he died, near East Oakland, Cal.

In addition to his two important works, mentioned above, Merrill also published *Galilee in the Time of Christ* (1881), *Greek Inscriptions Collected in the Countries East of the Jordan* (1885), *The Site of Calvary Identified* (1885), and collaborated in *Picturesque Palestine, Sinai and Egypt* (2 vols., 1881–84), edited by Sir Charles William Wilson. He lectured extensively, and wrote numerous popular articles on Palestine and the Bible; he was also an enthusiastic collector of antiquities, birds, and animals.

[*Annual of Am. Schools of Oriental Research,* vol. VIII (1928); Merrill's own books, especially *East of the Jordan*; Samuel Merrill, "A Merrill Memorial" (1917–28), 2 vols., mimeographed, in Lib. of Cong.; *Congreg. Year-Book,* 1910; *Who's Who in America,* 1908–09; *Congregationalist,* Jan. 30, 1909; *San Francisco Examiner,* Jan. 23, 1909.] W. F. A.

MERRILL, STEPHEN MASON (Sept. 16, 1825–Nov. 12, 1905) Methodist Episcopal bishop and writer, was born near Mount Pleasant, Jefferson County, Ohio, the fifth in a family of eleven children. His father, Joshua, was a farmer and shoemaker of New Hampshire birth and Revolutionary ancestry, descended from Nathaniel Merrill who settled at Newbury, Mass., in 1635; his mother, Rhoda (Crosson), was the daughter of a Revolutionary soldier of Bedford, Pa. Both were plain pioneers, with small school-learning, but characterized by sturdy moral fiber and strict Methodist piety. Stephen grew up in Clermont County, Ohio. His schooling ceased after a term or two in the rural academy at South Salem. He learned his father's trade of shoemaker, but did not stick to his last, for having "experienced religion," after the thorough Methodist manner, he joined the Methodist Society at Greenfield, Ohio, in 1842, and resolutely set about preparing himself to preach the gospel, working at his bench by day and toiling over his books far into the night. In his twentieth year, when he was teaching school, he was licensed to preach. Two weeks before he was twenty-one he was admitted to Ohio Conference on trial and appointed to Georgetown, a "hard-scrabble" circuit of twenty-two preaching places. On July 18, 1848, he married Anna Bellmire, who survived him by only a few days. They had one son.

Ordained deacon in 1849 and elder in 1851, Merrill rode hard circuits, read hard books, and meditated for eleven years. His salary was $216 and "table exercises." Then he was advanced to be pastor of a church, and from that position rose to the captaincy of a district, as presiding elder. In 1859 he was transferred to Kentucky Conference, but in 1863 returned to Ohio Conference. During these years he conquered a tendency to pulmonary disease and acquired rugged health. He also developed unusual gifts as a close student of the doctrines and especially the discipline of his denomination, and won recognition for power of lucid and logical statement in the public forum and in the church press.

Nor was he solely concerned with defending Arminian theology and Methodist polity against polemic Calvinists, Universalists, and others. In that seething ante-bellum period, his sound judgment, deep conviction, and knowledge of constitutional law were thrown into the discussions that sprang up wherever men gathered. Merrill, though not a radical agitator, was against slavery and for the Union. In his first General Conference (1868) he made his reputation as a Methodist leader, when his unanswerable argument defeated the popular project for admitting laymen to the Methodist legislature without duly amending the constitution. The General Conference was so impressed with his ability, "mental equipoise, mastery of constitutional principle and clearness of expression" that it elected him, though a new-comer, to the editorship of the *Western Christian Advocate* (Cincinnati). After four years in the editorial chair, where he gave ample demonstration of his intellectual resources, he was elected a bishop (1872). For eight years he resided in St. Paul, Minn. He was then assigned to Chicago, where he made his headquarters thereafter. In 1904 he retired from active duty at his own request, and died suddenly the following year while on a visit in Keyport, N. J.

Merrill's talents were rather solid than showy, and he had not the imaginative qualities essential to popularity as a preacher or occasional orator. He was no revivalist or stump speaker, but his power of massive argument, which his admirers likened to that of Daniel Webster, bore down all opposition. His knowledge of Methodist law was encyclopedic, and all his resources were at instant call. Physically he was tall and gaunt, with head of unusual size and the features of a Roman senator. He had a voice whose heavy tones were under complete control, and he pursued the course of his thought to its conclusion unruffled by contrary argument. As a bishop his calm judgment and dispassionate attachment to known principles of law made him a useful counselor. Only one man, Joshua Soule [*q.v.*], is rated his superior as an expounder of the Methodist constitution. In 1888 Merrill wrote the Episcopal Address to the General Conference, out of which came in substance those sections of the present constitution of the Methodist Episcopal Church which treat of the composition, powers, and limitations of the General Conference. He shone as a parliamentarian, and was a model presiding officer. In his handling of men in the appointive function of the episcopacy he was wise, sympathetic, and just. His quiet humor eased many difficult situations. His most valuable book was *A Digest of Methodist Law* (1885). Other works included: *Christian Baptism* (1876); *The New Testament Idea of Hell* (1878); *The Second Coming of Christ* (1879); *Aspects of Christian Experience* (copyright 1882); *Outline Thoughts on Prohibition* (1886); *The Organic Union of American Methodism* (1892); *Mary of Nazareth and Her Family* (1895); *The Crisis of This World* (1896); *Sanctification* (1901); *Atonement* (copyright 1901); *Discourses on Miracles* (copyright 1902).

[R. J. Cooke, "Bishop Stephen Mason Merrill," *Meth. Rev.,* May 1907; *Western Christian Advocate,* Sept. 2, 1896; *Christian Advocate* (N. Y.), Sept. 17, 1896; autobiographical statement in *Journal of the Twenty-fourth Delegated Gen. Conf. of the Meth. Episc. Ch.* (1904); *Minutes of the Ann. Conferences of the Meth. Episc. Ch., 1846–51* (1854); Samuel Merrill, "A Merrill Memorial" (1917–28), 2 vols., mimeographed, in Lib. of Cong.; J. B. Doyle, *20th Century Hist. of Steubenville and Jefferson County, Ohio* (1910); *N. Y. Daily Tribune,* Nov. 14, 1905.] J. R. J.

MERRILL, STUART FITZRANDOLPH (Aug. 1, 1863–Dec. 1, 1915), poet, was born at Hempstead, L. I., the eldest of three children. His father, George Merrill, a lawyer in New York City, came of a New England family. His name was originally Tibbetts, but he was adopted by an uncle by marriage, Nathaniel Wilson Merrill (Samuel Merrill, "A Merrill Memorial," 1917–28, mimeographed copy, in Library of Congress). Stuart's mother, Emma FitzRandolph Laing, was the daughter of William L. Laing of Virginia, who went north with his family about 1840 and settled at Hempstead. Her grandmother is said to have been French. In 1866 George Merrill was appointed counsellor to the American Legation in Paris. He was a man of strict and gloomy religious principles, and he obliged his family to lead in Paris, as far as possible, the same order of life they would have led in a New England village. When Stuart was twelve years old he was sent as a boarder to the Lycée at Vanves, a suburb of Paris. He stayed here till 1879, when he was removed to the Lycée Fontaines (now Condorcet). Here as at Vanves he proved a good scholar and obtained a high rank in his classes. He joined certain of his schoolfellows in starting a little magazine called *Le Fou.* One of the contributors was René Ghil, destined to be a leader of the Symbolist movement and to have some influence on Merrill's development as a poet. Merrill's contributions to the magazine reveal a poetic temperament and prove that he already possessed the technique of French versification.

He took his degree (*bachelier ès lettres*) in 1884. But whatever plans he had made to lead an artist's life in Paris were frustrated by his father who decided that the family must return to New York. There he became a very unwilling student at the Columbia Law School. His main interest was in literature, and in Washington Square, where he lived, he prepared his first book of poems, *Les Gammes,* and sent it to Paris. It was published in 1887 by Léon Vanier, and was dedicated to René Ghil, who saw it through the press, distributed it to the critics, and wrote a notice of it himself.

When he wrote *Les Gammes* and *Les Fastes,* which followed four years after, Merrill was interested only in exteriors and decoration, and for him to accept the noise and turmoil and passion of life at all they must come to him in symbols. It was not till much later that he gave expression to his vision of the world and to the love and anguish of his heart. In these two early books are some poems which he never surpassed. The influence of English poetry, which may be remarked in them, came principally from William Morris' "Defence of Guenevere," and in a much less degree from Rossetti and Swinburne and Wilde. Morris was Merrill's ideal man, and Morris' brand of socialism, with artistic beauty as a cure for all ills, Merrill kept all his life, though in his later years it became tinged with Tolstoyism. The youth of twenty had arrived in New York with his socialist convictions already strong. He campaigned for Henry George, and took up the defense of the eight Chicago anarchists condemned to death in 1886. Merrill's devotion to Henry George provoked his father to disinherit him; if he enjoyed easy financial circumstances all his life, he thenceforth owed it to his mother.

George Merrill died in 1888. The next year Mrs. Merrill and her sons went to Europe. From Vienna Stuart sent to America the only book he ever wrote in English, *Pastels in Prose* (1890), translations of short pieces by twenty-three French writers. The volume doubtless owed such trifling sale as it had to the preface by W. D. Howells. In the autumn of 1890 he returned to America to please his mother. On the way home he spent some weeks in London, where he came to know Oscar Wilde, then at the height of his fame. Their friendship continued till Wilde's downfall in 1895.

Merrill remained only five months in New York. Here he prepared his new book, *Les Fastes,* which was published in Paris at the end of

1891 with a dedication to Howells. During this winter he was an unfailing attendant upon Wagnerian opera. Wagner was one of the great influences of his life, as he was for most of the Symbolists. Another great influence was Walt Whitman. With him Merrill had an interview at a New York hotel. Whitman's humanitarian theory, his respect for individual freedom, Merrill entirely adopted. He returned to Paris in May 1891, and became one of the managers of the New Théâtre d'Art, founded as a protest against the commercial and realist theatres. He was back again in New York in the autumn, but in 1892 left America for the last time. As he was sailing, a letter from Howells was put into his hands, urging him to be an American poet and to write in English. Merrill did write some verses in English, but they have none of his special merits.

Upon his return to Paris, he fell in love with an artists' model known to her friends of the Latin Quarter as "Bob," and she became his wife in all but name. He now furnished an apartment on the Quai Bourbon which became famous in the annals of Symbolism, for therein gathered many of the young writers and painters. He began to lead the life of a poet of the Latin Quarter, and whenever this life became too much for him he retired to the country or traveled; fashionable social life he sedulously avoided. He lost all contact with America and in his later years had almost the same views about the United States as a Frenchman who has never been there. He had a house at Marlotte in the Forest of Fontainebleau. There he wrote *Petits Poèmes d'Automne* (1895) and *Les Quatre Saisons* (1900), which show a complete alteration in his conception of poetry and poetic expression.

In 1905 the woman who had lived with him so many years left him to marry another man. This departure threw Merrill into a state of demoralization. He cut himself off from general life. For some time he was hardly ever sober. He traveled at random. But out of this morbid condition arose his greatest work, *Une Voix dans la Foule* (1909). The section called *"Les Cris dans la Nuit"* contains some of the best poetry of the kind in French literature. Here he made what is perhaps the most stirring appeal for the wretched which had been heard in France since Victor Hugo. Pity for all who suffered had become the keynote of his life.

His wanderings took him to Belgium where he was extremely well received by the young writers, who regarded him as a master. He made the acquaintance of a family named Rion, who lived at Forêt, a suburb of Brussels, and in the summer of 1908 he married Claire Rion, who was about eighteen years old. After traveling for a while they settled permanently at Versailles in a beautiful house at 22 Boulevard de Roi. After his marriage Merrill published little, but his papers show that he had many projects, and he kept up a considerable correspondence with his friends. In 1913 he engaged in an unfortunate controversy with Guillaume Apollinaire concerning the morals of Walt Whitman, in which he made ferocious onslaughts on puritanism (*Mercure de France,* 16 avril, 16 novembre 1913).

The World War was the second crisis in his life, and this time he did not recover. It is necessary to realize Merrill's idealism, his dreams of human fraternity, to understand what the war meant to him. He thought of joining the French army, but his state of health made that impossible. He aided as he could several whom the war had reduced to misery, and wandered inconsolably in Versailles and Paris. The sight of the funeral of a British soldier at Versailles inspired his poem "Tommy Atkins," an entirely new expression of his art, which was published after his death, which occurred rather suddenly on Dec. 1, 1915. He had left instructions that he was to be buried without religious ceremonies.

In 1925 appeared *Prose et Vers,* an interesting volume containing some of his prose sketches and criticism and some hitherto unpublished poems. A great many of his prose contributions to magazines have never been reprinted. In 1929 a memorial tablet was placed on the outer wall of his house in Versailles, and the same year the Paris municipality gave the name of the American poet to a wide street near the Porte Champerret—*Place Stuart Merrill.*

Merrill performed the incredibly difficult feat of wringing out of French versification the soft far-away music of the English Pre-Raphaelites. More than any other he produced the nearest thing in words to Debussy's music. His amiable personality has become a legend. Not long before his death the great Belgian poet Verhaeren wrote to him: "For me you are as a flame and a glowing hearth at which I warm my hands." Although he spoke French like a Frenchman and German quite well he was generally recognized as an American.

[Marjorie Louise Henry, *Stuart Merrill* (Paris, 1927), written in French by an American, the chief authority on the subject; *Poètes d'Aujourd'hui* (1900), ed. by Adolphe Van Bever and Paul Léautaud, biographical notice by Léautaud; *Commemoration de Stuart Merrill à Versailles* (Paris, 1929), containing reminiscences by friends; Remy de Gourmont, *Promenades Littéraires 4me Série* (1912), and *Le Livre des Masques*

(1896); René Ghil, *Les Dates et les Œuvres* (1923); Ernest Raynaud, *La Mêlée Symboliste* (1918), André Barré, *Le Symbolisme* (1911), André Fontainas, *Mes Souvenirs du Symbolisme* (1928), and other books on the Symbolist period; scattered articles on Merrill in French magazines: by Charles Maurras in *Revue Encyclopédique*, Jan. 22, 1898, by Pierre Quillard in *Mercure de France*, Oct. 16, 1909, and many others listed in the bibliog. to Henry's *Stuart Merrill*; *Mercure de France*, Jan. 1, 1916, and July 15, 1929; T. B. Rudmose-Brown, *French Lit. Studies* (London, 1917); private information. V. O.

MERRILL, WILLIAM BRADFORD (Feb. 27, 1861–Nov. 26, 1928), newspaper editor and manager, descended from Nathaniel Merrill who settled at Newbury, Mass., in 1635, was born at Salisbury, N. H., the son of the Rev. Horatio Merrill, a Congregationalist minister, and Sarah Bradford (Whitman) Merrill. He studied at the Boston Latin School, 1874–76, preparing for Harvard, but instead of entering that institution he went to Paris, where he finished his education, devoting especial attention to art. While in Paris he wrote news letters for Philadelphia papers and on his return to the United States he took up newspaper work in Philadelphia, becoming a reporter for the *North American*. Within a year he was made its telegraph editor, despite his youth, and in another year became its dramatic critic. He gave up newspaper work for a time to make a study of American railroads, which took him into every part of the country and gave him an insight into railroad finance which was useful to him later, although the resulting publication, *Guide to Railways of the United States* (1881), was of temporary value only.

Returning to journalism, he became at the age of twenty-three managing editor of the Philadelphia *Press*. In a few years he developed to a marked degree the scope of the *Press* as a powerful and enterprising newspaper, gathering around him a staff of unusual efficiency, one of whose members was Richard Harding Davis [*q.v.*]. His success in Philadelphia attracted attention and at the age of thirty years he was called to be managing editor of the *New York Press*, being the youngest managing editor in the city which was the center of American journalism.

Merrill's versatility developed rapidly. His grasp included the problems of a publisher as well as those of an editor and in 1895 he became financial manager of the *Press*. In 1901 he transferred his services to the New York *World* and was made managing editor of the paper, then under the active control of Joseph Pulitzer. Later he became financial manager of the *World*, in which capacity he attracted the attention of William Randolph Hearst, who engaged him in 1908 as manager of the *New York American*. In 1917 he became general manager of all the Hearst papers, which was said to have been the fulfilment of an early ambition he had formed to be the director of a number of newspapers, at a time when newspaper "chains" did not exist. His favorite maxim was that "vigilance, enterprise and accuracy are the keynote of the successful newspaper," and he impressed that view upon editors and reporters.

As a member of the New York Publishers' Association, in which body he represented the *New York American* and the *New York Evening Journal*, he was active in negotiations with labor unions whose members were employed by newspapers, attaining a reputation for fairness to both sides. At the conclusion of a strike of pressmen, the publishers presented to him a memorial expressive of their appreciation, and the Pressmen's Union made him an honorary member. His zeal was centered intensely upon newspaper work, and only rarely could he be persuaded to take a vacation. A remark which he often made was that "all the rewards of life come in the day's work."

In his early days as a dramatic critic Merrill formed a lasting friendship with Charles and Daniel Frohman. He was one of the first to detect the latent abilities of Theodore Roosevelt and brought him to the attention of Mayor William L. Strong of New York City, who appointed him head of the police board, a stepping stone to his subsequent career.

Merrill continued active in the management of the Hearst papers until failing health caused him to give up work a year before his death. In appearance, he was slender and of medium height, with an expression of keenness and alertness. From his early twenties his hair was almost snow white. He married in 1882 Sara Louise Taylor, of Georgetown, D. C., who died in 1913. In 1922 he married Mrs. Josephine H. Bissell.

[Some information about Merrill may be found in J. K. Winkler's *W. R. Hearst* (1928) and Don C. Seitz's *Joseph Pulitzer, His Life and Letters* (1924). Other sources are *Who's Who in America*, 1928–29; Samuel Merrill, "A Merrill Memorial" (1917–28), 2 vols., mimeographed, in Lib. of Cong.; and the files of newspapers in Philadelphia and New York. A full obituary account prepared by one of his associates appeared in the *N. Y. American* of Nov. 27, 1928.]

A. S. W.

MERRILL, WILLIAM EMERY (Oct. 11, 1837–Dec. 14, 1891), soldier, engineer, was born at Fort Howard, Wis., the son of Capt. Moses E. Merrill and Virginia (Slaughter) Merrill. His father, born in Maine, was of New England ancestry, being descended from Nathaniel Merrill who settled at Newbury, Mass., in 1635; his mother came of an old Virginia family. When William was not quite ten, his father was killed while leading his troops in an attack at the battle of Molino del Rey, Mexico. Because of the father's services, President Pierce, in 1854, appointed the son a cadet at the United States Military Academy. He graduated at the head of his class in 1859 and was assigned to the Corps of Engineers.

Throughout the Civil War he served as a military engineer, first in the Department of the Ohio, subsequently in the Army of the Potomac and the Army of Kentucky, and finally, Jan. 27, 1864, to June 27, 1865, as chief engineer of the Army of the Cumberland. During McClellan's campaign in West Virginia he was captured (Sept. 12, 1861) and was a prisoner until the following February, except for two days in November when he escaped and was recaptured. Wounded in an engagement near Yorktown, Va., in April 1862, he was brevetted captain for gallantry. Subsequently, he served under Pope in the Cedar Mountain and Manassas campaigns, and was then transferred to the West to fortify Covington and Newport (September–October 1862) when threatened by Kirby-Smith's invasion of Kentucky. Promoted captain, Mar. 3, 1863, he served under Rosecrans in the Chickamauga campaign, under Thomas in the battle of Missionary Ridge, and under Sherman in the advance on Atlanta. He was specially charged with the construction of fortifications for the protection of the railways supplying Sherman's army. For his services in the battles of Chickamauga, Lookout Mountain and Missionary Ridge, and Resaca and New Hope Church, he received the brevets of major, lieutenant-colonel, and colonel. His military services closed in 1870 after three years of duty on Sherman's staff as chief engineer of the Division of the Missouri. As a military engineer he was excelled by none.

The second half of his career was devoted mainly to the river and harbor improvement work carried on by the Corps of Engineers. He originated one of the greatest projects for the development of American inland waterways—the canalization of the Ohio River from Pittsburgh to its mouth. In 1870 he was charged with the improvement of this river and in 1878, at his own request, he was sent to Europe to study the improvement of non-tidal rivers by means of locks and movable dams. On his return he advocated this method of improving the Ohio and, after overcoming great opposition, in 1879 succeeded in securing from Congress an appropriation for the Davis Island lock and dam below Pittsburgh. These were completed in 1885 and led to the approval of his project, with some modifications, for the entire river. He lived long enough to build only the first lock and dam; the entire project was not completed until 1929, when the President of the United States took part in the celebration which announced its accomplishment.

In 1870 Merrill published *Iron Truss Bridges for Railroads* and later he published studies of the improvement of non-tidal rivers and of inland navigation in France and the United States. In 1889 he was the United States representative at the Congress of Engineers in Paris. He was married in January 1873 to Margaret Spencer of Cincinnati. Two of their sons became officers of the United States Army.

[G. W. Cullum, *Biog. Reg. Officers and Grads. U. S. Mil. Acad.* (3rd ed., 1891); reports of the Chief of Engineers, U. S. Army, 1874–85, in annual reports of the Secretary of War; *Twenty-second Ann. Reunion Asso. Grads. U. S. Mil. Acad.* (1892); *Proc. Am. Soc. Civil Engineers,* vol. XVIII (1892); Samuel Merrill, "A Merrill Memorial" (1917–28), 2 vols., mimeographed, in Lib. of Cong.; *Army and Navy Jour.,* Dec. 19, 1891; *Cincinnati Enquirer,* Dec. 16, 1891.] G. J. F.

MERRIMON, AUGUSTUS SUMMERFIELD (Sept. 15, 1830–Nov. 14, 1892), jurist, was born at Cherryfields, in Buncombe (now in Transylvania) County, N. C. His father, Branch H. Merrimon, a Methodist minister and farmer, was a native of Virginia; his mother was Mary Paxton of North Carolina. His boyhood, spent in Haywood County, was one of hard labor on the farm and in a sawmill, with limited educational opportunity; but he "studied between the plow handles," and was able later to have more than a year at school in Asheville, serving part of the time as a junior teacher. He then began to study law, and in 1852 married Margaret J. Baird, the daughter of Israel Baird of Buncombe County. Receiving his license in 1853, he began practice at Asheville and was soon made a county attorney. In 1860 he went to the House of Commons and, as a Union Whig, opposed the secession movement, voting against submitting the question of a convention to the people and against all military preparation. After Lincoln's call for troops, however, he voted for calling the secession convention and at once enlisted. In May 1861 he was commissioned captain in the commissary department and was stationed successively at several posts in the state, but when later in that year he was appointed solicitor of a western district he accepted and served until 1865. The position was no sinecure during those years of war, with lawlessness flagrant and sedition common, and the performance of its duties took, perhaps, more courage than those of the field. He filled it with much credit and stanchly upheld the civil authority as superior to military power or to mob rule. He was instrumental in securing the candidacy of Vance for governor in 1862 and supported his administration loyally. In 1865 he was defeated for the "Johnson" convention, but the legislature elected him judge of the superior court. Here his task was perhaps as difficult as during the war, but he again proved his courage, decision, and initiative. He chafed under the interference of the army in judicial matters, and in 1867, when he was ordered to disregard the law and enforce military orders, he resigned, and moving to Raleigh began again the practice of law.

He vigorously opposed congressional reconstruction, cooperating with the Conservative party. For a short time he was chairman of its executive committee and was offered the nomination for governor in 1868, but declined and instead accepted one for associate justice of the supreme court. Defeated, he was quietly active in politics during the next four years. In 1871 he was one of the counsel of the board of managers in the impeachment trial of Gov. William Woods Holden [*q.v.*] and had charge of the examination of witnesses. The following year he was nominated for governor and covered the entire state in his campaign. North Carolina had the first state election that year and both national parties made a determined effort to win, sending their leading men to participate in the contest. Against Merrimon was employed the whole power of the Grant administration as well as that of the state, and, while he drove his opponent from the stump, he was defeated by a small majority.

He was promised by political leaders election to the Senate, but Vance was a candidate and secured the caucus nomination, which some of Merrimon's supporters in the legislature disregarded. After a deadlock both withdrew, but the caucus again nominated Vance, and the Republicans voted with Merrimon's supporters and elected Merrimon. He served until 1879 when he was defeated by Vance, who had, in the meantime, been elected governor. In 1883 Governor Jarvis appointed Merrimon associate justice of the supreme court, and he filled the place until 1889, when he was appointed chief justice. He served in this capacity until his death.

Merrimon was a straightforward, forceful, and magnetic man, a good speaker, and a warmly human person. He was an excellent trial judge and was highly regarded as an appellate judge, although he was in no sense a great one.

[Merrimon's decisions appear in 89–110 *N. C. Reports*. For estimates and biographical material see 111 *N. C. Reports*, 735 and 114 *N. C. Reports*, 930; S. A. Ashe and others, *Biog. Hist. of N. C.*, vol. VIII (1907); *News and Observer* (Raleigh, N. C.), Nov. 15, 16, 1892. See also *N. C. House Journal*, 1860–61; *Congressional Record*, 1873–79; J. G. deR. Hamilton, *Reconstruction in N. C.* (1914).]
J. G. deR. H.

MERRITT, ANNA LEA (Sept. 13, 1844–Apr. 7, 1930), painter and etcher, was born in Philadelphia, Pa. The daughter of Joseph and Susanna (Massey) Lea, she was descended through her father from John Lea, a Quaker who came from England to Philadelphia in 1699, and from Andrew Robeson, first chief-justice of Pennsylvania. She was educated privately. At the early age of seven she began the study of drawing under William H. Furness. After leaving school she traveled abroad for four years, and about 1865 she was studying painting under Heinrich Hoffman in Dresden. In 1871 she went to London, where she continued her training under Henry Merritt (see *Dictionary of National Biography*), artist and author, whose interest in his pupil was more than academic, for on Apr. 17, 1877, they were married.

Before this event took place she had begun to exhibit portraits and figure pieces at the Royal Academy, and had received some recognition. When she married she intended to give up her career as an artist, but her husband died soon afterward, and she then resumed painting. She was a fairly regular exhibitor at the Royal Academy exhibitions for nearly thirty years, and sent occasional contributions to exhibitions in Philadelphia and New York. She won a medal at the Centennial Exposition, Philadelphia, 1876; was elected a member of the Royal Society of Painter-Etchers; and wrote a memoir of her husband which was published with selections from his writings in *Henry Merritt: Art Criticism and Romance* (2 vols., London, 1879). She also made a series of twenty-three small etchings as illustrations for the same book. At a later period she etched a number of portraits, her subjects including likenesses of Sir Gilbert Scott, after the original by George Richmond; and Ellen Terry as Ophelia.

Among her more important paintings shown at the Royal Academy were "The Pied Piper of Hamelin," "Eve Overcome by Remorse" (which brought her a medal at the Chicago Exposition of 1893), "Camilla" (which appeared at the Paris exposition of 1889), and "Love Locked Out" (1890), which was purchased by the Chantrey Fund and hung in the National Gallery of British Art, commonly known as the Tate Gallery—the first work by a woman artist to be thus honored. Love, shown as a little boy, stands pushing at a golden door which is barred against him.

After 1890 she made her home in a tiny Hampshire village, Hurstbourne Tarrant. She made this village the theme of a book, illustrated by herself, called *A Hamlet in Old Hampshire* (1902); and her garden there was the subject of a magazine article published in 1908. The summers of 1893 and 1894 were devoted to mural paintings for St. Martin's Church, near Wanersh, Surrey. Another mural painting which she did was the large decoration in the vestibule of the Women's Building at the Chicago Exposition of 1893, for which she was awarded a medal. Her "Piping Shepherd" (1896) was bought by the Pennsylvania Academy of the Fine Arts, Philadelphia. Her portrait of James Russell Lowell belongs to Harvard University. Among other distinguished sitters were Gen. John A. Dix, United States minister to France, Lady Dufferin, General the Earl of Dundonald and Countess Dundonald, and Lord Walter Campbell. The group portrait of two children, Justine and Bayard Cutting, exhibited at the National Academy, New York, 1883, was entitled "Taming the Bird."

Mrs. Merritt was a versatile and accomplished woman; but her work lacks spontaneity. In the case of the etchings this defect is especially noticeable. When her death occurred, in London, she was eighty-five years old and for some time had been blind.

[Autobiographical data in *Henry Merritt . . .* (1879); J. H. and G. H. Lea, *The Ancestry and Posterity of John Lea* (1906), in which Anna Lea's name is given as Anna Massey Lea; K. H. Osbourne, *An Hist. and Geneal. Account of Andrew Robeson* (1916); *Who's Who* (British), 1920; *Who's Who in America*, 1920–21; *Am. Art Rev.*, Apr. 1880; *Art News*, Apr. 12, 1930; *Boston Transcript*, Apr. 9, 1930; the *Times* (London), Apr. 15, 17, 1930.] W. H. D.

MERRITT, ISRAEL JOHN (Aug. 23, 1829–Dec. 13, 1911), wrecker, inventor, eldest child of Hamilton and Elizabeth Merritt, was born in New York City. His father, seventh in descent from Thomas Merritt who came to America in the seventeenth century, was a merchant in moderate circumstances and had every intention of giving his son a good education, but in 1841 he was lost at sea and the boy was compelled to find work in order to help support his widowed mother and her family of children. After doing a number of odd jobs, including driving mules on a canal, Merritt went to sea until he was fifteen, then became associated with Capt. Thomas Bell salvaging wreckage from Long Island Sound and the waters about Manhattan Island. At the age of twenty he obtained command of a coasting schooner and some four years afterward was appointed agent for the Board of Marine Underwriters. In 1860 he became the general agent of the Coast Wrecking Company and from that time on his whole attention was given to salvage. In connection with this work Captain Merritt, as he came to be known, originated and employed many novel ideas and methods which to this day are successfully used by the company which bears his name. His greatest contribution probably was the pontoon patented by him in 1865. This was a specially constructed device for raising sunken vessels by displacement. Making possible the recovery of large vessels sunk with all decks submerged, it completely revolutionized the salvage business. In its various forms the pontoon is still an important and useful adjunct of modern salvage equipment. Merritt continued with the Coast Wrecking Company until 1880, when he organized the Merritt Wrecking Organization, with his eldest son as partner. The new company's operations quickly assumed immense proportions. Its fleet was one of the largest of the kind in the world, doing practically all the marine salvage on the Atlantic Coast. Offices were established in New York with storehouses and docks on Staten Island, and a similar establishment was set up at Norfolk, Va. In 1897 Merritt's organization and the Chapman Company, engaged in derrick and lighterage business about New York, united as the Merritt & Chapman Derrick & Wrecking Company, with Merritt as president and his son as treasurer. Merritt was active at the head of the combined organizations until his death. During the Civil War he took charge of the fitting out of many expeditions with surf boats and served under the secretary of the navy in an advisory capacity. He was for years an active volunteer fireman in New York City, and for many years foreman of Engine No. 17. He was married in March 1853 to Sarah L. Nichols of New York, who died on June 11, 1879. In 1890 he married Caroline Elizabeth Bull. He died in New York, survived by his widow and four children of his former marriage.

[Henry Hall, *America's Successful Men of Affairs*, vol. I (1895); Douglas Merritt, *Revised Merritt Records* (1916), pp. 121, 131; correspondence with Merritt & Chapman Holding Corporation, New York; Patent Office records; *N. Y. Times*, Dec. 15, 1911.] C. W. M.

MERRITT, LEONIDAS (Feb. 20, 1844–May 9, 1926), prospector, discoverer—with his brothers—of the Mesabi iron-ore deposit in Minnesota, was born on a farm in Chautauqua County, N. Y. His parents, Lewis Howell and Hepzibeth (Jewett) Merritt, later moved their family to Warren County, Pa., then to Ohio, and finally, in 1856, shortly after the opening of the canal at Sault Ste. Marie, to Duluth, Minn. They settled on a homestead claim at Oneota, a suburb of Duluth, where the father worked at his trade of millwright and sawyer. Of the ten children, eight sons survived to maturity and of these Alfred, Napoleon, Louis, and Cassius were actively associated with Leonidas in his iron-mining exploits. Although Leonidas, in his later years, was fond of writing narrative poems in the meter made popular by Longfellow's "Hiawatha," his formal education seems to have been limited to attendance upon the common-schools afforded by the frontier community and a brief term at Grand River Institute, Ashtabula, Ohio. In his late teens he enlisted in the Minnesota cavalry for service in the Civil War, and remained in the army through some of the Indian campaigns that followed.

From 1856 until 1890 the family was engaged in the usual pioneer ways of making a living, chiefly in connection with the lumbering industry, though Leonidas and Alfred built a sloop to engage in the carrying trade, wrecked it, worked as lumberman to pay off debts incurred, and built a schooner and operated it. Their most profitable adventures were in timber lands and at times they possessed considerable funds. After the first discovery of rich iron-ore fields in the Lake Superior region, nearly everyone who traversed the woods hoped to discover iron ore and thereby achieve a fortune. Lewis H. Merritt was early convinced that the Mesabi region was rich in iron-ore. Beginning in the seventies, it was repeatedly investigated, but without success because the explorers supposed its deposits would exhibit the same characteristics as those previously discovered, which were found in bold outcrops, whereas they were actually quite different, lying flat, buried beneath the surface. In 1887 the Merritts, who in connection with their work as "timber cruisers" had several times explored the field, made another survey, "running diagonals across the formation and mapping the lines of attraction with a dip-needle" (Van Brunt, *post,* p. 398). Their map conforms closely to later maps of the deposits. Leonidas Merritt filed claims for the land thus located, and in July 1890 the brothers organized the Mountain Iron Company to exploit the Mesabi range.

On Nov. 16 of that year, J. A. Nicols, who with a gang of men was working for Leonidas and Alfred Merritt in depressions, discovered high-grade ore at the bottom of a test pit. Other discoveries followed, and the Merritt family embarked on a program of mining and railroad and ore-dock building that required more capital than their local associates could provide. They therefore sought and secured the participation of John D. Rockefeller, who was shrewd enough to safeguard his own interests carefully, while the Merritts, engaging in enterprises that were of a magnitude entirely beyond their business and financial ability, were not so astute. As a result of the financial crisis of 1893 they lost their control of the mining and transportation enterprises they had initiated. Litigation ensued (1895), and, ultimately (1912), a congressional investigation. Leonidas apparently suffered a mental breakdown, at any rate he was not able to give the congressional committee any clear statement of what happened or even clearly to remember how and why, in 1897, he and some other members of the family transferred their holdings to Mr. Rockefeller for something over $500,000 in order to meet their other obligations. Louis Merritt took advantage of Mr. Rockefeller's offer to permit them to buy back their holdings at the price he paid, plus interest, and became very wealthy through their subsequent appreciation. During his later years Leonidas was commissioner of public utilities (1914–17) and commissioner of finance (1921–25) for the city of Duluth. He died there in May 1926, aged eighty-two years. On May 8, 1873, he had married Elizabeth E. Wheeler of Oneota, Minn. Three children survived him.

[*Who's Who in America,* 1924–25; Walter Van Brunt, *Duluth and St. Louis County, Minn.* (1921), vol. I; *Am. Mag.,* Sept. 1923; *Hearings before the Committee on Investigation of United States Steel Corporation* (8 vols., 1912), esp. III, 1885–1934, for Merritt's testimony; F. T. Gates, *The Truth about Mr. Rockefeller and the Merrits* (1912); Paul de Kruif, *Seven Iron Men* (1929); *Minneapolis Morning Tribune,* May 10, 1926; *Ely Miner* (Ely, Minn.), May 14, 1926.] T. T. R.

MERRITT, WESLEY (June 16, 1834–Dec. 3, 1910), soldier, seventh in descent from Thomas Merritt who came to America in the seventeenth century, was the fourth of eleven children born to John Willis Merritt and his wife Julia Anne (de Forest). The father was a lawyer, but in 1841, after financial reverses suffered during the crisis of 1837, abandoned his profession, and moved his family West to Illinois. After a few years of farming he turned to journalism, editing the Bellville *Advocate* and then the Salem *Advocate* and eventually being elected to the legislature. Wesley Merritt attended the school of the Christian Brothers and studied law with Judge Haynie in Salem, but when the opportunity came to him, in 1855, entered the United States Military Academy. The appointment had been tendered first to his younger brother, Edward, who did not wish to accept it, and it is the year of Edward's birth that still stands on the army records.

Upon graduation in 1860 Merritt was commissioned second lieutenant of dragoons. The following year, promoted first lieutenant, he served as aide-de-camp to Gen. Philip St. George Cooke [*q.v.*], commanding the cavalry of the Army of the Potomac. He was promoted captain in 1862, and on June 29, 1863, was commissioned brigadier-general of volunteers. He commanded the reserve cavalry brigade at Gettysburg, and received the brevet of major in the regular establishment for bravery there. Following continuous service in Virginia, he was brevetted major-general of volunteers in 1864, and commissioned in the same rank in 1865. In the meantime he was successively brevetted lieutenant-colonel, colonel, brigadier-general and major-general, United States Army, for meritorious services. He was present at Appomattox, then became chief of cavalry in the Department of Texas, and was mustered out of the voluntary service Feb. 1, 1866, resuming his regular rank. Later that year he became lieutenant-colonel, 9th Cavalry, and ten years later colonel, 5th Cavalry. Until 1879 his service was principally in the West in connection with Indian disturbances.

From Sept. 1, 1882, to June 30, 1887, he was superintendent of the United States Military Academy. Commissioned brigadier-general Apr. 10, 1887, he assumed command of the Department of the Missouri in July. He later commanded the Department of Dakota, and then the Department of the Missouri, with headquarters at Chicago from 1895 to 1897, being promoted to the grade of major-general, Apr. 25, 1895. The post at Chicago was considered a territorial command second in importance only to that of the Department of the East, and in 1897 Merritt succeeded to the latter command with headquarters at Governor's Island, New York.

The war with Spain brought larger responsibilities. On May 16, 1898, he was given command of the first Philippine Expedition. Sailing from San Francisco June 29, he arrived at Cavite, Manila Bay, July 25, where Dewey's fleet was anchored. Landing immediately, he assumed command of the American forces investing Manila, July 27, 1898. These forces, about two miles from the Spanish defenses, extended from the Bay to a point not far therefrom where the Philippine insurgents, under command of General Aguinaldo, continued the investment. The insurgents also had other forces between the American and Spanish lines. Since the American officers had been instructed to avoid all appearance of an alliance with the insurgents, and at the same time were hardly disposed to treat them as enemies, the situation presented extraordinary difficulties. On Aug. 6, Merritt and Dewey entered into communication with the Spanish commander, with a view to preventing suffering to non-combatants in case an attack should be necessary. Meanwhile, through one of his officers, Gen. F. V. Greene [*q.v.*], Merritt had tried to persuade the insurgents "to move out of the way" (Dewey, *post*, p. 270). On Aug. 9 a formal joint demand was made for the surrender of Manila. When this was refused Merritt decided, after consultation with Dewey, to try to carry the extreme right of the Spanish line of entrenchments without bombarding the city. Early in the morning of the 13th, after a short naval bombardment of the Spanish entrenchments, the attack was opened and was almost immediately successful, although there were numerous casualties on both sides. An exploitation of the attack brought the whole city into American possession, with the exception of the Walled City, which shortly after surrendered. Merritt's official report summarizes the operations as follows: "I submit that for troops to enter under fire a town covering a wide area, to rapidly deploy and guard all principal points in the extensive suburbs, to keep out the insurgent forces pressing for admission, to quietly disarm an army of Spaniards more than equal in numbers to the American troops, and finally by all this to prevent entirely all rapine, pillage, and disorder, and gain entire and complete possession of a city of 300,000 people filled with natives hostile to the European interests and stirred up by the knowledge that their own people were fighting in the outside trenches, was an act which only the law-abiding, temperate, resolute American soldier, well and skillfully handled by his regimental and brigade commanders, could accomplish."

On Aug. 14, the day after the capture of the city, Merritt issued a proclamation to the people of the Philippine Islands establishing military government therein, and entered on duty as military governor. Two days later he received the president's proclamation directing the cessation of hostilities. During his short governorship, in addition to setting up an administrative machine, he was under the necessity of conducting negotiations with Aguinaldo with regard to the location and conduct of the Philippine insurgents, who were much dissatisfied at not being permitted to occupy Manila. On Aug. 28 he was ordered to France, for conference with the Peace

Commission, and on completion of this duty, Dec. 10, returned to America, arriving Dec. 19. Relieved as military governor of the Philippines, he resumed his old command of the Department of the East, returning to Governor's Island, where he completed his military career. He retired at the statutory age of sixty-four, in June 1900.

In appearance as in character, Merritt was representative of the best in the United States Army of his day. A fine looking man of strong will and wide experience, he was highly competent, and at the same time modest and agreeable. He was twice married: in 1871, to Caroline Warren of Cincinnati, Ohio; and in 1898, at London, to Laura Williams of Chicago. He died at Natural Bridge, Va., and was buried at the United States Military Academy.

[Personnel files, War Dept.; files Army War College; G. W. Cullum, *Biog. Reg. Officers and Grads., U. S. Mil. Acad.* (3rd ed., 1891), and supplementary volumes; *Forty-Second Ann. Reunion Asso. Grads. U. S. Mil. Acad.* (1911); *Who's Who in America*, 1910–11; Douglas Merritt, *Revised Merritt Records* (1916); *Autobiog. of George Dewey* (1913); *Army and Navy Jour.*, Dec. 10, 1910; information as to certain facts from a cousin, Mrs. J. M. Chance, Kensington, Md.]

J. N. G.

MERRY, ANN BRUNTON (May 30, 1769–June 28, 1808), tragédienne, theatrical manager, was the daughter of John Brunton, a tea-dealer of London, and his wife, formerly a Miss Friend. In 1774 her father turned to the stage and after a few years joined the company at Bath and Bristol. Ann was educated by her mother's instruction and her father's Shakesperian readings, but no effort was made to direct her ambition toward the theatre. When, however, her father discovered that she had memorized several tragic rôles, he resolved to bring her before the public, and within a week she made her début at Bath, Feb. 17, 1785. She at once captured the town. Thomas Harris, manager of Covent Garden, engaged her for the coming season, and London bestowed on her its high favor until her retirement in 1792 after her marriage in August 1791 to Robert Merry, the Della-Cruscan poet.

In a few years Merry's extravagant living had so diminished his fortune that when Thomas Wignell, the Philadelphia director, made Mrs. Merry an offer in 1796, she readily accepted it and on Dec. 5 faced her first American audience as Juliet. Philadelphia remained the scene of her major efforts, though she occasionally played in other towns, especially New York, where she was a tremendous favorite. On Jan. 1, 1803, having been a widow for four years, she married Wignell, but his death followed seven weeks later. The theatre was now conducted by Mrs. Wignell and her late husband's partner, Alexander Reinagle, until, on Aug. 15, 1806, she married William Warren, a prominent comedian, to whom she committed the management of her affairs. When the company started its summer tour in 1808, Mrs. Warren, though pregnant, accompanied her husband, contrary to her physician's advice. At Alexandria, Va., she gave birth to a still-born son and died four days later. One child, the daughter of Wignell, survived her.

Mrs. Merry (by which name she is usually designated in theatrical histories) was one of the really notable players on the early American stage. As late as 1832 William Dunlap described her as one "who will long be entitled to the character of the most perfect actor America has seen" (*A History of the American Theatre*, 1832, p. 173). Despite her low stature and her lack of positive beauty, she made an irresistible appeal through gentleness, simplicity, and grace. John Bernard, the English comedian, found her less majestic than Mrs. Siddons but "equally perfect, and equally gifted to enrapture an audience. With a voice that was all music, and a face all emotion, her pathos and tenderness were never exceeded" (*Retrospections of America*, 1887, p. 269). Her character was as distinguished as her art. Her associates abundantly testified to the charm and beauty of her personality, and to the scrupulous honor of all her professional dealings. She was adored by her inferiors in the theatre and was on terms of social equality with some of the first families of Philadelphia. After her death her husband wrote in his diary "she has not left a better woman behind" (G. C. D. Odell, *Annals of the New York Stage*, II, 1927, p. 301).

[In addition to the works cited above, see: *The Thespian Dict.* (1802), which has been relied upon for the birth date; an anonymous article in the *Mirror of Taste*, Feb. 1810; Chas. Durang, "The Philadelphia Stage," published serially in the *Philadelphia Dispatch* (1854–60); W. B. Wood, *Personal Recollections of the Stage* (1855); J. N. Ireland, *Records of the N. Y. Stage*, vol. I (1866); John Genest, *Some Account of the English Stage* (1832), vols. VI and VII; *Gentleman's Mag.*, Sept. 1791, Aug. 1808.]

O. S. C.

MERRY, WILLIAM LAWRENCE (Dec. 27, 1842–Dec. 14, 1911), sea-captain, merchant, diplomat, was prominent as a supporter of the Nicaragua Canal project. He was born in New York City, the son of Thomas Henry and Candida Isbina (Xavier) Merry. His parentage helps to explain his interests and career, for his father came from a line of New York sea-captains and merchants of English descent, while his mother was a Latin American, apparently from Rio Grande do Sul in Brazil. At the age of seven he accompanied his father around Cape Horn to California, but returned east for an education in the schools of Massachusetts and at the Collegiate Institute of New York City. His maritime career was associated with the route between New York and San Francisco by way of Central America. At sixteen he was a junior officer on the steamship *George Law* between New York and Central America, and in 1862 he was commanding the New York clipper *White Falcon* on the Pacific Coast. In this year he visited Lake Nicaragua for the first time. Subsequently he had ample opportunity to study the rival canal routes of Panama and Nicaragua. In 1863 he was agent for the United States Mail Steamship Company on the Panama isthmus, making frequent trips over the Panama Railroad between Aspinwall and Panama City. A year later, he was given command of the steamship *America,* plying between San Francisco and Nicaragua. In 1867, he became general agent in charge of Nicaraguan transit for the Central American Transit Company and the North American Steamship Company, of which his father's old friend, William H. Webb [*q.v.*], of New York, was president. For three years Merry "practically lived" on the line of the projected Nicaragua Canal, passing over it "night and day, in steamers, boats and canoes" (*The Nicaragua Canal,* p. 46) and making a thorough study of the canal possibilities, which impressed him as superior to those of Panama. In the early seventies, he was with the Pacific Mail Steamship Company, and in 1874 he moved to San Francisco. There he engaged in business, becoming president of the North American Navigation Company, a Pacific Coast line, and serving as consul general of Nicaragua on the west coast. He was president of the San Francisco Chamber of Commerce for seven years.

"Captain Merry" was an active supporter of a strong navy and the maritime development of the Pacific ports, but he attracted particular attention between 1890 and 1895 as a protagonist of the Nicaragua Canal. He claimed credit for having *"first introduced the Canal question to the merchants of the United States from a commercial standpoint"* (*The Nicaragua Canal,* p. 46). It is said that his enthusiasm for the Nicaragua route arose partly from his financial interest in lands in that country, but the sincerity of his belief in its advantages was not questioned. He was appointed by McKinley on July 17, 1897, as minister to Nicaragua, Costa Rica, and Salvador. Residing at San Jose in Costa Rica, he held that position until, in 1907 and 1908 respectively, the increasing importance of Caribbean problems led to the appointment of separate ministers to Salvador and Nicaragua. Merry remained minister to Costa Rica until ill health forced him to resign in 1911. Though he was in such an important position when "dollar diplomacy" was spreading into Central America his printed dispatches in the *Papers Relating to the Foreign Relations of the United States* bear little trace of such methods, dealing mostly with perfunctory matters. Most of the important transactions seem to have been carried on at Washington. Merry's views, however, are set forth in several canal propaganda pamphlets including *The Nicaragua Canal, the Gateway between the Oceans* (1895), reprints of an article in the *California Bankers' Magazine,* October 1890, and a speech before the Trans-Mississippi Commercial Convention at St. Louis, Nov. 28, 1894. He argued that the nation that with the Nicaraguan Government on a joint agreement should control Lake Nicaragua, would then control the destiny of the Western Hemisphere. The decision in favor of Panama naturally thwarted his lifelong ambition to sail through a Nicaraguan canal before he died. His death occurred at the Battle Creek Sanitorium, shortly after he had retired from his post. He had married Blanche, daughter of William S. Hill of Scarsdale, N. Y., and he was buried in Scarsdale. He has been described as a "pure Yankee skipper" with quaint speech and ways, who spoke abominable Spanish with a nasal accent. He was generally liked and respected as an honest old gentleman who wanted to do his best both for his country and for Central America. In appearance he was undersized, spare, nervously built and wiry, acquiring some dignity from a remarkable pair of long, pointed side-whiskers.

[*Who's Who in America,* 1910–11; *Register* of the U. S. Dept. of State, 1897–1911; *Bull. Pan-Am. Union,* May 1912; *San Francisco Examiner,* Dec. 16, 1911.]

R. G. A.

MERVINE, WILLIAM (Mar. 14, 1791–Sept. 15, 1868), naval officer, was born at Philadelphia, Pa., the son of John and Zibia (Wright) Mervine. His grandfather, Philip Mervine, who wrote his name in German, "Marvine," although believed to be a Huguenot, settled in Germantown Township, near Philadelphia, before 1746. William was appointed midshipman from Jan. 16, 1809, and was assigned to duty at the Philadelphia naval station. Serving on board the *John Adams* at the outbreak of the War of 1812, he was on September 30 of that year transferred to the Black Rock flotilla on Lake Erie, and he remained on the Lakes until the end of the war. After the battle of Black Rock, in which he was wounded, he was transferred to the *Hamilton*. He was promoted to an acting lieutenancy on Aug. 25, 1813, and to a lieutenancy on Feb. 4, 1815. A tour of duty at Sacketts Harbor, N. Y., was followed by cruises on board the *Cyane* on the west coast of Africa, in the West Indies, and in the Mediterranean from 1820 to 1825. In 1827–28 he served with the *Natchez* of the West India Squadron. Having been promoted master-commandant in June 1834, he commanded the *Natchez* in 1836–37 during a cruise in the West Indies. From 1838 to 1845 he was on waiting orders. He saw his first sea service as captain, to which rank he was promoted from Sept. 8, 1841, in command of the *Cyane* from 1845 to 1846, and of the *Savannah* from 1846 to 1847, both of the Pacific Squadron. On July 7, 1846, with a detachment of sailors and marines he landed at Monterey, Cal., and took possession of the town, serving later as its military commandant. In October he commanded a landing party that engaged the Mexicans near Los Angeles with a loss of about a dozen men on each side and then retired.

From 1855 to 1857 he commanded the Pacific Squadron. During the last year of this tour of duty he was employed on the coast of Panama and Central America on account of the filibustering expedition of William Walker [*q.v.*]. He was on waiting orders when, on May 6, 1861, he was chosen to command the Gulf Blockading Squadron. With the *Colorado* as his flagship anchored off Fort Pickens, Fla., he established a blockade extending from Key West to Galveston. The destruction of the *Judah* by a boat expedition from the flagship was warmly commended by Gideon Welles, the secretary of the navy. Mervine, however, who was now more than seventy years old, impressed the secretary as lacking in energy and initiative, and he was therefore, in September 1861, relieved of his command. Later during the war he performed special duty at Washington and Philadelphia and served as president of the retiring board at New York. He was promoted commodore from July 16, 1862, and rear admiral from July 25, 1866, both on the retired list. He died at his home at Utica, N. Y. On Jan. 12, 1815, he was married to Amanda Maria Crane at Litchfield, N. Y.

[Letters of June 17, Sept. 2, 1930, from Mrs. Wm. M. Mervine; records of officers, bureau of navigation, Navy Department; records of the bureau of pensions; *War of the Rebellion, Official Records (Navy)*, ser. 1, vols. XVI, XXVII (1903–1917); *Register of the Commissioned and Warrant Officers of the Navy of the U. S.*, 1814–69; *Rept. of the Sec. of Navy*, 1855–57, 1861; H. H. Bancroft, *Hist. of Cal.* (1890), vol. V, esp. pp. 230–31, 318–20; *Diary of Gideon Welles* (1911), vol. I; *Utica Daily Observer*, Sept. 16 (misdated 15), 1868.]

C. O. P.

MERZ, KARL (Sept. 19, 1836–Jan. 30, 1890), musician, was born in Bensheim, Hesse, near Frankfort-on-the-Main. He was the third of nine children of Johannes Merz and Katharina (Werle). The father, a native of Steinheim, Prussia, was an excellent all-round musician who taught school and music for fifty years. He gave Karl his first lessons in violin and organ, enabling him to become a church organist at the age of eleven. The boy's schooling was not confined to music, however, but included excellent literary discipline; nor did his father continue long to teach him, but placed him with Franz Joseph Kunkel, a good musician though a less able schoolmaster.

Karl was graduated from the Gymnasium (in arts) in 1852 and the following year received a government appointment as school-teacher in a small town near Bingen-on-the-Rhine. His devotion to music caused him to weary of teaching school in so small a town and he remained only a year, coming to America in September 1854 and settling at once in Philadelphia. Since he could not speak English, he met with many obstacles. Through his friend Johann Heinrich Bonawitz he secured a position as violinist in a theatre orchestra and also an organ position in the Sixth Presbyterian Church of Philadelphia, where he remained for one year. From 1856 to 1859 he taught in a ladies' seminary near Lancaster, Pa., and played the organ associated with the school. Here he had much time for furthering his own study and growth, and for testing himself in musical composition. During the next two years, he was successively in Salem, Roanoke County, in Harrisonburg, at Hollins Institute, and at Botetourt Springs (all in Virginia), teaching music in schools for girls. While he was away on vacation in 1861 the Civil War began and he was obliged to seek another position. This circumstance was not really a misfortune, for he secured a much better place at Oxford Female College, Oxford, Ohio, where he remained twenty-one years. When this institution closed its doors temporarily in 1882 he was immediately called to Wooster University as director of the department of music and the arts, and here he remained until his death. He was a gifted lecturer, possessing personal charm which, combined with his thorough knowledge of his subject, won wide favor.

Besides his success as a teacher and lecturer, he achieved considerable reputation as a writer on musical topics. His "Musical Hints for the Million," published serially in *Brainard's Musical World* beginning in April 1868 (and in book form in 1875), gained immediate attention. He became a regular contributor to that journal and was made associate editor in 1871 and editor in 1873. His other works—useful in their time—include *The Modern Method for the Reed Organ* (1876); *Karl Merz' Piano Method* (1885), probably the best instruction books of the period; and his textbook, *The Elements of Harmony and Musical Composition* (copyright 1881). Probably his work most widely read by musicians is the posthumous volume, *Music and Culture* (1890), a collection of essays and articles, some of which were given as lectures before the students at Wooster University and some of which had appeared in musical periodicals. These writings were compiled by his son, Charles Hope Merz, in response to many requests for them made while the father was still living. Merz's compositions, now little remembered, included a trio for piano, violin, and 'cello, the three movements bearing the titles *"L'inquiétude," "Éloge," "La Belle Américaine"*; two nocturnes for piano entitled "Bitter Tears" and "Tranquility"; a piano sonata in C minor; and three operettas: *The Runaway Flirt* (1868), *The Last Will and Testament* (1877, produced at Oxford), and *Katie Dean* (1882, Oxford). He also wrote numerous quartets and choruses, organ and piano pieces, and songs. After his death, which occurred at Wooster, his valuable library was purchased and presented to the Carnegie Institute Library, Pittsburgh, Pa. His wife, whom he married in 1858, was Mary Louise Riddle of Paradise, Pa., a pupil. Their daughter, Bessie C. Merz, was, until her death in 1921, a well-known music teacher in New York City.

[W. S. B. Mathews and Granville Howe, *A Hundred Years of Music in America* (1889); letters from Merz's son, Charles Hope Merz, M.D.; *Grove's Dictionary of Music and Musicians, Am. Supp.* (1930); M. T. MacMillan, "The Wisdom of a Great Teacher, Karl Merz," *The Etude*, June 1930; *N. Y. Times*, Jan. 31, 1890.]

F. L. G. C.

MESERVE, NATHANIEL (*c.* 1705–June 28, 1758), colonial soldier, was the son of Clement Meserve (spelled variously), a carpenter of Newington, N. H., and of his wife, Elizabeth Jones. Shortly after his marriage in 1725, to Jane Libby, Nathaniel moved to Portsmouth, and during the next twenty years acquired a considerable fortune, a reputation as a prominent shipwright, and a character for probity and honesty which caused him to be named on numerous occasions as appraiser and executor. In 1746 he was one of the twelve chief inhabitants who purchased from Mason's heirs their claims to New Hampshire territory. After the death of his wife Jane on June 18, 1747, he married Mary (Odiorne) Jackson, a member of a leading Portsmouth family. He had eleven children, ten of whom survived him.

Meserve turned his carpentry training to good account in the siege of Louisbourg in 1745, when, as lieutenant-colonel of Moore's New Hampshire regiment, which he had helped to raise, he constructed sledges for the transportation of artillery across Cape Breton marshes. In compensation for his services he was selected, through the instrumentality of Sir Peter Warren and Sir William Pepperrell, to build a British frigate, one of the rare occasions when the British navy employed colonial shipyards. This vessel, the *America,* 44 guns, was launched from Portsmouth in 1749. In the trying summer of 1756 he served at Fort Edward as colonel of the New Hampshire regiment, and his readiness to obey all orders, the vigor which he instilled into his men, not scrupling himself to wield an axe when work did not progress to his satisfaction, his skill in constructing blockhouses, and perhaps his good-natured simplicity, marked him out definitely from the majority of provincial officers and gained him the esteem of his British superiors. Loudoun wrote of him in highest terms to Governor Wentworth and to the secretary of state, made him a present of a valuable piece of plate, properly inscribed, and later, with Pitt's authority, expressed to him "the gracious sense the King has of the Zeal and Diligence he has shewed the Service." In 1757 he was commissioned as captain of an independent company of sixty carpenters, paid, as were the ranging and Indian companies, out of British contingencies, and in that capacity, though still a New Hampshire colonel, he accompanied Loudoun to Halifax in the summer, where he built barracks and storehouses. Though Loudoun reëngaged him in 1758 for duty in New York, Pitt expressly ordered that he collect eighty carpenters to serve under Amherst at Louisbourg, and that he be urged to resign the command of the New Hampshire troops in order to devote his whole attention to the more essential service. Of his company of 108 men, ninety-two caught the smallpox at Louisbourg, and he and his son Nathaniel died there of the disease; "a very great loss," wrote Amherst, "to this Army." Another son, George, who as distributor of stamps was the target of Portsmouth rioters in 1765, petitioned for lands on account of his father's services, and put in claims as a Loyalist during the Revolution.

[Nathaniel Adams, *Annals of Portsmouth* (1825); *New Hampshire State Papers; Dover, N. H., Hist. Soc. Colls.*, I (1894), 130; *New-Eng. Hist. and Geneal. Reg.*, Oct. 1868, Apr. 1869; *Généalogie de la Famille Messervy* (Jersey, 1899); C. E. Potter, *The Mil. Hist. of the State of N. H.* (1866), also pub. in *Report of the*

Adjutant Gen. of . . . N. H., 1866; J. B. Meserve, in *Granite Monthly*, Jan. 1927; *Correspondence of William Pitt* (2 vols., 1906), ed. by G. S. Kimball; *Acts of the Privy Council of England, Colonial Ser.* (5 vols., 1908–12); the Loudoun Papers in the Henry E. Huntington Library; *N. H. Geneal. Record*, July 1903.]

S. M. P.

MESSER, ASA (May 31, 1769–Oct. 11, 1836), educator, for thirty-five years officially connected with Brown University and for twenty-four years its president, was born in Methuen, Essex County, Mass., the son of Asa and Abiah (Whittier) Messer. He grew up on his father's farm until he was thirteen years old, when he went to the nearby town of Haverhill and became a clerk in a wholesale grocery. Relinquishing this position, he prepared for college, partly, it is said, at an academy in Windham, N. H., but also under Rev. Hezekiah Smith [*q.v.*], pastor of the Baptist Church, Haverhill, who wrote in his diary under date of June 2, 1788, "Then Asa Messer quit his learning with me to go to college" (Guild, *post*, p. 455). Smith had labored zealously for the establishment of Rhode Island College, and presumably turned his pupil's footsteps toward that institution. At all events, Asa sought admission there, and so well prepared was he that he was admitted to the sophomore class in June 1788 and graduated in 1790. The following year he was elected tutor of the college; in 1798, professor of the learned languages; and in 1799, professor of natural philosophy. He had been licensed to preach by the First Baptist Church, Providence, in 1792 and was ordained in 1801, but never was a pastor. Upon the resignation of Jonathan Maxcy [*q.v.*], Sept. 2, 1802, Messer, at the age of thirty-three, was made president of the college *pro tempore* and two years later, president. He continued in this office until September 1826.

Although never attaining eminence in the field of scholarship, he was a most capable college president and as one of the leading citizens of the state came to be highly esteemed. His physical height and breadth were suggestive of the general solidity and catholicity of the man. He was hard-headed, sagacious, and practical, but withal kindly, not easily thrown off his balance, a good judge of men, and an excellent financier. His attainments were substantial and varied, but his taste was for mathematics, natural philosophy, and mechanics. Several inventions are credited to him, two of which were patented: "Flumes for Mill," Nov. 19, 1822, and "Waterwheel and Flume," May 18, 1826 (H. L. Ellsworth, *A Digest of Patents Issued by the United States from 1790 to Jan. 1, 1839*, 1840). The confidence people had in his judgment and honesty was evinced by the fact that he was offered a seat on the bench of the supreme court of Rhode Island. While he was no orator, his addresses were effective because of their common sense, sound reasoning, and terse, homely sayings. Under his wise leadership Rhode Island College made quiet but sure progress. Nicholas Brown [*q.v.*] became its generous patron and its name was changed to Brown University; a commodious dormitory was built; the number of students, professors, and courses increased; a medical school was established in 1811, for which an able faculty was secured. The students found Messer a good friend but a strict disciplinarian, and one difficult to outwit. He kept a bottle of picra in his office and anyone asking to be excused on account of a headache was obliged to take a dose.

Messer's breadth of mind and insistence on freedom of thought and speech finally brought his academic career to an end. He offered prayers in the First Congregational Church, Unitarian. Heretical Harvard conferred the degree of doctor of divinity upon him in 1820. While he held that Christ was preëminently the Son of God, he believed that he was such of himself and not from God. This alleged Arianism created much controversy and aroused such antagonism, variously expressed, that on Sept. 23, 1826, he presented his resignation with the accompanying remark that when his last hour came he hoped he might feel that he had served his God as faithfully as he had served Brown University. Through his business sagacity he had acquired one or two farms and an interest in a cotton-mill. He continued to reside in Providence, was for many years an alderman, and in 1830 was a candidate for governor of the state, but was defeated. On May 11, 1797, he married Deborah Angell, by whom he had a son who died in infancy and three daughters. One of the latter married Horace Mann [*q.v.*].

[*Vital Records of Methuen, Mass.* (1909); W. B. Sprague, *Annals Am. Pulpit*, vol. VI (1860); *The Brunonian*, July 1871; Romeo Elton, *The Lit. Remains of Rev. Jonathan Maxcy* (1844); R. A. Guild, *Early Hist. of Brown Univ., Including the Life, Times, and Correspondence of President Manning* (1897); W. C. Bronson, *The Hist. of Brown Univ., 1764–1914* (1914); E. M. Snow, *Alphabetical Index of Births, Marriages, and Deaths Recorded in Providence* (1879).]

H. E. S.

MESSLER, THOMAS DOREMUS (May 9, 1833–Aug. 11, 1893), railway official, sometimes regarded as the founder of the modern system of railway accounting, was born in Somerville, N. J., the first son of Rev. Abraham Messler and Elma (Doremus) Messler. He was of Dutch ancestry on both sides, his paternal ancestor, Jan Adamsen Metsalaer, having settled in New

Netherland about 1649. Educated at the Somerville Academy, he spent three years (1849–52) in a wholesale dry-goods house in New York City, then entered the auditor's office of the New York & Erie Railroad Company, now the Erie Railroad. In 1856 he became secretary and auditor at Pittsburgh of the Pittsburgh, Fort Wayne & Chicago Railway Company, whose line was then being completed between Pittsburgh and Chicago. He at once found that his department, like other railway departments of that time, was conducted with but little method and exactness. He thereupon evolved a system of railroad accounting having for its object simplicity, comprehensiveness, and classification, a system which subsequently became generally known as the "Messler System."

The principal object of this system was to consolidate in one department a uniform classification of revenues, expenses and operating statistics. The plan was outlined in the first annual report (1857) which Messler, as auditor, submitted to the president of the Pittsburgh, Fort Wayne & Chicago Railway Company. This system of accounts and statistics was carried out by the accounting department, the freight and passenger transportation departments, the treasurer of the company, and the general department, whose records and reports were interrelated. The chief accounting officer was made responsible for collecting all accounts due the company, and for making settlements with other companies. All operating expenses were classified, and a system of checks and balances was maintained, to furnish an accurate record of all transactions. The report was a model for its day, and many of its features have become standard practices in the uniform railway accounting system of today.

Messler continued with the Pittsburgh, Fort Wayne & Chicago Railway until July 1869, when it was leased to the Pennsylvania Railroad Company. At this time, by successive promotions, he had become assistant to the president. He was made comptroller of the Pennsylvania in 1871, and was promoted in 1876 to third vice-president. He was also chief executive officer of several auxiliary corporations controlled by the Pennsylvania company in the interest of the Pennsylvania Railroad. At his death, which occurred at Cresson, Pa., his total railroad service had covered a period of forty-one years. He was married on June 3, 1857, to Maria Remsen Varick of Poughkeepsie, N. Y. They had three sons, one of whom died in infancy.

[*Railroad Gazette*, Aug. 18, 1893; *The Biog. Dir. of the Ry. Officials of America*, 1887; *First Ann. Report . . . of the Pittsburgh, Fort Wayne & Chicago Railway Co.* (1857); J. B. Brittain, *A Financial Hist. of the Pa. Lines West of Pittsburgh . . .* (n.d.); L. F. Loree, *Railroad Freight Transportation* (1922), p. 211; R. V. Messler, *A Hist. or Geneal. Record of the Messler (Metselaer) Family* (1903); *Pittsburgh Post*, Aug. 12, 1893.]

J. H. P—e.

MESSMER, SEBASTIAN GEBHARD (Aug. 29, 1847–Aug. 4, 1930), Roman Catholic canonist and prelate, son of Sebastian Gebhard and Rosa (Baumgartner) Messmer, was born at Goldach, Switzerland. In 1866, after classical studies at the Seminary of St. George in St. Gall, he commenced to read philosophy and theology at the University of Innsbrück, Austria. Ordained to the priesthood July 23, 1871, he sailed for America in the fall, on the invitation of Bishop Bayley [*q.v.*], to take the chair of theology and canon law at Seton Hall College, South Orange, N. J. Here, during a professorship of eighteen years, he kept in touch with pastoral ministry, serving the German parish of St. Peter's in Newark for a number of years, St. Mary's Orphan Asylum, Newark, for eight years, and St. Leo's Church in Irvington for two. In the meantime, as assistant secretary of the Provincial Council of New York, he published *Praxis Synodalis* (1883). He was one of a commission of eight theologians who prepared a draft of decrees for consideration by the Plenary Council of Baltimore in 1884, acted as secretary of the Council, and in collaboration with Dr. Denis O'Connell edited the published decrees (1886). In recognition of his ability, in 1885 he was awarded an honorary doctorate in divinity by Pope Leo XIII. During the following year he edited an English translation of a German work by Franz Droste, *Canonical Procedure in Disciplinary and Criminal Cases of Clerics* (1887), which still remains an authoritative treatment of the subject. When the Catholic University of America was established in Washington he was called to the chair of canon law, and assumed his duties after two years of graduate work in Roman civil law at the Collegio Apollinare, Rome, where he earned the degree of D.C.L. Two years later, Dec. 14, 1891, he was appointed bishop of Green Bay in Wisconsin. Consecrated in St. Peter's Church, Newark, by Bishop Otto Zardetti of St. Cloud, Mar. 27, 1892, he served his diocese for ten years, during which a dozen parochial schools were established, as well as four academies, an Indian school, several asylums, and a number of hospitals.

On Nov. 28, 1903, he was translated to the prosperous archbishopric of Milwaukee. There was no modification in his democratic tastes. He continued to play the German card games of *skât* and *schafskopf* for relaxation and to chop wood for exercise. Approachable to priests and people to the extent of being easily imposed upon by place-seekers, he had no desire for luxuries. In traveling he sat bolt-upright in the smoking car, where his powerful physique, full beard, and affability made him a marked man. Racially broad-minded, alive to the problems of his people and his state, sympathetic with labor and trade unionism and with most of the progressive reforms though fearful of woman suffrage and of prohibition, he was a power in Wisconsin. His discreet pro-Germanism prior to 1917 and his loyalty after the United States entered the World War had a deep influence on Germans in America in general and German and Polish Catholics in particular. An active administrator, at least before old age left its mark upon him, he saw his archdiocese advance rapidly, although its extent was curtailed in 1905 when the separate diocese of Superior was created. Forty parochial schools, ten hospitals and sanitariums, and about fifteen additional charitable institutions for dependents were built during his régime; St. Francis Seminary was so developed in equipment and in staff that it attained first rank as a training school for priests; Marquette University became non-sectarian and one of the most progressive of Jesuit schools; and Mount Mary College for girls was established with a lay chancellor. While this growth cannot be directly ascribed to the archbishop, little could have been done without his active leadership and unstinted patronage.

Outside of his diocesan labors, he was a promoter of the American Federation of Catholic Societies, the National Catholic Welfare Conference, and the Deutsch Römisch Katholische Centralverein, and after 1925 an honorary president of the Catholic Hospital Association of the United States and Canada. His interest in the Catholic University continued till the end of his life; he was an active patron and trustee, rarely missing a meeting of the board even in his advanced years. His episcopal burdens did not end his scholarly activities. He edited *Spirago's Method of Christian Doctrine* (1901), *W. Devivier's Christian Apologetics* (1903), and the *Works of the Right Reverend John England* (7 vols., 1908), and contributed a number of articles to the *Catholic Encyclopedia, Ecclesiastical Review, Pastoral Blätt,* and *Catholic Historical Review.* At times, he permitted important diocesan matters to sleep in unanswered letters while he was busy with researches in county courthouses. The honors he earned included appointment as an Assistant at the Pontifical Throne (Nov. 16, 1906) and an elaborate religious and civic celebration to mark his golden jubilee (1921).

Death overtook him in his native Goldach, and here he was buried in his father's grave with religious services by local ecclesiastics, by representatives of the Vatican and Switzerland, and by Cardinal Piffl of Vienna in gratitude for his philanthropies on behalf of the starving Viennese after the war. By his will, which limited the cost of casket and grave marker, he bequeathed a small estate in books and life insurance to his diocese.

[*Am. Cath. Who's Who,* 1911; *Who's Who in America,* 1930–31; *Cath. Herald* (Milwaukee), Apr. 20, 1922, Apr. 25, 1929; official annual Catholic directories; *Cath. Citizen* (Milwaukee), Aug. 9, 1930; *N. Y. Times,* Aug. 5, 8, 1930; bulletin of Nat. Cath. Welfare Council news service, Aug. 4, 1930; *Milwaukee Jour.,* Aug. 4, 5, 1930; information from personal acquaintances.]

R. J. P.

METCALF, HENRY HARRISON (Apr. 7, 1841–Feb. 5, 1932), author and editor, son of Joseph P. and Lucy (Gould) Metcalf, was born at Newport, N. H., and received his early education at various public schools in his native state and at Mount Caesar Seminary. He graduated from the law school of the University of Michigan in 1865 and studied for the New Hampshire bar in the office of Edmund Burke, one of the prominent Democratic leaders of the state. He was admitted in 1866, but was too deeply interested in journalism and politics to continue in the profession. The next year he began his editorial career in charge of the *White Mountain Republic,* founded at Littleton partly at his suggestion by Chester E. Carey. In December 1869 he married Mary Jane Jackson of that town. During the next twenty-five years he conducted five different journals and acquired an encyclopedic knowledge of New Hampshire people and affairs. His most important editorship was that of the *New Hampshire People and Patriot* (Concord), 1882–92. He also acted for many years as New Hampshire correspondent of various New York papers. He was an active Democratic leader, rendering devoted service on sundry party committees and running several times for public office, though unsuccessfully, since his state was too strongly Republican during his active career to offer many opportunities for opposition candidates. As an editor he was intensely partisan and a vigorous critic of men and measures which aroused his antagonism.

In 1877 he founded the *Granite Monthly,* one of the pioneer state magazines, which he published until 1919, acting during several periods as editor. To its pages he contributed many articles on New Hampshire, historical, biographical, and descriptive. He was an organizer and active worker for the Patrons of Husbandry, and constantly endeavored to stimulate interest in agriculture and the rural life of the state. A life-long member of the Universalist Church, he was one of the outstanding laymen of that denomination, his influence extending far beyond the state boundaries.

In 1913 he was appointed state historian, and assisted in publishing some of the early records of New Hampshire, notably the second and third volumes of *Probate Records of the Province of New Hampshire* (1914, 1915), found in volumes XXXII and XXXIII of the State Papers. He also edited *New Hampshire Women* (1895), *Laws of New Hampshire* (vols. III–V, 1915–16), *One Thousand New Hampshire Notables* (1919), and wrote *New Hampshire in History* (1922) and several other historical articles or monographs. While he was neither a trained historical investigator nor a scholarly writer, his work in the field of state and local history was of considerable merit and his interest and loyalty to the social and educational interests of his state exercised a wholesome influence in its affairs.

[*Exercises at the Centennial Celebration of the Incorporation of the Town of Littleton, July 4, 1884* (1887); J. R. Jackson, *Hist. of Littleton, N. H.* (3 vols., 1905); Edmund Wheeler, *The Hist. of Newport, N. H.* (1879); *Manchester Union*, Feb. 6, 1932; *Concord Daily Monitor and N. H. Patriot*, Feb. 5, 6, 1932; *N. Y. Times*, Feb. 6, 1932; information from personal acquaintances.] W. A. R.

METCALF, JOEL HASTINGS (Jan. 4, 1866–Feb. 21, 1925), Unitarian clergyman, astronomer, was born in Meadville, Pa., the son of Lewis Herbert and Anna (Hicks) Metcalf. He graduated from the Meadville Theological Seminary in 1890, pursued graduate work for a time in the Harvard Divinity School, and continued at Allegheny College, where he obtained the degree of Ph.D. in 1892. In 1891 he married Elizabeth S. Lochman, of Cambridge, Mass. For ten years (1893–1903) he served a pastorate at Burlington, Vt., then went to England for rest and study at Oxford University. On his return, in much improved health, he assumed the duties of a pastorate in Taunton, Mass. From 1910 to 1920 he was minister of the Unitarian Society at Winchester, Mass., and from 1920 to the time of his death, of the First Parish, Portland, Me. Possessing "a wide tolerance side by side with an intense faith," he "met each man on his own plane and took him at his best" (Bailey, *post*, p. 493). Soon after the United States entered the World War, he took service in the Young Men's Christian Association, working by preference at the front, sharing the perils and privations of the soldiers, and distinguishing himself in getting food and supplies to men in exposed positions. He was cited for special courage at Château Thierry and later rendered commendable service during the reconstruction of Rumania.

Throughout his life, almost as deep as the interest in men that led him into the ministry was his devotion to astronomy. At the age of twelve he selected Proctor's *Other Worlds than Ours* to bring home from the Sunday-school library. An eclipse of the sun about the same time stimulated him to further investigation; he found a lens in an abandoned house and did odd jobs to earn the sixteen dollars needed to pay for materials for mounting. During his pastorate at Burlington he bought a second-hand photographic telescope and dome in New York State and brought it across Lake Champlain in winter on sledges, although the cost of the outfit—five hundred dollars—was a serious item in the budget of a minister on a small salary, with a wife and two children to support. While he was at Oxford, in addition to attending lectures on philosophy and religion, he became a frequent visitor at the observatory and spent much time on astronomical problems. Upon his return he built himself a private observatory at Taunton and both here and at Winchester made many astronomical observations of great value, discovering six comets, forty-one asteroids, and a number of variable stars. His observations are published in *Astronomische Nachrichten, Popular Astronomy,* and *Harvard College Observatory Bulletins.* His finest scientific work, however, was in applied optics. He combined in a remarkable degree the abilities to compute the lens curves necessary to perfect performance and the manual dexterity and skill to do the actual grinding. He made the telescope with which he himself observed; a ten-inch telescope and one of sixteen inches aperture of his make are in regular use at the Harvard College Observatory, while a thirteen-inch triplet, started by him shortly before his death and finished by C. A. R. Lundin the younger, was used in January 1930 at the Lowell Observatory in the discovery of the Trans-Neptunian planet. Metcalf was a fellow of the American Academy of Arts and Sciences and an active member of the American Astronomical Society. For many years he was chairman of the Committee to visit the Harvard Observatory, and a member of the Visiting Committee of the Ladd Observatory. He died in his sixtieth year, survived by his wife and two children.

[S. I. Bailey, "Joel Hastings Metcalf," *Pop. Astron.*, Oct. 1925; *Observatory*, May 1925; *Pubs. of the Astron. Soc. of the Pacific*, Apr. 1925; *Who's Who in*

America, 1924–25; *Press Herald* (Portland, Me.), Feb. 22, 1925.] R. S. D.

METCALF, THERON (Oct. 16, 1784–Nov. 13, 1875), Massachusetts jurist, was born in Franklin, Mass., the son of Hanan and Mary (Allen) Metcalf. The family was descended from Michael Metcalf who emigrated to New England and settled in Dedham. After graduating from Brown University in 1805 as valedictorian of his class, Metcalf studied law at Canterbury, Conn., then at Tapping Reeve's law school at Litchfield, Conn., and finally under Seth Hastings at Mendon, Mass. He was admitted to the bar of Litchfield County in 1807 and the following year began to practise in Massachusetts, first at Franklin and then at Dedham near-by. The region was one of Shaysites and Jeffersonians, with enough Federalists like Fisher Ames to keep politics boiling. Among these agrarian levelers Metcalf cast his lot and here in 1809 he brought his bride, Julia, daughter of Senator Uriah Tracy of Connecticut. Then and later, in the ferment of Jacksonian democracy, he was mistrustful of the "approaching reign of popular opinion, and the triumph of popular rights" (*An Address to the Phi Beta Kappa Society of Brown Univ. . . . 1832,* 1833, p. 24).

For many years Metcalf was county attorney. For two years, 1833–34, he sat in the lower house and in 1835 was a member of the state Senate. He edited the *Dedham Gazette* (1813–19) and in 1828 opened a law school. His *Law of Contracts* (1867) originated in one of his lecture courses. Every year a number of articles and reviews appeared in law journals over his name. He edited Sir Henry Yelverton's *Reports* (1820), Thomas Starkie's *Evidence,* and Sir William O. Russell's *Crimes.* But his chief claim to recognition lies in his *Reports of Cases Argued and Determined in the Supreme Judicial Court of Massachusetts* (13 vols., 1841–50), compiled when he was reporter to the court from 1840 to 1847, and in his indexes to the state statutes. On Feb. 25, 1848, he was appointed to the supreme bench. In his self-deprecating way he explained "that he was taken to fill a gap in the Court as people take an old hat to stop a broken window" (Hoar, *post,* II, p. 395). He retained his position until his resignation in August 1865, some ten years before his death. His opinions appear in 55–92 *Massachusetts Reports.* He was a quaint character, whose *bon mots* were repeated with zest. He enjoyed society, but was not especially given to hospitality. He was so steeped in the common law that he detested statutes and procedural innovations such as the abolition of special pleading. As a trial judge he was thought "fussy and interfering" (Hoar, *post,* II, p. 397), and by his misapplication of principles to facts he was often overruled, but his memory was a digest of the common law, and his opinions were clear and proverbially compact.

[G. S. Hale, "Memoir of the Hon. Theron Metcalf, LL.D.," *Proc. Mass. Hist. Soc.,* vol. XIV (1875–76); W. T. Davis, *Hist. of the Judiciary of Mass.* (1900); D. H. Hurd, *Hist. of Norfolk County, Mass.* (1884); G. F. Hoar, *Autobiog. of Seventy Years* (2 vols., 1903); *New-Eng. Hist. and Geneal. Reg.,* Apr. 1852, Oct. 1876; *Am. Law Rev.,* Jan. 1876; *Boston Evening Jour.,* Nov. 15, 1875.] C. F.

METCALF, WILLARD LEROY (July 1, 1858–Mar. 9, 1925), landscape and figure painter, born at Lowell, Mass., was the son of Greenleaf Willard and Margaret Jane (Gallop) Metcalf. His early education was obtained in the public schools of Lowell and Newton. At the age of twelve he went to Boston and found employment in a wholesale hardware store; in 1875 he was apprenticed to a wood engraver, then entered the studio of George L. Brown as an art student and remained there two years (1876–77), at the same time attending the life classes in the Lowell Institute. Later he continued his art studies at the Massachusetts Normal Art School, the school of the Museum of Fine Arts, and finally (1883) at the Académie Julien, Paris, studying under Boulanger and Lefebvre. Meanwhile he had spent two years in New Mexico and Arizona. The earlier years of his professional life were passed in Boston, and his first exhibition was held there in Chase's Gallery, about 1882, although he had previously sent his works to the exhibitions of the Boston Art Club and the Paint and Clay Club.

In these early years his paintings found few buyers, though his work was good from the first. In 1889, on his return to Boston from France, an exhibition of his pictures was held at the St. Botolph Club, which contained, besides landscapes painted in France, a number of excellent paintings from Tunis and Biskra. Shortly after this time he moved to New York, where he taught at Cooper Institute and the Art Students' League. He was subsequently an instructor at the Rhode Island School of Design. In 1892 he collaborated with William Hole in illustrating *The Wrecker* by Robert Louis Stevenson and Lloyd Osbourne.

Beginning in the nineties, fortune favored him; his paintings met with a brisk demand from private collectors and museums alike, and an impressive list of medals and prizes attest the high esteem in which his work was held. At the time of his death he was represented in fifteen public collections, including the museums of Philadelphia, Chicago, Boston, Washington, Pittsburgh, Cincinnati, St. Louis, and Buffalo. He became a member of the Ten American Painters, the National Institute of Arts and Letters, the American Society of Water Color Painters, and the Century Association.

Never surrendering his independence as an artist, Metcalf cannot be classified as a member of any esthetic sect. His personal talent was developed naturally, along congenial lines, unaffected by passing fashions in painting. He was not an impressionist; nor could he be fairly called a realist without some qualifications. He got very close to nature, however, and his point of view was modern, yet modest. His innate sensibility was kept in poise by his good sense; and he never erred in the way of extravagance or excess. His landscapes are noticeably free from mannerisms. His paintings were mostly of New England scenes, and he chose to depict the charm and beauty of his native region rather than its harsher aspect. The kind of subject that especially appealed to him, and in the treatment of which he was peculiarly felicitous, was an evanescent effect such as that in his "May Pastoral." This painting, now in the Boston Art Museum, is a landscape of great delicacy in which the signs of spring with its various hints of new life are indicated with rare and exquisite veracity. He was also happy in depicting the twinkling foliage of breeze-shaken birches and other delicate trees.

On Sept. 14, 1901, he was married, in New York, to Margaret Beaufort Hailé, and in 1911 he married Henriette A. McCrea of Chicago. Two children of his second marriage survived him.

[*Who's Who in America*, 1906–07, 1924–25; E. V. Lucas, in *Ladies' Home Journal*, June 1927; *Museum of Fine Arts Bull.* (Boston), Aug. 1908; W. H. Downes, in *Boston Sunday Courier*, Mar. 5, 1882; *Art Rev.*, Feb. 1912; Royal Cortissoz, in *Appleton's Booklovers Mag.*, Oct. 1905; Christian Brinton, in *Century Mag.*, Nov. 1908; F. W. Coburn, in *New Eng. Mag.*, Nov. 1908; C. B. Ely, in *Art in America*, Oct. 1925; Bernard Teevan, in *International Studio*, Oct. 1925; *Art News*, Mar. 14, 1925; *N. Y. Times*, Mar. 10, 1925.]

W. H. D.

METCALF, WILLIAM (Sept. 3, 1838–Dec. 5, 1909), metallurgist, steel manufacturer, was born in Pittsburgh, Pa. His father, Orlando Metcalf, was an attorney whose ancestor came from England in 1637; his mother was Mary Mehitabel (Knap) Metcalf. After attending the public schools of Pittsburgh, William went to Rensselaer Polytechnic Institute at Troy, N. Y., graduating in 1858. His first position was that of assistant engineer and draftsman at the Fort Pitt Foundry in his native city. Within a year he had become general superintendent of the company, a post he held until 1865. During this time, although not yet thirty years of age, he produced the largest castings and the heaviest machinery then known in the United States, and, perhaps, in the world. His foundry supplied more than three thousand heavy guns and projectiles for the United States during the Civil War. Two of the guns, the largest in the world, were of the twenty-inch variety and weighed eighty tons each. Not only were his deliveries prompt (in one instance General Grant received guns ordered only forty days before) but the quality was of the finest. His modest boast, many years later, was that "not one gun of Fort Pitt make was ever reported as failing in service" (Raymond, *post*, p. 866).

Following the war he entered the firm of his uncle, Charles Knap, which leased and operated the Fort Pitt foundry until late in 1867, when the firm became the Knap Fort Pitt Foundry Company. Then he became associated with Miller, Barr, & Parkin (after 1869 Miller, Metcalf, & Parkin), owners of the Crescent Steel Works, which was incorporated in 1889 as the Crescent Steel Company. As managing director of this organization he specialized in fine crucible steels, but after the company was taken over by the Crucible Steel Company of America in 1895 he left to become director of the Braeburn Steel Company (1897), a position he held at the time of his death.

Metcalf was not only a manufacturer of steel—one "of the generation of great steel-makers who made Pittsburg the Sheffield of America"—he was "one of the first practical experts to emphasize the importance of mechanical treatment and heat-treatment, as compared with chemical composition, and also the different effects of different kinds of tests of strength" (Raymond, p. 865). He read numerous papers before scientific societies on this subject. He was president of the Engineers' Society of Western Pennsylvania, 1880, and of the American Institute of Mining Engineers, 1881; vice-president of the American Society of Mechanical Engineers, 1882–84; and president of the American Society of Civil Engineers, 1893. He was also the author of a book, *Steel: A Manual for Steel Users*, which appeared in 1896 and served as a textbook in several technical schools.

Metcalf was married on Dec. 1, 1864, to Christiana, daughter of Aram Fries of Whitemarsh, Pa. They were the parents of three sons and three daughters. At the time of his death, Metcalf had been the senior warden of St. Peter's Protestant Episcopal Church, Pittsburgh, for thirty-five years. He was one of the most unassuming of men and it is for this reason, perhaps, that his name is not a household word. Greatness in his field came to him in spite of himself. He combined business ability with a love of research and knowledge but he found time for manifestation of character outside of his chosen field as well. He remained young in spirit in spite of age and was in the front ranks of those who welcomed change in a basic industry.

[*Trans. Am. Soc. of Civil Engineers,* vol. LXXIV (Dec. 1911), with portrait; R. W. Raymond, in *Trans. Am. Inst. of Mining Engineers,* vol. XLI (1911); *Trans. Am. Soc. Mech. Engineers,* vol. XXXII (1911); H. B. Nason, *Biog. Record Officers and Grads. Rensselaer Polytechnic Inst.* (1887); *Pittsburg Dispatch,* Dec. 6, 1909; *Pittsburgh Post,* Dec. 7, 1909.] A. I.

METCALFE, SAMUEL LYTLER (Sept. 21, 1798–July 17, 1856), chemist and physician, eldest of eleven children of Joseph and Rebecca (Littler or Sittler) Metcalfe, was born near Winchester, Va. Late in 1802 the family moved to Shelby County, Ky., and settled on a tract of land adjacent to an old Indian fort on Hickory Run, near Lynch's Station. In this primitive locality the boy received his early education. He entered the Medical School of Transylvania University, Lexington, Ky., in 1819, and four years later graduated with the degree of M.D., presenting a thesis entitled "The Malignant Fever of Louisville." While at Transylvania he wrote two books. The first was a choice collection of sacred music called *The Kentucky Harmonist,* which contained 130 pages of hymns and a long account of the origin, nature, and moral tendency of music. Two editions were issued within a short time (2nd ed., 1820). The success of this book enabled him to pay part of the cost of publishing the second, which was *A Collection of Some of the Most Interesting Narratives of the Indian Warfare in the West* (1821). It contained a description of every severe Indian fight which had taken place in Kentucky since its settlement by white men.

During the next seven years Metcalfe practised medicine, first at New Albany, Ind., and later at several places in Mississippi, though he lived most of the time at Natchez. From the latter place as a starting point, he walked over the greater portion of east Tennessee and North Carolina, and wrote several articles on the chemistry, geology, botany, and zoölogy of these regions. In 1831 he went to England where he continued his studies, specializing in chemistry and geology. On his return to the United States he settled in New York City, and for several years devoted himself to writing articles and books on chemistry and other sciences. Several of his scientific articles (signed merely "M") were published in the *Knickerbocker Magazine.* In 1835 he went to England again in order to conduct some researches in chemistry and geology. During this visit he was invited to become a candidate for the Gregorian chair in Edinburgh University, but declined in order to complete certain scientific books on which he had worked for several years. One phase of his chemical-geological studies is recorded in *A New Theory of Terrestrial Magnetism* (1833). Like many of his contemporaries he was attracted by the nature of heat, and after spending several years on the subject, expanded the views first set forth in his *New Theory* in a much more elaborate study, *Caloric: Its Mechanical, Chemical, and Vital Agencies in the Phenomena of Nature.* A portion of this work was issued in 1837; later it was enlarged into two volumes under the title given above and published in London in 1843; in 1853 a revised edition was issued in Philadelphia.

While in Mississippi Metcalfe was married, but his wife died after four years. In 1846, during a visit to England, he married Ellen Blondel of London, by whom he had one daughter. He died at Cape May, N. J.

[Personal communications from Transylvania College, Lexington, Ky.; E. M., "Dr. Metcalfe's Life," in *Caloric,* etc. (ed. of 1859), vol. I; H. A. Kelly and W. L. Burrage, *Am. Medic. Biogs.* (1920); J. N. McCormack, *Some of the Medical Pioneers of Ky.* (1917); *North American Medico-Chirurgical Rev.,* May 1857; *Pub. Ledger* (Phila.), July 18, 1856.] L. C. N.

METCALFE, THOMAS (Mar. 20, 1780–Aug. 18, 1855), Kentucky governor, representative, and senator, was born in Fauquier County, Va., the son of Sally and John Metcalfe, a militia officer in the Revolutionary War. About 1784 the family moved to Fayette County and later to Nicholas County, Ky. After attending the common-schools, young Thomas learned the trade of the stone-mason, which he followed for some years. About 1806 he married Nancy Mason. Entering politics, he served in the lower house of the legislature from 1812 to 1816. During the War of 1812 he raised a company of volunteers and led them at the battle of Fort Meigs. He served in Congress from 1819 to 1828, where he was a strong exponent of Western democracy. He opposed the banks, advocated making a two-thirds vote of the federal Supreme Court necessary to declare a state law unconstitutional, and disapproved of the discontinuance of credit to purchasers of public land. In 1821 he proposed to grant preëmption rights to squatters. He also favored protective tariffs and internal improvements, and he opposed restriction upon slavery in Missouri or in other parts of the Louisiana Purchase.

In 1825 he followed Henry Clay in voting for Adams for president and in 1827 was nominated for governor by the Adams-Clay convention, the first ever held in Kentucky. After an active contest with William T. Barry, the Jacksonian candidate, he was elected by a close vote, 38,940 to 38,231. He promised to disregard party affiliations in making appointments, but the Jacksonians asserted that he did not do so. As governor from 1828 to 1832, he indorsed protective tariffs and federal aid for internal improvements, and he denounced nullification, the spoils system, and Jackson's veto of the bill for federal aid for the Maysville-Lexington turnpike. He also favored the American Colonization Society, protection of the occupying claimants of Kentucky lands, simplification of the judicial system, district schools and additional aid for education, abolition of the branches of the bank of the commonwealth, improvement of rivers and roads, and prison reform. Most of his recommendations to the legislature became law. Later he was state senator from 1834 to 1838, president of the Kentucky board of internal improvements, and a member of the national Whig convention of 1839. During the debates over slavery, while he was United States senator from 1848 to 1849, he denounced secession and declared that Kentucky would uphold the Union. He retired to his farm in Nicholas County, Ky., where he died.

[Some of Metcalfe's letters and papers in Ky. State Hist. Soc. Coll.; *A Sketch of the Life of General Thomas Metcalfe* (1828?); Lewis Collins and R. H. Collins, *Hist. of Ky.*, revised ed. (1874), vol. II; W. E. Connelley and E. M. Coulter, *Hist. of Ky.* (1922), vol. II; *Biog. Directory Am. Cong.* (1928); J. T. McAllister, *Va. Militia in the Revolutionary War* (copr. 1913); *Register of the Ky. State Hist. Soc.*, Jan. 1904; *Niles' National Register*, Dec. 14, 1839.] W. C. M.

METTAUER, JOHN PETER (1787–Nov. 22, 1875), physician and surgeon, was the son of Francis Joseph Mettauer, an Alsatian surgeon, who came to America under Rochambeau and after the Revolution settled in Prince Edward County, Va., near Farmville. He married Jemimah Gaulding, probably *née* Crump. Their son, John Peter, born in Prince Edward County, attended the grammar school of Hampden-Sidney and in 1805 entered Hampden-Sidney College, but left before graduating and in 1807 entered the medical school of the University of Pennsylvania. There he heard the last lecture of the great Dr. Shippen and was a pupil of Rush, Wistar, and Physick. He received the degree of M.D. in 1809, and returned to Virginia to practise. During the War of 1812 he lived in Norfolk, and for one term, 1835–36, he was professor of surgery at Washington Medical College, Baltimore; but except for these brief intervals his long medical career was carried on entirely in his native county.

A daring and original surgeon, he soon became conspicuous for his skill, and patients flocked to him from all parts of the United States. He kept from forty-five to sixty surgical cases constantly under his care. Over 800 operations for cataract and over 200 for stricture of the urethra are recorded to his credit. A pioneer in genito-urinary surgery, he was also among the first in America to extirpate the parotid, ligate the carotid, and resect the superior maxilla. In lithotomy he was second only to Benjamin W. Dudley [*q.v.*], having operated seventy-nine times by 1853. His operation for cleft palate (1827), the third by an American surgeon, received widespread recognition (Smith, *post*, I, 407). Most of his work was done before the day of anesthesia, and most of his instruments he made himself. His chief technical innovation was the use of lead sutures in the treatment of vesico-vaginal fistula, an operation which he first performed, successfully, in August 1838, ten years before it was done by J. Marion Sims (*Boston Medical and Surgical Journal*, April 1840; *American Journal of the Medical Sciences*, July 1847). Sims [*q.v.*] himself called Mettauer one of two men who "stand out in bold relief amongst those who have devoted some time to this subject," the other being the famous French surgeon, Jobert (*Ibid.*, January 1852, p. 61).

Articles by Mettauer, appearing in nearly every medical journal in the country, prove that his interests extended beyond surgery. He wrote frequently on puerperal fever, and is said to have first suggested the use of iodine in scrofula. His paper on *Continued Fever in Middle Southern Virginia from 1816 to 1829* (1843) shows that he early recognized typhoid fever as a distinct disease. A scholarly 3,000-page manuscript work on surgery, in existence as late as 1905, is now lost. Most of his articles were signed "John Peter Mettauer, M.D., LL.D., of Virginia," but the source of the LL.D. is not known. In 1837 he organized the Prince Edward Medical Institute, which in 1847 became the Medical Department of Randolph-Macon College, with himself and his two elder sons constituting the faculty. His clinic was one of the most noted in the country. The prospectus for 1851–52 advertised a "handsome and chaste edifice," a ten months' course recognized by leading medical schools, and an infirmary where "surgical operations are frequently performed." The school was suspended at the outbreak of the Civil War, and never reopened.

Tall and austere, never attending either social or religious functions, Mettauer was eccentric but respected. He wore on all occasions, even while at meals and while operating, a high stovepipe hat. His daughter said she had never seen him without it, and he left instructions that he be buried in it. In spite of his peculiarities, four women married him: Mary Woodard, of Norfolk, by whom he had two sons; Margaret Carter, of Prince Edward County, Apr. 14, 1825; Louisa Mansfield, of Connecticut, 1833, who died in 1835; Mary E. Dyson, of Nottoway County, Va. He had at least ten children; three of his sons studied medicine. In the last week of his life, in his eighty-eighth year, he performed three successful operations: for cataract, stone, and amputation of the breast. He died of pneumonia and was buried in the College Church Cemetery at Hampden-Sidney.

[G. B. Johnston, *A Sketch of Dr. John Peter Mettauer* (1905), also pub. as presidential address in *Trans. Am. Surgic. Asso.*, vol. XXIII (1905); J. D. Eggleston, in *Wm. and Mary Coll. Quart.*, Apr. 1928; W. L. Harris, in *Va. Medic. Mo.*, Nov. 1926; A. M. Willis, in *Surgery, Gynecol. and Obstetrics*, Aug. 1926; *Va. Medic. Mo.*, Dec. 1875; *Richmond Dispatch*, Nov. 23, 1875; H. H. Smith, *A System of Operative Surgery* (2nd ed., 1855, I, 114, 407, II, 228, 273, 291, 297; A. J. Morrison, *College of Hampden-Sidney, Dict. of Biog., 1776–1825* (1921); Prince Edward County, Va., Deed Books 7, 15, 22, 26; Will Books 4, 14; files of medical journals, 1825–75.]

L. F. C.

METZ, CHRISTIAN (Dec. 30, 1794–July 27, 1867), religionist, a spiritual leader of the Community of True Inspiration, was born at Neuwied, Prussia, and with his parents removed to Ronneburg, Hesse, at the age of seven. His grandfather, Jakob Metz of Himbach, was a member of one of the early congregations of Inspirationists who traced their origin to the German Mystics and Pietists of the sixteenth and seventeenth centuries. By the close of the eighteenth century the Community of True Inspiration had suffered a spiritual decline: the founders, Gruber and Rock, were dead, and the gift of inspiration had ceased. But in 1817, when Christian Metz was twenty-three years old, the Community experienced a spiritual awakening and three members were recognized as "endowed with the miraculous gift of Inspiration," namely, Michael Krausert of Strassburg, Christian Metz of Ronneburg, and Barbara Heinemann of Leitersweiler, Alsace. Soon, however, Krausert "fell back into the world," and Barbara Heinemann, having married in 1823, temporarily lost the gift of inspiration. Thus spiritual guidance and temporal leadership devolved solely upon Christian Metz, who remained to the time of his death the recognized head of the Community. He was a man of profound piety and great sincerity, a successful organizer, and an executive of unusual ability. He it was who first conceived the idea of leasing estates in common as a refuge for the faithful; and while the original intention had been to live together simply as a Christian congregation or church, he foresaw that a system of communism would be the natural development of the mode of life which his people had been forced to adopt. He foresaw, also, that exorbitant rents and unfriendly governments would one day require them to seek a home in the New World.

Accordingly, with three other brothers he made the voyage to America in 1842 and purchased the Seneca Indian Reservation, a tract of five thousand acres near Buffalo, N. Y. This site, which he named Ebenezer, was the home of his people until 1854, when he led the brothers westward in search of cheaper and more abundant lands and greater seclusion. A tract of eighteen thousand acres was purchased in the frontier commonwealth of Iowa, and through inspiration Christian Metz christened it Amana. During the thirteen years of his leadership here he successfully organized and molded the community along the lines of his long-cherished hopes and dreams. In 1859 it was incorporated under the laws of Iowa as the Amana Society, with a constitution and by-laws which, with only minor changes, remained its fundamental law until the Reorganization of 1932, by which church and state were separated, ending spiritual authority in temporal affairs.

Christian Metz is remembered as a man of commanding presence and of great personal magnetism whose natural dignity and spiritual poise challenged admiration and respect everywhere. His voluminous writings, collected and preserved in the archives of the Community, reveal a penetrating mind, an earnest, eager spirit, an unusual patience with human frailties, toleration and a fine sense of justice in dealing with men and measures, a practical philosophy of life, a genuine feeling of humility, and a deep sense of the responsibility of his high office. He died at Amana in his seventy-third year and was buried in the cedar-bordered cemetery there. Only a tiny headstone marks his grave. His real monument is the Amana Society with its seven villages, its twenty-five thousand acres of land, its mills, factories, and stores, its barns and sheds, orchards, vineyards, and gardens, its homes and schools and churches—the most successful experiment in communism in America.

[MSS. in the *Archiv* at Amana; Bertha M. H. Shambaugh, *Amana, the Community of True Inspiration* (1908), "Amana the Church and Christian Metz the Prophet" (*The Midland,* Aug. 1915), "Amana Colony" (*The Midland Monthly,* July 1896), "Amana" (*The Palimpsest,* July 1921), "Amana," in James Hastings' *Encyc. of Religion and Ethics,* vol. I (Edinburgh, 1908), and *Amana That Was and Is* (1932); W. R. Perkins and B. L. Wick, *Hist. of the Amana Soc.* (1891); C. F. Noe, *A Brief Hist. of the Amana Soc., 1714–1900* (1904), also pub. in *Iowa Jour. of Hist. and Politics,* Apr. 1904.]
B. M. H. S.

MEYER, GEORGE VON LENGERKE (June 24, 1858–Mar. 9, 1918), diplomat and cabinet officer, was born on Beacon Hill of a good Bostonian family. Both his father and paternal grandfather had borne the name of George Augustus Meyer and both had been merchants in overseas trade. The elder, a native of Germany, had emigrated to New York in early manhood; the younger had moved to Boston and there married Grace Helen Parker. George von Lengerke Meyer was the eldest of his parents' three children. He prepared privately for college and was graduated from Harvard with the class of 1879. In 1885 he married Marian Alice Appleton. Within two decades after his graduation he stood near the center of the closely related inner group which dominated the banking and commercial activity of Boston, and at the same time he participated heartily in the social activity of Boston and Essex County. In 1890 the Meyers acquired "Rock Maple Farm" at Hamilton, which remained their dearest residence and was developed through a lifetime of attention into a show place of the region.

Although possessed of all that one of his group might consider sufficient for a full and contented life, Meyer was as much disturbed by the ambition and will "to make something out of life" as was his later chieftain, Theodore Roosevelt. Entering politics, he was elected as a Republican to the Boston Common Council, serving 1889–90, and in 1891 was chosen alderman. From 1892 to 1896 he was in the legislature, holding the speakership of the House during the last three years. Always a regular Republican and a conservative, he felt that government should be administered as efficiently as a paying business. He was probably especially useful to his party in his contacts with the business leaders who formed so important an element in Republican success (Roosevelt-Lodge *Correspondence, post,* II, 69, 136). In 1899 he was made national committeeman from Massachusetts.

His diplomatic career began with his appointment in December 1900 by President McKinley as ambassador to Italy. At Rome the King and the American Ambassador became warm friends, and the effective Meyer raised his embassy to a high standard of influence and popularity. He also formed valuable contacts in important circles throughout Europe. Especially with Emperor William II of Germany he made an acquaintance surprisingly intimate in nature. All the while he corresponded regularly with Henry Cabot Lodge and somewhat less frequently with President Roosevelt, assuming gradually the rôle of an important listening post in Europe for these two formulators of American foreign policy. During the Russo-Japanese War, when President Roosevelt was essaying the part of peacemaker, "I wish in St. Petersburg," he wrote, "a man who, while able to do all the social work, . . . can do, in addition, the really vital and important things" (Howe, *post,* pp. 110–11). Meyer was the man he selected and in March 1905 his Russian mission began. Cutting through the red tape of Russian bureaucracy without causing offense, he reached the Czar himself and effectively presented Roosevelt's proposals (Roosevelt-Lodge *Correspondence,* II, 187, *et passim*). It is said Meyer's skill at bridge did not prove a liability to his diplomacy.

Meanwhile Lodge as well as others were urging his appointment to the cabinet and Meyer himself was anxious for a cabinet post. On Mar. 5, 1907, he took office as postmaster-general under Roosevelt. Here again he gave evidence of efficient administrative ability. The department was conducted smoothly, postal savings banks were established, the parcel-post system was extended, a special-delivery system was started, and a two-cent postage convention was arranged between the United States and Great Britain and Ireland. Retained in the cabinet by Taft, who appointed him secretary of the navy, he held that office until 1913. He instituted naval aids to the Secretary to keep him more responsibly informed; he improved the gunnery and the direction of the active fleet; navy yards were administered to meet the needs of the fleet rather than as mere work-providers for local constituencies; engineering problems were better solved by his greater reliance upon naval engineers. Navy men speak of his tenure as one greatly increasing the efficiency of the department.

Meyer remained loyal to Taft in the political crisis of 1912, but his personal attachment to Roosevelt continued and after the World War began he was soon campaigning under Roosevelt's lead for preparedness and then for American participation. In 1916 he championed Roosevelt for the Republican nomination for the presidency. He died Mar. 9, 1918, in his sixtieth year.

[M. A. DeWolfe Howe, *George von Lengerke Meyer* (1919); *Selections from the Correspondence of Theodore Roosevelt and Henry Cabot Lodge, 1884–1918* (2 vols., 1925); *The Letters and Friendships of Sir Cecil Spring-Rice* (2 vols., 1929), ed. by Stephen Gwynn; *Taft and Roosevelt, The Intimate Letters of Archie Butt* (2 vols., 1930); *Harvard Coll., Class of 1879, Fiftieth Anniv., Ninth Report* (1929); *Harvard Grads. Mag.*, June 1918; *Boston Transcript*, Mar. 11, 1918.]

P. H. B.

MEYER, MARTIN ABRAHAM (Jan. 15, 1879–June 27, 1923), rabbi, Semitist, was born in San Francisco, Cal., the son of Charles and Louisa B. (Silberstein) Meyer. He attended the public schools of his native city, then entered Hebrew Union College, Cincinnati, having been prepared by Rabbi Jacob Voorsanger of San Francisco. He received the degree of A.B. in 1899 from the University of Cincinnati, and in 1901 graduated as rabbi from Hebrew Union College, honor man and valedictorian. Having won a fellowship in the American School of Oriental Study and Research in Palestine, he spent the winter 1901–02 in Jerusalem specializing in archeology, ethnology, and Semitic philology. Several articles which he contributed to American newspapers during that period indicate his disgust with Jewish conditions in the Holy Land. In 1902, he was elected rabbi of Congregation Beth Emeth at Albany, N. Y., where he remained four years. On June 19, 1905, he married Jennie May Haas of Cincinnati; two children, a son and a daughter, were born to them. He registered as a post-graduate student at Columbia University, majoring in Semitics, and received the degree of Ph.D. in 1910. His dissertation, *History of the City of Gaza* (1907), was a scholarly work in Arabic Semitic culture. In 1906, he was called to Temple Israel, Brooklyn, N. Y., and served there four years. As rabbi of the leading congregation in that large borough he wielded a wide influence along civic and philanthropic as well as religious lines. During this time he helped organize the Brooklyn Federation of Jewish Charities.

In 1910, he accepted the unanimous call of Temple Emanu El, the leading Reform congregation in San Francisco, where he served the remaining thirteen years of his life. He soon became an outstanding figure of the Pacific Coast. His scholarly training led to his appointment in 1911 as lecturer in Semitics at the University of California, a post he held with distinction until his death. He was in popular demand for lectures at western colleges, where he discussed scientific as well as religious topics. In addition to his doctoral thesis, he wrote the article "Jerusalem—Modern" for the *Jewish Encyclopedia* (1904); an introduction to *Sermons and Addresses by Jacob Voorsanger* (1913), edited by O. I. Wise; a noteworthy pamphlet, *Jew and Non-Jew* (1913), published by the Central Conference of American Rabbis; and a sketch of "The Jews of California," which appeared in A. W. Voorsanger's *Western Jewry* (1916). As a preacher, Meyer was direct, forceful, and effective. He brought his scholarly attainments into the preparation of his sermons, which were based invariably on the Bible and upon Jewish commentaries interpreted in the light of modern events. He was fearless, though usually tactful in discussing vital issues, and was one of the few Reform rabbis who openly spoke for and worked on behalf of Zionism.

He was most active in civic affairs along nonpartisan lines. Appointed in 1911 a member of the State Board of Charities and Corrections, he became chairman in 1912 and served with great credit until a reluctant governor accepted his resignation in 1920. Deeply interested in social-service problems and following reform ideas without being impractical, he became a recognized leader in western philanthropies. The most constructive achievement to his credit is the Jewish Committee for Personal Service in State Institutions, a society which he organized in cooperation with I. Irving Lipsitch, to care for Jewish wards under state supervision and to help them after their release. Another monument to him is the Martin A. Meyer Memorial Fund for needy Jewish students of the University of California, a sum of $25,000 collected by friends shortly after his death. In 1918 he volunteered for war service under the American Red Cross and returned in 1919 a chastened man, eager to uphold the principles of World Peace. He died in San Francisco.

[Files of *Emanu El* (San Francisco), esp. issues of June 29 and July 6, 1923; *The Am. Jewish Year Book*, vol. XXVII (1925); *Who's Who in America*, 1922–23; *Central Conf. of Am. Rabbis*, Yearbook, vol. XXXIII (1923); *San Francisco Examiner*, June 28, 1923; personal acquaintance.]

R. I. C.

MEZES, SIDNEY EDWARD (Sept. 23, 1863–Sept. 10, 1931), educator, was born at Belmont, Cal., the only son of Simon Monserrate and Juliet Janin (Johnson) Mezes. His father was a native of northern Spain who settled in California during the winter of 1849–50, was successful in business and became a large landowner. His mother, born in Florence, Italy, was the daughter of Sidney Law Johnson of New Haven, Conn. A graduate of Yale and a descendant of the second president of Yale College, this grandfather was a lawyer by profession, practising in New Orleans and San Francisco. Sidney Edward Mezes became an accomplished linguist at an early age, both through the help of his parents and in the course of protracted visits to Europe. Completing his preparatory studies at St. Matthew's Hall in San Mateo, he entered the University of California, from which he graduated in 1884 with the degree of B.S. In the early winter of 1884 his father died. For some years thereafter the son gave most of his attention to the affairs of his father's estate, meanwhile carrying on studies in the humanities at the universities of California and Berlin. Convinced at length that his major interest was in philosophy and attracted by the fame of Royce, James, and Palmer, he entered Harvard University as a senior in 1889.

At Harvard he remained four years, receiving the degrees of A.B. in 1890, A.M. in 1891, and Ph.D. in 1893. During the year 1893–94 he taught at Bryn Mawr and the University of Chicago. In the autumn of 1894 he was called to the University of Texas as adjunct professor of philosophy. He became associate professor in 1897, professor in 1900, dean in 1902, and president of the University in 1908. At the close of 1914 he resigned to accept the presidency of the College of the City of New York. It was at the University of Texas that Mezes spent the happiest years of his life. He was married at Austin (Dec. 10, 1896), to Annie Olive Hunter of that city; he formed at the University and in Austin many of his closest and most valued friendships; and his steady and rapid advancement bears witness alike to his ability and his popularity. In 1929, fifteen years after he left Texas, he had the honor of being elected president emeritus of the University.

The College of the City of New York under his administration entered upon a period of extraordinary growth, during which its development was carefully and skilfully guided, its internal organization nicely adjusted, its services to the community made more direct and valuable. Mezes was responsible for the establishment of the schools of Technology, Business, and Education, and for the expansion of evening, summer, and vocational courses; but he was responsible also for strengthening the discipline of the institution and raising its scholastic standards. It was his conscious aim to preserve and improve what was best in the old plan of instruction while introducing, with cautious moderation, what seemed to be good in the new.

While still at Texas he had declined the position of United States commissioner of education; but when in 1917 he was asked by his brother-in-law, Col. Edward M. House, at President Wilson's request, to gather a body of experts to collect data which might be needed eventually at the Peace Conference, he undertook the task at once. A first result of the studies carried on by this body, called The Inquiry, was the submission of a report "on the main outlines of an equitable settlement," which became "the basis from which the President started in formulating his Fourteen Points" (*What Really Happened at Paris,* p. 2). At the Paris Conference the members of The Inquiry were constituted into a Section of Territorial, Economic and Political Intelligence, still under Mezes, who was styled director of specialists and was also appointed United States delegate on the Central (*i.e.,* international) Territorial Commission. His great contribution to this enterprise was the selection and training of his staff of experts; to him belongs a considerable part of the credit for the able service which they rendered at Paris. In the summer of 1927, because of failing health, he retired from active service as president of the College of the City of New York. He died at Altadena, Cal., four years later.

Mezes contributed many articles dealing with philosophy or questions of college policy and administration to various scientific periodicals and was also the author of *Ethics, Descriptive and Explanatory* (1901), and of portions of *The Conception of God* (1895), by Josiah Royce, and *What Really Happened at Paris* (1921), edited by Charles Seymour and E. M. House. He was a tall, spare man, dark in complexion, dignified in his bearing. His most noteworthy qualities of mind and character were clarity in thought and speech, keenness in judgment whether of men or questions, an unusual range of learning and interest, cautious deliberation in planning combined with vigor and courage in execution, fairness, tolerance, and charity, and a modesty which almost reached the point of self-effacement.

[Papers and records of the Mezes family; letters and other writings of S. E. Mezes; records, faculty, and trustee minutes, etc., at Yale, the Univ. of Tex., College of the City of New York; *Who's Who in America,* 1930–31; Harvard classbooks, Class of 1890; E. M. House and Charles Seymour, *What Really Happened at Paris* (1921); *The Intimate Papers of Col. House* (4 vols., 1926–28); articles in *City Coll. Alumnus,* Oct. 1931; record of the City College Memorial Meeting, Nov. 12, 1931 (privately printed); *N. Y. Times,* Sept. 12, 1931; unpublished personal recollections of Mrs. Carmelita Mezes Wynne, Hon. D. F. Houston, Col. E. M. House, Dr. John H. Finley, Presidents H. Y. Benedict (Texas) and F. B. Robinson (C. C. N. Y), Provost Charles Seymour (Yale), Prof. W. J. Battle (Texas), Hon. Adolph C. Miller, and others, including the writer.]

C. L. B.

MIANTONOMO (d. 1643), Indian chief, was the son of Mascus and the nephew of Canonicus [*q.v.*]. Although he was presumably considerably younger than his uncle, the two divided the government of the Narragansett tribe between them. In 1632 Miantonomo visited Boston and was received by the governor. Two years later, when Stone and Norton were killed by the Indians, and again in 1636 when Oldham was killed, he did all he could to help the English catch the murderers. Nevertheless he was suspected by them and had to appear again at Boston in the latter year, when he cleared himself. In 1637 he joined the English and rendered them aid in the Pequot War. The following year both he and Uncas [*q.v.*] were summoned to Hartford to answer complaints regarding the Pequots in their charge and with the hope of bringing about peace between the two chiefs. As Miantonomo would have to cross the hostile Mohegan and Pequot territory, Roger Williams urged him not to risk his life, but, with his family and 150 warriors, he made the trip to Hartford and back in safety, although 600 Pequots were said to have lain in ambush for him. On the other hand, Uncas at first refused to appear, pleading lameness, but the English recognized the excuse as a subterfuge and forced him to come. Miantonomo agreed to a reconciliation but Uncas declined. On Sept. 21, 1638, however, the two chiefs signed a treaty of peace with the English and with each other.

In their Indian relations the English of Connecticut, and more particularly those of Massachusetts, were inclined to oppose the Narragansetts and favor the other tribes. In spite of his dissolute character, Uncas was less subject to suspicion than Canonicus and Miantonomo. Possibly the main reason was that the Rhode Island colonists were anathema to Massachusetts, and the stronger colonies, regardless of the faithfulness of the Indians, preferred to cultivate those on their own borders and to antagonize those who were closer to the Rhode Islanders. Miantonomo had signed a deed for Warwick to Samuel Gorton and his associates, whereupon in Massachusetts he was declared a usurper and the Indian Pumham was instigated to claim his territory. In March 1638 Miantonomo also signed a deed to William Coddington and his associates for the island of Rhode Island. In 1642, when it was said that he was plotting the destruction of the English, he was asked by the magistrates of Massachusetts to answer the charges through a hostile Pequot interpreter. He properly refused but offered to go to Boston if Williams should be allowed to go with him. Williams had tried to convince Winthrop of the Indian's friendliness. When this request was refused Miantonomo went to Boston alone. There, under duress, his accusers insisted upon his answering through the Pequot. He was insulted and forced to say that he had been at fault. In August 1643 Uncas made war on one of the Narragansett undersachems, Sequasson, and in the war following between the tribes, Miantonomo was taken prisoner by Uncas through treachery. He was delivered to the English at Hartford. In Boston the Commissioners of the United Colonies and a body of clergy considered the case and decided that Uncas might murder him within his own jurisdiction. The unfortunate Miantonomo was surrendered to Uncas for that purpose and killed with a hatchet near Norwich. He was buried where he fell, at Sachem's Plain. His wife, Wawaloam, survived him and was alive in 1661. A monument was erected to him in 1841.

[F. W. Hodge, *Handbook of Am. Indians*, pt. 1 (1907); S. G. Drake, *The Book of the Indians* (1841), which is the eighth edition of the *Indian Biography*; J. W. DeForest, *Hist. of the Indians of Conn.* (1851); J. K. Hosmer, *Winthrop's Jour.* (2 vols., 1908); "Acts of the Commissioners of the United Colonies of New England," vol. I (1859), which is vol. IX of the *Records of the Colony of New Plymouth*; J. R. Bartlett, *Letters of Roger Williams* (1874).]

J. T. A.

MICHAËLIUS, JONAS (b. 1584), first minister of the Dutch Reformed Church at New Amsterdam, was a son of the Rev. Jan Michielsz, one of those fighting preachers who fanned the hatred of Spanish rule and popery among the Reformed in Holland and Flanders. But he was also a man of affairs, for he was repeatedly employed in matters of state, both in England and Holland, by William of Orange, the Earl of Leicester, and Prince Maurice of Nassau. The son was born in 1584 in the village of Grootebroek in the north of the Province of Holland, to which Jan Michielsz had accepted a call in 1582. After the father's death in 1595, his widow moved to Hoorn, the town nearest to Grootebroek. Here the boy attended the Latin school until, at fifteen, he entered the Theological College at Leyden with a scholarship awarded him by the burgomasters of Hoorn. He graduated in 1605, and thereafter, for a period of twenty years, he ministered to various parishes in Brabant and Holland. In 1624, however, he asked to be transferred to Brazil, where the Hollanders were then trying to oust the Portuguese from their possessions. In March 1625 he sailed for his new destination in the fleet that was to clinch the Dutch hold on Bahia. During the voyage the commander, hearing from home-bound ships that the Portuguese had recaptured Bahia, changed his course and made for More on the coast of Guinea, West Africa.

They arrived on Nov. 19, 1625, and Michaëlius

went on shore and remained in the fort. By the end of the year 1627 he was again in Holland, for on Jan. 24, 1628, he sailed with his family from The Texel for New Netherland. They landed at New Amsterdam on Apr. 7. Five weeks later his wife died in childbed, leaving him three little children, one of whom, an only son, had stayed behind in Holland. Soon after his arrival he organized a church community, the beginning of the Collegiate Church in the City of New York and of the Reformed Church in America, of which Michaëlius may justly be called the founder. The Sunday services were held in Dutch, as the number of those who did not understand the language was very small, but for the benefit of those few he administered the Lord's Supper in French.

Michaëlius had a missionary's zeal to convert the Indians, whom he found to be "strangers to all decency." Two years later he wrote with greater bitterness about the men of his own congregation, including the Director-General Peter Minuit, an elder of his church, and the members of the Council, whom he condemned wholesale as a "pestilent kind of people." He accused them of defrauding the Company, of oppressing the innocent, and of leading immoral lives. Having returned to Holland in 1632, he repeated these charges in person before the Consistory of Amsterdam. The Directors of the West India Company, however, apparently did not appreciate the vehemence with which he had defended their interests. In 1637 the Classis of Amsterdam recommended Michaëlius for reappointment to the ministry in New Netherland, but the Assembly of the Nineteen unanimously rejected him. Their curt reply to the Classis contains the last record of his name. Three of the many letters that he sent from Manhattan to correspondents in Holland have fortunately been preserved. Two of these are written in forceful Dutch, the third is in somewhat florid Latin. They are among the earliest and most interesting records of New Amsterdam in its infancy. His character sketch of Peter Minuit and his Council, contained in the Latin letter to Joannes van Foreest, must be taken with reservations. Michaëlius was one of those who, not content with the care of souls, strove to meddle with things political and to sway the minds of the magistracy. He was, no doubt, an honest man, a fervid Christian, and a good Latin scholar, but intemperate in asserting his superiority in these respects over men of less conscience and less culture.

[*Ecclesiastical Records: State of N. Y.*, I (1901), 48–73; Albert Eekhof, *Jonas Michaëlius, Founder of the Church in New Netherland* (Leyden, 1926), *De Hervormde Kerk in Noord-Amerika* (2 vols., 1913), and an article in P. C. Molhuysen and P. J. Blok, *Nieuw Nederlandsch Biografisch Woordenboek*, vol. I (1911); *Narratives of New Netherland, 1609–1664* (1909), ed. by J. Franklin Jameson; I. N. P. Stokes, *The Iconography of Manhattan Island*, vol. IV (1922); Dingman Versteeg, *Manhattan in 1628* (1904).] A. J. B.

MICHAUX, ANDRÉ (Mar. 7, 1746–November 1802), explorer, silviculturist, and botanist, was born in the park of Versailles, France, at Satory, a royal domain which had long been managed by his ancestors. When ten years old he was sent to a pension but remained there only four years because his father wished to train him for the family tenancy. In October 1769 he married Cécile Claye, the daughter of a rich farmer near Beauce; she died eleven months later after the birth of their son, François André [*q.v.*]. To relieve his despondency, the young widower began the intensive study of botany and came under the instruction of Bernard de Jussieu. In 1779 he moved nearer the Jardin des Plantes and during the next two years herborized in England, the Auvergne, and the Pyrenees. Subsequently he was appointed secretary to the French consul at Ispahan, Persia, but, spurred by that zeal for exploration which was his most salient characteristic, he abandoned this connection in order to wander (1782–85) over much of the region between the Tigris and Euphrates rivers, in which he collected many seeds and plants. On his return to France his government directed him to make a study of the forest trees of North America, in order to ascertain the advisability of their introduction into France and their utility for naval construction.

On the first of October 1785 he arrived in New York with his young son and Paul Saulnier, a journeyman gardener who later brought the Lombardy poplar to the United States. The next year and a half he spent in a study of the local flora and in the establishment of a nursery near Hackensack, N. J. In 1787 he moved to Charleston, S. C., purchased a plantation about ten miles from the city, and continued his search for interesting plants, especially for those which might be successfully cultivated. In the same year he traveled extensively in the southern Appalachians and, during the next, invaded Spanish Florida. In 1789 he visited the Bahamas and also continued his explorations in the Carolina mountains. During this period he was interested in the distribution of ginseng and introduced among the mountaineers the idea of its commercial exploitation. Shortly afterward the French Revolution cut off his support from the home government although, despite family traditions, he appears to have espoused the republican cause. Perhaps the report of his son, who had previously returned to Paris, influenced him to some extent; half of the sixty thousand young trees which the Michaux had sent back had been presented by the Queen to the Austrian Emperor and the rest had been largely scattered or neglected. In 1792 the elder Michaux botanized in Canada and even visited the vicinity of Hudson Bay. On his return he interested the American Philosophical Society in a project for the exploration of the Far West by way of the Missouri; some money was subscribed for the purpose, and he received instructions for the proposed journey from Thomas Jefferson. But during these negotiations, Edmond Charles Genet arrived in Charleston and entrusted Michaux with a commission for George Rogers Clark [*q.v.*]. Genet had asked Jefferson to grant permission to Michaux to act as consul in Kentucky, but Jefferson declined to grant an exequatur, giving him instead letters of introduction as a traveling scientist.

On July 15, 1793, Michaux left Philadelphia for his famous mid-western travels; his manuscript journals were published almost a century later. In April 1796 he returned to Charleston, rich in botanical data but exhausted in finances. Four months later he sailed for France but was shipwrecked off Egmont, Holland, where some of his manuscripts were lost and his herbaria suffered damage. Despite a favorable reception in Paris, he failed to interest his government in further American explorations and finally accepted a commission as naturalist on the Australian expedition of Capt. Nicolas Baudin. They sailed from France on Oct. 18, 1800, visited Teneriffe, and reached Mauritius on Mar. 15, 1801. Michaux decided to leave the expedition in order to explore Madagascar. After some difficulty, he attained the larger island but trusted too well the physique which had withstood hardships in more temperate countries and succumbed to a tropical fever. His great contributions to botany were his explorations and collections. Neither adventures among Arabian bandits nor arduous travel by foot and canoe with only Indians or backwoodsmen as companions gave favorable training for literary attainment, and his journals (or field notes) are crudely laconic. Although largely based on his collections and data, the *Flora Boreali-Americana, sistens caracteres Plantarum quas in America Septentrionali collegit et detexit Andreas Michaux* (Paris, 1803) was prepared by Claude Richard, and Sargent has suggested that the *Histoire des Chênes de l'Amérique, ou descriptions et figures de toutes les espèces et variétés de Chênes de l'Amérique Septentrionale* (Paris, 1801) must have been the result of similar collaboration. His other publication is the "Mémoire sur les Dattiers," published in the *Journal de Physique, de Chemie et d'Histoire Naturelle* (vol. LII, 1801).

[J. P. F. Deleuze, "Notice Historique sur André Michaux," *Annales du Muséum National d'Histoire Naturelle*, vol. III (1804); Asa Gray, "Notes of a Botanical Excursion to the Mountains of N. C.," *Am. Jour. of Sci.*, Oct.–Dec. 1841; Ovide Brunet, *Notice sur les Plantes de Michaux et sur son Voyage au Canada et à la Baie d'Hudson* (1863); C. S. Sargent, "Portions of the Jour. of André Michaux, Botanist, written during his Travels in the U. S. and Canada, 1785 to 1796: With an Introduction and Explanatory Notes," *Proc. Am. Philos. Soc.*, vol. XXVI (1889); R. G. Thwaites, *Early Western Travels*, vol. III (1904) and *Original Jours. of the Lewis and Clark Expedition, 1804–06* (7 vols., 1904–05); F. J. Turner, "Correspondence of the French Ministers to the U. S., 1791–97," *Ann. Report of the Am. Hist. Asso. for the Year 1903* (1904); "Correspondence of Clark and Genet," *Ann. Report of the Am. Hist. Asso. for the Year 1896*, vol. I (1897); *North Am. Rev.*, July 1821; *S. C. Hist. and Geneal. Mag.*, Jan. 1928.]
H. B. B.

MICHAUX, FRANÇOIS ANDRÉ (Aug. 16, 1770–Oct. 23, 1855), silviculturist, traveler, and botanist, was born on the royal domain of Satory in the park of Versailles, France. His father was André Michaux [*q.v.*]; his mother, Cécile Claye, who died in the month after his birth. At the age of fifteen he accompanied his father to New York and later (1787) to Charleston, S. C. He also went on the trip to the sources of the Keovee River, Fla., but was mainly entrusted with the management of the nursery. On Sept. 20, 1789, he was accidentally shot in the left eye, which never entirely recovered. Early in 1790 he returned to France and entered ardently into the French Revolution, but he also found time to study medicine with Corvisart. In 1801 he was commissioned by his government to strip and sell the two tree-plantations which his father had established in the United States and to appoint instead native correspondents in the principal seaports; he reached Charleston Oct. 9 and spent the winter on the Atlantic seaboard. On June 27, 1802, he left Philadelphia for the summer of travels that are described in his *Voyage à l'ouest des monts Alléghanys dans les états de l'Ohio, et du Kentucky, et du Tennessée, et retour à Charleston par les Hautes-Carolines* (Paris, 1804), which went through several editions and was translated into English (London, 1805) and German (Weimar, 1805). After a winter in Charleston (Oct. 18, 1802–Mar. 1, 1803), he returned to France. In 1804 he published his report *Sur la Naturalisation des Arbres Forestiers de l'Amérique du Nord.* On Feb. 5, 1806, he again started for Charleston but was captured by the British and detained in the Bermudas, which resulted in his "Notice sur les Iles Bermudes, et particulièrement sur l'Ile Saint-

Georges" (*Annales du Muséum d'Histoire Naturelle,* vol. VIII, 1806). In May he reached the United States and spent three years in travel and study, mainly along the Atlantic Coast. Incidentally, he and another Frenchman were the only passengers on Robert Fulton's trial trip up the Hudson. On his return to France he published the *Histoire des Arbres forestiers de l'Amérique Septentrionale* (Paris, 3 vols., 1810–13), which is better known in this country as *The North American Sylva, or a Description of the Forest Trees of the United States, Canada, and Nova Scotia, Considered Particularly with Respect to their Use in the Arts and their Introduction into Commerce* (Paris, 3 vols., 1818–19), later supplemented by Thomas Nuttall [*q.v.*]. Parts of the larger work were also monographed separately. The remainder of his life was largely spent in the administration of an estate and experimental farm which belonged to the Société Centrale de l'Agriculture, although he published several short papers on a variety of subjects. When advanced in age, he married his housekeeper, a relative; they left no issue. He died quite suddenly from apoplexy. Part of his fortune was bequeathed to the American Philosophical Society. He was a chevalier of the Legion of Honor, a correspondent of the French Institute, and a member of the American Philosophical Society. Apparently he was far better known in the United States than in his native country.

[See Elias Durand, "Biog. Memoir of the late François André Michaux," *Trans. Am. Philos. Soc.,* vol. XI (1860); Michaux's account of his trip with Fulton in the *Bull. de la Soc. d'Encouragement pour l'Industrie Nationale,* Sept. 1848, reprinted in translation in the *Jour. of the Franklin Inst.,* July 1849; and the *Am. Jour. of Sci.,* July 1856. See also the bibliography of André Michaux.] H. B. B.

MICHEL, WILLIAM MIDDLETON (Jan. 22, 1822–June 4, 1894), physician, was born in Charleston, S. C., the son of Dr. William and Eugenia (Fraser) Michel. His father was of French ancestry and was educated entirely in France; his mother was of a family prominent in the colonial history of South Carolina. He was known familiarly by his second name which until about Civil War time he spelled Myddleton. For two years (1835–37) he studied at the Pension Labrousse in Paris. In 1842 he began to study medicine under eminent French instructors and for two years dissected for Jean Cruveilhier. After receiving a diploma in 1845 from the École de Médecine he returned to the United States and in 1846 was graduated from the Medical College of the State of South Carolina. The following year he opened the Summer Medical Institute of Charleston in which he lectured on anatomy, physiology, and obstetrics. The school attracted students from all over the South and continued in operation until 1860. In 1852 he had been offered a chair in Crosby Medical College of New York and was urged by his friend, Dr. Marion Sims, to accept the offer, but he refused it to remain in Charleston. In 1862 he was placed in charge of a Confederate hospital at Manchester, Va., and later became one of the consulting surgeons of the staff of the Richmond Hospital. He was the personal physician of Gen. Joseph E. Johnston.

Michel was professor of physiology and histology in the Medical College of South Carolina from 1868 until his death in 1894 and from 1880 until his death he was a member of the Charleston board of health. He was prominent in the Medical Society of South Carolina, serving as president from 1880 to 1883. He was a member of the Academy of Sciences of Philadelphia, of the American Association for the Advancement of Science, and a corresponding member of the Imperial Society of National History of Paris. For a time during the war (1863–64) he edited the *Confederate Medical and Surgical Journal,* in which he published a number of important case records. After the war he became associate editor, with Dr. F. Peyre Porcher, of the *Charleston Medical Journal and Review* and was also an associate editor of the *Boston Medical Journal.* His contributions to these and other medical magazines were numerous and considered of great value in his time. His study of the embryological development of the opossum, published in the *Proceedings of the American Association for the Advancement of Science* (vol. III, 1850), was the subject of much scientific discussion. In April 1866, Michel was married to Cecilia S. Inglesby, who with four children survived him.

[R. F. Stone, *Biog. of Eminent Am. Physicians and Surgeons* (1894); I. A. Watson, *Physicians and Surgeons of America* (1896); H. A. Kelly and W. L. Burrage, *Am. Medic. Biogs.* (1920); *Charleston News and Courier,* June 5, 1894.] A. R. C.

MICHELSON, ALBERT ABRAHAM (Dec. 19, 1852–May 9, 1931), physicist, was born at Strelno, a small Prussian town near the frontier of Poland. His parents, Samuel and Rosalie (Przlubska) Michelson, came to America in 1854. After a short stay in New York the family went by boat via Panama to San Francisco; thence the gold rush took them first to Murphy's camp in Calaveras County, Cal., and later to Virginia City, Nev., close to the bonanza silver mines. Michelson received his early schooling at Virginia City and, when his parents returned to San Francisco, completed his primary and secondary education in the schools of that city. Because of his evident interest and talent in science, his high-school teachers urged him to continue his education. He took the competitive examinations for congressional appointment to the United States Naval Academy, resulting in a tie between himself and another boy. The latter, through political influence, got the appointment. On the suggestion of the examining committee, Michelson then decided to try for one of the ten appointments at large, and, although only seventeen, set out for Washington to interview President Grant. He was successful in obtaining the interview, but unsuccessful in getting one of the appointments available. On the eve of Michelson's departure from Annapolis again to interview the President, the Commandant, in recognition of his ability and tenacity of purpose, made a place for him as an eleventh appointment.

He graduated from the Naval Academy in 1873. After the usual period of required service, he was appointed instructor in physics and chemistry there (1875–79). This service was followed by study in the University of Berlin in 1880, at Heidelberg the following year, and in Paris at the Collège de France and the École Polytechnique in 1882. Called to the Case School of Applied Science as professor of physics in 1883, he held this position until 1889. Thence he went to Clark University as professor of physics (1889–92). With the organization of the new University of Chicago in 1892 he was called by President Harper to be head of the department of physics, and this position he held until retirement to emeritus professor in 1931. He was made a "distinguished service" professor of physics at Chicago in 1925. He was Lowell lecturer in 1899, his lectures being later published under the title, *Light Waves and Their Uses* (1903); served on the Bureau International des Poids et Mesures, 1892–93; and on the International Committee of Weights and Measures in 1897. He was exchange professor at the University of Göttingen in 1911. On Apr. 10, 1877, he was married to Margaret McLean Heminway, from whom he was later divorced. By this marriage there were two sons and a daughter; one son predeceased him. On Dec. 23, 1899, he was married to Edna Stanton of Lake Forest, Ill., who bore him three daughters.

His career was rather unique in that, although he never received an academic degree in recognition of the completion of any course of study, he was the recipient of eleven honorary degrees from American and European universities. He was awarded the Rumford Medal of the Royal Society of London in 1889; the Grand Prize of the Paris Exposition in 1900; the Mattencci Medal of the Società Italiana, Rome, in 1904; the Copley Medal of the Royal Society and the Nobel Prize in 1907; the Cresson Medal of the Franklin Institute in 1912; the Draper Gold Medal of the National Academy of Sciences in 1916; the Franklin Medal in 1923; the Gold Medal of the Royal Astronomical Society in 1923; the Gold Medal of the Society of Arts and Sciences, New York, in 1929; the Duddell Medal of the Physical Society of London in 1930. In the war period in 1918 he was appointed lieutenant-commander, United States Naval Reserve. He was president of the National Academy of Sciences (1923–27); he served the American Association for the Advancement of Science as president in 1910; the American Physical Society as president (1901–03), and as a member of its editorial board (1915–17). He was vice-president of the American Philosophical Society during the years 1910, 1911, and 1913. Nearly all of the great scientific societies claimed him for membership. He was an honorary fellow of the Physical Society of London, foreign member of the Royal Society of London, honorary fellow of the Royal Society of Edinburgh, corresponding member of the British Association for the Advancement of Science, fellow of the Royal Astronomical Society, honorary member of the Royal Institution of Great Britain, honorary member of the Royal Irish Academy, foreign associate of the Académie Française, and also of the Académie des Sciences (Paris), and honorary fellow of the Optical Society of America. He was foreign member of the Reale Accademia dei Lincei (Rome) and held memberships in the American Astronomical Society, the American Academy, the Société Française de Physique, the Société Hollandaise des Sciences, the Deutschen Physicalische Gesellschaft, the Kungliga, Fysiografiska Sällskapet, Lund, and the Russian Academy of Sciences.

In *American Men of Science* Michelson's official field is succinctly summarized in one word, "Light." His entire scientific career, begun while a student at Annapolis and continued without pause until in his seventy-ninth year he suffered a cerebral hemorrhage that caused his death at Pasadena, Cal., on May 9, 1931, is summed up in some seventy-nine published papers. The first of these, printed in *The American Journal of Science* (May 1878), when he was twenty-six years of age, bears the title, "On a Method of Measuring the Velocity of Light"; the last, written shortly before he lost consciousness, but as yet unpublished, is on the same subject. In some aspect or other, light was the topic of all but twelve of these papers. His work in this field can be divided into two main categories, the first being the problem of the accurate determination of the velocity of light, and the second the study of optical interference. With respect to his work on the velocity of light, neither the young man of twenty-six nor the old man of seventy-nine ever had a rival. World-wide confidence in his ability, his judgment, and his honesty is indicated by the fact that, in this important work, no one ever attempted to repeat his experiments or check his results, excepting himself. In his first experiments, carried on at the Naval Academy, he conceived the idea of slightly modifying the optical path of an apparatus which had been used earlier by Léon Foucault. Foucault's unmodified experiment was at that time being carried on under the leadership of Prof. Simon Newcomb, of the Naval Academy, on a very elaborate scale supported by thousands of dollars of congressional appropriation. Michelson, by changing the position of one mirror, was able, with equipment designed and built by himself and costing less than ten dollars, to achieve precision equal to or superior to that of the official apparatus. This was the first instance of his ingenuity with respect to physical phenomena. In his last determination of the velocity of light, which embodies many refinements of his original plan, an accuracy of about three parts in a million is expected, which means that the journey of more than one hundred and eighty-six thousand miles made by light in one second will be known to within half a mile.

Michelson's work on the interference of light was also begun rather early in life, the first paper being published in *The American Journal of Science* in August 1881, under the title, "The Relative Motion of the Earth and the Luminiferous Ether." This title explains the fundamental object of all of this work, which was to detect, if possible, the absolute motion of the earth as, trailing along with the rest of the solar family, it follows the sun's plunging course through space. In common with his distinguished predecessors, and his contemporaries, Michelson held the idea that light consists of an electro-magnetic wave motion carried through a luminiferous ether, with respect to which, as a fixed system of reference, cosmical motions might be measured. It is well known now that these experiments and all others which have been designed to determine absolute motion have given completely negative results. It is equally striking testimony to confidence in his work that Michelson's first disclosure of the abortive character of this experiment was accepted without question by experimental and theoretical physicists the world over, and that a new philosophy with respect to the fundamentals of physical science was immediately attempted. This new philosophy reached its highest development in the hands of Einstein, first as the special theory of relativity, and later as the general relativity theory. Only within comparatively recent years when a somewhat more modern design of apparatus and many thousands of observations by another worker appeared to give a minute residual effect, was the experimental problem subjected to another rather widespread attack, not only by Michelson himself, but by other experimenters in America and Europe. The upshot of these latest experiments has been a complete confirmation of Michelson's earlier assertion. The constancy of the velocity of light, irrespective of the motion of either source or observer, is perhaps the keystone of the structure of modern physical theory.

As by-products of the interference experiments on ether drift, in which Edward W. Morley cooperated with Michelson, should be mentioned his contributions to fundamental apparatus and fundamental theory in spectroscopy. His echelon spectroscope was one of the earliest forms having sufficiently high resolution to disclose direct optical evidence of molecular motion which is identified with temperature. This same apparatus also, when used to study the effect of a magnetic field upon a source of radiation, did much to lay the foundation for the future of a field of investigation which even in the swiftly changing world of modern physics has maintained the same fundamental and important position with respect to new theories that it held with respect to the old. In July 1890 he published in *The London, Edinburgh, and Dublin Philosophical Magazine* a paper, "On the Application of Interference Methods to Astronomical Measurements." Thirty years later, this method was used by the astronomers in the attempt to measure the diameter of a star, and it achieved such striking success that it became front-page news, in the public press throughout the world.

Other by-products of his work in interference were his adoption of the wave length of cadmium light as a fundamental standard of length, and his calibration of the international meter which he found to contain 1,553,163½ wave lengths of the red radiation from this source. In collaboration with Thomas Chrowder Chamberlin and one or two other colleagues, Michelson applied the delicate methods of measurement by means of interference to the problem of the rigidity of the earth, using for this purpose the ebb and flow of such tiny tides as are engendered in a six-inch iron pipe five hundred feet long, filled with water and buried underground. This investigation confirmed early provisional estimates by Kelvin, based on celestial mechanics, that the earth possessed a rigidity of the same order of magnitude as that of steel. These experiments showed in addition that the earth's viscosity also was not much different from that of steel. In the ruling of diffraction gratings, which are of primary importance in the study of spectra, not only of terrestrial sources but also of the stars, Michelson laid noteworthy contributions on the foundations of work along these lines of his distinguished predecessor, Henry A. Rowland of Johns Hopkins. While failing to achieve his ideals in this direction, he established at the University of Chicago one of the very few centers in the world from which high-grade diffraction gratings may be produced for the benefit of scientific workers elsewhere.

No account of this great figure is complete without some reference to a few aspects of his personality, other than scientific. His life was a magnificent exhibition of singleness of purpose, unruffled by winds of favor or disfavor. Even the cosmic forces of love, hate, jealousy, envy, and ambition seemed to move him little. Possessed of an astonishing indifference to people in general because of his absorption in his scientific pursuits, he nevertheless had the capacity of making and cherishing a few devoted friends. As a teacher, his lectures were models of acute organization and clarity of exposition. Comparatively few students in his classes aroused his personal interest, but those who did found no end of patience and sympathetic and intelligent consideration for their scientific or their personal problems. As the executive head of a large and important department in a great university, it was his practice to delegate full responsibility with respect to all details to others. However, whenever his colleagues or his staff needed his support, no one was ever more quick to champion their cause as his own. In such situations his clarity of vision, fearlessness, and swift assumption of initiative usually won the desired results with little effective opposition.

Michelson's primitive simplicity of character showed itself in his intuitions with respect to natural phenomena and in the boldness and the brilliance of his attack upon those citadels wherein nature keeps her most carefully treasured secrets. His inquiries were of highly fundamental character. The man's artistic side might have been regarded as exhibiting versatility. He was a musician of some talent on the violin, and the musical instructor of some of his children; in water color and in oil he was an artist of unusual skill and feeling, for an amateur. All who knew him well realized that the feeling of the artist was the keynote of his scientific work as well. On one occasion in Chicago he had been prevailed upon to exhibit some of his water colors in one of the university halls. Physical force had been almost necessary to get him there in person. A lady came up to him and said that she felt he must have made a great mistake when he abandoned art for science. Michelson, with that characteristic grave courtesy that he always achieved when disagreeing with another's opinion, replied that he hoped she was mistaken; to his own way of thinking, he said, he felt he had never abandoned art. He said it was his conviction that in science alone was art able to find its highest expression.

F. R. Moulton, in an appreciation of Michelson published in *Popular Astronomy* (June–July 1931), admirably expresses the spirit of his work: "He was unhurried and unfretful. He was never rushed by University duties; he never drove himself to complete a laborious task; he never feared that science, the University, or mankind was at a critical turning point; he never trembled on the brink of a great discovery. . . . If I have correctly caught the dominant note of his life, Michelson was moved only by the æsthetic enjoyment his work gave him. In everything he did, whether it was work or play, he was an artist. . . . He pursued his modest serene way along the frontiers of science, entering new pathways and ascending to unattained heights as leisurely and as easily as though he were taking an evening stroll."

[J. M. and Jaques Cattell, eds., *Am. Men of Science* (4th ed., 1927); "Proc. of the Michelson Meeting of the Optical Soc. of America," in *Jour. of the Optical Society of America,* March 1929, containing an almost complete list of his published papers; R. A. Millikan, in *Science,* May 10, 22, 1931; F. R. Moulton, in *Popular Astronomy,* June–July 1931; H. G. Gale, in *Astrophysical Jour.,* July 1931; *N. Y. Times,* May 10, 11, 28, 1931, the last containing a letter signed Margaret Heminway Shepherd about his first marriage; *Who's Who in America,* 1930–31.]

H. B. L—n.

MICHENER, EZRA (Nov. 24, 1794–June 24, 1887), physician and botanist, the fourth and youngest child of Mordecai and Alice (Dunn) Michener, was born on a farm in London Grove Township, Chester County, Pa. The Micheners were Quakers and Ezra was brought up in this faith. His education began with reading lessons from the Bible taught by his maternal grandmother as she worked at her spinning wheel and was continued at the country school, where he learned writing and arithmetic. A neighbor, John Jackson, was an enthusiastic florist and botanist and taught the child much about the various plants. Young Michener responded eagerly and made good use of his friend's teaching and library. He pored over Rees's *Cyclopaedia* seeking familiar plants which he collected and classified—the beginning of his herbarium. Physically he was not robust. Realizing that he would not be able to carry on the heavy work of the farm he decided to study medicine and at the age of twenty-two entered the University of Pennsylvania at Philadelphia. In recognition of his ability and diligence he was chosen to be house student in the Philadelphia Dispensary and in his second year was given almost entire charge of the out-patient department. On Apr. 10, 1818, he received his diploma and began the practice of medicine in Chester County. He was married on Apr. 15, 1819, to Sarah Spencer. She died in 1843, and in the following year Michener was married to Mary S. Walton. He died at the age of ninety-two at his home near Toughkenamon, Pa.

Michener was one of the first medical men to use ergot as a uterine tonic. He invented an apparatus for the treatment of fracture of the femur which he used successfully for more than sixty years. In addition to his large practice he continued his investigations in botany, attending lectures, collecting specimens, and writing. He was an honorary member of the Medical Society of Pennsylvania; a correspondent of the Academy of Natural Sciences; and a founder of the Chester County Medical Society. His natural history collection included more than five hundred species of birds, animals, and reptiles. It was presented to Swarthmore College in 1869 but was destroyed in the fire occurring there some years later. An extensive herbarium of flowering and cryptogamous plants which he prepared by means of a press of his own invention was left to his heirs. His work brought him to the notice of the eminent scientists of his time, with many of whom he carried on a voluminous correspondence. His autobiography reveals him as a humorless, inflexibly upright man. He was an active member of the religious Society of Friends, and slavery, war, and the use of alcohol and tobacco were abhorrent to him. He overlooked no opportunity to denounce these evils and was one of the founders of the Guardian Society for Preventing Drunkenness. This was said to be the first temperance society in Pennsylvania and perhaps one of the first in the United States. His writings consist of fifteen books, twenty-three medical reports, and contributions to various publications. The more important of his works include the *Manual of Weeds* (1872); *Conchologia Cestrica* (1874), in collaboration with W. D. Hartman; *Handbook of Eclampsia* (1883); *Retrospect of Early Quakerism* (1860), and *The Christian Casket* (1869).

[*Autographical Notes from the Life and Letters of Ezra Michener, M.D.* (1893); J. S. Futhey and Gilbert Cope, *Hist. of Chester County, Pa.* (1881); J. W. Harshberger, *The Botanists of Phila. and Their Work* (1899); *Medic. and Surgic. Reporter*, Aug. 20, 1870; the *Friends' Intelligencer and Jour.*, Seventh Month 2, 1887; the *Phila. Press*, June 26, 1887.] F. E. W.

MICHIE, PETER SMITH (Mar. 24, 1839–Feb. 16, 1901), soldier, educator, son of William and Ann D. (Smith) Michie, was born at Brechin, County Forfar, Scotland. His family came to America in 1843 and settled in Cincinnati, Ohio. After graduating with honors from the Woodward High School he was appointed a cadet at the United States Military Academy from which he graduated second in his class in June 1863 and was assigned to the Corps of Engineers. A short time thereafter he received orders to report at Hiltonhead, S. C., where an army under General Gillmore was engaged in the siege of Charleston. As assistant engineer he was engaged for six months in the construction of batteries for the reduction of Fort Sumter and in the attack on Fort Wagner. In the latter operation he was employed in the hazardous work of laying out and constructing the parallels and approaches which caused the Confederates to abandon the fort. In the early part of 1864 he was selected as chief engineer of a division under General Seymour sent to Florida where he took part in the battle of Olustee and fortified various points on the Florida Coast. When, in the spring of 1864, Gillmore with his corps was ordered to southern Virginia to join the Army of the James under General Butler, he took Michie with him. Later Michie became its chief engineer. He took part in all the operations of this army during 1864 and 1865 and was present in its final advance upon Appomattox under General Ord.

For his services while still a lieutenant he received the brevets of captain, major, lieutenant-colonel, and brigadier-general. General Grant said he was "one of the most deserving young officers in the service" and that his services eminently entitled him to "substantial promotion" (*War of the Rebellion: Official Records, Army*, 1 ser. XLVI, pt. 2, pp. 947, 880). From 1867 to 1871 he served as instructor at the Military Academy and in 1870 as a member of a board of engineer officers sent to Europe to collect information on the development of sea-coast defenses to meet the increased power of artillery. In February 1871 he was appointed professor of natural and experimental philosophy at the Military Academy, which position he held until his death. By his engaging personality and genial manners he made many friends in military, political, and civil life and through them was able to win support for the Military Academy which he loved. He was largely instrumental in securing the necessary legislation for the enlargement of the reservation at West Point in 1889 which made possible the expansion of the Academy after the Spanish-American War. He was the author of textbooks on mechanics, physics, and astronomy and in addition wrote *The Life and Letters of Emory Upton* (1885), *The Personnel of Sea Coast Defenses* (1887), and *General McClellan* (1901). From 1871 to 1901 he was one of the overseers of the Thayer School of Civil Engineering of Dartmouth College. He died at West Point. In 1863 he had married Marie Louise Roberts of Cincinnati, Ohio. They had two sons and a daughter. His younger son, Dennis Mahan Michie, was killed in the battle of San Juan, Cuba, in the Spanish-American War.

[G. W. Cullum, *Biog. Reg. . . . U. S. Mil. Acad.*, vol. II (ed. 1891); *Thirty-second Ann. Reunion: Asso. Grads. U. S. Mil. Acad.* (1901); *N. Y. Times*, Feb. 17, 1901.]

G. J. F.

MICHIKINIKWA [See Little Turtle, *c.* 1752–1812].

MIDDLETON, ARTHUR (1681–Sept. 7, 1737), acting colonial governor, was the son of Edward Middleton and his second wife, Sarah Middleton, who had been the widow of Richard Fowell of Barbados. The elder Middleton was born in England, emigrated to Barbados, and thence to Carolina, where he became a lord's proprietary deputy, member of the council, and assistant justice. His son, Arthur, was born in Charlestown to the prestige surrounding a wealthy and enterprising father and was probably educated in England. He inherited estates in Carolina, England, and Barbados. He was not only born to public life but, in 1707, married into it, taking as his wife, Sarah, the daughter of Jonathan Amory, speaker of the South Carolina House of Commons. She was the mother of his son, Henry Middleton, 1717–1784 [*q.v.*]. After her death in 1722 he was married, on Aug. 3, 1723, to Sarah (Wilkinson) Morton, the widow of Joseph Morton, a landgrave of Carolina. They had no children. Middleton began his public career early. From 1706 to 1710, he was a member of the South Carolina House of Commons. He became Lord Carteret's deputy and a member of the council. During the Yemassee War in 1715 he was sent as an agent to obtain aid from Virginia and, successful in his mission, was voted a pipe of wine by a grateful House. A year later he left the council for the House of Commons, where he led a movement against the proprietors, became president of the convention into which the Assembly resolved itself when dissolved by the governor, and helped overthrow proprietary control in 1719. After the Crown, in 1720, accepted the revolution and appointed Sir Francis Nicholson to be governor, Middleton became president of Nicholson's council and administered the government after the governor sailed for England in April 1725. In this capacity he met representatives of Spain in a conference to settle the southern boundary of Carolina but accomplished nothing. Like his predecessors he was concerned with Indian relations, so vital to a border colony, and when the Yemassee were harassing the border he had them subdued and severely punished. He also followed the usual policy against the French by efforts to counteract their influence with the Creeks and Cherokee. However, he found it difficult to maintain amicable relations with his legislature. In 1726 he checked the lower house in its attempt to issue paper money for rebuilding a fort burned on the Altamaha. Rioting followed, the council was threatened, and arrests had to be made before order could be restored. The paper-money party later sent representatives to the council, were denied an audience, and rioted again. Disputes over this question, constantly recurring, persisted throughout his administration and prevented the proper functioning of government. Six times he tried the expedient of dissolving the legislature and ordering new elections only to find the new assembly as hostile as the last. He was accused of corruption and of denying a writ of *habeas corpus.* Alexander Hewatt (*post,* I, p. 312) characterized him as a man "of a reserved and mercenary disposition . . . a sensible man, and by no means ill-qualified for governing," who, however, found it difficult as an erstwhile revolutionary leader to inculcate loyalty to the king and who had as his principal ambition the accumulation of property. After the arrival of Governor Johnson to take over the tangled affairs of the colony he became a member of Johnson's council and again became president of the council, in which position he was serving when he died.

[*S. C. Geneal. and Hist. Mag.*, July 1900, Oct. 1903; Alexander Hewatt, *Hist. Account of . . . S. C.* (2 vols., 1779), esp. I, pp. 312–19; *S. C. Hist. Soc. Colls.*, vol. I

(1857), pp. 236–46, 291–307; Edward McCrady, *The Hist. of S. C. under the Proprietary Government* (1897) and *The Hist. of S. C. under the Royal Government* (1889); W. R. Smith, *S. C. as a Royal Province* (1903); A. H. Middleton, *Life in Carolina and New England* (1929), p. 66, for death date from tombstone.]

H. B—C.

MIDDLETON, ARTHUR (June 26, 1742–Jan. 1, 1787), Revolutionary leader and signer of the Declaration of Independence, the son of Mary (Williams) and Henry Middleton, 1717–1784 [*q.v.*], was born at "Middleton Place" on the Ashley River, near Charlestown, now Charleston, S. C. He was educated in the colony and in England, part of the time probably at the academy in Hackney. On Apr. 14, 1757, he was admitted to the Middle Temple to read law. In 1763 he sailed for home and arrived in time to spend Christmas with his family, in which many changes had taken place since his departure, the birth of at least three of his sisters, the death of his mother, and his father's remarriage. The next summer, on Aug. 19, he was married to Mary, the daughter of Walter Izard. That year he became a justice of the peace and in October was elected to the colonial House of Assembly, in which he soon became a member of the committee to correspond with the colonial agent in London, and served until 1768. In May 1768 he took his wife to London, where their son Henry was born, and where Benjamin West painted a charming portrait of the little family. Visiting southern Europe, they spent some time in Rome, and in September 1771 they returned to South Carolina to settle down at "Middleton Place," which he inherited through his mother.

The next year he was again elected a member of the Commons' House of Assembly. In the anxious days before the Revolutionary War actually broke out he sat in the first provincial congress. He served on the general committee, on the secret committee of five that arranged and directed the action of the three parties of citizens who seized powder and weapons from the public storehouses on the night of Apr. 21, 1776, and within a few days raised 1,000 guineas to support colonial resistance, and on the special committee appointed on May 5 after the receipt of a letter from Arthur Lee in London intimating the possibility of British instigation of insurrection among the slaves of the American colonies. After the arrival of the news of Lexington he continued his activity and on June 14 became a member of the first Council of Safety, upon which devolved the executive power of the colony already in the midst of revolution. In the second provincial Congress he was elected to the new Council of Safety, on Nov. 16, 1775. As a leader of the extreme party he advocated the excommunication of all those who refused to sign the Association and the attachment of the estates of those who fled the colony, and he looked without disfavor on such activities as the tarring and feathering of Loyalists. Constantly he urged the preparation of Charlestown harbor against attack. On Feb. 11, 1776, he was appointed to the committee of eleven to prepare a constitution for South Carolina. A few days later he was elected to the Continental Congress, but not until South Carolina's constitution was written and adopted and the council of safety superseded by a new government did he travel northward to claim his seat. The first record of his presence is for May 20, and he was present to sign the Declaration of Independence. In January 1777 he was reëlected and continued in the Congress until October of that year. He left little imprint on the records of that body and absented himself from sessions to which he was elected. He was reëlected in 1778 but declined the election, and he failed to attend in 1779 and in 1780, although he had been elected on Feb. 5, 1779, and on Feb. 1, 1780. In 1775, when President John Rutledge [*q.v.*] vetoed the bill to enact the new constitution for South Carolina and resigned his office, Middleton was chosen as successor, but declined. During the siege of Charlestown in 1780 he served in the militia, was taken prisoner at the capture of the city, and was sent to St. Augustine as a prisoner of war. Exchanged in July 1781, he presented his credentials to the Continental Congress on Sept. 24, was reëlected by the Jacksonborough Assembly, and sat in the session of 1782.

After the war he repaired the damages suffered by his properties, devoted himself to planting, became a member of the racing club and of the hunting club of St. George's parish, and was an original trustee of the College of Charleston. He died at Goose Creek, survived by his wife and eight of their nine children. His daughter Isabella married Daniel Elliott Huger [*q.v.*], and his two sons, Henry and John Izard Middleton [*qq.v.*], carried on the family tradition of distinguished achievement.

[A. S. Salley, Jr., "Delegates to the Continental Congress from S. C.," *Bull. Hist. Com. of S. C.*, no. 9 (1927); E. A. Jones, *Am. Members of the Inns of Court* (1924); John Hutchinson, *A Cat. of Notable Middle Templars* (1902); Langdon Cheves, "Middleton of S. C.," *S. C. Hist. and Geneal. Mag.*, July 1900; "Correspondence of Hon. Arthur Middleton," *Ibid.*, Oct. 1925, Jan., Apr., July 1926; *Ibid.*, Jan. 1905, Jan. 1914, Apr. 1916, Jan. 1917, Jan. 1920, Apr. 1927, Apr. 1928, July 1929; John Drayton, *Memoirs of the Am. Revolution* (1821), esp. vol. I, pp. 175, 221–22, 231, 255, 268–71, 273, 285, 304–07, 318, 320, vol. II, pp. 15, 18,

23, 174, 180; E. C. Burnett, *Letters of Members of the Continental Congress,* vols. I–V (1921–31); *Journals of the Continental Congress,* vols. IV–XXII (1906–14).]

K. E. C.

MIDDLETON, HENRY (1717–June 13, 1784), president of the Continental Congress, was the son of Sarah (Amory) and Arthur Middleton, 1681–1737 [*q.v.*]. It is probable that he was born at his father's plantation "The Oaks" near Charlestown, now Charleston, S. C., and that he was educated in England. At his father's death he inherited "The Oaks" and a good deal of other property in South Carolina as well as in England and Barbados. Through his marriage to Mary Williams he added the estate afterward known as "Middleton Place," where he made his home, laying out the beautifully proportioned grounds and gardens, which have been enjoyed and embellished by later generations and which remain a delight to the residents and visitors of Charleston. He became one of the greatest landowners in South Carolina, owning nearly twenty plantations with a total of 50,000 acres and about 800 slaves. His wealth was so great that tradition credits him with having raised and supported at his own expense an entire regiment to fight in the Revolution.

Like many other members of prominent Southern families of this period, he held many official positions, of which the most important were, perhaps, justice of the peace, member of the commons house, speaker in 1747 and again in 1754 and 1755, and member of His Majesty's council for South Carolina. In 1769 he was in accord with the rest of the council in opposition to the action of the Assembly in voting £1,500 sterling to the John Wilkes fund. Nevertheless, although a churchman and a conservative with social and political position as well as a fortune at stake, he resigned his seat in the council in September 1770 to become a leader of the opposition to the British policy. In July 1774 a mass convention in Charlestown chose him to represent the province in the Continental Congress. When Peyton Randolph resigned he became the second president of the Congress and served from Oct. 22, 1774, to May 10, 1775. He did not wish for independence but hoped that moderate resistance would hasten the arrival of British commissioners to make a reasonable peace. When the radicals began to obtain control, he resigned from Congress, in February 1776, and was succeeded by his son Arthur Middleton [*q.v.*], who was more radical than he. After his resignation from the Continental Congress he became president of the South Carolina Congress and a member of the Council of Safety after Nov. 16, 1775. On Feb. 11, 1776, he and his son Arthur were appointed members of a committee to frame a temporary constitution for the state, following the adoption of which he was made a member of the legislative council, and in January 1779 he became a member of the newly created state Senate.

After the surrender of Charlestown, he was among those who accepted defeat and "took protection" under the British flag. Although the triumph of the Revolutionists was followed by numerous confiscations of the estates of Loyalists, he did not suffer for his abandonment of the struggle, nor is there any evidence that his fellow citizens regarded him in any less favorable light. His public spirit is shown not only in the offices he held but in the deeds he performed. When, at the outset of the Revolution, there was a lack of money in the province he and four other wealthy citizens "issued joint and several notes of hand in convenient denominations payable to the bearer, and these readily went into circulation at face value" (Allan Nevins, *During and After the Revolution, 1775–1789,* 1924, p. 487).

He was a generous benefactor of the church and was active in advancing the agricultural, commercial, and educational interests of the state. His contributions to the new colleges in New Jersey, Rhode Island, and at Philadelphia were large. In 1741 he married Mary, the only daughter of John Williams, member of the House of Commons from St. George's. She died on Jan. 9, 1761. In 1762 he married Maria Henrietta, daughter of Lieut.-Gov. William Bull, who died on Mar. 1, 1772. In January 1776 he married Lady Mary Mackenzie, who was the daughter of George, third earl of Cromartie, and was the widow of John Ainslie. Of his five sons and seven daughters, all the children of his first wife, Arthur was the eldest and the heir, Thomas became a Revolutionary patriot and a generous public servant, Henrietta married Edward Rutledge [*q.v.*], and Sarah married Charles Cotesworth Pinckney [*q.v.*].

[*S. C. Hist. and Geneal. Mag.,* July 1900, Apr. 1919, pp. 118–19, July 1926; Edward McCrady, *The Hist. of S. C. under the Royal Government* (1901) and *The Hist. of S. C. in the Revolution* (1902); W. R. Smith, *S. C. as a Royal Province* (1903); "An Old-Time Carolina Garden," *Century Mag.,* Oct. 1910; A. H. Middleton, *Life in Carolina and New England* (1929), esp. pp. 65–66.]

J. G. V—D.

MIDDLETON, HENRY (Sept. 28, 1770–June 14, 1846), South Carolina Unionist, the son of Mary (Izard) and Arthur Middleton, 1742–1787 [*q.v.*], was born in London, reared in South Carolina, and educated there and in England. He traveled extensively both in Europe and America. On Nov. 13, 1794, he was married to Mary Helen Hering of Heybridge Hall, England. He inherited "Middleton Place," on which he lavished money and labor. Although the azaleas, so much a feature of the modern gardens, were set out by his son, it was he who planted the first of the camellias, the gift of his friend, André Michaux [*q.v.*]. He served in both houses of the state legislature for ten years and then as governor of South Carolina from 1810 to 1812. One of the accomplishments of his administration was the passage of an act to establish a system of free schools, which, however, failed of a part of its purpose in that no means were found to enforce the provisions of the law and to select able and conscientious officials. As governor and after the expiration of his term, he supported a war policy in 1812. He represented his state in the Fourteenth and Fifteenth congresses, from 1815 to 1819, and then became minister to Russia. With a good deal of skill he negotiated with Russia the convention of 1824 to regulate trade and fisheries in the Pacific.

In 1830 he returned to America with the thought that his days of public service were over, but the nullification controversy soon called him from his retirement. He was among those who disagreed with Calhoun as to the wisdom and the constitutionality of nullification and became one of the leaders of what was called the Union party. He was a delegate to an anti-tariff convention that assembled at Philadelphia on Sept. 30, 1831, and submitted a memorial to Congress proposing the rates of 1816 as a satisfactory compromise. When, in the fall of 1832, the South Carolina Nullifiers obtained the two-thirds of the state legislature constitutionally necessary to call a state convention, he was one of the few Union men elected to this convention and sought in vain to prevent the adoption of the Nullification Ordinance. In the December convention at Columbia, representing the strong Unionist minority, he became one of the vice-presidents, and he was appointed to solicit the legislature of Tennessee to attend a convention in which the other Southern states should participate in order to consider possible constitutional measures of resistance. He died at Charleston survived by eight of his twelve children. Of his children the most distinguished was Henry Middleton (1797–1876), who devoted his attention to writing on political and economic subjects; in *The Government and the Currency* (1844, 2nd ed., with alterations, 1850) he denied the right of the federal government to issue paper money, in *Four Essays* (1847) he advocated free trade, and later touched the vital problem of the South in *Economical Causes of Slavery in the United States, and Obstacles to Abolition* (1857).

[*S. C. Hist. and Geneal. Mag.*, July 1900, Apr. 1919, p. 119; *Life, Letters, and Speeches of James Louis Petigru*, ed. by J. P. Carson (1920); *Hist. of S. C.*, ed. by Yates Snowden (1920), vol. I; Mrs. St. Julien Ravenal, *Charleston* (copr. 1906); C. S. Boucher, *The Nullification Controversy in S. C.* (1916); *The Am. Secretaries of State*, ed. by S. F. Bemis, vol. IV (1928); "An Old-Time Carolina Garden," *Century Mag.*, Oct. 1910; *Charleston Courier*, June 15, 16, 1846.]

J. G. V—D.

MIDDLETON, JOHN IZARD (Aug. 13, 1785–Oct. 5, 1849), archeologist, was born at "Middleton Place" near Charleston, S. C., the son of Mary (Izard) and Arthur Middleton, 1742–1787 [*q.v.*]. His father died soon after the son's birth and John is said to have been educated in England at the University of Cambridge. Having inherited his mother's large fortune he was able to devote his time to painting, for which he had no small talent and in which he attained some reputation. He took up his residence in Italy and spent most of his life there and in France. Endowed by nature with uncommon gifts, which he had cultivated to advantage, he found ready access to good society and "was received on terms of intimacy in circles into which foreigners seldom gained entrance" (Norton, *post*, p. 4). He married on June 11, 1810, Eliza Augusta Falconet, the daughter of Jean Louis Theodore de Palazieu Falconet. By her he had three children, all of whom died young. Two years after his marriage, in 1812, he published in London a volume with numerous colored plates, *Grecian Remains in Italy, a description of Cyclopian Walls and of Roman Antiquities with Topographical and Picturesque Views of Ancient Latium.* In his introduction he wrote that in such a work as his the artist was perhaps more important than the scholar. Therefore, he had made a collection of very accurate drawings, which were published in the book not merely to accompany the text but as the principal object of the publication. He said that he wrote the book because he had drawn the pictures. He had made the sketches while traveling in Italy during 1808 and 1809 with two English gentlemen, one of whom was Edward Dodwell later distinguished as an archeologist. Appearing as it did in a year crowded with events and at a time when scholarly communication between the United States and Europe was interrupted by war, Middleton's volume received little notice. Some of the drawings were used in later work on archeology without acknowledgment to the investigator who produced them, and his name has been largely forgotten. Nevertheless the work deserves to be remembered not only for its pioneer place in the early history of the study of antiquity but also because the accuracy and precision of its detail are notable even in a later day. He died in Paris and his body was brought to America and laid in the family vault at "Middleton Place."

[*S. C. Hist. and Geneal. Mag.*, July 1900; Chas. Eliot Norton, "The First Am. Classical Archaelogist," *Am. Jour. of Archaeology*, vol. I (1885); A. H. Middleton, *Life in Carolina and New England* (1929).] E. L. G.

MIDDLETON, NATHANIEL RUSSELL (Apr. 1, 1810–Sept. 6, 1890), fifth president of the College of Charleston, was born in Charleston, S. C., the eldest son of Arthur and Alicia Hopton (Russell) Middleton. His paternal grandfather, Thomas Middleton, was the son of Henry Middleton, 1717–1784, and the brother of Arthur Middleton, 1742–1787 [*qq.v.*]. His maternal grandfather, Nathaniel Russell, a wealthy Charleston merchant, was born in Bristol, R. I., the son of Joseph Russell, for a time chief justice of Rhode Island. He thus united two representative but very diverse strains in early American life, that of the Southern planter and the New England man of business. In 1824 he entered the College of Charleston and graduated in 1828. Following a sojourn in Europe he was married, on Jan. 18, 1832, to Margaret Emma Izard by whom he had three sons. After her death in 1836 he was married, on Sept. 20, 1842, to Anna Elizabeth de Wolf, of Bristol, R. I., by whom he had four daughters and one son. For many years he managed "Bolton-on-the-Stono," a plantation of about 3,000 acres near Charleston, which he had inherited from his father. The property, however, had financial encumbrances, a result probably of his father's generous and lavish way of life, and in 1852 he found it advantageous to sell the plantation with its slaves. He was then appointed treasurer of the Northeastern Railroad Company and later served for several years as treasurer of Charleston. His interests, however, had always been literary and artistic, and he found very tempting the prospect that was offered in 1857 by the call to the presidency of the College of Charleston. His extreme conscientiousness made him hesitate since he thought that his experience as a planter had not prepared him for such a position. In reality he was admirably fitted for the post. The College of Charleston, founded in the eighteenth century and later transferred to the control of the city council, was largely patronized by the planters' families. Its calendar was made to accommodate the schedule of the planters; Commencement always took place the last week of March; there followed a spring vacation, after which work was resumed and continued till Aug. 1; and the holidays and session days for the rest of the year fitted into the planter's life. Its ante-bellum prosperity was the result of the interest and patronage of this influential section of the community represented by such men as Elias Horry, Langdon Cheves, James L. Petigru, William Aiken, and many others.

The historical and social prominence of his name and family and his sympathetic understanding of plantation life were recognized in ante-bellum Charleston as important considerations in the choice of Middleton as president of the college, but the records of the institution give evidence that his qualifications as an executive went far beyond this. His reports to the trustees are characterized by sound good sense and by a grasp of the true essentials of collegiate training. His sincere love of learning, his appreciation of art, and his firm religious convictions are reflected in the addresses, essays, and fugitive poems that were collected and published after his death by his son (*The Allegory of Plato and Other Essays*, 1891, and *Education*, 1893). It was these characteristics and interests that caused him to be put at the head of the Carolina art association and the Charleston Bible society. As president of the latter he was instrumental during the Civil War in importing Bibles from England for distribution among the men in the service of the Confederate armies. The College remained open throughout the Civil War, except for a few months following the evacuation of Charleston by the Confederate forces in 1865. This is an unusual record among the Southern colleges of the period, and attests the ability, tact, and resourcefulness of the president. As early as 1862 he so arranged the college curriculum that many of the students were able to enter the military service and to perform their duties in the hours free from college work. Throughout the stormy days of Reconstruction the work of the institution proceeded uninterruptedly and he remained in active service until 1880, when he retired at the age of seventy. He continued to divide his time between his winter home in Charleston and his summer residence in Bristol, R. I., and died ten years later at Charleston in the eighty-first year of his age.

[Minutes of the Trustees of the College of Charleston; Journal of the Faculty of the College of Charleston; *S. C. Hist. and Geneal. Mag.*, July 1900; A. H. Middleton, *Life in Carolina and New England* (1919); Wm. Way, *Hist. of the New England Soc. of Charleston* (1920); *News and Courier* (Charleston), Sept. 8, 1890.] H. R.

MIDDLETON, PETER (d. Jan. 9, 1781), New York physician, left no known record of his ancestry, though his obituary places his birth in "North Britain." His first appearance is on the records of the University of St. Andrews, Feb. 27, 1752, when Prof. Thomas Simson represented to the university that "one Peter Middleton, a practitioner of physick, had been with him, and desired the Degree of Doctor of Medicine." After an examination, "the University, being satisfied with his performances," conferred the degree on him. Although the date usually given is 1750, it seems probable that it was in 1752 or later when Middleton and Dr. John Bard [*q.v.*] made in New York one of the first dissections of a human body for purposes of medical instruction on record in America. It was not long before Middleton was one of the chief physicians of New York, with an extensive and remunerative practice among the rich, and a large gratuitous practice among the poor. During the French war he had the rank of surgeon-general of the provincial forces in the Crown Point expedition, and in 1770 he received a grant of five thousand acres of land on the Susquehanna (*Third Annual Report of the State Historian of the State of New York, 1897,* 1898, p. 766). In 1756 he was one of the founders of the St. Andrew's Society of New York City, and from 1767 to 1770 its president; he was also a prominent Freemason, holding the office of deputy grand-master of the province under Sir John Johnson.

On Aug. 14, 1767, letters were presented to the governors of King's College from Middleton and five other New York physicians, proposing "to institute a Medical School within this College for instructing Pupils in the most usefull and necessary Branches of Medicine," and offering to give a course of lectures the following winter. The governors thereupon established the medical school and appointed the six physicians to professorships, Middleton securing the chair of physiology and pathology, to which materia medica was added in 1770 (manuscript minutes of the governors). The school was opened Nov. 2, 1767, with "a very elegant and learned Discourse" delivered by Middleton in the college hall in the presence of the governor of the province and other notables (*New-York Mercury,* Nov. 9, 1767). The discourse was published in 1769 with the title *A Medical Discourse, or an Historical Inquiry into the Ancient and Present State of Medicine*; it is an able work, displaying considerable familiarity with medical history, but gives little on the American situation. His only other known publication is a letter on the croup to Dr. Richard Bayley (R. Bayley, *Cases of the Angina Trachealis,* 1781, pp. 19–23; *Medical Repository,* vol. XIV, 1811, pp, 345–50).

Middleton became a governor of King's College, Nov. 11, 1773 (manuscript minutes). In June 1771 a charter was granted to the New York Hospital and his name headed the list of incorporators. He was one of the first physicians elected to the staff in 1774, but the destruction of the building by fire, and the war postponed the opening of the hospital until ten years after his death. He was a Tory, and in April 1776, "from prudential motives," sailed suddenly for Bermuda, returning to New York when the British occupied the city (*Medical Register of the City of New York and Vicinity,* 1868–69, p. 306). Middleton married (marriage bond, Nov. 25, 1766, *Names of Persons for Whom Marriage Licenses were Issued by the Secretary of the Province of New York,* 1860, p. 262) Susannah, daughter of Richard Nicholls and widow of John Burges of New York, merchant. She died Dec. 6, 1771. They had one child, Susannah Margaret Middleton. The doctor left a large estate and a month after his death his "large valuable library" was sold at auction.

[See the *N.-Y. Gazette and the Weekly Mercury,* Jan. 15, Feb. 5, 1781; Robt. W. Reid, "Peter Middleton, M.D.," *Masonic Outlook,* May 1932; and Middleton's will in the *N. Y. Hist. Soc. Colls. for the Year 1901* (1902), pp. 20–22. The articles by Geo. A. Morrison, in *Hist. of the St. Andrew's Soc. of the State of N. Y.* (1906), pp. 61–64, and Wm. M. MacBean, in *Biog. of St. Andrew's Soc. of the State of N. Y.,* I (1922), 19, abound in errors.] M. H. T.

MIDDLETON, THOMAS COOKE (Mar. 30, 1842–Nov. 19, 1923), educator, was born in Philadelphia, Pa. The eldest of the nine children of Joseph and Lydia (Cooke) Middleton, he was reared in strict Quaker simplicity, although his father as a contractor and president of the Wissahickon Turnpike Company lived a manorial life at "Monticello" near Chestnut Hill. Somewhat unsettled in religious belief, the family turned to Catholicism and was received into the Church in 1854 by the Rev. Michael Domenec, later bishop of Pittsburgh. Joseph Middleton became a devout Catholic. He was instrumental in the erection of a church at Chestnut Hill, sold his estate to the Sisters of St. Joseph for a mother-house, and rejoiced when two daughters became Mercy nuns and his son, Thomas, entered the Augustinian order. After graduation from Villanova College in Pennsylvania (1858), Thomas entered the Italian novitiate at Tolentino and later made his theological studies in San Agostino, Rome, where he gained a reputation for scholarship and linguistic proficiency. Ordained in St. John Lateran's by

Cardinal Patrizi (Sept. 24, 1864), he was recalled the following autumn to Villanova College where he spent the remainder of his life as a teacher, prefect of discipline, vice-rector, rector (1876–81), associate provincial and secretary of the American province of the Augustinians (1878–1914), librarian, and historiographer of the order.

Middleton was a founder and first president (1884–90) of the American Catholic Historical Society and for many years he edited the *Records* of the society. Every moment spared from official duties he devoted to a study of the history of his order and to researches in the Catholic history of Pennsylvania. He delved into parish and local records as he industriously compiled a voluminous manuscript of notabilia of community life from 1866 to 1923 and contributed numerous articles and scrupulously exact abstracts from parochial registers to the *Records,* to Griffin's *American Catholic Historical Researches,* to the *American Catholic Quarterly,* and to the *Ecclesiastical Review.* Among his most serviceable brochures are the *Sketch of Villanova, 1842–92* (1893), *Augustinians in the United States* (1909), *Some Notes on the Bibliography of the Philippines* (1900), and a list of Catholic periodicals published in the United States from 1809 to 1892 (*Records of the American Catholic Historical Society of Philadelphia,* September 1893, March 1908).

[*Am. Cath. Who's Who* (1911); *Who's Who in America,* 1920–21; *America,* Dec. 1, 1923; *Records of the Am. Cath. Hist. Soc. of Phila.,* especially Mar.–Dec. 1901 and Mar. 1924; the *Evening Bulletin* (Phila.), Nov. 19, 20, 1923; information from Middleton's associates.] R. J. P.

MIELATZ, CHARLES FREDERICK WILLIAM (May 24, 1860–June 2, 1919), etcher, was born in Breddin, Germany, the son of Charles and Wilhelmine (Wolff) Mielatz. He came to America at the age of six, attended the schools of Chicago, and studied drawing at the Chicago School of Design and Painting with Frederic Rondel, the elder. About 1880 he went to New York and thence to Newport, where he was employed with the United States engineer corps for about five years. He then returned to New York, where he married Mary Stuart McKinney on Feb. 25, 1903, and where he remained until the day of his death. Active as an etcher in the days of the New York Etching Club, of which he was secretary for a number of years, he was also a prominent figure in the revival of original etching which set in about the turn of the century. He formed a link between the older and the younger men and remained one of the latter. His influence on etching was exerted both through his work and through his teaching at the National Academy, of which he became an associate member. A tireless experimenter, he advanced steadily and did some of his best work in his later days. His "Georgian Courts" (Lakewood, N. J.) series, among his best prints, were of a freedom, even vivaciousness, quite in contrast to the "firm, virile, lean, even ascetic" line which James G. Huneker found in his etchings. The definiteness in treatment which Huneker had in mind appeared especially in his scenes in New York, and this fact may serve to illustrate his aim to select the medium and handling best suited to the particular problem on hand.

In three series of views, in aquatint, lithography, and monotype, respectively, done for the Society of Iconophiles, Mielatz showed his judgment in choosing the proper medium and adapting himself to it. With a rich command of resources, subordinating the craft to the purpose, he occasionally combined various accessories of the etching process to gain results. He was his own printer and knew also the effect of variation in shades of ink. Technical problems and difficulties absorbed him, and he experimented in color-printing. Generally, when he departed from black-and-white, he applied color by way of suggestion, or at most in flat tints, but in his remarkable plate after "Woman and Macaws," by George B. Luks, over which he labored long, he strove for complete color rendition. The technical aspect of his plates makes perhaps the most immediate claim on the interest of students of prints. He was honest always in his intentions and in his work; there was no parade. His subjects were invariably American, and while he did at times seek them outside of Manhattan, it was with that city's picturesqueness that he was particularly identified and to which he gave most of his effort. He was held mainly by the interesting locality or structure, not by the general sweep of urban view, and such aspects of the city he presented with a sure eye for effect and for the spirit of old New York. Much that he showed might easily be passed unnoticed; even the familiar was seen with a freshness of view that gave his work an air of novelty. When he placed the old "Poe Cottage" in a setting of sombre night, E. C. Stedman avowed that he had caught some of "the quality of Poe's own mood and utterance." His plates include pictures of tarpon fishing and of yacht races, which showed swing of action, but as one writer pointed out, he was probably "best in static themes."

[The chief sources of information are "Etchings of New York City by C. F. W. Mielatz, with commentary by Frank Weitenkampf" (75 etchings), a manuscript in the N. Y. Pub. Lib., intended for early publication, and articles by F. Weitenkampf, *Internat. Studio*, Sept. 1911, and G. W. Harris, *Internat. Studio*, July 1922. See also: *Who's Who in America*, 1918–19; the *Am. Art News*, June 14, 1919, *N. Y. Tribune*, June 4, 1919, and *N. Y. Times*, June 5, 1919. With the last was a portrait from a photograph, and the *Evening Post* of Nov. 8, 1919 (magazine section), commented upon a brilliant portrait of Mielatz painted by George B. Luks.] F.W.

MIELZINER, MOSES (Aug. 12, 1828–Feb. 18, 1903), rabbi, teacher, and author, was born in Schubin, province of Posen, Germany, and died at Cincinnati, Ohio. His father, Benjamin Leib Mielziner, rabbi of Schubin, belonged to a long line of Jewish savants, and his mother, Rose Rachel Caro, was descended from the celebrated Jewish ritualistic authority, Joseph Caro (1488–1575). Moses Mielziner naturally obtained his elementary Jewish education from his father, to which additions were made by Moses' brother at Tremessen and by the Yeshivah at Exin. His subsequent secular and Talmudic knowledge was acquired in Berlin, whither he went in 1844. In the fall of 1848 he matriculated at the University of Berlin, where he studied philosophy and philology.

After having served as religious head at Waren, Mecklenburg (1852–54), with David Einhorn as chief rabbi, Mielziner, in 1854, went to Copenhagen, Denmark. In 1855 he became principal of a school. During this period he wrote, in both Latin and German, a dissertation, *Die Verhältnisse der Sklaven bei den Alten Hebräern, nach Biblischen und Talmudischen Quellen Dargestellt* (1859), for which he received the degree of Ph.D. at the University of Giessen (1859). This work, published in English under the title *Slavery among the Ancient Hebrews* (1861), proved of special interest in America during the Civil War. All of Mielziner's writings had a timely message. They were prompted by prevailing needs; but they were marked also by literary grace, clarity, and, above all, reliability. At Copenhagen, on May 19, 1861, he married Rosette Levald, by whom he had seven children.

By heredity and environment Mielziner had been made a conservative liberal. Owing to the dissensions between orthodoxy and liberalism in his Copenhagen constituency, he came to the United States in 1865. His first position was the pulpit of Anshe Chesed, then the oldest German Jewish congregation in New York. On account of internal congregational wrangles, he gave up his office and the congregation merged with Beth-El, of which his friend, David Einhorn [*q.v.*], was rabbi. For a few years Mielziner conducted a private school for boys. In 1879 he was called by Isaac M. Wise [*q.v.*], founder and president of the Hebrew Union College, to Cincinnati, where, in the first American rabbinical seminary, he held the chair of the Talmud until the time of his death. From among his writings growing out of his professional Jewish associations—more especially his particular professorial office—and including essays, reviews, sermons, Hebrew poems, and expert opinions, the following are worthy of note: *Jødisk Almanak for Skudaaret 5622* (1861, reprinted 1928); "A Paper on Neginoth: Hebrew Accents" (*Hebraica*, February–April, 1879); "On Translations of the Talmud" (*Hebrew Review*, vol. I, 1880); "The Talmudic Syllogism" (*Ibid.*); *The Jewish Law of Marriage and Divorce* (1884); *A Selection from the Book of Psalms for School and Family Use* (1888, 1890); *Introduction to the Talmud* (1894, 1903, 1925); and "Marriage Agenda" (*Year Book of the Central Conference of American Rabbis*, vol. I, 1891). The first edition of the *Union Prayer-book* (2 parts, 1892–94) was edited in 1891 by a committee of the Central Conference of American Rabbis, with Mielziner as chairman. He contributed the English translation of Chronicles to the English Bible projected by the Jewish Publication Society under the supervision of Marcus Jastrow [*q.v.*], in 1894. In 1901 he was appointed consulting editor of *The Jewish Encyclopedia*, and himself contributed articles to the first volume of this work.

In 1882, after the death of its rabbi, Dr. Max Lilienthal [*q.v.*], the B'nai Israel Congregation of Cincinnati elected Mielziner temporary rabbi until a regular successor could be appointed. He often occupied the pulpit of Isaac M. Wise in Temple B'nai Jeshurun, Cincinnati. From 1888 to 1889 he was president of the Hebrew Sabbath School Union. When Dr. Wise died, Mielziner was elected, Apr. 5, 1900, president of the Hebrew Union College, and served as such until his death.

[*Year Book of the Central Conference of Am. Rabbis*, vol. XIII (copr. 1904); William Rosenau, "A Tribute to Moses Mielziner," in *Am. Israelite*, Apr. 5, 1928; E. M. F. Mielziner, *Moses Mielziner, 1828–1903* (1931); Kaufmann Kohler, in *Hebrew Union Coll. and Other Addresses* (1916); *Who's Who in America*, 1901–02; *Jewish Comment*, Feb. 20, 1903.] W.R.

MIFFLIN, LLOYD (Sept. 15, 1846–July 16, 1921), painter and poet, was born in Columbia, Pa. His father, John Houston Mifflin, was a descendant of the John Mifflin who emigrated to the colonies from Wiltshire, England, before 1680 and settled on land now included in Fairmount Park, Philadelphia. His mother, who died while he was a child, was Elizabeth Anne

Bethel (Heise) Mifflin, daughter of Solomon Heise, a native of Frankfort, Germany. John Houston Mifflin was an artist by profession, having studied in the Pennsylvania Academy of the Fine Arts and in Europe. He was also the author of a small volume of poems privately printed in 1835. Lloyd attended the public schools of Columbia and completed his education at the Washington Classical Institute in the same town and at a private school conducted by Howard W. Gilbert. He was never robust and was encouraged to engage in horseback riding and rowing in the hope of improving his health. At fourteen he began to draw and sketch, and although his father at first endeavored to divert him from the pursuit of his own profession, he was sent to Philadelphia for instruction by Isaac Williams and then by the well-known artist Thomas Moran. In 1869 he went to Europe and continued his studies with Henry Herzog at Düsseldorf, Germany. He also traveled widely in Italy, France, and Great Britain, sketching and painting industriously. Another period of European travel and study followed in 1871–72. He exhibited in America and continued an active interest in his art until forced in 1872 to abandon it because of a decline in health, induced, it is said, by the fumes of paint.

Having been long an eager student of poetry he now turned to literary work, adopting the sonnet as his favorite form. His *At the Gates of Song,* a volume of 150 sonnets, was published in June 1897 and was so well received that a second edition was called for in the same year and another in 1901. For the next decade he devoted himself chiefly to the sonnet-form and published a succession of volumes, of which the most important are: *The Slopes of Helicon, and Other Poems* (1898); *Echoes of Greek Idyls* (1899), consisting of versions of Bion, Moschus, and Bacchylides; *The Fields of Dawn and Later Sonnets* (1900); *Castalian Days* (1903); *The Fleeing Nymph, and Other Verse* (1905), a volume containing a long blank-verse poem and some lyrics not in sonnet-form; *My Lady of Dream* (1906); *Toward the Uplands* (1908); and *Flower and Thorn* (1909). In 1905 Mifflin gathered into a volume entitled *Collected Sonnets,* a selection from his previously published works with some new verse, amounting to 309 sonnets in all. A second edition of this work appeared in 1907. In 1916 he issued his last book, *As Twilight Falls.* In November 1915 he had suffered a stroke of apoplexy, which kept him in bed for six months and left him in precarious health for the rest of his life. He died July 16, 1921, at his home "Norwood" in Columbia and was buried in Mt. Bethel Cemetery. He was never married. He was unique among American poets in his devotion to a single poetic form, and his work, which faithfully represents the poetic ideals of his period, was distinguished by serious and lofty purpose.

[E. H. Sneath, *America's Greatest Sonneteer* (1928); *Who's Who in America,* 1920–21; J. H. Merrill, *Memoranda Relating to the Mifflin Family* (1890); *N. Y. Times* and *Pub. Ledger* (Phila.), July 17, 1921.]

J. C. F.

MIFFLIN, THOMAS (Jan. 10, 1744–Jan. 20, 1800), merchant, member of the Continental Congress, Revolutionary soldier, governor of Pennsylvania, first son of John Mifflin and Elizabeth Bagnell, was born in Philadelphia, Pa., of a Quaker family. He was of the fourth generation in descent from John Mifflin who emigrated to Pennsylvania from Warminster, Wiltshire, England, before 1680. John, the father of Thomas, was a wealthy merchant, and during his lifetime held the public posts of councilman, alderman, justice of the peace, provincial councilor, and trustee of the College of Philadelphia. Thomas attended a Quaker school and graduated from the College of Philadelphia, now the University of Pennsylvania, at the early age of sixteen. On leaving college he spent four years in the counting-house of William Coleman, prosperous Philadelphia merchant, preparing for a mercantile career. At twenty he visited Europe for a year. The effects of this broadening experience in no wise diminished his ardor for America, for he wrote from London, Nov. 23, 1764: "I find myself as great a patriot for America as when I first left it" (J. H. Merrill, Memoranda Relating to the Mifflin Family, 1890, p. 18). The next year he entered business as a merchant in partnership with his brother, George, the connection continuing until after the outbreak of the Revolution. Their enterprise was thoroughly successful, but Thomas's ambition and talent as a speaker drew him into politics. Recognized as a champion of colonial rights, beginning with 1772 he was elected to the provincial assembly four successive years, in 1774 receiving 1,100 out of 1,300 votes, despite Quaker opposition to his ardent Whiggism. Conspicuous in opposing the Stamp Act, in fostering nonimportation agreements, and in organizing sentiment for a colonial congress, he was one of the youngest and most radical members of the First Continental Congress, and helped to draft the Association of 1774. During the Congress his large and luxuriously furnished home was a rendezvous for its principal delegates. He was elected to the Second Continental Congress, but after the battle of Lexington turned his attention to the more active business of recruiting and training troops. On his appointment as major, May 1775, John Adams declared that he "ought to have been a general" because he was the "animating soul" of the revolutionary movement (C. F. Adams, *Familiar Letters of John Adams and his Wife Abigail Adams during the Revolution,* 1876, p. 59). The Quakers, however, frowned upon his military activities and read him out of meeting because he refused to reform his conduct.

On June 23, 1775, Mifflin was appointed Washington's aide-de-camp and on Aug. 14 following, quartermaster-general of the Continental Army, holding the latter post, except for a brief period, until March 1778. At first he was a faithful and efficient quartermaster, though he preferred the front line to administrative duties. An eye-witness declared he "never saw a greater display of personal bravery" than Mifflin exhibited in his "cool and intrepid conduct" in leading an attack on a British foraging expedition at Lechmire's Point, Nov. 9, 1775 (Rawle, *post,* p. 111). In the following month, on Dec. 22, he was commissioned colonel. He was appointed brigadier-general, May 16, 1776, was relieved as quartermaster shortly thereafter, at his own request, and commanded the covering party in the withdrawal from Long Island. Despite his unusual activity for the patriot cause, he was slow to commit himself on independence and steadfastly opposed the overthrow of Pennsylvania's provincial charter by the radicals, though when separation was achieved he appeared enthusiastic. In the gloom of late 1776, when he was sent by Washington to Philadelphia to rouse the authorities and the people to the need for reinforcements, his spirited appeals in the city and back country bore good fruit. In the following year his animated speeches kept many men in the army after their terms had expired. He was present at the battles of Trenton and Princeton, was appointed major-general, Feb. 19, 1777, and assisted in the defenses at Philadelphia. Meanwhile dissatisfaction developed with his conduct as quartermaster, the duties of which he had reluctantly resumed in October 1776 at the urgent request of Washington and Congress. Chafing under criticism and at congressional interference he went home in the summer of 1777 pleading ill health, and, disappointed at his diminishing influence with the commander-in-chief, resigned both as quartermaster and major-general, Oct. 8, 1777. Congress pressed him to continue the quartermaster's duties temporarily, but, complaining and malcontent, he neglected them, and gross confusion characterized the affairs of the department until a successor was appointed in March 1778. He continued, however, to retain his rank of major-general without salary.

Mifflin was deeply involved in the cabal to advance Horatio Gates over Washington, intent apparently on his own advancement. A severe critic of Washington's "Fabian tactics," when the board of war was reorganized in November 1777 he was appointed a member by Congress ostensibly to weaken the commander-in-chief. It was largely because of his recommendations that Gates became president of the board (W. C. Ford, "Defences of Philadelphia in 1777," *Pennsylvania Magazine of History and Biography,* April 1896, pp. 90–92). On the exposure of the plot he sought cover, solemnly disavowed all connection with it, and is reported to have said publicly at a later date that he considered Washington "the best friend he ever had in his life" (G. W. Greene, *The Life of Nathanael Greene,* vol. II, 1871, p. 37). On Apr. 18, 1778, he left the board of war and rejoined the army, but, with his quartermaster's record under fire, took little active participation. His enemies accused him of peculation and a committee of Congress recommended that he be held responsible for the acts of his subordinates, to which he strenuously objected on the ground that congressional interference had prevented his proper direction of the department's affairs. Washington was directed to order an inquiry and to hold a court-martial if it appeared that the deficiencies were chargeable to him or to his assistants. Mifflin invited the investigation, but waiting vainly for it, indignantly insisted that Congress accept his resignation as major-general, Aug. 17, 1778. His wish was finally granted, Feb. 25, 1779. Thereafter Congress continued, nevertheless, to call upon him for advice, notably in 1780 when he assisted in framing recommendations for reorganizing the staff departments. While his negligence as quartermaster seems inexcusable, and his carelessness in money matters is a matter of record, the charge of peculation has never been sustained.

Out of the army, Mifflin turned to state politics. In the assembly, 1778–79, he advocated amendment of the constitution of 1776, opposed paper-money issues and measures to regulate prices, and fought to save the charter of the College of Philadelphia. From 1782 to 1784 he was again in Congress, was elected president in his absence, Nov. 3, 1783, actually serving in this capacity from Dec. 13, 1783, to June 3, 1784. Through the irony of fate, when Washington returned his commission, Dec. 23, 1783, it became Mifflin's duty as president to accept it. His felicitations showed no trace of his earlier feelings toward the commander-in-chief, and Washington's visits to his home in later years indicate a restoration of their friendship. He was a member of the Federal Convention in 1787, and though participating little in its debates, was in full sympathy with the new Constitution. He was elected to the supreme executive council of Pennsylvania in 1788, serving as its president until 1790, and in 1789–90 was chairman of the state constitutional convention. Displeased at his appointments while president of the state, the Republicans in selecting a gubernatorial candidate in 1790 passed him by for Arthur St. Clair. His friends, however, put him at the head of another ticket, and, supported solidly by the Constitutionalists and by many Republicans, he carried the state by the overwhelming majority of 27,118 to 2,819. During his three terms as governor, 1790–99, the limit set by the constitution, many laws were enacted for the construction of roads and the improvement of inland navigation, and others reforming the judicial and penal establishments and strengthening the militia. He sympathized with the rising tide of Jeffersonianism in Pennsylvania, sat at the banquet table with Genet, and openly favored war with England in 1793 (J. T. Scharf and Thompson Westcott, *History of Philadelphia,* I, 1884, p. 475). In the Whiskey Insurrection, 1794, apprehensive of endangering his influence with the Jeffersonians, he first evaded Washington's plea for support but later called the legislature into special session, urged speedy action against the insurgents, and harangued the militiamen as of old. Despite his pro-French and Jeffersonian sympathies, in 1798 he trimmed his sails to the popular breezes by encouraging preparations for the anticipated French war. His last three years as governor were marked by increasing negligence and moral laxity, his secretary of commonwealth, Alexander James Dallas, constituting the real head of the administration. After retiring from the governorship he was in the legislature until his death.

Mifflin was of medium height, athletic frame, and handsome. He dressed in the height of fashion. Of unusual refinement, he possessed a warm temperament and agreeable manners, his martial and dignified bearing revealing little trace of his Quaker education. In money matters he was extravagant and careless. Borrowing heavily in later life, he was, nevertheless, excessively generous, and entertained lavishly at his home at the falls of the Schuylkill and at his farm, "Angelica," near Reading. An action brought against him by one of his creditors in 1799 obliged him to leave Philadelphia. This unfortunate occurrence preying on his mind hastened his death. When he died he was penniless, and the state of Pennsylvania paid the expenses of his burial in the Lutheran graveyard at Lancaster. His wife, Sarah, daughter of Morris Morris, whom he married on Mar. 4, 1767, and whom John Adams described as "a charming Quaker girl" (*Familiar Letters,* p. 45), died in 1790.

[Mifflin is one of the important Pennsylvanians of whom an adequate study remains to be made. William Rawle, "Sketch of the Life of Thomas Mifflin," in the *Memoirs of the Hist. Soc. of Pa.,* vol. II, pt. 2 (1830), is unsatisfactory. Many Mifflin letters and other manuscripts are scattered through various collections in the Hist. Soc. of Pa., Philadelphia, and in the "Papers of the Continental Cong.," Library of Congress. Other more important sources are: *Autobiog. of Charles Biddle* (1883); E. C. Burnett, *Letters of Members of the Continental Cong.,* vols. I–V (1921–31); W. C. Ford and Gaillard Hunt, eds., *Jours. of the Continental Cong.,* vols. I–XXVII (1904–28); Alexander Graydon, *Memoirs of a Life, Chiefly Passed in Pa.* (1811); *Pa. Archives,* ser. 1, vols. I–XII (1852–56), ser. 4, vol. IV (1890); *Pa. Colonial Records* (16 vols., 1852–53); scattered references in the *Pa. Mag. of Hist. and Biog.*; and contemporary newspapers.] J. H. P—g.

MIFFLIN, WARNER (Oct. 21, 1745–Oct. 16, 1798), Quaker reformer, son of Daniel and Mary (Warner) Mifflin, was born in Accomac County, Va., whither his grandfather, Edward, had removed from Philadelphia, Pa. He was a descendant of John Mifflin who emigrated from Wiltshire, England, sometime before 1680 and finally settled at "Fountain Green," now a part of Fairmount Park, Philadelphia. On May 14, 1767, Warner married Elizabeth Johns, of Maryland, by whom he had nine children, and on Oct. 9, 1788, Ann Emlen, of Philadelphia, by whom he had three. During most of his mature life he lived on his farm, "Chestnut Grove," near Camden, Del. (Justice, *post,* pp. 16–19).

He was a man of mild manner, always charitably inclined, yet of intense convictions. As early as 1775 he was arguing against "the pernicious use of ardent spirits." During the American Revolution he adhered to the Quaker peace principles and shared in the obloquy thereby entailed. He refused to have the least part in supporting the war, even to the use of Continental paper money. Consequently, he was dubbed a Tory, and his patriot neighbors made serious threats against him. While General Howe was in Philadelphia and General Washington on the outskirts of the city, Mifflin was one of a committee of six appointed by the Friends' Yearly Meeting in 1777 to visit both commanders-in-chief and present printed copies of the "Testimonies" against participation in war. They went without passports through the lines of both armies and accomplished their mission.

When he was fourteen years old, on his father's plantation in Virginia, one of the younger slaves, talking with him in the fields, had convinced him of the injustice of the slave system. He soon determined never to be a slave-holder. Later, however, he came into possession of several slaves through his first wife and from his father and mother. After a period of indecision, in 1774–75 he manumitted all his slaves (Justice, p. 39). Supersensitive to the promptings of conscience, he even paid them for their services after the age of twenty-one years. Thereafter, he traveled much in Quaker communities urging Friends to free their slaves. In the same cause he appeared before various legislative bodies including, in 1782, that of Virginia, where a law was passed in May of that year removing the former prohibitions against the private manumission of slaves (W. W. Hening, *Statutes at Large,* vol. XI, 1823, p. 39). Between 1783 and 1797 he helped to draw up, or to present to the Congress of the United States various petitions against slavery and the slave trade. One, dated 1789, helped to start an important debate on the powers of Congress over slavery and the slave trade under the new Constitution. In 1793 he published over his own name, *A Serious Expostulation with the Members of the House of Representatives of the United States* (Phila. 1793 and various reprints), in which he presented with no little force the anti-slavery case. In 1796, his motives and methods having been attacked by his opponents, he published in Philadelphia *The Defence of Warner Mifflin against Aspersions Cast on Him on Account of his Endeavors to Promote Righteousness, Mercy and Peace, among Mankind.* In this pamphlet he sketched the activities of his life and defended his stand on such subjects as slavery, peace, and temperance.

In 1798 he attended the Yearly Meeting of Friends held in Philadelphia and at that time, apparently, contracted the yellow fever which was then so prevalent in that city. He died of the disease soon after returning to his home in Delaware, aged about fifty-three years.

[The most accessible and fullest source of information is Hilda Justice, *Life and Ancestry of Warner Mifflin* (1905), containing reprints of Quaker records and other important documentary material; the most important manuscript Quaker records for the period are at 304 Arch Street, Phila.; about a dozen letters by Mifflin are in the Hist. Soc. of Pa. The most reliable of contemporary accounts of Mifflin's life are his own memoir in *Defence of Warner Mifflin,* cited above, and a "Testimony" by his friend George Churchman, in *Friends' Miscellany,* June 1832. See also J. H. Merrill, *Memoranda Relating to the Mifflin Family* (privately printed, 1890).] R. W. K.

MIGNOT, LOUIS REMY (1831–Sept. 22, 1870), landscape painter, born at Charleston, S. C., was probably the son of Remy Mignot, a confectioner, who for a time conducted the French Coffee House in Charleston. The Mignots had been ardent Bonapartists and had left France at the time of the restoration of the Bourbons in 1815. Louis Mignot's boyhood was spent in the home of his wealthy grandfather near his birthplace. He manifested a marked love of art while a mere child, and at seventeen he had definitely chosen his career. He passed through a course of drawing with credit, and in 1851, at the age of twenty, he traveled to Holland and became the pupil of Andreas Schelfhout, the landscapist, at The Hague. His progress was rapid. He soon began to work from nature, making trips to several European countries for sketching purposes, and remained about four years. Returning to the United States in 1855, he opened a studio in New York, where his success was immediate and complete.

At that time Frederick E. Church's spectacular pictures of the Andean peaks and jungles were in high favor. He had made one trip to Ecuador in 1853 and was planning to make another in 1857. Mignot, whose admiration for the work of his senior colleague was fervent, and who was deeply interested in tropical scenery, gladly accepted the opportunity offered him to accompany Church on this second voyage to Guayaquil. The two painters, actuated by the same enthusiasm for the stupendous scenes among the Andes, made the most of their time in Ecuador, and brought home studies made at Quito and Riobamba which were destined to bring both of them notice. It was not unnatural that Mignot should have worked much in the spirit of Church, and that some of his tropical landscapes should have resembled those of the elder man. His own native talent and facility, however, appear to have been quite generally recognized by his contemporaries on both sides of the Atlantic.

Mignot was made an associate of the National Academy of Design in 1858 and a year later became an academician. He collaborated with his friend T. P. Rossiter, the historical painter, in making one of the latter's series of Mount Vernon scenes, "Washington and Lafayette at Mount Vernon," in which it is evident that Mignot's part consisted of the landscape background. The picture belongs to the Metropolitan Museum of Art, New York. On the outbreak of the Civil War, Mignot's Southern sympathies made his further stay in New York so repugnant to his feelings that on June 26, 1862, he set sail for England on board the *Great Eastern.* A few days prior to his departure he had sold a collection of his paintings at Leeds' auction-room for a total of something over $5,000. He made his way to London, where he remained, for the most part, during the remainder of his life, and where he was as successful as he had been in New York. He was a frequent exhibitor at the Royal Academy, and among the landscapes shown there in the sixties were several noteworthy Ecuadorian subjects painted from the studies made in 1857—the "Lagoon of Guayaquil," "Evening in the Tropics," "Under the Equator," and "Mount Chimborazo." In 1870 he was in France, and, either by accident or design, was shut up in Paris during the siege. He died of smallpox at Brighton, shortly after his return to England. He was only thirty-nine years old. His collected works were exhibited in London soon after his death and elicited favorable attention.

[*Art Jour.* (London), Nov. 1, 1870, Jan. 1, 1871; T. S. Cummings, *Hist. Annals of the Nat. Acad. of Design* (1865); H. T. Tuckerman, *Book of the Artists* (1867); S. G. W. Benjamin, *Art in America* (1880); Clara E. Clement and Laurence Hutton, *Artists of the Nineteenth Century* (1880); U. Thieme and F. Becker, *Allgemeines Lexikon der Bildenden Künstler,* vol. XXIV (1930).] W. H. D.

MILBURN, WILLIAM HENRY (Sept. 26, 1823–Apr. 10, 1903), Methodist Episcopal clergyman, son of Nicholas Milburn, was born in Philadelphia. The Milburn family came from the Eastern Shore of Maryland. William's early education was obtained in his native city and in Jacksonville, Ill., to which place, after financial losses, the family removed in 1838. When he was five years old, the sight of his left eye was destroyed by a piece of glass thrown by a playmate. Inflammation spread to the right eye, and after several years of bleeding, cupping, leeching, and burning with caustic, he was almost blind. He attempted, however, to secure an education, though able to read only by holding a book very close to his eye. In Jacksonville, while his father kept a store, he helped his mother with housework and studied. He entered Illinois College in 1841 but was obliged to leave in 1843 on account of ill health. Pioneer Methodist preachers frequented his father's house, among them the famous Peter Cartwright [*q.v.*]. From them he heard tales of circuit riding in the backwoods, with its dangers from weather, wild animals, and Indians, which strengthened his conviction, early reached, that it was his duty to become a preacher.

In 1843 he went as an exhorter with Rev. Peter Akers, to cover a 500-mile circuit with a dozen charges. Each week they held services from Saturday noon until Sunday evening, and the remainder of the time traveled on horseback, sleeping at night upon shuck mattresses laid on cabin floors, and partaking of the food those they tarried with could supply. Milburn said that he never thereafter liked fried chicken, hog, hominy, or corn bread. On Sept. 13, 1843, he was admitted to the Illinois Conference on trial and assigned to the Winchester circuit, with thirty charges extending over 300 miles, which he visited every four weeks. His yearly salary was $100 and presents of clothing. His own comment on his circuit life was: "The terms of tuition in Brush College and Swamp University are high, the course of study hard, the examinations frequent and severe, but the schooling is capital" (*Ten Years of Preacher-Life,* p. 82). In 1844 the trouble with his eye became worse and, though almost penniless, he went for treatment to St. Louis, where he lived for nine months in the home of a friendly lawyer. On Sept. 17, 1845, he was ordained deacon and appointed agent to raise money for a "Female Seminary" and for McKendree College. Traveling from Wheeling to Cincinnati by boat, he met a group of congressmen whom he reproved for drinking, card playing, and profanity. They raised a purse for him and shortly after secured his election as chaplain of Congress on the part of the House of Representatives (1845). He retained his position as church agent and after his marriage, Aug. 13, 1846, in Baltimore, made that city his headquarters.

Poor health sent him South in 1848 and he became pastor of a church in Montgomery, Ala., where he remained two years. A like term as pastor of St. Francis Street Church, Mobile, and two years as Mobile city missionary followed. At the Alabama Conference of 1852 he was under investigation for questionable conduct (he had attended a New Year's ball) and for heresy. The latter consisted in a sympathetic attitude toward the higher criticism, which he later deplored. The Conference was satisfied with his explanations and no action was taken. In 1853, at thirty, poor, totally blind, with four children to support, he broke down physically and nervously and returned North, settling in New York City. He supplied churches for longer or shorter periods, lectured widely throughout the country, and visited Canada and England. About 1862 he took orders in the Protestant Episcopal Church, but in 1878 was readmitted to the Illinois Conference of the Methodist Church. He was again elected chaplain of Congress (1853), later of the House of Representatives (1885), and finally of the Senate (1893). In 1902 he resigned this office because of failing health. He died in Santa Barbara, Cal.

Milburn was the author of *The Rifle, Axe, and*

Saddle-Bags, and Other Lectures (1857); *Ten Years of Preacher-Life: Chapters from an Autobiography* (1859); *The Pioneers, Preachers, and People of the Mississippi Valley* (1860); *The Lance, Cross, and Canoe; the Flatboat, Rifle, and Plough in the Valley of the Mississippi* (1892). His style as speaker and writer was simple and undecorated, but enlivened by humor and illustration. He was at his best when telling of the backwoods life he knew well. Philosophic cheerfulness and courage marked his spirit and he indulged in no complaints or pathetic allusions to his misfortune.

[John McClintock, D. D., introduction to *The Rifle, Axe, and Saddle-Bags and Other Lectures* (1857); C. M. Eames, *Historic Morgan and Classic Jacksonville* (1885); Anson West, *A Hist. of Methodism in Ala.* (1893); *Minutes of the Ill. Ann. Conference of the M. E. Church* (1903); *Who's Who in America*, 1901–02; *Congressional Record*, 57 Cong., 2 Sess., p. 13; *Zion's Herald*, Apr. 15, 1903; *Christian Advocate* (N. Y.), Apr. 16, 23, 1903; *Evening Star* (Washington, D. C.), Apr. 11, 1903.] S. G. B.

MILES, EDWARD (Oct. 14, 1752–Mar. 7, 1828), miniature painter, was born in Yarmouth, England, and, as an errand boy for Dr. Giles Wakeman, was found to have a remarkable talent for drawing, which his employer encouraged. Receiving enough patronage among his friends in Yarmouth, at nineteen he set off for London, where he received an introduction to Sir Joshua Reynolds, who was favorable to his plan to copy some of the great painter's pictures. Quite early he directed his talents to the field of miniature painting and soon achieved a reputation. He set up a studio in the fashionable Berkeley Street, Berkeley Square, and was rewarded by the patronage of the aristocracy of London. His contributions appeared regularly at the Royal Academy exhibitions from 1775 to 1797 and he attracted the attention of the Court. In 1792 he was appointed miniature painter to the Duchess of York, and in 1794, Queen Charlotte regularly appointed him "Our Miniature Painter during our pleasure." Either before or after this appointment he painted a portrait of his royal mistress, as well as many of the princesses. In 1797 he went to St. Petersburg, where he became court painter during the reign of the Emperor Paul. After the murder of his original patron, he remained as court painter to the succeeding Czar, Alexander I., whose portrait he painted very beautifully, as he did that of the Empress, Maria Louisa of Baden. His miniatures were distinguished for their good drawing and for the delicacy and exquisiteness of their finish.

In 1807 Miles arrived in Philadelphia, where he remained until the end of his life. He took an active interest in the artistic and social life of the city and became a fellow and one of the founders of the Society of Artists of the United States which was organized in 1810. He did not exhibit in the society's first annual exhibition in 1811, but he was represented in the third annual display, in 1813, by which time the organization was known as the Columbian Society of Artists. He was an academician of the society and probably a drawing master in its schools, for he was so described in the Philadelphia Directory for 1813 and continued to be so designated thereafter, as he was also in the exhibition catalogues.

After Miles came to the United States, his son is said to have lost considerable money. Apparently he then began to give instruction to a few chosen pupils. His work as a miniature painter in Philadelphia seems to have been confined to painting portraits of his friends. He is known to have painted a portrait of Bishop White. In 1809 he was described as "portrait painter in crayons." As the exhibited work of pupils in the schools of the Columbian Society was entirely in this medium, it is probable that Miles literally taught drawing, for which profession he was especially gifted, and not painting. Although his name appears as an exhibitor in the annual exhibition catalogues, no work by him is indicated. One of his pupils, who became noted as a portrait painter, was James Reid Lambdin [*q.v.*], who subsequently learned painting in the studio of Thomas Sully. Lambdin is said to have painted a portrait of Miles as his first exhibition piece. Sir William Beechey, who had been one of Miles's warmest friends in England, painted a portrait of him in 1782. Miles also was on intimate terms with Sir Thomas Lawrence, to whom Thomas Sully carried a letter of introduction from the miniaturist in 1809.

[See Anne Hollingsworth Wharton, *Heirlooms in Miniatures* (1898); Wm. Dunlap, *A Hist. . . . of the Arts of Design in the U. S.* (ed. 1918), vols. II and III; J. J. and Ethel M. Foster, *A Dict. of Painters of Miniatures* (1926); Theodore Bolton, *Early Am. Portrait Painters in Miniature* (1921); *Poulson's Am. Daily Advertiser*, Mar. 8, 1828. In the sketch of Miles, in the *Dict. Nat. Biog.* it is assumed that Miles died in 1798.] J. J.

MILES, GEORGE HENRY (July 31, 1824–July 24, 1871), poet, playwright, and teacher of English literature, was born in Baltimore, Md. On his father's side he was of English ancestry, the great-grandson of Col. Thomas Miles, of the British army, who lies buried at Wallingford, Conn. The poet's father, William Miles, a native of New York, was a Baltimore merchant, at one time a commercial agent of the United States to Haiti. His mother, Sarah Mickle

Miles, was the daughter of a Scotch settler in Baltimore, and his maternal grandmother, Elizabeth Etting Mickle, of Philadelphia, was of Hebrew ancestry. At the age of nine Miles was sent to Mount Saint Mary's College, Emmitsburg, Md., and graduated *summa cum laude* in 1843. After graduation he studied law with J. H. B. Latrobe in Baltimore, was admitted to the bar, and practised for a time in partnership with Edwin Henry Webster. On Feb. 22, 1859, he was married to Adaline Tiers, daughter of Edward Tiers, a New York merchant. Having found the law uncongenial, he abandoned practice and a few months after his marriage accepted appointment as a professor of English literature in Mount Saint Mary's College. There like his brother poet and coreligionist, Father Tabb, he combined teaching with literary work, with the exception of two years, 1863–65, until in 1867 he retired to give his whole time to writing. His residence was a pleasant country place, "Thornbrook," about four miles from Emmitsburg, built for the poet and his wife by his father-in-law, who had an estate in the neighborhood.

The literary aspirations that tempted Miles into academic life were encouraged by early successes. His first tragedy, *Michael di Lando, Gonfalonier of Florence,* was begun in September 1844. His novel *The Truce of God* appeared anonymously in the *United States Catholic Magazine* in 1847, and in 1850 and 1851 *Loretto, or The Choice* and *The Governess* appeared in the *Catholic Mirror.* In 1849 the actor Edwin Forrest offered a prize for the best original tragedy in five acts. Miles was awarded one thousand dollars for *Mohammed, the Arabian Prophet.* Forrest did not use the play but it was performed in 1851 at the Lyceum Theatre in New York. When in 1866 the *Ave Maria* announced a prize of one hundred dollars for the best poem on the Blessed Virgin, Miles competed and was again successful (*Ave Maria,* June 23, 1866). His *Mohammed,* though published in 1850 in Boston and highly praised as poetry, was not successful as an acting play. With other dramas, however, Miles achieved a certain degree of success on the stage. His *Hernando de Soto,* written for J. E. Murdock in 1850, was produced acceptably at the Chestnut Street Theatre in Philadelphia for the first time on Apr. 19, 1852. A comedy, *Señor Valiente,* written at the request of John T. Ford, owner of Ford's Theatre in Baltimore, was produced in Baltimore and New York in 1859, and on Feb. 11, 1861, "Uncle Sam's Magic Lantern" was added to a production of Laura Keene's called *The Seven Sisters* which enjoyed a long run in Laura Keene's Theatre in New York City.

Besides the three novels, already mentioned, Miles wrote numerous lyrics and narrative poems. Of these latter the most ambitious is *Christine,* a romantic legend of the time of the Crusades. His "Inkerman," published in October 1856 in *Brownson's Quarterly Review,* is a spirited description of a battle of the Crimean War. His lyrics are marked by lightness of touch and notable facility in rime. In 1866 he published a collection of his verse under the title: *Christine, A Troubadour's Song, and Other Poems.* He was deeply religious and his faith tinged all of his literary work. In 1870 in the *Southern Review* appeared unsigned Miles's most important critical work, a detailed study of Shakespeare's *Hamlet.* A projected series of similar critiques on other Shakespearean tragedies remained incomplete. He died at "Thornbrook," after a lingering illness, of nephritis, and was buried in the churchyard of Mount Saint Mary's at Emmitsburg.

[Information about Miles is scanty and widely scattered. See an editorial in the *Sun* (Baltimore), July 26, 1871; Esmerelda Boyle, *Biog. Sketches of Distinguished Marylanders* (1877); Thomas E. Cox, *Gems from George H. Miles* (1901), with introduction; Mary M. Meline and E. F. X. McSweeny, *The Story of the Mountain: Mount St. Mary's Coll. and Seminary, Emmitsburg, Md.* (1911), vol. II; A. H. Quinn, *A Hist. of the Am. Drama from the Beginning to the Civil War* (1923) and *A Hist. of the Am. Drama from the Civil War to the Present Day* (1927), vol. I; J. C. Collins, Introduction to Miles's *Said the Rose and Other Lyrics* (1907); *Current Lit.,* Jan. 1898; the *Magnificat,* May, June 1908, Jan. 1933.]

J. C. F.

MILES, HENRY ADOLPHUS (May 30, 1809–May 31, 1895), Unitarian clergyman, historian, was the sixth child of Rev. John and Mary (Denny) Miles, and a descendant of John Miles who in 1639 was a freeman of Concord, Mass. Born in Grafton, Mass., where his father was pastor, Henry graduated from Brown University in 1829. Espousing Unitarian doctrines, he attended the Harvard Divinity School, and was ordained at Hallowell, Me., Dec. 19, 1832. On May 28, 1833, he married Augusta Holyoke Moore of Cambridge, Mass. After serving as minister at Hallowell for four years he was called in December 1836 to be the second pastor of the South Congregational (Unitarian) Church, Lowell, Mass. An address to the people commending the young minister was delivered by Rev. John Pierpont [*q.v.*], of the Hollis Street Church, Boston, which was subsequently published as a model of its kind (*An Address to the People, Delivered at the Installation of H. A. Miles as Pastor of the South Congregational Society, Lowell,* 1837).

In the first years of his Lowell pastorate Miles wrote a history of that then new factory city, entitled *Lowell as It Was and Is.* The little book, published in 1845, went through several editions. It provoked a local controversy, in which the author's critics charged him with drawing an unduly roseate picture of industrial conditions at Lowell, presumably for the purpose of gaining the favor of the mill owners. "It was to repel the charge that large corporations led to oppression, corruption and nepotism, that Dr. Miles seems to have written his history. Fully half of the book is devoted to showing that the mills of Lowell were managed by wise and benevolent men, and in a manner calculated to promote the moral welfare and the highest good, not only of the operatives, but of the community at large" (Chase, *post,* p. 30). Later historians, however, have found in Miles's work a valuable sourcebook, even though it may be admitted that he was disposed to discover mainly what is right in any given social picture.

Miles remained at Lowell until 1853 when he became secretary of the American Unitarian Association, with headquarters at Boston. At this same time he began to edit the *Quarterly Journal,* a denominational periodical, of which he continued in charge until 1857. In 1859 he relinquished his secretarial service in order to have leisure for independent literary work and for travel. Periods of European residence occupied about ten years. From 1865 to 1871 he was settled over the Unitarian church at Longwood, Mass., and from 1876 until his death he was pastor and pastor emeritus at Hingham. He compiled *Genealogy of the Miles Family* (1840), and published a number of religious works, which reflect a gentle and optimistic spirit. Notable among them are: *Gospel Narratives* (1848); *Grains of Gold* (1854); *Channing's Thoughts* (1859); *Words of a Friend* (1870); *Traces of Picture Writing in the Bible* (1870); and *Birth of Jesus* (1877). He was buried in Mount Auburn Cemetery, Cambridge, Mass.

[C. C. Chase's sketch of Lowell, in D. H. Hurd, *Hist. of Middlesex County, Mass.* (1890); F. W. Coburn, *Hist. of Lowell and Its People* (1920); *Boston Herald,* June 3, 1895; *Year Book of the Unitarian Congregational Churches* (1896).] F. W. C.

MILES, MANLY (July 20, 1826–Feb. 15, 1898), agriculturist, naturalist, and physician, was born at Homer, Cortland County, N. Y., the son of Manly and Mary Cushman Miles. On his father's side he came from a long line of soldiers; through his mother he was a lineal descendant of Miles Standish and Thomas Cushman. When he was eleven the family moved to a farm near Flint, Mich. His common-school education was supplemented, through his own efforts, with studies covering the subjects of mathematics, history, and science. His interest at this time in birds, fishes, insects, and other living forms was the starting point of his exceptional work as a naturalist. As a young man he entered Rush Medical College and in 1850 received the degree of M.D. In 1851 he married Mary E. Dodge. He established himself in Flint, but even while practising medicine he roamed in the fields and woods collecting specimens and making accurate observations. In 1858 he became the zoölogist of the new State Geological Survey. During his two years' incumbency he made a remarkable collection of the fauna of the state with excellent descriptions. In 1861, four years after the founding of the Michigan State Agricultural College, he was appointed professor of zoölogy and animal physiology. He was an enthusiastic teacher, was thoroughly interested in what he taught, and was most resourceful in devising apparatus and making the subject matter intelligible.

In 1865 when it seemed imperative that an agricultural college should have a course in agriculture, he was urged to become the head of the department for he had had considerable practical farm experience. He accepted and thus has the distinction of being the first professor of practical agriculture in the first agricultural college in the United States. In 1874 he was given a leave of absence and spent some of the time in England with the celebrated field-crop experimenters, Lawes and Gilbert. Soon after his return to America, in 1875, he accepted the offer of the professorship of agriculture at the University of Illinois. Later, in 1878, he became experimentalist at the Houghton Farm, Mountainville, N. Y., and in 1883 became professor of agriculture at the Massachusetts Agricultural College. In 1886 he returned to Lansing, Mich., and established his office and laboratory in three large rooms over a drug store and took up once more, with vigor, the favorite pursuits of his earlier days in Michigan. This was the period in which his scientific writings were most prolific. He published several books, chief among which were *Stock Breeding* (1879), *Silos, Ensilage and Silage* (1889), and *Land Drainage* (1892). Besides writing for the popular press he was a regular contributor to scientific journals. Three extended reports on the fauna of Michigan appeared in the publications of the Michigan Geological Survey. As President Snyder said in his report of 1906, much of Miles's work was a quarter of a century in advance of his time. His ability was recognized widely throughout the United States and abroad. He kept up his habits of reading, studying, and experimenting until the time of his death.

[W. B. Barrows, "Dr. Manly Miles," *Bull. Mich. Ornithol. Club,* Apr. 1898, and "A Sketch of Dr. Manly Miles," *Second Ann. Report of the Mich. Acad. of Sci.* (1901); W. J. Beal, *Hist. of the Mich. Agric. Coll.* (1915); *Hist. Colls. . . . Mich. Pioneer and Hist. Soc.,* vol. XXVIII (1900); the *Detroit Tribune,* Feb. 16, 1898.] R. P. H.

MILES, NELSON APPLETON (Aug. 8, 1839–May 15, 1925), soldier, came of New England ancestors descended from a Baptist clergyman and educator, John Myles, who emigrated from Wales to New England, settled in Swansea, Mass., in 1664, and fought in King Philip's War in 1675. His son, Rev. Samuel Miles, received a degree from Oxford and was for twenty-nine years rector of King's Chapel, Boston. His son and grandson, Daniel and Joab Miles, fought in the Revolution from Bennington to Yorktown. Joab's son Daniel, a farmer, married Mary Curtis, a descendant of William Curtis who arrived in Boston harbor from England in 1632. Nelson Appleton Miles, son of Daniel and Mary, was born on his father's farm near Westminster, Mass. After attending the district school and a local academy, he ventured to Boston when he was seventeen years old, and, through the good offices of his uncles, George and Nelson Curtis, secured employment in John Collamore's crockery store. He attended night school and incidentally received the rudiments of a military education from Col. M. Salignac, a former officer of the French army.

When the Civil War broke out Miles recruited a company of one hundred volunteers which formed part of Col. Henry Wilson's 22nd Massachusetts Regiment. He was commissioned captain of infantry, but his superiors considered him too young to exercise command in battle, and he served through the Peninsula campaign as a member of Gen. O. O. Howard's staff. His opportunity came at the battle of Fair Oaks (May 31–June 1, 1862), where under heavy fire he led reinforcements to the aid of the 61st New York Volunteers, receiving his first wound and official commendation for gallantry in battle. He was rewarded with promotion to the lieutenant-colonelcy of this regiment, and at Antietam, on Sept. 17, when Colonel Barlow was carried from the field wounded, Miles assumed command, becoming colonel, Sept. 30, 1862. At Fredericksburg, Dec. 13, where he was shot through the throat, his conduct was characterized by General Hancock as "most admirable and chivalrous" (*Official Records,* 1 ser. XXI, 230). For distinguished gallantry at Chancellorsville (May 3, 1863), where he was shot from his horse while desperately holding a line of abattis and rifle-pits against the enemy in advance of the II Army Corps, he was awarded the brevet of brigadier-general (Mar. 2, 1867) and the Congressional Medal of Honor (July 23, 1892). For his services in the battles of the Wilderness and Spotsylvania, he received the Thanks of Congress; he was mentioned for gallantry at Reams's Station, and at Petersburg sustained his fourth wound. On May 12, 1864, he was promoted to the grade of brigadier-general of volunteers. He and his division took a prominent part in the final campaign, which culminated at Appomattox, and he received high praise from General Grant for his services. On Oct. 21, 1865, he was made major-general of volunteers, commanding the II Army Corps of some 26,000 officers and men when but twenty-six years of age. With one exception, he had fought in every important battle of the Army of the Potomac.

After the close of hostilities he became for a time custodian of Jefferson Davis at Fort Monroe. Despite his tactful handling of a difficult situation, and the fact that he was acting on the orders of superiors, he was censured by Southern sympathizers for alleged ill-treatment of the former President of the Confederacy. From these charges he was ultimately vindicated when the true facts became known and the bitterness engendered by the war had passed (*A Statement of Facts Concerning the Imprisonment and Treatment of Jefferson Davis While a Military Prisoner at Fort Monroe, Va., in 1865 and 1866,* 1902).

Appointed colonel, 40th Infantry, in the regular establishment, July 28, 1866, he was mustered out of the volunteer service, Sept. 1, and on Mar. 15, 1869, was transferred to command the 5th Infantry, a regiment which he made famous through long-continued field service. For some fifteen years following, he was constantly associated with difficult but successful campaigns against various hostile Indians west of the Mississippi. He accomplished the defeat of the Cheyennes, Kiowas, and Comanches on the border of the Staked Plains in 1875, and subsequently took a leading part in the pacification of hostile Sioux Indians in Montana, driving Sitting Bull across the border into Canada, and dispersing the bands of Crazy Horse [*q.v.*], Lame Deer, Spotted Eagle, Broad Trail, and other chiefs. In the fall of 1877, while in command of the District of the Yellowstone, he intercepted and captured Chief Joseph [*q.v.*] and his band of Nez Percé warriors after a forced march of more than one hundred and sixty miles, an exploit considered one of the most brilliant feats of arms in Indian warfare. Later, in 1878, he succeeded in pacifying Elk Horn and his band of Bannocks near the Yellowstone Park.

He was appointed brigadier-general, United States Army, Dec. 15, 1880, and until 1885 was in command of the Department of the Columbia. During 1885–86 he commanded the Department of the Missouri and until 1888, the Department of Arizona. In 1886, he succeeded Gen. George Crook [*q.v.*] in the arduous and difficult military operations against the bloodthirsty Chiricahua Apaches under Geronimo [*q.v.*] and Naiche, whom popular opinion credited with twenty-five hundred homicides and with holding back the development of Arizona for many years. Miles accomplished the surrender of these Indians and their incarceration at Mount Vernon, Ala., after a chase which involved occupations of Mexican soil. As a token of appreciation of his service in the cause of Indian pacification he received the thanks of the state legislatures of Kansas, Montana, New Mexico, and Arizona; and in November 1887 the citizens of Arizona presented him with a sword of honor. He commanded the Division of the Pacific, with headquarters at San Francisco, during the years 1888–90, and was promoted major-general Apr. 5, 1890. In a winter campaign in Dakota, 1890–91, he suppressed a serious outbreak of Sioux Indians, inflamed by the supposed coming of a Messiah, and effected their return to government control after but one serious engagement at Wounded Knee. In 1894, while commanding the Department of the Missouri with headquarters at Chicago, he was in command of troops charged by President Cleveland with quelling the industrial riots and disorders accompanying the Pullman strike. In 1894–95 he was commander of the Department of the East, with headquarters at Governor's Island, New York.

Upon the retirement of Maj.-Gen. John M. Schofield, Sept. 29, 1895, Miles became by seniority the commander-in-chief of the Army (order dated Oct. 2). In 1897 he represented the United States at the Jubilee Celebration of Queen Victoria—visiting as an observer the theatre of war between Turkey and Greece and witnessing the autumn maneuvers of the Russian, German, and French armies. The following year, with the declaration of war against Spain, he took a directing part in the organization and training of the regular and volunteer forces, and although not permitted to command the expeditionary force dispatched to Santiago de Cuba, he joined later with reinforcements and dictated the terms of the surrender of the Spanish garrison following the battles fought by Shafter's army. He then proceeded to Porto Rico with United States troops, landed successfully at Ponce and Guanica, and after a few engagements with Spanish troops attended by trifling losses among American units, succeeded in the complete pacification of the island. By appointment of President McKinley, confirmed Feb. 11, 1901, he was advanced to the grade of lieutenant-general, a rank hitherto rarely held. In December of the same year he was officially censured by President Theodore Roosevelt through the Secretary of War for public expressions of approval in connection with Admiral Dewey's report upon the case of Admiral Schley (*New York Tribune,* Dec. 17, 22, 1901). In 1902 he visited the Philippine Islands, then in a state of insurrection, and after an official inspection of troops and an investigation of complaints by Filipino officials, caused much controversy by his report of alleged abuses on the part of American officers and soldiers in their relations with Filipino insurgent forces (*The Philippines: Reports by Lieutenant-General Nelson A. Miles,* Anti-Imperialist League, Boston, 1909; reprinted from *Army and Navy Journal,* May 2, 1903).

On Aug. 8, 1903, having reached the age of sixty-four, Miles was retired from active service by operation of law. He thereafter made his home in Washington, D. C. In 1896 he had published *Personal Recollections and Observations of General Nelson A. Miles.* This was followed, after his trip abroad in 1897, by *Military Europe* (1898). He published a second autobiographical volume, *Serving the Republic,* in 1911. In 1912 he became head of a short-lived patriotic organization known as the Sons of Liberty, and in the ensuing years held office in many societies and associations. From 1918 until his death he was local commander of the Military Order of the Loyal Legion. In his eighty-sixth year, while he was attending a circus performance at Washington, he suffered a heart attack of which he died. His funeral was attended by the President and many distinguished officials as well as several thousand soldiers and sailors and the representatives of numerous patriotic societies. His body was laid to rest, with the highest civic and military honors, in a mausoleum, the erection of which he had supervised many years before, in Arlington Cemetery.

Miles was married, June 30, 1868, while serving in the West, to Mary Hoyt Sherman, daughter of Judge Charles Sherman of Ohio, and niece of Senator John Sherman and Gen. William T. Sherman [*qq.v.*]. He was survived by a son and a daughter. A natural soldier, suddenly transferred, while yet a young man, from the hum-drum of mercantile life to the cataclysm of a great war, and without the benefit of many signal advantages possessed by his military contemporaries, he attained outstanding leadership through his indefatigable industry, sound judgment, and personal bravery.

[Many details of Miles's life are to be found in his two volumes of memoirs, *Personal Recollections* and *Serving the Republic.* See also *War of the Rebellion: Official Records (Army)*; *Battles and Leaders of the Civil War*, vols. III, IV (1888); *Personal Memoirs of U. S. Grant*, II (1886), 451–53; *Personal Memoirs of P. H. Sheridan* (1888), II, 172–73; and H. E. Davies, *General Sheridan* (1895), pp. 235–36; J. M. Schofield, *Forty-six Years in the Army* (1897); J. H. Wilson, *Under the Old Flag* (1912), II, 440–72; H. L. Scott, *Some Memories of a Soldier* (1928); *Who's Who in America*, 1924–25; *Army and Navy Jour.*, May 23, 1925; *Evening Star* (Washington), May 15, 19, 1925.]
C. D. R.

MILES, RICHARD PIUS (May 17, 1791–Feb. 21, 1860), Catholic prelate, son of Nicholas and Ann (Blackloc) Miles, both descendants of old Maryland planter families, was born in Prince George's County, Md. His parents moved to Nelson County, Ky., in 1796, and Richard was reared in pioneer surroundings and inured to frontier privations. At the age of fifteen he entered the Dominican school connected with the priory of St. Rose of Lima near Springfield, Ky., where he came under the influence of Fathers Samuel Wilson, W. R. Tuite, and E. D. Fenwick [*q.v.*]. Upon the completion of a collegiate course in which French, Italian, and music were not neglected, he took final vows in the Order of St. Dominic on May 13, 1810. He then studied theology at St. Thomas' College and in September 1816 was ordained a priest. The young friar was retained as a teacher at the academy, where Jefferson Davis studied two years, as a master of novices, and as an assistant on the missionary circuit. In 1828 he was sent to Zanesville, Ohio, where he built a new church and one of the first parochial schools in the state and from which he ministered to a parish which comprised several counties. An agreeable person and a gentle controversialist, he found little difficulty in obtaining court rooms and Protestant meeting-houses in which he preached to Catholics and curious visitors. In 1833 he was named superior at St. Rose's Priory, Springfield, Ky., and in this capacity he established the Convent of St. Catherine nearby, the sisters of which soon founded an academy for girls. Three years later, he was selected as prior of St. Joseph's Priory in Somerset County, Ohio, remaining there until elected provincial by a chapter of his order (Apr. 22, 1837). A council of the Catholic hierarchy at Baltimore urged Rome to erect the diocese of Nashville and honored Miles as its nominee for bishop. Gregory XVI made the appointment, July 28, 1837, which Miles accepted only under obedience; for both he and his religious brethren believed that as provincial he could perform a greater service than as bishop of a destitute see.

Frontier and missionary work on horseback had no terrors for him, however, and as soon as he was consecrated at Bardstown, Ky., by Bishop Joseph Rosati (Sept. 16, 1838), he rode to Nashville, Tenn., on a horse donated by the Dominicans. Well received by the 300 Catholics in the state and by the Protestant people also, he found a boarding house, repaired a dilapidated church for his cathedral, and commenced an arduous visitation of his diocese, during which he attended Irish laborers on public works, drew isolated Catholics together, established mass stations, and preached everywhere. Soon Joseph Stokes, rector of the seminary at Cincinnati, volunteered as an aide; and in time Miles attracted a group of able, self-sacrificing priests of various nationalities, willing to serve in a primitive diocese where ease was unknown. In 1840, as one of the bishops who brought the decrees of the Council of Baltimore to Rome, he had an opportunity to seek aid in Vienna from the Leopoldine Association and in Paris and Lyons from the Society for the Propagation of the Faith. Toward the end of his life, he could point to the Seven Dolors Cathedral (1847), a Dominican church at Memphis, other churches and chapels, several thousand Catholics, a small seminary, St. John's Hospital and Orphanage in Nashville (1849), Catholic colonies of German and Irish immigrants which he founded in Morgan and Humphreys counties, several girls' academies, and a negro school. Even in the trying Know-Nothing days he retained the general good will of the community. Somewhat broken in health, he sought to have Father N. R. Young, O.P., as coadjutor bishop, but in 1858 James Whelan, Archbishop Purcell's candidate, was named. Miles's death occurred two years later.

[V. F. O'Daniel, *The Father of the Church in Tenn.: The Rt. Rev. Richard Pius Miles* (1926) is a detailed biography based on archival and printed materials; see also R. H. Clarke, *Lives of the Deceased Bishops of the Cath. Ch. in the U. S.*, vol. II (1888); *Guardian* (Louisville) and *Cath. Telegraph* (Cincinnati), Feb. 25, 1860; *Freeman's Journal* (N. Y.), Mar. 3, 1860; *Republican Banner* (Nashville), Feb. 23, 1860; *Nashville Union and American*, Feb. 22, 1860.] R. J. P.

MILES, WILLIAM PORCHER (July 4, 1822–May 11, 1899), United States and Confederate States congressman, was born at Walterboro, Colleton District, S. C., the second son of Sarah Bond (Warley) and James Saunders Miles. After spending a year at the noted Willington academy in Abbeville District, he entered the College of Charleston, where he graduated in 1842 with highest honors. He studied law in the office of Edward McCrady but soon abandoned the law to become a teacher. He was assistant professor of mathematics in the College of Charleston from 1843 to 1855. During this period his elegant manners, handsome appearance, and reputation for learning won him a notable position in the polite circles of Charleston. In 1855 an event occurred that changed the course of his career. He excited the admiration of the public by his heroic services as a volunteer nurse during the yellow-fever epidemic at Norfolk, Va. That city presented him with a medal, and the conservative faction of Charleston, seeking an available candidate for mayor to stem the tide of Know-Nothingism, offered him the nomination. He accepted and was elected by a good majority. During his administration the police force of the city was reorganized, and a system of tidal drains was inaugurated. In 1857 he was elected to Congress, where he served until his withdrawal in December 1860, championing slavery and secession in a series of impressive addresses. He took a prominent part in the Washington phase of the negotiations over the status of the Charleston forts and joined other Southern congressmen in signing a manifesto announcing that the organization of a Southern confederacy was necessary. He was active in the Southern independence movement. He was chairman of the committee on foreign relations of the South Carolina secession convention and signed the ordinance of secession. Beauregard made him one of the three to arrange with Anderson the terms of the surrender of Fort Sumter. He represented the Charleston district in the Confederate Congress during its entire existence. In that body he was chairman of the committee that devised the Confederate flag and chairman of the important committee on military affairs.

In 1863 the course of his career was again changed. He married Betty, the daughter of Oliver Beirne, a rich Virginia and Louisiana planter. From 1865 until his death, with one interruption, he was able to play the rôle most congenial to him, that of a country gentleman with the means and leisure to entertain distinguished guests, collect books, and attract attention by his polished addresses. For fifteen years he lived at Oakridge, Nelson County, Va. In 1874 he was an unsuccessful candidate for the presidency of The Johns Hopkins University. In 1880 he became the first president of the University of South Carolina on its reorganization under white control. In 1882 he resigned from the university to become manager of the plantations of his father-in-law located in Ascension Parish, La. There he became one of the largest planters in the state, controlling thirteen plantations, which produced twenty million pounds of sugar annually. He became president of the Ascension branch of the Louisiana Sugar Planters' Association, and he was one of the founders of a sugar-experiment station and of *The Louisiana Planter and Sugar Manufacturer,* a weekly newspaper published in New Orleans. "Houmas House," his home, was noted for its hospitality and for its collection of rare and beautiful books. Although he took no active part in the public life of his adopted state, he frequently delivered orations on public occasions and expressed himself positively on controverted questions. He opposed the state lottery and the tendency of the sugar planters to favor high tariffs, a sugar bounty, and other measures of the Republican party. He died at "Houmas House."

[Newspaper clippings from his daughter, Mrs. Henry Middleton, Hendersonville, N. C.; *Cyc. of Eminent and Representative Men of the Carolinas* (1892), vol. I; *Letters and Testimonials Recommending Mr. Wm. Porcher Miles for the Presidency of Hopkins Univ.* (1874); *Biog. and Hist. Memoirs of La.* (1892), II, pp. 253–54; *Hist. of S. C.,* ed. Yates Snowden (1920), vol. II; E. L. Green, *Hist. of the Univ. of S. C.* (1916); *News and Courier* (Charleston), May 12, 1899.]

F. B. S.

MILHOLLAND, INEZ [See BOISSEVAIN INEZ MILHOLLAND, 1886–1916].

MILLEDGE, JOHN (1757–Feb. 9, 1818), Revolutionary patriot, governor of Georgia, representative, senator, was associated with most of the noteworthy events in his state from the Revolution to the War of 1812, but is remembered today chiefly because of his connection with the founding of the University of Georgia. His father, John Milledge, was one of the passengers on the brig *Ann,* Capt. John Thomas, which brought Oglethorpe and his little band of colonists to the port of Charleston in January 1733. He is said to have enjoyed the advantage of friendship and close association with Oglethorpe, and later became one of the prominent citizens of the colony. In 1751 he was one of the four representatives of the Savannah district in the first Provincial Assembly held under President Henry Parker. Young John's mother was the daughter of Mrs. Frances Robe of Savannah. When he was about ten his father was married again, to Mrs. Anne Rasberry.

The boy had the best advantages the little colony afforded. Probably the greater part of his education was gained at Bethesda, the school founded by the evangelist George Whitefield [*q.v.*] and still in existence as an institution for orphan boys. His intimate associates were the leading young men of the colony. He studied law in the office of the King's Attorney, but at the opening of the Revolution threw in his lot with the patriots. In the excitement caused by the news from Lexington and Concord he joined Joseph Habersham, Noble Wymberly Jones, Edward Telfair, and two others in breaking into Governor Wright's magazine and carrying off six hundred pounds of powder, some of which is said to have been used at Bunker Hill. A few weeks later he aided in an attack on Governor Wright in person, making him a prisoner in his own home. After this episode Milledge served gallantly in various capacities throughout the Revolution. He took part in the defense of Savannah, escaped with James Jackson to South Carolina, where they narrowly missed being hanged as British spies, and later served at the siege of Augusta and in Benjamin Lincoln's attempt to retake Savannah.

In 1780 he became attorney-general, and was later a member of the General Assembly during several sessions. In 1792 he was elected to Congress, succeeding Anthony Wayne who had been ousted after defeating James Jackson [*q.v.*]. He also served in the Fourth, Fifth, and Seventh congresses, resigning in 1802 to become governor. After two terms, in 1806 he was sent to the United States Senate to fill the vacancy caused by the death of James Jackson. Reëlected for a full term in 1807, he resigned while president *pro tempore* in 1809 and retired, respected and admired by all, to a life of elegant leisure.

Milledge's service to the University of Georgia probably seemed to him a small and relatively trivial incident of his eventful life. In 1785 a charter was granted by the General Assembly, and forty thousand acres of land in two newly created counties carved out of the wilderness were set aside as an endowment. The grant, princely in prospect, proved disappointing in product—Gov. Wilson Lumpkin relates that his father once swapped four hundred acres of such land for a shotgun—and the building of the university was deferred. In 1800 a renewed effort was made, and a committee appointed to select a site. Its members included Milledge, Abraham Baldwin [*q.v.*], George Walton, John Twiggs, and Hugh Lawton, all prominent in local annals. The land upon which their choice fell lay outside the bounds of the state grant and had passed into private ownership, but Milledge now immortalized himself by buying it outright for four thousand dollars and presenting it to the university. The tract embraced more than six hundred acres, including land now occupied by the campus of the university as well as a large part of the city of Athens which gradually grew up around the college. The imagination of posterity, struck by the impulsive generosity of the gift, has identified Milledge with the origin of the state's highest institution of learning, and has honored his name in Milledgeville, the state capital from 1807 to 1867, in Milledge Avenue, the principal residence street of Athens, in the Milledge Chair of Ancient Languages at the University of Georgia, and in Milledge Street in the Sand Hills, the aristocratic suburb of Augusta where his declining days were spent and his mortal remains entombed.

Milledge was married twice. His first wife was Martha Galphin of Silver Bluff, S. C., daughter of George Galphin. She bore him one daughter and died in November 1811. In May of the following year he married Ann, daughter of Thomas and Ann (Gresham) Lamar, by whom he had three children.

[George White, *Hist. Colls. of Ga.* (1854); W. J. Northen, *Men of Mark in Ga.*, vol. I (1907); L. L. Knight, *A Standard Hist. of Georgia and Georgians* (1917), I, *passim*, VI, 3200, and *Georgia's Landmarks, Memorials and Legends* (2 vols., 1913–14); T. U. P. Charlton, *The Life of Maj. Gen. James Jackson* (1809), reprinted in 1897 with valuable letters of Jackson to Milledge; C. C. Jones, Jr., *The Hist. of Ga.* (2 vols., 1883); W. B. Stevens, *A Hist. of Ga. . . . to . . . MDCCXCVIII* (2 vols., 1847–59); H. C. White, *Abraham Baldwin* (1926); E. M. Coulter, *College Life in the Old South* (1928); *Biog. Dir. Am. Cong.* (1928); *Daily Savannah Republican*, Feb. 13, 1818; Record of Bonds, Bills of Sale, Deeds of Gift for the Years 1765–72 (Ga. State Archives), p. 418; information as to certain facts from Mrs. A. S. Salley, Columbia, S. C., a descendant.]

J. H. T. M.

MILLEDOLER, PHILIP (Sept. 22, 1775–Sept. 22, 1852), clergyman, educator, son of John and Anna (Mitchell) Muhlithaler, was born at Rhinebeck, N. Y., whither his parents had fled from their home in New York City at the time of its occupancy by the British. His father was a native of Bern, Switzerland, and had come to America about 1751; his mother's parents had emigrated from Zurich. The family was connected with the German Reformed Church and Philip early showed unusual religious tendencies. He was graduated from Columbia College in 1793 and began at once the study of theology under the pastor of his church, John D. Gros [*q.v.*], and of Hebrew under a Lutheran pastor. His proficiency and personal promise were such that, after only a year, having been examined by the German Reformed Synod at Reading, Pa., he was ordained to the ministry (May 21, 1794).

His pastor and preceptor desiring that he succeed him, and the congregation also desiring it, Milledoler became pastor of the Nassau Street German Reformed Church in 1795 when he was but twenty years old, his preaching to be in both German and English. In 1800 he became pastor of the Pine Street Presbyterian Church of Philadelphia. Other churches called him; his former parish in New York repeatedly sought his return; and in 1805 he became pastor of the Rutgers Street Presbyterian Church, New York City. In all these pastorates his ministry was deeply spiritual and very effectual. His preaching was fervid, he was especially gifted in prayer, and his churches were notable for their evangelical interest, for their growth in membership, and for their large congregations. From early in his ministry he was in sympathy with the Reformed (Dutch) Church and for a short time, about 1800, his ministerial membership was in that body. In 1813 he became pastor of the Collegiate Dutch Reformed Church of New York City, to remain with the denomination for the rest of his life. During these years of devoted and distinguished pastorate he was active and influential in many religious associations. He held various important offices under the General Assembly of the Presbyterian Church and was moderator of the Assembly in 1808. He was concerned in the forming and managing of the American Bible Society, the Society for Evangelizing the Jews, and the United Foreign Missionary Society.

He was learned in theology and positive in his convictions. His opposition to Hopkinsianism had something to do, no doubt, with his changing from the Presbyterian to the Dutch Reformed body. In 1811, before Princeton Theological Seminary was organized, he was appointed by the Presbytery of New York to instruct students in theology. The General Synod of the German Reformed Church, in 1820, chose him its professor of theology, an appointment which he finally declined. In 1825 the General Synod of the Dutch Reformed Church elected him professor of theology in its theological seminary at New Brunswick, N. J., and at the same time the trustees of Rutgers, up to that time known as Queen's College, chose him president. He accepted the two offices. The college, which had been weak and even inactive for some years, began at once an era of prosperity, strength, and distinguished service, and the enrollment of students in the seminary also greatly increased. A remarkable number of graduates of this period became leaders in church, state, and education. Remaining in these exacting and important offices for fifteen years, he resigned them both in 1840 and returned to New York City. During his career he delivered many sermons and addresses which were published. On Mar. 29, 1796, he married Susan, daughter of Lawrence Benson of Harlem; she died in 1815 and on Nov. 4, 1817, he married Margaret, daughter of General John Steele of Philadelphia. He had ten children. The day after his death, on Staten Island, his wife also died, and the two were buried in one grave.

[E. T. Corwin, *A Manual of the Reformed Church in America* (4th ed. 1902); W. B. Sprague, *Annals Am. Pulpit*, vol. IX (1869); W. H. S. Demarest, *A Hist. of Rutgers Coll., 1766–1924* (1924); *Centennial of the Theological Seminary of the Reformed Church in America* (1885); *Mag. of the Reformed Dutch Church*, Mar., Apr. 1827, Aug. 1828; *Christian Intelligencer*, Sept. 30, Nov. 4, 30, Dec. 23, 1852; *N. Y. Observer*, Sept. 30, 1852; *N. Y. Times*, Sept. 23, 1852.]

W. H. S. D.

MILLER, CHARLES HENRY (Mar. 20, 1842–Jan. 21, 1922), landscape painter, etcher, born in New York, was a descendant of Fernandus de Muldor, who came to New Amsterdam from Holland in 1664. His parents were Jacob and Jane (Taylor) Miller. He exhibited his first picture at the National Academy of Design when he was eighteen years of age, but it was not until some years later that he adopted painting as his profession. Meanwhile he attended the Mt. Washington Collegiate Institute and later the New York Homeopathic Medical College, graduating with the degree of M.D. in 1863. Upon graduation he made a voyage to Europe as ship's doctor on the Black Ball liner *Harvest Queen* which enabled him to pay brief visits to Paris, London, and Scotland. The impressions he received there strengthened his love of art, and on his return to New York he abandoned the medical profession. His earliest studies from nature were made on Long Island; Bayard Taylor called him "the artistic discoverer" of the island. In 1867 he went to Munich to take up the serious work of preparation for the career of a painter. He became a pupil of Adolf Lier (a pupil of Jules Dupré), at the Bavarian Royal Academy, and later continued his studies in Vienna, Leipzig, Dresden, Berlin, and Paris. After three years abroad he returned to New York. He became an academician in 1875; was president of the New York Art Club in 1879; member of the Society of American Artists, the Art Union, Municipal Art Society, New York Etching Club, Century, Lotos, and Republican clubs; and a welcome contributor to all the important exhibitions, including the Centennial, 1876, and two or three of the international expositions in Paris.

Miller's etchings, like his paintings, were Long Island motives. Five of his prints were in the Boston Art Museum exhibition of etchings in 1881, among them "Home, Sweet Home," the birthplace of John Howard Payne. As the direct expression of a painter of great power, said S. R. Koehler, every one of his plates has some point of interest to the lover of art, though many of them are but hasty memoranda, jotted down rudely, reminding one of Jongkind. His paintings are warm in tone, rich in surface, and of handsome pattern, somewhat reminiscent of the Barbizon school. His Long Island subjects constitute a record of the changing aspect of nature in the suburbs of a metropolis. A typical example is "A Bouquet of Oaks," given to the Metropolitan Museum, New York, in 1907, by W. T. Evans. It was painted in 1883 at Stewart's Pond, near Jamaica, L. I., in the autumn. The region about Queens, where Miller found most of his motives, comprises Jamaica, Garden City, Mineola, Creedmoor; its rural character is a thing of the past; thus his "Oaks at Creedmoor" (Paris exposition of 1878) and his "Sunset at Queens" (Paris exposition of 1882) are not merely effective landscapes, but historic documents as well. Under the pen name of Carl De Muldor the artist published in 1885 a book entitled *The Philosophy of Art in America.* He wrote occasional essays in criticism and lectured. On Oct. 3, 1900, he married Mrs. Elizabeth Dorothea Mosback. He died at his New York home in his eightieth year.

[S. R. Koehler, article in the *Am. Art Review,* vol. II (1881); C. M. Kurtz, *Nat. Acad. Notes* (1884); Samuel Isham, *The Hist. of Am. Painting* (1905); "The Works of Chas. Henry Miller," *Art-Jour.* (London), Dec. 1877; G. W. Sheldon, *Am. Painters* (1881); *Cat. of the Thos. B. Clarke Coll. of Am. Pictures* (1891); *Am. Art News,* Jan. 28, 1922; *N. Y. Times,* Jan. 22, 1922.] W. H. D.

MILLER, CHARLES RANSOM (Jan. 17, 1849–July 18, 1922), editor, newspaper director, was born at Hanover Center, N. H. His father, Elijah Tenney Miller, a farmer, was descended from early Massachusetts stock. His mother was Chastina Hoyt Miller. As a boy he showed no liking for farm work and in 1863 he became a pupil at Kimball Union Academy at Meriden, N. H., from which he was expelled in 1865 for hilarious conduct. He spent a year in helping his father on the farm and then entered Green Mountain Liberal Institute, South Woodstock, Vt., where he prepared for Dartmouth College. At the end of his sophomore year at Dartmouth he was expelled again for youthful exuberance but after working in a printing office during the summer he was allowed to reënter and was graduated in 1872. Both in preparatory schools and college he showed no zeal for regular studies, preferring private reading and being considered inattentive in classes.

At Dartmouth he had been a contributor, especially of verse, to the college monthly and had acquired a taste for writing which led him to seek a place on the staff of the *Springfield Daily Republican,* for which he was a reporter for three years under the elder Samuel Bowles. Through a college friend he learned of an opening with the *New York Times* and was engaged in July 1875 by George Jones as assistant telegraph editor of that paper. He was in charge of the telegraph news on election night in 1876 but did not participate in the act of John Reid, the managing editor, who persuaded the Republican National Committee to claim victory for Hayes when other newspapers conceded it to Tilden. Miller was then and remained throughout his life an independent Democrat. On Jan. 1, 1876, he was put in charge of the weekly edition of the *Times.* Later in the same year, on Oct. 10, he was married to Frances Daniels, of Plainfield, N. H., who survived until 1906. While in charge of the weekly edition he had begun to write occasional editorials, which he continued to do when he became foreign editor of the *Times* in 1879. He was made a regular editorial writer in 1880. On Apr. 13, 1883, at the age of thirty-four, he became editor in chief in succession to John Foord and retained that post until his death.

The *Times,* as a Republican paper, had exposed Tweed and the Star Route frauds and had developed independent tendencies. In 1884 it supported Cleveland for president. Miller and Cleveland became close friends. Jones having died in 1891, Miller raised $950,000 in subscriptions for the purchase of the paper from the Jones heirs and took control in 1893. Circulation and advertising had been declining and the panic of 1893 hastened that process. Through a complete reorganization in 1896 control and management of the paper were acquired by Adolph S. Ochs, proprietor and publisher of the *Chattanooga* (Tennessee) *Daily Times.* Miller continued as editor in chief and became vice-president of the new company. Freed from heavy financial burdens and in the prime of his intellectual powers, he then began his most productive period as an editorial writer. He had studied deeply after leaving college and became proficient in Latin, Greek, French, German, and Russian, besides acquiring a wide knowledge of history and international affairs. At the outbreak of the World War, he forecast future developments with insight, predicting sure defeat for Germany. When the United States entered the war, the editorials in the *Times* gave vigorous support to the cause of the Allies. A notable editorial appearing in the issue for Dec. 15, 1914, entitled, "For the German People, Peace with Freedom," attracted wide attention, and was republished in many languages in newspapers all over the world. The opening paragraph was most prophetic: "Germany is doomed to sure defeat. Bankrupt in statesmanship, overmatched in arms, under the moral condemnation of the civilized world, befriended only by the Austrian and the Turk, two backward-looking and dying nations, desperately battling against the hosts of three great Powers to which help and reinforcement from States now neutral will certainly come should the decision be long deferred, she pours out the blood of her heroic subjects and wastes her diminishing substance in a hopeless struggle that postpones but cannot alter the fatal decree." On Sept. 16, 1918, an editorial by Miller advised acceptance of the Austro-Hungarian proposal for a non-binding discussion of peace terms, for which public opinion was not then prepared. It created quite a furore, but later it was regarded as wise and judicious. Miller's style in editorials was marked by strong conviction, clarity of expression, and forceful reasoning. He was of medium height, heavily built, and had a large head. He enjoyed his friends, and in his personal relations he was unusually gracious.

[The principal source of information about Miller is the biography, *Mr. Miller of "The Times"* (1931) by F. Fraser Bond who was his editorial secretary. There is also valuable material in the *Hist. of the N. Y. Times* (1921) by Elmer Davis, who was an editorial writer on his staff. His personal letters in the possession of his family and those addressed to George Fred Williams, his classmate, and Solomon Bulkley Griffin, his former associate on the staff of the *Springfield Republican*, throw light upon his character. His editorials are preserved in the files of the *Times*. An account of his death accompanied by a full sketch of his career may be found in the *N. Y. Times*, July 19, 1922.]

A. S. W.

MILLER, CINCINNATUS HINER (Mar. 10, 1839–Feb. 17, 1913), poet, son of Hulings and Margaret (Witt) Miller, was born in Liberty, Ind. His middle name was given in honor of the country physician who was in attendance at his birth; the form "Heine" which appeared in his early books, may or may not have been a printer's error. His father, a Quaker schoolmaster, wandered ever westward, seeking a land of peace and plenty, from Ohio to Indiana, thence to Illinois, and finally, in 1852, across the Rockies and Cascades to Oregon. He settled near the forks of the Willamette not far from the present Eugene. At about the age of seventeen, his son "Nat," as he was called, ran away from home in company with another boy. They found their way to one of the mining camps in Northern California where Miller obtained employment as a cook. Being a rather delicate lad, he fell seriously ill with the scurvy as the result of the bad food and his own cooking. He was nursed back to health by a Dr. Ream in Yreka, Cal., and was subsequently befriended by a gambler named James Thompson, who figures attractively in his writings as "The Prince." Despite Miller's lifelong assertion that he was wounded in the battle of Castle Rocks against the Modocs, on June 15, 1855, residents of that vicinity scouted the claim that he had taken part in the skirmish. Probably in 1856 Miller made the acquaintance of Joseph De Bloney, known as "Mountain Joe." According to Miller's story, the mountaineer proposed to establish an Indian republic at the base of Mount Shasta. If so grandiose a scheme was planned, it went no further than the building of a road-house in which Miller did the cooking. In the spring of 1857 he went to live with an Indian tribe, the Diggers, and married one of their women, who bore him a daughter, Cali-Shasta. His native associates were noted horse-thieves, and Miller, as a preliminary to establishing the republic, fell in with their ways. He was captured, after an exciting chase, on July 8, 1859, but was rescued the same night by a friend who sawed through the bars of the jail window. Although he had no share in the Pit River massacre of this year, the Shasta region became very unsafe for any Indian sympathizer, and Miller, soon after it, wisely returned to Oregon.

He then for a time attended an academy named "Columbia College" in Eugene, taught school for a while in Clarke, Washington Territory, studied law on the side, and was admitted to the bar in Portland, Ore., in 1861. Instead of practising, he established in 1862, in company with one Isaac Mossman, a pony express between Washington Territory and Idaho. With its proceeds, he purchased in 1863 the *Democratic Register* in Eugene and became an editor. His first appearance in print had been a letter in defense of the Mexican bandit, Joaquin Murietta [*q.v.*], which had resulted in his friends nick-naming him "Joaquin"; the name pleased him better than his own more burdensome one and in time he adopted it as his pen name. Some verses of his attracted the attention of a poetically minded girl in Port Orford, Ore., named Minnie Theresa Dyer, who wrote to him enthusiastically about them. After some correspondence, Miller rode over to Port Orford and returned the same week with Minnie Myrtle, as he called her, as his bride. His newspaper being suppressed by the government because of its support of the Confederacy, the editor moved to Canyon City, Ore., where he soon won the favor of his fellow-townsmen by successfully leading a party of them against a band of hostile Indians. He was rewarded by being elected judge of the Grant County court in 1866. A little later his wife, now the mother of two children, separated from him. Miller solaced his loneliness by bringing out two volumes of poetry, *Specimens* (1868) and *Joaquin et al* (1869). These attracted some attention, and in 1870 he went down to San Francisco to enjoy his réclame and was there admitted to the circle which included Bret Harte, Charles Warren Stoddard, and Ina Coolbrith.

Thence he started on a literary pilgrimage to England. After visiting the Burns and Byron shrines, he attempted to find a London publisher for a compilation of his own verse, some of which had already appeared in newspapers, under the title, *Pacific Poems.* Failing in this, he printed the book privately and succeeded in gaining the attention of the critics. William Michael Rossetti took him up and introduced him to London literary circles, where his striking appearance in chaps and sombrero, which he wore indoors and out, soon made him the sensation of the season. In 1871 Longmans published his *Songs of the Sierras,* which in spite of its cheap rhythms and Byronic imitations was loudly acclaimed by the British. Its reception in America was less favorable, critics refusing to accept its romanticism as a genuine expression of the Far West. Attention was also unkindly called to the author's lack of learning which had led him into sundry errors in his poems, such as riming "Goethe" with "teeth." A brief visit to America convincing the poet of his unpopularity, he sought consolation in foreign travel. During the next few years he visited South America, Europe, and possibly the Near East. In 1873 he published *Songs of the Sun-lands,* and, in prose, *Life Amongst the Modocs* (republished with variations under other titles), regarded by Stuart Sherman as "his most interesting book." These were followed by *The Ship in the Desert* (1875), *The Baroness of New York* (1877), *Songs of Italy* (1878), showing the influence of Browning, and a prose Indian romance, *Shadows of Shasta* (1881). He also published several dramas, of which *The Danites in the Sierras* (1881), a Mormon play, was the most successful. In 1884 appeared *Memorie and Rime,* an autobiographical miscellany, and in 1886 *The Destruction of Gotham,* an unsuccesful novel. His last prose works were *An Illustrated History of Montana* (1894), a typical subscription history, and *The Building of the City Beautiful* (1897), showing Miller as a Utopist. In 1897, also, he published the *Complete Poetical Works of Joaquin Miller.* His narrative poem, *Light,* which was published in 1907, was his last bid for fame and represents his closest approach to full maturity as a poet.

Meanwhile, Miller had returned to America and tried living in New York, Boston, and Washington, all of which were too crowded for his taste. In 1883 he married Abbie Leland, and in 1886 he settled permanently in Oakland, Cal. There on the hills above the town he purchased an estate, known as "The Heights" (in Miller's spelling usually "The Hights"), which he adorned with trees and stone monuments to Frémont, Browning, and Moses, and with a funeral pyre to be used at his own death. For many years he was one of the landmarks of California. As a bearded sage and advocate of the simple life he was looked upon with a respect which was mingled with amusement at his eccentricities and horror at his theories of free love. In 1897–98 he found renewed adventures as correspondent of the New York *Journal* in the Klondike. By the time of his death in 1913 the West that he loved had vanished. The best of his work remains of significance as an attempt, never wholly successful, to celebrate on a heroic scale its freedom and its beauty.

[Miller's autobiographical writings mentioned above and his *Overland in a Covered Wagon* (1930), ed. by Sidney G. Firman, are useful but untrustworthy. See also: Harr Wagner, *Joaquin Miller and His Other Self* (1929); Stuart P. Sherman, introduction to *The Poetical Works of Joaquin Miller* (1923); the *Frontier,* May 1931, Jan.–May 1932; *Sunset,* June 1913; *Am. Mercury,* Feb. 1926; *San Francisco Examiner,* Feb. 18, 1913. Information as to certain facts was supplied by Dr. Martin S. Peterson of the University of Nebraska, who has prepared a doctoral dissertation on Miller.]

E. S. B.

MILLER, EDWARD (May 9, 1760–Mar. 17, 1812), physician, brother of Samuel Miller, 1769–1850 [*q.v.*], was the son of Rev. John and Margaret (Millington) Miller, and grandson of John Miller, a Scotchman, who emigrated to Boston in 1710, and married Mary Bass of *Mayflower* ancestry. Born near Dover, Del., where his father was pastor of the Presbyterian church, Edward received a good academic education and began the study of medicine with a local practitioner, Dr. Charles Ridgely. Two years later, in 1780, dissatisfied with his lack of clinical opportunities, he began to serve as surgeon's mate in the colonial military hospitals, being stationed chiefly at Basking Ridge, N. J. In 1781 he became surgeon on an armed ship sailing for France, and during 1782–83 pursued his medical studies at the University of Pennsylvania. At the close of the Revolutionary period, he settled at Frederica, Del., removing later to Somerset County, Md., and in 1786 to Dover, Del. He had been accustomed to spend a part of each year in Philadelphia in order to keep in touch with medical advance, and in 1785 he received the degree of bachelor of medicine, and in 1789, that of doctor from the University of Pennsylvania. He appears to have studied the epidemic of yellow fever in Philadelphia in 1793, and about this time he wrote a letter to Dr. Benjamin Rush [*q.v.*], with whom he had formed a friendship, in which he indorsed the latter's belief that the disease was not imported and not contagious from person to person. In 1796 he removed to New York City and at once began to identify himself with the life of the future metropolis. With Drs. Samuel L. Mitchill and Elihu H. Smith [*qq.v.*], he founded what is classed by some authorities as the earliest medical periodical of the United States—the *Medical Repository,* the first number of which appeared in August 1797. He was active in connection with the yellow-fever epidemic of 1798, and on account of his familiarity with the disease was made physician to the Port of New York in 1803.

In 1805 there was a new outbreak of yellow fever and Miller made a report on it to the governor of the state (*Report on the Malignant Disease which Prevailed in the City of New York in the Autumn of 1805: Addressed to the Governor of New York,* 1806), which was reprinted in England and translated into French and German. He rendered valuable aid in the establishment of the College of Physicians and Surgeons (1807), "joining with Dr. Romayne in extending his credit for the procurement of the funds needed" (John Shrady, *The College of Physicians and Surgeons, New York,* vol. I, 1903–04, p. 42). He became its first professor of the practice of physic, and in 1809 was made one of the physicians to the New York Hospitals, where he inaugurated the custom of holding clinical lectures. His death took place in the midst of an active career, due to an acute respiratory affection.

He was evidently a man with unusual vision or intuition. He advocated lengthening the period of undergraduate studies, clinical advantages, and the study of pathology. He correctly recognized an enlarged spleen as the best evidence of chronic malaria and was the first to prescribe small doses of calomel for the summer complaints of early childhood. He wrote no major work but his articles and pamphlets were collected by his brother, Rev. Samuel Miller, and published in a volume of more than 300 pages, entitled, *The Medical Works of Dr. Edward Miller* (1814). At the time of his death he was a member of the American Mineralogical and Philosophical societies and of the Friendly Club, limited to a dozen members. He never married.

[A biog. sketch of Miller is included in *Medical Works* mentioned above; see also, F. B. Lee, *Geneal. and Personal Memorial of Mercer County, N. J.* (1907), vol. I; *Am. Medic. and Philosophical Reg.,* July 1812; L. P. Bush, *Address Before the Medic. Soc. of Del.,* June 1855; *No. Am. Medic. and Surgic. Jour.,* Jan. 1828; *N. Y. Gazette and General Advertiser,* Mar. 18, 1812.]

E. P.

MILLER, EMILY CLARK HUNTINGTON (Oct. 22, 1833–Nov. 2, 1913), author, editor, educator, daughter of Dr. Thomas and Paulina (Clark) Huntington, was born in Brooklyn, Conn. Her father, clergyman and physician, and a graduate of Middlebury College, was the son of Jedediah Huntington [*q.v.*]. Emily Huntington was graduated from Oberlin College, Ohio, with the degree of A.B. in 1857. In September 1860 she was married to John Edwin Miller, a teacher, of Greentown, Ohio. She became the mother of four children, a daughter who died in infancy and three sons. After her marriage she lived in Granville, Ill., where her husband was principal of an academy, then in Plainfield, Ill., where he was professor of Latin and Greek in Northwestern College, then in Akron, Chicago, and Evanston. Her husband was prominent in Sunday-school and Y.M.C.A. activities, in which Mrs. Miller helped him. She also shared his work in connection with a juvenile magazine, the *Little Corporal,* which he published in coöperation with Alfred L. Sewell, and in 1871 she became its editor. In April 1872 the *Little Corporal* absorbed *Work and Play* and in 1875 it was merged into *St. Nicholas.* She had begun to write while she was still in school and her stories and verse were printed in religious papers and magazines. Throughout her life she continued to write, even when domestic affairs absorbed her and during the years when she was connected with Northwestern University. She contributed to leading magazines and was at one time an associate editor of the *Ladies' Home Journal.* Her published volumes include: *The Royal Road to Fortune* (1869); *The Parish of Fair Haven* (1876); a series of stories published by the Kirkwood Library in 1877; *Kathie's Experience* (1886); *Thorn Apples* (1887); *The King's Messengers* (1891); *For the Beloved* (1892), a book of poems; *Home Talks about the World* (1894); and *From Avalon* (1896), poems. Her stories are of the type known as Sunday-school stories. They are clearly and simply written, with natural conversation, some humor, bits of good description, and inevitable moral lessons. Her verse is usually spiritual in thought, not lacking in imagination, conventional in form, but possessing occasional lyrical values.

In 1871 Mrs. Miller was one of a group which secured a charter for the Evanston College for Ladies, at Evanston, Ill. For the two years of its existence as a separate institution she was a trustee and corresponding secretary. In 1873 the college, of which Frances Willard was president, was united with Northwestern University, and Mrs. Miller was a trustee of the University from 1873 to 1885. Friction arose over the question of separate control of the social life of the women students and Frances Willard resigned. Mrs. Miller was one of a committee to decide whether the resignation should be accepted. She was dean of women and assistant professor of English literature from 1891 to 1898. At that time the position of dean of women was not an administrative office. It involved little more than being at the head of a hall and implied no very important advisory contact with students. The years of her deanship were harmonious. She always believed that women should be considered as part of the general student body, without special treatment and rules on account of sex. Many university occasions were celebrated by her in poetry. Her later years were passed in St. Paul, Minn., and at her summer home in Englewood, N. J. She was always actively interested in temperance, missionary, and Sunday-school work and in the Chautauqua movement. She died at the home of her brother at Northfield, Minn.

[*Who's Who in America,* 1912–13; Frances E. Willard, *Woman and Temperance* (1883); Frances E. Willard and Mary A. Livermore, *Am. Women* (1897), vol. II; A. H. Wilde, *Northwestern Univ.: a Hist., 1855–1905* (1905); *The Huntington Family in America* (1915); obituaries in *N. Y. Times,* Nov. 5, 1913, and *St. Paul Pioneer Press,* Nov. 3, 1913.] S. G. B.

MILLER, EZRA (May 12, 1812–July 9, 1885), engineer, inventor, was born near Pleasant Valley, Bergen County, N. J. He was the son of Ezra Wilson Miller, a native of Westchester County, N. Y., and Hannah (Ryerson) Miller of Pompton, N. J. During his boyhood the family moved to New York City, then to Rhinebeck, and finally to Flushing, L. I., where he received his preparatory school education. His parents wished him to study medicine but Ezra preferred to take up topographical, mechanical, and hydraulic engineering, and became a civil engineer. For upwards of ten years he practised his profession in and about New York. As an avocation he engaged in military studies and was active in the state militia. In 1833 he enlisted in a company of artillery belonging to the 2nd New York Militia and became, by promotion, adjutant in 1839, lieutenant-colonel in 1840, and colonel in 1842. After his marriage in May 1841 to Amanda J. Miller of New York, he settled at Fort Hamilton, N. Y., where he continued the practice of his profession until 1848, when he removed to Rock County, Wis., to take part in the survey of public lands. After a period with the State Survey he engaged in railway survey and construction work.

While so employed in 1853 he became interested in the improvement of existing methods of coupling railway cars, and for some ten years studied and experimented quietly with the problem. His work resulted in the perfection of a car coupler for which he obtained patent No. 38,057 on Mar. 31, 1863. Continuing his experiments, he improved his basic idea and on Jan. 31, 1865, secured patent No. 46,126 for his combined railroad-car platform, coupler, and buffer. Two years later he succeeded in placing his coupler arrangement on three cars being built in the railroad shops at Adrian, Mich. It proved an immediate success and soon replaced the dangerous old railroad car platform with its loose-link coupling throughout the United States and was widely adopted in Europe. The Miller coupler continued in favor for about twenty years before it was superseded by the Janney coupler [see Janney, Eli Hamilton], and provided its inventor with a large income.

In 1867 Miller returned to the East and lived for three years in Brooklyn, N. Y., then purchased a farm near Mahwah, N. J., where he spent the rest of his life, devoting his time mainly to raising prize livestock. He had a natural capacity for making friends which led to his election to public office both in Wisconsin and in New Jersey. He was commissioned colonel in the Wisconsin militia in 1851, and in 1852 was elected to the Wisconsin Senate, serving one term. Under President Buchanan he was deputy postmaster of Janesville, Wis., for two years, and at another time was justice of the peace in Magnolia, Wis. After taking up his residence in New Jersey, he was elected to the state Senate in 1883, and held his seat at the time of his death. He was several times a candidate for Congress. He died in Mahwah, survived by his widow and five children.

[Henry Hall, *America's Successful Men of Affairs,* vol. II (1896); C. M. Depew, *One Hundred Years of Am. Commerce* (1895), vol. I; W. W. Clayton, *Hist. of Bergen and Passaic Counties, N. J.* (1882); *Manual of the One Hundred and Eighth Session of the Legis-*

lature of N. J. (1884); *Railroad Gazette*, July 17, 1885; *Sun* (N. Y.), July 10, 1885; *N. Y. Tribune*, July 10, 1885; Patent Office records.] C. W. M.

MILLER, GEORGE (Feb. 16, 1774–Apr. 5, 1816), Evangelical preacher, was born in Pottstown, Pa., the son of Jacob and Elizabeth Miller. He grew up in Alsace Township, Berks County, lost his father when he was ten years old, was much influenced by his devout Lutheran mother, and attended a Lutheran catechetical class in Reading. Revivalism was then spreading through backwoods Pennsylvania like a grass-fire, but the educated German clergy were relatively incombustible, and for some years Miller's yearning for experimental religion was kept in check. A millwright by trade, in 1798 he bought some land in Brunswick Township, Schuylkill County, and built himself a gristmill. In 1800 he married Magdalena Brobst, whose father was proprietor of an iron forge in Albany Township, Berks; and in the same year he heard Jacob Albright [*q.v.*] preach and was deeply moved by him. It was not until June 3, 1802, however, that he felt himself assuredly converted. Thereupon he identified himself with Albright's followers, later known as the Evangelical Association, was made a class leader, and became the object of attention of his orthodox neighbors, who filled his mill flume with rubbish, took their custom away from him, leaving their bills unpaid, and at times pelted him with clubs and stones. In April 1805, under the guidance of Albright and John Walter, he became an itinerant preacher. His preparation for the ministry, like that of the other leaders of the movement, was of the scantiest: he had had almost no schooling, he knew no language except his Pennsylvania-German dialect, he had read few books except the Bible. In person he was an uncouth countryman, large of limb and feature, his red eyebrows contrasting oddly with a mat of black hair; but he was earnest and courageous, developed rapidly as a preacher and leader, conducted many satisfactory revivals, and made some converts wherever he went. During four years of circuit-riding he traveled through nineteen counties in Pennsylvania, but this heroic labor proved too much for him. On Dec. 26, 1808, he became seriously ill, returned to his home in Albany Township, Berks, and never regained his health. In his enforced leisure he became the first author of the denomination. Basing his work on the German version of the Methodist Discipline, which Ignatius Roemer had made in 1808 under the direction of Martin Boehm [*q.v.*], he compiled the Book of Discipline for the "Albright people" (1809) and did most of the work on the second edition (1817). In consequence his influence on the Evangelical Association has been great and lasting. He also wrote a devotional book, *Thätiges Christenthum* (1814), the earliest life of Albright (1814), and a revealing autobiography. For the four years before his death he lived on his farm at Dry Valley, Union County, a few miles below New Berlin, where he is buried.

[*Jacob Albright and his Co-laborers* (1883), compiled by Reuben Yeakel, contains a translation of Miller's autobiography. See also R. Yeakel, *Hist. of the Evangel. Asso.*, vol. I (1894), and A. Stapleton, *Annals of the Evangel. Asso. of North America* (1896).] G. H. G.

MILLER, HARRIET MANN (June 25, 1831–Dec. 25, 1918), author, naturalist, better known under the pseunonym Olive Thorne Miller, was the daughter of Seth Hunt and Mary Field (Holbrook) Mann, and was born in Auburn, N. Y. Her father was a banker; her grandfather, James Mann, was an importing merchant of Boston. During her childhood the family removed to Ohio, where she was educated in private schools. She was married in 1854 to Watts Todd Miller, at Rock Island, Ill. For twenty years after marriage she lived in Chicago, then in Brooklyn, N. Y., and, after the death of her husband, for the last fourteen years of her life in Los Angeles. For many years she devoted herself to the care of her four children. It was only after they were fairly well grown, while she was still living in Chicago, that she began to write stories for young people, under her pseudonym. She was interested in birds and commenced writing magazine articles and books and lecturing about birds and their habits. Her summers were spent almost entirely out doors, where she studied birds in their natural surroundings. In her Brooklyn home she equipped a room as an aviary, and there she studied the life of her bird pets during the winter. She was a copious note-taker and filled many notebooks with her observations. Her published volumes include: *Little Folks in Feathers and Fur, and Others in Neither* (1875), always one of her most popular books; *Queer Pets at Marcy's* (1880); *Bird-Ways* (1885); *In Nesting Time* (1888); *A Bird-Lover in the West* (1894); *The First Book of Birds* (1899); *The Second Book of Birds: Bird Families* (1901); *True Bird Stories from my Note-book* (1903); *With the Birds in Maine* (1904); and *The Children's Book of Birds* (1915). Her other stories for children are pleasantly free from didacticism and full of informed interest in nature, but her books on birds are her best work. They are results of personal observations rather than of much study and are fairly free from scientific errors. They are written with so much enthusiasm and interesting detail that few children fail to enjoy them and many adults have found them instructive and readable. She retained mental activity throughout her long life and continued writing until within a short time of her death. She was a member of many organizations, among them the American Ornithologists' Union, the Linnæan Society, and the Audubon Society of California. She believed in the educational and social value of women's clubs and wrote a book on the subject, *The Woman's Club* (1891). As a bird lover, she strongly opposed the wearing of birds or plumage for adornment. She died at her home in Los Angeles.

[*Who's Who in America,* 1918–19; Frances E. Willard and Mary A. Livermore, *Am. Women* (1897), vol. II; G. S. Mann, *Geneal. of the Descendants of Richard Mann of Scituate, Mass.* (1884); obituaries in *N. Y. Times,* Dec. 27, 1918, and *Los Angeles Times,* Dec. 26, 1918.] S. G. B.

MILLER, HEINRICH [See MILLER, JOHN HENRY, 1702–1782].

MILLER, HENRY (Nov. 1, 1800–Feb. 8, 1874), pioneer Kentucky physician, was born in the town of Glasgow, Barren County, Ky. His father, Henry Miller, of German descent, came from Maryland as one of the first settlers of that village. His education, he says, "was not acquired in academic halls, but in the primitive schoolhouses of his native state, and upon the ample sward, shaded by forest trees, appurtenant thereunto." He began the study of medicine in his native town with Doctors Bainbridge and Gist and received his degree of M.D. in 1822 from the recently organized Transylvania University at Lexington. His dissertation, *An Inaugural Thesis: Relation between the Sanguiferous and the Nervous Systems* (1822), was deemed worthy of publication by the faculty. Shortly after his return to Glasgow he was offered the position of demonstrator of anatomy in his alma mater and in preparation for this duty he went to Philadelphia by horse-back, where he spent several months in the dissecting-room. Faculty opposition developing, he resigned from Transylvania and took up his practice at Glasgow where he remained until 1827, removing then to Harrodsburg. After nine years at this popular health resort he moved to Louisville, where he had been offered the chair of obstetrics and diseases of women and children in the projected Medical Institute of Louisville. It was not until 1837 that the school was opened and Miller was made professor of obstetrics in the reorganized faculty. In 1846 the Institute became the medical department of the University of Louisville. Miller remained until 1858 when he resigned. In 1867 he returned to the school as professor of medical and surgical diseases of women, but resigned after one year. In 1869 he accepted the corresponding chair in the newly established Louisville Medical College which he held for the rest of his life.

Starting as a general practitioner, Miller developed into one of the leading obstetricians of his state and an able gynecologist. He was a pioneer in the use of ether in obstetrical practice and always a strong advocate of anesthesia in labor. He is credited with being the first in Louisville and one of the first in the United States to make use of the vaginal speculum in gynecological practice. He was a clear forcible writer. In 1849 he published his *Theoretical and Practical Treatise on Human Parturition.* A larger and more complete edition was published in 1858 under the title *Principles and Practice of Obstetrics.* This work has a place among the standard treatises on obstetrics. It is characterized by independence of thought and sound judgment. Notable among his journal articles are those in support of obstetrical anesthesia and of the operation of ovariotomy. In contrast to his facility with the pen were his limitations as a speaker. He had a poor voice and a worse delivery. He spoke haltingly and only his great reputation and a proverbial punctuality with his classes made possible his undoubted success as a teacher. Physically he was tall and slight. He practised up to the time of his death in Louisville from chronic nephritis. Miller was married on June 24, 1824, to Clarissa Robertson (or Robinson). Two sons became physicians. The elder, William, lost his life in the Civil War and Edward followed his father in the practice of surgery.

[*Richmond and Louisville Medic. Jour.*, Jan. 1872; *Trans. Am. Medic. Asso.*, vol. XXVI (1875); J. N. McCormack, *Some Medic. Pioneers of Ky.* (1917); *Trans. Ky. State Medic. Soc.*, 1875; H. A. Kelly and W. L. Burrage, *Am. Medic. Biogs.* (1920); the *Louisville Commercial,* Feb. 11, 1874.] J. M. P.

MILLER, HENRY (Feb. 1, 1860–Apr. 9, 1926), actor-manager, was born in London, England, the child of John Miller, a railroad contractor, and Sophia (Newton) Miller. The family moved to Toronto, Canada, before Henry was thirteen, and he was but fifteen when he attended, in Montreal, a performance of *Romeo and Juliet* which determined his career. There and then he decided to be an actor; by eighteen he was on the stage; within thirteen years thereafter he had become "leading man" in support of such established "stars" as Helena Modjeska, Adelaide Neilson, Clara Morris, Mme. Janauschek, and Dion Boucicault. He then received from the best players and directors in America a thorough training both in the older classical tradition and in the heavily emotional, or sentimental, drama then in vogue. It was, however, to Dion Boucicault that he looked back with the truest admiration and affection almost as pupil to master, regarding him as the great example of all-around "man of the theatre"—actor, manager, director, playwright. It can hardly be questioned that Boucicault's varied career was the immediate inspiration of his own. Henry Miller was a "man of the theatre" in the fullest and most honorable sense of that phrase; his love for the theatre was as deep as his knowledge of it was profound. His career falls naturally into three main divisions: his connection as leading man with the Empire Theatre Stock Company of New York, in the early nineties; his period of stardom; and, finally, the fulfilment of his life's ambitions as an actor-manager.

As leading man of the Empire Theatre Stock Company, he first became nationally known as a forceful and finished actor, scoring one personal success after another in plays of such varying value as *The Younger Son, Sowing the Wind, The Masqueraders, Sweet Lavendar, The Importance of Being Earnest,* and *Michael and His Lost Angel.* The reputation thus gained could, in those days, when the individual "star" ruled the American stage, lead to but one result. In 1899, at the Herald Square Theatre, the name "Henry Miller" appeared in electric lights as star of *The Only Way,* a drama extracted from *A Tale of Two Cities,* in which Miller's performance of the romantically tragic rôle of Sidney Carton was widely admired. The play ran for three years, in New York and on the road, and was followed by other, less impressive, stellar vehicles, such as *D'Arcy of the Guards* and *Heartsease.* Up to this point Miller's career, while successful, had followed conventional lines; but he was now, in his maturity, to prove that his love for the theatre (and, more specifically, for the American theatre) was a deeper thing than the normal stellar desire for continued personal popularity in "vehicles" specially manufactured for him and his too easily contented public. In the autumn of 1906 he entered upon his final phase as actor-manager and director, producing at the Princess Theatre the first prose play of an American poet, William Vaughn Moody's *The Great Divide.* Never was play more happily named, for its production marked a new era in the history of the American stage. Leaving ultimate values out of the question, *The Great Divide* was an enormous advance artistically upon contemporary American play writing; it took insight and courage and taste to back and produce and direct it successfully; and if the American theatre owes much to William Vaughn Moody, it owes hardly less to his manager, director, and "star."

The amazing popularity of this play—then considered so daringly unconventional—firmly established Miller as actor-manager and made possible his excellent production of other dramas. In 1908 he dared greatly again, and brought forward Charles Rann Kennedy's symbolic drama *The Servant in the House*—which made, at the time, a profound impression and scored an emphatic popular success, and in 1910 he produced Moody's far less successful, though possibly more valuable, second play, *The Faith Healer.* The production of *The Great Divide, The Servant in the House,* and *The Faith Healer,* form unquestionably the climax of Henry Miller's career. He was to produce and appear in many another successful play—*The Rainbow, Daddy Longlegs, The Famous Mrs. Fair, The Changelings*—but he will be remembered longest and most justly and gratefully for his faith in and successful championship of *The Great Divide.* He made his first appearance in London in 1909, when he presented both *The Great Divide* and *The Servant in the House.* His last productions were made at the Henry Miller Theatre, designed and built under his personal supervision in 1918. His last illness, pneumonia, struck him down suddenly on the eve of a new production at this theatre; he rose from bed, hoping to play his part, but collapsed on reaching his dressing-room. Death followed within the week. He was survived by his wife, Helen (Stoepel) Miller, whom he married on Feb. 1, 1884, and by three children.

[*Who's Who in America,* 1924–25; J. B. Clapp and E. F. Edgett, *Players of the Present,* pt. 2 (1900); John Parker, *Who's Who in the Theatre* (1922); *N. Y. Times,* Apr. 2, 7, 1918, Apr. 10, 12, 18, 1926; *N. Y. Herald Tribune,* Apr. 18, 1926.] L. W. D.

MILLER, JAMES RUSSELL (Mar. 20, 1840–July 2, 1912), Presbyterian clergyman, editor, author, was born at Harshaville, Beaver County, Pa., the eldest of the seven children of James Alexander and Eleanor (Creswell) Miller who survived infancy. His father was a country miller and devout elder in the Associate Reformed Church. His mother's grandfather, Thomas McCarrell, a Scotch resident of Ireland, visited America in 1777 on his uncle's ship and remained to serve in the American army during the Revolution, and later to live in Washington

County, Pa., as an elder in the "Seceder" Church. Among McCarrell's descendants were seven clergymen. James Russell Miller attributed to his boyhood home the religious impulses which signally characterized his life. A significant influence was his parents' lifelong habit of visiting the homes of neighbors far and near on every occasion of trouble and sorrow.

His education was received at district schools in Beaver County, Pa., and near Calcutta, Ohio, to which state the family removed when he was about fourteen years old; at Beaver Academy; at Westminster College, New Wilmington, Pa., from which he was graduated in 1862; and at Allegheny Theological Seminary of the United Presbyterian Church, where he completed the course in 1867. Early revealing a deep religious nature, in 1857 he united with the Associate Reformed Church, which in 1858 joined with other groups in forming the United Presbyterian Church. During his academy course he taught a term of school at Industry, Pa., and one at Calcutta, Ohio. His seminary course was interrupted, 1863–65, by work among the soldiers for the United States Christian Commission, eventually as general field agent with scores of workers under his direction. Ordained a minister in 1867, he was in charge of the First United Presbyterian Church, New Wilmington, Pa., 1867–69, and of the following Presbyterian churches: Bethany, Philadelphia, 1869–78; Broadway, Rock Island, Ill., 1878–80; Hollond, Philadelphia, 1881–83 and 1886–97; and St. Paul's, Philadelphia, which he organized, 1898–1912. His work was marked by unusual success with young people, by building weak churches into strong organizations, by remarkably effective and numerous pastoral calls, most of which were made at night, and by extensive personal correspondence, which required the writing of thousands of letters during his lifetime.

In 1880 he began editorial work for the Presbyterian Board of Publication, Philadelphia. As the board's editorial superintendent from 1887 until his death, he edited hundreds of books and all the periodicals, to many of which he contributed regularly; he increased the number of Sunday-school publications from five to eighteen, and founded and edited the magazine *Forward,* which at his death had a weekly circulation of nearly half a million copies. His *Week-Day Religion,* published in 1880, was the first of more than sixty devotional books from his pen. One of the best known of these was his eight-volume *Devotional Hours with the Bible* (1909–13), which attained a sale of more than two million copies during his lifetime and was translated into many languages. He was widely regarded as the most popular religious writer of his day.

In all his activities he was known for his manifold and tireless labors, his sound judgment, simplicity, sympathy, and boundless faith. On June 22, 1870, he married Louise E. King of Argyle, N. Y.

[J. T. Faris, *The Life of Dr. J. R. Miller* (1912), includes a list of Miller's published books and the names of periodicals he edited; see also *Action of the Presbyterian Board of Publication—Life and Service of J. R. Miller, D.D.* (1912); *Who's Who in America,* 1910–11; the *Presbyterian,* July 10, 1912.] P. P. F.

MILLER, JOAQUIN [See MILLER, CINCINNATUS HINER, 1839–1913.]

MILLER, JOHN (Nov. 25, 1781–Mar. 18, 1846), congressman and governor of Missouri, was born in Berkeley County, Va. (now W. Va.). At the age of twenty-two he went to Steubenville, Ohio, where he became editor and publisher of the *Western Herald,* developed a superior literary style, and became deeply interested in all frontier problems, especially in military matters. Shortly before the War of 1812 he was appointed general in the Ohio militia, and then served during that war as colonel of the 19th United States Infantry. His regiment won special commendation for courage and discipline from General William Henry Harrison. At the close of the war he was ordered to duty in Missouri. In 1818 (Heitman, *post*) he resigned from the army and in 1821 (Houck, *post,* p. 184) became register of the land office at Franklin, Howard County, Mo., a position which he held until 1825.

On the death of Gov. Frederick Bates in 1825, he was elected to serve the unexpired term, and was reëlected in 1828 without opposition for the full four-year term. Thus he became the only governor of Missouri to serve more than one term. Although he deplored narrow partisanship he was ordinarily classed as a Jacksonian Democrat. He brought to the office of governor talents of a high order. His public policies and addresses manifested a grasp of frontier problems, social forces, legal principles, educational needs, and financial affairs. It was also his good fortune to be able to express his thoughts in clear and vigorous English. During his administration David Barton and Thomas H. Benton labored to draw party lines more closely and aspired to the political leadership of the state. Miller, however, disliked this emphasis on partisanship, and was, for several years, able to assert a leadership superior to theirs. Placing ability above political considerations, he appointed such men as Spencer Pettis, John C. Edwards, and Hamilton R. Gamble to the highest state offices. Among the major policies advocated by Miller were: a well-organized and trained militia, the withdrawal of state paper money from circulation, combined state and federal protection of trade and travel on the Santa Fé trail, the establishment of a state library and college, and the exclusion by the federal governments of all British traders from the Rocky Mountain fur-trading region. During his administration thousands of immigrants settled in the state, and Missouri grew prosperous. He proved to be an unusually faithful guardian of the state treasury.

After he retired from the governorship, he spent four years of quiet private life at Fayette. In 1836 he was elected to congress, and served three consecutive terms, at the end of which he voluntarily retired. Aside from advocating federal improvement and maintenance of the navigation facilities of the Missouri and the Mississippi rivers, and consistently opposing the growing tendency toward sectionalism and bitter partisanship, his congressional career was inconspicuous. He died near Florissant in St. Louis County. He was never married.

[*The Messages and Proclamations of the Gov. of . . . Mo.*, ed. by Buel Leopard and F. C. Shoemaker, esp. biog. by P. S. Rader, vol. I (1922); F. B. Heitman, *Hist. Register and Dict. of the U. S. Army* (1903), vol. I; H. L. Conard, *Encyc. of the Hist. of Mo.* (1901), vol IV; *Biog. Dir. Am. Cong.* (1928); Louis Houck, *A Hist. of Mo.* (1908), vol. III; *Jeffersonian Republican* (Jefferson, Mo.), Aug. 31, 1833, Jan. 30, 1836, Feb. 10, Sept. 22, 1838, June 4, 1842; *Jefferson City Inquirer*, Mar. 25, 1846; *Boonville Weekly Observer*, May 29, July 17, 1844, Mar. 24, 31, 1846; *Boonville Western Emigrant*, Jan. 24, 1839; *Boonville Weekly Advertiser*, Mar. 16, 1923, all of Missouri.]

H. E. N.

MILLER, JOHN (Apr. 6, 1819–Apr. 14, 1895), Presbyterian clergyman, son of Rev. Samuel [*q.v.*] and Sarah (Sergeant) Miller, was born at Princeton, N. J. On his father's side his ancestry went back to John Miller, a native of Scotland, who came to America in 1710 and married Mary Bass, great-grand-daughter of John and Priscilla Alden. It included a number of scholarly clergymen. On his mother's side he was descended from a line of patriots, his maternal grandfather being Jonathan Dickinson Sergeant [*q.v.*], a member of the Continental Congress and attorney-general of Pennsylvania. His father was the renowned first professor of church history at Princeton Theological Seminary. Consequently, the son was brought up in surroundings of earnest Christian piety, yet with intimate knowledge of the many forms in which that piety has been expressed through the ages. He secured his preparatory education at the Edgehill Boarding School, Princeton, and graduated from Princeton College in 1836. For a year he served with ability as an assistant to Prof. Joseph Henry [*q.v.*] in preparation for becoming a professor of natural philosophy. In later years he was the first person to urge the creation at Princeton of a research university, thereby initiating a movement out of which has grown the Princeton Graduate College.

As the result of his conversion at a revival, he decided to go into the ministry and in 1838 entered Princeton Theological Seminary, graduating in 1841, but remaining another year for special study. On Oct. 30, 1843, he was ordained by the Presbytery of Baltimore and served for five years as pastor of the Presbyterian Church at Frederick, Md. From 1850 to 1855 he was in charge of the West Arch Street Presbyterian Church, Philadelphia, and then for eight years he supplied churches in the Valley of Virginia while he devoted himself to study and writing, serving also in 1861–62 as captain of artillery and chaplain in the Confederate army. From 1863 to 1871 he was pastor of the Second Presbyterian Church of Petersburg, Va. In the latter year he took up his residence in Princeton, where he remained the rest of his life. As the result of his views on immortality, the human nature of Christ, and the nature of the Godhead which he expressed in *Questions Awakened by the Bible* (1877), he was suspended by the Presbytery of New Brunswick and the synod of New Jersey, and after the General Assembly refused to sustain an appeal he withdrew from the Presbyterian Church (1877). His defense at the Assembly was considered a masterpiece of argument and eloquence and he succeeded in retaining the personal friendship of his stanchest theological opponents because of the humility of his character and benevolence of his life.

In 1880 he built at Princeton an independent church, and later established several mission stations in connection with it, of which he served as pastor till his death in 1895. In 1893 he was received into the ministry of the Cumberland Presbyterian Church, giving to it his Princeton church and its missions. This denomination united with the Presbyterian Church in 1906, thus by implication restoring Miller to good standing in the latter. His tombstone in the cemetery at Princeton is a recumbent cross made of great blocks of stone on each of which is chiseled one article of his creed, carefully supported by a subsidiary statement.

Miller was a prolific writer, his chief works being: *Fetich in Theology* (2nd edition 1922); *Is God a Trinity?* (3rd edition 1922); *The Design of the Church* (1846); *A Commentary on Proverbs* (1872); *Metaphysics* (1875); *The Old*

Church Creed (1879); *Commentary on Romans* (1887); "Seven Failures of Ultra-Calvinism," *Cumberland Presbyterian Review,* 1892. In these works he taught the following doctrines: (1) that although Jesus Christ was incorrupt, yet, having the sin of Adam imputed to him, he needed for salvation a ransom as all sinners do—even that of his own death on the cross; (2) that Jesus Christ and Jehovah are one person, and the Godhead is not a Trinity; (3) that Jesus Christ has two consciousnesses—one omniscient and the other ignorant, and two wills—one sovereign and one dependent,—although they interact harmoniously in the execution of his work as one redeemer; (4) that God saves and damns not for his own glory, but for the sake of righteousness—why one sinner should be selected to accept salvation in Christ and be saved rather than another being left a mystery when viewed as an act of God, but as the result of the gradual improvement in the moral character of the sinner when viewed as an act of man; (5) that every soul goes out of existence between death and the return of Christ to judge the world, when misery and happiness will be proportioned to the characters of the souls. These doctrines he upheld by a great array of Biblical proof-texts, at times as translated by himself; by references to the great symbols of the Reformed faith of the Presbyterian Church, to which symbols he considered himself essentially loyal; and by a careful exposition of the contradiction inherent in the Reformed faith as set forth in the *Systematic Theology* of Dr. Charles Hodge [*q.v.*], then professor of systematic theology at Princeton Theological Seminary, the most authoritative exposition of that faith in the Presbyterian Church at the time. Unfortunately, Miller was not aware of the contradictions inherent in his own doctrines and often wrote in a style made obscure by condensations and by passion.

He was twice married: first, Sept. 24, 1844, to Margaret Benedict, who died Sept. 5, 1852; and second, Nov. 3, 1856, to Sally Campbell Preston McDowell, daughter of James McDowell [*q.v.*], governor of Virginia.

[*Necrological Report . . . Princeton Theological Seminary,* 1896; letters from Miller's daughter, Miss Margaret Miller, in the files of the Princeton University Alumni office; F. B. Lee, *Geneal. and Personal Memorial of Mercer County, N. J.* (1907), vol. I; *Records of the Presbytery of New Brunswick in the Case of Rev. John Miller* (1877); *Minutes of the General Assembly of the Presbyt. Church in the U. S. A.,* 1877–79, 1903–06; *Daily True American* (Trenton), Apr. 16, 1895.]

G. Y. R.

MILLER, JOHN FRANKLIN (Nov. 21, 1831–Mar. 8, 1886), United States senator, was born at South Bend, Ind., the eldest son of William and Mary (Miller) Miller. His father was of Swiss stock, which had established itself in Virginia in search of religious freedom as early as 1800. On the mother's side he came of Scotch ancestry, identified with American affairs as early as the War of 1812, in which his grandfather served as colonel. His boyhood was spent in South Bend where he entered the academy at the age of fourteen, devoting his summers to work on the farm. In 1848 he became a student in the Hatheway Mathematical and Classical School in Chicago and a year later returned to South Bend, where he began to read law with Judge Elisha Egbert. His law studies were continued in the State and National Law School at Ballston Spa, N. Y., and in 1852 the degree of LL.B. was conferred upon him. He was admitted to the bar and opened his first law office in South Bend in partnership with Joseph Defrees. When ill health made a change advisable Miller joined the emigrants bound for California by way of Nicaragua. In March 1853, he arrived in Napa where his legal ability won him much prestige and a partnership with Judge John Currey of San Francisco. Six months after his arrival in California he was made county treasurer, an office which he held for two years. In 1855 ill health again forced him to make a change, and he returned to South Bend. Here affiliating himself in his profession with Norman Eddy, he continued his practice until 1861, when he became state senator, and was with one exception the youngest member of that body. In 1857, during this period of residence in South Bend, he married Mary Chess of Pennsylvania. One son and one daughter were born of the marriage.

With the opening of the Civil War Miller resigned his seat in the legislature, and on Aug. 27, 1861, received his commission as colonel of the 29th Indiana Volunteers. He was wounded in the battle of Stone River and again at Liberty Gap, Tennessee, in both instances distinguishing himself by his ability and courage. On Jan. 5, 1864, he was made brigadier-general of volunteers, and later, following the battle of Nashville, in which he had been in command of a division, was brevetted a major-general "for gallant and meritorious services." At the close of the war he was offered a colonelcy in the United States army, but declined and returned to California. For the next four years he served under appointment from President Johnson as collector of the port of San Francisco, refusing reappointment to accept the presidency of the Alaska Commercial Company. For a period of twelve stormy years, beginning with its incorporation in 1869, he led this very active organization in its program of control of the fur industry of the Pribilof or Seal Islands. In spite of strong competitors, who fought the monopoly of the Alaska Commercial Company with bitter opposition, this company paid into the federal treasury more than twice the amount expected under the agreement and apparently complied scrupulously with the stipulations of its contract.

Miller served as a member of the California state constitutional convention of 1878–79. His eminence in his profession, coupled with his active interest in political affairs, led to his election as United States senator from California (Republican) in 1880, in which capacity he served until his death. He is chiefly known for the active part he took in the anti-Chinese legislation which reached its culmination during his term of office. His name is closely linked with the successful effort to modify the Burlingame Treaty with China and also with the Exclusion Bill of 1882. He died in Washington, D. C., in March 1886. His body was interred in Laurel Hill Cemetery, San Francisco, but in 1913 was removed to Arlington Cemetery, Virginia.

[*Biog. Dir. Am. Cong.* (1928); *Biog. and Geneal. Hist. of Wayne, Fayette, Union and Franklin Counties, Ind.* (1899), vol. II; *A Biog. Hist. of Eminent and Self-Made Men . . . of Ind.* (1880), vol. II; H. H. Bancroft, *Hist. of Alaska, 1730–1885* (1886); "The Alaska Commercial Company," *House Report 623*, 44 Cong., 1 Sess.; *Cong. Record*, 49 Cong., 1 Sess.; W. H. Miller, *Hist. and Geneals. of the Families of Miller, Woods, Harris* (1907); *Evening Star* (Wash., D. C.), Mar. 8, 1886.] R. G. C—d.

MILLER, JOHN HENRY (Mar. 12, 1702–Mar. 31, 1782), printer, editor, and publisher, was born at Rheden in the principality of Waldeck, Germany, where his parents then resided. When they returned to their native town, near Zürich, Switzerland, in 1715, young Miller was apprenticed to a printer in Basel. Completing his apprenticeship, he went to Zürich as a journeyman, but soon opened a printing office of his own there and began the publication of a newspaper. Abandoning the business after a few years, he spent some time in travel. In 1741 he accompanied Count von Zinzendorf [*q.v.*] to Pennsylvania and for a short period worked as a journeyman in Franklin's printing shop in Philadelphia. He was back in Europe in 1742, and in 1744 opened a printing office in Marienburg, West Prussia, marrying there in that year Johanna Dorothea Blanner, a Swiss. He was a scholarly man and a good printer; his wife was equally gifted, being a woman of culture, who "spoke French fluently and was an excellent painter in water-colors" (Thomas, *post*, p. 255).

In 1751 he made a second visit to America and associated himself with Samuel Holland in Lancaster, Pa. The two founded *Die Lancastersche Zeitung*, a bilingual paper, the second of its kind in America, the first being Franklin's *Deutsche und Englische Zeitung*. Soon afterward, however, Miller went to Philadelphia where he found work in the printing house of William Bradford, 1721/22–1791 [*q.v.*]. He was again in Europe in 1754, and remained until 1760, when he recrossed the Atlantic, bringing with him equipment with which to set up a printing establishment in Philadelphia. In 1762 he began the publication of a newspaper, *Der Wöchentliche Staatsbote*, which he edited under the successive titles *Der Wöchentliche Philadelphische Staatsbote*, *Der Wöchentliche Pennsylvanische Staatsbote*, and *Henrich Miller's Pennsylvanische Staatsbote* until 1779. From his shop, also, a German almanac was issued each year. He printed a few books in both the German and English languages, chief among those in English being *Juvenile Poems* (1765), by the younger Thomas Godfrey [*q.v.*], which included "The Prince of Parthia," the first native play to be produced professionally in America.

In 1765, when the Stamp Act became operative, Miller announced that he would suspend his newspaper "until it would appear whether means can be found to escape the chains forged for the people and from unbearable slavery" (Daniel Miller, *post*, p. 27). This suspension continued from Oct. 31 to Nov. 18. On July 5, 1776, *Henrich Miller's Pennsylvanische Staatsbote* had the privilege of being first to announce to the world the adoption of the Declaration of Independence. Through the accident of circumstances it was the only newspaper then published in Philadelphia on Fridays, and July 4th that year fell upon Thursday. Unfortunately Miller was not able to give the text of the historic document until the following Tuesday, but on that day he printed it in large type as an extra leaf to his journal. From Sept. 17, 1777, to Aug. 5, 1778, the occupation of Philadelphia by the British troops forced suspension again. The British seized his press and materials and removed them to New York, but after the enemy left Philadelphia Miller succeeded in reëstablishing himself and his paper. On May 26, 1779, he retired from business and removed to the Moravian settlement of Bethlehem, Pa., where he died. He was a pedestrian of note; even when he was advanced in years he would occasionally walk from Philadelphia to Bethlehem, a distance of fifty-three miles.

[C. S. R. Hildeburn, *A Century of Printing: The Issues of the Press in Pa., 1685–1784,* vol. II (1886); Daniel Miller, "Early German-American Newspapers," *The Pa.-German Soc., Proc. and Addresses,* vol. XIX (1910); Augustus Schultze, "The Old Moravian Cemetery of Bethlehem, Pa.," *Ibid.,* vol. XXI (1912); C. F. Dapp, "The Evolution of an American Patriot: Being an Intimate Study of the Patriotic Activities of John Henry Miller," *Ibid.,* vol. XXXII (1924); "William McCulloch's Additions to Thomas's Hist. of Printing," *Proc. Am. Antiquarian Soc.,* vol. XXI, pt. 1 (1922); Isaiah Thomas, *The Hist. of Printing in America* (2nd ed., 1874), I, 253–55; Oswald Seidensticker, *The First Century of German Printing in America, 1728–1830* (1893); C. F. Dapp, "Johann Heinrich Miller," *German American Annals,* May–Aug., 1916.] J. J.

MILLER, JOHN PETER (Dec. 25, 1709–Sept. 25, 1796), German Reformed clergyman, later head of the Ephrata Community of Seventh Day Baptists, was born in Germany, probably at Zweikirchen, near Zweibrücken, where his father, Johann Müller, was the Reformed pastor. In America he is best known by the anglicized form of his name, as given above; in the Ephrata Community he was called Brother Jabez. He matriculated Dec. 29, 1725, at the University of Heidelberg, his father then being pastor at Alsenborn, and on Aug. 29, 1730, he arrived at Philadelphia on the ship *Thistle* from Rotterdam.

The circumstances of his emigration are unknown, but it is likely that he was already somewhat heterodox, and that he had been in friendly relations with George Michael Weiss, who had come over earlier in 1730. Almost immediately on his arrival he was engaged as minister by the Reformed people of Philadelphia and Germantown and by the anti-Boehm faction at Skippack, and applied for ordination to the Presbyterian Synod. The Synod referred his case to the Presbytery of Philadelphia, the members of which were astonished by Miller's learning, especially by his ability to speak Latin and by the erudition displayed in his answer to a question on Justification. Meanwhile, on Oct. 19, Miller called on John Philip Boehm [*q.v.*], who curtly advised him to seek ordination from the Dutch Reformed clergy of New York; Miller, however, was in a hurry and denied that the Dutch church authorities had any jurisdiction in Pennsylvania. He was ordained Nov. 20, 1730, by three Presbyterian ministers, Jedediah Andrews, Adam Boyd, and Gilbert Tennent [*q.v.*]. In the fall of 1731 he withdrew into the interior and began ministering to the Reformed congregations at Goshenhoppen, Tulpehocken, and along the Conestoga. From the beginning he and Boehm were antagonistic.

Very early he came under the influence of Johann Conrad Beissel [*q.v.*], who was eager to make a convert of him. In May 1735 Miller publicly renounced the Reformed Church and was rebaptized by trine immersion. This event, which came as a surprise to everyone except Boehm, created a huge sensation, seriously threatening for a while the existence of the Reformed Church, for Miller was reputed to be the most learned theologian in the province, and his prestige was great. A number of families and individuals followed him into Beissel's society, among them no less a person than Johann Conrad Weiser [*q.v.*]. From May to November 1735 Miller lived as a hermit on the bank of the Mühlbach, a tributary of the Tulpehocken. Like the other solitary brethren, he was called in by Beissel as soon as the cloister at Ephrata was ready for occupancy, and from then till his death sixty-one years later he lived in the Ephrata Community. In the autumn of 1744 he went to Connecticut and Rhode Island to visit several groups of Rogerines. On Beissel's death July 6, 1768, he succeeded him as head of the Community. Apparently he acted as editor of the various books issued by the cloister press, translated J. T. V. Braght's famous work on the Mennonite martyrs from Dutch into German as *Der Blütige Schau-Platz oder Martyrer Spiegel* (1748), perhaps the largest book to come from the colonial press, and may have been part-author of the *Chronicon Ephratense* (1786). He became a member of the American Philosophical Society, counted Francis Hopkinson, Benjamin Franklin, and George Washington among his acquaintances, and was highly regarded for his attainments and character. He was engaged by the Continental Congress to translate the Declaration of Independence into several European languages. The Ephrata Community gained no new members under his régime, and as the infirmities of age crept upon the brethren it steadily declined. Miller died in his eighty-seventh year and was buried beside Beissel in the cloister cemetery.

[J. F. Sachse, *The German Sectarians of Pa., 1708–1800* (2 vols., privately printed, 1899–1900) is the fullest account, but for Miller's career prior to 1735, see W. J. Hinke, *Life and Letters of the Rev. John Philip Boehm* (1916). For autobiographical material, see *Chronicon Ephratense . . . Zusamen getragen von Br. Lamech u. Agrippa* (1786), tr. by J. Max Hark (1889), and Miller's letter in the *Hallesche Nachrichten,* vol. I (new ed., ed. by W. J. Mann and B. M. Schmucker, 1886). See also "Letter of Peter Miller . . . to James Read, 1776," *Pa. Mag.,* XXXVIII (1914), 227; "Description of the Grotto at Swatara," by the Rev. Peter Miller, communicated by Wm. Barton, *Trans. Am. Phil. Soc.,* II (1786), 177–78; "A Method of Preserving Pease from the Worms," . . . communicated by Charles Thomson, *Ibid.,* I (1789), 313–14; "Original Letters of Peter Miller," Samuel Hazard, *Hazard's Reg. of Pa.,* Mar. 28, Oct. 17, 1835.] G. H. G.

MILLER, JONATHAN PECKHAM (Feb. 24, 1796–Feb. 17, 1847), Greek sympathizer and anti-slavery advocate, was born in Randolph, Vt., the son of Heman and Deimia (Walbridge) Miller (Vital Records, Office of the Secretary of State, Montpelier, Vt.). Upon his father's death in 1799 he was taken in charge by an uncle, Jonathan Peckham, and on the latter's death, about 1805, by Capt. John Granger of Randolph. In 1813, having completed his common-school education, young Miller went to Woodstock, Vt., to learn the tanner's trade, but ill health soon caused him to return to the Granger home where he remained for the next four years. A love of adventure and military life, as well as patriotism, led him to join the town volunteers under Capt. Libbeus Egerton who marched to repel the British invasion that ended at Plattsburg. The Randolph forces arrived too late, however, to take part in the fighting. In 1817, he enlisted as a private in the United States army, in which he served for two years, being stationed on the northern frontier. A recurrence of ill health then caused his return to Randolph, where he attended the local academy and fitted for college. In the fall of 1821 he entered Dartmouth, but a few weeks later removed to the University of Vermont, where he pursued his studies until May 24, 1824, when fire destroyed the college buildings. Rather than wait to finish his college course at Vermont, or transfer elsewhere, he now determined to offer his services to the Greek revolutionists, inspired, no doubt, by his classical studies, by the wave of sympathy for Greece then at its height in western Europe and the United States, and by his own spirit of adventure. From Governor Van Ness he secured a letter introducing him to the Greek Association of Boston, which in turn gave him letters to the Greek government at Missolonghi, as well as $300 for his expenses.

He sailed for Malta Aug. 21, 1824, and from there made his way to Missolonghi, where he reported to Dr. Mayer and Gen. George Jarvis, on whose staff he became a colonel in the Greek service. During the next two years Miller's military exploits won for him the name of "The American Dare Devil." He was among those who took part in the valiant but futile defense of Missolonghi, escaping in the last sortie. A few months later he returned to the United States to lecture throughout the northern and middle states in the Greek cause. In February 1827, he returned to Greece as principal agent of the New York Greek Committee. In this service he spent about a year, turning over to the Greeks food and clothing to the value of more than $75,000. On returning to America, he published *The Condition of Greece in 1827 and 1828* (1828), being his journal as kept by order of the Greek Committee. At this time he brought back with him a Greek youth, Lucas Miltiades, whom he adopted and educated. He also brought to the United States the sword worn by Lord Byron in Greece, now in the possession of the Vermont Historical Society.

After his second return from Greece, he settled in Montpelier, Vt., studied law, was admitted to the bar, and opened a law office in company with Nicholas Baylies. For three years, 1831, 1832, and 1833, he served in the Vermont legislature, and in 1833 initiated the anti-slavery movement in the legislature by introducing a resolution calling upon the Vermont representatives in Congress to urge the abolition of slavery and the slave trade in the District of Columbia. From this time on, Miller devoted much of his energy and money to the anti-slavery cause, lecturing throughout the state. In 1840, as one of the two Vermont delegates, he attended the World's Anti-Slavery Convention in London where he took a prominent part in the debates.

As a public speaker, he was off-hand, bold and earnest. His private life was characterized by a fearless utterance of opinion and a straightforward, unstudied frankness. To these qualities he added a vigorous physical constitution and a soldierly bearing that some thought bordered on roughness. As a citizen he was public-spirited and benevolent. Samuel Gridley Howe [*q.v.*], with whom Miller was closely associated, describes him as "rather superficially than well educated, with an immense deal of good common sense, an acute mind, but self-opinionated, and bigoted in religion, which he reads and argues about rather to confirm his belief than to examine the subject" (Richards, *post,* p. 120). He died prematurely in Montpelier as the result of an accidental injury to his spine, leaving a wife and one child. He had married Sarah Arms, daughter of Capt. Jonathan Arms, on June 26, 1828.

[Material for the above was drawn in part from the sketch of Col. Miller's life found in D. P. Thompson, *Hist. of the Town of Montpelier* (1860); the same sketch appears in A. M. Hemenway, *Vt. Hist. Gazetteer,* vol. IV (1882), p. 457. For further light on Miller's Greek adventure consult his *Condition of Greece in 1827 and 1828* (1828) mentioned above, and *Letters from Greece* (1825) by Miller and others. See also L. E. Richards, *Letters and Journals of Samuel Gridley Howe: The Greek Revolution* (1906); M. A. Cline, *Am. Attitude toward the Greek War of Independence* (1930); E. M. Earle, "American Interest in the Greek Cause 1821–1827," in *Am. Hist. Rev.,* Oct. 1927; *Vt. Patriot* (Montpelier), Feb. 18, 1847.] W. R. W.

MILLER, LESLIE WILLIAM (Aug. 5, 1848–Mar. 7, 1931), educator in the field of industrial art, was born in Brattleboro, Vt., the son of Nathan and Hannah (Works) Miller. He was a descendant of James Miller, a Scotsman, who was admitted to the First Church, Charlestown, Mass., in 1676, and made a freeman in 1677. His grandson, Isaac, laid out the town of Dummerston, Windham County, Vt. Leslie went to work in his father's harness shop at the age of twelve, but continued his education by reading and study, acquiring a good knowledge of Latin and other high-school subjects. His early interest in art manifested itself in spirited drawings with which he decorated the pages of his textbooks.

Upon attaining his majority, he found work in a japanning factory in Orange, Mass., where he painted baby carriages and decorated sewing machines. This occupation marked the turning point in his career, and he soon went to Boston where he could work during the day and attend drawing school at night. He enrolled in the first classes held in the School of the Museum of Fine Arts, and in 1875 graduated from the Massachusetts Normal Art School. The year preceding, Oct. 29, he had married Maria Persons of Boston. His original intention was to devote himself to portrait painting and he did some excellent work in this field, but circumstances drew him into teaching. While still pursuing his studies he became connected with the Boston schools, and later was instructor in the Salem Normal School and in Adams Academy, Quincy. In 1879 he joined the staff of the Summer Institute, Martha's Vineyard, as teacher of painting.

In Boston he had been closely associated with Walter Smith who had come from London to start a school of industrial art under the auspices of the state of Massachusetts. In 1880 the trustees of the School of Industrial Art, Philadelphia, established four years before, asked Smith to name some one who could reorganize the institution along broader lines and Smith recommended Miller. In the fall of 1880 he took charge of the school, which then had but a handful of students and little equipment. During the forty years he was at its head, it became one of the leading institutions in its field, and he left it with a faculty of forty and some thirteen hundred students. He made occasional contributions to periodicals and in 1887 published *The Essentials of Perspective.* His enthusiasm not only for industrial but also for municipal art led him to assume leadership in various city organizations. He was a member of the Municipal Art Jury of Philadelphia from the time of its organization in 1912 until his retirement in 1920, serving as its secretary during its formative period and thereafter as vice-president, By addresses, articles, and personal labors he furthered many of the important improvements effected in the municipality during his long residence there. He was secretary of the Fairmount Park Association from 1900 to 1920, and "the present Fairmount Parkway and the improvements on the banks of the Schuylkill . . . are in large measure a monument to his devotion to the cause of civic betterment" (*Proceedings of the American Philosophical Society, post,* p. 401). For fourteen years he was secretary of the Art Club of Philadelphia, of which he was one of the founders, and for twelve years its vice-president. In 1899 he was elected to the American Philosophical Society and was long one of its curators. The Art Club of Philadelphia awarded him, in 1920, its gold medal for "distinguished services," and the University of Pennsylvania, the unusual degree of doctor of fine arts.

After his retirement in 1920, he made his home on Martha's Vineyard Island. Here before the fireplace of his home hidden among the pine trees, surrounded by his books and his pictures, he spent his last days, maintaining his interest in public affairs and his genial, philosophic spirit to the end. He died in his eighty-third year, survived by two sons, and was buried in Oak Grove Cemetery, Vineyard Haven.

[A. M. Hemenway, *Vt. Hist. Gazetteer,* vol. V (1891), pt. 2; *Pa. Museum Bull.,* Oct. 1920; *Proc. Am. Phil. Soc.,* vol. LXX (1931); *Who's Who in America,* 1928–29; *N. Y. Times,* Mar. 8, 1931; information from a son, P. C. Miller.] D. G.

MILLER, LEWIS (July 24, 1829–Feb. 17, 1899), inventor, manufacturer, philanthropist, a founder of the Chautauqua, was born in Greentown, Ohio. His grandfather, Abraham Miller, emigrated from Zweibrücken in the Palatinate about 1776 and settled in Maryland. He served in the Continental Army during the Revolutionary War, engaged in many battles, and was at Valley Forge under Washington. In 1813 he bought land in Stark County, Ohio, near Canton, and became a farmer there. His son, John Miller, was a farmer and also a carpenter and cabinet-maker. In 1823 he married Mary Elizabeth York (Jorg), who died at the age of twenty-two, after the birth of their son Lewis. Although he did not have a college education, Lewis Miller was early interested in education and read widely. He taught school and built up a Sunday school of which he was superintendent for forty-five years. Following his mechanical inclinations, he entered the employment of the Ball brothers in Greentown who were manufacturing mowing machines and reapers. In 1852 he became a member of the firm, which, as Ball, Aultman & Company, established its plant in

Canton, Ohio. On Sept. 16, 1852, Miller was married to Mary Valinda Alexander and for the next eleven years they made their home in Canton. Upon the withdrawal of Ephraim Ball the firm became C. Aultman & Company. Miller's inventive genius enabled him to design several improvements in the implements manufactured by the company. Probably the most important were the double-jointed cutting-bar of the mowing machine, the "low down" binder, and a device for binding reaped grain with twine. Thanks to these and other inventions, the "Buckeye Machine" became popular and the business expanded rapidly. In 1863 an additional plant was built in Akron, Ohio, known as Aultman, Miller & Company. Miller managed this plant and maintained his residence in Akron until his death.

Miller displayed his creative and administrative powers in all his activities in business, civic, and religious affairs. As an employer, he anticipated some of the later reforms in industrial relations. As a citizen he was active in the municipal affairs of Akron, serving as president of the board of education, in which capacity he introduced a number of new and now commonly accepted ideas both in public school-house design and in teaching methods. In religion he was a Methodist, and as a member of the church he organized a large teachers' class and introduced normal training and an organized course of instruction for the Sunday school. Although not a trained architect, he originated the so-called Akron plan for church buildings, which was widely adopted in the construction of churches making special provision for Sunday schools. He promoted Mount Union College both financially and educationally, by serving as a member of the board of trustees from 1865 until his death in 1899.

But it was in the development of the Chautauqua Institution in New York that he made his most original contribution to the cause of popular education. He had conceived the idea of combining recreation and some form of education and in 1874 invited John H. Vincent [*q.v.*] to join in organizing a general assembly, as distinct from a Sunday-school teachers assembly, to meet in a grove on Lake Chautauqua. Under the creative influence of the two men, the Assembly became a pioneer in the establishment of adult education. In it were combined summer study, correspondence work, supervised reading, and the combination of recreation, physical training, popular lectures, religion, and music. In the development of this institution the two founders supplemented each other and refused to claim any but joint credit for its development. Miller was especially responsible for its financial support and administration, but he was by no means limited to such activity. He was constantly suggesting new plans and methods. The respect in which he was held by all those with whom he came into contact contributed not only to the success of an institution, but to the general development of educational theory and practice. The pressure of all these enterprises proved too much for even his exceptionally vigorous health, and he died, in New York City, in February 1899. He was survived by his wife and nine of his eleven children. One of his daughters married Thomas Alva Edison.

[Ellwood Hendrick, *Lewis Miller: A Biog. Essay* (1925); J. H. Vincent, *The Chautauqua Movement* (1886); J. L. Hurlbut, *The Story of Chautauqua* (1921); *The Biog. Cyc. and Portrait Gallery . . . of Ohio*, vol. I (1883); the *N. Y. Times*, Feb. 18, 1899; Patent Office records; information as to certain facts from members of the family.]

S. M.

MILLER, OLIVE THORNE [See MILLER, HARRIET MANN, 1831–1918].

MILLER, OLIVER (Apr. 15, 1824–Oct. 18, 1892), jurist, was born in Middletown, Conn., the son of Clarissa Miller (G. T. Chapman, *Sketches of the Alumni of Dartmouth College*, 1867). He received his elementary education in the public schools of that place and at the age of twelve entered the academy at Frederick, Md., of which his brother-in-law, Mr. Converse, was principal. At that time he became closely attached to the Converse family and, in later years, during his sister Emily's widowhood, he supported her as long as he lived and educated her children. In 1845 he entered Dartmouth College, graduating with distinction in 1848. He began reading law in the office of Alexander Randall in Annapolis soon afterward, and in 1850 was admitted to the bar. His career as a practising attorney was brief however, for by nature he preferred more exacting though less remunerative public service. In 1850–51 he reported four volumes of Maryland chancery decisions and mastered the technique of the profession. In 1852 he became reporter of the court of appeals and, in the following decade, edited volumes III–XVIII of the *Maryland Reports, Containing Cases Argued and Determined in the Court of Appeals of Maryland* (1853–1862). His peculiar fitness for such tasks now evinced itself, and these *Reports,* marked by logic, vigorous language, and directness, and still regarded as models, brought him to the favorable attention of lawyers throughout the East.

Miller was chosen a member of the Maryland constitutional convention of 1864 and played a prominent part in drafting the new organic law of the state. He represented Anne Arundel County in the House of Delegates from 1865 to 1867 and became speaker of that body in the latter year. Political life, with its intrigues and harassments by constituents, proved uncongenial to him, however, and in the election of November 1867, the first held under the constitution of 1867, he became candidate for the position of chief judge of the fifth judicial circuit (Anne Arundel, Howard, and Carroll counties), which automatically brought membership in the state court of appeals as associate judge. He was an easy victor and, upon the expiration of his term in 1882, was reëlected. It was during his quarter of a century on the bench that Miller won lasting distinction. He possessed a robust and virile intellect, a coldly analytical mind, an amazing memory, and was a master stylist; his opinions are among the best known in the judicial annals of Maryland and contributed in a marked degree to the high reputation which the decisions of the state court of appeals enjoy throughout the nation. Although he was of stern and forbidding exterior, the justice rendered by him was always tempered with mercy. Dignified, patient, independent, and inflexibly just, he exerted a profound personal influence upon the younger members of the bar, among whom his memory has continued a living force through four decades.

In 1874, he married Adeline Dewees (Piper) Green, widow of Lieut. Charles Green of the United States Navy, and opened a second home in Ellicott City, because of its central location on his circuit. They had no children. His wife died there in 1890. In September 1892, while at Ellicott City, Miller was stricken with paralysis and, resigning as of Oct. 1, died three weeks later.

[*The Debates of the Constitutional Convention of the State of Maryland . . . 1864* (3 vols., 1864); *Proc. of the State Convention of Md. to Frame a New Constitution* (1864); M. R. Hodges, *General Index of Wills of Anne Arundel County, Md., 1771–1917* (n.d.), p. 89; *Baltimore American*, Sept. 29, Oct. 19, 1892; the *Sun* (Baltimore), June 20, 1890, Sept. 29, Oct. 18, 19, 20, 22, 1892; *Ellicott City Times,* issues for June 1890 and Oct. 1892; *Anne Arundel Advertiser* (Annapolis), Oct. 6, 20, 27, 1892; *Evening Capital* (Annapolis), Sept. 28 and Oct. 19, 20, 22, 1892; Dartmouth College records; legal and legislative manuals.] L. J. R.

MILLER, PETER [See MILLER, JOHN PETER, 1709–1796].

MILLER, SAMUEL (Oct. 31, 1769–Jan. 7, 1850), Presbyterian clergyman, educator, author, was a son of Rev. John and Margaret (Millington) Miller, and a brother of Edward Miller [*q.v.*]. His grandfather, John Miller, a Scotchman, had emigrated to America in 1710 and was later a sugar refiner and distiller. Samuel's paternal grandmother was a great-grand-daughter of John Alden. He was born near Dover, Del., received his education chiefly at home from his father and brothers, pursued the studies of the senior year in the University of Pennsylvania (1788–89), and then studied theology under his father and after his death in 1791, under Rev. Charles Nisbet, first principal of Dickinson College. On June 5, 1793, he was ordained to the Presbyterian ministry and became associated with Dr. John Rodgers and Dr. John McKnight in a collegiate pastorate of the Presbyterian congregations of New York City. For years he urged a separation of the three churches—Wall Street, Brick, and Rutgers Street—and he regarded his efforts to this end, achieved in 1809, as his most important service in New York. Thereafter, until 1813, he acted as sole pastor of the Wall Street congregation, which later became the First Presbyterian Church. After 1813 he was professor of church history and government in Princeton Theological Seminary, of which he had been one of the founders.

He owed much of his fame to his extraordinary energy and activity. For many years he delivered several long addresses a week, made frequent and prolonged pastoral calls, conducted a voluminous correspondence, and in addition contributed to the religious press and published dozens of books and pamphlets. His success in preserving his never robust health during these labors is ascribed to his exact and systematic ordering of every detail of each day. His literary activities made him widely known in America and Great Britain. Following the appearance of his *Brief Retrospect of the Eighteenth Century* (1803), a scholarly two-volume work published before he was thirty-five years old, he received the honorary degree of doctor of divinity from Union College and from the University of Pennsylvania, and was made a corresponding member of the Philological Society of Manchester, England. Though his larger literary productions were mainly historical and biographical, his writings covered a broad range. His early pamphlets discussed slavery, suicide, novel-reading, education of students for the ministry, and other diverse topics. At Princeton he wrote on such multifarious subjects as Free Masonry, sea kale, social amusements, religious fasting, domestic happiness, temperance, and the theatre. Notable among the books published by him during this period are *The Medical Works of Edward Miller, M.D.* (1814); "Life of Jonathan Edwards," in Sparks's *Library of American Biography,* vol. VIII (1837); *Memoir of the Rev. Charles Nisbet, D.D.* (1840); *Letters from a*

Father to His Sons in College (1843), and *Thoughts on Public Prayer* (1849).

In 1809 he became chaplain of the first regiment of New York State artillery, and he was long official historian of the Presbyterian General Assembly, which in 1806 made him its moderator. He was a trustee of Columbia College and of the College of New Jersey, a founder and later a president of the New York Bible Society, a founder and corresponding secretary of the New York Historical Society, and a corresponding member of the Massachusetts Historical Society. He impressed his contemporaries by his cultured and urbane manner; he was at home in any circle. Somewhat lacking in imagination, he had a quick perception, a retentive memory, sound judgment, and much common sense. He was an acceptable but not a striking preacher; his sermons were well considered and evenly balanced. At Princeton he left a tradition of clear and intelligent teaching and of ability to retain the confidence and affection of his students. On Oct. 24, 1801, he married Sarah, daughter of Jonathan Dickinson Sergeant [*q.v.*], attorney-general of Pennsylvania. They had ten children, one of whom was Rev. John Miller [*q.v.*].

[F. B. Lee, *Geneal. and Personal Memorial of Mercer County, N. J.* (1907), vol. I; Samuel Miller, *The Life of Samuel Miller, D.D., LL.D.* (1869); W. B. Sprague, *Annals Am. Pulpit*, vol. III (1858) and *A Discourse Commemorative of the Rev. Samuel Miller, D.D.* (1850); John DeWitt, *The Intellectual Life of Samuel Miller* (1906), reprinted from the *Princeton Theological Rev.*, Apr. 1906; Margaret Miller, "A List of the Writings of Samuel Miller," *Ibid.*, Oct. 1911; *No. Am. and U. S. Gazette* (Phila.), Jan. 9, 1850; *Christian Observer* (Phila.), Jan. 12, 1850.] P. P. F.

MILLER, SAMUEL (Oct. 4, 1820–Oct. 24, 1901), horticulturist, was born in Lancaster, Pa. While a young man, he moved to Avon, Lebanon County. Here he served as justice of the peace in 1840 and 1845, and in 1847 married Martha Isabel Evans, who became the mother of nine children. His horticultural work was begun probably several years before the Concord grape was introduced in 1854 (U. P. Hedrick, *Grapes of New York*, 1908, p. 488). Miller later stated that he was the first man in Pennsylvania to fruit the Concord grape before it was offered to the public, as well as the well-known seedling grapes introduced by Edward S. Rogers of Salem, Mass. (*40th Annual Report of the State Horticultural Society of Missouri, 1897*, 1898, p. 70).

In 1867, he moved to Bluffton, Montgomery County, Mo., where he lived until his death. Here his horticultural experiments were carried on with increased energy, and from his gardens many plants were disseminated, either of his own breeding or from selections he had made. His best known plant contribution is perhaps the Captain Jack strawberry, a chance seedling found on his farm about 1870 (U. P. Hedrick, *The Small Fruits of New York*, 1925, p. 411). Captain Jack soon became a standard sort, especially in the Rocky Mountain states. It was not only a hardy, drouth resistant variety but commonly served as a pollinizer for the much more famous strawberry Crescent. Most of his plant-breeding work was practised with grapes, and about a half-dozen varieties which he developed found a degree of prominence in the horticultural lists of the times. One particularly, Martha, was for a time the most popular of the green grapes. He also originated or introduced several minor sorts of raspberries. At the time of his death he was engaged in an attempt to improve the native persimmon and had selected a number of promising varieties.

His greatest contribution to horticulture and to the welfare of mankind lies not in the plants he bred so much as in his extensive testing of various types and varieties of fruits and ornamental plants sent him by their owners. His knowledge of varieties and values was considerable and his carefully considered opinions were frequently sought, particularly in the states adjacent to Missouri, concerning varietal adaptabilities to that region. Miller apparently was not concerned with attempting to secure either fame or financial gain from his plants. A contemporary observed in an obituary notice: "It never occurred to him to see 'if it would pay' in any of his experiments. . . . I really believe that he took more genuine enjoyment in finding a new flower or in the ripening of some new fruit which he was testing, than he would in the finding of a thousand dollars. He often said 'that he had no time to make money'" (*44th Annual Report of the State Horticultural Society of Missouri, 1901*, 1902, pp. 277–78). For about thirty years, Miller was an officer of the State Horticultural Society, but steadfastly declined to accept the presidency, which was often tendered him. The annual reports of the society contain many papers by him on all phases of horticulture. He was also a regular contributor, for a third of a century, to the horticultural column of *Colman's Rural World*. He was survived by seven of his children.

[In addition to sources cited above see *Colman's Rural World*, Oct. 30 1901; *Am. Gardening*, Nov. 23, 1901; *Trans. Iowa Hort. Soc.*, 1897; L. H. Bailey, *The Standard Cyc. of Horticulture*, III (1915), 1588; W. H. Egle, *Hist. of the Counties of Dauphin and Lebanon* (1883), p. 121.] R. H. S.

MILLER, SAMUEL FREEMAN (Apr. 5, 1816–Oct. 13, 1890), associate justice of the

United States Supreme Court, was born at Richmond in the blue-grass region of Kentucky. His father, Frederick Miller, was a Pennsylvania German who had gone west in 1812. His mother was Patsy Freeman, whose family had emigrated from North Carolina. In 1836, without formal education, Miller entered the medical department of Transylvania University, at Lexington. He attended lectures for one year and then settled at Barbourville, county seat of Knox County, on the road leading down from Cumberland Gap. The autumn of 1837 found him back at Transylvania, where on Mar. 9, 1838, he was "examined and received" for the degree of M.D. For the next twelve years he practised medicine in the mountain community about Barbourville. Here he married Lucy Ballinger, whose family was locally prominent. In the spring of 1837 the young men of the town formed a debating society. From the start Miller was its most active member. Here current political questions were threshed out, and Miller came to recognize that he had a *flair* for statecraft. He became a justice of the peace and a member of the county court. Surreptitiously he studied law, and on Mar. 22, 1847, he was admitted to the bar of Knox County.

Like most of his neighbors, Miller was a Whig. He favored the gradual abolition of slavery in Kentucky, and aspired, unsuccessfully, to membership in the constitutional convention of 1849 where slavery was to be a leading issue. When the peculiar institution was fastened more firmly upon the state, he decided to seek a more congenial sphere of action. In 1850 with his wife and children he moved to Keokuk, Iowa, and formed the law partnership of Reeves & Miller. Shortly afterward he was left a widower, and in 1857, his partner having died, he was married to the latter's widow, Elizabeth (Winter) Reeves. While his practice was increasing he found time to engage in the organization of the Republican party, and in projects for building plank roads and railroads. He was a candidate for the nomination for governor in 1861. During the early months of the war he drew upon his meager resources to advance funds to meet the state's unforeseen needs. In 1862 President Lincoln was under the necessity of making nominations for the Supreme Court. To him a sound view on public questions was a better recommendation than profundity of legal learning, and Miller was actively suported by the Iowa delegation, which circulated a recommendation among the members of both houses of Congress, and by the lawyers of several western states. On July 16, 1862, he was nominated and unanimously confirmed as an associate justice. He was at the time the chairman of the district Republican committee at Keokuk.

The development in power and authority of this self-made jurist is interesting. His training had been woefully unsystematic but was such as tended to develop independence of judgment and capacity for hard thinking. In later years he came to recognize the superiority in education and training enjoyed by leading eastern jurists. Yet with a certain self-satisfaction he insisted that it was "from some western prairie town . . . that future Marshalls and Mansfields shall arise and give new impulses and add new honor to the profession of the law" (*Albany Law Journal,* July 5, 1879, p. 29). His first term was Taney's last but one, and though Miller had cherished a hatred of the author of the Dred Scott opinion, the newest and the eldest of the justices parted fast friends. Throughout the war and reconstruction no judge was more stanch than Miller in the support of national authority. When in *Ex parte Garland* (4 *Wallace,* 333) the Court held that the requirement of a test oath of former loyalty from lawyers, teachers, and ministers amounted to an *ex post facto* law and a bill of attainder, Miller and the other Republicans argued that the measure was constitutional and proper. He was with the majority in the Legal Tender Cases (12 *Wallace,* 457) when by the advent of Justices Strong and Bradley this feature of the war program was narrowly saved from judicial repudiation.

A characteristic opinion is that in *Crandall* vs. *Nevada* (6 *Wallace,* 35). The legislature had imposed a tax on every person leaving the state. The Court was unanimous in holding the tax unconstitutional. Miller, as its spokesman, relied upon the broadest considerations of policy: "The people of these United States constitute one nation. They have a government in which all of them are deeply interested. . . . That government has a right to call to this point [the capital] any or all of its citizens to aid in its service. . . . The citizen also has correlative rights. He has the right to come to the seat of government to assert any claim he may have upon that government, or to transact any business he may have with it." Thus the tax was objectionable in that it conflicted with these implications of the nature of the union and of federal citizenship. In *Loan Association* vs. *Topeka* (20 *Wallace,* 655), a question of great contemporary importance was raised: Might a state or municipality grant public funds to aid a private enterprise? Miller approached the problem not in the light of constitutional provisions, but of his conception of natural law. "It must be conceded that there are . . . rights in every free government beyond the control of the State. A government which recognized no such rights, which held the lives, the liberty, and the property of its citizens subject at all times to the absolute disposition and unlimited control of even the most democratic depository of power, is after all but a despotism. . . . There are limitations on such [public] power which grow out of the essential nature of all free governments. Implied reservations of individual rights, without which the social compact could not exist, and which are respected by all governments entitled to the name. . . . There can be no lawful tax which is not laid for *a public purpose*."

A courageous and emphatic dissent was that in *Gelpcke* vs. *City of Dubuque* (1 *Wallace,* 175) in Miller's second year on the bench. The city had issued bonds for the purchase of railroad stock, under the authority of a state law which had been held good at the time of the issue. Subsequently the state supreme court reversed itself and held the statute *ultra vires.* A foreign bondholder brought suit on the bonds in the federal courts. Would the Supreme Court, as in most other cases, accept the jurisprudence of the state court as the rule of decision? The mischief seemed so great that the majority upheld the validity of the bonds. Two of Miller's deepest convictions united in compelling his dissent. First, he was always opposed to any tendency to allow a state to grant away its taxing power. Time and again in the next twenty years he dissented on this score. Then again, though a nationalist, he was impressed with the importance of maintaining an ample autonomy for state governments. He was strong in his belief that it was not the function of federal courts to sit in judgment on state courts expounding state law.

The latter conviction appears more maturely in the Slaughter House Cases (16 *Wallace,* 36). The Carpet-bag government of Louisiana granted a monopoly of the slaughtering business at New Orleans. Rival butchers contended that this action abridged their privileges and immunities as citizens of the United States and was a denial of due process of law and equal protection of the laws. Thus the Fourteenth Amendment came to receive its first authoritative construction at the hands of the Court. A majority of five, speaking through Miller, started from the proposition that there is a distinction between those rights which inhere in state citizenship and those which inhere in federal citizenship. It was only the latter with which the new amendment dealt. The monopoly might deny the plaintiffs some right conferred by the state constitution; but no federal privilege or immunity had been abridged. To hold otherwise, said Miller, "would constitute this court a perpetual censor upon all legislation of the States." The argument on due process and equal protection of the laws was briefly answered with the prophecy that "we doubt very much whether any action of a State not directed by way of discrimination against the negroes as a class . . . will ever be held to come within the purview of this provision."

This was not a scholastic discussion of state rights: it signified that the majority of the Court refused to read into the words of a Reconstruction amendment a promise of federal protection of vested property rights against the exertions of state power. Thus the nationalizing purposes of some of the Radical Republican authors of the amendment were frustrated. In the long run Miller's effort was somewhat unsuccessful, for those implications which he severed from the "privileges and immunities" clause were later grafted on to the "due process" clause of the same amendment.

Miller was more concerned with the practical result of a decision than with its doctrinal basis. Mere precedents were unimpressive aside from the authority of the judges who made them. He was disposed to let no technicalities stand in the way of what seemed right or just. Thus in *United States* vs. *Lee* (106 *U. S.,* 196) he held that "no man in this country is so high that he is above the law," adding that, notwithstanding a government's immunity to suit, an action of ejectment may be maintained against an officer who holds the possession of property under an invalid title claimed by the United States. In the case involving a federal marshal who was being held for the killing of a citizen who had attacked Justice Field on circuit (*In re Neagle,* 135 *U. S.,* 1), Miller held that it is an obligation of the President, fairly inferrible from the Constitution, to protect federal judges, and that the marshal had been acting in pursuance of "a law" of the United States, and was therefore entitled to be liberated on a writ of *habeas corpus* from the custody of the state authorities. Notwithstanding this tendency to view legal questions in the large, Miller could, on occasion, engage in minute hair-splitting (*Kring* vs. *Missouri,* 107 *U. S.,* 221; *Medley, Petitioner,* 134 *U. S.,* 160).

Of the nobility and generosity of Miller's nature there is ample evidence. Yet he felt that he was, as Chief Justice Chase said, "beyond question, the dominant personality . . . upon the bench" (Strong, *post,* p. 247). With this confidence came a certain blunt impatience with lesser minds and with futile arguments. The reference to him as "that damned old Hippopotamus" by one attorney in his circuit court was not unnatural (Gregory, *post,* p. 60). Miller was anxious to accelerate the administration of justice, and advocated a curtailment of the appellate jurisdiction of the Court (*United States Jurist,* January 1872, *Western Jurist,* February 1872). He never achieved the chief justiceship, though he was more than once considered for the position.

On the bench Miller retained his interest in the Republican party. He was one of the majority in the Electoral Commission of 1876. Yet he was content to rely upon his judicial labors to win his name immortality, and unlike Chase and Field refrained from gazing toward the presidency. Yet he would have been quite willing to become a compromise candidate if the convention of 1884 had become deadlocked. In stature he was tall and massive. He looked, dressed, and acted the part of a great magistrate. He enjoyed good living and bright company. In the midst of this satisfying life he found no opportunity to save money and died almost penniless. He was in active service on the supreme bench and as circuit justice until the day of his death, which occurred at his residence in Washington. During his tenure of office he participated in more than five thousand decisions of the Court. In more than six hundred cases he was its spokesman. Of 478 cases which required a construction of the federal Constitution, he was the organ of the Court in almost twice the normal quota for one justice.

[See C. N. Gregory, *Samuel Freeman Miller* (1907); Horace Stern, "Samuel Freeman Miller, 1816–1890," in W. D. Lewis, *Great Am. Lawyers,* vol. VI (1909); Henry Strong, "Justice Samuel Freeman Miller," in *Annals of Iowa,* Jan. 1894; *Proc. of the Bench and Bar of the Supreme Court of the U. S. in Memoriam Samuel F. Miller* (1891); *Miss. Valley Hist. Rev.,* Mar. 1931; Charles Warren, *The Supreme Court in U. S. Hist.* (1922), vol. III; the *Evening Star* (Wash., D. C.), Oct. 14, 1890. Information as to certain facts was supplied for this sketch by members of Miller's family. In 1891 a series of *Lectures on the Constitution* by Miller was posthumously published.] C. F.

MILLER, STEPHEN DECATUR (May 8, 1787–Mar. 8, 1838), representative and senator from South Carolina, Nullifier, was the son of William and Margaret (White) Miller. His ancestors were Scotch Presbyterians who emigrated to South Carolina from the north of Ireland and were among the first white settlers in Lancaster District, where he was born at the Waxhaw settlement. His father died early leaving little wealth. The few slaves the boy inherited were sold to pay for his education. He received the usual classical preparation of the time, in 1808 was graduated from the South Carolina College, and then studied law in the office of John S. Richardson of Sumter. He was admitted to the bar in 1811, was known as a good lawyer, and had a large practice. From 1817 to 1819 he was a member of the South Carolina delegation in the national House of Representatives. His next public service was as state senator for the Sumter District from 1822 to 1828. Then he became governor for two years. At the conclusion of his term he was elected, against William Smith, to the United States Senate and took his seat on Dec. 5, 1831. During this period he opposed most of the measures of President Jackson although, like Jackson, he was an enemy of the Bank.

When he entered Congress he was an anti-Calhoun Democrat, but repeated demands of the protectionists converted him to Calhoun's nullification doctrine. When the tariff of 1827 was under consideration, he was a member of a special committee of the state Senate that reported a series of resolutions announcing the compact theory of government and condemning the tariff acts of 1816, 1820, and 1824, federal appropriations for roads and canals, and federal support of the American Colonization Society as violations of the Constitution. As governor his speeches did much to crystallize nullification sentiment. There were, he insisted, three ways of reforming unequal congressional legislation, the ballot box, the jury box, and the cartridge box. It was the prerogative of the people to elect a convention to nullify the federal tariff laws, which all South Carolinians admitted were unconstitutional and oppressive. If the laws were once nullified, juries, regardless of the opinions of federal judges, would not sustain them. Yet, if all other means failed, there still remained the right of resistance. In the United States Senate he spoke and voted against the tariff of 1832, and, when it passed, he and nearly all the other members of the South Carolina delegation united in an "Address to the People of South Carolina." The addressers rejected the lower rates of that act as unsatisfactory, since protection still remained "the settled policy of the country." All hope of fair dealing from the federal government seemed to them to have vanished. The remedy, they declared, was in the sovereign power of the state. He was a member of the state conventions of 1832 and 1833, called to consider nullification. He voted for the nullification ordinance in 1832. In the convention of 1833 he opposed the measure to require of all office holders the test oath of paramount allegiance to the state, which was, nevertheless, passed with a good majority.

He resigned from the Senate on Mar. 2, 1833, on account of ill health and retired to Mississippi, where he had removed three years earlier and had set up as a cotton planter. He died at his nephew's house in Raymond, Miss. He was married twice. His first wife was a Miss Dick of Sumter whom he married about 1814. She died in 1819. Their three sons died in youth. In May 1821 he married Mary Boykin of Kershaw, S. C., who survived him with their son and three daughters.

[J. B. O'Neall, *Biog. Sketches of the Bench and Bar in S. C.* (1859), vol. II; *Cyc. of Eminent and Representative Men* (1892), vol. I; *Biog. Directory of the Am. Cong.* (1928).] J. G. V—D.

MILLER, WARNER (Aug. 12, 1838–Mar. 21, 1918), paper manufacturer and United States senator, of German descent, was born at Hannibal, Oswego County, N. Y., the son of Hiram and Mary Ann (Warner) Miller. In 1839 his parents moved to Millertown (now North Pittstown) and later to a farm near Northville, in Fulton County, where Warner grew up. He attended an academy in Charlotteville, in Schoharie County, N. Y., and for a time taught school near New Brunswick, N. J. From here he entered Union College at Schenectady and was graduated in 1860. He began to teach at Fort Edward Collegiate Institute in New York but upon the advent of the Civil War enlisted in the 5th New York Cavalry. His military experiences were varied and brief, as he was captured, paroled, and honorably discharged by September 1862. Not being able to reënter the army, and having lost interest in an academic career, he took a position in a paper-mill at Fort Edward, where he advanced to a foremanship and was sent to Belgium to study a new process for making paper. In 1865 Warner Miller & Company purchased the paper-mill of A. H. Laflin in Herkimer. In the same year, on July 13, Miller was married to Caroline Churchill. In his business he developed new processes for making paper from wood pulp and gained considerable reputation as a leader in the industry.

His financial success brought him to public notice and directed him into politics. For many years he was the leading Republican of Herkimer County, and in 1872 he was a delegate to the Republican National Convention at Philadelphia. During the next three years he served as state assemblyman. In 1878 he was chosen to represent his district in Congress, a position which he held until July 26, 1881, when he resigned to become United States senator. His election to this office came as the result of a split in the Republican party of his state. Miller became the successful candidate of the "Half Breeds," against the "Stalwarts," for the seat vacated by Thomas C. Platt. He remained in the Senate until Mar. 3, 1887, being denied reëlection because of the political adroitness of Platt, who rather than see Miller triumph over his own candidate, Levi P. Morton, threw his votes to a third candidate, Frank Hiscock. In the Senate Miller served on many committees, at one time being chairman of the committee on agriculture. He was particularly nationalistic in his attitudes and strongly favored Chinese exclusion, the development of the merchant marine, and the protective tariff. He also supported the Nicaraguan canal proposals. He had a simple though effective style of oratory which won for him a considerable reputation.

In 1884 Miller supported Blaine for the presidency and at the National Convention in 1888 was partly responsible for the nomination of Benjamin Harrison. His ability and service to his party were rewarded in August 1888 by his nomination by acclamation as the Republican candidate for governor of New York. During the campaign which followed he supported Harrison and spoke frequently on the merits of a protective tariff. It has often been stated that it was due to his opposition to the liquor interests that he lost the election, being defeated by David Bennett Hill, the Democratic candidate, by 19,171 votes. In 1892, as delegate at large at the Republican Convention, Miller worked for the nomination of Blaine, but he returned to work equally hard for the election of Harrison. In 1894 and 1895 he was an active leader at the state conventions and warmly approved of McKinley in 1896. After this date he gradually retired from politics, although in 1906 he was chairman of a special tax commission in New York. He was a leading and public-spirited citizen, a member of the Herkimer County Historical Society, and an active participant in the affairs of the local Methodist Episcopal Church. He died in New York City.

[*Biog. Dir. Am. Cong.* (1928); J. L. M'Millan, "Printing and Its Development in This Country," *Papers Read Before the Herkimer County Hist. Soc. During the Years 1896, 1897, and 1898* (1899); "Herkimer County People at the Nat. Capitol," *Ibid.*, vol. II (1902); C. M. Depew, *One Hundred Years of Am. Commerce* (1895), vol. I; R. Van V. Raymond, *Union Univ.* (1907), II, 56–59; G. A. Hardin, *Hist. of Herkimer County, N. Y.* (1893); R. B. Smith, *Pol. and Gov. Hist. of the State of N. Y.* (1922), vols. III and IV; D. S. Alexander, *Four Famous New Yorkers* (1923); *N. Y. Times*, Mar. 22, 1918.] W. F. G.

MILLER, WILLIAM (Feb. 15, 1782–Dec. 20, 1849), leader of the Adventist movement, the son of Capt. William Miller, a veteran of the Revolutionary War, was born at Pittsfield,

Mass., and grew to manhood in Low Hampton, Washington County, N. Y. His mother, Paulina, was the daughter of Elnathan Phelps, a Baptist preacher. His early education was limited to that afforded by a frontier school, but his deep thirst for further learning was partially satisfied by reading books borrowed from men of learning in the neighborhood. On June 29, 1803, he married Lucy P. Smith of Poultney, Vt., settled in the bride's home town, and became a farmer. Availing himself of the public library, he became a constant reader and student. His mother had taught him to revere the Bible as the word of God to man, but perplexed by certain apparently contradictory passages and influenced by his reading and certain skeptical friends, he became a deist. In his new home he grew into prominence, filling numerous offices of public trust, including those of justice of the peace and deputy sheriff. During the War of 1812 he served in the army, rising to the rank of captain.

Upon his return to civil life he settled in Hampton, N. Y., on a farm, where, in 1816, after great mental and spiritual struggle, he experienced conversion. Taunted by deist friends, he began a prayerful study of the Bible in an effort to meet their gibes. By pursuing a study of the prophecies, he discovered to his own satisfaction that the Bible revealed the return of Christ to earth about 1843. Fifteen years' further study only deepened this conviction. Along with it came a call to present his views. This he resisted for several years, fearing his calculations might be incorrect. In 1831, however, he accepted an invitation to give a public interpretation of the prophecies. Filled with the theme, and master of his subject, he soon became a power in the pulpit. Invitations poured in upon him and great crowds attended his lectures. Before long he was unable to answer half the calls for his services. In 1833 the Baptist church of which he was a member granted him a license to preach. In 1836 he published the chief Adventist writing of his time, a volume of sixteen lectures entitled *Evidence from Scripture and History of the Second Coming of Christ, about the Year 1843. Exhibited in a Course of Lectures.* Everywhere the Baptist, Methodist, and Congregational churches were thrown open, and pastors requested him to address their congregations. Hundreds were converted in the revivals that followed his work.

In 1839 Joshua Vaughan Himes [*q.v.*] accepted Miller's teaching and became one of the greatest publicity men of his day. Through his activities Adventist papers were published in the chief cities of the country and millions of pages of literature were circulated. A great tent was purchased for a tabernacle and Miller and his associates traveled over the country warning the people to prepare for the great day of the Lord. At least 120 camp meetings were held during the summer months of 1842, 1843, and 1844, with an estimated attendance of half a million. Miller expected Christ to come some time between March 1843 and March 1844. Consequently, his followers began to name different dates as probable times for the advent. Signs in the heavens of its coming were reported; a great meteoric shower which occurred in 1833 was regarded as an omen; strange rings were seen around the sun; crosses were discerned in the sky; and a great comet appeared at high noon and for days hung ominously over the earth like a huge sword threatening a guilty world. The entire country was astir. People began to lose their reason, Miller's followers were accused of donning ascension robes and assembling in graveyards and on high places to await their Saviour. These charges, according to the best evidence, are not based on facts, although tradition to this day readily affirms them. Certain other forms of fanaticism, such as speaking with strange tongues and possessing discerning spirits, did appear. These extravagances, although confined to a small minority, were sharply rebuked by the leaders. Disappointed in their expectation in 1843, the Millerites, as the Adventists were called by their enemies, again looked for Christ on Oct. 22, 1844. The intensity of their anticipation rose to flood tide at this time. Crops were left unharvested, stores closed, and positions were resigned. Men prepared, as though on their death beds, to meet their God. Again disappointed, Miller continued steadfast in the faith, looking for Christ in the immediate future but setting no date.

When he began preaching, he had no thought of forming a separate church. Bitter opposition to his followers, who were members of the principal Protestant churches, arose, however, and they began to withdraw from their several sects in 1843. Two years later the Adventist Church was organized with Miller at its head. Although nominally the leader, he handed over the reins to younger hands and spent the remainder of his days in comparative inactivity, going forth occasionally to preach or to grace a conference with his sage-like presence. His rise had been rapid. From the position of an obscure country preacher to that of a religious teacher of national prominence he rose in three years. Possessing a commanding personality and genial disposition, together with pious scholarship and the deepest sincerity, he was a mighty force in the religious world. In his old age he lost his eyesight and his career closed in darkness. He died at Hampton surrounded by his family.

[Everett Dick, "The Adventist Crisis 1831–1844," doctoral dissertation presented at the University of Wisconsin, 1930, is the most comprehensive study of Miller's work; see also Sylvester Bliss, *Memoirs of William Miller* (1853); I. C. Wellcome (*History of the Second Advent Message and Mission, Doctrine and People* (1874); James White, *Sketches of the Christian Life and Public Labors of William Miller* (1875); C. E. Sears, *Days of Delusion* (1924); *Littell's Living Age*, Jan. 19, 1850, *Advent Herald*, Jan. 1850; O. S. Phelps and A. T. Servin, *The Phelps Family of America* (2 vols., 1899); Crisfield Johnson, *Hist. of Washington Co., N. Y.* (1878).] E. N. D.

MILLER, WILLIAM HENRY HARRISON (Sept. 6, 1840–May 25, 1917), attorney-general of the United States, was born at Augusta, N. Y., the son of Lucy (Duncan) and Curtis Miller, a farmer. His ancestors were Scotch and English. After being graduated from Hamilton College in 1861, he taught school at Maumee, Ohio. In May 1862 he enlisted in the 84th Ohio Infantry but was mustered out in September with the rank of second lieutenant. He then began the study of law in the office of Morrison R. Waite [*q.v.*]; this he continued at Peru, Ind., while serving there as superintendent of schools. He was married to Gertrude A. Bunce in December 1863. In 1865 he was admitted to the bar and in 1866 moved to Fort Wayne. He attracted the attention of Benjamin Harrison at whose invitation he became a partner in the firm of Harrison and Hines at Indianapolis. He was a man of great industry, inclined to be somewhat impulsive at times, and well versed in the law. He took no active part in politics but was the trusted adviser of those Republicans who did; when cases came before the state supreme court involving political questions, he often argued the Republican side. The most dramatic case of this type was the lieutenant-governorship contest in 1886 (*Robertson* vs. *the State, ex rel. Smith,* 109 *Ind. Reports,* 79).

When Benjamin Harrison became president Miller became his attorney-general and one of his most trusted personal advisors. The appointment was a surprise to Republican leaders, for Miller was unknown outside of his state and had had practically no administrative experience. As attorney-general he endeavored to enforce the laws vigorously and impartially with a disregard of political influences that was often disconcerting to Republican leaders. His careful investigation into the records of men suggested for federal judicial appointments was responsible in part for the excellence of Harrison's judicial appointments. Among the more important cases that came before the United States Supreme Court and to which Miller gave his personal attention were those involving the anti-lottery law, the interstate commerce act, the Sherman anti-trust act, and the constitutionality of the McKinley tariff. In the spectacular case *in re Neagle* (135 *U. S. Reports,* 1) his position that it was the duty of the executive to protect federal judges against physical injury while on duty was upheld by the Supreme Court. (See article on Stephen Johnson Field.) Among his most able assistants was the solicitor-general, William Howard Taft. When Taft resigned to become United States circuit judge, he wrote of Miller: "To serve under a chief whose only requirement is that one shall do right and enforce the law without fear or favor is as delightful as it is exceptional" (draft of letter of resignation, *Taft Papers*). When Harrison's term ended in 1893, Miller rejoined his old law firm and engaged in active practice until 1910. He died in Indianapolis, survived by his wife and three of their seven children.

[Benjamin Harrison Papers and William Howard Taft Papers in the Lib. of Cong.; Letter Books and Registers of the firm of Harrison, Hines, and Miller and its successors at Indianapolis; *Indianapolis Star,* May 26, 1917; *Indianapolis News,* May 26, 28, 1917.] A. T. V.

MILLER, WILLOUGHBY DAYTON (Aug. 1, 1853–July 27, 1907), dentist, a son of John H. and Nancy L. (Sommerville) Miller, was born on a farm near Alexandria, Licking County, Ohio. His education began in the county public school; but in 1865 his parents removed to Newark, Ohio, where he graduated from the high school in 1871. In the same year he entered the University of Michigan at Ann Arbor, and received the degree of A.B. in 1875. He then took special courses in chemistry, mathematics, and physics at the University of Edinburgh, and in 1876 entered upon further study along these lines at the University of Berlin. Overwork resulted in a nervous breakdown in 1877, but during his convalescence he mingled in the social life of the American colony in Berlin and collaborated in some chemical researches with F. P. Abbot, a pioneer American dentist in Germany. Miller shortly became engaged to marry Abbot's daughter, and decided to adopt dentistry as his profession and settle in Berlin, so that his future wife could be near her parents. He served a few months as student assistant to Abbot, then, late in 1877, entered the Pennsylvania College of Dental Surgery, which became the Dental Department of the University of Pennsylvania in 1878 and graduated Miller with the degree of D.D.S. in 1879. Returning immediately to Berlin, he married Caroline L. Abbot on Oct. 26, 1879, and began the practice of dentistry with her father, at the same time continuing his studies at the University of Berlin.

From the beginning of his professional career to the time of his death, Miller was especially interested in bacteriology and chemistry as related to dental and oral diseases. The first of his many articles on micro-organisms in the etiology of dental caries appeared in German in 1881 and in English in 1882. In 1884 he was appointed professor of operative dentistry in the newly organized Dental Institute of the University of Berlin. In 1887 he graduated with the degree of M.D. from the medical school of the University of Berlin with the predicate *magna cum laude.* In 1894 he was made a professor extraordinary on the medical faculty of the same university, an honor rarely conferred upon a foreigner and never before upon a dentist; and about the same time he became a state examiner for dentistry in Berlin. His elevation to these coveted positions at first aroused much opposition from German dentists, some of whom repeatedly petitioned the minister of education to give the offices to Germans; but this opposition was soon overcome, and Miller was recognized everywhere as one of the leading dental authorities and bacteriologists of his day. As a practitioner of dentistry he stood second to none in Berlin, the Empress Augusta and other members of the imperial family being included among his many distinguished patients, while in 1906 the Emperor in a personal letter appointed him privy medical councilor. He served as president of the National Dental Association of Germany, the Association of Dental Faculties of that nation, the American Dental Society of Europe, and the Féderation Dentaire Internationale. He was also an honorary member of some forty dental societies in America and abroad.

Miller published more than a hundred articles in professional journals. The majority were in German, while some were in English, but many of the former were translated into English. In America, most of his contributions to dentistry appeared in the *Dental Cosmos* and the *Independent Practitioner.* He also published two extensive works in book form, the more notable of which is *Die Mikro-organismen der Mundhöhle* (1889 and 1892), translated into English as *The Micro-organisms of the Human Mouth* (1890). This was followed by his *Lehrbuch der Conservirenden Zahnheilkunde* (1896 and 1898). In his laboratory experiments, he produced caries in extracted human teeth by means of bacteria from the mouth, and demonstrated that tooth tissue is destroyed by fermentative acids formed by these micro-organisms. This is now generally accepted as the basic truth of the "chemicoparasitic theory"; but neither Miller nor his followers claimed that this theory could explain all the phenomena of dental caries. Miller's researches and writings also relate to various other subjects, such as the use of antiseptics in dentistry, diseased teeth and oral tissues as foci of infection, and the etiology of dental erosion and abrasion.

His practice was confined to Berlin; but such was his loyalty to his native land that he declined to become a naturalized citizen of Germany. In 1907 he accepted the position of dean of the Dental College of the University of Michigan, his alma mater. Efforts were made to have him remain in Berlin, a wealthy merchant even offering to build, equip, and support a research laboratory for him in that city; but he severed his connection with the University there and brought his family to the United States, expecting to begin his duties at Ann Arbor in October 1907. In the summer of that year however, while on a visit with his family to relatives in Alexandria, Ohio, near the place of his birth, he was stricken with appendicitis, and died after an operation at the City Hospital of Newark, Ohio. He was survived by his wife and their three children, one son and two daughters. Miller was of slight build and never robust. His life was devoted to his family, his professional duties, his researches, and his writings. For some years he was secretary of the non-sectarian American Church in Berlin, and he was an ardent golfer. In 1915 a life-size bronze statue of him was unveiled on the campus of the Ohio State University at Columbus.

[The chief sources are *Dental Cosmos,* Sept. 1907; *Index of Dental Periodical Literature,* and family information. See also *Dental Summary,* Apr. 1916, and *Detroit Free Press,* July 30, 1907. The biography of Miller by B. K. Thorpe in C. R. E. Koch's *Hist. of Dental Surgery* (1910), vol. III, is incomplete and unreliable.]

L. P. B.

MILLET, FRANCIS DAVIS (Nov. 3, 1846–Apr. 15, 1912), painter, author, war correspondent, illustrator, was born in Mattapoisett, Mass., the son of Dr. Asa and Huldah A. (Byram) Millet. In July 1864 he enlisted as a private in the 60th Massachusetts Militia Infantry and served as a drummer until Nov. 30, when he was honorably discharged. He graduated at Harvard in 1869 with the degree of M.A. in modern languages and literature. While working on the *Boston Advertiser* he learned lithography and so earned money to take him in 1871 to the Royal Academy, Antwerp, where in two years he won all the prizes the academy offered and was publicly crowned by the King. In 1873, as secretary of the Massachusetts commission to the Vienna exposition he formed a lasting friendship with Charles Francis Adams, cemented by travel and work together. He wandered through the Near East, becoming acquainted with the peoples of Turkey, Greece, and Hungary. Then he studied painting in Rome and Venice and returned to act as correspondent of the *Boston Advertiser* at the Philadelphia Centennial, where he was an exhibitor. He helped John La Farge decorate Trinity Church, Boston, and painted a portrait of Mark Twain.

In 1877 the *New York Herald* sent Millet as correspondent with the Russians in their war against Turkey. Later he succeeded Archibald Forbes on the *London Daily News* and as artist for the *London Graphic*. Whistling bullets gave vividness to his pencil, and hard rides to post dispatches taught him the country. So it happened that he daringly broke military etiquette and told the Russian officers of a ford unknown to them by which they might avoid crossing a deep river to attack the Turks. The flank movement succeeded. No notice was taken of Millet's temerity until he was summoned by the Russian general, who "dealt with an unprecedented action of a civilian in proffering advice on military matters" by presenting to him in the name of the Czar the Cross of St. Stanislaus. Next came the Cross of St. Anne for valuable and exceptional service to the Russian government. With his friend, General Gurko he rode into Adrianople and received the Iron Cross of Roumania. Of these decorations he spoke only to point some robust or pithy story.

In 1878 Millet was a member of the fine arts jury at the Paris exposition and an exhibitor in both the Salon and the British Royal Academy. On Mar. 11, 1879, he married Elizabeth Greely Merrill, the sister of William Bradford Merrill [*q.v.*]. For a time they lived in Boston, then New York. In 1884, Millet, with E. A. Abbey, J. S. Sargent, and Alfred Parsons made a Bohemian colony at Broadway, England. In *Picture and Text* (1893) Henry James has written of Broadway and Millet: "He has made pictures without words and words without pictures. He has written very clever ghost stories and drawn and painted some very immediate realities. . . . He has draped and distributed Greek plays at Harvard . . . and given publicity to English villages. . . . The old surfaces and tones, the stuffs and textures, the old silver and mahogany and brass—the old sentiment too, and the old picture-making vision are in the direct tradition of Terburg and DeHoogh and Metzu" (pp. 9–12). In 1891, for *Harper's Magazine,* he made a trip of seventeen hundred miles down the Danube with Poultney Bigelow. Their narratives, which appeared in *Harper's* from February to May 1892, later took book form (*From the Black Forest to the Black Sea,* 1893). Also he printed a sheaf of short stories, which still bubble up in anthologies. In 1887 he had published a translation of Tolstoi's *Sebastopol.* At the World's Columbian Exhibition of 1893 he was director of decorations of the White City and ended as master of ceremonies. His humorous ingenuity brought the fair to a brilliant end, notwithstanding the financial panic. *The Expedition to the Philippines* (1899) represents his war-correspondence for the *London Times, Harper's Weekly,* and the New York *Sun.* A journey through the Far East brought him back to the Paris Exposition of 1900 as representative of his country. Then he painted historical murals for the Minnesota and Wisconsin capitols, the Baltimore Custom House, the Cleveland Trust Company. In 1908 Secretary Root sent him on a special mission to Tokyo, whence he returned with the First Class Order of the Sacred Treasure. France had made him a chevalier of the Legion of Honor.

Millet was the creative spirit of the American Federation of Arts and of the National Commission of Fine Arts (1910). Reluctantly he accepted the directorship of the American Academy in Rome at a time of an academy crisis in 1911. In 1912 he and his Washington companion, Maj. Archie Butt, President Taft's aide, were in Rome, Millet on urgent Academy business. They took return passage on the *Titanic* and went down with the ship. Millet was last seen encouraging the Italian women and children to go into the lifeboats. In a shaded nook in the President's Park (White Lot) in Washington, stands a modest monument to Millet and Butt, the design a tribute of friendship by Daniel Chester French, sculptor, and Thomas Hastings, architect. Elihu Root said of Millet: "He never pushed himself forward. He never thought or cared where the spotlight was. . . . Yet from somewhere among his forbears in old New England there came into his make-up a firmness of fiber which made him modest, sensitive, beauty-loving as he was, a man of strength and force, decision of character, and executive capacity" (*Francis Davis Millet, Memorial Meeting, post,* p. 8).

[*Eleventh Report of the Class of 1869 of Harvard Coll.* (1919); *Harvard Grads.' Mag.*, Sept. 1909; *Francis Davis Millet: Memorial Meeting* (1912), published by the Am. Federation of Arts, and containing a bibliography of Millet's paintings and literary work; *Art* and Progress, July 1912, Sept., Nov. 1913; *Internat. Studio,* Oct. 1907, Dec. 1912; Leila Mechlin, "A Decorator of Public Buildings," *World's Work,* Dec. 1909; James Hunt, *A List of Paintings, Drawings, Mural Decorations and Designs . . . and Lit. Works of Francis Davis Millet* (n.d.); Thos. Hastings, "La Farge, Abbey, Millet," *Proc. Am. Acad. Arts and Letters,* vol. I (1913); Charles Moore, *Daniel H. Burnham, Architect, Planner of Cities* (2 vols. 1921) and *The Life and Times of Chas. Follen McKim* (1929); *Am. Art News,* Apr. 20, 1912; *N. Y. Times,* Apr. 16, 1912.] C. M.

MILLIGAN, ROBERT (July 25, 1814–Mar. 20, 1875), minister of the Disciples of Christ, educator, was born in County Tyrone, Ireland, the son of John and Margaret Milligan, who with their children emigrated to the United States about 1818 and settled in Ohio not far from Youngstown. Robert attended academies in Zelienople and Jamestown, Pa., and in 1837 opened a classical school of his own at Flat Rock, Bourbon County, Ky. He was at that time a member of the Associate Presbyterian Church, but a thorough study of the Greek New Testament resulted in his accepting the views of the Disciples of Christ as Scriptural, and in 1838 he united with that body. Entering Washington College, Pa., in 1839, he received the degree of A.B. the following year, and at once became professor of English in that institution. In 1842 he married Ellen Blaine Russell.

Milligan was ordained to the ministry in 1844 by Thomas Campbell, but although he preached frequently he held no regular pastorate. Among the Disciples he occupied a position of leadership, but his influence was exerted chiefly as an educator and writer. He was connected with Washington College for some twelve years, where, after teaching English and the classics, he became professor of chemistry and the natural sciences. In 1852 he was called to Indiana University, but two years later became professor of mathematics at Bethany College. While here he also served for some time as co-editor of the *Millennial Harbinger.* Becoming president of Kentucky University in 1859, and also professor of sacred history and mental and moral philosophy, he managed the institution successfully through the difficult days of the Civil War. When, after its removal from Harrodsburg to Lexington, it was united with Transylvania University in 1865, he voluntarily relinquished the presidency and became head of the College of the Bible, which position he held until his death. During the last decade of his life he published a number of religious works which include *Reason and Revelation, or the Province of Reason in Matters Pertaining to Divine Revelation Defined and Illustrated* (1868); *An Exposition and Defense of the Scheme of Redemption* (1869); *The Great Commission of Jesus Christ to the Twelve Apostles* (1871); *Analysis of the New Testament* (1874). A commentary on Hebrews (*The New Testament Commentary,* vol. IX, 1876), appeared after his death.

[W. T. Moore, *The Living Pulpit of the Christian Church* (1869); J. T. Brown, *Churches of Christ* (1904); G. T. Ridlon, *Hist. of the Families Millingas and Millanges . . .* (1907); W. T. Moore, *A Comprehensive Hist. of the Disciples of Christ* (1909); *Christian Standard,* Mar. 27, Apr. 10, 1875.] H. E. S.

MILLIGAN, ROBERT WILEY (Apr. 8, 1843–Oct. 14, 1909), naval officer, was born in Philadelphia, Pa., the son of James and Mary (Thornton) Milligan and a grandson of Robert Milligan who emigrated from County Down, Ireland, to Pennsylvania, sometime before 1840. After attending Philadelphia grammar and high schools he entered the navy as third assistant engineer, Mar. 3, 1863, and served through the remainder of the Civil War in the *Mackinaw,* participating in both attacks on Fort Fisher, the fall of Wilmington, and the subsequent campaign on the James River. Engineering duty on many ships and stations in the ensuing thirty years was broken by two assignments as Naval Academy instructor, 1879–82 and 1885–89, and service on the Board of Inspection and Survey, 1893–96. He went to the *Oregon* as chief engineer in January 1897, and was in this ship during her famous cruise around South America and her outstanding work at Santiago in the Spanish-American War. Both were essentially feats of engineering, justifying in a measure Admiral C. F. Pond's statement, made on "The Battleship Oregon Day" at the Panama-Pacific Exposition, that to Milligan, "more than to any other one man, was due the wonderful success of this . . . ship" (*Army and Navy News,* San Francisco, November 1915, p. 6).

Leaving San Francisco on Mar. 19, 1898, the *Oregon,* with a trial speed of 16.7 knots, averaged 11.16 on the fourteen-thousand-mile cruise, making Florida in sixty-eight days, fifty-four under way. That no machinery accidents or delays occurred was due primarily to the chief engineer and his devoted assistants, who both at sea and during the brief overhauls worked under great strain. On the Santiago blockade, Milligan "ran a sweat-shop" (J. R. Spears, *Our Navy in the War with Spain,* 1898, p. 294). As during the cruise, he insisted on fresh water only for the boilers, and his was the only ship to keep all four boilers constantly under steam. As a result, the *Oregon* in the battle shot "like an express train," in Capt. Robley D. Evans' words, past all her consorts but the *Brooklyn,* averaging 12.9 knots, whereas the 21-knot *Brooklyn* averaged only 13.2. The last spurt, which brought her in range of the *Cristobal*

Colon, was made with superior coal which Milligan brought from San Francisco and kept under lock and key. Milligan was advanced five numbers and after a year as fleet engineer was stationed at the Norfolk Navy Yard from July 1899 until his retirement as rear admiral on Apr. 8, 1905. He had been made captain in 1902 after the amalgamation of engineers with the line. He was a well-built man above medium height, slow-spoken, thoughtful, and whole-hearted in his work. He was married on Feb. 17, 1870, to Sarah Ann Du Bois of Annapolis, Md., and was survived by two daughters. His death occurred at Annapolis, where he had made his home after retirement, and he was buried there in the naval cemetery.

[F. F. Hemenway, "An Interview with Chief Engineer Milligan," *Machinery,* Oct. 1898; C. A. E. King, "Recent Performances of the U.S.S. Oregon," *Jour. Am. Soc. Naval Engineers,* Aug. 1898; C. E. Clark, *My Fifty Years in the Navy* (1917); L. R. Hamersly, *The Records of Living Officers of the U. S. Navy and Marine Corps* (7th ed., 1902); *Who's Who in America,* 1908–09; *Army and Navy Jour.,* Oct. 16, 1909; the *Sun* (Baltimore), Oct. 15, 1909.] A. W.

MILLINGTON, JOHN (May 11, 1779–July 10, 1868), engineer, scientific writer, and teacher, was born in Hammersmith, near London, the son of Thomas Charles Millington, an attorney, and his wife, Ruth Hill. Millington entered Oxford University but because of his father's poverty withdrew without a degree, studied law, and in the years following 1803 had a considerable practice as a patent agent. In some way, time and place unknown, he apparently acquired the degree of M.D. He never practised medicine, nor did he ever engage in general legal practice, but devoted himself to engineering and teaching. In 1806 he was admitted a fellow of the Society for the Encouragement of Arts (later the Royal Society of Arts). He is said to have been associated with McAdam in road-building, to have been engineer of the West Middlesex water works, and to have served as superintendent of "the royal grounds in London, or at Kew." In 1815 the Royal Institution engaged him to give a course of about twelve lectures on natural philosophy at three guineas a lecture. From this time until 1829, he gave annual courses of lectures on natural philosophy, mechanics, and astronomy before the Institution, and on July 7, 1817, was appointed professor of mechanics there. In 1820 he became one of the original fellows of the Astronomical Society of London and served as secretary for the three years 1823 to 1826. In December 1823 he was elected a member of the Linnean Society of London. Upon the organization of the University of London, he was appointed first professor of engineering but resigned before the university was opened (H. H. Bellot, *University College, London,* 1929, pp. 28, 40, 135).

During these busy years in London, Millington married Emily, daughter of Sir William Hamilton, the painter; invented and patented a ship's propeller; published in 1823 his *Epitome of the Elementary Principles of Mechanical Philosophy,* which had a second edition in 1830; taught chemistry in Guy's Hospital; and was vice-president of the London Mechanics' Institution. At the age of fifty, as an engineer and teacher of science in his native London, he had approached greatness, though at a respectful distance. He now set out upon a career of almost forty years of restless wandering. In 1830 and the year following he was in Mexico, employed by an English company as superintendent of a group of mines and of a mint. Here his wife Emily died leaving a number of small children. A few years later he was in Philadelphia, marrying Sarah Ann Letts and conducting a shop which professed to supply "all the various machines, instruments, apparatus and materials, required for mechanical, philosophical, mathematical, optical and chemical purposes" (Holmes, *post,* p. 28). In 1835 he accepted the chair of chemistry, natural philosophy, and engineering in the College of William and Mary at Williamsburg, Va. While there he wrote his *Elements of Civil Engineering,* published in 1839, possibly the first American textbook on the subject. In 1848 he was elected the first professor of the natural sciences in the newly organized University of Mississippi at Oxford, Miss. He also served as head of the geological survey of the state, though B. L. C. Wailes did the work. In 1853 he became professor of chemistry and toxicology in the Memphis Medical College. At the age of eighty he retired to his new home at La Grange, Tenn. The Civil War reduced him to poverty. He fled to Philadelphia, seeking a livelihood, and finally found a haven at the home of his daughter in Richmond, Va. He died in July 1868 and was buried in the churchyard of Bruton Parish in Williamsburg. In youth the friend of Herschel, Faraday, and Davy, he spent his old age teaching the natural sciences to the restless sons of the Old South.

[G. F. Holmes, "Prof. John Millington, M.D., 1779–1868," *William and Mary Coll. Quart.,* Jan. 1923; S. C. Gladden, "John Millington (1779–1868)," *Ibid.,* July 1933; sketch by R. B. Prosser in the *Dict. Nat. Biog.*; Bennett Woodcroft, *Alphabetical Index of Patentees of Inventions . . . 1617–1852* (1854), p. 380; *Richmond Enquirer,* June 23, 1848; *Daily Enquirer and Examiner* (Richmond), July 11, 1868.]

T. C. J., Jr.